.g.pdf

Software for Asset-Liability Management	www.olsonresearch.com
Chicago Board of Trade's Knowledge Center	www.cbot.com
Chicago Mercantile Exchange's New Center	www.cme.com
Federal Reserve's Trading and	www.federalreserve.gov/
Capital Markets Activity Manual	
Futures and Options Information	www.kesdee.com/events/brochures/cooption.html
	www.marketvolume.com/glossary
	financialservices.house.gov
Use of Futures Contracts by Banks	www.futuresweb.com
Employment of Options Trades	www.freddiemac.com
International Swaps and Derivatives	www.isda.org/index.html
Association	
Interest-Rate Swaps	www.economagic.com/fedbog.htm
	www.financewise.com/risk/
Swap Trading Activities of	financialservices.house.gov/banking
Nonbank Institutions	www.derivativesstrategy.com/magazine
	www.financialservicesfacts.org
Use of Interest-Rate Swaps	www.snl.com
	www.aei.org
Loan Securitizations/Loan Sales/	www.investorwords.com
Standby Credits/Credit Derivatives	www.mortgage101.com
Credit Derivatives Market	www.intltreasurer.com
	www.margrabe.com/creditderivatives.html
Jobs in the Derivatives Industry	www.streetjobs.com
	www.portfolioservices.com
Loan Securitization	www.key.com
Use of Standby Credit Letters	www.fleetcapital.com/products
	www.fhfb.gov/fhlb/fhlbp_loc.htm
Credit Derivative Contracts	www.credit-deriv.com
	www.margrabe.com
Risk/Return Data on Securities	www.wsrn.com
Managing a Bond Portfolio	www.investinginbonds.com
	www.munidirect.com
	www.riskgrades.com/retail/myportfolio/
	www.publicdebt.treas.gov/sec/secfaq
Statistics on Depository Institutions	www3.fdic.gov/sdi
Regulations for Permissible Bank Investments	www.fdic.gov/regulations/resources
Investment Manager Careers	www.banking-financejobs.com/jobs.html
Rules for Bank Investing in Securities Markets	www.occ.treas.gov
	www.thecommunitybanker.com
	www.bondmarkets.com
Asset- or Loan-backed Securities Market	www.fanniemae.com
Evaluating Securities	www.bondmarket.com
	www.investinginbonds.com
Trading and Capital-Markets	
Activity Manual	www.federalreserve.gov/boarddocs/supmanual/trading/trading.pdf
Liquidity Issues	www.firstcapitalbank.com/pages/products/sweep.html
Research Collections	research.stlouisfed.org/wp/
	www.ny.frb.org (Economic Research link)
	www.chicagofed.org/publications
Federal Reserve and 9/11 Terrorist Attacks	www.clevelandfed.org/research
	www.ny.frb.org/rmaghome/search.html

With the purchase of a New Book*

You Can Access the Real Financial Data that the Experts Use!

*If you purchased a used book, see other side for access information.

This card entitles the purchaser of a new textbook to six months of access to the Educational Version of Standard & Poor's Market Insight®, a rich online resource featuring hundreds of the most often researched companies in the Market Insight database.

For 650 companies, this website provides you:

- Access to six years' worth of fundamental financial data from the renowned Standard & Poor's COMPUSTAT® database
- 12 Excel Analytics Reports, including balance sheets, income statements, ratio reports and cash flow statements; adjusted prices reports, and profitability; forecasted values and monthly valuation data reports
- Access to Financial Highlights Reports including key ratios
- S & P Stock Reports that offer fundamental, quantitative and technical analysis
- EDGAR reports updated throughout the day
- Industry Surveys, written by S & P's Equity analysts
- Charting, providing powerful, interactive JavaCharts with price and volume data, incorporating over 100 different technical studies, user-specific watch lists, easy to customize parameters and drawing tools. Delayed real time pricing available.
- News feeds (updated hourly) for companies and industries.

See other side for your unique site ID access code.

Welcome to the Educational Version of Market Insight!

www.mhhe.com/edumarketinsight

Check out your textbook's website for details on how this special offer enhances the value of your purchase!

1. To get started, use your web browser to go to
www.mhhe.com/edumarketinsight

2. Enter your site ID exactly as it appears below.

3. You may be prompted to enter the site ID for future
use—please keep this card.

Your site ID is:

ma12m357

STANDARD
&POOR'S

ISBN#   0-07-297424-9

Mc Graw Hill **McGraw-Hill Irwin**

*If you purchased a used book, this site ID may have expired.
For new password purchase, please go to
www.mhhe.com/edumarketinsight.
Password activation is good for a 6 month duration.

Bank Management & Financial Services

The McGraw-Hill/Irwin Series in Finance, Insurance and Real Estate

Stephen A. Ross
Franco Modigliani Professor of Finance and Economics
Sloan School of Management
Massachusetts Institute of Technology
Consulting Editor

FINANCIAL MANAGEMENT

Adair
Excel Applications for Corporate Finance
First Edition

Benninga and Sarig
Corporate Finance: A Valuation Approach

Block and Hirt
Foundations of Financial Management
Eleventh Edition

Brealey and Myers
Principles of Corporate Finance
Seventh Edition

Brealey, Myers and Marcus
Fundamentals of Corporate Finance
Fourth Edition

Brooks
FinGame Online 4.0

Bruner
Case Studies in Finance: Managing for Corporate Value Creation
Fourth Edition

Chew
The New Corporate Finance: Where Theory Meets Practice
Third Edition

Chew and Gillan
Corporate Governance at the Crossroads: A Book of Readings
First Edition

DeMello
Cases in Finance

Grinblatt and Titman
Financial Markets and Corporate Strategy
Second Edition

Helfert
Techniques of Financial Analysis: A Guide to Value Creation
Eleventh Edition

Higgins
Analysis for Financial Management
Seventh Edition

Kester, Ruback, and Tufano
Case Problems in Finance
Twelfth Edition

Ross, Westerfield and Jaffe
Corporate Finance
Seventh Edition

Ross, Westerfield and Jordan
Essentials of Corporate Finance
Fourth Edition

Ross, Westerfield and Jordan
Fundamentals of Corporate Finance
Sixth Edition

Smith
The Modern Theory of Corporate Finance
Second Edition

White
Financial Analysis with an Electronic Calculator
Fifth Edition

INVESTMENTS

Bodie, Kane and Marcus
Essentials of Investments
Fifth Edition

Bodie, Kane and Marcus
Investments
Sixth Edition

Cohen, Zinbarg and Zeikel
Investment Analysis and Portfolio Management
Fifth Edition

Corrado and Jordan
Fundamentals of Investments: Valuation and Management
Third Edition

Farrell
Portfolio Management: Theory and Applications
Second Edition

Hirt and Block
Fundamentals of Investment Management
Seventh Edition

FINANCIAL INSTITUTIONS AND MARKETS

Cornett and Saunders
Fundamentals of Financial Institutions Management

Rose and Hudgins
Bank Management and Financial Services
Sixth Edition

Rose
Money and Capital Markets: Financial Institutions and Instruments in a Global Marketplace
Eighth Edition

Santomero and Babbel
Financial Markets, Instruments, and Institutions
Second Edition

Saunders and Cornett
Financial Institutions Management: A Risk Management Approach
Fourth Edition

Saunders and Cornett
Financial Markets and Institutions: A Modern Perspective
Second Edition

INTERNATIONAL FINANCE

Beim and Calomiris
Emerging Financial Markets

Eun and Resnick
International Financial Management
Third Edition

Levich
International Financial Markets: Prices and Policies
Second Edition

REAL ESTATE

Brueggeman and Fisher
Real Estate Finance and Investments
Twelfth Edition

Corgel, Ling and Smith
Real Estate Perspectives: An Introduction to Real Estate
Fourth Edition

Ling and Archer
Real Estate Principles: A Value Approach
First Edition

FINANCIAL PLANNING AND INSURANCE

Allen, Melone, Rosenbloom and Mahoney
Pension Planning: Pension, Profit-Sharing, and Other Deferred Compensation Plans
Ninth Edition

Crawford
Life and Health Insurance Law
Eighth Edition (LOMA)

Harrington and Niehaus
Risk Management and Insurance
Second Edition

Hirsch
Casualty Claim Practice
Sixth Edition

Kapoor, Dlabay and Hughes
Personal Finance
Seventh Edition

Williams, Smith and Young
Risk Management and Insurance
Eighth Edition

Bank Management & Financial Services

Sixth Edition

Peter S. Rose
Texas A & M University

Sylvia C. Hudgins
Old Dominion University

McGraw-Hill
Irwin

Boston   Burr Ridge, IL   Dubuque, IA   Madison, WI   New York   San Francisco   St. Louis
Bangkok   Bogotá   Caracas   Kuala Lumpur   Lisbon   London   Madrid   Mexico City
Milan   Montreal   New Delhi   Santiago   Seoul   Singapore   Sydney   Taipei   Toronto

Irwin

BANK MANAGEMENT & FINANCIAL SERVICES
Published by McGraw-Hill/Irwin, a business unit of The McGraw-Hill Companies, Inc., 1221 Avenue of the
Americas, New York, NY, 10020. Copyright © 2005, 2002, 1999, by The McGraw-Hill Companies, Inc. All
rights reserved. No part of this publication may be reproduced or distributed in any form or by any means, or
stored in a database or retrieval system, without the prior written consent of The McGraw-Hill Companies,
Inc., including, but not limited to, in any network or other electronic storage or transmission, or broadcast for
distance learning.
Some ancillaries, including electronic and print components, may not be available to customers outside the
United States.

This book is printed on acid-free paper.

1 2 3 4 5 6 7 8 9 0 CCW/CCW 0 9 8 7 6 5 4

ISBN 0-07-286163-0

Vice president and editor-in-chief: *Robin J. Zwettler*
Publisher: *Stephen M. Patterson*
Editorial assistant: *Meghan Grosscup*
Executive marketing manager: *Rhonda Seelinger*
Senior media producer: *Anthony Sherman*
Project manager: *Charlie Fisher*
Senior production supervisor: *Sesha Bolisetty*
Designer: *Artemio Ortiz Jr.*
Senior supplement producer: *Susan Lombardi*
Senior digital content specialist: *Brian Nacik*
Cover design: *Asylum Studios*
Typeface: *10/12 Goudy*
Compositor: *Shepherd Inc.*
Printer: *Courier Westford*

Library of Congress Cataloging-in-Publication Data

Rose, Peter S.
    Bank management and financial services / Peter S. Rose, Sylvia C. Hudgins.—6th ed.
      p. cm.
    Rev. ed. of: Financial institutions. 5th ed. 1995.
    Includes bibliographical references and index.
    ISBN 0-07-286163-0 (alk. paper)
    1. Financial institutions—United States. 2. Bank management—United States. 3. Financial
services industry—United States. 4. Banks and banking, International. I. Hudgins, Sylvia
Conway, 1956– II. Rose, Peter S. Financial institutions. III. Title.
HG181.R65 2005
332.1'068—dc22
                                              2003071072

www.mhhe.com

To my family.
—Peter S. Rose

To those encouraging and influencing my studies and research in banking and financial institutions, especially: George Emir Morgan, III, the SunTrust Professor of Finance at Virginia Tech and the best dissertation advisor ever, for introducing me to this exciting field of study and directing my first research efforts; all my coauthors for providing motivation and new perspectives in research; and Peter S. Rose, the founding author of this text, for having confidence in my abilities and sharing his wealth of knowledge and experience as we transformed this book to address today's issues.

—Sylvia C. Hudgins

Brief Contents

Contents

PART THREE
MANAGING THE INVESTMENT
PORTFOLIOS AND LIQUIDITY
POSITIONS OF BANKS AND SIMILAR
FINANCIAL FIRMS   305

Chapter 9
The Investment Function in Banking
and Financial Services Management   307

Chapter 10
Liquidity and Reserve Management:
Strategies and Policies   347

PART FOUR
MANAGING THE SOURCES OF
FUNDS FOR BANKS AND THEIR
CLOSEST COMPETITORS   387

Chapter 11
Managing and Pricing Deposit
Services   389

Chapter 12
Managing Nondeposit Liabilities and Other
Sources of Borrowed Funds   423

PART SIX
THE PATH OF EXPANSION FOR BANKS AND COMPETING FINANCIAL-SERVICE PROVIDERS   643

Chapter 18
Creating and Managing Service Outlets: New Charters, Branches, and Electronic Facilities   645

Chapter 19
Mergers and Acquisitions: Managing the Process   675

Chapter 20
International Banking Service Options   705

Preface

Banks are the leaders of the financial-services industry. They are the place where we often wind up when we are seeking a loan to purchase a new automobile, tuition for college or a professional school, financial advice on how to invest our savings, credit to begin a new business, a safe deposit box to protect our most valuable documents, a checking account to pay for purchases of goods and services, or a credit or debit card so we can conveniently keep track of when and where we spend our money. Increasingly today, financial firms other than banks are selling us these same services, but banks still head the list of financial-service providers in many markets.

The banking industry, composed of thousands of private and state-owned companies worldwide, affects the welfare of every other industry and the economy as a whole. As many nations in Asia, Europe, and Latin America have recently discovered, when banks stop lending and stop accepting the risks that go with it, the rest of the economy often falls apart, with plunging land and security prices, lengthening unemployment lines, failing businesses, and bankrupt households.

The United States experienced, albeit temporarily, the effects of banking breakdown and its consequences for the daily functioning of the financial system when the tragedy of 9/11 struck the nation's leading financial center, New York City. The destruction of the World Trade Center temporarily shut down the critical back-office operations of several leading banking and securities firms, creating uncertainty in the minds of thousands of investors about the timely recovery of their invested funds. Fortunately, both the banks and security dealers themselves and the U.S. central bank, the Federal Reserve System, responded quickly to the crisis and, within days, restored key services and a measure of calm to the financial marketplace. Still, the shock and uncertainty in the wake of the World Trade Center's collapse helped to push the slowing U.S. economy into a recession. Let's face it: *Healthy banks and healthy economies just seem to go together.*

Today banking is an industry in change. Rather than being something in particular, it is continually becoming something *new*—offering new services, merging and consolidating into much larger and more complex businesses no longer easily recognized as just banks, adopting new technologies that seem to change faster than most of us can comprehend, and facing a changing set of rules as more and more nations cooperate to regulate and supervise the banks and other financial-service firms that serve their citizens.

While banks are certainly important to the proper functioning of the economy and are the leaders of the financial-services industry as a whole, that position of leadership is no longer secure. Banking firms are being challenged on all sides today by aggressive financial-service competitors, including security brokers and dealers like Merrill Lynch and Charles Schwab, insurance companies like Axa and Prudential, finance companies like Beneficial and Household Finance, mutual funds like Vanguard and T. Rowe Price, and thrift institutions like Washington Mutual and the USA Federal Credit Union. Banking's share of the financial-services industry has been falling for decades as nonbank competitors invade banking's traditional service lines one by one.

Indeed, studying the banking industry in isolation from the rest of the financial-services marketplace is no longer sufficient. Literally, banks and their financial-services competitors are rushing toward each other in the services they offer—a phenomenon called *convergence*. As financial-service industries converge, this movement blurs the meaning of the term *bank*, forcing many bankers to rethink what their future role should be in the rapidly changing financial-services sector.

Banking and many of its closest financial competitors are among the most heavily *regulated* businesses in the world. After all, they handle the public's money and plenty of sensitive nerve endings surround our pocketbooks! No one can start a bank or other, closely related financial firm without some government's permission to do so, and no one can close one of these institutions without the government's approval. The extensive rules that constrain the services, behavior, and performance of banks and other financial-service businesses, however, are also changing. Regulators looking over the financial sector today are paying more attention to the industry's risk and to signals of possible trouble from the private marketplace. We now seem to recognize that government rules and regulations can only do so much, and that private decision makers—businesses and consumers—can do as much or more to determine which banks and other financial-service providers are most accommodating and efficient and which should be allowed to fail (or, perhaps, be absorbed by other, better-managed financial institutions).

Banking and the financial-services industry are also changing as a place to find a *job*. Traditionally, bankers and their most aggressive competitors hired one of the biggest shares of business, finance, and economics majors graduating from colleges and universities each year. To be sure, financial-service companies remain important sources of career opportunities for people of all ages and backgrounds, but employment in banking and financial services is no longer among the growth leaders in the job market. Fewer people are needed as machines, such as automated tellers and personal computers, take over routine financial transactions.

After all, banks and their key financial-service competitors are neither more nor less than *information gatherers*. Writing a check, transferring funds by wire, applying for an insurance policy, selling shares of stock, or spending the proceeds of a loan to buy a new car involve simply moving information from one computer file or account to another, and, increasingly, automated equipment is carrying out these tasks faster, more accurately, and more conveniently than people can do by hand. So rapid is the switch to computers and other electronic devices among banks and their competitors that their operating costs are becoming more and more like fixed costs (i.e., the cost of purchasing and maintaining equipment) and less and less like variable costs (i.e., labor time).

This shift in banking and financial services toward more fixed costs and fewer variable costs has had dramatic effects on the optimal size bank or nonbank financial firm needed to achieve maximum operating efficiency (in terms of lowest-cost production and delivery of financial services). In a world that is increasingly automating services, bankers and the managers of other financial firms interested in competitive and sustained profits must increase their volume of operations, often by acquiring smaller financial firms that are less able to keep abreast of rapidly changing technology.

Then, too, electronic media are rapidly broadening the geographic extent of financial-service markets, leaping over state and national boundaries and bringing continents closer together. This unfolding technological trend brings thousands of bank and nonbank financial firms into direct competition with each other, creating the need for fewer financial-service providers overall. The industry finds itself in a wave of *consolidation*—giant bank and nonbank service providers are emerging from numerous megamergers and smaller institutions are disappearing through consolidations and acquisitions. There is much less room today all over the globe for the small, locally owned bank or nonbank financial firm, though many of these institutions continue to survive and prosper by finding niches for fulfilling special service needs that the industry's giants ignore, overlook, or cannot do quite as well. Examples include personalized services for the aging consumer, small business financing, and personal financial advice from managers and employees willing to take the time to listen to each customer's unique service requirements.

Despite all the epic changes sweeping through this vital industry, some things in banking and financial services never seem to change. It is (and probably always will be) a service industry, producing an intangible product that is hard (some say, impossible) to differentiate from the products offered by competitors. One financial-service provider's deposit account, credit card, or loan looks pretty much like the deposit, credit card, and loan offered by another. However, accuracy, friendliness, and quality of service vary from financial institution to financial institution in most market areas.

Unlike many other jobs in private industry and government, the financial-services business requires both technical skills and people skills, rather than just one or the other. Bankers and many of their competitors are often heard to say: "It's a relationship business." People come to trust the bank or nonbank financial firm they deal with and rely upon its honesty, reliability, and stability when they need financial guidance, and they routinely expect courtesy no matter the nature or source of a problem.

Financial-service managers can never stop learning because their industry is literally becoming something *new* every day, and their customers expect them to be "ahead of the curve," financially speaking, no matter how fast things appear to be changing. What an exciting and dynamic area to study! What an adventure!

New and Continuing Developments in This Sixth Edition

As *Bank Management and Financial Services* enters its sixth edition, the changing world of financial services has compelled the authors to make important and significant changes in this new edition in a continuing race to keep up with (and sometimes look just ahead of) the dynamic financial-services industry. Among the most important new or expanded topics and instructional aids in the text are the following:

- The new text offers a significantly expanded discussion of the roles and services offered by banking's chief competitors—the *nonbank financial-service providers*, including security brokers and dealers, finance and insurance companies, thrift institutions, and financial conglomerates. Banks continue to lose market share to many of these aggressive nonbank service firms, and both bank and nonbank firms continue to invade each other's traditional service lines. No consideration of the great issues in the management and regulation of banks would be complete without a parallel discussion of the nonbank financial firms that challenge banks for leadership of the financial-services sector in thousands of local markets around the globe. Nonbank financial firms are discussed in nearly every chapter with a special emphasis on these aggressive competitors with banks in Chapters 1, 2, 3, 5, 11, 13, 16, 17, 19, and 20.

- An expanded discussion of the Gramm-Leach-Bliley (GLB or Financial Services Modernization) Act appears throughout the text. This 1999 law allows banking firms to form highly diversified (one-stop shopping) financial-service conglomerates, linking up with security brokers and dealers, insurance companies, and other financial firms under a single corporate umbrella. The GLB Act has opened up huge new issues of its own, such as how to efficiently and effectively regulate combinations of large bank and nonbank businesses and still preserve the safety net protecting depositors. GLB has also resulted in the creation of a new organizational form—the financial holding company (FHC), similar to the universal banking conglomerates that have existed in Europe for decades. Discussion of the Gramm-Leach-Bliley Act and its impact on banking and financial services appears in many places in the new edition, but especially in Chapters 2, 3, 13, and 19.

- An exploration of the increasingly important field of *ethics* in banking and financial services is introduced in multiple chapters of this new edition. The financial markets have been rocked by scandal in the most recent period as the CEOs and CFOs of several major corporations have been accused of preparing false or exaggerated financial reports and lining their own pockets at the expense of employees and investors, sometimes aided in these endeavors by the banking and security firms advising them. The result has been numerous federal and state investigations, stiff fines levied by the Securities and Exchange Commission, and passage of the *Sarbanes-Oxley Accounting Standards Act* in 2002 to require key officers of publicly traded companies (including banks and non-bank financial-service corporations) to attest to the accuracy of their firms' financial reports and avoid the dissemination of misleading information that might damage the interests of employees and investors in the firm's securities. The Sarbanes-Oxley law is discussed at some length in Chapter 2, and questions of ethics are raised throughout the text in a series of boxes, *"Ethics in Banking,"* which discuss banking and business practices and their moral implications.

- Along with the new accounting standards law, another new piece of legislation, the *Patriot Act* of 2001, has aroused controversy in the United States and in Europe where similar legislation has appeared. The Patriot Act is yet another consequence of the terrible 9/11 tragedy, which took so many lives and caused such great turmoil and uncertainty in the financial marketplace. The privacy of citizens and their dealings with banks and other financial-service providers has come under closer scrutiny. Banks and selected other financial firms are now compelled to establish the identities of customers opening new accounts, check their names against a government-supplied list of suspected terrorists and terrorist organizations, and report any suspicious activity on the part of customers to government authorities. The new law caught many financial-service providers by surprise and, for some institutions, necessitated substantial new investments in their recordkeeping and reporting functions. Issues raised by passage of the Patriot Act appear in several places in the text, but especially in Chapter 2 dealing with regulation.

- There is greater emphasis on *investment banking* and *security underwriting services*—one of the hottest topics in modern banking—in this new edition. Leading investment banking firms and their services are discussed and the possible conflicts of interest between commercial and investment banking are explored in greater depth than ever before. Among the most prominent of these additions surfaces in Chapter 13 where the investment banking industry is profiled and key ethical and regulatory issues are examined. Further discussion of investment banks and their interactions with commercial banks appear in Chapters 1, 2, 3, 19, and 20.

- There is expanded coverage of several uniquely important dimensions of today's bank environment, including trends in the demand for and profitability of *credit and debit cards* (Chapter 17), the controversial rise of *subprime lending* (Chapter 17), the increased use of *cash flow analysis* and *cash flow statements* in business lending decisions (Chapters 15 and 16), the expanding roles played by *futures, options, and credit derivatives* in risk management banking (Chapters 7 and 8), the increased reliance on such liquidity sources as the *Federal funds market, repurchase agreements (RPs)*, and *Federal Home Loan Bank (FHLB) loans* (Chapters 10 and 12), and the *spread of international banking activities into such key areas of the world as China, Japan, Latin America, and Russia* (Chapter 20).

- A major expansion of *new and updated problems and projects* stands out in this newest edition. A completely new set of projects and problems to solve, *"Real Numbers for Real Banks,"* spans multiple chapters, offering the reader interesting problems and issues to resolve as his or her knowledge of banking and financial services grows from chapter to chapter. The reader is asked to choose from a list of leading banking companies and, in subsequent chapters, to analyze that same banking firm's organization and structure, financial condition, behavior, and performance and to compare its financial profile to that of peer institutions.

- Also included in end-of-chapter material for all 20 chapters are problems and projects drawn from the Standard & Poor's Market Insight, Educational Version database, which contains the financial statements of leading banking and nonbank financial firms as well as major corporations outside the financial sector. The Market Insight questions and problems encourage the reader to gather detailed information about some of the largest financial firms in the world and to use that information to reach important conclusions.

- Not only have the boxes *Banking and Financial Services on the Net* been retained in every chapter of this newest edition, but also multiple key URLs are cited in the margins of every chapter. These important Web citations are supplemented by interesting facts about the banking and financial services industry, labeled *factoids*, and an intriguing set of questions and answers about banking and finance in popular movies, called *filmtoids*, that also appear in the margins of the chapters in this new edition.

- There is a renewed emphasis in the text on *real-world management actions, decisions,* and *problems,* illustrating the management principles presented in each chapter. Boxes throughout the text, *Real Banks, Real Decisions,* discuss actual problems banking and financial-service managers have been forced to deal with recently and how their decisions have worked out in practice.

- The continuing rush toward electronic banking is covered much more extensively in this new edition, reflecting the growing acceptance of online banking by millions of customers. Boxes titled *E-Banking and E-Commerce* appear in numerous chapters, discussing what banks and their closest competitors have accomplished in the electronic field and the benefits and costs of this rapidly unfolding movement. The services offered online and their production costs and risks are discussed, along with new information on Web-based banks. Among the most important chapters addressing the subject of electronic banking are Chapters 1, 2, 3, 17, and 18.

- The current issue of *reform of the federal deposit insurance system* and the proposed *restructuring of the federal regulatory system* is covered in this new edition, including a discussion of the recently proposed increase in U.S. deposit insurance coverage and its possible ramifications for the safety of depositors and the potential cost for taxpayers. The text discusses the links between proposals to more efficiently configure the regulatory system and the changing structure of the banking and financial services industry itself, marked by declining numbers of financial-service providers and greatly increased size of surviving financial firms. These issues are especially evident in Chapters 1, 2, 3, 11, and 14.

- The latest proposals for *reform of the international regulations surrounding bank capital* (known as *Basel II*) surface in Chapter 14 where the weaknesses of the existing capital rules are examined and the possible advantages and disadvantages of the new and revised Basel accord are explored.

- The text also examines the new rules for *borrowing from the Federal Reserve banks' discount window* and discusses the rationale for the Fed's recent opening of the discount window for greater access by financially sound depository institutions as laid out in a newly revised Regulation A of the Federal Reserve Board. This topic is discussed in Chapter 2 and, in more depth, in Chapter 12.

The changes and additions listed above are only part of the many differences between this new sixth edition and those editions that have gone before. The authors hope the new text will more fully meet the needs of teachers, students, professional bankers and financial-service managers, and others who have an interest in the banking and financial services industry and the sweeping changes that are rapidly transforming the financial sector of today's economy.

Pedagogical Features

Several unique and important educational aids are included in this new edition to assist readers and instructors in understanding and presenting the story of the banking and financial-services industry. Among them are the following:

- *Part openers* introduce each of the six major parts of the text. These openers explain the basic content and the goals of each part, summarizing a few key points that will emerge as the reader explores each of the chapters.

- An *Introduction* to each chapter explains why the chapter the reader is about to enter is important to understanding the management principles for banks and other closely related financial-service providers and for understanding the many trends sweeping through the industry.

- A box entitled "*Banking and Financial Services on the Net*" is positioned near the opening of every chapter, listing several websites that could help the reader more fully understand the information presented in each chapter.

- *Key URLs* also appear at various places in the margins of each chapter, providing the reader with the addresses of more finely tuned information sources available on the Web.

- *Factoids* are also margin notes, containing facts and interesting bits of background information about recent conditions or developments in the banking and financial-services sector. Supplementing these are *Filmtoids* that describe recent popular motion pictures that have banking and financial-service themes associated with the chapter where they are found.

- *Boxes of information* appear in every chapter of the new edition, providing more detail on recent developments shaping the structure and performance of banks and their financial-service competitors. These boxes of special information have several titles, including "*Real Banks, Real Decisions,*" which discuss banks and bankers faced with tough management decisions; "*Ethics in Banking,*" which explore moral dilemmas that bankers and other members of the financial-services community have faced; "*E-Banking and E-Commerce,*" which describe the many interesting problems banks and other financial firms have encountered as they offer more and more services online; and "*Insights and Issues,*" which cover a wide array of practical and conceptual issues that modern banking and the financial marketplace have encountered in recent years.

- In order to test the readers' understanding, *Concept Checks* appear at selected points in each chapter, raising questions and problems to ensure that readers have mastered what has been presented to that point. There are many more of these in the new edition.

- *Key Terms* are listed at the conclusion of each chapter along with the page numbers where these terms appear and where they are defined within the text. Very often the full understanding of banking and the financial-services sector depends heavily on knowing the terminology of the financial marketplace.

- To help master the key terms listed in each chapter, a *Dictionary of Banking and Financial-Service Terms* appears at the back of the book with definitions of each term.

- Immediately following each chapter's text material is a convenient and crisp bulleted *Summary* of the chapter's content and main conclusions. These chapter summaries allow readers to conduct a quick review of all they have learned and fill in any gaps that might have been left unexplored along the way.

- After the chapter summary and key terms list, an extensive group of *Problems and Projects* appears that offers both numerical problems and questions of management and policy. The collection of problems and projects has been greatly expanded in this new edition to include several new items that promote the use of key data banks, such as those provided in Standard & Poor's Market Insight, Educational Version and in the extensive website maintained by the Federal Deposit Insurance Corporation.

  A major new feature within this section is the *Real Numbers for Real Banks* series in which readers are asked to choose a representative firm from a list of leading banking and financial companies. They are then encouraged to analyze and evaluate that company's performance and behavior from several points of view as the chapters go by and new analytical tools are acquired. Assignments in the *Real Numbers for Real Banks* series in Chapters 1 through 5 provide the foundation for a semester-long project. Assignments from all other chapters are independent and reference only the foundational chapters. This gives instructors numerous opportunities to reaffirm what their students have learned about real-world banks and financial firms by assigning an ongoing project that gradually unfolds with each new chapter.

  Also within the problems and projects section at chapter's end are *Internet Exercises*, significantly expanded from the previous edition, where the reader is encouraged to visit the World Wide Web as often as possible and respond to problems and issues affecting banks and their financial-service competitors. Each Internet exercise supplies one or more key websites to help the reader get started toward resolving the questions raised.

- Numerous *diagrams*, *exhibits*, *tables*, and *real-world examples* from the banking and financial-services industry are integrated throughout the text to help clarify the most significant points.

- A list of *Selected References* appears on the final pages of each chapter, arrayed by topic so the reader can gain additional information from other sources and from different points of view about important subjects that were covered in the chapter just concluded.

- Finally, a new *Appendix on the use of a financial calculator* appears at the end of the text, illustrating for users of the book how to calculate the time value of money (TVM), present and future values of cash flows (PV and FV), and the annual percentage rate (APR) on a loan. These basic calculator routines will assist the reader in solving numerous problems that appear throughout the text.

The authors hope that the above-mentioned learning and teaching tools will prove to be of great service to the readers of this text and to those who carry the important responsibility of teaching others.

Supplementary Materials

Useful supplements increase the educational power of this new edition. Among the key supplementary educational materials available are the following:

- *Instructor's Manual and Test Bank,* which outlines each chapter and supplies hundreds of questions to answer and problems to solve that help greatly in the construction of exams and learning material for classroom activities.

- A *PowerPoint Presentation System*, which presents clear and concise slides to use in the classroom or as study notes outside the classroom. The PowerPoint slides include charts, graphs, and numerical examples along with summaries and outlines of key points made in the text. Users can rearrange or edit each slide to meet their own specific educational needs.

- A *website* that goes with the text and can be accessed by both students and teachers. The website includes chapter updates for users of *Bank Management & Financial Services* as the environment in the financial-services sector changes and new challenges appear. The chapter updates help keep the book fresh and new. The website's Internet address is www.mhhe.com/rose6e.

- *Standard & Poor's Market Insight, Educational Version*, which supplies extensive financial data and other items for 500 of the largest corporations, including leading commercial banks and other firms in the financial-services sector. This important database helps users solve several of the problem assignments in the new edition and do research on companies in which they have a special interest (for example: in order to prepare for a job interview or to put together a report for class). This website's Internet address is www.mhhe.com/edumarketinsight.

Acknowledgments

The authors have benefited in many ways from the criticisms and ideas of professionals and experts in the banking and financial services field. Several well-qualified professionals have read and criticized the text as it has progressed through this and earlier editions.

These committed and talented individuals include

Oliver G. Wood, Jr.
University of South Carolina

Edwin Cox
Boston University

James E. McNulty
Florida Atlantic University

Tony Cherin
San Diego State University

Edward C. Lawrence
The University of Missouri, St. Louis

James B. Kehr
Miami University

Emile J. Brinkmann
The University of Houston

David G. Martin
Bloomsberg University

David R. Durst
The University of Akron

Nelson J. Lacey
The University of Massachusetts–Amherst

William Sackley
The University of Southern Mississippi

Iqbal Memon
Fort Lewis College

David Rand
Northwest Tech College in Ohio

Jack Griggs
Abilene Christian University

Lyle L. Bowlin
University of Northern Iowa

George W. Kutner
Marquette University

Armand Picou
University of Central Arkansas

Sudhir Singh
Frostberg State University

The authors wish to express a special note of gratitude to those who helped with their comments and suggestions in the construction of this sixth edition, including Samuel Bulmash of Stockton College; David Stewart of Winston-Salem State University; George Kutner of Marquette University; Fuad Abdullah of University of Nebraska–Omaha; Young Kwak of Delaware State University; and James McNulty of Florida Atlantic University.

A special thank you also goes to Andreas Rauterkus of Siena College for the accompanying PowerPoint slides and for authoring the all-important *Instructor's Manual*. The authors also wish to thank George Kutner of Marquette University for developing the Test Bank.

A note of gratitude must also be extended to *The Canadian Banker* and the Canadian Bankers' Association for permission to use earlier articles, penned by one of the authors and published originally in *The Canadian Banker*.

The writers are likewise in debt to Steve Patterson, Jennifer Rizzi, Christina Kouvelis, and Meghan Grosscup as well as other Irwin/McGraw-Hill editors and editorial assistants for their first-class ideas, their inspired design and production work, and their high degree of professionalism in taking this new edition from its starting point to the finish line. Any demerits and deficiencies remaining in this text must be attributed to the authors.

A Note to the Student

The banking and financial-services sector of our economy represents one of those indispensable subjects about which few of us can afford to be ignorant. As recent problems in the domestic and global economies have demonstrated, our lifestyles and living standards often depend heavily on the willingness of banks and other financial-service firms to extend credit, deposits, savings and retirement plans, and other financial services to us as individuals and to the businesses and institutions we work for and trade with. But banking and the financial-services industry are changing so rapidly today that we cannot be content with merely a casual inquiry.

This book is designed to help you dig deeply into this fascinating and frequently trouble-plagued sector of the economy in order to master established management principles and to confront head-on the perplexing issues of risk, regulation, technology, and competition that bankers and other financial-service managers see as their greatest challenges for the future.

The text contains a number of pedagogical aids to help you accomplish this task, especially these:

1. Each major part of the text begins with a *Part Opener* to explain the goals and key topics covered by the chapters in that part. In a sense, each part opener provides a road map of what lies ahead in the following group of chapters.

2. Each chapter begins with its own *Introduction* to set the stage for you on what is to follow and to explain the importance of the topics and issues presented.

3. Numerous Internet references are provided in a box near the front of each chapter, "*Banking and Financial Services on the Net,*" and in the form of *Key URLs* that appear in chapter margins throughout the text.

4. Interesting facts and background information appear as *Factoids* and *Filmtoids* in the margins of all the chapters.

5. *Concept Checks* appear in every chapter at crucial points to allow you to determine whether you have reached a satisfactory level of understanding of the material presented thus far before you proceed onto another topic.

6. Each chapter ends with a bulleted *Summary* that lists the key points made and the conclusions reached in order to provide you with a convenient review of the material.

7. Following the chapter summary, *Key Terms* appear to help you learn the language of banking and the financial marketplace. Each term is followed by its page number in the text so you can readily discover where that term is discussed and defined.

8. A *Dictionary of Banking and Financial-Service Terms* can be found at the end of the book to supply brief definitions for all key terms. When you are assigned a specific chapter or set of chapters to read, you can double-check your understanding of the key terms in the text by using the dictionary.

9. Several types of problems and questions to resolve appear near the conclusion of each chapter, carrying various labels—*Problems and Projects*, *S&P Market Insight Challenge*, *Internet Exercises*, and *Real Numbers for Real Banks*. You will find these especially helpful in cementing what you have learned and in discovering new facets of the topics you have explored in the chapter just completed. Your instructor may assign some of these problems and projects to help you strengthen your knowledge and apply that knowledge to realistic situations.

10. Several boxes of information—for example, *"Issues and Insights," "Real Banks, Real Decisions," "E-Banking and E-Commerce,"* and *"Ethics in Banking"*—appear throughout the text, some of them in every chapter. Their purpose is to offer new ideas and raise practical issues that bankers and other financial-service managers must grapple with every day, thereby giving you a better feel for what happens in the real world.

11. Finally, a new appendix, *Using a Financial Calculator,* appears at the end of the book to aid in solving quickly many of the end-of-chapter problems and exercises in this new edition.

While this book presents several devices to help you along the way, like every other textbook it is locked in time. It presents a snapshot picture of an industry that is rapidly changing—a service industry that may soon be very different from what we understand it to be today. Therefore your journey toward understanding banks and their financial-service competitors cannot end here. A central mission of this book is to arouse your interest in banking and financial-service practices and problems. If *Bank Management & Financial Services* makes you want to read and understand more about this critical sector of the economy, it will have done its job.

This is a field where the amount of personal effort and your feeling of accomplishment are closely correlated, both in the near term and for a lifetime. Confidence, determination, and careful study usually pay off, no matter what twists and turns the future may bring. Best wishes for success on your journey into the fascinating marketplace of modern banking and financial services.

Peter S. Rose and Sylvia C. Hudgins

Bank Management & Financial Services

Introduction to the Business of Banking and Financial-Services Management

Opening this book launches us on a grand adventure, learning about one of the oldest and most important industries in the world. Banking includes some of the largest business firms ever created—behemoths like Citibank and Bank of America in the United States, Toronto-Dominion Bank in Canada, Deutsche Bank in Germany, and Barclays PLC in Great Britain—and also some of the smallest businesses to open their doors, such as Heritage Bank in Bozeman, Montana.

Banking has a profound effect on our lives, influencing the availability of jobs, the cost of living, and our savings for the future.

However, banking as we know it today is rapidly becoming a quite different industry than in the past. All over the world banks are converging with insurance companies, security dealers, finance companies, and other financial competitors into huge holding companies, proliferating the number of services they offer and capturing many new markets. Banks and many of their competitors are declining in number as the industry consolidates into fewer but larger companies that may be more efficient and more failure resistant. Although banking services are crucial elements of support for our financial system, the structure of firms offering these services is continuously changing. The banking industry has been invaded by firms from several other industries.

For example, if you want a credit card today to make purchases of goods and services you can find what you're looking for at such retail-oriented firms as Sears or from a major securities firm like Fidelity or Merrill Lynch. If you want a personal loan you can easily find one at thousands of credit unions, finance companies, savings associations, and scores of other lending institutions. If you are computer oriented and want to access financial services over the Internet, virtual banks and scores of other financial-service vendors wait there for you, reflecting the fact that the entire financial-services sector is undergoing a wave of technological change. Instead of focusing just on banking today, we must expand our focus somewhat to view banking within the financial-services industry.

Hang on, then, because this rapidly changing industry is about to unfold before us. In this part we discover banking's origins, explore its range of services, identify its key competitors, and see what career opportunities may await you if you enjoy learning about today's financial-services environment. We also explore the important role of government in regulating and interacting with banks and their competitors and discover how banking and other financial firms are organized today. We introduce you to the most important sources of financial-services information so you can explore well beyond the pages of this book. This opening part also dissects bank financial statements—how they are built and what they can tell us—and explains how to evaluate the financial condition and performance of banks and some of their closest competitors. We welcome you on this important journey and hope you find it interesting and useful for the future.

CHAPTER ONE

An Overview of Banks and the Financial-Services Sector

Key Topics in This Chapter

- Powerful Forces Reshaping the Industry
- What Is a Bank?
- Competing Financial-Service Institutions
- Old and New Services Offered
- Different Types of Banks
- Are Traditional Banks Dead?

Introduction

There is an old joke attributed to comedian Bob Hope that says "a bank is a financial institution where you can borrow money only if you can prove you don't need it." Although many of a bank's borrowing customers may get the impression that that old joke is more truth than fiction, the real story is that banks today readily provide hundreds of different services to millions of people, businesses, and governments all over the world. And many of these financial services are absolutely vital to our personal well-being, our future success, and the well-being of the communities and nations where we live.

Banks are the principal source of credit (loanable funds) for millions of individuals and families and for many units of government (school districts, cities, counties, etc.). Moreover, for small businesses ranging from grocery stores to automobile dealers, banks are often the major source of credit to stock the shelves with merchandise or to fill a dealer's lot with new cars. When businesses and consumers must make payments for purchases of goods and services, more often than not they use bank-supplied checks, credit or debit cards, or electronic accounts accessible through a bank's website. And when they need financial information and financial advice, it is the banker to whom they turn most frequently for advice and counsel.

Worldwide, banks grant more installment loans to consumers (individuals and families) than any other financial-service institution. In most years, they are among the leading buyers of bonds and notes governments issue to finance public facilities, ranging from auditoriums and football stadiums to airports and highways. Banks are among the most important sources of short-term working capital for businesses and have become increasingly active in recent years in making long-term business loans to fund the purchase of new plant and equipment. The assets held by U.S. banks represent about one-fifth of the total assets and a slightly larger proportion of the earnings of all U.S.-based financial-service institutions. In other nations—for example, in Japan—banks hold close to two-thirds of all assets in their domestic financial system. The difference is because in the United States, many different financial-service providers can and do compete to meet the needs of businesses, consumers, and governments.

Powerful Forces Are Reshaping the Banking Industry Today

As we begin our study of this important industry and its financial-service competitors, we should keep in mind the great forces that are reshaping both banking and the whole financial-services sector. Most banks today are profitable—and, in fact, in several recent quarters they have posted record earnings—but their *market share* of the financial-services marketplace is falling quite significantly. As the chairman of the Federal Deposit Insurance Corporation noted recently, in 1980 insured commercial banks and other depository financial institutions held more than 90 percent of Americans' money—a share that had dropped to only about 45 percent by 2001. Over the same time span, banks' and other depositories' share of U.S. credit market liabilities fell from about 45 percent of the grand total to only about 25 percent.[1]

Factoid
What nation has the greatest number of commercial banks?
Answer: The United States with about 8,000 commercial banks, followed by Germany.

The industry is also *consolidating* rapidly with substantially fewer, but much larger, banks and other financial firms. For example, the number of U.S. commercial banks fell from about 14,000 to just under 8,000 between 1980 and 2002. The number of separately incorporated commercial banks in the United States has now reached the lowest level in more than a century, and much the same pattern of industry consolidation appears around the globe in both bank and nonbank financial-service industries.

Moreover, banking is rapidly *globalizing* and facing *intense competition* in marketplace after marketplace around the planet, not only from other banks, but also from security dealers, insurance companies, credit unions, finance companies, and thousands of other financial-service competitors. These financial heavyweights are all *converging* toward each other, offering parallel services and slugging it out for the public's attention. If this were not enough to keep any industry in turmoil, banking and its financial-service neighbors are undergoing a *technological revolution* as the management of information and the production and distribution of financial services becomes increasingly electronic.

Clearly, if we are to understand this dynamic industry and its financial-service competitors and see where they all are headed, we have our work cut out for us. But, then, you always wanted to tackle a big challenge—right?

What Is a Bank?

As important as banks are to the economy as a whole and to the local communities they call home, there is still much confusion about what exactly a **bank** is. A *bank* can be defined in terms of (1) the economic functions it serves, (2) the services it offers its customers, or (3) the legal basis for its existence.

---

[1] See, for example, Donald E. Powell, Chairman of the Federal Deposit Insurance Corporation, "South America and Emerging Risks in Banking," Speech to the Florida Bankers Association, Orlando, FL, October 23, 2002.

Banking's presence on the World Wide Web has exploded recently, with thousands of banks utilizing their own individual websites and hundreds of websites tracking financial-service industry trends.

If, after reading this introductory chapter or after finishing this course, you think you might have an interest in a banking or financial-services career, you can check out several websites on the jobs available in this industry and just waiting for the right person to come along. For example, **www.careers-in-finance.com/cb.htm** not only contains a section about jobs in banking and related financial services, but also discusses the history of banking and important trends in the banking industry. See also the Bank Administration Institute Career Center at **www.bankjobsearch.com**.

You can find additional information about banking's history and changing makeup on the popular website maintained by the Federal Deposit Insurance Corporation (FDIC), **www.fdic.gov**, where you can learn about the history of deposit insurance and the FDIC itself.

If you want to know what services your bank or other financial-service provider offers, you can easily check its website by simply entering the full name (and city, state, and country if that name is not particularly unique). If this path isn't helpful for a particular bank operating inside the United States, you may wish to consult the FDIC's website on individual U.S.-insured banks at **www.fdic.gov/bank/index.html**, to determine the bank's correct name, headquarters location, and certificate number.

Banking's principal financial-service competitors have also entered cyberspace in large numbers. See, for example, the World Council of Credit Unions at **www.woccu.org**. Web-listed information about savings banks and savings and loan associations is available through their principal U.S. regulator, the Office of Thrift Supervision, at **www.ots.treas.gov**, and different money market funds can be explored by visiting **www.smartmoney.com**. Ample information about insurance companies is available from the American Council of Life Insurance at **www.acli.com** and the Insurance Information Institute at **www.iii.org**. Mutual funds (investment companies) also have an extensive Web presence and an educational organization, the Investment Company Institute that can be found at **www.ici.org**. Finally, you can learn much about one of the newest financial competitors, hedge funds, by consulting the Securities and Exchange Commission's website at **www.sec.gov/answers/hedge.htm**. As is the case with banks, you may also find a great deal of information about nonbank financial-service providers simply by calling up the name of each financial firm and the city of its headquarters location.

Certainly banks can be identified by the *functions* they perform in the economy. They are involved in transferring funds from savers to borrowers (financial intermediation) and in paying for goods and services.

Historically, banks have been recognized for the great range of financial services they offer—from checking accounts and savings plans to loans for businesses, consumers, and governments. However bank service menus are expanding rapidly today to include security trading and underwriting, insurance protection, financial planning, the management of pension plans, advice for merging companies, and numerous other innovative services. Banks no longer limit their service offerings to traditional banking services but have increasingly become general financial-service providers.

Unfortunately in our quest to identify what a bank is, we will soon discover that not only are the functions and services of banks changing within the global financial system, but their principal competitors are going through great changes as well. Indeed, many financial-service institutions—including leading security dealers, brokerage firms, credit unions, thrift institutions, mutual funds, and insurance companies—are trying to be as similar to banks as possible in the services they offer. Examples include Merrill Lynch, Dreyfus Corporation, and Prudential Insurance—all of which own banks or banklike firms. Moreover, if this were not confusing enough, several famous retailing and industrial companies have stepped forward in recent decades to offer loans, credit cards, savings plans,

EXHIBIT 1–1

The Different Kinds of Financial-Service Firms Calling Themselves *Banks*

Name of Banking-Type Firm	Definition or Description
Commercial banks: Sell deposits and make loans to businesses and individuals
Savings banks: Attract savings deposits and make loans to individuals and families
Cooperative banks: Help farmers, ranchers, and consumers acquire goods and services
Mortgage banks: Provide mortgage loans on new homes and housing projects
Community banks: Are smaller, locally focused commercial and savings banks
Money center banks: Are large commercial banks based in leading financial centers
Investment banks: Underwrite issues of new securities by their customers
Merchant banks: Supply both debt and equity capital to businesses
International banks: Are commercial banks present in more than one nation
Wholesale banks: Are larger commercial banks serving corporations and governments
Retail banks: Are smaller banks serving primarily households and small businesses
Bankers' banks: Supply services (e.g., check clearing and security trading) to banks
Minority banks: Focus primarily on customers belonging to minority groups
National banks: Function under a federal charter through the Comptroller of the Currency
State banks: Function under charters issued by banking commissions in the various states
Insured banks: Maintain deposits backed by federal deposit insurance plans (e.g., the FDIC)
Member banks: Belong to the Federal Reserve System
Affiliated banks: Are wholly or partially owned by a holding company
Fringe banks: Offer payday and title loans, cash checks, or operate as pawn shops and rent-to-own firms
Universal banks: Offer virtually all financial services available in today's marketplace.

and other traditional banking services. Examples of these giant banking-market invaders include General Motors Acceptance Corporation (GMAC), GE Capital, and Ford Motor Credit, to name only a few.

Bankers have not taken this invasion of their turf lying down. They are demanding relief from traditional rules and lobbying for expanded authority to reach into new markets all around the globe. For example, with large U.S. banks lobbying heavily, the United States Congress passed the Financial Services Modernization Act of 1999 (known more popularly as the Gramm-Leach-Bliley or GLB Act after its Congressional sponsors), allowing U.S. banks to enter the securities and insurance industries and permitting nonbank holding companies to acquire and control banking firms.

To add to the prevailing uncertainty about what a bank is, over the years literally dozens of organizations have emerged from the competitive financial marketplace proudly bearing the label of *bank*. As Exhibit 1–1 shows, for example, there are savings banks, investment banks, mortgage banks, fringe banks, merchant banks, bankers' banks, universal banks, and so on and on. In this text we will spend most of our time focused upon the most important of all banking institutions—the commercial bank—which serves both business and household customers all over the world. However, the management principles and concepts we will explore in the chapters that follow apply to many different kinds of "banks" as well as to other financial-service institutions that now provide banklike services.

One final note in our search for the definition of *banks* concerns the *legal basis* for their existence. When the federal government of the United States decided that it would regulate and supervise banks more than a century ago, it had to define what was and what was not a bank for purposes of enforcing its rules. After all, if you plan to regulate banks you have to write down a specific description of what they are—otherwise, the regulated firms can easily escape their regulators, claiming they aren't really banks at all!

The government finally settled on the definition still used by many nations today: A *bank is any business offering deposits subject to withdrawal on demand* (such as by writing a check or making an electronic transfer of funds) *and making loans of a commercial or business*

A BRIEF HISTORY OF BANKING AND OTHER FINANCIAL-SERVICE FIRMS

As best we can tell from historical records, *banking* is the oldest of all financial-service professions. Where did these powerful financial institutions come from?

Linguistics (the science of language) and *etymology* (the study of word origins) tell us that the French word *banque* and the Italian *banca* were used centuries ago to refer to a "bench" or "money changer's table." This describes quite well what historians have observed about the first bankers, who offered their services more than 2,000 years ago. They were money changers, situated usually at a table in the commercial district of a city, aiding travelers by exchanging foreign coins for local money or discounting commercial notes for a fee in order to supply other merchants with working capital.

The earliest bankers pledged a lot of their own money to support these early ventures, but it wasn't long before the idea of attracting deposits from wealthy customers and loaning out those same funds to other businesses emerged. Loans were granted to shippers, landowners, and others at interest rates as low as 6 percent to as high as 48 percent a month for the riskiest ventures! Most of the early banks were Greek in origin.

The banking industry gradually spread from the classical civilizations of Greece and Rome into northern and western Europe. It encountered religious opposition during the Middle Ages primarily because loans to the poor often carried high interest rates. However, as the Middle Ages drew to a close and the Renaissance began in Europe, the bulk of bank loans and deposits involved wealthy customers, which helped to reduce religious objections.

The development of new overland trade routes and improvements in navigation in the 15th, 16th, and 17th centuries gradually shifted the center of world commerce from the Mediterranean region toward Europe and the British Isles, where banking became a leading industry. During this period, the seeds of the Industrial Revolution, which demanded a well-developed financial system, were planted. The adoption of mass production required an expansion in global trade to absorb industrial output, which in turn required new methods for making payments and obtaining credit. Banks that could deliver on these needs grew rapidly, led by such institutions as the Medici Bank in Italy and the Hochstetter Bank in Germany.

The early banks in Europe were places for the safekeeping of valuables (such as gold and silver) as people came to fear loss of their assets due to war, theft, or expropriation by government. Merchants shipping goods across the seas found it safer to place their payments of gold and silver in the nearest bank rather than risking loss to pirates or storms at sea. In England government efforts to seize private holdings resulted in people depositing their valuables in goldsmiths' shops, which issued tokens or certificates indicating that the customer had made a deposit. Soon, goldsmith certificates began to circulate as money because they were more convenient and less risky to carry around than gold or other valuables. The goldsmiths also offered *certification of value* services—what we today might call property appraisal. Customers would bring in their valuables to have an expert certify that these items were, indeed, real and not fakes.

When colonies were established in North and South America, Old World banking practices were transferred to the New World. At first the colonists dealt primarily with established banks in the countries from which they had come. Later, state governments in the United States began chartering banking companies. The U.S. federal government became a major force in banking during the Civil War. The Office of the Comptroller of the Currency (OCC) was established in 1864, created by the U.S. Congress to charter *national banks*. This divided bank regulatory system, in which both the federal government and the states play key roles in the supervision of banking activity, has persisted in the United States to the present day.

Despite banking's long history and its successes, tough financial-service competitors have emerged over the past century or two mostly from Europe to challenge bankers at every turn. Among the oldest were life insurance companies, and the first American company was chartered in Philadelphia in 1759. Property-casualty insurers emerged at roughly the same time, led by the famous Lloyds of London in 1688, underwriting a wide range of risks to persons and property.

The 19th century ushered in a rash of new financial competitors, led by savings banks set up in Scotland in 1810. These institutions offered small savings deposits to individuals at a time when most commercial banks largely ignored this market segment. A similar firm, the savings and loan association, appeared in the midwestern United States during the 1830s, encouraging household saving and financing the construction of new homes. Credit unions were first chartered in Germany during the same era, providing savings accounts and low-cost credit to industrial workers, customers most banks avoided.

Mutual funds—one of banking's most successful competitors over the past two decades—appeared in Belgium in 1822. These investment firms entered the United States in significant numbers during the 1920s, but were devastated by the Great Depression of the 1930s, only to rise again and grow rapidly following World War II. A closely related institution—the money market fund—surfaced in the early 1970s to offer professional cash management services to households and institutions. These aggressive competitors attracted a huge volume of deposits away from banks and ultimately helped to bring about government deregulation of the banking industry. Finally, hedge funds appeared to offer investors a less regulated, more risky alternative to mutual funds. They grew explosively during the 1990s and into the new century.

nature (such as granting credit to private businesses seeking to expand the inventory of goods on their shelves or to purchase new equipment). Over a century later, during the 1980s, when hundreds of financial institutions and nonfinancial institutions (such as J.C. Penney and Sears) were offering either, but not both, of these two key services and, therefore, were claiming exemption from being regulated as a bank, the U.S. Congress decided to take another swing at the challenge of defining banking. Congress then defined a *bank* as *any institution that could qualify for deposit insurance administered by the Federal Deposit Insurance Corporation (FDIC)*.

A clever move indeed! Under federal law in the United States a *bank* had come to be defined, not so much by its array of service offerings, but by the government agency that happened to be insuring its deposits! Please stay tuned—this convoluted and complicated story undoubtedly will develop more interesting and bizarre twists as the 21st century unfolds.

The Financial System and Competing Financial-Service Institutions

As we noted at the opening of this chapter, bankers face challenges from all sides today as they reach out to their financial-service customers. Banks are only one part of a vast financial system of markets and institutions that circles the globe. The primary purpose of this ever-changing financial system is to *encourage individuals and institutions to save and to transfer those savings to those individuals and institutions planning to invest in new projects, products, and services*. This process of encouraging savings and transforming savings into investment spending causes the economy to grow, new jobs to be created, and living standards to rise.

But the financial system of markets and institutions does more than simply transform savings into investment. It also provides a variety of supporting services essential to modern living. These include *payment services* that make commerce and markets possible (such as checks, credit cards, and interactive websites), *risk protection services* for those who save and venture to invest (including insurance policies and derivative contracts), access to *liquidity services* (making it possible to convert property and possessions into immediately available spending power), and *credit services* for those who need loans to supplement their income and increase their standard of living.

Factoid
Did you know that the number of banks operating in the U.S. today represents only about one-third of the number operating 100 years ago? Why do you think this is so?

For many centuries banks were way out in front of other financial-service institutions in supplying savings and investment services, payment and risk protection services, liquidity, and loans. They dominated the financial system of decades past. But this is no longer as true today. As we noted at the beginning of this chapter, banking's financial market share has fallen sharply as other financial institutions have moved in to fight (often successfully) for the same turf. In the United States of a century ago, for example, banks accounted for more than two-thirds of the assets and revenues of all financial-service providers. However, as Exhibit 1–2 illustrates, that share has fallen to only about one-fifth of the assets of the U.S. financial marketplace.

Among the leading competitors with banks in wrestling for the loyalty of financial-service customers and a greater share of today's dynamic financial marketplace are such nonbank financial-service institutions as these:

Savings and loan associations: Specialize in selling savings deposits and granting home mortgage loans and other forms of credit to individuals and families, illustrated by such financial firms as Atlas Savings and Loan Association (**www.atlasbank.com**) and Flatbush Savings and Loan Association (**www.flatbush.com**) of Brooklyn, New York.

Savings banks: Sell savings deposits, grant consumer and home mortgage loans, and invest in high-quality securities under charters granted by the states and federal government,

EXHIBIT 1–2

Comparative Size
by Industry of
Commercial Banks
and Their Principal
Financial-Service
Competitors

Source: Board of Governors of
the Federal Reserve System,
*Flow of Funds Accounts of the
United States*. First Quarter
2003, June 2003.

Financial-Service Institutions	Total Financial Assets Held in 2003 (bill.)*	Percent of All Financial Assets Held in 2003
Depository Institutions:		
Commercial banks**	7,502	19.7%
Savings institutions***	1,408	3.7
Credit unions	589	1.5
Nondeposit Financial Institutions:		
Life insurance companies	3,358	8.8
Property/casualty and other insurers	925	2.4
Private pension funds	3,603	9.4
State and local govt. retirement funds	1,940	5.1
Money market funds	2,156	5.7
Investment companies (mutual funds)	3,587	9.4
Finance companies	1,188	3.1
Mortgage companies	32	0.1
Issuers of asset-backed securities	2,472	6.5
Real estate investment trusts	93	0.2
Security brokers and dealers	1,377	3.6
Other financial service providers (including government-sponsored enterprises, mortgage pools, payday lenders, etc.)	7,926	20.8
Totals	38,156	100.0%

Notes: Column figures may not add to totals due to rounding.
*Figures as of first quarter of 2003.
**Commercial banking as recorded here includes U.S. chartered commercial banks, foreign banking offices in the United States, bank holding companies, and banks operating in United States affiliated areas.
***Savings institutions include savings and loan associations, mutual and federal savings banks, and cooperative banks.

including such industry leaders as Washington Mutual (**www.washingtonmutual.com**) and American Federal Savings Bank (**www.americanfsb.com**).

Credit unions: Collect deposits from and make loans to their members as nonprofit associations of individuals sharing a common bond (such as the same employer), including such firms as American Credit Union of Milwaukee (**www.americancu.org**) and Chicago Post Office Employees Credit Union (**www.my-creditunion.com**).

Money market funds: Collect short-term, liquid funds from individuals and institutions buying shares in the fund and invest these monies in quality securities of short duration, including such firms as Franklin Templeton Tax-Free Money Fund (**www.franklintempleton.com**) and Scudder Tax-Free Money Fund (**www.scudder.com**).

Mutual funds (investment companies): Sell shares to the public representing an interest in the value of and returns from a professionally managed pool of stocks, bonds, and other securities, including such financial firms as Fidelity (**www.fidelity.com**) and The Vanguard Group (**www.vanguard.com**).

Hedge funds: Sell shares mainly to upscale investors in a broad group of different kinds of assets (including nontraditional investments in commodities, real estate, and other less liquid, more risky assets) and are largely unregulated; for additional information see such firms as Magnum Group (**www.magnum.com**) and Turn Key Hedge Funds (**www.turnkeyhedgefunds.com**).

Security brokers and dealers: Buy and sell securities on behalf of their customers and for their own investment accounts and provide professional advice to corporations and governments selling securities in the financial marketplace or seeking to make acquisitions, including such leading broker/dealer firms as Salomon Smith Barney (**www.smithbarney.com**) and Morgan Stanley (**www.morganstanley.com**).

Finance companies: Offer loans to commercial enterprises (such as auto and appliance dealers) and to consumers (individuals and families) using funds borrowed in the open market or from other financial institutions, including such well-known financial firms as Household Finance (**www.household.com**) and GMAC Financial Services (**www.gmacfs.com**).

Financial holding companies or conglomerates: Often include credit card companies, insurance and finance companies, and security broker/dealer firms under one corporate umbrella as highly diversified financial-service providers—and may or may not include a bank among the businesses whose stock they own, including such leading financial conglomerates as GE Capital (**www.gecapital.com**), UBS Warburg AG (**www.ubswarburg.com**) and Capital One Corporation (**www.capitalone.com**).

Life and property/casualty insurance companies: Protect against risks to persons or property through policies sold to the public and manage the pension plans of businesses and the retirement funds of individuals, including such industry leaders as Prudential Insurance (**www.prudential.com**) and State Farm Insurance Companies (**www.statefarm.com**).

Key URLs

You can learn more about the savings and loan and savings bank industries by exploring the sites of the Office of Thrift Supervision at **www.ots.treas.gov** and the Federal Deposit Insurance Corporation at **www.fdic.gov**.

All of these financial-service providers are converging in terms of the services they offer—rushing toward each other like colliding trains—and embracing each other's innovations. Moreover, recent changes in government rules, such as the Financial Services Modernization Act of 1999 in the United States, have allowed many of the financial firms listed above to offer the public one-stop shopping for financial services. To bankers the financial-services marketplace, as Exhibit 1–3 suggests, appears to be closing in from all sides as the list of aggressive competitors grows.

Thanks to more liberal government regulations, banks with quality management, adequate capital, and satisfactory community service records can now truly become conglomerate financial-service providers. The same is true for security firms, insurers, and other financially oriented companies that wish to acquire bank affiliates.

Thus, the historic legal barriers in the United States separating banking from other financial-service businesses have, like the walls of ancient Jericho, recently come tumbling down. The challenge of differentiating banks from other financial-service providers is greater than ever before. However, inside the United States, Congress (like the governments of many other nations around the globe) has chosen to limit severely banks' association with industrial and manufacturing firms, fearing that allowing banking-industrial combinations of companies might snuff out competition, threaten bankers with new risks, and possibly weaken the safety net that protects depositors and taxpayers from loss when the banking system gets into trouble.

As we noted earlier, the result of all these recent legal maneuverings is a state of confusion in the public's mind today over what is or is not a *bank*. The safest approach is probably to view these historic financial institutions in terms of the many key services—especially credit, savings, payments, financial advising, and risk protection services—they offer to the public. This multiplicity of services and functions has led to banks and their nearest competitors being labeled "financial department stores" and to such familiar advertising slogans as "Your Bank—a Full-Service Financial Institution" (see especially Exhibit 1–4).

Key URLs

Want to know more about credit unions? See **www.cujournal.com** and **www.cuna.org**.

EXHIBIT 1–3   The Most Important Nonbank Competitors for Banks

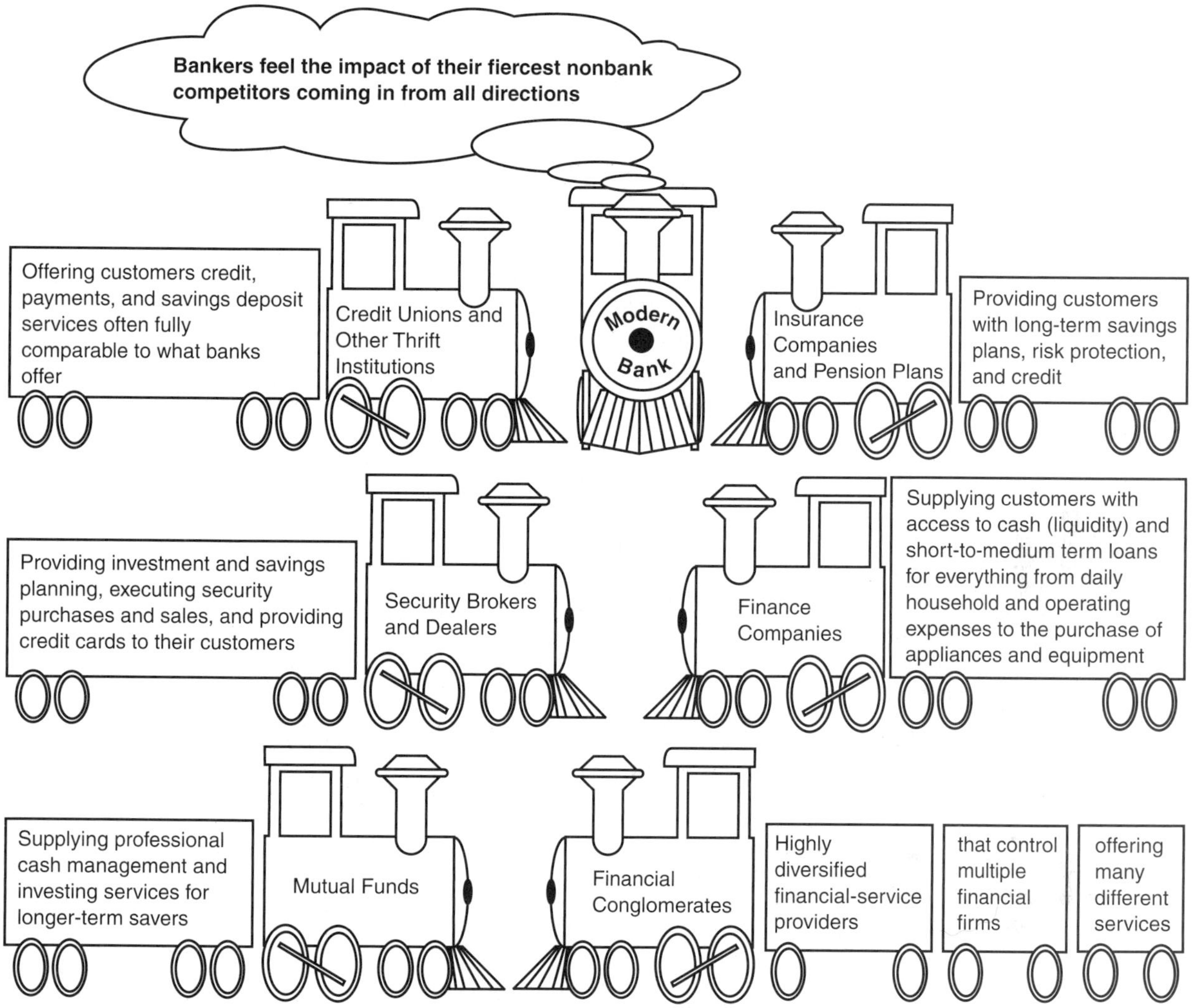

Bankers feel the impact of their fiercest nonbank competitors coming in from all directions

Offering customers credit, payments, and savings deposit services often fully comparable to what banks offer

Credit Unions and Other Thrift Institutions

Modern Bank

Insurance Companies and Pension Plans

Providing customers with long-term savings plans, risk protection, and credit

Providing investment and savings planning, executing security purchases and sales, and providing credit cards to their customers

Security Brokers and Dealers

Finance Companies

Supplying customers with access to cash (liquidity) and short-to-medium term loans for everything from daily household and operating expenses to the purchase of appliances and equipment

Supplying professional cash management and investing services for longer-term savers

Mutual Funds

Financial Conglomerates

Highly diversified financial-service providers

that control multiple financial firms

offering many different services

Concept Check

1–1. What is a *bank*? How does a bank differ from most other financial-service providers?

1–2. Under U.S. law what must a corporation do to qualify and be regulated as a *commercial bank*?

1–3. Why are some banks reaching out to become one-stop financial-service conglomerates? Is this a good idea, in your opinion?

1–4. Which businesses are banking's closest and toughest competitors? What services do they offer that compete directly with banks' services?

1–5. What is happening to banking's share of the financial marketplace and why? What kind of banking and financial system do you foresee for the future if present trends continue?

EXHIBIT 1–4 Service Areas in the Modern Bank

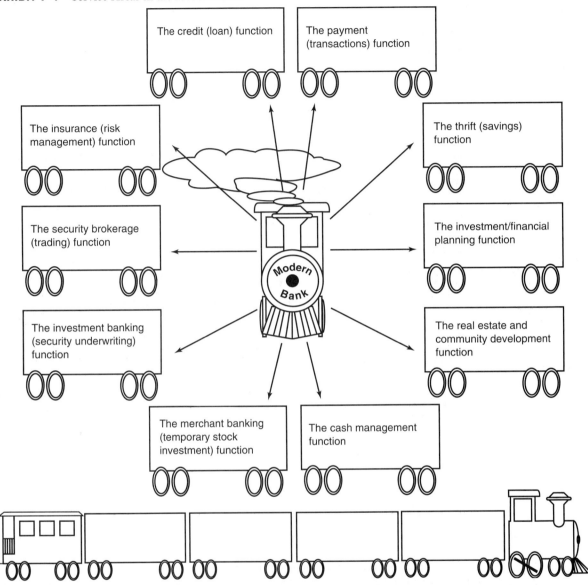

Services Banks and Many of Their Closest Competitors Offer the Public

Banks, like their closest competitors, are financial-service providers. As such, they create and play a number of important roles in the economy. (See Table 1–1.) Their success hinges on their ability to identify the financial services the public demands, produce those services efficiently, and sell them to the public at a competitive price. What services does the public demand from banks and their financial-service competitors today? In this section, we present an overview of both banking's traditional and its modern service menu.

TABLE 1–1
The Many Different
Roles Banks and
Their Closest
Competitors Play
in the Economy

The modern bank has had to adopt many new roles to remain competitive and responsive to public needs. Banking's principal roles (and the roles performed by many of its competitors) today include	
The intermediation role	Transforming savings received primarily from households into credit (loans) for business firms and others in order to make investments in new buildings, equipment, and other goods.
The payments role	Carrying out payments for goods and services on behalf of customers (such as by issuing and clearing checks, wiring funds, providing a conduit for electronic payments, and dispensing currency and coin).
The guarantor role	Standing behind their customers to pay off customer debts when those customers are unable to pay (such as by issuing letters of credit).
The risk management role	Assisting customers in preparing financially for the risk of loss to property and persons.
The savings/investment advisor role	Aiding customers in fulfilling their long-range goals for a better life by building, managing, and protecting savings.
The safekeeping/certification of value role	Safeguarding a customer's valuables and appraising and certifying their true market value.
The agency role	Acting on behalf of customers to manage and protect their property or issue and redeem their securities (usually provided through a trust department).
The policy role	Serving as a conduit for government policy in attempting to regulate the growth of the economy and pursue social goals.

Services Banks Have Offered throughout History

Carrying Out Currency Exchanges   History reveals that one of the first services banks offered was **currency exchange.** A bank stood ready to trade one form of coin or currency (such as dollars) for another (such as francs or pesos) in return for a service fee. Such exchanges were important to travelers over the centuries, as they are today, because the traveler's survival and comfort depend on gaining access to the local coin or currency. In today's financial marketplace, trading in foreign currency is conducted primarily by the largest financial-service firms due to the risks involved and the expense required to carry out such transactions.

Discounting Commercial Notes and Making Business Loans   Early in history, bankers began **discounting commercial notes**—in effect, making loans to local merchants who sold the debts (accounts receivable) they held against their customers to a bank to raise cash quickly. It was a short step from discounting commercial notes to making *direct loans to businesses* for purchasing inventories of goods or for constructing new facilities—a service that today is provided not only by banks, but also by finance companies, insurance firms, and other financial-service competitors.

Offering Savings Deposits   Making loans proved so profitable that banks (and later many of their financial-service competitors) began searching for ways to raise additional

THE ROLE OF BANKS AND OTHER FINANCIAL INTERMEDIARIES IN THEORY

Banks, along with insurance companies, mutual funds, finance companies, and similar financial-service providers, are *financial intermediaries*. The term *financial intermediary* simply means a business that interacts with two types of individuals and institutions in the economy: (1) *deficit-spending individuals and institutions,* whose current expenditures for consumption and investment exceed their current receipts of income and who, therefore, need to raise funds externally through borrowing; and (2) *surplus-spending individuals and institutions* whose current receipts of income exceed their current expenditures on goods and services so they have surplus funds that can be saved. Intermediaries perform the indispensable task of acting as a *bridge* between these two groups, offering convenient financial services to surplus-spending individuals and institutions in order to attract funds and then loaning those funds to deficit spenders. In so doing, intermediaries appear to accelerate economic growth by expanding the available pool of savings, lowering the risk of investments through diversification, and increasing the productivity of savings and investment.

Intermediation activities will take place (1) if there is a positive spread between the expected yields on loans that financial intermediaries make to deficit spenders and the expected interest rate (cost) on the funds intermediaries borrow from surplus spenders; and (2) if there is a positive correlation between the yields on loans and the interest rate paid for attracting funds provided by surplus-spending units. If an intermediary's loan rates and its borrowing costs are positively correlated, this will reduce uncertainty about its expected profits and allow it to expand.

An ongoing debate in the theory of finance and economics concerns *why* banks and other financial intermediaries exist. What services do they provide that other businesses and individuals cannot provide for themselves?

This question has proven difficult to answer. Research evidence showing that our financial markets are reasonably efficient has accumulated in recent yours. Funds and information flow readily to lenders and borrowers, and the prices of assets seem to be determined in highly competitive markets. In a perfectly competitive and efficient financial system, in which all participants have equal and open access to the financial marketplace, no one participant can exercise control over prices, all pertinent information affecting the value of various assets is available to all, transactions costs are not significant impediments to trading, and all assets are available in denominations anyone can afford, *why* would banks and many other financial-service competitors be needed at all?

Most current theories explain the existence of financial intermediaries by pointing to *imperfections* in our financial system. For example, all assets are *not* perfectly divisible into small denominations that everyone can afford. For example, marketable U.S. Treasury bonds—one of the most popular securities in the world—have minimum denominations of $1,000, which is beyond the reach of many small savers. Finan-

loanable funds. One of the earliest sources of these funds consisted of offering **savings deposits**—interest-bearing funds left with depository institutions for a period of weeks, months, or even years, sometimes bearing relatively high rates of interest. According to some historical records, banks in ancient Greece paid as high as 16 percent in annual interest to attract savings deposits from wealthy patrons and then made loans to ship owners sailing the Mediterranean Sea at loan rates double or triple the rate bankers were paying to their savings deposit customers. How's that for a nice profit spread?

Safekeeping of Valuables and Certification of Value During the Middle Ages, banks and other merchants (often called "goldsmiths") began the practice of holding gold, securities, and other valuables owned by their customers inside secure vaults, thus reassuring customers of their safekeeping. These financial firms would also, when asked, assay the market value of their customer's valuables, especially gold and jewelry, and certify whether or not these so-called "valuables" were worth what others had claimed.

Supporting Government Activities with Credit During the Middle Ages and the early years of the Industrial Revolution, governments in Europe noted bankers' and other service providers' ability to mobilize large amounts of funds and make loans. Frequently commercial banks were chartered under the proviso that they would purchase government bonds with a portion of the deposits they received. This lesson was not lost on the

cial intermediaries provide a valuable service in dividing up such instruments into smaller units that are readily affordable for millions of people.

Another contribution that banks and many of their competitors make is their willingness to accept risky loans from borrowers, while issuing low-risk securities to their depositors. These service providers engage in *risky arbitrage* across the financial markets.

Banks and other providers of money and near-money instruments satisfy the need of many customers for *liquidity*. Financial instruments are liquid if they can be sold quickly in a ready market with little risk of loss to the seller. Many households and businesses, for example, demand large precautionary balances of liquid funds to cover future cash needs. Banks and other intermediaries satisfy this customer need by offering high liquidity in the deposits and loans they provide, giving borrowers access to liquid funds precisely when they are needed.

Still another reason banks and other intermediaries have prospered is their *superior ability to evaluate information*. Pertinent data on financial investments is limited and costly. Some borrowers and lenders know more than others or possess inside information that allows them to choose profitable investments while avoiding the losers. This uneven distribution of information and the talent to analyze it is known as *informational asymmetry*. Asymmetries reduce the efficiency of markets, but provide a profitable role for intermediaries that have the expertise to evaluate financial instruments and to choose those with desirable risk-return features.

Yet another view of why banks and other lending institutions exist in modern society is called *delegated monitoring theory*. Most borrowers prefer to keep their financial records confidential. Banks and other lending institutions are able to attract borrowing customers, this theory suggests, because they pledge confidentiality. For example, a bank's own depositors are not privileged to review the records of its borrowing customers. Depositors often have neither the time nor the skill to choose good loans over bad. They turn the monitoring process over to a financial intermediary that has invested human and reputational capital in this process. Thus a depository institution serves as an *agent* on behalf of its depositors, monitoring the financial condition of those customers who do receive loans to ensure that depositors will recover their funds. In return for monitoring, depositors pay a fee to the lender that is probably less than the cost they would incur if they monitored borrowers themselves.

By making a large volume of loans, lending institutions acting as delegated monitors can diversify and reduce their risk exposure, resulting in increased safety for the funds savers contribute. Moreover, when a borrowing customer has received the stamp of approval of a lending institution it is easier and less costly for that customer to raise funds elsewhere. This signals the financial marketplace that the borrower is likely to repay his or her loans. This *signaling effect* seems to be strongest, not when a bank or other lending institution makes the first loan to a borrower, but when it renews a maturing loan.

fledgling American government during the Revolutionary War. The Bank of North America, chartered by the Continental Congress in Philadelphia in 1781, was set up to help fund the struggle to throw off British rule and make the United States a sovereign nation. Similarly, during the Civil War the U.S. Congress created a whole new federal banking system, agreeing to charter national banks provided these institutions purchased government bonds whose proceeds were used to help fund the war.

Factoid
What region of the United States contains the largest number of banks? The Midwest. The smallest number of banks? The Northeast. Why do you think this is so?

Offering Checking Accounts (Demand Deposits)   The Industrial Revolution in Europe and the United States ushered in new banking practices, new financial services, and new service providers. Probably the most important of the new services developed during this period was the demand deposit—a checking account that permitted the depositor to write drafts in payment for goods and services that the bank and other service providers had to honor immediately. **Demand deposit services** proved to be one of the financial-service industry's most important offerings because it significantly improved the efficiency of the payments process, making business transactions easier, faster, and safer. Today the checking account concept has been extended to the Internet, to the use of plastic debit cards that tap your checking account electronically, and to "smart cards" that electronically store spending money. Today payment-on-demand accounts are offered not only by banks, but also by savings associations, credit unions, securities firms, and other service providers.

Offering Trust Services For many years banks and a few of their competitors (such as insurance and trust companies) have managed the financial affairs and property of individuals and business firms in return for a fee that is often based on the value of properties or the amount of funds under management. This property management function is known as **trust services.** Providers of this service typically act as trustees for wills, managing a deceased customer's estate by paying claims against that estate, keeping valuable assets safe and productively invested, and seeing to it that the legal heirs receive their rightful inheritance. In their commercial trust departments, banks and other trust-service providers manage security portfolios and pension plans for businesses and act as agents for corporations issuing stocks and bonds. This requires the trust provider to pay interest or dividends to holders of the corporation's securities and to retire and pay off maturing corporate securities.

Services Banks and Many of Their Financial-Service Competitors Have Developed More Recently

Granting Consumer Loans Historically, banks did not actively pursue loan accounts from individuals and families, believing that the relatively small size of most consumer loans and their relatively high default rate would make such lending unprofitable. Accordingly, other financial-service providers—especially credit unions, savings and loans, and finance companies—soon moved in to focus on the consumer. Early in this century, however, bankers began to rely more heavily on consumers for deposits to help fund their large corporate loans. In addition, heavy competition for business deposits and loans caused bankers increasingly to turn to the consumer as a potentially more loyal customer. By the 1920s and 30s several major banks, led by one of the forerunners of New York's Citicorp and by the Bank of America, had established strong consumer loan departments. Following World War II, consumer loans were among the fastest-growing forms of bank credit. Their rate of growth has slowed somewhat recently, though, as bankers have run into stiff competition for consumer credit accounts from nonbank providers and the economy has slowed.

Key URLs
Interested in money market funds? Take a look at such sites as **www.smartmoney.com** and the Investment Company Institute at **www.ici.com**.

Financial Advising Customers have long asked bankers and their financial-service competitors for financial advice, particularly when it comes to the use of credit and the saving or investing of funds. Many banks as well as other service providers today offer a wide range of **financial advisory services,** from helping to prepare tax returns and financial plans for individuals to consulting about marketing opportunities at home and abroad for their business customers.

Filmtoid
What 2001 documentary recounts the creation of an internet company, GovWorks.com, using more than $50 million in funds provided by venture capitalists?
Answer: Startup.com.

Managing Cash Over the years, banks and similar institutions have found that some of the services they provide for themselves are also valuable for their customers. One of the most prominent examples is **cash management services,** in which a bank or other financial intermediary (such as a money market fund) agrees to handle cash collections and disbursements for a business firm and to invest any temporary cash surpluses in short-term, interest-bearing assets until the cash is needed to pay bills. Although banks tend to specialize mainly in business cash management services, many financial institutions are offering similar services to consumers. This trend began with brokerage companies (like Merrill Lynch) and other financial conglomerates offering consumers special brokerage accounts with a wide array of associated services, including investing in mutual funds, writing checks, and using credit cards for instant loans.

Offering Equipment Leasing Many banks and finance companies have moved aggressively to offer their business customers the option to purchase equipment through a lease arrangement in which the lending institution buys the equipment and rents it to the customer. These **equipment leasing services** benefit leasing institutions as well as their cus-

Leading Nonbank Financial Firms That Have Reached into Traditional Bank Service Markets

For several decades now bankers have watched as some of the world's most aggressive nonbank institutions have invaded banking's traditional marketplace and, in some cases, acquired a bank as a subsidiary. Among the most successful and aggressive of such companies are these:

Merrill Lynch & Co. (www.ml.com).* Merrill is one of the largest security trading and underwriting firms on the planet and serves as an adviser to corporations and governments on every continent. Beginning as an investment firm in 1885, Merrill now competes directly with banks in offering money market accounts and online banking services to both businesses and households. It was one of the first nonbank firms to adopt the holding company form and acquire or establish affiliates dealing in government securities, asset management, and the management of mutual funds. During the 1970s Merrill Lynch organized one of the largest of all money market funds.

American Express Company (www.americanexpress.com).* American Express was one of the first credit card companies in the United States and now serves millions of households and business firms. In addition to providing financial planning, securities trading, and insurance services, it also owns an FDIC-insured bank through which it offers home mortgage and home equity loans, savings deposits, checking and retirement accounts, and online bill paying. AEX also markets shares in mutual funds and is registered with the Federal Reserve Board as a financial holding company.

Household International (www.household.com).* Household is the largest finance company in the world, offering personal loans as well as financial assistance to businesses requiring inventory financing. Reaching over 50 million customers in Canada, the United States and Great Britain, Household competes directly with banks in offering credit cards, auto financing, home mortgages, and credit life insurance. It also operates a joint venture with an insurance company to offer term life and auto insurance coverage. On November 14, 2002, Household International announced its acquisition by HSBC of London, one of the world's largest banks.

Prudential Financial (www.prudential.com). Prudential is usually thought of as a life insurance company but it reaches into both banking and the securities business. The Pru offers stocks, bonds, and mutual funds; annuities; life and auto insurance policies; and retirement plans through its affiliates. In cooperation with its PruBank, this financial conglomerate markets personal trust accounts and credit cards. Prudential has offices around the globe with special emphasis on Europe, Asia, and the Americas.

*Indicates this financial firm is included in the Educational Version of S&P's Market Insight.

---

tomers because, as the real owner of the leased equipment, the lessor can depreciate it for additional tax benefits.

Making Venture Capital Loans   Increasingly, banks and competing institutions (such as security dealers and financial conglomerates) have become active in financing the start-up costs of new companies, particularly in high-tech industries. Because of the added risk involved in such loans, this is generally done through a separate venture capital firm—for example, a subsidiary of a bank holding company such as Citicorp Venture, Inc. Other investors may be brought in to help share the risk of these new ventures.

Key URLs
Is the growing role of finance companies within the financial marketplace of interest to you? See such web sites as **www.nacm.org.**, **www.household.com,** and **www .capitalone.com**.

Selling Insurance Services   For many years bankers have sold credit life insurance to their customers receiving loans, thus guaranteeing loan repayment if borrowers die or become disabled. Moreover, during the 19th and early 20th centuries, many bankers sold insurance and provided financial advice to their customers, literally serving as the local community's all-around financial-service store. However, beginning with the Great Depression of the 1930s when the Glass-Steagall Act was passed and later when the Bank Holding Company Act appeared, U.S. banks were prohibited from acting as insurance agents or underwriting **insurance policies.** For example, banks in most cases couldn't provide automobile or homeowners' coverage or general life and health insurance protection. Congress acted out of fear that selling insurance would increase bank risk, threaten depositors with losses, and lead to conflicts of interest in which customers asking for one service would be compelled to buy other services as well.

Many bankers arranged to have insurance companies sell policies to bank customers by renting space in bank lobbies or using customer lists furnished by bankers to generate insurance sales. This picture of extreme separation between banking and insurance changed dramatically in 1999 when Congress and President Bill Clinton tore down the legal barriers between the two industries, allowing bank holding companies to acquire control of insurance agencies and/or insurance underwriters and, conversely, permitting insurance companies to acquire bank affiliates. Today, these two industries are competing aggressively with each other and pursuing cross-industry mergers.

Selling Retirement Plans   Banks, trust departments, and insurance companies are active in managing the **retirement plans** that most businesses make available to their employees, investing incoming funds and dispensing payments to qualified recipients who have reached retirement or become disabled. Banks and other depository institutions sell deposit retirement plans (known as IRAs and Keoghs) to individuals holding these deposits until the funds are needed for income after retirement.

Dealing in Securities: Offering Security Brokerage and Security Underwriting Services

All over the world the largest banks have reached out to become "financial department stores," all-purpose financial firms that can fulfill all the financial service needs of their customers with one stop. One of the biggest of all banking service targets in recent years, particularly in the United States, has been dealing in securities, executing buy and sell orders for security trading customers (referred to as **security brokerage services**) and marketing new securities to raise funds for corporations and other institutions (referred to as **security underwriting** services). However, much of this security brokerage and underwriting activity was prohibited in the United States due to the separation of commercial and investment banking by the Glass-Steagall Act, passed in 1933. With the passage of the Gramm-Leach-Bliley Act in the fall of 1999, however, banks are now permitted to affiliate with securities firms and security firms can acquire banks (subject to regulatory approval). Two venerable old industries, long separated by law, especially in the United States, are now like two out-of-control locomotives rushing toward each other, pursuing many of the same customers.

Offering Mutual Funds and Annuities   Many customers have come to demand so-called *investment products* from their banker or other financial-service provider. Mutual fund investments and annuities that offer the prospect of higher yields than the returns often available on conventional bank deposits are among the most sought-after investment products. However, these product lines also tend to carry more risk than do bank deposits.

Annuities consist of long-term savings plans that promise the payment of a stream of income to the annuity holder beginning on a designated future date (e.g., at retirement). In contrast, mutual funds are professionally managed investment programs that acquire stocks, bonds, and other assets that appear to "fit" the funds' announced goals (such as to maximize current income or to achieve long-term capital appreciation). Recently many banking firms have organized special subsidiary organizations to market these services (e.g., Citigroup's Investment Services) or entered into joint ventures with security brokers and insurance companies. In turn, many of bankers' key competitors, including thrift institutions, insurance companies, and security firms, have moved aggressively to expand their public offerings of fixed and variable annuity plans and broaden their menu of mutual funds and other investment services in order to attract customers away from banks.

Banks and other financial-service firms have also experienced a rising tide of competition from leading manufacturing, retailing, and other businesses in recent decades. These companies based outside the financial sector nevertheless have often been successful in capturing financial-service customers. Among the best known of such nonfinancial-based entities are these:

GE Capital (www.gecapital.com).* The predecessor of GE Capital was set up during the 1930s as a captive finance company of its parent, General Electric, to provide financing so that consumers and appliance and equipment dealers could afford GE products. The firm branched out as it grew to finance more than just GE products. Today it offers such diverse services as leasing airplanes, autos, and oil tankers; credit cards; equity investments; and insurance. If GE Capital were a bank it would rank in the top 10 of all U.S. banks, having close to 90,000 employees and close to $70 billion in outstanding credit receivables. In 2002 GE announced that GE Capital would become four separate businesses—GE Commercial Finance, GE Consumer Finance, GE Equipment Management, and GE Insurance.

GMAC Financial Services (www.gmacfs.com). GMAC began in 1919 as a captive finance company, financing the vehicles produced by the plants of General Motors by lending to both dealers and consumers. Today GMAC Financial Services is a family of financial-service companies that not only finance purchases of motor vehicles, but extend home mortgage loans, provide real estate brokerage services, make commercial loans, sell insurance on homes and autos, and provide banking services through GMAC bank and a thrift institution. The company has nearly 30,000 employees in 40 countries.

Sears, Roebuck & Company (www.sears.com).* Sears began as a dry goods store offering catalogue sales to homes, farms, and ranches and ultimately sold goods through a chain of stores in shopping centers and malls. As the company grew it added Allstate Insurance Company, followed by Dean Witter Financial Services to provide investment planning and securities sales. The launching of Discover Card brought it into the payments and lending business. Sears acquired Coldwell Banker in 1981, giving it a presence in insurance, securities trading and management, consumer credit, and real estate brokerage. Recently Sears has retreated from its former lofty position in the financial marketplace to put more emphasis on its more traditional products, selling its huge credit card operation to Citigroup, Inc.

*Indicates this firm is included in the Educational Version of S&P's Market Insight.

Offering Merchant Banking Services U.S. bankers and other financial-service providers are following in the footsteps of leading financial institutions all over the globe (for example, Barclays Bank of Great Britain and Deutsche Bank of Germany) in offering **merchant banking services** to larger corporations. These services consist of the temporary purchase of corporate stock to aid the launching of a new business venture or to support the expansion of an existing company. Hence, a merchant banker becomes a temporary stockholder and bears the risk that the stock purchased may decline in value all the way to zero. In practice, merchant banking services often encompass the identification of possible merger targets for a corporate customer, providing that customer with strategic marketing advice, and offering hedging services to manage risk, especially the risk of loss due to changing currency prices and interest rates.

Convenience: The Sum Total of All Banking and Financial Services

It should be clear from the list of services we have described that not only are most banks and their financial-service competitors offering a wide array of comparable financial services today, but that service menu is growing rapidly. New service delivery methods like the Internet and smart cards with digital cash are expanding and whole new service lines

TABLE 1–2

Some of the Leading Banking and Nonbank Financial-Service Firms around the Globe

Sources: Bank for International Settlements, Bank of England, Bank of Japan, and Board of Governors of the Federal Reserve System.

Banking-Oriented Firms	**Security Dealers and Brokers**
Mizuho Financial Group Ltd., Japan**	Merrill Lynch, USA*
Mitsubishi Banking Corp, Japan*	Goldman Sachs, USA*
Deutsche Bank AG, Germany	Salomon Smith Barney, USA*
UBS AG, Switzerland	Nomura Securities, Japan
Citigroup, Inc., USA*	Daiwa Securities, Japan
HSBC Holdings PLC, Great Britain*	Morgan Stanley, USA*
Lloyds TSB, Great Britain	
Industrial and Commercial Bank of China	**Insurance Companies**
BNP Paribus Group, France	
Barclays PLC, London, Great Britain*	Nippon Life Insurance
Bank of Montreal, Canada	Compagnie UAP, France
Canadian Imperial Bank of Commerce	Axa/Equitable, Paris, France
J. P. Morgan Chase & Company, USA*	Metropolitan Life Insurance, USA*
Bank of America Corp., USA*	Prudential Insurance, USA
Agricultural Bank of China	Aetna Life and Casualty Insurance*
Australian & N.Z. Banking Group	
	Finance Companies
	Household International, USA*
	GE Capital, USA*
	Capital One Financial, USA*

*This financial firm appears in the Educational Version of S&P's Market Insight.
**Mizuho was formed from the combined merger of the Fuji, Dai-Ichi, and Industrial Banks of Japan.

Key URLs

You can expand your knowledge of mutual funds by exploring such sites as **CBSMarketWatch.com**, **Morningstar.com**, and **www.ici.com**.

are being launched every year. Viewed as a whole, the impressive array of services offered and the service delivery channels used by modern financial institutions add up to greater convenience for their customers, who can satisfy virtually all their financial-service needs at one financial firm in one location. Banks and some of their competitors have indeed become the financial department stores of the modern era, working to unify banking, fiduciary, insurance, and security brokerage services under one roof—a trend often referred to as *universal banking* in the United States and Great Britain, as *allfinanz* in Germany, and as *bancassurance* in France. Table 1–2 lists some of these financial department stores, including some of the very largest banks and competing nonbank financial firms in the world.

Concept Check

1–6. What different kinds of services do banks offer the public today? What services do their closest competitors offer?

1–7. What is a *financial department store?* A *universal bank?* Why do you think these institutions have become so important in the modern financial system?

1–8. Why do banks and other financial intermediaries exist in modern society, according to the theory of finance?

Key Trends Affecting Banks and Other Financial-Service Firms

The foregoing survey of financial services suggests that banks and many of their financial-service competitors are currently undergoing sweeping changes in function and form. In fact, the changes affecting the banking and financial-services business today are so important that many industry analysts refer to these trends as a *revolution*, one that may well leave banks and their nonbank service competitors of the next generation almost unrecognizable. What are the key trends reshaping banking and financial services today?

Service Proliferation   As the preceding section points out, banks and other leading financial firms have been rapidly expanding the menu of financial services they offer to their customers. This trend toward service proliferation has accelerated in recent years under the pressure of increasing competition from other financial firms, more knowledgeable and demanding customers, and shifting technology. It has also increased operating costs and posed greater risk of failure. The new services have had a positive effect, however, by opening up major new sources of revenue—noninterest service fees (called *fee income*), which are likely to continue to grow relative to more traditional sources of financial-service revenue (such as the interest earned on loans).

Rising Competition   The level and intensity of competition in the financial-services field have grown as banks and their competitors have proliferated their service offerings. The local bank offering business and consumer credit, savings and retirement plans, and financial counseling faces direct competition for all of these services today from other banks, thrift institutions like Washington Mutual, securities firms like Merrill Lynch, finance companies like GE Capital, and insurance companies and agencies like Prudential Insurance. This trend toward rising competition has acted as a spur to develop still more services for the future.

Government Deregulation   Rising competition and the proliferation of financial services have been spurred on by government deregulation—a loosening of government control—of the financial services industry that began more than two decades ago in the United States and has spread around the globe. As we will see more fully in the chapters ahead, deregulation began with the lifting of government-imposed interest rate ceilings on savings deposits in an effort to give the public a fairer return on their savings. Almost simultaneously, the services that many of banking's key competitors, such as savings and loans and credit unions, could offer were sharply expanded by legislation so they could remain competitive with banks. Such leading nations as Australia, Canada, Great Britain, and Japan have recently joined the deregulation movement, broadening the legal playing field for banks, security dealers, and other financial-service companies, and increasing exposure to risk in a freer and more competitive marketplace.

An Increasingly Interest-Sensitive Mix of Funds   Government deregulation of the financial sector, especially among depository institutions, has made it possible for customers to earn higher rates of return on their savings and payments accounts. However, only the public could translate that new opportunity created by government deregulation into action. And act the public did! Billions of dollars formerly deposited in older, low-yielding savings instruments and noninterest-bearing checking accounts flowed into new high-yielding accounts whose rates of return could be changed with market conditions. Thus, bankers and their closest competitors (especially thrift institutions) found themselves with an increasingly interest-sensitive mix of funds.

Bankers and other financial-service managers have discovered that they are facing a better-educated, as well as more interest-sensitive, customer today, whose loyalty can more easily be lured away by aggressive competitors. Financial-service providers must now strive to be more competitive in the returns they offer on the public's money and more sensitive to changing public preferences with regard to how savings are allocated.

Technological Change   Banks and many of their most serious competitors (for example, insurance companies) have been faced with higher operating costs in recent years and, therefore, have turned increasingly to automation and the installation of sophisticated electronic systems to replace older, labor-based production and delivery systems. This move toward greater technological change is especially evident in the delivery of such services as dispensing payments and making credit available to qualified customers.

The most prominent examples of major technological innovations in banking include automated teller machines (ATMs) and point of sale (POS) terminals. There are well over 140,000 ATMs in the United States today and a comparable number in Europe. These electronic terminals give customers 24-hour access to their accounts for cash withdrawals and deposits and to a widening menu of other services. Also accessible well beyond "bankers' hours" are POS terminals in stores and shopping centers that replace paper-based means of paying for goods and services with rapid computer entries. ATM and POS computer systems now process millions of transactions around the globe every day of the year with great speed and accuracy.

Thus, banking and financial services now comprise a more capital-intensive, fixed-cost industry and a less labor-intensive, variable-cost industry than in the past. Many experts believe that traditional brick-and-mortar buildings and face-to-face meetings with customers eventually will become relics of the past, replaced almost entirely by electronic communication. Service production and delivery will then be fully automated. Technological advances such as these will significantly lower the per-unit costs associated with high-volume transactions, but they will tend to depersonalize banking and financial services and result in further loss of jobs as capital equipment is substituted for labor. Recent experience suggests, however, that fully automated financial services for *all* customers may be a long time in coming. A substantial proportion of customers still prefer personalized service and the opportunity to consult personally, one to one, with their banker or financial advisor about a broad range of fiscal matters.

Consolidation and Geographic Expansion   Making efficient use of automation and other technological innovations requires a high volume of sales. So banks and other service providers have had to expand their customer base by reaching into new and more distant markets and by increasing the number of service units sold. The result has been a dramatic increase in branching activity in order to provide multiple offices (i.e., points of contact) for customers, the formation of financial holding companies that bring smaller institutions into larger conglomerates offering multiple services in multiple markets, and mergers between some of the largest bank and nonbank financial firms, such as Bank of America with Nations Bank, Citicorp with Travelers Insurance, and Deutsche Bank of Germany with Bankers Trust Company of New York.

The number of small, independently owned financial institutions is declining and the average size of individual banks, as well as thrift institutions, credit unions, finance companies, and insurance firms, has risen significantly—a phenomenon we call *consolidation*. The consolidation of financial-service providers has resulted in a decline in employment in the banking and financial-services sector.

Convergence   Service proliferation and greater competitive rivalry among banks and other financial firms have led to a powerful trend called *convergence*, particularly on the part of the largest financial institutions. *Convergence* refers to the movement of businesses across industry lines so that a firm formerly offering only one product line ventures into other product lines in order to broaden its sales base. This phenomenon has been most evident among larger banks, insurance companies, and security broker/dealer firms that have eagerly climbed into each other's backyard, offering the same or similar services. Clearly, competition intensifies in the wake of convergence as businesses previously separated into different industries now find that their former industry boundaries no longer discourage new competitors, Under these more intense competitive pressures, weaker firms will fail or be merged into companies that are ever larger and offer more diverse services.

E-BANKING AND E-COMMERCE

The world of banking and financial services is being turned upside down by the rapid spread of electronic banking systems. These electronic networks serve both businesses and households through computers at home, on the job, and wherever else a personal computer that can be linked to a financial firm's computer may be found.

As we will discover in future chapters, one of the most powerful factors propelling the rapid rise of e-banking and e-commerce is *operating costs*. Transactions conducted via the older service delivery systems (such as checks, telephones, and ATMs) appear to be several times more costly for a financial-service provider than are transactions conducted via the World Wide Web or through an automated clearinghouse.

Although some Web-based banking and other financial services are not profitable in and of themselves, many bankers appear to be looking ahead to a future time when the great majority of their customers *will be* electronically connected. Accordingly, financial-service providers are rapidly increasing the range of e-banking services they offer, giving their customers the ability to use the Web to check account balances, move money from one account to another, pay bills, and obtain forms to open new accounts and apply for loans, as well as to purchase securities, insurance, and other products and services.

Globalization The geographic expansion and consolidation of banking and other financial-service units have reached well beyond the boundaries of a single nation to encompass the whole planet—a trend we call *globalization*. The largest banks in the world compete with each other for business on every continent. For example, huge banks headquartered in France (led by BNP Paribus), Germany (led by Deutsche Bank), Great Britain (led by HSBC), and the United States (led by Citigroup and J. P. Morgan Chase) have become heavyweight competitors in the global market for corporate and government loans. Deregulation has helped all these institutions compete more effectively and capture growing shares of the global market for financial services.

Factoid
When did the greatest number of U.S. banks fail? Between 1929 and 1933 when about one-third (approximately 9,000) of all U.S. banks failed or were merged out of existence.

Increased Risk of Poor Performance and Failure While consolidation, convergence, and geographic expansion have helped to make many banks and their competitors less vulnerable to local economic conditions, increasing competition between banks and nonbank financial firms, coupled with problem loans when the economy is soft, have led to failures among banks and other financial firms all over the globe. Government deregulation of the financial sector has expanded the range of opportunities for bankers and their competitors, but only at the cost of creating a more treacherous financial marketplace in which poor performance and failures may be more likely to occur in a free market that offers little protection from or forgiveness of mistakes. The result is a tougher financial-services environment with increased risk of poor performance and failure.

Are Traditional Banks Dead?

Recently, with some depository institutions merging or failing in the United States, Europe, and Asia, greater concern has been expressed about the future of traditional banking. For example, between 1980 and 2003 more than 1,500 insured depository institutions failed and more than 9,000 mergers occurred in which many smaller banking firms were absorbed.

Even for those traditional banks that have survived failures and mergers (mostly located in smaller communities) there is evidence that banking's share of the market for financial services in declining. Security brokers and dealers, insurance companies, mutual funds, finance companies, and financial-service conglomerates have snared a growing share of

CONVERGENCE AND CONSOLIDATION IN FINANCIAL SERVICES SLOWS DOWN*

Although banks and their financial-service competitors have continued to move closer to each other, heating up competition in the financial-services sector, the pace of convergence and consolidation in financial services has slowed. As the 21st century opened, mergers were proceeding at about half the pace of the hectic 1990s. The formation of new financial holding companies, combining banking, insurance, and security services under one roof, paused and leveled out.

Perhaps most dramatic of all, the leading financial-services firm in the world—Citigroup—announced plans in 2002 to divest itself of its big Travelers Insurance property/casualty insurance unit. This was a big surprise because Citigroup has epitomized the expansion of "one-stop financial service shopping" around the world. Nor was Citigroup alone. FleetBoston Financial Company closed Robertson Stephens, its investment banking affiliate, while Bank of America disposed of its automobile leasing and subprime mortgage lending units at about the same time.

Why did these leading financial-service conglomerates take a step back from their highly publicized one-stop financial services strategies? Is the drive toward consolidation and convergence reversing itself, returning to traditional lines?

Not likely, but the pace of financial-services deregulation and diversification has slowed, at least for a time. One reason: We went from a high-flying economy in the 1990s to a more slowly growing, uncertain economy at the beginning of the 21st century. Moreover, in Europe and Asia government approval of badly needed financial-service mergers has been moving at a snail's pace due to political and economic problems, while in the United States efforts to further deregulate financial-service firms seem to have stalled for a time in the wake of new legislation enacted during the 1990s. Change in the financial-services industry proceeds by fits and starts, due principally to the ongoing interaction of changing economic conditions, legislation, and regulation.

*See, for example, Mark G. Guzman, "Slow but Steady Progress toward Financial Deregulation," *Southwest Economy,* Federal Reserve Bank of Dallas, January–February 2003; and Karen Couch, Robert Mahalik, and Robert R. Moore, "Banks as Real Estate Brokers—Letting Free Enterprise Work," *Southwest Economy,* Federal Reserve Bank of Dallas, May–June 2001.

available customers (with the possible exception of economic downturns when the public often seems more concerned about risk among nonbank financial institutions).

The Federal Reserve Bank of St. Louis calculates that the share of total assets held by banks and other depository institutions relative to the assets of all financial intermediaries combined fell from almost 60 percent in the 1980s to less than 40 percent during the 1990s—a drop attributed to "natural shrinkage" following government deregulation of the industry and greater financial sophistication on the part of customers. During roughly the same time period, the Federal Deposit Insurance Corporation reports that the volume of credit extended in the United States by mutual funds, asset pools, closed-end investment funds, and money market funds soared from less than 10 percent to about 35 percent of all credit market obligations (see especially Powell [7]). Some analysts (e.g., Beim [8]) have declared that banking, as we have known it, is either "dying or already dead."

Certainly as financial markets become increasingly efficient due to advances in technology and as larger business customers find ways to obtain credit other than borrowing from banks (such as by selling securities in the open market), traditional banks today appear to be less necessary to the effective functioning of our financial system. At the very least, there appear to be too many of those institutions we traditionally refer to as "banks." For example, the United States has close to 10,000 bank-like institutions (counting both commercial and savings banks) and Germany is not far behind.

It may be argued that many traditional banks continue to survive because they are being "propped up" by government support in the form of cheap deposit insurance and cheap government loans. Perhaps the huge number of mergers and failures worldwide are simply a sign that the banking industry is overcrowded and facing declining demand for many of its more traditional services. Then, too, banking faces a generally heavier burden of government regulation than many of the industry's financial-service competitors. The banking industry may, in some instances, be "regulated to death."

The decline in traditional banking's share of the financial-services marketplace has aroused concern among some government policymakers and bank customers. Among these concerns are fears that traditional banks' declining importance in the financial system could

- Weaken the central bank's ability to control the growth of the money supply and achieve the nation's economic goals.
- Damage those customers, mainly small businesses and families, who rely most heavily on banks for loans and other financial services.
- Make banking services less conveniently available to customers as bank offices are consolidated and closed.

Many economists have argued that excessive regulation of banks and little or no regulation of many of their competitors is a primary cause of these recent developments and that greater deregulation of the industry is a *must* if banking is to remain strong and viable and avoid being regulated to death. As we have seen in this chapter, many banks, especially the largest, are trying to fight back and preserve their market share by (1) offering new services (such as selling shares in mutual funds, annuities, and insurance policies); (2) charging higher user fees for many formerly free services (such as the use of ATMs); (3) offering more services through subsidiary businesses (such as security trading and underwriting) that are not as closely regulated as banks; or (4) entering into joint ventures with independent companies (such as insurers) and thereby avoiding at least some burdensome government regulations.

Other experts in the field (e.g., Kaufman and Mote [9]) argue that banking's decline may be more apparent than real. The nature of banking has changed so drastically in recent years with the development of new services, not all of which show up on bank balance sheets, that new measures of banking's size may be needed to determine if banks are really declining in importance relative to other financial-service institutions. At the same time, government programs to support and subsidize banks will probably have to be reformed. Undoubtedly some banks must be allowed to exit the industry in order to promote greater efficiency in using scarce resources.

Although many traditional banks won't survive, most banks should be able to live on if they are given broad service powers and deposit insurance is priced correctly to reflect the riskiness of each banking firm. In short, traditional banking *may* be dead or dying, but if banks are given freedom to respond to the public's changing demands for new services, they need not pass away merely from the blows of their financial-service competitors.

The Plan of This Book

This book has a twofold purpose: (1) to provide the reader with a comprehensive picture of the importance of banking and the financial-services industry to the economy and to our daily lives; and (2) to assist in educating tomorrow's managers of banks and other financial firms. Through its six major parts, we pursue these two key objectives both by presenting an overview of banking and the financial-service industry as a whole and by pointing the reader toward specific questions and issues that bankers and their principal competitors must resolve every day.

Part I provides a basic introduction to banking and financial services and their functions in the global economy and financial system. We define and explain the principal services offered by banks and their closest competitors and introduce the reader to their financial statements. We explore the various ways banks and other financial firms are organized to bring together human skill, capital equipment, and natural resources to produce and deliver their services. Part I also examines how and why banks and other financial-service providers are regulated and who their principal regulators are.

Part II explores the dynamic area of asset-liability management and hedging against risk. Chapters 6, 7 and 8 describe how bankers and other financial-service managers have changed their views on managing assets, liabilities, and capital and on controlling risk exposure in recent years. These chapters take a detailed look at the most important techniques for hedging against changing interest rates (including financial futures, options and swaps), recognizing that banks and other financial firms are among the most sensitive of all business firms to movements in market interest rates. Part II also explores some of the newer tools to deal with credit risk and the use of off-balance-sheet financing techniques, including securitizations and loan sales.

Part III addresses two ages-old problem areas for banks and their closest competitors: managing a portfolio of investment securities and maintaining enough liquidity to meet daily cash needs. We examine the different types of investment securities typically acquired and review the factors that an investment officer must weigh in choosing what investment securities to buy or sell. This part of the book also takes a critical look at why banks and their closest competitors (particularly thrift institutions) must constantly struggle to ensure that they have access to cash precisely when and where they need it.

Part IV directs our attention to the funding side of the balance sheet—raising money to support the acquisition of assets and to meet operating expenses. We present the principal types of deposits and nondeposit investment products and review recent trends in the mix and pricing of deposits for their implications for managing banks and other financial firms today and tomorrow. Next, we explore all the important nondeposit funding sources of short-term funds—federal funds, security repurchase agreements, Eurodollars, and the like—and assess their impact on profitability and risk for banks and similar institutions. This part also examines the rise of bank sales of nondeposit investment products, including sales of securities, annuities, and insurance and their implications for financial-firm return and risk. The final source of funds we review is equity capital—the source of funding provided by a financial firm's owners.

Part V takes up what many bankers and other financial-service managers regard as the essence of their business—granting credit to customers through the making of loans. The types of loans made by banks and their closest competitors, the regulations applicable to the lending process, and the procedures for evaluating and granting loans are all discussed. This portion of the text also includes expanded information about credit card services—one of the most successful, but challenging service areas for financial institutions today.

Part VI tackles an issue that other banking texts often ignore or pass over lightly—how banks and their closest financial-service competitors can organize their operations to achieve the goals most desired by management and the stockholders. Among the organizational issues we address in Part VI are electronic banking and establishing new service facilities, analyzing potential mergers and acquisitions, and engaging in international operations. This part—as well as material throughout this new edition—places a much heavier emphasis on electronic banking and e-commerce and how automation is rapidly changing banking and the financial-services arena. We conclude in this final part of the book that the future of banking and the financial-services marketplace it serves mirrors, in several important respects, our own future and the type of world we will all share as the 21st century unfolds.

Concept Check

1–9. How have banking and the financial-services market changed in recent years? What powerful forces are shaping financial markets and institutions today? Which of these forces do you think will continue into the future?

1–10. Can you explain why many of the forces you named in the answer to the previous question have led to significant problems for the management of banks and other financial firms and for their stockholders?

1–11. Is the traditional bank really dead? What evidence do you have for your answer?

1–12. What do you think the financial-services industry will look like 20 years from now? What are the implications of your projections for its management today?

Summary

In this opening chapter we have explored many of the roles played by modern banks and by their closest financial-service competitors. We have examined how and why the banking industry and the financial-services marketplace as a whole are rapidly changing, becoming something new and different as we move forward into the future.

Among the most important points presented in this chapter were these:

- Banks—the oldest and most familiar of all financial institutions—have changed greatly since their origins centuries ago, evolving from moneychangers and money issuers to become the most important gatherers and dispensers of financial information in the economy.

- Banking is by no means alone in the financial-services sector but increasingly is being pressured on all sides by key financial-service competitors—savings institutions (including savings and loan associations and savings banks), credit unions, money market funds, security brokers and dealers, investment companies (mutual funds), hedge funds, finance companies, insurance companies, and other financial conglomerates and holding companies.

- The leading nonbank businesses that compete with banks today in the financial sector offer many of the same services and, therefore, make it increasingly difficult to separate banks from other financial-service providers. Nevertheless, larger banks tend to offer the widest range of services of any financial-service firm today.

- The principal functions (and services) offered by banks and many of their financial-service competitors include these: (1) lending and investing money (the credit function); (2) making payments on behalf of customers to facilitate their purchases of goods and services (the payments function); (3) managing and protecting customers' cash and other forms of customer property (the cash management, risk management, and trust functions); and (4) assisting customers in raising new funds and investing those funds profitably (through the brokerage, investment banking, and savings functions).

- Major trends affecting the performance of banks and other financial firms today include the following: (1) widening service menus (i.e., greater product-line diversification); (2) the globalization of the financial marketplace and the spread of services worldwide (i.e., geographic diversification); (3) the easing or elimination of government rules affecting banks and other financial firms (i.e., deregulation); (4) the growing rivalry among banks themselves and with their closest financial-service competitors (i.e., intense competition); (5) the tendency for all financial firms increasingly to look alike, offering similar services (i.e., convergence); (6) the declining numbers and larger size of banks and other financial-service providers, (i.e., consolidation); and (7) the increasing automation of financial-service production and delivery (i.e., technological change) in order to offer greater convenience for customers, reach wider markets, and promote cost savings.

Key Terms

bank, *4*
savings and loan
associations, *8*
savings banks, *8*
credit unions, *9*
money market funds, *9*
mutual funds, *9*
hedge funds, *9*
security brokers and
dealers, *10*
financial holding
companies, *10*

finance companies, *10*
life and property/casualty
insurance companies, *10*
currency exchange, *13*
discounting commercial
notes, *13*
savings deposits, *14*
demand deposit services, *15*
trust services, *16*
financial advisory
services, *16*

cash management
services, *16*
equipment leasing
services, *16*
insurance policies, *17*
retirement plans, *18*
security brokerage
services, *18*
security underwriting, *18*
merchant banking
services, *19*

**Problems
and Projects**

1. You have just been hired as the marketing officer for the new First National Bank of
   Vincent, a suburban banking institution that will soon be serving a local community of
   120,000 people. The town is adjacent to a major metropolitan area with a total population of well over 1 million. Opening day for the newly chartered bank is just two
   months away, and the president and the board of directors are concerned that the new
   bank may not be able to attract enough depositors and good-quality loan customers to
   meet its growth and profit projections. (There are 18 other financial-service competitors in town, including two credit unions, three savings banks, four insurance agencies,
   and two security broker offices.) Your task is to recommend the various services the
   bank should offer initially to build an adequate customer base. You are asked to do the
   following:

   a. Make a list of all the services the new bank could offer, according to current
       regulations.

   b. List the types of information you will need about the local community to help you
       decide which of many possible services are likely to have sufficient demand to make
       them profitable.

   c. Divide the possible services into two groups: those that you think are essential to
       customers (which should be offered beginning with opening day) and those that can
       be offered later as the bank grows.

   d. Briefly describe the kind of advertising campaign you would like to run to help the
       public see how your bank is different from all the other financial-service providers in
       the local area. Which services offered by the nonbank service providers would be of
       most concern to the new bank's management?

2. Leading money center banks in the United States have accelerated their investment
   banking activities all over the globe in recent years, purchasing corporate debt securities and stock from their business customers and reselling those securities to investors
   in the open market. Is this a desirable move by banking organizations from a profit
   standpoint? From a risk standpoint? From the public interest point of view? How would
   you research there questions? If you were managing a corporation that had placed large
   deposits with a bank engaged in such activities, would you be concerned about the risk
   to your company's funds? What could you do to better safeguard those funds?

3. Many financial analysis have warned that the traditional bank—the maker of loans and
   acceptor of deposits—is doomed because competing nonbank financial institutions are
   pirating away the best and largest bank customers and because even modest-size businesses have a growing tendency to bypass banks for credit and borrow instead in the

open market. Do you agree with this assessment of traditional banking's future? See if you can develop good arguments on *both* sides of this issue—for and against the future survival of the traditional banking organization.

4. The term *bank* has been applied broadly over the years to include a diverse set of financial-service institutions, which offer different financial-service packages. Identify as many of the different kinds of "banks" as you can. How do the "banks" you have identified compare to the largest banking group of all—the commercial banks? Why do you think so many different financial firms have been called *banks*? How might this terminological confusion affect financial-service customers?

5. What advantages can you see to banks affiliating with insurance companies? How might such an affiliation benefit a bank? An insurer? Can you identify any possible disadvantages to such an affiliation? Can you cite any real-world examples of bank–insurer affiliations? How well do they appear to have worked out in practice?

6. Explain the difference between *consolidation* and *convergence*. Are these trends in banking and financial services related? Do they influence each other? How?

7. What is a *financial intermediary*? What are its key characteristics? Is a bank a type of financial intermediary? Why? What other financial-services companies are financial intermediaries? What important roles within the financial system do financial intermediaries play?

8. Four main types of financial-service firms—banks, security broker/dealers, insurance companies, and finance/credit card companies—are in intense competition with one another today. Using Standard & Poor's Market Insight, Educational Version, available to users of this McGraw-Hill book, describe the principal similarities and differences among these four types of companies. You may find it helpful in answering this question to examine the files on Market Insight devoted to such financial firms as Bank of America (BAC), Bear Stearns Companies (BSC), American International Group (AIG), and Capital One Financial Corp (COF).

Internet Exercises

1. The beginning of this chapter addresses the question, "What is a bank?" (That is a tough question!) A number of websites also try to answer the very same question. Explore the following websites and try to develop an answer from two different perspectives:

   http://money.howstuffworks.com/bank1.htm

   http://law.freeadvice.com/financial_law/banking_law/bank.htm

   http://www.pacb.org/pacb_h08.htm

   a. In the broadest sense, what constitutes a bank?

   b. In the narrowest sense, what constitutes a bank?

2. What services does the bank you use offer? Check out its website, either by surfing the Web using the bank's name and location or by checking the Federal Deposit Insurance Corporation's website for the bank's name, city, and state. How does your current bank seem to compare with neighboring banks in the range of services it offers? In the quality of its website? (See especially **www.fdic.gov**.)

3. In this chapter we discuss the changing character of the financial-services industry and the role of *consolidation*. Visit the website **http://www.financialservicesfacts.org/financial/** and look at consolidation for the financial-services industry. What do the numbers tell us? How have the numbers changed between the 1990s and this decade?

   a. Specifically, which sectors of the financial-services industry have increased the dollar amount of assets they control?

b. In terms of market share based on dollars of assets, which sectors have increased their shares (percentagewise) and which have decreased their shares?

4. As college students, we often want to know, How big is the job market? Visit the website **http://www.financialservicesfacts.org/financial/** and look at employment for the financial-services industry. Answer the following questions using the most recent data on this site.

   a. How many employees work at depository institutions? What is the share (percentage) of total financial-services employees?

   b. How many employees work in insurance? What is the share (percentage) of total financial-services employees?

   c. How many employees work in securities and commodities? What is the share (percentage) of total financial-services employees?

5. What kinds of jobs seem most plentiful in the banking industry today? Make a brief list of the most common job openings you find at various bank websites. Do any of these jobs interest you? (See, for example, **www.banking.about.com**.)

6. According to the sources mentioned earlier on the World Wide Web, how did banking get its start and why do you think it has survived for so long? What major event occurred in 1934 that has affected banking, not only in the United States, but in many countries around the world ever since then? (See **www.banking.about.com** and **www.fdic.gov**.)

7. In what ways do the following corporations resemble banks? How are they different from banks of about the same asset size?

   Charles Schwab Corporation (**www.schwab.com**)

   Household International (**www.household.com**)

   GMAC Financial Services (**www.gmacfs.com**)

STANDARD &POOR'S

S&P Market Insight Challenge

1. Use Standard & Poor's Market Insight website (**www.mhhe.com/edumarketinsight**) for this problem. GE Capital is a financial-services affiliate of General Electric. Reread the description of GE Capital in this chapter. Then, using the Educational Version of S&P's Market Insight, read and print the "Long Business Description" for GE. Describe any new developments concerning the company's financial-service affiliates. What is the most recent contribution of the financial-services affiliates to the total revenue received by the entire company? (This would be expressed as a percentage of total revenue.)

2. Use Standard & Poor's Market Insight website (**www.mhhe.com/edumarketinsight**) for this problem. Table 1–2 in this chapter provides a list of the leading banking and nonbanking financial-service providers around the globe. The left-hand column lists *banks* and the right-hand column lists several *nonbank financial-service firms*. (Those firms found in the Educational Version of S&P's Market Insight are noted in the table.) Choose one banking-oriented firm from the left-hand column and one nonbank financial-service firm from the right-hand column. Using Market Insight, print out the "Long Business Description" for your two selected financial firms. Compare and contrast the business descriptions of the two financial-service firms. What are the implications for these firms of any differences you detect in their business descriptions?

REAL NUMBERS FOR REAL BANKS — The Very First Assignment

Identification of a bank to follow throughout the semester (or perhaps for the rest of your life):

A. Choose a bank (financial) holding company (BHC) that is both among the 25 largest U.S. banking companies and in S&P's Market Insight. Do not choose National City Corporation because that BHC is used for examples throughout the text. (Your instructor may impose constraints to ensure that your class examines a significant number of institutions, rather than just a few.)

The list of the 50 largest U.S. BHCs is found at **www.ffiec. gov/nic.** Click on the link "Top 50 BHCs/Banks" and choose from the top 25.

B. Having chosen a BHC, check to make sure that your banking company is covered by Standard & Poor's Market Insight, Educational Version. (At last count, 21 of the 25 largest U.S. banking companies were included in Market Insight.) Using Market Insight, read and print the "Long Business Description" for your firm. In Chapter 1 we discussed the traditional financial services that have been associated with commercial banking for decades and then the services that have recently been added to banks' financial-service offerings. What does the Market Insight description for your chosen banking firm reveal regarding types of services?

C. The FDIC's website found at **http://www.fdic.gov/bank/ analytical/largest/index.html** contains quarterly reports highlighting the performance of the largest U.S. banking companies. Read the latest available report and see if the BHC you have chosen has changed its ranking. For each bank holding company, the website offers a one-page synopsis of financial information, in addition to summary information about the performance of the industry for the quarter. You will learn more about the meaning of "the financials" as the semester or term unfolds (something to look forward to!). This historical information provides some background concerning the BHC you have chosen to follow throughout this course.

D. In conclusion, write approximately one page on your chosen banking company and the focus of its operations.

Selected References

See the following for an overview and explanation of the services banks offer today:

1. Baughn, William H., and Charles E. Walker, eds. *The Banker's Handbook*. 4th ed. Homewood, IL: Business One Irwin, 1990.

2. Stavins, Joanna. "Checking Accounts: What Do Banks Offer and What Do Consumers Value?" *New England Economic Review*, Federal Reserve Bank of Boston, March/April 1999.

For a review of banking's history, see the following:

3. Kindleberger, Charles P. *A Financial History of Western Europe*. Boston: Allen and Unwin, 1984.

For a deeper exploration of the role of banks in modern financial theory, see the following:

4. Diamond, Douglas. "Financial Intermediation and Delegated Monitoring." *Review of Economic Studies* 51 (1984), pp. 393–414.

See the following for an analysis of key trends affecting banking and other financial-service institutions:

5. Jordan, Jerry L. "The Functions and Future of Retail Banking." *Economic Commentary*, Federal Reserve Bank of Cleveland, September 15, 1996.

6. Rose, Peter S. *Money and Capital Markets: The Financial System in the Economy*. 8th ed. Burr Ridge, IL: McGraw-Hill/Irwin, 2003. See especially Chapters 4, 15, and 18.

7. Powell, Donald E., Chairman of the Federal Deposit Insurance Corporation. "South America and Emerging Risks in Banking," Speech to the Florida Bankers Association, Orlando, FL, October 23, 2002.

For a discussion of the future of traditional banking, see:

8. Beim, David U. "Why Are Banks Dying?" *The Columbia Journal of World Business*, Spring 1992, pp. 1–12.

9. Kaufman, George G., and Larry R. Mote. "Is Banking a Declining Industry? A Historical Perspective." *Economic Perspectives*, Federal Reserve Bank of Chicago, May/June 1994, pp. 2–21.

10. Levonian, Mark E. "Why Banking Isn't Declining." *FRBSF Weekly Letter*, Federal Reserve Bank of San Francisco, No. 95-03 (January 20, 1995), pp. 1–3.

11. Stern, Gary H. "Managing Moral Hazard with Market Signals: How Regulation Should Change with Banking." *Region* 13, no. 3, Federal Reserve Bank of Minneapolis, pp. 28–31, 60–62.

For a useful model of banking's role as a key financial intermediary in the economy, see especially:

12. Rose, John T. "Commercial Banks as Financial Intermediaries and Current Trends in Banking: A Pedagogical Framework." *Financial Practice and Education* 3, no. 2 (Fall 1993), pp. 113–118.

For an analysis of the linkages between the development of the banking and financial-services sector and the growth of the economy, see:

13. Levine, Ross, Norman Loayza, and Thorsten Beck. "Financial Intermediation and Growth: Causality and Causes." *Journal of Monetary Economics* 46 (August 2000), pp. 31–77.

14. Valderrama, Diego. "Financial Development, Productivity and Economic Growth." *FRBSF Economic Letter*, Federal Reserve Bank of San Francisco, June 27, 2003.

For an analysis of the recent slowing in the expansion of conglomerate banks and other financial firms and its possible causes, see, in particular:

15. Guzman, Mark G. "Slow but Steady Progress toward Financial Deregulation." *Southwest Economy*, Federal Reserve Bank of Dallas, January–February 2003.

16. Couch, Karen, Robert Mahalik, and Robert R. Moore. "Banks as Real Estate Brokers—Letting Free Enterprise Work." *Southwest Economy*, Federal Reserve Bank of Dallas, May–June 2001.

Appendix

Career Opportunities in Banking and Financial Services

In this chapter, we have focused on the great importance of banks and their nonbank financial-service competitors in the functioning of the economy and financial system and on the many roles played by bank and nonbank financial firms in dealing with the public. But banks and their financial competitors are more than just financial-service providers. They can also be the place for a satisfying professional career, though this is more difficult to achieve than in the past due to industry automation and consolidation. What different kinds of professionals work inside most banks and other financial firms?

Loan Officers Many bankers and other financial managers begin their careers accepting and analyzing loan applications submitted by business and household customers. Loan officers make initial contact with potential new customers and assist them in filing loan requests and in developing a service relationship with the bank or other lending institution. Loan officers are needed in such important financial institutions as banks, credit unions, finance companies, and savings associations.

Credit Analysts The credit analyst backstops the work of the loan officer by preparing detailed written assessments of each loan applicant's financial position and advises management on the wisdom of granting any particular loan. Credit analysts and loan officers need professional training in accounting, financial statement analysis, and business finance.

Loan Workout Specialists With the substantial numbers of business failures in recent years, many loans to businesses and consumers have gone bad, requiring the services of skilled professionals to identify the causes of each problem loan situation and to find solutions that maximize the chances for recovering the lender's funds. This is the job of the loan workout specialist, who must have a strong background in accounting, financial statement analysis, business law, and economics, along with good negotiating skills.

Managers of Operations Managers in the operations division of a bank or other similar financial-services firm are responsible for processing checks and clearing other cash items on behalf of their customers, for maintaining and improving the institution's computer facilities and electronic networks, for supervising the activities of tellers, for handling customer problems with checking accounts and other services, for maintaining security systems to protect property, and for overseeing the operation of the personnel (human resources) department. Managers in the operations division need sound training in the principles of business and financial management and in computers and management information systems, and they must have the ability to interact with large groups of people.

Branch Managers When banks and their financial service competitors operate large branch systems, many of these functions are supervised by the manager of each branch office. Branch managers lead each branch's effort to attract new accounts, calling on business firms and households in their local area. They also approve loan requests and resolve customer complaints. Branch managers must know how to motivate employees and how to represent their institution well in the local community.

Systems Analysts These highly trained computer specialists work with officers and staff in all departments, translating their production and information needs into programming language. The systems analyst provides a vital link between financial-service managers and computer programmers in making the computer an effective problem-solving tool for management and an efficient, accurate, and safe channel for delivering customer services through websites and other electronic channels. Systems analysts need in-depth training in computer programming and mathematics as well as courses emphasizing business problem solving.

Auditing and Control Personnel Keeping abreast of the inflow of revenues and the outflow of expenses and track-

ing changes in the service provider's financial position are the responsibilities of auditors and accountants. These are some of the most important tasks within the financial institution because they help guard against losses from criminal activity and waste. Jobs as important as these require considerable training in accounting and auditing.

Trust Department Specialists Specialists in a trust department provide a wide variety of customer services. They aid companies in managing their employee retirement programs, issuing securities, maintaining business records, and investing funds. Consumers also receive help in managing their property and in building an estate for retirement. Men and women employed in trust departments usually possess a wide range of backgrounds in commercial and property law, real estate appraisal, securities investment strategies, financial statement analysis, and marketing.

Tellers One employee that many customers see and talk with at virtually all depository institutions is the teller— the individual who occupies a fixed station or location within a branch office or at a drive-in window, receiving deposits and dispensing cash and information. Tellers must sort and file deposit receipts and withdrawal slips, verify customer signatures, check account balances, and balance their own cash position at least once each day. Because of their pivotal role in communicating with customers, tellers must be friendly with customers, accurate, and knowledgeable about the other departments of the institution and the services they sell.

Security Analysts and Traders Security analysts and traders are usually found in a financial firm's bond department and in its trust department. All financial institutions have a pressing need for individuals skilled in evaluating the businesses and governments issuing securities that the institution might buy and in assessing financial market conditions. Such courses as economics, money and banking, money and capital markets, and investment analysis are usually the best fields of study for a person interested in becoming a security analyst or security trader.

Marketing Personnel With greater competition today, banks and other service providers have an urgent need to develop new services and to more aggressively sell existing services—tasks that usually fall primarily to the marketing department. This important function requires an understanding of the problems involved in producing and selling services and familiarity with service advertising techniques and cost accounting. Course work in economics, services marketing, statistics, and business management is especially helpful in this field.

Human Resources Managers A financial firm's performance in serving the public and its owners depends, more than anything else, on the talent, training, and dedication of its management and staff. The job of human resources (personnel) managers is to find and hire people with superior skills and to train them to fill the roles needed by the institution. Most large institutions operate intensive management training programs, lasting from 6 months to as long as 18 months, which typically are directed by the human resources division. Human resources managers keep records on employee performance and counsel employees on ways to improve their performance and opportunities for promotion.

Investment Banking Specialists Banks are becoming increasingly involved in assisting their business customers with the issue of bonds, notes, and stock to raise new capital, and they frequently render advice on financial market opportunities and on business mergers and acquisitions. This is the dynamic, fast-paced field of investment banking, one of the highest-paid and most challenging areas in the financial marketplace. Investment banking personnel must have intensive training in accounting, economics, strategic planning, investments, and international finance.

Bank Examiners and Regulators Because banks are among the most heavily regulated of all business firms, there is an ongoing need for men and women to examine the financial condition and operating procedures of banks and their closest competitors and to prepare and enforce banking regulations. Regulatory agencies hire examiners from time to time, often by visiting college cam-

Key URLs

Information about possible employment at key bank regulatory agencies may be found, for example, at **www.federal.reserve. gov/careers** or at **www.fdic.gov/about/ jobs**

puses or as a result of phone calls and letters from applicants. Examiners and regulators must have knowledge of accounting, business management, economics, and financial laws and regulations.

Training Specialists Employees hired into management positions typically go through training programs that vary considerably in length and content, though most seem to average a year to 18 months in length. Trainees are generally rotated through different departments and also are given classroom instruction. Most training programs also encourage their trainees to seek additional education, including computer classes, accounting and MBA programs, and foreign language instruction (reflecting the growing internationalization of the financial-services sector).

In summary, banking and financial services offer professional career opportunities for those who have received the necessary education and training. Moreover, with recent changes in services offered, technology, and regulation, the financial-services field can be an exciting and challenging career. However, finding a good job in this industry today will *not* be easy because of consolidation and convergence. Hundreds of smaller financial institutions are being absorbed by larger ones, with subsequent reductions in staff. Nevertheless, if such a career path sounds interesting to you, there is no substitute for further study of the industry: its history, services, and problems. It is also important to visit with current bank personnel and employees of other financially oriented businesses to learn more about the daily work environment inside a financial firm. Only then can you be sure that professional banking and financial services is really a good career target for you.

CHAPTER TWO

The Impact of Government Policy and Regulation on Banking and the Financial-Services Industry

Key Topics in This Chapter

- The Principal Reasons for Bank and Nonbank Financial-Services Regulations
- Major Bank and Nonbank Regulators and Laws
- The Riegle-Neal and Gramm-Leach-Bliley Acts
- Deregulation and Key Issues Left Unresolved
- The Central Banking System
- Organization and Structure of the Federal Reserve System
- The Central Bank's Principal Task: Making and Implementing Monetary Policy

Introduction

Some people fear banks and other financial institutions. They may be intimidated by the power and influence these institutions seem to possess. Thomas Jefferson, third President of the United States, once wrote in a letter: "I sincerely believe that banking establishments are more dangerous than standing armies." Partly out of such fears and concerns a complex web of laws and regulations has emerged.

This chapter is devoted to a study of the complex regulatory environment that governments around the world have created for banks and other financial-service firms in an effort to safeguard the public's savings, bring stability to the financial system, and prevent abuse of financial-service customers. Banks and selected other financial institutions operating in the United States and in most other countries must contend with some of the heaviest and most comprehensive rules applied to any industry. These government-imposed regulations are enforced by federal and state agencies that oversee the operations, service offerings, performance, and expansion of most financial-service firms.

Regulation is an ugly word to many people, especially the managers and stockholders of commercial banks and their financial-service competitors, who often see the rules imposed upon them by governments as burdensome, costly, and unnecessarily damaging to innovation and efficiency. But, as we will see in this chapter, the rules of the game are changing—more and more financial-service regulations are being set aside or weakened and the free marketplace, not government dictation, is increasingly being relied upon to shape and restrain what financial firms can do. One prominent example is the 1999 Gramm-Leach-Bliley (Financial Services Modernization) Act, which tore down the regulatory walls separating banking from security trading and underwriting and from the insurance industry, allowing these different types of financial firms to acquire each other, dramatically increasing financial-services competition inside the United States and around the world.

In this chapter we identify and discuss all the key regulatory agencies that supervise and examine banks and their closest competitors. The chapter concludes with a brief look at monetary policy and the two most powerful financial institutions in the world—the Federal Reserve System and the European Central Bank.

Banking Regulation

First, we turn to one of the most government regulated of all industries—commercial banking. As bankers work within the financial system to supply loans, accept deposits, and provide other financial services to their customers, they must do so within a climate of extensive federal and state rules designed primarily to protect the public interest.

A popular saying among bankers is that the letters FDIC (Federal Deposit Insurance Corporation) really mean Forever Demanding Increased Capital! To U.S. bankers, at least, the FDIC and the other bank regulatory agencies seem to be forever demanding something: more capital, more reports, more public service, and so on. No new bank can enter the industry in the United States, and in most other countries as well, without government approval (in the form of a charter to operate). The types of deposits and other financial instruments banks sell to the public to raise funds must be sanctioned by each bank's principal regulatory agency. The quality of a bank's loans and investments and the adequacy of its capital are carefully reviewed by bank examiners. When a bank seeks to expand by constructing a new building, merging with another bank, setting up a branch office, or acquiring or starting a nonbank business, regulatory approval must first be obtained. Finally, a bank's owners cannot even choose to close its doors and leave the industry unless they obtain explicit approval from the government agency that granted each bank's original charter of incorporation.

To encourage further thought concerning the process of regulatory governance, we can use an analogy between the regulation of financial firms and the experiences of youth. We were all children and teenagers before growing both physically, mentally, and emotionally into adults. As children and teenagers, we liked to have fun; however, we pursued this objective within the constraints set by our parents, and some kids had more lenient parents than others. Banks are financial firms that like to maximize shareholders' wealth (shareholders are having fun when they are making money); however, banks must operate within the constraints imposed by regulators. The banks are in essence the "kids" with the strictest parents on the block.

Bank Regulation—Pros and Cons of Strict Rules

Why are most banks so closely regulated—more so than virtually any other financial-service firm? A number of reasons can be given for this heavy burden of government supervision over banking, some of them centuries old.

Regulatory agencies and the federal and state laws that guide what they do have become prominent features on the World Wide Web. At literally dozens of sites, you can find out about banking's changing rules, including new legislation and new regulations. You can also find out how to contact a regulatory agency if you have a question about how a bank is or is not responding to your financial service needs.

For example, news concerning bank regulation and bank compliance with current rules can be found at **www.aba.com/compliance**. If you are interested in contacting regulatory agencies in your home state, one approach that is often useful is simply to enter your state's name and the words "banking commission."

The Federal Deposit Insurance Corporation (FDIC) has a nice summary on the Web of important banking laws in American history. Two key websites here are **www.fdic.gov/regulations/laws/important** and especially **www.fdic.gov/bank/historical/brief**.

Have you ever thought about becoming a bank examiner or securing another position with a regulator agency? For a glimpse of some of the job options in this area, you may wish to check out the site **www.fdic.gov/about/jobs** or **www.federalreserve.gov/careers**.

Just as key bank regulators are well represented on the Net, so are the regulators of financial firms that compete with banks. For example, the individual states, through boards and commissions, are heavily involved in the regulation of credit unions, savings and loans, savings banks, and insurance and finance companies. You can usually bring up these state regulator websites by typing in the name of each state followed by such phrases as "savings and loan board," "insurance commission," and the like. At the federal level several regulators' and trade associations' websites are useful for further information about banking's chief competitors, including the National Credit Union Administration (**www.ncua.gov**), the Office of Thrift Supervision (**www.ots.treas.gov**), the Insurance Information Institute (**www.iii.com**), the American Council of Life Insurance (**www.acli.com**), and the Securities and Exchange Commission (**www.sec.gov**).

First, banks are among the leading repositories of the public's savings, especially the savings of individuals and families. While most of the public's savings are placed in relatively short-term, highly liquid deposits, banks also hold large amounts of long-term savings in retirement accounts. The loss of these funds due to bank failure or crime would be catastrophic to many individuals and families. However, many savers lack the financial expertise and depth of information needed to correctly evaluate the riskiness of a bank. Therefore, regulatory agencies are charged with the responsibility of gathering and evaluating the information needed to assess the true financial condition of banks to protect the public against loss. Cameras and guards patrol bank lobbies to reduce the risk of loss due to theft. Periodic bank examinations and audits are aimed at limiting losses from embezzlement, fraud, or mismanagement. Government agencies stand ready to loan funds to banks faced with unexpected shortfalls of spendable reserves so that the public's savings are protected.

Banks are also closely watched because of their power to create money in the form of readily spendable deposits by making loans and investments. Changes in the volume of money created by banks and competing financial firms appear to be closely correlated with economic conditions, especially the growth of jobs and the presence or absence of inflation. However, the fact that banks and many of their nearest financial-service competitors create money, which impacts the vitality of the economy, is not necessarily a valid excuse for regulating them. As long as central banks as government policymakers can control a nation's money supply, the volume of money that individual banks and other financial firms create should be of no great concern to the regulatory authorities or to the public.

Banks are also regulated because they provide individuals and businesses with loans that support consumption and investment spending. Regulatory authorities argue that the

Insights and Issues

THE PRINCIPAL REASONS BANKS AND MANY OF THEIR FINANCIAL-SERVICE COMPETITORS ARE SUBJECT TO GOVERNMENT REGULATION

- To protect the safety of the public's savings.
- To control the supply of money and credit in order to achieve a nation's broad economic goals (such as high employment and low inflation).
- To ensure equal opportunity and fairness in the public's access to credit and other vital financial services.
- To promote public confidence in the financial system, so that savings flow smoothly into productive investment, and payments for goods and services are made speedily and efficiently.
- To avoid concentrations of financial power in the hands of a few individuals and institutions.

- To provide the government with credit, tax revenues, and other services.
- To help sectors of the economy that have special credit needs (such as housing, small business, and agriculture).

However, regulation must be balanced and limited so that: (*a*) banks and their financial-service competitors can develop new services that the public demands, (*b*) competition in financial services remains strong enough to ensure reasonable prices and an adequate quantity and quality of service to the public, and (*c*) private-sector decisions are not distorted in ways that misallocate and waste scarce resources (such as by governments propping up banks and other financial firms that should be allowed to fail).

public has a keen interest in an adequate supply of loans flowing from the financial system. Moreover, where discrimination in granting credit is present, those individuals who are discriminated against face a significant obstacle to their personal well-being and an improved standard of living. This is especially true if access to credit is denied because of age, sex, race, national origin, or other irrelevant factors. Perhaps, however, the government could eliminate discrimination in providing services to the public simply by promoting more competition among banks and other providers of financial services, such as by vigorous enforcement of the antitrust laws, rather than through regulation.

Finally, banks, in particular, have a long history of involvement with federal, state, and local government. Early in the history of the industry governments relied upon cheap bank credit and the taxation of banks to finance armies and to supply the funds they were unwilling to raise through direct taxation of their citizens. More recently, governments have relied upon banks to assist in conducting economic policy, in collecting taxes, and in dispensing government payments. This reason for banking regulation has come under attack recently, however, because banks and their competitors probably would provide financial services to governments if it were profitable to do so, even in the absence of regulation.

In the United States, banks are regulated through a **dual banking system;** that is, *both* federal and state authorities have significant regulatory powers. This system was designed to give the states closer control over industries operating within their borders, but also, through federal regulation, to ensure that banks would be treated fairly by individual states and local communities as their activities expanded across state lines. The key bank regulatory agencies within the U.S. government are the Comptroller of the Currency, the Federal Reserve System, and the Federal Deposit Insurance Corporation. The Department of Justice and the Securities and Exchange Commission have important, but smaller, federal regulatory roles in banking, while **state banking commissions** are the primary regulators of American banks at the state level, as shown in Table 2–1.

The Impact of Regulation on Banks—The Arguments for Strict Rules versus Lenient Rules

Although the reasons for the regulation of banks and other closely related financial firms are well known, the possible impacts of regulation on the banking industry are in dispute. One of the earliest theories about regulation, developed by economist George Stigler [8],

TABLE 2–1

Banking's Principal
Regulatory Agencies
and Their
Responsibilities

Federal Reserve System
- Supervises and regularly examines all state-chartered member banks and bank holding companies operating in the United States and acts as the "umbrella supervisor" for financial holding companies that are now allowed to combine banking, insurance, and securities firms under common ownership.
- Imposes reserve requirements on deposits (Regulation D).
- Must approve all applications of member banks to merge, establish branches, or exercise trust powers.
- Charters, supervises, and examines international banking corporations operating in the United States.

Comptroller of the Currency
- Issues charters for new national banks.
- Supervises and regularly examines all national banks.
- Must approve all national bank applications for new branch offices, trust powers, mergers, and acquisitions.

Federal Deposit Insurance Corporation
- Insures deposits of banks conforming to its regulations.
- Must approve all applications of insured banks to establish branches, merge, or exercise trust powers.
- Requires all insured banks to submit reports on their financial condition.

Department of Justice
- Must review and approve proposed bank mergers and holding company acquisitions for their effects on competition and file suit if competition would be significantly damaged by these proposed organizational changes.

Securities and Exchange Commission
- Must approve public offerings of debt and equity securities by banks or bank holding companies and oversee the activities of bank securities affiliates.

State Banking Boards or Commissions
- Issue charters for new banks.
- Supervise and regularly examine all state-chartered banks.
- Reserve the right to approve all applications of banks operating within state borders to form a holding company, acquire affiliates and subsidiaries, or establish branch offices.

---

contends that firms in regulated industries actually seek out regulation because it brings benefits in the form of monopolistic rents due to the fact that regulations often block entry into the regulated industry. Thus, some banks or other financial firms may lose money if regulations are lifted because they will no longer enjoy protected monopoly rents that increase their earnings. Samuel Peltzman [5], on the other hand, contends that regulation shelters a firm from changes in demand and cost, lowering its risk. If true, this implies that lifting regulations would subject individual banks to greater risk and eventually result in more failures.

More recently, Edward Kane [3] has argued that regulations can increase customer confidence, which, in turn, may create greater customer loyalty toward banks or other financial firms. Kane believes that regulators actually compete with each other in offering regulatory services in an attempt to broaden their influence among regulated firms and with the general public. Moreover, he argues that there is an ongoing struggle between regulated firms and the regulators, called the *regulatory dialectic*. This is much like the struggle between children (banks) and parents (regulators) over such rules as curfew and acceptable friends. Once regulations are set in place, bankers and other financial-service managers will inevitably search to find ways around the new rules through innovation in order to maximize the value of each financial firm. If they are successful in skirting existing rules, then new regulations will be created, encouraging bankers and other financial managers to seek further innovations in services and methods. Thus, the struggle between regulated firms and regulators goes on indefinitely. The regulated firms never really grow up. Kane also believes that regulations provide an incentive for less-regulated businesses to try to win customers away from more-regulated firms, something that appears to have happened in banking in recent years as mutual funds, financial conglomerates, and other less-regulated businesses have stolen away many of banking's best customers.

Concept Check

2–1. What key areas or functions of a bank are regulated today?

2–2. What are the *reasons* for regulating each of these key areas or functions?

Major Banking Laws—Where and When the Rules Originated

One useful way to see the potent influence regulatory authorities exercise on the banking industry is to review some of the major laws from which federal and state regulatory agencies receive their authority and direction. See Table 2–2 for a summary of these U.S. laws and major regulatory events in the history of American banking. Table 2–3 lists the number of U.S. banks by their regulators.

TABLE 2–2
Summary of Major Banking Laws and Their Provisions

Laws limiting bank lending and loan risk:
National Bank Act (1863–64)
Federal Reserve Act (1913)
Banking Act of 1933 (Glass-Steagall)
Laws restricting the services banks and thrifts can offer:
National Bank Act (1863–64)
Banking Act of 1933 (Glass-Steagall)
Competitive Equality in Banking Act (1987)
FDIC Improvement Act (1991)
Laws expanding the services banks and thrifts can offer:
Depository Institutions Deregulation and Monetary Control Act (1980)
Garn–St. Germain Depository Institutions Act (1982)
Gramm-Leach-Bliley Act (1999)
Laws prohibiting discrimination in offering banking services:
Equal Credit Opportunity Act (1974)
Community Reinvestment Act (1977)
Laws mandating increased information to the consumer of banking services:
Consumer Credit Protection Act (Truth in Lending, 1968)
Competitive Equality in Banking Act (1987)
Truth in Savings Act (1991)
Gramm-Leach-Bliley Act (1999)

Laws requiring more accurate financial reporting:
Sarbanes-Oxley Act (2002)
Laws regulating branch banking:
Banking Act of 1933 (Glass-Steagall)
Riegle-Neal Interstate Banking and Branching Efficiency Act (1994)
Laws regulating bank holding company activity:
Bank Holding Company Act of 1956
Riegle-Neal Interstate Banking and Branching Efficiency Act (1994)
Gramm-Leach-Bliley Act (1999)
Laws regulating bank mergers:
Bank Merger Act (1960)
Riegle-Neal Interstate Banking and Branching Efficiency Act (1994)
Laws assisting federal agencies in dealing with failing banks and thrifts:
Garn–St. Germain Depository Institutions Act (1982)
Competitive Equality in Banking Act (1987)
Financial Institutions Reform, Recovery, and Enforcement Act (1989)
Federal Deposit Insurance Corporation Improvement Act (1991)
Laws requiring the sharing of customer information with government:
USA Patriot Act (2001)

TABLE 2–3
Regulators of U.S. Insured Banks (Showing Numbers of U.S. Banks Covered by Deposit Insurance as of December 31, 2002)

Source: Federal Deposit Insurance Corporation.

Factoid
What is the oldest U.S. federal banking agency?
Answer: The Comptroller of the Currency, established to charter and regulate U.S. national banks during the 1860s.

Types of U.S. Insured banks	Number of U.S. Insured Banks (as of 12/31/02)	Number of Branch Offices of Insured Banks (as of 12/31/02)
Banks chartered by the federal government: U.S. insured banks with national (federal) charters issued by the Comptroller of the Currency	2,078	33,744
Banks chartered by state governments: State-chartered member banks of the Federal Reserve System and insured by the Federal Deposit Insurance Corporation	950	13,708
State-chartered nonmember banks insured by the Federal Deposit Insurance Corporation	4,859	18,733
Total of all U.S.-insured banks and branches	7,887	66,185

Primary Federal Regulators of U.S. Insured Banks (as of March 31, 2003):	Number of U.S. Insured Banks under Direct Regulation
Federal Deposit Insurance Corporation	4,849
Office of the Comptroller of the Currency	2,065
Board of Governors of the Federal Reserve System	950

Notes: The number of insured banks subject to each of the three federal regulatory agencies listed immediately above do not exactly match the numbers in the top portion of the table due to shared jurisdictions and other special arrangements among the regulatory agencies. Moreover, the figures in the bottom half of the table are for March 31, 2003, while those in the top portion were available only for year-end 2002.

Key URL
The supervision and examination of national banks is the responsibility of the Comptroller of the Currency in Washington, D.C., at **www.occ.treas.gov**.

Meet the Parents: The Legislation That Created Today's Bank Regulators

National Currency and Bank Acts (1863–64) The first major federal laws in U.S. banking were the National Currency and Bank Acts, passed during the Civil War. These laws set up a system for chartering national banks through a newly created division of the U.S. Treasury Department, the office of the **Comptroller of the Currency** (OCC). Any group of individuals could seek a federal bank charter provided they agreed to adhere to federal laws and regulations and pledged enough owners' (equity) capital to open for business.

The Comptroller of the Currency not only assesses the need for and charters new national banks, but also regularly examines those institutions. These examinations vary in frequency and intensity with the bank's financial condition. However, every national bank is examined by a team of federal examiners at least once every 12 to 18 months. In addition, the Comptroller's office must approve all applications for the establishment of new branch offices by national banks and any mergers where national banks are involved. The Comptroller can close a national bank that is insolvent or in danger of imposing substantial losses on its depositors.

The Federal Reserve Act (1913) A series of financial panics in the 19th and early 20th centuries led to the creation of a second federal bank regulatory agency, the **Federal Reserve System** (the Fed). Its principal roles vis-à-vis the banking industry are to serve as a lender of last resort—providing temporary loans to depository institutions facing financial emergencies—and to help stabilize the financial markets in order to preserve public confidence. The Fed also was created to provide important services to the banking industry, including the establishment of a nationwide network to clear and collect checks (supplemented later by an electronic funds transfer network). The Federal Reserve's most important job today, however, is to control money and credit conditions to promote economic stability. This final task assigned to the Fed is known as *monetary policy*, a topic we will examine again later in this chapter.

The Banking Act of 1933 (Glass-Steagall) Between 1929 and 1933, more than 9,000 banks failed and many Americans lost confidence in the U.S. banking system. The legislative response to this disappointing performance was to enact stricter rules and regulations in the **Glass-Steagall Act.** If as children we brought home failing grades, our parents may have reacted by revoking TV privileges and overseeing our homework more closely. Congress reacted in much the same manner. The Glass-Steagall Act defined commercial banking by providing constraints that were effective for more than 50 years. This legislation separated commercial banking from investment banking and insurance. The "kids" (banks) could no longer play with their friends, providers of insurance and investment banking services.

The most important part of the Glass-Steagall Act was Section 16, which prohibited national banks from investing in stock and from underwriting new issues of *ineligible securities* (especially corporate stocks and bonds). Several major New York banking firms split into separate entities—for example, J. P. Morgan, a commercial banking firm, split off from Morgan Stanley, an investment bank. Congress feared that underwriting privately issued securities (as opposed to underwriting government-guaranteed securities, which has been legal for many years) would increase the risk of bank failure. Moreover, banks might be able to coerce their customers into buying the securities they were underwriting as a condition for getting a loan (usually referred to as *tying arrangements*).

Factoid
What U.S. federal regulatory agency supervises and examines more banks than any other?
Answer: The Federal Deposit Insurance Corporation (FDIC).

Establishing the FDIC under the Glass-Steagall Act One of the Glass-Steagall Act's most important legacies was quieting public fears over the soundness of the banking system. The **Federal Deposit Insurance Corporation** (FDIC) was created to guarantee the public's deposits up to a stipulated maximum amount (initially $2,500; today up to $100,000 per account holder). Without question, the FDIC, since its inception in 1934, has helped to reduce the number of potential bank runs significantly, though it has not prevented bank failures. In fact, it may have contributed to individual bank risk taking and failure in some instances. Each insured bank is required to pay the federal insurance system an insurance premium based upon its volume of insurance-eligible deposits and its risk exposure. The hope was that, over time, the FDIC's pool of insurance funds would grow large enough to handle a considerable number of failures. However, the federal insurance plan was never designed to handle a rash of bank closings like the hundreds that occurred in the United States during the 1980s. This is why the FDIC was forced to petition Congress for additional borrowing authority in 1991, when the U.S. deposit insurance fund had become nearly insolvent.

Criticisms of the FDIC and Responses via New Legislation: The FDIC Improvement Act (1991) The FDIC became the object of strong criticism during the 1980s and early 1990s. Faced with predictions from the U.S. General Accounting Office that failing-bank claims would soon render the deposit insurance fund insolvent, the House and Senate passed the **Federal Deposit Insurance Corporation Improvement Act** in 1991. This legislation permitted the FDIC to borrow from the Treasury to remain solvent, called for risk-based deposit insurance premiums, and defined the actions to be taken when banks fall short of meeting capital requirements.

The debate leading to passage of the FDIC Improvement Act did not criticize the fundamental concept of deposit insurance, but it *did* criticize the way the federal deposit insurance system had been administered through most of its history. Prior to 1993, the FDIC levied fixed insurance premiums on all deposits eligible for insurance coverage, regardless of the riskiness of an individual bank's balance sheet. This fixed-fee system led to a *moral hazard* problem: it encouraged banks to accept greater risk because the government was pledged to pay off their depositors if they failed. Because all banks paid an identical insurance fee (unlike most private insurance systems), more risky banks were being supported by more conservative banks. The moral hazard problem created the need for regulation because it encouraged some institutions to take on greater risk than they otherwise would if no low-cost federal insurance system was available.[1]

Most depositors (except for the very largest) do not carefully monitor bank risk. Instead, they rely on the FDIC for protection. Because this results in subsidizing the riskiest banks—encouraging them to gamble with their depositors' money—a definite need developed for a risk-scaled insurance system in which the riskiest banks paid the highest insurance premiums. In response, Congress in 1991 ordered the FDIC to develop a risk-sensitive fee schedule under which the riskiest banks pay the highest insurance premiums and face the most restrictive regulations. In 1993, the FDIC implemented premiums differentiated on the basis of risk. Nevertheless, the federal government sells U.S. banks relatively cheap deposit insurance that may still encourage bank risk taking.

Congress also ordered the bank regulatory agencies to develop a new measurement scale for describing how well capitalized each bank and thrift institution is and to take "prompt corrective action" when a depository institution's capital begins to weaken, using such steps as slowing bank growth, requiring the owners to raise additional capital, or replacing management. If steps such as these do not solve the problem, the government can seize a bank whose ratio of tangible capital to total risk-adjusted assets falls to 2 percent or below and sell it to a healthy bank.

Under the law, regulators have to examine all banks over $100 million in assets on site at least once a year; for smaller banks, on-site examinations have to take place at least every 18 months. In a move toward "reregulating" the banking industry—bringing it under tighter control—federal banking agencies were required to develop new standards for the banks they regulate regarding loan documentation, internal management controls, risk exposure, and salaries paid to bank employees and to make sure that banks are not violating these guidelines. At the same time, in reaction to the debacle of the huge Bank of Credit and Commerce International (BCCI) of Luxembourg, which allegedly laundered drug money and illegally tried to secure control of U.S. banks, Congress ordered foreign banks to seek approval from the Federal Reserve Board before opening or closing any U.S. offices. They must also apply for FDIC insurance coverage if they wish to accept domestic deposits under $100,000. Moreover, foreign bank offices in the United States can be closed if their home countries do not adequately supervise their activities, and the FDIC is restricted from fully reimbursing uninsured and foreign depositors if their banks fail.

In an interesting final twist the Federal Reserve was restrained from propping up failing banks with long-term loans unless the Fed, the FDIC, and the current presidential administration agree that all the depositors of a bank should be protected in order to avoid damage to public confidence in the financial system. Congress's intent here was to bring the force of "market discipline" to bear on banks that have taken on too much risk and encourage problem banks to solve their own problems without government help.

One popular (but as yet unadopted) proposal for revamping or replacing the current federal deposit insurance system includes turning over deposit insurance to the private sector (privatization). Presumably, a private insurer would be more aggressive in assessing the riskiness of individual banks and would compel risky banks buying its insurance plan to pay much greater insurance fees. However, privatization of the deposit insurance system would not solve all the problems of trying to protect the public's deposits. For example, an effective private insurance system would be difficult to devise because, unlike most other forms

---

[1]For an in-depth discussion of the moral hazard problem see, for example, Kareken [4].

of insured risk, where the appearance of one claim does not necessarily lead to other claims, depositors' risks can be highly intercorrelated. The failure of a single bank can result in thousands of claims. Moreover, the failure of one bank may lead to still other failures. If a state's or region's economy turns downward, hundreds of failures may occur almost simultaneously. Could private insurers correctly price or even withstand that kind of risk?

In its earlier history, the FDIC's principal task was to restore public confidence in banks and avoid panic on the part of the public. Today, the challenge is how to *price* deposit insurance fairly so that risk is managed and the government is not forced to use excessive amounts of taxpayer funds to support private bank risk taking.

Raising the FDIC Insurance Limit? As the 21st century opened, the FDIC found itself embroiled in another public debate: *Should the federal deposit insurance limit be raised?* The FDIC pointed out that the $100,000 limit of protection for depositors was set more than two decades ago in 1980. In the interim, inflation in the cost of living had significantly reduced the real purchasing power of the FDIC's $100,000 insurance coverage limit. Accordingly, the FDIC and several other groups recommended a significant coverage hike, perhaps to $130,000 or even up to $200,000, along with an indexing of deposit insurance coverage to protect against inflation.

Proponents of the proposed insurance hike pointed out that during the previous decade banks and thrifts lost huge amounts of deposits to mutual funds, security brokers and dealers, retirement plans provided by insurance companies, and the like. Thus, it was argued, banks and other depositories needed a boost to make their deposits more competitive in the race for the public's savings.

Opponents of the proposed insurance increase also made several good arguments. For example, the original purpose of the federal insurance program was to protect the smallest and most vulnerable depositors. $100,000 seems to fulfill that purpose nicely (even with inflation taken into account). Moreover, the more deposits that are protected, the more likely it is that banks and other depositories will take advantage of a higher insurance limit and make high-risk loans that, if they pay off, reap substantial benefits for both stockholders and management (behavior we referred to earlier as *moral hazard*). On the other hand, if the risky loans are not repaid, the bank fails, but the government is there to rescue the depositors. With more risk taking, more depository institutions will probably fail, leaving a government insurance agency (and, ultimately, the taxpayers) to pick up the pieces and pay off the depositors.

Even if raising the FDIC's maximum insurance limit is not a good idea right now, a broader question remains: *Should we automatically adjust deposit insurance coverage every few years in order to offset the effects of inflation and raise the public's confidence in the banking system?* Not an easy question, but one that demands we be clear on the key *goal* envisioned. Are we trying to protect most depositors or just the most vulnerable who may have their whole life's savings at risk? Probably the latter. If deposit insurance is going to continue to be a government subsidy, do we really want to add to that subsidy or even protect its real value? Probably not, at least if inflation remains fairly modest. If deposit insurance provides an incentive for most depositors to simply ignore the true condition of their banks, is this really a healthy situation for our banking system? Shouldn't the marketplace, not the government, be allowed to play a greater role in disciplining bank risk taking? Probably so.[2]

---

[2]The FDIC is unique in one interesting aspect: While many nations collect funds from healthy banks to pay off the depositors of failed banks only when failure occurs, the FDIC collects funds each year to build up a reserve until these funds are needed to cover bank failures.

Some observers believe that the FDIC *may* need a larger reserve in the future due to ongoing consolidation in the banking industry. Instead of facing mainly small bank failures, as in the past, the FDIC may face record losses in the future from the failure of one or more very large banks.

ETHICS IN BANKING

The powers of the Federal Deposit Insurance Corporation (FDIC) to punish abuse at federally insured banks and to prevent damage to the federal insurance fund are awesome. It can remove the management or directors of an insured bank if it decides they have deliberately and recklessly weakened the bank or banks they control. It can even bar an individual from being involved in the operations of any FDIC-insured bank for a specific period of time or for life where there is a "demonstrated disregard" for bank safety and soundness. Finally, the FDIC can assess civil monetary penalties (CMPs) for violations of the Federal Deposit Insurance Act.

An interesting example of the latter action occurred in November 2002 when the FDIC issued a Notice of Charges to impose monetary penalties in excess of $5 million against some of the former officers and directors of Connecticut Bank

of Commerce in Stamford. The FDIC's notice alleged that certain key officers of that bank had used their positions of leadership to arrange large loans for their personal benefit, to conceal the true condition of those loans, and to cover up severe losses. The bank had failed in June 2002 and the FDIC had been appointed receiver to protect and liquidate whatever assets remained.

In addition to the monetary penalties, the FDIC also sought orders to prohibit some of the Connecticut bank's senior leadership from further participation in the banking industry and called for repayment to the bank of about $34 million.

See especially "FDIC Issues Notice of Charges against Certain Former Officers and Directors of the Failed Connecticut Bank of Commerce, Stamford, Connecticut," FDIC News Release, June 26, 2002.

Key URL
The Federal Deposit Insurance Corporation has several of the finest banking sites on the World Wide Web, all of which can be directly or indirectly accessed through **www.fdic.gov**.

Instilling Social Graces and Morals—Social Responsibility Laws of the 1960s, 1970s, 1980s and 1990s

The 1960s and 1970s ushered in a concern with the impact banks were having on the quality of life in the communities they served. Congress feared that banks were not adequately informing their customers of the terms under which loans were made and especially about the true cost of borrowing money. In 1968 Congress moved to improve the flow of information to the consumer of financial services by passing the Consumer Credit Protection Act (known as Truth in Lending), which required that lenders clearly spell out all the customer's rights and responsibilities under a loan agreement.

In 1974, Congress targeted possible discrimination in providing bank services to the public with passage of the Equal Credit Opportunity Act. Individuals and families could not be denied a loan merely because of their age, sex, race, national origin, or religious affiliation, or because they were recipients of public welfare. In 1977, Congress passed the Community Reinvestment Act (CRA), prohibiting U.S. banks from discriminating against customers residing within their trade territories merely on the basis of the neighborhood in which they lived. Further steps toward requiring fair and equitable treatment of customers and improving the flow of information from banks to consumers were taken in 1987 with passage of the Competitive Equality in Banking Act and in 1991 with the approval of the Truth in Savings Act. These federal laws required banks to more fully disclose their deposit service policies and the true rates of return offered on the public's savings.

Concept Check

2–3. What is the principal role of the Comptroller of the Currency?

2–4. What is the principal job performed by the FDIC?

2–5. What key roles does the Federal Reserve System perform in the banking and financial system?

2–6. What is the Glass-Steagall Act and why was it important in banking history?

2–7. Why did the federal insurance system run into serious problems in the 1980s and 1990s? Can the current federal insurance system be improved? In what ways?

2–8. How did the Equal Credit Opportunity Act and the Community Reinvestment Act address discrimination?

HOW THE FDIC USUALLY RESOLVES A BANK FAILURE

Most troubled bank situations are detected in a regular examination conducted by either federal or state banking agencies. If examiners find a serious problem, they ask the management and board of directors of the troubled bank to prepare a report, and a follow-up examination normally is scheduled several weeks or months later. If failure seems likely, FDIC examiners are called in to see if they concur that the bank is about to fail.

The FDIC then must choose among several different methods to resolve each failure. The two most widely used methods are *deposit payoff* and *purchase and assumption*. A deposit payoff is used when the closed bank's offices are not to be reopened, often because there are no interested bidders and the FDIC perceives that the public has other convenient banking alternatives. With a payoff, all insured depositors receive checks from the FDIC for up to $100,000, while uninsured depositors and other creditors receive a pro rata share of any funds generated from the eventual liquidation of the bank's assets. A purchase and assumption transaction, on the other hand, is employed if a healthy bank can be found to take over selected assets and the deposits of the failed institution.

When a purchase and assumption is employed, shortly before the bank's closing the FDIC will contact healthy banks in an effort to solicit bids for the failing institution. Interested buyers will negotiate with FDIC officials on the value of the failing bank's "good" and "bad" assets and on which assets and debts the FDIC will retain for collection and which will become the responsibility of the buyer.

On a predetermined date the state or federal agency that issued the bank's charter officially closes the troubled bank and its directors and officers meet with FDIC officials. After that meeting a press release is issued and local newspapers are contacted.

On the designated closing date the FDIC's liquidation team assembles at some agreed-upon location. When all team members are ready (and often just after the bank's offices are closed for the day), the liquidation team will enter the failed bank and place signs on the doors indicating that the bank has been seized by the FDIC. The team will move swiftly to take inventory of all assets and determine what funds the depositors and other creditors are owed. In subsequent days the liquidators may move their operations to rented office space nearby so the closed bank's facilities can open for business under the control of its new owners.

Legislation Aimed at Allowing Interstate Banking: Where Can the "Kids" Play?

Not until the 1990s was one of the most controversial subjects in the history of American banking—*interstate bank expansion*—finally resolved. Prior to the 1990s many states prohibited banking firms from entering their territory and setting up full-service branch offices. Banks interested in building an interstate banking firm usually had to form holding companies and acquire banks in other states as *affiliates* of those holding companies—not the most efficient way to get the job done because it led to costly duplication of capital and management. Moreover, many states as well as the federal government for a time outlawed an out-of-state bank holding company from acquiring control of a bank unless state law specifically granted that privilege.

The Riegle-Neal Interstate Banking Law (1994) In an effort to reduce the cost of duplicating banking companies and personnel in order to cross state lines and to provide more convenient services to millions of Americans who cross state lines every day, both houses of Congress voted in August 1994 to approve two new banking-related bills. The **Riegle-Neal Interstate Banking and Branching Efficiency Act** and the Riegle Community Development and Regulatory Improvement Act were both signed into law by President Clinton in September 1994, repealing provisions of the McFadden Act of 1927 and Douglas amendments of 1970 that prevented full-service interstate banking. These provisions are among the most notable:

- Adequately capitalized and managed holding companies can acquire banks anywhere in the United States.

- Interstate bank holding companies may consolidate their affiliated banks acquired across state lines into branch offices (unless a state acted to outlaw this branching activity). Branch offices established across state lines to take deposits from the public must also create an adequate volume of loans to support their local communities.[3]
- A Community Development Financial Institutions Fund was established in Washington, D.C., to provide funding and technical support to banks and other community organizations acting to promote local economic development in depressed communities and neighborhoods.

Thus, for the first time in U.S. history, these new banking laws gave a wide spectrum of American banks the power to take deposits and follow their customers across state lines. While the change undoubtedly enhanced banking convenience for some customers, some industry analysts feared that these new laws would increase the consolidation of the industry into larger banks and threaten the survival of many smaller banks. We will return to these issues in Chapter 3.

While U.S. banks still face at least some restrictions on their branching activity, even in the wake of the Riegle-Neal Interstate Banking Act, banks in most other industrialized countries usually do not face regulatory barriers to creating new branch offices. However, some nations, including Canada and the member states of the European Community (EC), either limit foreign banks' branching into their territory (in the case of Canada) or reserve the right to treat foreign banks differently if they so choose. Within the European Community, EC-based banks may offer any services throughout the EC that are permitted by each bank's home country.

Moreover, each European home nation must regulate and supervise its own banks, no matter in what markets they operate inside the EC's boundaries, a principle of regulation known as *mutual recognition*. Banks chartered by an EC member nation receive, in effect, a single banking license to operate wherever they wish inside the European Community. However, because EC countries differ slightly in the activities in which each country allows its banks to engage, some regulatory arbitrage may exist in which banks and other financial-service firms migrate to those areas inside Europe (or, for that matter, to any place on the globe) that permit the greatest span of activities and impose the fewest restrictions against bank expansion.

The Gramm-Leach-Bliley Act (1999): What Are Acceptable Activities for Playtime?

One of the most important banking laws of the 20th century in the United States was signed into law by President Bill Clinton in November of 1999. Overturning long-standing provisions of the Glass-Steagall Act, passed in the 1930s, and the Bank Holding Company Act, passed in the 1950s and amended in the 1960s and 70s, the new Financial

---

[3]Concern that interstate banking firms entering a particular state and buying up its banks and branches might drain deposits from that state led the U.S. Congress to insert Section 109 in the Riegle-Neal Interstate Banking Act. This section prohibits a bank from establishing or acquiring branch offices outside its home state *primarily for deposit production.* The same prohibition applies to interstate acquisitions of banks by holding companies. Interstate acquirers are expected to make an adequate volume of loans available in those communities outside their home state that they have entered with deposit-taking facilities.

Several steps are taken annually to determine if an interstate banking firm is in compliance with Section 109. First, an interstate bank's statewide loan-to-deposit ratio is computed for each state it has entered and that ratio is then compared to the entered state's overall loan-to-deposit ratio for all banks based in that state (excluding wholesale, limited-purpose, or credit card banks). The regulatory agencies look to see if the interstate bank's loan-to-deposit ratio in a given state is *less than half* of that state's overall loan-to-deposit ratio for banks calling that state home. If it is, an investigation ensues to determine if the banking firm's interstate branches are "reasonably helping to meet the credit needs of the communities served." A banking firm failing this investigation is subject to penalties imposed by its principal federal regulator.

Services Modernization Act (more commonly known as the **Gramm-Leach-Bliley Act** or GLB after its Senate and House sponsors) permitted well-managed and well-capitalized banking companies to affiliate with insurance and securities firms under common owner-ship. Conversely, securities and insurance companies could form financial holding compa-nies (FHCs) that also could control one or more banks. Banks were permitted to sell insurance provided they conform to state insurance rules. Eventually, bankers *may* be allowed to engage in real estate brokerage if the U.S. Treasury ultimately approves this activity.

GLB permits these banking-insurance-securities affiliations to take place either through (1) a financial holding company (FHC) type of organization, with banks, insurance com-panies or agencies, and securities firms each operating as separate companies but con-trolled by the same stock-holding corporation (if approved by the Federal Reserve Board), or (2) through subsidiary firms owned by a bank (if approved by the bank's principal regulator).

FHCs were also authorized, with regulatory approval, to set up *merchant banking* sub-sidiaries. These equity lenders take temporary ownership interests (holding stock) in com-mercial projects—a service already offered for many years by large European banks. However, merchant banks cannot actively manage the companies whose equity securities they hold.

The new law's purpose was to allow U.S. banks and other financial-service companies the ability to diversify their service offerings and thereby reduce their overall business risk exposure. Presumably, if the banking industry happened to be in a recession with declin-ing profits, the insurance or the securities business might be experiencing an economic boom with rising profits, thereby bringing greater overall stability to a fully diversified financial firm's cash flow and profitability.

Moreover, the new law seems to offer financial-service customers the prospect of "one-stop shopping," obtaining many, if not all, of their financial services from a single provider. While this type of *convergence* of different financial services may well increase customer convenience and reduce transactions costs, some financial experts believe that competi-tion may be reduced as well if larger financial-service providers continue to acquire smaller financial companies in greater numbers and merge them out of existence. In the long run the public may have fewer alternatives and conceivably could wind up paying higher financial-service fees.

One of the most controversial parts of the new Financial Services Modernization Act concerns *customer privacy*. GLB requires financial-service providers—including banks, credit unions, finance companies, thrift institutions, insurance companies and agencies, security brokers, and travel agencies—to disclose their policies regarding the sharing of their customers' private ("nonpublic") data with others. When customers open a new account, they must be told what the financial-service provider's customer privacy policies are and be informed at least once a year thereafter about the company's customer privacy rules.

GLB allows affiliates of the same financial-services company to share nonpublic cus-tomer information with each other. Under the new law, customers cannot prevent this type of *internal* sharing of their personal information. However, customers are permitted to "opt out" of any private information sharing by financial-service providers with third par-ties, such as telemarketers. The new law states that customers must notify their financial-service firm in writing if they do not want their personal information shared with "outsiders."

Although many customers appear to be concerned about protecting their privacy, many financial-service providers are fighting recent attempts that limit information sharing about customers. These companies point out that by sharing personal data, the financial firm can more efficiently design and market services that will benefit their customers.

(MODIFICATION AND REPEAL OF THE GLASS-STEAGALL ACT OF 1933)

- Commercial banks can affiliate with insurance companies and securities firms (either through the holding-company route or through a bank subsidiary structure), provided they are well capitalized and have regulatory approval from their principal federal supervisory agency.

- Protections must be put in place for consumers considering the purchase of insurance through a bank. Consumers must be reminded that nondeposit financial-service products, including insurance policies, are not FDIC-insured and the purchase of insurance cannot be imposed by a lender as a requirement for obtaining a loan from the same lending institution.

- Banks, thrifts, credit unions, insurance companies, security brokers, and other financial institutions must inform consumers about their *privacy policies* when accounts are opened and at least once a year thereafter, indicating whether consumers' nonpublic personal information can be shared with an affiliated firm or with outsiders. Customers are allowed to "opt out" of their financial institutions' plans for sharing personal customer information with unaffiliated parties.

- Fees to use an automated teller machine (ATM) must be clearly disclosed at the site where the machine is located so that customers can choose to cancel a transaction before they incur a fee.

- It is a federal crime (punishable with up to five years in prison) to use fraud or deception to steal someone else's account numbers or personal information (called *identify theft*) from a financial institution.

Factoid
What is the fastest growing crime in the United States?
Answer: Identity theft—a subject addressed with stiffer federal criminal penalties by the Gramm-Leach-Bliley Act.

Moreover, some financial-service providers argue that they can make better decisions and more effectively control risk if they can share consumer data with others. For example, if an insurer knows that a customer is in poor health or is a careless driver and would not be a good credit risk, this information could be especially helpful to a lender that is part of the same company in deciding whether this customer should be granted a loan. Undoubtedly, new amendments to GLB will be brought forward in the future to restrict the use of private customer information, especially customers' medical information, and perhaps limit data sharing with other financial and nonfinancial companies.

Tattling on the Bullies—The USA Patriot Act (2001)

Adverse political developments and news reports rocked the financial world as the 21st century began and gave rise to more financial-services regulation. Terrorists used commercial airliners to attack the World Trade Center in New York City and the Pentagon in Washington, D.C., with great loss of life on September 11, 2001. The U.S. Congress quickly responded with passage of the **USA Patriot Act** in the fall of that same year.

Among the numerous provisions of the Patriot Act, designed to find and prosecute terrorists, are requirements that banks and selected other financial-service providers operating inside the United States establish the *identity* of any customers opening new accounts or holding accounts whose terms are changed. This is usually accomplished, at minimum, by asking for a driver's license or other acceptable picture ID and obtaining the Social Security number of the customer, storing this information in the financial firm's records. Banks and selected other service providers are also required to check the customer's ID against a government-supplied list of possible terrorists or terrorist organizations and report to the U.S. Treasury any suspected terrorists or any suspicious activity in a customer's account. If the federal government requests this information, the financial firm involved must quickly supply it.

Recent evidence indicates that governments intend to enforce laws like the Patriot Act. For example, in the Fall of 2002 Western Union was fined $8 million for allegedly failing to fully comply with the requirements laid down in the Patriot Act and its support-ing regulations on money transfers. In Great Britain, which has a similar law, The Royal Bank of Scotland, second largest in the British Isles, was fined the equivalent of about $1.2 million for allegedly not taking enough care to establish customers' identities. The Patriot Act has aroused controversy among some bankers concerned about the cost of compliance and among some citizens concerned about their personal privacy.

Telling the Truth and Not Stretching It—The Sarbanes-Oxley Accounting Standards Act (2002)

On the heels of the terrorist attacks of 9/11 came disclosures in the financial press of wide-spread manipulation of corporate financial reports and questionable dealings among lead-ing corporations (such as Enron), commercial and investment bankers, and public accounting firms to the detriment of thousands of employees and market investors. Faced with deteriorating public confidence in the business community and the financial system, Congress moved quickly to pass the **Sarbanes-Oxley Accounting Standards Act** of 2002.

Sarbanes-Oxley creates a panel to enforce higher standards in the accounting profession and to promote accurate and objective audits of the financial reports of public companies (including banks and other financial-service corporations). Publishing false or misleading information about the financial performance and condition of banks and other publicly owned corporations is prohibited. Moreover, top corporate officers must vouch for the accu-racy of their companies' financial statements. Loans to senior management and directors (insiders) of a bank or other publicly owned lending institution are restricted to the same credit terms that regular customers of comparable risk receive. Extensive new regulations affecting the accounting practices of banks and other public companies are emerging in the wake of this new law. Beginning October 1, 2003, federal banking agencies acquired the power to bar accounting firms from auditing depository institutions if these firms displayed evidence of negligence, reckless behavior, or lack of professional qualifications.

Deregulation and the Key Issues Left Unresolved by Recent Legislation and Regulation

Recent decades have seen a movement to *deregulate* financial services and let the private marketplace, rather than the government, shape what banks and some of their closest competitors can and cannot do. For example, in 1980 the U.S. Congress passed the Depos-itory Institutions Deregulation and Monetary Control Act (DIDMCA), which lifted fed-eral government ceilings on bank and thrift deposit interest rates and allowed individuals and nonprofit institutions to receive interest on their checkable deposits. In 1982 the Garn–St. Germain Depository Institutions Act made banks and thrifts more alike in the financial services they could offer and granted depository institutions permission to offer flexible-rate money market deposit accounts to compete directly with money market mutual funds. Passage of the Financial Institutions, Reform, Recovery and Enforcement Act in 1989 allowed bank holding companies to acquire thrift institutions and, if desired, convert them into branch offices.

As impressive as the deregulation movement has been in recent decades, legislation and regulation have still left some important issues unresolved. For example, while most banks and thrifts now offer more services and expand over wider geographic areas than in the past, regulatory approval is still generally required before any *new* services can be offered. This restriction could become an even more serious problem because if depository institutions cannot respond fast enough to the rapidly changing demands of the financial marketplace, they could easily become outmoded and be overrun by their competitors.

BANKING AND COMMERCE: THE HOT REGULATORY ISSUE FOR THE 21st CENTURY?

Many observers of the financial-services marketplace believe that the key regulatory issue in banking in the 21st century will center on *banking versus commerce*—how far will banks and nonfinancial industrial firms be able to go in invading each other's territory in the future? How much overlap in ownership can we allow between financial and nonfinancial businesses and still adequately protect the public's savings?

Currently solid barriers *seem* to exist between banks and nonfinancial businesses, preventing their combining with each other. These legal and regulatory barriers include such laws as the Bank Holding Company Act and the National Bank Act, which define what banks can and cannot do. For those companies that do find clever ways to slip through these barriers, Section 23 of the Federal Reserve Act limits transactions between bank and nonbank firms owned by the same company in order to protect banks from being looted by their nonbank affiliates. For example, bank transactions with an affiliated business cannot exceed 10 percent of the bank's capital or a maximum of 20 percent of a bank's capital for all its nonbank affiliates combined.

Even with such tough rules, however, serious holes have been punched in the existing legal and regulatory barriers that prevent banks from affiliating with commercial and industrial firms over the years. For example, prior to passage of the Bank Holding Company Act (as amended in 1970) companies controlling a single bank could purchase or start virtually any other kind of business. After passage of this sweeping law, however, banking was confined essentially to the financial services sector with a couple of exceptions.

One of these exceptions was the *nonbank bank* route through which a commercial firm could purchase a bank, strip it of either its checking accounts or its commercial loans, and use it as a less-regulated conduit for selling a wide array of new services. The U.S. Congress closed this gap in the barriers in 1987 (except for those nonbank banks that had already sneaked through). A second exception centered around thrift institutions (such as savings and loans) that could get into the commercial sector by having a company acquire a single thrift and then add other businesses. Passage of the Gramm-Leach-Bliley Act of 1999 closed this *unitary thrift* device.

As the 21st century opened, still another crack in the barriers separating banking and commerce remained in the form of *industrial loan companies*. These state-chartered deposit and loan businesses are often affiliated with industrial firms and may provide credit to help finance the purchase of their parent company's products. Industrial loan companies raise funds by selling noncheckable deposits, and they can apply for FDIC insurance. These firms, centered mostly in California and Utah, currently play a small role in the financial sector, however, holding less then 2 percent of the total assets of all U.S. insured depository institutions.

The banking-commerce issue remains a hot one as creative financial minds look for (and often find) clever ways to invade new turf despite the barriers. For excellent expanded discussions of this issue see John R. Walter, "Banking and Commerce: Tear Down This Wall?" *Economic Quarterly,* Federal Reserve Bank of Richmond, 89, no. 2 (Spring 2003), pp. 7–31; and Donald E. Powell, Chairman of the Federal Deposit Insurance Corporation, Remarks before the Conference of State Bank Supervisors, Asheville, North Carolina, May 30, 2003.

Another key issue for the future centers upon the so-called *safety net* that most nations provide for their depositors, usually in the form of government-sponsored deposit insurance. A great deal of the complicated regulatory structure that surrounds banks and thrifts today is designed to support this safety net and to make sure depository institutions behave prudently so that governments and, most important, their taxpayers do not have to bail out failing banks and nonbank depository institutions. A key issue for the future, however, centers on whether the current regulatory structure will be able to effectively provide a safety net in a rapidly changing financial-services marketplace.

For example, how can we be reasonably sure a conglomerate financial firm that includes a bank will not loot the bank to prop up its other affiliated nonbank businesses? *Functional regulation*, in which each bank and nonbank business component of a financial-services company is regulated by a different government agency, seems to be settling in as the accepted approach to government overseeing financial-services production and delivery. If this is the case, will all the different regulators be able to cooperate successfully and maintain consistently high standards to protect the public adequately? What if the

1863–64—The U.S. government begins chartering and supervising national banks to expand the nation's supply of money and credit and to compete with state-chartered banks.

1913—The Federal Reserve Act is signed into law in December, setting up the Federal Reserve System to improve the payments mechanism, supervise banks, and regulate the supply of money and credit in the United States.

1933—The Glass-Steagall (Banking) Act creates the Federal Deposit Insurance Corporation (FDIC) and imposes interest-rate ceilings on deposits in an effort to keep bank costs low. It also separates commercial and investment banking into two different industries with no common ownership.

1934—The Securities and Exchange Act requires greater disclosure of information about securities sold to the public and creates the Securities and Exchange Commission (SEC) to prevent the use of fraudulent or deceptive information in the marketing of securities.

1935—The Banking Act expands the powers and length of terms of the Federal Reserve's Board of Governors as the chief administrative body of the Federal Reserve System and establishes the Federal Open Market Committee as the Fed's principal monetary policy decision-making group.

1956—The Bank Holding Company Act requires corporations controlling two or more banks to register with the Federal Reserve Board and seek approval for any new business acquisitions.

1960—The Bank Merger Act requires federal approval for any mergers involving federally supervised banks and, in subsequent amendments, subjects bank mergers and acquisitions to the antitrust laws.

1970—Bank Holding Company Act is amended to include one-bank companies that must register with the Federal Reserve Board and are then subject to examination. Permissible nonbank services that bank holding companies may offer are limited to services the Federal Reserve Board deems to be "closely related to banking."

1977—Community Reinvestment Act (CRA) is passed to outlaw banks from "redlining" certain neighborhoods, refusing to serve those particular areas.

1978—International Banking Act imposes federal regulation on foreign banks operating in the United States for the first time and requires deposit insurance coverage for foreign banks selling retail deposits inside the United States.

1980—Federal deregulation of deposit interest rates begins as half-century-old deposit interest-rate ceilings are gradually lifted and legal reserve requirements are imposed on all depository institutions offering checkable or nonpersonal time deposits under the terms of the Depository Institutions Deregulation and Monetary Control Act. Interest-bearing checking accounts are legalized nationwide for households and nonprofit institutions.

1982—Federal deregulation of deposit interest rates is accelerated through passage of the Garn–St. Germain Depository Institutions Act. Banks and other depositories may offer deposits competitive with money market fund share accounts, while thrift institutions were given new service powers that allowed them to compete more fully with commercial banks.

different regulators overseeing different parts of the same financial company—for example, the Securities and Exchange Commission (SEC) regulating the company's security brokerage unit and the Comptroller of the Currency regulating the company's bank—disagree? How is this disagreement to be resolved in a way that ensures maximum public benefit? Could the newly adopted functional regulatory system impose an undue regulatory burden on the companies involved?

Moreover, if all financial firms are becoming more like each other, do we really need *multiple regulators*? Why burden taxpayers and financial institutions with an extra financial burden in order to support many different regulatory agencies when *one* might do? Perhaps a single financial services regulatory agency could replace the bewildering collection of regulators we have today. After all, the financial industries being regulated are consolidat-

1987—Competitive Equality in Banking Act is passed, permitting the creation of nonbank banks to compete with commercial and savings banks, allowing some bank and thrift mergers to take place across state lines and requiring public disclosure of checking account deposit policies. The Federal Reserve Board rules that bank holding companies can establish securities underwriting subsidiaries subject to limits on the revenues they generate from selling corporate securities.

1988—The Basel Agreement imposes common minimum capital requirements on banks in leading industrialized nations based on the riskiness of their on-balance-sheet and off-balance-sheet assets.

1989—The Financial Institutions Reform, Recovery, and Enforcement Act (FIRREA) is enacted in order to resolve failures of thrifts and set up the Savings Association Insurance Fund (SAIF), under the FDIC's management. In addition, FIRREA launches the Office of Thrift Supervision inside the U.S. Treasury Department to regulate thrift institutions.

1991—The FDIC improvement Act mandates fees for deposit insurance based on a bank's risk exposure, grants the FDIC authority to borrow and raise funds, and creates the Truth in Savings Act to require greater public disclosure of the terms and fees associated with selling deposits to the public.

1994—The Riegle-Neal Interstate Banking and Branching Efficiency Act permits interstate full-service banking. Interstate mergers and acquisitions are permitted for adequately capitalized and managed banks provided concentration limits and state laws are not violated and CRA standards are met.

1999—The Gramm-Leach-Bliley Financial Services Modernization Act repeals key sections of the Glass-Steagall and Bank Holding Company Acts and allows banks to create securities and insurance subsidiaries, and financial holding companies (FHCs) can set up commercial banking, insurance, security, and merchant banking affiliates and engage in other "complementary" activities. Similarly, insurance and security firms can now acquire banks and form FHCs with Federal Reserve Board approval, Financial-service providers must protect the privacy of their customers and limit sharing their private information with other businesses.

2000—The European Monetary Union and central banking system expands in Western Europe, allowing both European and foreign banks greater freedom to cross national borders. A new central bank, the ECB, now operates to reshape money and credit policies in Europe and the European Community of nations adopts a common currency unit, the *euro*.

2001—The USA Patriot Act requires financial-service firms to collect and share information about customer identities with government agencies and to report suspicious activity in customer accounts to the U.S. Treasury Department.

2002—The Sarbanes-Oxley Accounting Standards Act requires publicly owned companies to strengthen their internal and external auditing practices and prohibits the publishing of false or misleading information about the financial condition or operations of a publicly held firm.

ing into fewer firms to regulate. Recognizing this, the United Kingdom and several other nations have already moved to simplify their financial-services regulatory structure.

And, what about *mixing banking and commerce*? Should the remaining regulatory barriers to bank control by industrial and manufacturing companies (or vice versa) be torn down? Should a bank be able to sell cars and trucks right alongside deposits and loans? Would these industrial-financial alliances create unfair competitive advantages in the industrial marketplace, the financial marketplace, or both? Would such an affiliation subject depositors and deposit insurers (like the FDIC) to greater risk of loss? Should bank examiners be allowed to fully examine industrial and manufacturing firms that have been permitted to acquire a depository institution? If so, how do you train a bank examiner to tackle that kind of job?

Another unresolved issue is what happens *when nations disagree about banking or financial-services regulation.* As we have seen, the trend today is toward the emergence of multinational financial-service conglomerates spanning countries and continents, like Citigroup and DeutscheBank. Oversight of what these behemoths do with the public's money and with customers' personal information is supposed to fall most heavily upon regulators in each financial firm's country of origin. But, what if that nation is weak and ineffective as a financial-services regulator? Who takes up the slack? Clearly nations must cooperate in financial-services regulation just as they do in the defense of their homelands.

Concept Check

2–9. How does the FDIC deal with most failures?

2–10. What changes have occurred in U.S. banks' authority to cross state lines?

2–11. How have bank failures influenced recent legislation?

2–12. What changes in regulation did the Gramm-Leach-Bliley (Financial Services Modernization) Act bring about? Why?

2–13. What new regulatory issues remain to be resolved now that interstate banking is possible and security and insurance services are allowed to commingle with banking?

2–14. Why must we be concerned about *privacy* in the sharing and use of a financial-service customer's information? Can the financial system operate efficiently if sharing nonpublic information is forbidden? How far, in your opinion, should we go in regulating who gets access to private information?

2–15. Why were the Sarbanes-Oxley and USA Patriot Acts enacted in the United States? What impact are these new laws and their supporting regulations likely to have on the financial-services sector?

The Regulation of Nonbank Financial-Service Firms Competing with Banks

Regulating the Thrift (Savings) Industry

While commercial banks rank at or near the top of the list in terms of government involvement and government control of their businesses, several other financial intermediaries—most notably credit unions, savings associations and savings banks, and money market funds—are not far behind. These so-called thrift institutions together attract a large proportion of the public's savings and grant a rapidly growing portion of consumer (household) loans. As such, even though they are privately owned, the thrifts are deemed to be "vested with the public interest" and, therefore, often face close supervision and regulation at both federal and state levels.

Key URLs

To find out more about credit unions, see the World Council of Credit Unions at **www.woccu.org** and the Credit Union National Association at **www.cuna.org**.

Credit Unions   These nonprofit associations of individuals accept savings and share draft (checkable) deposits from and make loans only to their members. Federal and state rules prescribe what is required to be a credit union member—you must share a "common bond" with other credit union members (such as working for the same employer). Credit union deposits may qualify for federal deposit insurance coverage up to $100,000, however, from the National Credit Union Share Insurance Fund (NCUSIF). During the 1930s the Federal Credit Union Act provided for federal as well as state chartering of qualified credit unions. Federal credit unions are supervised and examined by the **National Credit Union Administration** (NCUA). Several aspects of credit union activity are closely supervised to protect their members, including the services they are permitted to offer and how they allocate funds. Risk connected with granting loans to members must be counterbalanced by sizable investments in government securities, insured bank CDs, and other short-term money market instruments.

Key URL
To further explore the characteristics and services of savings and loan associations and savings banks, see the Office of Thrift Supervision at **www.ots.treas.gov.**

Savings Associations   These depository institutions include state and federal savings and loans and federal savings banks, created to encourage family savings and the financing of new homes. Government deregulation of the industry during the 1980s led to a proliferation of new consumer services to mirror many of those offered by commercial banks. Moreover, savings associations, like banks, face multiple regulators in an effort to protect the public's deposits. State-chartered associations are supervised and examined by state boards or commissions, whereas federally chartered S&Ls and savings banks fall under the jurisdiction of the **Office of Thrift Supervision**—a part of the U.S. Treasury Department. Deposits are insured by the Savings Association Insurance Fund (SAIF), administered by the FDIC, bringing savings-association balance sheets under FDIC supervision.

State Savings Banks   Savings banks were chartered exclusively by state governments until the 1970s, when the federal government began to charter federal savings banks subject to the same regulators and regulations as federal savings and loan associations. In recent years many have been allowed under federal and state law to convert from depositor (mutual) ownership to stock-issuing corporations and to offer a wide array of financial services, primarily to households. The FDIC insures the deposits of those savings banks willing to follow its rules, and both the FDIC and state commissions monitor their balance sheets and the quality of their investments of depositor funds.

Money Market Funds   Although many financial institutions regard government regulation as burdensome and costly, money market funds owe their existence to federal regulations limiting the rates of interest banks and thrifts could pay on deposits. Security brokers and dealers found a way to attract short-term savings away from depository institutions and invest in money market securities bearing higher interest rates, but low risk. Investment assets must be dollar denominated, have remaining maturities of no more then 397 days, and a dollar-weighted average maturity of no more then 90 days. There is no federal deposit insurance program for money funds, but they are regulated by the **Securities and Exchange Commission** (SEC) with the goal of keeping money fund share prices fixed at $1 each.

Key URLs
Additional information about life and property casualty insurers may be found at the website of the American Council for Life Insurance (**www.acli.com**) or the Insurance Information Institute (**www.iii.com**).

Life and Property/Casualty Insurance Companies   These sellers of risk protection for persons and property are one of the few financial institutions regulated almost exclusively at the state level. **State insurance commissions** generally prescribe the types and content of insurance policies sold to the public, often set maximum premium rates the public must pay, license insurance agents, scrutinize insurer investments for the protection of policyholders, charter new companies, and liquidate failing ones.

Recently the federal government has become somewhat more involved in insurance company regulation. For example, when these firms sell equity or debt securities to the public, they need approval from the Securities and Exchange Commission—a situation that is happening more frequently as many mutual insurers (which are owned by their policyholders) are converting to stockholder-owned companies. Similarly, when insurers form holding companies to acquire banks or other federally regulated financial businesses, they may come under the Federal Reserve's review.

Finance Companies   These business and consumer lenders have been regulated at the state government level for many decades, and state commissions look especially closely at their treatment of individuals and families borrowing money. Although the depth of state regulation varies across the United States, most states focus upon the types and contents of loan agreements they offer the public, the interest rates they charge (with some states setting maximum loan rates), and the methods they use to repossess property or to recover funds from delinquent borrowers. Relatively light regulation has led to a recent explosion in the number of small-loan companies (such as payday lenders and check-cashing firms).

Mutual Funds   These investment companies, which sell shares in a pool of income-generating assets (especially stocks, bonds, and asset-backed securities), have faced close federal and state regulation since the Great Depression of the 1930s when many failed. The U.S. Securities and Exchange Commission (SEC) requires these businesses to register with that agency, submit periodic financial reports, and provide investors with a prospectus that reveals the financial condition, recent performance, and objectives of each fund. Recently the SEC has cooperated closely with the FDIC in warning the public of the absence of federal deposit insurance behind these funds and with the Federal Reserve as more and more banks invade the mutual fund business.

Filmtoid
What 2001 romantic comedy begins with stockbroker Ryan Turner (played by Charlie Sheen) finding himself without a job and being investigated by the SEC for insider trading?
Answer: *Good Advice.*

Security Brokers and Dealers   A combination of federal and state supervision applies to these traders in financial instruments who buy and sell securities, underwrite new security issues, and give financial advice to corporations and governments. Security brokers and dealers have been challenging banks for big corporate customers for decades, but deregulation under the Gramm-Leach-Bliley Act of 1999 has encouraged banks to fight back and win a growing share of the market for security trading and underwriting. The chief federal regulator is the SEC, which requires these firms to submit periodic reports, limits the volume of debt they take on, and investigates insider trading practices. Recent corporate scandals have redirected the SEC to look more closely at the accuracy and objectivity of the research and investment advice these companies pass on to their clients.

Key URLs
Important information about mutual funds and security brokers and dealers may be found at such key sites as the Investment Company Institute (**www.ici.com**) and the Securities and Exchange Commission (**www.sec.gov**).

Financial Conglomerates   These highly diversified companies, which may combine banking, insurance, security dealing, and other services in *one* organization, have created something of a regulatory crisis because only parts of each firm may come under the purview of any one regulator, leaving room for highly risky ventures. Recently the state regulatory commissions (which oversee finance and insurance companies that may be part of a conglomerate), the SEC (responsible for securities firms), and the Federal Reserve Board (if banks are part of a conglomerate's product mix) have been cooperating more extensively in sharing oversight of these complex financial firms.

Are Regulations Really Necessary in the Financial-Services Sector?

A great debate is raging today about whether *any* of the remaining regulations affecting commercial banks and their financial-service competitors are really necessary. Perhaps, as a leading authority in this field, George Benston, suggests [1, p. 16], "It is time we recognize that financial institutions are simply businesses with only a few special features that require regulation." He contends that depository institutions, for example, should be regulated no differently from any other corporation with no tax subsidies or other special privileges.

Why? Benston argues that the historical reasons for regulation in the financial sector—taxation as monopolies in supplying money, prevention of centralized power, preservation of solvency to mitigate the impact of failures on the economy, and the pursuit of social goals (such as ensuring an adequate supply of financial services, supporting housing for families, and preventing discrimination and unfair dealing)—are no longer relevant today. Moreover, these regulations are *not* free: they impose real costs in the form of taxes on money users, production inefficiencies, and reduced competition.

In summary, the trend under way today all over the globe is to free banking and other financial-service firms from the rigid boundaries of regulation; however, much still remains to be done if we wish to enhance the benefits of free competition to financial institutions and the public they serve.

E-BANKING AND E-COMMERCE

THE RULES OF THE INTERNET BANKING GAME

Like all other aspects of financial-services activity, selling financial services over the Internet, through ATMs, or via other forms of electronic banking is subject to a comprehensive set of federal and state rules. To receive approval to offer Internet-based financial services, the institution involved must seek approval from its principal regulatory agency (for example, the Comptroller of the Currency for national banks and the state banking commission for state-chartered banks). The regulatory agencies involved must be convinced that the safety and security of customers' funds will be adequately protected and that the soundness of the offering institution will not be threatened.

Bankers are allowed to ally themselves with nonbank firms in developing and offering websites and other electronic prod-

ucts. However, the public must be clearly informed about which products offered come from a bank and which come from nonbank businesses. For their part, electronic customers must sign a contract with the offering institution that warns them of possible liability if they carelessly reveal their account numbers or identity codes to unauthorized persons.

One hopeful sign for the future is the general lack of regulatory restrictions against the types of electronic technology that can be utilized. The regulatory agencies seem to be more concerned with protecting the customer and the service-offering institution rather than putting walls around the development of new technology and slowing the pace of financial-services innovation.

The Central Banking System: Its Impact on the Decisions and Policies of Banks and Their Financial-Service Competitors

No discussion of the regulation of financial-service firms would be complete without a discussion of the activities of *central banks* around the world, including the central bank of the United States, the Federal Reserve System (the Fed). Like all central banks around the globe, the Fed probably has more impact on the day-to-day activities of banks than any other government agency. A central bank's primary job is to carry out **monetary policy,** which involves making sure the supply and cost of money and credit from the financial system contributes to the nation's economic goals. By controlling the growth of money and credit, the Fed and other central banks around the globe try to ensure that the economy grows at an adequate rate, unemployment is kept low, inflation is held down, and the value of the nation's currency in international markets is protected.

In the United States the Fed is relatively free to pursue these goals because it does not depend on the government for its funding. Instead, the Fed raises its own funds from sales of its services and from securities trading, and it passes along most of its earnings (after making small additions to its capital and paying dividends to member banks holding Federal Reserve bank stock) to the U.S. Treasury.

The nations belonging to the new European union also have a central bank, the **European Central Bank (ECB),** which is relatively free and independent of governmental control as it pursues its main goal of avoiding inflation. In contrast, central banks in Japan, China, and other parts of Asia are generally under close control by their governments, and these countries have experienced higher inflation rates, volatile currency prices, and other significant economic problems in recent years. Though the matter is still hotly disputed, recent research studies (e.g., Pollard [13] and Walsh [14]) suggest that more independent central banks have been able to come closer to their nation's desired level of long-run economic performance (particularly better control of inflation).

EXHIBIT 2–1
Organization Chart
for the Federal
Reserve System

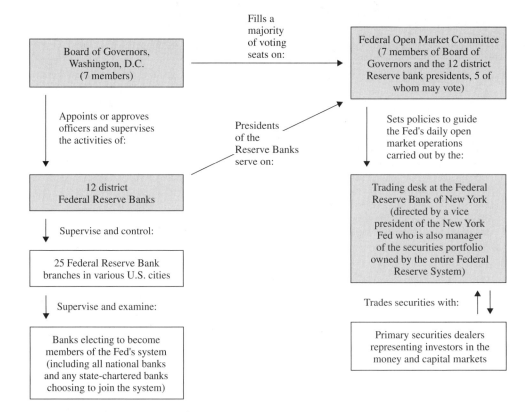

Organizational Structure of the Federal Reserve System

To carry out the objectives noted above, the Fed and many other central banks have evolved into large and complex quasi-governmental bureaucracies with many divisions and responsibilities. See Exhibit 2–1. The center of authority and decision making within the Federal Reserve System is the **Board of Governors** in Washington, D.C. By law, this governing body must contain no more than seven persons, each selected by the president of the United States and confirmed by the Senate for terms not exceeding 14 years. The board chairman and vice chairman are appointed by the president from among the seven board members, each for four-year terms (though these appointments may be renewed).

The board regulates and supervises the activities of the 12 district Reserve banks and their branch offices. It sets reserve requirements on deposits held by banks and other depository institutions, approves all changes in the discount rates posted by the 12 Reserve banks, and takes the lead within the system in determining open market policy to affect interest rates and the growth of money and credit.

The Federal Reserve Board members make up a majority of the voting members of the **Federal Open Market Committee (FOMC).** The other voting members are 5 of the 12 Federal Reserve bank presidents, who each serve one year in filling the five official voting seats on the FOMC (except for the president of the New York Federal Reserve Bank, who is a permanent voting member). While the FOMC's specific task is to set policies that guide the conduct of **open market operations (OMO)**—the buying and selling of securities by the Federal Reserve banks, this body actually looks at the whole range of Fed policies and actions to influence the economy and financial system.

The Federal Reserve System is divided into 12 districts, with a **Federal Reserve Bank** chartered in each district to supervise and serve member banks. Among the key services

Key URL
The central website for the Board of Governors of the Federal Reserve System is **www. federalreserve.gov**.

Key URL
All 12 Federal Reserve banks have their own websites which can be accessed from **www. federalreserve.gov/ otherfrb.htm**.

One of the most important of all financial institutions in any economy is the *central bank*. Just to name some of the world's best-known central banks, like the Federal Reserve System, the Bank of England, the European Central Bank (ECB), or the Bank of Japan, carries the image of great financial power and prestige.

Reflecting their importance, central banks around the globe have established websites to list their functions and services and provide other important information to the public. For example, the Federal Reserve has an introductory site addressed **www.federalreserve.gov**. Other central banks can be found on the Web simply by entering their name (e.g., Bank of Canada) and conducting a Web search. If you would like to know a lot more about the fascinating and relatively new European Central Bank (ECB) and the monetary system developing around it, you may want to check the site **www.ecb.int**.

the Federal Reserve banks offer to depository institutions in their districts are (1) issuing wire transfers of funds between banks and other depository institutions, (2) safe-keeping securities owned by depository institutions and their customers, (3) issuing new securities from the U.S. Treasury and selected other federal agencies, (4) making short-term loans to qualifying depository institutions through the "Discount Window" in each Federal Reserve bank, (5) maintaining and dispensing supplies of currency and coin, (6) clearing and collecting checks and other cash items moving between cities, and (7) providing information to keep bankers, other financial firm managers, and the public informed about regulatory changes and other developments affecting the welfare of their institutions.

All banks chartered by the Comptroller of the Currency (national banks) and those few state banks willing to conform to the Fed's supervision and regulation are designated **member banks.** Member institutions must purchase stock (up to 6 percent of their paid-in capital and surplus) in the district Reserve bank and submit to comprehensive examinations of their operations by Fed staff. There are few unique privileges stemming from being a member bank of the Federal Reserve System, because Fed services are also available on the same terms to other depository institutions keeping reserve deposits at the Fed. Many bankers believe, however, that belonging to the system carries prestige and the aura of added safety, which helps member banks attract and hold large deposits.

The Central Bank's Principal Task: Making and Implementing Monetary Policy

A central bank's principal function is to conduct money and credit policy to promote sustainable growth in the economy, avoid severe inflation, and achieve the nation's other economic goals. To pursue these important objectives, most central banks use a variety of tools to affect the *legal reserves of the banking system*, the *interest rates charged on loans* made in the financial system, and relative *currency values* in the global foreign exchange markets.

By definition, *legal reserves* consist of assets held by a depository institution that qualify in meeting the reserve requirements imposed on an individual depository institution by central banking authorities. In the Unites States legal reserves consist of cash that depository institutions keep in their vaults and the deposits these institutions hold in their legal reserve accounts at the district Federal Reserve banks. Each of the Fed's policy tools also affects the level and rate of change of interest rates. The Fed drives interest rates higher when it wants to reduce lending and borrowing in the economy and slow down the pace of economic activity; on the other hand, it lowers interest rates when it wishes to stimulate business and consumer borrowing. Central banks also can influence the demand for their home nation's currency by varying the level of interest rates and by altering the pace of domestic economic activity.

To influence the behavior of legal reserves, interest rates, and currency values, the Fed employs three main tools: open market operations, the discount rate, and legal reserve requirements on various bank liabilities. The policy tools used by other central banks vary. For example, the Bank of England uses open market operations in the form of purchases of short-term government and commercial bills and makes discount loans. The Bank of Japan conducts open market purchases and sales primarily in commercial bills, notes, and deposits and sets its discount rate on the loans it grants to banks that need to borrow reserves. The Swiss National Bank conducts open market operations in the currency markets (employing U.S. dollar–Swiss franc swaps), while Germany's Bundesbank trades security repurchase agreements and sets its preferred interest (discount and Lombard) rates on short-term loans. In contrast, the Bank of Canada uses both open market operations and daily transfers of government deposits between private banks and the central bank to influence credit conditions. The fundamental point is that while different central banks often use different tools, nearly all focus upon the reserves of the banking system, interest rates, and, to some extent, currency prices as key operating targets to help achieve each nation's most cherished economic goals.

The Open Market Policy Tool In the United States purchases and sales of securities that are designed to move the reserves of depository institutions and interest rates toward desired levels are called *open market operations* (OMO). Inside the United States, government securities (bills, notes, and bonds) are most commonly traded by the Federal Reserve, as are selected Federal agency securities.

OMO is considered the Fed's most flexible policy tool because (*a*) this tool can be used every day (and sometimes more than once on any given day), and (*b*) if the Fed makes a mistake, it can quickly reverse itself through an offsetting buy or sell transaction.

Central bank sales of securities tend to *decrease* the growth of deposits and loans within the financial system. When the Fed sells U.S. government securities, the dealers purchasing those securities authorize the Fed to deduct the dollar amount of the purchase from the reserve accounts dealers' banks hold at a district Federal Reserve bank. Banks and other depository institutions have less raw material for making loans and extending other types of credit. In contrast, central bank purchases of securities tend to *increase* the growth of deposits and loans. The Federal Reserve pays for its purchases of U.S. government securities simply by crediting the reserve deposits of the dealers' banks that are held at the district Federal Reserve banks. This means that the banks and dealers involved in the transaction have the proceeds of the securities' sale immediately available for their use. (See Exhibit 2–2.)

Today the Federal Reserve targets the *federal funds interest rate* attached to overnight loans of reserves between banks and other depository institutions. If the Fed wishes to nudge the federal funds rate higher to discourage some borrowing and spending, it will usually sell securities in the open market, reducing the reserves depository institutions have available to generate new loans and forcing them to borrow more reserves, which tends to drive up market interest rates and slow the economy. On the other hand, if the Fed wishes to push interest rates down to stimulate borrowing and spending in the economy, it will usually buy securities in the open market, expanding the reserves depository institutions have available to generate new loans and relieving them of some of the pressure to borrow more reserves in the federal funds market, which tends to lower prevailing interest rates and stimulate the economy.

The Discount Rate Policy Tool Most central banks are an important source of short-term funds for banks and other depository institutions, especially the largest banks, which tend to borrow frequently to replenish their legal reserves. Some U.S. banks place

EXHIBIT 2–2
Federal Reserve Open Market Operations

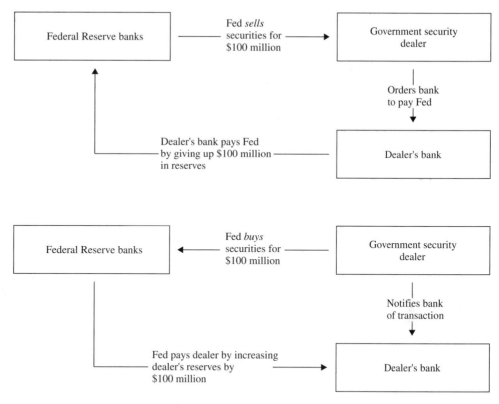

signed borrowing authorizations at the Federal Reserve bank in their district for this purpose. When the Fed loans reserves to borrowing institutions, the supply of legal reserves expands temporarily, which may cause loans and deposits to expand. Later, when the discount window loans are repaid, the borrowing institutions lose reserves and may be forced to curtail the growth of their deposits and loans.

The loan rate charged by the Fed, the *discount rate,* is set by each Reserve bank's board of directors (though any changes in this basic rate must also be approved by the Federal Reserve Board). Most discount window loans are for what historically has been called *adjustment credit* or for *seasonal credit* to meet temporary shortages of reserves and usually last only a few days. Longer-term *extended credit,* stretching over a month or more, historically has been designed to aid banks facing longer-term liquidity shortages and carries a higher discount rate.

In January 2003 the Fed implemented new rules for the use and administration of the discount window. The loan types known as *adjustment credit* and *extended credit* were replaced by primary and secondary credit. *Primary credit* is readily extended to sound borrowing institutions at an interest rate slightly higher than the Fed's target for the Federal funds interest rate (initially 100 basis points above the Fed funds rate). Depository institutions not qualifying for primary credit may apply for *secondary credit* to meet temporary funding needs at an interest rate above (initially 50 basis points higher than) the primary credit loan rate. The purpose of these changes in discount window policy and mechanics is to encourage greater use of the Fed's loan facility (due to fewer borrowing restrictions) and to bring greater stability to the key Federal funds interest rate and to the money market as a whole. Moreover, an above-the market discount rate looks less like a subsidy to borrowing depository institutions.

By raising the discount rate on primary and secondary credit, the Fed makes new loans from the discount window more costly. This discourages some depository institutions from borrowing reserves, which may lead to slower growth in credit. Lowering the discount rate, on the other hand, may act to stimulate borrowing from the Fed. Depository institutions may become more liberal in making credit available to their customers. Changes in the discount rate seem to affect other interest rates in the financial system, generally pushing them in the same direction as the move in the discount rate. Finally, changing the discount rate seems to have a psychological "announcement effect," bringing on investor expectations of higher or lower interest rates.

Changing Reserve Requirements on Deposits and Other Liabilities of Depository Institutions Banks and other depository institutions selling transaction deposits (such as checking accounts) must place a small percentage of each dollar of those deposits in reserve, either in the form of vault cash or in a deposit at the regional Federal Reserve bank. Selected other sources of funds, such as time deposits sold to businesses and institutions and Eurodollar deposits borrowed from abroad, are also subject to reserve requirements set by the Board of Governors of the Federal Reserve System, but at present only checkable (transaction) deposits carry reserve requirements.

Changes in the percentage of deposits and other funds sources that must be held in reserve can have a potent impact on credit expansion by banks and other depository institutions. Raising reserve requirements, for example, means that banks must set aside more of each incoming dollar of deposits into required reserves, and less money is available to support making new loans. Moreover, a higher required reserve tends to increase interest rates because depository institutions have fewer reserves available that they can use to make loans. Lowering reserve requirements, on the other hand, releases reserves for additional lending. Interest rates also tend to decline because depository institutions have more funds to loan.

Even though the Fed is empowered to do so, it rarely changes the percentage of deposits and other reservable liabilities that must be held in reserve form. Experience has shown that any such move can set in motion substantial changes in credit availability and interest rates. The Fed usually prefers to use open market operations and the discount rate to change credit policy and economic conditions. We should note that there is a trend around the globe to eliminate legally imposed deposit reserve requirements, as exemplified by recent central bank action in Canada and Switzerland.

Moral Suasion One other important policy tool the Federal Reserve (as well as the Bank of Japan and other central banks) uses to influence the economy and the behavior of banks and other financial firms is *moral suasion*. Through this policy tool the central bank tries to bring psychological pressure to bear on individuals and institutions to conform to its policies. Examples of moral suasion include central bank officials testifying before Congress to explain what the bank is doing and what its objectives are, letters and phone calls sent to those financial institutions that seem to be straying from central bank policies, and press releases from central bank officials urging the public to cooperate with their efforts to strengthen the economy.

A Final Note Clearly bankers and the managers of other financial firms must be fully aware of the impact of *both* government regulation and the central bank monetary policy on their particular institutions. No financial institution's management can ignore the effects of these key government activities upon the value of a financial-service provider's assets, liabilities, and equity capital and upon the magnitude of its revenues and expenses.

THE EUROPEAN CENTRAL BANK (ECB)

In January 1999, 11 member nations of the European Union launched a new monetary system based on a single currency, the euro, and surrendered leadership of their monetary policy-making to a single central bank, the ECB. This powerful central bank is taking leadership to control inflationary forces, promote a sounder European economy, and help stabilize the euro's value in international markets.

The ECB is similar in structure to the Federal Reserve System with a governing board or council (known as the Executive Board, composed of six members) and a policy-making council (similar to the Fed's Federal Open Market Committee). The ECB has a cooperative arrangement with each EC member nation's central bank (such as Germany's Bundesbank and the Bank of France, for example), just as the Fed's Board of Governors works with the 12 Federal Reserve banks that make up the Federal Reserve System. The ECB is the centerpiece of the European System of Central Banks, which includes

- The national central bank (NCB) of each member nation, and
- The ECB, headquartered in Frankfurt, Germany.

The chief administrative body for the ECB is its Executive Board, consisting of a president, vice president, and four bank directors and appointed by the European Council, which consists of the heads of state of each member nation. The key policy-making group is the Governing Council, which includes all members of the ECB's Executive Board plus the leaders of the national Central Banks of each member nation, each leader appointed by its home nation's government.

Unlike the U.S. Federal Reserve System, which has multiple policy goals—including pursuing greater price stability, low unemployment, sustainable economic growth, and a stronger balance of payments position—the ECB has a much simpler policy menu. Its central goal is to maintain *price stability*. Moreover, it is largely granted a free hand in the pursuit of this goal with minimal interference from the member states of the European Community. The principal policy tools of the ECB to help it achieve greater price stability are open market operations and reserve requirements.

Although it has a much simpler policy focus than the Federal Reserve, the ECB still has no easy task. It must pursue price stability across 11 member states (with more nations from both Eastern and Western Europe to join in the near future) with different economies, political systems, and social and economic problems. Like the Federal Reserve System, the ECB is a "grand experiment" in economic policy cooperation. How well it will work and how effective it can be in keeping the right balance of political and economic forces in Europe remains to be seen.

Concept Check

2–16. In what ways is the regulation of nonbank financial institutions different from the regulation of banks in the United States? How are they similar?

2–17. Which financial-service firms are regulated primarily at the federal level and which at the state level? Can you see problems in this type of regulatory structure?

2–18. Can you make a case for having only *one* regulatory agency for both bank and nonbank financial-service firms?

2–19. What is *monetary policy?*

2–20. What services does the Federal Reserve provide to banks and other depository institutions?

2–21. How does the Fed affect the banking and financial system through open market operations (OMO)? Why is OMO the preferred tool for the Fed and many other central banks around the globe?

2–22. How can changes in the discount rate and reserve requirements affect the operations of banks and other depository institutions? What happens to the legal reserves of the banking system when the Fed grants loans through the discount window? How about when these loans are repaid? What are the effects of an increase in reserve requirements?

2–23. How did the Federal Reserve change the policy and practice of the discount window recently? Why was this change made?

2–24. How does the structure of the European Central Bank (ECB) appear to be similar to the structure of the Federal Reserve System? How are these two powerful and influential central banks different from one another?

Summary

What banks and other financial-service firms can do within the financial system is closely monitored by *regulation*—government oversight of the behavior and performance of banks and other businesses. Indeed, banking and financial-service institutions inside the United States and in many other nations are among the most heavily regulated of all industries due, in part, to their key roles in attracting and protecting the public's savings, providing credit to a wide range of borrowers, and creating money to serve as the principal medium of exchange in a modern economy. The principal points in this chapter include these:

- Financial-services regulations are created to implement federal and state laws by providing practical guidelines for financial firms' behavior and performance. Among the key laws that have had a powerful and lasting impact on the regulation of banks and competing financial institutions are the National Bank Act (which authorized federal chartering of banks), the Glass-Steagall Act (which separated commercial and investment banking), the Riegle-Neal Interstate Banking and Branching Efficiency Act (which allowed U.S. banking firms to cross state lines), the Gramm-Leach-Bliley Act (which repealed restrictions against banks, security firms, and insurance companies affiliating with each other), the Sarbanes-Oxley Accounting Standards Act (which imposed new rules upon the financial accounting practices that financial firms and other publicly held businesses use), and the USA Patriot Act (which required banks and other financial-service providers to gather and report customer information to the government in order to help prevent terrorism).

- Regulation of banks and other financial firms takes place in a *dual system* in the United States—both federal and state governments are involved in chartering, supervising, examining, and closing financial-service companies.

- The key federal regulators of banks include the Federal Deposit Insurance Corporation (FDIC), the Federal Reserve System (FRS), and the Office of the Comptroller of the Currency (OCC). The OCC supervises and examines federally chartered (national) banks, while the FRS oversees state-chartered banks that have elected to join the Federal Reserve System. The FDIC regulates state-chartered banks that are *not* members of the Federal Reserve System. State regulation of banks is carried out in the 50 U.S. states by boards or commissions.

- Nonbank service providers competing with banks also are generally regulated and supervised either at the state or federal government level or both. Examples include credit unions, savings and loan associations, savings banks, and some security broker/dealer firms where state boards or commissions and federal agencies share regulatory responsibility. In contrast, finance and insurance companies are supervised chiefly by state agencies. The chief federal regulatory agency for credit unions is the National Credit Union Administration (NCUA), while the Office of Thrift Supervision (OTS) oversees savings and loans and federally chartered savings banks. Security brokers and dealers are usually subject to supervision by the Securities and Exchange Commission (SEC).

- *Deregulation* of financial institutions is a new and powerful force reshaping banks and other financial firms and their regulators today in an effort to encourage increased competition and greater discipline from the marketplace. Even as deregulation has made progress around the world, key regulatory issues remain unresolved. For example, should banking and industrial companies be kept separate from each other to protect the safety of the public's funds? Do we need fewer regulators as the number of independently owned financial firms continues to fall?

- One of the most powerful of all financial institutions in the financial system is the *central bank*, which regulates money and credit conditions, (i.e., conducts *monetary policy*) using such tools as open market operations, discount window loans, and legal reserve requirements. Central banks have a powerful impact upon the profitability, growth, and viability of banks and competing financial-service providers.

Key Terms

dual banking system, *38*
state banking commissions, *38*
Comptroller of the Currency, *41*
Federal Reserve System, *41*
Glass-Steagall Act, *42*
Federal Deposit Insurance Corporation, *42*
Federal Deposit Insurance Corporation Improvement Act, *42*

Riegle-Neal Interstate Banking and Branching Efficiency Act, *46*
Gramm-Leach-Bliley Act, *48*
USA Patriot Act, *49*
Sarbanes-Oxley Accounting Standards Act, *50*
National Credit Union Administration, *54*
Office of Thrift Supervision, *55*

Securities and Exchange Commission, *55*
state insurance commissions, *55*
monetary policy, *57*
European Central Bank (ECB), *57*
Board of Governors, *58*
Federal Open Market Committee (FOMC), *58*
open market operations (OMO), *58*
Federal Reserve Bank, *58*
member banks, *59*

Problems and Projects

1. For each of the actions described, explain which government agency or agencies a banker must deal with and what banking laws are involved:
   a. Chartering a new bank.
   b. Establishing new branch offices.
   c. Forming a bank or financial holding company.
   d. Completing a merger.
   e. Making holding company acquisitions of nonbank businesses.

2. See if you can develop a good case *for* and *against* the regulation of banking in the following areas:
   a. Restrictions on the number of new banks allowed to enter the industry each year.
   b. Restrictions on which banks are eligible for government-sponsored deposit insurance.
   c. Restrictions on the ability of banking firms to underwrite debt and equity securities issued by their business customers.
   d. Restrictions on the geographic expansion of banks, such as limits on branching and holding company acquisitions across state and international borders.
   e. Regulations on the failure process, defining when banks are to be allowed to fail and how their assets are to be liquidated.

3. Consider the issue of whether or not the government should provide a system of deposit insurance. Should it be wholly or partly subsidized by the taxpayers? What portion of the cost should be borne by depository institutions? by depositors? Should riskier banks pay higher deposit insurance premiums? Explain how you would determine exactly how big an insurance premium each depository institution should pay each year.

4. The Trading Desk at the Federal Reserve Bank of New York elects to sell $100 million in U.S. government securities to its list of primary dealers. If other factors are held constant, what will happen to the supply of legal reserves available to banks? To deposits and loans? To interest rates?

www.mhhe.com/rose6e

Suppose the Fed made $100 million available to the banking system by lending depository institutions that amount through the discount windows of the Federal Reserve banks. Would this decision affect the banking system differently from purchasing $100 million in securities from dealers? Please explain.

5. Suppose the Federal Reserve's primary-credit discount rate is 7 percent. This afternoon the Federal Reserve Board announces that it is approving the request of several of its Reserve banks to raise their primary-credit rates to 7.5 percent. What will happen to other interest rates (particularly money market rates) tomorrow morning? Carefully explain the reasoning behind your answer.

   Would the impact of the discount rate change described above be somewhat different if:
   a. Loan demand was increasing or decreasing?
   b. There existed a large or a very small spread between prevailing money market rates (especially the Federal funds rate) and the Fed's discount rate?
   c. The Fed simultaneously sold $100 million in securities through its Trading Desk at the New York Fed? What if it purchased $100 million in securities instead?

6. Suppose the Fed purchases $500 million in government securities from a security dealer. What will happen to the level of bank reserves and by how much will they change? If the Federal Reserve imposes a 10 percent reserve requirement on deposits and there are no other leakages from the banking and financial system, by how much will deposits and loans change as a result of the Fed's purchase of securities?

7. If the Fed loans banks or other depository institutions $200 million in reserves from the discount windows of the Federal Reserve banks, by how much will the legal reserves of the banking system change? What happens when these loans are repaid by the borrowing institutions?

Internet Exercises

1. Does the banking commission or chief bank regulatory body in your home state have a website? What functions does this regulatory agency fulfill? Do they post job openings?

2. What U.S. banking laws have been important in shaping American history? (See **www.fdic.gov**.)

3. Have you ever wanted to be a bank examiner? What do bank examiners do? See if you can prepare a job description for a bank examiner. (See, for example, **www.federalreserve.gov**.)

4. What does it take to become a central banker? What does the job entail and what kind of training do you think you should have (perhaps to become a member of the Federal Reserve Board)? (See **www.federalreserve.gov**.)

5. Can you describe the structure and mission of the new European Central Bank (ECB)? What central bank does it seem to most resemble? (See especially **www.ecb.int**.)

6. Compare the federal regulatory agencies that oversee the activities and operations of credit unions, savings and loan associations and savings banks, and security brokers and dealers. In what ways are these regulatory agencies similar and in what ways do they seem to differ from each other? (See, for example, the websites **www.ncua.gov**, **www.ots.treas.gov**, and **www.sec.gov**.)

STANDARD &POOR'S

S&P Market Insight Challenge

1. Use Standard & Poor's Market Insight website (**www.mhhe.com/edumarketinsight**) for this problem. Government regulations of financial-service companies continue to change and evolve. For timely information concerning changes in regulatory environments, utilize the Industry tab in S&P's Market Insight, Educational Version. The drop-down menu provides subindustry selections that may interest you, including Asset

REAL NUMBERS FOR REAL BANKS — Assignment for Chapter 2

THE REGULATORY INFLUENCE ON YOUR BANKING COMPANY

In Chapter 2, we focus on the *regulations* that created and empower today's regulators, govern how and where our banks or other financial institutions may operate, and what those operations may entail. For this segment of the project we will be developing a table (Excel sheet) of information, using some of the terminology from the regulations discussed in this chapter and becoming familiar with the FDIC's website.

A. Go to the FDIC's Institution Directory at **www3.fdic. gov/idasp/** and search for your bank holding company (BHC). When you find your BHC make a note of the "BHC ID" because you will be using this number in future assignments. We suggest including it in the name of this spreadsheet. If you click on the active bank holding company name link, you will also see a list of bank and thrift subsidiaries. (These are just the bank and thrift subsidiaries of the BHC and do not include nonbank subsidiaries.) List these individual institutions (subsidiaries) and their FDIC certificate numbers in the first column of your spreadsheet. The "class" column will give you information concerning the regulator that chartered each institution, whether the institution is a member of the Federal Reserve, and which regulator has primary supervisory authority. Create columns B through D on your spreadsheet with this information—Column B defines state/federal charter; Column C defines member/nonmember of the Fed; and Column D identifies the primary federal regulator. (For a commercial bank this would be the OCC, Fed, or FDIC.)

B. Go to the FDIC's Institution Directory at **www3.fdic. gov/idasp/** and do institution searches using the certificate numbers you found. You will again see information about individual institutions: charter, primary regulator, and primary Internet Web address (keep this for future reference). Collect the information for the date each institution was established and the date that federal deposit insurance was acquired. Enter this information in columns E and F. (Prior to the Riegle-Neal Interstate Banking Act in 1994, banks used the bank holding company structure and individual institutions to expand their markets, especially across state lines.)

C. Go to the FDIC's Institution Directory at **www3.fdic. gov/idasp/** and do office searches using the certificate numbers you found. Collect the information on the number of offices and the types of offices and include this in columns G and H. The branch structure has changed as the Riegle-Neal Act has allowed interstate branching.

What have we accomplished? We have begun to organize information and become familiar with the FDIC's website. (Make sure that you provide an appropriate title for the spreadsheet and label the columns.) In Chapter 3 we will be focusing on organization and structure and you will be able to relate your banking company to the industry as a whole. (We always have something to look forward to!)

www.mhhe.com/rose6e

Management & Custody Banks, Consumer Finance, Diversified Banks, Diversified Capital Markets, Insurance Brokers, Investment Banking and Brokerage, Life and Health Insurance, Multi-line Insurance, Property & Casualty Insurance, Regional Banks, and Thrifts & Mortgage Finance. Once you select an industry, you will find S&P Industry Surveys that can be downloaded in Adobe Acrobat and are updated frequently. The S&P Industry Surveys include Banking, Investment Services, Financial Services Diversified, Insurance: Property and Casualty, Insurance: Life and Health, and Savings and Loans. Download two industry surveys and explore the first section, "Current Environment." Identify recent regulatory changes that appear to be affecting the current environments of the two industries and write a summary of these changes and their apparent effects.

2. Use Standard & Poor's Market Insight website (**www.mhhe.com/edumarketinsight**) for this problem. Which of the financial-service (bank and nonbank) firms listed in the Educational Version of S&P's Market Insight appear to bear the heaviest level of government regulation, and which ones appear to be least government regulated? Why do you think these differences in the intensity of regulation exist? Which financial-service companies listed on Market Insight are regulated predominantly by the states? By the U.S. government? By foreign governments? Which are regulated at *both* federal and state levels? Do you think it makes a difference to the regulated firms?

Selected References

See the following for a good discussion of the reasons for and against the regulation of banking and other financial-service institutions:

1. Benston, George G. "Federal Regulation of Banks: Analysis and Policy Recommendations." *Journal of Bank Research*, Winter 1983, pp. 216–44.

2. Gande, Amar; Manju Puvi; Anthony Saunders; and Ingo Walter. "Bank Underwriting of Debt Securities: Modern Evidence." *The Review of Financial Studies* 10, no. 4 (Winter 1997), pp. 1175–202.

3. Kane, Edward J. "Metamorphosis in Financial-Services Delivery and Production." In *Strategic Planning of Economic and Technological Change in the Federal Savings and Loan.* San Francisco: Federal Home Loan Bank Board, 1983, pp. 49–64.

4. Kareken, John H. "Deposit Insurance Reform: Or Deregulation Is the Cart, Not the Horse." *Quarterly Review*, Federal Reserve Bank of Minneapolis, Winter 1990, pp. 3–11.

5. Peltzman, Samuel. "Toward a More General Theory of Regulation." *Journal of Law and Economics*, August 1976, pp. 211–40.

6. Rose, Peter S. *Banking across State Lines: Public and Private Consequences.* Westport, CT: Quorum Books, 1997.

7. Santomero, Anthony M., and Xavier Freixas. "An Overall Perspective on Banking Regulation." Working Paper 02-1, Federal Reserve Bank of Philadelphia, 2002.

8. Stigler, George J. "The Theory of Economic Regulation." *The Bell Journal of Economics and Management Science* II (1971), pp. 3–21.

For a review of the Gramm-Leach-Bliley (Financial Services Modernization) Act and other current regulatory issues, see the following:

9. Krainer, John. "The Separation of Banking and Commerce." *Economic Review*, Federal Reserve Bank of New York, 2000, pp. 15–25.

10. Stern, Gary H. "Managing Moral Hazard with Market Signals: How Regulation Should Change with Banking." *The Region*, Federal Reserve Bank of Minneapolis, June 1999, pp. 28–31.

11. Stiroh, Kevin J., and Jennifer P. Poole. "Explaining the Rising Concentration of Banking Assets in the 1990s." *Current Issues in Economics and Finance*, Federal Reserve Bank of New York VI, no. 9 (August 2000), pp. 1–6.

12. Thomson, James B. "Raising the Deposit Insurance Limit: A Bad Idea Whose Time Has Come?" *Economic Commentary*, Federal Reserve Bank of Cleveland, April 15, 2000.

For a discussion of the methods and procedures of monetary policy and its impact on banks and other financial institutions, see the following:

13. Pollard, Patrica S. "Central Bank Independence and Economic Performance." *Review*, Federal Reserve Bank of St. Louis, July/August 1993, pp. 21–36.

14. Walsh, Carl E. "Is There a Cost to Having an Independent Central Bank?" *FRBSF Weekly Letter*, Federal Reserve Bank of San Francisco, February 4, 1994, pp. 1–3.

15. Rose, Peter S. *Money and Capital Markets: Financial Institutions and Instruments in a Global Marketplace.* 8th ed. Burr Ridge, IL: Irwin, 2002.

16. Weinberg, John A. "Competition among Bank Regulators." *Economic Quarterly*, Federal Reserve Bank of Richmond 88, no. 4 (Fall 2002), pp. 19–36.

www.mhhe.com/rose6e

For an explanation of the recent changes made by the Federal Reserve in its discount window lending procedures, see especially the following:

17. DePrince, Albert E. Jr., and William F. Ford. "The Fed's New Discount Mechanism: Implications for Community Bank Funds Managers." *Special Report*, Sheshunoff Information Services, March 2003.

18. Stevens, Ed. "The New Discount Window." *Economic Commentary*, Federal Reserve Bank of Cleveland, May 15, 2003.

Recent moves toward deregulation of the financial-services arena are discussed in:

19. Guzman, Mark G. "Slow but Steady Progress toward Financial Deregulation." *Southwest Economy*, Federal Reserve Bank of Dallas, January/February 2003, pp. 1, 6–9, and 12.

The great debate over deposit insurance reform is outlined in:

20. Martin, Antoine. "A Guide to Deposit Insurance Reform." *Economic Review*, Federal Reserve Bank of Kansas City, First Quarter 2003, pp. 29–54.

The estimated burden of regulation on the banking industry is explored in:

21. Elliehausen, Gregory. "The Cost of Bank Regulation: A Review of the Evidence." Staff Study No. 171, Board of Governors of the Federal Reserve System, April 1998.

The great debate over the separation of banking and commerce and whether the walls between these sectors should be removed is discussed in:

22. Walter, John R. "Banking and Commerce: Tear Down This Wall?" *Economic Quarterly*, Federal Reserve Bank of Richmond 89, no. 2 (Spring 2003), pp. 7–31.

CHAPTER THREE

The Organization and Structure of Banking and the Financial-Services Industry

Key Topics in This Chapter

- The Organization and Structure of the Commercial Banking Industry
- Internal Organization of the Banking Firm: Smaller Community and Larger Money-Center Banks
- The Array of Organizational Structures in Banking: Unit, Branch, Holding Company and Electronic Banks
- Interstate Banking and the Riegle-Neal Act
- Two Alternative Types of Banking Organizations as the 21st Century Opened: The Financial Holding Company and Bank Subsidiaries Model
- The Changing Organization and Structure of Banking's Principal Competitors
- Efficiency and Size

Introduction

Chapter 1 of this text explored the many roles and services the modern bank and many of its financial-service competitors offer. In that chapter we viewed banks and their closest financial-service competitors as providers of credit, channels for making payments, repositories of the public's savings, managers of business and household cash balances, trustees of customers' property, providers of risk protection, and brokers charged with carrying out purchases and sales of securities and other assets to fulfill their customers' wishes. Over the years, bankers and the managers of other financial institutions have evolved different **organizational forms** to perform these various roles and to supply the services their customers demand.

Truly, organizational form follows function, for banks and other financial firms usually are organized to carry out the roles assigned to them by the marketplace as efficiently as possible. Because larger institutions generally play a wider range of roles and offer more services, *size* is also a significant factor in determining how banks and other financial institutions are organized. Indeed, the financial-services industry has the greatest disparity in size of firms of virtually any industry—from behemoths like J. P. Morgan Chase Bank, with offices all over the world and hundreds of billions of dollars in assets to manage, to the Big Sky Bank of Gallatin County, Montana, which knows most of its customers personally and has relatively modest assets to manage.

However, a financial institution's roles and size are not the only determinants of how it is organized or of how well it performs. As we saw in Chapter 2, government regulation, too, has played a major role in shaping the performance and diversity of banking and other financial-service organizations around the globe. In this chapter we will see clearly how changing public mobility and changing public demand for financial services, the rise of potent competition for the financial-service customer's business, and changing government rules have dramatically changed the structure, the size, and the types of organizations dominating the banking and financial services industry over time.

The Organization and Structure of the Commercial Banking Industry

Size and Concentration of Assets   In our exploration of the great impact of organization and structure on the behavior and performance of banks and their competitors we turn first to the leading financial-services industry: *commercial banking,* the dominant supplier of credit to business firms and of deposits payable on demand in the global financial system. Most commercial banks in the United States are *small* by world standards. As Exhibit 3–1 shows, about 53 percent of all U.S.-insured commercial banking organizations, or approximately 4,200 banks, held total assets of less than $100 million each in 2002. Yet the American banking industry also contains some of the largest banking organizations on the planet. For example, Citigroup of New York holds sufficient assets to place it among the very largest financial institutions in the world. Moreover, banking in the United States is becoming increasingly concentrated in the largest firms. For example, the 10 largest American banks controlled about a quarter of all industry assets, while the 100 largest U.S. banking organizations held about 75 percent of all industry assets. Interestingly enough, not only industry assets but also banking profits today seem to be concentrated in the largest banks: most U.S. banks that lost money at the opening of the 21st century were among the smallest organizations.

Factoid
What is the largest banking company in the United States and the fifth largest in the world (measured by total assets)?
Answer: Citigroup, Inc., based in New York City.

Although banking nationwide seems to have become more concentrated in the largest institutions, the concentration of bank assets and deposits at the local level—in the towns and cities where most people live and work—seems to have changed very little on average in recent years. There appears to have been little, if any, change in the average number of banks or in the percentage of assets banks control in most individual cities and rural areas across America. However, the great differences in bank size across the United States have led to greater differences in the way banks are organized internally and in the types and variety of financial services each bank offers in the markets it serves.

Internal Organization of the Banking Firm

Smaller Banks—Community and Retail Institutions   The influence of size upon internal organization can be seen most directly by looking at the "typical" organization chart supplied by the management of a small bank of about $150 million in assets located in a smaller community in the Midwest. (See Exhibit 3–2.) Like hundreds of banks serving smaller cities and towns, this bank is heavily committed to attracting smaller household deposits and making household and small business loans. A bank like this, with its primary efforts devoted to the markets for household and small business loans and deposits, is often called a *retail bank.* Moreover, because of its strong focus on the local area, it is also often labeled a *community bank.* Banks of this type stand in sharp contrast to *whole-*

EXHIBIT 3–1 The Structure of the U.S. Commercial Banking Industry, December 31, 2002

Source: Federal Deposit Insurance Corporation.

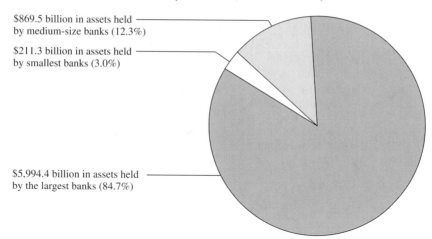

Assets Held by U.S. FDIC-insured Commercial Banks
(Total Industry Assets of $7,075 Billion in 2002)

$869.5 billion in assets held by medium-size banks (12.3%)

$211.3 billion in assets held by smallest banks (3.0%)

$5,994.4 billion in assets held by the largest banks (84.7%)

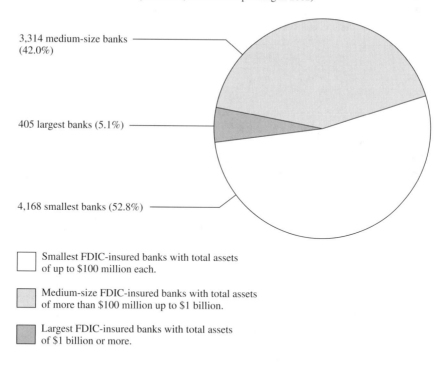

Number of U.S. FDIC-insured Banks
(Total of 7,887 Banks Operating in 2002)

3,314 medium-size banks (42.0%)

405 largest banks (5.1%)

4,168 smallest banks (52.8%)

☐ Smallest FDIC-insured banks with total assets of up to $100 million each.

▨ Medium-size FDIC-insured banks with total assets of more than $100 million up to $1 billion.

▨ Largest FDIC-insured banks with total assets of $1 billion or more.

sale banks, like J. P. Morgan Chase and First Union Corp., which concentrate mainly upon serving commercial customers and making large corporate loans all over the globe.

The service operations of a community bank are usually monitored by a cashier and auditor working in the accounting department and by vice presidents heading up the bank's loan, fund-raising, marketing, and trust departments. These officers report to the senior executives of the firm, consisting of the board chairman, the president (who usually runs the bank from day to day), and senior vice presidents (who are usually responsible for long-range planning and for assisting heads of the various departments in solving their most pressing problems). Senior management, in turn, reports periodically during the year to members of the **board of directors**—the committee selected by the **stockholders** (owners) to set policy and monitor the bank's performance.

The organization chart in Exhibit 3–2 is not complicated. Close contact between top management and the management and staff of each division is common. If smaller community banks have serious problems, they usually center upon trying to find competent new managers to replace aging administrators and struggling to afford the cost of new electronic equipment. Also, community banks are usually significantly impacted by changes in the health of the local economy. For example, many are closely tied to agriculture or to the condition of other locally based businesses, so when local sales are depressed, the bank often experiences slower growth and its deposits, loans, and earnings may fall.

Community banks usually present a relatively low-risk working environment, but one with limited opportunities for advancement or for the development of new banking skills. Nevertheless, banks of this size and geographic location represent attractive employment

EXHIBIT 3–2
Organization Chart
for a Smaller
Community or Retail
Bank

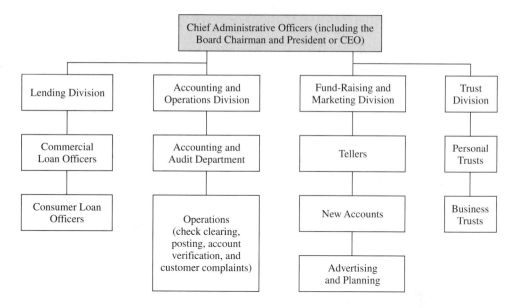

opportunities because they place the banker close to his or her customers and give bank employees the opportunity to see how their actions, especially the granting of loans, can have a real impact on the quality of life in local cities and towns.

Larger Banks—Money Center, Wholesale and Retail In comparison to smaller community and retail banks, the organization chart of a large (multibillion dollar) *money center bank*—located in a large city and wholesale or wholesale plus retail in its focus—typically looks far more complex than that of a smaller, community-oriented bank. A fairly typical organization chart from an eastern U.S. money-center bank with more than $20 billion in assets is shown in Exhibit 3–3. This bank is owned and controlled by a holding company whose stockholders elect a board of directors to oversee the bank and nonbank businesses allied with the same holding company. Selected members of the holding company's board of directors serve on the bank's board as well. The key problem in such an organization is often the *span of control*. Top management is often knowledgeable about banking practices but less well informed about the products and services offered by subsidiary companies. Moreover, because the bank itself offers so many different services in both domestic and foreign markets, serious problems may not surface for weeks or months. In recent years, a number of the largest banks have moved toward the profit-center approach, in which each major department strives to maximize its contribution to the bank's profitability and closely monitors its own performance.

The largest money center banks (wholesale or retail) possess some advantages over smaller, community-oriented institutions. Because the largest institutions serve many different markets with many different services, they are better diversified—both geographically and by product line—to withstand the risks of a fluctuating economy. These institutions are rarely dependent on the economic fortunes of a single industry or, in many cases, even a single nation. For example, such banking companies as Citigroup, Chase/J.P. Morgan, and Deutschebank often receive half or more of their net earnings from sources outside their home country. They also possess the important advantage of being able to raise financial capital at relatively low cost. As interstate banking spreads across the United States and global banking expands throughout Asia, Europe, and the Middle East, these banks should be well situated because of their greater capacity to accept the risks of entering new markets and their potentially greater access to new capital and managerial talent.

EXHIBIT 3–3
Organization Chart for a Money Center or Wholesale Bank Serving International Business Markets

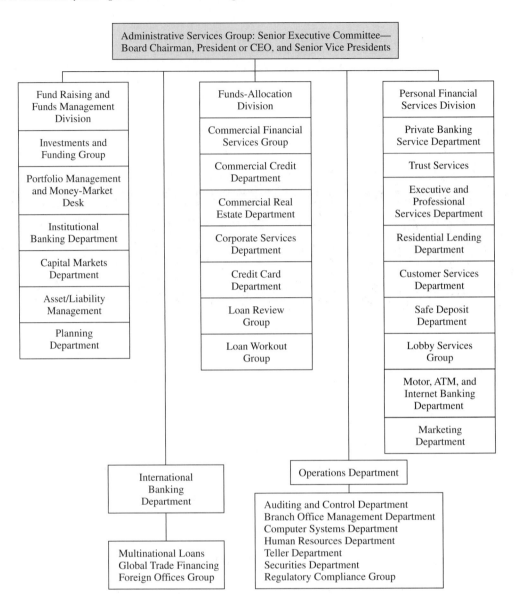

Key URL
Retail-oriented banks are represented in the industry by the Consumer Bankers Association at **www.cbanet.org**.

Key URL
For further information about community banks and their management see America's Community Bankers at **www.acbankers.org**.

Recent Trends in Bank Organization

The tendency in recent years has been for most banking institutions to become *more complex* organizations over time. When a bank begins to grow, it usually adds new services and new facilities. With them come new departments and new divisions to help management more effectively focus and control the bank's resources.

Another significant factor influencing banking organizations today is the changing makeup of the skills bankers need to function effectively and efficiently as market conditions and technology change. For example, with the global spread of government deregulation and the resultant increase in the number of competitors banks face in their major markets, more and more banking firms have become *market driven* and *sales oriented,* more alert to the changing service demands of their customers and also to the challenges that bank and nonbank competitors pose.

These newer activities require the appointment of bank management and staff who can devote more time to surveying customer service needs, developing new services based upon customer surveys, and modifying old service offerings to reflect changing customer needs. Similarly, as the technology of financial services production and delivery has shifted more and more in recent years toward computer-based systems, electronic service delivery, ATMs, and the Internet, banks have needed growing numbers of people with computer skills and the electronic equipment they work with. At the same time, automated book-keeping has reduced the time managers spend in routine operations, thus allowing greater opportunity for planning new services and new service delivery facilities that reflect the latest technology.

Concept Check

3–1. How would you describe the *size distribution* of American banks and the *concentration* of industry assets inside the United States? What is happening in general to the size distribution and concentration of banks in the United States and in other industrialized nations and why?

3–2. Describe the typical organization of both a smaller, community-oriented bank and a large, money-center bank. What does each major division or administrative unit within the banking organization do?

3–3. What trends are affecting the way banks are organized today?

The Array of Corporate Organizational Structures in Banking

Whatever financial services a banking organization offers to the public, it must make them available through one or more *customer service facilities*—physical locations or electronic networks through which bank personnel and equipment sell and deliver services to the public. These banking facilities may be placed under the control of either a single banking corporation or under multiple corporations linked to each other through a common group of stockholders.

Getting a New Charter of Incorporation

Before any services can be offered the bank must have a *charter of incorporation*. Where can a bank secure a charter to get its business off and running? In the United States, from one of two places—through a formal application submitted either (*a*) to the banking commission of the state where the bank is to be headquartered in order to form a *state-chartered bank* or (*b*) to the Comptroller of Currency, who is empowered to issue a certificate of association for a *national bank*. (See Chapter 18 for a more detailed discussion of the bank charter process.)

If a national bank is chartered, it must also join the Federal Reserve System and secure a certificate of approval for deposit insurance from the FDIC. However, a state-chartered bank is not necessarily obligated to join the Federal Reserve System and apply for federal deposit insurance, though the overwhelming majority of banks do seek federal deposit insurance in order to win public confidence. In fact, most U.S. states today require deposit insurance certification before they will grant a charter. Even so, the majority of U.S. banks have *not* joined the Federal Reserve System due to its tougher regulations. (See Exhibit 3–4 for a breakdown of the major types of U.S. banks and their relative importance within the U.S. banking system.)

Getting a federal or state bank charter is only the beginning. The organizers must select management for the bank and, jointly with management, decide such matters as the number of offices needed, types of physical and electronic facilities desired, and the preferred form of corporate organization. We will see in the discussion that follows that banks and many of their nonbank competitors around the world generally have moved toward larger organizations with many branch offices or automated service units, toward the formation of holding companies, and toward expansion across state and national boundaries to find greater opportunities for profit.

EXHIBIT 3–4 U.S. Commercial Banks with Federal and State Charters, Membership in the Federal Reserve System, and Deposit Insurance from the Federal Government (as of December 31, 2002)

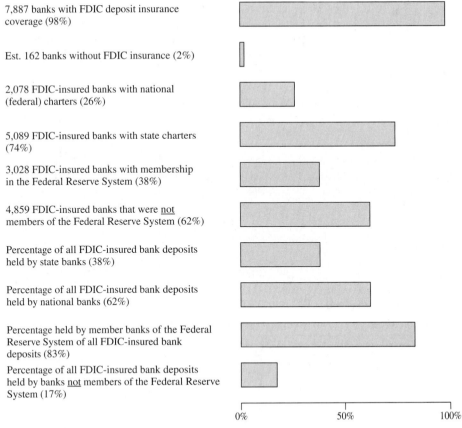

7,887 banks with FDIC deposit insurance coverage (98%)

Est. 162 banks without FDIC insurance (2%)

2,078 FDIC-insured banks with national (federal) charters (26%)

5,089 FDIC-insured banks with state charters (74%)

3,028 FDIC-insured banks with membership in the Federal Reserve System (38%)

4,859 FDIC-insured banks that were <u>not</u> members of the Federal Reserve System (62%)

Percentage of all FDIC-insured bank deposits held by state banks (38%)

Percentage of all FDIC-insured bank deposits held by national banks (62%)

Percentage held by member banks of the Federal Reserve System of all FDIC-insured bank deposits (83%)

Percentage of all FDIC-insured bank deposits held by banks <u>not</u> members of the Federal Reserve System (17%)

0%   50%   100%

Source: Board of Governors of the Federal Reserve System and the Federal Deposit Insurance Corporation.

Unit Banking Organizations

Unit banks, one of the oldest kinds of banking, offer all of their services from *one office*, though some services (such as taking deposits, cashing checks, or paying bills) may be offered from limited-service facilities, such as drive-in windows, automated teller machines, retail store point-of-sale terminals that are linked to the bank's computer system, and each bank's Internet website. These organizations are common in U.S. banking today. For example, in 2002 nearly 2,500 of the nation's commercial banks, about one-third, operated out of just one full-service office, compared to about 5,600 banks that had two or more offices in operation.

One reason for the comparatively large number of unit banks is the rapid formation of new banks, even in an age of electronic banking, consolidation, and megamergers among industry leaders. About 15 percent of all community banks are less than 10 years old. Many customers still seem to prefer small banks, which get to know their customers well and often provide personalized service. Between 1980 and 2002, more than 4,700 new banks were chartered in the United States, or an average of just over 200 per year—substantially more than the number of failing banks in most years, as Table 3–1 relates.

Most new banks start out as unit organizations, in part because their capital, management, and staff are severely limited until the bank can grow and attract additional resources and professional staff. However, most banks desire to create multiple service facilities—branch offices, electronic networks, websites, and other service outlets—to open up new markets and to diversify geographically in order to lower their overall risk exposure. Bankers know that relying on a single location from which to receive customers and income can be risky if the surrounding economy weakens and people and businesses move away to other market areas.

TABLE 3–1 Entry and Exit in U.S. Banking

Source: Board of Governors of the Federal Reserve System and the Federal Deposit Insurance Corporation.

Year	Newly Chartered Banks	Failures of FDIC-Insured Banks	Number of Mergers and Acquisitions	Bank Branches Opened	Bank Branches Closed
1980	267	10	126	2,397	287
1981	286	7	210	2,326	364
1982	378	32	256	1,666	443
1983	419	45	314	1,320	567
1984	489	78	330	1,405	889
1985	346	116	336	1,480	617
1986	283	141	341	1,387	763
1987	217	186	543	1,117	960
1988	234	209	598	1,676	1,082
1989	204	206	411	1,825	758
1990	165	158	393	2,987	926
1991	106	105	447	2,788	1,456
1992	94	98	428	1,677	1,313
1993	71	42	481	1,499	1,215
1994	66	11	548	2,461	1,146
1995	125	6	609	2,367	1,319
1996	146	5	554	2,487	1,870
1997	188	1	600	NA	NA
1998	190	3	561	1,436	NA
1999	255	8	442	1,450	NA
2000	51	2	109	1,286	NA
2001	129	3	360	1,010	NA
2002	91	10	281	1,285	NA

Key URL

One of the more interesting bankers' associations is the NBA or National Bankers Association—a trade group that serves to protect the interests of minority-owned banks, including those owned by African Americans, Native Americans, Hispanic Americans, and women. See especially **www.nba.org** for a fuller description.

Concept Check

3–4. What are unit banks?

3–5. What advantages might a unit bank have over banks of other organizational types? What disadvantages?

Branch Banking Organizations

As a unit bank grows larger in size it usually decides at some point to establish a **branch banking** organization, particularly if it serves a rapidly growing region and finds itself under pressure either to follow its business and household customers as they move into new locations or lose them to more conveniently located financial-service competitors. Branch banking organizations offer the full range of banking services from several locations, including a head office and one or more full-service branch offices. Such an organization is also likely to offer limited services through a supporting network of drive-in windows, automated teller machines, computers electronically linked to the bank's computers through mini-branches, point-of-sale terminals in stores and shopping centers, telephones, fax machines, the Internet, and other advanced communications systems.

Senior management of a branch banking organization is usually located at the home office, though each full-service branch has its own management team with limited authority to make decisions on customer loan applications and other facets of daily operations. For example, a branch manager may be authorized to approve a customer loan of up to $25,000. Larger loan requests, however, must be referred to the home office for a final decision. Thus, some services and functions in a branch banking organization are highly

EXHIBIT 3–5 The Branch Banking Organization

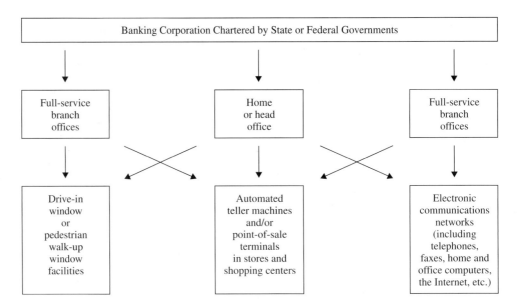

centralized, whereas others are decentralized at the individual service facility level. Exhibit 3–5 displays a typical branch banking organization.

Branching's Growth Most branch banks in the United States are small compared to other banks around the globe. For example, as the 21st century opened there were about 7,000 branch banking organizations in the United States, operating more than 60,000 full-service branch office facilities. As Table 3–1 reminds us, while the number of U.S. banks declined over this last half-century from around 14,000 to about 8,000 today, the number of all branch offices, including home offices, has soared from only about 3,000 to more than 70,000 full-service offices, not counting more than 150,000 computer-terminal banking facilities scattered across the United States in thousands of stores, shopping centers, and lobbies, and at more than 3,000 active Internet sites. Indeed, electronic banking facilities today are even more popular in Europe than they are in the United States.

During the Great Depression of the 1930s, only one in five American banks, on average, operated a full-service branch office. By the beginning of the 21st century the average U.S. bank operated about eight full-service branch offices, although some of the nation's leading banks, like Bank America and J. P. Morgan Chase, operate hundreds of branch offices. By and large, these limited numbers of U.S. branches per bank are small potatoes compared to leading banks in Canada, Great Britain, and Western Europe that often operate hundreds or thousands of branch outlets in addition to their computer terminal and Internet customer connections.

This wide disparity in national banking structures arises from differences in public attitudes toward branch banking. Early in the history of the United States, there was great fear of the power of branch banks to eliminate competition and charge their customers excessive prices for banking services. As a result, most states passed laws to limit branching activity to designated areas, such as the city or county of a bank's home office. Unfortunately, this antibranching attitude may have allowed some banks, freed from the danger of outside entry by other banking organizations, to act as monopolies, raising prices and restricting output. In recent years, however, bank branching has spread rapidly across the United Sates. Today all 50 states and the District of Columbia permit some form of branch facilities.

TABLE 3–2
Growth of Bank
Branch Offices in the
United States

Source: Federal Deposit
Insurance Corporation.

Year	Number of Bank Home (Main) Offices	Number of Branch Offices	Total of All U.S. Bank Offices	Average Number of Branches per U.S. Bank
1934	14,146	2,985	17,131	0.21
1940	13,442	3,489	16,931	0.26
1952	13,439	5,486	18,925	0.41
1964	13,493	14,703	28,196	1.09
1970	13,511	21,810	35,321	1.61
1982*	14,451	39,784	54,235	2.75
1988	13,137	46,619	59,756	3.55
1993	11,212	53,049	64,261	4.73
1999	8,551	63,684	72,265	7.45
2001	8,096	64,938	73,034	8.02
2002	7,887	66,185	74,072	8.39

*Beginning in 1982 remote service facilities (ATMs) were not included in the count of total branches. At year-end 1981, there were approximately 3,000 remote service banking facilities.

Reasons behind Branching's Growth   The causes of the rapid growth in branch banking are many. One factor has been the exodus of population over the past several decades from cities to suburban communities, forcing many large downtown banks to either follow or lose their mobile customers. The result has been the expansion of branch offices and automated tellers, radiating out from downtown areas of major cities like the spokes of a wheel, with the leading money center banks at the hub of the branching wheel, along with growing computer networks and Internet connections to serve distant and more mobile customers. Bank failures have also spawned branching activity as larger, healthier banks have been allowed to take over sick ones and convert them into branch offices. Business growth, too, has fueled the spread of branch banking; the credit needs of rapidly growing corporations necessitate larger and more diversified banks that can reach into many local markets for small deposits and pool those funds into large-volume loans. Table 3–2 demonstrates how the concentration of U.S. banking facilities has shifted from main offices to branch offices over the past half century.

The passage of the Riegle-Neal Interstate Banking and Branching Efficiency Act in 1994 (which we will explore more fully later in this chapter) provided the basis for an expansion of new bank branch offices nationwide (i.e., interstate banking). However, in recent years new bank branch office expansion appears to be slowing down and no single bank has yet established full-service branch offices nationwide. One reason is a recent rise in full-service office closings as the burgeoning cost of brick-and-mortar buildings has soared and some neighborhoods have declined and become less attractive to bankers. Then, too, the Internet, the telephone, plastic cards, and other electronic access media have taken over many routine financial transactions and there may be less need for extensive full-service branch offices. Finally, as we saw above, U.S. legislation in 1994 that allows branching anywhere in the country now permits bankers to buy *existing* branch networks in the most desirable communities, no matter where they are located, rather than always having to build new offices.

Advantages and Disadvantages of Branch Banking   Whether or not banks should be allowed to branch and, if so, over what areas has been one of the most controversial issues in banking history. Indeed, for most of the history of banking in the United States, few banks were allowed to set up branch offices due to federal and state restrictions. The U.S. bank branching movement didn't really take off until after World War II.

Opponents of full-service branch banking feared that it would drive out smaller competitors, giving customers fewer choices. Others argued that branching was likely to result in higher service fees (presumably due, in part, to forcing out competitors) so that customers would be confronted with more costly financial transactions. Still other opponents feared that branching would drain scarce capital from smaller cities and towns and divert funds into the biggest cities.

Proponents, on the other hand, argued that branch banking would result in greater operating efficiency (in part, because banks with branches would grow bigger), benefiting customers with lower-cost services. Still other supporters of branching thought it would offer customers greater convenience (more offices close by with a greater array of services) and provide banks with greater stability and stamina, especially during tough economic times.

Ultimately, the *proponents* in this debate came out the winners because branch banking is now legal, in one form or another, across the United States and in most other industrialized nations as well. Interestingly enough, however, few of the advantages or disadvantages claimed for branch banks have been convincingly supported by recent research evidence.

Branch banking organizations do often buy out smaller banks, converting them into branches and concentrating the industry's assets into the hands of fewer firms. However, there is little or no evidence that this necessarily lessens competition. Customer convenience seems to improve because more services are available at every branch location and branching areas tend to have more offices per unit of population, reducing transactions costs for the average customer. However, some service fees seem to be higher in branching areas, especially when branch banks acquire smaller institutions and boost service charges after these acquisitions are made. (See, for example, Rose [3].) However, the higher service fees may reflect greater knowledge on the part of larger banks concerning the true cost of each service.

We can say that setting up new brick-and-mortar full-service branches seems to be an especially costly way to grow in today's marketplace. With the continuing spread of computer-driven information technology, the need for old-fashioned "brick and mortar" branch offices seems to be diminishing and the demand instead for "electronic-style" branches (including websites and automated tellers), which appear to be more cost effective, is increasing. This development, however, would seem to favor bigger banks with more resources and greater technical expertise—characteristics that large branch banks often possess.[1]

Moreover, branch banks do appear to be less prone to failure than banks without full-service branch offices. For example, Canada—where the typical bank operates hundreds of branches—experienced not a single bank failure during the Great Depression of the 1930s, whereas the United States—a nation of predominantly modest-size banks—experienced thousands of bank failures.

Concept Check

3–6. What is a branch banking organization?

3–7. What trend in branch banking has been prominent in the United States in recent years?

3–8. Do branch banks seem to perform differently than unit banks? In what ways? Can you explain any differences?

---

[1]See, for example, Hunter and Timme [7], and Guzman [26].

Electronic Branching—Websites and Electronic Networks: An Alternative or a Supplement to Traditional Bank Branch Offices?

As we saw in the preceding section, traditional brick-and-mortar bank branch offices continue to expand across the United States and in many other countries as well. Growing somewhat faster today, however, are what some experts call "electronic branches." These include websites offering **Internet banking services, automated teller machines (ATMs)** and ATM networks dispensing cash and accepting deposits, **point of sales (POS) terminals** in stores and shopping centers to facilitate payment for goods and services, and personal computers and telephone systems connecting the customer to his or her bank. (See Exhibit 3–6.) Through many of these computer- and telephone-based systems, bank

EXHIBIT 3–6   Electronic Banking Systems, Computer Networks, and Web Banking

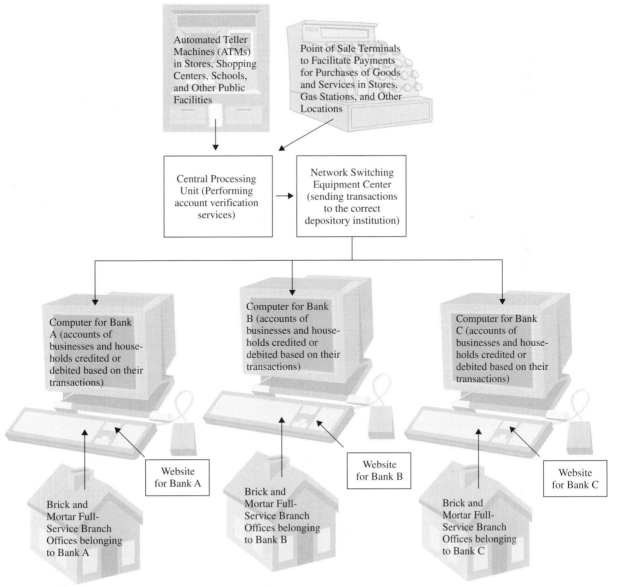

customers can check deposit balances, set up new accounts, move money from one account to another, pay bills, request approval for loans, and invest spare cash any time of the day or night.

Most electronic branches today operate at far lower cost to banks than do conventional brick-and-mortar branch offices. For example, a deposit made via the Internet may cost the bank as little as one one-hundredth the cost of a deposit made through a human teller at a local brick-and-mortar branch office and be more than 20 times cheaper than a deposit made through an ATM. Although most bank websites do not yet appear to be profitable by themselves, banks offering Internet banking services tend to have higher returns on invested capital than banks not offering Internet services, partially reflecting the operating cost advantage from providing services on the Web.

Many banks—especially **virtual banks,** like NetBank, that operate exclusively on the Web rather than through traditional branch offices—are moving today to pass some of the realized cost savings from electronic service delivery along to their customers, increasing the advantage to customers of "going electronic" rather than bearing the cost and inconvenience of driving to a local banking facility. One way the exclusively Web-based virtual banks have attracted customers away from traditional banks is to offer higher interest rates and lower service fees on deposits and cheaper rates on loans than many brick-and-mortar banks have been willing to offer.

Are electronic branches and virtual banks really an alternative to traditional brick-and-mortar bank branch offices or still mainly a supplemental channel for service delivery? Today most electronic systems in banking *supplement,* rather than fully replace, traditional, nonelectronic branch offices. Brick-and-mortar bank buildings provide a real point of contact between the banker and his or her customers, supplying personalized services, helping to straighten out problems that may have emerged with a customer's account (such as overdrafts), negotiating the terms of business and personal loans, and conveying to the customer a sense of stability and security. Few "electronic branches" today can offer the complete range of financial services that a modern bank offers through its brick-and-mortar branch system. However, this picture is changing as millions of new Internet-connected customers convert from older banking methods in favor of doing their banking business online.

True, most bank websites are not particularly profitable today, in part because the volume of Internet banking transactions is still relatively low. But many bankers are still willing to expand their Web-based services in the belief that this speedy and accurate approach to banking eventually will represent the wave of the future in the delivery of financial services.

Bank Holding Company Organizations

In earlier decades when states and other governments prohibited or severely restricted branch banking, the bank holding company often became the most attractive organizational alternative inside the United States and in several other countries as well. A **bank holding company** is simply a corporation chartered for the purpose of holding the stock (equity shares) of at least one bank.

Many holding companies hold only a small minority of the outstanding shares of one or more banks, thereby escaping government regulation. However, if a holding company operating in the United States seeks to *control* a bank whose shares it has acquired, it must seek approval from the Federal Reserve Board to become a registered bank holding company. Under the terms of the Bank Holding Company Act, control is assumed to exist if the holding company acquires 25 percent or more of the outstanding equity shares of at least one bank or can elect at least two directors of at least one bank. Once registered, the company must submit to periodic examinations of its records by the Federal Reserve Board and receive approval from the Fed when it reaches out to acquire other businesses.

E-BANKING AND E-COMMERCE

VIRTUAL BANKS

The rapid growth of Internet access and the millions of daily Web transactions by the public soon brought thousands of banks and other financial-service providers to the Internet. Most websites in the early years were *information-only sites*—for example, describing services offered or explaining how to reach the nearest branch office. As the 21st century began, however, the most rapidly growing financial-service websites were of the *transactions* variety where the customer could access basic services (e.g., checking account balances, transferring funds, and paying bills) and, in a growing number of cases, access extended services (including access to credit and the ability to make investments).

Initially, most of these websites were established by conventional banks that also operated brick-and-mortar, full-service branch offices. More recently, however, a cadre of *virtual banks* has emerged that do not operate conventional branches, but work exclusively over the Internet. Some have qualified for FDIC deposit insurance and offer an expanding menu of deposits, loans, and other services, though many remain unprofitable.

Some of the most prominent virtual banks are listed below along with their website addresses. You may want to explore how these banks are organized and what services they sell to the public.

E-Trade Bank (**www.etrade.com**)

Netbank (**www.netbank.com**)

First Internet Bank of Indiana (**www.firstib.com**)

National Interbank (**www.nationalinterbank.com**)

Bank of Internet USA (**www.bankofinternet.com**)

Juniper Bank (**www.juniper.com**)

Why Holding Companies Have Grown   The growth of bank holding companies has been rapid in recent decades. As long ago as 1971 these organizations controlled banks holding about half of U.S. bank deposits. By the 1990s, the nearly 6,000 bank holding companies operating in the United States controlled in excess of 90 percent of the industry's assets. Just over 6,300 U.S. commercial banks were affiliated with bank holding companies as 2002 drew to a close. (A list of the dozen largest U.S. bank holding companies appears in Table 3–3.) The principal reasons for this rapid upsurge in holding company activity include their greater ease of access to capital markets in raising funds, their ability to use higher leverage (more debt capital relative to equity capital) than nonaffiliated banking firms, their tax advantages in being able to offset profits from one business with losses generated by other firms that are part of the same company, and their ability to expand into businesses outside the banking industry.

One-Bank Holding Companies   Most registered bank holding companies in the United States are one-bank holding companies. By the beginning of the 21st century, about 5,000 of the roughly 6,000 bank holding companies in the United States controlled stock in just *one* bank.

However, these one-bank companies frequently owned and operated one or more nonbank businesses as well. Once a bank holding company registers with the Federal Reserve Board, any nonbank business activities it starts or acquires must first be approved by the Federal Reserve Board or the Federal Reserve banks. These nonbank businesses must offer services "closely related to banking" that also yield "public benefits," such as improved availability of financial services or lower service prices. (See Table 3–4 for examples of nonbank businesses that registered bank holding companies are allowed to own and control.)

Beginning in 2000, following passage of the Gramm-Leach-Bliley Act, a different type of holding company—financial-service holding companies (FHCs)—could offer an array of important new services (including insurance and security trading) through holding company affiliates or through bank subsidiaries. Today, the principal advantage for bank holding companies entering nonbank lines of business is the prospect of diversifying

TABLE 3–3

Leading Bank
Holding Companies
Operating in the
United States
Measured by Their
Total Deposits, 2002
(end of first quarter)

Source: Board of Governors of
the Federal Reserve System and
Federal Deposit Insurance
Corporation.

Holding Company Name	Location	Size of Organization Measured by Total Deposits Held (in billions of U.S. dollars)
Citigroup, Inc.	New York City, New York	$702
Bank of America Corporation	Charlotte, North Carolina	367
J. P. Morgan Chase & Co.	New York City, New York	282
Wells Fargo & Company	San Francisco, California	190
Wachovia Corporation	Charlotte, North Carolina	180
Bank One Corporation	Chicago, Illinois	159
FleetBoston Financial Corporation	Boston, Massachusetts	122
U.S. Bancorp	Minneapolis, Minnesota	102
HSBC North America, Inc.	Buffalo, New York	73
SunTrust Banks, Inc.	Atlanta, Georgia	70
Merrill Lynch Bank USA	Salt Lake City, Utah	60
National City Corp.	Cleveland, Ohio	58

TABLE 3–4   The Most Important Nonbank Financially Related Businesses Registered Bank Holding Companies Can Acquire under U.S. Regulations

Finance Companies
Lend short- and long-term funds to businesses and households.

Mortgage Companies
Provide short-term credit to improve real property for residential or commercial use.

Data Processing Companies
Provide computer processing services and information transmission.

Factoring Companies
Purchase short-term assets (mainly accounts receivable) from businesses in exchange for supplying temporary financing.

Security Brokerage Firms
Execute customer buy and sell orders for marketable securities, foreign exchange, and exchange-traded financial futures and option contracts and provide other full-service brokerage functions.

Financial Advising
Advise institutions and high-net-worth individual customers on investing funds, managing assets, mergers, reorganizations, raising capital, and feasibility studies.

Credit Insurance Underwriters
Supply life, accident, or health insurance coverage to customers borrowing money to guarantee repayment of a loan.

Merchant Banking
Invest in corporate stock as well as loan money to help finance the start of new ventures or to support the expansion of existing businesses.

Security Underwriting Firms
Purchase new U.S. government and municipal bonds, corporate stocks and bonds, asset-backed securities, and selected money market instruments from issuers and offer these securities for resale to buyers (permissible for well-managed and well-capitalized bank holding companies under the Gramm-Leach-Bliley Act).

Trust Companies
Manage and protect the property of businesses, individuals, and nonprofit organizations and place customers' securities with private investors.

Credit Card Companies
Provide short-term credit to individuals and businesses in order to support retail trade.

Leasing Companies
Purchase and lease equipment and other assets for businesses and individuals needing the use of these assets.

Insurance Companies and Agencies
Sell or underwrite insurance polices to businesses and individuals in order to provide risk protection.

Real Estate Services
Supply real estate appraisals, arrange for the financing of commercial and residential real estate projects, and broker real properties.

Savings Associations
Offer savings deposit plans and housing-related credit, predominantly to individuals and families.

EXHIBIT 3–7 The Multibank Holding Company

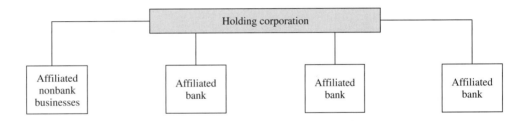

sources of revenue and profits (and, therefore, reducing risk exposure) from service lines that are not perfectly correlated with each other. (FHCs will be discussed in more detail later in this chapter.)

Multibank Holding Companies   A minority of bank holding company organizations are **multibank holding companies.** Multibank companies number just under 900 but control about 70 percent of the total assets of all U.S. banking organizations. Prior to the Riegle-Neal Act (1994), this form of banking organization appealed especially to bank stockholders and managers who wanted to set up an interstate banking organization composed of several formerly independent banking firms. One very dramatic effect of holding company expansion and acquisition has been a sharp decline in the number of independently owned banking organizations.

A bank holding company that wishes to acquire 5 percent or more of the equity shares of an additional bank must seek approval from the Federal Reserve Board and demonstrate that such an acquisition will not significantly damage competition in the local market, will promote public convenience, and will better serve the public's need for financial services. Banks acquired by holding companies are referred to as **affiliated banks.** (See Exhibit 3–7.) Banks that are not owned by holding companies are known as *independent banks*.

Advantages and Disadvantages of Holding Company Banking   Many of the advantages and disadvantages associated with branch banking have also been claimed by proponents and opponents of holding company banking. Thus, holding company banking has been blamed for reducing competition as its swallows up formerly independent banks, for overcharging customers (principally because holding-company affiliated banks allegedly reduce competition), for ignoring the credit needs of smaller towns and cities, and for accepting too much risk. In contrast, supporters of the holding company movement claim greater efficiency, more services available to customers, lower probability of organizational failure, and higher and more stable profits.

Today the holding company form permits the *de jure* (legal) separation between banks and nonbank businesses having greater risk, allowing these different firms to be owned by the same group of stockholders. Outside the United States, the holding company form is usually legal but is not often used in banking, except in the Netherlands and Italy. Most industrialized countries other than the United States allow banks themselves to offer more services or permit a bank to set up a subsidiary company under direct bank ownership and sell services that banks themselves are not allowed to offer.

Research on Holding Company Behavior   What are we to make of the claimed advantages and disadvantages for the holding company form of organization in banking? If holding companies actually reduce competition in banking, we might expect this to result in higher profits for holding company banks relative to other banks. There is, however, little convincing evidence that this has happened. However, several studies suggest that, while individual banks may not benefit from acquisition by holding companies, the holding company as a whole tends to be more profitable than banking organizations that

Key URL
Banks *not* affiliated with holding companies are represented in industry and legislative affairs by the Independent Community Bankers of America at www.ibaa.org.

do *not* form holding companies.[2] Moreover, the failure rate for holding company banks appears to be well below that of comparable-size independent banks.

As some have claimed, there is at least anecdotal evidence that multibank holding companies drain scarce capital from some communities and may sometimes weaken smaller towns and rural areas. We have no solid evidence on this claim, though a survey by Leonard M. Apcor and Buck Brown [4] of small towns in Texas suggests the issue may be worth further study. These reporters observed a tendency in some small cities for local funds to be siphoned away in an effort to shore up troubled lead banks of major holding companies. The result was less credit available for local community projects. Similarly, in a survey by John Helyon [6], some customers of holding-company banks in Florida complained about the rapid turnover of bank personnel, the lack of personalized service, and long delays when local office managers were forced to refer questions to the holding company's home office.

As we saw earlier, holding companies have reached outside the banking business in recent years, acquiring or starting finance companies, leasing firms, insurance companies and agencies, security underwriting firms, and other businesses. Have these nonbank acquisitions paid off? If added profitability was the goal, the results must be described as disappointing thus far. Frequently, acquiring companies have lacked sufficient experience with nonbank products to manage their nonbank firms successfully. However, not all nonbank business ventures of holding companies have been unprofitable. In fact, a study by Nellie Liang and Donald Savage [8] of nearly 300 bank holding companies with nonbank subsidiaries found that the average profitability of the nonbank firms was higher than that of banking firms belonging to the same company, though the nonbank firms also tended to make riskier loans and take riskier market positions than banks did. Certainly, the attractiveness of using nonbank firms as a vehicle for interstate expansion has declined somewhat with the continuing spread of full-service interstate banking across the United States in the wake of passage of the Riegle-Neal Interstate Banking Act in 1994.

Factoid
Which type of banking organization holds more than 90 percent of all U.S. banking assets?
Answer: Holding companies.

Concept Check

3–9. What is a bank holding company?

3–10. When must a holding company register with the Federal Reserve Board?

3–11. What nonbank businesses are bank holding companies permitted to acquire under the law?

3–12. Are there any significant advantages or disadvantages for holding companies from launching nonbank business ventures?

Interstate Banking and the Riegle-Neal Interstate Banking and Branching Efficiency Act of 1994

Many banking authorities today confidently predict that full-service interstate banking eventually will invade virtually every corner of the United States. Indeed, as we saw earlier in Chapter 2, the federal government took a giant step toward this goal when the U.S. Congress passed the Riegle-Neal Interstate Banking and Branching Efficiency Act of 1994—an action supported by most of the states. Riegle-Neal allows holding companies operating in the United States to acquire banks throughout the nation without needing any state's permission to do so and to establish branch offices across state lines in every state (except Montana, which opted out of interstate branching). No single company can

---

[2] See, for example, Rhoades and Savage [20], Varvel [9], and Frieder and Apilado [5].

hold more than 10 percent of insured deposits nationwide or more than 30 percent of insured deposits in a single state (unless a state waives this particular restriction).

Why did the federal government enact and the states support interstate banking/branching laws in 1994 after so many years of resistance, especially by community banks, to the very idea of interstate expansion.[3] Multiple factors were at work, including these:

- The need to bring in new capital to revive struggling local economies.
- The expansion of financial services by nonbank financial institutions that face few restrictions on their ability to expand nationwide.
- Competition with neighboring states that may have already liberalized their interstate banking laws.
- A strong desire (and extensive lobbying efforts) on the part of the largest banks to geographically diversify their operations and open up new marketing opportunities.
- The belief among regulators and many bankers that large banks may be more efficient and less prone to failure.
- Advances in the technology of financial-services delivery, permitting banks to serve customers over broader geographic areas.
- The opinion among the stockholders of many smaller banks that bank stock prices might rise if larger banks could cross state lines and buy out smaller competitors.

Proponents of interstate banking believe that it will bring new capital into states that are rapidly growing and short of investment capital, result in greater convenience for the customer (especially if the customer is traveling or changing residence to another state), and stimulate competitive rivalry that will promote greater efficiency in the use of scarce resources and lower prices for financial services. Interstate expansion may also bring greater stability to the U.S. banking system by allowing individual banking organizations to further diversify their operations across different markets and regions, offsetting losses that may arise in one market with gains in other markets. In the long run, interstate banking may improve the efficiency of the entire U.S. financial system by facilitating the flow of credit toward areas offering the highest expected rates of return at acceptable levels of risk.

Not everyone agrees, however, that interstate banking is an unmixed blessing. Some economists contend that it will lead to increases in banking concentration as smaller banks are merged into larger interstate organizations, possibly leading to less competition and higher prices and to the draining of funds from local areas into the nation's financial centers. Indeed, on a nationwide basis concentration of resources in the nation's largest banks has significantly increased since 1980 when the interstate banking movement began to take hold. The top 100 U.S. banks held only about half of all U.S. domestic banking assets in 1980, but by 2000 their proportion of the nation's domestic banking assets had climbed to more than 70 percent. At the same time the top 10 U.S. banking organizations rose sharply to capture close to half of all domestic banking assets. However, small banks seem to have little to fear from large interstate banks if the former are willing to compete aggressively for their customers' business.[4]

Doesn't this national concentration trend suggest possible damage to the consumer of financial services? Not necessarily. Many experts believe that those customers most likely to be hurt by a reduced number of competitors—the *potentially most damaged market*—are households and small businesses that trade for financial services mainly in smaller cities and towns. Interestingly enough, there has apparently been little change

[3] See especially Colburn and Hudgins [13].
[4] See especially Stiroh and Poole [30].

in the concentration of bank deposits at the local level in many metropolitan areas and rural counties. Therefore, it appears that in the interstate banking movement, thus far, many customers, particularly the smallest, have seen little change in their alternatives for obtaining banking services.

Concentration in the U.S. banking industry, measured by the share of assets and deposits held by the largest banks in the system, is among the lowest in the world. For example, while the three largest banking organizations in the United States hold about one-fifth of the U.S. banking industry's total assets, in most other industrialized countries, such as Canada, France, Germany, the Netherlands, Spain, Sweden, and Switzerland, half or more of all banking assets rest in the hands of the three largest banking companies. Germany typically posts the highest three-bank concentration ratio, with the largest three banks accounting for around 90 percent of industry assets, followed closely by Sweden and Switzerland, where the top three banks account for 80 percent or more of industry assets.

Research on Interstate Banking   Recent research suggests that the actual benefits the public and bank stockholders can expect from the coming of **full-service interstate banking** may be limited. For example, an interesting study by Goldberg and Hanweck [16] of the few early interstate banking organizations protected by grandfather provisions of federal law found that banks previously acquired across state lines did not gain on their instate competitors. In fact, these older interstate-controlled banks actually lost market share over time and were, on average, no more profitable than were neighboring banks serving the same states. Moreover, studies by Rose [21, 22] of interstate bank acquisitions early in the interstate banking era found that many of the banks acquired across state lines were in poor financial condition, with low or even negative earnings and high loan losses, which severely limited the growth and profitability of the interstate banking firms that acquired them. On average, interstate banks were generally *not* stellar performers in either profitability or growth.

Have the new interstate banking laws enacted in recent years resulted in any tangible benefits for the stockholders and employees of interstate banks? The evidence is mixed for both groups. Employees of interstate banking organizations would seem to have more opportunity for promotions in an expanding organization. However, many of the largest interstate firms (for example, J. P. Morgan Chase and Bank of America) frequently have laid off substantial numbers of employees in acquired businesses in an effort to cut expenses and increase efficiency. On the other hand, some interstate firms apparently have experienced an *increase* in the market value of their stock when laws were passed permitting interstate banking, suggesting that stock market investors regarded the trend toward nationwide banking as a positive event for the industry.

The most recent studies generally conclude that interstate mergers generate *positive* abnormal returns on bank stock for the stockholders of *both* acquiring and acquired banking firms, though the biggest gains in stock returns generally go to the acquired bank's shareholders. Research evidence is also beginning to emerge on whether interstate expansion can reduce the *risk* to a bank's earnings. In theory, if an interstate organization can acquire banks in states where bank earnings have a negative or low-positive correlation with bank earnings in those states where the interstate company is already represented, a "portfolio effect" could occur in which earnings losses at banks in one group of states offset profits earned at banks in other states, resulting in lower overall earnings risk for the interstate banking firm as a whole. However, research by Levonian [19] and Rose [24] suggests that reduction of bank earnings risk does not occur automatically simply because a banking organization crosses state lines. To achieve at least some reduction in earnings risk, Rose found, interstate banks must expand into a number of different states (at least

Key URL
The most important banking industry trade association, representing the industry as a whole, is the American Bankers Association at **www.aba.com**.

four) and different regions (at least two economically distinct regions of the nation). The bottom line is that *interstate banking organizations must be selective about which states they enter if risk reduction is an important consideration.*

Two Alternative Types of Banking Organizations Available as the 21st Century Opened

In 1999 the landmark Gramm-Leach-Bliley (GLB) Act moved U.S. banking closer to the concept of *universal banking,* in which commercial banking activities converge with investment banking and insurance as well as other financial services. To allow banks to offer selected nonbank financial services (particularly selling or underwriting insurance and trading in securities), the new law further opened the door to two forms of banking organizations. These two organizational forms—the financial holding company and the bank subsidiaries model—are illustrated in Exhibit 3–8.

Under the Gramm-Leach-Bliley Act, *financial services holding companies* (FHCs) may offer the broadest range of new services, at least initially. However, in future years the Federal Reserve and the Treasury are empowered to expand the list of new financial services that banking organizations can offer, through either FHCs or via the bank subsidiaries route, provided the new service offerings are "compatible" with banking and are "financial in nature."

For example, initially, GLB allows only FHCs to own and operate merchant banks that make temporary equity investments in commercial ventures. However, in future years the Comptroller of the Currency and the Federal Reserve Board may allow banks, rather than just FHCs, to own and operate merchant bank subsidiaries. Insurance policies, securities, and travel agency services can be sold through banking offices under both types of banking organizations—FHCs and bank subsidiaries—but they must be sold by licensed agents, and customers must be informed in writing that these services do not enjoy federal insurance protection through the FDIC.

Currently, the FHC organizational form seems to have an advantage over the bank subsidiaries model because size limits are imposed on how big banking subsidiaries can grow and still be small enough to avoid threatening the soundness of the bank that owns them.

EXHIBIT 3–8
Two New Bank Organization Models

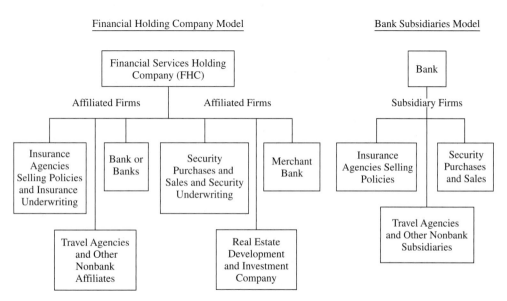

TABLE 3–5

Leading Financial Holding Companies (FHCs) Selling Financial Services in the U.S.

Source: Board of Governors of the Federal Reserve System.

Citigroup, Inc.	J. P. Morgan Chase & Co.
Bank of America Corp.	Wells Fargo & Company
Wachovia Corporation	Bank One Corporation
FleetBoston Financial Corp.	Mellon Financial Corp.
Deutsche Bank	U.S. Bancorp
PNC Financial Services	ABN AMRO Holding Co.

Key URLs
Educational organizations striving to teach bankers how to keep up with changing industry trends include the Bank Administration Institute at **www.bai.org** and the American Bankers Association at **www.aba.com**.

Moreover, more financial services can currently be offered through the FHC organizational form as Exhibit 3–8 illustrates.

Despite these advantages, the number of FHCs has expanded slowly. By Fall 2002 only 584 domestic banks (out of an industry population of about 8,000) and only 28 foreign financial institutions had received Federal Reserve Board approval to form an FHC. These approved institutions represented only about 12 percent of all registered U.S. bank holding companies. The reasons for the relatively modest expansion of FHCs include a slowly growing economy, corporate accounting and corporate governance scandals, and the slow drafting of new government regulations to guide the formation of these new entities. We should note, however, that the 20 biggest FHCs operating in the U.S., offering banking, insurance, and security dealing in one conglomerate, now control more than half the assets of all U.S. bank holding companies. (See Table 3–5 for a list of twelve of the largest financial holding companies approved by the Federal Reserve Board and operating inside the United States.)

Whereas earlier banking legislation gradually moved the American banking system toward greater *consolidation* into larger, but fewer banks, each serving a much wider geographic area, the GLB Act promotes the *convergence* of different types of financial institutions—bank and nonbank financial-service industries—moving them on a collision course toward each other and creating greater product line diversification. More and more financial-service customers will be able to enjoy the option of one-stop financial services shopping, buying all or most of their services through one financial firm. Perhaps these most recent and powerful banking trends—greater geographic and product line diversification through consolidation and convergence—will work together to reduce risk in financial services and, ultimately, better serve customers. Only the passage of time will tell us what benefits and what burdens we may ultimately encounter as a result of the recent passage of the Financial Services Modernization Act (more popularly known as GLB).

The Changing Organization and Structure of Banking's Principal Competitors

In the preceding sections of this chapter we have explored the great changes going on in the structure and organization of the banking industry. Propelled by powerful forces—including rising operating costs and rapidly changing technology—the banking industry of the future is likely to look quite different from what we see today.

Key URL
If you would like to learn more about one of banking's newest and fastest growing bank competitors, hedge funds, see especially **www.hedgefundcenter. com**.

But what about banking's principal *competitors*—the credit unions, savings associations, finance companies, insurance firms, security dealers, and financial conglomerates? Are they insulated from these same powerful forces for change? Is the structure of nonbank financial-service industries also changing?

Indeed, virtually all of banking's top competitors are experiencing much the same changes as banks are undergoing. For example, *consolidation* (fewer, but much larger service providers) is occurring at a rapid pace, particularly among savings associations, finance companies, security firms, and insurance companies, all of which are experiencing falling industry populations and the emergence of a handful of giant firms. Even credit unions in the United States have been declining in numbers, but increasing in asset and deposit size, for more than three decades.

Convergence (with all financial firms coming to look alike, especially in the menu of services offered) has been sweeping through virtually all of banking's competitors. For example, finance companies, security firms, and insurance companies have greatly broadened their service menus to challenge banks in both business and consumer credit markets, in some cases buying banks to aid them in their financial services expansion. At the same time, credit unions have moved to capture a growing share of such vital banking markets as checkable deposits, consumer installment credit, and small business loans.

In brief, the great structural and organizational changes we have unwrapped and examined in the pages of this chapter have "spilled over" onto nonbank financial firms. This dynamic structural and organizational revolution has occurred among nonbank firms for many of the same reasons it has happened to banks. But, whatever its causes, the *effects* are manifest around the world—intensifying financial-services competition, a widening gulf between the smallest and the largest firms in each industry, and greater exposure to the risks associated with larger and more cumbersome organizations striving to compete in an increasingly globally integrated financial marketplace.

Efficiency and Size: Do Bigger Financial Firms Operate at Lower Cost?

As commercial banks and their closest competitors have expanded from their origins as small unit (branchless) institutions into much larger corporate entities with many branch offices and holding-company affiliated firms, reaching across countries and continents with a growing menu of services, one question has emerged over and over again: *Do larger financial firms enjoy a cost advantage over smaller firms?* In other words, *Are bigger financial institutions simply more efficient than smaller ones?* If not, then why have some financial institutions (such as Citigroup and Deutsche Bank) become some of the largest businesses on the planet?

This is not an easy question to answer. There are two possible sources of cost savings due to growth in the size of financial firms. *Economies of scale,* if they exist, mean that doubling output of any one service or package of services will result in *less* than doubling production costs because of greater efficiencies in using the firm's resources to produce multiple units of the same service package. *Economies of scope* imply that a financial-service provider can save on operating costs when it expands the mix of its output because some resources, such as management skill and plant and equipment, are more efficiently used in jointly producing multiple services rather than just turning out one service from the same location. Fixed costs can be spread over a greater number of service outputs.

Efficiency in Producing Financial Services

The large majority of cost and efficiency studies in the financial sector have focused on the commercial banking industry, not only because of its great importance within the financial system, but also because extensive cost data is readily available for some banks. A few cost studies have appeared for nonbank firms (especially credit unions, savings associations, and insurance companies) and their conclusions are, in most cases, broadly similar to the banking studies with a few exceptions.

What do the banking studies tell us about costs and efficiency for big and small financial firms? Most recent research suggests that the average cost curve in the banking industry—the relationship between bank size (measured usually by total assets or total deposits) and the cost of production per unit of output—is roughly U-shaped, like that

EXHIBIT 3–9 The Most Efficient Sizes for Banks

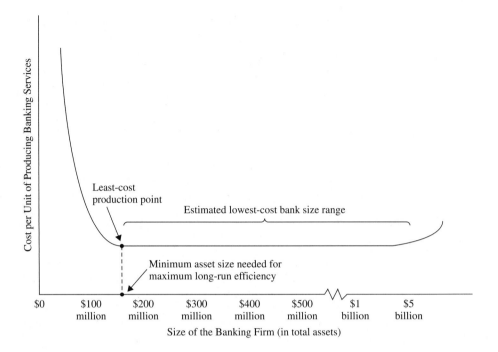

shown in Exhibit 3–9, but appears to have a fairly flat middle portion. This implies that a fairly wide range of banking firms lie close to being at maximally efficient size. However, recent studies also reveal that smaller banks tend to produce a somewhat different menu of services than do larger banks, with larger banks typically offering many more services. As a result, some cost studies have attempted to figure out the average costs for smaller banks separately from their cost calculations for larger banks. These newer studies suggest that smaller and middle-size banks tend to reach their lowest production costs somewhere between $100 million and $1 billion in aggregate assets. Larger banks, on the other hand, tend to achieve an optimal (lowest-cost) size at somewhere between $2 and $15 billion in total assets.[5]

Interestingly enough, studies of selected nonbank financial firms often reach conclusions that roughly parallel the results for banking firms. The U-shaped cost curve described above, with medium-size banks usually the most competitive costwise, also seems to prevail in the thrift industry (including savings and loans, savings banks, and credit unions). However, evidence suggests that the "U" in the cost curve for these near-bank competitors is somewhat deeper and more pronounced (i.e., a greater operating cost advantage for mid-size firms) than is true in the commercial banking industry—a situation frequently attributed to somewhat narrower and more restricted diversity of services among thrifts compared to the highly diverse service offerings of commercial banks.

Of course, the problem with these findings is that they leave unresolved the question of why many banks and other financial-service firms around the world are much larger than any of the calculated optimal size levels. For example, when Chase Manhattan and Chemical Banking Corporation of New York merged in the 1990s, their combined assets were almost $300 billion, and both banks claimed substantial "cost savings" flowing from their mergers. When Citicorp and Travelers Insurance merged in 1998, well over $700 billion in assets were involved. Indeed, it may be true that the optimal operating size in banking

[5]·See especially the studies by Berger, Hanweck, and Humphrey [10], Berger and Humphrey [11], Berger, Hunter, and Timme [12], Humphrey [17], Guzman [26], and Stiroh and Poole [30].

and for selected other financial institutions is really a moving target, changing all the time and probably getting bigger as technology moves forward.

For example, with banks and their closest competitors increasingly producing and delivering services via computer and through electronic networks, operating costs may have fallen substantially. At the same time new laws and regulations in the United States have made it possible for financial-service companies to establish smaller branches inside malls and retail stores, set up more limited-service facilities (such as ATMs and website offerings), and branch more freely within the territories of individual states. These lower-cost service delivery vehicles suggest that recent bank cost studies must be regarded with some suspicion unless, of course, larger banks are currently gaining something other than lower operating costs from their mergers and continuing growth. The larger institutions may reap higher operating revenues or bigger rewards for their managers at the expense of their shareholders.

One other important aspect of more recent cost studies asks a slightly different question than earlier cost studies: Is a bank or other financial-service firm, regardless of its size, operating as efficiently as it possibly can? This question raises an issue known to economists as *x-efficiency*. Given the size of a financial firm, is it operating near to or far away from its lowest possible operating cost? Another way of posing the same question is to ask if the financial firm is currently situated along what economists would label its *cost-efficient frontier,* with little or no waste. Research evidence to date is not encouraging, suggesting that most banks and other financial companies do not operate at their minimum possible cost. Rather, their degree of x-efficiency tends to be 20 to 25 percent greater in aggregate production costs than it should be under conditions of maximum efficiency.

This latter finding implies that most banks and other financial-service providers could gain more from lowering operating costs at their current size than they could from changing their scale of output (i.e., by shrinking or growing bigger) in order to reach a lower cost point on their average cost curve. Thus, x-efficiencies seem to override economies of scale for many financial firms. To be sure, larger banks seem to operate closer to their low-cost point than do smaller banks, probably because the larger institutions generally operate in more intensely competitive markets. Moreover, riskier banks and those in financial trouble appear to be less efficient than the average bank in the industry.

Either way, however, we must remain cautious about cost studies focused upon financial-service firms. The financial services business is changing rapidly in form and content. The statistical methodologies available today to carry out cost studies have serious limitations and tend to focus upon a single point in time rather than attempting to capture the dynamics of this ever-changing industry.

Banking and Financial Firm Goals: Their Impact on Operating Cost, Efficiency, and Performance

One of the reasons studies of banking and financial firm operating costs and efficiency are so mixed and sometimes confusing in their results and implications for the public and for financial management may lie in the motivations of managers and owners (stockholders). For example, pursuing minimum operating costs and maximum efficiency makes some sense for financial firms that seek maximum profitability and earnings for their owners. However, for those financial firms wanting minimum risk exposure, maximum growth, or the biggest market share, cost control and efficiency would seem to have a much lower priority.

Moreover, suppose the management of a financial-service firm decides that *benefits for managers* (and not the stockholders or the public) should be the primary objective of the company. In this case the *opposite* of cost control and efficiency—something called **expense preference** behavior—may come to shape the financial firm's performance.

Filmtoid
What 1991 comedy
casts Danny Devito as
Lawrence Garfield
—the disgruntled
shareholder—who
undertakes a hostile
takeover when he feels
the management of
New England Wire and
Cable is not making
decisions in his best
interest?
Answer: *Other People's
Money*

Expense-Preference Behavior   Recent research finds evidence of considerable expense-preference behavior among the managers of some bank and nonbank financial firms. These managers often appear to value fringe benefits, plush offices, and ample travel budgets over the pursuit of maximum returns for the stockholders. Such expense-preference behavior may show up in the form of staffs larger than required to maximize profits or excessively rapid growth, which causes expenses to get out of control. Some economists believe that expense-preference behavior is more likely in those institutions where management is dominant and the stockholders are not well organized. There, managers have more opportunity to enjoy a lavish lifestyle at the shareholder's expense. (See, for example, Hughes et al. [27].)

Agency Theory   The concept of expense-preference behavior is part of a much larger view of how modern financial and nonfinancial corporations operate, called **agency theory,** which analyzes relationships between a firm's owners (stockholders) and its managers, who are agents of the owners. Agency theory explores whether mechanisms exist in a given situation to compel managers to act to maximize the welfare of their firm's owners. For example, if a bank's owners do not have access to all the information its managers possess, they cannot fully evaluate how good management has been at making decisions. For many financial-service firms today, ownership is increasingly being spread out, and the dominance of individual stockholders in the industry appears to be decreasing. These two trends may worsen any agency problems that may already be present in the financial-services industry.

One way to reduce costs from agency problems is to develop better systems for monitoring the behavior of managers and to put in place stronger incentives for managers to follow the wishes of corporate owners. The latter *might* be accomplished by tying management salaries more closely to the firm's performance or giving management access to valuable benefits (such as stock options), though recent events suggest these steps may also encourage managers to take on greater risk. New research evidence (especially the Federal Reserve Bank of New York [33]) suggests, however, that banks (and perhaps other financial firms as well) are less likely than businesses in the manufacturing sector to tie management compensation to company performance and also less likely to offer stock options to management. This may be due to the heavier regulation and greater use of leverage (i.e., higher debt-to-equity ratios) in the financial sector compared to the manufacturing sector of the economy.

Many experts in the field believe that lower agency costs and better company performance depend upon the effectiveness of **corporate governance**—the relationships that exist among managers, the board of directors, and the stockholders and other stakeholders (such as creditors) of a corporation. (In banking and financial institutions management, governance relationships tend to be more complicated due to the presence of regulators and depositors who often have different goals than stockholders and management may have.) Hopefully, better governance leads to better performance for a firm, its owners, customers, and the public as a whole. Unfortunately, we cannot really validate this notion yet because we know very little to date about corporate governance in the financial sector. Recent research [33] does suggest that banking companies tend to have larger boards of directors and a higher proportion of outside directors than do manufacturing companies, on average, due in part to the influence of regulations. This *may* mean that managers of banks and similar financial firms are subject to greater monitoring and discipline than managers in other sectors of the economy, although there is some evidence that larger boards of directors also may lead to poorer firm performance.

In the long run, some economists believe, agency problems can be reduced by efficient labor and capital markets. Labor markets can reduce management's tendency to feather its own nest at the expense of the stockholders by rewarding better-performing managers with higher salaries and more job opportunities. Capital markets can help eliminate bad managers and poor performance with the threat of corporate takeovers (which could lead new owners to fire existing management) and by lowering the stock price of poorly managed firms. Because recent changes in laws and regulations in the financial sector have tended to allow more takeovers, we can entertain the hope that agency problems among bank and nonbank financial firms will diminish over time as the financial-services industry faces more intense competition.

Concept Check

3–13. What did the Riegle-Neal Interstate Banking Act do? Why was it passed into law?

3–14. Can you see any advantages to allowing interstate banking? What about potential disadvantages?

3–15. How is the structure of the nonbank financial-services industry changing? How do the organizational and structural changes occurring today among nonbank financial-service firms parallel those experienced by the banking industry?

3–16. What relationship appears to exist between bank size, efficiency, and operating costs per unit of service produced and delivered? How about among nonbank financial-service providers?

3–17. Why is it so difficult to measure output and economies of scale and scope in the financial ser-

vices industry? How could this measurement problem affect any conclusions reached about firm size, efficiency, and expense behavior?

3–18. What is *expense-preference* behavior? How could it affect the performance of a bank or other financial firm?

3–19. Of what benefit is *agency theory* in helping us understand the consequences of changing control of a financial-services firm? How can control by management as opposed to control by stockholders affect the behavior and performance of a financial-services provider?

3–20. What is *corporate governance* and how might it be improved for the benefit of the owners and customers of banks and other financial firms?

Summary

This chapter has highlighted the different ways banks and their closest financial-service competitors are organized to serve the public. Among the key points in the chapter are the following:

- Banks and their closest financial-service competitors have changed dramatically over time, often moving from relatively simple, single-office (unit) firms to more complex branching organizations with multiple offices to serve the public and ultimately financial holding companies that acquire the stock of one or more banks and nonbank businesses.

- When a bank or other financial firm starts out, it must secure a *charter of incorporation* from either state or federal authorities. In the case of banks and their closest competitors—credit unions and savings associations—a state charter may be obtained from a state board or commission, whereas at the federal level charters are issued for national (federal) banks from the Office of the Comptroller of the Currency (OCC) or, in the case of savings associations and credit unions, from the Office of Thrift Supervision (OTS) or the National Credit Union Administration (NCUA).

- Each organizational form adopted by a bank or other financial firm is usually a response to competitive pressures, to the demands of customers for better service, to the need to diversify geographically and by product line in order to reduce risk exposure, and to the pressure of government regulation.

- The rapid growth of today's financial-service firms also reflects a desire for a greater volume of service production and sales. With greater overall *size* of operations comes the possibility of *economies of scale* (lower cost) in the production of each individual financial service and *economies of scope* (lower cost) in producing multiple services using the same organization and resources. These economies, if achieved, can lead to reduced production costs and a stronger competitive presence in the financial marketplace.

- In the United States one of the most dramatic changes in the banking industry of the past two decades has been the spread of interstate banking as state and federal laws (especially the Riegle-Neal Interstate Banking Act of 1994) paved the way for banking companies to acquire banks and purchase or start branch offices in different states. Riegle-Neal makes possible nationwide banking for the first time in U.S. history. This interstate banking law reflects the need for banking firms to diversify into different geographic markets and the demands of the public for financial-service providers that can follow businesses and individuals as they move across the landscape.

- Another major change in law and regulation was the passage of the Gramm-Leach-Bliley (Financial Services Modernization) Act in 1999. This new law permitted U.S. banks to affiliate with insurance firms and underwriters, security firms, and selected other nonbank businesses. The GLB law has led to the formation of new organizational types in banking—financial holding companies (FHCs) and bank subsidiaries are entering into product lines (such as security underwriting services for corporations) previously prohibited or restricted under federal law. GLB paves the way for American banks, as well as insurance companies, security firms, and other financial conglomerates, to become one-stop financial-service providers.

- All of these sweeping changes in organization within the banking and financial-services industry are contributing to fundamental changes in the production and delivery of financial services. Banks and their competitors are *consolidating*—resulting in fewer, but much larger surviving service providers—and *converging*—the survivors offer a wider menu of services that permit them to invade new industries and reach for the possible risk-reducing benefits of product-line diversification.

- As banks and the financial-services industry consolidate and converge, public and regulatory concern about their *operating efficiency* (to keep operating costs as low a possible) and *corporate governance* (the relationships between management, stockholders, and depositors) has increased. Perhaps the management of some banks and other service providers today is focusing on the wrong target, striving to better management's position at the expense of stockholders and depositors, creating *agency* problems and giving rise to *expense-preference behavior* where operating costs are higher than necessary. Interest in how efficient banks and their competitors are and especially how well they are managed is definitely on the rise.

- Finally, *concentration* is intensifying as a few large financial firms come to dominate banking, insurance, security brokerage, and other key product lines, perhaps offering greater customer *convenience* but possibly also decreasing *competition* in some markets. Governments and the public will need to be vigilant in the years ahead to ensure that customer convenience is fully served, but not at the cost of decreasing competitive rivalry among those financial-service providers that survive.

Key Terms

organizational forms, *71*
board of directors, *74*
stockholders, *74*
unit banks, *78*
branch banking, *79*
Internet banking
services, *83*

automated teller machines
(ATMs), *83*
point-of-sale (POS)
terminals, *83*
virtual banks, *84*
bank holding company, *84*
multibank holding
companies, *87*

affiliated banks, *87*
full-service interstate
banking, *90*
expense preference, *96*
agency theory, *96*
corporate governance, *96*

Problems and Projects

1. Suppose you owned a bank holding company headquartered in California. Into what other states could you enter and acquire banks through your holding company today?

2. Of the business activities listed here, which activities can be conducted through U.S. regulated financial-service holding companies today?

    a. Data processing companies

    b. Office furniture sales

    c. Auto and truck leasing companies

    d. General life insurance and property-casualty insurance sales

    e. Savings and loan associations

    f. Mortgage companies

    g. General insurance underwriting activities

    h. Professional advertising services

    i. Underwriting of new common stock issues by nonfinancial corporations

    j. Real estate development companies

    k. Merchant banks

3. You are currently serving as president and chief executive officer of a unit bank that has been operating out of its present location for five years. Due to the rapid growth of households and businesses in the market area served by the bank and the challenges posed to your share of this market by several aggressive competitors, you want to become a branch bank by establishing two satellite offices. Please answer the following questions:

    a. How would you go about deciding (1) where to locate the new offices and (2) which services each office should make available?

    b. How are you going to evaluate each new office's performance in deciding whether to keep it open?

    c. Based on the content of this chapter, what advantages would your branch be likely to have over the old unit bank? What disadvantages are likely to come with adding branch offices? Any ideas on how you might minimize these disadvantages?

    d. Would it be a good idea to form a holding company at the same time or perhaps before or after setting up the new branches? Based on the material in this chapter, what advantages could a holding company bring to your bank? Disadvantages?

4. Suppose you are managing a medium-size branch banking organization (holding about $10 billion in assets) with all of its branch offices located within the same state. The board of directors has asked you to look into the possibility of the bank offering limited security underwriting and trading services as well as insurance sales and insurance underwriting. What federal law opens up the possibility of offering the foregoing

services and under what circumstances may they be offered? What do you see as the principal benefits from and the principal stumbling blocks to successful pursuit of such a project?

5. First Security Trust National Bank of Boston is considering making aggressive entry into the People's Republic of China, possibly filing the necessary documents with the government in Bejing in the coming year to establish future physical and electronic service facilities. What advantages might such a move bring to the management and shareholders of First Security? What potential drawbacks should be considered by the management and board of directors of this Boston bank?

Internet Exercises

1. Suppose you wanted to determine if the top 10 banks in the United States were capturing a growing share of the banking industry's resources. Where can you go on the Web to answer that question? What are the implications of the trend in banking concentration that you observe? Should the public be concerned? Why or why not? (See, for example, **www.fdic.gov**.)

2. What has been happening to the structure of banking in your home town? Which banks in your home town belong to holding companies? How could you figure this out? Can the Web help you here? (See, in particular, **www.federalreserve.gov** and **www. fdic.gov**.)

3. How many U.S.-insured banks have failed in recent years? Where would you look on the Web for this information? Do these failures concern you or are they the sign of a relatively healthy industry? Please explain. (See, for example, **www.fdic.gov/bank/historical**.)

4. How are mergers changing the shape of banking? In what ways can the Web help you answer that question? (Consider such sites as **www.snl.com** and **www.federalreserve.gov**.)

5. Several educational and trade associations service the banking industry in the United States and around the globe. Among the most active associations are the American Bankers Association (at **www.aba.com**), the Bank Administration Institute (at **www.bai.org**), and the Japanese Bankers Association (at **www.zenginkyo.or.jp/en**). What are the principal goals of these institutions? What services do they offer?

6. Smaller banks in recent years have been under intense pressure from the aggressive competition posed by leading money center banks, both domestic and foreign. In response bankers serving predominantly local areas have formed associations to represent their interests before the public and before law-making bodies. What are the names, objectives, and services of these associations? (See especially America's Community Bankers at **www.acbankers.org** and Independent Community Bankers of America at **www.ibaa.org**.)

7. If you wanted to learn more about electronic banking and its future scope in the financial-services industry where could you go on the Web to find out? (See, in particular, the ATM Industry Association at **www.atmia.com** and the American Bankers Association at **www.aba.com**.)

8. What kinds of services are offered by *virtual banks?* What advantages do they seem to have in competing against traditional banking organizations? What disadvantages? (See for example, **www.netbank.com** and **www.bankofinternet.com**.)

S&P Market Insight Challenge

STANDARD &POOR'S

1. Use Standard & Poor's Market Insight website (**www.mhhe.com/edumarketinsight**) for this problem. As the organization and structure of individual financial firms change, the operations of entire industries change. For up-to-date information concerning recent changes in financially oriented industries please use the Industry tab in S&P's

REAL NUMBERS FOR REAL BANKS

Assignment for Chapter 3

YOUR BANK'S CORPORATE ORGANIZATION, NETWORK OF BANKS AND BRANCHES AND THE HOLDING COMPANY STRUCTURE

A. Your bank was chosen from the largest 25 banking companies in America. It is a big bank, rather than a community bank. Some of the corporate offices of these banking companies are located in global money centers such as New York and others are not, such as Bank of America located in Charlotte, North Carolina. Some have focused on wholesale banking, whereas others are more retail oriented and then some balance their efforts in both retail and wholesale banking. In Chapter 3, we first examine the internal organization of the banking firm. To get a better feel for your bank's internal organization, go to your bank's primary website. (If you do not have this, review the assignment for Chapter 2.) Because we rarely find an explicit organization chart, we will look at the lists of boards of directors and senior management to provide some insights. This information is almost always provided in the Web pages "About the Company" and "Investor Relations" and is often titled "Officers and Directors." (If you have trouble locating this information, try exploring the site map of the banking company's website.) Think about the designated role of the board of directors. Write one paragraph characterizing the composition of this board. Then turn your attention to the officers and senior management. Their titles and bio-sketches provide some insights regarding the internal organization of the banking company. Try to characterize the internal organization in one paragraph.

B. You have the spreadsheet you created in Chapter 2's assignment. Often finance folks are asked to tell the story of the data. You are being given this task.

a. First focus on regulatory organization. Your banking company is a bank holding company (BHC) and, as such, it is registered and overseen by the Federal Reserve Board. Within your BHC, you have at least one institution (bank) chartered by either state or federal governments. How many bank/thrift subsidiaries does the BHC have and what are their charters? Are the individual institutions members of the Fed? How long have they been in operation? What about FDIC Insurance? Write a page about your banking company with the focus on regulatory supervision. The above questions provide some structure for the coverage of your written comments.

b. Second, in this chapter we discussed unit and branch banking operations. Write a paragraph or so describing your banking company's use of branching by its affiliated institutions. Include the types of offices it operates and some reference to the number of offices.

C. As of 1999 the Gramm-Leach-Bliley (GLB) Act allowed banks to extend their nonbank financial services (particularly insurance and investment banking services). They can achieve this by utilizing the financial holding company model or the bank subsidiaries model. Go to the Federal Reserve website at **http://www.federalreserve.gov/generalinfo/fhc/** and determine whether your banking company has registered as a financial holding company (FHC). Having completed Assignment 1 and Part A of this assignment, you have some idea about how much your bank has become involved in nonbanking financial services. Write a paragraph about how the GLB Act appears to have affected your bank's organization.

Market Insight, Educational Version. The drop-down menu provides subindustry selections that may be of interest, including such industry categories as Asset Management & Custody Banks, Consumer Finance, Diversified Banks, Diversified Capital Markets, Insurance Brokers, Investment Banking and Brokerage, Life and Health Insurance, Multi-Insurance, Property & Casualty Insurance, Regional Banks, and Thrifts & Mortgage Finance. For any of the foregoing financial-service industry categories, S&P Industry Surveys may be downloaded in Adobe Acrobat. These industry surveys cover such financial-service groups as Banking, Investment Services, Financial Services Diversified, Insurance: Property and Casualty, Insurance: Life and Health, and Savings and Loans. Download the S&P Industry Survey for Banking and for one other financial-services industry. Then read the section titled "How the Industry Operates," focusing particularly upon organization and structure. Compare and contrast these two industries along the lines of organization and structure.

2. Use Standard & Poor's Market Insight website (**www.mhhe.com/edumarketinsight**) for this problem. Of the nonfinancial companies listed on S&P's Market Insight, Educational Version, which appear to be most closely linked to banks and other financial firms (through holding companies, subsidiary relationships, or other organizational ties)? Please list the nonfinancial companies in the Market Insight list that seem most closely connected to banks and other financial-service providers. Why do you believe these close financial-nonfinancial ties exist for the firms you have listed but not for other nonfinancial companies? Are there advantages for the firms involved and for the public stemming from such financial-nonfinancial organizational ties?

Selected References

See the following for good discussions of recent trends in banking structure and organization:

1. Phillips, Dave, and Christine Pavel. "Interstate Banking Game Plans: Implications for the Midwest." *Economic Perspectives*, Federal Reserve Bank of Chicago, 1986.
2. Powell, Donald E., Chairman, Federal Deposit Insurance Corporation, Speech to the American Bankers Association Annual Meeting, Phoenix, Arizona, October 8, 2002.
3. Rose, Peter S. *The Changing Structure of American Banking*. New York: Columbia University Press, 1987.

Information on the advantages and disadvantages of bank holding companies and branch banking may be found in the following:

4. Apcor, Leonard M., and Buck Brown. "Branch Bullying: Small Texas Towns Are the Latest Victims of Big Banks' Crisis." *The Wall Street Journal*, May 25, 1988, pp. 1 and 8.
5. Frieder, Larry A., and Vincent P. Apilado. "Bank Holding Company Research: Classification, Synthesis, and New Directions." *Journal of Bank Research*, Summer 1982, pp. 80–95.
6. Helyon, John. "Multistate Banks Rile Many Customers." *The Wall Street Journal*, April 20, 1988, p. 22.
7. Hunter, William C., and Stephen G. Timme. "Concentration and Innovation: Striking a Balance in Deregulation." *Economic Review*, Federal Reserve Bank of Atlanta, January/February 1987, pp. 11–20.
8. Liang, Nellie, and Donald Savage. *New Data on the Performance of Nonbank Subsidiaries of Bank Holding Companies*. Staff Study No. 159, Board of Governors of the Federal Reserve System, February 1990.
9. Varvel, Walter A. "A Valuation Approach to Bank Holding Company Acquisitions." *Economic Review*, Federal Reserve Bank of Richmond, July/August 1975, pp. 9–15.

See the following for a discussion of the benefits, costs, and characteristics of interstate banking and economies of scale in banking and other financial firms:

10. Berger, Allen N.; Gerald A. Hanweck; and David B. Humphrey. "Competitive Viability in Banking: Scale, Scope, and Product Mix Economies." *Journal of Monetary Economics* 20, no. 4 (December 1987).
11. Berger, Allen N., and David B. Humphrey. "The Dominance of Inefficiencies Over Scale and Product Mix Economies in Banking." Finance and Economics Discussion Series No. 107, Board of Governors of the Federal Reserve System, January 1990.
12. Berger, Alan N.; W. C. Hunter; and S. G. Timme. "The Efficiency of Financial Institutions: A Review and Preview of Research Past, Present, and Future." *Journal of Banking and Finance* 17 (1993), pp. 221–49.

13. Colburn, Christopher B., and Sylvia C. Hudgins. "The Intersection of Business, State Government and Special Interests in Federal Legislation: An Examination of Congressional Votes on the Road to Interstate Branching." *Economic Inquiry* 41 (2003), pp. 620–38.

14. Doherty, Neil A. "The Measurement of Output and Economies of Scale of Property-Liability Insurance." *Journal of Risk and Insurance*, September 1982, pp. 390–402.

15. Geehan, Randall. "Returns to Scale in the Life Insurance Industry." *Bell Journal of Economics*, Autumn 1977, pp. 497–514.

16. Goldberg, Lawrence G., and Gerald A. Hanweck. "What Can We Expect from Interstate Banking?" *Journal of Banking and Finance* 12 (1988), pp. 51–67.

17. Humphrey, David B. "Why Do Estimates of Bank Scale Economies Differ?" *Economic Review*, Federal Reserve Bank of Richmond 76 (September/October 1990), pp. 38–50.

18. Jayaratne, Jith, and Philip E. Strahan. "The Benefits of Branching Deregulation." *Economic Policy Review*, Federal Reserve Bank of New York, December 1997, pp. 13–29.

19. Levonian, Mark E. "Interstate Banking and Risk." *FRBSF Weekly Letter,* July 22, 1994, pp. 1–2.

20. Rhoades, Stephen A., and Donald T. Savage. "The Relative Performance of Bank Holding Companies and Branch Banking Systems." *Journal of Economics and Business,* Winter 1981, pp. 132–41.

21. Rose, Peter S. "The Firms Acquired by Interstate Banks: Testable Hypotheses and Consistent Evidence." *Journal of Business and Economic Perspectives* 15, no. 2 (1989), pp. 127–35.

22. ———. "The Banking Firms Making Interstate Acquisitions: Theory and Observable Motives." *Review of Business and Economic Research* 25, no. 1 (Fall 1989), pp. 1–18.

23. ———. *Banking across State Lines: Public and Private Consequences*. Westport, CT: Quorum Books, 1997.

24. ———. "Diversification and Cost Effects of Interstate Banking." *The Financial Review* 33, no. 2 (May 1996).

For a discussion of the consolidation and convergence of bank and nonbank financial service industries, see especially these resources:

25. Basset, William F., and Egon Zakrajsek. "Profits and Balance Sheet Developments at U.S. Commercial Banks in 1999." *Federal Reserve Bulletin*, June 2000, pp. 367–98.

26. Guzman, Mark G. "The Economic Impact of Bank Structure: A Review of Recent Literature." *Economic and Financial Review*, Federal Reserve Bank of Dallas, Second Quarter 2000, pp. 11–25.

27. Hughes, Joseph P., William L. Lang, Loretta J. Mester, Choon-Ged Moon, and Michael S. Pagano. "Do Bankers Sacrifice Value to Build Financial Empires?" Working Paper 02-2, Federal Reserve Bank of Philadelphia, 2002.

28. Kiser, Elizabeth. "Households Switching Behavior at Depository Institutions: Evidence from Survey Data." Working Paper, Board of Governors of the Federal Reserve System, Washington, D.C., August 14, 2002.

29. Krainer, John. "The Separation of Banking and Commerce." *Economic Review*, Federal Reserve Bank of San Francisco, 2000, pp. 15–25.

30. Stiroh, Kevin J., and Jennifer P. Poole. "Explaining the Rising Concentration of Banking Assets in the 1990s." *Current Issues in Economics and Finance*, Federal Reserve Bank of New York 6, no. 4 (August 2000), pp. 1–6.

www.mhhe.com/rose6e

31. Wenninger, John. "The Emerging Role of Banks in E-Commerce." *Current Issues in Economics and Finance*, Federal Reserve Bank of New York 6, no. 3 (March 2000), pp. 1–6.

For a discussion of the formation of financial holding companies (FHCs), see especially:

32. Guzman, Mark G. "Slow but Steady Progress toward Financial Deregulation." *Southwest Economy*, Federal Reserve Bank of Dallas, January/February 2003, pp. 1, 6–9, and 12.

To learn more about corporate governance issues in banking and financial services, see especially:

33. Federal Reserve Bank of New York. "Corporate Governance: What Do We Know and What Is Different about Banks?" *Economic Policy Review*, Special Issue, April 2003, pp. 1–142.

CHAPTER FOUR

The Financial Statements of Banks and Some of Their Closest Competitors

Key Topics in This Chapter

- An Overview of Bank Balance Sheets and Income Statements
- The Bank's Balance Sheet
- Bank Assets
- Bank Liabilities
- Recent Expansion of Off-Balance Sheet Items
- The Problem of Book-Value Accounting
- Components of the Income Statement

Introduction

The particular services that each bank and each nonbank financial firm chooses to offer and the overall size of each financial-service organization are reflected in its *financial statements*. Financial statements are literally a "road map" telling us where a bank or other financial firm has been in the past, where it is now, and, perhaps, where it is headed in the future. They are invaluable guideposts that can, if properly constructed and interpreted, signal success or signal disaster. Unfortunately, much the same problems with faulty and misleading financial statements that visited Enron, Global Crossings, and other troubled nonbank firms in recent years have also visited some banks and their financial-service competitors, teaching us to be cautious in reading and interpreting the financial statements that bank and nonbank financial companies routinely publish.

The two main financial statements that bank managers, customers (particularly large depositors not fully protected by deposit insurance), and the regulatory authorities look at are the *balance sheet (Report of Condition)* and the *income statement (Report of Income)*. We will examine these two important bank financial reports in depth in this chapter. In addition, we will explore briefly the makeup of two other key financial statements that credit

TABLE 4–1
Financial Outputs and
Inputs in the Two
Key Bank Financial
Statements

The Balance Sheet (Report of Condition)	
Financial Outputs **(uses of bank funds or assets)**	**Financial Inputs** **(sources of bank funds or** **liabilities plus equity capital)**
Cash and deposits in other institutions	Deposits from the public
Investments in securities	Nondeposit borrowings
Loans and leases	Equity capital from stockholders
As with any firm's balance sheet, total sources of bank funds must equal total uses of bank funds (i.e., total assets = total liabilities + equity capital).	

The Income Statement (Report of Income)	
Financial Outputs **(revenues from making use of** **bank funds and other resources** **to produce and sell services)**	**Financial Inputs** **(the cost of acquiring funds** **and other resources the bank needs** **to produce its services)**
Loan income	Deposit costs
Security income	Costs of nondeposit borrowings
Income from deposits in other institutions	Employee costs
Fee income from miscellaneous services	Overhead expenses
	Taxes
As with any firm's income statement, total revenues minus total costs must equal net earnings (income) of the bank.	

analysts and managers often use to assess changes in a bank's funds-using and funds-raising activities: the *Sources and Uses of Funds Statement* (also known as the Funds-Flow Statement) and the *Statement of Stockholders' Equity.* Finally, we examine some of the similarities and some of the differences between bank financial statements and those of nonbank financial firms that are their closest competitors.

An Overview of Bank Balance Sheets and Income Statements

The two most important financial statements for a banking firm—its balance sheet, or Report of Condition, and its income statement, or Report of Income—may be viewed as a list of financial inputs and outputs, as Table 4–1 shows. The Report of Condition shows the amount and composition of funds sources (financial inputs) the bank has drawn upon to finance its lending and investing activities and how much has been allocated to loans, securities, and other funds uses (financial outputs) at any given point in time.

In contrast, the financial inputs and outputs on the Report of Income show how much it has cost the bank to acquire its deposits and other funds sources and to generate revenues from the uses the bank has made of those funds. These costs include interest paid to depositors and other creditors of the institution, the expenses of hiring management and staff, overhead costs in acquiring and using office facilities, and taxes paid for government services. The Report of Income also shows the revenues (cash flow) generated by selling services to the public, including making loans and leases and servicing customer deposits. Finally, the Report of Income shows a bank's net earnings after all costs are deducted from the sum of all revenues, some of which will be reinvested in the business for future growth and some of which will flow to bank stockholders as dividends.

The publicly available sources of bank balance sheets (Reports of Condition) and income statements (Reports of Income) have exploded in recent years as more and more customers have become interested in the condition of their banks and the ease of access to information now made possible by the World Wide Web.

For example, suppose you wanted to find the total assets of a local bank or needed a detailed breakdown of what's listed on its balance sheet. Where could you go? One obvious source is the name of the bank itself. Most banks can be found by typing their name into a Web browser followed by .com. Because many banks have similar names, you also may need to enter the city where their headquarters is located to find the website you are seeking. This usually will get you their address, a list of their key services, access to some online services, and, frequently, an annual report or at least an abbreviated balance sheet.

Even better is the Federal Deposit Insurance Corporation's website, **www.fdic.gov**, which supplies quarterly individual bank and bank holding company data. To access this data you need to know either the FDIC certificate number or the bank holding company ID number; however, you can also do a search based on the name, city, or state of the bank's headquarters to acquire the needed information. The bank holding company data found here is an aggregation of all FDIC-insured subsidiaries and excludes nondeposit subsidiaries or parent companies. The National Information Center of the Federal Financial Institutions Examination Council at **http://www.ffiec.gov/nic/** provides financial and performance reports for individual banks, bank holding companies, savings associations, and credit unions.

If you would like to learn more about the financial statements of banking's closest competitors, you can use a number of excellent sources. Most of the financial firms that compete with banks are regulated by a federal or state regulatory board or commission—indeed, sometimes, *both* federal and state regulatory agencies share rule making for the same financial-service providers. These regulators often display for public viewing the financial statements of the entire industry and/or firms they regulate. Examples include the National Credit Union Administration (NCUA) at **www.ncua.gov**, the Office of Thrift Supervision (OTS) at **www.ots.treas.gov**, and the Securities and Exchange Commission (SEC) at **www.sec.gov** for such tough bank competitors as credit unions, savings and loan associations, insurance companies, registered security brokers and dealers, and money market funds. You can also call up state regulatory agencies by name, such as the Texas Savings and Loan Commission (**www.tsld.state.tx.us**) or the New York Insurance Department (**www.ins.state.ny.us**).

Finally, each leading nonbank financial firm will have its own website bearing the name of the corporation you are seeking and often containing the firm's most recent financial statement. It is usually quite interesting, for example, to search for the financial reports of such leading bank competitors as the IBM Credit Union (at **www.thinkcu.com**), Dreyfus Money Market Funds (at **www.dreyfus.com**), Washington Mutual Savings Bank (at **www.wamu.com**), Merrill Lynch & Company (**www.ml.com**), and Aetna Life and Casualty Company (**www.aetna.com**) simply by entering the name of each of these companies into your Web browser.

The Bank's Balance Sheet (Report of Condition)

The Principal Types of Accounts

A bank's balance sheet, or **Report of Condition,** lists the assets, liabilities, and equity capital (owners' funds) held by or invested in the institution on any given date. Because banks are simply business firms selling a particular kind of product, the basic balance sheet identity

$$\text{Assets} = \text{Liabilities} + \text{Equity capital} \tag{1}$$

must be valid for banks, nonbank financial-service providers, and any other business firm.

TABLE 4–2
Key Items on Bank
Financial Statements

The Balance Sheet (Report of Condition)	
Assets (accumulated uses of funds)	**Liabilities and Equity** (accumulated sources of funds)
Cash (primary reserves)	Deposits:
Investment securities: The liquid portion	Demand
(secondary reserves)	NOWs
Investment securities: The income-	Money market
generating portion	Savings
Loans:	Time
Consumer	Nondeposit borrowings
Real estate	Equity capital:
Commercial	Stock
Agriculture	Surplus
Financial institutions	Retained earnings
Miscellaneous loans and leases	(undivided profits)
Miscellaneous assets (buildings, equipment, etc.)	

Income Statement or Statement of Earnings and Expenses (Report of Income)
Revenues (revenues from the bank's service outputs)
Loan income
Investment income
Noninterest sources of income (such as deposit service fees)
Expenses (cost of the bank's inputs of resources needed to produce its services)
Interest paid on deposits
Interest paid on nondeposit borrowings
Salaries and wages (employee compensation)
Provision for loan losses (allocations to the reserve for possible losses on any loans made)
Other expenses
Income before taxes and securities transactions
Taxes
Gains or losses from trading in securities
Net income after taxes and securities gains or losses

In banking, the *assets* on the balance sheet are of four major types: cash in the vault and deposits held at other depository institutions (C), government and private interest-bearing securities purchased in the open market (S), loans and lease financings made available to customers (L), and miscellaneous assets (MA). *Liabilities* fall into two principal categories: deposits made by and owed to various customers (D) and nondeposit borrowings of funds in the money and capital markets (NDB). Finally, *equity capital* represents long-term funds the owners contribute to the bank (EC). (See Table 4–2.) Therefore, the bank's balance sheet identity can be written as follows:

$$C + S + L + MA = D + NDB + EC \qquad \textbf{(2)}$$

Cash assets (C) are designed to meet the bank's need for *liquidity* (i.e., immediately spendable cash) in order to meet deposit withdrawals, customer demands for loans, and other unexpected or immediate needs for cash. Security holdings (S) are a backup source of liquidity and provide another source of income. Loans (L) are made principally to supply income, while miscellaneous assets (MA) are usually dominated by the fixed assets owned by the bank (its plant and equipment) and investments in subsidiaries (if any). Deposits (D) are typically the main source of funding for banks, with nondeposit borrowings (NDB) carried out mainly to supplement deposits and provide the additional liquidity that cash assets and securities cannot provide. Finally, equity capital (EC) supplies the long-term, relatively stable base of financial support upon which the bank will rely to grow and to cover any extraordinary losses it incurs.

One useful way to view this balance sheet identity is to note that bank liabilities and equity capital represent *accumulated sources of funds,* which provide the needed spending power to acquire assets. A bank's assets, on the other hand, are its *accumulated uses of funds,* which are made to generate income for its stockholders, pay interest to its depositors, and compensate its employees for their labor and skill. Thus, the bank's balance sheet identity can be pictured simply as follows:

$$\begin{array}{ccc} \text{Accumulated uses} & & \text{Accumulated sources} \qquad \textbf{(3)} \\ \text{of bank funds} & = & \text{of bank funds} \\ \text{(assets)} & & \text{(liabilities and equity capital)} \end{array}$$

Clearly, each use of funds must be backed by a source of funds, so that accumulated uses of funds must equal accumulated sources of funds.

Of course, in the real world, bank balance sheets are more complicated than this simple sources and uses statement because each item on a balance sheet usually contains several component accounts. A more inclusive balance sheet, or Report of Condition, contains many more accounts. This is illustrated by the balance sheet of a large midwestern banking organization, National City Corporation, shown in Table 4–3. Let's take a closer look at its principal components.

Bank Assets

Cash and Due from Depository Institutions   The first asset item normally listed on a bank's Report of Condition is *cash and due from depository institutions.* This item, which includes cash held in the bank's vault, any deposits the bank has placed with other depository institutions (usually called *correspondent deposits*), cash items in the process of collection (mainly uncollected checks), and the bank's reserve account held with the Federal Reserve bank in the region, is often labeled *primary reserves.* This means that these cash assets are the bank's first line of defense against deposit withdrawals and the first source of funds to look to when a customer comes in with a loan request. Normally, banks strive to keep the size of this account as low as possible, because cash balances earn little or no interest income. Note that the $4,252 million in cash and due from other depository institutions listed in Table 4–3 for National City Corporation represents less than 4 percent of its total assets of $134,982 million as of December 31, 2002.

Investment Securities: The Liquid Portion   A second line of defense to meet demands for cash and serve as a quick source of funds is the bank's liquid security holdings, often called *secondary reserves* or referenced on the balance sheet as "available for sale." These typically include holdings of short-term government securities and privately issued money market securities, including interest-bearing time deposits held with other banks and commercial paper. Secondary reserves occupy the middle ground between cash assets and loans, earning some income but held mainly for the ease with which they can be converted into cash on short notice. In Table 4–3, some portion of the $8,285 million shown as investment securities held by this bank will serve as a secondary reserve to help deal with liquidity needs.

Investment Securities: The Income-Generating Portion   Bonds, notes, and other securities the bank holds primarily for their expected rate of return or yield are known simply as *investment securities.* (These are called held-to-maturity securities on regulatory

TABLE 4–3
Report of Condition (Balance Sheet) for National City Corporation

Financial data is from the FDIC website for the Bank Holding Company. The dollar amounts represent combined amounts for all FDIC-insured bank and thrift subsidiaries, and do *not* reflect nondeposit subsidiaries or parent companies.

National City Corporation
(Note: Dollar figures in thousands)

Date	12/31/02	12/31/01
Total assets	**134,982,014**	**118,468,882**
Cash and due from depository institutions	4,251,967	4,605,576
Securities	8,284,705	8,588,292
Federal funds sold and reverse repurchase agreements	3,905,950	6,726,421
Gross loans and leases	109,733,683	90,850,415
(less) Loan loss allowance	1,098,588	997,329
Trading account assets	299,705	515,289
Bank premises and fixed assets	957,791	1,032,236
Other real estate owned	114,507	64,134
Goodwill and other intangibles	1,596,130	2,135,175
All other assets	6,936,164	4,948,673
Total liabilities and capital	**134,982,014**	**118,468,882**
Total liabilities	**125,610,394**	**110,186,939**
Total deposits	66,324,088	63,879,592
Federal funds purchased and repurchase agreements	8,839,291	18,681,781
Trading liabilities	0	41,053
Other borrowed funds	43,378,774	21,867,607
Subordinated debt	1,796,099	1,654,855
All other liabilities	5,272,142	4,062,051
Total equity capital	**9,371,620**	**8,281,943**
Perpetual preferred stock	0	0
Common stock	277,324	277,324
Surplus	3,871,354	3,266,023
Undivided profits	5,222,942	4,738,596

Key URLs
The most complete sources for viewing the financial statements of individual banks in the United States are at www.fdic.gov and www.ffiec.gov/nic/.

reports.) Frequently these are divided into *taxable securities*—for example, U.S. government bonds and notes, securities issued by various federal agencies (such as the Federal National Mortgage Association, known as Fannie Mae), and corporate bonds and notes—and *tax-exempt securities*, which consist principally of state and local government (municipal) bonds. The latter generate interest income that is exempt from federal income taxes.

Investment securities may be recorded on a bank's books at their original cost or at market value, whichever is lower. Of course, if interest rates rise after the securities are purchased, their market value will be less than their original cost (book value). Therefore, banks that record securities on their balance sheets at cost often include a parenthetical note giving the securities' current market value. However, accounting rules for U.S. banks are changing—the trend is toward replacing original or historical cost figures with current market values.

Trading Account Assets Securities purchased to provide short-term profits from short-term price movements are not included in "Securities" on the Report of Condition. They are reported as trading account assets. In Table 4–3, about $300 million is reported for National City Corporation. If the bank serves as a security dealer, the securities acquired for resale are included here. The amount recorded in the trading account is valued at market.

Federal Funds Sold and Reverse Repurchase Agreements Another type of loan account listed as a separate item on the Report of Condition is federal funds sold and reverse repurchase agreements. This item includes mainly temporary loans (usually extended overnight, with the funds returned the next day) made to other depository institutions, securities dealers, or even major corporations. The funds for these temporary loans often come from the reserves a bank has on deposit with the Federal Reserve Bank in its district—hence the name *federal funds*. Some of these temporary credits are extended in the form of reverse repurchase (resale) agreements (RPs) in which the bank acquires temporary title to securities owned by the borrower and holds those securities as collateral until the loan is paid off (normally after a few days).

Loans and Leases By far the largest asset item is *loans and leases*, which generally account for half to almost three-quarters of the total value of all bank assets. A bank's loan account typically is broken down into several groups of similar type loans. For example, one commonly used breakdown is by the *purpose* for borrowing money. In this case, we may see listed on a bank's balance sheet the following loan types:

1. Commercial and industrial (or business) loans.
2. Consumer (or household) loans.
3. Real estate (or property-based) loans.
4. Financial institutions loans (such as loans made to other depository institutions as well as to finance and insurance companies and other nonbank financial institutions).
5. Foreign (or international) loans (extended to foreign governments, agencies, and institutions).
6. Agricultural production loans (extended primarily to farmers and ranchers to raise and harvest crops and raise and round up livestock).
7. Security loans (to aid investors and security brokers and dealers in their trading activities).
8. Leases (usually consisting of the bank buying equipment for business firms and then making that equipment available for the firms' use for a stipulated period of time in return for a series of rental payments—the functional equivalent of a regular loan).

As we will see in Chapter 15, bank loans can be broken down in other ways, too, such as by maturity (i.e., short-term versus long-term), by collateral (i.e., secured versus unsecured), or by their pricing terms (i.e., floating-rate versus fixed-rate loans).

The two loan figures—gross loans and leases and net loans and leases—nearly always appear on bank balance sheets. The larger of the two, *gross loans and leases*, is the sum of all outstanding IOUs owed to the bank. In Table 4–3 gross loans and leases amounted to $109,734 million in the most recent year, or about 81 percent of total assets.

Factoid
Did you know that the total financial assets of the commercial banking industry operating in the United States in 2002, totaling more than $6.8 trillion, was more than three times the financial assets held by the entire thrift industry (including savings and loan associations, savings banks, and credit unions combined)?

Loan Losses However, loan losses, both current and projected, are deducted from the amount of this total (gross) loan figure. Under current U.S. tax law, banks and other depository institutions are allowed to build up a reserve for future loan losses, called the *allowance for loan losses* (ALL), from their flow of income based on their recent loan-loss experience. The ALL, which is a contra-asset account, represents an accumulated reserve against which loans declared to be uncollectible can be charged off. This means that bad loans normally do not affect current income. Rather, when a loan is considered uncollectible, the accounting department will write (charge) it off the books by reducing the ALL account by the amount of the uncollectible loan while simultaneously decreasing the asset account for gross loans. For example, suppose a bank granted a $10 million loan to a property development company to build a shopping center and the company

Another Way of Classifying Banks: By the Types of Assets They Hold

Recently the Federal Deposit Insurance Corporation and other bank regulatory agencies have been grouping banks and thrift institutions by the make-up of their assets. The table below illustrates the different types of U.S. banking firms grouped by the types of assets they hold (Asset Concentrations):

Type of Bank	Definition	Number of U.S. Banks in 2003
International	Assets over $10 billion with more than 25% of assets in foreign offices	6
Agricultural	Over 25% of total loans and leases in agricultural loans and real estate loans secured by farmland	1796
Credit Card	Credit-card loans and securitized receivables over 50% of assets plus securitized receivables	38
Commercial Lenders	Commercial and industrial loans and loans secured by commercial real estate over 25% of total assets	3755
Mortgage Lenders	Residential mortgage loans and mortgage-backed securities over 50% of total assets	254
Consumer Lenders	Loans to individuals (including residential mortgages and credit-card loans) over 50% of total assets	129
Other Specialized	Assets under $1 billion and loans and leases less than 40% of total assets	434
All Other	Assets under $1 billion with no identified asset concentrations	81
Total of All U.S. Insured Banks, First Quarter 2003		7864

Source: Federal Deposit Insurance Corporation, Quarterly Banking Profile, First Quarter 2003.

subsequently went out of business. If the bank could reasonably expect to collect only $1 million of the original $10 million owed, the unpaid $9 million would be subtracted from total (gross) loans and from the ALL account.

The allowance for possible loan losses is built up gradually over time by annual deductions from current income. These deductions appear on the bank's income and expense statement (or Report of Income) as a noncash expense item called the *provision for loan losses* (PLL). For example, suppose a bank anticipated loan losses this year of $1 million and held $100 million already in its ALL account. It would take a noncash charge against its current revenues, entering $1 million in the provision for loan-loss account (PLL) on its Report of Income. Thus:

Amount reported on the bank's income and expense statement

Annual provision for loan-loss expense (PLL) = $1 million, a noncash expense item deducted from current revenues

↓   Then adjust the bank's balance sheet, in its ALL account, as follows:

Allowance for loan losses (ALL) = $100 million + $1 million (from PLL on the current income and expense statement)

= $101 million

Now suppose the bank subsequently discovers that its truly worthless loans, which must be written off, total only $500,000. Then we would have:

Beginning balance in the allowance
for loan loss account (ALL) = $100 million
+
This year's provision for loan losses (PLL) = + $1 million
= Adjusted allowance for loan losses (ALL) = $101 million
− Actual charge-offs of worthless loans − $500,000
= Net allowance for loan losses (ALL) = $100.5 million
after all charge-offs

At about the same time suppose that management discovers it has been able to recover some of the funds (say $1.5 million) that it had previously charged off as losses on earlier loans. Often this belated cash inflow arises because the bank was able to take possession of and then sell the collateral that a borrower had pledged behind his or her defaulted loan. These so-called *recoveries*, then, are added back to the allowance for loan-loss account (ALL) as follows:

Net allowance for loan losses (ALL) after all charge-offs = $100.5 million
+ Recoveries from previously charged-off loans = + $ 1.5 million
= Ending balance in the allowance for loan loss account (ALL) = $102.0 million

If writing off a large loan reduces the balance in the ALL account too much, management of a bank will be called upon (often by examiners representing its principal regulatory agency) to increase the annual PPL deduction (which will lower its current net income) to restore the ALL to a safer level. Additions to ALL are usually made as the loan portfolio grows in size, when any sizable loan is judged to be completely or partially uncollectible, or when an unexpected loan default occurs that has not already been reserved. The required accounting entries simply increase the contra-asset ALL and the expense account PLL. The total amount in the loan-loss reserve (ALL) as of the date of the Report of Condition is then deducted from gross loans to help derive the account entry called *net loans* on the bank's balance sheet—a measure of the net realizable value of all loans outstanding.

Specific and General Reserves   Many banking firms divide the ALL account into two parts: specific reserves and general reserves. *Specific reserves* are set aside to cover a particular loan or loans expected to be a problem or that present the bank with above-average risk. Management may simply designate a portion of the reserves already in the ALL account as specific reserves or add more reserves to cover specific loan problems. The remaining reserves in the loan-loss account are called *general reserves*. This division of loan-loss reserves helps bank managers better understand their bank's need for protection against current or future loan defaults. (See especially Walter [9].)

Reserves for loan losses are determined by management; however, they are influenced by tax laws and government regulations. The Tax Reform Act of 1986 mandated that only loans actually declared worthless could be expensed through the loan-loss provision (PLL) expense item for large banking companies (with assets over $500 million) for tax purposes. This has tended to depress ALL accounts by encouraging a backward-looking rather than a forward-looking process. In Chapter 14, we will see that total loan loss reserves (the ALL account) are counted as part of bank capital up to 1.25 percent of a bank's total risk-weighted assets. However, while the regulations define retained earnings (undivided profits) as permanent capital, loan-loss reserves are not considered permanent capital; hence, managers are further encouraged to build retained earnings at the cost of the ALL account.

The tax laws and government regulations have discouraged allocations to loan-loss reserves relative to allocations made prior to the mid-80s. (See especially O'Toole [6].)

International Loan Reserves   The largest U.S. banks that make international loans to lesser-developed countries are required to set aside so-called *allocated transfer-risk reserves* (ATRs). ATRs were created to help American banks prepare to deal with possible losses on loans made to lesser-developed countries. Like the ALL account, the ATR total is deducted from a bank's gross loans to help determine its net loans. These international-related reserve requirements are established by the Intercountry Exposure Review Committee (ICERC), which consists of representatives from the Federal Deposit Insurance Corporation, the Federal Reserve System, and the Comptroller of the Currency.

Unearned Discount Income   This item consists of interest income on loans that has been received from customers, but not yet earned under the accrual method of accounting banks use today. For example, if a customer receives a loan and pays all or some portion of the interest up front, the bank cannot record that interest payment as earned income because the customer involved has not yet had use of the loan for any length of time. Over the life of the loan, the bank will gradually earn the interest income and will transfer the necessary amounts from unearned discount to the bank's interest income account.

Nonperforming (noncurrent) Loans   Banks have another loan category on their books called *nonperforming (noncurrent) loans*, which are credits that no longer accrue interest income for the bank or that have had to be restructured to accommodate a borrower's changed circumstances. Under current regulations, a loan is placed in the nonperforming category when any scheduled loan repayment is past due for more than 90 days. (This situation is often discussed in the memoranda to the balance sheet.) Once a loan is classified as "nonperforming," any accrued interest recorded on the bank's books, but not actually received, must be deducted from loan revenues. The bank is then forbidden to record any additional interest income from the loan until a cash payment actually comes in.

Key URL
To view the services offered and the recent financial history of the Bank of America, one of the best known and largest banks in the United States, see **www.bankofamerica.com**.

Bank Premises and Fixed Assets   Bank assets also include the net (adjusted for depreciation) value of bank buildings and equipment. A bank usually devotes only a small percentage (between 1 and 2 percent) of its assets to the institution's physical plant—that is, the fixed assets represented by buildings and equipment needed to carry on daily operations. In Table 4–3 National City Corporation has less than 1 percent of its assets ($958 million) in premises and fixed assets. Indeed, as we have seen, the great majority of a bank's assets are financial claims (loans and investment securities) rather than fixed assets. However, fixed assets typically generate fixed operating costs in the form of depreciation expenses, property taxes, and so on, which provide *operating leverage*, enabling the bank to boost its operating earnings if it can increase its sales volume to a high enough level and earn more from using its fixed assets than those assets cost. But with so few fixed assets relative to other assets, banks cannot rely heavily on operating leverage to increase their earnings; they must instead rely mainly upon *financial leverage*—the use of borrowed funds—to boost their earnings performance and remain competitive with other industries in attracting capital.

Other Real Estate Owned (OREO)   This asset category includes the bank's direct and indirect investments in real estate. When bankers speak of OREOs, they are not talking about two chocolate cookies with sweet white cream in the middle. The principal component of OREO is commercial and residential properties obtained to compensate for nonperforming loans. While "kids" may want as many Oreos as possible, bankers like to keep the OREO account small by lending funds to borrowers that will make payments in a timely fashion.

SHAPING LOAN LOSS RESERVES TO MEET CHANGING MARKET CONDITIONS

Banks and selected other financial firms that compete with them (such as savings and loan associations and credit unions) set aside reserves to protect themselves against bad loans and other "nonperforming" assets. There is some judgment needed in this process because no lending institution knows for sure how many loan losses it will actually incur. Moreover, setting aside more loss reserves creates additional expense that can lower earnings and possibly stock prices as well.

As the 21st century opened, Citigroup, Inc., of New York City—the largest financial firm in the United States and one of the top five banking companies in the world—set its loan-loss reserve ratio at one of the lowest levels for major banks in the United States. Why did Citigroup's management decide to keep its loan-loss reserve so low relative to many other money-center banks? One reason was management's belief in the underlying strength of the U.S. economy. Although a recession prevailed for much of the period, management expressed confidence that the American economy would recover. Moreover, the U.S. economy seemed far stronger than the economies of many other areas of the world, such as Japan and Germany. Loan losses are highly sensitive to economic conditions; a stronger economy generally means fewer loan losses.

At the same time, Citigroup had the advantage of considerable product-line and geographic diversification. One of the largest players in the international market, it has a presence all over the globe and offers a wider range of services than virtually any other bank. If revenues fall off in one particular area, other service revenues may take up the slack. With lower risk to revenues, there appeared to be less need for more loan-loss reserves. Of course, only time will tell if Citigroup's confidence in its people and in its market position turns out to be justified.

Goodwill and Other Intangible Assets   Most banks have some purchased assets lacking physical substance. Goodwill occurs when a firm acquires another firm and pays more than the market value of its net assets (assets less liabilities). Other intangible assets include mortgage servicing rights and purchased credit card relationships. In Table 4–3, Goodwill and Other Intangible Assets account for just over 1 percent of the bank's assets.

All Other Assets   This group of assets accounts for just over 5 percent of National City's assets in Table 4–3. This account includes investments in subsidiary firms, customers' liability on acceptances outstanding, income earned but not collected on loans, net deferred tax assets, excess residential mortgage servicing fees receivable, and all other assets.

Bank Liabilities

Deposits   The principal liability of any bank is its *deposits*, representing financial claims held by businesses, households, and governments against the bank. In the event a bank is liquidated, the proceeds from the sale of its assets must first be used to pay off the claims of its depositors (along with the IRS!). Other creditors and bank stockholders receive whatever funds remain. There are five major types of deposits:

1. *Noninterest-bearing demand deposits*, or regular checking accounts, generally permit unlimited check writing. But, under federal regulations, they cannot pay any explicit interest rate (though many banks offer to pay postage costs and offer other "free" services that yield the demand deposit customer an implicit rate of return on these deposits).
2. *Savings deposits* generally bear the lowest rate of interest offered to depositors by a bank but may be of any denomination (though most banks impose a minimum size requirement) and permit the customer to withdraw at will.
3. *NOW accounts*, which can be held only by individuals and nonprofit institutions, bear interest and permit drafts (checks) to be written against each account to pay third parties.

Factoid
What U.S. financial-service industry comes closest in total financial assets to the banking industry?
Answer: Pension funds with about $6.4 trillion in combined financial assets in 2002, followed by mutual funds with about $4.2 trillion in assets.

4. *Money market deposit accounts* (MMDAs) can pay whatever interest rate the offering bank feels is competitive and have limited check-writing privileges attached. No minimum denomination or maturity is required by law, though depository institutions must reserve the right to require seven days' notice before any withdrawals are made.

5. *Time deposits* (mainly certificates of deposit, or CDs), usually carry a fixed maturity (term) and a stipulated interest rate but may be of any denomination, maturity, and yield agreed upon by the bank and its depositor. Included are large ($100,000-plus) *negotiable CDs*—interest-bearing deposits that banks use to raise money from their most well-to-do customers.

The bulk of bank deposits are held by individuals and business firms. However, governments (federal, state, and local) also hold substantial deposit accounts, known as *public fund deposits*. Any time a school district sells bonds to construct a new school building, for example, the proceeds of the bond issue will flow into its deposit in a local bank. Similarly, when the U.S. Treasury collects taxes or sells securities to raise funds, the proceeds normally flow initially into public deposits that the Treasury has established in thousands of banks across the United States. Major banks also draw upon their foreign branch offices for deposits and record the amounts received from abroad simply as *deposits at foreign branches*.

Clearly, as Table 4–3 suggests, banks are heavily dependent upon their deposits, which today often support between 70 and 80 percent of their total assets. In the case of the bank we have been analyzing, total deposits of $66,324 million funded 49 percent of its assets in the most recent year. Because these financial claims of the public are often volatile and because they are so large relative to the owners' capital (equity) investment in the bank, the average banking institution has considerable exposure to failure risk. It must continually stand ready (be liquid) to meet deposit withdrawals. These twin pressures of risk and liquidity force bankers to exercise caution in their choices of loans and other assets. Failure to do so threatens the bank with collapse under the weight of depositors' claims.

Borrowings from Nondeposit Sources   Although deposits typically represent the largest portion of bank sources of funds, sizable amounts of funds also stem from miscellaneous liability accounts. All other factors held equal, the larger the depository institution, the greater use it tends to make of *nondeposit sources of funds*. One reason borrowings from nondeposit funds sources have grown rapidly in recent years is that there are no reserve requirements or insurance fees on most of these funds, which lowers the cost of nondeposit funding. Also, borrowings in the money market usually can be arranged in a few minutes and the funds wired immediately to the depository institution that needs them. One drawback, however, is that interest rates on nondeposit funds are highly volatile. If there is even a hint of financial problems at an institution trying to borrow from these sources, its borrowing costs can rise rapidly, or money market lenders may simply refuse to extend it any more credit.

The most important nondeposit funding source for most U.S. banks, typically, is represented by *federal funds purchased and repurchase agreements*. This account tracks the bank's temporary borrowings in the money market, mainly from reserves loaned to it by other banks (federal funds purchased) or from repurchase agreements in which the bank has borrowed funds collateralized by some of its own securities from another bank or from a large nonbank corporate customer. Other borrowed funds the bank may draw upon include both short-term and long-term borrowings. Short-term funds usually consist of *borrowing reserves from the discount windows of the Federal Reserve banks, issuing commercial paper,* or *borrowing in the Eurocurrency market from multinational banks or from the borrowing bank's own overseas branches*. In the worldwide banking system, *Eurocurrency borrowings* (i.e.,

E-BANKING AND E-COMMERCE

THE IMPACT OF GROWING ELECTRONIC BANKING ON BANK FINANCIAL STATEMENTS

Electronic banking facilities (including automated teller machines, point-of-sale terminals, websites, and other computer-based service delivery systems) have begun to replace and to slow the growth of full-service brick-and-mortar branch offices. This is true not only in the commercial banking industry but also in the thrift industry (including savings and loans, savings banks, and credit unions) where, among the thrifts, the number of full-service branch offices appears to be falling.

Indeed, the impact of the trend toward greater automation in banking was first detectable beginning in the 1980s when the annual rate of growth of new full-service banking offices began to rise less steeply. While the total number of full-service bank branch offices continues to rise inside the United States, reaching more than 66,000 in 2002, the annual *net* change in the number of branch offices (i.e., new branches minus established offices that are closing), though still positive, appears to have slowed somewhat.

This ongoing shift from brick and mortar buildings to electronic service production and delivery systems might be expected to have an impact on bank financial statements. And so it has!

One important indicator is the asset item on the industry's balance sheet titled "bank premises and fixed assets." Normally quite small to begin with (generally falling in the one to two percent of total assets range) the value of bank premises and fixed assets relative to total industry assets has been declining through most of the past decade. For example, in 1996 the ratio of premises and fixed assets to total bank assets stood at 1.411 percent but then steadily fell to reach only 1.120 percent of all banking assets in 2002. With more efficient and less costly electronic equipment available banks simply need to spend less on buildings and real estate. Partly as a result, the industry's profitability has risen in recent years as its operating expenses have declined relative to its revenues.

transferable time deposits denominated in a variety of currencies) represent the principal source of short-term borrowings by banks. Many banks also issue *long-term debt*, including real estate mortgages, for the purpose of constructing new office facilities or modernizing plant and equipment. Subordinated debt (notes and debentures) are yet another source of funds that are identified on the Report of Condition. This category includes *limited-life preferred stock* (that is, preferred stock that eventually matures) and any noncollateralized borrowings of the bank. The *other liabilities* account serves as a catch-all of miscellaneous amounts owed by the bank, such as a deferred tax liability and obligations to pay off investors who hold bankers' acceptances.

Equity Capital Accounts   The equity capital accounts on a bank's Report of Condition represent the owners' (stockholders') share of the business. Every new bank or other corporate financial firm begins with a minimum amount of owners' capital and then borrows funds from the public to "lever up" its operations. In fact, banks and many nonbank financial institutions are among the most heavily leveraged (debt-financed) of all businesses. Their capital accounts normally represent less than 10 percent of the value of their total assets. In the case of the bank whose balance sheet appears in Table 4–3, the *stockholders' equity capital* of $9,372 million in the most recent year accounted for just 6.9 percent of its total assets.

Bank capital accounts typically include many of the same items that other business corporations display on their balance sheets. They list the total par (face) value of *common stock outstanding*. When that stock is sold for more than its par value, the excess market value of the stock flows into a *surplus* account. Few banks issue *preferred stock*, which guarantees its holders an annual dividend before common stockholders receive any dividend payments. Perpetual preferred stock is part of equity capital, while limited-life preferred stock is usually listed as debt capital. Preferred stock is generally viewed in the banking community as expensive to issue, principally because the annual dividend is not tax deductible, and a drain on the earnings that normally would flow to the bank's common stockholders, though the largest bank holding companies have issued substantial amounts of preferred shares in recent years in order to open up a new source of capital.

Usually, the largest item in the capital account is *retained earnings* (undivided profits), which represent accumulated net income left over each year after payment of stockholder dividends. There may also be a *contingency reserve* held as protection against unforeseen losses and *treasury stock* that has been retired.

Comparative Balance Sheet Ratios for Different Size Banks The items discussed previously generally appear on all bank balance sheets, regardless of the bank's size. But the relative importance of each balance sheet item varies greatly with bank size. A good illustration of how bank size affects the mix of balance sheet items is shown in Table 4–4. For example, larger banks tend to hold more total (net) loans relative to their assets than smaller, community-oriented banks. Smaller banks hold more investment securities and often make fewer loans relative to their assets than larger firms. Smaller community banks rely more heavily on deposits to support their assets than do larger banks, while the larger institutions make heavier use of money market borrowings (such as the purchase of Eurocurrencies or federal funds). Clearly, the analyst examining a bank's financial condition must consider the *size* of the bank and compare it to other institutions of the same size and, preferably, serving a similar market area as well.

Recent Expansion of Off-Balance-Sheet Items in Banking

As we will see in much greater detail in Chapters 7 and 8, recently banks have converted many of their customer services into fee-generating transactions not fully disclosed on their balance sheets. Prominent examples of these *off-balance sheet items* include:

1. *Standby credit agreements*, in which a bank pledges to guarantee repayment of a customer's loan received from a third party.
2. *Interest rate swaps*, in which a bank promises to exchange interest payments on debt securities with another party.
3. *Financial futures and option interest-rate contracts*, in which a bank agrees to deliver or to take delivery of securities from another party at a guaranteed price.
4. *Loan commitments*, in which a bank pledges to lend up to a certain amount of funds in the future until the commitment matures.
5. *Foreign exchange rate contracts*, in which a bank agrees to deliver or accept delivery of foreign currencies.

The problem with these off-balance-sheet transactions is that they often expose a bank to added risk even though they may not appear in adequate detail in conventional financial reports. This is particularly true of standby credit agreements issued to back a loan that a customer has received from another lender. If the customer defaults on the loan, the bank is pledged to pay off the customer's IOU. Moreover, as Table 4–5 illustrates, off-balance-sheet items have grown so rapidly that they exceed total bank assets several times over! These contingent contracts are heavily concentrated in the largest banks—those institutions holding more than $1 billion in total assets—where their nominal value recently was more than eight times larger than the total of all reported bank assets.

Reflecting growing concern about bank risk exposure from off-balance-sheet items, the Financial Accounting Standards Board (FASB) recently issued FASB Statement No. 133, labeled Accounting for Derivative Instruments and Hedging Activities. This new rule, implemented in 2000, impacts any firm that conducts virtually any type of risk protection (hedging) activity. The new rules were designed to make derivatives and hedging transac-

TABLE 4–4 The Composition of Bank Balance Statements (Percentage Mix of Bank Sources and Uses of Funds for Year-End 2002)

Source: Federal Deposit Insurance Corporation

Assets, Liabilities, and Equity Capital Items	Percentage of Total Assets for:			
	All U.S. Insured Banks	U.S. Banks with Less than $100 Million in Total Assets	U.S. Banks with $100 Million to $1 Billion in Total Assets	U.S. Banks with More than $1 Billion in Total Assets
Assets:				
Cash and deposits due from depository institutions	5.43%	6.00%	4.68%	5.51%
Investment securities	18.85	23.97	23.01	18.07
Federal funds sold and securities purchased under agreements to resell	4.41	5.45	3.49	4.51
Total loans and leases (net)	57.71	60.15	63.88	56.73
Commercial and industrial loans	21.92	16.80	16.99	22.92
Consumer loans	16.91	11.44	9.61	18.30
Real estate loans	49.71	60.20	68.95	46.28
Loans to depository institutions	3.21	0.08	0.30	3.80
Loans to foreign governments	0.14	0.00*	0.00*	0.17
Agricultural loans	1.13	10.28	2.92	0.49
Other loans	3.15	0.94	1.21	3.55
Leases	3.91	0.34	0.62	4.57
Assets held in trading accounts	5.61	0.00	0.01	6.62
Bank premises and fixed assets	1.12	1.84	1.79	1.00
Other assets	6.87	2.59	3.13	7.57
Total Assets	100.0%	100.0%	100.0%	100.0%
Liabilities and Equity Capital:				
Interest-bearing deposits	53.04	71.46	68.66	50.13
Noninterest-bearing (demand) deposits	13.24	12.98	12.66	13.33
Federal funds purchased and securities sold under agreements to repurchase	8.07	0.77	2.39	9.16
Other liabilities	16.49	3.70	6.40	18.40
Total equity capital	9.16	11.13	9.88	8.98
Total Liabilities and Equity Capital	100.0%	100.0%	100.0%	100.0%

*Less than 0.005 percent. Totals may not exactly equal 100% due to rounding.

Filmtoid
What 1999 British drama tells the story of how one trader's risk exposure resulted in losses that closed the doors of England's oldest merchant bank, Barings?
Answer: *Rogue Trader.*

tions more publicly visible on corporate financial statements and to capture and publish the impact of hedging transactions on corporate earnings.

Gains or losses on derivative contracts must be marked to market value as they accrue, which affects a firm's report of income and, perhaps, increases the volatility of its earnings. Moreover, firms like banks that are heavily regulated in the interest of public safety must connect their use of hedging contracts to actual risk exposures in their operations (thereby prohibiting speculative use of derivatives). The fundamental purpose of all these provisions is to make corporate accounting more transparent to the public and to prevent businesses, including financial-service firms, from concealing risky transactions by using creative accounting techniques. Fundamentally, FASB 133 aims to restore badly shaken public confidence in the wake of accounting fiascos visible to the public from such firms as Enron, Global Crossings, and J. P. Morgan Chase.

TABLE 4–5   Off-Balance-Sheet Items Reported by U.S. Banks

Source: Federal Deposit Insurance Corporation.

Off-Balance-Sheet Items	Total Off-Balance-Sheet Items Reported by U.S. Banks Arranged by Size Group (in Billions of Dollars) on December 31, 2002:			
	Total Volume in Billions of Dollars at All U.S. Insured Banks	**U.S. Insured Banks under $100 Million in Total Assets**	**U.S. Insured Banks $100 Million to $1 Billion in Total Assets**	**U.S. Insured Banks $1 Billion or More in Total Assets**
Standby credit agreements (letters of credit)	$ 268.0	$ 0.4	$ 3.6	$ 264.1
Interest-rate swaps (notional value)	31,189.5	0.0*	2.9	31,186.6
Credit derivatives	641.5	0.0	0.1	641.4
Financial futures and forward contracts	7,379.5	0.0*	1.0	7,378.5
Purchased option contracts	4,660.0	0.0*	1.3	4,658.7
Loan commitments (unused)	5,315.0	93.5	618.1	4,603.4
Foreign exchange contracts	6,271.5	0.0	0.0*	6,271.5
Other off-balance-sheet items	1,009.2	0.0*	0.1	1,009.1
Total off-balance-sheet items	$56,734.2	$93.9	$627.1	$51,873.3
Total assets reported on U.S. insured banks' balance sheets	7,075.2	211.3	869.5	5,994.4
Off-balance-sheet items as a percent of on-balance-sheet assets	801.9%	44.4%	72.1%	865.4%

*Less than $50 million

The Problem of Book-Value Accounting in Banking

A broader public confidence issue concerns how bankers have recorded the value of their assets and liabilities for, literally, generations. The industry has generally followed the practice of recording assets and liabilities at their *original cost* on the day they are posted or received. This accounting practice, known as *book-value, historical,* or *original cost accounting,* has come under severe attack in recent years. The book-value accounting method assumes that all loans and other balance-sheet items will be held to maturity. It does not reflect the impact on a bank's balance sheet of changing interest rates and changing default risk, which affect both the value and cash flows associated with loans, security holdings, and debt.

While we usually say that most assets are valued at historical or original cost, the traditional bank accounting procedure should really be called *amortized cost.* For example, if a loan's principal is gradually paid off over time, a bank will deduct from the original face value of the loan (i.e., its original historical recorded value) the amount of any repayments of loan principal, thus reflecting the fact that the amount owed by the borrowing customer is being amortized downward over time as loan payments are received. Similarly, if a security is acquired at a discounted price below its par (face) value, the spread between the security's original discounted value and its value at maturity will be amortized upward over time as additional income until the security finally reaches maturity.

For example, if market interest rates on government bonds maturing in one year are currently at 10 percent, a $1,000 par-value bond held by a bank and promising an annual interest (coupon) rate of 10 percent would sell at a current market price of $1,000. However, if market interest rates rise to 12 percent, the value of the bond must fall to about $980 so that the investment return from this asset is also about 12 percent.

Similarly, changes in the default risk exposure of borrowers will affect the current market value of loans. Clearly, if some loans are less likely to be repaid than was true when they were granted, their market value must be lower. For example, a $1,000 loan for a year granted to a borrower at a loan rate of 10 percent clearly must fall in market value if the borrower's financial situation deteriorates and he or she becomes more risky. If interest rates applicable to other borrowers in the same higher risk class stand at 12 percent, the $1,000, one-year loan will decline to only $982 in market value. Recording assets at their original (or historical) cost and never changing that number to reflect current market conditions does not give depositors, stockholders, and other investors interested in buying bank-issued stock or debt a true picture of the firm's real financial condition. Investors could easily be deceived.

Under the historical or book-value accounting system, interest rate changes do not affect the value of bank capital because they do not affect the values of bank assets and liabilities recorded at cost. Moreover, only realized capital gains and losses affect the book values shown on a bank's balance sheet under traditional accounting practices. Banks and other financial firms can increase their current income and their capital, for example, by selling assets that have risen in value while ignoring the impact of any losses in value experienced by other assets still held on the books.

In the summer of 1992, FASB issued Rule 115, which focuses primarily upon investments in marketable securities, probably the easiest balance sheet item for a banker to value at market. The FASB asked banks to divide their security holdings into two broad groups: those they planned to hold to maturity and those that may be traded before they reach maturity. Securities that a bank plans to hold to maturity could be valued at their original cost while tradable securities would be valued at their current market price. At the same time the Securities and Exchange Commission (SEC) asked leading banks that were actively trading securities to put any securities they expected to sell into a special balance sheet account labeled *assets held for sale*. These reclassified assets must be valued at cost or market, whichever is lower at the time. The FASB and the SEC seem determined to eradicate "gains trading," a practice in which managers sell any securities that have appreciated in order to reap a capital gain, but hold onto those securities whose prices have declined and continue to value these lower-priced instruments at their higher historical cost.

Currently, for regulatory purposes you will find securities identified as *held-to-maturity* or *available-for-sale* on the Report of Condition. The available-for-sale securities are reported at their fair market value. When we examine the schedule for securities for a bank or bank holding company, we find that both the amortized cost and the market value are often reported.

As the 21st century began, the market-value accounting controversy heated up to a fever pitch. U.S. and international accounting regulatory bodies, especially the FASB and the International Accounting Standards Committee (IASC), proposed for implementation a new *fair value rule* under which all financial assets held by banks would be valued not at their face value, but at the price they would bring in the financial marketplace. Declining asset values would not only reduce the accumulated value of a bank's balance sheet, but also result in reduced earnings and possibly lead to the erosion of capital if a banker had not already set aside adequate reserves to handle the problem.

Opposition to the FASB–IASC market-value proposal came flying in from all directions, including trade associations in several countries and the Federal Reserve Board.

Insights and Issues

WHAT SHOULD BE DONE ABOUT LOST INTEREST FROM TROUBLED LOANS?

A long-standing accounting controversy has centered on how banks should deal with the interest income they lose when customers stop paying on their loans. Realizing that the industry was for the most part ignoring this issue, the U.S. Financial Accounting Standards Board recently issued an important accounting rule, known as FASB 114.

Under FASB 114, banks and other financial institutions must account for the *expected loss of interest income on nonperforming loans* when calculating their loan-loss provisions. Many banks still base their loan-loss reserves only upon their projected loss of principal from a troubled loan, not including the expected loss or delay in receiving interest payments. A similar problem arises when the terms of a loan must be renegotiated to a longer payout schedule or the bank agrees to reduce or delay interest payments because the borrower cannot successfully handle the originally negotiated terms of a loan. Currently, many banks do not report lost interest if they expect eventual repayment of the principal of a troubled loan. Statement 114 requires banks to reduce the value of a loan on their books in order to reflect any reduction in expected interest payments as well as loss of principal. While both secured and unsecured loans are covered, certain loans (such as credit card loans and home mortgages) are exempt.

When the adjustment for loss of interest is made, the result is likely to be an increase in loan-loss provisions at those banks not already recognizing interest losses on nonperforming loans. In figuring the value of impaired loans, banks are required by FASB 114 to measure the value of loans by the present value of their expected future cash flows discounted at the loan's effective interest rate (which is the contractual loan rate adjusted for any deferred loan fee, costs, premiums, or discounts that prevailed when the loan was extended or acquired). Each quarter bankers must estimate when their troubled loans are likely to be repaid, if ever.

Among the objections posed from different groups were the possible danger of increasingly volatile bank earnings, greater instability in stock prices, loss of at least a part of bank capital cushions (which protect against failure), slower expansion of commercial banks into the investment banking business where lending capacity is important, higher-cost loans (especially for small businesses), and lack of active resale markets for many types of bank assets (particularly smaller loans), thus making it more difficult to assign market values to these assets. In fact, it is conceivable that bankers could have widely different values attached to essentially the same kinds and quality of loans.

Nevertheless, many experts think the adoption of these new market pricing rules is just a matter of time. Indeed, the European Commission of the European Union of nations recently ruled that all listed European-based companies must adopt IASC accounting standards by 2005. Inside the United States, the SEC now requires mutual funds that purchase bank loans as investments to value these loans at market, not original, cost.

In addition to requiring greater disclosure of the market value of bank assets, federal regulatory agencies began in 1994 to require the largest U.S. banks (holding $500 million or more in assets) to file financial statements audited by an independent public accountant with the Federal Deposit Insurance Corporation (FDIC) and with the federal or state agency that chartered the bank within 90 days of the end of their fiscal year. Along with audited financial statements, each bank must also submit a statement by its management concerning the effectiveness of the bank's internal controls over financial reporting in preserving its safety and soundness. An independent accountant must also evaluate and give an opinion on the quality of the bank's internal controls and its compliance with safety and soundness laws. Moreover, an audit committee consisting entirely of outside directors must review and evaluate a bank's annual audit with its management and with an independent public accountant.

Larger U.S. banks, with $3 billion or more in total assets, must meet even more stringent requirements for setting up outside audit committees, including requiring at least two audit committee members to have prior banking experience, prohibiting the most signifi-

Factoid
Did you know that the volume of FDIC-insured deposits reached a record high in 2002 at more the $3.3 trillion?

cant bank customers from serving on such a committee, and mandating that bank audit committees must have access to legal counsel that is independent of bank management. These tough reporting rules were a consequence of the FDIC Improvement Act, passed by the U.S. Congress in 1991 and designed to prevent the FDIC's insurance reserves from being drained away by bank failures.

Even tougher accounting and reporting rules emerged in 2002 in the wake of the collapse of energy-trader Enron and dozens of reports of corporate mismanagement and fraud. The Sarbanes-Oxley Accounting Standards Act mandates that the CEOs and CFOs of publicly traded banks and other corporations certify the accuracy of their institutions' financial reports. The publication of false or misleading information may be punished with heavy fines and even jail sentences. Internal auditing and audit committees of each institution's board of directors are granted greater authority and independence in assessing the accuracy and quality of their institutions' accounting and financial reporting practices.

Concept Check

4–1. What are the principal accounts that appear on a bank's balance sheet (Report of Condition)?

4–2. Which accounts are most important and which are least important on the asset side of a bank's balance sheet?

4–3. What accounts are most important on the liability side of a bank's balance sheet?

4–4. What are the essential differences among demand deposits, savings deposits, and time deposits?

4–5. What are primary reserves and secondary reserves and what are they supposed to do?

4–6. Suppose that a bank holds cash in its vault of $1.4 million, short-term government securities of

$12.4 million, privately issued money market instruments of $5.2 million, deposits at the Federal Reserve banks of $20.1 million, cash items in the process of collection of $0.6 million, and deposits placed with other banks of $16.4 million. How much in primary reserves does this bank hold? In secondary reserves?

4–7. What are off-balance-sheet items and why are they important to some banks and other financial firms?

4–8. Why are bank accounting practices under attack right now? In what ways could banks and similar financial institutions improve their accounting methods?

Components of the Income Statement (Report of Income)

A bank's income statement, or **Report of Income,** indicates the amount of revenue received and expenses incurred over a specific period of time, such as the current year. There is usually a close correlation between the size of the principal items on a bank's balance sheet (Report of Condition) and its income statement. After all, assets on the balance sheet account for the majority of operating revenues, while liabilities generate most of a bank's operating expenses.

The principal source of bank revenue is the interest income generated by the bank's *earning assets*—mainly its loans and investments. Additional revenue is provided by the *fees* charged for specific services (such as processing checks). The major expenses incurred in generating this revenue include interest paid out to depositors; interest owed on nondeposit borrowings; the cost of equity capital; salaries, wages, and benefits paid to bank employees; overhead expenses associated with the bank's physical plant; funds set aside for possible loan losses; taxes owed; and miscellaneous expenses.

The difference between all revenues and expenses is *net income*. Thus:

$$\text{Net income} = \text{Total revenue items} - \text{Total expense items} \qquad \textbf{(4)}$$

where:

Revenue Items

↓

cash assets × average yield on cash assets
+
security investments × average yield on security investments
+
loans outstanding × average yield on loans
+
miscellaneous assets × average yield on miscellaneous assets
+
income from fiduciary activities + fee income + trading account gains

Minus (−) **Expense Items**

↓

Total deposits × average interest cost on deposits
+
nondeposit borrowings × average interest cost on nondeposit borrowings
+
owners' capital × average cost of owners' capital
+
employee salaries, wages, and benefits expense
+
overhead expense
+
provision for possible loan losses
+
miscellaneous expenses
+
taxes owed

The above chart on revenue and expense items reminds us that banks and many other financial firms interested in increasing their net earnings (income) have a number of options available to achieve this goal: (1) increase the net yield on each asset held; (2) redistribute earning assets toward those assets that carry higher yields; (3) increase the volume of services that provide fee income; (4) increase the fees associated with various services; (5) shift their funding sources toward less-costly deposits and other borrowings; (6) find ways to reduce their employee overhead, loan-loss, and miscellaneous operating expenses; or (7) reduce their taxes owed through improved tax management practices.

Of course, management does not have full control of all of these items that affect a bank or nonbank firm's net income. The yields earned on various assets, the revenues generated by sales of services, and the interest rates that must be paid to attract deposits and nondeposit borrowings are determined by demand and supply forces in the market the financial firm serves. Over the long run, the public will be the principal factor shaping what types of loans the bank or nonbank financial-service provider will be able to make and what types of deposit services it will be able to sell in its market area. Within the broad boundaries allowed by competition in the marketplace, by regulation, and by the pressures exerted by public demand, however, management decisions are still a major factor in determining the particular mix of loans, securities, cash, and deposits each bank and nonbank financial firm holds and the size and composition of its revenues and expenses.

Key URL
One of the most complete bank websites in the world, packed with information on service offerings, the bank's financial condition, and other information, is maintained by Wells Fargo Bank of San Francisco at **www.wellsfargo.com**.

Financial Flows and Stocks

Income statements of banks and other financial companies are a record of *financial flows* over time, in contrast to the balance sheet, which is a statement of *stocks* of assets, liabilities, and equity held at any given point in time. Therefore, we can represent the bank's income statement as a report of *financial outflows* (expenses) and *financial inflows* (revenues):

The Income Statement (Report of Income)	
Financial Inflows	**Financial Outflows**
Interest income on loans and investments	Deposit costs
Income from fiduciary activities	Nondeposit borrowing costs
Income from service charges	Salaries and wages expense
Trading account gains and fees	Miscellaneous expenses
Miscellaneous income	Tax expense
Total financial inflows – Total financial outflows = Net income	
(all) revenues) (all expenses)	

Actual bank income reports are usually more complicated than this simple statement because each item may have several component accounts. Most bank income statements closely resemble the income statement shown in Table 4–6 for a large midwestern banking organization, the same institution whose balance sheet we examined earlier. Table 4–6 is divided into four main sections: (1) interest income, (2) interest expenses, (3) noninterest income, and (4) noninterest expenses.

TABLE 4–6
Report of Income (Income Statement) for National City Corporation

Financial data is from the FDIC website for the bank holding company. (The dollar amounts represent combined amounts for all FDIC-insured bank and thrift subsidiaries, and do *not* reflect nondeposit subsidiaries or parent companies.) Note: all figures are expressed in thousands of dollars.

Report of Income	12/31/2002	12/31/2001	
Total interest income	$6,107,245	$6,714,097 }	Financial inflows
Total interest expense	$2,043,003	$3,188,188 }	Financial outflows
Net interest income	$4,064,242	$3,525,909	
Provision for loan and lease losses	$681,917	$605,297 }	Noncash financial outflows
Total noninterest income	$2,656,643	$2,556,444	
Fiduciary activities	$282,024	$331,491	
Service charges on deposit accounts	$507,978	$465,037	
Trading account gains and fees	$44,021	$5,088	Financial inflows
Additional noninterest income	$1,822,620	$1,754,828	
Total noninterest expense	$3,612,002	$3,527,287	
Salaries and employee benefits	$1,695,181	$1,506,614	
Premises and equipment expense	$374,398	$371,296	Financial outflows
Additional noninterest expense	$1,542,423	$1,649,377	
Pretax net operating income	$2,426,966	$1,949,775	
Securities gains (losses)	$4,275	$21,445 }	Financial inflows
Applicable income taxes	$847,478	$683,289 }	Financial outflows
Income before extraordinary items	$1,583,763	$1,287,931	
Extraordinary gains—net	$0	–$1,059 }	Financial inflows
Net Income	**$1,583,763**	**$1,286,872**	

E-BANKING AND E-COMMERCE

BALANCE SHEETS, INCOME STATEMENTS, AND THE FAILURE OF AN INTERNET-ONLY BANK

The strength of a bank's balance sheet and income statement is an indicator of its probability of survival or failure. Most bank failures appear to spring from weaknesses in the loan portfolio on the balance sheet, accompanied by declining loan revenues on the income statement and by inadequate equity capital to stem these losses.

Most of us are quite familiar with the failures of traditional brick-and-mortar banks—some traditional banks fail every year. But what about Internet-only banks? They are relatively new. Have any net banks failed? Yes, due to many of the same balance-sheet and income-statement weaknesses that we see in the failures of traditional banks.

For example, in February 2002, the Office of the Comptroller of the Currency (OCC) closed Nextbank, N.A.—a national Internet-only bank chartered in Phoenix, Arizona. Nextbank marketed credit cards, credit card receivables, and deposits through its website until its losses and expenses overwhelmed the institution's capital. The FDIC was appointed receiver and attempted to sell the failed bank's deposits to other institutions but received no bids. Accordingly, the FDIC paid off all of the insured depositors, sending them checks by mail. The failed institution's remaining assets (credit card receivables) were sold by an auction conducted over the Internet. The FDIC's losses from this failure have been estimated at $300 to $350 million.

Interest Income Not surprisingly, interest and fees generated from loans account for most bank revenues (normally two-thirds or more of the total) as well as most of the revenues received by nonbank thrift institutions, such as savings and loan associations and credit unions. In the case of the bank we have been following, the $6,107 million in loan revenues represents about 70 percent of total interest and noninterest income. Loan revenues are usually followed in importance by investment earnings from taxable and tax-exempt securities, interest earned on federal funds loans and repurchase (resale) agreements, and interest received on time deposits placed with other depository institutions. The relative importance of these various income items fluctuates from year to year with shifts in interest rates and loan demand, though loan income is nearly always the dominant revenue source. It must be noted, however, that the relative importance of loan revenue versus noninterest revenue sources (so-called *fee income*) is changing rapidly, with fee income today growing much faster than interest income on loans as bankers and other financial managers work to develop fee-based services.

Interest Expenses The number one expense item for a bank or other depository institution normally is *interest on deposits*. For the banking company we have been following, National City Corporation, interest on deposits accounted for almost 60 percent of this bank's total interest costs. Another important and rapidly growing interest expense item in recent years is the interest owed on short-term borrowings in the money market—mainly borrowings of federal funds (reserves) from other depository institutions and borrowings backstopped by security repurchase agreements—plus any long-term borrowings that have taken place (including mortgages on bank property and subordinated notes and debentures outstanding).

Net Interest Income Total interest expenses are subtracted from total interest income to yield *net interest income*. This important item is often referred to as the *interest margin*, the gap between the interest income the bank or other financial firm receives on loans and securities and the interest cost of its borrowed funds. It is usually a key determinant of profitability. When the interest margin falls, the stockholders of banks and other financial firms will usually see a decline in their bottom line—net after-tax earnings—and the dividends they receive on each share of stock held may decrease as well.

Loan-Loss Expense   As we saw earlier in this chapter, another expense item that banks and selected other financial institutions can deduct from current income is known as the *provision for loan and lease losses*. This provision account is really a *noncash expense*, created by a simple bookkeeping entry. Its purpose is to shelter a portion of current earnings from taxes to help prepare for bad loans. The annual loan-loss provision is deducted from current revenues before taxes are applied to earnings.

Under today's tax laws, U.S. banks calculate their loan-loss deductions using either the *experience method* (in which the amount of deductible loan-loss expense would be the product of the average ratio of net loan charge-offs to total loans in the most recent six years times the current total of outstanding loans) or the *specific charge-off method*, which allows them to add to loan-loss reserves from pretax income each year no more than the amount of those loans actually written off as uncollectible. Expensing worthless loans usually must occur in the year that troubled loans are judged to be worthless. Large banking companies are required to use the specific charge-off method. Smaller banks and banking companies (under $500 million in assets) can use either the experience method or the specific charge-off approach.

Noninterest Income   Sources of income other than earnings from loans and security investments are called simply *noninterest income* and usually include fees earned from providing fiduciary services (such as trust services), service fees assessed on deposit accounts, trading account gains or losses, and miscellaneous fees and charges stemming from other services sold to customers. Recently bankers and many of their competitors have targeted noninterest income, or *fee income*, as a key source of future revenues. By more aggressively selling services other than loans, such as security brokerage, insurance, and trust services, bankers and other financial service-providers have found a promising channel for boosting the bottom line on their income statements, for diversifying their income sources, and for insulating their institutions more adequately from fluctuations in interest rates. The $2,657 million of noninterest income reported by the bank in Table 4–6 was more than 30 percent of its total revenue for the annual reporting period. (Please see the box on the next page for several examples of important fee income sources today.)

Noninterest Expenses   The key noninterest expense item for most banks and other financial institutions is *wages, salaries, and employee benefits*, which has been a rapidly rising expense item in recent years, as leading financial firms have pursued top-quality college graduates to head their management teams and lured experienced senior management away from their competitors. The costs of maintaining a financial institution's properties and rental fees on office space show up in the *premises and equipment expense*. The cost of furniture and equipment also appears under the noninterest expense category, along with numerous small expense items including legal fees, office supplies, and repair costs.

Net Income   The sum of *net interest income* (interest income − interest expense) and *net noninterest income* (noninterest income − noninterest expense) is called *pretax net operating income*. Applicable federal and state income tax rates are applied to pretax net operating income plus *securities gains or losses* to derive *income before extraordinary items*.

Securities gains (losses) are usually small, but can be substantial for some banks and financial firms. For example, banks purchase, sell, or redeem securities during the year, and this activity often results in gains or losses above or below the original cost (book value) of the securities. The regulators require that banks report securities gains or losses as a separate item; however, other income statements may record these gains or losses as a component of noninterest income. A bank can use these gains or losses on securities to help smooth out its net income from year to year. If earnings from loans decline, securities gains

Principal Types of Noninterest ("Fee") Income Received by Banks and Competing Financial Firms Today

Fees arising from credit transactions:	Charges for membership in a credit card plan
	Charges for late loan payments
	Charges for exceeding credit limits
	Servicing fees for collecting mortgage payments for another lender
	Fees for refinancing home loans
Fees arising from deposit transactions:	Checking account maintenance fees
	Checking account overdraft fees
	Fees for writing excessive checks
	Savings account overdraft fees
	Fees for stopping payment of checks
	Surcharges for use of ATMs
Fees arising from securities transactions:	Security brokerage commissions
	Commissions for sales of annuities and mutual funds
	Commissions and fees for underwriting the sale of new stocks and bonds
Fees arising from fiduciary activities:	Fees for managing and protecting a customer's property
	Fees for record keeping for corporate security transactions and dispensing interest and dividend payments
	Fees for managing corporate and individual pension and retirement plans
Fees for miscellaneous financial services:	Data processing service fees
	Advisory service fees for managing mergers and acquisitions

may offset all or part of the decline. In contrast, when loan revenues (which are fully taxable) are high, securities losses can be used to reduce taxable income.

Another method for stabilizing the earnings of banks and other financial institutions consists of *nonrecurring sales of assets*. These one-time-only (*extraordinary income or loss*) transactions often involve financial assets, such as common stock, or real property pledged as collateral behind a loan upon which the lender has foreclosed. A financial firm may also sell real estate or subsidiary firms that it owns. Such transactions frequently have a substantial effect on current earnings, particularly if a lender sells property it acquired in a loan foreclosure. Such property is usually carried on the lender's books at minimal market value, but its sale price may turn out to be substantially higher.

The key bottom-line item on any financial firm's income statement is *net income*, which the firm's board of directors usually divides into two categories. Some portion of net income may flow to the stockholders in the form of *cash dividends*. Another portion (usually the larger part) will go into *retained earnings* (also called *undivided profits*) in the capital accounts in order to provide a larger capital base to support future growth. We note in

Table 4–6 that the bank we are studying in this chapter reported net income of $1,584 million for the year just ended.

Comparative Income Statement Ratios for Banks of Different Sizes

Like bank balance sheets, income statements usually contain much the same items for both large and small banks, but the relative importance of individual income and expense items varies substantially with the size of a bank. For example, as shown in Table 4–7, larger banks receive more of their total income from noninterest fees (e.g., service charges and commissions) than do small banks, while smaller banks rely more heavily on deposits than on money market borrowings for their funding and, thus, pay out relatively more deposit interest per dollar of assets than many larger banks. Any meaningful analysis of an individual bank's income statement requires comparisons with other banks of comparable size and location.

Other Useful Bank Financial Statements

Many bankers and analysts like to supplement the information provided on the balance sheet and the income statement with two other financial statements that display balance sheet and income statement items in a different and frequently revealing format. These are (*a*) the Funds-Flow, or Sources and Uses of Funds, Statement and (*b*) the Statement of Stockholders' Equity. Let's look briefly at these two useful sources of financial information.

The Funds-Flow Statement (Sources and Uses of Funds Statement)

The *Funds-Flow Statement*, also called the Sources and Uses of Funds Statement, answers two questions: Where did the funds a financial institution used over a certain period of time come from? How were those funds used? It is based upon the following relationships:

Funds provided to the financial institution over a specific period of time

= Funds provided from operations
+ Decreases in financial institution assets
+ Increases in financial institution liabilities

Funds used by the financial institution during a specific period of time

= Dividends paid out to stockholders
+ Increases in financial institution assets
+ Decreases in financial institution liabilities

TABLE 4–7 The Composition of Bank Income Statements (Percentage of Total Assets Measured as of Year-End 2002)

Source: Federal Deposit Insurance Corporation.

Income and Expense Items	Percentage of Total Assets for:			
	All U.S. Insured Banks	U.S. Banks with Less than $100 Million in Total Assets	U.S. Banks with $100 Million to $1 Billion in Total Assets	U.S. Banks with $1 Billion or More in Total Assets
Total interest and fee income:	5.06%	5.84%	5.83%	4.92%
Loan income	3.77	4.56	4.63	3.61
Security income	0.85	1.12	1.06	0.81
Federal funds sold and repurchase agreements	0.09	0.09	0.06	0.09
Other interest income	0.35	0.08	0.08	0.40
Total interest expense:	1.71	2.07	2.00	1.65
Deposit interest	1.16	1.93	1.74	1.05
Federal funds purchased and repurchase agreements	0.15	0.01	0.04	0.17
Other interest expenses	0.40	0.12	0.22	0.43
Net interest income	3.35	3.77	3.83	3.26
Provision for loan losses	0.68	0.29	0.37	0.74
Noninterest (fee) income	2.42	0.97	1.52	2.61
Service charges on deposits	0.42	0.41	0.41	0.42
Other fee income	2.00	0.56	1.11	2.19
Noninterest expense	3.29	3.24	3.33	3.28
Salaries and employee benefits	1.42	1.71	1.63	1.38
Other noninterest expenses	1.87	1.53	1.70	1.90
Net noninterest income	−0.87	−2.27	−1.81	−0.67
Pretax net operating income	1.81	1.21	1.65	1.85
Gains (or losses) on securities not in trading accounts	0.09	0.03	0.03	0.10
Income before taxes	1.90	1.24	1.68	1.95
Income taxes	0.62	0.28	0.47	0.66
Income before extraordinary items	1.27	0.97	1.21	1.29
Extraordinary items, net	−0.00*	−0.00*	−0.01	0.00*
Net income after taxes	1.27	0.97	1.20	1.29

*Less than 0.005 percent.

And, of course:

Funds provided to the financial institution over a specific time period = Funds used by the financial institution during the same time period

While regulatory agencies do not require a Funds-Flow Statement, it can usually be found in the bank or other financial firm's annual report.

Statement of Stockholders' Equity

A second useful supplemental financial report is the *Statement of Stockholders' Equity*. This financial report reveals changes in the all-important capital account, showing how the owners' investment of funds in a financial institution (i.e., their claim on the institution's assets) has changed over time (usually during a recent year). Because stockholders' equity represents a cushion of financial strength for banks and other financial institutions that can be used to absorb losses and protect the depositors and other creditors, changes in a

ETHICS IN BANKING

THE DISTORTIONS CAUSED BY "WINDOW-DRESSING" ACTIVITY AND "CREATIVE ACCOUNTING"

Financial institutions, like other businesses, are notorious for manipulating their financial statements in order to look stronger or more successful in exploiting their market opportunities. "Window-dressing" behavior can occur at any time, but is most common at the end of the fiscal year and at the end of a quarter.

For example, managers may decide they want their institution to look "bigger" in asset or deposit size, giving it an apparent increase in market share. This can be accomplished by simple bookkeeping entries in which two depository institutions, for example, agree to exchange deposits with each other. Total deposits and total assets temporarily increase at each institution as the new deposits are recorded.

Alternatively, management may decide they want their financial firm to look "financially stronger" at year's end. The firm can temporarily sell off some of its riskier assets and purchase high-quality government securities, reversing the transaction after the year-end financial statement is recorded.

Security dealers often engage in a similar practice called "painting the tape," which usually consists of temporarily buying or selling securities that have a relatively thin market and, therefore, tend to be more volatile in price. A few sales or purchases can have a significant impact on price in such a market. Thus, such a transaction may dress up the firm's financial statement at the end of the quarter or fiscal year and may be reversed shortly thereafter. Other financial firms may elect to temporarily sell off some of their worst-performing assets so the shareholders won't complain. Within minutes, the transaction can be undone.

More than just a harmless game, window dressing, painting the tape, or, more commonly, so-called creative accounting can do real harm to investors and to the overall efficiency of the financial marketplace. Activities of this sort work to conceal the true financial condition of the firms involved. Financial decision making may be flawed because investors must work with poor quality information. Regulators like the Securities and Exchange Commission and the Federal Reserve System tend to discourage such activity whenever they find evidence that financial statements contain misleading information.

financial institution's capital account are closely followed by regulators and by its creditors (including large depositors in the case of a bank or thrift institution).

The Financial Statements of Leading Nonbank Financial Firms: A Comparison to Bank Statements

While the balance sheet, income statement, and other financial reports of banks are unique, the financial statements of nonbank firms have, in recent years, come closer and closer to what we normally see on bank statements. This is particularly true of the *nonbank thrift institutions*—including credit unions and savings associations. Like banks, the thrifts' balance sheet is dominated by loans (especially home mortgage loans and consumer installment loans), deposits from customers, and borrowings in the money market. Also paralleling the banking sector, the thrifts' income statements are heavily tilted toward revenue from loans (normally two-thirds or more of annual revenue flows) and by the interest they must pay on deposits and money market borrowings.

As we move away from the thrift group of financial firms into such financial-service industries as finance companies, life and property/casualty insurers, investment companies (mutual funds), and security brokers and dealers, the financial statements include sources and uses of funds unique to the functions of these industries and to their often unusual accounting systems. For example, *finance company* balance sheets, like those of banks, are dominated by loans, but these credit assets are usually labeled "accounts receivable" and include business receivables, consumer receivables, and real estate receivables, reflecting loans made to these customer segments. Moreover, on the sources of funds side, finance company financial statements show heavy reliance, not on deposits for funding, but on

Key URLs

To learn more about commercial bank similarities and differences with their major competitors in the insurance and securities industries, see **www.acli.com**, **www.iii.org**, and **www.ici.org**.

borrowings from the money market (commercial paper), borrowings from banks, and borrowings from parent companies in those cases where a finance company is controlled by a larger firm (e.g., as GMAC is controlled by General Motors).

Life and property/casualty insurance companies also make loans, especially to the business sector. But these usually show up on insurance company balance sheets in the form of holdings of bonds, stocks, mortgages, and other securities, many of which are purchased in the open market. Key sources of funds for insurers include policyholder premium payments to buy insurance protection, returns from investments made, and borrowings in the money and capital markets. Most of the insurance industry's profits come from the investments they make, not policyholder premiums.

Among banks' most potent competitors in recent years, *mutual funds* hold primarily corporate stocks, bonds, asset-backed securities, and money market instruments that are financed principally by their net sales of fund shares to the public and in the form of occasional borrowings. Security dealers and brokers—also a tough bank competitor—tend to hold a similar range of investments in stocks and bonds, financing these acquisitions by borrowings in the money and capital markets and equity capital contributed by their owners. The dealers also generate large amounts of revenue from buying and selling securities for their customers, by charging underwriting commissions to businesses needing assistance with new security offerings, and by assessing customers fees for advice. Increasingly, banks are offering the same services, and their consolidated financial reports look very much like those of these tough nonbank competitors.

Key URLs

The regulatory agencies that oversee banking's closest competitors are the Office of Thrift Supervision at **www.ots.treas.gov** and the National Credit Union Administration at **www.ncua.gov**.

An Overview of Key Features of Financial Statements and Their Consequences

We have explored a substantial number of details about the content of bank financial statements and the comparable statements of some of their closest competitors in this chapter. Table 4–8 provides a useful overview of the key features of bank and closely related institutions' financial statements and their consequences for the managers of banks and similar financial firms.

Concept Check

4–13. What types of information does a Funds-Flow or Sources and Uses of Funds Statement provide?

4–14. What does the Statement of Stockholders' Equity reveal about how well a bank is being managed and what stresses it is under?

4–15. Suppose a bank has an initial balance in its capital account of $26 million, receives net income during the year of $3 million, pays out stockholder dividends of $2 million, and issues $1 million in new

stock during the year. What balance remains in the bank's capital account at the end of the year?

4–16. Who are banking's chief competitors in the financial-services marketplace and how do their financial statements resemble or differ from bank financial statements? Why do these similarities and differences exist? What major trend is changing the content of bank and nonbank financial statements?

Summary

This chapter presents us with an overview of the types and content of bank financial statements, which provide us with vital information that managers, investors, regulators, and other interested parties can use to assess each firm's performance. The reader also is given a glimpse at how selected nonbank financial-service firms' financial statements compare with those issued by banks. Several key points emerge in the course of the chapter:

TABLE 4–8

Features and Consequences of the Financial Statements of Banks and Similar Financial Firms

Key Features of the Financial Statements of Banks and Similar Financial Institutions	Consequences for the Managers of Banks and Similar Financial Institutions
• Heavy dependence on borrowed funds supplied by others (including deposits and nondeposit borrowings); thus, banks and similar financial firms make heavy use of financial leverage (debt) in an effort to boost their stockholders' earnings.	• The earnings and the very existence of banks and similar institutions are exposed to significant risk if those borrowings cannot be repaid when due. Thus, banks and similar institutions must hold a significant proportion of high-quality and readily marketable assets to meet their most pressing debt obligations.
• Most revenues stem from interest and dividends on loans and securities. The largest expense item is often the interest cost of borrowed funds, followed by personnel costs.	• Management must choose loans and investments carefully to avoid a high proportion of earning assets that fail to pay out as planned, damaging expected revenue flows. Because revenues and expenses are sensitive to changing interest rates, management must be competent either at interest-rate forecasting or, more practically, at protecting against losses due to interest-rate movements by using interest-rate hedging techniques.
• The greatest proportion of assets is devoted to financial assets (principally loans and securities). A relatively small proportion of assets is devoted to plant and equipment (fixed assets); thus, banks and similar financial institutions tend to make very limited use of operating leverage in most cases.	• With only limited resources devoted to fixed assets and, therefore, few fixed costs stemming from plant and equipment, banks' and similar financial firms' earnings are less sensitive to fluctuations in sales volume (operating revenues) than those of many other businesses, but this also limits a bank's or similar financial institution's potential earnings. (Banking thus tends to be a moderately profitable industry.)

- The two most important financial statements issued by banks and their closest deposit-type competitors include the balance sheet or Report of Condition and the income and expense statement or Report of Income. Two additional financial statements that can reveal important but somewhat more limited information about financial firms include the Sources and Uses of Funds Statement and the Statement of Stockholders' Equity.

- Bank balance sheets report the value of assets held (usually broken down into such categories as cash assets, investment security holdings, loans, and miscellaneous assets), liabilities outstanding (including deposits and nondeposit borrowings), and capital or stockholders' equity. The values recorded on the balance sheet are measured at a single moment in time (such as the last day of the quarter or year).

- In contrast, the income and expense statement or Report of Income includes key sources of revenue and operating expenses. Revenue sources for banks and closely related firms typically include loan and investment income and revenue from the sale of fee-generating services. Major sources of operating expense include interest payments on deposits and other borrowed funds, employee wages, salaries and benefits, taxes, and miscellaneous expenses.

- A Sources and Uses of Funds (or Funds-Flow Statement) tracks where a bank or similar financial firm raises funds and how it allocates those funds. In contrast, the Statement of Stockholders' Equity describes any changes that may have occurred in the owners' stake in the business and what factors contributed to those changes.

- The financial statements of nonbank financial firms (including thrift institutions, finance companies, life and property/casualty insurers, and security firms) are increasingly coming to resemble bank financial statements and vice versa as these different industries rush toward each other. Among the common features are heavy use of financial leverage (debt) to finance their operations, the dominance of financial assets over real (physical) assets, and the concentration of revenues from making loans and assisting businesses in selling their securities. For most financial firms the key expense is usually interest expense on borrowings, followed by personnel costs.

- By carefully reading the financial statements of banks and their competitors, we learn more about the services these institutions provide and how their financial condition changes with time. These statements, when accurately prepared, provide indispensable information to managers, owners, creditors, and regulators of banks and other financial-service providers. Unfortunately, some financial institutions engage in "window dressing" and other forms of data manipulation, which can send misleading information to their shareholders, creditors, customers, and the regulatory community, sometimes resulting in serious damage.

Key Terms

Report of Condition, *107*   Report of Income, *123*

Problems and Projects

1. Evergreen National Bank has just submitted its Report of Condition and Report of Income to its principal government regulator, the Comptroller of the Currency. Please fill in the missing items from its statement shown below (all figures in millions of dollars):

Report of Condition			
Assets		**Liabilities and Equity Capital**	
Cash and deposits due from banks	?	Noninterest-bearing demand deposits	$107
Investment securities	$ 87	Savings deposits and NOW accounts	?
Trading account securities	6	Money market deposit accounts	49
Federal funds sold	11	Time deposits	227
Loans, gross	?	Deposits at foreign branches	21
Allowance for loan loss	(19)	Total deposits	440
Unearned discount on loss	(6)	Nondeposit borrowings	41
Loans, net	348	Other liabilities	19
Bank premises and equipment	10	Stockholders' equity capital	?
Customers' liability on acceptances	18		
Miscellaneous assets	43		
Total assets	$550	Total liabilities and equity capital	$550

Report of Income

Interest and fees on loans	?	Service charges on customer deposits		?
Interest on investment securities	$ 7	Trust department income		$ 8
Other interest income	5	Other operating income		20
Total interest income	$180	Total noninterest income		39
Total interest expense	$159	Wages, salaries, and employee benefits		?
Net interest income	?	Net occupancy and equipment expense		7
Provision for possible loan losses	4	Other expenses		5
		Total noninterest expenses		54
		Net noninterest income		?

Provision for income taxes   2
Net income (or loss) after taxes   ?

2. If you know the following figures:

Total interest income	$271	Provision for loan losses	$ 13
Total interest expenses	205	Income taxes	5
Total noninterest income	23	Dividends to common stockholders	11
Total noninterest expenses	40		

Please calculate these items:

Net interest income	____	Total operating revenues	____
Net noninterest income	____	Total operating expenses	____
Net income before income taxes	____	Increases in bank's undivided profits	____
Net income after taxes	____		

3. If you know the following figures:

Gross loans	$294	Trading-account securities	$ 2
Allowance for loan losses	13	Federal funds sold	26
Unearned discount on loans	5	Savings deposits	12
Common stock	12	Total liabilities	380
Surplus	19	Preferred stock	3
Total equity capital	49	Nondeposit borrowings	10
Cash and due from banks	9	Time deposits	160
Miscellaneous assets	38	Money market deposits	88
Bank premises and equipment, gross	34	Bank premises and equipment, net	29
		Other real estate owned	4
		Goodwill and other intangibles	3

Please calculate these items:

Total assets	____	Investment securities	____
Net loans	____	Depreciation	____
Undivided profits	____	Total deposits	____

4. To test your understanding of the basic bank financial statements presented in this chapter, consider the account entries listed here in random order. See if you can use these to create a balance sheet and income statement for this bank. All figures are in thousands of dollars. Consider using Excel, or a similar software program, to assist you in constructing the required balance sheet and income statement.

Cash and due from depository institutions	$ 4,261,234
Securities	10,123,678
Other borrowed funds	33,378,779
Premises and equipment expense	$564,398
Service charges on deposit accounts	$507,045
Loan loss allowance	2,098,598
Additional noninterest expense	1,542,675

Trading account assets	504,705
Securities gains (losses)	6,345
Trading account gains and fees	67,021
Additional noninterest income	2,822,620
All other assets	7,936,164
Total interest expense	3,043,563
Applicable income taxes	878,976
Provision for loan and lease losses	681,717
Common stock	300,000
Surplus	5,346,354
Total deposits	79,737,777
Salaries and employee benefits	2,875,181
Fiduciary activities	372,024
Unearned income	9,164
Subordinated debt	2,036,099
All other liabilities	5,543,142
Gross loans and leases	113,541,458
Total interest income	7,207,221
Bank premises and fixed assets	863,791
Perpetual preferred stock	0
Goodwill and other intangibles	1,705,130
Federal funds purchased and repurchase agreements	8,839,291
Trading liabilities	0
Other real estate owned	114,986
Pretax net operating income	2,268,397
Undivided profits	5,666,942
Federal funds sold and reverse repurchase agreements	3,905,000
Extraordinary gains—net	0

5. First National Bank of Irwin reports loan losses and eligible (reservable) total loans over the past five years as shown below. First National currently holds total assets of $465 million. Which method of figuring this bank's deductible loan-loss expense should management use? Why?

	Loan Losses	Total Eligible Loans
Current year	$1.34 million	$279 million
One year ago	$1.19 million	$258 million
Two years ago	$1.08 million	$249 million
Three years ago	$0.85 million	$240 million
Four years ago	$0.71 million	$235 million
Five years ago	$0.59 million	$228 million

Suppose that next year First National of Irwin holds total assets of $507 million. Would this development require a change in its method of expressing loan losses? Please explain. On what basis would management then have to determine the bank's annual loan-loss expense?

6. For each of the following transactions, which items on a bank's statement of income and expenses (Report of Income) would be affected?

a. Office supplies are purchased so the bank will have enough deposit slips and other necessary forms for customer and employee use next week.

b. The bank sets aside funds to be contributed through its monthly payroll to the employee pension plan in the name of all its eligible employees.

c. The bank posts the amount of interest earned on the savings account of one of its customers.

d. Management expects that among a series of real estate loans recently granted the default rate will probably be close to 3 percent.

e. Mr. and Mrs. Harold Jones just purchased a safety deposit box to hold their stock certificates and wills.

f. The bank collects $1 million in interest payments from loans it made earlier this year to Intel Composition Corp.

g. Hal Jones's checking account is charged $30 for two of Hal's checks that were returned for insufficient funds.

h. The bank earns $5 million in interest on the government securities it has held since the middle of last year.

i. The bank has to pay its $5,000 monthly utility bill today to the local electric company.

j. A sale of government securities has just netted the bank a $290,000 capital gain (net of taxes).

7. For each of the transactions described here, which of at least two accounts on a bank's balance sheet (Report of Condition) would be affected by each transaction?

a. Sally Mayfield has just opened a time deposit in the amount of $6,000 and these funds are immediately loaned to Robert Jones to purchase a used car.

b. Arthur Blode deposits his payroll check for $1,000 in the bank and the bank invests the funds in a government security.

c. The bank sells a new issue of common stock for $100,000 to investors living in its community and the proceeds of that sale are spent on the installation of new ATMs.

d. Jane Gavel withdraws her checking account balance of $2,500 from the bank and moves her deposit to a credit union; the bank employs the funds received from Mr. Alan James, who has just paid off his home equity loan, to provide Ms. Gavel with the funds she withdrew.

e. The bank purchases a bulldozer from Ace Manufacturing Company for $750,000 and leases it to Cespan Construction Company.

f. Signet National Bank makes a loan of reserves in the amount of $5 million to Quesan State Bank and the funds are returned the next day.

g. The bank declares its outstanding loan of $1 million to Deprina Corp. to be uncollectible.

8. See if you can construct a simple balance sheet for River's Edge National Bank from the following information (all figures in millions of dollars) for the year-end date just concluded. What item is clearly missing from the above accounts that you need to add in so that the bank's balance sheet will be fully in balance?

Municipal bonds	$12
Time deposits	25
Federal funds sold and securities purchased under repurchase agreements	5
Subordinated notes and debentures	20
Leases of assets to business customers	3
Automobile loans	21
Loans to commercial and industrial firms	64
Demand deposits	55

U.S. Treasury bills	10
Cash	13
Credit card loans	22
Deposits due from other banks	25
Savings deposits	15
Bank building and equipment	7
Money market deposits	31
Federal funds purchased	34
Mortgage against the bank's building	26
Real estate loans	42
Deposits due to other banks	5
Securities sold under repurchase agreements	4

9. See if you can determine the amount of Rosebush State Bank's current net income after taxes from the figures below (stated in millions of dollars) and the amount of its retained earnings from current income that it will be able to reinvest in the bank. (Be sure to arrange all the figures given in correct sequence to derive the bank's Report of Income.)

Effective tax rate of 25%	
Interest and fees on loans	$62
Employee wages, salaries, and benefits	13
Interest and dividends earned on government bonds and notes	9
Provision for loan losses	10
Overhead expenses	3
Service charges paid by depositors	4
Capital gains on securities sold, net of taxes	1
Interest paid on federal funds purchased	6
Payment of dividends of $2 per share on 1 million outstanding shares to be made to common stockholders	
Interest paid to customers holding time and savings deposits	32
Trust department fees	1

10. Which of these account items or entries would normally occur on a bank's balance sheet (Report of Condition) and which on a bank's income and expense statement (Report of Income)?

Federal funds sold	Deposits due to banks
Retained earnings	Leases of business equipment to
Credit card loans	customers
Utility expense	Interest received on credit card loans
Vault cash	Employee benefits
Allowance for loan losses	Savings deposits
Depreciation on bank plant	Provision for loan losses
and equipment	Service charges on deposits
Commercial and industrial loans	Undivided profits
Repayments of credit card loans	Mortgage owed on the bank's
Common stock	buildings
Interest paid on money market deposits	Other real estate owned
Securities gains or losses	

11. Suppose you were informed that a bank's latest income and expense statement contained the following figures:

Net interest income	= $750 million
Net noninterest income	= –$300 million
Net income before income taxes	= $45 million
Net income after taxes	= $20 million
Total operating revenues	= $2,400 million
Total operating expenses	= $2,000 million
Increases in bank's undivided profits	= $10 million

Suppose you also were told that the bank's total interest income is twice as large as its total interest expense and its noninterest income is three-fourths of its noninterest expense. Imagine that its provision for loan losses equals 1 percent of its total interest income, while its taxes generally amount to 25 percent of its net income before income taxes. Finally, suppose the bank routinely pays out 50 percent of the amount of its net income to its common stockholders as dividends. Calculate the following items for this bank's income and expense statement:

Total interest income	_____
Total interest expenses	_____
Total noninterest income	_____
Total noninterest expenses	_____
Provision for loan losses	_____
Income taxes	_____
Dividends paid to common stockholders	_____

12. Why do the financial statements issued by banks and by nonbank financial-service providers look increasingly similar today? Which nonbank financial firms have balance sheets and income statements that closely resemble those of commercial banks (especially community banks)?

13. What principal types of assets and funds sources do nonbank thrifts (including savings banks, savings and loans, and credit unions) draw upon? Where does the bulk of their revenue come from and what are their principal expense items?

14. How are the balance sheets and income statements of finance companies, insurers, and securities firms similar to those of banks, and in what ways are they different? What might explain the differences you observe?

Internet Exercises

1. This exercise involves exploring the data you will find at regulatory sites for bank holding companies (BHCs). The FDIC's website is the source of National City's Report of Condition and Report of Income presented in Tables 4–3 and 4–6. At the FDIC's website we may search under the category of Bank Holding Company to acquire analogous data for all U.S. bank holding companies. The data for bank holding companies found at the FDIC site represent combined amounts for all FDIC-insured bank and thrift subsidiaries, and do *not* reflect nondeposit subsidiaries or parent companies. This indicates that the data provided here is an aggregation of the banking subsidiaries for the BHC being analyzed.

   Go to **www.fdic.gov** and explore the link for Bank Data for Individual Banks. If you go to the Institution Directory, you will be able to "Find a Bank Holding Company,"

"Find an Institution," or "Find an Office." Use "Find a Bank Holding Company" and search for information for December 31, 2002, for Wachovia Corporation. What are the dollar amounts of Total Assets, Total Liabilities, Total Deposits, Net Interest Income, and Net Income?

More comprehensive holding company information can be found at the website for the Federal Reserve System—National Information Center (NIC). Go to **www.ffiec.gov/nic/** and select the link for "Financial and Performance Reports." Again, search for information for December 31, 2002, for Wachovia. What are the dollar amounts of Total Assets, Total Liabilities, Total Deposits (you will need to sum the different types of deposits), Net Interest Income, and Net Income?

You will see that there is more information available at this site, but it is a bit more challenging to sort through. You are interested in the Schedule HC—Consolidated Balance Sheet and Schedule HI—Consolidated Income Statement. Compare and contrast the information found for Wachovia at both websites.

2. This exercise involves exploring the data you will find at regulatory sites for individual banks (institutions). Go to **www.fdic.gov** and explore the link for Bank Data for Individual Banks. If you go to the Institution Directory, you will be able to "Find a Bank Holding Company," "Find an Institution," or "Find an Office." Use "Find a Bank Holding Company" and search for information for December 31, 2002, for Wachovia Bank (you want the bank located in Charlotte, North Carolina). What are the dollar amounts of Total Assets, Total Liabilities, Total Deposits, Net Interest Income, and Net Income?

Another source for bank data is the website for the Federal Reserve System—National Information Center (NIC). Go to **www.ffiec.gov/nic/** and select the link for Financial and Performance Reports. Click on the link for Banks. Once again, search for information for December 31, 2002, for Wachovia Bank. What are the dollar amounts of Total Assets, Total Liabilities, Total Deposits (you will need to sum the different types of deposits), Net Interest Income, and Net Income? You are interested in the Schedule RC—Balance Sheet and Schedule RI—Income Statement. Compare and contrast the information found for Wachovia at both websites.

3. In this exercise, we will further explore the items on the Report of Condition. Go to the FDIC website, **www.fdic.gov**, and pull up the Assets and Liabilities as of December 31, 2002, for Bank of America as described in Internet Exercise 1.

   a. Using the link for Other Real Estate Owned (OREO), identify and describe the dollar composition of this item.

   b. Using the link for Goodwill and Other Intangibles, identify and describe the dollar composition of this item.

4. In this exercise, we will further explore Net Interest Income on the Report of Income. Go to the FDIC website, **www.fdic.gov**, and pull up the annual Income and Expense as of December 31, 2002, for Bank of America as described in Internet Exercise 1.

   a. Using the link for Total Interest Income, identify and describe the dollar composition of this item.

   b. Using the link for Total Interest Expense, identify and describe the dollar composition of this item.

5. In this exercise, we will further explore Noninterest Income and Expenses on the Report of Income. Go to the FDIC website, **www.fdic.gov**, and pull up the annual Income and Expense as of December 31, 2002, for Bank of America as described in Internet Exercise 1.

    a. What components are combined to create the dollar amount of Noninterest Income? You will need to use the links for Trading Account Gains & Fees and Additional Noninterest Income to describe the dollar composition of this item.

    b. What components are combined to create the dollar amount of Noninterest Expense? You will need to use the link for Additional Noninterest Expense to describe the dollar composition of this item.

6. What similarities do you see between the balance sheets and income statements of smaller community banks versus major money-center banks? What are the principal differences? For comparison purposes you may wish to view the most recent financial reports of one or more community banks in your hometown or local area and compare them to the financial reports filed most recently by such industry leaders as Bank One Corporation (**www.bankone.com**) and the Bank of New York (**www.bankofnew york.com**). You can call up community-oriented banks in your local area either by entering their name and city of location or by consulting the Federal Deposit Insurance Corporation's data site accessible through that agency's main website at **www.fdic.gov**.

7. Consulting the websites posted by Atlantic Commercial Credit Corporation (**www.atlanticcommercial.com**), Salomon Smith Barney (at **www.smithbarney.com**), State Farm Insurance Companies (at **www.statefarm.com**) and Wells Fargo Bank (at **www.wellsfargo.com**), what differences do you observe between the financial reports of the finance company Commercial Credit Corporation, the security dealer Salomon Smith Barney, the insurance industry leader State Farm Insurance Companies, and one of the leaders of the domestic U.S. banking industry, Wells Fargo? Are there any important similarities among the financial statements of these different financial-service providers?

STANDARD &POOR'S

S&P Market Insight Challenge

1. Use Standard & Poor's Market Insight website (**www.mhhe.com/edumarketinsight**) for this problem. Becoming familiar with the names and types of banks makes the study of banking a little more interesting. In the S&P Industry Survey on Banking, banks are currently categorized as Diversified Banks, Regional Banks, and Other Companies with Significant Commercial Banking Operations. For up-to-date information concerning the size and profitability of banks, use the industry tab in S&P's Market Insight. The drop-down menu provides subindustry selections of Diversified Banks and Regional Banks. Upon selecting one of these subindustries, you will find a recent S&P Industry Survey on Banking. Download the Banking Survey and view the Comparative Company Analysis at the back. Focus on the most recent year's data and answer the following questions, providing the relevant dollar amounts in each category, that is, Diversified Banks, Regional Banks, and Other Companies with Significant Commercial Banking Operations: (1) Which company has the highest operating revenues? (2) The highest net income? (3) The largest asset total? (4) The most loans? (5) The largest volume of deposits?

2. Use Standard & Poor's Market Insight website (**www.mhhe.com/edumarketinsight**) for this problem. Examine the most recent balance sheets and income statements provided by S&P's Market Insight, Educational Version for a large bank holding company (such as Bank of America or Bank One). (Hint: remember that Table 1–2 in Chapter 1 has a list of leading banking firms with those appearing on Market Insight clearly marked.) Do the same for a leading manufacturing firm or nonfinancial service provider listed on Market Insight (such as Ford Motor Company or United Airlines). How do these bank–nonbank balance sheets and income statements compare to each other? What major differences do you observe and why?

REAL NUMBERS FOR REAL BANKS

Assignment for Chapter 4

YOUR BANK'S FINANCIAL STATEMENTS

In Chapter 4, we focus most heavily on the financial statements for banking companies. As you read this chapter, you progress through a lengthy, yet interesting, discussion of the items found on the Report of Condition (balance sheet) and the Report of Income (income statement). The discussion is applied to National City Corporation's Financial Statements within the chapter, and Tables 4–3 and 4–6 were created using the information from the FDIC's website for Bank Holding Companies to provide the necessary data. For this segment of the project, we will be developing analogous financial statements

(Excel™ Spreadsheet) for your chosen banking company, using them to explore the interrelationships of financial statement items, and developing a comparative analysis.

A. Create an Excel™ Spreadsheet, identical in format to Tables 4–3 and 4–6, for your chosen banking company. This spreadsheet will become known as Spreadsheet One and will be referenced as such in future assignments. Below is the format for the spreadsheet with cell locations identified in parentheses.

Name of Banking Company (A1)		
Report of Condition (A2)		
(A3)	12/31/yy	12/31/yy
Total assets (A4)	$	$
Cash and due from depository institutions (A5)		
Securities (A6)		
Federal funds sold and reverse repurchase agreements (A7)		
Gross loans and leases (A8)		
(less) Loan loss allowance (A9)		
(less) Unearned income (A10)		
Net loans and leases (A11)		
Trading account assets (A12)		
Bank premises and fixed assets (A13)		
Other real estate owned (A14)		
Goodwill and other intangibles (A15)		
All other assets (A16)		
Total liabilities and capital (A18)	$	$
Total liabilities (A19)		
Total deposits (A20)		
Federal funds purchased and repurchase agreements (A21)		
Trading liabilities (A22)		
Other borrowed funds (A23)		
Subordinated debt (A24)		
All other liabilities (A25)		
Total equity capital (A27)		
Perpetual preferred stock (A28)		
Common stock (A29)		
Surplus (A30)		
Undivided profits (A31)		

Report of Income (A33)		
Total interest income (A34)	$	$
Total interest expense (A35)		
Net interest income (A36)		
Provision for loan and lease losses (A37)		
Total noninterest income (A38)		
Fiduciary activities (A39)		
Service charges on deposit accounts (A40)		
Trading account gains and fees (A41)		
Additional noninterest income (A42)		
Total noninterest expense (A43)		
Salaries and employee benefits (A44)		
Premises and equipment expense (A45)		
Additional noninterest expense (A46)		
Pretax net operating income (A47)		
Securities gains (losses) (A48)		
Applicable income taxes (A49)		
Income before extraordinary items (A50)		
Extraordinary gains—net (A51)		
Net income (A52)	$	$

To fill in the dollar amounts, go to **www.fdic.gov** and then explore the link for Bank Data for Individual Banks. If you enter the link labeled Institution Directory, you will be able to "Find a Bank Holding Company," "Find an Institution," or "Find an Office." Use "Find a Bank Holding Company" and search for Information for December 31, yyyy. (Use the two most recent year-end reports.) A pull-down menu allows you to access information from these reports.

For the Report of Condition you will be able to enter most data directly from the Assets and Liabilities report generated at the FDIC website; however, you will have to explore the Net Loans and Leases link to get Gross Loans and Leases and Unearned Income. For the Report of Income, you will find the information you need in Income and Expense.

B. For comparative purposes we want to standardize these reports for size, as in Tables 4–4 and 4–7 in this chapter. In columns D and E report each item as a percentage of total assets. (Excel hint: This can be accomplished very quickly by doing the calculation for Cell D5 (=B5/total assets) and then using the fill handle for that cell (tiny square in the lower left hand corner of D5) to drag the series down the column.) Then write one paragraph describing how the Report of Condition has changed between the two years examined and one paragraph describing changes in the Report of Income.

C. To develop an understanding of the relationships on the Reports of Condition and Income and to double-check for errors, we will use our formula functions to calculate total assets, total liabilities and capital, total liabilities, total equity capital, net interest income, pretax net operating income, income before extraordinary items, and net income. First Step: copy Columns B and C to Columns F and G. Second Step: clear the values in the cells containing total assets (i.e., Cells F4 and G4), total liabilities and capital, total liabilities, total equity capital, net interest income, pretax net operating income, income before extraordinary items, and net income. Then use the formula functions in Excel to create entries for the empty cells. For example, the formula for total liabilities would be =SUM(B20:B25). If the formulas and entries are correct, you will get the same numerical values as in columns B and C and you can be reassured that you are developing an understanding of the financial statements of banks and similar financial firms.

Selected References

See the following for an overview of bank and similar financial firms' financial statements and their components:

1. Carlson, Mark, and Roberto Perli. "Profits and Balance Sheet Developments at U.S. Commercial Banks in 2002." *Federal Reserve Bulletin*, June 2003, pp. 243–270.

2. Cocheo, Steve. "If You Liked FASB 115, You'll Love FASB 114." ABA *Banking Journal*, January 1994, pp. 44–45.

3. Federal Deposit Insurance Corporation. *The Quarterly Banking Profile*. Washington, D.C., Third Quarter 2002.

4. Giroux, Gary A., and Peter S. Rose. *Financial Forecasting in Banking: Methods and Applications*. Ann Arbor, MI: UMI Research Press, 1981.

5. Morris, Charles S., and G. H. Sellon, Jr. "Market Value Accounting for Banks: Pros and Cons." *Economic Review*, Federal Reserve Bank of Kansas City 76, March/April 1991, pp. 5–19.

6. O'Toole, Randy. "Recent Developments in Loan Loss Provisioning at U.S. Commercial Banks." *FRBSF Economic Letter*, Federal Reserve Bank of San Francisco, No. 97-21, July 25, 1997.

7. Rose, Peter S. *Money and Capital Markets*. 8th ed. New York: McGraw-Hill/Irwin, 2002, chap. 4.

8. Shaffer, Sherrill. "Marking Banks to Market." *Business Review*, Federal Reserve Bank of Philadelphia, July/August 1992, pp. 13–22.

9. Walter, John R. "Loan Loss Reserves." *Economic Review*, Federal Reserve Bank of Richmond, July/August 1991, pp. 20–30.

CHAPTER FIVE

Measuring and Evaluating the Performance of Banks and Their Principal Competitors

Key Topics in This Chapter

- Stock Values and Profitability Ratios
- Measuring Credit, Liquidity, and Other Risks
- Measuring Operating Efficiency
- Performance of Competing Financial Firms
- Size and Location Effects
- The UBPR and Comparing Performance

Humorist and poet Ogden Nash once wrote, "Bankers are just like anybody else, except richer." It turns out that statement may or may not be true; a lot depends upon how successful their banks are as performers in the financial marketplace. Indeed, in today's world, bankers and their competitors are under great pressure to *perform* well all the time.

What do we mean by the word *perform* when it comes to banks and other financial-service providers? In this case *performance* refers to how adequately a bank or other financial firm meets the objectives its stockholders (owners), employees, depositors and other creditors, and borrowing customers identify. At the same time, these financial firms must find a way to keep government regulators satisfied that their operating policies, loans, and investments are sound, protecting the public interest. The success or lack of success of these institutions in meeting the expectations of others is usually revealed by a careful and thorough analysis of their financial statements.

Why are bank financial statements (and the financial reports of their principal competitors) under such heavy scrutiny today? One key reason is that banks and similar institutions now depend heavily upon the open market to raise the funds they need, selling stocks, bonds, and short-term IOUs (including deposits). Entry into the open market to raise money means that a bank's financial statements will be gone over "with a fine tooth comb" by stock and bond market investors, credit rating agencies (such as Moody's and Standard & Poor's), regulators, and scores of other people.

This development has placed the management of banks (and many of their competitors) under great pressure to set and meet the institution's performance goals or suffer serious financial and reputational losses. In 2002 J. P. Morgan Chase, the second largest banking company in the United States, became a prominent example. The firm's credit rating came under review and, for a time, it faced rising borrowing costs as major depositors and other creditors reacted negatively to the bank's potential loan losses and adverse publicity from its involvement with Enron Corporation and other troubled companies. Subsequently, J. P. Morgan Chase's position strengthened and improved.

At the same time, as we saw earlier in Chapters 1, 2, and 3, competition for bankers' traditional loan and deposit customers has increased dramatically. Credit unions, money market funds, insurance companies, brokerage firms and security dealers, and even chain stores are fighting for a bigger slice of nearly every credit or deposit market traditionally served by banks. Bankers have been called upon to continually reevaluate their loan and deposit policies, review their plans for growth and expansion, and assess their returns and risk exposure in light of this new competitive environment.

In this chapter we take a detailed look at the most widely used indicators of the quality and quantity of bank performance and at some of the performance indicators used to measure banking's principal competitors. The chapter centers on the most important dimensions of performance—*profitability* and *risk*. After all, banks and other financial institutions are simply businesses organized to maximize the value of the shareholders' wealth invested in the firm at an acceptable level of risk. The objectives of maximum (or at least satisfactory) profitability with a level of risk acceptable to the institution's owners is not easy to achieve, as recent bank and other institutional failures around the globe suggest. Aggressive pursuit of such an objective requires a financial firm to be continually on the lookout for new opportunities for further revenue growth, greater efficiency, and more effective planning and control. The pages that follow examine the most important measures of a bank's rate of return and risk. We also make note of several performance measures applicable to some of banking's toughest competitors.

Evaluating a Bank's Performance

How can we use a bank's financial statements, particularly its Report of Condition (balance sheet) and Report of Income (income statement), to evaluate how well the bank is performing? What do we look at to help decide if a bank is facing serious problems that its management should deal with?

Determining the Bank's Long-Range Objectives

The first step in analyzing any bank's financial statements is to decide what objectives the bank is seeking. Bank performance must be directed toward *specific objectives*. A fair evaluation of any financial firm's performance should start by evaluating whether it has been able to achieve the objectives its management and stockholders have chosen.

Certainly many banks and other financial institutions have their own unique objectives. Some wish to grow faster and achieve some long-range growth objective. Others seem to prefer the quiet life, minimizing risk and conveying the image of a sound institution, but with modest rewards for their shareholders.

Maximizing the Value of the Firm: A Key Objective for Nearly All Financial-Service Institutions

While all of the foregoing goals have something to recommend them, increasingly banks and other financial-service corporations are finding they must pay close attention to the *value of their stock*. Indeed, the basic principles of financial management, as that science is practiced today, suggest strongly that attempting to maximize a financial corporation's stock value is the key objective that should have priority over all others. If the stock fails to rise in value commensurate with stockholder expectations, current investors may seek to unload their shares and the bank or other financial institution will have difficulty raising new capital to support its future growth. Clearly, then, management should pursue the objective of maximizing the value of the financial firm's stock.

Let us focus on commercial banking, the largest of all corporate-dominated financial-service industries. What will cause a bank's stock to *rise* in value? Each institution's stock price is a function of the

$$
\begin{array}{c}
\text{Value of the} \\
\text{bank's stock} \\
(P_0)
\end{array}
=
\frac{
\begin{array}{c}
\text{Expected stream of future} \\
\text{stockholder dividends}
\end{array}
}{
\begin{array}{c}
\text{Discount factor (based on} \\
\text{the minimum required market} \\
\text{rate of return on equity capital} \\
\text{given each bank's} \\
\text{perceived level of risk)}
\end{array}
}
=
\sum_{t=0}^{\infty} \frac{E(D_t)}{(1 + r)^t}
\tag{1}
$$

Key URLs
The most comprehensive sites on the World Wide Web for the financial statements of individual banks and for the industry as a whole are **www.fdic.gov** and **www.ffiec.gov**.

where $E(D_t)$ represents stockholder dividends expected to be paid in future periods, discounted by a minimum acceptable rate of return (r) tied to the bank's perceived level of risk. The minimum acceptable rate of return, r, is sometimes referred to as an institution's *cost of capital* and has two main components: (1) the risk-free rate of interest (often proxied by the current yield on government bonds) and (2) the equity risk premium (which is designed to compensate an investor for accepting the risk of investing in a bank or other corporation's stock rather than in risk-free securities).

The value of the bank's stock will tend to *rise* in any of the following situations:

1. The value of the stream of future stockholder dividends is expected to increase, due perhaps to recent growth in some of the markets served or perhaps because of profitable acquisitions the organization has made.

Concept Check

5–1. Why should banks and other corporate financial firms be concerned about their level of profitability and exposure to risk?

5–2. What individuals or groups are likely to be interested in these dimensions of performance for a bank or other financial institution?

5–3. What factors influence the stock price of a bank or other financial corporation?

5–4. Suppose that a bank is expected to pay an annual dividend of $4 per share on its stock in the current period and dividends are expected to grow 5 percent a year every year, and the minimum required return to equity capital based on the bank's perceived level of risk is 10 percent. Can you estimate the current value of the bank's stock?

Measuring the performance of banks and their competitors has become big business for major corporations and other large-size financial-service customers around the world. Many of these large customers find that their millions of dollars in deposits are not adequately protected by most government-sponsored insurance plans, so they must monitor continuously the condition and performance of the financial firms that hold their money. Moreover, the biggest customers of a bank or other financial firm often need to borrow large amounts of money and want to know if their financial-service provider can supply the credit they need exactly when they need it.

Not surprisingly, then, the search for performance data on banks and their competitors is going on all the time, all around the globe. Where could you go to find this performance data about the banks and other financial firms you trade with?

For example, suppose you want a detailed breakdown by dollar volume and percentages of the composition of the balance sheet of a particular bank. If it happens to be located in the United States, one excellent source is the Federal Deposit Insurance Corporation's website, **www.fdic.gov**. If you know the bank's correct name, headquarters' city and state, or its ID (certificate) number, you can find a great deal of information about its security and loan totals, noncurrent (nonperforming) loans, equity capital, off-balance-sheet commitments, and insider loans.

For performance comparisons you can use the FDIC's Statistics on Depository Institutions (SDI) at **www3.fdic.gov/sdi/main.asp**. At this site you can create peer groups for comparisons using the FDIC's Standard Groups defined by size and/or charter type or develop your own custom peer groups. Another possibility is to compare the bank you might be interested in with industry averages. This can be accomplished by calling up industry statistics on the FDIC's industry websites, **http://www.fdic.gov/bank/analytical/index.html** or **http://www.fdic.gov/bank/statistical/index.html**.

The Uniform Bank Performance Reports (UBPRs), discussed later in this chapter, are among the most complete individual bank financial statements available today. They allow financial analysts not only to carry out detailed studies of how a bank is performing across multiple dimensions of its operations, but also to find causes for any performance variations observed. These UBPR reports are compiled through the cooperation of various federal regulatory agencies and are issued under the sponsorship of the Federal Financial Institutions Examination Council (FFIEC), accessible at **www.ffiec.gov**.

Tracing the performance of nonbank financial institutions that compete with banks is somewhat more difficult than assessing performance in the banking industry. Fortunately, many of the largest nonbank financial firms have their own websites that post their most recent financial statistics—for example, see Merrill Lynch at **www.ml.com** or Washington Mutual Savings Bank at **www.washingtonmutual.com**. Another alternative is to gather individual financial firm information through regulatory agencies and trade associations, such as the Office of Thrift Supervision at **www.ots.treas.gov**, the Securities and Exchange Commission at **www.sec.gov**, and the Insurance information Institute at **www.iii.org**.

2. The banking organization's perceived level of risk falls, due perhaps to an increase in equity capital, a decrease in its loan losses, or the perception of investors that the institution is less risky overall (perhaps because it has further diversified its service offerings and expanded the number of markets it serves) and, therefore, has a lower equity risk premium.

3. Market interest rates decrease, reducing shareholders' acceptable rates of return via the risk-free rate of interest component of all market interest rates.

4. Expected dividend increases are combined with declining risk, as perceived by investors in the bank's stock.

Research evidence over the years has found the stock values of banks and other corporate financial institutions to be especially sensitive to changes in market interest rates, currency exchange rates, and the strength or weakness of the economy that each serves. Clearly, management can work to achieve policies that increase future earnings, reduce risk, or pursue a combination of both actions in order to raise its company's stock price.

The formula for the determinants of a bank or other financial firm's stock price presented in equation (1) above assumes that the stock may pay stockholder dividends of varying amounts over time. However, if the dividends paid to stockholders are expected to grow at a constant rate over time, perhaps reflecting steady growth in earnings, the stock price equation can be greatly simplified into the form

$$P_0 = D_1/(r - g) \tag{2}$$

where D_1 is the expected dividend on stock in period 1, r is the rate of discount reflecting the perceived level of risk attached to investing in the stock, g is the expected constant growth rate at which stock dividends will grow each year, and r must be greater than g.

For example, suppose that a bank is expected to pay a dividend of $5 per share in period 1, dividends are expected to grow by 6 percent a year thereafter, and the appropriate discount rate to reflect shareholder risk is 10 percent. Then the bank's stock price must be valued at

$$P_0 = \$5/(0.10 - 0.06) = \$125 \text{ per share}$$

The two stock-price formulas discussed above assume the bank or other financial-service corporation will pay dividends indefinitely into the future. Most capital-market investors have a limited time horizon, however, and plan to sell the stock at the end of their planned investment horizon. In this case the current value of a bank or nonbank financial corporation's stock is determined from

$$P_0 = \frac{D_1}{(1 + r)^1} + \frac{D_2}{(1 + r)^2} + \cdots + \frac{D_n}{(1 + r)^n} + \frac{P_n}{(1 + r)^n} \tag{3}$$

where we assume the investor will hold the stock for n periods, receiving the stream of dividends $D_1 D_2, \ldots, D_n$, and sell the stock for price P_n at the end of the planned investment horizon. For example, suppose investors expect a bank to pay a $5 dividend at the end of period 1, $10 at the end of period 2, and then plan to sell the stock for a price of $150 per share. If the relevant discount rate to capture risk is 10 percent, the current value of the bank's stock should approach:

$$P_0 = \frac{\$5}{(1 + 0.10)^1} + \frac{\$10}{(1 + 0.10)^2} + \frac{\$150}{(1 + 0.10)^2} = \$136.78 \text{ per share}$$

(A financial calculator can be used to help solve the above equation for stock price per share where N = 2, I/Y = 10, PV = (?), Pmt = 5, FV = 155.)

Profitability Ratios: A Surrogate for Stock Values

While the behavior of a stock's price is, in theory, the best indicator of a firm's performance because it reflects the market's evaluation of that firm, this indicator is often not available for smaller banks, thrifts, and other relatively small financial-service corporations because the stock issued by smaller institutions is frequently not actively traded in international or national markets. This fact forces the financial analyst to fall back on surrogates for market-value indicators in the form of various *profitability ratios*.

E-BANKING AND E-COMMERCE

OUTSOURCING COMPUTER SERVICES MAY LOWER COST AND IMPROVE BANKING PERFORMANCE

As bankers and the managers of other financial firms increasingly recognize that they deal in information and that computers can handle the information side of nearly every service they offer, electronics continue to expand and to take over more and more functions of the banking and financial-services industry. However, this doesn't mean that all electronic equipment and all electronic processing needs to be *inside* the financial firm.

Recently J. P. Morgan Chase, American Express, Bank of America, and other leading financial firms concluded service contracts with such computer leaders as International Business Machines (IBM) and Electronic Data Systems (EDS). These arrangements call for transferring bank data processing to these two computer giants. By outsourcing computer facilities and people, financial-service providers hope to save money and time while improving accuracy. The plan is to save not only on personnel and equipment costs, which should improve earnings performance, but also to avoid "dead time" each week when computer equipment and staff are not being utilized. Thus, banks and other financial firms are basically "renting" IBM and EDS (including their computers, help desks, networks, and software) on an "as needed" basis. As a result, some former bank employees will join computer-company staffs.

Factoid
Contrary to popular opinion, the largest banks in the industry are not always the most profitable. The same is true for the smallest banks. The highest ROAs and ROEs often lie among medium-size institutions.

Key Profitability Ratios   Among the most important ratio measures of **profitability** used today are the following:

$$\text{Return on equity capital (ROE)} = \frac{\text{Net income after taxes}}{\text{Total equity capital}} \tag{4}$$

$$\text{Return on assets (ROA)} = \frac{\text{Net income after taxes}}{\text{Total assets}} \tag{5}$$

$$\text{Net interest margin} = \frac{\begin{array}{c}(\text{Interest income from loans and} \\ \text{security investments} - \text{Interest} \\ \text{expense on deposits and on other} \\ \text{debt issued})\end{array}}{\text{Total assets}^1} \tag{6}$$

$$\text{Net noninterest margin} = \frac{(\text{Noninterest revenues} - \text{Noninterest expenses})}{\text{Total assets}^1} \tag{7}$$

$$\text{Net operating margin} = \frac{(\text{Total operating revenues} - \text{Total operating expenses})}{\text{Total assets}} \tag{8}$$

$$\text{Earnings per share of stock (EPS)} = \frac{\text{Net income after taxes}}{\text{Common equity shares outstanding}} \tag{9}$$

Like all financial ratios, each of these profitability measures varies substantially over time and from market to market.

---

[1] Many authorities prefer to use total *earning assets* in the denominator of the net interest margin and the noninterest margin. Earning assets are those generating interest or fee income, principally the loans and security investments the bank or other financial firm has made. The reasoning is that net interest income as well as net noninterest income should be compared, not to all assets, but rather to those assets—principally loans and security holdings—that account for the majority of all income.

Interpreting Profitability Ratios   Each of the foregoing ratios looks at a slightly different aspect of bank profitability. Thus, return on assets **(ROA)** is primarily an indicator of *managerial efficiency*; it indicates how capably the management of the bank has been converting the institution's assets into net earnings. Return on equity **(ROE),** on the other hand, is a measure of the *rate of return flowing to the bank's shareholders.* It approximates the net benefit that the stockholders have received from investing their capital in the financial firm (i.e., placing their funds at risk in the hope of earning a suitable profit).

The net operating margin, net interest margin, and net noninterest margin are **efficiency** measures as well as profitability measures, indicating how well management and staff have been able to keep the growth of revenues (which come primarily from loans, investments, and service fees) ahead of rising costs (principally the interest on deposits and other borrowings and employee salaries and benefits). The **net interest margin** measures how large a spread between interest revenues and interest costs management has been able to achieve by close control over earning assets and the pursuit of the cheapest sources of funding. The **net noninterest margin,** in contrast, measures the amount of noninterest revenues stemming from deposit service charges and other service fees the financial firm has been able to collect (called fee income) relative to the amount of noninterest costs incurred (including salaries and wages, repair and maintenance costs of facilities, and loan-loss expenses). For most banks, the net noninterest margin is *negative:* Noninterest costs generally outstrip fee income, though fee income has been rising rapidly in recent years as a percentage of all bank revenues.

Another traditional measure of the earnings efficiency with which a bank is managed is called the *earnings spread*, or simply the *spread*, calculated as follows:

$$\frac{\text{Earnings}}{\text{spread}} = \frac{\text{Total interest income}}{\text{Total earning assets}} - \frac{\text{Total interest expense}}{\substack{\text{Total interest-bearing} \\ \text{bank liabilities}}} \qquad \textbf{(10)}$$

Concept Check

5–5. What is return on equity capital and what aspect of bank performance is it supposed to measure? Can you see how this performance measure might be useful to the managers of nonbank financial firms?

5–6. Suppose a bank reports that its net after-tax income for the current year is $51 million, its assets total $1,144 million, and its liabilities amount to $926 million. What is its return on equity capital? Is the ROE you have calculated good or bad? What information do you need to answer this last question?

5–7. What is the return on assets (ROA), and why is it important in banking? Might the ROA measure be important to banking's key competitors?

5–8. A bank estimates that its total revenues from all sources will amount to $155 million and its total expenses (including taxes) will equal $107 million this year. Its liabilities total $4,960 million while its equity capital amounts to $52 million. What is the bank's return on assets? Is this ROA high or low? How could you find out?

5–9. Why do bankers and the managers of competing financial firms often pay close attention today to the net interest margin and noninterest margin? To the earnings spread?

5–10. Suppose a banker tells you that his bank in the year just completed had total interest expenses on all borrowings of $12 million and noninterest expenses of $5 million, while interest income from earning assets totaled $16 million and noninterest revenues totaled $2 million. Suppose further that assets amounted to $480 million, of which earning assets represented 85 percent of that total while total interest-bearing liabilities amounted to 75 percent of the bank's total assets. See if you can determine this bank's net interest and noninterest margins and its earnings base and earnings spread for the most recent year.

The spread measures the effectiveness of a financial firm's intermediation function in borrowing and lending money and also the intensity of competition in the firm's market area. Greater competition tends to squeeze the difference between average asset yields and average liability costs. If other factors are held constant, the spread will decline as competition increases, forcing management to try to find other ways (such as generating fee income from new services) to make up for an eroding earnings spread.

Useful Profitability Formulas for Banks and Other Financial-Service Companies

In analyzing how well any given bank or other financial-service firm is performing, it is often useful to break down some of these profitability ratios into their key components. For example, it is easy to see that ROE and ROA, two of the most popular profitability measures in use today, are closely related. Both use the same numerator: *net income*. Therefore, these two profit indicators can be linked directly:

$$\text{ROE} = \text{ROA} \times \frac{\text{Total assets}}{\text{Total equity capital accounts}} \tag{11}$$

Or, in other words:

$$\frac{\text{Net income after taxes}}{\text{Total equity capital accounts}} = \frac{\text{Net income after taxes}}{\text{Total assets}} \tag{12}$$
$$\times \frac{\text{Total assets}}{\text{Total equity capital accounts}}$$

But we note that net income is equal to total revenues minus operating expenses and taxes. Therefore,

$$\text{ROE} = \frac{\text{Total revenues} - \text{Total operating expenses} - \text{Taxes}}{\text{Total assets}} \times \frac{\text{Total assets}}{\text{Total equity capital accounts}} \tag{13}$$

The relationships in Equations (12) and (13) remind us that the return to a financial firm's shareholders is highly sensitive to how its assets are financed—whether more debt or more owners' capital is used. Even a financial institution with a low ROA can achieve a relatively high ROE through heavy use of debt (leverage) and minimal use of owners' capital.

In fact, the ROE–ROA relationship illustrates quite clearly the fundamental trade-off the managers of banks and other financial-service providers face between risk and return. For example, a bank whose ROA is projected to be about 1 percent this year will need $10 in assets for each $1 in capital to achieve a 10 percent ROE. That is, following Equation (11):

$$\text{ROE} = \text{ROA} \times \frac{\text{Total assets}}{\text{Total equity capital accounts}}$$
$$= \frac{0.01 \times \$10 \times 100}{\$1} = 10 \text{ percent}$$

If, however, the bank's ROA is expected to fall to 0.5 percent, a 10 percent ROE is attainable only if each $1 of capital supports $20 in assets. In other words:

$$\text{ROE} = \frac{0.005 \times \$20 \times 100}{\$1} = 10 \text{ percent}$$

Indeed, we could construct a risk-return trade-off table like the one shown below that would tell us how much leverage (debt relative to equity) must be used to achieve a finan-

Risk-Return Trade-Offs for Return on Assets (ROA) and Return on Equity (ROE)

Ratio of Total Assets to Total Equity Capital Accounts	ROE with an ROA of:			
	0.5%	1.0%	1.5%	2.0%
5:1	2.5%	5.0%	7.5%	10.0%
10:1	5.0%	10.0%	15.0%	20.0%
15:1	7.5%	15.0%	22.5%	30.0%
20:1	10.0%	20.0%	30.0%	40.0%

cial institution's desired rate of return to its stockholders. For example, the trade-off table shown above indicates that a bank with a 5-to-1 assets-to-capital ratio can expect (*a*) a 2.5 percent ROE if ROA is 0.5 percent and (*b*) a 10 percent ROE if ROA is 2 percent. In contrast, with a 20 to 1 assets-to-capital ratio a bank or other financial firm can achieve a 10 percent ROE simply by earning a modest 0.5 percent ROA.

Clearly, as earnings efficiency represented by ROA declines, the firm must take on more risk in the form of higher leverage to have any chance of achieving its desired rate of return to its shareholders (ROE).

Breaking Down Equity Returns for Closer Analysis

Another highly useful profitability formula focusing upon ROE is this one:

$$\text{ROE} = \frac{\text{Net income after taxes}}{\text{Total operating revenue}} \times \frac{\text{Total operating revenue}}{\text{Total assets}} \qquad \textbf{(14)}$$
$$\times \frac{\text{Total assets}}{\text{Total equity capital accounts}}$$

or

$$\text{ROE} = \text{Net profit margin} \times \text{Asset utilization ratio} \times \text{Equity multiplier}$$

where:

$$\text{The bank's } \textbf{net profit margin (NPM)} = \frac{\text{Net income after taxes}}{\text{Total operating revenues}} \qquad \textbf{(15)}$$

$$\text{The bank's degree of } \textbf{asset utilization (AU)} = \frac{\text{Total operating revenues}}{\text{Total assets}} \qquad \textbf{(16)}$$

$$\text{The bank's } \textbf{equity multiplier (EM)} = \frac{\text{Total assets}}{\text{Total equity capital accounts}} \qquad \textbf{(17)}$$

Each component of this simple equation is a telltale indicator of a different aspect of a bank or other financial firm's operations. (See Exhibit 5–1.)

For example:

The net profit margin (NPM)	reflects ⟶	effectiveness of expense management (cost control) and service pricing policies.
The degree of asset utilization (AU)	reflects ⟶	portfolio management policies, especially the mix and yield on assets.
The equity multiplier (EM)	reflects ⟶	leverage or financing policies: the sources chosen to fund the financial institution (debt or equity).

EXHIBIT 5–1 Elements that Determine the Rate of Return Earned on the Stockholders' Investment (ROE) in a Bank or Other Financial Firm

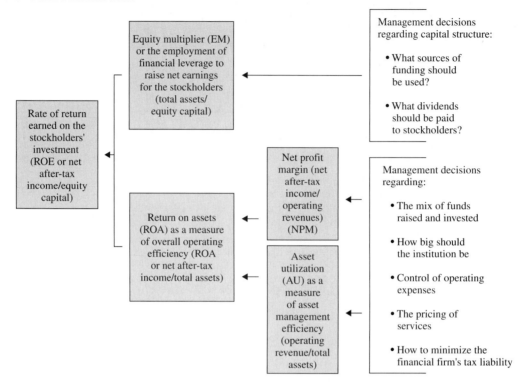

If any of these ratios begins to decline, management needs to pay close attention and assess the reasons behind that change. For example, of these three financial ratios the equity multiplier (EM), or assets to equity ratio, is normally the largest, averaging about 15X or larger for most commercial banks. Bigger banks often operate with multipliers of 20X or more. The multiplier is a direct measure of financial leverage—how many dollars of assets must be supported by each dollar of equity (owners') capital and how much of the financial firm's resources, therefore, must rest on debt. Because equity must absorb losses on assets, the larger the multiplier, the more exposed to failure risk the bank or other financial institution is. However, the larger the multiplier, the greater the potential for high returns for the stockholders.

The net profit margin (NPM), or the ratio of net income to total revenues, is also subject to some degree of management control and direction. It reminds us that banks and other financial-service corporations can increase their earnings and the returns to their stockholders by successfully controlling expenses and maximizing revenues. Similarly, by carefully allocating assets to the highest-yielding loans and investments while avoiding excessive risk, management can raise the average yield on assets (AU, or asset utilization).

An interesting case in point is the recent track record of average ROE for all U.S. insured commercial banks between 1991 and 2003, shown in Table 5–1. Careful perusal of the figures in that table reveals that the ROE for all U.S. insured banks began the period with one of the lowest equity returns in U.S. history, when ROE dropped well below 10 percent, due almost entirely to an unusually low profit margin. U.S. banks were finding their earnings squeezed by rising expenses, and this problem was exacerbated by large deductions from current revenues to cover heavy loan losses. At about the same time, the U.S. economy was mired in a "double dip" recession, which stifled revenues and loan demand. However, banking industry earnings as measured by ROE roared back as the U.S.

TABLE 5–1

Components of
Return on Equity
(ROE) for All
FDIC-Insured U.S.
Commercial Banks
(1991–2003)

Source: Federal Deposit
Insurance Corporation.

Year	Return on Equity Capital (ROE)	=	Net Profit Margin (NPM) (Net After-Tax Income/Total Revenues)	×	Asset Utilization (AU) (Total Revenues/ Total Assets)	×	Equity Multiplier (EM) (Total Assets/ Total Equity Capital)
2003*	14.85%	=	19.47%	×	7.01%	×	10.87×
2002	14.51	=	17.03	×	7.48	×	11.40×
2000	14.48	=	12.20	×	9.32	×	12.74×
1999	15.31	=	14.01	×	8.91	×	11.95×
1997	11.94	=	13.32	×	8.86	×	11.94×
1995	14.19	=	12.68	×	8.93	×	12.53×
1993	15.13	=	13.47	×	8.87	×	12.66×
1991	8.00	=	5.32	×	10.17	×	14.77×

*Figures for 2003 are for first quarter only and include both FDIC-insured banks and thrift institutions.

economy recovered in the mid-1990s and began what turned out to be the longest continuous (recession free) economic expansion in American history. Returns to U.S. bank stockholders (ROE) ultimately soared to new heights before leveling out over the 2000–2003 period as the economy slowed.

What caused such a dramatic earnings turnaround in the decade of the 1990s? Table 5–1 shows clearly the primary cause—the banking industry's net profit margin (NPM) surged upward (particularly noninterest revenues, or fee income), expanding significantly faster than operating expenses. So powerful was the rise in U.S. banking's net profit margin (NPM), basking in the sunshine of a growing economy for most of the 1991–2003 period as well as enjoying the benefits of tough industry cost-cutting moves, that banking's expanding net profit margin more than offset decreases in the industry's asset utilization (AU) ratio and in its equity multiplier (EM).

Why did these latter two ratios decline? The industry's asset utilization (AU), or average yield on assets, ratio fell because market interest rates fell and stayed low most of the time. Almost simultaneously, banking's equity multiplier, the ratio of its total assets to its equity capital, declined primarily because industry regulators demanded that banks use more equity capital and less debt to finance the acquisition of their assets in hopes of protecting depositors and the government's deposit insurance reserves. At the same time banks managed to slow their asset growth on the balance sheet by making much heavier use of off-balance-sheet transactions (as we saw in Chapter 4) and by getting more of their revenues from sales of fee-generating services rather than from booking new assets.

A slight variation on this simple ROE model produces an efficiency equation useful for diagnosing problems in four different areas in the management of banks and competing financial-service firms:

$$\text{ROE} = \frac{\text{Net income after taxes}}{\text{Net income before taxes and securities gains (or losses)}} \times \frac{\text{Net income before taxes and securities gains (or losses)}}{\text{Total operating revenue}} \quad \textbf{(18)}$$

$$\times \frac{\text{Total operating revenue}}{\text{Total assets}} \times \frac{\text{Total assets}}{\text{Total equity capital accounts}}$$

ETHICS IN BANKING

QUESTIONABLE ACCOUNTING PRACTICES CAN TURN BANK PERFORMANCE SOUR

In 2001 Superior Bank of Chicago—a federal savings bank—failed and was taken over by the Federal Deposit Insurance Corporation (FDIC). This failed banking firm provides a classic example of how misleading accounting practices that inflate asset values and revenues and deflate liabilities and expenses can hurt a bank's performance and ultimately bring it down.

In 2002 the FDIC, acting as receiver and liquidator of the assets of Superior Bank, filed suit against the public accounting firm of Ernst and Young LLP, claiming that the firm's auditors detected flawed accounting practices at the bank, but did not report their findings to the regulatory agencies until months later. Allegedly, this delay on the part of the outside auditors prevented regulators from acting quickly to minimize losses to the government's insurance fund.

Ernst and Young allegedly had both an auditor–client and a consultant–client relationship with Superior. The FDIC charged that this dual relationship compromised the auditors' judgment and discouraged them from "blowing the whistle" on the bank's accounting problems. The delay in reporting overvaluation of the bank's mortgage-related assets allegedly caused the FDIC's loss to eventually balloon to about three-quarters of a billion dollars. Federal law, the Sarbanes-Oxley Accounting Standards Act of 2002, now restricts combined auditing and consulting relationships in order to promote auditor objectivity and independence. However, that law was passed after the Superior Bank failure occurred.

In short, strong performance on the part of financial-service providers depends on honest reporting that fairly values current and expected revenues, operating costs, assets, and liabilities so that both insiders and outsiders get a clear picture of how well a financial firm is performing and where it seems to be headed.

Source: Federal Deposit Insurance Corporation.

or:

$$\text{ROE} = \underset{\text{efficiency}}{\overset{\text{Tax}}{\text{management}}} \times \underset{\text{efficiency}}{\overset{\text{Expense}}{\text{control}}} \times \underset{\text{efficiency}}{\overset{\text{Asset}}{\text{management}}} \times \underset{\text{efficiency}}{\overset{\text{Funds}}{\text{management}}} \qquad (19)$$

In this case we have merely split the net profit margin (NPM) into two parts: (1) a tax-management efficiency ratio, reflecting the use of security gains or losses and other tax-management tools (such as buying tax-exempt bonds) to minimize tax exposure, and (2) the ratio of before-tax income to total revenue as an indicator of how many dollars of revenue survive after operating expenses are removed—a measure of operating efficiency and expense control. For example, suppose a commercial bank's Report of Condition and Report of Income show the following figures:

$$\text{Net income after taxes} = \$1.0 \text{ million}$$
$$\text{Net income before taxes and securities gains (or losses)} = \$1.3 \text{ million}$$
$$\text{Total operating revenue} = \$39.3 \text{ million}$$
$$\text{Total assets} = \$122.0 \text{ million}$$
$$\text{Total equity capital accounts} = \$7.3 \text{ million}$$

Its ROE must be

$$\text{ROE} = \frac{\$1.0 \text{ mil}}{\$1.3 \text{ mil}} \times \frac{\$1.3 \text{ mil}}{\$39.3 \text{ mil}} \times \frac{\$39.3 \text{ mil}}{\$122.0 \text{ mil}} \times \frac{\$122.0 \text{ mil}}{\$7.3 \text{ mil}}$$

$$\text{ROE} = 0.769 \times 0.033 \times 0.322 \times 16.71 = 0.137, \text{ or } 13.7 \text{ percent}$$

Clearly, when any one of these four ratios begins to drop, management needs to reevaluate the financial firm's efficiency in that area. In the banking example shown above, if the ratio of after-tax net income to income before securities gains or losses falls from 0.769 to 0.610 next year, management will want to look closely at how well the bank's tax exposure is being monitored and controlled. If after-tax net income before special transactions to operating revenue drops from 0.033 to 0.025 in the coming year, the bank's effectiveness in controlling operating expenses needs to be reviewed. And if the ratio of operating revenues to assets plummets from 0.322 to 0.270, a careful reexamination of asset portfolio policies is warranted to see if the decline in asset yields is due to factors within management's control.

Breakdown Analysis of the Return on Assets

We can also divide a financial firm's return on assets (ROA) into its component parts, as shown in Table 5–2. Actually, ROA is based on three simple component ratios:

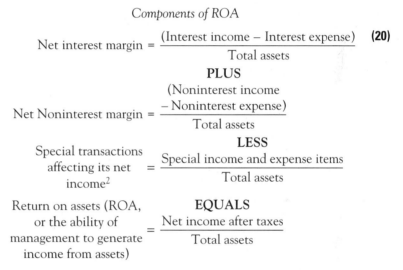

$$\text{Components of ROA}$$

$$\text{Net interest margin} = \frac{(\text{Interest income} - \text{Interest expense})}{\text{Total assets}} \quad \textbf{(20)}$$

$$\textbf{PLUS}$$

$$\text{Net Noninterest margin} = \frac{(\text{Noninterest income} - \text{Noninterest expense})}{\text{Total assets}}$$

$$\textbf{LESS}$$

$$\text{Special transactions affecting its net income}^2 = \frac{\text{Special income and expense items}}{\text{Total assets}}$$

$$\textbf{EQUALS}$$

$$\text{Return on assets (ROA, or the ability of management to generate income from assets)} = \frac{\text{Net income after taxes}}{\text{Total assets}}$$

Such a breakdown of the components of return on assets (ROA) can be very helpful in explaining some of the recent changes that banks and other financial-service providers have experienced in their financial position. For example, as shown in Table 5–3, the average ROA for all U.S. insured commercial banks between 1991 and 2003 rose from about 0.5 percent at the beginning of this decade—among the lowest asset returns in U.S. banking history—to record levels as the 1990s drew to a close and the 21st century opened.

Why did this dramatic rise in ROA occur for most of the 1991–2003 period? As Table 5–3 reveals, early in the period the banking industry struggled with heavy loan losses, increasing the provision for loan-loss expense to almost unprecedented levels. Yet, remarkably, the ROA measure of bank profitability recovered dramatically as the period unfolded. Better control over expenses, led by advances in automation and mergers that

---

2 The special income and expense items include provision for loan losses, taxes, securities gains or losses, and extraordinary income or losses.

TABLE 5–2
Calculating Return on Assets (ROA)

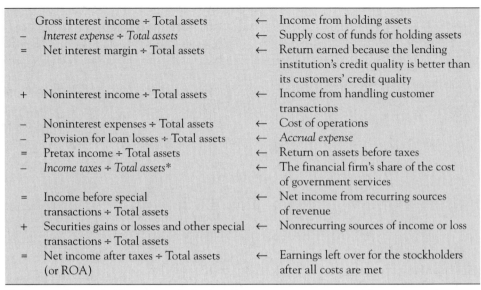

	Gross interest income ÷ Total assets	← Income from holding assets
−	*Interest expense ÷ Total assets*	← Supply cost of funds for holding assets
=	Net interest margin ÷ Total assets	← Return earned because the lending institution's credit quality is better than its customers' credit quality
+	Noninterest income ÷ Total assets	← Income from handling customer transactions
−	Noninterest expenses ÷ Total assets	← Cost of operations
−	Provision for loan losses ÷ Total assets	← *Accrual expense*
=	Pretax income ÷ Total assets	← Return on assets before taxes
−	*Income taxes ÷ Total assets**	← The financial firm's share of the cost of government services
=	Income before special transactions ÷ Total assets	← Net income from recurring sources of revenue
+	Securities gains or losses and other special transactions ÷ Total assets	← Nonrecurring sources of income or loss
=	Net income after taxes ÷ Total assets (or ROA)	← Earnings left over for the stockholders after all costs are met

*Both income and taxes applicable to income need to be adjusted for any tax-exempt earnings received. One can restate such income on a fully tax-equivalent basis by multiplying the amount of tax-exempt income by the expression $1 + (1 - t)$ where t is the firm's tax bracket rate.

eliminated many overlapping facilities, along with an expanding economy, which propelled upward the public's demand for financial services, resulted in a rapid expansion of fee (noninterest) income and loan revenues. All this occurred in the face of falling market interest rates, which lowered banking's ratio of gross interest income to total assets and reduced its net interest margin. The decline in banks' net interest earnings was more than made up for, however, by dramatic increases in their fee (noninterest) income and improved loan quality as reflected in somewhat smaller loan-loss expenses. By 1999 the industry's ROA, averaging 1.25 percent, represented the biggest average rate of return on bank assets since the FDIC began its operations in 1934, only to be topped again in 2003 when U.S. banking's ROA climbed over 1.30 percent.

However, between these interludes of record earnings, U.S. bank profitability fell back slightly during the years 2000 and 2001. This slight pause in the upward earnings trend reflected a business recession as the 21st century began. Thousands of jobs were eliminated and many businesses stopped investing in new plant and equipment. The downturn in the economy lowered the public's demand for financial services, and the revenues of banks and many of their financial-service competitors fell or grew more slowly. At the same time, many business and consumer loans went sour, forcing banks to increase their loan-loss reserves, which put a drag on industry profitability. Several leading banks (including Wachovia of Winston-Salem, North Carolina, J.P. Morgan Chase in New York, and Bank of America in Charlotte, North Carolina) announced sharp cuts in their payrolls as several thousand workers were scheduled to be laid off. Still the banking industry continued to provide employment for close to 1.5 million people in the United States alone.

TABLE 5–3 Components of Return on Assets (ROA) for All Insured U.S. Commercial Banks (1991–2003)

Source: Federal Deposit Insurance Corporation.

Income Statement Items	2003*	2002*	2001	2000	1999	1997	1995	1993	1991
Interest income/Total assets	4.78%	5.06%	6.13%	6.86%	6.41%	6.77%	7.02%	6.62%	8.59%
− Interest expense/Total assets	−1.53	−1.71	−2.86	−3.59	−3.05	−3.29	−3.44	−2.85	−4.98
= Net interest income/Total assets	3.25	3.35	3.27	3.27	3.35	3.48	3.58	3.77	3.61
+ Noninterest income/Total assets	2.23	2.42	2.39	2.46	2.52	2.08	1.91	2.02	1.81
− Noninterest expense/Total assets	−3.13	−3.29	−3.38	−3.46	−3.56	−3.39	−3.47	−3.77	−3.74
= Net noninterest income/Total assets	−0.90	−0.87	−0.99	−1.00	−1.04	−1.31	−1.56	−1.75	−1.93
− Provision for loan losses/Total assets	−0.48	−0.68	−0.66	−0.48	−0.38	−0.40	−0.29	−0.45	−1.02
= Pretax operating income/Total assets	1.87	1.81	1.62	1.79	1.25	1.78	1.73	1.57	0.66
− Taxes paid/Total assets	−0.68	−0.62	−0.56	−0.61	−0.69	−0.64	−0.62	−0.54	−0.25
+ Security gains or losses/Total assets	+0.17	+0.09	+0.07	−0.04	+0.00**	+0.04	+0.01	+0.14	+0.11
= Net after-tax income/Total assets	1.36	1.27	1.13	1.14	1.25	1.18	1.13	1.17	0.52

Notes: Figures may not add exactly to totals due to rounding and the exclusion of extraordinary items. *2003 figures are for first quarter of year only and include both FDIC-insured banks and thrifts. **Less than 0.05 percent.

Concept Check

5–11. What are the principal components of ROE and what does each of these components measure?

5–12. Suppose a bank has an ROA of 0.80 percent and an equity multiplier of 12×. What is its ROE? Suppose this bank's ROA falls to 0.60 percent. What size equity multiplier must it have to hold its ROE unchanged?

5–13. Suppose a bank reports net income after taxes of $12, pretax net income of $15, operating revenues of $100, assets of $600, and $50 in equity capital. What is the bank's ROE? Tax-management effi-

ciency indicator? Expense control efficiency indicator? Asset management efficiency indicator? Funds management efficiency indicator?

5–14. What are the most important components of ROA and what aspects of a financial institution's performance do they reflect?

5–15. If a bank has a net interest margin of 2.50%, a non-interest margin of –1.85%, and a ratio of provision for loan losses, taxes, security gains, and extraordinary items of –0.47%, what is its ROA?

Factoid
Which banks in the industry tend to have the biggest net interest margins between their interest income from loans and securities and the interest cost of borrowed funds?
Answer: The smallest banks do.

What a Breakdown of Profitability Measures Can Tell Us

Clearly, breaking down profitability measures into their respective components tells us much about the causes of earnings difficulties and suggests where management needs to look for possible cures for any earnings problems that do surface. The foregoing analysis reminds us that achieving superior profitability for a financial institution depends upon several crucial factors:

1. Careful use of financial leverage (or the proportion of assets financed by debt as opposed to equity capital).
2. Careful use of operating leverage from fixed assets (or the proportion of fixed-cost inputs used to boost operating earnings as output grows).
3. Careful control of operating expenses so that more dollars of sales revenue become net income.
4. Careful management of the asset portfolio to meet liquidity needs while seeking the highest returns from any assets acquired.
5. Careful control of exposure to risk so that losses don't overwhelm income and equity capital.

Measuring Risk in Banking and Financial Services[3]

Risk to a banker or to the manager of a nonbank financial institution means the perceived uncertainty associated with a particular event. For example, will the customer renew his or her loan? Will deposits and other sources of funds grow next month? Will the financial firm's stock price rise and its earnings increase? Are interest rates going to rise or fall next week, and will a bank or other financial institution lose income or value if they do?

Bankers, for example, may be interested in achieving high stock values and high profitability, but none can fail to pay attention to the risks they are accepting as well. A volatile economy and recent problems with loans have led bankers in recent years to focus increased attention on how risk can be measured and kept under control. Bankers and the managers of other financial institutions are concerned with six main types of risk:

1. Credit risk
2. Liquidity risk
3. Market risk
4. Interest rate risk
5. Earnings risk
6. Capital risk

Each of these forms of risk can threaten a bank's solvency and long-run survival.

[3] This section is based, in part, on Peter S. Rose's 1987 article in the *Canadian Banker* [6] and is used with permission.

HOW TOP-EARNING BANKS GET THAT WAY

A large number of research studies over the years have examined the top-earning firms in the banking industry in an effort to answer a simple question: *What distinguishes a bank with above-average profitability from banks that are only average performers?* How did top-earning banks get that way?

Bank size is clearly one factor. The top-earning banks in the industry, at least as measured by their ROA and ROE, are often medium-size or larger institutions (for example, in 2003 those with over $10 billion in assets) that seem to benefit from lower overall operating costs and greater operating efficiency.

Expense control stands out as the most important discriminator between top performers and the also-rans. For example, high-profit banks manage their operating expenses better, generally posting lower average interest costs, and especially lower personnel expenses and overhead. Their ratios of operating expenses to operating revenues tend to be significantly below the expense-to-revenue ratios of low-profit institutions.

The *deposit structure* of banks also appears to influence their profit performance. Top-earning banks often hold more demand deposits than other banks; these checkable deposits pay little or no interest and carry customer service fees that help bring in more revenues. Relatedly, many highly profitable banks hold a large volume of *core deposits*—smaller denomination deposits from individuals and small businesses that pay low interest rates and are more loyal to the bank than larger deposit accounts.

Employee productivity tends to be higher among top earners. For example, banks with the best profits seem to generate and manage more assets and income per employee and often pay their more productive employees higher salaries.

Leverage (lower equity capital and greater use of debt) also emerges as a profit motivator. Top-earning banks, for example, generally economize on using high-cost owners' capital and rely on the earnings-leveraging effects of cheaper short- and long-term debt.

The *expansion of fee income* has become a key element in bank strategies to increase profits in recent years. Government deregulation has put added pressure on banks and competing financial institutions to charge fees for many formerly "free" services and to develop new fee-generating services, such as offering security management and underwriting services.

Growth in assets, deposits, and loans seems to play a role because top-earning banks seem to grow faster than average, possibly reflecting the presence of more aggressive management or greater customer acceptance of their services. However, growth should not become a substitute for profits. Top-earning banks seem to recognize that growth can be overdone, resulting in uncontrolled expansion that increases operating expenses faster than revenues. Moderate growth is usually a better route to high profits.

For further information on the characteristics and features of high-profit banks see especially Robert E. Goudreau, "FYI—Commercial Bank Profitability Rises as Interest Margins and Securities Sales Increase," *Economic Review,* Federal Reserve Bank of Atlanta, May–June 1992, pp. 33–52; and William F. Bassett and Egon Zakrajsek, "Profits and Balance Sheet Developments at U.S. Commercial Banks in 2000," *Federal Reserve Bulletin,* June 2002, pp. 243–270.

Credit Risk　　The probability that some of a financial institution's assets, especially its loans, will decline in value and perhaps become worthless is known as **credit risk.** Because banks, for example, hold little owners' capital relative to the aggregate value of their assets, only a relatively small percentage of total loans needs to turn bad to push any bank to the brink of failure. The following are four of the most widely used indicators of credit risk:

- The ratio of nonperforming assets to total loans and leases.
- The ratio of net charge-offs of loans to total loans and leases.
- The ratio of the annual provision for loan losses to total loans and leases or to equity capital.
- The ratio of allowance for loan losses to total loans and leases or to equity capital.
- The ratio of nonperforming assets to equity capital.

Nonperforming assets are income-generating assets, including loans, that are past due for 90 days or more. *Charge-offs,* on the other hand, are loans that have been declared worthless and written off the lender's books. If some of these loans ultimately generate income for the lender, the amounts recovered are deducted from gross charge-offs to yield net charge-offs. As both of the above ratios rise, exposure to credit risk grows, and failure of a bank or other lending institution may be just around the corner. The final two credit risk indicator ratios reveal the extent to which a bank or other lender is preparing for loan losses by building up its loan-loss reserves (the allowance for loan losses) through annual charges against current income (the provision for loan losses).

Another popular and long-standing credit risk measure, especially for banks and thrift institutions, is

- The ratio of total loans to total deposits.

As this ratio grows, examiners representing the regulatory community may become more concerned because loans are usually among the riskiest of all assets for banks and other depository institutions, and, therefore, deposits must be carefully protected. A rise in bad loans or declining market values of otherwise good loans relative to the amount of deposits creates greater depositor risk.

Liquidity Risk   Bankers and other financial-firm managers are also concerned about the danger of not having sufficient cash and borrowing capacity to meet customer withdrawals, loan demand, and other cash needs. Faced with **liquidity risk** a financial institution may be forced to borrow emergency funds at excessive cost to cover its immediate cash needs, reducing its earnings. Very few financial firms ever actually run out of cash because of the ease with which liquid funds can be borrowed from other banks. In fact, so rare is such an event that when a small Montana bank in the early 1980s had to refuse to cash checks for a few hours due to a temporary "cash-out," there was a federal investigation of the incident!

Somewhat more common is a shortage of liquidity due to unexpectedly heavy deposit withdrawals, which forces a bank or other depository institution to borrow funds at an elevated interest rate, higher than the interest rates other institutions are paying for similar borrowings. For example, significant decline in its liquidity position often forces a bank to pay higher interest rates to attract negotiable money market CDs, which are sold in million-dollar units and therefore are largely unprotected by deposit insurance. One useful measure of liquidity risk exposure is the ratio of

- Purchased funds (including Eurodollars, federal funds, security RPs, large CDs, and commercial paper) to total assets.

Heavier use of purchased funds increases the chances of a liquidity crunch in the event deposit withdrawals rise or loan quality declines. Other indicators of exposure to liquidity risk include the ratios of

- Cash and due-from balances held at other depository institutions to total assets.
- Cash assets and government securities to total assets.

Cash assets include vault cash held on the financial firm's premises, deposits held at the Federal Reserve bank in the region, deposits held with other depository institutions to compensate them for clearing checks and other interbank services, and cash items in the process of collection (mainly uncollected checks). Standard remedies for reducing a financial institution's exposure to liquidity risk include increasing the proportion of funds committed to cash and readily marketable assets, such as government securities, or using longer-term liabilities to fund the institution's operations.

Market Risk   In market-oriented economies, where most of the world's banks and other leading financial institutions offer their services today, the market values of assets, liabilities, and net worth of banks and other financial-service providers are constantly in a state of flux, creating **market risk.** Changes in market interest rates and currency prices, shifting public demands for bank services and the services offered by nonbank financial firms, sudden alterations in central bank monetary policies, and changing investor perceptions of the riskiness of banks and nonbank financial firms cause the value of institutional assets, liabilities, and equity to move up or down frequently, depending on the direction financial winds are blowing. Especially sensitive to these market-value movements are bond portfolios and stockholders' equity (net worth), which can dive suddenly as market prices move against a bank or other financial firm.

Among the most important indicators of market risk in banking and financial institutions' management are

- The ratio of book-value assets to the estimated market value of those same assets.
- The ratio of book-value equity capital to the market value of equity capital.
- The market value of bonds and other fixed-income assets held relative to their value as recorded on a bank or other financial institution's books.
- The market value of common and preferred stock per share, reflecting investor perceptions of a bank's or other financial institution's risk exposure and earnings potential.

Interest Rate Risk   Movements in market interest rates can also have potent effects on the margin of revenues over costs for both banks and their competitors. For example, rising interest rates can lower a bank's margin of profit if the structure of the institution's assets and liabilities is such that interest expenses on borrowed money increase more rapidly than interest revenues on loans and security investments. However, if a bank or other financial firm has an excess of flexible-rate assets over flexible-rate liabilities, falling interest rates will erode its profit margin. In this case, asset revenues will drop faster than borrowing costs.

The impact of changing interest rates on a bank's or other financial institution's margin of profit is usually called **interest rate risk.** Among the most widely used measures of interest-rate risk exposure are these:

- The ratio of interest-sensitive assets to interest-sensitive liabilities: when interest-sensitive assets exceed interest-sensitive liabilities in a particular maturity range, a financial firm is vulnerable to losses from falling interest rates. In contrast, when rate-sensitive liabilities exceed rate-sensitive assets, losses are likely to be incurred if market interest rates rise.
- For a depository institution, the ratio of uninsured deposits to total deposits, where uninsured deposits are usually government and corporate deposits that exceed the amount covered by insurance and are usually so highly sensitive to changing interest rates that they will be withdrawn if yields offered by competitors rise even slightly higher.

With more volatile market interest rates in recent years, bankers and their competitors have developed several new ways to defend their earnings margins against interest-rate changes, including interest-rate swaps, options, and financial futures contracts. We will examine these and other risk-management tools in Chapters 6, 7, and 8.

Earnings Risk   The risk to a financial institution's bottom line—its net income after all expenses are covered—is known as **earnings risk.** Earnings may decline unexpectedly due to factors inside the financial firm or due to external factors, such as changes in economic conditions or in laws and regulations. For example, recent increases in banking competition have tended to narrow the spread between earnings on a bank's assets and the cost of raising bank funds. Thus, a bank's stockholders always face the possibility of a

FINDING UNIQUE WAYS TO IMPROVE BANK PERFORMANCE

Bankers often find unique ways to improve their performance, especially in periods when earnings are weak. One of the more popular "rabbit out of the hat" techniques some banks and other financial-service companies use centers on selling property that they hold—for example, property that a bank acquired when a borrower defaults on a loan or even selling some of the bank's offices! This latter step has often been used after periods of significant inflation when office space frequently sells for relatively high prices, enabling the seller to reap substantial capital gains.

A classic example occurred in New York City where, in 2002, Citigroup Inc., the largest bank holding company in the United States, announced that it had sold its headquarters to a Boston-based real estate investment trust (REIT). The buyer paid the bank in excess of $600 per square foot for the building. Citigroup recorded a gain of more than $300 million after taxes from the sale, boosting its earnings by more than 20 percent. Sales of offices as a performance-enhancer may become more common in the future in order to reduce overhead costs and replace brick-and-mortar service facilities with electronic networks.

decline in their earnings per share of stock, which would cause the value of the bank's stock to fall, eroding its resources for future growth.

Among the more popular measures of earnings risk are the following:

- Standard deviation (σ) or variance (σ^2) of after-tax net income.
- Standard deviation or variance of the return on equity (ROE) and return on assets (ROA).

The higher the standard deviation or variance of a bank's or other financial institution's income, the more risky the institution's earnings picture is. For example, if investors in the bank's securities expect higher earnings risk to persist into the future, they will seek compensation for that added risk in the form of higher yields from the bank or go elsewhere with their money.

Capital Risk Bankers and their competitors must be directly concerned about risks to their institutions' long-run survival, often called **capital risk.** For example, if a bank takes on an excessive number of bad loans or if a large portion of its security portfolio declines in market value, generating serious capital losses when sold, then its equity capital account, which is designed to absorb such losses, may be overwhelmed. If investors and depositors become aware of the problem and begin to withdraw their funds, regulators may have no choice but to declare the institution insolvent and close its doors.

The failure of a bank or other financial-service corporation may leave its stockholders with none of the capital funds they committed to the institution. For example, in the case of banks and thrift institutions, depositors not covered by insurance also risk losing a substantial portion of their funds. For this reason, the prices and yields on bank capital stock and on large uninsured deposits can serve as an early warning sign of bank solvency problems. When investors believe that a bank or other financial firm has an increased chance of failing, the market value of its capital stock usually begins to fall and it must post higher interest rates on its borrowings in order to attract needed funds. Economists call this phenomenon *market discipline:* interest rates and security prices in the financial marketplace move against the troubled firm, forcing it to make crucial adjustments in policies

Filmtoid
What 2000 film stars
Paul Newman as an
incarcerated bank
robber who had stolen
millions from the banks
to which he sold and
installed security
systems and then
returned to rob them?
Answer: *Where the
Money Is.*

and performance in order to calm investors' worst fears.[4] This suggests that default or failure risk can be measured approximately by such factors as

- The interest rate spread between market yields on debt issues (such as capital notes and CDs issued by banks and thrifts) and the market yields on government securities of the same maturity. An increase in that spread indicates that investors in the market expect increased risk of loss from purchasing and holding the financial institution's debt.
- The ratio of stock price per share to annual earnings per share. This ratio often falls if investors come to believe that a bank or other financial firm is undercapitalized relative to the risks it has taken on.
- The ratio of equity capital (net worth) to total assets, where a decline in equity funding relative to assets may indicate increased risk exposure for shareholders and debtholders.
- The ratio of purchased funds to total liabilities. For example, bank purchased funds usually include uninsured deposits and borrowings in the money market from other banks, corporations, and governmental units that fall due within one year.
- The ratio of equity capital to risk assets, reflecting how well the current level of a financial institution's capital covers potential losses from those assets most likely to decline in value.

Risk assets consist mainly of loans and securities and exclude cash, plant and equipment, and miscellaneous assets. Some authorities also exclude holdings of short-term government securities from risk assets because the market values of these securities tend to be stable and there is always a ready resale market for them. Concern in the regulatory community over the risk of banks and thrift institutions has resulted in heavy pressure on their management to increase capital. In general, as we saw earlier in this chapter, banking capital has moved significantly higher relative to the industry's assets and liabilities in recent years.

Other Forms of Risk in Banking and Financial Services

Certainly credit, liquidity, market, interest rate, earnings, and capital risk are not the only forms of risk affecting banks and other financial firms today. Other important types of risk include

Inflation risk—the probability that an increasing price level for goods and services (inflation) will unexpectedly erode the purchasing power of a financial institution's earnings and the return to its shareholders.

Currency or exchange rate risk—the probability that fluctuations in the market value of foreign currencies (the dollar, pound, yen, etc.) will create losses by altering the market value of a bank's or other financial institution's assets and liabilities.

Political risk—the probability that changes in government laws or regulations, at home or abroad, will adversely affect a bank's or other financial firm's earnings, operations, and future prospects.

Crime risk—the possibility that a bank's or other institution's owners, employees, or customers may choose to violate the law and subject the institution to loss from fraud, embezzlement, theft, or other illegal acts.

We will look more closely at these other forms of risk later in this book, examining the threat they pose to institutional well-being and how management can respond to each of these risk factors.

---

[4] For further discussion of market discipline and its possible effectiveness in getting banks and other depository institutions to reduce their exposure to capital and other forms of risk, see Baer and Brewer (1) and Brewer and Cheng (2).

Concept Check

5–16. To what different kinds of risk are banks and their financial-service competitors subjected today?

5–17. What items on a bank's balance sheet and income statement can be used to measure its risk exposure? To what other financial institutions do these risk measures seem to apply?

5–18. A bank reports that the total amount of its net loans and leases outstanding is $936 million, its assets total $1,324 million, its equity capital amounts to $110 million, and it holds $1,150 million in deposits, all expressed in book value. The estimated market

values of the bank's total assets and equity capital are $1,443 million and $130 million, respectively. The bank's stock is currently valued at $60 per share with annual per-share earnings of $2.50. Uninsured deposits amount to $243 million and money-market borrowings total $132 million, while nonperforming loans currently amount to $43 million and the bank just charged off $21 million in loans. Calculate as many of the bank's risk measures as you can from the foregoing data.

Key URLs

Performance data on banking's closest competitors—nonbank depository institutions—can most easily be found at such websites as **www.ots.treas.gov**, **www.fdic.gov**, and **www.ncua.gov**.

Other Goals in Banking and Financial-Services Management

In an effort to maximize profitability and the value of the shareholders' investment in a bank or other corporate financial institution, many institutions recognize the need for greater *efficiency* in their operations. This usually means reducing operating expenses and increasing the productivity of their employees through the use of automated equipment and improved employee training. The government deregulation movement has forced banks and thrifts, for example, to pay higher interest costs for their funds and encouraged management to reduce noninterest costs, especially employee salaries and benefits and overhead costs. Among the most revealing measures of operating efficiency and employee productivity for a bank or other financial institution are its

$$\text{Operating efficiency ratio} = \frac{\text{Total operating expenses}}{\text{Total operating revenues}} \qquad \textbf{(21)}$$

$$\text{Employee productivity ratio} = \frac{\text{Net operating income}}{\text{Number of full-time-equivalent employees}}$$

Factoid
Which banks tend to be most efficient in controlling costs and revenues? **Answer:** Usually medium-size and larger institutions (over $100 million in assets).

Not all banks or their competitors pursue high profitability, maximum stock values, increased growth, or greater efficiency as key goals, however. There is considerable evidence that some institutions prefer greater *market power* in the markets they serve, not only because it gives them increased control over prices and customer relationships, but also because a financial-service provider with greater market influence can enjoy a more "quiet life," or face less risk of losing earnings or market share. Several recent studies have found, for example, that some commercial banks in this situation display expense preference behavior: They spend more on salaries and wages of management and staff, enjoy more fringe benefits, or build larger and more sumptuous offices. Unfortunately for the stockholders of these institutions, a preference for expenses sacrifices profits and limits potential gains in stock values.

Performance Indicators among Banking's Key Competitors

Many of the bank performance indicators discussed in the foregoing sections apply equally well for measuring the performance of many of their nonbank competitors. This is especially true of those nonbank financial institutions that are private, profit-making corporations, including stockholder-owned thrift institutions, insurance companies, finance and credit-card companies, security broker and dealer firms, and mutual funds.

Among the key bank performance indicators that often are equally applicable to privately owned, profit-making nonbank financial firms are these:

Prices on common and preferred stock

Return on assets (ROA)

Net interest margin

Asset utilization ratio

Nonperforming assets to equity capital ratio

Book-value assets to market-value assets

Equity capital to risk-exposed assets

Earnings per share of stock

Return on equity capital (ROE)

Net operating margin

Equity multiplier

Cash accounts to total assets

Interest-sensitive assets to interest-sensitive liabilities

Interest-rate spread between yields on the financial firm's debt and market yields on government securities

Some performance indicators are unique to each nonbank financial-service industry. For example, among life and property/casualty insurance companies, key performance measures include the growth of net premiums written (a measure of total sales) and the size of life and pension reserves (their chief liabilities) relative to total assets. Property/casualty insurers also pay close attention to an efficiency measure—the combined ratio of claims paid out plus operating expenses relative to premiums earned from policyholders.

Among mutual funds, one of banking's toughest competitors, key performance markers include the growth of net sales (i.e., gross sales of shares less share redemptions by the public), service fees relative to average assets, and the rate of return on funds invested. Another key competitor, finance and credit-card companies, often pay close attention to the growth of their outstanding debt and their gross receivables (a measure of total loans extended to customers). Finally, among competing depository institutions, such as credit unions and mutual savings associations, key performance measures include total loans to members relative to capital reserves (a measure of risk), home mortgage loans to total assets (a rapidly growing credit service), and the number of actual members (customers) relative to potential members (customers).

No financial institution can safely ignore its level of performance today relative to its past performance and relative to its competitors. Even if some financial-service institutions don't seem to care about performance, both the public and the regulatory community clearly do.

Factoid

In recent years FDIC-insured savings associations (savings and loans and savings banks) have had lower assets and equity returns than insured commercial banks, but not by much. For example, for all of 2002 commercial banks reported an average ROA of 1.33 percent versus 1.22 percent for savings associations and an average ROE of 14.51 percent versus 13.65 percent for savings associations.

The Impact of Size on Performance

When the performance of one bank or other financial firm is compared to that of another, *size*—often measured by total assets or, in the case of a bank or thrift institution, total deposits—becomes a critical factor. Most of the performance ratios presented in this chapter are highly sensitive to the size group in which a financial institution finds itself.

Thus, "size bias" is especially evident in the banking industry. For example, as Table 5–4 shows, key earnings and risk measures change dramatically as we move from the smallest banks (those in the table with assets of less than $100 million) to the largest banking firms

TABLE 5–4 Important Performance Indicators Related to the Size and Location of U.S. Insured Depository Institutions (2003)*

Source: Federal Deposit Insurance Corporation.

Performance Indicators	Average for All Insured U.S. Depository Institutions	Depository Institutions Arranged by Total Assets in the Size Range of:				Depository Institutions in Selected Regions of the United States			
		Under $100 Million	$100 Million to $1 Billion	$1 Billion to $10 Billion	Greater than $10 Billion	Southwest Region	Northeast Region	Midwest Region	West Coast and Mountain West Region
ROA (return on assets)	1.38%	1.02%	1.19%	1.33%	1.44%	1.39%	1.26%	1.54%	1.64%
ROE (return on equity capital)	15.00	8.95	11.93	13.23	16.42	14.49	14.22	14.65	16.42
Net operating margin to total assets (total operating revenues less total operating expenses ÷ total assets)	1.26	0.95	1.12	1.17	1.32	1.28	1.16	1.46	1.50
Net interest margin (net interest income ÷ earning assets)	3.80	4.08	4.01	3.75	3.75	4.08	3.51	4.61	4.25
Net noninterest margin (net noninterest income ÷ earning assets)	−0.91	−2.28	−1.86	−1.28	−0.59	−1.66	−0.63	−1.28	−0.89
Operating efficiency ratio (operating expenses ÷ operating revenues)	55.92	70.99	63.11	58.48	53.69	63.07	57.25	55.60	49.57
Annual loan-loss provision to net charge-offs of bad loans	99.29	183.12	142.74	118.81	94.17	122.19	91.89	112.01	111.79
Net charge-offs of bad loans/total loans and leases	0.81	0.19	0.27	0.49	1.03	0.38	1.25	1.04	0.65
Allowance for loan losses/total loans and leases	1.67	1.41	1.37	1.48	1.79	1.38	2.06	1.82	1.35
Noncurrent assets + other real estate owned ÷ total assets	0.86	0.92	0.76	0.69	0.92	0.83	0.94	0.82	0.72
Net loans and leases/total deposits	88.76	71.16	78.50	89.49	92.07	78.70	77.21	99.43	106.66
Equity capital/total assets	9.20	11.36	10.02	10.09	8.76	9.60	8.88	10.61	9.97
Yield on earning assets	5.59	6.08	6.02	5.64	5.46	5.74	5.43	6.44	5.81
Cost of funding earning assets	1.79	2.00	2.01	1.89	1.71	1.66	1.92	1.83	1.56

Notes: Data for all U.S. commercial banking and savings institutions whose deposits are FDIC insured.
*Figures shown are for the first quarter of 2003 and are annualized.

(with assets exceeding $10 billion). For example, the most profitable banks in terms of ROA tend to be among the largest banks over $1 billion in assets. These larger institutions also reported the largest equity returns (ROE) early in 2003.

On the other hand, middle-size and large banks with assets ranging from $100 million to more than $10 billion in total assets often display the most favorable net operating margins and the best operating efficiency (often with the lowest operating-expense-to-revenue ratio). Similarly, the largest banks generally report the highest (least negative) noninterest margins because they charge fees for so many of their services. Smaller and medium-size banks frequently display larger net interest margins and, therefore, greater spreads between interest revenue and interest costs because most of their deposits are small-denomination accounts with lower average interest costs. Moreover, a larger proportion of small and medium-size banks' loans tend to be higher interest consumer loans.

In terms of balance-sheet ratios, many of which reflect the various kinds of risk exposure banks face, the smallest banks usually report higher ratios of equity capital to assets while the largest, billion-dollar-plus institutions usually have much thinner capital-to-asset ratios. Some bank analysts argue that larger banks can get by with lower capital-to-asset cushions because they are more diversified across many different markets and have more risk-hedging tools at their disposal. Smaller banks appear to be more liquid, as reflected in their lower ratios of total (net) loans to total deposits, because loans are often among a bank's least liquid assets. The biggest banks also appear to carry greater credit risk as revealed by their higher loan-loss (net charge-offs to total loans and leases) ratios.

Size, Location, and Regulatory Bias in Analyzing the Performance of Banks and Competing Financial Institutions

As we saw in the preceding section, the *size* of a bank (often measured by its assets, deposits, or equity capital) and of competing financial-service institutions can have a highly significant impact on profitability and other performance measures. For example, when we compare the performance of one bank with another, it is best to compare institutions of similar size. One reason is that similar-size financial firms tend to offer the same or similar services, so you can be a bit more confident that your performance comparisons have some validity.

To conduct even more valid performance comparisons, we should also compare banks and competing financial firms serving the same or similar market areas. Performance is usually greatly influenced by whether a financial-service provider operates in a major financial center, smaller city, or rural area. The best performance comparison of all is to choose institutions of similar size serving the *same* market area. Unfortunately, in some smaller communities it may be difficult, if not impossible, to find another financial firm comparable in size. The financial analyst will then usually look for another community with a similar-size financial institution, preferably a community with comparable business and households because the character of a financial firm's customer base significantly impacts how it performs.

Finally, where possible, it's a good idea to compare financial institutions subject to *similar regulations* and regulatory agencies. For example, in the banking community each regulator has a somewhat different set of rules banks must follow, and these government-imposed rules can have a profound impact on performance. This is why comparisons of banks and other financial firms in different countries is often so difficult and must be done with great caution.

Even in the United States, with so many different regulatory agencies, analysts often stress the importance of comparing member banks of the Federal Reserve System against other member banks or nonmember banks against other nonmember banks. Similarly, the

Insights and Issues

CREDIT RATINGS BY THOMSON'S BANKWATCH, INC.

One of the most widely respected private institutions that rates the credit quality of banks and selected other financial institutions is Thomson's BankWatch, Inc. Thomson's rates both short-term debt and long-term obligations (debt and preferred stock), assessing the likelihood that the institutions issuing these obligations may not be able to pay. BankWatch's credit ratings are among the most widely followed risk indicators anywhere, particularly by large depositors and those who purchase the stock and capital notes of banks and some other firms.

Examples of Thomson's BankWatch ratings of credit worthiness include these:

Short-Term Ratings	Long-Term Ratings
TBW-1: Very high likelihood of timely repayment of principal and interest.	AAA: Extremely high capacity to repay.
TBW-2: Strong likelihood of timely repayment of principal and interest.	AA: Strong ability to repay.
TBW-3: Adequate capacity to service principal and interest in a timely way.	A: Relatively strong ability to repay.
TBW-4: Noninvestment grade and speculative in nature.	BBB: Lowest investment grade rating with an acceptable capacity to repay.
	BB: Likelihood of default just above investment grade with some significant uncertainties affecting the capacity to repay.
	B: Higher degree of uncertainty and greater likelihood of default than for higher-rated issues.
	CCC: High likelihood of default.
	CC: Subordinated to CCC obligations with less risk protection.
	D: Defaulted obligation.

The long-term credit ratings may be marked with a + or a − depending upon whether the rated institution appears to lie nearer the top or nearer the bottom of each rating category.

Key URLs

If you wanted to compare the overall profitability of the insurance industry to that of the banking industry, where would you look? The data supplied by the American Council of Life Insurance at **www.acli.org** and by the Insurance Information Institute at **www.iii.org** would be helpful.

performance of national banks, where possible, should be compared against that of other national banks, and state-chartered institutions should be compared against other state banks. If a bank is an affiliate of a holding company, it can be revealing to compare its performance with other holding company affiliates rather than with independently owned institutions. There is an old saying about avoiding comparing apples and oranges because of their obvious differences; the same is true in banking and the financial-services field. No two financial firms are ever exactly alike in size, location, service menu, or customer base. The performance analyst must make his or her best effort to find the most comparable institutions—and then proceed with caution.

Using Financial Ratios and Other Analytical Tools to Track Bank Performance—The UBPR

Compared to other financial institutions, more information is available about individual banks than any other type of financial firm. For example, during the 1980s, bankers and other financial analysts received an important new tool to aid them in analyzing the financial condition of a bank operating in the United States. This new tool, the cooperative effort of four federal banking agencies—the Federal Reserve System, the Federal Deposit Insurance Corporation, the Office of Thrift Supervision, and the Office of the Comptroller of the Currency—is called the Uniform Bank Performance Report (UBPR). The **UBPR,** which is sent quarterly to all federally supervised banks, reports each bank's assets, liabilities, capital, revenues, and expenses.

Supplementary items in the UBPR include breakdowns of loan and lease commitments, analysis of problem loans and loan losses, and a profile of each bank's exposure to risk and its sources of capital. Bankers can also obtain *peer group reports,* which allow them to compare their bank with other institutions of comparable size; *average reports,* which provide mean ratio values for each peer group of banking firms; and *state reports,* which permit comparisons between an individual bank and the combined financial statements of all banks in a given state. An important added feature is that a banker can acquire the UBPR report for any other federally supervised bank, thus enabling comparison of banks in the same market area subject to the same environmental conditions.

To get a better picture of the type of information in the UBPR, we present an example based on the 2002 and 2001 UBPRs of the lead bank for National City Corporation, National City Bank (NCB). In Chapter 4, we examined the aggregate numbers for all the banks in this bank holding company, using data found at the FDIC's website. The financial statements we see in this analysis, however, are focused on a single bank. The format of the UBPR is more detailed and extensive, but similar to the financial statements presented in the last chapter, Chapter 4.

NCB is a large national bank located in Cleveland, Ohio, which has total assets that exceeded $43 billion on December 31, 2002. How well or how poorly has NCB performed in recent years? We will examine the financials for 2001 and 2002 to provide some insights regarding this question. To put this analysis in context, we recall that the year 2001 was characterized by a slowdown in economic activity, the devastating effects of September 11th, increased uncertainty in the capital markets, and monetary policies focused on lowering interest rates to stimulate the economy. The reduction in interest rates continued into 2002—a year when investor confidence was shaken by the discovery of corporate wrongdoings and the intensification of geopolitical risks prior to the Iraqi War. The effects on the minimum acceptable rates of return to stockholders were that (1) the risk-free rate of interest decreased and (2) the equity risk premium increased.

Tables 5–5 through 5–9, taken from UBPR reports for 2002 and 2001, are used to assess the performance of NCB. Tables 5–5 and 5–6 indicate the principal assets, liabilities, and capital held by the bank and show how those items and their components have increased or decreased in volume since the same time one year earlier. In terms of growth, NCB's assets increased by more than $4.5 billion for an annual rate of growth of close to 11.5 percent (Table 5–5, line 26). If we examine the aggregate asset items having the largest dollar increases, we find that net loans and leases (item 10) increased by $2.21 billion (7.1 percent); total investments (item 18) increased by $1.14 billion (31.06 percent); and other assets (item 25) increased by $1.20 billion (53.48 percent). The sources of funds (Table 5–6) supporting this asset growth include a $2.31 billion increase (10.77 percent) in total deposits (item 9), a $0.73 billion increase (10.24 percent) in other borrowings with maturities less than one year (item 11), and a $1.36 billion increase (105.75 percent) in acceptances and other liabilities (item 14).

Table 5–5 indicates that NCB focuses on traditional banking with $33.4 billion in net loans and leases (item 10). During the year 2002, NCB increased its real estate loans (item 1) by 27.14 percent, or $3.5 billion, while decreasing the balances in most other loan categories (items 2–5). NCB provided what consumers wanted—financing for housing at a time when prices in the equity markets were declining and securities (i.e., bonds and Treasury bills) were offering very low returns. The increased proportion of real estate loans in the loan portfolio would most likely increase the average maturity of the loan portfolio and may increase NCB's interest-rate risk exposure, a concept introduced earlier in this chapter and discussed in detail in Part Two of the text.

NCB's deposit growth more than covered the loan growth. In Table 5–6, we see that core deposits (item 6) increased by 19.4 percent. Core deposits is a sum of items 1–5 in

TABLE 5–5 The Assets Section from the Balance Sheet for National City Bank*

Source: Uniform Bank Performance Reports (**www.ffiec.gov**).

Items (dollar amounts in thousands)	12/31/2002	12/31/2001	$ Change	Percentage Change
Assets: (dollar amounts in thousands)				
1. Real estate loans	$16,511,167	$12,986,420	$3,524,747	27.14%
2. Commercial loans	10,216,130	10,717,916	−501,786	−4.68
3. Individual loans	6,755,747	6,963,811	−208,064	−2.99
4. Agricultural loans	12,692	18,873	−6,181	−32.75
5. Other loans and leases in domestic offices	305,808	789,505	−483,697	−61.27
6. Loans and leases in foreign offices	156,674	154,174	2,500	1.62
7. Gross loans and leases	**33,958,218**	**31,630,699**	**2,327,519**	**7.36**
8. Less: Unearned income	31,956	30,278	1,678	5.54
9. Less: Loan and lease loss allowance	537,134	424,464	112,670	26.54
10. Net loans and leases	**33,389,128**	**31,175,957**	**2,213,171**	**7.10**
11. U.S. Treasury and agency securities	1,772,928	2,229,887	−456,959	−20.49
12. Municipal securities	22,840	25,703	−2,863	−11.14
13. Foreign debt securities	66	68	−2	−2.94
14. All other securities	1,997,875	367,862	1,630,013	443.10
15. Interest-bearing bank balances	850	7,249	−6,399	−88.27
16. Federal funds sold and resale agreements	697,385	810,251	−112,866	−13.93
17. Trading account assets	299,702	215,028	84,674	39.38
18. Total investments	4,791,646	3,656,048	1,135,598	31.06
19. Total earning assets	38,180,774	34,832,005	3,348,769	9.61
20. Noninterest-bearing cash and deposits due from other banks	1,642,543	1,707,449	−64,906	−3.80
21. Acceptances	19,802	18,753	1,049	5.59
22. Premises, fixed assets, capital leases	416,516	400,784	15,732	3.93
23. Other real estate owned	7,757	4,632	3,125	67.47
24. Investments in unconsolidated subsidiaries	0	0	0	0.00
25. Other assets	3,454,119	2,250,545	1,203,574	53.48
26. Total assets	**$43,721,511**	**$39,214,168**	**$4,507,343**	**11.49%**
Memoranda:				
27. Noninvestment other real estate owned	7,757	4,632	3,125	67.47
28. Loans held for sale	371,401	1,559,961	−1,188,560	−76.19
29. Held-to-maturity securities	0	0	0	0.00
30. Available-for-sale securities	3,793,709	2,623,520	1,170,189	44.60

Table 5–6, representing stable funds that are most unlikely to be removed from the bank. Core deposits also tend to be among the least expensive sources of funds. Overall, total deposits (item 9) increased by 10.77 percent or $2.3 billion while its component—core deposits—increased by almost $3.3 billion. The difference between the dollar increase in core deposits and the dollar increase in total deposits is mostly attributed to the more than $1.4 billion decrease in large time deposits (item 7). The replacement of interest-rate-sensitive large CDs by core deposits is a positive change because the acquired core deposits are less expensive and a more reliable source of funds. This change has the potential to help offset the increase in interest-rate risk exposure associated with the rise in real estate loans.

In addition to loan growth, Table 5–5 indicates that total investments (item 18) increased by 31.06 percent or more than $1.14 billion. This aggregate number includes significant decreases in U.S. Treasury and agency securities (item 11) and federal funds sold and resale agreements (item 16) and a whopping 443.10 percent increase in all other securities (item 14). All other securities include asset-backed securities (i.e., securities backed

TABLE 5–6 The Liabilities and Capital Section from the Balance Sheet for National City Bank

Source: Uniform Bank Performance Reports (**www.ffiec.gov**).

Items (dollar amounts in thousands)	12/31/2002	12/31/2001	$ Change	Percentage Change
Liabilities and Capital				
1. Demand deposits	$4,526,479	$4,263,798	$262,681	6.16%
2. All NOW and ATS accounts	205,964	295,736	−89,772	−30.36
3. Money market deposit accounts	7,777,538	6,001,881	1,775,657	29.59
4. Other savings deposits	4,272,506	3,048,548	1,223,958	40.15
5. Time deposits under $100,000	3,237,386	3,149,081	88,305	2.80
6. Core deposits	**20,019,873**	**16,759,044**	**3,260,829**	**19.46**
7. Time deposits of $100,000 or more	2,261,245	3,704,844	−1,443,590	−38.96
8. Deposits in foreign offices	1,502,078	1,007,072	495,006	49.15
9. Total deposits	**23,783,205**	**21,470,960**	**2,312,245**	**10.77**
10. Federal funds purchased and REPOs	2,022,784	2,053,431	−30,647	−1.49
11. Other borrowings with maturities less than 1 year	7,826,898	7,099,982	726,916	10.24
12. Memo: Short-term noncore funding	11,690,414	11,832,195	−141,781	−1.20
13. Other borrowings with maturities greater than 1 year	3,188,052	3,438,694	−250,642	−7.29
14. Acceptances and other liabilities	2,642,942	1,284,532	1,358,410	105.75
15. Total liabilities (including mortgages)	**39,463,881**	**35,347,599**	**4,116,282**	**11.65**
16. Subordinated notes and debentures	1,366,829	1,251,887	114,942	9.18
17. All common and preferred capital	2,890,801	2,614,682	276,119	10.56
18. Total liabilities and capital	**43,721,511**	**39,214,168**	**4,507,343**	**11.49**

by credit card receivables or home equity lines) and domestic debt securities. This replacement of marketable Treasury and agency securities with other securities may be viewed as a decrease in liquidity given the time and cost needed to liquidate the other securities group.

The $1.20 billion increase in other assets (item 25 in Table 5–5) is more than covered by the $1.36 billion increase in acceptances and other liabilities (item 14 in Table 5–6). Both accounts contain a mix of miscellaneous items. One item that we find in other assets is derivatives with a positive fair value held for purposes other than trading, while in other liabilities we find derivatives with a negative fair value held for purposes other than trading. Hence the growth in these accounts may pertain to off-balance-sheet activities (discussed earlier in Chapter 4). We would need to move beyond Tables 5–5 and 5–6 to confirm this hypothesis. In Chapter 7 we will see how derivatives can be used to offset interest-rate risk exposure.

Table 5–7 shows the composition of assets and liabilities held by NCB using averages across the four quarters of the year and the analogous information for a peer group of banks. The peer group used for NCB is all national banks with average assets in excess of $10 billion. The peer group includes the largest 71 banks in 2002 and the largest 69 banks in 2001. The changes in assets and liabilities that we discussed in Tables 5–5 and 5–6 are based on year-end numbers whereas the percentages in Table 5–7 represent averages that would reduce the effects of seasonality and window dressing. From this point on, our discussion will focus on *average* data.

For NCB we see very small changes in composition in Table 5–7. Net loans and leases as a percentage of average assets (line 4) decreased from 79.89 percent at the end of 2001 to 78.53 percent at the end of 2002—a meager 1.7 percent decrease in net loans and leases to average assets. However, in both years larger percentages of assets were accounted for as loans by NCB than by the peer group of banks that reported net loans and leases-to-average total assets of 63.60 percent and 61.32 percent for 2001 and 2002. Because loans usually represent the highest-yielding assets a bank can hold, NCB's higher

TABLE 5–7 Percentage Composition of Assets and Liabilities for National City Bank and Its Peer Group (all figures are percentages of average total assets*)

Source: Uniform Bank Performance Reports (**www.ffiec.gov**).

Items	NCB 12/31/2002	Peer Group 12/31/2002	NCB 12/31/2001	Peer Group 12/31/2001
Assets: Percentage of average assets				
1. Total loans	79.60%	59.10%	80.86%	61.27%
2. Lease financing receivables	0.08	2.42	0.08	2.61
3. Less: Loan and lease allowance	1.15	0.93	1.05	0.99
4. Net loans and leases	**78.53**	**61.32**	**79.89**	**63.60**
5. Interest-bearing bank balances	0.01	0.95	0.00	0.81
6. Federal funds sold and resales	0.97	3.75	0.75	3.29
7. Trading account assets	0.59	1.34	0.45	1.14
8. Held-to-maturity securities	0.00	0.55	0.00	0.75
9. Available-for-sale securities	7.84	17.34	8.17	15.42
10. Total earning assets	**87.94**	**88.91**	**89.26**	**88.19**
11. Noninterest-bearing cash and deposits due from other banks	4.13	3.60	4.30	4.14
12. Premises, fixed assets, and capital leases	0.99	1.04	0.98	1.02
13. Other real estate owned	0.02	0.05	0.02	0.04
14. Acceptances and other assets	6.91	6.21	5.44	6.25
15. Subtotal	**12.05**	**11.09**	**10.73**	**11.81**
16. Total assets	**99.99%**	**100.00%**	**99.99%**	**100.00%**
Liabilities				
17. Demand deposits	9.62%	7.51%	8.64%	8.24%
18. All NOW and ATS accounts	0.43	1.33	0.85	1.35
19. Money market deposit accounts	16.39	22.05	14.28	19.64
20. Other savings deposits	8.75	8.73	8.25	7.26
21. Time deposits under $100,000	8.39	9.70	8.71	10.78
22. Core deposits	**43.58**	**53.42**	**40.73**	**51.27**
23. Time deposits of $100,000 or more	6.02	6.70	9.47	7.58
24. Deposits in foreign offices	3.44	4.25	3.68	5.02
25. Total deposits	**53.04**	**66.65**	**53.87**	**66.43**
26. Federal funds purchased and repurchase agreements	6.39	8.62	7.85	8.80
27. Other borrowings (including maturities less than 1 year)	17.09	4.13	12.95	4.69
28. Memo: Short-term noncore funding	**28.03**	**23.52**	**27.69**	**27.03**
29. Other borrowings with maturities more than 1 year	8.67	5.63	12.38	4.99
30. Acceptances and other liabilities	4.75	3.18	3.20	3.00
31. Total liabilities (including mortgages)	**89.94**	**90.11**	**90.25**	**89.86**
32. Subordinated notes and debentures	3.22	1.33	2.11	1.41
33. All common and preferred capital	6.84	8.40	7.47	8.54
34. Total liabilities and capital	**100.00%**	**100.00%**	**100.00%**	**100.00%**

*Average total assets for National City Bank are $39,014,282 thousand for 2002 and $37,249,495 thousand for 2001.

loan-asset ratio would be expected to produce relatively higher earnings than the average earnings for the peer group.

NCB has maintained its composition of liquid assets (short-term securities and cash assets). If we sum the percentages for items 5, 6, 7, 9, and 11 in Table 5–7, we find that interest-bearing liquid assets and cash assets accounted for 13.67 percent of assets in 2001 and 13.44 percent of assets in 2002. In contrast, the peer group has about twice the portion of liquid assets relative to total assets. In 2001 and 2002, liquid assets accounted for 24.80 percent and 26.98 percent of assets at peer institutions. Could NCB's management be accepting greater liquidity risk (i.e., the possibility of a cash-out) than is warranted?

Banks, like other firms, want to have enough liquid assets to meet their needs without oppressing profitability with excessive funds invested in relatively low-yielding instruments. Their needs for funds are usually derived from their customers' needs for funds where the customer draws down loan commitments (off-balance-sheet items that become on-balance-sheet assets) or withdraws deposits.

On the sources of funds side, we note from Table 5–7 that NCB holds a significantly smaller proportion of core deposits (item 22) than the peer group of banks. Core deposits, as reported in the UBPR, include demand deposits, negotiable order of withdrawal (NOW) accounts, regular savings deposits, money market deposits, and time deposits of less than $100,000. The difference is derived for the most part from money market deposit accounts (MMDAs) (in item 19). The cost of MMDAs is comparable to the cost of many nondeposit sources of funds. Given that their checkable deposits are comparable—NCB has 10.05 percent (sum of items 17 and 18) and the peer group reports 8.84 percent—the lower proportion of core deposits does not necessarily indicate excessive funding costs and may be an unimportant observation. When we look at nondeposit liabilities, we see that short-term (maturity less than one year) other borrowings are significantly higher for NCB than for the peer group. To some extent, NCB has substituted nondeposit borrowings for money market deposits compared to its peers.

Turning to NCB's statement of earnings and expenses (Table 5–8), we must recall the changing interest rate environment over the years 2001 and 2002. If we disregard this, Table 5–8 produces "red flags" at first glance because we see so many negative signs in front of the figures for percentage changes. This was a period of declining interest rates—the federal funds rate dropped from 6.40 percent in December 2000 to 1.26 percent in December 2002 and the 30-year mortgage rate fell from 7.38 percent to 5.84 percent over the same period according to data provided by the Federal Reserve System. While total interest income (item 16) dropped by 16.37 percent, a somewhat disappointing but expected result, total interest expense (item 24) dropped by 41.89 percent—a favorable result. In the world of ideals, we like income to go up and expenses to go down. This ideal is similar to the directive to "buy low and sell high"—simplistic in theory yet hard to apply, especially when we are talking about interest income and expenses and both items are correlated to market interest rates. (We will be exploring the effects of such correlations in Chapter 6.) All interest expense items (17–23) went down as market rates fell; however, so did most of the interest income categories with the notable exceptions of income from all other securities (item 9) and other interest income (item 15). These two items are characterized by high growth rates in Table 5–5. Hence one would expect the dollar amount of income produced by these items to increase, even as interest rates declined.

NCB's net interest income (item 25) increased by 4.83 percent during the year. When net interest income is measured relative to average total assets, the net interest margin (NIM) remains unchanged as illustrated by the following:

$$\frac{\text{Interest income from loans and security investments} - \text{Interest expense on borrowed funds}}{\text{Average assets}} = \text{Net interest margin}^5$$

$$\begin{array}{cc} 2002 & 2001 \\ \dfrac{\$1,492,181}{\$39,014,282} = 3.82\% & \dfrac{\$1,423,386}{\$37,249,495} = 3.82\% \end{array}$$

[5] The numbers in the numerator are taken from Table 5–8, items 16 and 24. The denominator is average assets based on quarterly totals for 2002 of $39,014,282 thousand and for 2001 of $37,249,495 thousand.

TABLE 5–8
National City Bank
Income Statement
(Revenues and
Expenses)

Source: Uniform Bank
Performance Reports
(www.ffiec.gov).

Items (dollar amounts in thousands)	12/31/2002	12/31/2001	Percentage Change
1. Income and fees on loans	$1,975,545	$2,408,124	−17.96%
2. Income from lease financing	134	217	−38.25
3. Tax-exempt income	2,277	2,654	−14.20
4. Estimated tax benefit	900	614	46.58
5. Income on loans and leases (tax-equivalent basis)	1,976,579	2,408,955	−17.95
6. Income from U.S. Treasury and agency securities (excluding MBS)	9,288	23,935	−61.19
7. Mortgage-backed securities (MBS) income	105,791	130,311	−18.82
8. Estimated tax benefit	14	13	7.69
9. Income from all other securities	69,801	23,461	197.52
10. Tax-exempt securities income	35	55	−36.36
11. Investment income (tax-equivalent basis)	184,894	177,720	4.04
12. Interest due from other banks	109	19	473.68
13. Interest on federal funds sold and resales	10,405	14,871	−30.03
14. Trading account income	2,031	3,456	−41.23
15. Other interest income	5,289	839	530.39
16. Total interest income (tax-equivalent basis)	**2,179,307**	**2,605,859**	**−16.37**
17. Interest on deposits in foreign offices	44,860	61,051	−26.52
18. Interest on time deposits over $100,000	63,323	161,059	−60.68
19. Interest on all other deposits	243,399	357,513	−31.92
20. Interest on federal funds purchased and repurchase agreements	63,927	132,348	−51.70
21. Interest on trading liabilities and other borrowings	240,991	435,770	−44.70
22. Interest on mortgages and leases for property and equipment			0.00
23. Interest on subordinated notes and debentures	30,626	34,732	−11.82
24. Total interest expense	**687,126**	**1,182,473**	**−41.89**
25. Net interest income (tax-equivalent basis)	**1,492,181**	**1,423,386**	**4.83**
26. Noninterest income (tax-equivalent basis)	866,025	912,648	−5.11
27. Adjusted operating income (tax-equivalent basis)	**2,358,206**	**2,336,034**	**0.95**
28. Noninterest expense	1,114,101	1,161,795	−4.11
29. Provision: Loan and lease losses	422,440	343,895	22.84
30. Pretax operating income (tax-equivalent basis)	**821,665**	**830,344**	**−1.05**
31. Realized gains/losses on held-to-maturity securities	0	0	0.00
32. Realized gains/losses on available-for-sale securities	2,330	3,053	−23.68
33. Pretax net operating income (tax-equivalent basis)	**823,995**	**833,397**	**−1.13**
34. Applicable income taxes	283,144	286,806	−1.28
35. Current tax equivalent adjustments	914	626	46.01
36. Other tax-equivalent adjustments	0		0.00
37. Applicable income taxes (tax-equivalent basis)	284,058	287,432	−1.17
38. Net operating income	**539,937**	**545,965**	**−1.10**
39. Net extraordinary items	0	−1,059	−100.00
40. Net income	**539,937**	**544,906**	**−0.91**
41. Cash dividends declared	445,000	250,000	78.00
42. Retained earnings	94,937	294,906	−67.81

Factoid
Beginning in 1997
federal law allowed
banks and other
corporate financial
institutions that
qualify to become
Subchapter S
corporations, which are
treated like partnerships
for federal tax purposes.
This generally means
they are exempt from
income taxes as a
corporation, but their
shareholders usually pay
taxes on their share of
earnings paid out by the
bank or other financial
firm. For the financial
institution with
Subchapter S status,
reported taxes tend to
fall and earnings tend to
rise, while stockholders
may pay more in
personal income taxes
(though the
Subchapter S firm may
pay its shareholders
more in dividends to
help offset higher
personal taxes).

TABLE 5–9   Relative Income Statement and Margin Analysis for National City Bank and Its Peer Group (all figures are percentages of average total assets*)

Source: Uniform Bank Performance Reports (**www.ffiec.gov**).

Items	NCB 12/31/2002	Peer Group 12/31/2002	NCB 12/31/2001	Peer Group 12/31/2001
1. Total interest income (tax-equivalent basis)	5.59%	5.18%	7.00%	6.36%
2. Less: Interest expense	1.76	1.70	3.17	2.93
3. Equals: Net interest income (tax-equivalent basis)	**3.82**	**3.45**	**3.82**	**3.39**
4. Plus: Noninterest income	2.22	1.96	2.45	2.00
5. Minus: Noninterest expense	2.86	3.05	3.12	3.23
6. Minus: Provision for loan and lease losses	1.08	0.43	0.92	0.51
7. Equals: Pretax operating income (tax-equivalent basis)	**2.11**	**1.99**	**2.23**	**1.69**
8. Plus realized gains/losses on securities	0.01	0.08	0.01	0.06
9. Equals: Pretax net operating income (tax-equivalent basis)	**2.11**	**2.09**	**2.24**	**1.77**
10. Net operating income	**1.38**	**1.37**	**1.47**	**1.15**
11. Adjusted net operating income	**1.67**	**1.41**	**1.61**	**1.24**
12. Net income adjusted for Subchapter S status		1.37		1.15
13. Net income	**1.38%**	**1.37%**	**1.46%**	**1.15%**

*Average total assets for National City Bank are $39,014,282 thousand for 2002 and $37,249,495 thousand for 2001.

As Table 5–9 illustrates, NCB's 3.82 percent is above the average for peer group banks, which reported net interest margins of 3.45 percent in 2002 and 3.39 percent in 2001. Staying in front of one's peers is positive. However, management may be concerned that the margin between NCB and the peer group of banks is narrowing. While the percentage change in net interest margin is 0 percent for NCB, comparable banks increased their average NIM by 1.77 percent, indicating improvement in the management of the spread between interest revenue and interest expense.

NCB's *net operating margin* (line 10 in Table 5–9)—the gap between its operating revenues and operating expenses—has changed as follows:

$$\frac{\text{Net operating income}}{\text{Average assets}} = \text{Net operating margin}^6$$

$$\begin{array}{cc} 2002 & 2001 \\ \dfrac{\$539,937}{\$39,014,282} = 1.38\% & \dfrac{\$545,965}{\$37,249,495} = 1.47\% \end{array}$$

Once again, NCB's net operating margin is above that of the peer group, 1.38 percent versus 1.37 percent in 2002, and that is "good." However the lead is very small and, once again, the margin between NCB and the peer group has narrowed. While NCB's net operating margin dropped by 6.12 percent, the peer group's ratio increased by 19.13 percent. The peer group appeared to be gaining on NCB.

NCB's stockholders will probably be most concerned about their earnings per share (EPS) of stock held. National City Corporation (the bank holding company) had

---

[6] The numerator is based on item 38 in Table 5–8 and the denominator is average assets as given above.

607,354,727 shares outstanding in 2001 and 611,491,359 shares of stock in 2002 (according to its annual report submitted to the SEC and accessible using the student version of S&P's Market Insights and the associated Edgar link). Using this data we can calculate the EPS on a bank basis (using net income from NCB). Its EPS changed as follows between year-end 2001 and 2002:

$$\text{EPS} = \frac{\text{Net income after taxes}}{\text{Common equity shares outstanding}}$$

$$\begin{array}{cc} 2002 & 2001 \\ \dfrac{539,937,000}{611,491,359 \text{ shares}} = \$0.88 \text{ per share} & \dfrac{544,906,000}{607,354,727 \text{ shares}} = \$0.90 \text{ per share} \end{array}$$

The bank suffered a small decline in stockholders' earnings per share. Remember this calculation is based on the net income for the lead bank divided by the number of shares of National City Corporation, the bank holding company. Hence, caution in interpreting these results is important. Keeping this in mind, management would like to reverse this change by either expanding revenues from assets and services sold or moving toward a less-expensive mix of deposits and nondeposit sources of funds.

As we move further down the income and expense statement in Table 5–8, we see that while net interest income increased in 2002, net income (item 40) decreased by a small amount (–.91 percent). This was due to decreases in noninterest income (item 26) and realized gains and losses on available-for-sale securities (item 32) and increases in the provision for loan and lease losses (item 29). With a bank that focuses on lending, such as NCB, changes in the report of income's provision for loan and lease losses (item 29) and the related loan and lease allowance for losses account (item 9 in Table 5–5) from the Report of Condition may provide some insights into the quality of the loan portfolio. (Note: If you are a bit confused about what these accounts represent, review the discussion in Chapter 4.) The provision account increased by 22.84 percent to $422,440 thousand. The allowance account increased by 26.54 percent or by $112,670 thousands. This tells us that their annual expense was more than net charge-offs, creating a build-up in the Report of Condition's allowance account. According to Table 5–7, the loan and lease loss allowance to average assets (item 3) went from 1.05 percent in 2001 to 1.15 percent in 2002. Management's actions are consistent with preparation for future loan losses or possibly increasing credit risk.

How did NCB do relative to its peer group with regard to income and expenses? Table 5–9 provides a glimpse of an answer for this question. It outperformed its peer group on every item except provision for loan and lease losses (item 6) and realized gains/losses on securities (item 8). *Outperformed* means income was higher as a percentage of average assets and expenses were lower as a percentage of average assets. NCB's noninterest income as a percentage of average total assets is higher than that of the peer group for both 2001 and 2002, while its noninterest expense is lower. The lower noninterest expense indicates that management has succeeded in controlling overhead costs. Overall, the superior performance illustrated in the upper portion of Table 5–9 has resulted in higher net operating income to average total assets (item 10) and net income-to-average total assets (item 13) for NCB versus the peer group for both 2001 and 2002.

NCB looks good relative to its peers, but it experienced a downward trend in its net income when 2002 is compared to 2001. Net income decreased by 0.91 percent. We can explore NCB's earnings further using Equations 11, 14, and 18 discussed earlier in this chapter. Equation 11 provides the following breakdown using quarterly average figures for Report of Condition items:

$$\begin{array}{c} \text{NCB's} \\ \text{ROE in 2002}[7] \end{array} = \text{ROA} \times \frac{\text{Average assets}}{\text{Average equity capital}}$$

$$= .0138 \times 14.62$$

$$= .2023 \text{ or } 20.23\%$$

$$\begin{array}{c} \text{NCB's} \\ \text{ROE in the} \\ \text{previous year}[7] \end{array} = \text{ROA} \times \frac{\text{Average assets}}{\text{Average equity capital}}$$

$$= .0146 \times 13.39$$

$$= .1962 \text{ or } 19.62\%$$

Clearly, NCB's ROE increased because its use of leverage (i.e., the proportion of assets supported by debt capital) increased, offsetting the decline in ROA, a measure of managerial efficiency. If the bank can get by with less equity capital and not significantly increase its borrowing costs, it can increase its ratio of assets to equity capital and boost its ROE. We may be seeing NCB's effort to do just that illustrated by the 78 percent increase in cash dividends declared (item 41 in Table 5–8) that resulted in an increase in the year-end equity multiplier, rather than a decrease in the equity multiplier if NCB had maintained the dollar amount of cash dividends declared in 2001.

We can expand this analysis a bit further using Equation 14 for ROE:

$$\begin{array}{c} \text{NCB's} \\ \text{ROE in 2002}[8] \end{array} = \frac{\begin{array}{c}\text{Net income}\\\text{after taxes}\end{array}}{\begin{array}{c}\text{Total operating}\\\text{revenues}\end{array}} \times \frac{\begin{array}{c}\text{Total operating}\\\text{revenues}\end{array}}{\text{Average assets}} \times \frac{\text{Average assets}}{\begin{array}{c}\text{Average equity}\\\text{capital}\end{array}}$$

$$= \frac{\$539,937}{\$3,045,332} \times \frac{\$3,045,332}{\$39,014,282} \times \frac{\$39,014,282}{\$2,668,577}$$

$$= 0.1773 \times 0.0781 \times 14.62$$

$$= 0.2023 \text{ or } 20.23\%$$

$$\begin{array}{c} \text{NCB's} \\ \text{ROE in 2001}[8] \end{array} = \frac{\begin{array}{c}\text{Net income}\\\text{after taxes}\end{array}}{\begin{array}{c}\text{Total operating}\\\text{revenues}\end{array}} \times \frac{\begin{array}{c}\text{Total operating}\\\text{revenues}\end{array}}{\text{Average assets}} \times \frac{\text{Average assets}}{\begin{array}{c}\text{Average equity}\\\text{capital}\end{array}}$$

$$= \frac{\$544,906}{\$3,518,507} \times \frac{\$3,518,507}{\$37,249,495} \times \frac{\$37,249,495}{\$2,782,537}$$

$$= 0.1549 \times 0.0945 \times 13.39$$

$$= 0.1962 \text{ or } 19.62\%$$

What factors in these earnings relationships caused NCB's return to its stockholders (ROE) to rise? The key factors are (1) NCB's rising net profit margin, which increased by 14.46 percent and (2) the increase in the equity multiplier from 13.39 times to 14.62 times, a 9.19 percent increase. These positive effects were mitigated to some degree by the 17.35 percent decline in NCB's asset utilization ratio (operating revenues to average assets), which dropped from 9.45 percent in 2001 to 7.81 percent in 2002. This reflects

---

[7] ROA is item 13 from Table 5–9, and for balance sheet items we use average assets as reported in the UBPR and derive average equity capital from item 33 in Table 5–7. For 2002, average equity capital equals 6.84 percent of average assets where average assets is $39,014,282 thousand.

[8] Total operating revenue is item 16 plus item 26 from Table 5–8.

the decline in average asset yields that, in part, may be attributed to the downward trend in market interest rates as monetary policy was utilized to stimulate the economy.

Analysis of ROE using Equation 18 reiterates the bank's issues with asset management efficiency and applauds NCB's control of expenses that was illustrated above in its rising net profit margin.

$$\begin{aligned}
\text{NCB's ROE in 2002}^9 &= \frac{\text{Net income after taxes}}{\text{Net income before taxes and security gains (or losses)}} \times \frac{\text{Net income before taxes and security gains (or losses)}}{\text{Total operating revenues}} \\
&\quad \times \frac{\text{Total operating revenues}}{\text{Average assets}} \times \frac{\text{Average assets}}{\text{Average equity capital}} \\
&= \frac{\$539,937}{\$821,665} \times \frac{\$821,665}{\$3,045,332} \times \frac{\$3,045,332}{\$39,014,282} \times \frac{\$39,014,282}{\$2,890,801} \\
&= 0.6571 \times .2698 \times .0781 \times 14.62 \\
&= 0.2023 \text{ or } 20.23\%
\end{aligned}$$

$$\begin{aligned}
\text{NCB's ROE in 2001}^9 &= \frac{\text{Net income after taxes}}{\text{Net income before taxes and security gains (or losses)}} \times \frac{\text{Net income before taxes and security gains (or losses)}}{\text{Total operating revenues}} \\
&\quad \times \frac{\text{Total operating revenues}}{\text{Average assets}} \times \frac{\text{Average assets}}{\text{Average equity capital}} \\
&= \frac{\$545,965}{\$830,344} \times \frac{\$830,344}{\$3,518,507} \times \frac{\$3,518,507}{\$37,249,495} \times \frac{\$37,249,495}{\$2,782,537} \\
&= 0.6575 \times .2360 \times .0945 \times 13.39 \\
&= 0.2084 \text{ or } 20.84\%
\end{aligned}$$

Examining the breakdown of ROE indicates essentially no change in tax-management efficiency as captured by net after-tax income to net income before taxes and securities gains or losses. The measure of expense-control efficiency (net income before taxes and securities gains or losses to total operating revenue) increased by more than 14 percent, illustrating better control of expenses.

In conclusion, we have utilized the tools developed in this chapter and NCB's UBPR to get a better picture of the operations and management of this bank. NCB is more focused on the traditional business of lending than the average large bank. NCB's operations have generated higher revenues and lower expenses than its peer group. Its edge over its contemporaries narrowed between 2002 and 2001, which may reflect increased competition or may indicate that NCB has the potential to do better than the performance figures reported in 2002.

---

[9] Net income before taxes and security gains (or losses) is item 30 from Table 5–8.

Summary

The principal focus of this chapter has been on how well banks perform in serving their customers and in providing acceptable returns to their owners. We have also noted that many of the measures of performance banks employ also provide key insights regarding their closest nonbank competitors, including thrift institutions, security brokers and dealers, mutual funds, finance companies, and insurance firms. Increasingly, bankers and their competitors are being forced to assess their performance over time, analyze the reasons for any performance problems that appear, and find ways to strengthen their performance in the future.

Among the key points made in the chapter are these:

- The two key dimensions of performance among banks and most other financial-service firms are *profitability* and *risk*. Satisfactory profits and adequate risk controls preserve capital, providing a basis for a financial firm's survival and future growth.

- For the largest banks and other profit-oriented financial institutions the market value of their stock (equities) is usually the best overall indicator of profitability and risk exposure.

- For smaller financial firms whose stock is not actively traded every day a number of key *profitability ratios* (such as return on assets, return on equity capital, net interest margin, noninterest margin, and earnings spread) become important performance measures and significant managerial targets.

- Pursuit of profitability must always be tempered with concern for *risk exposure*, including the management and control of credit or default risk, liquidity or cash-out risk, market risk to the value of assets and liabilities held, interest-rate risk, earnings risk, and capital risk which focuses upon the probability of ultimate failure if a financial firm is undercapitalized relative to the risks it faces.

- Increasingly banks and other financial-service firms are adding operating *efficiency* to their list of performance criteria, focusing upon measures of expense control and the productivity of employees in managing assets, revenues, and income.

- The chapter concludes with a discussion of the Uniform Bank Performance Report (UBPR) available from the Federal Financial Institutions Examination Council. This financial report on individual FDIC-insured commercial and savings banks has become one of the most widely used performance summaries available to bankers, regulators, customers, and the general public.

Key Terms

profitability, *150*	net profit margin, *153*	market risk, *163*
ROA, *151*	asset utilization, *153*	interest rate risk, *163*
ROE, *151*	equity multiplier, *153*	earnings risk, *163*
efficiency, *151*	credit risk, *161*	capital risk, *164*
net interest margin, *151*	liquidity risk, *162*	UBPR, *170*
net noninterest margin, *151*		

Problems and Projects

1. An investor holds the stock of First National Bank of Inseco and expects to receive a dividend of $12 per share at the end of the year. Stock analysts have recently predicted that the bank's dividends will grow at approximately 8 percent a year indefinitely into the future. If this is true, and if the appropriate risk-adjusted cost of capital (discount rate) for the bank is 15 percent, what should be the current price per share of Inseco's stock?

2. Suppose that stockbrokers have projected that Price State Bank and Trust Company will pay a dividend of $3 per share on its common stock at the end of the year; a dividend of $4.50 per share is expected for the next year, and $6 per share in the following year. The risk-adjusted cost of capital for banks in Price State's risk class is 12 percent. If an investor holding Price State's stock plans to hold that stock for only three years and hopes to sell it at a price of $60 per share, what should the value of the bank's stock be in today's market?

3. Depositors Savings Association has a ratio of equity capital to total assets of 7.5 percent. In contrast, Newton Savings reports an equity-capital-to-asset ratio of 6 percent. What is the value of the equity multiplier for each of these institutions? Suppose that both institutions have an ROA of 0.85 percent. What must each institution's return on equity capital be? What do your calculations tell you about the benefits of having as little equity capital as regulations or the marketplace will allow?

4. The latest balance sheet and income statements for Gilcrest Merchants National Bank are as shown in the following tables. Using these statements, calculate for Gilcrest Merchants National Bank all the performance measures discussed in this chapter that you can. What strengths and weaknesses are you able to detect in this bank's performance?

GILCREST MERCHANTS NATIONAL BANK
Report of Income
(in millions of dollars)

Interest and fees on loans	$61	Noninterest income and fees	$ 7
Interest and dividends on securities	12	Salaries and employee benefits*	10
Interest paid on deposits	49	Overhead expenses	5
Interest paid on nondeposit		Other noninterest expenses	3
borrowings	6	Securities gains (or losses), net of taxes	1
Provision for loan losses	2	Taxes	1

*The bank has 40 full-time-equivalent employees.

GILCREST MERCHANTS NATIONAL BANK
Report of Condition
(in millions of dollars)

Assets		Liabilities	
Cash and deposits due from banks	$120	Demand deposits*	$210
Investment securities	150	Savings deposits*	180
Federal funds sold	10	Time deposits*	470
Net loans	670	Federal funds purchased	60
(Allowance for loan losses 25)		Total liabilities	$920
(Unearned income on loans 5)		**Equity Capital**	
Plant and equipment	50		
Total assets	$1,000	Common stock	20
		Surplus	25
		Retained earnings	35
		Total capital	$ 80

*Interest-bearing deposits totaled $650, while noninterest-bearing deposits amounted to $210.

5. The following information is for Shadowwood National Bank:

Interest income	$1,875 million	Shares of common stock	
Interest expenses	$1,210 million	outstanding	145,000
Total assets	$15,765 million	Noninterest income	$501 million
Securities gains (or losses)	$21 million	Noninterest expenses	$685 million
Earning assets	$12,612 million	Provision for loan losses	$381 million
Total liabilities	$15,440 million		
Taxes	$16 million		

Please calculate:

a. ROE.

b. ROA.

c. Net interest margin.

d. Earnings per share.

e. Net noninterest margin.

f. Net operating margin.

g. Net returns before special transactions.

Alternative scenarios:

(1) Suppose interest income, interest expenses, noninterest income, and noninterest expenses each increase by 5 percent while all other revenue and expense items shown in the preceding table remain unchanged. What will happen to Shadowwood's ROE, ROA, and earnings per share?

(2) On the other hand, suppose Shadowwood's interest income and expenses as well as its noninterest income and expenses decline by 5 percent, again with all other factors held constant. How would the bank's ROE, ROA, and per-share earnings change?

6. Farmers and Merchants National Bank holds total assets of $1.69 billion and equity capital of $139 million and has just posted an ROA of 0.0076. What is the bank's ROE?

Alternative scenarios:

(1) Suppose Farmers and Merchants Bank finds its ROA climbing by 50 percent, with assets and equity capital unchanged. What will happen to its ROE? Why?

(2) On the other hand, suppose the bank's ROA drops by 50 percent. If total assets and equity capital hold their present positions, what change will occur in ROE?

(3) If ROA at Farmers and Merchants National remains fixed at 0.0076 but both total assets and equity double, how does ROE change? Why?

(4) How would a decline in total assets and equity by half (with ROA still at 0.0076) affect the bank's ROE?

7. Granite Dells State Bank reports total operating revenues of $135 million, with total operating expenses of $121 million, and owes taxes of $2 million. It has total assets of $1.17 billion and total liabilities of $989 million. What is the bank's ROE?

Alternative scenarios:

(1) How will the ROE for Granite Dells State Bank change if total operating expenses, taxes, and total operating revenues each grow by 10 percent while assets and liabilities remain fixed?

(2) Suppose Granite Dells' total assets and total liabilities increase by 10 percent, but its revenues and expenses (including taxes) are unchanged. How will the bank's ROE change?

(3) Can you determine what will happen to ROE if both operating revenues and expenses (including taxes) decline by 10 percent, with the bank's total assets and liabilities held constant?

(4) What does ROE become if Granite Dells' assets and liabilities decrease by 10 percent, while its operating revenues, taxes, and operating expenses do not change?

8. Suppose a stockholder-owned nonbank thrift institution is projected to achieve a 1.25 percent ROA during the coming year. What must its ratio of total assets to equity capital be if it is to achieve its target ROE of 12 percent? If ROA unexpectedly falls to 0.75 percent, what assets-to-capital ratio must it then have to reach a 12 percent ROE?

9. Blythe County National Bank presents us with these figures for the year just concluded. Please determine the net profit margin, equity multiplier, asset utilization ratio, and ROE.

Net income after taxes	$16 million
Total operating revenues	$215 million
Total assets	$1,250 million
Total equity capital accounts	$111 million

10. Lochiel Commonwealth Bank and Trust Company has experienced the following trends over the past five years (all figures in millions of dollars):

Year	Net Income after Taxes	Total Operating Revenues	Total Assets	Total Equity Capital
1	$2.7	$26.5	$293	$18
2	3.5	30.1	382	20
3	4.1	39.8	474	22
4	4.8	47.5	508	25
5	5.7	55.9	599	28

Determine the figures for ROE, profit margin, asset utilization, and equity multiplier for this bank. Are any adverse trends evident? Where would you recommend that management look to deal with the bank's emerging problem(s)?

11. Wilmington Hills State Bank has just submitted its Report of Condition and Report of Income to its principal supervisory agency. The bank reported net income before taxes and securities transactions of $27 million and taxes of $6 million. If its total operating revenues were $780 million, its total assets $2.1 billion, and its equity capital $125 million, determine the following for Wilmington:

a. Tax management efficiency ratio.

b. Expense control efficiency ratio.

c. Asset management efficiency ratio.

d. Funds management efficiency ratio.

e. ROE.

Alternative scenarios:

(1) Suppose Wilmington Hills State Bank experienced a 20 percent rise in net before-tax income, with its tax obligation, operating revenues, assets, and equity unchanged. What would happen to ROE and its components?

(2) If total assets climb by 20 percent, what will happen to Wilmington's efficiency ratio and ROE?

(3) What effect would a 20 percent higher level of equity capital have upon ROE and its components?

12. Using this information for Laredo International Bank and Trust Company (all figures in millions), calculate the bank's net interest margin, noninterest margin, and ROA.

Interest income	$55	Noninterest expense	$ 8
Interest expense	$38	Noninterest income	$ 5
Provision for loan losses	$ 3	Special income and expense	
Security gains (or losses)	$ 2	(including taxes)	$ 1
		Total assets	$986

13. Valley Savings reported these figures (in millions) on its income statement for the past five years. Calculate the institution's ROA in each year. Are there any adverse trends? Any favorable trends? What seems to be happening to this institution?

	Current Year	One Year Ago	Two Years Ago	Three Years Ago	Four Years Ago
Gross interest income	$ 40	$ 41	$ 38	$ 35	$ 33
Interest expenses	24	23	20	18	15
Noninterest income	4	4	3	2	1
Noninterest expenses	8	7	7	6	5
Provisions for loan losses	2	1	1	0*	0*
Income taxes owed	1	1	0	1	0
Net securities gains (or losses)	(2)	(1)	0	1	2
Total assets	$385	$360	$331	$319	$293

*Less than 0.5.

14. An analysis of the UBPR reports on NCB was presented in this chapter. We examined a wide variety of profitability measures for that bank, including ROA, ROE, net profit margin, net interest and operating margins, and asset utilization. However, the various measures of earnings risk, credit risk, solvency risk, liquidity risk, market risk, and interest rate risk were not discussed in detail. Using the data in Tables 5–5 through 5–9, calculate each of these dimensions of risk for NCB for the most recent two years and discuss how the bank's risk exposure appears to be changing over time. What steps would you recommend to management to deal with any risk exposure problems you observe?

15. Today banks, securities firms, insurance companies, and finance/credit-card businesses are battling for many of the same customers and for many of the same sources of capital to support their growth and expansion. As a result there is keen interest today in the comparative financial performance of firms in these four competing industries. Using S&P's Market Insight, Educational Version, see if you can determine which of these financial-service industries are outperforming the others in terms of returns on

equity capital and risk exposure. You may find it useful to select certain firms from the Market Insight file to compare performances across these industries. For example, you can compare the financial statements of such companies as MetLife Insurance Inc. (MET), Capital One Financial Group (COF), Goldman Sachs Group (GS), and FleetBoston Financial Corp. (FBF).

Internet Exercises

1. You have been asked to compare the growth rate in assets and deposits of several banks that are regarded as takeover targets for your growth-oriented company. These banks include

    Wells Fargo Bank, San Francisco (**www.wellsfargo.com**)

    Bank One Corp., Columbus, Ohio (**www.bankone.com**)

    Comerica Banks, Detroit (**www.comerica.com**)

    Using the above company websites and other appropriate sites, determine which of these banks seems to be growing faster and why. Which would you recommend as a possible takeover target and why?

2. A guest speaker visiting your class contends that Bank of America is one of the most profitable banks of its size in the United States. Your instructor says that's really not true; it tends to be a middle-of-the-road performer. Check these claims out on the web (for example, at **www.bankofamerica.com** and **www.fdic.gov**). Who is right and what makes you think so?

3. The Uniform Bank Performance Reports (UBPRs) provide detailed financial performance data on all federally supervised U.S. banks. Using the website of the Federal Financial Institutions Examination Council (at **www.ffiec.gov**), see if you can determine what happened to the net earnings and credit risk exposure of BankOne Corp. (**www.bankone.com**) and Wells Fargo Bank (**www.wellsfargo.com**) in the most recent year for which data is available.

STANDARD &POOR'S

S&P Market Insight Challenge

Use Standard & Poor's Market Insight website (**www.mhhe.com/edumarketinsight**) for this problem. S&P Industry Surveys always conclude with the sections "How to Analyze a Company" and a "Comparative Company Analysis." For timely information on the analysis of financial firms use the Industry tab in Market Insight, Educational Version. The drop-down menu supplies several subfinancial-service industry selections, such as Asset Management & Custody Banks, Consumer Finance, Diversified Banks, Diversified Capital Markets, Insurance Brokers, Investment Banking and Brokerage, Life & Health Insurance, Multiline Insurance, Property & Casualty Insurance, Regional Banks, and Thrifts & Mortgage Finance.

Once an industry has been selected you will find downloadable S&P Industry Surveys, covering such key financial services sectors as Banking, Investment Services, Financial Services Diversified, Insurance: Property and Casualty, Insurance: Life and Health, and Savings and Loans. Please download S&P Industry Surveys for two of these financial sectors and review the How to Analyze and Comparative Company Analysis write-ups on each. In each category of financial firms found in the Comparative Company Analysis, identify the firm with the highest return on equity capital (ROE). How do the ROEs compare across categories and subindustries? Are there any other performance measures that could be compared across financial-service sectors?

REAL NUMBERS
FOR REAL BANKS   Assignment for Chapter 5

EVALUATION OF YOUR BANK'S PROFITABILITY

In Chapter 5, we focus on the evaluation of financial statements. Key profitability ratios are introduced and ROE and ROA are broken down into component ratios to aid interpretation. We used the UBPR for National City Bank, the lead bank of National City Corporation, to illustrate trends (comparison of December 2002 with December 2001 bank data) and for comparative analysis (comparison of bank data with peer group data). You will be evaluating your bank by (1) expanding the holding company data you collected in Chapter 4 for your bank; (2) comparing this to data for a group of peer banks; and (3) utilizing the profitability ratios discussed in this chapter to evaluate management's performance.

Part One: A Performance Comparison to Peers

A. Open the Excel Workbook containing Spreadsheet One that you developed in Chapter 4's assignment. Insert another spreadsheet for comparing the performance and character of your bank with a group of peer institutions. This spreadsheet will be called Spreadsheet Two, and it will be used in forthcoming assignments. Copy Column A from Chapter 4's assignment to Column A in the newly created spreadsheet. This gives you the income and balance sheet items to direct the collection of further information. You will collect percentage data from the FDIC website to create a spreadsheet similar in form to Tables 5–7 and 5–9 in this chapter. Instead of using the bank UBPR you will continue to work with the holding company data that aggregates all the banks in your banking company.

	Components Expressed as Percentages of Total Assets			
	Your Bank	Peer Group	Your Bank	Peer Group
	12/31/yy	12/31/yy	12/31/yy	12/31/yy
Name of banking company (A1)				
Report of condition (A2)				
Date (A3)				
Total assets (A4)	%	%	%	%
Cash and due from depository institutions (A5)				
Securities (A6)				
Federal funds sold and reverse repurchase agreements (A7)				
Gross loans and leases (A8)				
(less) Loan loss allowance (A9)				
(less) Unearned income (A10)				
Net loans and leases (A11)				
Trading account assets (A12)				
Bank premises and fixed assets (A13)				
Other real estate owned (A14)				
Goodwill and other intangibles (A15)				
All other assets (A16)				
Total liabilities and capital (A18)	%	%	%	%
Total liabilities (A19)				
Total deposits (A20)				
Federal funds purchased and repurchase agreements (A21)				
Trading liabilities (A22)				
Other borrowed funds (A23)				
Subordinated debt (A24)				
All other liabilities (A25)				
Total equity capital (A27)				
Perpetual preferred stock (A28)				
Common stock (A29)				
Surplus (A30)				
Undivided profits (A31)				

www.mhhe.com/rose6e

Components Expressed as Percentages of Total Average Assets				
Report of income (A33)				
Total interest income (A34)	%	%	%	%
Total interest expense (A35)				
Net interest income (A36)				
Provision for loan and lease losses (A37)				
Total noninterest income (A38)				
Fiduciary activities (A39)				
Service charges on deposit accounts (A40)				
Trading account gains and fees (A41)				
Additional noninterest income (A42)				
Total noninterest expense (A43)				
Salaries and employee benefits (A44)				
Premises and equipment expense (A45)				
Additional noninterest expense (A46)				
Pretax net operating income (A47)				
Securities gains (losses) (A48)				
Applicable income taxes (A49)				
Income before extraordinary items (A50)				
Extraordinary gains—net (A51)				
Net income (A52)	%	%	%	%

To fill in the percentages: Go to the FDIC's Statistics on Depository Institutions (SDI) at **www3.fdic.gov/sdi/main .asp**.[1] Now you can create a report. The process asks you to "Select the Number of Columns." You want to select "**4**" to develop the format to collect data for your bank and for a peer group for the two most recent year-end (December 31, yyyy) reports. This provides four pull-down menus, each labeled Select One, where you define the information to be collected. In column 1 select Bank Holding Company from the menu, type in your bank's BHC ID # (you collected this information in Chapter 2's assignment), and choose the most recent year-end date available for your Report Date. Go to column 2 and select Standard Peer Group.

After that selection, some additional choices become available. Since we are dealing with large banks, choose Banks with Assets more than 10B from the pull-down menu and then choose either National or State, depending on your

bank's charter. The second column should have the same report date as the first column. Repeat this process for columns 3 and 4 using the same selection process, but choosing the prior year's date for the Report Date. After defining the four columns click on Next. At this point you focus on Report Selection, choosing to View and to do calculations in Percentages. Then you get to identify the information you want before creating the report by clicking Next.

For the Report of Condition, you will be able to enter most data directly from the Assets and Liabilities report generated at the FDIC website; however, you will have to explore the Net Loans and Leases link to get Gross Loans and Leases and Unearned Income, just as you did in the Chapter 4 assignment.

For the Report of Income you will find the information you need in Income and Expense. Print the reports and use them to enter the data in Columns B, C, D, and E in your most recently created Excel spreadsheet. By working with these statements, you will be familiarizing yourself with real-world financial statements and developing the language to talk with finance professionals from all types of financial institutions.[2]

[1] As regulatory agencies update and improve their sites, the addresses of particular pages will change. If this link does not take you to SDI use the following procedure: Enter the FDIC's website at **www.FDIC.gov** and then explore the link for Bank Data for Individual Banks. If you go to the Institution Directory, you will be able to Click on "Advanced Features"—a button on a tool bar at the top of the web page. This takes you to the Advanced Features Page where you choose the link Statistics on Depository Institutions (SDI). From this web page you will be able to "Enter SDI" by clicking on the button labeled just that.

[2] Notice that the SDI (as of the writing of this text) creates percentage data for the Report of Condition (balance sheet) items using quarter-end total assets; however, for the Report of Income (income statement) items, average assets over the year are used to calculate percentages.

B. Once you have collected the data, you will focus on a comparative analysis, comparing your bank's Report of Condition and Report of Income with those of the banks in its peer group. Write approximately one page comparing the assets, one page comparing the sources of funds (liabilities and capital), and one page comparing income and expenses. Describe similarities and differences between your bank and the group of comparable banks. Then provide any inferences you can make on the basis of the data.

Part Two: A Breakdown of Returns for Closer Analysis

A. Open Spreadsheet One. Immediately below the rows you created in Chapter 4's assignment, add the rows illustrated at the cell locations identified in parentheses.

B. Calculate the ratios for the most recent year in Column B and then the prior year in Column C using the formula functions in Excel and the data in Rows 1 through 52 to create

the entries. For example, the formula for ROE entered in cell B55 would be: "=B52/B26".

C. In rows 55 through 59, calculate the key profitability ratios from Equations 4–8 in the chapter. Write one paragraph comparing profitability across years.

D. Rows 60 through 63 provide the framework for a breakdown of equity returns, Equations 14–17 in this chapter. Write one paragraph discussing the change in ROE using this breakdown. Explain the equation and interpret the information for your bank.

E. Rows 64 through 66 call for a breakdown of the net profit margin, as illustrated by Equation 18. Write one paragraph discussing the components of net profit margin for your bank and the implications of the changes occurring across the years.

F. Rows 67 through 70 provide the framework for a breakdown of ROA (Equation 20 in this chapter). Write one paragraph discussing the change in ROA and its components for your bank.

	12/31/yyyy	12/31/yyyy
(A53)		
Profitability ratios (A54)		
Return on equity (A55)		
Return on assets (A56)		
Net interest margin (A57)		
Net noninterest margin (A58)		
Net operating margin (A59)		
Breakdown of ROE (A60)		
Net profit margin (A61)		
Asset utilization ratio (A62)		
Equity multiplier (A63)		
Breakdown of NPM (A64)		
Tax-management efficiency ratio (A65)		
Expense control efficiency ratio (A66)		
Breakdown of ROA (A67)		
Net interest margin (A68)		
Noninterest margin (A69)		
Special transactions affecting its net income (A70)		

Selected References

For an explanation of measuring and evaluating risk in banking and financial services, see the following:

1. Baer, Herbert, and Elijah Brewer. "Uninsured Deposits as a Source of Market Discipline: Some New Evidence." *Economic Perspectives*, Federal Reserve Bank of Chicago, September/October 1986, pp. 23–31.

2. Brewer, Elijah, III, and Cheng Few Lee. "How the Market Judges Bank Risk." *Economic Perspectives*, Federal Reserve Bank of Chicago, November/December 1986.

3. Gilbert, R. Alton, Andrew P. Meyer, and Mark D. Vaughn. "How Healthy Is the Banking System? Funneling Financial Data into Failure Probability." *Regional Economist*, Federal Reserve Bank of St. Louis, April 2001, pp. 12–13.

4. Nelson, William R., and Ann L. Owen. "Profits and Balance Sheet Developments at U.S. Commercial Banks in 1996." *Federal Reserve Bulletin*, June 1997, pp. 475–89.

5. Rose, Peter S. *Bank Mergers in a Deregulated Environment.* Rolling Meadows, IL: Bank Administration Institute, 1987.

6. ———. "Risk—Taking the Temperature and Finding a Cure." *The Canadian Banker*, November/December 1987, pp. 54–63.

7. Short, Eugenia D. "Bank Problems and Financial Safety Nets." *Economic Review*, Federal Reserve Bank of Dallas, March 1987, pp. 17–28.

8. Siems, Thomas F., and Kelly Klemme. "Banking in a Changing World." *Financial Industry Issues*, Federal Reserve Bank of Dallas, Second Quarter 1997, pp. 1–6.

9. Wright, David M., and James V. Houpt. "An Analysis of Commercial Bank Exposure to Interest Rate Risk." *Federal Reserve Bulletin*, February 1996, pp. 116–28.

For information on how to read bank financial statements and make comparisons among banks, see the following:

10. Bassett, William F., and Egon Zakrajsek. "Profits and Balance Sheet Developments at U.S. Commercial Banks in 1999." *Federal Reserve Bulletin*, June 2000, pp. 367–95.

11. Federal Financial Institutions Examination Council. *A User's Guide for the Uniform Bank Performance Report*, Washington, D.C., 2002.

12. Gilbert, R. Alton, and Gregory E. Sierra. "The Financial Condition of U.S. Banks: How Different Are Community Banks?" *Review*, Federal Reserve Bank of St. Louis, January/February 2003, pp. 43–56.

13. Gunther, Jeffrey W., and Robert R. Moore. "Financial Statements and Reality: Do Troubled Banks Tell All?" *Economic and Financial Review*, Federal Reserve Bank of Dallas, Third Quarter 2000, pp. 30–35.

14. Rose, Peter S. *Money and Capital Markets.* 8th ed. New York: McGraw-Hill/Irwin, 2002, chaps. 4–6.

15. Wetmore, Jill L., and John R. Brick. "The Basis Risk Component of Commercial Bank Stock Returns." *Journal of Economics and Business* 50 (1998), pp. 67–76.

Appendix

Improving the Performance of Banks and Other Financial Firms through Knowledge: Sources of Information on the Banking and Financial-Services Industry

Chapter 5 focused on how to measure the performance of banks and the performance of some of their closest competitors in today's financial marketplace. However, mere measurement of the dimensions of performance is not enough. Managers must have the tools and the knowledge necessary to improve performance over time. The chapters that follow this one will provide many of the tools needed for successful management of a bank or other financial institution, but managers will always need more information than textbooks can provide. Their problems and solutions may be highly technical and specific and will shift over time, often at a faster pace than the one at which textbooks are written. The same difficulty confronts regulators and customers. They must often reach far afield to gather vital information in order to evaluate their financial-service providers and get the most service from them.

Where do bankers and the managers of other financial institutions find the information they need? One good source is the professional schools in many regions of the nation. Among the most popular of these have been the Stonier Graduate School of Banking and the School of Bank Marketing and Management, both sponsored by the American Bankers Association. Other professional schools are often devoted to specific problem areas, such as marketing, consumer lending, and commercial lending. Each offers educational materials and often supplies homework problems to solve.

Beyond the professional schools, selected industry trade associations annually publish a prodigious volume of written studies and management guidelines for wrestling with important performance problems, such as developing and promoting new services, working out problem assets, designing a financial plan, and so on. Among the most popular trade associations publishing problem-solving information in the financial services field are these:

- The American Bankers Association at **www.aba.com**.
- Bank Administration Institute at **www.bai.org**.
- Risk Management Association (RMA), Association of Risk Management and Lending Professionals at **www.rmahq.org**.
- America's Community Bankers at **www.acbankers.org**.
- Credit Union National Association (CUNA) at **www.cuna.org**.
- American Council of Life Insurance (ACLI) at **www.acli.org**.

- Investment Company Institute (ICI) at **www.ici.org**.
- Insurance Information Institute (III) at **www.iii.org**.

In addition to the material provided by these and numerous other trade associations, dozens of journals, news releases, and books are released each year by book publishing houses, magazine publishers, and government agencies. Among the most important of these recurring sources are the following:

General Information on Banking and Competing Financial-Service Industries

- *ABA Banking Journal* (published by the American Bankers Association at **www.banking.com** and **www.aba.com/Products**).
- *Risk Management and Lending Professionals Journal* (published by the Risk Management Association at **www.rmahq.org**).
- *The Canadian Banker* (published by the Canadian Bankers Association and discussed at **www.cba.ca**).
- *ABA Bank Marketing Magazine* at **www.aba.com/MarketingNetwork**.

Sources of Data on Individual Banks and Competing Financial Firms

- Uniform Bank Performance Reports (UBPR) (published quarterly by the Federal Financial Institutions Examination Council at **www.fiec.gov**).
- Historical Bank Condition and Income Reports (available from the National Technical Information Service and discussed at **www.ntis.org**).
- *American Banker Online* (banking industry newspaper published by the American Bankers Association and discussed at **www.americanbanker.com**).
- *The Wall Street Journal* (published by Dow Jones & Co., Inc., and online at **www.wsj.com**).

Economic and Financial Trends Affecting Banking and the Financial Services Sector

- *Survey of Current Business* (published by the U.S. Department of Commerce and discussed at **www.bea.doc.gov**).
- *Federal Reserve Bulletin* (published by the Board of Governors of the Federal Reserve System. Information from the *Bulletin* also available at **www.federalreserve.gov/pubs/bulletin**).

- *National Economic Trends* and *Monetary Trends* (all published by the Federal Reserve Bank of St. Louis and discussed at **www.stls.frb.org**).

Books and Journals Focusing on Laws and Regulations and International Developments Affecting Banks and Other Financial-Service Providers

- *International Economic Conditions* (published by the Federal Reserve Bank of St. Louis and accessible by mail and via **www.stls.frb.org**).
- *The Economist* (London) (available by subscription; information may be found at **www.economist.com**).
- *Banking and Financial Institutions Law* by William A. Lovett, 5th ed., published by West Group, St. Paul, Minnesota, 2001.

Key Regulatory Agencies

- Office of the Comptroller of the Currency (OCC) at **www.occ.treas.gov**.
- Board of Governors of the Federal Reserve System at **www.federalreserve.gov**.
- Federal Deposit Insurance Corporation (FDIC) at **www.fdic.gov**.
- Office of Thrift Supervision at **www.ots.treas.gov**.

Basic Education in Banking and Financial Services for Both Bankers and Their Customers

- Consumer Action at **www.consumeraction.org**.
- Federal Reserve System at **www.federalreserve.gov**.
- Federal Reserve Bank of Minneapolis at **www.minneapolisfed.org**.

Industry Directories

Directories for many industries give lists of businesses in an industry by name, city, state, and country of location. Some of the more complete directories provide essential avenues of contact for directory users, such as the names of key officers within a firm and the company's mailing address, telephone number, and e-mail address. More detailed directories have abbreviated financial statements of the firms listed and may even have a historical sketch about each firm. One common use of these directories is to pursue possible employment opportunities. Among the best-known industry directories are these:

- *Thomson/Polk Bank Directory* (see **www.finance.tfp.com**).
- *Almanac World Bankers Directory* (see **www.cd-directories.com**).
- *International Insurance Directory* (also described at **www.cd-directories.com**).

Asset-Liability Management Techniques and Hedging against Interest Rate and Credit Risk

Interest rates—the prices paid for obtaining credit—are one of the most important variables the managers of financial-service firms must work with every day. Adverse changes in market interest rates can both erode a financial institution's profitability and wipe out all or a substantial portion of the stockholders' investment in the institution. Banks' sensitivity to interest rate changes is especially severe because of the mismatch between their volatile short-term liabilities (mainly deposits) and their longer-term assets (mainly loans).

Equally troublesome is the fact that financial-service managers do not control interest rates—these rates are determined in national and international markets. Financial-service providers must learn how to manage no matter how high or low interest rates are and no matter how those rates are changing every day. The critical forces driving market interest rates include the demands of thousands of borrowers, the many suppliers of savings, and the forces of inflation, credit risk, demands for liquidity, maturity, and hundreds of other factors. Because of the tremendous number of factors shaping interest rates, they are difficult—indeed virtually impossible—to predict. However, some managers try to do so and often get into serious trouble.

Take one example: Japan's huge money center banks, which recently had taken on more than 40 trillion yen in interest rate swaps and could profit if long-term interest rates stayed low. The obvious danger that concerned many market analysts centered on the risk that interest rates might, in fact, rise more quickly than anticipated, subjecting these banks to substantial losses in their swap positions. Japanese banks were already struggling with well-publicized losses in their loan portfolios due to a weak, deflationary economy.

Clearly, the managers of financial institutions must avoid interest-rate speculation and, instead, learn how to *hedge* against interest rate movements. Managers need to learn to use the tools of interest-rate hedging, including gap analysis, duration, financial futures and options, and interest rate swaps. They must also be conscious of their exposure to interest-rate risk from their growing off-balance-sheet activities (such as loan securitizations, standby credits, and credit derivatives).

The foregoing hedging tools and off-balance-sheet activities are explored in depth in this part of the book. Here we learn that managers must know about so much more than just one or a few departments within their financial institutions. The important management technique known as asset-liability management (ALM) teaches us that every department and activity within a bank or other financial firm affects its overall performance. Good financial-service managers must learn how to take into account in their decisions both those departments that are raising funds and those that are using funds. Only then can a financial-service manager hope to effectively deal with the risk of damage from changing market interest rates and other risk factors that may impact a financial institution's survival.

Asset-Liability Management: Determining and Measuring Interest Rates and Controlling Interest-Sensitive and Duration Gaps

Key Topics in This Chapter

- Asset, Liability, and Funds Management
- Market Rates and Interest-Rate Risk
- The Goals of Interest-Rate Hedging
- Interest-Sensitive Gap Management
- Duration Gap Management
- Limitations of Hedging Techniques

Introduction

Banks and many of their financial-service competitors today are highly complex organizations, offering multiple financial services through multiple departments and divisions, each staffed by specialists in making different kinds of financial decisions.[1] Thus, different groups of individuals inside each modern financial firm usually make the decisions about which customers are to receive credit, which securities should be added to or subtracted from the financial institution's portfolio, which terms should be offered to the public on

[1] Portions of this chapter are based upon Peter S. Rose's article in *The Canadian Banker* (7) and are used with the permission of the publisher.

Asset-liability management is one of the most useful analytical tools developed in modern banking and financial-services management. Bankers and the managers of other financial institutions recognize this growing body of knowledge, usually referred to as ALM, as a series of management tools to help reduce risk exposure (particularly to the susceptibility to loss from changing market interest rates).

The most significant websites in the asset-liability management field include a network built to help ALM professional practicioners, known as ALM Professional, at **www.ALMprofessional.com**. This website is devoted to articles and discussions that cover several different facets of the asset-liability management field. You can also find information designed to help in the preparation of ALM committee reports and forecasts, as well as aids in measuring a financial firm's risk exposure, on such websites as BancWare! at **www.risk.sunguard.com/bancware**. In addition, several consultants have recently established themselves on the Internet to aid financial-service managers in applying ALM tools to their particular situation, including such websites as **www.profitstar.com, www.raterisk.com, www.iris.ch,** and **directory.google.com**—see business (finance).

Duration gap management is a powerful analytical tool for protecting net worth (owner's equity capital) of a bank from damage due to shifting interest rates. Professionals in banking and financial services, particularly those employees working in the asset-liability management (ALM) field, have found this tool surprisingly resilient and robust even when its basic assumptions are not fully met. Among the more interesting sites on the Web dealing with the use of duration and duration gaps are **www.tcs.com, www.alamols.com** and **www.aba.com**.

There has also been rapid expansion in asset-liability management tools available through various business websites for credit unions, savings associations, insurance companies, finance companies, mutual funds, investment banking houses, and selected other financial institutions. A prominent example includes **www.kesdee.com**.

loans, deposits, investment advice, and other services, and which sources of capital the institution should draw upon.

Yet, all of the foregoing management decisions are intimately linked to each other. For example, decisions on which customer credit requests should be fulfilled are closely related to the ability of the financial firm to raise deposit and nondeposit borrowed funds in order to support the requested new loans. Similarly, the amount of risk that a bank or other financial firm accepts in its portfolio is closely related to the adequacy and composition of its capital (net worth), which protects its stockholders, depositors, and other creditors against loss. Even as a financial institution takes on more risk it must protect the value of its net worth from erosion, which could result in ultimate failure.

In a well-managed financial institution all of these diverse management decisions must be coordinated across the whole institution in order to insure that they do not clash with each other, leading to inconsistent actions that damage earnings and net worth. Today bankers and other financial-service managers have learned to look at their asset and liability portfolios as an *integrated whole*, considering how their institution's whole portfolio contributes to the firm's broad goals of adequate profitability and acceptable risk. This type of coordinated and integrated decision making is known today as **asset-liability management** (ALM). The collection of managerial techniques that we call asset-liability management provides financial institutions with defensive weapons to handle such challenging events as business cycles and seasonal pressures and with offensive weapons to shape portfolios of assets and liabilities in ways that promote each institution's goals. The key purpose of this chapter is to give the reader a picture of how this integrated approach to managing assets, liabilities, and equity really works.

Asset-Liability Management Strategies

Asset Management Strategy

Financial institutions have not always possessed a completely integrated view of their assets and liabilities. Through most of the history of banking, for example, bankers tended to take their sources of funds—liabilities and equity—largely for granted. This so-called **asset management** view held that the amount and kinds of deposits a bank held and the volume of other borrowed funds it was able to attract were largely determined by its customers. Under this view, the public determined the relative amounts of checkable deposits, savings accounts, and other sources of funds available to depository institutions. The key decision area for management was not deposits and other borrowings but assets. The banker could exercise control only over the allocation of incoming funds by deciding who was to receive the scarce quantity of loans available and what the terms on those loans would be. Indeed, there was some logic behind this asset management approach because, prior to deregulation of the banking and thrift industries, the types of deposits, the rates offered, and the nondeposit sources of funds banks and thrifts could draw upon were closely regulated. Managers had only limited discretion in reshaping their sources of funds.

Liability Management Strategy

The 1960s and 1970s ushered in dramatic changes in asset-liability management strategies. Confronted with soaring interest rates and intense competition for funds, bankers and many of their competitors began to devote greater attention to opening up new sources of funding and monitoring the mix and cost of their deposit and nondeposit liabilities. The new strategy was called **liability management.** Its goal was simply to gain control over funds sources comparable to the control financial managers had long exercised over their assets. The key control lever was *price,* the interest rate and other terms banks and their competitors could offer on their deposits and borrowings to achieve the volume, mix, and cost desired. For example, a bank faced with heavy loan demand that exceeded its available funds could simply raise the offer rate on its deposits and money market borrowings relative to its competitors, and funds would flow in. On the other hand, a bank flush with funds but with few profitable outlets for those funds could leave its offer rate unchanged or even lower that price, letting competitors outbid it for whatever funds were available in the marketplace. Exhibit 6–1 charts the goals of asset-liability management.

Funds Management Strategy

The maturing of liability management techniques, coupled with more volatile interest rates and greater risk, eventually gave birth to the **funds management** approach, which dominates banking and the activities of many competitors today. This view is a much more balanced approach to asset-liability management that stresses several key objectives:

1. Management should exercise as much control as possible over the volume, mix, and return or cost of *both* assets and liabilities in order to achieve the financial institution's goals.

2. Management's control over assets must be coordinated with its control over liabilities so that asset management and liability management are internally consistent and do not pull against each other. Effective coordination in managing assets and liabilities will help to maximize the spread between revenues and costs and control risk exposure.

3. Revenues and costs arise from both sides of the balance sheet (i.e., from both assets and liabilities). Management policies need to be developed that maximize returns and minimize costs from supplying services.

EXHIBIT 6–1
Asset-Liability
Management
in Banking and
Financial Services

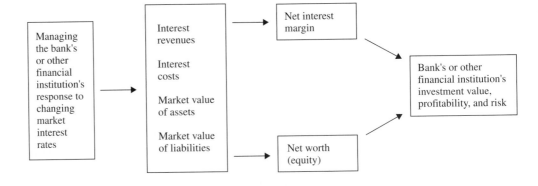

Thus, the traditional view that all income received by banks and many of their competitors must come from loans and investments has given way to the notion that financial institutions today sell a *bundle of financial services*—credit, payments, savings, financial advice, and the like—that should each be priced to cover their cost of production. *Income from managing the liability side of the balance sheet can help achieve profitability goals as much as revenues generated from managing loans and other assets.*

Interest Rate Risk: One of the Greatest Asset-Liability Management Challenges

No financial manager can completely avoid one of the toughest and potentially most damaging forms of risk that all banks and many of their competitors must face—**interest rate risk.** When interest rates change in the financial marketplace, the sources of revenue banks and their closest competitors receive—especially interest income on loans and securities—and their most important source of expenses—interest cost on deposits and other borrowings—must also change. Moreover, changing market interest rates also change the market value of assets and liabilities, thereby changing the financial institution's net worth—that is, the value of the owner's investment in the firm. Thus, changing market interest rates impact both the balance sheet and the statement of income and expense of banks and other financial-service institutions.

Forces Determining Interest Rates

The problem with interest rates is that although they are critical to every bank and to many other financial institutions, the managers of these financial firms simply cannot control either the level of or the trend in market rates of interest. The rate of interest on any particular loan or security is ultimately determined by the financial marketplace where suppliers of loanable funds (credit) interact with demanders of loanable funds (credit) and the interest rate (price of credit) tends to settle at the point where the quantities of loanable funds (credit) demanded and supplied are equal, as shown in Exhibit 6–2.

In granting loans, bankers and their competitors are on the *supply* side of the loanable funds (credit) market, but each lending institution is only one supplier of credit in an

EXHIBIT 6–2
Determination of the
Rate of Interest

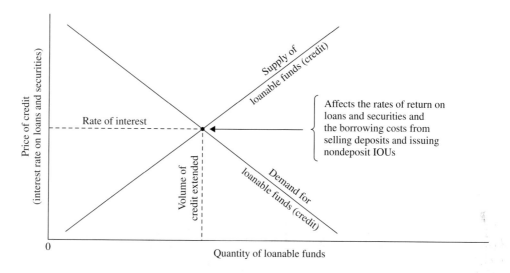

international market for loanable funds that includes many thousands of lenders. Similarly, bankers and comparable financial firms come into the financial marketplace as demanders of loanable funds (credit) when they offer deposit services to the public or issue nondeposit IOUs to raise funds for lending and investing. But, again, each financial institution, no matter how large it is, is only *one* demander of loanable funds in a market containing thousands of borrowers.

Thus, whether bankers and their principal competitors are on the supply side or the demand side of the loanable funds (credit) market at any given moment (and banks and other financial intermediaries are usually on *both* sides of the credit market simultaneously), they cannot determine the level, or be sure about the trend, of market interest rates. Rather, the individual financial institution can only react to the level of and trend in interest rates in a way that best allows it to achieve its goals. In other words, most bankers and other financial managers must be *price takers*, not price makers, and must accept interest rates as a given and plan accordingly.

As market interest rates move, bankers and their competitors face at least two major kinds of interest rate risk—price risk and reinvestment risk. *Price risk* arises when market interest rates rise, causing the market values of most bonds and fixed-rate loans to fall. If a financial institution wishes to sell these financial instruments in a rising rate period, it must be prepared to accept capital losses. *Reinvestment risk* rears its head when market interest rates fall, forcing a financial firm to invest incoming funds in lower-yielding earning assets, lowering its expected future income. A big part of managing assets and liabilities consists of finding ways to deal effectively with these two forms of risk from changing market interest rates.

The Measurement of Interest Rates

When we use the term *interest rates* exactly what do we mean? How are interest rates measured?

Most of us understand what interest rates are because we have borrowed money at one time or another and know that interest rates are the *price of credit*, demanded by lenders as compensation for the use of borrowed funds. In simplest terms the interest rate is a ratio of the fees we must pay to obtain the use of credit divided by the amount of credit obtained. However, over the years a bewildering array of interest-rate measures have been developed as we will see in future pages of this book.

One of the most popular rate measures is the **yield to maturity (YTM),** which is the discount rate that equalizes the current market value of a loan or security with the expected stream of future income payments that the loan or security will generate. In terms of a formula, the yield to maturity may be found from

$$\text{Current market price of a loan or security} = \frac{\text{Expected cash flow in Period 1}}{(1 + YTM)^1} + \frac{\text{Expected cash flow in Period 2}}{(1 + YTM)^2} \tag{1}$$

$$+ \cdots + \frac{\text{Expected cash flow in Period n}}{(1 + YTM)^n} + \frac{\text{Sale or redemption price of security or loan in Period n}}{(1 + YTM)^n}$$

For example, a bond purchased today at a price of $950 and promising an interest payment of $100 each over the next three years, when it will be redeemed by the bond's issuer for $1,000, will have a promised interest rate, measured by the yield to maturity, determined by:

$$\$950 = \frac{\$100}{(1 + YTM)^1} + \frac{\$100}{(1 + YTM)^2} + \frac{\$100}{(1 + YTM)^3} + \frac{\$1000}{(1 + YTM)^3}$$

This bond's yield to maturity is determined to be 12.10 percent.[2]

Another popular interest rate measure is the **bank discount rate,** which is often quoted on short-term loans and money market securities (such as U.S. Treasury bills). The formula for calculating the discount rate (DR) is as follows:

$$DR = \left(\frac{100 - \text{Purchase price on loan or security}}{100} \right) \tag{2}$$

$$\times \frac{360}{\text{Number of days to maturity}}$$

For example, suppose a money market loan or security can be purchased for a price of $96 and has a face value of $100 to be paid at maturity. If the loan or security matures in 90 days, its interest rate measured by the bank DR must be

$$DR = \frac{(100 - 96)}{100} \times \frac{360}{90} = 0.16, \text{ or } 16 \text{ percent}$$

We note that this interest rate measure ignores the effect of compounding of interest and is based on a 360-day year, unlike the yield to maturity measure, which assumes a 365-day year and assumes as well that interest income is compounded at the calculated yield to maturity (YTM).

In addition, the DR uses the *face value* of a financial instrument to calculate its yield or rate of return, a simple approach that makes calculations easier but is theoretically incorrect. The purchase price of a financial instrument, rather than its face amount, is a much better base to use in calculating the instrument's true rate of return, according to the theory of finance.

To convert a DR to the equivalent yield to maturity we can use the formula:

$$\text{YTM equivalent yield} = \frac{(100 - \text{Purchase price})}{\text{Purchase price}} \times \frac{365}{\text{Days to maturity}} \tag{3}$$

---

[2] Financial calculators and spreadsheets such as Excel will give this yield to maturity figure directly after entering the bond's purchase price, promised interest payments, sales or redemption price, and number of time periods covered. (See appendix on using financial calculators at the end of the book for details concerning these applications.) Note: the YTM for bonds is equivalent to the APR for loans.

For the money market security discussed previously, its equivalent yield to maturity would be

$$\text{YTM equivalent} = \frac{(100 - 96)}{96} \times \frac{365}{90} = 0.1690, \text{ or } 16.90 \text{ percent}$$

While the two interest rate measures listed above are very popular, we should keep in mind that there are literally dozens of other measures of "the interest rate," many of which we will encounter in later chapters of this book.

The Components of Interest Rates

Over the years many bankers and other financial managers have tried to forecast future movements in market interest rates as an aid to combating interest rate risk. However, the fact that interest rates are determined by the interactions of thousands of credit suppliers and demanders makes consistently accurate rate forecasting virtually impossible. Adding to the forecasting problem is the fact that any particular interest rate attached to a loan or security is composed of multiple elements or building blocks, including

$$
\begin{array}{ccc}
\text{Market} & \text{Risk-free real} & \text{Risk premiums to compensate} \\
\text{interest rate} & \text{interest rate} & \text{lenders who accept risky} \\
\text{on a risky} = & \text{(such as the} & + \text{IOUs for their default (credit)} \\
\text{loan or} & \text{inflation-adjusted} & \text{risk, inflation risk, term or} \\
\text{security} & \text{return on} & \text{maturity risk, marketability} \\
& \text{government bonds)} & \text{risk, call risk, and so on}
\end{array}
\qquad (4)
$$

Not only does the *risk-free real interest rate* change over time with shifts in the demand and supply for loanable funds, but the perceptions of lenders and borrowers in the financial marketplace concerning each of the *risk premiums* that make up any particular market interest rate on a risky loan or security also change over time, causing market interest rates to move up or down, often erratically.

Risk Premiums To cite some examples, when the economy goes into a recession with declining business sales and rising unemployment, many lenders will conclude that some businesses will fail and some individuals will lose their jobs, increasing the risk of borrower default. The *default-risk premium* component of the interest rate charged a risky borrower will increase, raising the borrower's loan rate (all other factors held constant). Similarly, an announcement of rising prices on goods and services may trigger lenders to expect a trend toward higher inflation, reducing the purchasing power of their loan income unless they demand from borrowers a higher *inflation-risk premium* to compensate for their projected loss in purchasing power. Many loan and security interest rates also contain a premium for *liquidity risk*, because some of these financial instruments are more difficult to sell quickly at a favorable price to another lender, and for *call risk*, which arises when a borrower has the right to pay off a loan early, reducing the lender's expected rate of return.

Yield Curves Another key component of each interest rate is the *maturity*, or *term*, *premium*. Longer-term loans and securities often carry higher market interest rates than shorter-term loans and securities due to maturity risk because of greater opportunities for loss over the life of a longer-term loan. The graphic picture of how interest rates vary with different maturities of loans viewed at a single point in time (and assuming that all other factors, such as credit risk, are held constant) is called a *yield curve*.

Exhibit 6–3 charts three different U.S. Treasury security yield curves plotted in December of 2001, November 2002, and for the week ending December 13, 2002. The maturities

EXHIBIT 6–3

Yield Curves for U.S. Treasury Securities (December 2001 and 2002)

Source: Federal Reserve Bank of St. Louis, *Monetary Trends*, January 2003.

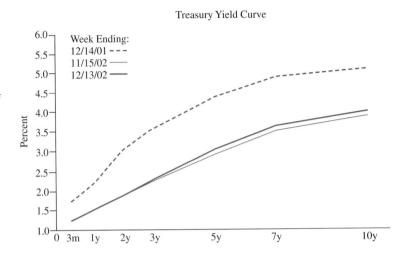

Treasury Yield Curve

of Treasury securities (in months and years) are plotted along the horizontal axis and the yields to maturity (YTM) for each maturity of Treasury security appear along the vertical axis. Yield curves are constantly changing shape because the yields on the securities included in each curve change every day. Moreover, different yields change at different speeds with short-term interest rates tending to rise or fall faster than long-term rates, though this is not always the case.

Occasionally long-term interest rates will move over a wider range than short-term rates for brief periods. For example, we notice in Exhibit 6–3 that the steeply upward-sloping yield curve prevailing in December of 2001 had become a somewhat flatter, less precipitous yield curve one year later. Long-term interest rates (along the right-hand portion of the yield curve) had moved downward by more than a percentage point, while short-term interest rates (along the left-hand portion of the curve) also fell but by less than the decline in long-term rates.

The relative changes in short-term interest rates versus long-term interest rates varies greatly over time. This is very evident in the picture presented in Exhibit 6–4, which plots the 3-month U.S. Treasury bill rate compared to the 10-year Treasury bond rate. We notice, for example, that in periods of recession (the shaded areas in Exhibit 6–4), with the economy struggling, short-term interest rates tend to fall relative to long-term interest rates and the gap between the two tends to widen. In contrast, a period of economic prosperity usually begins with a fairly wide gap between long- and short-term interest rates, but that interest-rate gap tends to narrow and sometimes becomes negative.

In summary, yield curves will display an *upward* slope (i.e., a rising yield curve) when long-term interest rates exceed short-term interest rates. This often happens when all interest rates are rising but short-term rates have started from a lower level than long-term rates. Yield curves can also slope *downward* (i.e., a negative yield curve), with short-term interest rates higher than long-term interest rates. Finally, *horizontal* yield curves prevail when long-term interest rates and short-term rates are at approximately the same level so that investors receive the same yield to maturity no matter what maturity of security they buy.

The Maturity Gap and the Yield Curve Typically bankers and the managers of many nonbank financial institutions fare somewhat better with an *upward-sloping yield curve*, where longer-term interest rates are higher than shorter-term interest rates, than they do under a horizontal or downward-sloping yield curve. The upward-sloping yield curve is

EXHIBIT 6–4   Spread between Short-Term and Long-Term Interest Rates
(based on 3-month and 10-year U.S. Treasury yields)

Source: Federal Reserve Bank of St. Louis, *Monetary Trends*, January 2003.

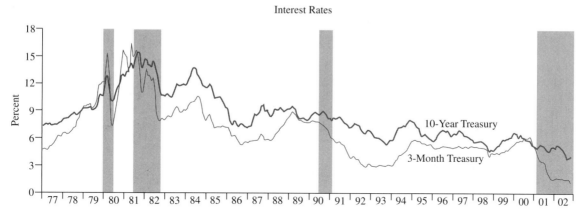

Note: Shaded areas reflect periods of economic recession.

usually more favorable for the profitability of banks and similar lending institutions be-cause their loans and security holdings on the asset side of their balance sheet tend to have longer maturities than their sources of funds (liabilities), such as deposits and money-market borrowings.

Thus, most banks and similar type lending institutions experience a positive **maturity gap** between the average maturity of their assets and the average maturity of their liabilities. If the yield curve is upward sloping, then revenues from longer-term assets will out-strip expenses from shorter-term liabilities. The result will normally be a *positive* net interest margin (interest revenues greater than interest expenses), which tends to gener-ate higher earnings. In contrast, a relatively flat (horizontal) or negatively sloped yield curve often generates a small or even negative net interest margin, putting downward pres-sure on the earnings of banks and other financial firms that borrow short and lend long.

The Response of Banks and Other Financial Firms to Interest Rate Risk

As we noted at the outset, changes in market interest rates can damage a bank or other financial firm's profitability by increasing its cost of funds, lowering its returns from earn-ing assets, and reducing the value of the owners' investment (net worth or equity capital). Moreover, recent decades have ushered in a period of volatile interest rates, confronting financial managers with an entirely new and more unpredictable environment to work in. A dramatic example of the huge losses associated with interest-rate risk exposure occurred in Minnesota when First Bank System, Inc., of Minneapolis bought unusually large quan-tities of government bonds. First Bank's management had forecast a decline in interest rates. Unfortunately, bond prices fell as interest rates rose, and First Bank reported a loss of about $500 million, resulting in the sale of its headquarters building (see Bailey [2]).

In recent decades bankers have aggressively sought ways to insulate their asset and lia-bility portfolios and their profits from the ravages of changing interest rates. For example, many banks now conduct their asset-liability management strategies under the guidance of an *asset-liability committee*, which usually meets daily. Such a committee not only chooses strategies to deal with interest rate risk but also participates in both short- and long-range planning, in preparing strategies to handle the institution's liquidity needs, and in dealing with other management issues.

Factoid

As the 21st century opened and market interest rates fell to record lows, interest-rate risk threatened to severely impact the net asset values of what major competitor of banks?

Answer: Money market funds, which were often forced to lower their fees in order to avoid reducing the net value of their assets below the accepted market standard of $1.00 per share.

One of the Goals of Interest Rate Hedging

In dealing with interest rate risk, one important goal is to insulate *profits*—net income after taxes and all other expenses—from the damaging effects of fluctuating interest rates. No matter which way interest rates go, managers of financial institutions want profits that achieve the level desired and are stable.

To accomplish this particular goal, management must concentrate on those elements of the institution's portfolio of assets and liabilities that are most sensitive to interest rate movements. Normally this includes loans and investments on the asset side of the balance sheet—earning assets—and interest-bearing deposits and money market borrowings on the liability side. In order to protect profits against adverse interest rate changes, then, management seeks to hold fixed the financial firm's **net interest margin** (NIM), expressed as follows:

$$\text{NIM} = \frac{\left(\begin{array}{cc} \text{Interest income} & \text{Interest expense on} \\ \text{from loans} & - \text{ deposits and other} \\ \text{and investments} & \text{borrowed funds} \end{array} \right)}{\text{Total earning assets}} \tag{5}$$

$$= \frac{\text{Net interest income after expenses}}{\text{Total earning assets}}$$

For example, suppose a large international bank records $4 billion in interest revenues from its loans and security investments and $2.6 billion in interest expenses paid out to attract deposits and other borrowed funds. If this bank holds $40 billion in earning assets, its net interest margin is

$$\text{NIM} = \frac{(\$4 \text{ billion} - \$2.6 \text{ billion})}{\$40 \text{ billion}} \times 100 = 3.50 \text{ percent}$$

Note how narrow this net interest margin (which is fairly close to the average for the banking industry) is at just 3.5 percent, which is not this bank's profit from borrowing and lending funds because we have not considered noninterest expenses (such as employee salaries and overhead expenses). Once these expenses are also deducted, the manager of this bank generally has very little margin for error in protecting against interest rate risk. If management does find this 3.5 percent net interest margin acceptable, it will probably use a variety of interest-rate risk hedging methods to protect this NIM ratio value, thereby helping to stabilize the bank's net earnings.

If the interest cost of borrowed funds rises faster than income from loans and securities, a bank's NIM will be squeezed, with adverse effects on bank profits.[3] If interest rates fall and cause income from loans and securities to decline faster than interest costs on borrowings, the NIM will again be squeezed. In other words, yield curves do not usually move in parallel fashion over time, so that the yield spread between borrowing costs and interest revenues is never perfectly constant. Management must struggle continuously to find ways to ensure that borrowing costs do not rise significantly relative to interest income and threaten the margin of a bank or other financial intermediary.

---

[3] In recent years, as noted by Alden Toevs [8], the net interest income of U.S. banks has accounted for about 60 to 80 percent of their net earnings. Toevs also found evidence of a substantial increase in the volatility of net interest income over time, encouraging managers of financial institutions to find better methods for managing interest-rate risk.

6-3. What forces cause interest rates to change? What kinds of risk do bankers and other financial firms face when interest rates change?

6-4. What makes it so difficult to correctly forecast interest rate changes?

6-5. What is the yield curve and why is it important to know about its shape or slope?

6-6. What is it that a bank or other lending institution wishes to protect from adverse movements in interest rates?

6-7. What is the goal of *hedging?*

6-8. First National Bank of Bannerville has posted interest revenues of $63 million and interest costs from all of its borrowings of $42 million. If this bank possesses $700 million in total earning assets, what is First National's net interest margin? Suppose the bank's interest revenues and interest costs double, while its earning assets increase by 50 percent. What will happen to its net interest margin?

Interest-Sensitive Gap Management

The most popular interest rate hedging strategy in use today is often called **interest-sensitive gap management.** Gap management techniques require management to perform an analysis of the maturities and repricing opportunities associated with interest-bearing assets and with deposits and other borrowings. If management feels its institution is excessively exposed to interest rate risk, it will try to match as closely as possible the volume of assets that can be repriced as interest rates change with the volume of deposits and other liabilities whose rates can also be adjusted with market conditions during the same time period.

For example, a bank can hedge itself against interest rate changes—no matter which way rates move—by making sure for each time period that the

$$\text{Dollar amount of repriceable} \atop \text{(interest-sensitive)} \atop \text{assets} \quad = \quad \text{Dollar amount of repriceable} \atop \text{(interest-sensitive)} \atop \text{liabilities} \qquad \textbf{(6)}$$

In this case, the revenue from earning assets will change in the same direction and by approximately the same proportion as the interest cost of liabilities.

What is a repriceable asset? A repriceable liability? The most familiar examples of repriceable assets are loans that are about to mature or are coming up for renewal. If interest rates have risen since these loans were first made, the lender will renew them only if it can get an expected yield that approximates the higher yields currently expected on other financial instruments of comparable quality. Similarly, loans that are maturing will provide the lender with funds to reinvest in new loans at today's interest rates, so they represent repriceable assets as well. Repriceable liabilities include a depository institution's CDs about to mature or be renewed, where the financial firm and its customers must negotiate a new deposit interest rate to capture current market conditions; floating-rate deposits whose yields move automatically with market interest rates; and money-market borrowings whose rates are often adjusted daily to reflect the latest market developments.

What happens when the amount of repriceable assets does not equal the amount of repriceable liabilities? Clearly, a *gap* exists between these interest-sensitive assets and interest-sensitive liabilities. The gap is the portion of the balance sheet affected by interest rate risk:

$$\text{Interest-sensitive gap} = \text{Interest-sensitive assets} \atop - \text{Interest-sensitive liabilities} \qquad \textbf{(7)}$$

Examples of Repriceable Assets and Liabilities and Nonrepriceable Assets and Liabilities			
Repriceable Assets	**Repriceable Liabilities**	**Nonrepriceable Assets**	**Nonrepriceable Liabilities**
Short-term securities issued by governments and private borrowers (about to mature) Short-term loans made to borrowing customers (about to mature) Variable-rate loans and securities	Borrowings from the money market (such as federal funds or RP borrowings) Short-term savings accounts Money-market deposits (whose interest rates are adjustable every few days)	Cash in the vault and deposits at the Central Bank (legal reserves) Long-term loans made at a fixed interest rate Long-term securities carrying fixed rates Buildings and equipment	Demand deposits (which pay no rate or a fixed interest rate) Long-term savings and retirement accounts Equity capital provided by the financial institution's owners

If interest-sensitive assets in each planning period (day, week, month, etc.) exceed the volume of interest-sensitive liabilities subject to repricing, the financial firm is said to have a *positive gap* and to be *asset sensitive*. Thus:

$$\text{Asset-sensitive (positive) gap} = \text{Interest-sensitive assets} - \text{Interest-sensitive liabilities} > 0 \qquad (8)$$

For example, suppose a commercial bank with interest-sensitive assets of $500 million and interest-sensitive liabilities of $400 million is asset sensitive with a positive gap of $100 million. If interest rates rise, this bank's net interest margin will increase because the interest revenue generated by assets will increase more than the cost of borrowed funds. Other things being equal, the bank will experience an increase in its net interest income. On the other hand, if interest rates fall when the bank is asset sensitive, this bank's NIM will decline as interest revenues from assets drop by more than interest expenses associated with liabilities. The bank with a positive gap will lose net interest income if interest rates fall.

In the opposite situation, suppose an interest-sensitive bank's liabilities are larger than its interest-sensitive assets. This bank then has a *negative gap* and is said to be *liability sensitive*. Thus:

$$\text{Liability-sensitive (negative) gap} = \text{Interest-sensitive assets} - \text{Interest-sensitive liabilities} < 0 \qquad (9)$$

A bank holding interest-sensitive assets of $150 million and interest-sensitive liabilities of $200 million is liability sensitive, with a negative gap of $50 million. Rising interest rates will lower this bank's net interest margin, because the rising cost associated with interest-sensitive liabilities will exceed increases in interest revenue from interest-sensitive assets. Falling interest rates will generate a higher interest margin and probably greater earnings as well, because borrowing costs will decline by more than interest revenues.

Actually, there are several ways to measure the interest-sensitive gap (IS GAP). One method is called simply the Dollar IS GAP. For example, as we saw above, if interest-sensitive assets (ISA) are $150 million and interest-sensitive liabilities (ISL) are $200 million, then the Dollar IS GAP = ISA − ISL = $150 million − $200 million = −$50 million. Clearly, an institution whose Dollar IS GAP is positive is asset sensitive, while a negative Dollar IS GAP describes a liability-sensitive condition.

An Asset-Sensitive Financial Firm Has:	A Liability-Sensitive Financial Firm Has:
Positive Dollar IS GAP	Negative Dollar IS GAP
Positive Relative IS GAP	Negative Relative IS GAP
Interest Sensitivity Ratio greater than one	Interest Sensitivity Ratio less than one

We can also form the Relative IS GAP ratio:

$$\text{Relative IS GAP} = \frac{\text{IS GAP}}{\substack{\text{Size of financial institution} \\ \text{(measured, for example,} \\ \text{by total assets)}}} = \frac{-\$50 \text{ million}}{\$150 \text{ million}} = -0.33 \qquad \textbf{(10)}$$

A Relative IS GAP greater than zero means the institution is asset sensitive, while a negative Relative IS GAP describes a liability-sensitive financial firm. Finally, we can simply compare the ratio of ISA to ISL, sometimes called the Interest Sensitivity Ratio (ISR). Based on the figures in our previous example,

$$\substack{\text{Interest Sensitivity Ratio} \\ \text{(ISR)}} = \frac{\text{ISA}}{\text{ISL}} = \frac{\$150 \text{ million}}{\$200 \text{ million}} = 0.75 \qquad \textbf{(11)}$$

In this instance an ISR of less than 1 tells us we are looking at a liability-sensitive institution, while an ISR greater than unity points to an asset-sensitive institution.

Only if interest-sensitive assets and liabilities are *equal* is a financial institution relatively insulated from interest rate risk. In this case, interest revenues from assets and funding costs will change at the same rate. The interest-sensitive gap is *zero*, and the net interest margin is protected regardless of which way interest rates go. As a practical matter, however, a zero gap does not eliminate all interest rate risk because the interest rates attached to assets and liabilities are not perfectly correlated in the real world. Loan interest rates, for example, tend to lag behind interest rates on many money market borrowings. So interest revenues often tend to grow more slowly than expenses during economic expansions, while interest expenses tend to fall more rapidly than revenues during economic downturns.

Gapping methods used today vary greatly in complexity and form. All methods, however, require financial managers to make some important decisions:

1. Management must choose the time period during which the net interest margin (NIM) is to be managed (e.g., six months, one year) to achieve some desired value and the length of subperiods ("maturity buckets") into which the planning period is to be divided.

2. Management must choose a target level for the net interest margin—that is, whether to freeze the margin roughly where it is or perhaps increase the NIM.

3. If management wishes to increase the NIM, it must either develop a correct interest rate forecast or find ways to reallocate earning assets and liabilities to increase the spread between interest revenues and interest expenses.

4. Management must determine the dollar volume of interest-sensitive assets and interest-sensitive liabilities it wants the financial firm to hold.

Computer-Based Techniques Many institutions use computer-based techniques in which their assets and liabilities are classified as due or repriceable today, during the coming week, in the next 30 days, and so on. Management tries to match interest-sensitive assets with interest-sensitive liabilities in each of these maturity buckets in order to improve the chances of achieving the financial firm's earnings goals. For example, a commercial bank's latest computer run might reveal the following:

Maturity Buckets	Interest-Sensitive Assets	Interest-Sensitive Liabilities	(dollars in millions)	
			Size of Gap	Cumulative Gap
1 day (next 24 hours)	$ 40	$ 30	+10	+10
Day 2–day 7	120	160	−40	−30
Day 8–day 30	85	65	+20	−10
Day 31–day 90	280	250	+30	+20
Day 91–day 120	455	395	+60	+80
•	•	•	•	•
•	•	•	•	•
•	•	•	•	•

It is obvious from this table that the *time period* over which the gap is measured is crucial to understanding this bank's true interest-sensitive position. For example, within the next 24 hours, the bank in this example has a positive gap; its earnings will benefit if interest rates rise between today and tomorrow. However, a forecast of rising money market interest rates over the next week would be bad news because the cumulative gap for the next seven days is negative, which will result in interest expenses rising by more than interest revenues. If the interest rate increase is expected to be substantial, management should consider taking countermeasures to protect the bank's earnings. These might include selling longer-term CDs right away or using futures contracts to earn a profit that will help offset the margin losses that rising interest rates will almost surely bring in the coming week. Looking over the remainder of the table, it is clear the bank will fare much better over the next several months if market interest rates rise, because its cumulative gap eventually turns positive again.

The foregoing example reminds us that the net interest margin of a bank or other financial service provider is influenced by multiple factors:

1. Changes in the level of interest rates, up or down.
2. Changes in the spread between asset yields and liability costs (often reflected in the changing shape of the *yield curve* between long-term rates and short-term rates because many liabilities are short-term while a significant portion of a financial firm's assets may bear longer maturities).
3. Changes in the volume of interest-bearing (earning) assets a financial institution holds as it expands or shrinks the overall scale of its activities.
4. Changes in the volume of interest-bearing liabilities that are used to fund earning assets as a financial institution grows or shrinks in size.
5. Changes in the mix of assets and liabilities that management draws upon as it shifts between floating and fixed-rate assets and liabilities, between shorter and longer maturity assets and liabilities, and between assets bearing higher versus lower expected yields (e.g., a shift from less cash to more loans or from higher-yielding consumer and real estate loans to lower-yielding commercial loans).

Table 6–1 provides a more detailed example of interest-sensitive gap management techniques as they are applied to asset and liability data for an individual bank. In it, management has arrayed (with the help of a computer) the amount of all the bank's assets and

E-BANKING AND E-COMMERCE

INTEREST-RATE RISK IS BIG IN BANKING, BUT IT ISN'T THE ONLY RISK OUT THERE!

There is no question that banks, thrifts, and many of their competitors carry powerful interest-rate risk and, unmediated, that risk can lead to a series of losses in income and in the value of the banking firm. As potent as interest-rate risk is for most financial institutions, however, other risks in this business can occasionally shoot up into the stratosphere and command the industry's attention.

A good example happened a few hours before Super Bowl XXXVII in January 2003. The electronic banking system took a big hit for several hours as a rapidly spreading virus spread from computer to computer, disrupting several global information networks. In addition to those systems being hammerlocked by the fast-spreading electronic disease, thousands of e-mail transmissions were also delayed for hours.

Several leading banks in the United States and Canada found their service offerings, especially their automated teller machines (ATMs), under vigorous assault. For example, the

Bank of America, headquartered in Charlotte, North Carolina, reported that customers were running into an electronic roadblock when they attempted to draw out spending money through that bank's network of about 13,000 ATMs. Through hard work by the bank's employees, B of A's automated teller system—one of the largest in the United States—came back online later the same day without apparent loss to the Charlotte bank's customers. One comforting observation is that computer-service firms seem to be constantly at work developing new software to protect bank and nonbank computer systems from disruption or, at least, to speed their recovery. This is absolutely vital in the financial-services sector because this is one industry that literally everyone relies upon.

In short, interest-rate risk is a powerful force in banking, shaping the performance of individual banks and competing financial institutions. However, it is not the only important risk facing the financial-services industry and must be balanced against other risks impacting the industry at the same time.

liabilities, grouped by the future time period when those assets and liabilities will reach maturity or their interest rates will be subject to repricing. Note that this bank is liability sensitive during the coming week and over the next 90 days and then becomes asset sensitive in later periods. Consciously or unconsciously, management has positioned this bank for falling interest rates over the next three months and for rising interest rates over the longer horizon.

At the bottom of Table 6–1, we calculate the bank's net interest income and net interest margin to see how they will change if interest rates rise. The bank's net interest income can be derived from the following formula:

$$\text{Net interest income} = \text{Total interest income} - \text{Total interest cost} \qquad \textbf{(12)}$$
$$= \text{Average interest yield on rate-sensitive assets} \times \text{Volume of rate-sensitive}$$
$$\text{assets} + \text{Average interest yield on fixed (non-rate-sensitive) assets} \times \text{Volume}$$
$$\text{of fixed assets} - \text{Average interest cost on rate-sensitive liabilities}$$
$$\times \text{Volume of interest-sensitive liabilities} - \text{Average interest cost on fixed}$$
$$\text{(non-rate-sensitive) liabilities} \times \text{Volume of fixed}$$
$$\text{(non-rate-sensitive) liabilities}$$

For example, suppose the yields on rate-sensitive and fixed assets average 10 percent and 11 percent, respectively, while rate-sensitive and non-rate-sensitive liabilities cost an average of 8 percent and 9 percent, respectively. During the coming week the bank holds $1,700 million in rate-sensitive assets (out of an asset total of $4,100 million) and $1,800 million in rate-sensitive liabilities. Suppose, too, that these annualized interest rates remain steady. Then this bank's net interest income on an annualized basis will be

$$0.10 \times \$1,700 + 0.11 \times [4,100 - 1,700] - 0.08 \times \$1,800 - 0.09$$
$$\times [4,100 - 1,800] = \$83 \text{ million}$$

TABLE 6–1   Sample Interest-Sensitivity Analysis (GAP management) for a Commercial Bank

Asset and Liability Items	**Volume of Asset and Liability Items Maturing or Subject to Repricing within the Following Maturity Buckets (in millions of dollars)**					
	One Week	Next 8–30 Days	Next 31–90 Days	Next 91–360 Days	More than One Year	Total for All Assets, Liabilities, and Net Worth on the Bank's Balance Sheet
Assets						
Cash and deposits owned	$ 100	—	—	—	—	$ 100
Marketable securities	200	$ 50	$ 80	$110	$ 460	900
Business loans	750	150	220	170	210	1,500
Real estate loans	500	80	80	70	170	900
Consumer loans	100	20	20	70	90	300
Farm loans	50	10	40	60	40	200
Buildings and equipment	—	—	—	—	200	200
Total repriceable (interest-sensitive) assets	**$1,700**	**$310**	**$440**	**$480**	**$1,170**	**$4,100**
Liabilities and Net Worth						
Checkable deposits	$ 800	$100	—	—	—	$ 900
Savings accounts	50	50	—	—	—	100
Money market deposits	550	150	—	—	—	700
Long-term time deposits	100	200	450	150	300	1,200
Short-term borrowings	300	100	—	—	—	400
Other liabilities	—	—	—	—	100	100
Net worth	—	—	—	—	700	700
Total repriceable (interest-sensitive) liabilities and net worth	**$1,800**	**$600**	**$450**	**$150**	**$1,100**	**$4,100**
Interest-sensitive gap (repriceable assets–repriceable liabilities)	–$100	–$290	–$ 10	+$330	+$70	
Cumulative gap	–$100	–$390	–$400	–$ 70	–0	
Ratio of interest-sensitive assets to interest-sensitive liabilities	94.4%	51.7%	97.8%	320%	106.4%	
This bank is	liability sensitive	liability sensitive	liability sensitive	asset sensitive	asset sensitive	
The bank's net interest margin will be squeezed if	Interest rates rise	Interest rates rise	Interest rates rise	Interest rates fall	Interest rates fall	

However, if the market interest rate on rate-sensitive assets rises to 12 percent and the rate on rate-sensitive liabilities rises to 10 percent during the first week, this liability-sensitive institution will have an annualized net interest income of only

$$0.12 \times \$1,700 + 0.11 \times [4,100 - 1,700] - 0.10 \times \$1,800 - 0.09 \times [4,100 - 1,800] = \$81 \text{ million}$$

Therefore, this bank will lose $2 million in net interest income on an annualized basis if market interest rates rise in the coming week. Management must decide whether to accept that risk or to counter it with hedging strategies or tools.

A useful overall measure of interest rate risk exposure is the *cumulative gap*, which is the total difference in dollars between those assets and liabilities that can be repriced over a designated period of time. For example, suppose that a commercial bank has $100 million

TABLE 6–1 *Continued*

Suppose that interest yields on interest-sensitive assets currently average 10%, while interest-sensitive liabilities have an average cost of 8%. In contrast, fixed assets yield 11% and fixed liabilities cost 9%. If interest rates stay at these levels, this bank's net interest income and net interest margin measured on an annualized basis will be as follows:

	One Week	Next 8–30 Days	Next 31–90 Days	Next 91–360 Days	More than One Year
Total interest income on an annualized basis	$0.10 \times \$1,700$ $+ 0.11 \times$ $[4100 - 1,700]$	$0.10 \times \$310$ $+ 0.11 \times$ $[4,100 - 310]$	$0.10 \times \$440$ $+ 0.11 \times$ $[4,100 - 440]$	$0.10 \times \$480$ $+ 0.11 \times$ $[4,100 - 480]$	$0.10 \times \$1,170$ $+ 0.11 \times$ $[4,100 - 1,170]$
Total interest costs on an annualized basis	$-0.08 \times \$1,800$ $-0.09 \times$ $[4,100 - 1,800]$	$-0.08 \times$ $\$600 - 0.09 \times$ $[4,100 - 600]$	$-0.08 \times$ $\$450 - 0.09 \times$ $[4,100 - 45]$	$-0.08 \times$ $\$150 - 0.09 \times$ $[4,100 - 150]$	$-0.08 \times$ $\$1,100 - 0.09 \times$ $[4,100 - 1,100]$
Annualized net interest income	$= \$83$	$= \$84.9$	$= \$82.10$	$= \$80.20$	$= \$81.30$
Annualized net interest margin	$\$83 \div 4,100$ $= 2.02\%$	$\$84.9 \div 4,100$ $= 2.07\%$	$\$82.10 \div 4,100$ $= 2.00\%$	$\$78.7 \div 4,100$ $= 1.92\%$	$\$81.3 \div 4,100$ $= 1.98\%$

Suppose the interest rates attached to rate-sensitive assets and liabilities rise two full percentage points on an annualized basis to 12% and 10%, respectively.

	One Week	Next 8–30 Days	Next 31–90 Days	Next 91–360 Days	More than One Year
Total interest income on an annualized basis Total interest cost on an annualized basis	$0.12 \times \$1,700$ $+ 0.11 \times [4,100 -$ $1,700] - 0.10 \times$ $\$1,800 - 0.09 \times$ $[4,100 - 1,800]$	$0.12 \times \$310$ $+ 0.11\times$ $[4,100 - 310]$ -0.10×600 $- 0.09 \times$ $[4,100 - 600]$	0.12×440 $+ 0.11 \times$ $[4,100 - 440]$ $- 0.10 \times 450$ $- 0.09 \times$ $[4,100 - 450]$	$0.12 \times \$480$ $+ 0.11 \times$ $[4,100 - 480]$ -0.10×150 $- 0.09 [4,100$ $- 150]$	$0.12 \times \$1,170$ $+ 0.11 \times$ $[4,100 - 1,170]$ $- 0.10$ $\times 1,100$ $- 0.09 [4,100$ $- 1,100]$
Annualized net interest income	$= \$81$	$= \$79.10$	$= \$81.90$	$= \$85.30$	$= \$82.70$
Annualized net interest margin	$\$81 \div 4,100$ $= 1.98\%$	$\$79.1 \div 4,100$ $= 1.93\%$	$\$81.9 \div 4,100$ $= 2.00\%$	$\$85.3 \div 4,100$ $= 2.08\%$	$\$82.7 \div 4,100$ $= 2.02\%$

We note by comparing annualized interest income and margins for each time period (maturity bucket) that this bank's net interest income and margin fall if it is liability sensitive when interest rates go up. When the bank is asset sensitive and market interest rates rise, the bank's net interest income and margin increase.

in earning assets and $200 million in liabilities subject to an interest rate change each month over the next six months. Then its cumulative gap must be –$600 million—that is, ($100 million in earning assets per month × 6) – ($200 million in liabilities per month × 6) = –$600 million. The cumulative gap concept is useful because, given any specific change in market interest rates, we can calculate approximately how net interest income will be affected by an interest rate change. The key relationship is this:

$$\begin{matrix} \text{Change in} \\ \text{net interest} \\ \text{income} \end{matrix} = \begin{matrix} \text{Overall change in} \\ \text{interest rate (in} \\ \text{percentage points)} \end{matrix} \times \begin{matrix} \text{Size of the} \\ \text{cumulative gap} \\ \text{(in dollars)} \end{matrix} \qquad \textbf{(13)}$$

For example, suppose market interest rates suddenly rise by 1 full percentage point. Then the bank in the example given above will suffer a net interest income loss of approximately

$$(+ 0.01) \times (-\$600 \text{ million}) = -\$6 \text{ million}$$

Aggressive Interest-Sensitive GAP Management

Expected Changes in Interest Rates (Management's Forecast)	Best Interest-Sensitive GAP Position to Be in:	Aggressive Management's Most Likely Action
Rising market interest rates	Positive IS GAP	Increase interest-sensitive assets Decrease interest-sensitive liabilities
Falling market interest rates	Negative IS GAP	Decrease interest-sensitive assets Increase interest-sensitive liabilities

If management anticipates an increase in interest rates, it may be able to head off this pending loss of income by shifting some assets and liabilities to reduce the size of the cumulative gap or by using hedging instruments (such as financial futures contracts, to be discussed in Chapter 7). In general, financial institutions with a negative cumulative gap will benefit from falling interest rates but lose net interest income when interest rates rise. Institutions with a positive cumulative gap will benefit if interest rates rise, but lose net interest income if market interest rates decline.

Some banks and competing financial firms shade their interest-sensitive gaps toward either asset sensitivity or liability sensitivity, depending on their degree of confidence in their own interest rate forecasts. This is often referred to as *aggressive GAP management*. For example, if management firmly believes interest rates are going to fall over the current planning horizon, it will probably allow interest-sensitive liabilities to climb above interest-sensitive assets. If interest rates do fall as predicted, liability costs will drop by more than revenues and the institution's NIM will grow. Similarly, a confident forecast of higher interest rates will trigger many financial firms to become asset sensitive, knowing that if rates do rise, interest revenues will rise by more than interest expenses. Of course, such an aggressive strategy creates greater risk. Consistently correct interest rate forecasting is impossible; most financial managers have learned to rely on hedging against, not forecasting, changes in market interest rates. Interest rates that move in the wrong direction can magnify losses. (See Table 6–2.)

TABLE 6–2
Eliminating an Interest-Sensitive Gap

With Positive Gap	The Risk	Possible Management Responses
Interest-sensitive assets > interest-sensitive liabilities (asset sensitive)	Losses if interest rates fall because the net interest margin will be reduced.	1. Do nothing (perhaps interest rates will rise or be stable). 2. Extend asset maturities or shorten liability maturities. 3. Increase interest-sensitive liabilities or reduce interest-sensitive assets.

With Negative Gap	The Risk	Possible Management Responses
Interest-sensitive assets < interest-sensitive liabilities (liability sensitive)	Losses if interest rates rise because the net interest margin will be reduced.	1. Do nothing (perhaps interest rates will fall or be stable). 2. Shorten asset maturities or lengthen liability maturities 3. Decrease interest-sensitive liabilities or increase interest-sensitive assets.

Many bankers and other financial-service managers have chosen to adopt a purely defensive GAP management strategy:

Defensive Interest-Sensitive GAP Management
Set interest-sensitive GAP as close to zero as
possible to reduce the expected volatility of
net interest income

While interest-sensitive gap management works beautifully in theory, practical problems in its implementation always leave banks and other financial institutions using this technique with at least *some* interest-rate risk exposure. For example, interest rates paid on liabilities (which often are predominantly short term) tend to move faster than interest rates earned on assets (many of which are long term). Then, too, changes in interest rates attached to assets and liabilities do not necessarily move at the same speed as do interest rates in the open market. In the case of a bank or thrift institution, for example, deposit interest rates typically lag loan interest rates.

Some financial institutions have developed a *weighted* interest-sensitive gap approach that takes into account the tendency of interest rates to vary in speed and magnitude relative to each other and with the up and down cycle of business activity. The interest rates attached to assets of various kinds often change by different amounts and by different speeds than many of the interest rates attached to liabilities—a phenomenon called *basis risk*.

For example, suppose that a commercial bank has the current amount and distribution of interest-sensitive assets and liabilities shown in the table below with rate-sensitive assets

The Weighted Interest-Sensitive Gap: Dealing with Basis Risk

	Original Balance Sheet Entries	Interest-Rate Sensivity Weight	Balance Sheet Refigured to Reflect Interest Rate Sensitivities
Asset items sensitive to interest rate movements:			
Federal funds loans	$ 50	× 1.0 =	$ 50.00
Government securities and other investments	25	× 1.3 =	32.50
Loans and leases	125	× 1.5 =	187.50
Total rate-sensitive assets	$200		$270.00
Liability items sensitive to Interest rate movements:			
Interest-bearing deposits	$159	× 0.86 =	$137.00
Other borrowings in the money market	64	× 0.91 =	58.00
Total rate-sensitive liabilities	$223		$195.00
The bank's interest-sensitive GAP	–$23		+$75

How net interest income would change if the federal funds rate in the money market increases by 2 percentage points:

	Original Balance Sheet	Refigured Balanced Sheet
Predicted movement in net interest income	–$0.46	+$1.50
	(=–$23 × .02)	(= +$75 × .02)

Concept Check

6–9. Can you explain the concept of *gap management?*

6–10. When is a bank or other financial intermediary asset sensitive? Liability sensitive?

6–11. Commerce National Bank reports interest-sensitive assets of $870 million and interest-sensitive liabilities of $625 million during the coming month. Is the bank asset sensitive or liability sensitive? What is likely to happen to the bank's net interest margin if interest rates rise? If they fall?

6–12. Peoples' Savings Bank, a thrift institution, has a cumulative gap for the coming year of +$135 million and interest rates are expected to fall by two and a half percentage points. Can you calculate the expected change in net interest income that this thrift institution might experience? What change

will occur in net interest income if interest rates rise by one and a quarter percentage points?

6–13. How do you measure the dollar interest-sensitive gap? The relative interest-sensitive gap? What is the interest sensitivity ratio?

6–14. Suppose Carroll Bank and Trust reports interest-sensitive assets of $570 million and interest-sensitive liabilities of $685 million. What is the bank's dollar interest-sensitive gap? Its relative interest-sensitive gap and interest-sensitivity ratio?

6–15. Explain the concept of *weighted interest-sensitive gap.* How can this concept aid management in measuring a financial institution's real interest-sensitive gap risk exposure?

totaling $200 million and rate-sensitive liabilities amounting to $223 million, yielding an interest-sensitive GAP of –$23 on its present balance sheet. Its federal funds loans generally carry interest rates set in the open market, so these loans have an interest rate sensitivity weight of 1.0—that is, we assume the bank's fed funds rate tracks market rates one for one. In this bank's investment security portfolio, however, suppose there are some riskier, somewhat more rate-volatile investments than most of the security interest rates reported daily in the financial press. Therefore, its average security yield moves up and down by somewhat more than the interest rate on federal funds loans; here the interest-rate sensitivity weight is estimated to be 1.3. Loans and leases are the most rate-volatile of all with an interest-rate sensitivity weight half again as volatile as federal funds rates at an estimated 1.5. On the liability side, deposit interest rates and some money-market borrowings (such as borrowing from the central bank) may change more slowly than market interest rates. In this example, we assume deposits have a rate-sensitive weight of 0.86 and money-market borrowings are slightly more volatile at 0.91, close to but still less than the volatility of federal funds interest rates.

We can simply multiply each of the rate-sensitive balance-sheet items by its appropriate interest-rate sensitivity indicator, which acts as a weight. More rate-volatile assets and liabilities will weigh more heavily in the refigured (weighted) balance sheet we are constructing in the previous table. Notice that after multiplying by the interest rate weights we have created, the new weighted balance sheet has rate-sensitive assets of $270 and rate-sensitive liabilities of $195. Instead of a negative (liability-sensitive) interest rate gap of –$23, we now have a positive (asset-sensitive) rate gap of +$75.

Thus, this bank's interest-sensitive gap has changed direction and, instead of being hurt by rising market interest rates, for example, this financial firm would actually benefit from higher market interest rates. Suppose the federal funds interest rate rose by 2 percentage points (+.02). Instead of declining by –$0.46, this bank's net interest income increases by $1.50. Clearly, management would have an entirely different reaction to a forecast of rising interest rates with the new weighted balance sheet than it would have with its original, conventionally constructed balance sheet. Indeed, when it comes to assessing interest rate risk, things are not always as they appear!

Key URLs
If you want to learn more about asset-liability management techniques in the banking industry, see such useful websites as **www.fmsinc.org/cms** and **directory.google.com**.

Moreover, the point at which certain assets and liabilities can be repriced is not always easy to identify. And the choice of planning periods over which to balance interest-sensitive assets and liabilities is highly arbitrary. Some items always fall between the cracks in setting planning periods, and they could cause trouble if interest rates move against the financial-service institution. Wise asset-liability managers use several different lengths of planning periods ("maturity buckets") in measuring their possible exposure to changing market interest rates.

Finally, interest-sensitive gap management does *not* consider the impact of changing interest rates on the owners' (stockholders') position in the financial firm as represented by the institution's *net worth*. Managers choosing to pursue an aggressive interest-rate sensitive gap policy may be able to expand their institution's net interest margin, but at the cost of increasing the volatility of net earnings and reducing the value of the stockholders' investment (net worth). Effective asset-liability management demands that financial managers must work to achieve desirable levels of both net interest income and net worth.

Duration Gap Management

In the preceding sections of this chapter we examined a key management tool—*interest-sensitive gap management*—that enables the managers of financial institutions to combat the possibility of losses to their institution's *net interest margin* or spread due to changes in market interest rates. Unfortunately, changing interest rates can also do serious damage to another aspect of a financial firm's performance—its *net worth*, the value of the stockholders' investment in a financial institution. Just because the net interest margin is protected against interest-rate risk doesn't mean an institution's net worth is also sheltered from loss. This requires the application of yet another managerial tool—**duration gap management.** We turn now to look at the concept of duration and its many valuable uses in the world of banks and other financial institutions.

The Concept of Duration

Duration is a value- and time-weighted measure of maturity that considers the timing of all cash inflows from earning assets and all cash outflows associated with liabilities. It measures the average maturity of a promised stream of future cash payments (such as the payment streams that a bank or thrift institution expects to receive from its loans and securities or the stream of interest payments it must pay out to its depositors). In effect, duration measures the average time needed to recover the funds committed to an investment.

The standard formula for calculating the duration (D) of an individual financial instrument, such as a loan, security, deposit, or nondeposit borrowing, is

$$D = \frac{\sum_{t=1}^{n} \text{Expected CF in Period } t \times \text{Period } t \, / \, (1 + \text{YTM})^t}{\sum_{t=1}^{n} \frac{\text{Expected CF in Period } t}{(1 + \text{YTM})^t}} \qquad \textbf{(14)}$$

D stands for the instrument's duration in years and fractions of a year; t represents the period of time in which each flow of cash off the instrument, such as interest or dividend income, is to be received; CF indicates the volume of each expected flow of cash in each time period (t); and YTM is the instrument's current yield to maturity. We note that the denominator of the above formula is equivalent to the instrument's current market value (price). So, the duration formula can be slightly abbreviated to this form:

$$D = \frac{\sum_{t=1}^{n} \text{Expected CF} \times \text{Period } t / (1 + \text{YTM})^t}{\text{Current Market Value or Price}} \qquad (15)$$

For example, suppose that a commercial bank grants a loan to one of its customers for a term of five years. The customer promises the bank an annual interest payment of 10 percent (that is, $100 per year). The face (par) value of the loan is $1,000, which is also its current market value (price) because the loan's current yield to maturity is 10 percent. What is this loan's duration? The formula with the proper figures entered would be this:

$$D_{\text{Loan}} = \frac{\sum_{t=1}^{5} \$100 \times t / (1 + .10)^t + \$1,000 \times 5 / (1 + .10)^5}{\$1,000}$$

$$D_{\text{Loan}} = \frac{\$4,169.87}{\$1,000}$$

$$D_{\text{Loan}} = 4.17 \text{ years}$$

We can calculate duration of this loan a little more simply by setting up the table below to figure the components of the formula. As before, the duration of the loan is $4,169.87/$1,000.00, or 4.17 years.

We recognize from Chapter 4 that the net worth (NW) of any business or household is equal to the value of its assets less the value of its liabilities:

$$NW = A - L \qquad (16)$$

As market interest rates change, the value of both a financial institution's assets and liabilities will change, resulting in a change in its net worth (the owner's investment in the institution):

	Period of Expected Cash Flow	Expected Cash Flow from Loan	Present Value of Expected Cash Flows (at 10% YTM in this case)	Time Period Cash Is to Be Received (t)	Present Value of Expected Cash Flows × t
Expected interest income from loan	1	$ 100	$ 90.91	1	$ 90.91
	2	100	82.64	2	165.29
	3	100	75.13	3	225.39
	4	100	68.30	4	273.21
	5	100	62.09	5	310.46
Repayment of loan principal	5	1,000	620.92	5	3,104.61
		Price or Denominator of Formula = $1,000.00		PV of Cash Flows = × t	$4,169.87

$$\Delta NW = \Delta A - \Delta L \qquad\qquad \textbf{(17)}$$

Portfolio theory in finance teaches us that

A. A rise in market rates of interest will cause the market value (price) of both fixed-rate assets and liabilities to decline.
B. The longer the maturity of a financial firm's assets and liabilities, the more they will tend to decline in market value (price) when market interest rates rise.

Thus, a change in net worth due to changing interest rates will vary depending upon the relative maturities of a financial institution's assets and liabilities. Because duration is a measure of maturity, a bank or other financial firm with longer-duration assets than liabilities will suffer a greater decline in net worth when market interest rates rise than a financial institution whose asset duration is relatively short term or one that matches the duration of its liabilities with the duration of its assets. By equating asset and liability durations, management can balance the average maturity of expected cash inflows from assets with the average maturity of expected cash outflows associated with liabilities. Thus, duration analysis can be used to stabilize, or *immunize*, the market value of a financial institution's net worth (NW).

The important feature of duration from a risk management point of view is that it measures the sensitivity of the market value of financial instruments to changes in interest rates. The percentage change in the market price of an asset or a liability is roughly equal to its duration times the relative change in interest rates attached to that particular asset or liability. That is,

$$\frac{\Delta P}{P} \approx -D \times \frac{\Delta i}{(1 + i)} \qquad\qquad \textbf{(18)}$$

where $\Delta P \div P$ represents the percentage change in market price and $\Delta i \div (1 + i)$ is the relative change in interest rates associated with the asset or liability. D represents duration, and the negative sign attached to it reminds us that market prices and interest rates on financial instruments move in opposite directions. For example, consider a bond held by a thrift institution that carries a duration of four years and a current market value (price) of $1,000. Market interest rates attached to comparable bonds are about 10 percent currently, but recent forecasts suggest that market rates may rise to 11 percent. If this forecast turns out to be correct, what percentage change will occur in the bond's market value? The answer is:

$$\frac{\Delta P}{P} = -4 \text{ years} \times (0.01) / (1 + 0.10) = -0.0364 \text{ or } -3.64 \text{ percent}$$

Equation 18 tells us that the interest-rate risk of financial instruments is directly proportional to their durations. A financial instrument whose duration is 2 will be twice as risky (in terms of price volatility) as one with a duration of 1.

The relationship between a bond's (or other asset's) change in price and its change in yield or interest rate is captured by another term in finance related to duration. This term is **convexity.** Convexity increases with the duration of an asset. The concept of convexity for interest-bearing assets tells us that the rate of change in any interest-bearing asset's price (value) for a given change in its interest rate or yield varies according to the prevailing level of interest rates or yields. For example, an interest-bearing asset's price change is greater at low interest rates or yields than it is at high interest rates or yields. To express this idea another way, price risk is greater at lower interest rates or yields than at higher interest rates or yields.

As an illustration, suppose the interest rate or yield attached to a 30-year bond held by a financial institution decreases from 6.5 percent to 6 percent. Then, this bond's price will rise by about 8 points (i.e., by about $8 per $1,000 in face value). In contrast, suppose the bond's interest rate or yield falls from 10 percent to 9.5 percent; then its market price will rise by just slightly more than 4 points (about $4 per $1,000 in face value). Moreover, if we hold the maturity and yield of an asset constant, the convexity of that asset will fall as the asset's promised return (or coupon rate) rises. Bankers and other financial managers using asset-liability management techniques to protect the value of their assets must keep in mind that asset values change differently according to their duration, their promised (or coupon) rates of return, and the prevailing level of market interest rates.

Using Duration to Hedge against Interest Rate Risk

A bank or other financial-service provider interested in fully hedging against interest rate fluctuations wants to choose assets and liabilities such that

$$\begin{matrix} \text{The dollar-weighted duration} \\ \text{of the asset portfolio} \end{matrix} \approx \begin{matrix} \text{The dollar-weighted duration} \\ \text{of liabilities} \end{matrix} \qquad (19)$$

so that the **duration gap** is as close to zero as possible (see Table 6–3):

$$\text{Duration gap} = \begin{matrix} \text{Dollar-weighted} \\ \text{duration} \\ \text{of asset} \\ \text{portfolio} \end{matrix} - \begin{matrix} \text{Dollar-weighted} \\ \text{duration} \\ \text{of liability} \\ \text{portfolio} \end{matrix} \qquad (20)$$

Because the dollar volume of assets usually exceeds the dollar volume of liabilities (otherwise the financial firm would be insolvent!), a financial institution seeking to minimize the effects of interest rate fluctuations would need to adjust for *leverage*:

$$\begin{matrix} \text{Leverage-} \\ \text{adjusted} \\ \text{duration} \\ \text{gap} \end{matrix} = \begin{matrix} \text{Dollar-weighted} \\ \text{duration} \\ \text{of asset} \\ \text{portfolio} \end{matrix} - \begin{matrix} \text{Dollar-weighted} \\ \text{duration of} \\ \text{liabilities} \\ \text{portfolio} \end{matrix} \times \frac{\text{Total liabilities}}{\text{Total assets}} \qquad (21)$$

Equation (21) tells us that the value of liabilities must change by slightly more than the value of assets to eliminate a financial firm's overall interest-rate exposure.

The larger the leverage-adjusted duration gap, the more sensitive will be the net worth (equity capital) of a financial institution to a change in market interest rates. For example, if we have a positive leverage-adjusted duration gap, a parallel change in all market interest rates will result in the value of liabilities changing by less (up or down) than the value of assets. In this case, a rise in interest rates will tend to lower the market value of net worth as asset values fall further than the value of liabilities. The owner's equity in the institution will decline in market value terms. On the other hand, if a financial firm has a negative leverage-adjusted duration gap, then a parallel change in all interest rates will generate a larger change in liability values than asset values. If interest rates fall, liabilities will increase more in value than assets and net worth (owners' equity) will decline. Should interest rates rise, however, liability values will decrease faster than asset values and the net worth position will increase in value.

We can calculate the change in the market value of a bank or other financial institution's equity (net worth) if we know its dollar-weighted average asset duration, its dollar-weighted average liability duration, the original rate of discount applied to the institution's cash flows, and how interest rates have changed during the period we are concerned about. The relevant formula is based upon the balance-sheet relationship we discussed earlier in Equation (17):

$$\Delta NW = \Delta A - \Delta L$$

TABLE 6–3
Use of Duration
Analysis to Hedge
Interest Rate
Movements

A. Calculate the dollar-weighted average duration of a financial firm's earning assets and liabilities from the following:

$$\text{Dollar-weighted asset duration in years} = \frac{\text{Time-weighted distribution of expected cash inflows from loans and securities}}{\text{Present value of loans and securities held}}$$

$$D_A = \frac{\displaystyle\sum_{t=1}^{n} \frac{(\text{Expected cash inflows} \times \text{Time period received})}{(1 + \text{Discount rate})^t}}{\displaystyle\sum_{t=1}^{n} \frac{\text{Expected cash inflows}}{(1 + \text{Discount rate})^t}}$$

$$\text{Dollar-weighted liability duration in years} = \frac{\text{Time-weighted distribution of expected cash outflows due to interest expenses}}{\text{Present value of liabilities}}$$

$$D_L = \frac{\displaystyle\sum_{t=1}^{n} \frac{(\text{Expected cash outflows} \times \text{Time period paid out})}{(1 + \text{Discount rate})^t}}{\displaystyle\sum_{t=1}^{n} \frac{\text{Expected cash outflows}}{(1 + \text{Discount rate})^t}}$$

B. Plan the acquisition of earning assets and liabilities so that, as closely as possible,

$$\text{Dollar-weighted asset duration} - \text{Dollar-weighted liabilty duration} \times \frac{\text{Total liabilities}}{\text{Total assets}} \approx 0$$

in order to protect the value of net worth (equity capital).

Because $\Delta A/A$ is approximately equal to the product of asset duration times the change in interest rates $\left[-D_A \times \dfrac{\Delta i}{(1 + i)} \right]$ and $\Delta L/L$ is approximately equal to liability duration times the change in interest rates $\left[-D_L \times \dfrac{\Delta i}{(1 + i)} \right]$, it follows that:

$$\Delta NW = \left[-D_A \times \frac{\Delta i}{(1 + i)} \times A \right] - \left[-D_L \times \frac{\Delta i}{(1 + i)} \times L \right] \tag{22}$$

In words,

$$\begin{aligned}
\text{Change in value of net worth} &= \left[-\text{Average duration of assets} \times \frac{\text{Change in interest rate}}{(1 + \text{Original discount rate})} \times \text{Total assets} \right] \\
&\quad - \left[-\text{Average duration of liabilities} \times \frac{\text{Change in interest rates}}{(1 + \text{Original discount rate})} \times \text{Total liabilities} \right]
\end{aligned} \tag{23}$$

For example, suppose that a commercial bank has an average duration in its assets of three years, an average liability duration of two years, total liabilities of $100 million, and total assets of $120 million. Interest rates were originally 10 percent, but suddenly they rise to 12 percent.

In this example:

$$\begin{array}{l} \text{Change in the} \\ \text{value of} \\ \text{net worth} \end{array} = \left[-3 \times \frac{+0.02}{(1 + 0.10)} \times \$120 \text{ million} \right]$$

$$- \left[-2 \times \frac{+0.02}{(1 + 0.10)} \times \$100 \text{ million} \right] = -\$2.91 \text{ million}$$

Clearly, this bank faces a substantial decline in the value of its net worth unless it can hedge itself against the projected loss due to rising interest rates.

Let's consider an example of how duration can be calculated and used to hedge a financial firm's asset and liability portfolio. We take advantage of the fact that the duration of a portfolio of assets and of a portfolio of liabilities equals the value-weighted average of the duration of each instrument in the portfolio. We can start by (1) calculating the duration of each loan, deposit, and the like; (2) weighting each of these durations by the market values of the instruments involved; and (3) adding all the value-weighted durations together to derive the duration of a financial institution's entire portfolio.

For example, suppose the management of a bank finds that it holds a U.S. Treasury $1,000 par bond with 10 years to final maturity, bearing a 10 percent coupon rate with a current price of $900. Based on the formula shown in Equation (15), this bond's duration is 7.49 years.

Suppose this bank holds $90 million of these Treasury bonds, each with a duration of 7.49 years. The bank also holds other assets with durations and market values as follows:

Key URLs
Like banking firms, nonbank financial-service providers frequently make use of asset-liability management techniques, often working with consulting firms that have software programs designed to aid management in making effective use of these techniques. See, for example, **www.cyfi.com** and **www.olson research.com**.

Assets Held	Actual or Estimated Market Values of Assets	Asset Durations
Commercial loans	$100 million	0.60 years
Consumer loans	50 million	1.20 years
Real estate loans	40 million	2.25 years
Municipal bonds	20 million	1.50 years

Weighting each asset duration by its associated dollar volume, we calculate the duration of the asset portfolio as follows:

(24)

$$\begin{array}{l} \text{Dollar-weighted} \\ \text{asset portfolio} \\ \text{duration} \end{array} = \frac{\displaystyle\sum_{i=1}^{n} \begin{array}{l} \text{Duration of} \\ \text{each asset in} \\ \text{the portfolio} \end{array} \times \begin{array}{l} \text{Market value} \\ \text{of each asset} \\ \text{in the portfolio} \end{array}}{\begin{array}{l} \text{Total market value} \\ \text{of all assets} \end{array}}$$

$$= \frac{\begin{array}{l} (7.49 \text{ years} \times \$90 \text{ million in Treasury bonds} \\ + 0.60 \text{ years} \times \$100 \text{ million in commercial loans} \\ + 1.20 \text{ years} \times \$50 \text{ million in consumer loans} \\ + 2.25 \text{ years} \times \$40 \text{ million in real estate loans} \\ + 1.50 \text{ years} \times \$20 \text{ million in municipal bonds}) \end{array}}{\begin{array}{l} (\$90 \text{ million} + \$100 \text{ million} + \$50 \text{ million} \\ + \$40 \text{ million} + \$20 \text{ million}) \end{array}}$$

$$= \frac{\$914.10 \text{ million}}{\$300 \text{ million}}$$

$$= 3.047 \text{ years}$$

A DURATION GAP REPORTED BY THE WORLD'S LARGEST MORTGAGE BANK

One of the most dramatic real-world examples of the use and application of duration gap analysis appeared as 2002 drew to a close. The world's leading mortgage banking institution—the Federal National Mortgage Association (FNMA or Fannie Mae)—announced that it faced a *widening duration gap*.

Fannie Mae is a crucial institution supporting the U.S. housing market. It issues notes and bonds to raise new capital and then uses the proceeds to purchase residential mortgages from private lenders and to package home loans into pools that support the issuance of mortage-backed securities. Fannie Mae has contributed greatly to making many more families eligible to receive loans to purchase new homes.

As market interest rates worldwide plunged toward record lows early in the 21st century and the volume of home mortgage refinancings soared, Fannie Mae experienced a significant shift in the average maturity of its assets and liabilities. Lengthening liabilities and shorter-term assets generated a *negative duration gap* of about 14 months. FNMA's assets were rolling over into cash over a year sooner than its liabilities. If market interest rates continued to fall, the value of Fannie Mae's net worth would also decline as longer-term liabilities increased in value relative to its assets. Investors in the financial markets reacted negatively to FNMA's announcement of its widening duration gap and its stock price fell for a time.

If Fannie Mae's duration gap and, therefore, its interest-rate risk exposure were to continue growing, government regulators and investors in the marketplace could demand that this venerable institution raise more equity capital. The net effect might well be to reduce this mortgage bank's overall support of the American housing market.

Sources: Federal National Mortgage Association and Federal Home Loan Mortgage Corporation.

Duration is a measure of *average maturity*, which for this bank's portfolio of assets is about three years. The bank can hedge against the damaging effects of rising deposit interest rates by making sure the dollar-weighted average duration of its deposits and other liabilities is also approximately three years.[4] In this way the present value of bank assets will balance the present value of liabilities, approximately insulating the bank from losses due to fluctuating interest rates.

The calculation of duration for this bank's liabilities proceeds in the same way as asset durations are calculated. For example, suppose this same bank has $100 million in negotiable CDs outstanding on which it must pay its customers a 6 percent annual yield over the next two calendar years. The duration of these CDs will be determined by the distribution of cash payments made by the bank over the next two years in present-value terms. Thus:

$$\text{Duration of negotiable CDs} = \frac{\frac{\$6 \times 1}{(1.06)^1} + \frac{\$6 \times 2}{(1.06)^2} + \frac{\$100 \times 2}{(1.06)^2}}{\$100} = 1.943 \text{ years}$$

We would go through the same calculation for the remaining liabilities of the bank in this example, as illustrated in Table 6–4. This institution has an average liability duration of 2.669 years, substantially *less* than the average duration of its asset portfolio, which is 3.047 years. Because the average maturity of its liabilities is shorter than the average

---

[4] As noted earlier, we must adjust the duration of the liability portfolio by the value of the ratio of total liabilities to total assets because asset volume usually exceeds the volume of liabilities. For example, suppose the bank described in the example above has an asset duration of three years and its total assets are $100 million while total liabilities are $92 million. Then management will want to achieve an approximate average duration for liabilities of 3.261 years (or asset duration × total assets + total liabilities = 3 years × $100 million ÷ $92 million = 3.261 years).

TABLE 6–4 Calculating the Duration of a Bank's Assets and Liabilities (dollars in millions)

Composition of Assets (uses of funds)	Market Value of Assets	Interest Rate Attached to Each Category of Assets	Average Duration of Each Category of Assets (in years)	Composition of Liabilities and Equity Capital (sources of funds)	Market Value of Liabilities	Interest Rate Attached to Each Liability Category	Average Duration of Each Liability Category (in years)
U.S. Treasury Securities	$ 90	10.00%	7.490	Negotiable CDs	$100	6.00%	1.943
Municipal bonds	20	6.00	1.500	Other time deposits	125	7.20	2.750
Commercial loans	100	12.00	0.600	Subordinated notes	50	9.00	3.918
Consumer loans	50	15.00	1.200	Total liabilities	275		
				Stockholders' equity capital			
Real estate loans	40	13.00	2.250		25		
			Average in Years				Average in Years
Total	$300		3.047	Total	$300		2.669

$$\text{Duration of assets} = \frac{\$90}{\$300} \times 7.49 + \frac{\$20}{\$300} \times 1.50 + \frac{\$100}{\$300} \times 0.60 + \frac{\$50}{\$300} \times 1.20 + \frac{\$40}{\$300} \times 2.25$$

$$= 3.047 \text{ years}$$

$$\text{Duration of liabilities} = \frac{\$100}{\$275} \times 1.943 + \frac{\$125}{\$275} \times 2.750 + \frac{\$50}{\$275} \times 3.198 = 2.669 \text{ years}$$

$$\frac{\text{Current leverage-adjusted}}{\text{duration gap}} = \frac{\text{Average asset}}{\text{duration}} - \frac{\text{Average liability}}{\text{duration}} \times \frac{\text{Total liabilities}}{\text{Total assets}}$$

$$= 3.047 \text{ years} - 2.669 \text{ years} \times \frac{\$275}{\$300} = +0.60 \text{ years}$$

Management Interpretation

The positive duration gap of .60 years means that the bank's net worth will decline if interest rates rise and increase if interest rates fall. Management may be anticipating a decrease in the level of interest rates. If there is significant risk of rising market interest rates, however, the asset-liability management committee will want to use hedging tools to reduce the exposure of net worth to interest rate risk.

How much will the value of this bank's net worth change for any given change in interest rates? The appropriate formula is as follows:

$$\frac{\text{Change in value}}{\text{of net worth}} = -D_A \cdot \frac{\Delta r}{(1+r)} \cdot A - \left[-D_L \cdot \frac{\Delta r}{(1+r)} \cdot L \right],$$

where A is total assets, D_A the average duration of assets, r the initial interest rate, Δr the change in interest rates, L the total liabilities, and D_L the average duration of liabilities.

Example: Suppose interest rates on both assets and liabilities *rise* from 8 to 10 percent. Then filling in the asset and liability figures from the table above gives this result:

$$\frac{\text{Change in value of}}{\text{net worth}} = -3.047 \text{ years} \times \frac{(+0.02)}{(1+0.08)} \times \$300 \text{ million} - \left[-2.669 \text{ years} \times \frac{(+0.02)}{(1+0.08)} \times \$275 \text{ million} \right]$$

$$= -\$16.93 \text{ million} + \$13.59 \text{ million} = -\$3.34 \text{ million}$$

This bank's net worth would fall by approximately $3.34 million if interest rates increase by 2 percentage points.

TABLE 6–4 *Continued*

Suppose interest rates *fall* from 8 percent to 6 percent. What would happen to the value of the above institution's net worth? Again, substituting in the same formula:

$$\text{Change in value of net worth} = -3.047 \text{ years} \times \frac{(-0.02)}{(1 + 0.08)} \times \$300 \text{ million}$$

$$- \left[-2.669 \text{ years} \times \frac{(-0.02)}{(1.08)} \times \$275 \text{ million} \right]$$

$$= \$16.93 \text{ million} - \$13.59 \text{ million} = +\$3.34 \text{ million}.$$

In this instance, the value of net worth would *rise* by about $3.34 million if all interest rates fell by 2 percentage points.

The above formula reminds us that the impact of interest rate changes on the market value of net worth (or owners' equity) depends upon three crucial size factors:

A. The size of the duration gap ($D_A - D_L$), with a larger duration gap indicating greater exposure of a financial firm to interest rate risk.
B. The size of a financial institution (A and L), with larger-size institutions experiencing a greater change in net worth for any given change in interest rates.
C. The size of the change in interest rates, with larger rate changes generating greater interest-rate risk exposure.

Management can reduce a financial firm's exposure to interest rate risk by closing up the firm's duration gap (changing D_A, D_L, or both) or by changing the relative amounts of assets and liabilities (A and L) outstanding.

For example, suppose in the previous example the bank's leverage-adjusted duration gap, instead of being +0.60 years, is *zero*. If the average duration of assets (D_A) is 3.047 years (and assets and liabilities equal $300 and $275 million respectively) this would mean the institution's average liability duration (D_L) must be as follows:

$$\text{Current leverage-adjusted duration gap} = \text{Average asset duration } (\bar{D}_A) - \text{Average liability duration } (\bar{D}_L) \times \frac{\text{Total liabilities}}{\text{Total assets}}$$

or,

$$0 = 3.047 - \text{Average liability duration } (\bar{D}_L) \times \frac{\$275}{\$300}$$

Then:

$$\text{Average liability duration } (\bar{D}_L) = 3.324 \text{ years}$$

Suppose, once again, market interest rates all rise from 8 percent to 10 percent. Then the change in the value of this bank's net worth would be as shown below:

$$\text{Change in value of net worth} = -3.047 \text{ years} \times \frac{(-0.02)}{(1 + 0.08)} \times \$300 \text{ million} - \left[-3.324 \text{ years} \times \frac{(+0.02)}{(1 + 0.08)} \times \$275 \text{ million} \right]$$

$$= -\$16.93 \text{ million} + \$16.93 \text{ million} = 0$$

As expected, with asset and liability durations perfectly balanced (and adjusted for differences in the amounts of total assets versus total liabilities), the change in net worth must be *zero*. Net worth doesn't move despite the rise in market interest rates.

(continued)

TABLE 6–4 *Concluded*

It shouldn't surprise us to discover that if market interest rates drop from, say, 8 percent to 6 percent, net worth will also not change if asset and liability durations are perfectly balanced. Thus:

$$\text{Change in value of net worth} = -3.047 \text{ years} \times \frac{(-0.02)}{(1 + 0.08)} \times \$300 \text{ million} - \left[-3.324 \text{ years} \times \frac{(-0.02)}{(1.08)} \times \$275 \text{ million} \right]$$

$$= +\$16.93 \text{ million} - \$16.93 \text{ million} = 0$$

The change in the value of the financial firm's net worth must be zero because assets and liabilities, adjusted for the difference in their dollar amounts, exhibit a similar response to interest rate movements.

maturity of its assets, this financial firm's net worth will decrease if interest rates rise and increase if interest rates fall. Clearly, management has positioned this institution in the hope that interest rates will fall in the period ahead. If there is a substantial probability interest rates will rise, management may want to hedge against damage from rising interest rates by lengthening the average maturity of its liabilities, shortening the average maturity of its assets, or employing hedging tools (such as financial futures or swaps, as discussed in the next chapter) to cover this duration gap.

In summary, the impact of changing market interest rates on net worth is indicated by entries in the following table:

If the Financial Institution's Leverage-Adjusted Duration Gap Is:	And If Interest Rates:	The Financial Institution's Net Worth Will:
Positive $\left(D_A > D_L \times \dfrac{\text{Liabilities}}{\text{Assets}} \right)$	Rise Fall	Decrease Increase
Negative $\left(D_A < D_L \times \dfrac{\text{Liabilities}}{\text{Assets}} \right)$	Rise Fall	Increase Decrease
Zero $\left(D_A = D_L \times \dfrac{\text{Liabilities}}{\text{Assets}} \right)$	Rise Fall	No Change No Change

In the final case, with a leverage-adjusted duration gap of zero, the financial firm is *immunized* against changes in the value of its net worth. Changes in the market values of assets and liabilities will simply offset each other and the net worth will remain where it is.

Of course, more aggressive financial-service managers may not like the seemingly "wimpy" strategy of **portfolio immunization** (duration gap = 0). They may be willing to take some chances to maximize the shareholders' position. For example,

Expected Change in Interest Rates	Management Action	Possible Outcome
Rates will rise	Reduce D_A and increase D_L (moving closer to a negative duration gap).	Net worth increases (if management's rate forecast is correct).
Rates will fall	Increase D_A and reduce D_L (moving closer to a positive duration gap).	Net worth increases (if management's rate forecast is correct).

The Limitations of Duration Gap Management

While duration is simple to interpret, it has several limitations. For one thing, finding assets and liabilities of the same duration that fit into a financial-service institution's portfolio is often a frustrating task. It would be much easier if the maturity of a loan or security equaled its duration; however, for financial instruments paying out gradually over time, duration is always less than calendar maturity. Only in the case of instruments like zero-coupon securities, single-payment loans, and Treasury bills does the duration of a financial instrument equal its calendar maturity. The more frequently a financial instrument pays interest or pays off principal, the shorter is its duration. One useful fact is that the shorter the maturity of an instrument, the closer the match between its maturity and its duration is likely to be.

Some accounts held by banks and thrift institutions, such as checkable deposits and passbook savings accounts, may have a pattern of cash flows that is not well defined, making the calculation of duration difficult. Moreover, customer prepayments distort the expected cash flows from loans and so do customer defaults (credit risk) when expected cash flows do not happen. Moreover, duration gap models assume that a linear relationship exists between the market values (prices) of assets and liabilities and interest rates, which is not quite true.

A related problem with duration analysis revolves around the concept of convexity. Duration gap analysis tends to be reasonably effective at handling interest rate risk problems if the yield curve (i.e., the maturity structure of interest rates) changes by relatively small amounts and moves in parallel steps with short-term and long-term interest rates changing by about the same proportion over time. However, if there are major changes in interest rates and different interest rates move at different speeds, the accuracy and effectiveness of duration gap management decreases somewhat. Moreover, yield curves in the real world typically do *not* change in parallel fashion—short-term interest rates tend to move more drastically than long-term interest rates, for example—and a *big* change in market interest rates (say, by 100 to 200 basis points, or one or two percentage points) can result in a distorted reading of how much interest rate risk a banker or other financial manager is really facing. Duration itself can shift as market interest rates move, and the durations of different financial instruments can change at differing speeds with the passage of time.

Concept Check

6–16. What is *duration?*

6–17. How is a financial institution's *duration gap* determined?

6–18. What are the advantages of using duration as an asset-liability management tool as opposed to interest-sensitive gap analysis?

6–19. How can you tell if you are fully hedged using duration gap analysis?

6–20. What are the principal limitations of duration gap analysis? Can you think of some way of reducing the impact of these limitations?

6–21. Suppose that a thrift institution has an average asset duration of 2.5 years and an average liability duration of 3.0 years. If the thrift holds total assets of $560 million and total liabilities of $467 million, does it have a significant leverage-adjusted duration gap? If interest rates rise, what will happen to the value of its net worth?

6–22. Stilwater Bank and Trust Company has an average asset duration of 3.25 years and an average liability duration of 1.75 years. Its liabilities amount to $485 million, while its assets total $512 million. Suppose that interest rates were 7 percent and then rise to 8 percent. What will happen to the value of the Stilwater bank's net worth as a result of a decline in interest rates?

Fortunately, recent research suggests that duration balancing can still be effective, even with moderate violations of the technique's underlying assumptions. We need to remember, too, that duration gap analysis helps a financial manager better manage the value of the firm to its shareholders (i.e., its net worth). In this age of mergers and continuing financial-services industry consolidation, the duration gap concept remains a powerful and valuable managerial tool despite its limitations.

Summary

Bankers and the managers of other financial-service companies focus heavily today on the *management of risk*—attempting to control their exposure to loss due to changes in market rates of interest, the inability or unwillingness of borrowers to repay their loans, regulatory changes, and other risk-laden factors. Successful risk management requires effective tools that provide financial managers with the weapons they need to achieve their institution's goals. In this chapter several of the most important risk management tools for banks and other financial firms were discussed. The most important points in the chapter include these:

- Early in the history of the banking industry, managers focused principally upon the tool of *asset management*—emphasizing control and selection of assets, such as loans and security investments, to achieve institutional goals because liabilities were assumed to be dominated by customer decisions and government rules.

- Later, during the 1960s and 1970s, *liability management* tools emerged in which bankers and their closest competitors discovered they could achieve a measure of control over the liabilities on their balance sheet by changing interest rates and other terms offered to the public relative to the terms offered by their competitors.

- More recently, banks and many of their rivals have practiced *funds management*, discovering how to *coordinate* the management of *both* assets and liabilities in order to achieve institutional goals, especially those related to profitability and risk.

- One of the strongest risk factors financial-service managers have to deal with every day is *interest rate risk*. Managers cannot control market interest rates, but instead they must learn how to react to interest-rate changes in order to control their risk exposure and achieve their objectives.

- One of the most popular tools for handling interest-rate risk exposure is *interest-sensitive gap management*. This technique focuses upon protecting or maximizing each financial firm's *net interest margin* or spread between interest revenues and interest costs. For example, a bank's assets and liabilities may be divided using specialized computer software into those items that are *interest-rate sensitive* (that is, whose revenue or expense flow changes with movements in market interest rates) and those that are not rate sensitive. Managers determine for any given time period (maturity bucket) whether their institution is *asset sensitive* (with an excess of interest-rate sensitive assets) or *liability sensitive* (with more rate-sensitive liabilities than rate-sensitive assets). These interest-sensitive gaps are then compared with the financial firm's interest rate forecast, and management takes appropriate action (such as the use of futures contracts or the shifting of asset and/or liability portfolios) in order to protect the firm's net interest margin.

- Managers soon discovered that interest-sensitive gap management didn't necessarily protect another important dimension of their financial firm's performance—its *net worth* or value of shareholder's investment in the institution. This job required the development of another asset-liability management tool—*duration gap management*.

- Based on the concept of *duration*—a value- and time-weighted measure of maturity— the managers of banks and many of their competitors learned how to assess their exposure to loss in net worth from relative changes in the value of assets and liabilities when market interest rates changed. This technique points to the importance of avoiding large gaps between the duration of a financial firm's asset portfolio compared to the duration of its portfolio of liabilities.

- Finally, financial-service managers have discovered that *risk* in all of its forms—interest rate risk, market risk, default risk, regulatory risk, and so on—cannot be eliminated. Rather it must be *managed* properly if the financial firm is to survive and prosper.

Key Terms

asset-liability management, *196*
asset management, *197*
liability management, *197*
funds management, *197*
interest rate risk, *198*
yield to maturity (YTM), *199*

bank discount rate, *200*
maturity gap, *203*
net interest margin, *204*
interest-sensitive gap management, *205*
duration gap management, *215*

duration, *215*
convexity, *217*
duration gap, *218*
portfolio immunization, *224*

Problems and Projects

1. A government bond is currently selling for $900 and pays $80 per year in interest for five years when it matures. If the redemption value of this bond is $1,000, what is its yield to maturity if purchased today for $900?

2. Suppose the government bond described in problem 1 above is held for three years and then the thrift institution acquiring the bond decides to sell it at a price of $950. Can you figure out the average annual yield the thrift institution will have earned for its three-year investment in the bond?

3. U.S. Treasury bills are available for purchase this week at the following prices (based upon $100 par value) and with the indicated maturities:

   a. $97.25, 182 days.
   b. $96.50, 270 days.
   c. $98.75, 91 days.

   Calculate the bank discount rate (DR) on each bill if it is held to maturity. What is the equivalent yield to maturity (sometimes called the bond-equivalent or coupon-equivalent yield) on each of these Treasury bills?

4. The First State Bank of Ashfork reports a net interest margin of 3.25 percent in its most recent financial report, with total interest revenues of $88 million and total interest costs of $72 million. What volume of earning assets must the bank hold? Suppose the bank's interest revenues rise by 8 percent and its interest costs and earning assets increase 10 percent. What will happen to Ashfork's net interest margin?

5. If a bank's net interest margin, which was 2.85 percent, doubles and its total assets, which stood originally at $545 million, rise by 40 percent, what change will occur in the bank's net interest income?

6. The cumulative interest rate gap of Commonwealth Federal Savings and Loan doubles from an initial figure of −$35 million. If market interest rates fall by 25 percent from an initial level of 6 percent, what changes will occur in this thrift's net interest income?

7. Merchants State Bank has recorded the following financial data for the past three years (dollars in millions):

	Current Year	Previous Year	Two Years Ago
Interest revenues	$ 57	$ 56	$ 55
Interest expenses	49	42	34
Loans (excluding nonperforming loans)	411	408	406
Investment securities and interest-bearing deposits in other banks	239	197	174
Total deposits	487	472	467
Money market borrowings	143	118	96

What has been happening to the bank's net interest margin? What do you think caused the changes you have observed? Do you have any recommendations for Merchants' management team?

8. The First National Bank of Wedora, California, finds that its asset and liability portfolio contains the following distribution of maturities and repricing opportunities:

	Dollar Volume of Assets and Liabilities Maturing or Subject to Repricing Within:			
	Coming Week	Next 8–30 Days	Next 31–90 Days	More than 90 Days
Loans	$144	$110	$164	$184
Securities	29	19	29	8
Transaction deposits	232	—	—	—
Time accounts	98	84	196	35
Money market borrowings	36	6	—	—

When and by how much is the bank exposed to interest rate risk? For each maturity or repricing interval, what changes in interest rates will be beneficial to the bank and which will be damaging, given its current portfolio position?

9. First National Bank of Barnett currently has the following interest-sensitive assets and liabilities on its balance sheet:

Interest-Sensitive Assets		Interest-Sensitive Liabilities	
Federal funds loans	$ 65	Interest-bearing deposits	$185
Security holdings	42	Money-market borrowings	78
Loans and leases	230		

What is the bank's current interest-sensitive gap? Suppose its federal funds loans carry an interest-rate sensitivity index of 1.0 while its investments have a rate-sensitivity index of 1.15 and its loans and leases display a rate-sensitivity index of 1.35. On the liability side First National's rate-sensitivity index is 0.79 for interest-bearing deposits and 0.98 for its money-market borrowings. Adjusted for these various interest-rate sensitivity weights, what is the bank's weighted interest-sensitive gap? Suppose the federal funds interest rate increases or decreases one percentage point. How will the bank's net interest income be affected (a) given its current balance sheet makeup and (b) reflecting its weighted balance sheet adjusted for the foregoing rate-sensitivity indexes?

10. Hilltop Savings Association has interest-sensitive assets of $225 million and interest-sensitive liabilities of $168 million. What is the bank's dollar interest-sensitive gap? What is Hilltop's relative interest-sensitive gap? What is the value of its interest-sensitivity ratio? Is it asset sensitive or liability sensitive? Under what scenario for market interest rates will Hilltop experience a gain in net interest income? A loss in net interest income?

11. Casio Merchants and Trust Bank, N.A., has a portfolio of loans and securities expected to generate cash inflows for the bank as follows:

Expected Cash Inflows of Principal and Interest Payments	Annual Period in Which Cash Receipts Are Expected
$ 1,385,421	Current year
746,872	Two years from today
341,555	Three years from today
62,482	Four years from today
9,871	Five years from today

Deposits and money market borrowings are expected to require the following cash outflows:

Expected Cash Outflows of Principal and Interest Payments	Annual Period during Which Cash Payments Must Be Made
$ 1,427,886	Current year
831,454	Two years from today
123,897	Three years from today
1,005	Four years from today
—	Five years from today

If the discount rate applicable to the previous cash flows is 8 percent, what is the duration of Casio's portfolio of earning assets and of its deposits and money market borrowings? What will happen to the bank's total returns, assuming all other factors are held constant, if interest rates rise? If interest rates fall? Given the size of the duration gap you have calculated, in what type of hedging should Casio engage? Please be specific about the hedging transactions that are needed and their expected effects.

12. Given the cash inflow and outflow figures in problem 11 for Casio Merchants and Trust Bank, N.A., suppose that interest rates began at a level of 8 percent and then suddenly rise to 9 percent. If the bank has total assets of $125 million, and total liabilities of $110 million, by how much would the value of Casio's net worth change as a result of this movement in interest rates? Suppose, on the other hand, that interest rates decline from 8 percent to 7 percent. What happens to the value of Casio's net worth in this case and by how much in dollars does it change? What is the size of its duration gap?

13. Leland Thrift Association reports an average asset duration of 4.5 years and an average liability duration of 3.25 years. In its latest financial report, the association recorded total assets of $1.8 billion and total liabilities of $1.5 billion. If interest rates began at 7 percent and then suddenly climbed to 9 percent, what change will occur in the value of Leland's net worth? By how much would Leland's net worth change if, instead of rising, interest rates fell from 7 percent to 5 percent?

14. A bank holds a bond in its investment portfolio whose duration is 5.5 years. Its current market price is $950. While market interest rates are currently at 8 percent for

REAL NUMBERS FOR REAL BANKS — Assignment for Chapter 6

YOUR BANK'S INTEREST RATE SENSITIVITY

In Chapter 6, the focus is interest-rate risk management. Regulatory agencies began to collect relevant information in the 1980s when large numbers of thrifts failed due to their interest rate risk exposure at a time when market rates were increasing both in level and volatility. You will find Interest Rate Risk Analysis or Interest Sensitivity Reports included in both the UBPR (introduced in Chapter 5) and the Uniform Bank Holding Company Performance Report (UBHCPR). Both reports are available at **www.ffiec.gov.** This is one area where measurement within banks and BHCs is more sophisticated than the measures used by regulatory agencies. For instance, to date none of the regulatory agencies require their financial institutions to submit measures of duration gap.

Part One: NIM: A Comparison to Peers

A. Open your Excel Workbook and access Spreadsheet Two (created for Part One of Chapter 5's assignment). On line 36,

you find net interest income (NII) as a percentage of total assets (TA). This is one calculation of NIM. You may have noticed from a footnote in Chapter 5 that sometimes NIM is calculated using total assets as the denominator and sometimes total earning assets (TEA) is used as the denominator as illustrated in Chapter 6's Equation 5. To transform the first measure of NIM(NII/TAA) to the second measure using TEA, we need to collect one more item from the FDIC's website. Using the directions in Chapter 5's assignment, go to the FDIC's Statistics for Depository Institutions, **www3.fdic.gov/sdi/main.asp,** and collect from the Memoranda Section of Assets and Liabilities the Earning Assets as a percentage of Total Assets for Your Bank Holding Company and its Peer Group for the two periods. We will add this information to this spreadsheet to calculate NIM (NII/TEA) as follows:

Memoranda (A53)	Your Bank	Peer Group	Your Bank	Peer Group
Date (A55)	12/31/yy	12/31/yy	12/31/yy	12/31/yy
Earning Assets (A56)	%	%	%	%
NIM using TEA as denominator (A57)				

comparable quality securities, an increase in interest rates to 10 percent is expected in the coming weeks. What change (in percentage terms) will this bond's price experience if market interest rates change as anticipated?

15. A savings bank's dollar-weighted asset duration is six years. Its total liabilities amount to $750 million, while its assets total $900 million. What is the dollar-weighted duration of the bank's liability portfolio if it has a zero leverage-adjusted duration gap?

16. Commerce National Bank holds assets and liabilities whose average duration and dollar amount are as shown in this table:

Asset and Liability Items	Average Duration	Dollar Amount
Investment-grade bonds	8.0 years	$ 60 million
Commercial loans	3.6	320
Consumer loans	4.5	140
Deposits	1.1	490
Nondeposit borrowings	0.1	20

Use your formula functions to generate the percentages in row 57. For instance, cell B57=B36/B56.

B. Once you have collected the data on NIM, write one paragraph discussing interest rate sensitivity for your bank relative to the peer group across the two time periods based on the NIM. Discuss what is revealed by the variation of NIM across time. Review the discussion of NIM in this chapter for further direction.

Part Two: Interest-Sensitive Gaps and Ratios

While the FDIC's website is powerful in providing basic data concerning assets, liabilities, equity, income, and expenses for individual banks and the banking component of BHCs, it does not provide any reports on interest sensitivity. For individual banks such information is available in the UBPR, and for BHCs information is available in the BHCPR. (Note that this data is for the entire BHC and not an aggregation of the chartered bank and thrifts that we have used to this point.) We will use the information in Schedule HC-H-Interest Sensitivity of the BHCPR to create one-year interest-sensitive gaps (Equation 7) and one-year interest-sensitive ratios (Equation 11) for the two most recent years. We will add our information to Spreadsheet One as follows:

Interest-sensitivity data from UBHCPR (A71)	12/31/yyyy	12/31/yyyy
Interest-sensitive assets (1-year planning period) (A72)		
Interest-sensitive liabilities (1-year planning period) (A73)		
Interest-sensitive gap (A74)		
Interest sensitivity ratio (A75)		

A. To collect the data for Cells B72, B73, C72, and C73, go to **www.ffiec.gov** and select the link Bank Holding Company Performance Report (BHCPR). This web page provides two pull-down menus, one for the date (you want to do this for the two most recent year-end dates) and one for the type of financial report (HC-H-Interest Sensitivity). After submitting the information request for this page, you will be requested to provide the name of your bank holding company. Finally, you will be able to display Schedule HC-H-Interest Sensitivity. The schedule will be opened using Adobe Acrobat, and you will find five items listed there. Allocate each item to either the category of Interest-Sensitive Assets or Interest-Sensitive Liabilities and sum within each category, providing entries for cells B72 and B73 for the most recent year and C72 and C73 for the prior year.

B. Having acquired the above information, you will now be able to compute interest-sensitive gaps and ratios for your BHC.

C. Write one paragraph discussing the interest rate risk exposure for your BHC. Is it asset or liability sensitive at the conclusion of each year? What are the implications of the changes occurring across the years? Using Equation 13, discuss the effects on net interest income if market interest rates increase or decrease by one full percentage point.

What is the dollar-weighted duration of Commerce's asset portfolio and liability portfolio? What is its leverage-adjusted duration gap?

17. A government bond currently carries a yield to maturity of 12 percent and a market price of $940. If the bond promises to pay $100 in interest annually for five years, can you calculate its current duration?

18. Dewey National Bank holds $15 million in government bonds having a duration of six years. If interest rates suddenly rise from 6 percent to 7 percent, what percentage change should occur in the bonds' market price?

Internet Exercises

1. Suppose you wanted to know what type of banks make the greatest use of asset-liability management tools and what their biggest ALM problems are. Where could you go on the Web in order to help find answers to questions like these?

2. If a new model to apply ALM techniques to a bank's risk exposure is developed, where on the Web could you look and most likely find a discussion of that new ALM model? (See, for example, **www.ALMprofessional.com**.)

3. If you need guidance on how to prepare forecasts and measure risk as part of a financial firm's ALM activities, which kinds of websites could be the most helpful? (See, for example, **www.bancware.com**.)

4. If you wanted to uncover a useful definition of what duration is, where on the Web would you likely find such information?

5. See if you can find the meaning of *modified duration* on the World Wide Web.

6. How can ALM techniques aid key nonbank competitors of banks, such as credit unions, savings and loan associations, finance and insurance companies, and mutual funds? (See, for example, **www.kesdee.com**, **www.ncfcorp.com**, and **www.olson research.com**.)

STANDARD &POOR'S

S&P Market Insight Challenge

1. Use Standard & Poor's Market Insight website (**www.mhhe.com/edumarketinsight**) for this problem. Changing market interest rates affect the profitability of banks and many other financial-service firms. For up-to-date information concerning the current interest-rate environment, use the Industry tab and drop-down menu in S&P's Market Insight, Educational Version. Several subindustry categories should appear, including Consumer Finance, Diversified Banks, Diversified Capital Markets, Regional Banks, and Thrifts and Mortgage Finance. Once an industry group has been chosen, you can download one or more S&P Industry Surveys using Adobe Acrobat. The Industry Surveys associated with the above categories include Banking, Financial Services Diversified, and Savings and Loans. Please download these particular surveys and read the information on Interest Rates in the Key Industry Ratios and Statistics section. Write a paragraph concerning recent developments in short-term market interest rates and a paragraph covering long-term interest rates.

2. Use Standard & Poor's Market Insight website (**www.mhhe.com/edumarketinsight**) for this problem. Which banks listed on S&P's Market Insight, Educational Version, appear to have the greatest exposure to damage from interest-rate risk? Why do you think so? What damages could these banking firms incur on their income and expense statements? Their balance sheets? What does this chapter suggest might be appropriate remedies to help reduce the possible damages you have described?

Selected References

The following studies provide an overview of the effectiveness of risk-hedging techniques:

1. Akert, Lucy. "Derivative Securities' Use Grows as Banks Strive to Hedge Risk." *Financial Update*, Federal Reserve Bank of Atlanta, January–March 1999, pp. 8–9.

2. Bailey, Jess. "Minnesota Bank Begins to Shed Its U.S. Bonds." *The Wall Street Journal*, December 20, 1988, p. 3.

3. Bassett, William F., and Egon Zakrajsek. "Profits and Balance Sheet Development at U.S. Commercial Banks in 1999." *Federal Reserve Bulletin*, June 2000, pp. 367–95.

4. Edwards, Gerald A., and Gregory E. Eller. "Derivative Disclosures by Major U.S. Banks, 1995." *Federal Reserve Bulletin*, September 1996, pp. 791–801.

5. Jackson, Patricia; David T. Maude; and William Perraudin. "Bank Capital and Value at Risk." *Journal of Derivatives* 4 (Spring 1997), pp. 73–89.

6. King, Robert G., and Andre Kurmann. "Expectations and the Term Structure of Interest Rates: Evidence and Implications." *Economic Quarterly*, Federal Reserve Bank of Richmond 88, no. 4 (Fall 2002), pp. 49–95.

For additional information about the technique of gap management, see these studies:

7. Rose, Peter S. "Defensive Banking in a Volatile Economy—Hedging Loan and Deposit Interest Rates." *The Canadian Banker* 93, no. 2 (April 1986), pp. 52–59.

8. Toevs, Alden L. "Gap Management: Managing Interest Rate Risk in Banks and Thrifts." *Economic Review,* Federal Reserve Bank of San Francisco, no. 2 (Spring 1983), pp. 20–35.

9. Wright, David M., and James V. Houpt. "An Analysis of Commercial Bank Exposure to Interest-Rate Risk." *Federal Reserve Bulletin,* February 1996, pp. 115–28.

For useful descriptions of measuring and interpreting duration, see these studies:

10. Cherin, Antony C., and Robert C. Hanson. "Consistent Treatment of Interest Payments in Immunization Examples." *Financial Practice and Education,* Spring/Summer 1997, pp. 122–26.

11. Shaffer, Sherrill. "Interest Rate Risk: What's a Bank to Do?" *Business Review,* Federal Reserve Bank of Philadelphia, May/June 1991, pp. 17–27.

12. Sundaresan, Suvesh. *Fixed Income Markets and Their Derivatives.* Cincinnati, Ohio: South-Western College Publishing, 1997.

13. Wright, David M., and James V. Houpt, "An Analysis of Commercial Bank Exposure to Interest-Rate Risk." *Federal Reserve Bulletin,* February 1996, pp. 115–28.

CHAPTER SEVEN

Using Financial Futures, Options, Swaps, and Other Hedging Tools in Asset-Liability Management

Key Topics in This Chapter

- Use of Derivatives by Commercial Banks
- Financial Futures Contracts: Purpose and Mechanics
- Short and Long Hedges
- Interest-Rate Options: Nature and Types of Contracts
- Interest-Rate Swaps
- Regulations and Accounting Rules
- Caps, Floors, and Collars

Introduction

The American humorist James Thurber once wrote: "A pinch of probably is worth a pound of perhaps." Modern bankers have learned how to live in a new kind of world today—a world, not of perhapses, but one of *probabilities*. A world of *calculated risk* rather than one of simple uncertainty.

What is the probability that interest rates in the economy will rise or fall tomorrow? What is the probability that the expected outcome for market interest rates simply won't materialize? How can a bank or other financial firm protect itself if "probably" turns out to be wrong?

In the preceding chapter we introduced one of the most important topics in the field of banking and financial-services management—the concept of risk and the risk-management tool known as *asset-liability management*. As we saw in Chapter 6, the techniques and tools of asset-liability management are designed principally to control the threat of significant losses due to unexpected changes in interest rates in the financial markets. Asset-liability managers are especially concerned about stabilizing their institution's *margin*—the spread between its interest revenues and interest expenses—and about protecting a financial firm's *net worth*—the value of the stockholders' investment in the institution. This chapter explores several of the most widely used weapons for dealing with a bank or other financial firm's exposure to interest-rate risk—financial futures contracts, interest-rate options, interest-rate swaps, and the use of interest-rate caps, collars and floors.

As we enter this interesting and important chapter we should keep a few key points in mind. First, the asset-liability management tools we explore here are useful, not just for banks, but also across a broad range of financial-service providers sensitive to the risk of changes in market interest rates. This includes credit unions, finance companies, insurance and investment companies, savings associations, and financial-service conglomerates. In fact, one of the most vulnerable financial industries as the 21st century began was the life insurance business, which soon began to wish it had made even heavier use of risk-management tools such as futures and options. Some of the largest life insurers in Asia (especially China and Japan) and in Western Europe and the United States had promised their customers high-interest yields on their savings, only to be confronted subsequently with record low market interest rates that made it close to impossible to deliver on promises.

Second, many of the risk management tools we study in this part of the book are not only used by financial firms to cover their own interest-rate risk, but also are sold to customers who need risk protection and generate important *fee income* for banks and other financial-service providers. And, finally, we need to be aware that most of the financial instruments we will be discussing in the following pages are *derivatives*—that is, they derive their value from the value and terms of underlying instruments such as Treasury bills and bonds and Eurodollar deposits. Not only do derivatives help financial managers deal with interest-rate and other risks, but also they present some of their own risks and challenges for the managers of banks and other financial institutions.[1]

Commercial Banks' Use of Derivative Contracts

Due to their high exposure to interest-rate risk, banks are among the heaviest users of derivative contracts in the financial system. Moreover, due to the presence of heavy regulation of this industry, bank usage of these hedging instruments is among the best documented of all financial firms. According to a recent survey by the Office of the Comptroller of the Currency,[2] approximately 5 percent of all banks surveyed reportedly employ the use of derivative contracts. As of the third quarter of 2002, 408 banks operating in the United States held derivatives having a combined notional (face) value of $53.2 trillion. The dollar amount of derivatives employed by banks in the United States has increased more than 500 percent over the preceding 10 years. Exhibit 7–1, derived from the Comptroller's report, illustrates the growth of derivative contracts by type of contract for all commercial banks over the period from the fourth quarter of 1991 through the first quarter of 2003. In this chapter we focus on futures, options, and swap contracts and then examine the possible uses of credit derivatives—the newest of derivative contracts—in Chapter 8.

---

[1] Portions of this chapter are based on Peter S. Rose's article in *The Canadian Banker* (5) and are used with the permission of the publisher.

[2] See especially the website posted by the Office of the Comptroller of the Currency (**www.occ.treas.gov**), which contains the "OCC Bank Derivatives Report, Third Quarter 2002."

EXHIBIT 7–1 Derivative Contracts by Product, All U.S. Commercial Banks, Year Ends 1991–2002, Most Recent Quarters

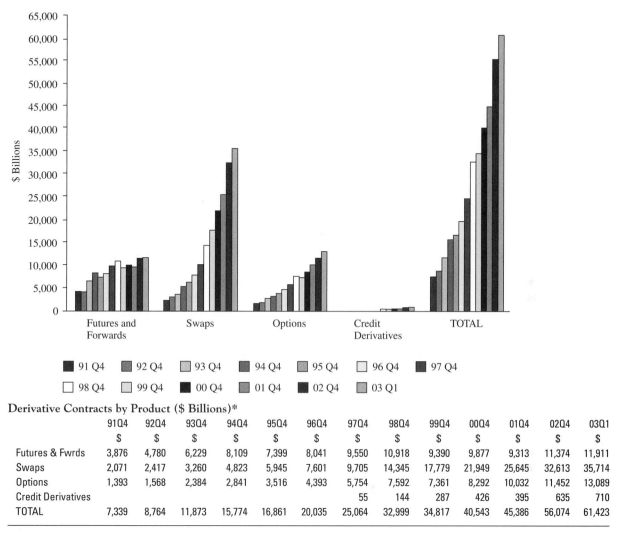

Derivative Contracts by Product ($ Billions)*

	91Q4	92Q4	93Q4	94Q4	95Q4	96Q4	97Q4	98Q4	99Q4	00Q4	01Q4	02Q4	03Q1
	$	$	$	$	$	$	$	$	$	$	$	$	$
Futures & Fwrds	3,876	4,780	6,229	8,109	7,399	8,041	9,550	10,918	9,390	9,877	9,313	11,374	11,911
Swaps	2,071	2,417	3,260	4,823	5,945	7,601	9,705	14,345	17,779	21,949	25,645	32,613	35,714
Options	1,393	1,568	2,384	2,841	3,516	4,393	5,754	7,592	7,361	8,292	10,032	11,452	13,089
Credit Derivatives							55	144	287	426	395	635	710
TOTAL	7,339	8,764	11,873	15,774	16,861	20,035	25,064	32,999	34,817	40,543	45,386	56,074	61,423

*In billions of dollars; notional amount of futures, total exchange traded options, total over-the-counter options, total forwards, and total swaps. Note that data after 1994 do not include spot fx in the total notional amount of derivatives.
Credit derivatives were reported for the first time in the first quarter of 1997. Currently, the call report does not differentiate credit derivatives by product and thus they have been added as a separate category. As of 1997, credit derivatives have been included in the sum of total derivatives in this chart.
Note: numbers may not add due to rounding.
Data Source: Call Reports assembled by the Office of the Comptroller of the Currency, Washington, D.C.

Recent information supplied by the Comptroller of the Currency, the Federal Reserve Board, and other regulatory agencies reveals that the bulk of trading in derivatives is centered in the very largest banks. For example, the Comptroller's survey discussed above disclosed that the 25 largest U.S. banking companies accounted for more than 99 percent of derivatives activity, employing nearly $2.5 trillion in contracts for risk-management activities as of the third quarter of 2002. We now turn to explore how futures, options, swaps, and other derivatives aid in the control of interest-rate risk exposure for banks and other financial-service providers.

Financial Futures Contracts: Promises of Future Security Trades at a Set Price

In Chapter 6 we explored the nature of *gaps* between assets and liabilities that are exposed to interest-rate risk. For example, we developed the concept of an interest-sensitive gap:

$$\text{Interest-sensitive gap} = \text{Interest-sensitive assets} - \text{Interest-sensitive liabilities} \tag{1}$$

where interest-sensitive assets and liabilities are those items on a balance sheet whose associated interest rates can be changed, up or down, during a given interval of time. As we saw earlier, for example, a bank that is *asset sensitive* (whose interest-sensitive assets exceed its interest-sensitive liabilities) will suffer a decline in its net interest margin if market interest rates fall. On the other hand, a financial firm that is *liability sensitive* (whose interest-sensitive liabilities are greater than its interest-sensitive assets) will experience a decrease in its net interest margin when interest rates rise.

The preceding chapter developed one other measure of the difference between risk-exposed assets and liabilities—the leverage-adjusted *duration gap*, which measures the difference in weighted-average maturity between a financial institution's assets and its liabilities. Specifically:

$$\text{Duration gap} = \text{Average (dollar-weighted) duration of assets} - \text{Average (dollar-weighted) duration of liabilities} \times \frac{\text{Total liabilities}}{\text{Total assets}} \tag{2}$$

For example, a bank whose asset portfolio has an average duration longer than the average duration of its liabilities has a positive duration gap. A rise in market interest rates will cause the value of the bank's assets to decline faster than its liabilities, reducing the institution's net worth. On the other hand, if a financial firm has a negative duration gap, falling interest rates will cause the value of its liabilities to rise faster than the value of its asset portfolio; its net worth will decline, lowering the value of the stockholders' investment. One of the most popular methods for neutralizing these gap risks is to buy and sell financial futures and options contracts.

Key URLs

Among the more interesting websites dealing with the use of futures contracts by banks and thrift institutions are **www.futuresweb.com** and **www.expert witnessron.com.**

Background on Futures   A **financial futures** contract is an agreement between a buyer and a seller reached today that calls for the delivery of a particular security in exchange for cash at some future date.

Financial futures trade in futures markets and are usually accounted for as off-balance-sheet items in the financial statements of banks and other financial service firms. To put this in perspective, in our financial markets there are both *cash* (sometimes referred to as *spot*) markets and *futures* markets. In cash financial markets, financial assets are exchanged between buyers and sellers. Sellers of financial assets remove the assets from their balance sheet and account for the losses/gains on their income statements. Buyers of financial assets add the item purchased to their balance sheet. In cash markets, the buyers and sellers exchange the financial asset for cash at the time the price is set. In futures markets, the buyers and sellers exchange a contract calling for delivery of the underlying financial asset at a specified date in the future. When the contract is created, neither the buyer nor the seller is making a purchase or sale at that point in time.

When a bank or other investor buys or sells futures contracts at a designated price, it must deposit an *initial margin*. The initial margin is a minimum dollar amount per contract that is specified by the exchange where the trading occurs. This deposit may be in cash or in a financial security, such as a Treasury bill. The initial margin is the investor's equity in the position when he or she buys (or sells) the contract. At the end of the first trading day, the settlement price for that day (a price determined by the exchange, based on the trades that day) is compared with the price at which the trade occurred. If the price has increased, the buyer of the contract has profited while the seller has lost an equal amount. Each trader's account is *marked-to-market.* This means the equity account of the buyer increases by the change in price, while the seller's equity position decreases by the same amount. When a trader's equity position falls below the maintenance margin (the minimum specified by the exchange) the trader must deposit additional funds to the equity account to maintain his or her position, or the futures position is closed out within 24 hours. If profits have accrued, the excess margin may be withdrawn. The mark-to-market process takes place at the end of each trading day. This mechanism allows traders to take a position with a minimum investment of funds.

Purpose of Financial Futures Trading   The financial futures markets are designed to shift the risk of interest-rate fluctuations from risk-averse investors, such as commercial banks and thrift institutions, to speculators willing to accept and possibly profit from such risks. Futures contracts are traded on organized exchanges (such as the Chicago Board of Trade, the Chicago Mercantile Exchange, or the London Futures Exchange).

On the exchange floor, individuals known as *floor brokers* execute orders received from the public to buy or sell these contacts at the best prices available. For example, when a bank or other institution contacts an exchange broker and offers to *sell* futures contracts (i.e., the bank or other institution wishes to "go short" in futures), this means it is promising to deliver the securities underlying the contract to the buyer of those contracts on a stipulated date at a predetermined price. Conversely, a bank or other institution may enter the futures market as a *buyer* of contracts (i.e., the bank or other institution chooses to "go

Chicago Board of Trade (CBT)

Financial Exchange (FINEX) and New York Futures Exchange (NYFE)

Marche a Terme International De France (MATIF)

Singapore Exchange Ltd (SGX)

Chicago Mercantile Exchange (CME)

London International Financial Futures Exchange (LIFFE)

Sydney Futures Exchange (SFE)

Toronto Futures Exchange (TFE)

long" in futures), agreeing to accept delivery of the underlying securities named in each contract or to pay cash to the exchange clearinghouse the day the contracts mature, based on their price at that time.

Futures contracts are also traded over the counter (OTC), without the involvement of an exchange, which is often less costly for traders. However, over-the-counter futures trades generally are more risky because an exchange guarantees the settlement of each contract even if one or the other party to the contract defaults. Moreover, liquidity risk is usually less for exchange-traded futures, options, and other financial instruments because of the presence of substantial numbers of speculators and specialists on the exchanges who are always ready to make a market for the instruments traded there.

Exhibit 7–2 contains the quotes for interest-rate futures contracts traded on American exchanges. The quotes are from the December 19, 2002, edition of *The Wall Street Journal* for trades made on December 18 of that year. A description of the most popular financial futures contracts is given below.[3]

1. The U.S. *Treasury bond futures contract* calls for the delivery of a $100,000-denomination bond (measured at its par value) carrying a minimum maturity of 15 years and a promised (coupon) rate of return of 6 percent.[4] To trade a Treasury bond futures contract, the buyer and seller must deposit the margin specified by the Chicago Board of Trade. For the hedger, the initial margin and the maintenance margin are $2,000 per contract, whereas for the speculator the initial margin is higher at $2,700 per contract.

   Exhibit 7–2 provides quotes for the December 2002, March 2003, and June 2003 Treasury bond contracts. These are the months each contract will expire and delivery will be made if the futures contract has not been offset prior to delivery. If we look at the "Mr03" contract, we see that the first trade (OPEN) on December 18, 2002, took place at 109 8/32nds (percent of par value). (Note that Treasury bond quotes are in 32nds rather than decimals.) An increase in price of 1/32nd is equivalent to $31.25 in profits or losses per contract depending on whether the trader has a short or long posi-

---

[3] The initial and maintenance margins were applicable as of January 2003 and were obtained from the websites of the CBOT and CME.

[4] If a contract is not offset prior to delivery, the seller has some freedom regarding the Treasury bond that is delivered to the buyer of the futures contract. Bonds whose coupon rates lie above or below the 6 percent standard and have at least 15 years until maturity are deliverable to the buyer. The price the buyer pays the seller is adjusted by a prespecified conversion factor depending on the coupon rate and maturity of the delivered bond.

EXHIBIT 7–2

Interest-Rate Futures

Source: *The Wall Street Journal*, December 19, 2002, p. C12. Reprinted by permission of *The Wall Street Journal*, © 2002 Dow Jones & Company, Inc. All Rights Reserved Worldwide.

Interest Rate Futures

	OPEN	HIGH	LOW	SETTLE	CHG	YIELD	CHG	OPEN INT

Treasury Bonds (CBI)-$100,000; pts 32nds of 100%

	OPEN	HIGH	LOW	SETTLE	CHG			OPEN INT
Dec	110-21	111-13	110-20	111-06	21	115-04	96-06	40,884
Mr03	109-08	110-04	109-04	109-27	21	113-28	100-05	388,585
June	107-31	108-24	107-31	108-18	21	111-00	105-00	23,519

Est vol 133,369; vol Tue 157,798; open int 453,155, –3,087.

Treasury Notes (CBT)-$100,000; pts 32nds of 100%

Dec	114-03	14-155	14-015	114-11	17.0	116-14	99-31	29,689
Mr03	12-145	113-04	12-145	12-315	17.5	115-09	105-16	701,795
June	111-08	111-08	111-08	111-18	17.0	113-15	109-10	6,167

Est vol 273,516; vol Tue 329,813; open int 737,651, –13,303.

10 Yr Agency Notes (CBT)-$100,000; pts 32nds of 100%

Dec	...	...	...	110-26	18.0	111-23	106-24	239
Mr03	109-05	109-17	109-05	109-12	18.0	109-25	106-13	10,802

Est vol 1,077; vol Tue 91; open int 11,041, +5

5 Yr Treasury Notes (CBT)-$100,000; pts 32nds of 100%

Dec	13-075	13-085	13-065	113-08	13.0	14-185	106-03	44,922
Mr03	111-18	112-00	11-175	111-30	13.5	113-05	09-255	651,190

Est vol 128,649; vol Tue 165,311; open int 696,113, +3,773.

2 Yr Treasury Notes (CBT)-$200,000; pts 32nds of 100%

Dec	107-15	107-18	107-15	07-177	3.7	09-167	106-23	9,431
Mr03	106-31	109-11	06-307	07-017	4.2	109-11	106-03	103,695

Est vol 9,065; vol Tue 14,405; open Int 113,126, –1,804.

30 Day Federal Funds (CBT)-$5,000,000; 100 - daily avg.

Dec	98.765	98,275	98.760	98.760	–.005	98.780	96.290	77,485
Ja03	98.76	98.77	98.76	98.77	...	98.78	96.29	43,880
Feb	98.78	98.79	98.78	98.79	.01	98.81	97.366	58,897
Mar	98.78	98.80	98.78	98.79	.01	98.81	98.00	36,360
Apr	98.79	98.81	98.79	98.80	.02	98.82	98.12	41,054
May	98.76	98.78	98.75	98.77	.01	98.78	98.42	1,704
June	98.73	98.74	98.72	98.74	.02	98.74	98.40	1,363
July	98.69	98.72	98.68	98.72	.03	98.72	98.48	285
Sept	98.53	98.58	98.50	98.57	.09	98.58	98.21	700

Est vol 33,822; vol Tue 30,914; open Int 262,179, +2,935.

10 Yr Interest Rate Swaps (CBT)-$100,000; pts 32nds of 100%

Mar	110-26	110-30	110-23	110-29	17	111-14	107-22	35,488

Ests vol 1,753; vol Tue 2,305; open int 35,488, –292.

Muni Bond Index (CBT)-$1,000 X The Bond Buyer 40 Index

Dec	108-10	108-14	108-05	108-14	15	111-13	104-00	1,652

Est vol 244; vol Tue 588; open int 3,881, –39.
Index: Close 107-28; Yield 5.18.

13 Week Treasury Bills (CME)-$1,000,000; pts of 100%

	OPEN	HIGH	LOW	SETTLE	CHG	YIELD	CHG	OPEN INT
Mar	...	...	...	98.86	.02	1.14	–.02	95

Est vol 0; vol Tue 1; open int 95, –531.

1 Month Libor (CME)-$3,000,000; pts of 100%

Jan	98.64	98.66	98.64	98.65	.01	1.35	–.01	23,363
Feb	98.66	98.68	98.66	98.66	.01	1.34	–.01	14,608
Mar	98.68	98.68	98.68	98.68	.04	1.32	–.04	1,395
Apr	98.66	98.66	98.66	98.67	.03	1.33	–.03	563
June	98.60	98.61	98.60	98.60	.04	1.40	–.04	2,152

Est vol 1,282; vol Tue 3,212; open int 43,743, –10.025.

Eurodollar (CME)-$1,000,000; pts of 100%

Jan	98.61	98.64	98.61	98.64	.03	1.36	–.03	59,458
Feb	98.62	98.64	98.62	98.64	.03	1.36	–.03	11,272
Mar	98.60	98.64	98.59	98.63	.03	1.37	–.03	756,974
May	98.54	98.58	98.54	98.58	.05	1.42	–.05	652
June	98.46	98.53	98.46	98.52	.06	1.48	–.06	563,533
Sept	98.19	98.28	98.19	98.26	.08	1.74	–.08	498,382
Dec	97.80	97.92	97.80	9790	.11	2.10	–.11	355,136
Mr04	97.45	97.54	97.41	97.51	.11	2.49	–.11	252,776
June	97.03	97.13	97.02	97.10	.12	2.90	–.12	191,982
Sept	96.67	96.76	96.64	96.74	.12	3.265	.12	165,172
Dec	96.40	96.48	96.38	96.46	.10	3.654	–.10	121,035
Mr05	96.19	96.26	96.19	96.24	.09	3.76	–.09	120,761
June	96.00	96.05	96.00	96.05	.09	3.95	–.09	90,736
Sept	95.85	95.90	95.85	95.90	.09	4.10	–.09	98,647
Dec	95.69	95.74	95.69	94.73	.09	4.27	–.09	64,774
Mr06	95.56	95.59	95.56	95.59	.09	4.41	–.09	59,930
June	95.41	95.45	95.41	95.44	.08	4.56	–.08	54,490
Sept	95.27	95.31	95.27	95.31	.08	4.69	–.08	48,444
Dec	95.15	95.17	95.14	95.17	.08	4.83	–.08	35,498
Mr07	94.98	95.04	94.98	95.03	.07	4.97	–.07	29,900
June	94.85	94.91	94.85	94.90	.07	5.10	–.07	27,386
Sept	94.75	94.80	94.75	94.79	.07	5.21	–.07	22.212
Dec	94.63	94.68	94.63	94.66	.06	4.34	–.06	12,879
Mr09	94.14	94.15	94.14	94.15	.06	5.85	–.06	8,814

Est vol 534,747; vol Tue 476,157; open int 3,724,058, –392,688.

---

tion. The price agreed upon by the buyer and seller is $109,250 for the first contract initiated on December 18. The highest quote for a March contract on December 18 was 110-04 or 110 4/32nds, while the lowest quote was 109-04 or 109 4/32nds.

The settlement price (SETTLE) determined by the clearinghouse and used to mark-to-market equity accounts was 109-27. The column following the SETTLE is labeled CHG and means that the settlement price increased 21 points since the prior trading day (December 17, 2002). Hence, on December 17 the settlement price was 109-06. The next two columns give the lifetime high (113-28) and low (100-05) prices for the contract calling for delivery of Treasury bonds in March 2003. The last column, on the far right, identifies the open interest as 388,585 contracts. This is the number of contracts that has been established and not yet offset or exercised.

2. The U.S. *Treasury bill futures contract* is quoted for the future delivery of 90-day T-bills in denominations of $1 million each. For hedgers, the initial margin and the maintenance margin are $325 per contract, whereas for speculators the initial margin is $439. As with Treasury bonds, the expiration/delivery months are March, June, September, and December of each year. If the futures contract expires and delivery occurs, 90-, 91-, and 92-day bills are deliverable. Whereas at one time, the Treasury bill futures contract was the most popular, its liquidity as measured by the open interest has declined.

In Exhibit 7–2, we see illustrated the recent lack of activity for the 13-week Treasury Bills futures contracts traded on the Chicago Mercantile Exchange. The only contract information is for the March 2003 futures contract. The blank OPEN, HIGH, and

LOW columns indicate that no trading occurred on December 18. The settlement price is quoted using the convention of the IMM index. This index price is based on $100 of Treasury bills and is 100 minus the yield on a bank discount basis. (As we saw in Chapter 6, this means the yield is calculated using the convention of a 360-day year.) The (SETTLE) IMM index of 98.86 is consistent with an annualized discount yield of 1.14 percent (100 − 98.86), which is referred to as YIELD in *The Wall Street Journal* quote. This is indicative of a price for the underlying 90-day T-bills of $997,150 (1,000,000 ×[1−(1.14/100) ×(90/360)]). The change in the settlement IMM index (CHG) on December 18, as compared to December 17, is .02. From this information we can infer that the SETTLE for December 17 was 98.84. If you were "long" one March 2003 Treasury bill contract, then you realized a 2 index point gain or $50.00 in profits ($25 times 2) on December 18. (Note that every basis point or index point change translates to $25.00 in profits or losses.) Likewise, if you were "short" the March contract, then $50 was deducted from your equity account for each contract that you held at the close of trading on the Chicago Mercantile Exchange on December 18. The change in YIELD always has an opposite sign to the change in the IMM Index. (Recall that when prices increase, yields decrease.) At the close of trading on December 18, the number of March T-bill contracts that had been established and not yet offset was 95.

3. Futures contracts on *three-month Eurodollar time deposits* are traded in million-dollar units at exchanges in Chicago (The Chicago Mercantile Exchange), London, Tokyo, Singapore, and elsewhere around the globe, offering banks and other investors the opportunity to hedge against interest rate changes attached to bank deposits, money market borrowings, and commercial loans. Currently this is the most actively traded futures contract in the world. The underlying instrument is the Eurodollar CD, which pays the London Interbank Offer Rate (LIBOR). Note that the LIBOR is the rate on short-term deposits set daily based on a survey of leading international banks. To trade Eurodollar CD futures, hedgers must provide an initial margin and a maintenance margin of $600 per contract, whereas for speculators the initial margin is $810.

   As with Treasury bill futures, prices are quoted using the IMM Index. Exhibit 7–2 provides the opening, high, low, and settlement quotes for 24 Eurodollar Futures Contracts extending out to more than six years. If a Eurodollar futures position is not offset before expiration, it is settled in cash based on the LIBOR at expiration. Cash settlement means that Eurodollar deposits are never actually delivered. On December 18, 2002, the cumulative open interest for all Eurodollar contracts traded on the Chicago Mercantile Exchange was 3,724,058. This large open interest makes Eurodollar futures a very liquid instrument for trading.

4. The 30-day *Federal funds futures contracts* are traded at the Chicago Board of Trade in units of $5 million with an index price equal to 100 less the Federal funds futures interest rate. This is essentially the same as the IMM Index the Chicago Mercantile Exchange uses for Treasury bill futures and Eurodollar deposit futures. The quotes from *The Wall Street Journal* provide index information for the opening, high, low, and settlement prices for that trading day (December 18) and the index information for the highs and lows over the life of the particular contract. The initial and maintenance margins for hedgers are $400 per contract, with speculators having an initial margin requirement of $540 per contract. These contracts are settled in cash, based on the monthly average of the daily interest rate quoted by Federal funds brokers.

5. The *one-month LIBOR futures contract* is traded in $3 million units on the Chicago Mercantile Exchange and quotes are in the form of an IMM index. The initial and maintenance margins for hedgers are $300 per contract, while speculators must provide

E-BANKING AND E-COMMERCE

ELECTRONIC BANKING SERVICES INCREASE THE NEED FOR EFFECTIVE USE OF DERIVATIVES AND OTHER HEDGING TECHNIQUES

Banks and their closest competitors must live everyday with "unbalanced" balance sheets—assets mature on different schedules than their liabilities. For most banks, thrifts, and similar financial-service providers, many of their assets take far longer to mature and "cash out" than do their liabilities. This is especially true of such liability items as checking accounts, which are immediately withdrawable, and savings accounts, which usually have no required maturities. The result is a *gap*—in maturity, duration, or interest sensitivity—and the threat of a liquidity crisis.

Many observers believe that the rise of electronic banking has worsened this gap problem and increased the necessity for employing derivatives to deal with the risks associated with changing market interest rates and security values.

Today a growing number of banks and their closest competitors permit the transfer of funds electronically in seconds between savings-type instruments into transactions-type instruments where the transferred funds can be spent immediately. Moreover, an increasing number of depository institutions offer electronic bill paying services that, in microseconds, can move funds from depositors' accounts to merchants' accounts. These electronic devices appear to shorten the time interval between financial decision making and the movement of money. Other factors held constant, maturity gaps may grow, spawning even greater exposure to interest-rate risk on the part of banks and their competitors. More financial firms have reached out to financial futures, options, swaps, and other derivatives to more effectively deal with the "unbalancing" of financial institutions' assets and liabilities.

an initial margin of $405. These contracts are settled in cash rather than through actual delivery of Eurodeposits.[5]

Today's selling price on a futures contract presumably reflects what investors in the market expect cash prices to be on the day delivery of the securities underlying the contract must be made. A futures hedge against interest rate changes generally requires a bank or other financial institution to take an *opposite* position in the futures market from its current position in the cash (immediate delivery) market. Thus, a bank planning to buy bonds ("go long") in the cash market today may try to protect the bonds' value by selling bond contracts ("go short") in the futures market. Then if bond prices fall in the cash market there will be an offsetting profit in the futures market, minimizing the loss due to changing interest rates. While banks and selected other financial institutions make heavy use today of financial futures in their security dealer operations and in bond portfolio management, futures contracts can also be used to protect returns and costs on loans, deposits, and money market borrowings.

---

[5] Other regularly traded interest-rate futures contracts include a $100,000 denomination Treasury note contract and two-year and five-year T-note contracts (with $100,000 and $500,000 denominations respectively), and a Municipal Bond Index contract, all traded on the Chicago Board of Trade (CBT). Added to these are several foreign-related contracts on non-U.S. financial instruments, including Euroyen deposits; British sterling accounts; the long-gilt British bond; Euromark, EuroSwiss, and EuroLira deposits; Canadian, German, French, and Italian government bonds; and Canadian bankers' acceptances. The appearance of the new euro deposit and currency unit in the European Community (EC) has also spawned a three-month Euribor contract traded in units of 1 million euros on the London International Futures Exchange and another three-month Euribor contract (also with a face value of 1 million euros) bought and sold on France's Marche a Termine International (MATIF). In addition, an array of euro-denominated bond contracts includes a 10-year euro bond contract (traded in 100,000 euro units) and 2-, 5-, and 10-year German euro-government bond contracts (all expressed in 100,000 euro units).

The Short Hedge in Futures

Let us illustrate how the *short hedge* in financial futures contracts works. Suppose interest rates are expected to rise, boosting the cost of selling deposits or the cost of borrowing in the money market and lowering the value of any bonds or fixed-rate loans that a bank or other financial institution holds or expects to buy. In this instance a short hedge in financial futures can be used.

This hedge would be structured to create profits from futures transactions to offset losses experienced on a bank's or other financial institution's balance sheet if interest rates do rise. The asset-liability manager will sell futures contracts calling for the future delivery of the underlying securities. The manager will choose contracts expiring around the time new borrowings will occur, when a fixed-rate loan is made, or when bonds are added to a financial firm's portfolio. Later, as borrowings and loans approach maturity or securities are sold and before the first futures contract matures, a like amount of futures contracts will be purchased on a futures exchange. If market interest rates have risen significantly, the interest cost of borrowings will increase and the value of any fixed-rate loans and securities held will decline.

For instance, suppose the securities portfolio of a commercial bank contains $10 million in 6 percent, 15-year bonds and market yields increase from 6 percent to 6.5 percent. The market value of these bonds decreases from $10 million to $9,525,452.07. That is a loss in the cash market of $474,547.73. However, this loss will be approximately offset by a price gain on the futures contracts. Moreover, if the bank makes an offsetting sale and purchase of the *same* futures contracts on a futures exchange, it then has no obligation either to deliver or to take delivery of the securities named in the contracts. The clearinghouse that keeps records for each futures exchange will simply cancel out the two offsetting transactions. (See the box "Management in Action: Hedging Deposit Costs with Financial Futures" on page 247 for an example of how banks and other depository institutions can protect themselves from rising deposit rates using futures contracts.)

The Long Hedge in Futures

We turn now to describe the *long hedge* in futures. While banks and most other financial institutions are generally more concerned about the potentially damaging effects of rising interest rates, there are times when a financial firm wishes to hedge itself against falling interest rates. Usually this occurs when a *cash inflow* is expected in the near future.

For example, suppose the management of a bank expects to receive a sizable inflow of deposits a few weeks or months from today but forecasts lower interest rates by that time. This sounds favorable from a cost-of-funds point of view, but it is not favorable for the future growth of bank revenues. If management takes no action and the forecast turns out to be true, the bank will suffer an *opportunity loss* (i.e., reduced potential earnings) because those expected deposits will have to be invested in loans and securities bearing lower yields or having increased prices. For instance, if the bank was going to buy $1 million (par value) of 15-year, 6 percent bonds and interest rates dropped from 6 percent to 5.5 percent, the price of these bonds would increase from $1 million to $1,050,623.25, forcing the bank to pay a higher price to acquire the bonds. To offset this opportunity loss, management can use a *long hedge:* Futures contracts can be purchased today and then sold in like amount at approximately the same time deposits come flowing in. The result will be a profit on the futures contracts if interest rates do decline because those contracts will rise in value.

Using Long and Short Hedges to Protect Income and Value Table 7–1 provides examples of other short and long hedges using financial futures. In general, the three most typical interest rate hedging problems banks and many of their competitors face are (1) protecting the value of securities and fixed-rate loans from losses due to rising inter-

Factoid
Has any financial firm ever failed due to losses on derivatives? **Answer:** Yes. One of the best-known examples occurred in 1994 when Community Bankers U.S. Government Money Market Fund closed its doors due to derivatives-related losses, paying off its shareholders (mainly smaller community banks) about 94 cents on the dollar.

TABLE 7–1
Examples of Popular
Financial Futures
Transactions Used by
Banks and Other
Financial Institutions

The Short, or Selling, Hedge to Protect against Rising Interest Rates

Fearing *rising* interest rates over the next several months, which will lower the value of its bonds, the management of a bank takes the following steps:

Today—contracts are *sold* through a futures exchange to another investor, with the bank promising to deliver a specific dollar amount of securities (such as Treasury bills) at a set price six months from today.

Six months in the future—contracts in the same denominations are *purchased* through the same futures exchange, according to which the bank promises to take delivery of the same or similar securities at a future date at a set price.

Results—the two contracts are canceled out by the futures exchange clearinghouse ("zero out"), so the bank no longer has a commitment to sell or take delivery of securities—the position has been offset.

However, if interest rates rise over the life of the first futures contracts that are sold, security prices will fall. When the bank then purchases future contracts at the end of the six-month period, they will be obtainable for a lower price than when it sold the same futures contracts six months earlier. Therefore, a *profit* will be made on futures trading, which will offset some or all of the *loss* in the value of any bonds still held by the bank

The Long, or Buying, Hedge to Protect against Falling Interest Rates

A bank's economist has just predicted *lower* interest rates over the next six months, and management fears a decline in bank profits as interest rates on loans fall relative to deposit rates and other operating costs. Moreover, incoming funds must be invested in lower-yielding assets, thus incurring an opportunity loss for the bank. Management elects to do the following:

Today—contracts are *purchased* through a futures exchange, committing the bank to take delivery of a specific amount of securities (such as Treasury bills) at a set price six months from today.

Six months in the future—contracts are *sold* on the same futures exchange, committing the bank to deliver the same amount of securities at a set price on the same future date.

Results—the two contracts are canceled by the clearinghouse, so the bank is not obligated to either make or take delivery of the securities involved. The position has been offset.

However, if interest rates do fall while the futures contracts are in force, security prices must rise. Therefore the bank will be able to sell futures contracts for a higher price than it paid for them six months earlier. The resulting *profit* from trading in financial futures will offset some or all the *loss* in revenue due to lower interest rates on loans.

Filmtoid
What 1980s comedy, starring Dan Aykroyd and Eddie Murphy, illustrated the shorts and longs of futures trading, not to mention the devastating effects of a margin call?
Answer: *Trading Places*

est rates, (2) avoiding a rise in borrowing costs, and (3) avoiding a fall in the interest rates expected from loans and security holdings. In most cases, the appropriate hedging strategy using financial futures is as follows:

Avoiding higher borrowing costs and declining asset values	→	Use a short (or selling) hedge: sell futures and then cancel with a subsequent purchase of similar futures contracts
Avoiding lower than expected yields from loans and security investments	→	Use a long (or buying) hedge: buy futures and then cancel with a subsequent sale of similar contracts

Where the financial institution faces a positive interest-sensitive gap (interest-sensitive assets > interest-sensitive liabilities), it can protect against loss due to falling interest rates by covering the gap with a long hedge (buy and then sell futures) of approximately the same dollar amount as the gap. On the other hand, if the institution is confronted with a negative interest-sensitive gap (interest-sensitive liabilities > interest-sensitive assets), it can avoid unacceptable losses from rising interest rates by covering with a short hedge (sell and then buy futures) approximately matching the amount of the gap.

Active trading in futures contracts for a wide variety of securities (discussed earlier) now takes place on several exchanges worldwide. One distinct advantage of this method of hedging interest rates is that only a *fraction* of the value of a futures contract must be pledged as collateral: in the form of initial and maintenance margins, due to the daily mark-to-market process.

Moreover, brokers commissions for trading futures are relatively low. Thus, traders of financial futures can hedge large amounts of deposits, money market borrowings, loans, and securities with only a small outlay of cash.

Basis Risk   However, there are some limitations to financial futures as interest rate hedging devices, among them a special form of risk known as *basis risk*. *Basis* is the difference in interest rates or prices between the cash (immediate-delivery) market and the futures (postponed-delivery) market. Thus

$$\text{Basis} = \text{Cash-market price (or interest rate)} \qquad \textbf{(3)}$$
$$- \text{Futures market price (or interest rate)}$$

when both are measured at the same moment in time. For example, suppose 10-year U.S. government bonds are selling today in the cash market for $95 per $100 bond while futures contracts on the same bonds calling for delivery in six months are trading today at a price of $87. Then the current basis must be

$$\$95 - \$87 = \$8 \text{ per contract}$$

If the basis changes between the opening and closing of a futures position, the result can be a significant loss, which subtracts from any gains a trader might make in the cash market. Fortunately, basis risk is usually less than interest-rate risk in the cash market, so hedging reduces (but usually does not completely eliminate) overall risk exposure.

The dollar return from a hedge is the sum of changes in prices in the cash market and changes in prices in the futures market. Let's take a look at the essence of basis risk for both a short and long hedge.

Basis Risk with a Short Hedge   For instance, if you are concerned about the interest-rate risk exposure for bonds in a financial institution's securities portfolio, then you fear increasing interest rates that would decrease the value of these bonds. The change in the cash market prices ($C_t - C_0$) would be negative. You have a long position in the cash market. To hedge this possible increase in interest rates, you would take a short position in the futures market. If your concerns are realized, then your dollar return is the sum of the loss in the cash market ($C_t - C_0$) and the gain in the futures market ($F_0 - F_t$). In a short position, you sell at F_0 and you buy at F_t; hence, your gain (loss) is calculated as the sell price minus the buy price.

$$\$\text{ Return from a combined cash and futures position} \qquad \textbf{(4)}$$
$$= (C_t - C_0) + (F_0 - F_t)$$

HEDGING DEPOSIT COSTS WITH FINANCIAL FUTURES

The Problem

Suppose the management of a bank or thrift institution is expecting a *rise* in interest rates over the next three months. Currently deposits can be sold to customers at a promised interest rate of 10 percent. However, management is fearful that deposit interest rates may rise at least one-half of a percentage point (50 basis points) in the next three months, eroding the profit margin of loan revenues over deposit costs.

For example, if a commercial bank needed to raise $100 million from sales of deposits over the next 90 days, its marginal cost of issuing the new deposits at a 10 percent annual rate would be as follows:

$$\begin{array}{c}\text{Amount of new}\\\text{deposits to be}\\\text{issued}\end{array} \times \begin{array}{c}\text{Annual}\\\text{interest rate}\end{array} \times \dfrac{\text{Maturity of deposit in days}}{360} = \begin{array}{c}\text{Marginal}\\\text{deposit interest}\\\text{cost}\end{array}$$

$$\$100 \text{ million} \times 0.10 \times 90 \div 360 = \$2,500,000$$

However, if deposit interest rates climb to 10.50 percent, the marginal deposit cost becomes

$$\$100 \text{ million} \times 0.1050 \times 90 \div 360 = \$2,625,000$$

Amount of added fund-raising costs (and potential loss in profit) $= \$2,625,000 - \$2,500,000 = \$125,000$

An Offsetting Financial Futures Transaction

To counteract the potential profit loss of $125,000, management might select the following financial futures transaction:

Today: Sell 100 90-day Eurodollar futures contracts trading at an IMM Index of 91.5.
Price per $100 = 100 − ((100-IMM Index) × 90 ÷ 360)
Price per $100 = 100 − (8.5 × 90 ÷ 360) = 97.875
100 contracts = $97,875,000
Within next 90 days: Buy 100 90-day Eurodollar futures contracts trading on the day of purchase at an IMM Index of 91.
Price per $100 = 100 − (9 × 90 ÷ 360) = 97.75
100 contracts = $97,750,000
Profit on the completion of sale and purchase of futures = $125,000
Result: Higher deposit cost has been offset by a gain in futures.

This can be rearranged as:

$$\$ \text{ Return from a combined cash and futures position} \qquad \textbf{(5)}$$
$$= (C_t - F_t) - (C_0 - F_0)$$

Thus, with a short hedge in futures,

$$\text{Dollar return} = \text{Basis at termination of hedge} \qquad \textbf{(6)}$$
$$- \text{Basis at initiation of hedge}$$

Basis Risk with a Long Hedge Increasing interest rates are often the concern of bankers and managers of other financial institutions. However, declining interest rates can also weigh on profitability.

If you have concerns about declining interest rates, you would create a long hedge. For instance, you anticipate an inflow of cash in three months that will be used to purchase bonds at that time. In opportunity terms, you have essentially "gone short" in these bonds. To hedge the decrease in interest rates, you would take a long position in the futures market. Your dollar return is the sum of the loss (gain) in the cash market $(C_0 - C_t)$ and the gain (loss) in the futures market $(F_t - F_0)$.

$$\text{\$ Return from a combined cash and futures position} \tag{7}$$
$$= (C_0 - C_t) + (F_t - F_0)$$

This can be rearranged as:

$$\text{\$ Return from a combined cash and futures position} \tag{8}$$
$$= (C_0 - F_0) - (C_t - F_t)$$

$$\text{Dollar return} = \text{Basis at initiation of hedge} \tag{9}$$
$$- \text{Basis of termination of hedge}$$

With an effective hedge, the positive or negative returns earned in the cash market will be approximately offset by the profit or loss from futures trading. The real risk the user faces from hedging with futures stems from the movement in basis that may occur over the life of a futures contract because cash and futures prices are not perfectly synchronized with each other. Futures market prices and interest rates may change more or less than cash-market prices or rates, resulting in gains or losses for the trade as illustrated above.

The sensitivity of the market price of a financial futures contract depends, in part, upon the duration of the security to be delivered under the futures contract. (See Chapter 6 for a discussion of calculating duration for individual securities.) That is,

$$\frac{\text{Change in futures price}}{\text{Initial futures price}} = - \begin{bmatrix} \text{Duration of the} \\ \text{underlying security} \\ \text{named in the} \\ \text{futures contract} \end{bmatrix} \tag{10}$$
$$\times \begin{bmatrix} \dfrac{\text{Change expected in}}{\text{interest rates}} \\ \dfrac{}{\text{1 + Original}} \\ \text{interest rate} \end{bmatrix}$$

If we rewrite this equation slightly we get an expression for the gain or loss from the use of financial futures:

$$\begin{matrix} \text{Positive or negative} \\ \text{change in futures} \\ \text{position value} \end{matrix} = - \begin{bmatrix} \text{Duration of the} \\ \text{underlying security} \\ \text{named in the} \\ \text{futures contract(s)} \end{bmatrix} \times \begin{bmatrix} \text{Initial} \\ \text{futures} \\ \text{price} \end{bmatrix} \times \begin{bmatrix} \text{Number} \\ \text{of futures} \\ \text{contracts} \end{bmatrix} \tag{11}$$
$$\times \begin{bmatrix} \dfrac{\text{Change expected in}}{\text{interest rates}} \\ \dfrac{}{\text{1 + Original}} \\ \text{interest rate} \end{bmatrix}$$

EXHIBIT 7–3
Trade-Off Diagrams
for Financial Futures
Contracts

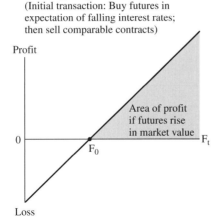

The Long Hedge in Financial Futures
(Initial transaction: Buy futures in
expectation of falling interest rates;
then sell comparable contracts)

Purpose: Protect against falling yields on
assets (such as current loans and future
loans and investments in securities).

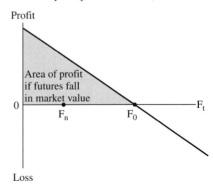

The Short Hedge in Financial Futures
(Initial transaction: Sell futures in
expectation of rising interest rates;
then buy comparable contracts)

Purpose: Protect against rising deposit
and other borrowing costs and falling
market values of assets (such as
security investments and loans).

The negative sign in this equation clearly shows that when interest rates rise, the market value (price) of futures contracts must fall.

For example, suppose a $100,000 par value Treasury bond futures contract is traded at a price of $99,700 initially but then interest rates on T-bonds increase a full percentage point from 7 to 8 percent. If the T-bond has a duration of nine years, then the change in the value of the T-bond futures contracts would be

$$\text{Change in market value of futures contracts} = -9 \text{ years} \times \$99{,}700 \times \frac{+0.01}{1 + 0.07} = -\$8{,}385.98$$

In this case the one percentage point rise in interest rates lowered the price of a $100,000 futures contract for Treasury bonds by almost $8,386.

Exhibit 7–3 summarizes how trading in financial futures contracts can help protect a bank or competing financial-service provider against loss due to interest rate risk. The *long hedge* in financial futures consists of first buying futures contracts (at price F_0) and, then, if interest rates fall, selling comparable futures contracts (in which case the futures price moves toward F_t). The decline in interest rates will generate a gross profit of $F_t - F_0 > 0$, less, of course, any taxes or broker commissions that have to be paid to carry out the long-hedge transaction. In contrast, the *short hedge* in futures consists of first selling futures contracts (at price F_0) and, then, if interest rates rise, buying comparable futures contracts (whose price may move to F_n). The rise in interest rates will generate a profit of $F_0 - F_n > 0$, net of any tax obligations created or traders' commissions. These profitable trades can be used to help offset any losses resulting from a decline in the market value of a financial institution's assets or a decline in its net worth or in its net interest income due to adverse changes in market interest rates.

Number of Futures Contracts Needed   How many futures contracts does a bank or other financial firm need to cover a given size risk exposure? The objective is to offset the loss in net worth due to changes in market interest rates with gains from trades in the futures market. From Chapter 6, we quantify the change in net worth from an increase in interest rates as follows:

$$
\begin{array}{l}
\text{Change} \\
\text{in net} \\
\text{worth}
\end{array}
= - \left(D_{\text{assets}} - \frac{\text{Total liabilities}}{\text{Total assets}} \times D_{\text{liabilities}} \right)
$$

$$
\times \left(\begin{array}{l} \text{Total} \\ \text{assets} \end{array} \right) \times \left(\frac{\begin{array}{l} \text{Change expected} \\ \text{in interest rates} \end{array}}{1 + \begin{array}{l} \text{original} \\ \text{interest rate} \end{array}} \right)
\qquad \textbf{(12)}
$$

where, for example, a bank may have an average asset duration represented by D_{assets} and the average duration of the bank's liabilities is labeled $D_{\text{liabilities}}$. (See Chapter 6 for a description of how to calculate the average duration of a financial institution's assets and liabilities.) If we set the change in net worth equal to the change in the futures position value (Equation 12), we can solve for the number of futures contracts needed to fully hedge a financial firm's overall interest rate risk exposure and protect its net worth (owners' equity):

$$
\begin{array}{l}
\text{Number of} \\
\text{futures} \\
\text{contracts} \\
\text{needed}
\end{array}
= \frac{\left(D_{\text{assets}} - \dfrac{\text{Total liability}}{\text{Total assets}} \times D_{\text{liabilities}} \right) \times \text{Total assets}}{\begin{array}{l} \text{Duration of the} \\ \text{underlying security} \\ \text{named in the} \\ \text{futures contract} \end{array} \times \begin{array}{l} \text{Price of the} \\ \text{futures} \\ \text{contract} \end{array}}
\qquad \textbf{(13)}
$$

For example, suppose a bank has an average asset duration of four years, an average liability duration of two years, total assets of $500 million, and total liabilities of $460 million. Suppose, too, that the bank plans to trade in Treasury bond futures contracts. The T-bonds named in the futures contracts have a duration of nine years and the T-bonds current price is $99,700 per $100,000 contract. Then this bank would need about

$$
\begin{array}{l}
\text{Number of} \\
\text{futures} \\
\text{contracts} \\
\text{needed}
\end{array}
= \frac{\left(\text{four years} - \dfrac{\$460 \text{ million}}{\$500 \text{ million}} \times \text{two years} \right) \times \$500 \text{ million}}{\text{nine years} \times \$99,700}
$$

$$
\approx 1,200 \text{ contracts}
$$

We note that this bank has a positive duration gap of +2.16 years (or 4 years − $460/$500 million × 2 years), indicating that its assets have a longer average maturity than its liabilities. Then if market interest rates rise, its assets will decline in value by more than its liabilities, reducing the stockholder's investment (net worth). To protect against an interest rate rise, this bank would probably want to adopt a short hedge in T-bond futures contracts, selling about 1,200 of these contracts initially. An interest rate decline, on the other hand, usually would call for a long hedge, purchasing contracts on T-bonds or other securities.

Concept Check

7–1. What are *financial futures* contracts? Which banks and other financial institutions use futures and other derivatives for risk management?

7–2. How can financial futures help banks and competing financial service firms deal with interest-rate risk?

7–3. What is a long hedge in financial futures? A short hedge?

7–4. What financial futures transactions would most likely be used in a period of rising interest rates? Falling interest rates?

7–5. How do you interpret the quotes for financial futures in *The Wall Street Journal*?

7–6. A futures contract calling for delivery of Treasury bills in 90 days is currently selling at an interest yield of 4 percent, while yields on Treasury bills available for immediate delivery currently stand at 4.60 percent. What is the *basis* for the T-bill futures contracts?

7–7. Suppose a bank wishes to sell $150 million in new deposits next month. Interest rates today on comparable deposits stand at 8 percent but are expected to rise to 8.25 percent next month. Concerned about the possible rise in borrowing costs, management wishes to use a futures contract. What type of contract would you recommend? If the bank does not cover the interest-rate risk involved, how much in lost potential profits could the bank experience?

7–8. What kind of futures hedge would be appropriate in each of the following situations?

   a. A bank fears that rising deposit interest rates will result in losses on fixed-rate loans.

   b. A bank holds a large block of floating-rate loans and market interest rates are falling.

   c. A projected rise in market rates of interest threatens the value of a bank's bond portfolio.

Interest-Rate Options

The **interest-rate option** grants a holder of securities the right to either (1) place (put) those instruments with another investor at a prespecified exercise price before the option expires or (2) take delivery of securities (call) from another investor at a prespecified price before the option's expiration date. In the put option, the option writer must stand ready to accept delivery of securities from the option buyer if the latter requests. In the call option, the option writer must stand ready to deliver securities to the option buyer upon request. The fee that the buyer must pay for the privilege of being able to put securities to or call securities away from the option writer is known as the *option premium.*

How do options differ from financial futures contracts? Unlike futures contracts, options do not obligate any party to deliver securities. They grant the *right* to deliver or take delivery, but not the obligation to do so. The option buyer can (1) exercise the option, (2) sell the option to another buyer, or (3) simply allow the option to expire. Interest-rate options are traded mostly in over-the-counter markets where the exercise date and price can be tailored to the needs of the option buyer. For standardized exchange-traded interest-rate options, the most activity occurs using options on futures, which is referred to as the futures options market.

The buyer of a *call* futures option has the right, but not the obligation, to take a long position in the futures market at the exercise (strike) price any time prior to expiration of the options contract. The buyer of a put futures option has the right, but not the obligation, to take a short position in the futures market at the exercise (strike) price any time prior to expiration of the options contract. The futures price is highly correlated with the

Key URL
The employment of option trades by banks, thrifts, and other mortgage-lending institutions is discussed at **www.freddiemac .com**.

TABLE 7–2

Put Options to Offset Rising Interest Rates

Put Option

Buyer receives from an option writer the right to sell and deliver securities, loans, or futures contracts to the writer at an agreed-upon *strike price* up to a specified date in return for paying a fee (*premium*) to the option writer. If interest rates *rise*, the market value of the optioned securities, loans, or futures contracts will fall. Exercise of the put results in a gain for the buyer, because he or she can now purchase the optioned securities, loans, or contracts at a lower market price and deliver them to the option writer at the higher strike price. Commissions and any resulting tax liability will reduce the size of the buyer's gain.

Example of a Put Option Transaction: A bank plans to issue $150 million in new 180-day interest-bearing deposits (CDs) at the end of the week but is concerned that CD rates in the market, which now stand at 6.5 percent (annual yield), will rise to 7 percent. An increase in deposit interest rates of this magnitude will result in an additional $375,000 in interest costs on the $150 million in new CDs, possibly eroding any potential profits from lending and investing the funds provided by issuing the CDs. In order to reduce the potential loss from these higher borrowing costs, the bank's asset-liability manager decides to buy put options on Eurodollar deposit futures contracts traded at the Chicago Mercantile Exchange. For a strike price of 9500 the quoted premium for the put option is .50, which is (50 × $25) or $1,250. If interest rates rise as predicted, the market index of the Eurodollar futures will fall below 95.00, perhaps to 94.00. If the market index of the futures contract drops far enough, the put option will be exercised because it is now "in the money" since the futures contract named in the put option has fallen in value below its strike price (9500). The bank's asset-liability manager can exercise a put option, receiving a short position in the futures market at 95.00 and then offset the short position by buying a futures contract at the current index of 94.00. The profit from exercising the option is $2,500 (100 × $25) per contract.

The bank's before tax profit on this put option transaction could be found from:

$$
\begin{array}{l} \text{Before-tax} \\ \text{profit on put} \\ \text{option} \end{array} = \left[\begin{array}{l} \text{Option} \\ \text{strike} \\ \text{price} \end{array} - \left(\begin{array}{l} \text{Futures} \\ \text{market} \times 100 \\ \text{price} \end{array} \right) \right] \times 25 - \text{Option premium} \qquad \textbf{(14)}
$$

The before-tax profit on each million-dollar Eurodollar futures contract would be:

$$
\begin{array}{l} \text{Before-tax} \\ \text{profit on put} \end{array} = [9500 - (94.00 \times 100)] \times \$25.00 - \$1,255 = \$1,250 \text{ per contract}
$$

The $1,250 option profit per futures contract will at least partially offset the higher borrowing costs should interest rates rise.

If you bought 150 puts, you would have partially offset the additional $375,000 in interest costs by $187,500 in futures options profits.

If interest rates don't rise, the option will likely remain "out of the money" and the bank will lose money equal to the option premium. However, if interest rates do not rise, the bank will not face higher borrowing costs and, therefore, has no need of the option. Put options can also be used to protect the value of bank-held bonds and loans against rising interest rates.

underlying cash price; hence, futures on options can be used to hedge interest-rate risk. For example, the buyer of a T-bond futures option at the Chicago Board of Trade is granted the right for a long position (call) or short position (put) in a T-bond futures contract at the exercise (strike) price until the option expires. If interest rates rise, *put* (sell) options are most likely to be exercised. If interest rates fall, holders of *call* (buy) options will be more inclined to exercise their option right and demand delivery of bond futures at the agreed-upon *strike price*. The reason is that falling interest rates can push bond prices higher than the strike price specified in the option contract. (See Tables 7–2 and 7–3.)

Exchange-traded futures options are generally set to expire in March, June, September, or December to conform to most futures contracts. The option on a futures contract

TABLE 7–3

Call Options to Offset
Falling Interest Rates

Call Option

Buyer receives the right from an option writer to buy and take delivery of securities, loans, or futures contracts from the writer at a mutually agreeable *strike price* on or before a specific expiration date in return for paying a *premium* to the writer. If interest rates *fall,* the market value of the optioned securities, loans, or contracts must rise. Exercising the call option gives the buyer a gain, because he or she will acquire securities, loans, or contracts whose value exceeds the strike price that the buyer must pay. Of course, commissions and taxes will reduce the size of the buyer's gain.

Example of a Call Option Transaction: A bank plans to purchase $50 million in Treasury bonds in a few days and hopes to earn an interest return of 8 percent. The bank's investment officer fears a drop in market interest rates before she is ready to buy, so she asks a security dealer to write a call option on Treasury bonds at a strike price of $95,000 for each $100,000 bond. The investment officer had to pay the dealer a premium of $500 to write this call option. If market interest rates fall as predicted, the T-bonds' market price may climb up to $97,000 per $100,000 bond, permitting the investment officer to demand delivery of the bonds at the cheaper price of $95,000. The call option would then be "in the money" because the securities' market price is above the option's strike price of $95,000.

What profit could the bank earn from this call option transaction? On a before-tax basis the profit formula for a call option is

$$\begin{array}{c} \text{Before-tax} \\ \text{profit} \\ \text{on call} \\ \text{option} \end{array} = \text{Security market price} - \text{Strike price} - \text{Option premium} \qquad (15)$$

The before-tax profit on each $100,000 bond would be:

$$\begin{array}{c} \text{Before-tax} \\ \text{profit on call} \end{array} = \$97,000 - \$95,000 - \$500 = \$1,500 \text{ per bond}$$

The projected profit per bond will at least partially offset any loss in interest return experienced on the bonds traded in the cash market if interest rates fall. If interest rates rise instead of fall, the option would likely have dropped "out of the money" as Treasury bond prices fell below the strike price. In this case the T-bond option would likely expire unused and the bank would suffer a loss equal to the option premium. However, the rise in interest rates would permit the bank to come closer to achieving its desired interest return on any newly purchased T-bonds. A call option could also be used to help combat falling interest returns on loans.

expires on or just a few days before the first delivery date of the futures contract. The exception to this rule is the serial contracts for the nearest expiration month. For example, if it is currently January and the nearest expiration month in the futures market is March, futures options trades may expire in January and February, in addition to the March futures options. This is exemplified in Exhibit 7–4.

The exchange's clearinghouse normally guarantees fulfillment of any option agreements traded on that exchange just as the exchange also stands behind any exchange-traded futures contracts. Interest-rate options offer the buyer added leverage—control of large amounts of financial capital with a limited investment and limited risk. The maximum loss to the option buyer is the premium paid to acquire the option.

Exhibit 7–4 shows quotes for options on futures found in the December 19, 2002 edition of *The Wall Street Journal.* We will discuss the details and information provided by these quotes for the two most popular futures options contracts traded today.

1. *U.S. Treasury bond futures options* grant the options buyer the right to a short position (put) or a long position (call) involving one T-bond futures contract for each option.

EXHIBIT 7–4

Futures Options Prices

Source: *The Wall Street Journal,* December 19, 2002. Reprinted by permission of *The Wall Street Journal,* © 2002 Dow Jones & Company, Inc. All Rights Reserved Worldwide.

STRIKE	CALLS-SETTLE			PUTS-SETTLE		
Interest Rate						
T-Bonds (CBT)						
$100,000; points and 64ths of 100%						
Price	Jan	Feb	Mar	Jan	Feb	Mar
109	1-17	2-10	2-47	0-27	1-20	1-57
110	0-44	1-39	2-13	0-54	1-49	2-23
111	0-20	1-11	1-48	1-30	2-20	2-58
112	0-08	0-53	1-23	2-18	2-63	3-33
113	0-03	0-36	1-03	3-13	3-46	4-12
114	0-01	0-24	0-50	4-11	4-33	4-59

Est vol 20,923;
Tu vol 27,000 calls 14,667 puts
Op int Tues 288,919 calls 265,988 puts

T-Bonds (CBT)						
$100,000; points and 64ths of 100%						
Price	Jan	Feb	Mar	Jan	Feb	Mar
112	1-09	1-44	2-07	0-10	0-45	1-08
113	0-29	1-06	1-34	0-30	1-07	1-35
114	0-08	0-42	1-04	1-09	...	2-05
115	0-02	0-23	0-45	2-03	...	2-45
116	0-01	0-11	0-29	...	...	3-29
117	0-01	0-05	0-17	...	...	4-17

Est vol 77,766 Tu 33,939 calls 53,428 puts
Op int Tues 620,353 calls 743,860 puts

5 Yr Treas Notes (CBT)						
$100,000; points and 64ths of 100%						
Price	Jan	Feb	Mar	Jan	Feb	Mar
11250	0-07	0-30	0-48	0-43	...	1-20
11300	0-02	0-20	0-36	1-06	...	1-40
11350	0-01	0-13	0-27	1-37	...	....
11400	0-01	...	0-19	2-04	...	....
11450	0-01	...	0-13	...	...	....
11500	0-01	...	0-09	...	...	....

Est vol 21,191 Tu 5,445 calls 5,495 puts
Op int Tues 119,876 calls 153,923 puts

Eurodollar (CME)						
$ million; pts. of 100%						
Price	Jan	Feb	Mar	Jan	Feb	Mar
9825	3.82	...	3.92	0.02	0.10	0.12
9850	1.40	1.55	1.70	0.10	0.25	0.40
9875	0.20	0.32	0.50	1.40	1.52	1.70
9900	0.02	...	0.15	...	...	...
9925	...	...	0.05	...	...	...
9950	...	...	0.02	...	...	...

Est vol 186,273;
Tu vol 66,834 calls 101,775 puts
Op int Tues 3,017,425 calls 2,316,604 puts

STRIKE	CALLS-SETTLE			PUTS-SETTLE		
Interest Rate						
1 Yr. Mid-Curve Eurodlr (CME)						
$1,000,000 contract units; pts. of 100%						
Price	Jan	Feb	Mar	Jan	Feb	Mar
9700	5.30	5.75	6.07	0.20	0.65	1.00
9725	3.10	3.80	4.35	0.50	1.20	1.75
9750	1.50	2.27	2.85	1.40	2.17	2.75
9775	0.50	...	1.60	...	...	4.00
9800	0.10	0.50	0.87	...	...	...
9825	0.00	...	0.30	...	...	7.67

Est vol 49,130 Tu 17,912 calls 4,831 puts
Op int Tues 458,988 calls 269,273 puts

2 Yr Mid-Curve Eurodlr (CME)						
$1,000,000 contract units; pts. of 100%						
Price	Jan	Feb	Mar	Jan	Feb	Mar
9575	5.87	5.72	5.75	0.95	2.70	...
9600	4.15	4.22	4.40	1.70	3.67	5.40
9625	2.70	2.85	...	2.75	...	...
9650	...	1.85	...	...	...	...
9675	0.75	1.10	...	...	...	...
9700	0.30	0.60	...	...	...	...

Est vol 550 Tu 2,250 calls 0 puts
Op int Tues 64,636 calls 44,938 puts

Euribor (LIFFE)						
Euro 1,000,000						
Price	Jan	Feb	Mar	Jan	Feb	Mar
96875	0.41	0.41	0.42	...	0.00	0.01
97000	0.28	0.29	0.30	...	0.01	0.01
97125	0.16	0.18	0.19	0.00	0.02	0.03
97250	0.06	0.09	0.12	0.03	0.06	0.08
97375	0.02	0.05	0.07	0.11	0.14	0.16
97500	0.00	0.02	0.04	0.22	0.23	0.25

Vol Wd 52,483 calls 3,878 puts
Op int Tues 2,511,309 calls 1,167,470 puts

Euro-BUND (EUREX)						
100,000; pts. in 100%						
Price	Jan	Feb	Mar	Jan	Feb	Mar
11150	1.22	1.50	1.71	0.01	0.28	0.49
11200	0.72	1.15	1.37	0.01	0.43	0.65
11250	0.22	0.84	1.09	0.01	0.62	0.87
11300	0.01	0.60	0.85	0.28	0.88	1.13
11350	0.01	0.41	0.64	0.78	1.19	1.42
11400	0.01	0.28	0.48	1.28	1.56	1.76

Vol Wd 28,869 calls 22,404 puts
Op int Tues 267,914 calls 336,026 puts

In Exhibit 7–4, the premiums for six strike prices ranging from 109 to 114 are quoted. Three months—January, February, and March—are listed for both the call and put premiums at the Chicago Board of Trade. These options are on the nearest T-bond futures contract, which happens to be the March contract. The T-bond futures options contract expires just a few days prior to the first delivery date of the underlying futures contract for March, June, September, and December.

The premium quote for the March call is 2-47 for a strike (exercise) price of 109. This means that you would pay 2 and 47/64ths (percent of par value) or $2,734.38 as a premium to have the right to a long position in the T-bond futures contract at $109,000. If in March, when this call option expires, the futures price is above the strike price of 109, then the option will be exercised. For instance, if the futures price is 112, then the buyer of the option would exercise that option, resulting in a long position for one March T-bond futures contract. The exerciser would have his or her equity account immediately marked-to-market for a gain of $3,000. The exerciser will have to meet the margin requirements of the futures exchange or offset his position in futures immediately.

2. *Eurodollar futures options* give the buyer the right to deliver (put) or accept delivery (call) of one Eurodollar deposit futures contract for every option exercised. In Exhibit 7–4, six strike prices are quoted in the first column ranging from 9825 to 9950 in 25 basis point intervals for three call options and three put options on the March

Eurodollars futures contract. The March puts and calls expire on the same day as the March Eurodollar futures contract. Both the futures contracts and the options on futures trade at the Chicago Mercantile Exchange.

The premium quote for the March put is .12. As with the underlying futures contract, one basis point or index point is equivalent to $25.00; hence a quote of .12 is indicative of a premium of $300 (12 basis points × $25.00). For $300, you can purchase the right to a short position for one Eurodollar futures contract. Your exercise (strike price) is 98.25 in IMM index terms. If you hold your put until expiration and the final settlement IMM index is 97.50 then you will receive $1,875 (75 basis points × $25.00) at the time the put is exercised. (Recall that all Eurodollar futures contracts are settled for cash.)

In addition to those futures options that trade on the Chicago Board of Trade, the Chicago Mercantile Exchange, and other exchanges, all types of interest-rate options can be tailored specifically to a bank's or other financial institution's needs in the over-the-counter-market.[6]

Most options today are used by money center banks. They appear to be directed at two principal uses:

1. Protecting a security portfolio through the use of put options to insulate against falling security prices (rising interest rates); however, there is no delivery obligation under an option contract so the user can benefit from keeping his or her securities if interest rates fall and security prices rise.

2. Hedging against positive or negative gaps between interest-sensitive assets and interest-sensitive liabilities; for example, put options can be used to offset losses from a negative gap (interest-sensitive liabilities > interest-sensitive assets) when interest rates rise, while call options can be used to offset a positive gap (interest-sensitive assets > interest-sensitive liabilities) when interest rates fall.

Banks and their closest competitors can both buy and sell (write) options, but they are usually buyers of puts and calls rather than sellers of these instruments. The reason is the much greater risk faced by option writers compared to that faced by option buyers; an option seller's potential profit is limited to the premium charged the buyer, but the potential loss if interest rates move against the seller is much greater. Regulations in the United States prohibit banks and selected other regulated financial firms from writing put and call options in some high-risk areas and generally require any options purchased to be directly linked to specific risk exposures.

Exhibits 7–5 and 7–6 provide us with a convenient summary of how banks and other financial firms can profit or at least protect their current position through the careful use of options. A bank concerned about possible losses in net earnings due to falling interest rates, for example, may elect to purchase a call option from an option writer, such as a securities dealer. The call option grants the bank the right to demand delivery of securities or futures contracts at price S (as shown in the left panel of Exhibit 7–5). If interest rates do fall, the securities or futures contracts will rise in price toward F_t, opening up the opportunity for profit equal to $F_t - S$ (less the premium that must be paid to buy the call option and any taxes that may be owed). Conversely, as the right panel in Exhibit 7–5 suggests, an expectation of rising interest rates may lead management to purchase a put option on

---

[6] Among the newest exchange-traded option contracts is the Chicago Board of Trade's options on Federal funds futures contracts, which began trading in March 2003. This new options contract assists bankers and others to gauge the public's expectations (as expressed through changes in the Federal funds market interest rate) regarding possible future monetary policy actions by the Federal Reserve System—a key decision-making institution shaping the money and credit decisions that banks and competing financial-service providers must make everyday. For further details on this new Fed-funds options contract see especially **http://www.cbot.com/**.

EXHIBIT 7–5

Payoff Diagrams for Put and Call Options Purchased by a Bank or Other Financial Institution

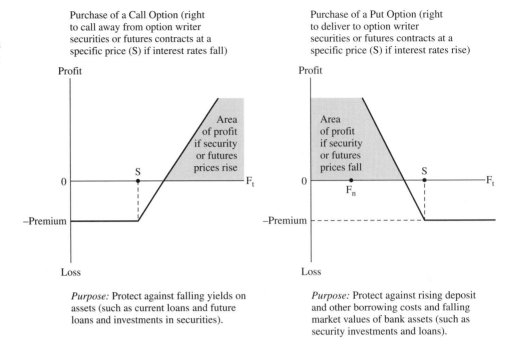

Purchase of a Call Option (right to call away from option writer securities or futures contracts at a specific price (S) if interest rates fall)

Purchase of a Put Option (right to deliver to option writer securities or futures contracts at a specific price (S) if interest rates rise)

Purpose: Protect against falling yields on assets (such as current loans and future loans and investments in securities).

Purpose: Protect against rising deposit and other borrowing costs and falling market values of bank assets (such as security investments and loans).

securities or futures contracts. The upward movement in interest rates will perhaps be large enough to send market prices down to F_n, below strike price S. The bank will purchase the securities or futures contracts mentioned in the put option at current price F_n and deliver them to the writer of the option at price S, pocketing the difference $S - F_n$ (less the premium charged by the option writer and any tax payments due).

Banks and their competitors can also be option writers, offering to sell calls or puts to option buyers. For example, as illustrated in Exhibit 7–6, suppose a bank sells a call option to another institution and the option carries a strike price of S. As shown in the left panel of Exhibit 7–6, if interest rates rise, the call option's market value may fall to F_n and the option will have no value to the buyer. It will go unused and the bank will pocket the option's premium as a profit to help offset any damaging losses due to a trend of rising market interest rates. On the other hand, a banker or other financial manager fearful of losses because of falling interest rates may find another institution interested in purchasing a put option at strike price S. If market interest rates do, in fact, decline, the market price of the securities or futures contracts mentioned in the option will rise, and the put will be of no value to its buyer. The option writer will simply pocket the option's premium, helping to offset any losses that might occur due to falling interest rates.

Regulations and Accounting Rules for Bank Futures and Options Trading

All three federal banking agencies in the United States have guidelines for the risk management of financial derivatives, of which financial futures and options are an important part. For instance, the Office of the Comptroller of the Currency (OCC) has a 186-page document, "Risk Management of Financial Derivatives: Comptrollers Handbook," outlining the necessary elements for such a system. The regulators expect a bank's board of directors to provide oversight while senior management is responsible for the development of an appropriate risk-management system. The risk-management system is to be comprised of

EXHIBIT 7–6

Payoff Diagrams for Put and Call Options Written by a Bank or Other Financial Firm

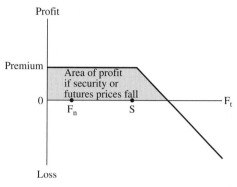

Bank Sells a Call Option to a Buyer (giving the buyer the right to call away securities or futures contracts from the bank at the price (S) specified in the option if interest rates rise)

Purpose: Protect against rising deposit and other borrowing costs and falling market values of bank assets (such as security investments and loans).

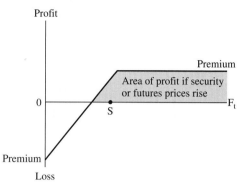

Bank Sells a Put Option to a Buyer (giving the buyer the right to deliver securities or futures contracts to the bank at the price specified (S) in the option if interest rates fall)

Purpose: Protect against falling yields on bank assets (such as current loans and future loans and investments in securities).

1. Policies and procedures to control financial risk taking.
2. Risk measurement and reporting systems.
3. Independent oversight and control processes.

The OCC requires banks to measure and set limits with regards to nine different aspects of risk associated with derivatives. These risks include strategic risk, reputation risk, price risk, interest-rate risk, liquidity risk, foreign exchange risk, credit risk, transaction risk, and compliance risk.

Debilitating losses due to derivative activities of hedge funds and companies such as Enron point to the need for comprehensive accounting guidelines for derivatives. In 1998 the Financial Accounting Standards Board (FASB) introduced Statement 133 (FAS 133) "Accounting for Derivative Instruments and Hedging Activities." This statement became applicable to all publicly traded firms in the year 2000.

FAS 133 requires that all derivatives be recorded on the balance sheet as assets or liabilities at their fair value. With regard to interest-rate risk, FAS 133 recognized two types of hedges: a fair value hedge and a cash flow hedge. Of course, the accounting treatment is defined based on the type of hedge. The objective of a fair value hedge is to offset losses due to changes in the value of an asset or liability. The change in the fair value of the derivative (i.e., the change in the underlying price of the futures contract) plus the change in the fair value of the hedged item must be reflected on the income statement. Cash flow hedges try to reduce the risk associated with future cash flows (interest on loans or interest payments on debt). For cash flow hedges, the change in the fair value of the derivative (for futures, the change in the underlying price) is divided into the effective portion and the ineffective portion. The effective portion must be claimed on the balance sheet as equity, identified as Other Comprehensive Income. Meanwhile, the ineffective portion must be reported on the income statement. The new derivatives regulation can have a significant impact on the earnings of banks by compelling them to reveal the potential profit or loss from their current holdings of futures and options contracts and other derivatives.

Concept Check

7–9. Explain what is involved in a *put option.*

7–10. What is a *call option?*

7–11. What is an option on a futures contract?

7–12. What information do T-bond and Eurodollar futures option quotes contain?

7–13. Suppose market interest rates were expected to rise. What type of option would normally be used?

7–14. If market interest rates were expected to fall, what type of option would a bank or other financial institution's manager be likely to employ?

7–15. What rules and regulations have recently been imposed on the use of futures, options, and other derivatives by banks? What does the Financial Accounting Standards Board (FASB) require banks and other publicly traded firms to do in accounting for derivative transactions?

Interest-Rate Swaps

Early in the 1980s, an interest-rate hedging device was developed in the Eurobond market that enables two borrowers of funds, including banks and other financial institutions, to aid each other by exchanging some of the most favorable features of their loans. For example, one borrower may be small or have a relatively low credit rating so that it cannot go into the open market and sell bonds at the lowest fixed rates of interest. This borrower may be forced to use short-term credit and accept relatively high-cost, variable-rate loans. The other borrower, in contrast, may have a very high credit rating and be able to borrow long term in the open market at a relatively low fixed interest rate. However, the highly rated company, which is often a large bank, may desire a more flexible short-term loan if the interest rate can be made low enough. These two borrowers, often with the help of a bank, security dealer, or other intermediary, can simply agree to *swap interest payments*, tapping the best features of each other's borrowings. (See Exhibit 7–7.)

EXHIBIT 7–7
The Interest-Rate Swap

Lower Credit-Rated Bank or Nonbank Corporate Borrower (known as the *swap buyer*)		Higher Credit-Rated Bank or Nonbank Corporate Borrower (known as the *swap seller*)
Wants lower credit costs	Pays long-term, fixed interest rate, usually based on recently offered Treasury securities	Wants lower credit costs
Prefers fixed-rate, longer term loans due to substantial holdings of long-term assets or short-run uncertainties, but is prevented by size or credit rating from having access to cheap, long-term funds (must borrow short-term instead at a higher interest rate)	The net difference paid by one or the other borrower, often through an intermediary Pays interest rate on short-term loan tied perhaps to the prime bank rate or the London Interbank Offered Rate (LIBOR)	Can borrow at low long-term bond interest rate, but prefers flexible, short-term interest rate in place of long-term fixed rate due to large holdings of short-term assets or because of long-run uncertainties
Often has a positive duration gap (Duration of assets > Duration of liabilities)		Often has a negative duration gap (Duration of liabilities > Duration of assets)

Commercial bank, security dealer, insurance company, or other financial institution acts as a broker to arrange the swap and, perhaps, guarantee performance by each party to the swap for a fee.

Introduced in 1981, *interest-rate swaps* are relative newcomers in the field of derivatives, but they have risen in total face (nominal) value to become one of the largest of all financial instruments in the world. In contrast, caps, floors, and collars are among the oldest of all interest-rate management tools and remain popular with many lending and borrowing institutions.

Detailed websites devoted to these asset-liability management tools are growing. One of the better ones is **www.finpipe.com**, which provides an excellent glossary of derivatives' terminology. This particular website provides good overall descriptions of different types of interest-rate swaps available in the financial marketplace today.

Another potentially useful website in this area is supplied by the International Swaps and Derivatives Association (ISDA) at **www.isda.org/index.html**. Twice a year this organization surveys its members concerning the amount of swaps and options outstanding and helps us determine how these instruments are growing and changing over time.

Just recently, Internet sites that contain relatively new information regarding interest-rate swaps, including swap data, are beginning to multiply. Examples include the economic and financial data bank compiled by the Federal Reserve Board (at **www.economagic.com/fedbog.htm**) and Finance Wise (at **www.financewise.com/risk/**) which supplies more than 350 links to sites discussing risk-management techniques utilizing swaps, caps, floors, futures, and options. One problem website researchers should be aware of, however, is that change occurs rapidly in this field. New websites appear and existing sites disappear with considerable speed.

While commercial banks historically have made the greatest use of interest-rate swaps of any financial institution, nonbank financial firms are expanding their beachhead in this market. Among the key users are some of the largest savings and loans and savings banks, life insurance firms, and security brokers and dealers. Key websites dealing with the swap trading activities of nonbank institutions include **http://financialservices.house.gov/banking**, **www.derivativesstrategy.com/magazine**, and **www.financialservicesfacts.org**.

An **interest-rate swap,** then, is a way to change an institution's exposure to interest-rate fluctuations and achieve lower borrowing costs. Swap participants can convert from fixed to floating interest rates or from floating to fixed interest rates and more closely match the maturities of their liabilities to the maturities of their assets. In addition, a bank or other financial intermediary arranging a swap for its customers earns fee income (usually amounting to 0.25 to 0.50 percent of the amount involved) for serving as an intermediary and may earn additional fees if it agrees to guarantee a swap agreement against default.

Under the terms of an agreement called a *quality swap*, a borrower with a lower credit rating (perhaps with a credit rating of A) enters into an agreement to exchange interest payments with a borrower having a higher credit rating (perhaps with a top-quality rating of AAA). In this case the lower credit-rated borrower agrees to pay the higher credit-rated borrower's fixed long-term borrowing cost. In effect, the lower credit-rated borrower receives a long-term loan from the financial markets at a much lower effective interest cost than the lower-rated borrower could obtain without the swap agreement. At the same time, the borrower with the higher credit rating covers all or a portion of the lower-rated borrower's short-term floating loan rate, thus converting a fixed long-term interest rate into a more flexible and possibly cheaper short-term interest rate.

In summary, the higher credit-rated borrower gets a long-term fixed-rate loan, but pays a floating interest rate to the lower credit-rated borrower. The lower credit-rated borrower gets a short-term, floating rate loan, but pays a fixed interest rate to the higher credit-rated borrower. Often the lower-rated borrower, such as a savings and loan or insurance company, has longer duration assets than liabilities, while the higher-rated borrower may have

Factoid
Most derivatives (measured by their notional value) used by banks and thrifts are traded on organized exchanges, like the Chicago Board of Trade. True or false? **Answer:** False; on average more than 80 percent are over-the-counter (OTC) contracts.

longer duration liabilities than assets (such as a commercial bank). Through the swap agreement just described, each party achieves cash outflows in the form of interest costs on liabilities that more closely match the interest revenues generated by its assets.

The most popular short-term, floating rates used in interest rate swaps today include the London Interbank Offered Rate (LIBOR) on Eurodollar deposits, Treasury bill rates, the prime bank rate, the Federal funds rate, and interest rates on bank and thrift CDs and commercial paper. Each swap partner simply borrows in that market in which it has the greatest comparative cost advantage, and then the two parties exchange interest payments owed on the funds they have each borrowed. In total, the cost of borrowing is lower after a swap is arranged, even though one of the parties (the borrower with the highest credit rating) can usually borrow more cheaply in *both* short-term and long-term markets than the borrower with the lower credit rating.

Notice that neither firm lends money to the other. The principal amount of the loans, usually called the *notional* amount, is not exchanged.[7] Each party to the swap must still pay off its own debt. In fact, only the *net* amount of interest due usually flows to one or the other party to the swap, depending on how high short-term interest rates in the market rise relative to long-term interest rates on each interest-due date. The swap itself normally will not show up on a swap participant's balance sheet, though it can reduce interest-rate risk associated with the assets and liabilities on that balance sheet.[8]

As noted earlier, swaps are often employed to deal with asset-liability maturity mismatches. For example, as shown in Exhibit 7-7, one firm may have short-term assets with flexible yields and long-term liabilities carrying fixed interest rates. Such a firm fears that a decline in market interest rates will reduce its earnings. In contrast, a company having long-term assets with fixed rates of return, but facing shorter-term liabilities, fears rising interest rates. These two firms are likely candidates for a swap. The one with long-term fixed-rate assets can agree to take over the interest payments of the one with long-term fixed-rate liabilities, and vice versa.

A bank or other financial firm can use swaps to alter the effective duration of its assets and liabilities. It can shorten asset duration by swapping out a fixed interest-rate income stream in favor of a variable interest-rate income stream. If the duration of liabilities is too short the financial firm can swap out a variable interest-rate expense in favor of a fixed interest-rate expense. Thus, interest-rate swaps can help immunize a portfolio by moving closer to a balance between asset and liability durations.

Why use swaps for these problem situations? Wouldn't refinancing outstanding debt obligations, or perhaps using financial futures, accomplish the same thing? In principle, yes, but practical problems frequently favor swaps. For example, retiring old debt and issuing new securities with more favorable characteristics can be expensive and risky. New borrowing may have to take place in an environment of higher interest rates. Underwriting costs, registration fees, time delays, and regulations often severely limit how far any business firm can go in attempting to restructure its balance sheet. Financial futures also present problems for hedgers because of their rigid maturity dates (they usually fall due within a few weeks or months) and the limited number of financial instruments they cover.

---

[7] Swaps in which the notional amount is constant are called *bullet swaps.* In *amortizing* swaps, notional amount declines over time, and in *accruing* swaps, notional principal accumulates during their term. *Seasonal* swaps have notional principals that vary according to the seasonal cash flow patterns the swap parties experience.

[8] If a bank or other financial institution agrees to guarantee a swap agreement negotiated between two of its customers or if it participates in a swap with another firm, it usually merely marks the transaction down as a contingent liability. Because such arrangements may become real liabilities for a financial firm, many financial analysts seek out information on any outstanding swaps in evaluating individual banks or other financial-service firms as possible investments for their clients.

Insights and Issues

DERIVATIVES STABILIZE BANKS, THE FINANCIAL SYSTEM, AND THE WHOLE ECONOMY?

Financial futures, options, swaps, and other derivatives have been getting a lot of positive publicity lately. Government officials in the United States and Europe, security traders, and the managers of banks and other financial-service firms have claimed that these contracts have literally showered financial firms and the public with ample benefits. Curiously enough, the claims made coincided closely with public hearings and calls from several quarters that more regulation is needed to deal with the risks in the derivatives field. After all, if something is really so beneficial for so many, why should it be regulated at all?

Arguments heard up and down Wall Street allege that individual bank earnings (and the earnings of other financial firms) have become less volatile as derivative usage has grown. Some recent evidence from federal banking agency reports indicates that the growth of bank earnings, assets, deposits, and capital *have* become somewhat more stable in recent years. This appears especially to be the case among the largest banking firms, which tend to be the heaviest users of derivative contracts.

However, some financial analysts and members of the regulatory community have gone much further, alleging that derivatives have become low-cost "shock absorbers" for the entire economy and financial system. With derivatives, risk-averse banks and other investors are able to slough off much of their risk exposure, transferring that risk to other investors willing to carry it. In turn, the entire financial marketplace allegedly becomes better able to absorb shocks generated by changing interest rates, stock prices, currency values, inflation, and other factors.

Is there any proof for these claims? Allegedly the greater stability in national output, incomes, employment, and inflation that seemed to emerge in the 1990s and continued (albeit with some pauses) into this new century is at least consistent with the foregoing claims. Real proof, however, must await the verdict afforded by time and experience.

For more information about the role of derivatives in the financial system, see especially Jeffrey W. Gunther and Thomas F. Siems, "Debunking Derivatives Delirium," *Southwest Economy,* Federal Reserve Bank of Dallas, March/April 2003, pp. 1, 5–9.

In contrast, swaps can be negotiated to cover virtually any period of time or borrowing instrument desired, though most fall into the 3-year to 10-year range. They are also easy to carry out, usually negotiated and agreed to over the telephone through a broker or dealer. During the 1980s, several large American and British banks developed a communications network to make swap trading relatively easy, even for small-denomination, short-maturity swaps. Another key innovation was the development of *master swap agreements*, which spell out the rights and responsibilities of each swap partner, thereby simplifying the negotiation of an agreement and significantly improving the liquidity and smoothness of the international swap market.

Reverse swaps can also be arranged, in which a new swap agreement offsets the effects of an existing swap contract. Many swap agreements today contain termination options, allowing either party to end the agreement for a fee. Other swaps carry interest-rate ceilings (caps), interest-rate minimums (floors), or both ceilings and floors (collars), which limit the risk of large changes in interest-rate payments. There may also be escape clauses and "swaptions," which are options for one or both parties to make certain changes in the agreement, take out a new option, or cancel an existing swap agreement.

On the negative side, swaps may carry substantial brokerage fees, credit risk, basis risk, and interest rate risk. With *credit risk*, either or both parties to a swap may go bankrupt or fail to honor their half of the swap agreement (though the loss would be limited to promised interest payments, not repayment of loan principal). Moreover, a third party with a top credit rating, such as a commercial bank or security dealer, may be willing to *guarantee* the agreed-upon interest payments through a letter of credit if the swap partner seeking the guarantee pays a suitable fee (usually 10 to 50 basis points). The most heavily used intermediaries in arranging and guaranteeing swap contracts include the largest U.S., Canadian, Japanese, and European commercial banks and securities firms (such as J. P. Morgan Chase, Merrill Lynch, and Salomon Brothers). Sometimes the lower-rated swap

Key URLs

The use of interest-rate swaps by banks and nonbank financial firms may be explored further using such sites as **www.snl.com**, **www.scotiacapital.com**, and **www.aei.org**.

partner may be asked to post collateral to strengthen the contract. Indeed, the posting of collateral is increasing in this market, even among high-credit-quality participants.

In fairness to swaps, we should note that actual defaults on these contracts are rare.[9] Credit quality in this marketplace is relatively high, with swap parties usually carrying credit ratings of A or higher. If a swap partner is rated BBB or lower it may be impossible to find a counterparty to agree to the swap or the low-rated partner may be required to agree to a *credit trigger clause*, which allows the other partner to the swap to terminate the contract should the lower-rated borrower's credit rating deteriorate.

One element that significantly reduces the potential damage if a swap partner does default on its obligation to pay is called *netting*. Remember that on each payment due date the swap parties exchange only the net difference between the interest payments each owes the other. This amount is much smaller than either the fixed or floating interest payment itself and would be the actual amount subject to default. Moreover, when a bank or other financial intermediary is involved in several swap contracts with another party, it will often calculate only the *net* amount owed across all swap contracts, which further reduces the actual amount of credit risk.

Basis risk arises because the particular interest rates that define the terms of a swap, such as a long-term bond rate and a floating short-term rate like LIBOR, are not exactly the same interest rates as those attached to all the assets and liabilities that either or both swap partners hold. This means that as a swap's reference interest rate changes, it may not change in exactly the same proportion as the interest rates attached to the swap buyer's and seller's various assets and liabilities. Thus, an interest-rate swap cannot hedge away all interest-rate risk for both parties to the agreement; some risk exposure must remain in any real-world situation.

Indeed, swaps may carry substantial *interest-rate risk*. For example, if the yield curve slopes upward, the swap buyer, who pays the fixed interest rate, normally would expect to pay a greater amount of interest cost during the early years of a swap contract and to receive greater amounts of interest income from the swap seller, who pays the floating interest rate, toward the end of the swap contract. This could encourage the seller to default on the swap agreement near the end of the contract, possibly forcing the swap buyer to negotiate a new agreement with a new partner under less-favorable market conditions. Swap dealers, which account for most contracts in the market, work to limit their interest-rate risk exposure by setting up offsetting swap contracts with a variety of partners.

In general, if short-term market interest rates are expected to fall and stay low, this will be a plus for the short-term rate payer and a disadvantage to the long-term rate payer whose swap rate will consistently be higher. The fixed-rate paying partner will have to pay out the difference between short-term and long-term interest rates whenever a payment is owed. On the other hand, if the yield curve becomes negatively sloped, the long-term fixed-rate payer may benefit if the short-term rate rises above the long-term fixed swap rate. In the latter case the short-rate payer must now pay out a stream of interest payments to the swap partner as long as the short-term (variable) interest rate stays above the fixed interest rate. Obviously, *changing interest-rate expectations* are likely to impact the market appeal of swaps.

---

[9] In addition to conventional interest-rate swaps, banks and other intermediaries today engage in several other types of swaps, including commodity swaps, equity swaps, and currency swaps. *Commodity* swaps are designed to hedge against price fluctuations in oil, natural gas, copper, and selected other commodities where one party fears rising prices and the other fears falling prices. *Equity* swaps are designed to convert the interest flows on debt into cash flows related to the behavior of a stock index, which allows swap partners to benefit from favorable movements in stock prices. *Currency* swaps are discussed in Chapter 20 on international banking.

AN EXAMPLE OF A SWAP TRANSACTION

This example shows how two businesses can each save on borrowing costs by agreeing to swap interest payments with each other. The savings arise principally because interest rate spreads, often called *quality spreads,* are normally much wider in the long-term credit market than in the short-term market.

Parties to the Swap	Fixed Interest Rates Parties Must Pay if They Issue Long-Term Bonds	Floating Interest Rates Parties Must Pay if They Receive a Short-Term Loan	Potential Interest Rate Savings of Each Borrower
A lower credit-rated bank or nonbank corporate borrower	11.50%	Prime + 1.75%	0.50%
A higher credit-rated bank or nonbank corporate borrower	9.00	Prime interest rate	0.25%
Difference in interest rates due to differences in borrower's credit ratings (*quality spread*)	2.50%	1.75%	0.75%

FINANCING METHODS USED

The higher-rated borrower issues long-term bonds at 9 percent, while the lower-rated borrower gets a loan at prime plus 1.75 percent. They then swap interest payments.

A swap transaction might be arranged in which the lower-rated borrower agrees to pay the higher-rated borrower's 9 percent interest cost, thus saving 2.5 percent in long-term borrowing costs because it would have had to pay 11.5 percent for long-term credit. The higher-rated borrower pays the lower-rated borrower's prime interest rate minus 0.25 percent, thus saving the higher-rated borrower, who normally would borrow at prime, a quarter of a percentage point (−0.25 percent) on a short-term loan. Notice that the lower credit-rated borrower saves a *net* interest rate of 0.50 percent (that is, 2.50 percentage points saved on the long-term rate minus the 2 percent additional it must pay above the amount of the prime rate less 0.25 percent contributed by the higher-rated borrower). Thus:

Low credit-rated borrower pays .... 9 percent (fixed rate)

High credit-rated borrower pays .... Prime rate less 0.25 percent (floating rate)

Low credit-rated borrower saves .... [(11.5 percent − 9 percent) − (1.75 percent more than the prime rate + 0.25 percent less than the prime rate)] = 0.50 percent

High credit-rated borrower saves .... 0.25 percent (below the prime rate)

The lower-rated borrower may also agree to pay the underwriting costs associated with the higher-rated borrower's issue of long-term bonds so that both ultimately wind up with roughly equal savings of about 0.5 percent.

Clearly, both parties save as a result of this interest rate swap. They also benefit from a closer matching of cash inflows and outflows from their respective portfolios of assets and liabilities.

Some authorities argue, however, that these savings are illusory, that an efficient financial marketplace will rapidly eliminate such arbitrage opportunities between long-term and short-term markets except for possible market imperfections, such as those introduced by government regulations. Others contend that the supposed savings from a swap are counterbalanced by the surrender of valuable options by the swap parties, who, were it not for the swap agreement, could refinance their loans if interest rates move in a favorable direction. However, they must honor the terms of a swap contract regardless of how interest rates subsequently behave unless they can work out a revised contract.

The Interest-Rate Swap Yield Curve

Recently the Federal Reserve Board began releasing a series of interest rates for swap contracts of varying maturities from 1 year to 30 years. Collected under the auspices of the International Swaps and Derivatives Association, Inc., the reported rates represented the interest rates that a fixed-rate partner to a swap would pay based on swap rates collected by survey at 11 A.M. each business day. Each swap agreement in the survey assumes that the variable-rate partner to the swap would pay the fixed-rate partner the prevailing three-month London Interbank Offer Rate (LIBOR).

An example of the fixed interest rates attached to swaps of varying maturities is reported for July 7, 2003:

Maturity of Swap Contract Reported in Survey	Prevailing Interest Rate Paid by Fixed-Rate Swap Partner in Return for Receiving the 3-Month LIBOR Rate
1 year	1.18%
2 years	1.55
3 years	2.03
4 years	2.48
5 years	2.88
7 years	3.46
10 years	4.04
30 years	4.97

At the time these interest rates were obtained by survey, the variable-rate party in each of these swap contracts was paying a money market interest rate at or close to 1.04 percent. Two key points stand out from this data source:

1. The long-term rate payer, at least at the beginning of the swap, paid the higher interest rate compared to the short-term rate payer.
2. The swap yield curve generally slopes upward, suggesting that the longer the term of a swap contract, the higher the fixed interest rate tends to be.

What accounts for these differences in swap interest rates? The key factor tends to be *risk*—the risk of changing market interest rates and shifts in the term structure of interest rates (the yield curve).

For example, if short-term market interest rates are expected to remain relatively low, it will benefit the short-term rate payer in a swap and be a disadvantage to the long-term rate payer whose swap rate will consistently be higher. In this instance the fixed-rate-paying partner will have to pay out the difference between short-term and long-term interest rates whenever a payment is due. On the other hand, if the yield curve gets flatter or becomes negatively sloped, the long-term fixed-rate payer may benefit if the short-term (variable) rate rises above the long-term fixed swap rate. In the latter case the short-rate payer must now pay out a stream of interest payments to the swap partner as long as the short-term (variable) interest rate stays above the fixed interest rate. Clearly, shifting interest-rate expectations can play a key role in the attractiveness of swaps to either or both swap partners.

For more information on the interest-rate swap yield curve, see especially the International Swaps and Derivatives Association at **www.isda.org** and the Federal Reserve Board, Statistical Release H.15 at **www.federalreserve.gov**.

The swap market's growth has been truly phenomenal. Starting from zero in the early 1980s, outstanding swap contracts denominated in U.S. dollars and measured by their notional (face) value approached $20 trillion as the 21st century began. Further testimony to the swap market's rapid growth is provided by the substantial breadth of market participants today. Among the most important are banks and thrifts; insurance companies; finance companies; nonfinancial corporations; dealers in government, corporate, and asset-backed securities; hedge funds; and government-related enterprises, including U.S. federal agencies (such as Fannie Mae) and the World Bank.

Concept Check

7–16. What is the purpose of an interest-rate swap?

7–17. What are the principal advantages and disadvantages of interest-rate swaps?

7–18. How can a bank or other financial institution get itself out of an interest-rate swap agreement?

Caps, Floors, and Collars

Finally, among the most familiar hedging devices developed by banks and other lenders for themselves and their customers are interest-rate caps, floors, and collars.

An **interest-rate cap** protects its holder against rising market interest rates. In return for paying an up-front premium, borrowers are assured that institutions lending them money cannot increase their loan rate above the level of the cap. Alternatively, the borrower may purchase an interest-rate cap from a third party, with that party promising to reimburse borrowers for any additional interest they owe their creditors beyond the cap. If a bank or other lending institution sells a rate cap to one of its borrowing customers, it takes on interest-rate risk from that customer but earns a fee (premium) as compensation for added risk taking. If a bank takes on a large volume of cap agreements it can reduce its overall risk exposure by using another hedging device, such as an interest-rate swap.

Interest-rate caps are administered simply. Consider the following example: A bank purchases a cap of 11 percent from another financial institution on its borrowings of $100 million in the Eurodollar market for one year. Suppose interest rates in this market rise to 12 percent for the year. Then the financial institution selling the cap will reimburse the bank purchasing the cap the additional 1 percent in interest costs due to the recent rise in market interest rates. In terms of dollars, the bank will receive a rebate of

$$\left(\begin{matrix} \text{Market} \\ \text{interest rate} \end{matrix} - \begin{matrix} \text{Cap} \\ \text{rate} \end{matrix} \right) \times \begin{matrix} \text{Amount} \\ \text{borrowed} \end{matrix} = \tag{16}$$

$$(12 \text{ percent} - 11 \text{ percent}) \times \$100 \text{ million} = \$1 \text{ million}$$

for one year. Thus, the bank's effective borrowing rate can float over time but it will never exceed 11 percent. Banks and other financial firms buy interest rate caps when conditions arise that could generate losses, such as when a financial institution finds itself funding fixed-rate assets with floating-rate liabilities, possesses longer-term assets than liabilities, or perhaps holds a large portfolio of bonds that will drop in value when interest rates rise.

Interest-Rate Floors

Financial-service providers can also lose earnings in periods of falling interest rates, especially when rates on floating-rate loans decline. For example, a bank or thrift institution can insist on establishing an **interest-rate floor** under its loans so that, no matter how far loan rates tumble, it is guaranteed some minimum rate of return.

Another popular use of interest-rate floors arises when a financial firm sells an interest rate floor to its customers who hold securities but are concerned that the yields on those securities might fall to unacceptable levels. For example, a bank's customer may hold a 90-day negotiable CD promising 6.75 percent but anticipates selling the CD in a few days. Suppose the customer does not want to see the CD's yield drop below 6.25 percent. In this instance, the customer's bank may sell its client a rate floor of 6.25 percent, agreeing to pay the customer the difference between the floor rate and the actual CD rate if interest rates fall too far at the end of the 90 days.

How can banks and other financial institutions benefit from trading in interest-rate floors? To cite one example, suppose a bank extending a $10 million floating-rate loan to one of its corporate customers for a year at prime insists on a minimum (floor) interest rate on this loan of 7 percent. If the prime rate drops below the floor to 6 percent for one year, the customer will pay not only the 6 percent prime rate (or $10 million $\times$ 0.06 = $600,000 in interest) but also pay out an interest rebate to the bank of

$$\left(\begin{array}{c} \text{Floor} \\ \text{rate} \end{array} - \begin{array}{c} \text{Current loan} \\ \text{interest rate} \end{array} \right) \times \begin{array}{c} \text{Amount} \\ \text{borrowed} \end{array} = (7\% - 6\%) \quad\quad \textbf{(17)}$$
$$\times \; \$10 \text{ million} = \$100,000$$

Through this hedging device the bank is guaranteed, assuming the borrower doesn't default, a minimum return of 7 percent on its loan. Banks and other financial intermediaries use interest-rate floors most often when their liabilities have longer maturities than their assets or when they are funding floating-rate assets with fixed-rate debt.

Interest-Rate Collars

Lending institutions and their borrowing customers also make heavy use of the **interest-rate collar,** which combines in one agreement a rate floor and a rate cap. Many banks, security firms, and other institutions sell collars as a separate fee-based service for the loans they make to their customers. For example, a customer who has just received a $100 million loan may ask the lender for a collar on the loan's prime rate between 11 percent and 7 percent. In this instance, the lender will pay its customer's added interest cost if prime rises above 11 percent, while the customer reimburses the lender if prime drops below 7 percent. In effect, the collar's purchaser pays a premium for a rate cap while receiving a premium for accepting a rate floor. The net premium paid for the collar can be positive or negative, depending upon the outlook for interest rates and the risk aversion of borrower and lender at the time of the agreement.

Normally, caps, collars, and floors range in maturity from a few weeks out to as long as 10 years. Most such agreements are tied to interest rates on government securities, commercial paper, prime-rated loans, or Eurodollar deposits (LIBOR). Banks and other lenders often make heavy use of collars to protect their earnings when interest rates appear to be unusually volatile and there is considerable uncertainty about the direction in which market interest rates may move.

Caps, collars, and floors are simply special types of options designed to deal with interest rate risk exposure from assets and liabilities held by lending institutions and their customers. Sales of caps, collars, and floors to customers have generated a large volume of fee income (up-front revenues) in recent years, but these special options carry both credit risk (when the party is obligated to pay defaults) and interest-rate risk that must be carefully weighed by financial managers when making the decision to sell or use these rate-hedging tools.

Concept Check

7–19. How can banks and other financial-service providers make use of interest-rate *caps, floors,* and *collars* to generate revenue and help manage interest-rate risk?

7–20. Suppose a bank enters into an agreement to make a $10 million, three-year floating-rate loan to one of its best corporate customers at an initial rate of 8 percent. The bank and its customer agree to a cap and a floor arrangement in which the customer reimburses the bank if the floating loan rate drops below 6 percent and the bank reimburses the customer if the floating loan rate rises above 10 percent. Suppose that at the beginning of the loan's second year, the floating loan rate drops to 5 percent for a year and then, at the beginning of the third year, the loan rate increases to 12 percent for the year. What rebates must each party to the agreement pay?

Summary

In this chapter we have focused upon the principal types of *derivatives*—financial futures contracts; options; swaps; and interest-rate caps, collars, and floors—designed to deal with the exposure of banks and other financial-service institutions to losses due to changing market interest rates. The key points which surfaced in this chapter include these:

- *Financial futures contracts* are agreements to deliver or take delivery of securities or other financial instruments, such as bonds, bills, and deposits, at a stipulated price on a specific future date. This brand of derivatives has grown rapidly in recent years because of their relatively low cost and ready availability in a variety of types and maturities.

- *Option contracts* give their holders the right to deliver (put) or to take delivery of (call) specified financial instruments at a prespecified (strike) price on or before a stipulated future date. Options are widely traded on organized exchanges and can be particularly effective when the managers of banks and other financial-service institutions wish to have downside risk protection but do not want to restrict potential gains should market interest rates move in a favorable direction.

- *Interest-rate swaps* are agreements between parties to exchange interest payments so that each participating institution can achieve a better match of its cash inflows and cash outflows. Swaps also can help to lower interest costs because each party to the agreement normally borrows in that credit market offering the greatest cost advantage.

- *Interest-rate caps* place an upper limit on a borrower's loan rate, while *interest-rate floors* protect a lender from declining loan yields should market interest rates fall too far. *Collars* combine caps and floors, freezing loan rates or security yields within the limits spelled out by the accompanying contractual agreement between borrower and lender.

- Derivative usage is heavily centered in the largest commercial banks and among some of their biggest competitors, such as security firms and insurance companies. This size bias in the employment of interest-rate hedging tools stems from the huge market risk exposures leading banks and competing financial firms experience, as well as the highly technical skills needed to use derivatives successfully as an asset-liability management tool. Moreover, it is the biggest banks, security dealers, and other financial firms that most corporations and governments turn to when they require effective risk protection.

Key Terms

Problems and Projects

1. You hedged your bank's exposure to declining interest rates by buying one March Treasury bond futures contract at the opening price on December 18, 2002 (see Exhibit 7–2). It is now Monday, January 6, and you discover that on Friday, January 3, March T-bond futures opened at 110-08 and settled at 110-09.

   a. What are the profit/losses on your long position as of settlement on January 3?

   b. If you deposited the required initial margin on 12/18 and have not touched the equity account since making that cash deposit, what is your equity account balance?

2. Use the quotes of Eurodollar futures contracts traded on the Chicago Mercantile Exchange on January 3, 2002, to answer the following questions:

	Open	High	Low	Settle	Chg	Yield	Chg	Open Int
Eurodollar (CME)-$1,000,000; pts of 100%								
Jan	98.61	98.61	98.61	98.61	. . .	1.39	. . .	63,517
Feb	98.62	98.62	98.62	98.62	. . .	1.38	. . .	13,792
Mar	98.62	98.64	98.61	98.63	. . .	1.37	. . .	740,349
May	98.58	98.58	98.58	98.58	.01	1.42	−.01	382
June	98.52	98.53	98.49	98.52	.01	1.48	−.01	573,271

Source: *The Wall Street Journal*, January 06, 2002, p. C10.

   a. What is the dollar price for the underlying securities ($1 million in 90-day Eurodollar time deposits) based on the low IMM index for the nearest June contract?

   b. If your bank took a short position at the high price for the day for 15 contracts, what would be the dollar gain/loss at settlement on January 3, 2003?

   c. If you deposited the initial required hedging margin in your equity account upon taking the position described in *b*, what would be the marked-to-market value of your equity account at settlement?

3. What kind of futures or options hedges would be called for in the following situations?

   a. Market rates are expected to increase and First National Bank's asset and liability managers expect to liquidate a portion of their bond portfolio to meet depositors' demands for funds in the upcoming quarter.

   b. Silsbee Savings Bank has interest-sensitive assets of $79 million and interest-sensitive liabilities of $88 million over the next 30 days and market interest rates are expected to rise.

   c. A survey of Tuskee Bank's corporate loan customers this month (January) indicates that on balance, this group of firms will need to draw $165 million from their credit lines in February and March, which is $65 million more than the bank's management has forecasted and prepared for. The bank's economist has predicted a significant increase in money market rates over the next 60 days.

   d. Monarch National Bank has interest-sensitive assets greater than interest-sensitive liabilities by $24 million. If interest rates fall (as suggested by data from the Federal

Reserve Board), the bank's net interest margin may be squeezed due to the decrease in loan and security revenue.

e. Caufield Thrift Association finds that its assets have an average duration of 1.5 years and its liabilities have an average duration of 1.1 years. The ratio of liabilities to assets is .90. Interest rates are expected to increase by 50 basis points during the next six months.

4. Your bank needs to borrow $300 million by selling time deposits with 180-day maturities. If interest rates on comparable deposits are currently at 2 percent, what is the cost of issuing these deposits? Suppose interest rates rise to 3 percent. What then will be the cost of these deposits? What position and types of futures contracts could be used to deal with this cost increase?

5. In response to the above scenario, management sells 300 90-day Eurodollar time deposit futures contracts trading at an IMM Index of 98. Interest rates rise as anticipated and your bank offsets its position by buying 300 contracts at an IMM index of 96.98. What type of hedge is this? What before-tax profit or loss is realized from the futures position?

6. It is March and Cavalier Financial Services Corporation is concerned about what an increase in interest rates will do to the value of its bond portfolio. The portfolio currently has a market value of $101.1 million and Cavalier's management intends to liquidate $1.1 million in bonds in June to fund additional corporate loans. If interest rates increase to 6 percent, the bond will sell for $1 million with a loss of $100,000. Cavalier's management sells 10 June Treasury bond contracts at 109-05 in March. Interest rates do increase, and in June Cavalier's management offsets its position by buying 10 June Treasury bond contracts at 100-03.

a. What is the dollar gain/loss to Cavalier from the combined cash and futures market operations described above?

b. What is the basis at the initiation of the hedge?

c. What is the basis at the termination of the hedge?

d. Illustrate how the dollar return is related to the change in the basis from initiation to termination.

7. By what amount will the market value of a Treasury bond futures contract change if interest rates rise from 5 to 6 percent? The underlying Treasury bond has a duration of 10.36 years and the Treasury bond futures contract is currently being quoted at 110-14. (Remember that Treasury bonds are quoted in 32nds.)

8. Tiger National Bank reports that its assets have a duration of 10 years and its liabilities average 2 years in duration. To hedge this duration gap, management plans to employ Treasury bond futures, which are currently quoted at 110-09 and have a duration of 10.36 years. Tiger's latest financial report shows total assets of $110 million and liabilities of $97 million. Approximately how many futures contracts will the bank need to cover its overall exposure?

9. You hedged your bank's exposure to declining interest rates by buying one March call on Treasury bond futures at the premium quoted on December 18, 2002 (see Exhibit 7–4).

a. How much did you pay for the call in dollars if you chose the strike price of 110? (Remember that premiums are quoted in 64ths.)

b. Using the following information for trades on January 3, 2003, if you sold the call on 01/03/03 due to a change in circumstances would you have reaped a profit or loss? Determine the amount of the profit/loss.

Interest Rate

T-Bonds (CBT)

$100,000; points and 64ths of 100%

Price	Feb	Mar	Apr	Feb	Mar	Apr
108	2-49	3-24	. . .	0-31	1-07	. . .
109	2-03	2-47	. . .	0-49	1-29	2-38
110	1-28	2-09	. . .	1-10	1-56	3-10
111	0-62	1-43	. . .	1-44	2-25	. . .
112	0-39	1-16	. . .	2-21	2-62	. . .
113	0-23	0-59	. . .	3-05	3-41	. . .

Source: *The Wall Street Journal*, January 06, 2002, p. C10

10. Refer to the information given for problem 9. You hedged your bank's exposure to increasing interest rates by buying one March put on Treasury bond futures at the premium quoted on December 18, 2002 (see Exhibit 7–4).

    a. How much did you pay for the put in dollars if you chose the strike price of 110? (Remember that premiums are quoted in 64ths.)

    b. Using the following information for trades on January 3, 2003, if you sold the put on 01/03/03 due to a change in circumstances would you have reaped a profit or loss? Determine the amount of the profit/loss.

11. You hedged your thrift institution's exposure to declining interest rates by buying one March call on Eurodollar deposit futures at the premium quoted on December 18, 2002 (see Exhibit 7–4).

    a. How much did you pay for the call in dollars if you chose the strike price of 9,850? (Remember that premiums are quoted in IMM Index terms.)

    b. If March arrives and Eurodollar Deposit Futures have a settlement index at expiration of 99.00, what is your profit or loss? (Remember to include the premium paid for the call option.)

12. You hedged your bank's exposure to increasing interest rates by buying one March put on Eurodollar deposit futures at the premium quoted on December 18, 2002 (see Exhibit 7–4).

    a. How much did you pay for the put in dollars if you chose the strike price of 9,850? (Remember that premiums are quoted in IMM Index terms.)

    b. If March arrives and Eurodollar Deposit Futures have a settlement index at expiration of 99.00, what is your profit or loss? (Remember to include the premium paid for the call option.)

13. A commercial bank is considering the use of options to deal with a serious funding cost problem. Deposit interest rates have been rising for six months, currently averaging 5 percent, and are expected to climb as high as 6.75 percent over the next 90 days. The bank plans to issue $60 million in new money market deposits in about 90 days. It can buy put or call options on 90-day Eurodollar time deposit futures contracts for a quoted premium of .31 or $775.00 for each million-dollar contract. The strike price is quoted as 9,500. We expect the futures to trade at an index of 93.50 within 90 days. What kind of option should the bank buy? What before-tax profit could the bank earn for each option under the terms described?

14. Hokie Savings Bank wants to purchase a portfolio of home mortgage loans with an expected average return of 8.5 percent. The bank's management is concerned that

interest rates will drop and the cost of the portfolio will increase from the current price of $50 million. In six months when the funds become available to purchase the loan portfolio, market interest rates are expected to be in the 7.5 percent range. Treasury bond options are available today at a quoted price of $79,000 (per $100,000 contract), upon payment of a $700 premium, and are forecast to rise to a market value of $87,000 per contract. What before-tax profits could the bank earn per contract on this transaction? How many options should Hokie buy?

15. A savings and loan's credit rating has just slipped, and half of its assets are long-term mortgages. It offers to swap interest payments with a money center bank in a $100 million deal. The bank can borrow short term at LIBOR (8.05 percent) and long term at 8.95 percent. The S&L must pay LIBOR plus 1.5 percent on short-term debt and 10.75 percent on long-term debt. Show how these parties could put together a swap deal that benefits both of them about equally.

16. A bank plans to borrow $55 million in the money market at a current interest rate of 8.5 percent. However, the borrowing rate will float with market conditions. To protect itself, the bank has purchased an interest-rate cap of 10 percent to cover this borrowing. If money market interest rates on these funds sources suddenly rise to 11.5 percent as the borrowing begins, how much interest in total will the bank owe and how much of an interest rebate will it receive, assuming the borrowing is for only one month?

17. Suppose that Exeter Savings Association has recently granted a loan of $3.6 million to Fairhills Farms at prime plus 0.5 percent for six months. In return for granting Fairhills an interest-rate cap of 12 percent on its loan, this thrift has received from this customer a floor rate on the loan of 7.5 percent. Suppose that, as the loan is about to start, the prime rate declines to 6.25 percent and remains there for the duration of the loan. How much (in dollars) will Fairhills Farms have to pay in total interest on this six-month loan? How much in interest rebates will Fairhills have to pay due to the fall in the prime rate?

Internet Exercises

1. Bank trading in futures and options is subject to strict regulations. You can find out about the rules and regulatory supervision of banks (BHCs) in the Federal Reserve's *Trading and Capital-Markets Activity Manual*, found at **www.federalreserve.gov/boarddocs/supmanual/trading/trading.pdf.** Using the index locate "Regulation, Compliance with." After reading this page, discuss which banking regulations and regulators are involved with futures, options, and swap activities.

2. All three federal banking regulators have guidelines for the risk management of financial derivatives (futures and options). In this chapter we have provided some of the details from the *Comptrollers Handbook for National Banks*. Go to the FDIC's website, **www.fdic.gov/regulations/laws/rules/** and search the index under *D* for *derivatives*. Under the heading of Risk Management, click on the link for FDIC Statement of Policy, which will provide the Supervisory Policy Statement on Investment Securities and End-User Derivatives Activities. Print and read the eight pages of this statement. In terms of managing the specific risks involved in investment activities, compare and contrast the types of risks listed in this statement with those identified by the OCC and listed in the chapter's discussion.

3. The *Federal Reserve's Trading and Capital-Markets Activity Manual* found at **www.federalreserve.gov/boarddocs/supmanual/trading/trading.pdf** includes the section, "Instrument Profiles." Read the descriptions of options (section 4330), financial futures (section 4320), and swaps (section 4325). Compare and contrast the risks associated with these instruments based on the Federal Reserve document.

REAL NUMBERS FOR REAL BANKS — Assignment for Chapter 7

YOUR BANK'S USE OF INTEREST-RATE DERIVATIVE CONTRACTS

Chapter 7 explores how banks and many of their competitors can use interest-rate derivatives to hedge interest-rate risk and increase noninterest income (fee income). The derivative contracts discussed in this chapter include interest-rate futures, options, options on futures, swaps, caps, floors, and collars. Early in the chapter, data provided from the Office of the Comptroller of the Currency (OCC) illustrates that the largest banks account for the bulk of trading activity. The banking company you selected in earlier chapters was chosen from the largest 25 banking companies in the United States. This assignment is designed to explore your bank's usage of derivative contracts, how its usage compares to other large banks, and the composition of its interest-rate derivatives portfolio.

For this assignment, you will once again access data at **www3.fdic.gov/sdi/main.asp** for your BHC (the bank and thrift chartered component) and its peer group of banks with more than $10 billion in assets. Follow the directions in Chapter 5's assignment to create the four columns of your bank's information and the peer group information over the two-year period. In this assignment, for Report Selection use the pull-down menu to select Derivatives and view this in Percentages of Average Assets. For Interest Rate Contracts, you are interested in Items 6–10. This includes all the interest-rate derivatives discussed here in Chapter 7 plus a few more. Caps, floors, and collars are part of the Purchased and Written Option Contract categories. Enter the percentage information for Interest Rate Contracts as an addition to Spreadsheet 2 as follows:

	Your Bank	Peer Group	Your Bank	Peer Group
Derivatives (interest rate) (A59)				
Date (A60)	12/31/yy	12/31/yy	12/31/yy	12/31/yy
Interest-rate contracts (A61)	%	%	%	%
Notional value of interest rate swaps (A62)				
Futures and forward contracts (A63)				
Written option contracts (A64)				
Purchased option contracts (A65)				

YOUR BHC'S USE OF DERIVATIVE CONTRACTS ACROSS PERIODS

A. Compare columns of row 61. How has the use of derivative contracts changed across periods? Is your bank more or less involved than the group of comparable institutions?

B. Use the chart function in Excel and the data by columns in rows 62 through 63 to create four pie charts illustrating the break-down of the type of interest-rate contracts held by your BHC and its peer group. Your pie charts should include titles and labels. For instance, what follows is a pie chart for National City Corp for 12/31/02.

C. Utilizing the above information, write approximately one page about your bank's usage of interest-rate derivatives and how it compares to its peers. Use your pie charts as graphics and incorporate them in the discussion. The pie chart on the right was included by creating a text box and copying the Excel spreadsheet into the text box.

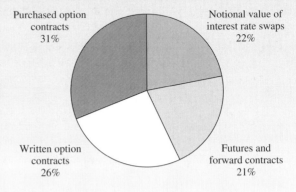

Interest Rate Contracts for NCC (12-31-02)

Purchased option contracts 31%

Notional value of interest rate swaps 22%

Written option contracts 26%

Futures and forward contracts 21%

4. What do the following terms mean in financial futures and options trading?

Basis	Daily trading limit
Carrying charge	Limit order
Clearing margin	Managed futures
Convergence	Market order

(To answer this question, see especially the Knowledge Center of the Chicago Board of Trade at **www.cbot.com.**)

5. If you want to become more familiar with swaps and other derivatives, visit **www.finpipe.com** and click on the Derivatives link. Explore the swap links. Discuss the example provided for a firm using an interest-rate swap to hedge changing interest rates.

STANDARD &POOR'S

S&P Market Insight Challenge

1. Use Standard & Poor's Market Insight website (**www.mhhe.com/edumarketinsight**) for this problem. The S&P Industry Survey on Banking discusses commercial banking's role in the derivatives market. For an up-to-date description use the Industry tab in S&P's Market Insight. The drop-down menu provides subindustry selections for Diversified Banks and Regional Banks. Upon selecting one of these subindustries, you will find a recent downloadable S&P Industry Survey on Banking. View the section, "How to Analyze a Bank," looking particularly at derivatives. Describe the advantages and the risks associated with derivative usage by banks and other financial-service providers.

2. Use Standard & Poor's Market Insight website (**www.mhhe.com/edumarketinsight**) for this problem. Which financial firms in the Market Insight group appear to make the heaviest use of financial futures? Interest-rate options? Interest-rate swaps? Why and how can you tell? What industries do these firms represent?

Selected References

For excellent readings on the use of financial futures and options in risk management, see the following studies:

1. Ackert, Lucy. "Derivative Securities Use Grows as Banks Strive to Hedge Risks." *Financial Update*, Federal Reserve Bank of Atlanta, January–March 1999, pp. 8–9.

2. Ardalan, Kavous. "Textbook Treatment of Volatility in Valuing Options and Corporate Liabilities." *Financial Practice and Education*, Spring/Summer 1997, pp. 103–12.

3. Brealey, Richard A., and Stewart C. Myers. *Principles of Corporate Finance*, 7th ed. New York: McGraw-Hill/Irwin, 2003, Chapters 21 and 27.

4. Sundaresan, Suresh. *Fixed Income Markets and Their Derivatives*. Cincinnati: South Western College Publishing, 1997.

5. Rose, Peter S. "Defensive Banking in a Volatile Economy: Hedging Loan and Deposit Interest Rates." *The Canadian Banker* 93, no. 2 (April 1986), pp. 52–59.

6. Wall, Larry, D.; John J. Pringle; and James E. McNultz. "Capital Requirements for Interest-Rate and Foreign-Exchange Hedges." *Economic Review,* Federal Reserve Bank of Atlanta, 75 (May/June 1990), pp. 14–28.

These studies give a more detailed view of interest rate swaps:

7. Abken, Peter A. "Beyond Plain Vanilla: A Taxonomy of SWAPs." *Economic Review,* Federal Reserve Bank of Richmond, March/April 1991.

8. Ackert, Lucy. "Derivative Securities Use Grows as Banks Strive to Hedge Risks." *Financial Update*, Federal Reserve Bank of Atlanta, January–March 1999, pp. 8–9.

www.mhhe.com/rose6e

For further information on interest rate caps, floors, and collars, see in particular:

9. Rose, Peter S. "Interest Rate Forecasting and Hedging against Interest Rate Risk," in *Money and Capital Markets: Financial Institutions and Instruments in a Global Marketplace*, 8th ed. Burr Ridge, IL: Irwin/McGraw Hill, 2003, Chapter 9.

For a review of the controversy over the alleged benefits and risks of derivatives, see especially:

10. Gunther, Jeffery W., and Thomas F. Siems. "Debunking Derivatives Delirium." *Southwest Economy*, Federal Reserve Bank of Dallas, March/April 2003, pp. 1, 5–9.

11. Peek, Joe, and Eric Rosengren. "Derivatives Activity at Troubled Banks." *Financial Services Research* 12, no. 2/3 (October/December 1997), pp. 287–302.

For an analysis of some of the newest financial futures and options contracts, involving Federal funds loans and borrowings, of interest to bankers and other financial-service providers that trade daily in the money market, see especially:

12. Carlson, John B., William R. Melick, and Erkin Y. Sabinoz. "An Option for Anticipating Fed Action." *Economic Commentary*, Federal Reserve Bank of Cleveland, September 1, 2003.

CHAPTER EIGHT

Asset-Backed Securities, Loan Sales, Credit Standbys, and Credit Derivatives: Important Risk-Management Tools for Banks and Competing Financial-Service Firms

Key Topics in This Chapter

- The Securitization Process
- Securitization's Impact and Risks
- Sales of Loans: Nature and Risks
- Standby Credits: Pricing and Risks
- Credit Derivatives and CDOs
- Benefits and Risks of Credit Derivatives

Introduction

As we have seen in preceding chapters, banks and many of their competitors face several different kinds of risk exposure.[1] Interest rates change in the financial marketplace and both interest revenues and interest costs are affected, as is the value of many assets, especially the securities portfolio of a bank, insurance company, securities dealer, or other

---

[1] Portions of this chapter are taken from Peter S. Rose's articles focusing on off-balance-sheet financing in *The Canadian Banker* (10, 11, and 15) and are used with permission.

The rapid rise of off-balance-sheet transactions and derivatives trading has transformed the banking and financial services industry in just a few short years. The loan securitizations and sales, credit letters, and credit derivatives discussed in this chapter have created new sources of funding, new sources of revenue, and new kinds of risk challenges for banks and other financial firms making use of them. One of the key indicators of financial health and stability among banks and their competitors today is the size and composition of each financial firm's off-balance-sheet position and the promises it has made to support that position as market conditions change.

One of the more complete sources to consult for additional information on banking and thrift activity in the markets for interest-rate and credit derivatives, as well as for the rules that govern such activity, is the Federal Deposit Insurance Corporation. You may access most of their data simply by working through their main website at **www.fdic.gov**. Users of FDIC information on off-balance-sheet activity in banking will be able to compare the growth of derivatives trading and other off-balance-sheet activities, for example, against the growth of bank assets, equity capital, loans, and other financial-statement items.

Numerous websites have also begun to appear that define, explain, and track loan securitizations, loan sales, standby credits, and the rapidly expanding use of credit derivatives. Examples of such sites include **www.investorwords.com**, **www.mortgage101.com**, and **www.finpipe.com**. Another useful approach to learning about the use of loan securitizations and sales, credit letters, and derivatives is to consult the websites of leading players in these market specialties, including Citibank and Citigroup, J. P. Morgan, Bank of America, Wells Fargo, and, in Europe, National Westminster Bank and Deutsche Bank.

The rapidly expanding credit derivatives market, which today is led by the largest banks, insurance companies, securities dealers, and funds-management companies, may be sampled through such sites as **www.intltreasurer.com**, **www.margrabe.com/creditderivatives.html**, **www.statestreet.com**, and **www.vankampen.com**.

As the structuring and trading of the instruments discussed in this chapter have expanded in recent years, so have jobs in this field. Among the more useful sites to check for possible job opportunities is **www.streetjobs.com**. You may also want to check out informational websites among private companies serving the derivatives industry such as **www.portfolioservices.com**, and **www.thecapitalgroup.com**. It is truly an exciting area to explore!

financial institution. Borrowing customers may default on their loans, confronting banks and other lenders with serious credit losses and diminishing their expected earnings. Added to these problems are the demands of the regulatory community to strengthen capital—the most expensive source of funds for most financial-service institutions—in order to protect the financial firm against interest-rate risk, credit risk, and other forms of risk exposure. Bankers and many of their competitors have actively sought out newer, more efficient, and less costly ways to deal with these kinds of risks.

In earlier chapters in this section we explored the workings of such risk-management tools as interest sensitivity analysis, duration gap management, financial futures and options contracts, interest-rate swaps, and interest-rate caps and collars. However, the foregoing tools focus principally upon combating interest-rate risk—fending off damage to each financial firm as market interest rates change. True, that kind of protection is very important, but other costs and risks also have to be dealt with if you are going to successfully manage a financial institution today, including credit risk and the burden of having to raise new capital to meet the funding needs of your customers and satisfy regulatory standards. These management problem areas have spawned whole new weapons to help bankers and other financial-service managers do their job, including such devices as securitizing loans, selling loans off balance sheets, issuing standby letters of credit, and pursuing credit derivative contracts of various kinds.

Not only have these newer tools helped bankers and many of their competitors manage risk more effectively, but they have also opened up new sources of fee income and helped serve customers better, even during those times when available funding is scarce and costly to obtain. Among the leaders in this field are such innovative companies as J. P. Morgan Chase in the banking industry, Bear Stearns in the securities field, and Prudential Inc. from the insurance industry. We take a close look at each of these risk-management and fee-generating tools in the sections that follow.

Securitizing Bank Loans and Other Assets

The growth of securitizations of loans and other assets around the world has been truly awesome, particularly among the largest, billion-dollar-plus banks and thrift institutions. The securitization of mortgage loans placed in pools or trusts with government agency sponsorship—the largest, but not the only segment of the asset-securitization market—reached more than $4 trillion in 2002, nearly doubling from just over $2 trillion five years earlier. What has led to such enormous growth? What are securitizations and why are they so popular among banks, thrifts, and other financial-service firms?

Securitization of loans and other assets is a simple idea for raising new funds and for reducing risk exposure—so simple, in fact, that one wonders why it was not fully developed until the 1970s and 1980s. Securitizing assets requires a lending institution to set aside a group of income-earning assets, such as mortgages or consumer loans, and to sell securities (financial claims) against those assets in the open market. As the assets pay out—for example, as borrowing customers repay the principal and interest owed on their loans—that income stream flows to the holders of the securities. In effect, loans are transformed into publicly traded securities. For its part, the securitizing institution receives the money it originally expended to acquire the assets and uses those funds to acquire new assets or to cover operating expenses.

The bank, thrift institution, or other lender whose loans are pooled is called the *originator* and the loans are then passed on to (acquired by) an *issuer,* who is usually a *special purpose entity* (SPE). (See Exhibit 8–1.) The SPE is completely separate from the originator so that if the originating lender goes bankrupt, this event will not affect the credit status of the loans in the pool. A *trustee* is appointed to ensure that the issuer fulfills all the

EXHIBIT 8–1
Key Players in the Securitization Process

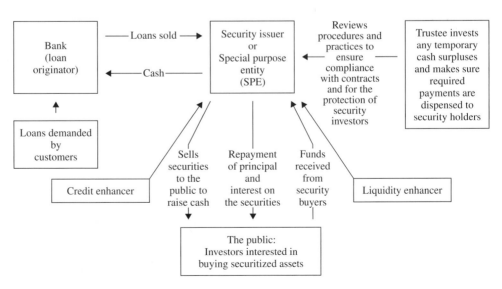

requirements of the transfer of loans to the pool and provides all the services promised (including, where stipulated, fulfilling any guarantees or collateral requirements in case a significant proportion of the pooled loans are defaulted). The trustee collects and disburses to investors any cash flows generated by the pooled loans and temporarily invests any cash generated by the loans between required investor payment dates. Investors in the securities normally receive added protection that they will be repaid in the form of credit guarantees (enhancements) and liquidity guarantees (enhancements), usually supplied under contract by an independent financial institution, such as a bank or an insurance company.

Pooling loans through securitization helps to diversify a lender's credit risk exposure and reduces the need to monitor each individual loan's payment stream. It creates liquid assets out of relatively illiquid, expensive-to-sell assets and transforms these assets into new sources of capital.

Securitizations permit banks and other lenders subject to economic downturns in their local areas to, in effect, hold a more geographically diversified loan portfolio, perhaps countering local losses with higher returns available from loans originating from different geographic areas with more buoyant economic conditions.

Securitization is also a tool for managing interest rate risk, making it easier for any individual financial firm to adjust its asset portfolio so that the maturity (duration) of its assets more closely approximates the maturity (duration) of its liabilities.

Moreover, a lending institution can earn added fee income by agreeing to *service* the packaged assets. Usually this means monitoring the borrowers' performance in repaying their loans, collecting payments due, and making sure adequate collateral is posted to protect holders of any securities issued against those loans. While the lender may continue to service any assets pledged, it can remove those assets from its balance sheet, eliminating the risk of loss if the loans are not repaid or if interest rate movements lower their value.[2] (Securitization tends to shorten the maturity of a lender's assets, reducing its overall sensitivity to interest rate movements.) A lender may also secure additional earnings based on the spread between the interest rate being earned on the securitized assets and the interest rate paid to security holders, which usually is lower. Moreover, taxes may be reduced because of the deductibility of the interest expense incurred when assets are securitized and there is no regulatory tax in the form of deposit reserve requirements. However, the assets packaged to back any securities issued must be uniform in quality and purpose and carry investment features (such as high yields or ready marketability) that are attractive to investors.

As the foregoing paragraph suggests, securitization of loans creates numerous opportunities for revenue for a bank or other lender choosing this fund-raising alternative. A lender can benefit from the normal positive spread between the average yield on the packaged loans and the coupon (promised) rate on the securities issued, capturing at least a portion of the difference in interest rates between the loans themselves and the securities issued against the loans in the form of *residual income*. The securitizing institution may be able to gain additional income by servicing the loans pledged behind the securities, collecting interest from the loans and monitoring their performance. Many financial firms have also gained added income by selling guarantees (*credit enhancements*) to protect investors who hold loan-backed securities, by advising institutions securitizing their loans on the correct procedures, and by providing backup liquidity (*liquidity enhancements*) in

---

[2] This step—removing loans in the securitized pool from the lender's balance sheet—can be a real plus from a regulatory point of view. Regulations generally limit the proportion of a lender's assets committed to loans in order to control risk exposure. A lender with a relatively high loan-asset ratio can bundle a group of loans and move them off its books to make the institution look financially stronger. Total assets will decline while capital remains the same, so the lender's protective capital-to-assets ratio improves.

case a securitizing institution runs short of cash to meet its obligations to investors. Here is an illustration of a typical securitization transaction and the fees it might generate:

Average expected yield on the pooled loans
(as a percent of the total value of the securitized loans) 15%

Promised fees and payments on these securitized loans might include the following (expressed as a percent of the total value of the securitized loans):

- Coupon rate promised to investors who buy
  the securities issued against the pool of loans 9%
- Default rate on the pooled loans—often covered
  by a government or private guarantee
  (enhancement) or the placement of some revenues
  generated by the pooled loans in a special reserve
  to ensure security holders against default 5%
- Fees to compensate a servicing institution for
  collecting payments from the loans in the pool
  and for monitoring the performance of the pooled loans 0.25%
- Fees paid for advising on how to set up the
  securitized pool of loans 0.25%
- Fees paid for providing a liquidity facility
  (enhancement) to cover any temporary shortfalls
  in cash needed to pay security investors 0.25%
- Residual interest income for the securitizing
  institution (left over after payment of all fees
  and payment of the coupon rate promised to
  investors) 0.25%
- Sum of all fees, promised payments, and residual
  interest income 15%

The Beginnings of Securitization—The Home Mortgage Market

The concept of securitization began in the residential mortgage market of the United States. (See Exhibit 8–2.) In this huge home loan marketplace, three federal agencies—the Government National Mortgage Association (GNMA), the Federal National Mortgage Association (FNMA), and the Federal Home Loan Mortgage Corporation (FHLMC)—have worked to greatly improve the salability of residential mortgage loans. For example, GNMA sponsors a mortgage loan-backed securities program under which banks, thrifts, and other lenders can pool their home mortgages that are insured against default by the Federal Housing Administration (FHA), Veterans Administration (VA), and the Farmers Home Administration (FMHA) and issue securities against the pooled loans. GNMA insures the interest and principal payments owed to holders of those securities it has agreed to sponsor. While GNMA sponsors and guarantees the issuance of securities by private lenders, FNMA creates its own mortgage-backed securities, which it sells to individual investors and to major institutional investors like life insurance companies and retirement plans, using the proceeds of these sales to purchase packages of both conventional and government-insured home mortgage loans from banks and other lending institutions.

EXHIBIT 8–2
The Home Mortgage
Loan-Backed
Securities Market

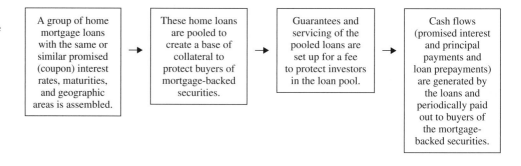

For its part, FHLMC purchases pools of both conventional and government-insured home mortgage loans from private lending institutions and pays for these by issuing FHLMC-guaranteed mortgage-backed securities. Beginning in the 1980s with the cooperation of First Boston Corporation, a major security dealer, FHLMC developed a new mortgage-backed instrument—the CMO, or collateralized mortgage obligation—in which investors are offered different classes of mortgage-backed securities with different expected cash flow patterns. CMOs typically are created from a multistep process in which home mortgage loans are first pooled together, and then GNMA-guaranteed securities are issued against the mortgage pool that may be purchased by a bank or other investor. These securities are placed in a trust account off the lender's balance sheet and several different classes of CMOs are issued as claims against the security pool in order to raise new funds. The lender as issuer of CMOs hopes to make a profit by packaging the loan-backed securities in a form that appeals to many different types of investors. Each class (tranche) of CMOs promises a different coupon rate of return to investors and carries a different maturity and risk that some of the mortgage loans in the underlying pool will be paid off early, reducing the investor's expected yield.[3] (See Exhibit 8–3.)

With a CMO the different tiers (tranches) in which securities are issued receive the interest payments to which they are entitled, but all loan principal payments flow first to securities issued in the top tier until these top-tier instruments are fully retired. Subsequently received principal payments then go to investors who purchased securities belonging to the next tier until all securities in that tier are paid out, and so on until the point is reached where all CMO tiers are finally paid off. The upper tiers of a CMO carry shorter maturities, which reduces their reinvestment risk exposure. In contrast, the lower tiers carry lengthier maturities, and, hence, have more prepayment protection and promise higher expected returns.

Certain CMO instruments include a special Z tranche with the highest degree of risk exposure because this particular tranche generates no principal or interest payments until all other CMO tiers are paid off. Among the more exotic CMOs developed recently are floaters (whose rate of return is related to a particular interest rate index), superfloaters (which yield a multiple change in return based upon a particular interest rate index), and so-called "jump Z tranches" that may suddenly catapult to first place among the tiers of a CMO depending upon events in the market. These and other complex loan-backed security instruments in recent years have become so complicated that even sophisticated traders have stumbled at times with sizable losses.

During the 1990s a new market for home equity loan-backed securities appeared and grew rapidly. *Home equity loans* permit home owners to borrow against the residual value of their residence—that is, the difference between the current market value of their home

Key URLs
To learn more about loan securitizations see especially **www.key.com**, **www.lucent.com** (which presents an example of a real transaction), and **www.fdic.gov.**

---

[3] See Chapter 9 for a discussion of *prepayment risk* and its implications for investors in loan-backed securities, such as CMOs and pass-throughs.

EXHIBIT 8–3
The Structure of
Collateralized
Mortgage Obligations
(CMOs)

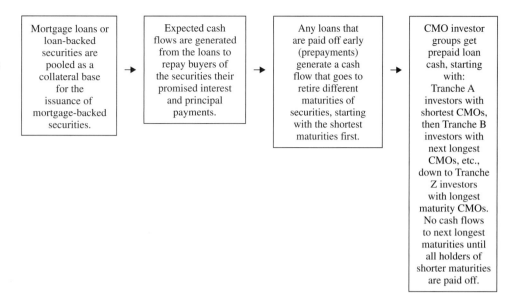

Mortgage loans or loan-backed securities are pooled as a collateral base for the issuance of mortgage-backed securities.

→

Expected cash flows are generated from the loans to repay buyers of the securities their promised interest and principal payments.

→

Any loans that are paid off early (prepayments) generate a cash flow that goes to retire different maturities of securities, starting with the shortest maturities first.

→

CMO investor groups get prepaid loan cash, starting with: Tranche A investors with shortest CMOs, then Tranche B investors with next longest CMOs, etc., down to Tranche Z investors with longest maturity CMOs. No cash flows to next longest maturities until all holders of shorter maturities are paid off.

and the amount of the mortgage loan against that property. Bonds backed by pools of home equity loans often carry higher yields than other loan-backed securities because of their substantial prepayment risk when interest rates fall and homeowners pay off their home equity loans early. Competition in this market has become intense among banks, thrifts, and other lending institutions trying to attract as many home equity borrowers as possible, increasing the risk of home-equity-backed securities for investors buying them.

Yet another securitization device to help raise funds has appeared in recent years in the form of *loan-backed bonds*. Bankers and other lenders can set aside a group of loans on their balance sheet, issue bonds, and pledge the loans as collateral to backstop the bonds. Unlike CMOs and similar loan-backed instruments, which allow lenders to remove loans from their balance sheets, loan-backed bonds usually stay on the lenders balance sheet as liabilities. Moreover, while the loans backing these bonds provide the collateral for borrowing (so that if the bond-issuing institution fails, the bondholders will have a priority claim against the pledged loans), the cash flow from the pooled loans is not the sole source of cash to pay the bonds' interest and principal. Rather, monies owed on loan-backed bonds can come from *any* revenues generated by the issuing financial firm. Because the market value of the loans pledged as collateral is normally greater in amount than the volume of bonds issued, loan-backed bonds may actually carry higher credit ratings than the issuing institution itself.

What does a bank, thrift institution, or other lending institution gain from issuing loan-backed bonds? First, the cost of raising funds may go down because investors consider the bonds to have low default risk due to the greater dollar value of the loans that back the bonds. In fact, it is often cheaper to issue such bonds than it is to sell large-denomination deposits that are not fully covered by government deposit insurance, suggesting that some depository institutions can replace uninsured deposits with bonds backed by selected assets. Moreover, the bonds generally have longer maturities than deposits, so a depository institution can extend the maturity of the liability side of its balance sheet by issuing loan-backed bonds, perhaps to better match the longer maturities (durations) of its assets. Unfortunately, a portion of this double benefit from loan-backed bonds stems from a depository institution's ability to sell insured deposits at low interest rates because of government-supplied deposit insurance, resulting in a potential moral hazard problem in which the tax-paying public may wind up stuck with losses.

Of course, there are some disadvantages from issuing loan-backed bonds. For example, any loans pledged behind these bonds must be held on a lender's balance sheet until the bonds reach maturity, which decreases the overall liquidity of a loan portfolio. Moreover, with these loans remaining on its balance sheet the lender must meet regulatory-imposed capital requirements to back the loans. At the same time, since a depository institution must hold more loans as collateral than the amount of bonds it issues, more deposits and other borrowings must be used to make up the difference, increasing the amount of liabilities taken on and possibly increasing its legal reserve requirements.

Examples of Other Assets That Have Been Securitized

In addition to securitized home mortgages there are many other examples of securitized assets. For example, in October 1986, First Boston Corp., one of the world's leading investment banking firms, announced plans to sell $3.2 billion of securities backed by low-interest automobile loans granted originally by General Motors Acceptance Corporation (GMAC). One unusual twist was the tiered structure of this security offering, which consisted of a combination of short-term, medium-term, and long-term bonds, each with a different priority of claim to the income from the packaged auto loans (labeled *CARs,* or certificates of automobile receivables). A subsidiary of First Boston actually owned the loans after purchasing them from GMAC; therefore, investors acquiring the associated bonds were not given recourse to either First Boston or GMAC in the event some of the loans defaulted. However, GMAC did promise to repurchase up to 5 percent of the loans securitized in order to cover any loans that turned sour.

Another prominent example of securitized loans is the market for participations in discounted debt issued by less-developed countries (LDCs) and syndicated Euroloans. These international loans, extended mainly to governments and multinational companies, frequently have not paid out as planned. In addition, many domestic securitizations have arisen out of adverse loan-loss situations faced by banks and other lenders that have been battered by losses on energy, farm, and real estate loans and see securitization as a way to clean up their portfolios. With fewer risky and nonperforming loans on the books, a lender looks financially stronger and may be able to lower its borrowing costs.

In the United States, loan-backed securities have been issued against an ever-widening range of loans, including commercial mortgages, Small Business Administration loans, mobile home loans, credit card receivables, truck leases, and computer leases. A new dimension was added to the market in the late 1980s when banks and other intermediaries began to help their corporate customers securitize credit and lease receivables and issue asset-backed commercial paper in order to provide these customers with low-cost, stable funding sources.

Securitization is *not* a funds source available to all lenders. Recent estimates suggest that the minimum-size loan-backed securities offering likely to be successful is at least $50 million. However, smaller institutions are often active investors in these securities, and it is possible for several small lenders to pool their loans and jointly issue securities.

Loan-backed securities closely resemble traditional bonds, promising a fixed interest rate payable monthly, quarterly, or semiannually. These securities often carry various forms of **credit enhancement** to give buyers the impression that they are low-risk investments. These credit enhancers may include a credit letter from another financial institution willing to guarantee repayment of the securities. Another popular credit enhancement is for the issuer to set aside a cash reserve, created from the excess returns earned by the securitized loans over the amount of interest paid to security holders, in order to cover losses from any defaulted loans.

One exciting innovation that entered the securitization market as the new century began was the appearance of loan-backed subordinated securities of varying credit ratings.

For example, in the fall of 2000 Citibank of New York came forward with plans to sell $875 million of credit-card-backed triple-B and single-A rated securities. These so-called *subordinated securitizations* were designed to provide extra protection for those investors who want to purchase top-rated (AAA) senior loan-backed securities, but also offer investors who are willing to accept somewhat lower credit-rated loan-backed securities a shot at higher market yields. While senior quality and subordinated loan-backed securities are normally issued together, Citibank led the market with a new approach, proposing to sell the subordinated loan-backed securities first and the related senior-quality securities later as more funds are needed.

One trend in the securitization and loan-backed securities sales market that must be borne in mind is its *rapid international expansion* today. This market owes most of its origins to the United States, but it exploded on the international scene as the 1990s progressed and the 21st century opened. Nowhere was this more the case than in the unfolding European Community, where new groups of investors and new loan-backed security issuers appeared in droves, freely adopting innovations from the U.S. market and hiring away securitization specialists from U.S. banks and other investment firms. More recently many Asian lenders have also entered the securitization marketplace.

The Impact of Securitization on Banks and Other Lending Institutions

Securitization is likely to affect the management of banks and other lending institutions in several different ways. Certainly it raises the level of competition for the best-quality loans between lending institutions. Securitization may also raise the level of competition among lenders trying to attract deposits because knowledgeable depositors may find that they can get a better yield by purchasing loan-backed securities from security dealers than by buying deposits. Securitization has made it possible for many corporations to bypass their banks and other traditional lenders for loans and, instead, seek credit in the open market through securities sales, thereby diminishing the growth rate of loans—the prime revenue source for most banks and other lenders.

A good example of banks and other traditional lenders being bypassed by their best corporate customers is occurring today in the *commercial paper market*. Many companies are pooling their accounts receivable from credit sales and issuing commercial paper—short-term notes—against those receivables. The issuance of this "asset-backed commercial paper," like most securitizations, takes place through an SPE (special purpose entity), which buys the company's receivables by using the cash raised from selling securities that will be backed by the receivables. Unlike other securitizations, asset-backed commercial paper is of short maturity (less than nine months) but the deal doesn't necessarily end when the receivables mature or the securities are paid off. Rather, new receivables may be sold to the same SPE to replace those paid off and new commercial notes can be issued to replace the commercial paper that is maturing.

Banks and other business lenders have been able to benefit indirectly from securitizations conducted by their corporate customers by providing, for a fee, *credit letters* to enhance the credit rating of corporations selling their securities in the public market. Moreover, banks and competing financial firms can generate added fee income by providing backup liquidity in case the securitizing company runs short of cash and by acting as underwriters for new asset-backed security issues. Banks also find they can use securitization to assist a good corporate customer in finding financing without having to make any direct loans to that customer, which would inflate the lender's risky assets and require it to raise more capital. The net result of all these changes is probably to decrease lenders' revenues somewhat and possibly to increase funding costs. Faced with intense competition on both sides of their balance sheets, recently many lenders have more aggressively pursued service areas where securitization is less of a factor, such as loans to small business firms and households.

Concept Check

8–1. What does *securitization* of assets mean?

8–2. What kinds of assets are most amenable to the securitization process?

8–3. What advantages does securitization offer for banks and other lending institutions?

8–4. What risks of securitization should the managers of lending institutions be aware of?

8–5. Suppose that a bank securitizes a package of its loans that bear a gross annual interest yield of 13 percent. The securities issued against the loan package promise interested investors an annual-ized yield of 8.25 percent. The expected default rate on the packaged loans is 3.5 percent. The bank agrees to pay an annual fee of 0.35 percent to a security dealer to cover the cost of underwriting and advisory services and a fee of 0.25 percent to Arunson Mortgage Servicing Corporation to process the expected payments generated by the packaged loans. If the above items represent all the costs associated with this securitization transaction, can you calculate the percentage amount of *residual income* the bank expects to earn from this particular transaction?

Sales of Loans to Raise Funds

Filmtoid

What 1993 made-for-HBO movie finds investment bankers scurrying for funds to support the leveraged buyout of RJR Nabisco?
Answer: *Barbarians at the Gate.*

Not only can loans issued by banks and other lenders be used as collateral for issuing securities to raise new funds, but the loans themselves can be sold in their entirety to a new owner. Indeed, **loan sales**—often done in the past by the world's largest banks—now involve banks, finance companies, security dealers, and other financial firms of widely varying sizes. Included among the principal buyers of loans are banks (including foreign banking firms seeking a solid foothold in the domestic market), insurance companies, pension funds, nonfinancial corporations, mutual funds (including vulture and hedge funds that choose to concentrate on purchasing troubled loans), and large security dealers (such as Goldman Sachs and Merrill Lynch). Among the leading sellers of these loans are Deutsche Bank, J. P. Morgan Chase, the Bank of America, and ING Bank of the Netherlands. (See Exhibit 8–4.)

The loans sold by commercial banks usually mature within 90 days and may be either new loans or loans that have been on the seller's books for some time. The loan sale market received a boost during the 1980s when a wave of corporate buyouts led to the creation of thousands of loans to fund *highly leveraged transactions* (HLTs). The market for such loans in the United States expanded more than tenfold during the 1980s, but then fell dramatically in the 1990s as many corporate buyouts cooled off and federal regulatory agencies tightened their rules regarding the acceptability of such loans. Generally, HLT-related loans are secured by the assets of the borrowing company and, typically, are long-term, covering in some cases up to eight years, and carrying floating loan rates tied to the prime rate or some other widely publicized interest rate. In contrast, most other loans sold carry maturities of only a few weeks or months, have minimum denominations of at least a million dollars, are generally extended to borrowers with investment-grade credit ratings, and carry interest rates that usually are connected to short-term corporate loan rates (such as the prevailing market interest rate on commercial paper).

Typically, the seller retains **servicing rights** on the sold loans. These rights enable the selling institution to generate fee income (often one-quarter or three-eighths of a percentage point of the amount of the loans sold) by collecting interest and principal payments from borrowers and passing the proceeds along to loan buyers. Servicing institutions also monitor the performance of borrowers and act on behalf of loan buyers to make sure borrowers are adhering to the terms of their loans.

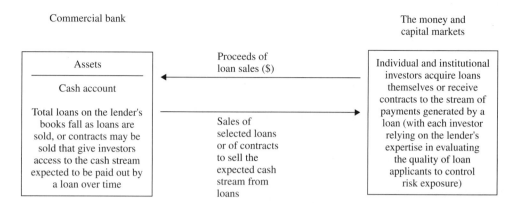

EXHIBIT 8–4
The Impact of Loan Sales

Source: Peter S. Rose, "New Benefits, New Pitfalls," *The Canadian Banker,* September/October 1988.

Most loans are purchased in million-dollar units by banks and corporations that already operate in the loan marketplace and have special knowledge of the debtor. During the 1990s a multibillion-dollar market for floating-rate corporate loans arose as some insurance companies and mutual funds that had purchased ordinary bonds in the past switched some of their money into corporate loans. These salable loans appear to have several advantages over bonds for many investors due to their strict loan covenants, floating interest rates, and the availability of both short-term and long-term financial instruments.

Loan sales occur in several different forms. For example, two of the most popular types are: (*a*) **participation loans** and (*b*) **assignments.** In a participation loan the purchaser is an outsider (i.e., not a partner) to the loan contract between the lender selling the loan and the borrower. Only if there are significant alterations in the terms of the original loan contract can the buyer of a participation in a loan exercise any influence over the terms of the loan contract. Thus, the buyer of a participation in an existing loan faces substantial risks: the loan seller may fail or the borrower may fail, presenting the participation purchaser with substantial losses. This means that the buyer of a loan participation must watch both the borrower and the seller closely. As a result of these and other limitations of participations, many loan sales today are by *assignment.* Under an assignment, ownership of a loan is transferred to the buyer, who thereby acquires a direct claim against the borrower. This means that, in some cases, the borrower has to agree to the sale of his or her loan before an assignment can be made.

A third type of loan sale is the **loan strip.** Loans strips are short-dated pieces of a longer-term loan and often mature quickly—in a few days or weeks. The buyer of a strip is entitled to a fraction of the expected income from a loan. With strips, the selling institution retains the risk of borrower default and usually has to put up some of its own funds to support the loan until it reaches maturity.

Reasons behind Loan Sales

There are many reasons why banks and selected other lenders in many countries have turned to loan sales as an important method of funding operations. One reason is the opportunity loan sales provide for getting rid of lower-yielding assets in order to make room for higher-yielding assets when market interest rates rise. Selling loans and replacing them with more marketable assets, such as government securities, can increase a lender's liquidity, better preparing the institution for deposit withdrawals or other cash needs. Moreover, disposing of loans removes both credit risk and interest-rate risk from the lender's balance sheet and may generate fee income up front rather than having to wait until the loans the lender is thinking of selling accrue some interest. Then, too, loan sales slow the growth of assets, which helps management maintain a better balance between the growth of capital and the acceptance of risk in the lending function. In this way loan sales help bankers and other lenders please regulators, who have put considerable pressure on banks and thrifts to get rid of their riskiest assets and strengthen their capital in recent years. A few studies, such as Benveniste and Berger [12] and Hassan [3], suggest that investors in the capital markets generally view loan sales as a way to reduce risk for the selling institution, helping to lower its cost of capital and diversify its asset portfolio by selling old loans and replacing them with new ones. Buyers purchasing these loans receive help in diversifying their loan portfolio, acquiring loans from new regions and new industries outside their traditional trade areas. Diversification of this sort can lower risk exposure and result in lower borrowing costs for the loan buyer.

Researchers Haubrich and Thomson [6] have argued that the development of the loan sales market has profound implications for the future of lending institutions. The growth of this market means that banks, for example, can make loans without taking in deposits and cover deposit withdrawals merely by selling loans. Moreover, if this market grows in the future, banks may have less need for deposit insurance or for borrowing from the discount windows of the Federal Reserve banks. Because loan sales are so similar to issuing securities, this financing device blurs the distinction between financial intermediaries, like banks and finance companies, that make loans and other financial institutions that trade securities.

The Risks in Loan Sales

Loan sales are just another form of investment banking, in which the seller trades on his or her superior ability to evaluate the creditworthiness of a borrower and sells that expertise (represented by the content of the loan contract itself) to another investor. Investors are willing to purchase loans that a bank or other trusted lender originates because they have confidence in the seller's ability to identify good-quality borrowers and write an advantageous loan contract. Nevertheless, loan sales as a source of funds for lenders are not without their problems. For example, the best-quality loans are most likely to find a ready resale market. But if the seller isn't careful, it will find itself selling off its soundest loans, leaving its portfolio heavily stocked with poor-quality loans, which may result in more volatile earnings. This development is likely to trigger the attention of regulators, and the bank or other lending institution may find itself facing demands from regulatory agencies to acquire more capital.

Moreover, a sold loan can turn sour just as easily as a direct loan from the originating lender to its own customer. Indeed, the seller may have done a poor job of evaluating the borrower's financial condition. Buying an existing loan, therefore, obligates the purchasing institution to review the financial condition not only of the seller but also of the borrower.

In some instances, the seller will agree to give the loan purchaser *recourse* to the seller for all or a portion of those sold loans that become delinquent. In effect, the purchaser gets a *put option*, allowing him or her to sell a troubled loan back to its originator. This arrangement forces buyer and seller to share the risk of loan default. Recourse agreements are not common in today's loan market, in part because federal regulations require a bank selling loans with recourse to hold reserves behind those loans and to count them as part of its assets when determining the bank's required level of capital. However, many banks and other lenders seem to feel obligated to reacquire the troubled loans they sold to a customer, even if there is no legal requirement to do so, simply to protect an established customer relationship.

Often loans themselves are not sold. Instead, the originating lender sells claims to the expected stream of cash from a loan, and the purchaser of rights to that cash stream has no recourse to either the lender or its borrowing customer if the loan fails to pay out as planned.

INVESTMENT BANK AND AUTOMOBILE MANUFACTURER FIND GOOD REASONS TO SELL AUTO LOANS

Recently two of the world's best-known companies—Ford Motor Credit, the huge finance company that helps finance the purchase of autos produced by Ford Motor Company, and a subsidiary of Bear Stearns, a leading investment bank and security dealer—put together a record-setting deal in the loan sales market. Ford Motor Credit bundled up about $3 billion in loans it had extended to customers of Ford and sold the bundle of auto loans to an affiliate of Bear Stearns, which, in turn, began selling the loans in the financial marketplace to other investors.

While there's certainly nothing unusual about selling loans today, this deal was unique in at least one major respect: Ford Motor Credit sold the loans off its balance sheet to Bear Stearns "without any strings attached." Normally a sale of this sort would include a pledge by the seller (in this case, Ford Motor Credit) to post a reserve of capital (usually more than $200 million on a sale of this size) to make good any losses incurred by purchasing investors when some of the loans went bad. Not this time, however. Ford cleared the loans off its balance sheet without recourse for buyers in case of loan defaults.

The new deal enabled Ford to raise in the neighborhood of $3 billion in new funds at a price that was actually cheaper than it would have paid had it ventured into the corporate bond market and floated a new bond issue. Moreover, Ford avoided adding more debt to its balance sheet, making the company look financially stronger. The Bear Stearns organization, on the other hand, secured commissions and fees from the deal.

Finally, banks and other lending institutions must recognize that raising funds by selling loans is likely to be affected by a strong *cyclical* factor. In some years, particularly when the economy is expanding rapidly, there may be an abundance of salable loans, while in other years the volume of salable loans may decline significantly, particularly during recessions when loan demand is at a low ebb and there are fewer originations of new loans.

Indeed, the loan sales market declined sharply in the closing years of the 20th century and continued depressed as the new century opened. A number of factors appear to have accounted for the decline: more businesses are bypassing banks and other traditional financial intermediaries for the loans they need, which has led to a decrease in the availability of quality loans that are the easiest to sell; corporate merger and acquisition activity has slowed; and other sources of funds have opened up through deregulation (such as fewer restrictions on deposit terms and broader powers for U.S. banks to underwrite commercial paper issues). However, some authorities expect a future rebound in loan sales due to the trend toward market-value accounting, which may cause better-informed buyers to view loans more favorably as investment vehicles; due to tougher capital-adequacy requirements, which may encourage banks, in particular, to continue to sell off selected loans and lower their capital requirements; and also due to the continued swing of many international banks (such as Deutsche Bank of Germany and the Netherlands' ING) toward more market trading in place of traditional lending activities.

Concept Check

8–6. What advantages do *sales of loans* have for banks and other lending institutions trying to raise funds?

8–7. Are there any disadvantages to using loan sales as a significant source of funding for banks and other financial institutions?

8–8. What is *loan servicing?*

8–9. How can loan servicing be used to increase income?

Standby Credit Letters

One of the most rapidly growing of all markets in recent years has been the market for **financial guarantees**—instruments used to enhance the credit standing of a borrower to help insure lenders against default on the borrower's loans and to reduce the borrower's financing costs. In short, financial guarantees are designed to ensure the timely repayment of the principal and interest from a loan even if the borrower goes bankrupt or cannot perform a contractual obligation. One of the most popular guarantees in the banking and insurance communities is the **standby letter of credit (SLC).** The growth of standby letters of credit has been substantial in recent years, rising from $210 billion to $320 billion among U.S.-insured commercial banks during the six-year period ending 2002. However, this remains a large-bank market; more than 98 percent of standby letters issued by U.S.-insured commercial banks came from those banking firms above a billion dollars in total assets each.

Standby letters of credit may include (1) *performance guarantees*, in which a bank or other financial firm guarantees that a building or other project will be completed on time, or (2) *default guarantees*, under which a financial institution pledges the repayment of defaulted corporate notes and state and local government bonds when the borrowers cannot pay. These standby letters enable borrowing customers to get the credit they require at lower cost and on more flexible terms. In order to sell these guarantees successfully, however, the bank or other service provider must have a higher credit rating than its customer.

A standby credit letter is a **contingent obligation** of the letter's issuer. The issuing bank or nonbank firm, in return for a fee, agrees to *guarantee* the credit of its customer or to guarantee the fulfillment of a contract made by its customer with a third party. The key advantages to a financial institution issuing standbys are the following:

1. Letters of credit earn a fee for providing the service (usually around 0.5 percent to 1 percent of the amount of credit involved).
2. They aid a customer, who can usually borrow more cheaply when armed with the guarantee, without using up the guaranteeing institution's scarce reserves.
3. Such guarantees usually can be issued at relatively low cost because the issuer may already know the financial condition of its standby credit customer (e.g. when that customer applied for his or her last loan).
4. The probability is low that the issuer of the credit guarantee will ever be called upon to pay.

Standby credit letters have grown in recent years for several reasons:

1. The rapid growth of *direct finance* worldwide, with borrowers selling their securities directly to investors rather than going to a bank or other traditional intermediary to borrow money; direct financing has increased investor concerns about borrower defaults and resulted in increased demand for credit guarantees.
2. The risk of economic fluctuations (recessions, inflation, etc.), which has led to demand for risk-reducing devices.
3. The opportunity standbys offer banks and other lenders to use their credit evaluation skills to earn additional fee income by underwriting credit risk without the immediate commitment of funds.
4. The relatively low cost of issuing standbys—unlike deposits, they carry zero reserve requirements and no insurance fees.

Key URLs
It's fun to explore the use of standby credit letters at such sites as **www.fleetcapital.com/products** and **www.fhfb.gov/fhlb/FHLBP_loc.htm**.

The Structure of Standby Letters of Credit (SLCs)

SLCs contain three essential elements: (1) a commitment from the **issuer** (usually a bank or insurance company today), (2) an **account party** (for whom the letter is issued), and (3) a **beneficiary** (usually a bank or other lender concerned about the safety of funds committed to the account party). The key feature of SLCs is that they are usually *not* listed on the issuer's or beneficiary's balance sheet. This is because a standby agreement is only a *contingent liability*. In most cases, it will expire unexercised. Delivery of funds to the beneficiary can occur only if something unexpected happens to the account party (such as bankruptcy or nonperformance). Moreover, the beneficiary can claim funds from the issuer only if the beneficiary meets *all* the conditions laid down in the credit letter. If any of those conditions are not met, the issuer is not obligated to pay. (See Exhibit 8–5.)

The Value and Pricing of Standby Letters

Under the terms of an SLC, the issuer of the letter will pay any interest or principal to the beneficiary that is owed and left unpaid by its customer, the account party. In effect, the letter issuer agrees for a fee to take on a risk that, in the absence of the SLC, would be carried fully by the beneficiary. Therefore, the beneficiary may be willing to lend the account party more money or provide the same amount of funds but at a lower interest rate than if there were no standby credit.

In general, an account party will seek a standby guarantee if the issuer's fee for providing the guarantee is less than the value assigned to the guarantee by the beneficiary. Thus, if P is the price of the standby guarantee, NL is the cost of a nonguaranteed loan, and GL is the cost of a loan backed by a standby guarantee, then a borrower is likely to seek a standby guarantee if

$$P < (NL - GL)$$

For example, a borrower can get a nonguaranteed loan at an interest cost of 7.50 percent, but is told that a quality standby credit guarantee would reduce the loan's interest cost to 6.75 percent. If a bank offers the borrower a standby guarantee for 0.50 percent of the loan's face value, it will pay the borrower to get the guarantee because the savings on the loan of (7.50 percent – 6.75 percent) or 0.75 percent exceeds the 0.50 percent guarantee fee.

In turn, the value to the beneficiary of an SLC is a function of the credit ratings of the issuer and the account party and the information cost of assessing their credit standing. Clearly, beneficiaries will value highly the guarantee of a bank or other letter issuer with a superior credit rating. Account parties will be less likely to seek out a weak institution to issue a credit letter, because such a guarantee gives them little bargaining power in obtaining

EXHIBIT 8–5
The Nature of a
Standby Credit
Agreement

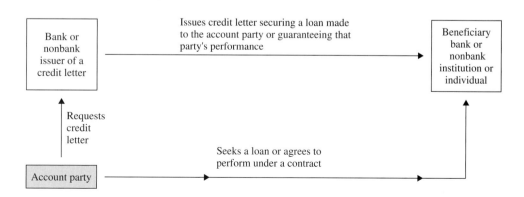

better terms from the beneficiary. If the cost of obtaining relevant information about the condition of the guaranteeing institution or about the account party is high, the beneficiary also may find little or no value in a standby credit agreement.

Sources of Risk with Standby Credits

What kinds of risk do banks and other investors who become the beneficiaries of standby credit letters have to bear? Standby credits carry several forms of risk exposure for the bank or other lending institution relying upon them. For example, the issuing institution may not be able to cover its commitment, resulting in default. Because credit letters do not qualify as insured deposits, a bank holding the credit letter as beneficiary will probably receive little or nothing if the letter's issuer fails. Also, some jurisdictions have held that an issuing institution cannot be forced to pay off on a credit letter if doing so would force it to violate regulations (e.g., if the amount to be paid exceeds a bank's legal lending limit).

Banks relying on standby credit assurances received from other institutions must take considerable care that such agreements are fully documented so they know how to file a valid claim for payment. Banks and other institutions with beneficiary rights cannot legally obtain reimbursement from the issuer unless all of the conditions required for successful presentation of a credit letter are met. In addition, bankruptcy laws present a potential hazard for banks as beneficiaries trying to collect on letters of credit. In some court jurisdictions, it has been held that any payments made upon presentation of a valid credit letter are "preference items" under the federal bankruptcy code and, therefore, must be returned to the account party if bankruptcy is declared.

Do the banks or other financial firms issuing standby credits face any risk exposure? There may be substantial interest rate and liquidity risks. If the issuer is compelled to pay under a credit letter without prior notice, it may be forced to raise substantial amounts of funds at unfavorable interest rates. Indeed, if the letter is for a substantial sum of money relative to the lender's credit capacity, the institution may find itself in an adverse borrowing position. Bankers and other financial managers can use various devices to reduce risk exposure from the standby credit letters they have issued, such as

1. Frequently renegotiating the terms of any loans extended to customers who have standby credit guarantees so that loan terms are continually adjusted to the customer's changing circumstances and there is less need for the beneficiaries of those guarantees to press for collection.
2. Diversifying standby letters issued by region and by industry to avoid concentration of risk exposure.
3. Selling participations in standbys in order to share risk with a variety of other lending institutions.

Regulatory Concerns about Standby Credit Arrangements

Recent rapid growth of contingent obligations among major banks and other guarantors has raised the specter of more institutional failures if more standby credits than expected are presented for collection. For example, many regulators fear that investors in bank securities, including holders of uninsured deposits, may be lulled to sleep (i.e., will tend to underprice bank risk) if a bank books fewer loans but at the same time takes on a large volume of standby credits. Unfortunately, there is ample incentive for banks and other lenders to take on more standbys due to their relatively low production costs and the added leverage they generate because no cash reserves are required, at least at the beginning of the agreement.

Examiners and regulatory agencies are working to keep bank and nonbank financial firm risk exposure from credit standbys under control. Several new regulatory rules are in use today. For example, in the banking community,

1. Banks must apply the same credit standards for approving credit letters as they do for approving direct loans.
2. Banks must count standbys as loans when assessing how risk-exposed the institution is to a single credit customer.
3. Since the adoption of international capital agreements between the United States and other leading nations (discussed in Chapter 14), banks have been required to post capital behind most standbys as though these contingent agreements were loans.

Research Studies on Standbys, Loan Sales, and Securitizations

Several studies have addressed the issue of the relative riskiness of direct loans versus standby credits, loan sales, and securitizations for banks and other lenders. For example, Bennett [1] observed that direct loans carry substantially higher market risk premiums than do credit letters. This supports the idea that investors as a whole believe standby credits carry significantly less risk than loans themselves. One reason may be that such credit letters are usually requested by prime-quality borrowers. Another factor may be the market's expectation that most credit letters will never be presented for collection. These suppositions were supported by an earlier study conducted by Goldberg and Lloyd-Davies [2], who found that issuing SLCs had essentially no impact on the deposit costs of banks.

More recently, Hassan [5] finds evidence from option-pricing models that both bank stockholders and creditors view off-balance-sheet standby credit letters as reducing bank risk by increasing the overall diversification of a bank's assets. Hassan argues that imposing capital requirements on standby letters of credit, therefore, may not be appropriate because standbys, if properly used, can reduce risk for the issuers of these letters. Moreover, Pennacchi [8], Pavel and Phillis [7], and Pyle [9] have argued that standby credits, loan sales, and securitizations are principally *defensive* reactions by bankers and other financial managers to regulation. These off-balance-sheet activities can be viewed simply as attempts by banks and other lenders to increase their financial leverage, thereby augmenting returns to their shareholders. Contingent obligations will be substituted for bank assets and deposits whenever regulation increases the cost of more traditional intermediation activities.

But according to James [4], regulation is not the only motivation for loan sales, standby credits, and other nontraditional fund-raising devices. James believes that these transactions are better viewed as substitutes for collateralized debt because banks and thrift institutions are prohibited from selling collateralized deposits (with the exception of government deposits where specific assets are pledged to protect these deposits). He argues that both regulations and the cost of deposit insurance can be incentives for banks, for example, to pursue off-balance-sheet activities. However, if these new services and instruments increase the value of banks and other service providers (i.e., raise their stock prices), it might be a mistake to severely restrict them by government regulation.

Concept Check

8–10. What are *standby credit letters?* Why have they grown so rapidly in recent years?

8–11. Who are the principal parties to a standby credit agreement?

8–12. What risks accompany a standby credit letter for *(a)* the issuer and *(b)* the beneficiary?

8–13. How can a bank or other lending institution mitigate the risks inherent in issuing standby credit letters?

Credit Derivatives: Contracts for Reducing Credit Risk Exposure on the Balance Sheet

Securitizing assets, loan sales, and standby credit letters can help reduce the credit risk associated with a loan or security portfolio as well as help with interest-rate risk exposure. For example, removing and securitizing a pool of loans from a bank or thrift's balance sheet reduces or disposes of the credit risk exposure from those loans. Similarly, a lending institution that has just made loans to some of its customers can sell those loans to other investors, who now may take on the credit risks inherent in those loans.

However, securitizations and loan sales are usually not feasible for groups of loans that do not have some common features—that is, loans (such as many business loans) that do not have the same cash-flow schedules or comparable risk exposures. For these common types of loans **credit derivatives**—financial contracts offering protection to their beneficiary in case of loan default—can be helpful in reducing a financial firm's exposure to credit risk and, in some cases, interest rate risk as well. The credit derivative market is today one of the fastest growing in the world. Among U.S.-insured banks alone, the volume of credit derivatives rose to $640 billion in 2002 from only negligible amounts just five years earlier. Not surprisingly, the biggest banks have led the way in their issuance and use—99 percent of credit derivatives outstanding involve billion-dollar-plus U.S.-insured banks.

Credit Swaps

One prominent example of a credit derivative is the **credit swap,** where two lenders simply agree to exchange a portion of their customers' loan repayments. For example, Banks A and B may find a swap dealer, such as a large insurance company, that agrees to draw up a credit swap contract between the two banks. Bank A then transmits an amount (perhaps $100 million) in interest and principal payments that it collects from its credit customers to the dealer. Bank B also sends all or a portion of the loan payments its customers make to the same dealer. The swap dealer will ultimately pass these payments along to the other bank that signed the swap contract. (See Exhibit 8–6.) Usually the dealer levies a fee for the service of bringing these two swap partners together. The swap dealer may also guarantee each swap partner's performance under the agreement in return for an additional charge.

What is the advantage for each swap partner in participating in such an agreement? Clearly, in the example shown below each bank is granted the opportunity to further spread out the risk in its loan portfolio, especially if the banks involved are located in different market areas. Because each bank's loan portfolio may come from a different market, a credit swap permits each institution to broaden the number of markets from which it collects loan revenues and loan principal, thus reducing each bank's dependence on one or a narrow set of market areas.

A popular variation on the credit swap just described—a *total return swap*—may involve a financial institution (dealer) that guarantees the swap parties a specific rate of return on their credit assets. For example, a swap dealer may guarantee Bank A a return on its small

EXHIBIT 8–6
Example of a Credit Swap

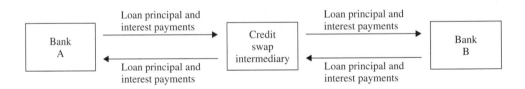

business loans that is 3 percentage points higher than the long-term government bond rate. In this instance Bank A would have exchanged the risky return from a portion of its loans for a much more stable rate of reward based upon the return from a government security (unless, of course, the swap dealer promising that more predictable source of income goes out of business).

Another example of a total return swap might rest upon a loan that Bank A has recently made to one of its commercial customers. Bank A then agrees to pay Bank B the total return earned on the loan (including interest and principal payments plus any increase [appreciation] in the loan's market value that occurs). Bank B, for its part, agrees to pay A the London InterBank Offer Rate (LIBOR) plus a small interest rate spread and to compensate A for any depreciation that occurs in the loan's market value. In essence, Bank B bears the credit risk (and also the interest-rate risk if the loan involved is a floating-rate loan or its market value is highly sensitive to market interest rate movements) associated with Bank A's loan just as though it actually owned Bank A's loan, even though it is not the owner. This swap may terminate early if the borrower defaults on the loan. (See Exhibit 8–7.)

Credit Options

Another popular credit risk derivative today is the **credit option,** which guards against losses in the value of a credit asset or helps to offset higher borrowing costs that may occur due to changes in credit ratings. For example, a thrift institution worried about default on a large $100 million loan it has just made might approach an options dealer about an option contract that pays off if the loan declines significantly in value or completely turns bad. If the borrowing customer pays off as promised, the lender collects the loan revenue it expected to gather and the option issued by the dealer (option-writer) will go unused. The thrift involved will, of course, lose the premium it paid to the dealer writing the option. Many financial institutions will take out similar credit options to protect the value of securities held in their investment portfolios should the securities' issuer fail to pay or should the securities decline significantly in value due to a change in credit standing. (See Exhibit 8–8.)

Another type of credit option can be used to hedge against a rise in borrowing costs due to a change in the borrower's default risk or credit rating. For example, a bank holding company may fear that its credit rating will be lowered just before it plans to issue some long-term notes or bonds to raise new capital. This would force the banking firm to pay a higher interest rate for its borrowed funds. One possible solution is for the banking

EXHIBIT 8–7
Example of a Total Return Swap

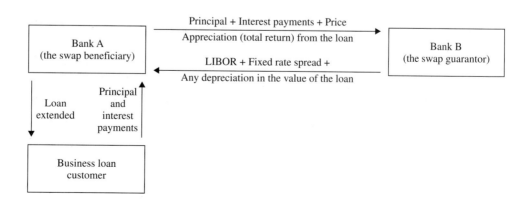

ETHICS IN BANKING

ILLEGAL TRADING IN CREDIT DERIVATIVES?

Institutions and individuals who trade *credit derivatives* are not immune to ethical problems. An example of what might possibly be violations of commonly accepted ethical principles occurred in the wake of an economic recession and the bankruptcies of leading corporations, such as Enron and WorldCom Inc., in 2001 and 2002.

Under both law and tradition customers seeking loans are promised confidentiality by lenders when they fill out a loan application and disclose inside information about their financial status. However, charges of improper use of this kind of private information spread across the credit markets like wildfire as the 21st century began.

Allegedly, some loan officers may have disclosed to security brokers and dealers inside the same institution details about the financial status of their borrowing customers. If so, this inside disclosure gave the security dealers involved the opportunity to employ insider information to make profitable deals in the credit derivatives market before the same information reached the public. One indicator of a possible insider-trading problem was the tendency of credit-derivative prices to change significantly just before news was released about large corporate loan requests.

Interestingly enough, the credit derivatives market may represent a loophole in the regulatory net administered by the Securities and Exchange Commission (SEC) and the bank regulatory agencies. It is not clear yet whether credit derivatives really qualify as *securities* under prevailing law and regulation.

EXHIBIT 8–8

Example of a Credit Option

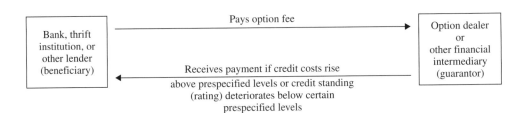

company to purchase a call option on the default-risk interest-rate spread prevailing in the market for debt securities similar in quality to its own securities at the time it needs to borrow money. Like other types of options, the credit risk option would have a *base rate spread* and would pay off if the market's default-risk rate spread over riskless securities climbs upward beyond the base rate spread specified in the option.

For example, suppose the banking company expected to pay a borrowing cost that was one percentage point over the five-year government bond rate. In this instance, the base rate spread is one percentage point. If the banking firm's credit rating were lowered or a recession in the economy occurred, the default risk rate spread the bank must pay might balloon upward from one percentage point to perhaps two percentage points above the government bond rate. The call option becomes profitable if this happens and helps cover the borrower's higher borrowing costs, in effect lowering the default risk interest rate spread back to the neighborhood of one percentage point over the five-year government security rate. On the other hand, if default risk rate spreads fall (perhaps due to a rise in the bank's credit rating or a strengthening in the economy), this option will not be profitable and the bank will lose the option premium that it paid.

Credit Default Swaps

Related to the credit option is the **credit default swap,** usually aimed at lenders able to handle comparatively limited declines in value, but wanting insurance against truly serious losses. In this case a lender may seek out a dealer willing to write a put option on a

EXHIBIT 8–9

Example of a Credit
Default Swap

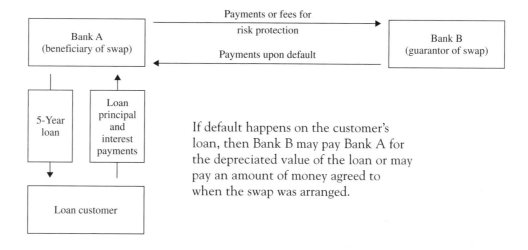

If default happens on the customer's
loan, then Bank B may pay Bank A for
the depreciated value of the loan or may
pay an amount of money agreed to
when the swap was arranged.

portfolio of loans or other assets. Suppose, for example, that a savings bank has recently
made a total of 100 million-dollar commercial real estate loans to support the building
of several investment projects in various cities. Fearing that several of these 100 loans
might turn sour because of weakening local economic conditions, it purchases a put
option that pays off if more than two of these commercial real estate loans default. Thus,
for each commercial real estate loan that fails to pay out above the bad-loan threshold
of two, the lender will receive $1 million less the resale value of the building used to
secure the loan.

In another example of a credit default swap, a commercial bank may seek out a guarantor institution to unload the risk on one of its loans in case of default. For example,
suppose Bank A swaps the credit risk from a five-year, $100 million construction loan to
Bank B. Typically, A will pay B a fee based upon the loan's par or face value (for example,
1/2 percent of $100 million, or $500,000). For its part, B agrees to pay A a stipulated
amount of money or a fixed percentage of the value of the loan *only if default occurs*.
There may be a so-called *materiality threshold*, a minimum amount of loss required before
any payment occurs. If the swap ends in an actual default, the amount owed is normally
the face value of the loan less the current market value of the defaulted asset. (See
Exhibit 8–9.)

Credit-Linked Notes

Another credit derivative instrument, *credit-linked notes*, has recently appeared that fuses
together a normal debt instrument, such as a note or bond, plus a credit option contract
to give a borrower of funds greater payment flexibility. A credit-linked note grants its
issuer the privilege of lowering the amount of loan repayments it must make if some significant factor changes. For example, suppose a finance company borrows through a bond
issue in order to support a group of real estate loans it intends to make and agrees to pay
the investors buying these bonds a 10 percent annual coupon payment (e.g., $100 a year
for each $1,000 par-value bond). However, the credit-linked note agreement carries the
stipulation that if defaults on the loans made with the borrowed funds rise significantly
(perhaps above 7 percent of all the loans outstanding), then the note-issuing lender will
only have to pay a 7 percent coupon rate (e.g., $70 a year per $1,000 bond). Therefore,
the lender has taken on credit-related insurance from the investors who bought into its
bond issue.

Factoid
What U.S. bank is one
of the world's leaders in
the market for
structuring credit
derivatives?
Answer: J. P. Morgan
Chase with a staff of
nearly 200 working on
structuring credit
derivatives worldwide.

Factoid
The principal buyers of risk protection through credit derivatives today include banks, finance companies, thrift institutions, and other lending institutions, while the principal sellers of risk protection via credit derivatives include insurance companies, securities dealers, and funds-management firms.

Key URLs
Among the best sites to read about CDOs—the newest and most rapidly growing of credit derivative instruments—are, **www.statestreet.com** and **www.fsa.com**.

Collateralized Debt Obligations (CDOs)

As the economy weakened in 2001 and 2002, coupled with worries about global terrorism, concern over credit quality and credit risk soared in the financial markets. Not surprisingly, credit derivatives became much more popular as risk-hedging devices and their outstanding volume skyrocketed around the world. This strong demand led to innovation as important new types of credit derivatives appeared. Among the most popular were **collateralized debt obligations** or **CDOs.**

While there are several types of these particular credit risk–hedging instruments, they are basically very similar to loan securitizations discussed earlier in this chapter except that CDOs may contain pools of high-yield bonds, equities, or other financial instruments contributed by companies interested in improving their balance sheets and raising new funds. Notes (claims) of varying grade are sold to investors interested in earning income from the pooled assets.

Unlike traditional securitizations, income-earning assets can be contributed to the same CDO pool by more than one corporate customer. The collateral contributed must be sufficient to cover any debt service payments to investors. The biggest challenge presented by CDOs lies in trying to evaluate their credit risk exposure to investors should some of the assets pledged go bad. To aid investors interested in this market, both Moody's and Standard & Poor's assign credit ratings to large CDOs.

Risks Associated with Credit Derivatives

Credit derivatives are not without risk, though they can do much to protect a lender's loan, investment, or borrowing risk exposure. The partner to each swap or option may fail to perform, in which case the lender has to find a new swap partner to hedge its credit risk exposure. Courts may rule that credit risk agreements are not legal or are improperly drawn and the lender may lose all or a portion of its risk protection. A good example of the possibility of losing some or all of a credit derivative's risk protection in a legal battle occurred in 2003 when the Royal Bank of Canada was sued by Rabobank NV, the latter seeking to avoid reimbursing Royal Bank under a total return swap after Enron Corporation collapsed. The relative newness surrounding these more exotic derivatives has left many legal issues in this field unresolved. In the case of Royal Bank, it settled for less than half of the amount claimed under its total return swap with Rabobank.

Such agreements are still relatively small in volume compared to such popular hedging devices as financial futures contracts, interest rate and currency options, and interest rate and currency swaps, meaning that resale markets for these agreements are thinner and more volatile. In fact, the still relatively small credit derivatives market may, at times, leave a bank or other lender seeking risk protection with few attractive options.

Major issues also remain for banks, thrifts, and other heavily regulated institutions that employ credit derivatives today. These contracts are largely unregulated right now, but they could become subject to regulation at any time. Capital regulations for these instruments are currently being closely studied by the bank regulatory agencies, and no one knows for sure how regulators' attitudes toward these instruments might change with time.

The FDIC has announced that "only those arrangements that provide virtually complete credit protection to the underlying asset will be considered effective guarantees for purposes of asset classification and risk-based capital calculations. On the other hand, if the amount of credit risk transferred by the beneficiary is severely limited or uncertain, then the limited credit protection the derivative provides the beneficiary should not be taken into account for these purposes" (FDIC [18], p. 3).

Should the regulatory community decide to lower the amount of capital needed by banks and other financial firms using these derivatives, this step would certainly cause the market to grow rapidly. If credit derivatives come to be regarded as inherently destabilizing and risky, however, forcing bankers and other financial managers using them to pledge even more capital, the market could flounder and become less efficient. Many unknowns currently plague this relatively new risk-management arena.

Concept Check

8–14. Why were *credit derivatives* developed? What advantages do they have over loan sales and securitizations, if any?

8–15. What is a *credit swap?* For what kinds of situations was it developed?

8–16. What is a *total return swap?* What advantages does it offer the swap beneficiary institution?

8–17. How do *credit options* work? What circumstances result in the option contract paying off?

8–18. When is a *credit default swap* useful? Why?

8–19. Of what use are *credit-linked notes?*

8–20. What are CDOs? How do they differ from other credit derivatives?

8–21. What risks do credit derivatives pose for banks and other financial institutions using them? What is the attitude of the regulatory community, thus far, toward banks and their closest competitors using these credit-related instruments? In your opinion what should regulators do about the recent rapid growth of this market, if anything?

Summary

This chapter has explored some of the newer sources of funding and risk management that banks and many of their leading financial-service competitors draw upon today. Among the key management tools explored in the chapter were the following:

- *Securitizing assets* in which loans are packaged into sets or pools and moved off the balance sheet into a special purpose account, and securities are issued against the loan pool, thus providing new capital and freeing up space on a bank or other financial institution's balance sheet for stronger or higher-yielding assets.

- *Selling loans* or pieces of loans to other investors, such as insurance companies, mutual funds, and foreign banks, thus sharing the loans' risk exposure and raising new funds for other ventures.

- *Issuing standby credit letters,* which help a borrowing customer raise funds more cheaply by pledging to guarantee the customer's loan, while helping the financial institution issuing the letter (usually a bank or insurance company) because it does not have to give up scarce funds in order to support the customer's loan request.

- *Utilizing credit derivatives,* which are contracts involving lenders who wish to slough off some of the default risk in their loan portfolios and investors who are willing to bear that risk and hope the derivatives will subsequently rise in value.

The foregoing tools have promised a number of advantages and some possible disadvantages for financial institutions that use them, including these:

- Greater flexibility in managing assets on the balance sheet in order to achieve a more balanced, more liquid, and more risk-resistant portfolio for financial firms skilled in the use of these new tools.

- Making more efficient use of a financial institution's existing stock of capital and avoiding having to sell stock or other instruments to raise new capital when market conditions are unfavorable.

- Generating new sources of income for a bank or other financial firm in the form of fees and commissions from helping customers more efficiently raise new funds and deal with risk exposures.

- Presenting their own risks for banks and other financial institutions, however, because of the greater skills required in their design and trading and their uncertain reception in the regulatory community, which is increasingly concerned about speculative activity and increased volatility in these highly specialized markets.

Key Terms

securitization, *277*
credit enhancement, *282*
loan sales, *284*
servicing rights, *284*
participation loans, *285*
assignments, *285*
loan strip, *285*

financial guarantees, *288*
standby letter of credit (SLC), *288*
contingent obligation, *288*
issuer, *289*
account party, *289*
beneficiary, *289*

credit derivatives, *292*
credit swap, *292*
credit option, *293*
credit default swap, *294*
collateralized debt obligation (CDO), *296*

Problems and Projects

1. Deltone National Bank has placed a group of 10,000 consumer loans bearing an average expected gross annual yield of 14.5 percent in a package to be securitized. The investment bank advising Deltone estimates that the securities will sell at a slight discount from par that results in a net interest cost to the issuer of 10.08 percent. Based on recent experience with similar types of loans, the bank expects 2.67 percent of the packaged loans to default without any recovery for the lender and has agreed to set aside a cash reserve to cover this amount of anticipated loss. Underwriting and advisory services provided by the investment banking firm will cost 0.65 percent. Deltone will also seek a liquidity facility, costing 0.45 percent, and a credit guarantee if actual loan defaults should exceed the expected loan default rate, costing 0.55 percent. Please calculate the estimated *residual income* for Deltone from this loan securitization.

2. Ryfield Corporation is requesting a loan for repair of some assembly line equipment in the amount of $5 million. The nine-month loan is priced by Farmers Financial Corporation at a 9.25 percent rate of interest. However, the finance company tells Ryfield that if it obtains a suitable credit guarantee the loan will be priced at 9 percent. Quinmark Bank agrees to sell Ryfield a standby credit guarantee for $10,000. Is Ryfield likely to buy the standby credit guarantee Quinmark has offered? Please explain.

3. The Monarch Bank Corp. has placed $100 million of GNMA-guaranteed securities in a trust account off the balance sheet. A CMO with four tranches has just been issued by Monarch using the GNMAs as collateral. Each tranche has a face value of $25 million and makes monthly payments. The annual coupon rates are 4 percent for Tranche A, 5 percent for Tranche B, 6 percent for Tranche C, and 7 percent for Tranche D.

   a. Which tranche has the shortest maturity and which tranche has the most prepayment protection?

   b. Every month, principal and interest are paid on the outstanding mortgages and some mortgages are paid in full. These payments are passed through to Monarch and the trustee uses the funds to pay coupons to the CMO bondholders. What are the coupon payments owed for each tranche for the first month?

   c. If scheduled mortgage payments and early prepayments bring in $1 million, how much will be used to retire the principal of CMO bondholders and which tranche will be affected?

   d. Why does Tranche D have a higher expected return?

4. First Security National Bank has been approached by a long-standing corporate customer, United Safeco Industries, concerning a $30 million *term loan* for five years to purchase new stamping machines that would further automate the company's assembly line operations in the manufacture of metal toys and metal containers. The company also plans to use at least half the loan proceeds to facilitate its buyout of Calem Corp., which imports and partially assembles video recorders and cameras. Additional funds for the buyout will come from a corporate note issue that will be underwritten by an investment banking firm not affiliated with First Security National Bank.

   The problem the bank's commercial credit division faces in assessing this customer's loan request is a management decision reached several weeks ago that the bank should gradually work down its leveraged buyout loan portfolio due to recent quality problems, including a significant rise in nonperforming credits. Moreover, the prospect of sharply higher interest rates has caused the bank to revamp its loan policy toward more short-term loans (under one year) and fewer term (over one year) loans. Senior management has indicated it will no longer approve loans that require a commitment of the bank's resources beyond a term of three years, except in special cases.

   Does the bank have any *service option* in the form of off-balance-sheet instruments that could help this customer meet its credit needs while avoiding committing $30 million in reserves for a five-year loan? What would you recommend that management do to keep United Safeco happy with its current banking relationship? Could the bank earn any fee income if it pursued your idea?

   Suppose the current interest rate on Eurodollar deposits (three-month maturities) in London is 8.40 percent, while federal funds and six-month CDs are trading in the United States at 8.55 percent and 8.21 percent, respectively. Term loans to comparable-quality corporate borrowers are trading at one-eighth to one-quarter percentage point above the three-month Eurodollar rate or one-quarter to one-half point over the secondary-market CD rate. Is there a way First Security National could earn at least as much fee income by providing United Safeco with support services as it could from making the loan the company has asked for (after all loan costs are taken into account)? Please explain how the customer could also benefit even if the bank does not make the loan requested.

5. What type of credit derivative contract would you recommend for each of these situations?

   a. A bank plans to issue a group of bonds backed by a pool of credit card loans but fears that the default rate on these credit card loans will rise well above 6 percent of the portfolio—the default rate it has projected. The bank wants to lower the interest cost on the bonds in case the loan default rate rises too high.

   b. A commercial finance company is about to make a $50 million project loan to develop a new gas field and is concerned about the risks involved if petroleum geologists' estimates of the field's potential yield turn out to be much too high and the borrowing developer cannot repay.

   c. A bank holding company plans to offer new capital notes in the open market next month, but knows that the company's credit rating is being reevaluated by two credit-rating agencies. The holding company wants to avoid paying sharply higher credit costs if its rating is lowered by the investigating credit-rating agencies.

   d. A savings bank is concerned about possible excess volatility in its cash flow off a recently made group of commercial real estate loans supporting the building of several apartment complexes. Moreover, many of these loans were made at fixed interest rates, and the thrift institution's economics department has forecast a

www.mhhe.com/rose6e

substantial rise in capital market interest rates. The savings bank's management would prefer a more stable cash flow emerging from this group of loans if it could find a way to achieve it.

e. First National Bank of Ashton serves a relatively limited geographic area centered upon a moderate-size metropolitan area. It would like to diversify its loan income based upon loans from other market areas it does not presently serve, but does not wish to make loans itself in these other market areas due to its lack of familiarity with loan markets outside the region it has served for many years. Is there a credit derivative contract that could help the bank achieve the loan portfolio diversification it seeks?

Internet Exercises

1. Using the National Information Center, identify the four largest BHCs in the top 50 at **www.ffiec.gov/nic/.** Then go to Statistics on Depository Institutions (SDI) at the FDIC's website (**http://www3.fdic.gov/sdi/main.asp**) and, after looking up the BHC identification numbers for the four largest BHCs, compare the notional amount of credit derivatives as a percentage of total assets for each using the most recent year-end data. What is the difference between the bank acting as a guarantor and the bank acting as a beneficiary? This information is available in "Derivatives: report."

2. Using the same institutions and the same websites as in the previous exercise, compare the credit standbys-to-total assets for the four BHCs. This information is found in the Letters of Credit report.

3. As a stock analyst following the banking industry, you are especially concerned about the growth of off-balance-sheet activities in the large institutions. Your argument is that these off-balance-sheet financial tools have, in fact, increased rather than decreased bank risk in many cases. Using the data at **http://www3.fdic.gov/sdi/main.asp**, compare the percentages obtained in Exercises 1 and 2 with data for the same institutions 10 years earlier.

4. The market for credit derivatives is one of the most rapidly growing financial markets in the world. What factors seem to explain this rapid expansion? (See especially **www.finpipe.com** and **www.investorwords.com**.)

S&P Market Insight Challenge

STANDARD & POOR'S

1. Use Standard & Poor's Market Insight website (**www.mhhe.com/edumarketinsight**) for this problem. In the S&P Industry Survey entitled "Financial Services: Diversified," *securitization* is a key measure of financial performance for consumer finance companies. For an up-to-date description of how consumer finance companies use securitization use the Industry tab in Market Insight and through the drop-down menu select the subindustry Consumer Finance. You will encounter a recent S&P Industry survey on Financial Services: Diversified. Please download this survey and review the section entitled "How to Analyze a Financial Services Company" with a particular focus on securitization activity. What does securitization mean for a consumer finance company? What are its advantages and disadvantages?

2. Use Standard & Poor's Market Insight website (**www.mhhe.com/edumarketinsight**) for this problem. The largest banks and thrift institutions are heavy users of the risk-management devices discussed in this chapter, including securitization, loan sales, standby credits, and credit derivatives. Using the most recent financial reports of and news stories about bank and thrift institutions found in S&P's Market Insight, see if you can determine the extent to which the largest banks and thrifts are utilizing each of the risk-management devices discussed in this chapter. Measured by dollar volume, which of these financial instruments are most heavily used and why? For what specific purposes? Do you think this scale of usage is proper given the risks and costs discussed in this chapter?

REAL NUMBERS FOR REAL BANKS

Assignment for Chapter 8

YOUR BANK'S USE OF ASSET SECURITIZATION AND LOAN SALES AS RISK-MANAGEMENT TOOLS AND FEE INCOME GENERATORS

Chapter 8 describes a number of off-balance-sheet activities (asset-backed securities, loan sales, standby letters of credit, and credit derivatives) that can be used for risk management and fee generation. Some financial institutions have used asset securitization and loan sales to focus on loan brokerage where the institutions (1) make loans, (2) remove the loans from their balance sheets by either securitizing or selling the loans, and then (3) use the cash generated in the transfer to repeat the cycle time and time again. This process, as discussed in Chapter 8, can generate income at the time of the loan transfer and over the lives of the loans if the institution continues to service the loans it created and sold or securitized. In this assignment we will examine to what degree your bank's income is generated using this means.

Part One: Collecting the Data

For this part, we will visit the FDIC's website located at **www3.fdic.gov/sdi/main.asp** where you will use SDI to create a four-column report of your bank's information and the peer group information across years. This is familiar because you have been here before. In this part of the assignment, for Report Selection use the pull-down menu to choose Additional Noninterest Income and view this in Percentages of Total Assets. Collect the percentage information for the items listed below and include this as an addition to Spreadsheet 2 as follows:

Income from loan securitization and sales (A67)	Your Bank	Peer Group	Your Bank	Peer Group
Date (A68)	12/31/yy	12/31/yy	12/31/yy	12/31/yy
(A69)	Percentage of Total Assets			
Net servicing fees (A70)	%	%	%	%
Net securitization income (A71)				
Net gains (losses) on sales of loans (A72)				

Part Two: Analyzing the Data for Interpretation

A. Compare the columns of rows 70–72, which have been standardized for size by using the Percentages of Total Assets. Is your bank involved in loan brokerage and to what degree?

B. Extend this portion of the spreadsheet to columns F, G, H, and I, where you will calculate each item as a percentage of Total Operating Income (Interest Income plus Noninterest Income). To calculate these ratios from the data you have collected, divide each entry in columns B–E (rows 70–72) by Total Operating Income/Total Assets. Note this is equivalent to Item/Total Assets × Total Assets/Total Operating Income = Item/Total Operating Income. (A little algebra makes life worth living.) For example the formula for cell F70 would be B70/(B34+B38) and the formula for cell I72 would be E72/(E34+E38). Columns F–I should appear as follows:

Your Bank	Peer Group	Your Bank	Peer Group
12/31/yy	12/31/yy	12/31/yy	12/31/yy
Percentage of Total Operating Income			
%	%	%	%

C. Write one or two paragraphs interpreting your data and discussing your bank's involvement in loan securitization and sales relative to other large institutions (its peer group). How has income from these activities contributed to total operating income? What inferences can you make concerning the potential effects on risk exposure? You can incorporate tables using the Excel spreadsheets and reference these in your discussion.

Selected References

For a discussion of the characteristics of standby credit letters, see the following studies:

1. Bennett, Barbara. "Off Balance Sheet Risk in Banking: The Case of Standby Letters of Credit." *Economic Review*, Federal Reserve Bank of San Francisco, no. 1 (1986), pp. 19–29.

2. Goldberg, Michael, and Peter Lloyd-Davies. "Standby Letters of Credit: Are Banks Overextending Themselves?" *Journal of Bank Research*, Spring 1985, pp. 28–39.

3. Hassan, M. Kabir. "The Off-Balance-Sheet Banking Risk of Large U.S. Commercial Banks." *The Quarterly Review of Economics and Finance* 33, no. 1 (Spring 1993), pp. 51–69.

4. James, Christopher. "Off-Balance-Sheet Banking." *Economic Review*, Federal Reserve Bank of San Francisco, no. 4 (Fall 1987), pp. 21–36.

The following studies review the developing market for selling commercial loans:

5. Hasaan, M. Kabir. "Capital Market Tests of Risk Exposure of Loan Sales Activities of Large U.S. Commercial Banks." *Quarterly Journal of Business and Economics* 32, no. 1 (Winter 1993), pp. 27–49.

6. Haubrich, Joseph G., and James B. Thomson. "The Evolving Loan Sales Market." *Economic Commentary*, Federal Reserve Bank of Cleveland, July 14, 1993, pp. 1–6.

7. Pavel, Christine, and David Phillis. "Why Commercial Banks Sell Loans: An Empirical Analysis." *Economic Perspectives*, Federal Reserve Bank of Chicago, no. 11 (1987), pp. 3–14.

8. Pennacchi, George. "Loan Sales and the Cost of Bank Capital." Working paper, University of Pennsylvania, 1987.

9. Pyle, David. "Discussion of Off-Balance-Sheet Banking." In *The Search for Financial Stability: The Past Fifty Years*. Federal Reserve Bank of San Francisco, 1985.

10. Rose, Peter S. "New Benefits, New Pitfalls." *The Canadian Banker* 95, no. 5 (September/October 1988), pp. 52–57.

11. ———. "The Search for Safety in an Uncertain Market." *The Canadian Banker* 97, no. 1 (January/February 1990).

For a discussion of securitization, see these studies:

12. Benveniste, Lawrence M., and Allen N. Berger. "Securitization with Recourse: An Investment That Offers Uninsured Bank Depositors Sequential Claims." *Journal of Banking Research*, September 1987, pp. 190–201.

13. Board of Governors of the Federal Reserve System. *Interagency Advisory on Accounting Treatment of Accrued Interest Receivables Related to Credit Card Securitizations*, Washington, D.C., December 9, 2002.

14. Katz, Jane. "Securitization." *Regional Review*, Federal Reserve Bank of Boston, Summer 1997, pp. 13–17.

15. Rose, Peter S. "The Quest for Funds: New Directions in a New Market." *The Canadian Banker* 94, no. 5 (September/October 1987), pp. 46–55.

For a review of different types of credit derivatives see especially these sources:

16. Ackert, Lucy. "Derivative Securities Use Grows as Banks Strive to Hedge Risks." *Financial Update*, Federal Reserve Bank of Atlanta, January–March 1999, pp. 8–9.

17. Das, Sanjiv. "Credit Risk Derivatives." *Journal of Derivatives*, Spring 1995, pp. 7–230.

18. Federal Deposit Insurance Corporation. "Credit Derivatives." FIL-62-96, Supervisory Guidance for Credit Derivatives, Office of the Director, Division of Supervision, August 19, 1996.

19. Neal, Robert S. "Credit Derivatives: New Financial Instruments for Controlling Credit Risk." *Economic Review,* Federal Reserve Bank of Kansas City, Second Quarter 1996, pp. 15–27.

20. Rose, Peter S. *Money and Capital Markets: Financial Institutions and Instruments in a Global Marketplace,* 8th ed. New York: McGraw-Hill, 2003, Chapters 8 and 15.

Managing the Investment Portfolios and Liquidity Positions of Banks and Similar Financial Firms

Bankers and other financial-service managers are not so very different from you and me really—they sometimes spend more cash than they have on hand, take on more debt than they can afford, or acquire more risky assets than they really should.

For example, during the 1980s a small-town bank in Montana, just a few miles from the Canadian border, suddenly ran out of cash—only small coins remained in its drawers. This is a relatively rare event—so rare that government investigators inquired into the situation. Fortunately, however, for the curious customers and worried employees, the bank's president hopped in his car and drove several hundred miles to pick up some cash, stuffing it in his trunk for the ride home!

This little bank is not alone. More recently, numerous banks and other financial institutions stuffed their asset portfolios with investment securities they should have evaluated more closely and wound up taking losses they had not considered possible. In a period of relatively low interest rates, for example, many bankers bought securities backed by pools of home mortgage loans and credit card loans. With the economy softening, market interest rates headed toward record lows, and thousands of homeowners refinanced their mortgages, retiring the old loans upon which many of these investment securities rested for their value. The cash flow off these loan-backed investments sagged and their market values plummeted. At the same time a sluggish economy led to rising defaults on credit-card-backed securities, reducing their value as well.

We tend to think of the cash position of a bank or other financial firm and its investment portfolio, composed of marketable securities like Treasury notes and bonds, as a stodgy old place, neither exciting nor trendy. How wrong we can be! Really, the liquidity (cash position) of a financial firm and its portfolio of investment securities are all about *managing risk*. Investment securities help balance the greater risk banks and other lenders usually take on in their loan portfolios, generating a relatively steady income when loans are in trouble. Liquidity managers, for their part, keep a watchful eye on the cash available to the institution to make sure liquidity is available when it is needed.

Because most banks and other depository institutions have a huge volume of short-term deposits and other borrowings supporting assets that often carry far longer maturities than do their borrowings, managing the cash position, like managing the investment portfolio, is one of the most important areas within a financial firm. Moreover, rules and regulations in this area are constantly changing, new financial instruments (such as trust-preferred securities and equity-linked CDs) are constantly appearing to tempt investment managers, and new tax laws often show up over the horizon affecting what investment securities a banker or other financial manager should buy. So hang on for a while! You may find this section of the book far more important and more interesting than you ever dreamed.

CHAPTER NINE

The Investment Function in Banking and Financial Services Management

Key Topics in This Chapter

- Nature and Functions of Investments
- Investment Securities Available: Advantages and Disadvantages
- Measuring Expected Returns
- Taxes, Credit, and Interest-Rate Risks
- Liquidity, Prepayment, and Other Risks
- Investment Maturity Strategies
- Maturity Management Tools

Introduction

An investments officer of a large money-center bank was once overheard to say: "There's no way I can win! I'm either buying bonds when their prices are the highest or selling bonds when their prices are the lowest. Who would want this kind of a job?" In this chapter we will discover exactly what that bank officer really meant.

To begin our journey, we need to keep in mind that the primary function of most banks and many of their closest competitors is *not* to buy and sell bonds, but rather to make loans to businesses and individuals. After all, loans support business investment and consumer spending in the local community. Such loans ultimately provide jobs and income to thousands of community residents, many of whom are not borrowers of funds from the financial system but are certainly indirect beneficiaries of a financial institution's willingness to lend in its local community.

Yet buying and selling bonds has its place because not all of a financial institution's funds can be allocated to loans. For one thing, many loans are illiquid—they cannot easily be sold prior to maturity if a bank or other lending institution needs cash in a hurry. Another problem is that loans are among the riskiest assets, generally carrying the highest customer default rates of any form of credit. Moreover, for small and medium-size banks and thrift institutions, at least, the majority of loans typically come from the local area. Therefore, any significant drop in local economic activity weakens the quality of a major

307

portion of the average lender's loan portfolio, Then, too, loan income is usually taxable for commercial banks and selected other financial institutions in the United States and in many other countries as well, necessitating the search for tax shelters in years when earnings from loans are high.

For all these reasons, commercial banks and thrift institutions, for example, have learned to devote a significant portion of their asset portfolios—usually somewhere between a fifth to a third of all assets—to another major category of earning asset: investments in securities that are under the management of investments officers. Moreover, several nonbank financial-service providers—insurance companies, pension funds, and mutual funds, for example—often devote an even bigger portion of their assets to investment securities. Indeed, for several of the aforementioned nonbank financial firms the large majority of their financial assets are usually held in the form of investment securities. These instruments typically include government bonds and notes; corporate bonds, notes, and commercial paper; asset-backed securities arising from lending activity; domestic and Eurocurrency deposits; and certain kinds of common and preferred stock where permitted by law.

As we will see as this chapter unfolds, these security holdings perform a number of vital functions in the asset portfolios of banks and their closest competitors, providing income, liquidity when cash is most needed, diversification to reduce risk, and shelter for at least a portion of earnings from taxation. Investments also tend to stabilize the earnings of banks and other lenders, providing supplemental income when other sources of revenue (especially interest on loans) are in decline. See Exhibit 9–1 and Table 9–1 for a summary of the principal roles investment portfolios play on the balance sheets of banks and other financial firms.

Investment Instruments Available to Banks and Other Financial Firms

The number of financial instruments available for financial institutions to add to their securities portfolio is both large and growing. Moreover, each financial instrument has different characteristics with regard to risk, sensitivity to inflation, and sensitivity to shifting government policies and economic conditions. To examine the different investment vehicles available, it is useful to divide them into two broad groups: (1) **money market instruments,** which reach maturity within one year and are noted for their low risk and ready

EXHIBIT 9–1   Investments: The Crossroads Account on a Bank's or Other Depository Institution's Balance Sheet

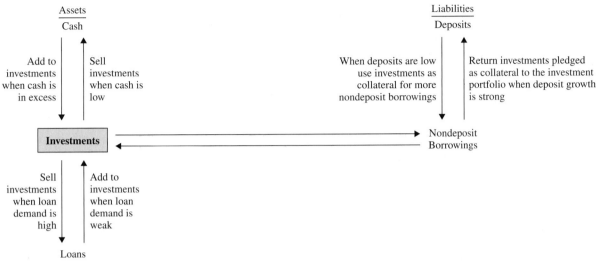

TABLE 9–1

Functions of the
Investment Security
Portfolio

Investment security portfolios help to

a. *Stabilize income,* so that revenues level out over the business cycle—when loan revenues fall, income from investment securities may rise.

b. *Offset credit risk exposure in the loan portfolio.* High-quality securities can be purchased and held to balance out the risk from loans.

c. *Provide geographic diversification.* Securities often come from different regions than the sources of loans, helping diversify a financial firm's sources of income.

d. *Provide a backup source of liquidity,* because securities can be sold to raise needed cash or used as collateral for borrowing additional funds.

e. *Reduce tax exposure,* especially in offsetting taxable loan revenues.

f. *Serve as collateral* (pledged assets) to secure federal, state, and local government deposits held by a bank or thrift institution.

g. *Help hedge* against losses due to changing interest rates.

h. *Provide flexibility* in a financial firm's asset portfolio because investment securities, unlike most loans, can be bought or sold quickly to restructure assets.

i. *Dress up the balance sheet* and make a financial institution look financially stronger due to the high quality of most marketable securities.

Federal regulations stress the need for every regulated depository institution to develop a *written* investment policy giving specific guidelines on the following:

a. The quality or degree of default risk exposure the institution is willing to accept.

b. The desired maturity range and degree of marketability sought for all securities purchased.

c. The goals sought for its investment portfolio.

d. The degree of portfolio diversification to reduce risk the institution wishes to achieve with its investment portfolio.

In the banking field examiners review a bank's investment portfolio and its written investment policy to be sure speculation has not replaced more acceptable investment goals.

marketability, and (2) **capital market instruments,** which have remaining maturities beyond one year and are generally noted for their higher expected rate of return and capital gains potential. See Table 9–2 for a summary of the advantages and disadvantages of the principal types of investment securities available.

Some authorities refer to investments as the *crossroads account.* Investments literally stand between cash, loans, and deposits. When cash is low, some investments will be sold

TABLE 9–2 Key Advantages and Disadvantages of Popular Investment Securities Often Purchased by Banks and Other Financial Firms

Money Market Instruments

	Treasury Bills	Short-Term Treasury Notes and Bonds	Federal Agency Securities	Certificates of Deposit	International Eurocurrency Deposits	Bankers' Acceptances	Commercial Paper	Short-Term Municipal Obligations
Key advantages:	Safety and high liquidity Ready marketability Good collateral for borrowing Can pledge behind government deposits Taxable income	Safety Good resale market Good collateral for borrowing Offer yields usually higher than bill yields	Safety Good to average resale market Good collateral for borrowing Higher yields than on U.S. government securities	Safety (insured to $100,000) Yields higher than on T-bills Over $100,000 denomination is often marketable through dealers	Low risk Higher yields than on many domestic CDs	Low risk due to multiple credit guarantees	Low risk due to high quality of borrowers	Tax-exempt interest income
Key disadvantages:	Low yields relative to other financial instruments Taxable income	More price risk than T-bills Taxable gains and income	Less marketable than Treasury securities Taxable gains and income	Limited resale market on longer-term CDs Taxable income	Volatile interest rates Taxable income	Limited availability at specific maturities Issued in odd denominations Taxable income	Volatile market Poor to nonexistent resale market Taxable income	Limited to nonexistent resale market Taxable capital gains

Capital Market Instruments

	Treasury Notes and Bonds	Municipal (State and Local Government) Bonds	Corporate Notes and Bonds	Asset-Backed Securities (Including CMOs)
Key advantages:	Safety Good resale market Good collateral for borrowing May be pledged behind government deposits	Tax-exempt interest income High credit quality Liquidity and marketability of selected securities	Higher pretax yields than on government securities Aid in locking in long-term rates of return	Higher pretax yields than on Treasury securities Safety Adequate resale market Good collateral for borrowing
Key disadvantages:	Low yields relative to long-term private securities Taxable gains and income Limited supply of longer-term issues	Volatile market Some issues have limited resale possibilities Taxable capital gains	Limited resale market Inflexible terms Taxable gains and income	Less marketable and more unstable in price than Treasury securities Taxable gains and income

in order to raise more cash. On the other hand, if cash is too high, some of the excess cash will be placed in investment securities. If loan demand is weak, investments will rise in order to provide more earning assets and maintain profitability. But, if loan demand is strong, some investments will be sold to accommodate the heavy loan demand. Finally, when deposits are not growing fast enough, some investment securities will be used as collateral to borrow nondeposit funds. No other account on the balance sheet occupies such a critical intersection position as do investments, fulfilling so many important roles.

Popular Money Market Investment Instruments

Treasury Bills

One of the most popular of all short-term investments is the **U.S. Treasury bill,** a debt obligation of the United States government that, by law, must mature within one year from date of issue. Bills are issued in weekly and monthly auctions and are particularly attractive to banks and other financial firms because of their high degree of *safety.* Bills are supported by the taxing power of the federal government, their market prices are relatively stable, and they are readily marketable. Moreover, T-bills can serve as collateral for attracting loans from other institutions through repurchase agreements and other borrowing instruments. Bills are issued and traded at a discount from their par (face) value. Thus, the investor's return consists purely of price appreciation as the bill approaches maturity. The rate of return (yield) on T-bills is figured by the bank discount method, which uses the bill's par value at maturity as the basis for calculating its return, ignores the compounding of interest, and is based on a 360-day year, as we discussed in Chapter 6.

Short-Term Treasury Notes and Bonds

At the time they are issued, **Treasury notes** and **Treasury bonds** have relatively long maturities: 1 to 10 years for notes and over 10 years for bonds. However, when these securities come within one year of maturity, they are considered money market instruments. While Treasury notes and bonds are more sensitive to interest rate risk and less marketable than Treasury bills, their expected returns (yields) are usually higher than for bills with greater potential for capital gains. Treasury notes and bonds are *coupon instruments,* which means they promise investors a fixed rate of return, though the expected return may fall below or climb above the promised coupon rate due to fluctuations in the security's market price.

All negotiable Treasury Department securities are issued by electronic book entry, with no registered or engraved certificates issued. This system, known as Treasury Direct, provides bank and nonbank owners of U.S. Treasury securities with a statement showing the bills, notes, and bonds they hold. Any interest and principal payments earned are deposited directly into the owners' checking or savings account. This approach means not only greater convenience for financial institutions and other investors purchasing and selling Treasury securities but also increased protection against theft.

Federal Agency Securities

Marketable notes and bonds sold by agencies owned by or started by the federal government are known as **federal agency securities.** Familiar examples include securities issued by the Federal National Mortgage Association (FNMA, or Fannie Mae), the Farm Credit System (FCS), the Federal Land Banks (FLBs), the Federal Home Loan Mortgage Corporation (FHLMC, or Freddie Mae), and the Student Loan Marketing Association (SLMA, or Sallie Mae). Most of these securities are not formally guaranteed by the federal government, though many financial analysis believe Congress would move to rescue any agency

Factoid
Which federal agency in the United States has more securities outstanding in the financial marketplace for banks and other investors to buy than any other agency? **Answer:** The Federal National Mortgage Association (Fannie Mae), followed by the Federal Home Loan Banks (which are lenders to banks and thrifts) and the Federal Home Loan Mortgage Corporation (Freddie Mac).

in trouble. This implied government support keeps agency yields close to those on Treasury securities (normally within one percentage point) and contributes to the high liquidity of many agency securities.

Among the most popular of all federal agency securities are *discount notes*. These short-term agency borrowings are sold at prices below their face value and usually have a maturity range of overnight to one year. Most discount notes are issued in book entry form, though a few are still available as bearer certificates, with yields figured (as with Treasury bills) on a 360-day basis. Interest income on agency-issued discount notes is federally taxable and, in most cases, subject to state and local taxation as well.

Certificates of Deposit

A **certificate of deposit (CD)** is simply an interest-bearing receipt for the deposit of funds in a bank or thrift institution. Thus, the primary role of CDs is to provide banks and other depository institutions with an additional source of funds. However, banks often buy the CDs issued by other depository institutions, regarding them as an attractive, lower-risk investment. CDs carry a fixed term, and there is a federally imposed penalty for early withdrawal. Banks and thrifts issue both small *consumer-oriented CDs*, ranging in denomination from $500 to $100,000, and large *business-oriented* or *institution-oriented CDs* (often called *jumbos* or *negotiable CDs*) with denominations over $100,000 (though only the first $100,000 is federally insured). CDs have negotiated interest rates that, while normally fixed, may be allowed to fluctuate with market conditions. Securities dealers make an active secondary market for $100,000-plus CDs maturing within six months.

International Eurocurrency Deposits

The 1950s in Western Europe ushered in the development of high-quality international bank deposits, sold in million-dollar units and denominated in a currency other than the home currency of the country in which they are deposited. *Eurocurrency deposits* are not checking accounts, but time deposits of fixed maturity issued by the world's largest banks headquartered in financial centers around the globe, though the heart of the Eurocurrency deposit market is in London. Most of these international deposits are of short maturity— 30, 60, or 90 days—to correspond with the funding requirements of international trade. They are *not* insured, and due to their perceived higher credit risk, lower liquidity, and greater sensitivity to foreign economic and political developments, they normally carry slightly higher market yields than domestic time deposits issued by comparable-size U.S. banks. (For a detailed discussion of the role and creation of Eurocurrency deposits, see Chapter 12.)

Bankers' Acceptances

Because they represent a bank's promise to pay the holder a designated amount of money (indicated on the face of the acceptance) on a designated future date, **bankers' acceptances** are considered to be among the safest of all money market instruments. Most acceptances arise from a bank or other financial firm's decision to guarantee the credit of one of its customers who is exporting, importing, or storing goods or purchasing currency. In legal language, the bank agrees to be the *primary obligor*, committed to paying off the customer's debt regardless of what happens subsequently, in return for a fee. Through the acceptance vehicle, the issuing institution supplies its name and credit standing so that its customer will be able to obtain credit from someone else more easily and at lower cost.

The holder of the acceptance on its maturity date may be another bank, a financial institution, or a money market investor attracted by its safety and active resale market. Because acceptances have a ready resale market, they may be traded from one investor to another before reaching maturity. If the current holder sells the acceptances, this does not erase the issuer's obligation to pay off its outstanding acceptances at maturity. However, by selling an acceptance, a bank or other holder adds to its reserves and transfers interest rate risk to another investor. The acceptance is a discount instrument and, therefore, is always sold at a price below par before it reaches maturity. As with Treasury bills, the investor's expected return comes solely from the prospect that the acceptance will rise in price as it gets closer to maturity. Rates of return on acceptances generally lie between the yield on Eurocurrency deposits and the yield on Treasury bills. One other important advantage of acceptances is that they may qualify for discounting (borrowing) at the Federal Reserve Banks, provided they qualify as *eligible* acceptances. To be eligible as collateral for borrowing from the Fed, the acceptance must be denominated in dollars, normally cannot exceed six months to maturity, and must arise from the export or import of goods or from the storage of marketable commodities.

Commercial Paper

Many smaller banks, money market funds, and other financial firms find **commercial paper**—short-term, unsecured IOUs offered by major corporations—an attractive investment that is safer than most types of loans. Commercial paper sold in the United States is of relatively short maturity—the bulk of it matures in 90 days or less—and generally is issued by borrowers with the highest credit ratings. A growing market in western Europe and in Japan for Europaper has attracted participation by major international banks, finance companies, and other leading institutions. Europaper generally carries longer maturities and higher interest rates than U.S. commercial paper due to its greater perceived credit risk; however, there is a more active resale market for Europaper than for most U.S. commercial paper issues whose market has weakened in recent years. Most commercial paper is issued at a discount from par, like T-bills and acceptances, though some paper bearing a promised rate of return (coupon) is also issued today.

Short-Term Municipal Obligations

State and local governments, including counties, cities, and special districts, issue a wide variety of short-term debt instruments to cover temporary cash shortages. Two of the most common are tax-anticipation notes (TANs), issued in lieu of expected future tax revenues, and revenue-anticipation notes (RANs), issued to cover expenses from special projects, such as the construction of a toll bridge, highway, or airport, in lieu of expected future revenues from those projects. All interest earned on such municipal notes is exempt from federal income taxation, so they are attractive to investors bearing relatively high income tax rates, such as commercial banks. However, as we will see later in this chapter, the tax savings associated with municipal securities has been sharply limited for U.S. banks in recent years, reducing their attractiveness relative to federal and privately issued securities. At the same time, many state and local governments have encountered serious financial problems that have weakened the credit quality of their notes recently, forcing bankers and other investing institutions to take a closer look at the quality of the municipals they choose to buy.

Popular Capital Market Investment Instruments

Treasury Notes and Bonds

Among the safest and most liquid long-term investments that banks and their competitors can make are U.S. Treasury notes and bonds. U.S. Treasury notes are available in a wide variety of maturities (ranging from 1 year to 10 years when issued) and in large volume.

Treasury bonds (with original maturities of more than 10 years) are traded in a more limited market with wider price fluctuations than is usually the case with Treasury notes. Treasury bonds and notes carry higher expected returns than bills, but present a bank or other investing institution with greater price risk and liquidity risk. They are issued normally in denominations of $1,000, $5,000, $10,000, $100,000, and $1 million.

Municipal Notes and Bonds

Long-term debt obligations issued by states, cities, and other governmental units are known collectively as **municipal bonds.** As with short-term municipal notes, interest on the majority of these bonds is exempt from federal income tax provided they are issued to fund public, rather than private, projects. Capital gains on municipals are fully taxable, however, except for bonds sold at a discounted price, where the gain from purchase price to par value is considered a portion of the investor's tax-exempt interest earnings. Banks and other investing institutions often submit competitive bids for or purchase after private negotiation the debt issued by local cities, counties, and school districts as a way of demonstrating support for their local communities and to attract other business. They also purchase municipal securities from brokers and dealers in the national market for reasons strictly related to after-tax return and risk because most municipal bonds have high credit ratings. Unfortunately, municipals are not very liquid—few issues trade on any given day and those that do trade often report only one transaction per day.

Many different types of municipal bonds are issued today, but the majority fall into one of two categories: (1) *general obligation (GO) bonds*, backed by the full faith and credit of the issuing unit of government, which means they may be paid from any available source of revenue (including the levying of additional taxes); and (2) *revenue bonds*, which can be used to fund long-term revenue-raising projects and are payable only from certain stipulated sources of funds. U.S. banks have long possessed the authority to deal in and underwrite general obligation (GO) municipal bonds, but for many years they faced restrictions on directly underwriting municipal revenue bonds until this power was extended with passage of the Gramm-Leach-Bliley Act in 1999.

Corporate Notes and Bonds

Long-term debt securities issued by corporations are usually called **corporate notes** when they mature within five years or **corporate bonds** when they carry longer maturities. There are many different varieties, depending on the types of security pledged (e.g., mortgages versus debentures), purposes of issue, and terms of issue. Corporate notes and bonds generally are more attractive to insurance companies and pension funds than to banks because of their higher credit risk relative to government securities and their more limited resale market. However, they do offer significantly higher average yields than government securities of comparable maturity, and their yield spread over government securities widens when investors become more concerned about corporate credit quality.

Factoid
Which U.S. Treasury security is the most popular (measured by volume outstanding)—Treasury bills, notes, or bonds?
Answer: T-notes (with an original maturity of 1 to 10 years), followed by T bills. (See, for example, **www.treas.gov**.)

Concept Check

9–1. Why do banks and their closest competitors, the thrift institutions, choose to devote a significant portion of their assets to investments in securities?

9–2. What key roles do investments play in the management of a bank or other depository institution?

9–3. What are the principal money market and capital market instruments available to banks and competing financial institutions today? What are their most important features or characteristics?

Other Investment Instruments Developed More Recently

The range of investment opportunities for banks and other financial institutions has expanded in recent years. Many new securities have been developed; some of these are variations on traditional notes and bonds, while others represent entirely new investment vehicles. Examples include structured notes, securitized assets, and stripped securities.

Structured Notes   In their search to protect themselves against shifting interest rates, many banks added *structured notes* to their investment portfolios during the 1990s. Most of these notes arose from security brokers and dealers who assembled pools of federal agency securities (issued by such well-known agencies as the Federal Home Loan Banks) and offered investment officers of banks and thrift institutions a package investment whose interest yield could be periodically reset (perhaps every quarter, semiannually, or after a certain number of years) based on what happened to a stated reference rate, such as the U.S. Treasury bill or bond rate. A guaranteed floor rate and cap rate could be added in which the bank's promised investment return could not drop below a stated (floor) level or rise above some maximum (cap) level. Some structured notes carried multiple coupon (promised) rates that periodically were given a boost ("step-up") to give investors a higher yield; others carried adjustable coupon (promised) rates determined by a specific formula. The complexity of these notes resulted in substantial losses for some banks and thrift institutions, not from credit risk since few of these notes are actually defaulted upon, but from substantial interest rate risk.

Securitized Assets   In recent years hybrid securities based upon pools of loans have been one of the most rapidly growing investments for banks and selected other firms, such as thrifts, insurance companies, and mutual funds. These **securitized assets** are backed by selected loans of uniform type and quality, such as FHA- and VA-insured home mortgages, automobile loans, and credit card loans.[1] The most popular securitized assets that banks and thrift institutions buy as investments today are based upon mortgage loans.

There are three main types of mortgage-backed securitized assets: (1) pass-through securities, (2) collateralized mortgage obligations (CMOs), and (3) mortgage-backed bonds. *Pass-through securities* arise when a bank, thrift institution, or other lender pools a group of similar home mortgage loans appearing on its balance sheet, removes them from the balance sheet into an account controlled by a legal trustee, and issues securities to interested investors using the mortgage loans as collateral. As the mortgage loan pool generates principal and interest payments, these payments are "passed through" to investors holding the mortgage-backed securities. Repayment of principal and interest on the calendar dates promised is guaranteed by the Government National Mortgage Association (GNMA, or Ginnie Mae), an agency of the U.S. government, in return for a small fee (currently 6 basis points or 0.06 percent of the total amount of loans placed in the pool).

The Federal National Mortgage Corporation (FNMA, or Fannie Mae), which was chartered by Congress but is legally separate from the U.S. government, also helps create pass-through securities by purchasing packages of mortgage loans from banks and thrift institutions. While GNMA aids in the creation of mortgage-loan-backed securities for government-insured home loans, FNMA securitizes both conventional (noninsured) and government-insured home mortgages. Banks and other investors who acquire pass-through securities issued against pools of government-insured home mortgages are protected against default on those securities because the Federal Housing and Veterans Administrations

---

[1] See Chapter 8 for a discussion of how banks and other financial firms use securitized assets to raise new funds and to restructure their sources and uses of funds.

ensure that the pooled loans will be repaid even if the homeowner abandons his or her home. Moreover, GNMA and FNMA may add their own guarantees of timely repayment of principal and interest.

In 1983 another government-sponsored agency, the Federal Home Loan Mortgage Corporation (FHLMC, or Freddie Mac), now legally separate from the U.S. government, developed the *collateralized mortgage obligation* (CMO). A CMO is a pass-through security divided into multiple classes (tranches), each with a different promised (coupon) rate and level of risk exposure. CMOs arise either from the securitizing of mortgage loans themselves or from the securitizing of pass-through securities, taking these instruments off the balance sheet of the firm holding them.

Closely related to CMOs are REMICs—Real Estate Mortgage Investment Conduits, which also partition the principal cash flow from a pool of mortgage loans or mortgage-backed securities into multiple maturity classes in order to help reduce the cash-flow uncertainty of investors active in the mortgage market. As we will see later in this chapter, the principal risk to a bank or other investor buying these securities is *prepayment risk* because some borrowers will pay off their home mortgages early or default on their loans, meaning that the holder of these securities may receive diminished income and declining value in the future.

The final type of mortgage-related security is the **mortgage-backed bond.** Unlike pass-throughs and CMOs where mortgage loans are removed from the balance sheet, mortgage-backed bonds (MBBs) and the mortgage loans backing them stay on the issuer's balance sheet, and there is no direct connection between the principal and interest payments coming from the mortgage loans themselves and the interest and principal payments owed on the MBBs. The financial institution issuing these bonds will separate the mortgage loans held on its balance sheet from its other assets and pledge those loans as collateral to support the MBBs. A trustee acting on behalf of the mortgage bondholders keeps track of the dedicated loans and checks periodically to be sure that the market value of the loans is greater than what is owed on the bonds.

Pass-throughs, CMOs, and other securitized assets have been among the most rapidly growing financial instruments in bank and thrift institution investment portfolios in recent years. Several factors appear to account for the popularity of these asset-backed investment securities:

1. Guarantees from federal agencies (in the case of home-mortgage-related securities) or from private institutions (such as banks or insurance companies pledging to back credit card loans).
2. The higher average yields available on securitized assets than on U.S. Treasury securities.
3. The lack of good-quality loans and securities of other kinds in some markets around the globe.
4. The superior liquidity and marketability of securities backed by loans compared to the liquidity and marketability of the loans themselves.

Key URLs
For a close look at the rules for bank investments in securities markets, see **www.occ.treas.gov, www.thecommunity banker.com,** and **www.bondmarkets.com.**

Stripped Securities In the early 1980s, security dealers developed and marketed a hybrid instrument known as the **stripped security,** a claim against either the principal or interest payments associated with a debt security, such as a U.S. Treasury bond. Dealers create stripped securities by separating the principal and interest payments from an underlying debt security and selling separate claims to these two promised income streams. Claims against only the principal payments from a security are called *PO (principal-only) securities,* while claims against only the stream of interest payments promised by a security are referred to as *IO (interest-only) securities.*

Stripped securities often display markedly different behavior from the underlying securities from which they come. In particular, some stripped securities offer interest-rate hedging possibilities to help protect a portfolio of bonds and other traditional security holdings against loss from interest-rate changes. The two securities whose interest and principal payments are most likely to be stripped today are longer-term (10 years and longer) U.S. Treasury bonds and mortgage-backed securities. Treasury bonds were first offered in stripped form by security dealers early in the 1980s, and the U.S. Treasury itself agreed to strip long-term bonds on its books beginning in 1985.

Both PO and IO bond strips are really *zero coupon bonds* with no periodic interest payments; they therefore carry zero reinvestment risk. Each stripped security is sold at a discount from its par value, so the investor's rate of return is based solely on the security's price appreciation. Because bonds normally pay interest twice a year, an investor can lock in a fixed rate of return for a holding period as short as six months out to several years up to the time to maturity of the original bond. POs tend to be *more* price sensitive to interest-rate changes than regular bonds, whereas IO strips tend to be *less* price sensitive than the original bonds.

Investment Securities Actually Held by Banks

We have now examined the principal investment opportunities available to banks and competing institutions, but which of these investments do banks actually prefer? Table 9–3 provides an overview of investment securities held by all U.S.-insured banks as of year-end 2001. Clearly just a few types of securities dominate U.S. bank investment portfolios:

1. Obligations of the U.S. government and of various federal agencies such as the Federal National Mortgage Association (FNMA), the Federal Home Loan Mortgage Corporation (FHLMC), and the Government National Mortgage Association (GNMA).
2. State and local government obligations (municipals).
3. Nonmortgage-related asset-backed securities (such as obligations backed by credit card and home equity loans).

Federal-government-related IOUs account for just over 60 percent of the U.S. commercial bank investment total, counting various types of U.S. government and federal agency–guaranteed mortgage-backed instruments. In fact, mortgage-loan-backed securities account for just over half of all U.S. bank investment holdings (with the heaviest concentrations of these mortgage-related instruments held by the largest banks in the industry) due to their ready marketability and comparatively high market yields. Non-government-guaranteed asset-backed securities (such as instruments backed by auto and commercial loans) fall into a distant second place followed by holdings of tax-exempt state and local government IOUs.

As reflected in Table 9–3, we can see that commercial banks hold relatively few private-sector securities, such as corporate bonds, notes, and commercial paper or corporate stock. They would prefer to make direct loans to customers rather than to buy their securities because the yield is normally lower on investment securities than on loans and because purchasing securities usually generates no new deposits for a bank.

Table 9–3 also tells us that management targets most bank-held investments for eventual resale rather than planning to hold them until they reach maturity. These investments will generally be sold when a bank or other financial firm needs cash to cover customer withdrawals of funds, to make loans, or to take advantage of more lucrative investment opportunities. About a quarter of the U.S. commercial-bank investment portfolio consists of *trading account securities*, and the largest banks perform the role of security dealers by

TABLE 9–3   Investment Securities That FDIC-Insured U.S. Banks Hold (year-end 2001; billions of dollars at all U.S.-insured banks)

Source: Federal Deposit Insurance Corporation, *Statistics on Banking*, 2001.

Types of Securities Held	All FDIC-Insured U.S. Commercial Banks	Percent of all Invest-ment Holdings	Percent Held at Banks with Total Assets of		
			Less than $100 Mill.	$100 Mill. to $1 Bill.	$1 Billion or More
U.S. Treasury securities	$45,055	3.8%	5.5%	4.9%	3.5%
U.S. government obligations:					
U.S. government issued nonmortgage-backed securities	5,642	0.5	1.0	0.6	0.4
U.S. government enterprise issued nonmortgage-backed securities	190,146	16.1	44.9	33.3	11.1
Mortgage-backed pass-through securities issued by FNMA and FHLMC	256,286	21.7	11.0	13.5	24.0
Mortgage-backed pass-through securities issued by GNMA	101,832	8.6	5.7	7.0	9.1
Collateralized mortgage obligations (CMOs and REMICs)	166,725	14.1	7.5	12.2	14.9
All U.S. government obligations	$720,632	61.1	70.1	66.6	59.5
Securities issued by states and political subdivisions (municipals)	96,489	8.2	18.4	18.6	5.5
Asset-backed securities:					
Credit-card-loan-backed securities	39,013	3.3	0.0*	0.2	4.1
Home-equity-loan-backed securities	32,447	2.8	0.0*	0.1	3.4
Auto-loan-backed securities	15,275	1.3	0.0*	0.0*	1.6
Securities backed by other consumer loans	1,290	0.1	0.0*	0.1	0.1
Securities backed by commercial loans	6,726	0.6	0.0*	0.0*	0.7
Other asset-backed securities	13,426	1.1	0.0*	0.0*	1.4
Total asset-backed securities	$108,177	9.2	0.2	0.5	11.4
Other domestic debt securities	$128,133	10.9	4.8	7.3	11.9
Foreign debt securities	60,359	5.1	0.0*	0.3	6.4
Equity securities	20,717	1.8	1.1	1.8	1.8
Total investment securities	$1,179,562	100.0%	100.0%	100.0%	100.0%
Memo items:					
Total investments to total assets	–	18.0%	24.0%	22.6%	17.0%
Investment securities held to maturity (amortized cost)	–	8.2%	19.4%	15.6%	6.1%
Investment securities available for sale (fair value)	–	91.8	80.6	84.4	93.9
Pledged securities as a percent of all investments	–	47.0%	35.8%	43.0%	48.5%
Mortgage-backed securities as a percent of all investments	–	52.0%	24.8%	34.8%	57.0%
Structured notes as a percent of all investments (fair value)	–	0.4%	0.6%	0.6%	0.4%
Assets held in trading accounts	–	25.7%	0.0%*	0.2%	32.2%
Securities with maturities of:					
Under one year		14.7%	13.4%	11.8%	18.3%
One to five years		18.7	39.1	30.3	15.3
More than five years		66.6	47.5	57.9	66.4

Note: * indicates figure is less than 0.05 percent.

Factoid

After loans, what is the greatest source of revenue for most banks around the world?
Answer: Interest and dividends on investment securities.

purchasing investments and reselling them to their customers. We also note that most bank investments during the period examined were relatively long term—more than five years to maturity—as banks sought higher market yields during a period of record low market interest rates.

As might be expected, the smallest banks tend to invest more heavily in U.S. Treasury and other government securities than do the largest. The smaller institutions tend to be more heavily exposed to risk of loss from economic problems in their local areas and, therefore, tend to use the lowest-risk securities to offset the high risk often inherent in their loans. In contrast, the largest banks tend to be more heavily invested in foreign securities and private debt and equity obligations, especially corporate bonds and commercial paper, all of which tend to carry greater risk exposure than government securities.

In total, investment securities represent just under a fifth of all U.S. bank assets nationwide. But this proportion of total bank assets varies with bank size and location. Banks operating in areas with weak loan demand usually hold significantly greater percentages of investment securities relative to their total assets. Moreover, as Table 9–3 suggests, bank size also plays a key role. The smallest size group of banks holds nearly a quarter of its assets in the form of investments, while the largest multi-billion-dollar banks hold only about 17 percent of their assets in investment securities, reflecting the relatively heavy loan demand most large banks face. In contrast, loans represent over half of all bank assets and a majority of bank revenues come from loans; no surprise, bank loans generally carry significantly higher average yields than investments. But as we have already seen, the investment portfolio is expected to do several jobs in addition to generating income, such as tax sheltering, reducing overall risk exposure, and serving as sources of additional cash and collateral for borrowing funds.

Concept Check

9–4. What types of investment securities do commercial banks seem to prefer the most? Can you explain why?

9–5. What are securitized assets? Why have they grown so rapidly in recent years?

9–6. What special risks do securitized assets present to banks and other financial institutions investing in them?

9–7. What are structured notes and stripped securities? What unusual features do they contain?

Factors Affecting Choice of Investment Securities

The investments officer of a bank or other financial institution must consider several factors in deciding which investment securities to buy, sell, or hold. The principal factors bearing on which investments are chosen include the following:

1. Expected rate of return
2. Tax exposure
3. Interest-rate risk
4. Credit risk
5. Business risk
6. Liquidity risk
7. Call risk
8. Prepayment risk
9. Inflation risk
10. Pledging requirements

We will briefly review each of these factors.

Filmtoid

What 1987 film busted Michael Douglas and Charlie Sheen's characters for insider trading when the expected rates of return in the market were not enough to satisfy their greed?
Answer: *Wall Street*

Expected Rate of Return

The investments officer must determine the total rate of return that can reasonably be expected from each security, including the interest payments promised by the issuer of that security and possible capital gains or losses. For most investments, this requires the investment manager to calculate the **yield to maturity (YTM)** if a security is to be held to maturity or the planned **holding period yield (HPY)** between point of purchase and point of sale.

As we saw in Chapter 6, *the yield to maturity formula determines the rate of discount (or yield) on a loan or security that equalizes the market price of the loan or security with the expected stream of cash flows (interest and principal) that loan or security will generate*. To illustrate how the YTM formula can be useful to an investments officer, suppose the officer is considering purchasing a $1,000 par-value U.S. Treasury note that promises an 8 percent coupon rate (or $1,000 $\times$ 0.08 = $80) and is slated to mature in five years. If the T-note's current price is $900, we have

$$\$900 = \frac{\$80}{(1 + \text{YTM})^1} + \frac{\$80}{(1 + \text{YTM})^2} + \cdots + \frac{\$80}{(1 + \text{YTM})^5} + \frac{\$1,000}{(1 + \text{YTM})^5} \qquad \textbf{(1)}$$

Solving using a financial calculator reveals that the yield to maturity (YTM) is 10.74 percent. The calculated YTM should be compared with the expected yields on other loans and investments that might be acquired in order to determine where the best possible rate of return lies.

However, banks and several of their closest competitors (such as savings and loans and credit unions) frequently do not hold all their security investments to maturity. Some securities must be sold off early to accommodate new loan demand or to cover deposit withdrawals. To deal with this situation, the investments officer needs to know how to calculate the holding period yield (HPY) earned by his or her institution. *The HPY is simply the rate of return (discount factor) that equates a security's purchase price with the stream of income expected from that security until it is sold to another investor*. For example, suppose the 8 percent Treasury note described above and currently priced at $900 was sold at the end of two years for $950. Its holding period yield could be found from

$$\$900 = \frac{\$80}{(1 + \text{HPY})^1} + \frac{\$80}{(1 + \text{HPY})^2} + \frac{\$950}{(1 + \text{HPY})^2} \qquad \textbf{(2)}$$

In this case, the note's HPY would be 11.51 percent.[2]

Tax Exposure

Interest and capital gains income from investments held by U.S. banks are taxed as *ordinary income* for tax purposes, just as are the wages and salaries earned by most U.S. citizens. Because of their relatively high tax exposure, banks are more interested in the after-tax rate of return on loans and securities than in their before-tax return. This situation contrasts with such institutions as credit unions and mutual funds, which are generally tax-exempt.

The Tax Status of State and Local Government Bonds   For banks in the upper tax brackets, tax-exempt state and local government (municipal) bonds and notes have been attractive from time to time, depending upon their status in tax law.

For example, suppose that Aaa-rated corporate bonds are carrying an average gross yield to maturity of about 7 percent, the prime rate on top-quality corporate loans is about 6

---

[2] Using a financial calculator such as the TI BA II Plus™, N = 2, i=?, PV = −900, Pmt = 80, FV = 950.
Solving for the interest rate (HPY) gives i = 11.51%.

percent, and Aaa-rated municipal bonds have a 5.5 percent gross yield to maturity. The investments officer for a bank or other financial firm subject to the corporate income tax could compare each of these potential yields using this formula:

$$\frac{\text{Before-tax}}{\text{gross yield}} \times (1 - \text{Firm's marginal income tax rate}) \tag{3}$$

$$= \text{After-tax gross yield}$$

This comparison yields the following expected after-tax gross returns for a bank or other taxed financial firm in the top 35 percent federal income tax bracket:

$$\frac{\text{Aaa-rated corporate bonds}}{7.00 \text{ percent} \times (1 - 0.35) = 4.55 \text{ percent}}$$

$$\frac{\text{Prime-rated loans}}{6 \text{ percent} \times (1 - 0.35) = 3.90 \text{ percent}}$$

$$\frac{\text{Aaa-rated municipal bonds}}{5.50 \text{ percent} \times (1 - 0) = 5.50 \text{ percent before and after taxes}}$$

Under the assumptions given, the municipal bond is the most attractive investment in gross yield. However, other considerations do enter into this decision, such as the need to attract and hold deposits and other customer accounts, management's desire to keep good loan customers, and recent changes in tax laws.

For example, tax reform in the United States has had a major impact on the relative attractiveness of state and local government bonds as investments for commercial banks. Prior to federal tax reform legislation during the 1980s, commercial banks held close to 30 percent of all state and local government debt outstanding. But their share of the municipal market has fallen substantially since that time, due to (1) declining tax advantages for banks, (2) lower corporate tax rates, and (3) fewer qualified tax-exempt municipal securities.

Bank Qualified Bonds   Prior to 1986, the federal tax code allowed significant tax deductions for interest expenses incurred when banks borrow funds to buy municipal securities. Today banks buying *bank qualified bonds*—those issued by smaller local governments (governments issuing no more than $10 million of public securities per year)—are allowed to deduct 80 percent of any interest paid to fund these acquisitions. This tax advantage is *not* available for nonbank-qualified bonds.

Prior to the 1986 Tax Reform Act, the highest corporate tax bracket was 46 percent. Today the top bracket is 35 percent for corporations earning more than $10 million in annual taxable income or 34 percent otherwise. Lower tax brackets reduce the tax savings associated with the tax-exemption feature.[3]

Fewer state and local bonds qualify for tax exemption today. If 10 percent or more of the proceeds of a municipal bond issue is used to benefit a private individual or business, it is considered a private activity issue and fully taxable. In addition, Congress placed ceilings on the amount of industrial development bonds (IDBs) local governments could issue to provide new facilities or tax breaks in order to attract new industry to their municipalities. These laws reduced the supply of tax-exempt securities for investors to purchase and contributed to the lower proportion of municipals in the securities portfolios of many financial institutions.

---

[3] Under current federal law, U.S. banks must calculate their income taxes in two different ways—using a normal tax rate schedule (maximum 35 percent tax rate) and using an alternative minimum tax rate of 20 percent, and then must pay the greater of the two different amounts. Interest income from municipals has to be added in to determine each bank's alternative minimum tax, making municipal income subject to at least some taxation.

CRISIS IN THE INVESTMENTS MARKET: WHAT THE 9–11 TERRORIST ATTACKS DID TO THE DELIVERY OF SECURITIES TO BANKS AND OTHER INVESTORS

The market for investment securities is not only one of the largest markets in the world, but also one of the deepest and most efficient of all marketplaces. Trillions of dollars in funds exchange hands daily and both payments and the delivery of securities purchased generally occur on time. Now consider what happened following the terrorist attacks on 9–11, 2001. Within hours the system for delivering U.S. Treasury securities—the most popular financial investment in the world—to banks and other purchasers began to unravel. Many sellers of Treasuries were unable to meet their promises to deliver securities and some buyers couldn't execute payments for them on the scheduled date. These so-called settlement fails soared from an average of less than $2 billion a day before the terrorist attacks to as much as $190 billion a day immediately following the attacks.

The "settlement fails" occurred initially because some vital communications systems linking dealers, banks, and their customers were destroyed or damaged when the twin towers of the World Trade Center collapsed. Moreover, several key securities-market institutions experienced destruction of their records. A severe shortage of certain normally available Treasury securities developed, and the usual remedy for such shortages—borrowing securities through special collateral repurchase agreements—became as costly as failure to deliver what was promised.

Fortunately, two critical government agencies reacted quickly. The Federal Reserve poured liquid funds into the banking system so that emergency money was available. The U.S. Treasury, even though it didn't need to borrow additional funds at the time, announced the reopening of a key security issue—the 10-year T-note that was currently "on the run." The Treasury's same day ("snap") auction expanded the supply of these particular notes by 50 percent, which helped to make borrowing these securities a superior alternative than simply failing to settle.

An excellent article prepared by two staff officers at the Federal Reserve Bank of New York, Michael J. Fleming and Kenneth D. Garbade, offers some proposals for the future, should a tragedy of comparable magnitude happen again. These proposals include setting up a special facility inside the Treasury that would be able to lend securities experiencing excess demand. Moreover, in order to provide an incentive to avoid settlement fails, a special penalty fee might be imposed. Fails are of particular concern because they threaten securities market participants with serious loss and even bankruptcy.

Source: Michael J. Fleming and Kenneth D. Garbade, "When the Back Office Moved to the Front Burner: Settlement Fails in the Treasury Market After 9/11," *Economic Policy Review,* Federal Reserve Bank of New York, November 2002, pp. 35–58.

To evaluate the attractiveness of municipals, financial firms calculate the net after-tax returns and/or the tax-equivalent yields to enable comparisons with other investment alternatives. The net after-tax return of bank-qualified municipals is calculated as follows:

$$
\begin{array}{l}
\begin{array}{l}\text{Net after-tax}\\\text{return on}\\\text{municipals}\\\text{(in percent)}\end{array} =
\left[
\begin{array}{l}\text{Nominal return}\\\text{on municipals}\\\text{after taxes}\\\text{(in percent)}\end{array} -
\begin{array}{l}\text{Interest expense incurred}\\\text{in acquiring the}\\\text{municipals}\\\text{(in percent)}\end{array}
\right] \qquad \textbf{(4)}\\[3em]
\qquad\qquad\qquad +\ \begin{array}{c}\text{Tax advantage}\\\text{of a}\\\text{qualified bond}\end{array}
\end{array}
$$

where the tax advantage of a qualified bond is determined like this:

$$
\begin{array}{c}
\text{Tax advantage} \\
\text{of} \\
\text{qualified} \\
\text{bond}
\end{array}
=
\begin{bmatrix}
\text{The bank's} & \text{Percentage of} & \text{Interest} \\
\text{marginal} & \text{interest expense} & \text{expense of} \\
\text{income} & \times \quad \text{that is still} & \times \text{ acquiring the} \\
\text{tax rate} & \text{tax deductible} & \text{municipals} \\
\text{(in percent)} & \text{(if any)} & \text{(in percent)}
\end{bmatrix}
\tag{5}
$$

Suppose a bank purchases a bank-qualified bond from a small city, county, or school district issuing no more than $10 million in securities annually, and the bond carries a nominal (published) gross rate of return of 7 percent. Assume also that the bank had to borrow the funds needed to make this purchase at an interest rate of 6.5 percent and is in the top (35 percent) income tax bracket. Because this bond comes from a small local government that qualifies for special tax treatment under the 1986 Tax Reform Act, the bond's net annual after-tax return to the bank (after all funding costs and taxes) must be as follows:

$$
\begin{array}{l}
\text{Net after-tax return} \\
\quad \text{on a qualified} \\
\text{municipal security}
\end{array}
\begin{array}{l}
= (7.0 - 6.50) + (0.35 \times 0.80 \times 6.50) \\[4pt]
= 0.50 \text{ percent} + 1.82 \text{ percent} \\[4pt]
= 2.32 \text{ percent}
\end{array}
\tag{6}
$$

The investments officer would want to compare this calculated net after-tax rate of return to the net returns after taxes available from other securities and loans, both taxable and tax-exempt.

Notice, however, that if the municipal bond described previously had come from a larger state or local government not eligible for special treatment under the Tax Reform Act, *none* of the interest expense would have been tax deductible and the tax advantage would be zero. In this case, the bank's net after-tax return from the municipal bond is:

$$
\begin{array}{l}
\text{Net after-tax} \\
\quad \text{return on} \\
\text{municipals}
\end{array}
= 7.00 - 6.50 = 0.50 \text{ percent, or 50 basis points}
$$

As we saw earlier, it is often useful to translate a tax-exempt bond's expected return into the tax-equivalent yield (TEY). In other words, we want to find the before-tax return on taxable bonds (TEY) that provides the investor with the same after-tax return as a particular investment in tax-exempt securities. The equation that expresses this is

$$\text{TEY} \times (1 - \text{marginal tax rate}) = \text{after-tax return on municipals}$$

$$
\text{TEY} \times (1 - \text{marginal tax rate}) =
\boxed{
\begin{array}{c}
\text{Nominal} \\
\text{return on} \\
\text{municipals}
\end{array}
}
+
\boxed{
\begin{array}{c}
\text{Tax-advantage of} \\
\text{qualified bonds}
\end{array}
}
\tag{7}
$$

$$
\text{TEY} \times (1 - \text{marginal tax rate}) =
\boxed{
\begin{array}{c}
\text{Nominal} \\
\text{return on} \\
\text{municipals}
\end{array}
}
\tag{8}
$$

$$
+
\begin{bmatrix}
\text{The bank's} & \text{Percentage of} & \text{Interest} \\
\text{marginal} & \text{interest expense} & \text{expense of} \\
\text{income tax} & \times \quad \text{that is} & \times \quad \text{acquiring} \\
\text{bracket} & \text{deductible} & \text{the security}
\end{bmatrix}
$$

RISKY AND COMPLEX INVESTMENTS ON THE RISE: RANGE NOTES, BANK OFFICER LIFE INSURANCE (BOLI), EQUITY-LINKED CDS, AND TRUST-PREFERRED SECURITIES

In recent years banks and other depository institutions have had the tendency to accept greater risk and complexity in their investment portfolios. New instruments have appeared that are intended to do more than just provide liquidity and income, especially when loan demand is weak. Four prominent examples of this trend include range notes, bank officer life insurance (BOLI), equity-linked CDs, and trust-preferred securities.

Range notes are callable securities that usually promise relatively high coupon interest rates contingent on which way the market moves. These notes pay out interest provided an agreed-upon market index stays within a specified range. If the market index moves outside the designated range, there is no payoff. For example, a range note might call for paying its holder interest only if LIBOR stays between 2 and 4 percent.

Banks and other institutions in recent years have often purchased *life insurance on their officers and directors (BOLI)*, with the purchasing firm designated as beneficiary. As long as the purchaser continues to pay the annual premiums, the BOLI is recorded as an asset on its books. If the officer or director dies during the policy's term the purchasing institution receiving the funds has several options, including donating the proceeds to a charity and securing a tax deduction.

Equity-linked CDs contain features of both debt and stock. They promise guaranteed interest income and provide an embedded option, offering an additional bonus based on a market index (most often the Standard & Poor's 500 stock index). For example, a bull CD with an embedded call option scores additional returns if the market index rises above a designated strike price. Alternatively, a bear CD contains a put option that pays off only if the market index falls below the strike price.

Finally, *trust-preferred securities* also have both stock and debt characteristics. Generally these instruments are created with the help of an investment banker who sets up a special purpose entity (SPV) that issues preferred shares. In return, the participating financial institution issues long-term debentures (usually 30 or more years to maturity) to support the new stock. Multiple possible payoffs include that the debentures are considered new capital, the interest paid out is tax deductible, and the risk of shareholder dilution is reduced.

Regulatory agencies (e.g., the FDIC and the Comptroller of the Currency) have expressed serious concern in recent years that many such investments carry considerable credit and liquidity risk (often the resale market is poor), with subpar yields. Regulators today insist that purchasing institutions do a careful *prepurchase analysis* of these investments and employ *stress testing* to determine what the possible risk exposure would be under different market conditions. See, for example, such informative websites as **www.fdic.gov**, **www.emis.de/journals**, **www.wib.org**, and **www.aba.com**.

Using the example of bonds issued by small cities and other small local units of government, we find the TEY on the 7 percent municipal bond discussed previously to be

$$\text{TEY} = \frac{7.00 + 1.82}{(1 - .35)}$$

$$= \frac{8.82}{0.65}$$

$$= 13.57 \text{ percent.}$$

If other factors are held constant, a taxable security, such as a corporate bond or U.S. government bond, would have to carry a yield of at least 13.57 percent to have the same after-tax return to a bank as the tax-exempt municipal bond described previously.

The Tax Swapping Tool   The size of a bank's or other lender's revenue from loans in any given year also plays a key role in how its security investments are handled. In years when loan revenues are high, it is often beneficial to engage in tax swapping. In a **tax swap,** the bank or other lending institution usually sells lower-yielding securities at a loss in order to reduce its current taxable income, while simultaneously purchasing new high-yielding securities in order to boost future expected returns on its investment portfolio.

Tax considerations in choosing securities to buy or sell tend to be more important for larger lending institutions than for smaller ones. Usually the larger lending institutions are in the top income-tax bracket and have the most to gain from security portfolio trades that minimize their tax exposure. The security portfolio manager tries to estimate the institution's projected net taxable income under alternative portfolio choices.

This involves, among other things, estimating how much tax-exempt income the taxed lending institution can use. No bank or other lending institution can use unlimited amounts of tax-exempt income. For banks and thrift institutions, at least some taxable income will be necessary to offset the allowable annual deduction for possible loan losses. However, once these conditions are met, the basic decision between purchasing tax-exempt securities or purchasing taxable securities and loans comes down to the relative after-tax returns of the two.

The Portfolio Shifting Tool   Banks and other lending institutions also do a great deal of **portfolio shifting** in their holdings of investment securities, with both taxes and higher returns in mind. Banks, for example, often sell off selected securities at a loss in order to offset large amounts of loan income, thereby reducing their tax liability. They may also shift their portfolios simply to substitute new, higher-yielding securities for old security holdings whose yields are well below current market levels. The result may be to take substantial short-run losses in return for the prospect of higher long-run profits.

For example, the investments officer of First National Bank may be considering the following shift in its municipal bond portfolio:

Find a buyer for $10 million in 10-year New York City bonds bearing a 7 percent coupon rate that the bank currently holds.	→	Current market price Value recorded on the bank's balance sheet Annual interest income	= = =	$9.5 million $10 million $0.7 million
Then acquire $10 million in 10-year Orange County (City of Los Angeles) bonds bearing a 9 percent coupon rate to add to the bank's investment portfolio.	→	Current market price Annual interest income	= =	$10 million $0.9 million

Clearly, this bank takes an immediate $500,000 loss before taxes ($10 million − $9.5 million) on selling the 7 percent New York City bonds. But if First National is in the 35 percent tax bracket, its immediate loss after taxes becomes only $500,000 × (1 − 0.35), or $325,000. Moreover, it has swapped this loss for an additional $200,000 annually in tax-exempt income for 10 years. This portfolio shift is probably worth the immediate loss the bank must absorb from its current earnings. Moreover, if the bank has high taxable income from its loans, that near-term loss can be used to lower current taxable income and perhaps even increase this year's after-tax profits.

Interest-Rate Risk

Changing interest rates create real risk for investments officers and their institutions. Rising interest rates lower the market value of previously issued bonds and notes, with the longest-term security issues generally suffering the greatest losses. Moreover, periods of rising interest rates are often marked by surging loan demand. Because a lender's first priority is to make loans, many security investments must be sold off to generate cash for lending. Such sales frequently result in substantial capital losses, which the lender hopes to counteract by a combination of tax benefits and the relatively higher yields available on loans. A growing number of tools to hedge (counteract) **interest-rate risk** have appeared in recent years, including financial futures, options, interest-rate swaps, gap management, and duration, as we saw earlier in Chapters 6–8.

Credit or Default Risk

The security investments made by banks and by their closest competitors are closely regulated due to the **credit risk** displayed by many securities, especially those issued by private corporations and some local governments. The risk that the security issuer may default on the principal or interest owed on a bond or note has led to regulatory controls that prohibit the acquisition of speculative securities—those rated below Baa by Moody's or BBB on Standard & Poor's bond-rating schedule. (See Table 9–4 for definitions of the various credit rating symbols used today on debt securities.) U.S. banks generally are allowed to buy only *investment-grade securities*, rated at least Baa or BBB, in order to protect the depositors against excessive risk. Moreover, banks through their securities affiliates or through the formation of a financial holding company are permitted to underwrite (i.e., purchase for resale) government and privately issued securities (including corporate bonds, notes, and stock). (See Chapters 1, 2, and 3 for a review of legislative, regulatory, and court decisions that have significantly expanded the security underwriting powers of banking organizations in recent years.)

In January 1997 Moody's Investors Service announced significant modification in its credit rating system for bonds issued by state and local (municipal) governments. Specif-

TABLE 9–4 Default Risk Ratings on Marketable Securities

Investment securities sold by corporations and state and local governments must be assigned credit ratings that assess their probability of default before they can be successfully marketed. Over the past century, the two most popular private security rating companies have been Moody's Investor Service and Standard & Poor's Corporation. Their credit quality rating symbols have served as general guides for assessing the credit quality of investment securities for bankers and other financial institutions for decades:

| Credit Quality of Securities | Rating Symbols | | |
	Moody's Rating Category	Standard & Poor's Rating Category	
Best quality/smallest investment risk	Aaa	AAA	Investment quality or
High grade or high quality	Aa	AA	investment grade/
Upper medium grade	A	A	considered acceptable
Medium grade	Baa	BBB	for most banks
Medium grade with some speculative elements	Ba	BB	
Lower medium grade	B	B	Speculative quality and
Poor standing/may be in default	Caa	CCC	junk bonds/not considered
Speculative/often in default	Ca	CC	suitable for most banks
Lowest-grade speculative securities/ poor prospects	C	C	
Defaulted securities and securities issued by firms that have declared bankruptcy	Not rated	DDD DD D	

Most depository institutions are limited to investment-grade securities—that is, they must purchase securities rated AAA to BBB (by Standard & Poor's) or Aaa to Baa (by Moody's). Unrated securities may also be acquired, but the investing institution must be able to demonstrate that they are of investment-grade quality.

ically, securities in selected categories (such as Aa, A, and Baa) have a 2 or 3 numerical modifier added to their rating to differentiate securities slightly different in quality that carry similar letter credit grades. In 1981 Moody's added the number 1 to the letter grades attached to some A- and B-rated municipals. Now, with the numbers 2 and 3 also added to some letter grades, an investments officer is alerted that a 1 means the municipal security in question ranks at the upper end of its letter rating category, while 2 implies the issue lies in the middle range of its letter rating group and 3 suggests the security in question lies at the low end of the letter grade category. These 1, 2, and 3 numerical modifiers were also added to corporate bond ratings from Aa to B a number of years ago:

Moody's Investor Service's
New Credit Rating Symbols for
State and Local Government Securities

Aaa	
Aa1	Ba1
Aa2	Ba2
Aa3	Ba3
A1	B1
A2	B2
A3	B3
Baa1	Caa
Baa2	Ca
Baa3	C

The new rating modifiers reflect growing concern about recent trends in the municipal market, especially increased credit risk and volatility.

There has been a fluctuating, but general, uptrend in municipal defaults over the past three decades. In 1991 a record 258 municipal bond defaults occurred, involving about $5 billion in total defaulted IOUs. While the number of defaulted issues annually has since fallen somewhat, many state and local governments are under great stress today due to declining federal monies to support local welfare, health (including medicare), and other programs; rising needs for street, sewer, bridge, and other infrastructure repairs; higher energy costs; and local taxpayer resistance to higher taxes. Moreover, with many local areas opposing new taxes and spending programs, more state and local governments have turned to more risky revenue bonds to supplement their financing options.

As we saw in the preceding chapter, bankers and other financial-service managers have helped develop new methods for dealing with credit risk in both their investments and their loans in recent years. Credit options and swaps can be used to protect the expected yield on investment securities. For example, bank investment officers may be able to find another financial institution, often an insurance company, willing to swap an uncertain return on securities the bank holds for a lower but more certain return based upon a standard reference interest rate, such as the market yield on Treasury bills. Credit options are also available in today's markets that help to hedge the value of a corporate bond, for example. If the bond issuer defaults, the option holder receives a payoff from the credit option that at least partially offsets the bond's loss. Investment officers can also use credit options to protect the price (market value) of a bond in case its credit rating is lowered, dropping its value. In this instance the option holder receives a payoff from the option writer if the bond's credit rating falls.

Business Risk

Banks and other financial institutions of all sizes face significant risk that the economy of the market area they serve may turn down, with falling business sales and rising bankruptcies and unemployment. These adverse developments, often called **business risk,** would be reflected quickly in the loan portfolio, where delinquent loans would rise as borrowers struggled to generate enough cash flow to pay the lender. Because business risk is always present, many banks and other financial institutions rely heavily on their security portfolios to offset the impact of economic risk on their loan portfolios. This usually means that many of the investment securities purchased will come from borrowers located outside the principal market for loans. For example, a bank located in Dallas or Kansas City will probably purchase a substantial quantity of municipal bonds from cities and other local governments outside the Midwest (e.g., Los Angeles or New York debt securities). Bank and thrift examiners encourage out-of-market security purchases to balance risk exposure in the loan portfolio.

Liquidity Risk

Banks and competing financial institutions must be ever mindful of the possibility they will be required to sell investment securities in advance of their maturity due to liquidity needs and be subjected to **liquidity risk.** Thus, a key issue that a portfolio manager must face in selecting a security for investment purposes is *the breadth and depth of its resale market.* Liquid securities are, by definition, those investments that have a ready market, relatively stable price over time, and high probability of recovering the original amount invested (i.e., the risk to principal is low). U.S. Treasury securities are generally the most liquid and have the most active resale markets, followed by federal agency securities, municipal bonds, and mortgage-backed securities. Unfortunately, the purchase of a large volume of liquid, readily marketable securities tends to lower the average yield from a financial institution's earning assets and, other factors held constant, tends to reduce its profitability. Thus, management faces a trade-off between profitability and liquidity that must be reevaluated daily as market interest rates and exposure to liquidity risk change.

Call Risk

Many corporations and some governments that issue investment securities reserve the right to call in those instruments in advance of their maturity and pay them off. Because such calls usually take place when market interest rates have declined (and the borrower can issue new securities bearing lower interest costs), the financial firm investing in callable bonds and notes runs the risk of an earnings loss because it must reinvest its recovered funds at today's lower interest rates. Investments officers generally try to minimize this **call risk** by purchasing bonds bearing longer call deferments (so that a call cannot occur for several years) or simply by avoiding the purchase of callable securities. Fortunately for bank investments officers and other active investors, call privileges attached to bonds have been declining significantly in recent years due to the availability of other tools to manage interest-rate risk.

Prepayment Risk

A form of risk specific to certain kinds of investment securities—especially asset-backed securities—that financial firms buy for their investment portfolios is known as **prepayment risk.** This form of risk arises because the realized interest and principal payments (cash flow) from a pool of securitized loans, such as GNMA or FNMA pass-throughs, collateralized mortgage obligations (CMOs), or securitized packages of auto or credit card loans, may be quite different from the payments (cash flow) expected originally. Indeed, having to price the prepayment option associated with asset-backed securities distinguishes these investments from any other investment securities.

For example, consider what can happen to the planned interest and principal payments from a pool of home mortgage loans that serve as collateral for the issuance of mortgage-backed securities. Variations in cash flow to holders of the securities backed by these loans can arise from

A. *Loan refinancings*, which tend to accelerate when market interest rates fall significantly and yield curves achieve a substantial positive slope (in this case, borrowers may come to believe that they will save on loan payments if they replace their existing loan with a new lower-rate loan).
B. *Turnover of the assets behind the loan* (in this case borrowers may sell out and move away or some borrowers may not be able to meet their required loan payments and default on their loans).

In either or both of these cases some loans will be terminated or paid off ahead of schedule, generating smaller or larger cash flows sooner than expected that can lower the expected rate of return to a bank or other investing institution that has purchased loan-backed securities.

The pace at which loans that underlie asset-backed investment securities are terminated or paid off depends heavily upon the interest rate spread between current interest rates on similar type loans and the interest rates attached to loans in the securitized pool. When market interest rates drop below the interest rates attached to loans in the pool far enough to cover refinancing costs, more and more borrowers will call in their loans and pay them off early. This means that the market value of a loan-backed security depends not only upon the promised cash flows (interest and principal payments) it will generate, but also on the projected prepayments and loan defaults that occur—that is,

$$
\begin{array}{c}
\text{Market value} \\
\text{(price) of a} \\
\text{loan-backed} \\
\text{security}
\end{array}
=
\frac{
\begin{array}{c}
\text{Expected cash flows} \\
\text{adjusted for any} \\
\text{prepayments or} \\
\text{defaults of} \\
\text{existing loans in} \\
\text{the pool in Period 1}
\end{array}
}{(1 + y/m)^1}
+ \cdots +
\frac{
\begin{array}{c}
\text{Expected cash flows} \\
\text{adjusted for any} \\
\text{prepayments or} \\
\text{defaults of} \\
\text{existing loans in} \\
\text{the pool in Period n} \times \text{m}
\end{array}
}{(1 + y/m)^{n \times m}}
\qquad \textbf{(9)}
$$

where n is the number of years required for the last of the loans in the pool to be paid off or retired, m represents the number of times during the year interest and principal must be paid to holders of the loan-backed securities, and y is the expected yield to maturity from these securities.

In order to properly value an asset-backed security, the investments officer needs to make some reasonable assumptions about what volume of loans might be prepaid or terminated while his or her institution is holding the security. In making estimates of loan prepayment behavior, the investments officer must consider such factors as expected market interest rates, future changes in the shape of the yield curve, the impact of seasonal factors (e.g., in the case of home-mortgage-backed securities, most homes are bought and sold in the spring of each year), the condition of the economy and the availability of jobs, and how old the loans in the pool are (because new loans are less likely to be repaid than older loans).

One commonly employed way of making loan prepayment estimates is to use the prepayment model developed by the Public Securities Association (PSA), which calculates an average loan prepayment rate based upon past experience. The so-called PSA model assumes, for example, that insured home mortgages will prepay at an annual rate of 0.2 percent the first month and the prepayment rate will grow by 0.2 percent each month for the first 30 months. Loan prepayments are then assumed to level off at a 6 percent annual rate for the remainder of the loan pool's life. When an investments officer adopts the PSA model without any modifications, he or she is said to be assuming a 100 percent PSA repayment rate. However, the investments officer may decide to alter the PSA model to 75 percent PSA, 110 percent PSA, or some other percentage multiplier based upon his or her special knowledge of the nature of loans in the pool, such as their geographic location, distribution of maturities, or the average age of borrowers.

It must be noted that while prepayment of securitized loans tends to accelerate in periods of falling interest rates, this is not always an adverse development for banks and other holders of asset-backed securities. For example, as prepayments accelerate, a bank or thrift institution investing in these assets recovers its invested cash at a faster rate, which can be a favorable development if it has other profitable uses for those funds, such as making direct loans to customers. Moreover, lower interest rates increase the present value of all projected cash flows from a loan-backed security so that its market value could rise. The investments officer must compare these potential benefits to the potential losses from falling interest payments in the form of lower reinvestment rates and lost future income from loans that are prepaid. In general, asset-backed securities will fall in value when interest rates decline if the expected loss of interest income from prepaid loans and reduced reinvestment earnings exceeds the benefits that arise from recovering cash more quickly from prepaid loans and from the higher present values attached to expected cash flows.

Inflation Risk

Key URLs
To explore the recent growth of the asset or loan-backed securities market and bank activity in that market see especially **www .dresdnerbank.lu** and **www.fanniemae .com**.

While there is less of a problem today than in some earlier periods, banks and other investing institutions must be alert to the possibility that the purchasing power of both the interest income and repaid principal from a security or loan will be eroded by rising prices for goods and services. Inflation can also erode the value of the stockholders' investment in a bank or other institution—its *net worth*. Some protection against **inflation risk** is provided by short-term securities and those with variable interest rates, which usually grant the investments officer greater flexibility in responding to any flare-up in inflationary pressures.

One new inflation risk hedge that may aid some banks and other financial firms is the United States Treasury Department's new TIPS, or Treasury Inflation-Protected Securities. Beginning in January 1997 the Treasury began issuing 5–, 10–, and 30-year marketable notes and bonds and later announced the offering of inflation-protected small-denomination savings bonds. Both the coupon interest rate and the principal (face) value of a TIPS are adjusted annually to match changes in the consumer price index (CPI). Thus far, TIPS have met with limited enthusiasm, in part because they represent only one of many possible inflation-hedging instruments and pay a relatively low real rate of return. To date, banks and most other financial institutions have not been especially heavy investors in these inflation-adjusted instruments due to the relatively subdued inflation rate the U.S. economy has experienced in recent years.

Concept Check

9–8. How is the expected yield on most bonds determined?

9–9. If a government bond is expected to mature in two years and has a current price of $950, what is the bond's YTM if it has a par value of $1,000 and a promised coupon rate of 10 percent? Suppose this bond is sold one year after purchase for a price of $970. What would this investor's holding period yield be?

9–10. What forms of risk affect security investments?

9–11. How has the tax exposure of various U.S. bank security investments changed in recent years?

9–12. Suppose a corporate bond an investments officer would like to purchase for her bank has a before-tax yield of 8.98 percent and the bank is in the 35 percent federal income tax bracket. What is the bond's after-tax gross yield? What after-tax rate of return must a prospective loan generate to be competitive with the corporate bond? Does a loan have some advantages for a bank or other lending institution that a corporate bond would not have?

9–13. What is the net after-tax return on a qualified municipal security whose nominal gross return is 6 percent, the cost of borrowed funds is 5 percent, and the bank holding the bond is in the 35 percent tax bracket? What is the tax-equivalent yield (TEY) on this tax-exempt security?

9–14. Spiro Savings Bank currently holds a government bond valued on the day of its purchase at $5 million, with a promised interest yield of 6 percent, whose current market value is $3.9 million. Comparable quality bonds are available today for a promised yield of 8 percent. What are the advantages to Spiro Savings from selling the government bond bearing a 6 percent promised yield and buying some 8 percent bonds?

9–15. What is tax swapping? What is portfolio shifting? Give an example of each.

9–16. Why do banks and other depository institutions face pledging requirements when they accept government deposits?

9–17. What types of securities are used to meet collateralization requirements?

Pledging Requirements

Depository institutions in the United States cannot accept deposits from federal, state, and local governments unless they post collateral acceptable to these governmental units in order to safeguard the deposit of public funds. The first $100,000 of these public deposits is covered by federal deposit insurance; the rest must be backed up by holdings of U.S. Treasury and federal agency securities valued at par. Some municipal bonds (provided they are at least A-rated) can also be used to secure the federal government's deposits in banks and other depository institutions, but these securities must be valued at a discount from par (usually only 80 to 90 percent of their face value) in order to give governmental depositors an added cushion of safety. State and local government deposit **pledging** requirements differ widely from state to state, though most allow banks to use a combination of federal and municipal securities to meet government pledging requirements. Sometimes the government owning the deposit requires that the pledged securities be placed with a trustee not affiliated with the institution receiving the deposit.

Pledging requirements also exist for selected other bank liabilities. For example, when a bank borrows from the discount window of the Federal Reserve bank in its district, it must pledge either federal government securities or other collateral acceptable to the Fed. If a bank or other financial institution uses repurchase agreements (RPs) to raise money, it must pledge some of its securities (usually U.S. Treasury and federal agency issues) as collateral in order to receive funds at the low RP interest rate.

Investment Maturity Strategies

Once the investments officer chooses the type of securities he or she believes a financial firm should hold, based on their expected return and risk, pledging requirements, tax exposure, and other factors, there remains the question of how to distribute those security holdings over time. That is, what *maturities* of securities should the bank or other investing institution hold? Should it purchase mainly short-term bills and notes, or only long-term bonds, or perhaps some combination of the two? Several alternative maturity distribution strategies have been developed over the years, each with its own unique set of advantages and disadvantages. (See Exhibits 9–2 and 9–3.)

EXHIBIT 9–2

Alternative Maturity Strategies for Managing Investment Portfolios

STRATEGY: Divide investment portfolio equally among all maturities acceptable to the bank or other investing institution.
ADVANTAGES: Reduces investment income fluctuations/requires little management expertise.

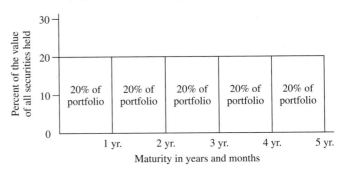

The Ladder or Spaced-Maturity Policy

STRATEGY: All security investments are short-term.
ADVANTAGES: Strengthens the financial firm's liquidity position and avoids large capital losses if market interest rates rise.

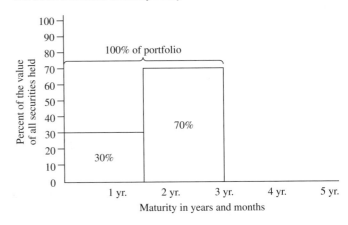

The Front-End Load Maturity Policy

STRATEGY: All security investments are long-term.
ADVANTAGES: Maximizes the financial firm's income potential from security investments if market interest rates fall.

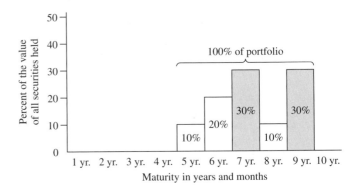

The Back-End Load Maturity Policy

The Ladder, or Spaced-Maturity, Policy   One popular approach to the maturity prob-lem, particularly among smaller financial institutions, is to choose some maximum ac-ceptable maturity and then invest in an equal proportion of securities in each of several maturity intervals until the maximum acceptable maturity is reached.

For example, suppose the management of a bank decided that it did not want to pur-chase any bonds or notes with maturities longer than five years. This bank might then decide to invest 20 percent of its investment portfolio in securities one year or less from maturity, another 20 percent in securities maturing within two years but no less than one year, another 20 percent in the interval of two to three years, and so forth, until the five-year point is reached. This strategy certainly does *not* maximize investment income, but it has the advantage of reducing income fluctuations and requires little management expertise to carry out. Moreover, this ladder approach tends to build in investment flexi-bility. Because some securities are always rolling over into cash, the bank can take advan-tage of any promising opportunities that may appear.

The Front-End Loan Maturity Policy   Another popular strategy is to purchase only short-term securities and place all investments within a certain brief interval of time. For example, the investments officer may decide to invest 100 percent of his or her institu-tion's funds not needed for loans or cash reserves in securities three years or less from ma-turity. This approach stresses using the investment portfolio primarily as a source of *liq-uidity* rather than as a source of income.

The Back-End Load Maturity Policy   An opposite approach would stress the invest-ment portfolio as a source of *income*. A bank or other investing institution following the so-called *back-end load* approach might decide to invest only in bonds in the 5- to

EXHIBIT 9–3
Additional Maturity
Strategies for
Managing Bank
Investment Portfolios

STRATEGY:
Security holdings
are divided between
short-term and
long-term.
ADVANTAGES:
Helps to meet a
financial institution's
liquidity needs with
short-term securities
and to achieve earnings
goals due to higher
potential earnings from
the long-term
portfolio.

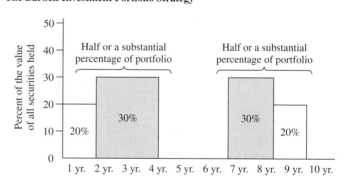

The Barbell Investment Portfolio Strategy

STRATEGY:
Change the mix of
investment maturities
as the interest-rate
outlook changes.
ADVANTAGES:
Maximizes the
potential for earnings
(and also for losses).

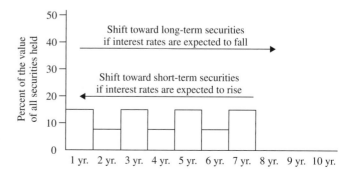

The Rate-Expectations Approach

10-year maturity range. This institution would probably rely heavily on borrowing in the money market to help meet its liquidity requirements.

The Barbell Strategy A combination of the front-end and back-end load approaches is the *barbell strategy*, in which a bank or other investing institution places most of its funds in a short-term portfolio of highly liquid securities at one extreme and in a long-term portfolio of bonds at the other extreme, with minimal or no investment holdings in intermediate maturities. The short-term portfolio provides liquidity, while the long-term portfolio is designed to generate income.

The Rate Expectations Approach The most aggressive of all maturity strategies is one that continually shifts maturities of securities held in line with current forecasts of interest rates and the economy. This *total performance*, or *rate expectation*, approach calls for shifting investments toward the short end of the maturity spectrum when interest rates are expected to rise and toward the long end when falling interest rates are expected. Such an approach offers the potential for large capital gains, but also raises the specter of substantial capital losses. It requires in-depth knowledge of market forces, presents greater risk if expectations turn out to be wrong, and carries greater transactions costs because it may require frequent security trading and switching.

Banks, in particular, do not hesitate to trade their unpledged security holdings whenever there is the prospect of significant gains in expected returns or the opportunity to reduce asset risk without a significant loss in expected yield. They are particularly aggressive when loan revenues are down and the sale of securities whose market value has risen will boost net income and shareholder returns. However, because losses on security trades reduce before-tax net income, portfolio managers do not like to take such losses unless they can demonstrate to the institution's board of directors that the loss will be more than made up by higher expected returns on any new assets acquired from the proceeds of the security sale. In general, banks and other investing institutions are inclined to trade securities if (*a*) their expected after-tax returns can be raised through effective tax management strategies, (*b*) higher yields can be locked in at the long-term end of the yield curve when the forecast is for falling interest rates, (*c*) the trade would contribute to an overall improvement in asset quality that would enable the institution to better weather an economic downturn, or (*d*) the investment portfolio can be moved toward higher-grade securities without an appreciable loss in expected return, especially if problems are developing in the loan portfolio.

Maturity Management Tools

In choosing among various maturities of short-term and long-term securities to acquire, investments officers need to consider carefully the use of two key maturity management tools—the *yield curve* and *duration*. These two tools help the investments officer understand more fully the consequences and potential impact upon earnings and risk of his institution from any particular maturity mix of securities he chooses.

The Yield Curve

As we saw in Chapter 6, the **yield curve** is simply a picture of how market interest rates differ across loans and securities of varying term or time to maturity. Each yield curve, such as the one drawn in Exhibit 9–4, assumes that all interest rates (or yields) included along the curve are measured at the same time and that all other rate-determining forces are held constant. While the curve in Exhibit 9–4 slopes upward as we move to the right, yield

EXHIBIT 9–4
The Yield Curve

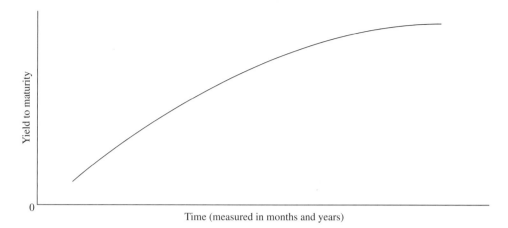

curves may also slope downward or be horizontal, indicating that short- and long-term interest rates at that particular moment are about the same.

Yield curve shapes have several critical implications for the decisions an investments officer must make. For example, the yield curve contains an *implicit forecast of future interest rate changes*. Positively sloped yield curves reflect the average expectation in the market that future short-term interest rates will be higher than they are today. In this case, investors expect to see an upward interest-rate movement, and they translate this expectation into action by shifting their investment holdings away from longer-term securities (which will incur the greatest capital losses when market interest rates do rise) toward shorter-term securities. Thus, banks and other investing institutions following the interest-rate expectations approach to security management will tend to avoid purchasing long-term securities because their market prices are expected to fall, generating future losses, and will place more emphasis on shorter-term securities. Conversely, a downward-sloping yield curve points to investor expectations of declining short-term interest rates in the period ahead. The investments officer will probably consider lengthening the maturities of at least some portion of his or her institution's security portfolio, because falling interest rates offer the prospect of substantial capital gains income from longer-term securities.

In the short run, yield curves provide the investments officer with a clue about over-priced and underpriced securities. Because the yield curve indicates what the yield to maturity should be for each maturity of security, a security whose yield lies above the curve at a particular maturity represents a tempting *buy* situation; its yield is temporarily too high (and, therefore, its price is too low). On the other hand, a security whose yield lies below the curve represents a possible *sell* or "don't buy" situation because its yield, momentarily, is too low for its maturity (and, thus, its price is too high). In the long run, yield curves send signals about what stage of the business cycle the economy presently occupies. They generally rise in economic expansions and fall in recessions.

The yield curve is also useful because it tells the investments officer something important about the *current trade-offs between seeking greater returns and accepting greater risks*. The yield curve's shape determines how much additional yield the investments officer can earn by replacing shorter-term securities with longer-term issues, or vice verse. For example, a steeply sloped positive yield curve that rises 150 basis points between 5-year and 10-year maturity bonds indicates that the investments officer can pick up 1.5 percentage points in extra yield (less broker or dealer commissions and any tax liability incurred) by switching from 5-year bonds to 10-year bonds. However, 10-year bonds are generally more volatile in price than 5-year bonds, so the investments officer must be willing to accept greater risk of a capital loss on the 10-year bonds if interest rates rise. Longer-term bonds are also generally less liquid, with a thinner market in case cash must be raised quickly by selling them. The investments officer can measure along the curve what gain in yield will result from maturity extension and compare that gain against the likelihood a bank or other financial firm will face a liquidity crisis ("cash out") or suffer capital losses if interest rates go in an unexpected direction.

If the yield curve has a sufficiently strong positive slope, a bank or other investing institution may be able to score significant portfolio gains with a maneuver known as *riding the yield curve*. The investments officer looks for a situation in which some securities are approaching maturity and their prices have risen significantly while their yields to maturity have fallen. If the yield curve's slope is steep enough to more than cover transactions costs, the investing institution can sell those securities, scoring a capital gain due to the rise in their prices, and reinvest the proceeds of that sale in longer-term securities carrying higher rates of return. If the riding maneuver works (i.e., the slope of the yield curve does not fall significantly), the bank or other investing institution will reap both higher current income and greater future returns on its security portfolio.

Duration

While the yield curve presents the investments officer with valuable information and occasionally the opportunity for substantial gains in income, it has several limitations, such as uncertainty over exactly how and why the curve appears the way it does at any particular moment and the possibility of a change in the curve's shape at any time, Moreover, the yield curve concept is based on a crude, but traditional, measure of the maturity of a security—the amount of calendar time in days, weeks, months, or years remaining until any particular security will be paid off and retired. This traditional maturity measure counts only clock time, not the income or cash flow expected from a security. The most critical information for the investments officer is usually not how long any particular security will be around but, rather, *when* it will generate cash flow or income and *how much* cash will be generated each month, quarter, or year that the investment security is held.

The need for this kind of information gave rise to the concept of **duration**, a present value–weighted measure of maturity of an individual security or portfolio of securities. As we saw in Chapter 6, duration measures the average amount of time it takes for all of the cash flows from a security to reach the institution that holds it.

To illustrate how to calculate the duration of an investment security that a bank or one of its competitors might wish to buy, we use the equation illustrated in Chapter 6, Equation (1) and the example of the Treasury note presented earlier in this chapter. Recall that this was a $1,000 par value T-note scheduled to mature in five years and paying $80 per year in interest. Earlier we found that this note's yield to maturity was 10.73 percent and its current market price was $900. If interest is paid just once each year at year-end, what is this note's duration?

$$
D = \frac{\left[\begin{array}{c} \dfrac{\$80 \times 1}{(1 + 0.1073)^1} + \dfrac{\$80 \times 2}{(1 + 0.1073)^2} + \dfrac{\$80 \times 3}{(1 + 0.1073)^3} \\[2ex] + \dfrac{\$80 \times 4}{(1 + 0.1073)^4} + \dfrac{\$1,080 \times 5}{(1 + 0.1073)^5} \end{array}\right]}{\$900}
\tag{10}
$$

$$
= \frac{\$72.75 + \$130.50 + \$176.77 + \$212.85 + \$3,243.83}{\$900} = \frac{\$3,836.20}{\$900}
$$

$$
D = 4.26 \text{ years}
$$

Thus, this Treasury note will pay itself out in present value terms in 4.26 years (or about 4 years and 3 months), which is its *average* maturity considering the amount and timing of all of its expected cash flows of principal and interest.

We recall from Equation (18) in Chapter 6 that there is an important linear relationship between the duration of an investment security and its price sensitivity to interest rate changes. Specifically, the percentage change in the price of an investment security is equal to the negative of its duration times the change in interest rates divided by one plus the initial interest rate or yield.[4] To illustrate how this relationship can provide the investments officer with valuable information, consider the Treasury note whose duration we calculated to be 4.26 years. Suppose market interest rates rose from the note's current yield of 10.73 percent to 12 percent, a change in yield of 1.27 percentage points. The approximate change in the T-note's price then would be as follows:

$$\text{Percentage change in security's price} = -4.26 \times \left(\frac{0.0127}{1 + 0.1073} \right) \times 100\% = -4.89\% \tag{11}$$

In this instance, a rise in interest rates of just over one percentage point produces almost a 5 percent decline in the security's price. The investments officer must now decide how much chance there is that interest rates will rise, whether this kind of price sensitivity is acceptable, and whether other investment securities would better suit the institution's current needs.

Duration also suggests a way to minimize the damage to a bank or other institution's earnings that changes in market interest rates may cause. That is, *duration gives the investment officer a tool to reduce his or her institution's exposure to interest-rate risk*. It suggests a formula for minimizing and possibly eliminating rate risk:

$$\begin{matrix} \text{Duration of} \\ \text{an individual} \\ \text{security or a} \\ \text{security portfolio} \end{matrix} = \begin{matrix} \text{Length of the investor's} \\ \text{planned holding period} \\ \text{for a security or a} \\ \text{security portfolio} \end{matrix} \tag{12}$$

For example, suppose a bank is interested in buying U.S. Treasury notes and bonds today, perhaps because loan demand currently is weak, fears that it may be required to sell those securities at this time next year in order to accommodate its best customers when loan demand recovers. Faced with this prospect and determined to minimize interest rate risk, the investments officer could choose those government notes and bonds with a duration of one year. The effect of this step is to immunize the securities purchased from loss of return, no matter which way market interest rates go.

Duration works to immunize a security or portfolio of securities against interest rate changes because the two key forms of risk—*interest rate risk,* or the danger of falling security prices, and *reinvestment risk,* or the possibility that cash flows received from securities must be invested at lower and lower interest rates—offset each other when duration is set equal to the investing institution's planned holding period. If interest rates rise after the securities are purchased, their market price will decline, but the bank or other financial institution can reinvest the cash flow those securities are generating at higher market

---

[4] The formula described in this sentence (and presented in Chapter 6) applies if a security pays interest once each year. If interest is paid more than once each year the appropriate formula is this:

$$\text{Percentage change in price} = -\text{Duration} \times \left[\frac{\text{Change in interest rate}}{1 + (1 / m)(\text{Initial rate})} \right]$$

where m is the number of times during a year that the security pays interest. For example, most bonds pay interest semiannually, in which case m = 2.

interest rates. Similarly, if interest rates fall, the institution will be forced to reinvest the cash flow from its securities at lower interest rates but, correspondingly, the prices of those securities will have risen. The net result is to *freeze the total return from investment security holdings*. Capital gains or losses are counterbalanced by falling or rising reinvestment yields when duration equals the investing institution's planned holding period.

Concept Check

9–18. What factors affect a bank or other financial-service institution's decision regarding the different maturities of securities it should hold?

9–19. What maturity strategies do financial firms employ in managing their investment portfolios?

9–20. Bacone National Bank has structured its investment portfolio, which extends out to four-year maturities, so that it holds about $11 million each in one-year, two-year, three-year, and four-year securities. In contrast, Dunham National Bank and Trust holds $36 million in one- and two-year securities and about $30 million in 8- to 10-year maturities. What investment maturity strategy is each bank following? Why do you believe that each of these

banks has adopted the particular strategy it has as reflected in the maturity structure of its portfolio?

9–21. How can the yield curve and duration help an investments officer choose which securities to acquire or sell?

9–22. A bond currently sells for $950 based on a par value of $1,000 and promises $100 in interest for three years before being retired. Yields to maturity on comparable-quality securities are currently at 12 percent. What is the bond's duration? Suppose interest rates in the market fall to 10 percent. What will be the approximate percent change in the bond's price?

Summary

This chapter has focused on *investments* in the banking and financial-services field. What is involved in making investments and why is it important?

- For most banks and other financial-service firms, *investments* refer to the buying and selling of marketable securities, such as government bonds and notes, federal agency securities, asset-backed notes and bonds, municipal (state and local government) bonds, domestic certificates of deposit and Eurocurrency deposits, and corporate securities (including commercial paper, corporate bonds and notes, and corporate stock).

- Investments fulfill multiple roles in the management of a bank, thrift institution, or other lending institution. These roles include (*a*) supplementing income from loans and stabilizing total income; (*b*) supplying extra liquidity when cash is low; (*c*) serving as collateral for borrowings; (*d*) reducing a financial firm's tax exposure; (*e*) offsetting risks inherent in other parts of the balance sheet, such as in the loan portfolio; (*f*) dressing up the balance sheet to attract customers and capital; (*g*) helping to hedge against interest-rate risk; and (*h*) providing greater flexibility in the management of assets and liabilities.

- Some experts in the banking field refer to investments as the *crossroads account* because the investment portfolio interacts in crucial ways with most other parts of a bank's or financial firm's balance sheet, especially its cash account, loan portfolio, and liabilities.

- The *investments officer* of a bank or competing financial institution must choose what kinds of investment securities best contribute to the goals established for each institution's investment portfolio and for the financial firm as a whole. In lending-type institutions, such as banks, savings and loan associations, and credit unions, the investments portfolio normally plays "second fiddle" to the loan portfolio and the investments officer is usually charged with the responsibility of backstopping loans— providing more income when loan demand is weak and more cash (and fewer investments) when loan demand is high.

- In choosing which investment securities to acquire and hold, investments officers must weigh multiple factors: (*a*) the goal or purpose of the investments portfolio within each institution; (*b*) expected rates of return (yields) available on different financial instruments; (*c*) the financial firm's tax exposure and how any investment security might affect its current and future tax obligations; (*d*) the risks associated with changing market interest rates and the changing maturity structure of interest rates (interest-rate risk), with possible default by issuers of securities (credit risk), with the possible need for liquidity (cash) at any time (liquidity risk), with the impact of inflation and business cycle risk upon interest rates and the demand for financial services, and with the prepayment of loans pledged behind asset-backed securities that can reduce their expected returns (prepayment risk).

- An additional factor that investments officers of banks and other financial institutions must consider is the *maturity* or *duration* of different investment securities. Maturity refers to the term structure of interest rates or the spread between rates attached to shorter-term versus longer-term securities, often represented by the *yield curve*. Yield curves convey information about the market's outlook for market interest rates and graphically illustrate the trade-off between risk and return that confronts the investments officer at a moment in time. Duration, on the other hand, provides a picture of the time distribution of expected cash flows from investments and can be used to help reduce a financial firm's exposure to interest-rate risk.

- Most banks and other financial firms have a preferred range of maturities and durations for the investments they make, with banks and other depository institutions tending to focus upon comparatively short and midrange maturities or durations, and many of their competitors, such as insurance companies and pension funds, tending to reach heavily into the longest maturities or durations of investments available. Investment decisions about the desired maturity structure or duration of instruments inside the investment portfolio affect that portfolio's sensitivity to risk and its capacity for generating income for the investing institution.

- Clearly, investments officers have one of the toughest jobs inside a bank or other investing institution, with multiple tasks to perform and multiple factors to weigh each time they buy or sell investment instruments. Often investments officers working for a lending institution, such as a bank or savings and loan association, feel that they "cannot win" because they are often compelled to *sell* bonds and other investment securities for cash when loan demand is high, but security prices are falling, and to *buy* bonds and other securities to generate income when loan demand is low, but, unfortunately, security prices are high. Sometimes it's a thankless task!

Key Terms

money market instruments, 308
capital market instruments, 309
U.S. Treasury bill, 311
Treasury notes, 311
Treasury bonds, 311
federal agency securities, 311
certificate of deposit (CD), 312
bankers' acceptances, 312

commercial paper, 313
municipal bonds, 314
corporate notes, 314
corporate bonds, 314
securitized assets, 315
mortgage-backed bond, 316
stripped security, 316
yield to maturity (YTM), 320
holding period yield (HPY), 320
tax swap, 324

portfolio shifting, 325
interest-rate risk, 326
credit risk, 326
business risk, 328
liquidity risk, 328
call risk, 328
prepayment risk, 328
inflation risk, 330
pledging, 331
yield curve, 334
duration, 336

www.mhhe.com/rose6e

Problems and Projects

1. A 10-year U.S. Treasury bond with a par value of $1,000 is currently selling for $775 from various security dealers. The bond carries a 9 percent coupon rate. If purchased today and held to maturity, what is its expected yield to maturity?

2. A state government bond is selling today for $962.77 and has a $1,000 face (par) value. Its yield to maturity is 6 percent, and the bond promises its holders $55 per year in interest for the next 10 years before it matures. What is the bond's duration?

3. Calculate the yield to maturity of a 10-year U.S. government bond that is selling for $800 in today's market and carries a 10 percent coupon rate with interest paid semiannually.

4. A corporate bond being seriously considered for purchase by First Security Savings Bank will mature 20 years from today and promises a 12 percent interest payment once a year. Recent inflation in the economy has driven the yield to maturity on this bond to 15 percent, and it carries a face value of $1,000. Calculate this bond's duration.

5. Tiger National Bank regularly purchases municipal bonds issued by small rural school districts in its region of the state. At the moment, the bank is considering purchasing an $8 million general obligation issue from the Youngstown school district, the only bond issue that district plans this year. The bonds, which mature in 15 years, carry a nominal annual rate of return of 7.75 percent. Tiger National, which is in the top corporate tax bracket of 35 percent, must pay an average interest rate of 7.38 percent to borrow the funds needed to purchase the municipals. Would you recommend purchasing these bonds?

   a. Calculate the net after-tax return on this bank-qualified municipal security. What is the tax advantage for being a qualified bond?

   b. What is the tax-equivalent yield for this bank-qualified municipal security?

6. Tiger National Bank also purchases municipal bonds issued by the city of Cleveland. Currently the bank is considering a nonqualified general obligation municipal issue. The bonds, which mature in 10 years, provide a nominal annual rate of return of 8.1 percent. Tiger National Bank has the same cost of funds and tax rate as stated in the previous problem.

   a. Calculate the net after-tax return on this nonqualified municipal security.

   b. What is the tax-equivalent yield for this nonqualified municipal security?

   c. Discuss the pro's and con's of purchasing the nonqualified rather than the bank-qualified municipal described in the previous problem.

7. Lakeway Thrift Savings and Trust is interested in doing some investment portfolio shifting. This institution has had a good year thus far, with strong loan demand; its loan revenue has increased by 16 percent over last year's level. Lakeway is subject to the 35 percent corporate income tax rate. The thrift's investments officer has several options in the form of bonds that have been held for some time in its portfolio:

   a. Selling $4 million in 12-year City of Dallas bonds with a coupon rate of 7.5 percent and purchasing $4 million in bonds from Bexar County (also with 12-year maturities) with a coupon of 8 percent and issued at par. The Dallas bonds have a current market value of $3,750,000 but are listed at par on the thrift institution's books.

   b. Selling $4 million in 12-year U.S. Treasury bonds that carry a coupon rate of 12 percent and are recorded at par, which was the price when the institution purchased them. The market value of these bonds has risen to $4,330,000.

   Which of these two portfolio shifts would you recommend? Is there a good reason for not selling these Treasury bonds? What other information is needed to make the best decision? Please explain.

8. Current market yields on U.S. government securities are distributed by maturity as follows:

    3-month Treasury bills = 7.69 percent
    6-month Treasury bills = 7.49 percent
    1-year Treasury notes = 7.77 percent
    2-year Treasury notes = 7.80 percent
    3-year Treasury notes = 7.80 percent
    5-year Treasury notes = 7.81 percent
    7-year Treasury notes = 7.86 percent
    10-year Treasury bonds = 7.87 percent
    30-year Treasury bonds = 7.90 percent

    Draw a *yield curve* for these securities. What shape does the curve have? What significance might this yield curve have for a bank or other investing institution with 75 percent of its investment portfolio in 7-year to 30-year U.S. Treasury bonds and 25 percent in U.S. government bills and notes with maturities under one year? What would you recommend to management?

9. A bond possesses a duration of 5.82 years. Suppose that market interest rates on comparable bonds were 7 percent this morning, but have now shifted upward to 7.5 percent. What percentage change in the bond's value occurred when interest rates moved 0.5 percent higher?

10. The investments officer for Sillistine Savings is concerned about interest rate risk lowering the value of the thrift institution's bonds. A check of the bond portfolio reveals an average duration of 4.5 years. How could this bond portfolio be altered in order to minimize interest rate risk should interest rates change significantly within the next year?

11. A commercial bank's economics department has just forecast accelerated growth in the economy, with GDP expected to grow at a 4.5 percent annual growth rate for at least the next two years. What are the implications of this economic forecast for a bank's investments officer? What types of securities should the investments officer think most seriously about adding to the bank's investment portfolio? Why? Suppose the bank holds a security portfolio similar to that described in Table 9–3 for all insured U.S. banks. Which types of securities might the bank's investments officer want to think seriously about selling if the projected economic expansion takes place? What losses might occur and how could these losses be minimized?

12. Contrary to the exuberant economic forecast described in problem 11, suppose a bank's economics department is forecasting a significant recession in economic activity. Output and employment are projected to decline significantly over the next 18 months. What are the implications of this forecast for a bank's investment portfolio manager? What is the outlook for interest rates and inflation under the foregoing assumptions? What types of investment securities would you recommend as good additions to the bank's portfolio during the period covered by the recession forecast and why? What other kinds of information would you like to have about the bank's current balance sheet and earnings report in order to help you make the best quality decisions regarding the investment security portfolio?

13. Arrington Hills Savings Bank, a $3.5 billion asset institution, holds the investment security portfolio outlined in the following table. This savings bank serves a rapidly growing money center into which substantial numbers of businesses are relocating their corporate headquarters. Suburban areas around the city are also growing rapidly as large numbers of business owners and managers along with retired professionals are purchasing new homes and condominiums. Would you recommend any changes in the makeup of this investment portfolio? Please explain why.

www.mhhe.com/rose6e

Types of Securities Held	Percent of Total Portfolio	Types of Securities Held	Percent of Total Portfolio
U.S. Treasury securities	38.7%	Securities available for sale	45.6%
Federal agency securities	35.2	Securities with maturities:	
State and local government obligations	15.5	Under one year	11.3
Domestic debt securities	5.1		
Foreign debt securities	4.9	One to five years	37.9
Equities	0.6	Over five years	50.8

Internet Exercises

1. As the investments officer for Bank of America, you have been informed by a member of the bank's board of directors that the investment policies you have followed over the past year have been substandard relative to your competitors, including Citigroup, Wells Fargo, and BankOne. You protest and observe that all financial institutions have faced a tough market and, in your opinion, your bank has done exceptionally well. Challenged, your CEO asks you to prepare a brief memo with comparative investment facts, defending your bank's relative investment performance against the other BHCs mentioned. Use the FDIC's Statistics on Depository Institutions at **www3.fdic.gov/sdi/main.asp** to develop a reply. What conclusion did you reach after examining your bank's relative investment performance over the last complete calendar year?

2. A number of websites are available to help in evaluating the merits and demerits of different types of securities that banks are allowed to hold in their investment portfolios. See **www.bondmarket.com** and **www.investinginbonds.com**. Find one additional website on your own and compare and contrast the usefulness of these three websites.

3. If you want a summary of regulations applying to bank and thrift security portfolios, you would turn to the regulators' websites. The Federal Reserve's *Trading and Capital-Markets Activity Manual* found at **www.federalreserve.gov/boarddocs/supmanual/trading/trading.pdf** has a section on "Capital Market Activities." Read and briefly outline the first two pages on "Limitations and Restrictions on Securities Holdings." See if you can find similar information for thrifts at **www.ots.treas.gov**.

STANDARD &POOR'S

S&P Market Insight Challenge

1. Use Standard & Poor's Market Insight website (**www.mhhe.com/edumarketinsight**) for this problem. In the S&P Industry Survey on Banking, commercial banks' earning assets are categorized as loans and securities.

    For a timely description of the banking industry's use of investment securities, click on the Industry tab in S&P's Market Insight, Educational Version, using the drop-down menu to select one of the subindustry categories, Diversified Banks or Regional Banks. Download the S&P Industry Survey on Banking and review the section "How the Industry Operates." Describe the importance of investment securities to a bank's earnings. What does the typical bank's investment securities portfolio contain? What is the most recent total amount of investment securities held in all FDIC-insured commercial banks?

2. Use Standard & Poor's Market Insight website (**www.mhhe.com/edumarketinsight**) for this problem. This chapter reminds us of the importance of investment securities in the asset portfolios of banks and closely related nonbank financial firms. The leading banks whose financial reports are represented on Market Insight tend to be heavy investors in marketable securities. Why? See if you can determine the percentage of total assets that investment securities represent for the Market Insight–listed commercial banks. Which banks show the highest proportion of investment security holdings (relative to total assets)? The lowest proportion? What factors would help explain these differences?

www.mhhe.com/rose6e

REAL NUMBERS FOR REAL BANKS   Assignment for Chapter 9

YOUR BANK'S INVESTMENT FUNCTION: AN EXAMINATION OF THE SECURITIES PORTFOLIO

Chapter 9 explores how the investments officer manages a bank or other financial firm's securities portfolio and describes the portfolio's purpose and composition. A significant portion of the chapter outlines and describes the different types of money market and capital market instruments that often make up the securities portfolio. Part One of this assignment examines the types of securities in your bank's portfolio and asks you to make some inferences about factors that played a role in the selection of securities for that portfolio. The possible factors are discussed midchapter. Part Two of this assignment examines the maturity structure of your bank's securities portfolio. This topic is covered in the latter part of the chapter. Chapter 9's assignment is designed to focus on the issues of importance to investments officers in large commercial banks or similar competing institutions.

Part One: The Composition of Your Bank's Securities Portfolio—Trend and Comparative Analysis

A.   **Data Collection:** For this part, you will once again access data at the FDIC's website located at **www3.fdic.gov/ sdi/main.asp** for your BHC. Use SDI to create a four-column report of your bank's information and the peer group information across years. In this part of the assignment for Report Selection use the pull-down menu to select Securities and view this in Percentages of Total Assets. For the relative size of the securities portfolio to total assets, see Item 1—the components of the securities portfolio are listed as Items 4–10. Enter the percentage information for these items as an addition to Spreadsheet 2 as follows:

Composition of Securities Portfolio (A75)	Your Bank	Peer Group	Your Bank	Peer Group
Date (A76)	12/31/yy	12/31/yy	12/31/yy	12/31/yy
Securities (A77)%	%	%	%	%
U.S. Treasury securities (A78)				
U.S. government obligations (A79)				
Securities issued by states and political subdivisions (A80)				
Asset-backed securities (A81)				
Other domestic debt securities (A82)				
Foreign debt securities (A83)				
Equity securities (A84)				

B.   Compare columns of row 77. How has the relative size of your bank's securities portfolio-to-total assets changed across periods? Does your bank have more or less liquidity than the group of comparable institutions?

C.   Use the Chart function in Excel and the data by columns in rows 78 through 84 to create four pie charts illustrating the profile of securities held by your BHC and its peer group.

With these pie charts provide titles, labels, and percentages. If you save these as separate sheets, they do not clutter the spreadsheets that you use most frequently, yet they are available to insert in Word documents. To give you an example, the Charts for NCC and its peer group would appear as follows:

(continued)

REAL NUMBERS FOR REAL BANKS

Assignment for Chapter 9 *(continued)*

Composition of Securities Portfolio for Peer Group (12-31-02)

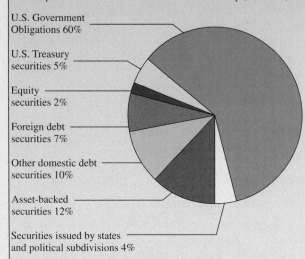

U.S. Government Obligations 60%

U.S. Treasury securities 5%

Equity securities 2%

Foreign debt securities 7%

Other domestic debt securities 10%

Asset-backed securities 12%

Securities issued by states and political subdivisions 4%

Composition of Securities Portfolio for NCB (12-31-02)

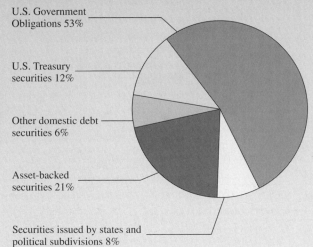

U.S. Government Obligations 53%

U.S. Treasury securities 12%

Other domestic debt securities 6%

Asset-backed securities 21%

Securities issued by states and political subdivisions 8%

D. Utilizing the above information, write approximately one page about your bank's securities portfolio and how it compares to its peers. Use your pie charts as graphics and incorporate them in the discussion. Provide inferences concerning the factors (e.g., expected rate of return, tax exposure, interest rate risk) affecting the choice of investment securities.

Part Two: Investment Maturity Strategies

A. **Data Collection:** The chapter concludes with a discussion of investment maturity strategies. The SDI at **www3.fdic.gov/sdi/main.asp** contains maturity data for debt securities for banks and BHCs. You will follow the process used to collect data for Part One; however, this time you will focus on the dollar year-end information for your BHC only. You will collect information in the two-column format. For Report Selection, use the pull-down menu to select Total Debt Securities and view this in Dollars. For maturity and repricing data for debt securities (all securities but equities), you are inter-

ested in Items 6–10. This includes a breakdown by maturity of (1) mortgage pass-throughs backed by closed-end first lien 1–4 residential mortgages, (2) CMOs, REMICs, and stripped MBs, and (3) other debt securities. Groups 1 and 3 are partitioned into six maturity periods, whereas Group 2, given the prepayment risk, has its expected average life partitioned into two more general categories. Our objective is to aggregate the data for all the debt securities based on maturities and enter our sums in Spreadsheet One as outlined below. For simplification we will include CMOs, REMICs, and stripped MBs with expected average lives of three years or less in the aggregation for row 82 and CMOs, REMICs, and stripped MBs with expected average lives of more than three years in row 84. Enter the aggregated data using dollar information for Debt Securities as an addition to Spreadsheet One as follows: for Example, Cell B80 would be the sum of mortgage pass-throughs and other debt securities with maturity and repricing of three months or less.

Maturity and repricing data for debt securities: (A78)	12/31/yyyy	12/31/yyyy
Total debt securities (A79)		
Three months or less (A80)		
Over 3 months through 12 months (A81)		
Over 1 year through 3 years (A82)		
Over 3 years through 5 years (A83)		
Over 5 years through 15 years (A84)		
Over 15 years (A85)		

B. Use the Chart function in Excel and the data by columns in rows 78 through 85 of Spreadsheet One to create two bar charts that graphically portray the maturity characteristics of your bank's securities portfolio. With these bar charts provide titles and labels and save for insertion in Word documents. To give you an example, one chart for NCC appears as follows:

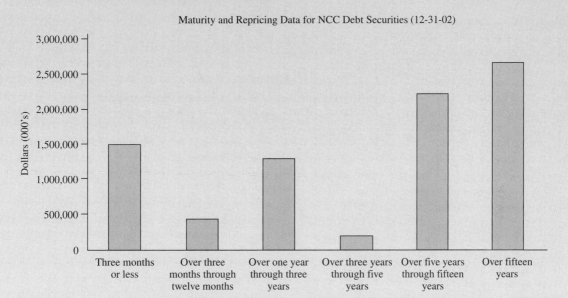

Maturity and Repricing Data for NCC Debt Securities (12-31-02)

C. Interpreting the above information, write approximately one page about your bank's maturity strategy and how it has changed between the two year-ends. Use your bar charts as graphics and incorporate them in the discussion. Tie your discussion to the types of strategies discussed in the latter part of Chapter 9.

Selected References

See below for a discussion of securitized assets and security stripping:

1. Beckettii, Sean. "The Role of Stripped Securities in Portfolio Management." *Economic Review*, Federal Reserve Bank of Kansas City, May 1988, pp. 20–31.

2. Dupont, Dominique, and Brian Sack. "The Treasury Securities Market: Overview and Recent Developments." *Federal Reserve Bulletin* 85, no. 12 (1999), pp. 785–806.

3. Smith, Stephen D. "Analyzing Risk and Return for Mortgage-Backed Securities." *Economic Review*, Federal Reserve Bank of Richmond, January/February 1991, pp. 2–10.

For a review of tax management issues in banking and financial institutions management, see the following:

4. French, George E. "Tax Reform and Its Effects on the Banking Industry." *Issues in Bank Regulation*, Summer 1987, pp. 3–10.

The following review yield to maturity and other investment yield measures:

5. Carlson, John B., and Erkin Y. Sahinoz. "Measures of Corporate Earnings: What Number is Best?" *Economic Commentary*, Federal Reserve Bank of Cleveland, February 1, 2003.

6. King, Robert G., and André Kurmann. "Expectations and the Term Structure of Interest Rates: Evidence and Implications." *Economic Quarterly*, Federal Reserve Bank of Richmond, Fall 2002, pp. 49–95.

7. Rose, Peter S. *Money and Capital Markets*, 8th ed. Burr Ridge, IL: McGraw-Hill Irwin, 2003. (See especially Chapter 6, "Measuring and Calculating Interest Rates and Financial Asset Prices.")

For a thorough discussion of investment strategies involving many securities purchased by banks and other financial institutions, see these resources;

8. Bassett, William F., and Mark Carlson. "Profits and Balance Sheet Developments at U.S. Commercial Banks in 2001." *Federal Reserve Bulletin*, June 2002, pp. 254–288.

9. Federal Deposit Insurance Corporation. *Law, Regulation, and Related Acts*. Washington, D.C., 2000.

10. Fleming, Michael J., and Kenneth Garbade. "When the Back Office Moved to the Front Burner: Settlement Fails in the Treasury Market after 9/11." *Economic Policy Review*, Federal Reserve Bank of New York, November 2002, pp. 35–58.

11. Kopcke, Richard W., and Ralph C. Kimball. "Inflation-Indexed Bonds: The Dog That Didn't Bark." *New England Economic Review*, Federal Reserve Bank of Boston, January/February 1999, pp. 3–24.

12. Sundaresan, Suresh M. *Fixed Income Markets and Their Derivatives*. Cincinnati, OH: South-Western, 1997.

For a description of key investment securities markets see the following:

13. Downing, Chris, and Frank Zhang. "Trading Activity and Price Volatility in the Municipal Bond Markets." *Finance and Economics Discussion Series No. 2002-39*, Federal Reserve Board, 2002.

14. Fleming, Michael. "The Round-the-Clock Market for U.S. Treasury Securities." *Economic Policy Review*, Federal Reserve Bank of New York, vol. 3, no. 2 (July 1997).

15. ———. "Are Larger Treasury Issues More Liquid? Evidence from Bill Reopenings." *Journal of Money, Credit and Banking* 34, no. 3 (2002), pp. 707–35.

16. Sack, Brian, and Robert Elsasser. "Treasury Inflation-Indexed Debt: A Review of the U.S. Experience." *Finance and Economics Discussion Series No. 2002-32*, Federal Reserve Board, 2002.

CHAPTER TEN

Liquidity and Reserve Management: Strategies and Policies

Key Topics in This Chapter

- Sources of Demand for and Supply of Liquidity
- Why Financial Firms Have Liquidity Problems
- Liquidity Management Strategies
- Estimating Liquidity Needs
- The Impact of Market Discipline
- Legal Reserves and Money Management

Introduction

Not long ago, as a recent article published by the Federal Reserve Bank of St. Louis [13] tells the story, a savings bank headquartered in the northeastern United States experienced a real liquidity crisis. Acting on rumors of a possible embezzlement of funds, some worried depositors launched an old-fashioned "run" on the bank. Flooding into the institution's Philadelphia and New York City branches, some frightened customers yanked out close to 13 percent of the savings bank's deposits in less than a week, sending management scrambling to find enough cash to meet the demands of concerned depositors and support the institution's asset portfolio. While the bank appeared to weather the storm in time, aided by federal deposit insurance, the event reminded us of at least two important things: (1) how much banks and other financial institutions depend upon public confidence to survive and prosper, and (2) how quickly the essential item called "liquidity" can be eroded when the public, even temporarily, loses its confidence in one or more financial institutions.

One of the most important tasks the management of any bank or other financial-service provider faces is ensuring adequate **liquidity** at all times, no matter what emergencies may suddenly appear. A financial institution is considered to be "liquid" if it has ready access to immediately spendable funds at reasonable cost at precisely the time those funds are needed. This suggests that a liquid bank or other financial firm either has the right amount of immediately spendable funds on hand when they are required or can raise liquid funds in a timely fashion by borrowing or by selling assets.

Indeed, lack of adequate liquidity can be one of the *first* signs that a bank or other financial institution is in real trouble. For example, a troubled bank or thrift that is losing deposits will likely be forced to dispose of some of its safer, more liquid assets. Other lending institutions may become increasingly reluctant to lend the troubled firm any new funds without additional security or the promise of a higher rate of interest, which may reduce the earnings of the beleaguered institution and threaten it with ultimate failure.

The cash shortages that banks and other financial-service providers in trouble often experience make clear that liquidity needs cannot be ignored. A bank or thrift institution can be closed if it cannot raise sufficient liquidity even though, technically, it may still be solvent. For example, during the 1990s, the Federal Reserve forced the closure of the $10 billion Southeast Bank of Miami because it couldn't come up with enough liquidity to repay the loans it had already received from the Fed. Moreover, the competence of liquidity managers is an important barometer of management's overall effectiveness in achieving any financial institution's goals. So, let's begin our journey and see how really important quality liquidity management is to the success of a bank or other financial firm.

The Demand for and Supply of Liquidity

A bank or other financial institution's need for liquidity—immediately spendable funds—can be viewed within a demand–supply framework. What activities give rise to the demand for liquidity? And what sources can be relied upon to supply liquidity when spendable funds are needed?

For most banks and other depository institutions, the most pressing demands for spendable funds come from two sources: (1) customers withdrawing money from their deposits, and (2) credit requests from customers the institution wishes to keep, either in the form of new loan requests, renewals of expiring loan agreements, or drawings upon existing credit lines. Other sources of liquidity demand include paying off previous borrowings, such as loans the institution may have received from other financial firms or from the central bank (e.g., the Federal Reserve, the Bank of England, or the European Central Bank). Similarly, payment of income taxes or cash dividends to the stockholders periodically gives rise to a demand for immediately spendable cash. (See Table 10–1.)

To meet the foregoing demands for liquidity, banks and other financial firms can draw upon several potential sources of supply. The most important source for a depository institution normally is receipt of new customer deposits, both from newly opened accounts and from new deposits placed in existing accounts. These deposit inflows are heavy the first of each month as business payrolls are dispensed, and they may reach a secondary peak toward the middle of each month as bills are paid and other payrolls are met. Another important element in the supply of liquidity comes from customers repaying their loans, which provides fresh funds for meeting new liquidity needs, as do sales of assets, especially marketable securities, from the investment portfolio. Liquidity also flows in from revenues generated by selling nondeposit services and from borrowings in the money market.

TABLE 10–1

Sources of Demand and Supply for Liquidity for a Depository Institution

Supplies of Liquid Funds Come From:	Demands for Liquidity Typically Arise From:
Incoming customer deposits	Customer deposit withdrawals
Revenues from the sale of nondeposit services	Credit requests from quality loan customers
Customer loan repayments	Repayment of nondeposit borrowings
Sales of assets	Operating expenses and taxes incurred in producing and selling services
Borrowings from the money market	Payment of stockholder cash dividends

Banking and Financial Services on the Net

The extensive information provided by the World Wide Web also includes important data sources concerning the liquidity of banks and other financial institutions and explores recent trends in liquidity management. One of the most important Web information sources is supplied by the Federal Deposit Insurance Corporation (FDIC), where you can get financial data on the liquid assets and borrowed liquidity positions of U.S.-insured banks and thrift institutions.

Quarterly data on the liquidity position of an individual bank or thrift and quarterly comparisons of the liquidity positions of two or more banks or thrift institutions can easily be called up through the FDIC's Statistics for Depository Institutions at **www3.fdic.gov/sdi/main.asp**. Be sure to specify the institution's name, city and state, or certificate (ID) number or bank holding company (BHC) number.

Banks, thrifts, and selected other financial firms also provide liquidity management services for their customers, helping those customers manage their cash positions, usually in return for a management fee. Most large institutions describe these services on their websites (e.g., **www.uboc.com**). Websites that periodically take up issues in the liquidity field include a site dealing with sweep accounts at **www.firstcapitalbank.com/pages/products/sweep.html**; Grant Thornton LLP's newsletter devoted to financial institutions at **www.grantthornton.com**; and collections of research papers or articles through such prominent institutions as the Federal Reserve Bank of St. Louis at **research .stlouisfed.org/wp/**; the Federal Reserve Bank of New York at **www.ny.frb.org/** (see Economic Research link); and the Federal Reserve Bank of Chicago at **www.chicagofed.org/publications/**.

As we will also see in this chapter, one of the most challenging aspects of liquidity management is managing a bank or thrift institution's *money position*—its legal reserve requirements, normally set by the central bank or other agency of government. In the United States the primary authority on legal reserve requirements is the Federal Reserve System. You can check on U.S. legal reserve requirements through **www.federalreserve.gov/regulations/default.htm** (see Regulation D). You can also find out about the new European Central Bank's reserve requirement powers through **www.ecb.int** or by entering into your Web search engine the name of any other central bank you wish (such as the Bank of Japan) and asking about its legal reserve rules.

These various sources of liquidity demand and supply come together to determine each financial firm's **net liquidity position** at any moment in time. That net liquidity position (L) at time t is as follows:

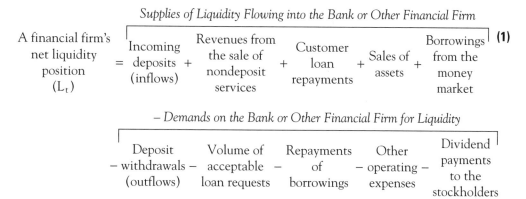

When the total demand for liquidity exceeds its total supply (i.e., $L_t < 0$), management must prepare for a *liquidity deficit*, deciding when and where to raise additional liquid funds. On the other hand, if at any point in time the total supply of liquidity exceeds all liquidity demands (i.e., $L_t > 0$), management must prepare for a *liquidity surplus*, deciding when and where to profitably invest surplus liquid funds until they are needed to cover future liquidity needs.

Liquidity has a critical time dimension. Some liquidity needs are *immediate* or nearly so. For example, in the case of a bank or thrift institution several large CDs may be due to mature tomorrow, and the customers may have indicated that they plan to withdraw these deposits rather than simply rolling them over into new deposits. Sources of funds that can be accessed immediately, such as borrowing reserves from another institution, must be used to meet these near-term liquidity pressures.

Longer-term liquidity demands arise from seasonal, cyclical, and trend factors. For example, liquid funds are generally in greater demand during the fall and summer coincident with school, holidays, and customer travel plans. Anticipating these longer-term liquidity needs, liquidity managers can draw upon a wider array of alternative sources of funds than is true for immediate liquidity needs, such as selling off accumulated liquid assets, aggressively advertising the institution's current menu of deposits or other services, or negotiating long-term borrowings of reserves from other financial firms. Of course, not all demands for liquidity need to be met by selling assets or borrowing new money. For example, just the right amount of new deposits may flow in, or loan repayments from borrowing customers may occur very close to the date new funds are needed. Timing is critical to liquidity management: Bankers and other financial managers must plan carefully how, when, and where needed liquid funds can be raised.

Most liquidity problems arise from outside the financial firm as a result of the financial activities of the firm's customers. In effect, customers' liquidity problems gravitate toward their liquidity suppliers. If a business is short on liquid reserves, for example, it will ask for a loan or draw down its deposit balances, either of which may require the firm's financial institution to come up with additional funds. A dramatic example of this phenomenon occurred in the wake of the worldwide stock market crash in October 1987. Investors who had borrowed heavily to buy stock on margin were forced to come up with additional funds to secure their stock loans. They went to their lending institutions in huge numbers, turning a liquidity crisis in the capital market into a liquidity crisis for banks and other suppliers of liquid funds.

The essence of the liquidity management problem for a financial institution may be described in two succinct statements:

1. Rarely are the demands for liquidity equal to the supply of liquidity at any particular moment in time. The financial firm must continually deal with either a liquidity deficit or a liquidity surplus.

2. There is a trade-off between liquidity and profitability. The more resources are tied up in readiness to meet demands for liquidity, the lower is that financial firm's expected profitability (other factors held constant).

Thus, ensuring adequate liquidity is a never-ending problem for management that will always have significant implications for profitability. Liquidity management decisions cannot be made in isolation from all the other service areas and departments of the bank or other financial firm.

Moreover, resolving problems subjects a financial institution to costs, including the interest cost on borrowed funds, the transactions cost of time and money in finding adequate liquid funds, and an *opportunity cost* in the form of future earnings that must be forgone when earning assets are sold in order to help meet liquidity needs. Clearly, management must weigh these costs against the immediacy of the institution's liquidity needs. If a financial institution winds up with excess liquidity at any time, its management must be prepared to invest those excess funds immediately to avoid incurring an opportunity cost from idle funds that are not generating any earnings.

From a slightly different vantage point, we could say that the management of liquidity is subject to the risk that market interest rates will change (*interest-rate risk*) and the risk that liquid funds will not be available in the volume needed (*availability risk*). If interest rates rise, financial assets that the financial firm plans to sell to raise liquid funds, such as government bonds, will decline in value, and some must be sold at a loss. Not only will

Factoid
Did you know that a serious liquidity crisis inside the United States in 1907, which followed several other liquidity crises in the 19th century, led to the creation of the U.S. central bank, the Federal Reserve System, to prevent or moderate similar liquidity problems in the future?

fewer liquid funds be raised from the sale of those assets, but the losses incurred will reduce earnings as well. Then, too, raising liquid funds by borrowing will cost more as interest rates rise, and some forms of borrowed liquidity may no longer be available. If the lenders of liquidity perceive a financial institution to be more risky than before, it will be forced to pay higher interest rates to borrow liquidity, and some lenders will simply refuse to make liquid funds available at all.

Why Banks and Many of Their Closest Competitors Face Significant Liquidity Problems

It should be clear from the foregoing discussion that banks and several other types of financial institutions face major liquidity problems. This significant exposure to liquidity pressures arises from several sources.

In the case of banks and thrift institutions, for example, these depository institutions borrow large amounts of short-term deposits and reserves from individuals and businesses and from other lending institutions and then turn around and make long-term credit available to their borrowing customers. Thus, most banks and thrifts face an imbalance between the maturity dates attached to their assets and the maturity dates of their liabilities. Rarely will incoming cash flows from assets exactly match the cash flowing out to cover liabilities.

A problem related to the maturity mismatch situation is that banks and many thrifts hold an unusually high proportion of liabilities subject to immediate payment, such as demand deposits, NOW accounts, and money market borrowings. Thus, they must always stand ready to meet immediate cash demands that can be substantial at times, especially near the end of a week, at the first of each month, and during certain seasons of the year.

Another source of liquidity problems is sensitivity to changes in interest rates. When interest rates rise, for example, some depositors of banks and thrifts will withdraw their funds in search of higher returns elsewhere. Many loan customers may postpone new loan requests or speed up their drawings on those credit lines that carry lower interest rates. Thus, changing interest rates affect both customer demand for deposits and customer demand for loans, each of which has a potent impact on a depository institution's liquidity position. Moreover, movements in market interest rates affect the market values of assets the bank or other financial firm may need to sell in order to raise additional liquid funds, and they directly affect the cost of borrowing in the money market.

Concept Check

10–1. What are the principal sources of *liquidity demand* for a bank or other financial firm?

10–2. What are the principal sources from which the *supply of liquidity* comes?

10–3. Suppose that a bank faces the following cash inflows and outflows during the coming week: (a) deposit withdrawals are expected to total $33 million, (b) customer loan repayments are expected to amount to $108 million, (c) operating expenses demanding cash payment will probably approach $51 million, (d) acceptable new loan requests should reach $294 million, (e) sales of bank assets are projected to be $18 million, (f) new deposits should total $670 million, (g) borrowings from the money market are expected to be about $43 million, (h) nondeposit service fees should amount to $27 million, (i) previous bank borrowings totaling $23 million are scheduled to be repaid, and (j) a dividend payment to bank stockholders of $140 million is scheduled. What is this bank's projected net liquidity position for the coming week?

10–4. When is a bank or other financial institution *adequately liquid?*

10–5. Why do banks and many of their closest financial-service competitors face significant liquidity management problems?

Beyond these factors, banks and similar financial firms must give high priority to meeting demands for liquidity. To fail in this area may severely damage public confidence in the institution. We can imagine the reaction of a bank's customers, for example, if the teller windows and teller machines had to be closed one morning because the bank was temporarily out of cash and could not cash checks or meet deposit withdrawals (as happened to a bank in Montana several years ago, prompting a federal investigation, as we discussed in the opener to Part Three). One of the most important tasks of a liquidity manager is to keep close contact with the largest depositors and holders of large unused credit lines to determine if and when withdrawals of funds will be made and to make sure adequate funds will be available when the demand for funds occurs.

Strategies for Liquidity Managers

Over the years, experienced liquidity managers have developed several broad strategies for dealing with liquidity problems: (1) providing liquidity from assets (asset liquidity management), (2) relying on borrowed liquidity to meet cash demands (liability management), and (3) balanced (asset and liability) liquidity management.

Asset Liquidity Management (or Asset Conversion) Strategies

Key URLs
To find out how the Federal Reserve System dealt with the 9/11 terrorist attacks and helped to stabilize the U.S. financial system, see especially **www.clevelandfed.org** and **www.ny.frb.org/ research/search.html**.

The oldest approach to meeting liquidity needs is known as **asset liquidity management.** In its purest form, this strategy calls for storing liquidity in the form of holdings of liquid assets, predominantly in cash and marketable securities. When liquidity is needed, selected assets are sold for cash until all demands for cash are met. This liquidity management strategy is often called *asset conversion* because liquid funds are raised by converting noncash assets into cash.

What is a **liquid asset?** It must have three characteristics:

1. A liquid asset must have a *ready market* so that it can be converted into cash without delay.
2. It must have a reasonably *stable price* so that, no matter how quickly the asset must be sold or how large the sale is, the market is deep enough to absorb the sale without a significant decline in price.
3. It must be *reversible,* meaning the seller can recover his or her original investment (principal) with little risk of loss.

Among the most popular liquid assets are Treasury bills, federal funds loans, deposits, municipal bonds, federal agency securities, bankers' acceptances, and Eurocurrency loans. (See the box entitled "Storing Liquidity in Assets—The Principal Options" for brief descriptions of these liquid assets.) Although a bank or other financial firm can strengthen its liquidity position by holding more liquid assets, it will not necessarily be a liquid institution if it does so, because each institution's liquidity position is also influenced by the demands for liquidity made against it. Remember: A financial firm is liquid only if it has access, at reasonable cost, to liquid funds in exactly the amounts required at the time they are needed.

Asset liquidity management strategy is used mainly by smaller banks and thrifts that find it a less risky approach to liquidity management than relying on borrowings. But asset conversion is not a costless approach to liquidity management. First, selling assets means the loss of the future earnings those assets would have generated had they not been sold off. Thus, there is an **opportunity cost** to storing liquidity in assets when those assets must be sold. Most asset sales also involve transactions costs (commissions) paid to security brokers. Moreover, the assets in question may need to be sold in a market experiencing

The principal options open to liquidity managers for holdings of liquid assets that can be sold when additional cash is needed are

1. *Treasury bills*—direct obligations of the United States government or of foreign governments issued at a discount and redeemed at par (face value) when they reach maturity; T-bills have original maturities of 3, 6, and 12 months, with an active resale market through security dealers.
2. *Federal funds loans to other institutions*—loans of reserves held by depository institutions with short (often overnight) maturities.
3. *Purchase of liquid securities under a repurchase agreement (RP)*—using high quality securities as collateral to secure loans from dealers and other lending institutions.
4. *Placing of correspondent deposits with banks and thrift institutions*—these interbank deposits can be borrowed or loaned in minutes by telephone or by wire.
5. *Municipal bonds and notes*—debt securities issued by state and local governments that range in maturity from a few days to several years.
6. *Federal agency securities*—short- and long-term debt instruments sold by federally sponsored agencies such as FNMA (Fannie Mae) or FHLMC (Freddie Mac).
7. *Bankers' acceptances*—liquid claims against a bank arising from credit extended to customers, normally coming due within six months.
8. *Commercial paper*—short-term debt issued by large corporations with excellent credit ratings.
9. *Eurocurrency loans*—the lending of deposits accepted by banks and bank branches located outside a particular currency's home country for periods stretching from a few days to a few months.

Filmtoid
What 1980s thriller, starring Kris Kristofferson and Jane Fonda, aligned murder with the liquidity problems of Borough National Bank created by Arab withdrawals of Eurodeposits?
Answer: *Rollover*

declining prices, increasing the risk of substantial capital losses. Management must take care that those assets with the least profit potential are sold first in order to minimize the opportunity cost of future earnings forgone. Selling assets to raise liquidity also tends to weaken the appearance of the balance sheet because the assets sold are often low-risk government securities that give the impression the financial firm is financially strong. Finally, liquid assets generally carry the lowest rates of return of all financial assets. Investing heavily in liquid assets means forgoing higher returns on other assets that might be acquired.

Borrowed Liquidity (Liability) Management Strategies

In the 1960s and 1970s, many commercial banks, led by the largest in the industry, began to raise more of their liquid funds through borrowings in the money market. This borrowed liquidity strategy—often called *purchased liquidity* or **liability management**—in its purest form calls for borrowing enough immediately spendable funds to cover all anticipated demands for liquidity. Today many different financial institutions use this liquid strategy.

Borrowing liquid funds has a number of advantages. A bank or other financial firm can choose to borrow only when it actually needs funds, unlike storing liquidity in assets where a storehouse of at least some liquid assets must be held at all times, lowering potential return because liquid assets usually have such low yields. Then, too, using borrowed funds permits a bank or other financial institution to leave the volume and composition of its asset portfolio unchanged if it is satisfied with the assets it currently holds. In contrast, selling assets to provide liquidity for liability-derived demands, such as deposit withdrawals, shrinks the size of a financial firm as its total asset holdings decline. Finally, as we saw in Chapter 6, liability management comes with its own *control lever*—the interest rate offered to borrow funds. If the borrowing institution needs more funds, it merely raises its *offer rate* until the requisite amount of funds flow in. If fewer funds are required, the financial firm's offer rate may be lowered.

The principal sources of borrowed liquidity for a depository institution include jumbo ($100,000+) negotiable CDs, federal funds borrowings, repurchase agreements (in which securities are sold temporarily with an agreement to buy them back), Eurocurrency borrowings, advances from the Federal home loan banks, and borrowings at the discount window of the central bank in each nation or region. (See the box entitled "Borrowing Liquidity—The Principal Options" for a description of these instruments.) Liability management techniques are used most extensively by the largest commercial banks, which often borrow close to 100 percent of their liquidity needs.

Borrowing liquidity is the most risky approach to solving liquidity problems (but also carries the highest expected return) because of the volatility of money market interest rates and the rapidity with which the availability of credit can change. Often financial-service providers must purchase liquidity when it is most difficult to do so, both in cost and in availability. The borrowing cost is always uncertain, which adds greater uncertainty to the bank's net earnings. Moreover, a bank that gets into financial trouble is usually most in need of borrowed liquidity, particularly because knowledge of the bank's difficulties spreads and depositors begin to withdraw their funds. At the same time, other financial institutions become less willing to lend to the troubled bank due to the risk involved.

Balanced (Asset and Liability) Liquidity Management Strategies

Due to the risks inherent in relying on borrowed liquidity and the costs of storing liquidity in assets, most banks and many of their financial-service competitors compromise by using both asset management and liability management. Under a **balanced liquidity management** strategy, some of the expected demands for liquidity are stored in assets (principally holdings of marketable securities and deposits), while other anticipated liquidity needs are backstopped by advanced arrangements for lines of credit from banks or other suppliers of funds. Unexpected cash needs are typically met from near-term borrowings. Longer-term liquidity needs can be planned for and the funds to meet these needs can be parked in short-term and medium-term loans and securities that will provide cash as those liquidity needs arise.

10–6. What are the principal differences among *asset management, liability management,* and *balanced liquidity management?*

10–7. What guidelines should management keep in mind when it manages a bank or other financial firm's liquidity position?

Guidelines for Liquidity Managers

Over the years, liquidity managers have developed several rules of thumb that guide their activities. First, the liquidity manager must keep track of the activities of all departments using and/or supplying funds while coordinating his or her department's activities with theirs. Whenever the loan department grants a new credit line to a customer, for example, the liquidity manager must prepare for possible drawings against that line. If the savings account division expects to receive several large deposits in the next few days, this information should be passed on to the liquidity manager.

Second, the liquidity manager should know in advance, wherever possible, when the biggest credit or deposit customers plan to withdraw their funds or add to their deposits. This allows the manager to plan ahead to deal more effectively with emerging liquidity surpluses and deficits.

Third, the liquidity manager, in cooperation with senior management and the board of directors, must make sure the bank or other financial firm's priorities and objectives for liquidity management are clear. For example, in the past, a bank or thrift institution's liquidity position was often assigned top priority when it came to allocating funds. A typical assumption was that a depository institution had little or no control over its sources of funds—those were determined by the public—but the bank or thrift could control its uses of funds. In addition, because the law usually requires depository institutions to set aside liquid funds at the central bank to cover deposit reserve requirements and because the depository must be ready at all times to handle deposit withdrawals, liquidity management and the diverting of sufficient funds into liquid assets were given the highest priority. Today, liquidity management has generally been relegated to a supporting role compared to most financial firms' number one priority—making loans and supplying other fee-generating services to all qualified customers. All profitable loans should be granted, leaving to the liquidity manager the task of finding sufficient cash to fund them.

Fourth, liquidity needs and liquidity decisions must be analyzed on a continuing basis to avoid both excess and deficit liquidity positions. Excess liquidity that is not reinvested the same day it occurs results in lost income, while liquidity deficits must be dealt with quickly to avoid dire emergencies where the hurried borrowing of funds or sale of assets results in excessive losses for the bank or other financial firm involved.

Estimating Liquidity Needs

Several methods have been developed in recent years for estimating a bank or other financial institution's liquidity requirements: the sources and uses of funds approach, the structure of funds approach, and the liquidity indicator approach. Each method rests on specific assumptions and yields only an approximation of actual liquidity requirements at any given time. This is why a liquidity manager must always be ready to fine-tune estimates of liquidity requirements as new information becomes available. In fact, most banks and competing financial firms make sure their liquidity reserves include both a *planned component,* consisting of the reserves called for by the latest liquidity forecast, and a *protective component,* consisting of an extra margin of liquid reserves over those dictated by the most recent forecast. The protective liquidity component may be large or small, depending on management's philosophy and attitude toward risk—that is, how much chance of running a cash-out management wishes to accept.

Let us turn now to the most popular methods for estimating a bank or other financial firm's liquidity needs. For illustrative purposes, we will focus on the problem of estimating a commercial bank's liquidity needs because commercial banks typically face the greatest liquidity management challenges of any financial firm. However, the key principles we will explore apply to other financial-service providers as well.

The Sources and Uses of Funds Approach

The **sources and uses of funds method** for estimating liquidity needs begins with two simple facts:

1. In the case of a bank, for example, liquidity rises as deposits increase and loans decrease.
2. Alternatively, liquidity declines when deposits decrease and loans increase.

Whenever sources and uses of liquidity do not match, there is a **liquidity gap,** measured by the size of the total difference between sources and uses of funds. When sources of liquidity (e.g., increasing deposits or decreasing loans) exceed uses of liquidity (e.g., decreasing deposits or increasing loans), the bank or other financial firm will have a *positive liquidity gap.* Its surplus liquid funds must be quickly invested in earning assets until they are needed to cover future cash needs. On the other hand, when uses of liquidity exceed sources of liquidity, the bank or competing financial institution faces a liquidity deficit, or *negative liquidity gap.* It now must raise funds from the cheapest and most timely sources available.

The key steps in the sources and uses of funds approach, using a commercial bank as an example, are as follows:

1. Loans and deposits must be forecast for a given liquidity planning period.
2. The estimated change in loans and deposits must be calculated for that same planning period.
3. The liquidity manager must estimate the net liquid funds' surplus or deficit for the planning period by comparing the estimated change in loans (or other use of funds) to the estimated change in deposits (or other funds source).

Banks, for example, use a wide variety of statistical techniques, supplemented by management's judgment and experience, to prepare forecasts of deposits and loans. For example, the bank's economics department or its liquidity managers might develop the following forecasting models:

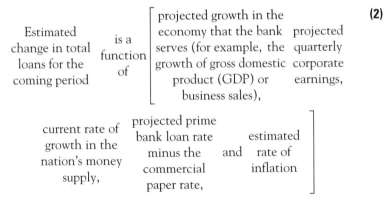

$$
\begin{array}{l}
\begin{array}{c}
\text{Estimated} \\
\text{change in total} \\
\text{loans for the} \\
\text{coming period}
\end{array}
\begin{array}{c}
\text{is a} \\
\text{function} \\
\text{of}
\end{array}
\left[
\begin{array}{cc}
\text{projected growth in the} \\
\text{economy that the bank} \quad \text{projected} \\
\text{serves (for example, the} \quad \text{quarterly} \\
\text{growth of gross domestic} \quad \text{corporate} \\
\text{product (GDP) or} \quad \text{earnings,} \\
\text{business sales),}
\end{array}
\right.
\end{array}
\tag{2}
$$

$$
\left.
\begin{array}{ccc}
\text{current rate of} & \text{projected prime} & \\
\text{growth in the} & \text{bank loan rate} & \text{estimated} \\
\text{nation's money} & \text{minus the} \quad \text{and} & \text{rate of} \\
\text{supply,} & \text{commercial} & \text{inflation} \\
& \text{paper rate,} &
\end{array}
\right]
$$

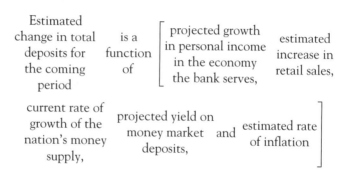

Using the forecasts of loans and deposits generated by the foregoing models, management could then estimate the bank's need for liquidity by calculating as follows:

$$\begin{array}{c}\text{Estimated liquidity} \\ \text{deficit } (-) \text{ or surplus } (+) = \\ \text{for the coming period}\end{array} \begin{array}{c}\text{Estimated change in} \\ \text{total deposits}\end{array} - \begin{array}{c}\text{Estimated} \\ \text{change in} \\ \text{total loans}\end{array} \qquad \textbf{(3)}$$

A somewhat simpler approach for estimating future deposits (or other funds sources) and loans (or other funds uses) is to divide the forecast of future deposit and loan growth into three key components:

1. A *trend component*, which the bank can estimate by constructing a trend (constant-growth) line using as reference points year-end, quarterly, or monthly deposit and loan totals established over at least the last 10 years (or some other base period sufficiently long to define a trend or long-run average growth rate).

2. A *seasonal component*, which measures how deposits (or other funds sources) and loans (or other funds uses) are expected to behave in any given week or month due to seasonal factors, as compared to the most recent year-end deposit or loan level.

3. A *cyclical component*, which represents positive or negative deviations from a bank's total expected deposits and loans (measured by the sum of trend and seasonal components), depending upon the strength or weakness of the economy in the current year.

For example, suppose we are managing liquidity for a bank whose trend growth rate in total deposits over the past decade has averaged about 10 percent a year. Loan growth has been slightly less rapid, averaging 8 percent a year for the past 10 years. Our bank's total deposits stood at $1,200 million and total loans outstanding reached $800 million at year-end. Table 10–2 presents a forecast of weekly deposit and loan totals for our bank for the first six weeks of the new year. Each weekly loan and deposit *trend* figure shown in column 1 accounts for a one-week portion of the projected 10 percent annual increase in deposits and the expected 8 percent annual increase in loans. To derive the appropriate *seasonal* element shown in column 2, we compare the ratio for the average (trend) deposit and loan figure for each week of the year to the average deposit and loan level during the final week of the year for each of the past 10 years. We assume the seasonal ratio of the current week's level to the preceding year-end level applies in the current year in the same way as it did for all past years, so we simply add or subtract the calculated seasonal element to the trend element.

The *cyclical* element, given in column 3, compares the sum of the estimated trend and seasonal elements with the actual level of deposits and loans the previous year. The dollar gap between these two numbers is presumed to result from cyclical forces, and we assume that roughly the same cyclical pressures that prevailed last year apply to the current year. Finally, column 4 reports the estimated *total* deposits and loans, consisting of the sum of trend (column 1), seasonal (column 2), and cyclical components (column 3).

TABLE 10–2 Forecasting Deposits and Loans with the Sources and Uses of Funds Approach
(figures in millions of dollars)

Deposit Forecast for	Trend Estimate for Deposits	Seasonal Element*	Cyclical Element**	Estimated Total Deposits
January, Week 1	$1,210	−4	−6	$1,200
January, Week 2	1,212	−54	−58	1,100
January, Week 3	1,214	−121	−93	1,000
January, Week 4	1,216	−165	−101	950
February, Week 1	1,218	+70	−38	1,250
February, Week 2	1,220	+32	−52	1,200

Loan Forecast for	Trend Estimate for Loans	Seasonal Element*	Cyclical Element**	Estimated Total Loans
January, Week 1	$799	+6	−5	$ 800
January, Week 2	800	+59	−9	850
January, Week 3	801	+174	−25	950
January, Week 4	802	+166	+32	1,000
February, Week 1	803	+27	−80	750
February, Week 2	804	+98	−2	900

*The seasonal element compares the average level of deposits and loans for each week over the past 10 years to the average level of deposits and loans for the final week of December over the preceding 10 years.

**The cyclical element reflects the difference between the expected deposit and loan levels in each week during the preceding year (measured by the trend and seasonal elements) and the actual volume of total deposits and total loans the bank posted that week.

Table 10–3 shows how we can take estimated deposit and loan figures, such as those given in column 4 of Table 10–2, and use them to estimate a bank's expected liquidity deficits and surpluses in the period ahead. In this instance, the liquidity manager has estimated expected liquidity needs for the next six weeks. Columns 1 and 2 in Table 10–3 merely repeat the estimated total deposit and total loan figures from column 4 in Table 10–2. Columns 3 and 4 in Table 10–3 calculate the *change* in total deposits and total loans from one week to the next. Column 5 shows the differences between the change in loans and the change in deposits each week. When deposits fall and loans rise, a liquidity deficit is more likely to occur. When deposits grow and loans decline, a bank usually moves toward a liquidity surplus position.

As Table 10–3 reveals, our bank has a projected liquidity *deficit* over the next three weeks—$150 million next week, $200 million the third week, and $100 million in the fourth week—because its loans are growing while its deposit levels are declining. Due to a forecast of rising deposits and falling loans in the fifth week, a liquidity surplus of $550 million is expected then, followed by a $200 million liquidity deficit in week 6. What liquidity management decisions must be made over the six-week period shown in Table 10–3? The liquidity manager must prepare to raise new funds in weeks 2, 3, 4, and 6 from the cheapest and most reliable funds sources available and to profitably invest the expected funds surplus in week 5.

Management can now begin planning which sources of liquid funds to draw upon, first evaluating the bank's stock of liquid assets to see which assets are likely to be available for use and then determining if adequate sources of borrowed funds are also likely to be available. For example, the bank probably has already set up lines of credit for borrowing from its principal correspondent banks. The liquidity manager wants to be sure these credit lines are still in place and adequate to meet the projected amount of borrowing that will be needed.

TABLE 10–3 Forecasting Liquidity Deficits and Surpluses with the Sources and Uses of Funds Approach (figures in millions of dollars)

Time Period	Estimated Total Deposits	Estimated Total Loans	Estimated Deposit Change	Estimated Loan Change	Estimated Liquidity Deficit (–) or Surplus (+)
January, Week 1	$1,200	$ 800	$___	$___	$___
January, Week 2	1,100	850	–100	+50	–150
January, Week 3	1,000	950	–100	+100	–200
January, Week 4	950	1,000	–50	+50	–100
February, Week 1	1,250	750	+300	–250	+550
February, Week 2	1,200	900	–50	+150	–200

The Structure of Funds Approach

Another approach to estimating a financial institution's liquidity requirements is the **structure of funds method.** Once again we will illustrate this liquidity estimation procedure using some figures provided by a commercial bank that frequently faces substantial liquidity demands. In the first step in the structure of funds approach, the bank's deposits and other funds sources are divided into categories based upon their estimated probability of being withdrawn and, therefore, lost to the banking firm. As an illustration, we might divide the bank's deposit and nondeposit liabilities into three categories:

1. *"Hot money" liabilities* (often called volatile liabilities)—deposits and other borrowed funds (such as federal funds) that are very interest sensitive or that management is sure will be withdrawn during the current period.
2. *Vulnerable funds*—customer deposits of which a substantial portion, perhaps 25 to 30 percent, will probably be removed from the bank sometime during the current time period.
3. *Stable funds* (often called *core deposits* or *core liabilities*)—funds that management considers most unlikely to be removed from the bank (except for a minor percentage of the total).

Second, the liquidity manager must set aside liquid funds according to some desired *operating rule* for each of these three funds sources. For example, the manager may decide to set up a 95 percent liquid reserve behind all hot money funds (less any required legal reserves held behind hot money deposits). This liquidity reserve might consist of holdings of immediately spendable deposits in correspondent banks plus investments in Treasury bills and repurchase agreements where the committed funds can be recovered in a matter of minutes or hours.

A common rule of thumb for vulnerable deposit and nondeposit liabilities is to hold a fixed percentage of their total amount—say, 30 percent—in liquid reserves. For stable (core) funds sources, this bank may decide to place a small proportion—perhaps 15 percent or less—of their total in liquid reserves. Thus, the liquidity reserve behind the bank's deposit and nondeposit liabilities would be as follows:

$$\text{Liability liquidity reserve} = 0.95 \times (\text{Hot money deposits and nondeposit funds} - \text{Legal reserves held}) + 0.30 \times (\text{Vulnerable deposit and nondeposit funds} - \text{Legal reserves held}) + 0.15 \times (\text{Stable deposits and nondeposit funds} - \text{Legal reserves held}) \qquad (4)$$

In the case of loans, the bank, like any other lender, must be ready at all times to make good loans—that is, to meet the legitimate credit needs of those customers who satisfy the lender's loan quality standards. The bank in this example must have sufficient liquid reserves on hand because, once a loan is made, the borrowing customer will spend the proceeds, usually within hours or days, and those funds will flow out to other depository institutions. However, this bank does not want to turn down any good loan, because loan customers bring in new deposits and normally are the principal source of bank earnings from interest and fees.

Indeed, a substantial body of current thinking in banking suggests that any lending institution should make all good loans, counting on its ability to borrow liquid funds, if necessary, to cover any pressing cash needs. This is known as the *customer relationship doctrine:* management should strive to make all good loans that walk in the door in order to build lasting customer relationships that will continue to generate deposits and loans into the future. Under today's concept of *relationship banking,* once the customer is sold a loan, the bank making that loan can then proceed to sell that customer other services, establishing a multidimensional relationship that will bring in additional fee income and increase the customer's dependence on (and, therefore, loyalty to) the institution. This reasoning suggests that management must try to estimate the maximum possible figure for total loans and hold in liquid reserves or borrowing capacity the full amount (100 percent) of the difference between the actual amount of loans outstanding and the maximum potential for total loans.

Combining both loan and deposit liquidity requirements, this bank's *total liquidity requirement* would be derived as follows:

Total liquidity requirement for a bank = = Deposit and nondeposit liability liquidity requirement and loan liquidity requirement = $0.95 \times$ (Hot money funds − Required legal reserves held behind hot money deposits) + $0.30 \times$ (Vulnerable deposits and nondeposit funds − Required legal reserves) + $0.15 \times$ (Stable deposits and nondeposit funds − Required legal reserves) + $1.00 \times$ (Potential loans outstanding − Actual loans outstanding)

Admittedly, the deposit and loan liquidity requirements that make up the above equation are subjective estimates that rely heavily on management's judgment, experience, and attitude toward risk.

A brief numerical example of this liquidity management method is shown in Table 10–4. First National Bank has broken down its deposit and nondeposit liabilities into hot money, vulnerable funds, and stable (core) funds, amounting to $25 million, $24 million, and $100 million, respectively. The bank's loans total $135 million currently, but recently have been as high as $140 million, and loans are projected to grow at a 10 percent annual rate. Thus, within the coming year, the bank's total loans might reach as high as $154 million, or $140 million + (0.10 × $140 million), which would be $19 million higher than they are now. Applying the percentages of deposits that management wishes to hold in liquid reserves, we find that the bank needs more than $63 million in total liquidity, consisting of both liquid assets and borrowing capacity.

Many banks, thrifts, and other financial firms like to use *probabilities* in deciding how much liquidity to hold behind their deposits and loans. Under this refinement of the structure of funds approach, the liquidity manager will want to define the best and the worst possible liquidity positions his or her financial institution might find itself in and assign probabilities to as many of these situations as possible. For example,

LIQUIDITY SHORTAGES IN THE WAKE OF THE SEPTEMBER 11, 2001, TERRORIST ATTACKS

The terrorist attacks of 9/11 in New York City assaulted the banking system as well as the twin towers of the World Trade Center. Banks with facilities for making payments located in or near the World Trade Center experienced temporary, intense shortages of funds due to their inability to collect and record payments they were owed and to dispense payments they were obligated to make. The problems banks at or near "ground zero" in Lower Manhattan faced soon spread to outlying banks in domino fashion. Banks whose electronic communications systems were destroyed or damaged couldn't make timely payment of their obligations to other banks that, in turn, could not make good on their own promises to pay. Within hours many banks faced a full-blown *liquidity crisis.*

One of the first signs of trouble was a sharp reduction in the movement of funds through Fed Wire—the Federal Reserve's electronic funds transfer network—as the banks hit hardest by the attacks stopped transferring reserves to other banks because they could not be sure they themselves would receive incoming funds they expected. Several banks that borrowed reserves from other institutions on September 10 were unable to return the borrowed funds on the 11th. Moreover, many banks near ground zero were unable to communicate with their customers to explain what was happening. Nor could they update their records or make deliveries of securities they had promised to their clients. Also, the economy began to feel the 9/11 attack's effects as several banks became fearful about lending out their funds, preferring to hold onto their cash lest they too were confronted with a liquidity squeeze.

Within hours, however, the system began to recover and was approaching near-normal operating levels by September 14. Why did recovery from such a serious liquidity crisis come about so quickly? The Federal Reserve—the proverbial "lender of last resort"—stepped in aggressively. At 10:00 A.M. on September 11, the Fed announced, "The Federal Reserve System is open and operating. The discount window is available to meet liquidity needs." At the same time, the Fed temporarily suspended penalties against banks running overdrafts and cranked up its open market operations to pour new funds into the federal funds market. Discount window loans jumped from a daily average of about $100 million to more than $45 billion on September 12, while the Fed's open-market trading desk accelerated its trading activity from a relatively normal $3.5 billion a day to about $38 billion that same day. The Fed's quick reaction and injection of liquidity into the banking system, along with the determination of many bankers to restore communications links to their customers, soon quelled the liquidity crisis.

Source: Federal Reserve Bank of New York, *Economic Policy Review,* November 2002; and Bruce Champ, "Open and Operating: Providing Liquidity to Avoid a Crisis," *Economic Commentary,* Federal Reserve Bank of Cleveland, February 15, 2003.

1. *The worst possible liquidity position.* Suppose deposit growth at the bank we have been following falls significantly below management's expectations, so that actual deposit totals sometimes go below the lowest points on the bank's historical minimum deposit growth track. Moreover, suppose loan demand from qualified credit customers rises significantly above management's expectations, so that loan demand sometimes goes beyond the high points of the bank's loan growth track. In this instance, the bank would face maximum pressure on its available liquid reserves because deposit growth would not likely be able to fund all the loans customers were demanding. In this worst situation the liquidity manager would have to prepare for a sizable *liquidity deficit* and develop a plan for raising substantial amounts of liquid funds.

2. *The best possible liquidity position.* Suppose deposit growth turns out to be significantly above management's expectations, so that it touches the highest points in the bank's deposit growth track record. Moreover, suppose loan demand turns out to be significantly below management's expectations, so that loan demand grows along a minimum path that touches the low points in the bank's loan growth track. In this case, the bank

TABLE 10–4
Estimating Liquidity
Needs with the
Structure of Funds
Method

A. First National Bank estimates that its current deposits and nondeposit liabilities break down as follows:

Hot money	$ 25 million
Vulnerable funds (including the largest deposit and nondeposit liability accounts)	$ 24 million
Stable (core) funds	$100 million

First National's management wants to keep a 95% reserve behind its hot money deposits (less the 3% legal reserve requirement behind many of these deposits) and nondeposit liabilities, a 30% liquidity reserve in back of its vulnerable deposits and borrowings (less required reserves), and a 15% liquidity reserve behind its core deposit and nondeposit funds (less required reserves).

B. First National Bank's loans total $135 million but recently have been as high as $140 million, with a trend growth rate of about 10 percent a year. The bank wishes to be ready at all times to honor customer demands for all those loans that meet its quality standards.

C. The bank's total liquidity requirement is as follows:

Deposit/Nondeposit Funds plus Loans

$$0.95 \,(\$25 \text{ million} - 0.03 \times \$25 \text{ million})$$
$$+0.30 \,(\$24 \text{ million} - 0.03 \times \$24 \text{ million})$$
$$+0.15 \,(\$100 \text{ million} - 0.03 \times \$100 \text{ million})$$
$$+\$140 \text{ million} \times 0.10 + (\$140 - \$135 \text{ million})$$
$$= \$23.04 \text{ million} + \$6.98 \text{ million} + \$14.55 \text{ million} + \$19 \text{ million}$$
$$= \$63.57 \text{ million (held in liquid assets and additional borrowing capacity)}$$

would face minimum pressure on its liquid reserves because deposit growth probably could fund nearly all the quality loans that walk in the door. In this "best" situation, it is highly likely that a *liquidity surplus* will develop. The liquidity manager must have a plan for investing these surplus funds in order to maximize the bank's return.

Of course, neither the worst nor the best possible outcome is likely for both deposit and loan growth. The most likely outcome lies somewhere between these extremes. Many banks, thrifts, and other financial firms like to calculate their *expected liquidity requirement*, based on the probabilities they assign to different possible outcomes. For example, suppose the liquidity manager of the bank we have been following considers the bank's liquidity situation next week as likely to fall into one of three possible situations:

Possible Liquidity Outcomes for Next Week	Estimated Average Volume of Deposits Next Week (millions)	Estimated Average Volume of Acceptable Loans Next Week (millions)	Estimated Liquidity Surplus or Deficit Position Next Week (millions)	Probability Assigned by Management to Each Possible Outcome
Best possible liquidity position (maximum deposits, minimum loans)	$170	$110	+$60	15%
Liquidity position with the highest probability of occurrence	$150	$140	+$10	60%
Worst possible liquidity position (minimum deposits, maximum loans)	$130	$150	−$20	25%

Thus, management sees the worst possible situation next week as one characterized by a $20 million liquidity deficit, but this least desirable outcome is assigned a probability of only 25 percent. Similarly, the best possible outcome would be a $60 million liquidity surplus, which the bank could invest in profitable loans and security investments; however, this is judged to have only a 15 percent probability of occurring. Much more likely is the middle ground—a $10 million liquidity surplus—with a management-estimated probability of 60 percent.

What, then, is the bank's expected liquidity requirement? We can find the answer from this formula:

$$
\begin{aligned}
\text{Expected liquidity requirement} =\ & \text{Probability of Outcome A} \times \left(\begin{array}{c}\text{Estimated liquidity} \\ \text{surplus or} \\ \text{deficit in} \\ \text{Outcome A}\end{array}\right) \quad \textbf{(5)} \\
& + \text{Probability of Outcome B} \times \left(\begin{array}{c}\text{Estimated liquidity} \\ \text{surplus or} \\ \text{deficit in} \\ \text{Outcome B}\end{array}\right) \\
& + \cdots + \cdots
\end{aligned}
$$

for all possible outcomes, subject to the restriction that the sum of all probabilities assigned by management must be 1.

Using this formula, this bank's expected liquidity requirement must be as follows:

$$
\begin{aligned}
\text{Expected liquidity requirement} =\ & 0.15 \times (+\$60 \text{ million}) + 0.60 \times (+\$10 \text{ million}) \\
& + 0.25 \times (-\$20 \text{ million}) \\
=\ & +\$10 \text{ million}
\end{aligned}
$$

On average, management should plan for a $10 million liquidity surplus next week and begin now to review the options for investing this expected surplus. Of course, management would also do well to have a contingency plan ready in case the worst possible outcome does occur.

Liquidity Indicator Approach

Many financial-service institutions estimate their liquidity needs based upon experience and industry averages. This often means using certain bellwether financial ratios or **liquidity indicators.** For example, for banks and other depository institutions the following are popular liquidity indicator ratios:

1. *Cash position indicator:* Cash and deposits due from depository institutions ÷ total assets, where a greater proportion of cash implies the depository institution is in a stronger position to handle immediate cash needs.

2. *Liquid securities indicator:* U.S. government securities ÷ total assets, which compares the most marketable securities an institution can hold with the overall size of its asset portfolio; the greater the proportion of government securities, the more liquid the depository institution's position tends to be.

3. *Net federal funds and repurchase agreements position:* (Federal funds sold and reverse repurchase agreements – Federal funds purchased and repurchase agreements) ÷ total assets, which measures the comparative importance of overnight loans relative to overnight borrowings of reserves; liquidity tends to increase when this ratio rises. (Repurchase agreements are essentially collateralized Federal funds.)

4. *Capacity ratio:* Net loans and leases ÷ total assets, which is really a negative liquidity indicator because loans and leases are often among the most illiquid assets a depository institution can hold.

5. *Pledged securities ratio:* Pledged securities ÷ total security holdings, also a negative liquidity indicator because the greater the proportion of securities pledged to back government deposits, the fewer securities are available to sell when liquidity needs arise.[1]

6. *Hot money ratio:* Money market (short-term) assets ÷ volatile liabilities = (Cash and due from deposits held at other depository institutions + holdings of short-term securities + Federal funds loans + reverse repurchase agreements) ÷ (large CDs + Eurocurrency deposits + Federal funds borrowings + repurchase agreements), a ratio that reflects whether the institution has roughly balanced the volatile liabilities it has issued in the money market with the volume of money market assets it holds that could be sold quickly to cover those money market liabilities.

7. *Deposit brokerage index:* Brokered deposits ÷ total deposits, where brokered deposits consist of packages of funds (usually $100,000 or less to gain the advantage of deposit insurance) placed by securities brokers for their customers with banks and thrift institutions paying the highest yields. Brokered deposits are highly interest sensitive and may be quickly withdrawn; the more a depository institution holds, the greater the chance of a liquidity crisis.

8. *Core deposit ratio:* Core deposits ÷ total assets, where core deposits are defined as total deposits less all deposits over $100,000. Core deposits are primarily small-denomination accounts from local customers that are considered unlikely to be withdrawn on short notice and so carry lower liquidity requirements.

9. *Deposit composition ratio:* Demand deposits ÷ time deposits, where demand deposits are subject to immediate withdrawal via check writing, while time deposits have fixed maturities with penalties for early withdrawal. This ratio measures how stable a funding base each depository institution possesses; a decline in the ratio suggests greater deposit stability and, therefore, a lessened need for liquidity.

Table 10–5 indicates recent trends in a few of these liquidity indicators among U.S.-insured banks. In general, most indicators seem to show a gradual decline in bank liquidity, particularly in liquid assets. One reason is a gradual shift in bank deposits toward longer-maturity instruments that are more stable and have fewer unexpected withdrawals. Another important factor is a recent decline in the legal reserve requirements levied by the Federal Reserve, which has reduced the legal reserves U.S. banks need to hold behind their deposits. There are also more ways to raise liquidity today, and advancing technology has made it somewhat easier to anticipate liquidity needs and to prepare for them.

The first five liquidity indicators discussed previously focus principally upon *assets*, or *stored liquidity*. The last four focus mainly on *liabilities*, or *purchased liquidity*. Each liquidity indicator needs to be compared with the average value of that indicator for banks and other financial firms of comparable size in a similar location. These indicators are highly sensitive to the season of the year and the stage of the business cycle. Liquidity indicators often decline in a boom period under pressure from heavy loan demand, only to rise again during the ensuing business recession. Therefore, industrywide averages are often misleading. Each financial institution's liquidity position must be judged relative to peer institutions of similar size operating in similar market environments. Moreover, liquidity managers usually focus on *changes* in their institution's liquidity indicators rather than on the level of each indicator. They want to know whether liquidity is rising or falling and why.

---

[1] See Chapter 9 for a discussion of the nature and use of pledged securities.

TABLE 10–5   Recent Trends in Liquidity Indicators for FDIC-Insured U.S. Banks

*Source: Federal Deposit Insurance Corporation.

Selected Liquidity Indicators	1985	1987	1989	1991	1993	1996	1998	2001	2002	2003
Cash Position Indicator: Cash and deposits due from depository institutions ÷ total assets	12.5%	11.9%	10.6%	8.9%	6.3%	7.3%	6.6%	6.0%	5.4%	4.6%
Net Federal Funds Position: (Federal funds sold − Federal funds purchased) ÷ total assets	−3.3	−3.7	−3.9	−2.4	−3.4	−3.4	−2.9	−2.8	−3.7	−1.2
Capacity Ratio: Net loans and leases ÷ total assets	58.9	59.3	60.7	57.0	56.6	60.2	58.5	58.2	57.7	58.6
Deposit Composition Ratio: Demand deposits ÷ Time deposits	68.4	55.8	44.8	44.7	52.4	58.2	50.2	44.4	41.2	NA

The Ultimate Standard for Assessing Liquidity Needs: Signals from the Marketplace

Many analysts believe there is really only one ultimately sound method for assessing a financial institution's liquidity needs and how well it is fulfilling them. This method centers on *the discipline of the financial marketplace.* For example, consider this question: Does a bank or other financial-service company really hold adequate liquidity reserves? The answer depends upon the financial firm's standing in the market. No bank or other financial-service provider can tell for sure if it has sufficient liquidity until it has passed the *market's test.*

For example, liquidity managers for banks should closely monitor the following signals:

1. *Public confidence.* Is there evidence the bank is losing deposits because individuals and institutions believe there is some danger it will run out of cash and be unable to pay its obligations?

2. *Stock price behavior.* Is the banking corporation's stock price falling because investors perceive the bank has an actual or pending liquidity crisis?

3. *Risk premiums on CDs and other borrowings.* Is there evidence that the bank is paying significantly higher interest rates on its offerings of time and savings deposits (especially on large negotiable CDs) and money market borrowings than other depository institutions of similar size and location? In other words, is the market imposing a *risk premium* in the form of higher borrowing costs because it believes the bank is headed for a liquidity crisis?

4. *Loss sales of assets.* Has the bank recently been forced to sell assets in a hurry, with significant losses, in order to meet demands for liquidity? Is this a rare event or has it become a frequent occurrence?

5. *Meeting commitments to credit customers.* Has the bank been able to honor all reasonable and potentially profitable requests for loans from its valued customers? Or have liquidity pressures compelled management to turn down some otherwise acceptable loan applications?

6. *Borrowings from the central bank.* Has the bank been forced to borrow in larger volume and more frequently from the central bank in its home territory (such as the Federal Reserve, Bank of England, or Bank of Japan) lately? Have central bank officials begun to question the bank's borrowings?

If the answer to any of the foregoing questions is *yes*, management needs to take a close look at its liquidity management policies and practices to determine whether changes are in order.

Concept Check

10–8. How does the sources and uses of funds approach help a manager estimate a financial institution's need for liquidity?

10–9. Suppose that a bank estimates its total deposits for the next six months in millions of dollars will be, respectively, $112, $132, $121, $147, $151, and $139, while its loans (also in millions of dollars) will total an estimated $87, $95, $102, $113, $101, and $124, respectively, over the same six months. Under the sources and uses of funds approach, when does this bank face liquidity deficits, if any?

10–10. What steps are needed to carry out the structure of funds approach to liquidity management?

10–11. Suppose that a thrift institution's liquidity division estimates that it holds $19 million in hot money deposits and other IOUs against which it will hold an 80 percent liquidity reserve, $54 million in vulnerable funds against which it plans to hold a 25 percent liquidity reserve, and $112 million in stable or core funds against which it will hold a 5 percent liquidity reserve. The thrift expects its loans to grow 8 percent annually; its loans currently total $117 million but have recently reached $132 million. If reserve requirements on liabilities currently stand at 3 percent, what is this depository institution's total liquidity requirement?

10–12. What is the liquidity indicator approach to liquidity management?

10–13. First National Bank posts the following balance sheet entries on today's date: Net loans and leases, $3,502 million; cash and deposits held at other banks, $633 million; Federal funds sold, $48 million; U.S. government securities, $185 million; Federal funds purchased, $62 million; demand deposits, $988 million; time deposits, $2,627 million; and total assets, $4,446 million. How many liquidity indicators can you calculate from these figures?

10–14. How can the discipline of the marketplace be used as a guide for making liquidity management decisions?

Legal Reserves and Money Position Management

The Money Position Manager   Management of a financial institution's liquidity position can be a harrowing job, requiring quick decisions that may have major long-run consequences for profitability. Nowhere is this more evident than in the job of **money position manager.**

Most large banks and thrift institutions have designated an officer of the firm as *money position manager.* Smaller banks and thrifts often hand this job over to larger depository institutions with which they have a correspondent relationship (that is, that hold deposits to help clear checks and meet other liquidity needs).

Legal Reserves   The manager of the money position is responsible for ensuring that the institution maintains an adequate level of **legal reserves**—assets the law and central bank regulation say must be held in support of the institution's deposits. In the United States, only two kinds of assets can be used for this purpose: (1) *cash in the vault;* (2) *deposits held in a reserve account at the Federal Reserve bank in the region* (or, for smaller banks and thrift institutions, deposits held with a Fed-approved depository institution that passes reserves through to the Fed). Incidentally, the smallest U.S. depository institutions in the year 2003 (those holding $6 million or less in reservable deposits) are generally

EXHIBIT 10–1
Federal Reserve Rules
for Calculating a
Weekly Reporting
Bank's Required
Legal Reserves

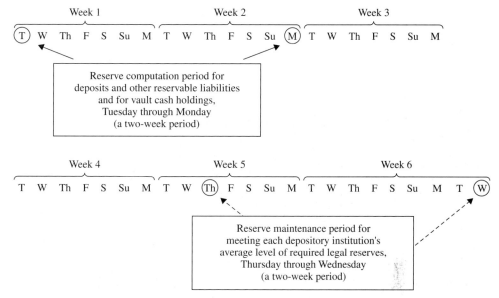

Federal Reserve rules for calculating and maintaining required legal reserves
(Regulation D):

exempt from legal reserve requirements. This exemption amount is adjusted annually to help reduce the impact of inflation on deposit growth. Legal reserve requirements apply to all qualified depository institutions, including commercial and savings banks, savings and loan associations, credit unions, agencies and branches of foreign banks, and Edge Act corporations that offer transaction deposits or nonpersonal (business) time deposits or borrow through Eurocurrency liabilities.

Regulations on Calculating Legal Reserve Requirements

Reserve Computation Exhibit 10–1 illustrates the timing associated with calculating reserve requirements and maintaining reserves that the Federal Reserve has set up for all depository institutions holding deposits and other liabilities subject to legal reserve requirements. As the exhibit shows, under the current system of accounting for legal reserves—sometimes called **lagged reserve accounting (LRA)**—the daily average amount of deposits and other reservable liabilities are computed using information gathered over a two-week period stretching from a Tuesday to a Monday two weeks later. This interval of time is known as the **reserve computation period.** The daily average amount of *vault cash* each bank or other depository institution holds is also figured over the same two-week computation period. Exhibit 10–1 illustrates one cycle. For large institutions another cycle begins immediately.[2]

---

[2] The process used for calculating legal reserve requirements described here applies to the largest U.S. banks, known as *weekly reporters,* that must report their cash positions and other data to the Federal Reserve banks on a weekly basis. The more numerous, but smaller U.S. banks and qualifying thrift institutions are known as *quarterly reporters.* This latter group of institutions have their daily average deposit balances figured over a seven-day computation period beginning on the third Tuesday in the months of March, June, September, and December, each representing one-quarter of the calendar year. These smaller U.S. depository institutions, then, must settle their reserve position at the required level weekly based on a legal reserve requirement determined once each quarter of the year. In contrast, the largest U.S. banks must meet (settle) their legal reserve requirement over successive two-week periods (biweekly).

Reserve Maintenance   After the money position manager calculates daily average deposits and the institution's required legal reserve, he or she must maintain that required legal reserve on deposit with the Federal Reserve bank in the region (less the amount of daily average vault cash held), on average, over a 14-day period stretching from a Thursday to a Wednesday. This is known as the **reserve maintenance period.** Notice from Exhibit 10–1 that this period begins 30 days after the beginning of the reserve computation period for deposits and other reservable liabilities. Using LRA, the money position manager has a 16-day lag following the computation period and preceding the maintenance period. This period provides time for planning.

Reserve Requirements   How much money must be held in legal reserves? That answer depends upon the volume and mix of each bank's deposits and also on the particular time period, since the amount of deposits subject to legal reserve requirements changes each year. For transaction deposits—checking accounts, NOWs, and other deposits that can be used to make payments—the reserve requirement in 2003 was 3 percent of the end-of-the-day daily average amount held over a two-week period, up to $42.1 million. Transaction deposits over $42.1 million held at the same bank carried a 10 percent reserve requirement.

The $42.1 million figure, known as the *reserve tranche*, is changed once each year based upon the annual rate of U.S. bank deposit growth. Under the dictates of the Depository Institutions Deregulation and Monetary Control Act of 1980, the Federal Reserve Board must calculate the June-to-June annual growth rate of all deposits subject to legal reserve requirements. The dollar cut-off point above which reserve requirements on transaction deposits become 10 percent instead of 3 percent is then adjusted by 80 percent of the calculated annual deposit growth rate. This annual legal reserve adjustment is designed to offset the impact of inflation, which over time would tend to push banks into higher and higher reserve requirement categories.

Calculating Required Reserves   The largest depository institutions must hold the largest amount and percentage of legal reserves, reflecting their great importance as funds managers for themselves and for thousands of smaller financial institutions within the financial system. However, whether large or small, the total required legal reserves of each depository institution are figured by the same basic method of calculation. Each reservable liability item is multiplied by the stipulated reserve requirement percentage set by the central bank (in the United States, the Federal Reserve Board) to derive each depository's total legal reserve requirement. Thus:

Total required legal reserves = Reserve requirement on transaction deposits   **(6)**
× Daily average amount of net transaction deposits over the computation period
+ Reserve requirement on nontransaction reservable liabilities × Daily average amount of nontransaction reservable liabilities over the computation period.

A sample calculation of a U.S. bank's total required legal reserves is shown in Table 10–6. The bank illustrated has daily averages over the computation period of $100 million in net transaction deposits and $200 million in nontransaction reservable liabilities.[3]

---

[3] *Net transaction deposits* include the sum total of all deposits on which a depositor is permitted to make withdrawals by check, telephone, or other transferable instrument minus any cash items in the process of collection, and deposits held with other depository institutions. Nonpersonal time deposits include savings deposits, CDs, and other time accounts held by a customer who is not a natural person (i.e., not an individual, family, or sole proprietorship). Eurocurrency liabilities are mainly the sum of net borrowing by domestic banking offices from foreign offices.

TABLE 10–6

Sample Calculation of Legal Reserve Requirements in the United States

Source: Board of Governors of the Federal Reserve System.

The applicable percentage reserve requirements imposed by the Federal Reserve Board are as follows:*

First $42.1 million of net transaction deposits: 3% legal reserve requirement. Amount over $42.1 million of net transaction deposits: 10% legal reserve requirement. Nontransaction reservable liabilities (including nonpersonal time deposits and Eurocurrency liabilities): 0% reserve requirement.**

First National's net transaction deposits averaged $100 million over the 14-day computation period while its nontransaction reservable liabilities had a daily average of $200 million over the same period.

Then First National's daily average required legal reserve level = 0.03 × $42.1 million + 0.10X ($100 million − $42.1 million) + 0.0X $200 million = 1.263 million + $5.79 million + $0.00 million = $7.053 million.

First National held a daily average of $5 million in vault cash over the required two-week computation period. Therefore, it must hold at the Federal Reserve Bank in its district the following amount, on average, over its two-week reserve maintenance period:

$$\begin{matrix} \text{Daily average level} \\ \text{of required legal} \\ \text{reserves to hold on} \\ \text{deposit at the Fed} \end{matrix} = \begin{matrix} \text{Total} \\ \text{required} \\ \text{legal} \\ \text{reserves} \end{matrix} - \begin{matrix} \text{Daily} \\ \text{average} \\ \text{vault} \\ \text{cash holdings} \end{matrix} = \text{\$7.053 million} - \text{\$5.00 million} = \text{\$2.053 million}$$

Federal Reserve officials today differentiate between so-called *bound* and *nonbound* depository institutions. Bound institutions' required legal reserves are larger than their vault cash holdings, meaning that they must hold additional legal reserves beyond the amount of their vault cash at the Federal Reserve Bank in their district. Nonbound institutions hold more vault cash than their total required legal reserves and therefore are not required to hold legal reserves at the Fed. As reserve requirements have been lowered in recent years, the number of nonbound depositories has increased.

---

*As of March 2003.

**Net transaction deposits are gross demand deposits less cash items in process of collection and deposits due from other banks. The percentage reserve requirement on nonpersonal time deposits with an original maturity of less than 18 months and on Eurocurrency liabilities was reduced to zero in 1991. Nonpersonal time deposits 18 months or longer to maturity were assigned a zero reserve requirement in 1983.

Key URL

To learn more about the latest legal reserve requirement rules under Regulation D, see http://www.frbservices.org/

Once a depository institution determines its required reserve amount, it compares this figure against its actual daily average holdings of legal reserve assets—vault cash and the size of its reserve deposit at the central bank. If total legal reserves held are greater than required legal reserves, the depository institution has *excess reserves.* Management will move quickly to invest the excess, because excess reserves pay no interest. Excess reserves carry an opportunity cost in the form of interest income that is not earned because management failed to invest them, even overnight.

If, on the other hand, the calculated required reserve figure exceeds the amount of legal reserves actually held on a daily average basis, the depository institution has a *reserve deficit.* The law requires that the depository institution cover this deficit by acquiring additional legal reserves. Actually, current regulations allow the depository institution to run up to a 4 percent deficit from its required daily average legal reserve position, provided this shortfall is balanced out by a corresponding excess during the next required reserve maintenance period. (The current Federal Reserve rule allows a depository institution to carry over from one reserve maintenance period to another the larger of $50,000 or 4 percent of the sum of a bank's required level of legal reserves plus the net amount of its clearing balance requirement (see the explanation below) at the Federal Reserve bank in its district.

Penalty for a Reserve Deficit Any deficit above 4 percent may be assessed an interest penalty equal to the Federal Reserve's discount (primary credit) rate at the beginning of the month plus 2 percentage points (measured as an annual rate), which is applied to the amount of the reserve deficiency. Increased surveillance costs may also be assessed if repeated reserve deficits lead regulators to examine and monitor the bank's operations more closely, possibly interfering with daily routine and perhaps damaging its efficiency.

Clearing Balances In addition to holding a legal reserve account at the central bank, many banks and thrift institutions also hold a **clearing balance** with the Fed to cover any checks or other debit items drawn against them. In the United States any depository institution using the Federal Reserve's check-clearing facilities must maintain a minimum-size clearing balance—an amount that is set by agreement between each institution and its district Federal Reserve bank, based on its estimated check-clearing needs and its recent record of overdrafts.

Clearing balance rules work much like legal reserve requirements, with banks and other depositories required to maintain a minimum daily average amount in their clearing account over the same two-week maintenance period as applies to legal reserves. When they fall more than 2 percent or $25,000 (whichever is greater) below the minimum balance required, they must provide additional funds to bring the balance up to the promised level. If a clearing balance has an excess amount in it, this can act as an extra cushion of reserves to help a depository institution avoid a deficit in its legal reserve account.

A bank or thrift earns credit from holding a clearing balance that it can apply to help cover the cost of using Fed services (such as the clearing and collection of checks or making use of Fed Wire, the Federal Reserve's electronic funds wire transfer service). The amount of credit earned from holding a Fed clearing balance depends on the size of the average account balance and the level of the Federal funds interest rate over the relevant period. For example, suppose a bank had a clearing balance averaging $1 million during a particular two-week maintenance period and the Federal funds interest rate over this same period averaged 5.50 percent. Then it would earn a Federal Reserve credit of

$$\text{Average clearing balance} \times \text{Annualized Fed funds rate} \times 14 \text{ days}/360 \text{ days} \qquad \textbf{(7)}$$
$$= \$1,000,000 \times .055 \times .0389 = \$2,138.89$$

Assuming a 360-day year for ease of computation, this bank could apply up to $2,138.89 to offset any fees charged the bank for the use of Federal Reserve services.

Factors Influencing the Money Position

A depository institution's money position, especially the size of its legal reserve account at the central bank in its nation or district, is influenced by a long list of factors, some of which are included in the following table. Among the most important of these factors are the volume of checks and other drafts cleared each day, the amount of currency and coin shipments back and forth between each depository and the central bank's vault, purchases and sales of government securities, and borrowing and lending in the Federal funds (interbank) market. Some of these factors are largely *controllable* by management, while others are essentially *noncontrollable*, and management needs to anticipate and react quickly to them.

Factoid
The oldest kind of sweep account offered by depository institutions are business-oriented sweep programs that convert business checking accounts, usually overnight, into savings deposits or off-balance-sheet interest-bearing investments.

Controllable Factors Increasing Legal Reserves	**Controllable Factors Decreasing Legal Reserves**
• Selling securities. • Receiving interest payments on securities. • Borrowing reserves from the Federal Reserve bank. • Purchasing Federal funds from other banks. • Selling securities under a repurchase agreement (RP). • Selling new CDs, Eurocurrency deposits, or other deposits to customers (with the new funds coming into the bank's reserve account by check or by wire).	• Purchasing securities. • Making interest payments to investors holding the bank's securities. • Repaying a loan from the Federal Reserve bank. • Selling Federal funds to other institutions in need of reserves. • Security purchases under a repurchase agreement (RP). • Receiving into the bank's vault currency and coin shipments from the Federal Reserve bank.
Noncontrollable Factors Increasing Legal Reserves	**Noncontrollable Factors Decreasing Legal Reserves**
• Surplus position at the local clearinghouse due to receiving more deposited checks in its favor than checks drawn against it. • Credit from cash letters sent to the Fed, listing drafts received by the bank. • Deposits made by the U.S. Treasury into a tax and loan account held at the bank. • Credit received from the Federal Reserve bank for checks previously sent for collection (deferred availability items, which the Fed credits to the bank's reserve account each day according to a fixed schedule).	• Deficit position at the local clearinghouse due to more checks drawn against the bank than in its favor. • Calls of funds from the bank's tax and loan account by the U.S. Treasury. • Debits received from the Federal Reserve bank for checks drawn against the bank's reserve account. • Withdrawal of large deposit accounts (such as CDs and Eurodollar deposits), often immediately by wire.

In recent years the volume of legal reserves held at the Federal Reserve banks by depository institutions operating in the United States has declined sharply. Today, for example, legal reserves held by depository institutions at all 12 Federal Reserve banks are less than half their volume in the mid-1990s. The significant decline in legal reserves is largely due to the development of **sweep accounts**—a service that the Federal Reserve permitted depository institutions to offer during the 1990s and that results in bankers shifting their customers' deposited funds out of accounts that carry reserve requirements (currently checkable or transaction accounts), usually overnight, into repurchase agreements, shares in money market funds, and savings accounts (not currently bearing reserve requirements). Such sweeps yield an advantage to the offering bank or other depository institution because they lower its overall cost of funds, while still preserving depositor access to his or her checking account and the ability to make payments or execute withdrawals.

Key URLs
For more information on sweep accounts see especially **www.research.stlouisfed.org/aggreg/swdata.html** and **www.treasurystrategies.com**.

These sweep arrangements have ballooned in size today to cover well over $500 billion in deposit balances, substantially lowering bankers' total required reserves. Bankers have been aided in their sweep activities by access to online sites made available from the Federal Reserve banks that track on a real-time basis any large dollar payments flowing into or out of their reserve balances at the Fed each day, allowing money managers to better plan what happens to their banks' legal reserve positions on a daily basis. Today the sweep accounts depository institutions offer include *retail sweeps*, involving the checking and savings accounts of individuals and families, and *business sweeps*, where commercial checkable deposit balances are changed overnight into commercial savings deposits or moved off depository institutions' balance sheets into interest-bearing investments and then quickly returned within hours.

The key goal of money position management is to keep legal reserves at the required level, with no excess reserves and no reserve deficit large enough to incur a penalty. If the bank or other depository institution has an *excess* reserve position, it will sell Federal funds to other banks short of legal reserves, or if the excess appears to be longer lasting, purchase securities or perhaps make new loans. If the depository institution has a legal reserve *deficit*, it will usually purchase Federal funds or borrow from the Federal Reserve bank in the district. If the deficit appears to be especially large or long lasting, the institution may sell some of its marketable securities and cut back on its lending.

An Example Table 10–7 illustrates how a bank, for example, can keep track of its reserve position on a daily basis. This example also illustrates the money desk manager's principal problem—trying to keep track of the many transactions each day during the reserve maintenance period that will affect this particular bank's legal reserves held at the district Federal Reserve bank. In this example, the money desk manager had estimated that his bank needed to average $500 million per day in its reserve account at the district Federal Reserve bank. However, at the end of the first day (Thursday) of the new reserve maintenance period, it had a $550 million reserve position. The bank's money manager tried to take advantage of this excess reserve position the next day (Friday) by purchasing $100 million in U.S. Treasury securities. The result was a reserve deficit of $130 million, much deeper than expected, due in part to an $80 million adverse clearing balance (that is, the bank had more checks presented for deduction from its customers' deposits than it received from other depository institutions for crediting to its own customers' accounts).

To help offset this steep decline in its reserve account, the money manager borrowed $50 million from the Federal Reserve bank's discount window on Friday afternoon. This helped a little because Friday's reserve position counts for Saturday and Sunday as well, when most banks and other depository institutions are closed, so the $130 million reserve deficit on Friday resulted in a $390 million (3 × $130 million) cumulative reserve deficit for the whole weekend. If the money desk manager had not borrowed the $50 million from the Fed, the deficit would have been $180 million for Friday and thus $540 million (3 × $180 million) for the entire weekend.

The bank depicted in Table 10–7 continued to operate below its required daily average legal reserve of $500 million through the next Friday of the reserve maintenance period, when a fateful decision was made. The money manager decided to borrow $100 million in Federal funds, but at the same time to sell $50 million in Federal funds to other depository institutions. Unfortunately, the manager did not realize until day's end on Friday that the bank had suffered a $70 million adverse clearing balance due to numerous checks written by its depositors that came back for collection. On balance, the bank's reserve deficit increased another $10 million, for a closing balance on Friday of $480 million. Once again, because Friday's balance carried over for Saturday and Sunday, the money desk manager faced a cumulative reserve deficit of $410 million on Monday morning, with only that day plus Tuesday and Wednesday to offset the deficit before the reserve maintenance period ended. As we noted earlier, Federal Reserve regulations require a depository institution to be within 4 percent of its required daily average reserve level or pay a penalty on the amount of the deficit. Trying to avoid the penalty, the money manager swung into high gear, borrowing $250 million in Federal funds on Monday and $100 million on Tuesday. Over two days this injected $350 million in new reserves. With an additional

TABLE 10–7 An Example: Daily Schedule for Evaluating a Bank's Money Position (all figures in millions of dollars)

Days in the Reserve Maintenance Period	Required Daily Average Balance at the Fed	Federal Funds Transactions Purchases (+)	Sales (−)	Fed's Discount Window Borrow (+)	Repay (−)	Treasury Securities Redeem (+)	Purchase (−)	Check Clearing Credit (+)	Debit (−)	Closing Daily Average Balance at the Federal Reserve Bank	Excess or Deficit in Legal Reserve Position	Cumulative Excess or Deficit in Legal Reserves	Cumulative Closing Balance at the Fed
Carryover excess (+) or deficit (−) in legal reserves from previous period:											0		
Thursday	$ 500	+50	−25		−25			+50		$550	+50	+50	$ 550
Friday	500			+50			−100		−80	370	−130	−80	920
Saturday	500			+50			−100		−80	370	−130	−210	1,290
Sunday	500			+50			−100		−80	370	−130	−340	1,660
Monday	500		−25		−50			+40		465	−35	−375	2,125
Tuesday	500	+50							−25	525	+25	−350	2,650
Wednesday	500					+50			−60	490	−10	−360	3,140
Thursday	500							+10		510	+10	−350	3,650
Friday	500	+100	−50						−70	480	−20	−370	4,130
Saturday	500	+100	−50						−70	480	−20	−390	4,610
Sunday	500	+100	−50						−70	480	−20	−410	5,090
Monday	500	+250					−25	+15		740	+240	−170	5,830
Tuesday	500	+100								600	+100	−70	6,430
Wednesday	500	+70								570	+70	0	7,000
Cumulative	$7,000												7,000
Daily average	$ 500												500

EXHIBIT 10–2

Movements in the Effective Federal Funds Rate and Its Target Interest Rate: Key Data Items for Money Position Managers to Watch

Source: Federal Reserve Bank of San Francisco, *Economic Letter*, No. 2002-30 (October 11, 2002).

Effective daily Federal funds rate and target rate

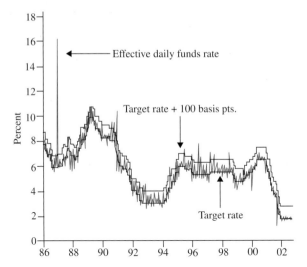

borrowing of $70 million in the Federal funds market on Wednesday, the last day of the reserve maintenance period (known as "bank settlement day"), the bank in our example ended the period with a zero cumulative reserve deficit.

Use of the Federal Funds Market   In the foregoing example, the money position manager had a large reserve deficit to cover in a hurry. This manager elected to borrow heavily in the **Federal funds market**—usually one of the cheapest places to borrow legal reserves, but also frequently quite volatile.

The effective interest rate on Federal funds changes minute by minute so money position managers must stay abreast of both the level and upward or downward movements in the effective daily Fed funds rate. One factor that aids the manager in anticipating changes in the cost of borrowing in the funds market is the fact that the Federal Reserve sets a target Fed funds rate and intervenes periodically (usually only once per day) to move the current funds rate closer to its target. As Exhibit 10–2 indicates, the effective daily funds rate hovers close to the Fed's target interest rate, generally within a few basis points of that target. The most volatile day in terms of trying to anticipate which way and by how much the funds rate will move is during *bank settlement day* (usually a Wednesday), when many depository institutions may find themselves desperately short of required reserves with the door (i.e., the reserve maintenance period) about to slam shut on them at day's end.

Other Options besides Fed Funds   While the Federal funds market is usually the most popular route for solving immediate shortages of legal reserves, the money position manager usually has a fairly wide range of options to draw upon from both the asset (stored liquidity) and liability (purchased liquidity) sides of the balance sheet. These include selling Treasury bills or other liquid securities the institution may already hold, drawing upon any excess correspondent balances placed with other depository institutions, entering into repurchase agreements for temporary borrowing, selling new time deposits to the largest customers, and borrowing in the Eurocurrency market. The money position manager's job is to find the best options in terms of cost, risk, and other factors.

Overdraft Penalties   Banks and other depository institutions operating inside the U.S. financial system run the risk of modest penalties if they run an intraday overdraft and possibly a stiffer penalty if overnight overdrafts occur in their reserves. Avoiding intraday and overnight overdrafts is not easy for most depository institutions because they have only partial control over the amount and timing of inflows and outflows of funds from their reserves, as we saw earlier. Because of possible overdraft penalties, many banking institutions hold "precautionary balances" (extra supplies of reserves) to help prevent overdrafting of their reserve account.

Factors in Choosing among the Different Sources of Reserves

In choosing which source of reserves to draw upon in order to cover a legal reserve deficit, money position managers must carefully consider several aspects of their institution's need for liquid funds:

1. *Immediacy of need.* If a reserve deficit comes due within minutes or a few hours, the money position manager will normally tap the Federal funds market for an overnight loan or contact the central bank for a loan from its discount window. In contrast, the bank or other depository institution can meet its nonimmediate reserve needs by selling deposits or assets, which may require more time to arrange than immediately available borrowings normally do.

2. *Duration of need.* If the liquidity deficit is expected to last for only a few hours, the Federal funds market or the central bank's discount window is normally the preferred source of funds. Liquidity shortages lasting days, weeks, or months, on the other hand, are often covered with sales of assets or long-term borrowings.

3. *Access to the market for liquid funds.* Not all depository institutions have equal access to all markets for funds. For example, smaller depositories cannot, as a practical matter,

---

Concept Check

10–15. What is *money position* management?

10–16. What is the principal *goal* of money position management?

10–17. Exactly how is a depository institution's legal reserve requirement determined?

10–18. First National Bank finds that its net transaction deposits average $140 million over the latest reserve computation period. Using the reserve requirement ratios imposed by the Federal Reserve as given in the textbook, what is the bank's total required legal reserve?

10–19. A U.S. savings bank has a daily average reserve balance at the Federal Reserve bank in its district of $25 million during the latest reserve maintenance period. Its vault cash holdings averaged $1 million and the savings bank's total transaction deposits (net of interbank deposits and cash items in collection) averaged $200 million daily over the latest reserve maintenance period. Does this depository institution currently have a legal reserve defi-

ciency? How would you recommend that its management respond to the current situation?

10–20. What factors should a money position manager consider in meeting a deficit in a depository institution's legal reserve account?

10–21. What are clearing balances? Of what benefit can clearing balances be to a bank or other depository that uses the Federal Reserve System's check-clearing network?

10–22. Suppose a bank maintains an average clearing balance of $5 million during a period in which the Federal funds rate averages 6 percent. How much would this bank have available in credits at the Federal Reserve Bank in its district to help offset the charges assessed against the bank for using Federal Reserve services?

10–23. What are *sweep accounts?* Why have they led to a significant decline in the total legal reserves held at the Federal Reserve banks by depository institutions operating in the United States?

draw upon the Eurocurrency market or sell commercial paper. Liquidity managers must restrict their range of choices to those their institution can access quickly.

4. *Relative costs and risks of alternative sources of funds.* The cost of each source of reserves changes daily, and the availability of surplus liquidity is also highly uncertain. Other things being equal, the liquidity manager will draw on the cheapest source of reliable funds and, therefore, must maintain constant contact with the money and capital markets to be aware of how interest rates and credit conditions are changing.

5. *Interest rate outlook and the shape of the yield curve.* When planning to deal with a future liquidity deficit, the liquidity manager wants to draw on those funds sources whose interest rates are expected to be the lowest. Often, with an upward-sloping yield curve, this means borrowing liquidity cheaply in the short-term market and loaning out any funds raised at a higher long-term interest rate. Management must be cautious here, however, because this strategy opens a depository institution up to additional interest-rate risk.

6. *Outlook for central bank monetary policy and for government borrowing.* Central bank and government borrowing operations should be studied carefully to determine which way credit conditions and interest rates in the financial markets are moving. A heavy government borrowing schedule or restrictive money and credit policy implies higher interest rates and reduced credit availability, making the raising of liquid funds more costly and more difficult for a liquidity manager.

7. *Hedging capability.* Banks and other depository institutions that make heavy use of borrowed sources of liquidity must wrestle with the problem of interest cost uncertainty. They do not know what their future borrowing costs will be. If management has sufficient skill, it can use hedging techniques (such as trading in options or financial futures) to reduce that uncertainty.

8. *Regulations applicable to a liquidity source.* Sources of liquidity cannot be used indiscriminately. For example, reserve requirements on deposits and a few remaining restrictions on borrowing from the discount windows of the central bank, limit banks and other depository institutions from drawing upon these sources and force liquidity managers to look elsewhere.

The liquidity manager must carefully weigh each of these factors in order to make a rational choice among alternative sources of reserves.

Central Bank Reserve Requirements beyond U.S. Borders

We should note that not all central banks impose legal reserve requirements on the banks and other depository institutions they regulate. For example, the Bank of England has not established official legal reserve requirements for its banks, and there is a trend among central banks around the globe to eliminate, suspend, or at least make less and less use of the legal reserve requirement tool, in part because it is so difficult to control. Moreover, while the United States imposes legal reserve requirements on deposits, many central banks impose required reserves on loans or on selected nondeposit liabilities. Finally, it is important to recognize that even if central banks like the Federal Reserve imposed no reserve requirements at all, bankers themselves would still hold some cash reserves because they need those immediately available funds to handle customer deposit withdrawals, meet new loan demand, and satisfy other cash-emergency needs.

Summary

Managing the *liquidity* position for a bank or other financial institution can be one of the most challenging jobs in the financial marketplace. In this chapter we reviewed several fundamental principles of liquidity management and looked at several of the liquidity manager's best tools. The key points in the chapter are listed below:

- A *liquid* bank or other financial firm is one that can raise cash in the amount required at reasonable cost precisely when the need for liquidity arises.

- Among depository institutions the two most common needs for cash arise when depositors withdraw their funds and when requests for loans come in the door.

- Liquidity needs are generally met either by selling assets (i.e., disposing of *stored liquidity*) or by borrowing in the money market (i.e., using *purchased liquidity*) or by a combination of these two approaches.

- Bankers and many of their competitors have developed several different methods to estimate what their institution's true liquidity needs are likely to be today and in the future. One of these estimation methods is the *sources and uses of funds method* in which total sources and uses of funds are projected over a desired planning horizon and liquidity deficits and surpluses are calculated from the difference between funds sources and funds uses.

- Another popular liquidity estimation method is the *structure of funds method*. This requires each financial firm to classify its funds uses and sources according to their probability of withdrawal or loss, particularly due to changes in market interest rates. Assigning probabilities of withdrawal or loss makes it possible to give a quantitative estimate of future liquidity needs.

- Still another liquidity estimation approach focuses on *liquidity indicators*, in which selected financial ratios measuring a bank or other financial firm's liquidity position on both sides of its balance sheet are calculated with the liquidity manager looking for any evidence of adverse trends in liquidity for his or her institution.

- Banks and their financial-service competitors today can draw upon multiple sources of liquid assets and borrowed liquidity. Key sources of liquidity on the asset side of the balance sheet include correspondent balances held with depository institutions and sales of government securities and other highly liquid money market instruments. Important borrowed liquidity sources include borrowing from the central bank's discount window, purchasing Federal funds, employing repurchase agreements (RPs), issuing CDs or other deposits, borrowing Eurocurrency deposits, and issuing commercial paper.

- One of the most challenging areas of funds management among depository institutions centers upon the *money position manager* who oversees the *legal reserve account* of a bank or competing depository institution. These legal reserves include vault cash held on a depository institution's premises and a deposit account kept with the central bank, which must be controlled to achieve a target level of legal reserves over each reserve maintenance period. Failure to hold adequate legal reserves can incur monetary penalties and greater surveillance by regulatory authorities.

- Liquidity and money position managers choose their sources of liquidity based on several key factors, including (1) immediacy of the liquidity need; (2) duration of the liquidity need; (3) market access; (4) relative costs and risks; (5) the outlook for market interest rates; (6) the outlook for monetary policy and government borrowing; (7) hedging capacity or capability; and (8) government regulations.

Key Terms

liquidity, *347*
net liquidity position, *349*
asset liquidity
management, *352*
liquid asset, *352*
opportunity cost, *352*
liability management, *353*
balanced liquidity
management, *354*

sources and uses of funds
method, *356*
liquidity gap, *356*
structure of funds
method, *359*
liquidity indicators, *363*
money position
manager, *366*
legal reserves, *366*

lagged reserve accounting
(LRA), *367*
reserve computation
period, *367*
reserve maintenance
period, *368*
clearing balance, *370*
sweep account, *371*
federal funds market, *374*

Problems and Projects

1. Caesar Hills State Bank estimates that over the next 24 hours the following cash inflows and outflows will occur (all figures in millions of dollars):

Deposit withdrawals	$ 47
Deposit inflows	87
Scheduled loan repayments	55
Acceptable loan requests	102
Borrowings from the money market	61
Sales of bank assets	16
Stockholder dividend payments	178
Revenues from sale of nondeposit services	33
Repayments of bank borrowings	67
Operating expenses	45

What is this bank's projected net liquidity position in the next 24 hours? From what sources can the bank cover its liquidity needs?

2. See if you can determine from the following information the volume of deposit withdrawals that Hillpeak Savings Bank is expecting to occur next week. Hillpeak is projecting a net liquidity surplus of $2 million next week partially as a result of expected quality loan demand of $24 million, necessary repayments of previous bank borrowings of $15 million, disbursements to cover operating expenses of $18 million, planned stockholder dividend payments of $5 million, expected deposit inflows of $26 million, revenues from nondeposit service sales of $18 million, scheduled repayments of previously made customer loans of $23 million, bank asset sales of $10 million, and money market borrowings of $11 million. How much must this savings bank's expected deposit withdrawals be for the coming week?

3. First National Bank of Los Alamos has forecast its checkable deposits, time and savings deposits, and commercial and household loans over the next eight months. The resulting estimates (in millions) are as shown in the following table. Use the sources and uses of funds approach to indicate which months are likely to result in liquidity deficits and which in liquidity surpluses if these forecasts turn out to be true. Explain carefully what you would do to deal with each month's projected liquidity position.

	Checkable Deposits	Time and Savings Deposits	Commercial Loans	Consumer Loans
January	$111	$543	$682	$137
February	102	527	657	148
March	98	508	688	153
April	91	491	699	161
May	101	475	708	165

June	87	489	691	170
July	84	516	699	172
August	99	510	672	156

4. Hamilton Security Savings and Thrift Association of Houston is attempting to determine its liquidity requirements today (the last day in August) for the month of September. This is usually a month of heavy business and consumer loan demand due to the beginning of the school term and the buildup of business inventories of goods and services for the fall season and the winter. This thrift institution has analyzed its deposit accounts thoroughly and classified them as follows (in millions).

   Management has elected to hold a 75 percent reserve in liquid assets or borrowing capacity (0.75) for each dollar of hot money deposits, a 20 percent reserve behind the vulnerable deposits, and a 5 percent reserve for its holdings of core funds. The estimated reserve requirements on most deposits are 3 percent, except that savings deposits carry a zero percent reserve requirement and all checkable deposits above $42.2 million carry a 12 percent reserve requirement. Hamilton currently has total loans outstanding of $2,389 million, which two weeks ago were as high as $2,567 million. Its loans' mean annual growth rate over the past three years has been about 8 percent. Carefully estimate Hamilton's total liquidity requirement for September.

	Checkable Deposits	Savings Deposits	Nonpersonal Time Deposits
Hot money funds	$132	$___	$782
Vulnerable funds	207	52	540
Stable (core) funds	821	285	72

5. Using the following financial information for Wilson National Bank, calculate as many of the *liquidity indicators* discussed in this chapter for Wilson as you can. Do you detect any significant liquidity trends at this bank? Which trends should management investigate?

	Most Recent Year	Previous Year
Assets:		
Cash and due from depository institutions	$ 358,000	$ 379,000
U.S. Treasury securities	178,000	127,000
Other securities	343,000	358,000
Pledged securities	223,000	202,000
Federal funds sold	131,000	139,000
Loans and leases net	1,948,000	1,728,000
Total assets	3,001,000	2,941,000
Liabilities:		
Demand deposits	$ 456,000	$ 511,000
Savings deposits	721,000	715,000
Time deposits	853,000	744,000
Transaction accounts	644,000	630,000
Nontransaction accounts	1,349,000	1,328,000
Brokered deposits	37,000	12,000
Federal funds purchased	237,000	248,000
Other money market borrowings	16,000	84,000

6. The Bank of Your Dreams has a very simple balance sheet. The figures are in millions of dollars as follows:

Assets		Liabilities and Equity	
Cash	$ 100	Deposits	$4,000
Securities	1,000	Other liabilities	500
Loans	4,000	Equity	600
Total Assets	5,100	Total liabilities and equity	5,100

Although the balance sheet is simple, the liquidity manager encounters a liquidity challenge when depositors withdraw $500 million.

a. If asset liquidity management is used and securities are sold to cover the deposit drain, what happens to the size of the Bank of Your Dreams?

b. If liability liquidity management is used to cover the deposit drain, what happens to the size of the Bank of Your Dreams?

7. The liquidity manager for the Bank of Your Dreams needs cash to meet some unanticipated loan demand. The loan officer has $600 million in loans that he/she wants to make. Use the simplified balance sheet provided in the previous problem to answer the following questions:

a. If asset liquidity management is used and securities are sold to provide money for the loans, what happens to the size of the Bank of Your Dreams?

b. If liability liquidity management is used to provide funds for the loans, what happens to the size of the Bank of Your Dreams?

8. Suppose a savings bank's liquidity manager estimates that the bank will experience a $550 million liquidity deficit next month with a probability of 10 percent, a $700 million liquidity deficit with a probability of 40 percent, a $230 million liquidity surplus with a probability of 30 percent, and a $425 million liquidity surplus bearing a probability of 20 percent. What is this savings bank's *expected liquidity requirement?* What should management do?

9. United Savings of Pierce, Iowa, reported transaction deposits of $75 million (the daily average for the latest two-week reserve computation period). Its nonpersonal time deposits over the most recent reserve computation period averaged $37 million daily, while vault cash averaged $0.978 million over the vault-cash computation period. Assuming that reserve requirements on transaction deposits are 3 percent of the total amount outstanding up to $42.1 million and 12 percent for all transaction deposits over $42.1 million while time deposits carry a 3 percent required reserve, calculate this thrift and savings institution's required daily average legal reserve at the Federal Reserve Bank in the district.

10. Elton Harbor National Bank has a cumulative legal reserve deficit of $44 million at the Federal Reserve bank in the district as of the close of business this Tuesday. The bank must cover this deficit by the close of business tomorrow (Wednesday).

Charles Tilby, the bank's money desk supervisor, examines the current distribution of money market and long-term interest rates and discovers the following:

Money Market Instruments	Current Market Yield
Federal funds	8.46%
Borrowing from the central bank's discount window	7.00
Commercial paper (one-month maturity)	8.40
Bankers' acceptances (three-month maturity)	8.12
Certificates of deposit (one-month maturity)	8.35
Eurodollar deposits (three-month maturity)	8.38
U.S. Treasury bills (three-month maturity)	7.60
U.S. Treasury notes and bonds (one-year maturity)	7.64
U.S. Treasury notes and bonds (five-year maturity)	7.75
U.S. Treasury notes and bonds (10-year maturity)	7.83

One week ago, the bank borrowed $20 million from the Federal Reserve's discount window, which it paid back yesterday. The bank had a $5 million legal reserve deficit during the previous reserve maintenance period. From the bank's standpoint, which sources of reserves appear to be the most promising? Which source would you recommend to cover the bank's legal reserve deficit? Why?

11. Eckhardt County Building and Loan Association estimates the following information regarding this thrift institution's legal reserve position at the Federal Reserve for the reserve maintenance period that begins today (Thursday):

Calculated required daily average balance at the Federal Reserve bank	=	$750 million
A loan received from the Fed's discount window a week ago that comes due next Friday	=	$70 million
Planned purchases of U.S. Treasury securities on behalf of the thrift institution and its customers:		
Tomorrow (Friday)	=	$80 million
Next Wednesday	=	$35 million
Next Friday	=	$18 million

Eckhardt County also had a $750 million required daily average reserve requirement during the preceding reserve maintenance period. What problems are likely to emerge as this thrift institution tries to manage its legal reserve position over the next two weeks? Relying on the Federal funds market and loans from the Federal Reserve's discount window as tools to manage its legal reserve position, carefully construct a pro forma daily worksheet for this thrift's money position over the next two weeks. Insert your planned adjustments in discount window borrowing and Federal funds purchases and sales over the period to show how you plan to manage Eckhardt County's legal reserve position and hit your desired reserve target.

Check-clearing estimates over the next 14 days are as follows:

Day	Credit Balance in Millions (+)	Debit Balance in Millions (−)
1	+10	
2		−60
3	Closed	
4	Closed	
5		−40
6		−25
7	+30	
8		−45
9		−5
10	Closed	
11	Closed	
12	+20	
13		−70
14	+10	

Closing reserve position in the previous reserve maintenance period = −$5 million.

12. NCA Savings Bank and Trust Co. has calculated its daily average deposits and vault cash holdings for the most recent two-week computation period as follows:

Net transaction deposits	= $ 81,655,474
Nonpersonal time deposits under 18 months to maturity	= $147,643,589
Eurocurrency liabilities	= $ 5,840,210
Daily average balance in vault cash	= $ 1,002,031

Suppose the reserve requirements posted by the Board of Governors of the Federal Reserve System are as follows:

Net transaction accounts:	
$0 to $42.1 million	3%
More than $42.1 million	12%
Nonpersonal time deposits:	
Less than 18 months	3%
18 months or more	0%
Eurocurrency liabilities—all types	3%

What is this savings bank's total required level of legal reserves? How much must the bank hold on a daily average basis with the Federal Reserve bank in its district?

13. Frost Street National Bank currently holds $750 million in transaction deposits subject to legal reserve requirements but has managed to enter into sweep account arrangements with its transaction deposit customers affecting $150 million of their deposits. Given the current legal reserve requirements applying to transaction deposits (as mentioned in this chapter), by how much would Frost Street's total legal reserves

decrease as a result of these new sweep account arrangements, which stipulate that transaction deposit balances covered by the sweep agreements will be moved overnight into savings deposits?

14. Lindberg Thrift and Savings Association maintains a clearing account at the Federal Reserve Bank in its district and agrees to keep a minimum balance of $22 million in its clearing account. Over the two-week reserve maintenance period ending today Lindberg managed to keep an average clearing account balance of $24 million. If the Federal funds interest rate has averaged 5.25 percent over this particular maintenance period, what maximum amount would Lindberg have available in the form of Federal Reserve credit to help offset any fees the Federal Reserve bank might charge the bank for using Federal Reserve services?

Internet Exercises

1. Evaluate the cash assets, including legal reserves, held by the Bank of America and Citigroup. How has their liquidity position changed recently? One website that provides this information for all the depository institutions in a bank holding company (BHC) is **www3.fdic.gov/sdi/main.asp**. You are particularly interested in the items identified as "Cash and Due from Depository Institutions."

2. With reference to the BHCs mentioned in exercise 1, what was their ratio of cash and due from depository institutions to total assets at last year's year-end? Do you notice any significant trends in their liquidity position that you think have also affected the banking industry as a whole? Examine the ratios for all FDIC-insured banks. This can also be accomplished at **www3.fdic.gov/sdi/main.asp**.

3. In describing reserve management, we referenced some numbers that change every year based on U.S. bank deposit growth. The reservable liabilities exemption determines which banks are exempt from legal reserve requirements, and the low reserve tranche is used in calculating reserve requirements. Go to **www.federalreserve.gov/ regulations/default.htm** and explore information concerning Regulation D. Find and report the low reserve tranche adjustment and the reservable liabilities exemption adjustment that are being used this year.

STANDARD &POOR'S

S&P Market Insight Challenge

1. Use Standard & Poor's Market Insight website (**www.mhhe.com/edumarketinsight**) for this problem. In the S&P Industry Survey entitled "Banking," *liquidity* is a key measure of financial condition for banking firms. For an up-to-date description of how banks measure liquidity, use the Industry tab in Market Insight and the drop-down menu to select Diversified Banks or Regional Banks. Upon selecting one of these subindustries, you will find the S&P Industry Survey on Banking. Please download this survey and view the section, "How to Analyze a Bank." Describe what it means to be "liquid." When is a bank "loaned up," and how does this relate to liquidity?

2. Use Standard & Poor's Market Insight website (**www.mhhe.com/edumarketinsight**) for this problem. Of all the businesses that are represented in S&P's Market Insight, bank thrift institutions typically face the most critical liquidity problems. Examining closely the most recent financial reports of such banks as Barclays PLC, J. P. Morgan Chase & Company, Washington Mutual, and other leading depositories, can you see any significant trends in liquidity among these institutions? Is banking's liquidity really declining, as some financial experts claim, or have banks and thrifts simply discovered new ways to manage cash and raise additional liquidity? Are structural changes under way in the industry that might explain its recent liquidity trends?

REAL NUMBERS FOR REAL BANKS   Assignment for Chapter 10

YOUR BANK'S LIQUIDITY REQUIREMENT: AN EXAMINATION OF ITS LIQUIDITY INDICATORS

Chapter 10 describes liquidity and reserve management. Within the chapter we explore how liquidity managers evaluate their institution's liquidity needs. Four methodologies are described: (1) the sources and uses of funds approach, (2) the structure of funds approach, (3) the liquidity indicator approach, and (4) signals from the marketplace. In this assignment we will calculate and interpret the nine ratios associated with the liquidity indicators approach. By comparing these ratios across time and with a group of contemporary banks, we will examine the liquidity needs of your BHC. In doing so, you will familiarize yourself with some new terms and tools associated with real data. This assignment involves some data exploration that is best described as a financial analyst's "treasure hunt."

Application of the Liquidity Indicator Approach: Trend and Comparative Analysis

A. **Data Collection:** To calculate these ratios, we will use some data collected in prior assignments and revisit the Statistics for Depository Institutions website (**www3.fdic.gov/sdi/main.asp**) to gather more information for your BHC and its peer group. Use SDI to create a four-column report of your bank's information and the peer group information across years. In this part of the assignment, for Report Selection you will access a number of different reports. We suggest that you continue to collect percentage information to calculate your liquidity indicators. The additional information you need to collect before calculating the indicators is denoted by **. All data is available in SDI by the name given next to the **. As you collect the information, enter the percentages for items marked ** in Columns B–E as an addition to Spreadsheet 2.

Liquidity indicators (A87)	Your Bank	Peer Group	Your Bank	Peer Group
Date (A88)	**12/31/yy**	**12/31/yy**	**12/31/yy**	**12/31/yy**
(1) Cash position indicator (A89)	%	%	%	%
(2) Liquid securities indicator (A90)				
** U.S. Government securities (A91)				
(3) Net Fed funds and RP indicator (A92)				
(4) Capacity ratio (A93)				
(5) Pledged securities ratio (A94)				
** Pledged securities (A95)				
(6) Hot money ratio (A96)				
** Fixed and floating rate debt securities with remaining maturity of one year or less (A97)				
** Volatile liabilities (A98)				
(7) Deposit brokerage index (A99)				
** Brokered deposits (A100)				
(8) Core deposit ratio (A101)				
** Core deposits (A102)				
(9) Deposit composition ratio (A103)				
** Demand deposits (A104)				
** Total time deposits (A105)				

B. Having collected the additional data needed, use the newly collected and previously collected data to calculate the liquidity indicators. For instance, the percentage data you have can be used to calculate the pledged securities ratio. The formula to enter for Cell B94 is B95/B6.

C. The first five liquidity indicators focus upon assets or stored liquidity. Write one paragraph describing your bank's use of asset liquidity management and describe any changes you observe across the two years.

D. Compare and contrast the first five ratios for the peer group in Columns C and E to your bank's asset liquidity ratios. Write one paragraph describing your observations.

E. The last four liquidity indicators focus upon liabilities or purchased liquidity. Write one paragraph describing your bank's use of liabilities liquidity management and describe any changes you observe across the two years.

F. Compare and contrast the last four ratios for the peer group in Columns C and E to your bank's liabilities liquidity ratios. Write one paragraph describing your observations.

Selected References

The following studies discuss the instruments often used to manage the liquidity positions of banks, competing institutions, and their customers:

1. Anderson, Richard G. "Retail Sweep Programs and Money Demand." *Monetary Trends*, Federal Reserve Bank of St. Louis, November 2002.

2. Bassett, William F., and Egon Zakrajesk. "Profits and Balance Sheet Developments at U.S. Commercial Banks in 2001." *Federal Reserve Bulletin*, June 2002.

3. Bennett, Paul, and Spence Hilton. "Falling Reserve Balances and the Federal Funds Rate." *Current Issues in Economics and Finance*, Federal Reserve Bank of New York, vol. 3, no. 5 (April 1997), pp. 1–6.

4. Champ, Bruce. "Open and Operating: Providing Liquidity to Avoid a Crisis." *Economic Commentary*, Federal Reserve Bank of Cleveland, February 15, 2003.

For a review of the rules for meeting Federal Reserve deposit reserve requirements, see the following:

5. Board of Governors of the Federal Reserve System. Press Release, December 11, 2002, Notice 02-66.

6. Bartolini, Leonardo, Giuseppe Bestda, and Alessandro Prati. "Day to Day Monetary Policy and Volatility of the Federal Funds Rate." *Journal of Money, Credit and Banking* 34(1), February 2002, pp. 137–159.

7. Coleman, Stacy P. "The Evolution of the Federal Reserve's Intraday Credit Policies." *Federal Reserve Bulletin* 88 (February 2002), pp. 67–84.

8. Cyree, Ken B., Mark D. Griffiths, and Drew B. Winters. "On the Pervasive Effects of Federal Reserve Settlement Regulations." *Review*, Federal Reserve Bank of St. Louis, March/April 2003, pp. 27–46.

For an examination of market discipline as a force in the liquidity management of banks and competing institutions, see these sources:

9. Board of Governors of the Federal Reserve System. *Study Group on Subordinated Notes and Debentures.* Staff Study 172, Washington, D.C., December 1999.

10. Jordan, John S. "Depositor Discipline at Failing Banks." *New England Economic Review*, Federal Reserve Bank of Boston, March/April 2000, pp. 15–28.

11. Krainer, John, and Jose A. Lopez. "How Might Financial Information Be Used for Supervisory Purposes?" *FRBSF Economic Review*, Federal Reserve Bank of San Francisco, 2003, pp. 29–45.

12. Madigan, Brian, and William Nelson. "Proposed Revision to the Federal Reserve's Discount Window Lending Programs." *Federal Reserve Bulletin* 88(7), July 2002, pp. 313–319.

13. Stackhouse, Julie L., and Mark D. Vaughan. "Navigating the Brave New World of Bank Liquidity." *The Regional Economist*, Federal Reserve Bank of St. Louis, July 2003, pp. 12–13.

www.mhhe.com/rose6e

PART FOUR

Managing the Sources of Funds for Banks and Their Closest Competitors

To fund their operations and to grow, banks and competing financial-service institutions have learned to seek out multiple sources of funds, including checkable and savings deposits sold to the public and nondeposit borrowings from other banks, thrifts, security firms, and even industrial corporations. They have also unearthed new funds sources from the sale of nontraditional services that add to revenues and, ultimately, to earnings, such as fee income from providing investment banking services, brokerage commissions for executing the sale of stocks, bonds, and mutual funds on behalf of their customers, sales revenue and underwriting profits from insurance policies, fees from managing their customers' property (trust services), and numerous other sources of fee income that, historically, have been outside banking's conventional boundaries. Finally, the owners of banks and other financial-service corporations are always expected to contribute some of their own funds (equity capital or net worth) to reduce risk and provide protection for depositors and others who hold claims against a financial-service provider.

This broadening of funds sources for banks and their closest competitors reflects multiple forces at work within the financial system. One of the most important is *competition* among a wide variety of financial firms, especially money market funds, stock and bond mutual funds, security broker/dealer firms and other financial-service providers that frequently seem to offer the prospect of higher returns for those customers willing to withdraw their funds from one type of financial-service firm and place them with another. This was evident during the 1990s when billions of dollars in deposits at banks and thrift institutions flowed into the stock market and the managers of these depository institutions had to scramble to find other ways to fund their assets.

Moreover, bank managers and many of their competitors have found that the *condition of the economy* matters greatly in raising new money and in holding onto the funds you already have. For example, when the economy dips into a recession and unemployment

management emerged, reminding banks and other financial-service managers that their sources of funds needed to be closely managed just as they closely manage the asset side of the balance sheet.

In this part of the book we explore some critical topics for banks and a number of their closest financial-service competitors. For example, how should a bank or other financial firm determine the cost of each funding source? How can we measure the impact of various funds sources on a financial institution's risk exposure and capital requirements? And why is the funding base of a bank or other financial firm (especially its owner's capital) such a critical determinant of its ability to expand today and in the future?

CHAPTER ELEVEN

Managing and Pricing Deposit Services

Key Topics in This Chapter

- Types of Deposit Accounts Offered
- The Changing Mix of Deposits and Deposit Costs
- Pricing Deposit Services and Deposit Interest Rates
- Conditional Deposit Pricing
- Disclosure of Deposit Terms
- Lifeline Banking

Introduction

Barney Kilgore, one of the most famous presidents in the history of Dow Jones & Company and publisher of *The Wall Street Journal,* once cautioned his staff: "Don't write banking stories for bankers. Write for the bank's customers. There are a hell of a lot more depositors than bankers." Kilgore was a wise man, indeed. For every banker in this world there are thousands upon thousands of depositors. Deposit accounts are a banker's number one source of funds.

Deposits are a key element in defining what a banking firm really does and what critical roles it plays in the economy. The ability of management and staff to attract checking and savings deposits from businesses and consumers is an important measure of a depository institution's acceptance by the public. Moreover, deposits provide most of the raw material for making loans and, thus, usually represent the ultimate source of profits and growth for a bank or thrift institution. Important indicators of management's effectiveness are whether or not funds deposited by the public have been raised at the lowest possible cost and whether sufficient deposits are available to fund all those loans the management of a bank or thrift wishes to make.[1]

This last point highlights the two key issues that every bank or other depository institution must deal with in managing the public's deposits: (1) Where can funds be raised at the lowest possible cost? and (2) How can management ensure that the institution always has enough deposits to support the volume of loans and other investments and services the public demands? Neither question is easy to answer, especially in today's intensely competitive financial marketplace. Both the cost and amount of deposits banks and other depository institutions can sell to the public are heavily influenced by the pricing

---

[1] Portions of this chapter are based upon articles by Peter S. Rose in *The Canadian Banker* [5, 6] and are used with permission of the publisher.

Information on deposit products offered by banks and other depository institutions has mushroomed on the World Wide Web. Not only can we use the Web today to find the best terms available on checking and savings-type services, but we can also analyze how well individual banks and other depositories are performing in reaching the public with their deposit services.

Among the most popular sites in this field are the "scanner sites" that survey banks and thrift institutions across the nation or around the world to find those offering the best terms available on savings and checking accounts. Examples include the Federally Insured Savings Network (FISN), which publishes a daily table listing the top rate-paying depository institutions at **www.fisn.com**. Another popular site in this same area is the Bank CD Rate Scanner FAQ at **bankcd.com**, which scans more than 3,000 U.S. banks for the best terms available on checking accounts, money market and savings deposits, and CDs bearing maturities as short as one month out to 15 years. These sites not only perform a valuable service in helping customers find the best deposit yields and lowest fees available, they also give bankers and other financial-service managers the opportunity to assess what their competition is doing.

Issues in the deposit field also show up periodically in such sources as the Financial Institutions Center at **fic.wharton.upenn.edu/fic/** and Bank Security Publications at **www.banksecurity.com/products.html**. Because deposit banking increasingly involves the electronic transfer of funds, it is also helpful to be familiar with the Federal Trade Commission's new site on electronic funds transfer services (EFTS) at **www.ftc.gov/bcp/conline/pubs/credit/elbank.htm**.

Customers curious about the degree of insurance protection for their deposits can check with a site maintained by the Federal Deposit Insurance Corporation (FDIC), which helps to explain the rules of insurance coverage, at **www2.fdic.gov/edie** and also the FDIC's new Learning Bank site at **www.fdic.gov/about/learn/learning/index.html**. Finally, if you want to track the changing deposit growth of any FDIC-insured institution, go to **www3.fdic.gov/sdi/main.asp**. This source will not only help you find figures for measuring quarterly and annual deposit growth at individual banks, but also let you compare one bank against another or relative to the industry as a whole.

schedules and competitive maneuverings of scores of other financial institutions offering similar services, such as share accounts in money market mutual funds and credit unions, cash management accounts offered by brokerage firms and insurance companies, and interest-bearing checkable deposits offered by many security firms. Innovation in the form of new types of deposits, new service delivery methods (increasingly electronic in design), and new pricing schemes is accelerating today. Bankers and other financial-service managers who fail to stay abreast of changes in their competitors' deposit pricing and marketing programs stand to lose both customers and profits.

In this chapter we explore the types of deposits banks and their competitors sell to the public. We also examine how deposits are priced, the methods for determining their cost to the offering institution, and the impact of government regulation on the deposit function.

Types of Deposits Offered by Banks and Other Depository Institutions

The number and range of deposit services offered by banks and their chief competitors is impressive indeed and often confusing for customers. Like a Baskin-Robbins ice cream store, deposit plans designed to attract customer funds today come in 31 flavors and more, each plan having features intended to closely match business and household needs for saving money and making payments for goods and services.

Transaction (Payments) Deposits

One of the oldest services offered by banks and other depository institutions has centered on making *payments* on behalf of customers. This **transaction,** or *demand,* **deposit** service requires the bank or other financial-service provider to honor immediately any withdrawals made either in person by the customer or by a third party designated by the customer to be the recipient of the funds withdrawn. Transaction deposits include *regular noninterest-bearing demand deposits,* which do not earn an explicit interest payment but provide the customer with payment services, safekeeping of funds, and recordkeeping for any transactions carried out by check, and *interest-bearing demand deposits* that provide all of the foregoing services and pay interest to the depositor as well.

Noninterest-Bearing Demand Deposits   Interest payments have been prohibited on regular checking accounts in the United States since passage of the Glass-Steagall Act of 1933. Congress feared at the time that paying interest on immediately withdrawable deposits endangered bank safety—a proposition that researchers have subsequently found to have little support. However, demand deposits are among the most volatile and least predictable of a depository institution's sources of funds, with the shortest potential maturity, because they can be withdrawn without prior notice. Most noninterest-bearing demand deposits are held by business firms.

Interest-Bearing Demand Deposits   Many consumers today have moved their funds into other types of checkable deposits that pay at least some interest. Beginning in New England during the 1970s, hybrid checking–savings deposits began to appear in the form of *negotiable order of withdrawal* **(NOW) accounts.** NOWs are interest-bearing savings deposits that give the bank or other service provider the right to insist on prior notice before the customer withdraws funds. Because this notice requirement is rarely exercised, the NOW can be used just like a checking account to pay for purchases of goods and services. NOWs were permitted nationwide beginning in 1981 as a result of passage of the Depository Institutions Deregulation Act of 1980. However, they can be held only by individuals and nonprofit institutions. When NOWs became legal nationwide, the U.S. Congress also sanctioned the offering of automatic transfers (ATS), which permit the customer to preauthorize a bank or other depository institution to move funds from a savings account to a checking account in order to cover overdrafts. The net effect was to pay interest on transaction balances roughly equal to the interest earned on a savings account.

Key URLs
Among the best sources for the current deposit interest rates offered by many banks and thrift institutions are www.Bankrate.com and www.iMoneyNet .com.

Two other important interest-bearing transaction accounts were created in the United States in 1982 with passage of the Garn–St Germain Depository Institutions Act. Banks and nonbank thrift institutions could offer deposits competitive with the share accounts offered by money market funds that carried higher, unregulated interest rates and were backed by a pool of high-quality securities. The result was the appearance of **money market deposit accounts** (MMDAs) and **Super NOWs** (SNOWs), offering flexible money market interest rates but accessible via check or preauthorized draft to pay for goods and services.

MMDAs are short-maturity deposits that may have a term of only a few days, weeks, or months, and the bank or thrift institution can pay any interest rate that is competitive enough to attract and hold the customer's deposit. Up to six preauthorized drafts per month are allowed, but only three withdrawals may be made by writing checks. There is no limit to the personal withdrawals the customer may make (though banks and other service providers reserve the right to set maximum amounts and frequencies for personal withdrawals). Unlike NOWs, MMDAs can be held by businesses as well as individuals.

Super NOWs were authorized at about the same time as MMDAs, but they may be held only by individuals and nonprofit institutions. The number of checks the depositor may write is not limited by regulation. However, banks and thrift institutions post lower yields on SNOWs than on MMDAs because the former can be drafted more frequently by customers. Incidentally, federal regulatory authorities classify MMDAs today not as transaction (payments) deposits, but as savings deposits. They are included in this section on transaction accounts because they carry check-writing privileges.

Nontransaction (Savings or Thrift) Deposits

Savings deposits, or **thrift deposits,** are designed to attract funds from customers who wish to set aside money in anticipation of future expenditures or financial emergencies. These deposits generally pay significantly higher interest rates than transaction deposits do. While their interest cost is higher, thrift deposits are generally less costly to process and manage.

Just as banks and thrift institutions for decades offered only one basic transaction deposit—the regular checking account—so it was with savings plans. **Passbook savings deposits** were sold to household customers in small denominations (frequently a passbook deposit could be opened for as little as $5), and withdrawal privileges were unlimited. While legally a bank or other depository institution could insist on receiving prior notice of a planned withdrawal from a passbook savings deposit, few institutions have insisted on this technicality because of the low interest rate paid on these accounts and because passbook deposits tend to be stable anyway, with little sensitivity to changes in interest rates. Individuals, nonprofit organizations, and governments can hold savings deposits, as can business firms, but in the United States businesses cannot place more than $150,000 in such a deposit.

Some banks and thrifts offer *statement savings deposits*, evidenced only by computer entry. The customer can get monthly printouts showing deposits, withdrawals, interest earned, and the balance in the account. Many banks and thrift institutions, however, still offer the more traditional passbook savings deposit, where the customer is given a booklet showing the account's balance, interest earnings, deposits, and withdrawals, as well as the rules that bind both depository institution and depositor. Usually the depositor must present the passbook to a teller in order to make deposits or withdrawals.

For many years, wealthier individuals and businesses have been offered **time deposits,** which carry fixed maturity dates (usually covering 30, 60, 90, or 180 days) with fixed interest rates. More recently, time deposits have been issued with interest rates that are adjusted periodically (such as every 90 days, known as a *leg* or *roll period*). Time deposits must carry a minimum maturity of seven days and cannot be withdrawn before that. They come in a wide variety of types, ranging from negotiable certificates of deposit or CDs (to be discussed later) to Christmas and vacation club deposits. CDs are issued in *negotiable* form—the $100,000-plus instruments bought principally by corporations and wealthy individuals—and in *nonnegotiable* form (which cannot be traded prior to maturity), usually purchased by individuals. In the late 1990s brokerage houses and a few commercial banks developed a "callable" CD whose value fluctuates with market conditions and may be retired by the issuing financial institution if interest rates fall significantly. This new instrument soon aroused a storm of controversy after several buyers lost money, however.

In 1981, with passage of the Economic Recovery Tax Act, Congress opened the door to yet another deposit instrument—retirement savings accounts. Wage earners and salaried individuals were granted the right to make limited contributions each year, tax free, to an *individual retirement account* (IRA), offered by banks, savings institutions, brokerage firms,

E-BANKING AND E-COMMERCE

CHECK IMAGING: THE KEY ADVANTAGES AND USES

The technology of processing checks is changing rapidly with the availability of *check imaging* to reduce production costs. The Federal Reserve banks have recently set up online check image retrieval services over the Internet, called FedLine. With check imaging any staff member of a bank or other depository institution can search online for a check or other document by account number, date, dollar amount, or check or document number, with the item appearing onscreen in minutes or seconds, aiding in such common tasks as verifying that a correct signature appears on the imaged item.

This imaging service carries wire transfers for customers who need checkable funds moved the same day, provides connections to automated clearinghouses to process checks electronically, and permits online orders of cash by depository institutions. The Federal Reserve banks are also offering Image Enhanced MICR Presentment Plus, which allows a depository institution to bring up images of the front and back of checks and other funds transmittal items on its PCs. This makes it faster and easier for each depository to post checks

and other cash items to each customer's account. This service also makes it easier to handle a common customer request—a depositor comes to a branch office or contacts his depository institution via e-mail and asks to view a check he or she wrote several days or weeks ago. Internet retrieval of such a requested item becomes fairly easy to accomplish. The customer can walk out with an image of the check he or she wanted to see or view the image of the check on his or her home monitor. Copies can also be faxed from the Fed the same day.

If a customer's checking account is overdrawn and another check shows up, the participating depository institution's staff can ask the Fed to supply a copy of the insufficient-funds item. If the participating bank elects not to pay the check on the customer's behalf, the item can be returned through the Fed's system. Thus, check imaging speeds the process of deposits and withdrawals to customers' accounts. Normally, a few days later paper checks themselves are returned to the depositories on which they are drawn (sorted by account number) to be mailed out in original or image form in monthly account statements to customers.

insurance companies, and mutual funds, or by employers with qualified pension or profit-sharing plans. There was ample precedent for the creation of IRAs; in 1962, Congress had authorized financial institutions to sell *Keogh plan* retirement deposits, which are available to self-employed persons. Unfortunately for banks and other depository institutions and their customers interested in IRAs, the Tax Reform Act of 1986 restricted the tax deductibility of additions to an IRA account, which sharply reduced their growth, though Keogh deposits retained full tax benefits.

Then, in August 1997 the U.S. Congress, in an effort to encourage greater saving for retirement, purchases of new homes, and childrens' future education, modified the rules for IRA accounts, allowing individuals and couples with higher incomes to make annual tax-deductible contributions to their retirement accounts and individuals and families to set up new education savings accounts that could grow tax free until needed to cover college tuition and other qualified educational expenses. Finally, the Tax Relief Act of 1997 created the *Roth IRA*, which allows individuals and couples to accumulate investment earnings tax free and also pay no tax on their investment earnings when withdrawn.

Today depository institutions in the United States hold about a quarter of all IRA and Keogh retirement accounts outstanding, ranking second only to mutual funds. The great appeal for bankers and the managers of other depository institutions is the high degree of stability of IRA and Keogh deposits—financial managers can generally rely on having these funds around for several years. Moreover, many IRAs and Keoghs carry fixed interest rates—an advantage if market interest rates are rising—allowing banks and other depositories to earn higher returns on their loans and investments that more than cover the interest costs associated with IRAs and Keoghs.

Interest Rates Offered on Different Types of Deposits

Each of the different types of deposits we have discussed typically carries a different rate of interest. In general, the longer the maturity of a deposit, the greater the yield that must be offered to depositors because of the time value of money and the frequent upward slope of the yield curve. For example, NOW accounts and savings deposits are subject to immediate withdrawal by the customer; accordingly, their offer rate to customers is among the lowest of all deposits. In contrast, negotiable CDs and deposits of a year or longer to maturity often carry the highest deposit interest rates that banks and other depositories offer.

The size and perceived risk exposure of offering institutions also play an important role in shaping deposit interest rates. For example, banks in New York and London, due to their greater size and strength, are able to offer deposits at the lowest average interest rates, while deposit rates posted by other banks and thrift institutions are generally scaled upward from that level. Other key factors are the marketing philosophy and goals of the offering institution. Banks and other depository institutions that choose to compete for deposits aggressively usually will post higher offer rates to bid deposits away from their competitors. In contrast, when a bank or other depository institution wants to discourage or deemphasize a type of deposit, it will allow its posted rate to fall relative to interest rates offered by competing institutions.

The Composition of Bank Deposits

Factoid

Virtual (Web-centered) banks generally offer higher deposit interest rates than do traditional brick-and-mortar banks. This is probably due to the somewhat greater perceived risk of the Web-based banks and their frequent lack of a complete menu of services.

The largest of all depository institutions are *commercial banks*, whose $4.5 trillion in deposits in 2002 exceeded the total deposits held by all nonbank depository institutions (such as thrifts and credit unions) by a ratio of four to one. By examining recent trends in bank deposits we can get a pretty good idea of recent changes in the mix of deposits at all types of depository institutions in recent years.

In recent years, banks have been most able to sell *time and savings deposits*—interest-bearing thrift accounts—to the public. As Table 11–1 shows, time and savings deposits represented about four-fifths of the total deposits held by all U.S.-insured commercial banks at year-end 2002. Not surprisingly, then, interest-bearing deposits and nontransaction deposits, both of which include time and savings deposits, have captured the majority share of all U.S. bank deposit accounts. In contrast, regular demand deposits,

TABLE 11–1   The Changing Composition of Bank Deposits in the United States

Source: Federal Deposit Insurance Corporation

Deposit Type or Category	Percentages for All U.S. Insured Banks at Year's End							
	1983	1987	1991	1993	1996	1998	2001	2002
Noninterest-bearing deposits	37.9%	20.5%	17.9%	20.8%	19.8%	19.5%	19.9%	20.0%
Interest-bearing deposits	62.1	79.5	82.1	79.2	80.2	80.5	80.1	80.0
Total deposits	100.0%	100.0%	100.0%	100.0%	100.0%	100.0%	100.0%	100.0%
Transaction deposits	31.9%	32.3%	29.7%	33.4%	29.3%	24.3%	21.2%	17.6%
Nontransaction deposits	68.1	67.7	70.3	66.6	70.7	75.7	78.8	82.4
Total domestic office deposits	100.0%	100.0%	100.0%	100.0%	100.0%	100.0%	100.0%	100.0%
Demand deposits	25.4%	22.9%	19.1%	20.2%	22.1%	18.9%	19.0%	13.2%
Savings deposits*	30.2	36.2	38.3	41.2	39.8	43.5	48.0	54.8
Time deposits	44.4	40.9	42.6	38.6	38.1	37.6	33.0	32.0
Total domestic office deposits	100.0%	100.0%	100.0%	100.0%	100.0%	100.0%	100.0%	100.0%

*The savings deposit figures shown include money market deposit accounts (MMDAs). Components may not add to column totals due to rounding errors.

Filmtoid

What Christmastime ritual finds James Stewart playing the manager of a small town thrift with funding problems so severe (and core depositors lined up to make withdrawals) they drive him to consider suicide?
Answer: *It's a Wonderful Life.*

which generally pay no interest and make up the majority of transaction and noninterest-bearing deposits, have declined significantly to less than a fifth of total bank deposits inside the United States.

Indeed, as Gerdes and Walton [3] observed, the value of checks paid in the United States fell from about $49 billion in 1995 to only about $42 billion by the year 2000 due mainly to the rise of electronic payments media, including credit and debit cards, Web-based payments systems, and electronic wire transfers. However, most authorities argue that checks written against demand (transaction) deposits will continue to be important in the American payments system, though in parts of Europe (particularly in Finland, Germany, and the Netherlands) electronics payments devices are rapidly taking over.

Bankers, if left to decide for themselves about the best mix of deposits, would generally prefer a high proportion of transaction deposits (including regular checking or demand deposit accounts) and low-yielding time and savings deposits. These accounts are among the least expensive of all bank sources of funds and often include a substantial percentage of **core deposits**—a stable base of deposited funds that is not highly sensitive to movements in market interest rates (i.e., bears a low interest rate elasticity) and tends to remain with the bank. While many core deposits (such as small savings accounts) could be withdrawn immediately, they have an effective maturity often spanning several years. Thus, the availability of a large block of core deposits increases the duration of a bank's liabilities and makes the institution less vulnerable to swings in interest rates. The presence of substantial amounts of core deposits in smaller banks helps explain why large banks and bank holding companies in recent years have acquired so many smaller banking firms—to gain access to a more stable and less-expensive deposit base. However, the combination of inflation, deregulation, stiff competition, and better-educated customers has resulted in a dramatic shift in the mix of deposits banks and many of their competitors are able to sell.

Bank operating costs in offering deposit services have soared in recent years. For example, interest payments on deposits (both foreign and domestic) for all insured U.S. commercial banks amounted to $10.5 billion in 1970, but had jumped to more than $80 billion by 2002. At the same time the new, higher-yielding deposits proved to be more interest sensitive than the older, less-expensive deposits, thus putting pressure on the management of banks and other depository institutions to pay competitive interest rates on their deposit offerings. Depository institutions that didn't keep up with market interest rates had to be prepared for extra liquidity demands—substantial deposit withdrawals and fluctuating deposit levels. Faced with substantial interest cost pressures, many bankers have pushed hard to reduce their noninterest expenses (e.g., by automating their operations and reducing the number of employees on the payroll) and to increase operating efficiency.

As Table 11–2 shows, the dominant holder of bank deposits inside the United States is the private sector—individuals, partnerships, and corporations (IPC), accounting for about 90 percent of all U.S. bank deposits. The next largest deposit owner is state and local governments (4 percent of the total), representing the funds accumulated by counties, cities, and other local units of government. These deposits are often highly volatile, rising sharply when tax collections roll in or bonds are sold, and falling precipitously when local government payrolls must be met or construction begins on a new public building. Many depository institutions accept state and local deposits as a service to their communities even though these deposits frequently are not highly profitable.

Banks also hold small amounts of U.S. government deposits. In fact, the U.S. Treasury keeps most of its operating funds in domestic banking institutions in *Treasury Tax and Loan (TT&L) Accounts.* When taxes are collected from the public or Treasury securities are sold to investors, the federal government usually directs these funds into TT&L deposits first, in order to minimize the impact of government operations on the banking and financial system. The Treasury then makes periodic withdrawals of these funds

TABLE 11–2   The Changing Ownership Composition of Bank Deposits in the United States

Source: Federal Deposit Insurance Corporation

Deposit Owner Group	1983	1987	1991	1993	1996	1998	2001	2002
Individuals, partnerships, and corporations (IPC)	73.5%	77.0%	82.2%	89.2%	88.5%	89.1%	91.0%	90.0%
U.S. government	0.2	0.3	0.3	0.3	0.3	0.2	0.3	0.6
States and political subdivisions in the United States	4.5	4.5	3.7	3.5	3.7	3.8	4.0	4.3
Foreign deposits	16.7	14.6	11.3	4.1	4.5	4.0	2.6	2.9
All other deposits (including correspondent deposits with other banks)	5.1	3.6	2.5	2.9	3.0	2.9	2.1	2.2
Total deposits	100.0%	100.0%	100.0%	100.0%	100.0%	100.0%	100.0%	100.0%

Note: Totals may not add exactly to sum of components in each column due to rounding error.

Factoid
The more rapid the turnover of population in a given market area, the more intensive tends to be the competition among banks and other depository institutions in the sale of deposit services and the more favorable loan and deposit interest rates tend to be, unless the relocation of depositors doesn't require a change of depository institution.

(directing the money into its accounts at the Federal Reserve banks) when it needs to make expenditures. Today the Treasury pays fees to depository institutions to help lower the cost of handling government deposits and the Treasury receives interest income on many of the balances held with depository institutions.

Another deposit category of substantial size held by U.S. banks is deposits held by foreign governments, businesses, and individuals, many of which are received in offshore offices. Foreign-owned deposits rose rapidly during the 1960s and 1970s, climbing to nearly one-fifth of total U.S. bank deposits in 1980, reflecting the rapid growth in world trade and investments by U.S. businesses abroad. However, foreign-owned deposits then declined as a proportion of U.S. bank funds as U.S. domestic interest rates proved to be significantly cheaper for banks. Moreover, international crises and a stronger economy at home encouraged American banks to scale down their overseas expansion plans.

The final major deposit category is deposits of other banks, which include *correspondent deposits*, representing funds that depository institutions hold with each other to pay for correspondent services. For example, large metropolitan banks provide data processing and computerized recordkeeping, investment and tax counseling, participations in loans, and the clearing and collection of checks for smaller urban and outlying depository institutions. A bank or other depository institution that holds deposits received from other banks will record them as a liability on its balance sheet under the label *deposits due to banks and other depository institutions*. The bank that owns such deposits will record them as assets under the label *deposits due from banks and other depository institutions*.

The Functional Cost Analysis of Different Deposit Accounts

Other factors held constant, the managers of banks and other depositories would prefer to raise funds by selling those types of deposits that cost the least amount of money or, when revenues generated by the use of deposited funds are considered, generate the greatest net revenue after all expenses. If a bank or other depository institution can raise all of its capital from sales of the cheapest deposits and then turn around and purchase the highest-yielding assets, it will maximize its spread and, possibly, maximize the net income flowing to its stockholders. But what are the cheapest deposits? And which deposits generate the highest net revenues?

The Federal Reserve banks provide important clues about the costs and revenues from various types of deposits via their cost accounting system, known as Functional Cost

E-BANKING AND E-COMMERCE

PROBLEMS WITH ONLINE BANK BILL-PAYING SERVICES

The paper check is one of the most successful banking innovations in history—more convenient and safer than cash or most other payments instruments. Bankers, with some success lately, have been urging the public to convert to online banking, including bypassing conventional checks and using the computer to authorize and execute payments for purchases of goods and services. Electronic bill paying lowers bank operating costs significantly, and customers who use the service appear to be more loyal and tend to buy other banking services. Unfortunately, bankers still have some problems to work out with online bill paying before they can convince most customers to throw their checkbooks away.

For one thing, many merchants are not set up to receive electronic payments. When the customer authorizes a draft on his or her checking account through a website or other electronic means, the bank or thrift institution involved may still have to cut a check and mail it to the merchant expecting payment. This takes time and some customers are surprised to discover extra fees have been assessed against their account.

Moreover, many merchants have trouble linking up electronic payments received with the correct customer account. As a result bills may go unpaid or payment credit may be granted too late. Yet, most banking experts agree that online bill payment will eventually replace paper checks and other more cumbersome payment methods, especially after ironing out the most serious problems.

Analysis (FCA). The FCA program generates information about the earnings and costs associated with many different services, based upon data that selected depository institutions voluntarily supply to the Fed each year. FCA data reveal that *checkable* (demand) *deposits*—including regular checking accounts and special checkbook deposits (which usually pay no interest to the depositor) and interest-bearing checking accounts—are typically among the cheapest deposits that banks and other depositories sell to the public. While check processing and account maintenance costs are major expense items, the absence of interest payments on demand deposit accounts and the low interest rate usually paid on interest-bearing checking accounts help keep the cost of these deposits down relative to the cost of time and savings deposits and other sources of funds.

Moreover, check processing costs should move substantially lower in the period ahead as *check imaging* services become more widely used. Paper checks are gradually being supplanted with electronic images, permitting greater storage capacity and much faster retrieval, cutting costs and improving customer services.

Checkbook volume has been falling in the United States for several years now (from about 50 billion annually during the mid-1990s to about 40 billion during 2002) and even faster in Europe. Instead, alternative payments devices (such as credit and debit cards and point-of-sale terminals) have grabbed a growing share of the payments market. So significant has been the recent decline in checkbook volume that the Federal Reserve System announced in 2003 that it was reducing the number of check processing regions in the United States from 44 to 32. This trend has generally gotten a favorable reception from banks and thrift institutions in the hope of reducing operating costs. However, checking accounts have generated substantial fee income for most depository institutions—a key source of revenue that will have to be replaced with new revenue sources.

Thrift deposits—particularly money market accounts, time deposits, and savings accounts—generally rank second to demand deposits as the least costly deposits. Savings deposits are relatively cheap because of the low interest rate they carry—one of the lowest annual interest yields (APY) offered to the public—and, in many cases, the absence of monthly statements for depositors. However, many passbook savings accounts have substantial deposit and withdrawal activity; some savers attempt to use them as checking accounts. Many depository institutions have moved to discourage rapid turnover in their savings deposits by limiting withdrawals and charging activity fees.

WHO OFFERS THE HIGHEST DEPOSIT INTEREST RATES AND WHY?

Customers interested in purchasing the highest-yielding interest-bearing deposits and the managers of depository institutions interested in discovering what deposit interest yields their competitors are offering can consult daily newspapers or go online to key websites—for example, The BanxQuote Bank Center at **www.wsj.com** or **www.banx.com**.

Among the key types of deposit rate information available (with interest rates usually measured by the APY or annual percentage yield) are these:

- The average yields offered by major banks in leading states (e.g., California, Florida, Illinois, Texas, and New York) on money market deposits and certificates of deposit (CDs) out to 5 years to maturity.
- The average yields (APY) offered on CDs purchased through security brokers who search the marketplace every day for the highest yields available on large deposits (usually close to $100,000 in size).
- A list of those banks and thrift institutions around the United States offering the highest yields (APYs) on retail deposits (typically $500 to $25,000 minimum denomination) and jumbo CDs (usually carrying an opening balance of $95,000 or more).

Among the depository institutions offering the highest deposit yields are usually leading credit-card and household lenders, such as MBNA America, AIG Bank, ING DIRECT in Wilmington, Delaware, and CapitalOne.com of Glen Allen, Virginia, along with several virtual (Internet) banks, including NetBank.com of Alpharetta, Georgia, and VirtualBank of Palm Beach, Florida.

Why are the foregoing institutions generally among the leaders in offering the public the highest deposit interest rates? One reason is that these institutions generally expect to earn relatively high returns on their consumer and credit card loans, giving them an ample margin over deposit costs.

In the case of virtual (Internet-based) banking institutions these unique electronic firms must attract the public away from more traditional financial institutions and often provide very few services, so they must offer exceptional deposit rates to attract the funds they need. Moreover, virtual banks typically have relatively low fixed (overhead) costs, allowing these financial firms to bid higher for the public's deposits.

On the negative side, however, virtual banks have not been as successful in attracting customers as have traditional depository institutions in recent years. Indeed, the most successful firms at attracting customer deposits recently have been *multichannel banks*—offering both traditional and online services through the same institution—indicating that many customers are more likely to use the online services of financial firms that also are accessible in person through traditional branch offices and automated teller machines.

While demand (checking) deposits have about the same gross expenses (including interest and operating expenses) per dollar of deposit as time deposits do, the higher service fees levied against checking account customers help to lower the net cost of checkable deposits (after service revenues are netted out) below the net cost of most time (thrift) accounts. When we give each type of deposit credit for the earnings it generates through the making of loans and investments, checkable (demand) deposits appear to be substantially more profitable than thrift (time) deposits for the average bank or thrift institution. On average, checking-account service fees offset about one-third of a checking account's cost. In contrast, service fees on time (thrift) deposits make only a negligible contribution to offsetting their cost. Moreover, the interest expense per dollar of time deposits averages about triple the interest expense associated with each dollar of demand (checking) deposits.

To be sure, demand deposits incur much greater operating expenses due to the high employee and equipment costs associated with processing checks and recording deposits, while these "activity expenses" are far less for thrift (time) deposits. The critical difference in terms of the profitability of banks and other depository institutions, as we observed previously, is the service fees most checkable accounts generate. This fact helps explain why, faced with rising operating costs in recent years, depository institutions have more aggressively priced their checkable deposits, asking depositors to pay a bigger share of the activity costs they create when they write checks.

If checkable (demand) deposits tend to be more profitable, what particular types of checking accounts yield the greatest profits? Interest-bearing checking accounts generate about twice the volume of net returns (after earnings from loan and investment portfolios are added in) that regular (noninterest-bearing) checking accounts generate. For depository institutions of all sizes, special checking accounts, which charge the customer a fee for each check written but generally require low or no minimum balances, tend to be the least profitable of all demand deposits principally because the average special checking account generates a very small volume of investable funds at most depository institutions.

Commercial checking accounts, generally speaking, are considerably more profitable than personal checking accounts for banks and thrifts of all sizes that reported their deposit revenues and expenses to the Federal Reserve's FCA program. One reason is the lack of a significant interest expense with commercial deposits, while personal checking accounts carry an average interest expense that often exceeds the amount of fee income these deposits generate. Thus, even though the cost per dollar of funds raised is almost the same for both commercial and personal checking accounts, the added interest costs attached to many personal demand deposits often drive their return for a typical bank or other depository institution below the net return from commercial demand deposits. Moreover, the average size of a personal checking account normally is less than one-third the average size of a commercial account, so a bank or thrift institution receives substantially more investable funds from commercial demand deposits. However, competition posed by foreign financial service firms for commercial checking accounts has become so intense that the profit margins on these accounts tend to be razor thin in today's market.

Time deposits, retirement accounts, CDs, and money market accounts generally display low account activity in terms of deposits and withdrawals compared to savings accounts. However, the higher interest costs on most time and money market accounts come close to erasing their slight cost advantage over savings deposits. Smaller depository institutions often incur higher costs on savings and money market deposits than do larger ones, but they offset this by issuing time deposits and retirement accounts at a lower average cost than the average cost of time and retirement deposits issued by larger institutions. Nevertheless, larger depository institutions generate more revenue from checkable and thrift deposits because of the greater average size of these deposits at the biggest institutions.

Concept Check

11–1. What are the major types of deposit plans banks and other depository institutions offer today?

11–2. What are *core deposits* and why are they so important today?

11–3. How has the composition of deposits changed in recent years?

11–4. What are the consequences for the management and performance of depository institutions resulting from recent changes in deposit composition?

11–5. Which deposits are the least costly for banks and other depositories? The most costly?

11–6. First State Bank of Pine is considering a change of marketing strategy in an effort to lower its cost of funding and to maximize the bank's profitability. The new strategy calls for aggressive advertising of new commercial checking accounts and interest-bearing household checking accounts and for deemphasizing regular and special checking accounts. What are the possible advantages and possible weaknesses of this new marketing strategy?

While bankers and the managers of other depository institutions would prefer to sell only the cheapest deposits to the public, it is predominantly *public preference* that determines which types of deposits will be created. Banks and other depositories that do not wish to conform to customer preferences will simply be outbid for deposits by those who do. In recent years, the public has demanded both higher-yielding (more costly) thrift accounts and checkable deposits that pay interest rates comparable to returns available in the open market. At the same time, deregulation of the financial markets has made it possible for more kinds of financial-service firms to respond to the public's deposit preferences.

Pricing Deposit-Related Services

We have examined the different types of deposit plans offered today and how the composition of deposits has been changing over time. An equally important issue remains: How should banks and other depository institutions price their deposit services in order to attract new funds and make a profit? We turn now to that critical management issue.

In pricing deposit services, management is caught between the horns of an old dilemma. It needs to pay a high enough interest return to customers to attract and hold their funds, but must avoid paying an interest rate that is so costly it erodes any potential profit margin from using customer funds. Intense competition in today's markets compounds this dilemma because competition tends to raise deposit interest costs while lowering expected returns from putting deposits and other funds to work.

In fact, in a financial marketplace that closely approaches perfect competition, the individual bank or other depository institution has little control over its prices in the long run. It is the marketplace, not the individual financial firm, that ultimately sets all prices. In such a market, management must decide if it wishes to attract more deposits and hold all those it currently has by offering depositors at least the market-determined price, or whether it is willing to lose funds by offering customers terms different from what the market requires. Often managers must choose between growth and profitability. Aggressive competition for costly deposits and other sources of funds will help the depository institution grow faster, but often at the price of severe profit erosion.

Pricing Deposits at Cost Plus Profit Margin

Key URL
Each year under law the Federal Reserve Board must conduct a survey of retail fees charged by depository institutions on deposits and other services. For an example of recent survey data on bank and thrift service fees, see **www.federalreserve.gov/boarddocs/rptcongress/**.

The idea of charging the customer for the full cost of deposit-related services is relatively new. In fact, until a few years ago the notion that customers should receive most deposit-related services free of charge was hailed as a wise innovation—one that responded to the growing challenge posed by other financial intermediaries that were invading traditional deposit markets. Many managers soon found reason to question the wisdom of this new marketing strategy, however, because they were flooded with numerous low-balance, high-activity accounts that ballooned their operating costs.

The development of interest-bearing checkable deposits, particularly NOWs, offered bankers and other financial managers the opportunity to reconsider the pricing of deposit services. Unfortunately, many of the early entrants into this new market moved aggressively to capture a major share of the customers through *below-cost pricing*. Customer charges were set below the true level of operating and overhead costs associated with providing checkable deposits and other deposit plans. The result was a substantially increased rate of return to the customer, known as the *implicit interest rate*—the difference between the true cost of supplying fund-raising services and the service charges actually assessed the customer.

In the United States, variations in the implicit interest rate paid to the customer were the principal way most banks competed for deposits over the 50 years stretching from the Great Depression to the beginning of the 1980s. This was due to the presence of regulatory ceilings on deposit interest rates, beginning in 1933 with passage of the Glass-Steagall Act. These legal interest rate ceilings were designed to protect banks and thrift institutions from excessive interest rate competition for deposits, which could allegedly cause them to fail. Prevented from offering higher explicit interest rates, U.S. banks and thrifts competed instead by offering higher implicit returns with bank-by-mail services in which the depository institution promised to pay the postage both ways, by tempting depositors with gifts ranging from teddy bears to toasters, and by building convenient neighborhood branch office systems.

Unfortunately, such forms of *nonprice competition* tended to distort the allocation of scarce resources in the banking and thrift sector. Congress finally responded to these problems with passage of the Depository Institutions Deregulation Act of 1980, a federal law that called for a gradual phaseout of deposit interest-rate ceilings. Today, the responsibility for setting deposit prices in the United States (and in other leading industrialized nations as well) has been transferred from public regulators to private decision makers—that is, to depository institutions and their customers.

Deregulation has brought more frequent use of *unbundled* service pricing as greater competition has raised the average real cost of a deposit for bankers and other deposit-service providers. This means, for example, that deposits are usually priced separately from loans and other services. And each deposit service is often priced high enough to recover all or most of the cost of providing that service. Thus, the price of deposit services would conform to the following **cost-plus pricing** formula:

$$
\begin{array}{c}
\text{Unit price} \\
\text{charged the} \\
\text{customer for each} \\
\text{deposit service}
\end{array}
=
\begin{array}{c}
\text{Operating} \\
\text{expense} \\
\text{per unit of} \\
\text{deposit service}
\end{array}
+
\begin{array}{c}
\text{Estimated overhead} \\
\text{expense allocated} \\
\text{to the} \\
\text{deposit-service function}
\end{array}
+
\begin{array}{c}
\text{Planned profit} \\
\text{from each deposit-} \\
\text{service unit sold}
\end{array}
\quad \textbf{(1)}
$$

Tying deposit pricing to the cost of deposit-service production, as Equation 11–1 above does, has encouraged bankers and other deposit providers everywhere to match prices and costs more closely and to eliminate many formerly free services. In the United States, for example, more and more depositories are now levying fees for excessive withdrawals from savings deposits, charging for customer balance inquiries, increasing fees on bounced checks and stop-payment orders, assessing charges on cash withdrawals and balance inquiries made through ATMs, charging monthly maintenance fees even on small savings deposits, and raising required minimum deposit balances. The results of these trends have generally been favorable to banks and thrift institutions, with increases in service fee income generally outstripping losses from angry customers closing their accounts.

Estimating Average Deposit Service Costs

Cost-plus pricing demands an accurate calculation of the cost of each deposit service. How can this be done? One popular approach, discussed by Simonson and Marks [19, 20], is to base deposit prices on the estimated cost of raising funds. This requires the banker (1) to calculate the cost rate of each source of funds (adjusted for reserves required by the central bank, deposit insurance fees, and float); (2) to multiply each cost rate by the relative proportion of all funds coming from that particular source; and (3) to sum all resulting products to derive the weighted average cost of all funds raised. This so-called pooled-funds approach is based on the assumption that it is not the cost of each type of deposit that matters, but rather the weighted average cost of all funding sources for each depository institution.

Insights and Issues

SUMMARY OF DEPOSIT INSURANCE COVERAGE PROVIDED BY THE FDIC

A major reason commercial banks and thrift institutions (such as savings and loans and savings banks) are able to sell deposits at relatively low rates of interest compared to interest rates offered on other financial instruments is because of the existence of government-supplied deposit insurance. The **Federal Deposit Insurance Corporation (FDIC)** was established by the U.S. Congress in 1933 to insure deposits and protect the nation's money supply in those cases where banks and other depository institutions having FDIC membership failed. Today this federal corporation insures the deposits of banks through its Bank Insurance Fund (BIF) and insures the deposits of savings associations through its Savings Association Insurance Fund (SAIF), both of which are backed by the full faith and credit of the U.S. government. Insured depository institutions must display an official sign at each teller window or teller station, indicating that they hold an FDIC membership certificate.

FDIC insurance covers only those deposits payable in the United States, though the depositor does *not* have to be a U.S. citizen or resident to receive FDIC protection. All types of deposits normally are covered up to $100,000 for each single account holder. Savings deposits, checking accounts, NOW accounts, Christmas Club accounts, time deposits, cashiers' checks, money orders, officers' checks, and any outstanding drafts normally are protected by federal insurance. Certified checks, letters of credit, and travelers' checks for which an insured depository institution is primarily liable also are insured if these are issued in exchange for money or in return for a charge against a deposit. On the other hand, U.S. government securities, shares in mutual funds, safe deposit boxes, and funds stolen from an insured depository institution are *not* covered by FDIC insurance. Banks and thrift institutions gen-

erally carry private insurance against losses due to fire; storm damage; and theft, fraud, or other crimes.

Deposits placed in separate financial institutions (including different banks and thrifts that belong to the same holding company) are insured separately, each eligible for insurance coverage up to $100,000 per depositor. However, deposits held in more than one branch office of the *same* depository institution are added together to determine the total amount of insurance protection available. In this case the individual depositor can receive no more than $100,000 in total insurance protection. If two formerly independent banks or thrifts merge, for example, and a depositor holds $100,000 in each of these two merging institutions, the total protection afforded this depositor would then be a maximum of $100,000, not $200,000, as it was before the merger. However, the FDIC normally allows a grace period so that, for a short time, a depositor with large deposits in two institutions that merge can receive expanded coverage up to $200,000 until arrangements can be made to transfer some of the depositor's funds to other depository institutions in order to gain more insurance protection.

Insurance coverage may also be increased at a single institution by placing funds under different categories of legal ownership. For example, a depositor with $100,000 in a savings deposit and another $100,000 in a time deposit might achieve greater insurance coverage by making one of these two accounts a joint ownership account with his or her spouse. Also, if a family is composed of husband and wife plus one child, for example, each family member could own an account and each pair of family members (e.g., husband and wife, husband and child, and wife and child) could also hold joint accounts, resulting in insurance coverage up to $600,000 in total. Only natural persons, not corporations or partnerships, can set up FDIC insurance-eligible joint accounts, however.

Key URL

For more information on the findings of recent research about the factors depositors consider in choosing depository institutions see, for example, such websites as **www.federalreserve.gov/pubs/feds/**.

An Example of Pooled-Funds Costing

Let's consider an example of the pooled-funds cost approach. Suppose a commercial bank has raised a total of $400 million, including $100 million in checkable deposits, $200 million in time and savings deposits, $500 million borrowed from the money market, and $50 million from its owners in the form of equity capital. Suppose that interest and noninterest costs spent to attract the checkable deposits total 10 percent of the amount of these deposits, while thrift deposits and money market borrowings each cost the bank 11 percent of funds raised in interest and noninterest expenses. Owners' equity is the most expensive funding source for most banks and thrift institutions; assume that equity capital costs the bank an estimated 22 percent of any new equity raised. Suppose reserve requirements, deposit insurance fees, and uncollected balances (float) reduce the amount of money actually available to the bank for investing in interest-bearing assets by 15 percent for checkbook deposits, 5 percent for thrift deposits, and 2 percent for borrowings in the money market. Therefore, this bank's weighted average before-tax cost of funds would be as follows:

Each co-owner of a joint account is assumed to have equal right of withdrawal and is also assumed to own an equal share of a joint account unless otherwise stated in the account record. No one person's total insured interest in all joint accounts at the same insured depository institution can exceed $100,000. For example, suppose Mr. Jones has a joint account with Mrs. Jones amounting to $120,000. Then each is presumed to have a $60,000 share and each would have FDIC insurance coverage of $60,000 unless the deposit record at the bank specifically shows that, for example, Mrs. Jones owns $100,000 of the $120,000 balance and Mr. Jones owns just $20,000. In this instance Mrs. Jones would receive the full $100,000 in insurance protection and Mr. Jones would be covered for a maximum of $20,000.

After December 1993, IRA and Keogh retirement deposits became separately insured from nonretirement deposits. All retirement accounts are added together for a maximum amount of insurance protection of $100,000. Deposits belonging to pension and profit-sharing plans receive "pass-through insurance" up to $100,000 per beneficiary, provided the individual participants' beneficial interests are ascertainable and the depository institution involved is at least "adequately capitalized" and is eligible to take deposits placed by brokers on behalf of their customers. Otherwise, "pass-through insurance" is not available on pension and profit-sharing plans, which then would receive no more than $100,000 in total FDIC insurance protection for all participants.

Funds deposited by a corporation, partnership, or unincorporated business or association (including all of its departments or divisions) are insured up to $100,000 and are insured separately from the personal accounts of the company's stockholders, partners, or members. Funds deposited by a sole proprietor of a business are considered to be personal funds,

however, and are added to any other single-owner accounts the individual business owner has, and are protected only up to $100,000 in total.

The amount of insurance premiums that each FDIC-insured depository institution must pay is determined by the volume of deposits it receives from the public and by the insurance rate category in which each institution falls. Under the new risk-based deposit insurance system begun in the United States in 1993 (as mandated by the FDIC Improvement Act of 1991), more risky banks and thrift institutions (that is, those that present greater risk of loss to the FDIC) must pay higher insurance premiums. The degree of risk exposure is determined by the interplay of two factors: (1) the adequacy of capital maintained by each depository institution, and (2) the risk class is which the institution is judged to be by its regulatory supervisors. There are three classes of capitalization—well capitalized, adequately capitalized, and undercapitalized—and three supervisory risk categories—A, B, and C. The well-capitalized, A-rated depositories pay the lowest deposit insurance fee per each $100 of deposit they hold, while the undercapitalized, C-rated institutions pay the greatest insurance fees.

Twice each year the board of directors of the FDIC must decide what deposit insurance rates to assess each insured bank and thrift institution. The FDIC must hold a reserve of at least $1.25 per each $100 of insured deposits. If the federal insurance fund falls below $1.25 in reserves per $100 in covered deposits (known as the Designated Reserve Ratio [DRR]), the FDIC will raise its insurance assessment fees. When the amount of reserves exceeds the $1.25 per $100 standard, fees will be lowered or eliminated.

Source: Federal Deposit Insurance Corporation.

(Checkbook deposits ÷ Total funds raised)

$$\times \left(\frac{\text{Interest and noninterest fund-raising costs}}{100 \text{ percent } - \text{ Percentage reserve requirements and float}} \right)$$

+ (Time and savings deposits ÷ Total funds raised)

$$\times \left(\frac{\text{Interest and noninterest fund-raising costs}}{100 \text{ percent } - \text{ Percentage reserve requirements and float}} \right)$$

+ (Owner's capital ÷ Total funds raised)

× (Interest and noninterest costs ÷ 100 percent)

= $100 million ÷ $400 million × 10 percent ÷ (100 percent − 15 percent)

+ $200 million ÷ $400 million × 11 percent ÷ (100 percent − 5 percent)

+ $50 million ÷ $400 million × 11 percent ÷ (100 percent − 2 percent)

+ $50 million ÷ $400 million × 22 percent ÷ 100 percent

= 0.1288, or 12.88 percent of funds raised

In this example, the bank's management will want to make sure it earns at least a before-tax rate of return of 12.88 percent on its portfolio of loans and other earning assets. If this particular bank can earn more from its loans and investments than 12.88 percent before taxes, the extra return (less taxes) will flow to the stockholders in the form of increased dividends and into retained earnings to strengthen the bank's capital.

The pooled-funds cost approach provides managers with a way to calculate the effects of any change in funding costs or deposit prices. For example, management can experiment with alternative deposit terms (interest rates, fees, and minimum balance requirements) for any deposit plan offered and estimate their impact on funding costs. Of course, the managers of depository institutions cannot safely price deposits without knowing how low customer balances can go and still be profitable. Overly generous pricing terms can set in motion substantial account shifting by customers, leading to a sharp increase in the cost of funds without significantly increasing total funds available to the financial firm.

Using Marginal Cost to Set Interest Rates on Deposits

Many financial analysts would argue that, whenever possible, *marginal cost*—the added cost of bringing in new funds—and not weighted average cost, should be used to help price deposits and other funds sources for a financial-service institution. The reason is that frequent changes in interest rates will make average cost a treacherous and unrealistic standard for pricing. For example, if interest rates are declining, the added (marginal) cost of raising new money may fall well below the average cost over all funds raised. Some loans and investments that looked unprofitable when compared to average cost will now look quite profitable when measured against the lower marginal interest cost we must pay today to make those new loans and investments. Conversely, if interest rates are on the rise, the marginal cost of today's new money may substantially exceed the average cost of funds. If management books new loans based on average cost, they may turn out to be highly unprofitable when measured against the higher marginal cost of raising new funds in today's market.

Economist James E. McNulty [17] has suggested a way to use the marginal, or new money, cost idea to help a bank or thrift institution set the interest rates it will offer on new deposit accounts.[2] To understand McNulty's recommended marginal cost pricing method, suppose a commercial bank expects to raise $25 million in new deposits by offering its depositors an interest rate of 7 percent. Management estimates that if the bank offers a 7.50 percent interest rate, it can raise $50 million in new deposit money. At 8 percent, $75 million is expected to flow in, while a posted deposit rate of 8.5 percent will bring in a projected $100 million. Finally, if the bank promises an estimated 9 percent yield, management projects that $125 million in new funds will result from both new deposits and existing deposits that customers will keep in the bank to take advantage of the higher rates offered. Let's assume as well that management believes it can invest the new deposit money at a yield of 10 percent. This new loan yield represents *marginal revenue*, the added operating revenue the bank will generate by making new loans from the new deposits. Given these facts, what deposit interest rate should the bank offer its customers?

As Table 11–3 shows, based on McNulty's [17] method, we need to know at least two crucial items to answer this deposit rate question: the *marginal cost* of moving the deposit rate from one level to another and the *marginal cost rate*, expressed as a percentage of the volume of additional funds coming into the bank. Once we know the marginal cost rate,

---

[2] See also Watson [21] for a further discussion of marginal cost pricing.

TABLE 11–3 Using Marginal Cost to Choose the Interest Rate to Offer Customers on Deposits

Example of a Commercial Bank Attempting to Raise New Funds							
Expected Amounts of Deposits That Will Flow In	Average Interest the Bank Will Pay on New Funds	Total Interest Cost of New Funds Raised	Marginal Cost of New Deposit Money	Marginal Cost as a Percentage of New Funds Attracted (marginal cost rate)	Expected Marginal Revenue (return) from Investing the New Funds	Difference between Marginal Revenue and Marginal Cost Rate	Total Profits Earned (after interest cost)
$ 25	7.0%	$ 1.75	$1.75	7.0%	10.0%	+3%	$0.75
50	7.5	3.75	2.00	8.0	10.0	+2%	1.25
75	8.0	6.00	2.25	9.0	10.0	+1%	1.50
100	8.5	8.50	2.50	10.0	10.0	+0	1.50
125	9.0	11.25	2.75	11.0	10.0	−1%	1.25

Note: Figures in millions except percentages.

we can compare it to the expected additional revenue (marginal revenue) the bank expects to earn from investing its new deposits. The two items we need to know are the following:

Marginal cost = Change in total cost = New interest rate × Total funds raised at new rate − Old interest rate × Total funds raised at old rate

and

$$\text{Marginal cost rate } = \frac{\text{Change in total cost}}{\text{Additional funds raised}}$$

For example, if the bank raises its offer rate on new deposits from 7 percent to 7.5 percent, Table 11–3 shows the marginal cost of this change: Change in total cost = $50 million × 7.5 percent − $25 million × 7 percent = $3.75 million − $1.75 million = $2.00 million. The marginal cost rate, then, is the change in total cost divided by the additional funds raised, or

$$\frac{\$2 \text{ million}}{\$25 \text{ million}} = 8 \text{ percent}$$

Notice that the marginal cost rate at 8 percent is substantially above the average deposit cost of 7.5 percent. This happens because the bank must not only pay a rate of 7.5 percent to attract the second $25 million, but it must also pay out the same 7.5 percent rate to those depositors who were willing to contribute the first $25 million at only 7 percent.

Because the bank expects to earn 10 percent on these new deposit funds, marginal revenue exceeds marginal cost by 2 percent at a deposit interest cost of 8 percent. Clearly, the new deposits will add more to revenue than they will add to cost. The bank is justified (assuming its projections are right) in offering a deposit rate at least as high as 7.5 percent. Its total profit will equal the difference between total revenue ($50 million × 10 percent = $5 million) and total cost ($50 million × 7.5 percent = $3.75 million), for a profit of $1.25 million.

Scanning down Table 11–3, we note that the bank continues to improve its total profits, with marginal revenue exceeding marginal cost, up to a deposit interest rate of 8.5 percent. At that rate the bank raises an estimated $100 million in new deposit money at a marginal cost rate of 10 percent, matching its expected marginal revenue of 10 percent.

THE TRUTH IN SAVINGS ACT

In November 1991, the U.S. Congress passed the **Truth in Savings Act,** which requires depository institutions to make greater disclosure of the fees, interest rates, and other terms attached to the deposits they sell to the public. On September 14, 1992, the Federal Reserve Board issued Regulation DD to spell out the rules that banks and other depositories must follow to conform with this new law.

The Fed's regulation stipulates that consumers must be fully informed of the terms on deposit plans before they open a new account. If the consumer is not physically present when the account is opened, disclosure of the terms of the deposit account must be sent to him or her within 10 business days of the initial deposit. A depository institution must disclose the amount of the minimum balance that is required to open the account, how much must be kept on deposit to avoid paying fees or to obtain the promised yield, how the balance in each account is figured, when interest actually begins to accrue, any penalty provisions for early withdrawal, options available at maturity, reinvestment and disbursement options, any grace periods, advance notice of the approaching end of the deposit's term if it has a fixed maturity, and any bonuses available.

When a consumer asks for the current interest rate the offering institution is promising to pay, it must provide that customer with the interest rate that was offered within the most recent seven calendar days and also provide a telephone number so consumers can call and get the latest offered rate if interest rates have changed. On fixed-rate accounts the offering institutions must disclose to its customers for what period of time the fixed rate will be in effect. On variable-rate deposits banks and thrift institutions must warn consumers that interest rates can change, inform them how frequently interest rates can change, explain how a variable interest rate is determined, and specify if there are limits on how far deposit rates can move over time. For all interest-bearing accounts the bank or thrift must disclose the frequency with which interest is compounded and credited, both in writing and in advertising.

If a customer decides to renew a deposit that would not be automatically renewed on its own, the renewed deposit is considered a *new* account, requiring full disclosure of fees and other terms. Customers must also be told if their account is automatically renewed and, if not, what will happen to their funds (e.g., will they be placed in a noninterest-bearing account?) if the customer does not remember to renew his or her deposit. (Generally, customers must receive at least

---

There, total profit tops out at $1.5 million. It would *not* pay the bank to go beyond this point, however. For example, if it offers a deposit rate of 9 percent, the marginal cost rate balloons upward to 11 percent, which exceeds marginal revenue by a full percentage point. Attracting new deposits at a 9 percent offer rate adds more to this bank's cost than to its revenue. Note, too, that total profits at a 9 percent deposit rate fall back to $1.25 million. The 8.5 percent deposit rate is clearly the *best* choice for this bank, given all the assumptions and forecasts it has made.

The marginal cost approach provides valuable information to the managers of banks and other depository institutions, not only about setting deposit interest rates, but also about deciding just how far the institution should go in expanding its deposit base before the added cost of deposit growth catches up with additional revenues, and total profits begin to decline. When profits start to fall, management needs either to find new sources of funding with lower marginal costs, or to identify new loans and investments promising greater marginal revenues, or both.

Conditional Pricing

The appearance of interest-bearing checking accounts in the New England states during the 1970s led to fierce competition for customer transaction deposits among banks and nonbank thrift institutions across the United States. Out of that boiling competitive cauldron came widespread use of **conditional pricing,** where a bank or other depository sets up a schedule of fees in which the customer pays a low fee or even no fee if the deposit balance remains *above* some minimum level, but faces a higher fee if the average balance falls *below* that minimum. Thus, the customer pays a price conditional on how much he or she uses the deposit.

10 days' advance notice of the approaching maturity date for deposits over one year to maturity that are not automatically renewed.) If a change is made in fees or other terms of a deposit that could reduce a depositor's yield, a 30-day advance notice of the terms must be sent to the depositor.

Depository institutions must also include information in each statement sent to their customers on the amount of interest earnings the depositor has received, along with a statement of the annual percentage yield the deposit has earned. The *annual percentage yield* (or *APY*) must be calculated using the following formula:

APY earned $= 100[(1 + \text{Interest earned/Average account balance})^{(365/\text{Days in period})} - 1]$

where the account balance in the formula is the average daily balance kept in the deposit for the period covered by the account statement sent to the customer. Customers must be informed of the impact of early withdrawals on their account's expected APY.

For example, suppose a bank depositor had $1,500 on deposit in an interest-bearing account for the first 15 days and $500 in the account for the remaining 15 days of a 30-day period. The average daily balance in this case is clearly $1,000,

or [($1,500 × 15 days + $500 × 15 days)/30 days]. Suppose the bank has just credited the account with $5.25 in interest for the latest 30-day period. Then the APY earned by this depositor would be

$$\text{APY} = 100[(1 + 5.25/1000)^{365/30} - 1] = 6.58 \text{ percent}$$

In determining the balance on which interest earnings are figured, the depository institution must use the *full* amount of the principal in the deposit for each day, rather than, for example, counting only the minimum balance that was in the account on one day during the statement period. (Depository institutions may use either the exact daily balance or the average daily balance in calculating interest owed the customer.) Methods that do not pay interest on the full principal balance are prohibited. The daily rate earned by the depositor must be at least 1/365 of the normal interest rate quoted on the deposit.

In 1994 the U.S. Congress passed the Riegle Community Development and Regulatory Improvement Act of 1994, which narrowed the scope of deposit plans covered by the Truth in Savings Act to those accounts held by individuals for a personal, family, or household purpose. Deposits held by unincorporated, nonbusiness associations of individuals are no longer subject to the disclosure requirements of the Truth in Savings Act.

Conditional pricing techniques vary deposit prices according to one or more of these factors:

1. The number of transactions passing through the account (e.g., number of checks written, deposits made, wire transfers, stop-payment orders, or notices of insufficient funds issued).
2. The average balance held in the account over a designated period (usually per month).
3. The maturity of the deposit in days, weeks, or months.

The customer selects the deposit plan that results in the lowest fees possible and/or the maximum yields, given the number of checks he or she plans to write, the number of deposits and withdrawals expected, and the planned average balance. Of course, the bank or competing depository institution must also be acceptable to the customer from the standpoint of safety, convenience, and service availability.

Economist Constance Dunham [15] classified checking account conditional price schedules observed in the New England area into three categories: (1) flat-rate pricing, (2) free pricing, and (3) conditionally free pricing. In *flat-rate pricing*, the depositor's cost is a fixed charge per check, per time period, or both. Thus, there may be a monthly account maintenance fee of $2, and each check written against that account may cost the customer 10 cents, regardless of the level of account activity.

Free pricing, on the other hand, refers to the absence of a monthly account maintenance fee or per-transaction charge. Of course, the word *free* can be misleading. Even if a deposit-service provider does not charge an explicit fee for deposit services, the customer may incur an implicit fee in the form of lost income (opportunity cost), because the effective interest rate paid on the deposit may be less than the going rate on investments of

HOW U.S. DEPOSITORY INSTITUTIONS SHOULD DISCLOSE THE TERMS ON THEIR DEPOSIT SERVICES TO CUSTOMERS

In order to help banks and thrift institutions selling deposit services in the United States conform to the Truth in Savings Act, passed in 1991, the Federal Reserve Board now provides the managers of depository institutions with examples of proper disclosure forms to use in order to inform customers of the terms being quoted on their deposits. For example, the Fed has provided banks with an example of a proper disclosure form for certificates of deposit accounts as shown below.

Sample Disclosure Form for XYZ Savings Bank
One-Year Certificate of Deposit

Rate Information   The interest rate for your account is *5.20%* with an annual percentage yield of *5.34%*. You will be paid this rate until the maturity date of the certificate. Your certificate will mature on September 30, 2002. The annual percentage yield assumes interest remains on deposit until maturity. A withdrawal will reduce earnings.

Interest for your account will be compounded daily and credited to your account on the last day of each month. Interest begins to accrue on the business day you deposit any non-cash item (for example, checks).

Minimum Balance Requirements   You must deposit $1,000 to open this account. You must maintain a minimum balance of $1,000 in your account every day to obtain the annual percentage yield listed above.

Balance Computation Method   We use the daily balance method to calculate the interest on your account. This method applies a daily periodic rate to the principal in the account each day.

Transaction Limitations   After the account is opened, you may not make deposits into or withdrawals from the account until the maturity date.

Early Withdrawal Penalty   If you withdraw any principal before the maturity date, a penalty equal to three months' interest will be charged to your account.

Renewal Policy   This account will be automatically renewed at maturity. You have a grace period of ten (10) calendar days after the maturity date to withdraw the funds without being charged a penalty.

Factoid

Who cares most about the location of a bank or other depository institution—high-income or low-income consumers? Recent research suggests that low-income consumers care more about location in choosing a bank or other institution to hold their deposit, while high-income customers appear to be more influenced by the size of the financial firm holding their deposit account.

---

comparable risk. Many banks and thrifts have found free pricing decidedly unprofitable because it tends to attract many small, highly active deposits that earn positive returns for the offering institution only when market interest rates are very high.

Conditionally free deposits have come to replace both flat-rate and free deposit pricing systems in many financial-service markets. Conditionally free pricing favors large-denomination deposits because services are free if the account balance stays above some minimum figure. One of the advantages of this pricing method is that the customer, not the offering institution, chooses which deposit plan is preferable. This self-selection process is a form of *market signaling* that can give the depository institution valuable data on the behavior and cost of its deposits. Conditionally free pricing also allows a bank or thrift institution to divide its deposit market into high-balance, low-activity deposits and low-balance, high-activity accounts.

As an example of the use of *conditional pricing* techniques for deposits, the fees for regular checking accounts and savings accounts posted recently by two banks in the United States are given in Exhibit 11–1.

We note that Bank A in Exhibit 11–1 appears to favor high-balance, low-activity checking deposits, while Bank B is more lenient toward smaller checking accounts. For example, Bank A begins assessing a checking-account service fee when the customer's balance falls below $600, while Bank B charges no fees for checking-account services until the customer's account balance drops below $500. Moreover, Bank A assesses significantly higher service fees on low-balance checking accounts than does Bank B—$5 to $10 per month versus $3.50 per month. On the other hand, Bank A allows unlimited check writing from its regular accounts, while B assesses a fee if more than 10 checks or withdrawals occur in any month. Similarly, Bank A assesses a $3 per month service fee if a customer's savings account dips below $200, while Bank B charges only a $2 fee if the customer's savings balance drops below $100.

Both the Truth in Savings Act and the Federal Reserve's Regulation DD stipulate that advertising of deposit terms may not be misleading. If interest rates are quoted in an advertisement, the depository institution must also tell the public what the other relevant terms of the deposit are, such as the minimum balance needed to earn the advertised yield and whether any fees charged could reduce the depositor's overall yield.

The Federal Reserve has recently developed sample advertisements to guide managers of depository institutions in making sure that advertising contains all the essential information the consumer needs. For example, the sample advertisement form for CDs shown to the right was developed recently by the Federal Reserve Board.

The sample advertisement illustrates the basic requirements for legitimate advertising of deposits under the Truth in Savings Act: *(a)* deposit rates must be quoted as annual percentage yields (APY), *(b)* the dates and minimum balance required must be stated explicitly, and *(c)* the depositor must be warned of penalties or fees that could reduce his or her yield.

Bank XYZ
Always Offers You Competitive CD Rates!!

Certificate of Deposit	Annual Percentage Yield (APY)
5-year	6.31%
4-year	6.07%
3-year	5.72%
2-year	5.25%
1-year	4.54%
6-month	4.34%
90-day	4.21%

APYs are offered on accounts from 5/9/01 through 5/18/06

The minimum balance to open an account and obtain the APY is $1,000. A penalty may be imposed for early withdrawal.

For more information call: (202) 123-1234

EXHIBIT 11–1

Example of the Use of Conditional Deposit Pricing by Two U.S. Banks Serving the Same Market Area

Bank A		Bank B	
Regular checking account:		*Regular checking account:*	
Minimum opening balance	$100	Minimum opening balance	$100
If minimum daily balance is		If minimum daily balance is	
$600 or more	No fee	$500 or more	No fee
$300 to $599	$5.00 per mo.	Less than $500	$3.50 per mo.
Less than $300	$10.00 per mo.		
If the depositor's collected monthly balance averages $1,500, there is no fee		If checks written or ATM transactions (debits) exceed 10 per month and balance is below $500	$0.15 per debit
No limit on number of checks written			
Regular savings account:		*Regular savings account:*	
Minimum opening balance	$100	Minimum opening balance	$100
Service fees:		Service fees:	
If balance falls below $200	$3.00 per mo.	If balance falls below $100	$2.00 per mo.
Balance of $200 or more	No fee	Balance above $100	No fee
Fee for more than two withdrawals per month	$2.00	Fee for more than three withdrawals per month	$2.00

Key URLs

A new Internet technology called *aggregation* allows consumers to monitor their checking and savings accounts, their other financial investments, personal borrowings, and recent online purchases through a single website. See, for example, **www.bankofamerica .com** and **www.yodlee .com**.

These price differences reflect differences in the philosophy of the management and owners of these two banks and the types of customers each bank is seeking to attract. Bank A in Exhibit 11–1 is located in an affluent neighborhood of homes and offices and is patronized primarily by high-income individuals and businesses who usually keep high deposit balances, but also write many checks. Bank B, on the other hand, is located across the street from a large university and actively solicits student deposits, which tend to have relatively low balances. Bank B's pricing schedules are set up to accept low-balance deposits, but the bank also recognizes that it needs to discourage excessive check writing by numerous small depositors, which would run up its costs. It does so by charging higher per-check fees than Bank A. In these two instances depicted in Exhibit 11–1, we can see that deposit pricing policy is generally sensitive to two factors:

1. *The types of customers each depository institution plans to serve*—each institution establishes price schedules that appeal to the needs of individuals and businesses representing a significant portion of its market area.
2. *The cost that serving different types of depositors will present to the institution*—most banks and thrift institutions today price deposit plans in such a way as to cover all or at least a significant portion of anticipated service costs.

Pricing Deposits Based on the Total Customer Relationship

Related to the idea of targeting the best customers for special treatment is the notion of pricing deposits according to the *number of services the customer uses*. Customers who purchase two or more services may be granted lower deposit fees or have some fees waived compared to the fees charged customers having only a limited relationship to the offering institution. The idea is that selling a customer multiple services increases the customer's dependence on the institution and makes it harder for that customer to go elsewhere because of the strong relationship between customer and depository institution. Thus, in theory at least, **relationship pricing** promotes greater customer loyalty and makes the customer less sensitive to the interest rates offered on deposits or the prices posted on other services offered by competing financial-service firms.

The Role That Deposit Pricing and Other Factors Play When Customers Choose a Bank or Thrift Institution to Hold Their Deposit Accounts

Factoid

There is some research evidence today that the interest rates banks pay on deposits and the account fees they charge for deposit services do influence which depository institution a customer chooses to hold his or her account. Interestingly, rural financial-service markets appear to be more responsive to interest rates and fees than do urban markets, on average.

To be sure, deposit pricing is important to banks and other financial firms offering this service. But how important is it to the customer? Are interest rates and fees the most critical factors a customer considers when choosing a bank or thrift institution to hold his or her deposit account? The correct answer appears to be *no*.

Both households and businesses consider multiple factors, not just price, in deciding where to place their deposits, recent studies conducted at the Federal Reserve Board, the University of Michigan, and elsewhere suggest. As shown in Table 11–4, these studies contend that households generally rank *convenience, service availability,* and *safety* above price in choosing which financial firm will hold their checking account. Moreover, *familiarity,* which may represent not only *name recognition* but also safety, ranks above the interest rate paid as an important factor in how individuals and families choose a depository institution to hold their savings account.

Indeed, a recent U.S. survey by Kiser [4] indicates that household customers tend to be extremely loyal to their depository institutions—about a third reported *never* changing their principal bank of deposit. When a banking affiliation is changed, it appears to be due mainly to customer relocation, though once a move occurs many customers seem to pay

TABLE 11–4 Factors in Household and Business Customers' Choice of a Bank for Their Deposit Accounts (ranked from most important to least important)

Source: Based on studies by the Federal Reserve Board, *Survey of Consumer Finances*, 1983; Glenn B. Canner and Robert D. Kuntz, *Service Charges as a Source of Bank Income and Their Impact on Consumers*, Board of Governors of the Federal Reserve System, 1986; Greenwich Associates, *Commercial Banking*, Greenwich, CT, 1987; and Elizabeth K. Kiser, "Household Switching Behavior at Depository Institutions," *Finance and Economics Discussion Series*, Board of Governors of the Federal Reserve System, 2002–44.

In Choosing a Bank to Hold Their Checking Accounts, Households Consider	In Choosing a Bank to Hold Their Savings Deposits, Households Consider	In Choosing a Bank to Supply Their Deposits and Other Services, Business Firms Consider
1. Convenient location.	1. Familiarity.	1. Financial health of lending institution.
2. Availability of many other services.	2. Interest rate paid.	2. Whether bank will be a reliable source of credit in the future.
3. Safety.	3. Transactional convenience (not location).	3. Quality of bank officers.
4. Low fees and low minimum balance.	4. Location.	4. Whether loans are competitively priced.
5. High deposit interest rates.	5. Availability of payroll deduction.	5. Quality of financial advice given.
	6. Fees charged.	6. Whether cash management and operations services are provided.

Concept Check

11–7. Describe the essential differences between the following deposit pricing methods in use today: cost-plus pricing, market-penetration pricing, conditional pricing, upscale target pricing, and relationship pricing.

11–8. A bank determines from an analysis of its cost-accounting figures that for each $500 minimum-balance checking account it sells, account processing and other operating costs will average $4.87 per month and overhead expenses will run an average of $1.21 per month. The bank hopes to achieve a profit margin over these particular costs of 10 percent of total monthly costs. What monthly fee should it charge a customer who opens one of these checking accounts?

11–9. To price deposits successfully, service providers must know their costs. How are these costs determined using the historical average cost approach? The marginal cost of funds approach? What are the advantages and disadvantages of each approach?

11–10. How can the historical average cost and marginal cost of funds approaches be used to help select assets (such as loans) that a depository institution might wish to acquire?

11–11. What is meant by the statement, "Deposits are quasi-fixed factors of production for banks and other depository institutions"? Does this statement have any bearing on how deposit services are marketed?

11–12. What factors do household depositors rank most highly in choosing a bank or thrift institution for their checking account? Their savings account? What about business firms?

11–13. What does the 1991 Truth in Savings Act require financial firms selling deposits inside the United States to tell their customers?

11–14. Use the APY formula required by the Truth in Savings Act for the following calculation. Suppose that a customer holds a savings deposit in a savings bank for a year. The balance in the account stood at $2,000 for 180 days and $100 for the remaining days in the year. If the Savings bank paid this depositor $8.50 in interest earnings for the year, what APY did this customer receive?

greater attention to competing banks and thrifts and the relative advantages and disadvantages they offer as well as pricing. Three-quarters of the households surveyed recently by the University of Michigan's Survey Research Center cited *location* as the primary reason for staying with the banking firm they first chose.

Business firms, on the other hand, prefer to leave their deposits with financial institutions that will be reliable sources of credit and, relatedly, are in good financial shape. They also rate highly the quality of officers and the quality of advice they receive from the banker or other financial-service manager. Recent research suggests that bankers and other financial-service providers need to do a better job of letting their customers know about the cost pressures they face today and why they need to charge fully and fairly for any services that customers use.

Basic (Lifeline) Banking: Key Services for Low-Income Customers

Our overview of deposit services in this chapter would not be complete without a brief look at a controversial consumer and social issue—the issue of **basic (lifeline) banking.** Should every adult citizen be guaranteed access to certain basic financial services, such as a checking account or personal loan? Is there a basic minimum level of financial service to which everyone is entitled? Can an individual today really function—secure adequate shelter, food, education, a job, and health care—without access to certain key financial services?

Some authorities refer to this issue as *lifeline banking* because it originated in the controversy surrounding electric, gas, and telephone services. Many people believe that these services are so essential for health and comfort that they should be provided at reduced prices to those who could not otherwise afford them. The basic, or lifeline, banking issue catapulted to nationwide attention during the 1980s and 1990s when several consumer groups, such as the Consumers Union and the American Association of Retired Persons, first studied the problem and then campaigned actively for resolution of the issue. Some banks have been picketed and formal complaints have been lodged with federal and state regulatory agencies.

The dimensions of the basic banking issue have been hinted at in several recent consumer surveys conducted at the Federal Reserve Board, the Federal Deposit Insurance Corporation, and the FNMA Foundation (see, for example, references [7] and [8]). Recent studies by the Federal Reserve indicate that about 15 percent of U.S. households have no checking accounts and about 12 percent hold neither checking nor savings accounts. Other estimates suggest there may be more than 10 million "unbanked" people in the United States. Most of these people are among the lowest-income groups (e.g., annual incomes below $25,000), have little formal education, often live in households headed by single parents, and lack trust of the banking system. Many of these individuals and families appear to be turning increasingly to high-cost "fringe" financial institutions (such as pawnshops, title and payday lenders, check-cashing firms, and wire transfer companies) for the financial services they need.

Many members of the unbanked population represent potentially profitable customers for banks and other traditional financial-service providers. Among the financial services most in demand are *wire transfers* or *remittances* of money sent to loved ones elsewhere. For example, thousands of documented and undocumented workers regularly wire more than $10 billion annually from the United States to their families and friends in Mexico and the rest of Latin America. It has been estimated that the wire-transfer or remittance market generates well over $100 billion in business annually for those banks and other financial firms willing to provide the service.

THE EXPEDITED FUNDS AVAILABILITY ACT

Responding to thousands of complaints from depositors across the United States that many depository institutions were delaying too long in giving their customers credit in their accounts after checks were deposited, Congress passed the Expedited Funds Availability Act in 1987. Congress mandated a time schedule that set maximum delays for receipt of deposit credit that deposit-service institutions could use, and it required these institutions to *inform* their customers about their policies for making funds available for customer use. Specifically,

1. All depository institutions must let customers use funds deposited in checking, share draft, or NOW accounts within a fixed number of days. The number of days must be spelled out in writing and displayed in the lobby.
2. The longest permissible time delays under federal law and regulation before customers can use deposited funds are as follows:

a. The next business day after deposits are made—applies to deposits of cash; the first $100 of deposited checks; government, certified, or cashier's checks; checks drawn on another account at the same institution; deposits made electronically or otherwise made directly into the customer's account (unless deposited after a specific closing time, in which case the deposit is considered as being made the next day).
b. The second business day after the deposit is made—applies to checks drawn on local institutions.
c. The fifth business day after the deposit is made—applies to checks drawn on nonlocal institutions.
d. Deposits made at an ATM not belonging to the customer's depository institution must be available on the same time schedule as other deposits.

One of the most serious problems individuals and families outside the financial mainstream face is lack of access to a *deposit account*. Many of these potential deposit customers do not have Social Security numbers or other acceptable ID required to open an account under current U.S. law (especially the USA Patriot Act of 2001). Others who can submit acceptable ID find most conventional deposit accounts too expensive to meet their needs.

Without a checking or savings account, few people can get approval for *credit* because most banks and thrift institutions prefer to make loans to those customers who keep deposits with them. Yet access to credit is essential for most families to secure adequate housing, medical care, and other important services. Several banks and thrifts have responded to this problem with *basic deposit plans* that allow users to cash some checks (such as Social Security checks), make a limited number of personal withdrawals or write a small number of checks (such as 10 free checks per month), or earn interest on even the smallest balances. As yet, few laws compel financial institutions to offer basic banking services, except in selected states—for example, Illinois, Massachusetts, Minnesota, Pennsylvania, and Rhode Island—though many states have recently debated such legislation.

Another component was added to the dilemma when the U.S. Congress passed the Debt Collection Improvement Act in 1996 and, when the U.S. Treasury launched its Electronic Funds Transfer program in 1999. Both of these events required that government payments to recipients, such as paychecks and Social Security checks, eventually be delivered via *electronic* means. This, of course, implies that some sort of deposit account be available in the check recipient's name in which these funds can be placed.

What, if anything, should government do? Even if new legislation is not forthcoming, do banks and other financial institutions have a responsibility to serve *all* customers within their local communities? These are not easy questions to answer. Banks and most other financial-service providers are privately owned corporations responsible to their stockholders to earn competitive returns on invested capital. Providing financial services at prices so low they do not cover production costs interferes with that important goal.

However, the issue of lifeline banking may not be that simple because banks, thrift institutions, and selected other financial firms are not treated in public policy like other private firms. For example, entry into the banking industry is regulated, with federal and state regulatory agencies compelled by law to consider "public convenience and needs" in permitting new banks to be established. Moreover, the Community Reinvestment Act of 1977 requires regulatory agencies to consider whether a banking or thrift organization applying to set up new branch offices or merge with another institution has really made an "affirmative effort" to serve all segments of the communities in which it operates.

This most recent legal requirement to fully serve the local community may include the responsibility to offer lifeline financial services. Moreover, banks and thrifts receive important aid from the government that grants them a competitive advantage over other financial institutions. One of the most important of these aids is *deposit insurance*, in which the government guarantees most of the deposits these financial institutions sell. If banks and thrift institutions benefit from deposit insurance backed ultimately by the public's taxes, do they have a public responsibility to offer some services that are accessible to all? If yes, how should they decide which customers should have access to low-price services? Should they insist on imposing a means test on their customers? Someone must bear the cost of producing services. Who should bear the cost of lifeline banking services? Answers to these questions are not readily apparent, but one thing is certain: These issues are not likely to go away. They may become even more important in the future.

Concept Check

11–15. What is *lifeline banking?* What pressures does it impose on the managers of banks and other financial institutions?

11–16. What does the Expedited Funds Availability Act require U.S. depository institutions to do?

Summary

Deposits are the vital input for banks and their closest competitors, the thrift institutions—the principal source of financial capital to fund loans and security investments and help generate profits to support long-term growth. The most important points this chapter has brought forward include the following:

- In managing their deposits, bankers and the managers of other depository institutions must grapple with two key questions centered upon *cost* and *volume*. Which types of deposits will help minimize the cost of fund-raising? How can a depository institution raise sufficient deposits to meet its fund-raising needs?

- The principal types of deposits offered by banks and other depository institutions today include (1) *transaction* (or *payments*) accounts, which customers use primarily to pay for purchases of goods and services; and (2) *nontransaction* (*savings* or *thrift*) deposits, which are held primarily as savings to prepare for future emergencies and for the expected yield they promise the depositor. Transaction deposits include regular checking accounts, which often bear no interest return, and interest-bearing transaction deposits (such as NOWs), which pay a low interest yield and, in some cases, limit the number of checks that can be written against the account. Nontransaction deposits include certificates of deposit (CDs), savings accounts, and money market accounts.

- Transaction deposits often are among the most profitable deposit services because of their nonexistent or low interest rates and the higher service fees these accounts usually carry. In contrast, nontransaction, or thrift, deposits generally have the advantage of a more stable funding base that allows a depository institution to reach for longer-term and higher-yielding assets. However, many nontransaction deposits carry relatively high interest costs, reducing potential profits.

- Unfortunately for many depository institutions today, deposit composition is shifting toward more costly nontransaction and interest-bearing transaction accounts, forcing their managers to become more sensitive to cost of production and the pricing of deposit services.

- Recent government deregulation of the banking and financial-services industry has encouraged bankers and other financial-service managers to think creatively about their deposit pricing policies—the interest rates and fees they post when offering deposit services. The key deposit-pricing models in use today fall into four broad categories: (1) cost-plus deposit pricing; (2) marginal cost pricing; (3) conditional or price schedule pricing; and (4) relationship pricing.

- The most popular of these deposit-pricing methods today is *conditional pricing.* In this case the interest rate the customer may earn on his or her deposit and the fees he or she will be asked to pay are conditional on the intensity of use of deposit services and the balance in the account. In contrast, the *cost-plus* pricing method calls for estimating all the operating and overhead costs incurred in providing each deposit service and adds a margin for profit. Under *marginal cost pricing,* a bank or thrift institution will set its price at a level just sufficient to attract *new* deposits and still earn a profit on the last dollar of *new* funds raised. Finally, *relationship pricing* calls for assessing lower fees or promising more generous yields on the deposits of customers who buy the most services and are the most loyal.

- Recently new rules have entered the deposit market. The Truth in Savings Act requires U.S. banks, thrift institutions, and foreign-owned banks selling deposits to U.S. customers to make full and timely disclosure of the terms under which each deposit service is offered. This includes information on minimum-balance requirements, how deposit balances are determined, what yield is promised, what the depositor must do to earn the promised rate of return, and any penalties or extra fees that might be assessed. A 30-day advance notice of any planned changes in deposit terms must be sent to the deposit customer.

- Finally, one of the most controversial issues in modern banking—*lifeline banking*—continues to be debated in and outside the deposit-services industry. Banks, thrifts, and their competitors have been asked in several states to offer low-cost financial services, especially deposits and loans, for those customers unable to afford conventional credit and deposit services. Some banking institutions have responded positively with limited-service accounts, while others argue that most financial-service institutions are profit-making corporations that must pay close attention to the potential profitability and cost of each new service.

Key Terms

Problems and Projects

1. Exeter National Bank reports the following figures in its current Report of Condition:

Assets (millions)		Liabilities (millions)	
Cash and interbank deposits	$ 50	Core deposits	$ 50
Short-term security investments	15	Large negotiable CDs	150
Total loans, gross	375	Deposits placed by brokers	65
Long-term securities	150	Other deposits	140
Other assets	10	Money market liabilities	95
Total assets	$600	Other liabilities	70
		Equity capital	30
		Total liabilities and equity capital	$600

   a. Evaluate the funding mix of deposits and nondeposit sources of funds employed by Exeter. Given the mix of its assets, do you see any potential problems? What changes would you like to see the management of this bank make? Why?

   b. Suppose market interest rates are projected to rise significantly. Does Exeter appear to face significant losses due to liquidity risk? Due to interest rate risk? Please be as specific as possible.

2. Kalewood Savings Bank has experienced recent changes in the composition of its deposits (see the following table; all figures in millions of dollars). What changes have recently occurred in Kalewood's deposit mix? Do these recent changes suggest possible problems for management in trying to increase profitability and stabilize its earnings?

Types of Deposits Held by the Savings Bank	This Year	One Year Ago	Two Years Ago	Three Years Ago
Regular and special checking accounts	$235	$294	$337	$378
Interest-bearing checking accounts	392	358	329	287
Regular (passbook) savings deposits	501	596	646	709
Money market deposit accounts	863	812	749	725
Retirement deposits	650	603	542	498
CDs under $100,000	327	298	261	244
CDs $100,000 and over	606	587	522	495

3. First Metrocentre Bank posts the following schedule of fees for its household and small business checking accounts:

   • For average monthly account balances over $1,500, there is no monthly mainte-nance fee and no charge per check.

   • For average monthly account balances of $1,000 to $1,500, a $2 monthly mainte-nance fee is assessed and there is a 10¢ charge per check cleared.

   • For average monthly account balances of less than $1,000, a $4 monthly mainte-nance fee is assessed and there is a 15¢ per check fee.

   What form of deposit pricing is this? What is First Metrocentre trying to accomplish with its pricing schedule? Can you foresee any problems with this pricing plan?

4. Emerald Isle Savings Association finds that it can attract the following amounts of deposits if it offers new depositors and those rolling over their maturing CDs the interest rates indicated below:

Expected Volume of New Deposits	Rate of Interest Offered Depositors
$ 5 million	5.0%
15 million	5.5
19 million	6.0
22 million	6.5
23 million	7.0

Management anticipates being able to invest any new deposits raised in loans yielding 8 percent. How far should this thrift institution go in raising its deposit interest rate in order to maximize total profits (excluding interest costs)?

5. Silverton Bank plans to launch a new deposit campaign next week in hopes of bringing in from $100 million to $600 million in new deposit money, which it expects to invest at an 8.75 percent yield. Management believes that an offer rate on new deposits of 5.75 percent would attract $100 million in new deposits and rollover funds. To attract $200 million, the bank would probably be forced to offer 6.25 percent. Silverton's forecast suggests that $300 million might be available at 6.8 percent, $400 million at 7.4 percent, $500 million at 8.2 percent, and $600 million at 9 percent. What volume of deposits should the institution try to attract to ensure that marginal cost does not exceed marginal revenue?

6. Needles Savings Bank finds that its basic checking account, which requires a $400 minimum balance, costs this savings bank an average of $3.13 per month in servicing costs (including labor and computer time) and $1.18 per month in overhead expenses. The savings bank also tries to build in a $0.50 per month profit margin on these accounts. What monthly fee should the bank charge each customer?

   Further analysis of customer accounts reveals that for each $100 in average balance maintained in its checking accounts, Needles Savings saves about 5 percent in operating expenses associated with each account. For a customer who consistently maintains an average balance of $1,000 per month, how much should the bank charge in order to protect its profit margin?

7. Clyde Appleton maintains a savings deposit with Santa Paribe Credit Union. This past year Clyde received $12.24 in interest earnings from his savings account. His savings deposit had the following average balance each month:

January	$400	July	$350
February	250	August	425
March	300	September	550
April	150	October	600
May	225	November	625
June	300	December	300

What was the annual percentage yield (APY) earned on Clyde Appleton's savings account?

8. First and Merchants National Bank of Leetown quotes an APY of 7 percent on a one-year money market CD sold to one of the small businesses in town. The firm posted a balance of $2,500 for the first 90 days of the year, $3,000 over the next 180 days, and

$2,750 for the remainder of the year. How much in total interest earnings did this small business customer receive for the year?

Internet Exercises

1. Your education has paid off. You have stepped five years into the future and are reviewing your bank accounts. The money has just piled up. You have a joint account with your fianceé containing $175,000 to be used for your first home. You have a joint account with your mother containing $125,000, and you have an account in your own name with $55,000 for the necessities of life. All three accounts are at the Monarch National Bank. Go to the following FDIC website **www2.fdic.gov/edie** and have Edie determine the insurance coverage for the $355,000. How much is uninsured? Can you describe the rules determining coverage?

2. How has the composition of deposits changed at your favorite local bank or thrift over the past 10 years? You can find this deposit information for banks and savings institutions at the FDIC's website. Utilize the link Statistics on Depository Institutions at **www3.fdic.gov/sdi/main.asp.** Using the points made in this chapter, explain why your local institution's mix of deposits is changing the way it is. How can depository institution managers influence the trends occurring in the composition of their deposits?

3. Which depository institutions currently quote the highest interest rates on checking accounts? Savings accounts? Money market deposits? Three- and six-months CDs? Visit **www.fisn.com, www.bankcd.com,** and **www.banx.com** for the answers.

4. Compare your local depository institution's interest rates on six-month and one-year certificates of deposit (check newspaper ads, call its customer service line, or visit its website) with the best rates on these same savings instruments offered by depository institutions quoting the highest deposit interest rates in the United States. (See websites listed in Exercise 3.) Why do you think there are such large interest-rate differences between your local institution and those posting the highest interest rates?

S&P Market Insight Challenge

STANDARD &POOR'S

1. Use Standard & Poor's Market Insight website (**www.mhhe.com/edumarketinsight**) for this problem. Deposits are normally the most important source of funds for all depository institutions. For an up-to-date view of deposit growth use the Industry tab in S&P's Market Insight and employ the drop-down menu to select among the subindustry categories Diversified Banks, Regional Banks, and Thrifts & Mortgage Finance. By selecting these subindustry groups, you will be able to access the S&P Industry Surveys on Banking and on Savings and Loans. Download both surveys and read the sections "Industry Trends" and "How the Industry Operates." Using this information, describe recent trends in deposit availability and deposit growth for commercial banks and thrifts.

2. Use Standard & Poor's Market Insight website (**www.mhhe.com/edumarketinsight**) for this problem. The proportion of deposits versus other sources of funding that individual banks and thrift institutions draw upon varies greatly from institution to institution. To prove this to yourself, take advantage of the information S&P's Market Insight provides and try to determine the percentage of total assets represented by deposits at each of the leading banks the website covers. Which banks, in particular, have the highest deposit-to-asset ratios? Which report the lowest deposit-to-asset ratios? Can you explain these differences? Do you see any significant trends in deposit mix going on? What do they imply for the management of the banks involved?

REAL NUMBERS FOR REAL BANKS — Assignment for Chapter 11

YOUR BANK'S DEPOSITS: VOLATILITY AND COST

Chapter 11 examines the major source of funds for depository institutions—*deposits*. The importance of attracting and maintaining deposits as a stable and low-cost source of funds cannot be overstated. This chapter begins by describing the different types of deposits, then explains that when it comes to deposits, the depository institution's management is most concerned with cost, volatility (risk of withdrawals), and the trade-off between the two. In this assignment, you will be comparing the character of your bank's deposits across time and with its peer group of banks to glean information concerning the cost and stability of this source of funds. Chapter 11's assignment is designed to develop your deposit-related vocabulary and to emphasize the importance of being able to attract funds in the form of deposits, which is unique to banks and thrift institutions.

The Character and Cost of Your Bank's Deposits—Trend and Comparative Analysis

A. **Data Collection:** Once again the FDIC's website located at **www3.fdic.gov/sdi/main.asp** will provide access to the data needed for your analysis. Use Statistics on Depository

Institutions (SDI) to create a four-column report of your bank's information and peer group information across years. In this part of the assignment, for Report Selection use the pull-down menu to select Total Deposits and view this in Percentages of Total Assets. To assess the overall importance of deposits as a source of funding, focus on total deposits to total assets. From the Total Deposits report you will collect information to break down deposits in several ways: (1) total deposits into domestic deposits versus foreign; (2) total deposits into interest bearing deposits versus noninterest bearing deposits; and (3) domestic deposits into their basic types. All the data for rows 109–123 is available from the Total Deposits report; however, you will have to derive NOW accounts in Row 120 by subtracting demand deposits from transaction deposits. Finally we will go to the Interest Expense report and gather information on the proportion of interest paid for foreign and domestic deposits to total assets. Enter the percentage information for these items as an addition to Spreadsheet 2 as follows:

	Your Bank 12/31/yy %	Peer Group 12/31/yy %	Your Bank 12/31/yy %	Peer Group 12/31/yy %
Deposits (A107)				
Date (A108)				
Total deposits (A109)				
Deposits held in domestic offices (A110)				
Deposits held in foreign offices (A111)				
Total deposits (A112)				
Interest-bearing deposits (domestic) (A113)				
Interest-bearing deposits (foreign) (A114)				
Noninterest-bearing deposits (domestic) (A115)				
Noninterest-bearing deposits (foreign) (A116)				
(A117)	Bank (yyyy)	Peer (yyyy)	Bank (yyyy)	Peer (yyyy)
Total domestic deposits (A118)				
Demand deposits (A119)				
NOW accounts* (A120)				
Money market deposit accounts (MMDAs) (A121)				
Other savings deposits (excluding MMDAs) (A122)				
Total time deposits (A123)				
Domestic office deposits (interest expense) (A124)				
Foreign office deposits (interest expense) (A125)				
Average interest cost on domestic office interest-bearing deposits (A126)				
Average interest cost on foreign office interest-bearing deposits (A127)				

*NOW Accounts = Transaction Accounts – Demand Deposits

(continued)

B. Having collected all the data for Rows 109–125, you will calculate the entries for Rows 126 and 127. For example, the entry for Cell B126 is created using the formula function B124/B113.

C. Compare the columns of row 109. How has the reliance on deposits as a source of funds changed across periods? Has your bank relied more or less on depositors than the average bank in the peer group?

D. Use the chart function in Excel and the data by columns in rows 117 through 123 to create a group of four bar charts illustrating the types of domestic deposits supporting assets for your BHC and its peer group. You will be able to select the block and create the chart with just a few clicks of the mouse, saving it as a separate spreadsheet. Remem-ber to provide titles, labels, and percentages; otherwise, we have something reminiscent of abstract art. To give you an example, the chart containing information for NCC and its peer group would appear as shown below. (Note that if you have access to a color printer you will not have to transform graphics to be effective in black and white as we have done below.)

E. Utilizing the information below, write approximately one page about your bank's use of deposits as a source of funds and how it compares to its peers. Use your bar charts as a graphic and incorporate tables from your Excel spreadsheets as references for the discussion. Provide inferences concerning interest costs and deposit volatility (withdrawal risk) based on the data you have to interpret.

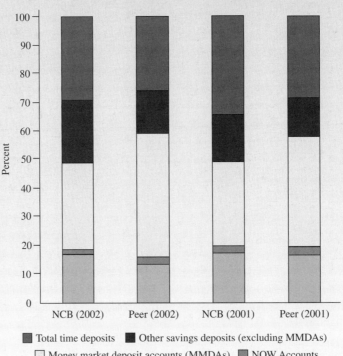

Types of Domestic Deposits: A Comparison

Selected References

For a discussion of recent trends in deposit services, see these sources:

1. Dick, Astrid A. "Demand Estimation and Consumer Welfare in the Banking Industry." *Finance and Economics Discussion Series*, Board of Governors of the Federal Reserve System, 2002-58.

2. Federal Reserve Banks. *Functional Cost and Profit Analysis. National Average Report*, 1996. Federal Reserve Bank of San Francisco, 1997.

3. Gerdes, Geoffrey R., and Jack K. Walton. "The Use of Checks and Other Noncash Payment Instruments in the United States." *Federal Reserve Bulletin*, August 2002, pp. 360–370.

4. Kiser, Elizabeth K. "Household Switching Behavior at Depository Institutions." *Finance and Economics Discussion Series*, Board of Governors of the Federal Reserve System, 2002-44.

5. Rose, Peter S. "Pricing Deposits in an Era of Competition and Change." *The Canadian Banker* 93, no. 1 (February 1986), pp. 44–51.

6. ———. "Defensive Banking in a Volatile Economy." *The Canadian Banker* 92, no. 5 (April 1986), pp. 44–49.

For a discussion of the issues surrounding lifeline banking services, see:

7. Canner, Glenn B., and Ellen Maland. "Basic Banking." *Federal Reserve Bulletin*, April 1987, pp. 255–69.

8. Good, Barbara A. "Bringing the Unbanked Aboard." *Economic Commentary*, Federal Reserve Bank of Cleveland, January 15, 1999.

For a discussion of the role of depositors in disciplining bank risk taking and bank behavior, see especially:

9. Jordan, John S. "Depositor Discipline at Failing Banks." *New England Economic Review*, Federal Reserve Bank of Boston, March/April 2000, pp. 15–28.

10. Marino, James A., and Rosalind L. Bennett. "The Consequences of National Depositor Preference." *FDIC Banking Review*, 1999, pp. 19–38.

11. Thompson, James B. "Raising the Deposit Insurance Limit: A Bad Idea Whose Time Has Come?" *Economic Commentary*, Federal Reserve Bank of Cleveland, April 15, 2000.

12. Vaughn, Mark D., and David C. Wheelock. "Deposit Insurance Reform: Is It Deja Vu All Over Again?" *The Regional Economist*, Federal Reserve Bank of St. Louis, October 2002, pp. 5–9.

For a discussion of deposit pricing techniques and issues, see these studies:

13. Canner, Glenn B., and Robert D. Kuntz. *Service Charges as a Source of Bank Income and Their Impact on Consumers*. Staff Economic Study No. 145, Board of Governors of the Federal Reserve System, 1984.

14. Crane, Dwight B., and Michael J. Reily. *NOW Deposits*. Lexington, MA: Lexington Books, 1978.

15. Dunham, Constance. "Unravelling the Complexity of NOW Account Pricing." *New England Economic Review*, Federal Reserve Bank of Boston, May/June 1983, pp. 30–45.

16. Flannery, Mark. "Retail Bank Deposits as Quasi-Fixed Factors of Production." *American Economic Review* 72, no. 3, pp. 527–36.

17. McNulty, James E. "Do You Know the True Cost of Your Deposits?" *Review*, Federal Home Loan Bank of Atlanta, October 1986, pp. 1–6.

18. Murphy, Neil B., and Lewis Mandell. *The NOW Account Decision: Profitability and Pricing Strategy*. Rolling Meadows, IL: Bank Administration Institute, 1981.

www.mhhe.com/rose6e

19. Simonson, Donald G., and Peter C. Marks. "Pricing NOW Deposits and the Cost of Bank Funds—Part One: Break-Even Analysis of NOW Deposits." *The Magazine of Bank Administration*, November 1980, pp. 28–31.

20. ———. "Pricing NOW Deposits and the Cost of Bank Funds—Part Two." *The Magazine of Bank Administration*, December 1980, pp. 21–24.

21. Watson, Ronald D. "Estimating the Cost of Your Bank's Funds." *Business Review*, Federal Reserve Bank of Philadelphia, May/June 1978.

For a discussion of recent trends in service availability and service fees levied by banks and thrift institutions see:

22. Anderson, Richard G., "Retail Sweep Programs and Money Demand." *Monetary Trends*, Federal Reserve Bank of St. Louis, November 2002.

23. Hannan, Timothy H. "Recent Trends in Retail Fees and Services of Depository Institutions." *Federal Reserve Bulletin*, September 1994, pp. 771–81.

24. Stavins, Joanna. "Checking Accounts: What Do Banks Offer and What Do Consumers Value?" *New England Economic Review*, March/April 1999, pp. 3–13.

For a discussion of factors influencing deposit growth in recent years, see especially:

25. Laderman, Elizabeth. "Deposits and Demographics?" *FRBSF Economic Letter*, Federal Reserve Bank of San Francisco, No. 97-19 (June 27, 1997).

For a discussion of the impact of the Truth in Savings Act on the cost of bank compliance, see:

26. Elliehausen, Gregory, and Barbara R. Lowrey. *The Cost of Implementing Consumer Financial Regulations: An Analysis of the Experience with the Truth in Savings Act.* Staff Study No. 170, Board of Governors of the Federal Reserve System, December 1997.

For a review of the impact of thrift institutions (such as credit unions) on the interest rates offered on deposits by banks, see, for example:

27. Hannan, Timothy H. "The Impact of Credit Unions on the Rates Offered for Retail Deposits by Banks and Thrift Institutions." *Finance and Economics Discussion Series*, 2003-06, Federal Reserve Board, Washington, D.C., September 10, 2002.

Managing Nondeposit Liabilities and Other Sources of Borrowed Funds

Key Topics in This Chapter

- Liability Management
- Customer Relationship Doctrine
- Alternative Nondeposit Funds Sources
- Measuring the Funds Gap
- Choosing among Different Funds Sources
- Determining the Overall Cost of Funds

Introduction

The traditional source of funds for banks and their closest competitors, the thrift institutions, is deposits. The public's demand for checking and savings deposits supplies most of the raw material for lending and investing and, ultimately, for the profits earned by banks and competing lenders.[1] But what does management do when deposit volume and growth are inadequate to support all the loans and investments the financial firm would like to make? The largest banks and thrifts—institutions like J. P. Morgan Chase, Wells Fargo & Company, and Washington Mutual—learned long ago that another source of funds, one that is usually more reliable, was needed to supplement deposit money. In this chapter we take a detailed look at such a funding source—the so-called nondeposit liabilities that banks and other depository institutions, particularly the largest institutions, draw upon every day.

Liability Management and the Customer Relationship Doctrine

Managers of banks and other lending institutions learned over the years that turning down a profitable loan request with the excuse, "we don't have enough deposits to support the loan," is not well received by their customers. Denial of a credit request often means the

---

[1] Portions of this chapter are based on an article by Peter S. Rose in *The Canadian Banker* [10] and are used with permission.

The slow growth of deposits, especially checking accounts, in recent years has caused many of the world's leading banks and depository institutions to turn more heavily to nondeposit borrowings in the money and capital markets. Banks and other lenders need to find funds for loans and investments, for daily operations, and for working capital. Not surprisingly, heavier usage of the open market for funding purposes has caused the markets for nondeposit instruments, such as Federal funds, Euro-deposits, repurchase agreements, commercial paper, and so on, to grow rapidly. The presence of descriptions and data about these financial instruments on the World Wide Web has grown apace; Web users today can learn a lot about the nondeposit funds market by going online.

First, it is fairly easy to check on how much in nondeposit borrowings, such as Federal funds and Repurchase Agreements, individual U.S. banks and thrift institutions are drawing upon by entering each institution's name, city, and state in the FDIC's website at **www.fdic.gov**. For banks or other financial firms headquartered overseas it is usually best to type in their name and country of origin in order to find their financial data. The need for nondeposit borrowings by a bank or other lender is heavily influenced by the strength of the economy—especially by the strength of loan demand. The economy's status can more easily be tracked today through such sites as Federal Reserve Board Browse Data at **www.economagic.com/fedbog.htm**.

Other key websites where information related to nondeposit borrowings is often found include **www.federalreserve.gov/boarddocs/RptCongress/** and **www.ny.frb.org/markets/**. Moreover, as this chapter will explain, banks and other lenders frequently manage their nondeposit liabilities using a technique referred to as *liability management*. The techniques and challenges of liability management can be tracked through a website devoted to news for professional asset-liability managers, called ALM Professional, at **www.almprofessional.com**. This site includes articles and models that asset-liability managers might use.

Filmtoid
What 2003 drama casts Philip Seymour Hoffman as an assistant bank manager with authority over sources and uses of funds at the bank who cannot resist the allure of Atlantic City?
Answer: *Owning Mahowny.*

immediate loss of a deposit and perhaps the loss of any future business from the disappointed customer. On the other hand, granting a loan request—even when deposit flows are inadequate—usually brings in both new deposits and the demand for other financial services as well. And the benefits may reach far beyond the borrowing customer alone. For example, a loan made to a business firm often brings in personal deposits from the firm's owners and employees.

The banking community learned long ago the importance of the **customer relationship doctrine**, and managers of other lending institutions have picked it up in recent years. This doctrine proclaims that the *first* priority of a lending institution is to make loans to all those customers from whom the lender expects to receive positive net earnings. Thus, lending decisions often *precede* funding decisions; all loans and investments whose returns exceed their costs and whose quality meets the lending institution's credit standards should be made. If deposits are not immediately available to cover these loans and investments, then management should seek out the lowest-cost source of borrowed funds available to meet its customers' credit needs.

During the 1960s and 1970s, the customer relationship doctrine spawned the liquidity management strategy known as **liability management,** introduced in Chapters 6 and 10. Liability management consists of *buying funds*, mainly from other financial institutions, in order to cover good-quality credit requests and satisfy any legal reserve requirements on deposits and other borrowings that law or regulation may require. As we saw in Chapter 10, a bank or other lending institution may acquire funds by borrowing short-term in the domestic Federal funds market, borrowing abroad through the Eurocurrency market, selling money market or jumbo ($100,000+) negotiable CDs to customers, securing a loan from the central bank or other government agency, negotiating security repurchase agreements with individuals and institutions having temporary surpluses of funds, issuing

TABLE 12–1

Sample Use of Nondeposit Funds Sources to Supplement Deposits and Make Loans

First National Bank and Trust Company Balance Sheet (Report of Condition)	
Assets	**Liabilities and Equity**
Loans: New loans to be made, $100,000,000	Funding sources found to support the new loans: Newly deposited funds expected today $ 50,000,000 Nondeposit funds sources: Federal funds purchased 19,000,000 Borrowings of Eurodollars abroad 20,000,000 Securities sold under agreements to repurchase (RPs) 3,000,000 Borrowings from a nonbank subsidiary of the bank's holding company that sold commercial paper in the money market +8,000,000 Total new deposit and nondeposit funds raised to cover the new loans $100,000,000

commercial paper through a subsidiary that is part of the same holding company, or even selling debentures (long-term debt) to raise capital for the long haul.

Table 12–1 illustrates the basic idea behind liability management. In this instance, one of a bank's business customers has requested a new loan for today amounting to $100 million. However, the bank's deposit division reports that only $50 million in new deposits are expected today. If management wishes to fully meet the loan request of $100 million from one of its customers, it must find another $50 million, mainly from nondeposit sources. Some quick work by the bank's money market division, which called correspondent banks inside the United States and in London and negotiated with nonbank institutions carrying temporary cash surpluses, resulted in raising the entire $50 million by borrowing domestic Federal funds, borrowing funds from a subsidiary part of the same holding company that sold notes (commercial paper) in the open market, selling bank-held securities under a security repurchase agreement, and borrowing Eurodollars from branches abroad.

Unfortunately, the money market and deposit divisions of the bank cannot rest on their laurels. They know that most of the $50 million just raised will be available only until tomorrow when many of the borrowed funds must be returned to the owners. These departing borrowed funds will need to be replaced quickly to continue to support the new loan. Customers who receive loans spend their funds quickly (otherwise, why get a loan?) by writing checks and wiring funds to other financial institutions. This bank, therefore, must find sufficient new funds to honor all those checks and wire transfers of funds away from the bank that its borrowing customers initiate.

Clearly, liability management is an essential tool lenders need to sustain the growth of their lending programs. However, liability management also poses real challenges for bankers and other financial-service managers, who must keep abreast of the market every day to make sure their institution is fully funded. Moreover, liability management is an *interest-sensitive* approach to raising funds. If interest rates rise and our bank is unwilling to pay those higher rates, funds borrowed from the money market will be gone in minutes. Money market lenders typically have a highly elastic response to changes in market interest rates.

Yet, viewed from another perspective, funds raised by the use of liability management techniques are *flexible:* the banker or other institutional borrower can decide exactly how

IS THIS REALLY THE TIME TO BORROW SO MUCH MONEY SHORT-TERM?

We note in the example of liability management in Table 12–1 that all of the nondeposit borrowings are short-term rather than long-term debt. Why would the liability manager in this situation rely so heavily upon short-term debt, especially overnight loans? Hasn't she heard about interest-rate risk and the danger that the lender may be forced to borrow over and over again at higher and higher interest rates to fund this loan?

Yes, certainly, but there are some good reasons for "going short" in this and similar cases. For one thing, the borrowing customer likely is standing there waiting for his loan. Today there may not be enough time to find and negotiate long-term debt contracts; tomorrow may be another story and longer-term deposits may soon roll in.

Second, remember that in the example above we are dealing with funding just one loan. A glance at the lender's whole loan portfolio may reveal a better overall balance between short and long-term debt.

Third, banks and many of their financial-service neighbors have gotten much better at managing interest-rate risk than used to be the case. As we saw in Part Two, they now have a lot of risk-management tools to work with.

Moreover, many assets depository institutions hold are also short-term, including some overnight and intraday loans. Bankers and other financial-service managers have learned to keep a rough balance between their shorter-term assets and shorter-term liabilities in order to protect against liquidity crises. Finally, should the current interest-rate forecast call for declining market interest rates, perhaps this liability manager is in a good position after all. With falling interest rates, tomorrow's borrowing costs should be lower than today's costs. Much depends on the outlook for changing interest rates and overall market conditions.

much he or she needs and for how long and usually find a source of funds that meets those requirements. In contrast, when a bank or thrift institution sells deposits to raise funds, it is the depositor who decides how much and how long funds will be left with the individual financial firm. With liability management, banks and other institutions in need of more funds to cover expanding loan commitments or deficiencies in required reserves can simply raise their *offer rate* until money market lenders offer them enough funds. Lending institutions confronted with declining loan demand and excess reserves can simply *lower* their offer rate in order to reduce their volume of money market borrowing. Thus, the hallmarks of liability management are (1) buying funds by selling liabilities in the money market and (2) using price (the interest rate offered) as the control lever to regulate the volume and timing of incoming funds.

Alternative Nondeposit Sources of Funds

As Table 12–2 suggests, the dollar usage of nondeposit sources of funds and money market jumbo ($100,000+) CDs has fluctuated in recent years, but generally it has risen to provide a bigger share of funds for depository institutions, particularly the largest commercial banks. While smaller banks and thrift institutions usually rely most heavily on deposits for their funding needs, leading money-center banks around the globe and depository institutions facing heavy customer demand for credit have come to regard the nondeposit funds market as a key source of short-term money to meet both loan demand and unexpected cash emergencies.

Table 12–3 shows the approximate relationship between the size of banks and thrifts and their affinity for nondeposit borrowing. Clearly, the smallest-size banks and thrift institutions (each under $100 million in assets) support only a small share of their assets by nondeposit borrowings. For example, the smallest U.S.-insured banks supported less than 4 percent of their assets with nondeposit borrowings, while the smallest thrift institutions met just under 7 percent of their funding needs using these funding sources at year-end 2002. Among the largest depository institutions (over $1 billion in assets), however,

TABLE 12–2   Recent Growth in Nondeposit Sources of Borrowed Funds at FDIC-Insured Banks and Thrifts

Sources: Board of Governors of the Federal Reserve System and Federal Deposit Insurance Corporation.

Nondeposit Sources of Borrowed Funds	Billions of Dollars at Year-End:							
	1990	1992	1994	1996	1998	2000	2002	2003*
Money market negotiable (jumbo) CDs ($100,000+)	$ 431.8	$ 366.5	$ 344.9	$ 476.9	$ 671.4	$ 821.3	$ 794.0	$ 819.3
Eurodollar borrowings from own foreign offices	168.0	160.4	185.9	177.3	148.8	194.3	227.9	233.4
Federal funds borrowings and security RPs	180.1	149.9	221.1	199.8	206.1	235.5	328.4	318.6
Commercial paper issued**	200.0	171.6	207.7	229.7	322.0	312.8	217.8	232.9
Borrowings from the Federal Reserve Banks	0.3	0.1	0.5	0.2	0.1	0.2	0.1	0.1
Total nondeposit funds raised by U.S.-insured banks and thrifts	$ 980.2	$ 848.5	$ 960.1	$1,083.9	$1,348.4	$1,564.1	$1,568.2	$1,604.3
Total deposits of FDIC-insured depository institutions	$3,637.3	$3,527.1	$3,611.6	$3,925.2	$4,386.1	$4,914.8	$5,568.7	$5,678.6
Ratio of nondeposit funds to total deposits for all FDIC-insured banks and thrifts	26.9%	24.1%	26.6%	27.6%	30.7%	31.8%	28.2%	28.3%

Notes: *Figures for 2003 are through the first quarter. **Includes all finance-company paper issued directly to investors by banks and other financial-service providers.

TABLE 12–3

The Relationship between the Size of Depository Institutions and Their Use of Nondeposit Borrowings (2002 figures for FDIC-insured banks and thrifts)

Source: Federal Deposit Insurance Corporation.

Size Group and Type of Depository Institution	Percent of Assets Supported by Nondeposit Borrowings
The largest U.S. commercial banks (over $1 billion in assets)	23.9%
The smallest U.S. commercial banks (under $100 million in assets)	3.7
The largest U.S. thrift institutions (over $1 billion in assets)	27.1%
The smallest U.S. thrift institutions (under $100 million in assets)	6.3

Notes: Thrift institutions include savings and loan associations and savings banks insured by the Federal Deposit Insurance Corporation.

nondeposit borrowings covered nearly 24 percent of large commercial bank assets and more than a quarter of the assets of large thrift institutions.

Overall, nondeposit borrowings have often outstripped the growth of traditional deposits, as Table 12–2 suggests, in part because of the greater flexibility of nondeposit borrowings, which are less regulated, and the loss of some deposits in recent years to competing financial institutions, such as mutual funds, insurance companies, hedge funds, and pension funds, which are competing aggressively to attract the public's savings.

In the sections that follow we examine the most popular nondeposit funds sources banks and selected other financial firms use today.

Federal Funds Market

The most popular domestic source of borrowed reserves among depository institutions is the **Federal funds market.** Originally, Federal funds consisted exclusively of deposits U.S. banks hold at the Federal Reserve banks. These deposits are owned by banks and other depository institutions and are held at the Fed primarily to satisfy legal reserve requirements, clear checks, and pay for purchases of government securities. These Federal Reserve balances can be transferred from one institution to another in seconds through the Fed's wire transfer network (Fedwire), linking all Federal Reserve banks across the United States. Today, however, correspondent deposits that depository institutions hold with each other also can be moved around the banking system the same day a request is made. The same is true of large collected demand deposit balances that securities dealers and governments own, which also can be transferred by wire. All three of these types of deposits make up the raw material that is traded in the market for Federal funds. In technical terms, Federal funds are simply short-term borrowings of immediately available money.

It did not take bankers and the managers of other financial institutions long to realize the potential source of profit inherent in these *same-day monies*. Because reserves deposited with the Federal Reserve banks and most demand deposits held by business firms pay no interest, banks and nonbank firms have a strong economic incentive to lend excess reserves or any demand deposit balances not needed to cover immediate cash needs. Moreover, there are no legal reserve requirements on Federal funds borrowings currently and few regulatory controls, features that have stimulated the growth of the market and helped keep the cost of borrowing down. Banks, thrifts, securities houses, and other firms in need of immediate funds can negotiate a loan with a holder of surplus interbank deposits or reserves at the Fed, promising to return the borrowed funds the next day if need be.

The main use of the Federal funds market today is still the traditional one: a mechanism that allows banks and other depository institutions short of reserves to meet their legal reserve requirements or to satisfy customer loan demand by tapping immediately usable funds from other institutions possessing temporarily idle funds. Fed funds are also used to supplement deposit growth and give lenders a relatively safe outlet for temporary cash surpluses on which interest can be earned (even for a loan lasting only a few hours). Moreover, the Federal funds market serves as a conduit for the policy initiatives of the Federal Reserve System designed to control the growth of money and credit in order to stabilize the economy.

By performing all of these functions, the Federal funds market efficiently distributes reserves throughout the financial system to areas of greatest need. To help suppliers and demanders of Federal funds find each other, funds brokers soon appeared to trade Federal funds in return for commissions. Large correspondent banks, known as *accommodating banks*, play a role similar to that of funds brokers for smaller depository institutions in their region. An accommodating bank buys and sells Federal funds simultaneously in order to make a market for the reserves of its customer institutions, even though the accommodating bank itself may have no need for extra funds.

The procedure for borrowing and lending Federal funds is a simple one. Borrowing and lending institutions communicate either directly with each other or indirectly through a correspondent bank or funds broker. Once borrowing and lending institutions agree on the terms of a Federal funds loan—especially its interest rate and maturity—the lending institution arranges to transfer reserves from a deposit it holds, either at the Federal Reserve bank in its district or with a correspondent bank, into a deposit controlled by the borrowing institution. This may be accomplished by wiring Federal funds if the borrowing and lending institutions are in different regions of the country. If both lender and borrower hold reserve deposits with the same Federal Reserve bank or with the same correspondent bank, the lending institution simply asks that bank to transfer funds from its reserve account to the borrower's reserve account—a series of bookkeeping entries accomplished in seconds via computer. When the loan comes due, the funds are automatically transferred back to the lending institution's reserve account. (See Table 12–4 for a description of the bookkeeping entries involved.) The interest owed may also be transferred at this time, or the borrower may simply send a check to the lender to cover any interest owed.

Key URL
If you would like to study the Federal funds market in greater detail see **http://econpapers .hhs.se/article**.

TABLE 12–4   The Mechanics of Borrowing and Lending Federal Funds (in millions of dollars)

Step 1. Lending Reserve Balances Held at the Federal Reserve Banks

Lender's Balance Sheet		**Borrower's Balance Sheet**	
Assets	Liabilities and Net Worth	Assets	Liabilities and Net Worth
Federal funds sold (loaned) +100		Reserves on deposit at the Fed +100	Federal funds purchased (borrowed) +100
Reserves on deposit at the Fed −100			

Step 2. Borrower Uses the Federal Funds It Obtains to Make Loans

	Borrower's Balance Sheet	
	Assets	Liabilities and Net Worth
	Reserves on deposit at the Fed −100	
	Loans +100	

Step 3. Repaying the Loan of Federal Funds

Lender's Balance Sheet		**Borrower's Balance Sheet**	
Assets	Liabilities and Net Worth	Assets	Liabilities and Net Worth
Reserves on deposit at the Fed +100		Reserves on deposit at the Fed −100	Federal funds purchased −100
Federal funds sold (loaned) −100			

Step 4. Lending Federal Funds by a Respondent (usually smaller) Depository Institution to a Correspondent (usually larger) Depository Institution

Lender's (respondent's) Balance Sheet		**Borrower's (correspondent's) Balance Sheet**	
Assets	Liabilities and Net Worth	Assets	Liabilities and Net Worth
Deposits held with correspondent −100			Federal funds purchased +100
Federal funds loaned +100			Respondent's deposit −100

(continued)

TABLE 12–4   The Mechanics of Borrowing and Lending Federal Funds (*concluded*)

Step 5. The Corespondent Institution May Use the Federal Funds Borrowed to Meet Its Own Reserve Needs or Loan Those Funds to Another Institution (usually located in a major money center where credit demands are heavy)

Correspondent Lender's Balance Sheet		Money Center Borrower's Balance Sheet	
Assets	Liabilities and Net Worth	Assets	Liabilities and Net Worth

Reserves −100
Federal funds
    loaned +100
		Reserves +100	Federal funds
			    purchased +100

Step 6. Repaying the Loan to the Respondent Institution

Respondent Institution		Correspondent Institution	
Assets	Liabilities and Net Worth	Assets	Liabilities and Net Worth

Deposits held
  with
    correspondent +100
Federal funds
    loaned −100
			Federal funds
			    purchased −100
			Respondent's
			    bank deposit +100

Key URL
For a look at the rapidly developing Fed funds futures market, see **www.cbot.com/** and explore "Interest Rate Product Information" in the CBOT's Knowledge Center.

The interest rate on a Federal funds loan is subject to negotiation between borrowing and lending institutions. While the interest rate attached to each Federal funds loan may differ from the rate on any other loan, most of these loans use the *effective interest rate* prevailing each day in the national market—a rate of interest posted by Federal funds brokers and major accommodating banks operating at the center of the funds marketplace. In recent years, tiered Federal funds rates (i.e., interest-rate schedules) have appeared at various times, with banks in trouble paying higher interest rates or simply being shut out of the market completely.

The Federal funds market uses three types of loan agreements: (1) overnight loans, (2) term loans, and (3) continuing contracts. *Overnight loans* are unwritten agreements, negotiated via wire or telephone, with the borrowed funds returned the next day. Normally these loans are not secured by specific collateral, though where borrower and lender do not know each other well or there is doubt about the borrower's credit standing, the borrower may be required to place selected government securities in a custody account in the name of the lender until the loan is repaid. *Term loans* are longer-term Federal funds contracts lasting several days, weeks, or months, often accompanied by a written contract. *Continuing contracts* are automatically renewed each day unless either the borrower or the lender decides to end this agreement. Most continuing contracts are made between smaller respondent banks and thrift institutions and their larger correspondents, with the correspondent automatically investing the smaller institution's deposits held with it in Federal funds loans until told to do otherwise.

Repurchase Agreements as a Source of Bank Funds

Repurchase agreements (RPs) are very similar to Federal funds transactions and are often viewed as collateralized Federal funds transactions. In a Federal funds transaction, the seller (lender) is exposed to credit risk via the uncertainty that the borrowing institution

TABLE 12–5 Raising Loanable Funds through a Repurchase Agreement Involving the Borrower's Securities (in millions of dollars)

Step 1. Bank Sells Some of Its Securities under an RP Agreement

Commercial Bank		Temporary Buyer of the Bank's Securities	
Assets	Liabilities and Net Worth	Assets	Liabilities and Net Worth
Securities −100 Reserves +100		Securities +100 Cash account −100	

Step 2. The RP Agreement Ends and the Securities Are Returned

Commercial Bank		Temporary Buyer of the Bank's Securities	
Assets	Liabilities and Net Worth	Assets	Liabilities and Net Worth
Securities +100 Reserves −100		Securities −100 Cash account +100	

Key URLs
Additional information about RPs may be found at **www.rich.frb.org/pubs/intruments/** and at **www.treasurypoint.com/knowledge/** (see the short-term investing link).

may not have the funds to repay. If the purchaser of federal funds were to provide collateral in the form of marketable securities, it would reduce the credit risk. The reduction in credit risk is exemplified in the lower cost of RPs when compared to Federal funds rates. Most RPs are transacted across the Fed Wire system, just as are Federal funds transactions. RPs may take a bit longer to transact because the seller of funds (the lender) must be satisfied with the quality and quantity of securities provided as collateral.[2]

Repurchase agreements get their name from the process involved—the institution purchasing funds (the borrower) is temporarily exchanging securities for cash. RPs involve the temporary sale of high-quality, easily liquidated assets, such as Treasury bills, accompanied by an agreement to buy back those assets on a specific future date at a predetermined price. (See Table 12–5.) An RP transaction is often for overnight funds; however, it may be extended for months.

The interest cost for both Federal funds transactions and repurchase agreements can be calculated from the following formula:

$$\frac{\text{Interest}}{\text{cost of RP}} = \frac{\text{Amount}}{\text{borrowed}} \times \frac{\text{Current}}{\text{RP rate}} \times \frac{\text{Number of days in RP borrowing}}{360 \text{ days}}$$

For example, suppose that a commercial bank borrows $50 million through an RP transaction collateralized by government bonds for three days and the current RP rate in the market is 6 percent. Then this bank's total interest cost would be as follows:

$$\frac{\text{Interest}}{\text{cost of RP}} = \$50,000,000 \times 0.06 \times \frac{3}{360} = \$24,995$$

Recently a major innovation occurred in the RP market with the invention of *General Collateral Finance (GCF) RPs*, inaugurated in 1998 under the leadership of the Bank of

[2] As a result of the losses on RPs associated with the collapse of two government securities dealers in 1985, Congress passed the Government Securities Act, which requires dealers in U.S. government securities to report their activities and requires borrowers and lenders to put their RP contracts in writing, specifying the nature and location of collateral.

New York, J. P. Morgan Chase, and the Fixed Income Clearing Corporation (FICC) of New York. What is a GCF RP? How does it differ from the traditional RP?

Conventional (fixed-collateral) repurchase agreements designate specific securities to serve as collateral for a loan, with the lender taking possession of those particular instruments until the loan matures. In contrast, the general-collateral GCF RP permits relatively easy and low-cost *collateral substitution*. Borrower and lender can agree upon a variety of securities, any of which may serve as loan collateral. This agreed-upon array of eligible collateral might include, for example, any Treasury securities maturing within five years or any obligation of the U.S. Treasury or a federal agency. Thus, the same securities pledged at the beginning do not have to be delivered at the end of a loan. Moreover, GCF RPs are settled on the books of the FICC, which allows *netting* obligations between lenders, borrowers, and brokers so that less money and securities must be transferred. Finally, GCF RPs are reversed early in the morning and settled late each day, giving borrowers greater flexibility during daylight hours in deciding what to do with collateral securities. Overall, GCF RPs make more efficient use of collateral, lower transactions cost, and help make the RP market more liquid, helping to explain their recent explosive growth. (For further discussion of this important RP innovation, see especially Fleming and Garbade [15].)

Concept Check

12–1. What is *liability management?*

12–2. What advantages and risks does the pursuit of liability management bring to a bank or other borrowing institution?

12–3. What is the *customer relationship doctrine,* and what are its implications for fund-raising by lending institutions?

12–4. For what kinds of funding situations are Federal funds best suited?

12–5. Chequers State Bank loans $50 million from its reserve account at the Federal Reserve Bank of Philadelphia to First National Bank of Smithville, located in the New York Federal Reserve Bank's district, for 24 hours, with the funds returned the next day. Can you show the correct accounting entries for making this loan and for the return of the loaned funds?

12–6. Hillside Savings Association has an excess balance of $35 million in a deposit at its principal correspondent, Sterling City Bank, and instructs the latter institution to loan the funds today to another bank or thrift institution, returning them to its correspondent deposit the next business day. Sterling loans the $35 million to Imperial Security National Bank for 24 hours. Can you show the proper accounting entries for the extension of this loan and for the recovery of the loaned funds by Hillside Savings?

12–7. Compare and contrast Federal funds transactions with RPs.

12–8. What are the principal advantages to the borrower of funds under an RP agreement?

Borrowing from the Federal Reserve Bank in the District

For a depository institution with immediate reserve needs, a viable alternative to the Federal funds and RP markets is negotiating a loan from a Federal Reserve bank for a short period of time (in most cases, no more than two weeks). The Fed will make the loan through its **discount window** by crediting the borrowing institution's reserve account held at the Federal Reserve bank in its district. (See Table 12–6 for an overview of the typical accounting entries associated with a discount window loan and its repayment.)

Each loan made by the 12 Federal Reserve Banks must be backed by collateral acceptable to the Fed. Most banks and other loan-eligible depository institutions keep U.S. government securities in the vaults of the Federal Reserve banks for this purpose. The Fed will

CHARGING U.S. DEPOSITORY INSTITUTIONS A "LOMBARD RATE"? WHAT'S THAT?

The Federal Reserve's recent changes in the rules (Regulation A) governing its discount window loans to banks and other depository institutions brings this aspect of U.S. central banking much closer to what central banks in Europe do.

Before 2003 the Federal Reserve's discount rate was frequently the lowest interest rate in the money market and often below the Federal funds interest rate. With the discount rate so low, many bankers and other depository institutions were tempted to borrow from the Fed and relend the money in the Federal funds market. Some did!

Today the U.S. primary-credit discount rate is now set *higher* than the Federal funds interest rate on overnight loans, which the Federal Reserve is using as a target rate to stabilize the economy. Setting the Fed's discount rate above market mirrors the so-called "Lombard" credit facilities used by several European central banks. (Incidentally, the term *Lombard* owes its origin to a German word for *collateralized loan.* One of the earliest users of above-market loan rates for banks in need of funds was the Bundesbank, Germany's central bank.) Today these Lombard loan rates are employed by the European Central Bank (ECB) and the central banks of Austria, Belgium, France, Germany, Italy, and Sweden. Similar lending rules were adopted recently by the Bank of Canada and the Bank of Japan.

With the discount or Lombard rate set *above* market levels for similar loans, central banks are less inclined to restrict borrowing from the discount window and less concerned about what borrowers do with the money. Moreover, recent evidence suggests that an above-market Lombard loan rate tends to act as a ceiling on overnight borrowing rates and may well serve as an effective ceiling for the U.S. Federal funds interest rate in the years ahead. (See especially Brian F. Madigan and William R. Nelson, "Proposed Revision to the Federal Reserve's Discount Window Lending Programs," *Federal Reserve Bulletin,* July 2002, pp. 313–319.)

---

also accept certain federal agency securities, high-grade commercial paper, and other assets judged satisfactory by the Federal Reserve banks.

Three types of Federal Reserve loans are available from the discount window:

1. **Primary credit**—loans available for very short terms (usually overnight but occasionally extending over a few weeks) to depository institutions in sound financial condition. Primary credit carries an interest rate slightly above the Federal Reserve's target Federal funds interest rate. (Initially the primary credit rate was set at 100 basis points above the Fed funds target rate.) The primary credit loan rate is established at least every two weeks, subject to review by the Board of Governors of the Federal Reserve System.

   Users of primary credit do not have to show (as they did in the past) that they have exhausted other sources of funds before asking the Fed for a loan. Moreover, the borrowing institution is no longer prohibited from borrowing from the Fed and then loaning that money to other depository institutions in the Federal funds market. By lifting earlier restrictions and charging an above-market discount rate, the Fed believes there will be fewer administrative costs associated with borrowing from the discount window, making it easier to deal with crises in the financial system. Moreover, depository institutions should be less reluctant to borrow from the Federal Reserve's discount window when there is a real need for backup funding.

2. **Secondary credit**—loans available at a higher interest rate to depository institutions not qualifying for primary credit. These loans are subject to monitoring by the Federal Reserve banks to make sure the borrower is not taking on excessive risk. The interest rate on secondary credit normally is set 50 basis points above the primary credit rate. Such a loan can be used to help resolve financial problems, to strengthen the borrowing institution's ability to find additional funds from private-market sources, and to

Key URLs

For further information about borrowing from the Federal Reserve's discount window, see **www.kc.frb.org/CRM/ DiscountWindow/ Discountwindow.htm,** **www.clevelandfed.org/ DiscountWindow,** and **www.frbdiscount window.org.**

TABLE 12–6 Borrowing Reserves from the Federal Reserve Bank in the District (in millions of dollars)

Securing a Loan from the District Reserve Bank

Borrowing Depository Institution		Federal Reserve Bank	
Assets	Liabilities and Net Worth	Assets	Liabilities and Net Worth
Reserves on deposit at the Federal Reserve Bank +100	Notes Payable +100	Loan and advances +100	Bank reserve accounts +100

Repaying a Loan from the District Reserve Bank

Borrowing Depository Institution		Federal Reserve Bank	
Assets	Liabilities and Net Worth	Assets	Liabilities and Net Worth
Reserves on deposit at the Federal Reserve bank −100	Notes Payable −100	Loan and advances −100	Bank reserve accounts −100

reduce its debt to the Fed. However, secondary credit cannot be used to fund the expansion of a bank's assets.

3. **Seasonal credit**—loans covering longer time periods than primary credit for small and medium-sized depository institutions experiencing seasonal (intrayear) swings in their deposits and loans (such as those swings experienced by farm banks during planting and harvesting time). The seasonal credit interest rate is set as an average of the effective Federal funds rate and the secondary market rate on 90-day certificates of deposit.

As noted above, each type of discount-window loan carries its own loan rate, with secondary credit generally posting the highest interest rate and seasonal credit the lowest. For example, in January 2003 the Federal Reserve's discount window loan rates were 2.25 percent for primary credit, 2.75 percent for secondary credit, and 1.25 percent for seasonal credit.

In 1991 the U.S. Congress passed the FDIC Improvement Act, which places limits on how far the Federal Reserve banks can go in supporting a troubled bank or thrift institution with loans. Generally speaking, undercapitalized institutions cannot be granted discount window loans for more than 60 days in each 120-day period. Long-term Fed support is only permissible if the borrowing institution is a "viable entity." If the Federal Reserve exceeds these limitations, it could be held liable to the FDIC for any losses incurred by the insurance fund should the troubled institution ultimately fail.

Advances from the Federal Home Loan Banks

Recently another government agency—the Federal Home Loan Bank System—has been lending banks and thrift institutions large amounts of funds. The FHLB system was created by federal government charter in 1932 to improve the liquidity of the market for home mortgage loans. It supplies funds to banks and thrifts that grant (originate) mortgage loans, and those loans are used as collateral for FHLB advances. As noted by Thomson [4], man-

Key URLs

You can learn more about FHLB advances from such websites as **www.fhlbboston.com/ productsandservices/ creditproducts/index.jsp** and **http://stlouisfed .org/publications/re/ 2000/d/pages/ lead-article.html**.

agers of banks and thrifts are attracted to FHLB loans because they are a stable source of funds at below-market lending rates. Loan maturities range from overnight to more than 20 years and can carry either fixed or variable interest rates.

Stojanovic, Vaughan, and Yeager [3] point out that between 1992 and 1999 membership in the FHLB system by banks and thrifts rose four-fold and the amount of loans increased 16-fold. By 2002, 7 of 10 U.S. banks were FHLB members and close to half of the industry had FHLB advances outstanding. The FHLB can extend generous loan terms, even to depository institutions in trouble, because its federal charter allows it to borrow money cheaply and its loans are heavily collateralized (the market value of collateral usually amounts to 125 to 170 percent of its advances). However, there is no record of any loss on an FHLB advance to depository institutions seeking its support. Should a borrowing institution fail, the FHLB, legally, is first in line (even ahead of the FDIC) in recovering its funds.

Development and Sale of Large Negotiable CDs

The concept of liability management and short-term borrowing to supplement deposit growth was given a significant boost early in the 1960s with the development of a new kind of deposit, the **negotiable CD.** This funding source is really a *hybrid* account: legally, it is a deposit, but, in practical terms, the negotiable CD is just another form of IOU issued to tap temporary surplus funds held by large corporations, wealthy individuals, and governments. A CD is an interest-bearing receipt evidencing the deposit of funds in the accepting bank or thrift institution for a specified time period at a specified interest rate or specified formula for calculating the contract interest rate.

There are four main types of negotiable CDs today. *Domestic* CDs are issued by U.S. banks inside the territory of the United States. Dollar-denominated CDs issued by banks outside the United States are known as *EuroCDs.* The largest foreign banks active in the United States sell CDs through their U.S. branches, called *Yankee* CDs. Finally, large savings and loan associations and other nonbank savings institutions sell *thrift* CDs.

Key URLs

For a closer look at the market for negotiable CDs, see such Web locations as **www.rich.frb.org/pubs/ instruments** and **www.ameritrade.com/ education/html/ encyclopedia** (see the Debt Securities link).

During the 1960s, faced with slow or nonexistent growth in checkbook deposits held by their largest customers because these customers had found higher-yielding outlets for their cash surpluses elsewhere, U.S. money center banks began to search the market for new sources of funds. First National City Bank of New York (now Citigroup), one of the most innovative banks in the world, was the first to develop the large ($100,000+) negotiable CD in 1961. Citigroup designed this marketable deposit to compete for funds with government bills and other well-known money market instruments. It was made large enough—generally sold in multiples of $1 million—to appeal to major corporations holding large quantities of liquid funds. Negotiable CDs would be confined to short maturities, ranging from seven days to one or two years in most cases, but concentrated mainly in the one- to six-month maturity range for the convenience of the majority of CD buyers. And the new instrument would be *negotiable*—able to be sold in the secondary market any number of times before reaching maturity—in order to provide corporate customers with liquidity in case their cash surpluses proved to be smaller or less stable than originally forecast. To make the sale of negotiable CDs in advance of their maturity easier, they were issued in *bearer* form. Moreover, several securities dealers agreed to make a market in negotiable CDs carrying maturities of six months or less.

The negotiable CD was an almost instant success. Large-denomination CDs grew from zero in the early 1960s to nearly $100 billion by the end of the 1960s and then surged upward during the high interest rate period of the 1970s and early 1980s. By the close of 2002, time accounts of $100,000+ at U.S. banks totaled more than $700 billion. Thrift institutions issued another $115 billion of these large CDs. As with all liability management instruments, management can control the quantity of CDs outstanding simply by varying the yield offered to CD customers.

Interest rates on *fixed-rate* CDs, which represent the majority of all large negotiable CDs issued, are quoted on an interest-bearing basis, and the rate is computed assuming a 360-day year. For example, suppose a bank promises an 8 percent annual interest rate to the buyer of a $100,000 six-month (180-day) CD. The depositor will have the following at the end of six months:

$$
\begin{aligned}
\text{Amount due CD customer} &= \text{Principal} + \text{Principal} \times \frac{\text{Days to maturity}}{360 \text{ days}} \times \text{Annual rate of interest} \\
&= \$100,000 + \$100,000 \times \frac{180}{360} \times 0.08 \\
&= \$100,000 + \$4,000 \\
&= \$104,000
\end{aligned}
$$

CDs that have maturities over one year normally pay interest to the depositor every six months. *Variable-rate* CDs have their interest rates reset after a designated period of time (called a *leg* or *roll* period). The new rate is based on a mutually accepted reference interest rate, such as the London Interbank Offer Rate (LIBOR) attached to borrowings of Eurodollar deposits or the average interest rate prevailing on prime-quality CDs traded in the secondary market.

The net result of CD sales to customers is often a simple transfer of funds from one deposit to another within the same depository institution, particularly from checkable deposits into CDs. The selling institution gains loanable funds even from this simple transfer because, in the United States at least, legal reserve requirements are currently zero for CDs, while checking accounts at the largest depository institutions carry a reserve requirement of 10 percent. Also, deposit stability is likely to be greater for the receiving bank or thrift institution because the CD has a set maturity and normally will not be withdrawn until maturity. In contrast, checkable (demand) deposits can be withdrawn at any time. However, the sensitive interest rates attached to the largest negotiable CDs mean that depository institutions making heavy use of negotiable CDs and other liability management techniques must work harder to combat volatile net earnings, including aggressive use of rate-hedging techniques, discussed in Chapters 6–8.

The cost of negotiable CDs, measured by their market interest rates, is sensitive to competition among depository institutions, the credit rating of the offering institutions, and economic conditions. As shown below, in an expanding economy, as in the year 2000, CD rates tend to move higher and increase with maturity (i.e., an upward-sloping CD yield curve) as offering banks and thrifts compete more aggressively to attract new CD money in order to satisfy rising customer loan demand. In contrast, when the economy is weak and bogged down in a recession, as in 2001 and 2002, CD rates typically average lower and sometimes may decline with maturity (i.e., a downward-sloping CD yield curve) due, in part, to falling loan demand that dampens bidding for new CDs.

Interest Rates Attached to Negotiable CDs Sold in the United States

Maturities	Average Annual Rate for the Year			
	2000	2001	2002	2003*
1-Month	6.35%	3.84%	1.72%	1.26%
3-Month	6.46	3.71	1.73	1.22
6-Month	6.59	3.66	1.81	1.19

Note: * Figures for 2003 are an average for the month of May.
Source: Board of Governors of the Federal Reserve System

Eurocurrency Deposit Market

The development of the U.S. negotiable CD market came on the heels of another deposit market that began in Europe in the 1950s—the **Eurocurrency deposit** market. Eurocurrency deposits were developed originally in Western Europe to provide liquid funds that could be swapped among multinational banks or loaned to the banks' largest customers. Most of such international borrowing and lending has occurred in the Eurodollar market.

Eurodollars are dollar-denominated deposits placed in bank offices outside the United States. Because they are denominated on the receiving banks' books in dollars rather than in the currency of the home country and consist of bookkeeping entries in the form of *time deposits*, they are *not* spendable on the street like currency.[3]

The banks accepting these deposits may be foreign banks, branches of U.S. banks overseas, or international banking facilities (IBFs) set up on U.S. soil but devoted to foreign transactions on behalf of a parent U.S. bank. The heart of the worldwide Eurodollar market is in London, where British banks compete with scores of American and other foreign banks for Eurodollar deposits. The Eurocurrency market is the largest unregulated financial marketplace in the world, which is one reason it has been one of the faster-growing financial markets.

A domestic bank or other financial firm can tap the Euromarket for funds by contacting one of the major international banks that borrow and lend Eurocurrencies every day. The largest U.S. banks also use their own overseas branches to tap this market. When one of these branches lends a Eurodeposit to its home office in the United States, the home office records the deposit in an account labeled *liabilities to foreign branches*. When a U.S. bank borrows Eurodeposits from a bank operating overseas, the transaction takes place through the correspondent banking system. The lending bank will instruct a U.S. correspondent bank where it has a deposit to transfer funds in the amount of the Eurocurrency loan to the correspondent account of the borrowing institution. These borrowed funds will be quickly loaned to qualified borrowers or, perhaps, used to meet a reserve deficit. Later, when the loan falls due, the entries on the books of correspondent banks are reversed. This process of borrowing and lending Eurodollars is traced out in Tables 12–7 and 12–8.

Key URLs

For more information about the Eurocurrency deposit markets, see **www.ny.frb.org/ education/index.html** and **http://rre .worldbank.org/**.

Most Eurodollar deposits are *fixed-rate time deposits*. Beginning in the 1970s, however, floating-rate CDs (FRCDs) and floating-rate notes (FRNs) were introduced in an effort to protect banks and their Eurodepositors from the risk of fluctuating interest rates. FRCDs and FRNs tend to be medium term to long term, stretching from 1 year to as long as 20 years. The offer rates on these longer-term negotiable deposits are adjusted, usually every three to six months, based upon interest rate movements in the interbank Eurodollar market. The majority of Eurodollar deposits mature within six months; however, some are as short as overnight. Most are interbank liabilities whose interest yield is tied closely to LIBOR, which is the interest rate money center banks quote each other for the loan of short-term Eurodollar deposits. Large-denomination EuroCDs issued in the interbank market are called *tap CDs*, while smaller-denomination EuroCDs sold to a wide range of investors are called *tranche CDs*. As with domestic CDs, there is an active resale market for these deposits.

Considerable evidence exists (e.g., Kreichen [8]) that both major banks and their large corporate customers practice arbitrage between the Eurodollar and American CD markets. For example, if domestic CD rates were to drop significantly below Eurodollar interest rates on deposits of comparable maturity, a bank or its corporate customers could borrow in the domestic CD market and lend those funds offshore in the Euromarket. Similarly, an

---

[3] In general, whenever a deposit is accepted by a bank denominated in the units of a currency other than the home currency, that deposit is known as a *Eurocurrency deposit*. While the Eurocurrency market began in Europe (hence the prefix *Euro*), it reaches worldwide today.

TABLE 12–7   U.S. Bank Borrowing Eurodollars from Foreign Banks (in millions of dollars)

Step 1. The Loan Is Made to a U.S. Bank from the Eurodollar Market

U.S. Bank Borrowing Eurodollars		U.S. Bank Serving as Correspondent to Foreign Bank		Foreign Bank Lending Eurodollars	
Assets	Liabilities	Assets	Liabilities	Assets	Liabilities
Deposits held at other banks +100	Deposits due to foreign bank +100 (Eurodollars borrowed)		Deposits due to foreign bank −100 Deposits of U.S. correspondent bank doing the borrowing +100 (Eurodollars borrowed)	Deposits at U.S. correspondent bank −100 Eurodollar loan to U.S. bank +100	

Step 2. The Loan Is Repaid by the Borrowing U.S. Bank

U.S. Bank Borrowing Eurodollars		U.S. Bank Serving as Correspondent to Foreign Bank		Foreign Bank Lending Eurodollars	
Assets	Liabilities	Assets	Liabilities	Assets	Liabilities
Deposits held at other banks −100	Deposits due to foreign bank −100 (Eurodollars borrowed)		Deposits due to foreign bank +100 Deposits of U.S. correspondent bank doing the borrowing −100 (Eurodollars borrowed)	Deposits at U.S. correspondent bank +100 Eurodollar loan to U.S. bank −100	

interest rate spread in the opposite direction might well lead to increased Eurodollar borrowings, with the proceeds flowing into CD markets inside the United States.

Commercial Paper Market

Late in the 1960s, large banks faced with intense demand for loans found a new source of loanable funds—the **commercial paper market.** Commercial paper consists of short-term notes, with maturities ranging from three or four days to nine months, issued by well-

TABLE 12–8 U.S. Bank Borrowing Eurodollars from Its Own Foreign Branch Office (in millions of dollars)

Step 1. U.S. Bank Home Office Credits Its Foreign Branch for a Deposit

Home Office of U.S. Bank			Foreign Branch Office of U.S. Bank		
Assets		Liabilities and Net Worth	Assets		Liabilities and Net Worth
Reserves	+100	Liabilities to foreign branches +100	Deposit at home office	+100	Deposit from branch office customers +100

Step 2. U.S. Bank Home Office Makes a Loan with the Newly Borrowed Reserves

Home Office of U.S. Bank		
Assets		Liabilities and Net Worth
Reserves	−100	
Loans	+100	

Step 3. The Loan Is Repaid, Funds Are Returned to the Branch Office, and the Deposits of Branch Office Customers Are Withdrawn

Home Office of U.S. Bank			Foreign Branch Office of U.S. Bank		
Assets		Liabilities and Net Worth	Assets		Liabilities and Net Worth
Reserves	−100	Liabilities to foreign branches −100	Deposit at home office	−100	Deposit from branch office customers −100

Key URL
Want to learn more about the commercial paper market? See the websites at **www .wallstreetsystems.com/ products/debt.htm**.

known companies to raise working capital. Most such paper is designed to finance the purchase of inventories of goods or raw materials, cover taxes, or meet other immediate corporate cash needs. The notes are sold at a discount from their face value through dealers or through direct contact between the issuing company and interested investors.

Most bank-related commercial paper today is issued by holding companies or by nonbank firms they control. Once it is sold, the proceeds can be used to purchase loans off the books of banks or other financial firms in the same organization, giving these institutions additional funds to make new loans. Table 12–9 summarizes this process of indirect bank borrowing through commercial paper issued by affiliated firms.

Long-Term Nondeposit Funds Sources

The nondeposit sources of funds discussed to this point are mainly short-term borrowings. The loans involved range from hours to days, occasionally stretching into weeks or months with term Federal funds contracts, commercial paper, and similar funding instruments. However, banks and other financial firms also tap longer-term nondeposit funds stretching well beyond one year. Examples include *mortgages* issued to fund the construction of buildings and *capital notes and debentures*, which usually range from 7 to 12 years in maturity and are used to supplement equity (owners') capital. Capital notes and debentures are discussed in greater detail in Chapter 14.

TABLE 12–9 Commercial Paper Borrowing by a Holding Company That Channels the Borrowed Funds to One of Its Banks or Other Affiliated Lending Institutions (in millions of dollars)

Step 1. Commercial Paper Is Sold by an Affiliated Nonbank Corporation in the Money Market				
Commercial Bank or Other Lending Institution			**Affiliated Corporation**	
Assets	Liabilities and Net Worth		Assets	Liabilities and Net Worth
			Cash account +100	Commercial paper +100

Step 2. The Affiliated Corporation Purchases Loans from Banks or Other Lenders That Are Part of the Same Organization				
Commercial Bank or Other Lending Institution			**Affiliated Corporation**	
Assets	Liabilities and Net Worth		Assets	Liabilities and Net Worth
Loans −100 Reserves +100			Cash account −100 Loans purchased from bank +100	

These longer-term nondeposit funds sources have remained relatively modest over the years due to regulatory restrictions and the augmented risks associated with long-term borrowing. Also, since most assets and liabilities held by banks and other depository institutions are short- to medium-term, issuing long-term indebtedness creates a significant maturity mismatch. Nevertheless, the favorable leveraging effects of such debt have made it attractive to large banking organizations and other financial firms in recent years.

Concept Check

12–9. What are the advantages of borrowing from the Federal Reserve banks or other central bank? Are there any disadvantages? What is the difference between primary, secondary, and seasonal credit? What is a Lombard rate and why might such a rate be useful in achieving monetary policy goals?

12–10. How is a discount window loan from the Federal Reserve secured? Is collateral really necessary for these kinds of loans?

12–11. Posner State Bank borrows $10 million in primary credit from the Federal Reserve Bank of Cleveland. Can you show the correct entries for granting and repaying this loan?

12–12. Which institutions are allowed to borrow from the Federal Home Loan Banks? Why is this source of funds becoming increasingly popular for many banks and thrifts?

12–13. Why were negotiable CDs developed?

12–14. What are the advantages and disadvantages of CDs as a funding source?

12–15. Suppose a customer purchases a $1 million 90-day CD, carrying a promised 6 percent annualized yield. How much in interest income will the customer earn when this 90-day instrument matures? What total volume of funds will be available to the depositor at the end of 90 days?

12–16. Where do Eurodollars come from?

12–17. How does a bank gain access to funds from the Eurocurrency markets?

12–18. Suppose that J. P. Morgan Chase Bank in New York elects to borrow $250 million from one of its London branches, loans the borrowed funds for a week to a security dealer, and then returns the borrowed funds to its branch office in London. Can you trace through the resulting accounting entries? What if the bank had decided to borrow the $250 million from a foreign bank not related to Chase? How do the accounting entries differ in these two cases?

12–19. What is *commercial paper?* What types of organizations issue such paper?

12–20. Suppose that the finance company affiliate of Citigroup issues $325 million in 90-day commercial paper to interested investors and uses the proceeds to purchase loans from Citibank. What accounting entries should be made on the balance sheets of Citibank and Citigroup's finance company affiliate?

12–21. What long-term nondeposit funds sources do banks and some of their closest competitors draw upon today? How do these interest costs differ from those costs associated with most money market borrowings?

Key URLs

For a further look at debentures and other types of long-term debt issued by banks and other depository institutions, see especially **www.frbsf .org/publications/ economics/letter/index .html** and **www.fannie- mae.com/ir/issues financial**.

Because of the long-term nature of these funding sources, they are a sensitive barometer of the perceived risk exposure (particularly the risk of default) of their issuing institutions. In 1990, for example, when there were fears of major bank defaults, the capital notes of troubled Southeast Banking Corp. and the Bank of Boston carried annual yields of close to 20 percent, while notes issued by the Bank of New England were trading at a discount equal to only about one-fifth of their face value. By March 2003 just over $100 billion in capital notes and debentures (subordinated to the claims of depositors) had been issued by all U.S. insured banks, who paid out about $5 billion in annual interest on these long-term debt obligations.

Choosing among Alternative Nondeposit Sources

With so many different nondeposit funds sources to draw on, managers of banks and other depository institutions must make choices among them. In using nondeposit funds, funds managers must answer the following key questions:

1. How much in total must be borrowed from these sources to meet funding needs?
2. Which nondeposit sources are best, given the borrowing institution's goals, at any given moment in time?

Measuring a Financial Firm's Total Need for Nondeposit Funds: The Funds Gap

Each depository institution's demand for nondeposit funds is determined basically by the size of the *gap* between its total credit demands and its deposits. Managers responsible for the asset side of the institution's balance sheet must choose which of a wide variety of customer credit requests they will meet by adding direct loans and investment securities to the institution's asset portfolio. Management must be prepared to meet, not only today's credit requests, but also all those it can reasonably anticipate in the future. This means that projections of current and anticipated credit demands must be based on knowledge of the current and probable future funding needs of each institution's customers, especially its largest borrowers. Such projections should not be wild guesses; they should be based on information gathered from frequent contacts between the financial firm's officers and both existing and potential customers.

The second decision that must be made is how much in deposits is likely to be attracted in order to finance the desired volume of loans and security investments. Again, projections must be made of customer deposits and withdrawals, with special attention to the largest depositors. Deposit projections must take into account current and future economic conditions, interest rates, and the cash flow requirements of the largest depositors.

The difference between current and projected credit and deposit flows yields an estimate of each institution's **funds gap.** Thus,

$$\text{The funds gap} = \begin{array}{l}\text{Current and projected loans}\\\text{and investments the lending institution}\\\text{desires to make} - \text{Current and}\\\text{expected deposit inflows}\end{array}$$

For example, suppose a commercial bank has new loan requests that meet its quality standards of $150 million; it wishes to purchase $75 million in new Treasury securities being issued this week and expects drawings on credit lines from its best corporate customers of $135 million. Deposits received today total $185 million, and those expected in the coming week will bring in another $100 million. This bank's estimated funds gap (FG) for the coming week will be as follows (in millions of dollars):

$$\begin{aligned}\text{FG} &= (\$150 + \$75 + \$135) - (\$185 + \$100)\\&= \$360 - \$285\\&= \$75\end{aligned}$$

Most institutions will add a small amount to this funds gap estimate to cover unexpected credit demands or unanticipated shortfalls in deposit inflows. Various nondeposit funds sources then may be tapped to cover the estimated funds gap.

Nondeposit Funding Sources: Factors to Consider

Which nondeposit sources will management use to cover a projected funds gap? The answer to that question depends largely upon five factors:

1. The *relative costs* of raising funds from each nondeposit source.
2. The *risk* (volatility and dependability) of each funding source.
3. The *length of time* (maturity or term) for which funds are needed.
4. The *size of the institution* that requires nondeposit funds.
5. *Regulations* limiting the use of alternative funds sources.

Relative Costs   Managers of financial institutions practicing liability management must constantly be aware of the going market interest rates attached to different sources of borrowed funds. Major lenders post daily interest rates at which they are willing to commit funds to banks and other financial firms in need of additional reserves. In general, managers would prefer to borrow from the cheapest sources of funds, although other factors do play a role.

A sample of interest rates on money market borrowings, averaged over selected years, is shown in Table 12–10. Note that the various funds sources vary significantly in *price*—the interest rate the borrowing institution must pay for use of the money. Usually the cheapest short-term borrowed funds source is the prevailing *effective interest rate on Federal funds* loaned overnight between depository institutions. In most cases the interest rates attached to domestic CDs and Eurocurrency deposits are slightly higher than the Federal funds rate. Commercial paper (short-term unsecured notes) normally may be issued at interest rates slightly above the Fed funds and CD rates, depending upon their maturity and time of issue. Today the discount rate attached to loans from the Federal Reserve banks (known as

TABLE 12–10 **Money Market Interest Rates Attached to Nondeposit Borrowings and Large ($100,000+) CDs**

Source: Board of Governors of the Federal Reserve System.

Sources of Borrowed Funds	Interest Rate Averages Quoted for the Years:							
	1990	**1992**	**1994**	**1996**	**1998**	**2000**	**2002**	**2003****
Federal funds borrowings	8.10%	3.52%	4.47%	5.30%	5.35%	6.24%	1.34%	1.25%
Borrowings from the Federal Reserve banks*	6.98	3.25	3.76	5.00	4.98	5.50	1.25	2.25
Selling commercial paper (1-month, directly placed)	8.15	3.71	4.65	5.43	n.a.	6.27	1.34	1.23
Issuing negotiable CDs (secondary market, 1-month)	8.15	3.64	4.60	5.35	5.49	6.35	1.39	1.25
Selling Eurodollar deposits (3-month maturities)	8.16	3.70	4.80	5.38	5.44	6.45	1.39	1.21

Notes: *Averages for the year as posted by the Federal Reserve banks. Beginning in 2003 the quoted discount rate on loans from the Federal Reserve banks is the primary credit rate, initially set at 100 basis points above the Fed's target Federal funds interest rate.
**2003 figures are for March.

the primary credit rate) is generally among the highest short-term borrowing rates because this form of Federal Reserve credit is generally priced at least one full percentage point above the central bank's target for the Fed funds rate.

Although low compared to most other borrowing rates, the effective Federal funds rate prevailing in the marketplace at any given moment tends to be volatile, fluctuating around the central bank's target (intended) Fed funds rate, but rising or falling several times each day. Thus, borrowers and lenders in this market must stay in frequent touch with major banks and Fed funds brokers to determine where the market for overnight loans of reserves lies when they most need to trade money.

The key advantage of Federal funds is their ready availability through a simple phone call or online computer request. Moreover, their maturities often are flexible and may be as short as a few hours or last as long as several months. The key disadvantage of Federal funds, as we noted above, is their volatile market interest rate—its often wide hour-by-hour fluctuations (especially during the last or settlement day that depository institutions are trying to meet their legal reserve requirements on deposits) make planning difficult.

In contrast, market interest rates on negotiable CDs and commercial paper interest rates are usually somewhat more stable, but generally hover close to and slightly above the Fed funds rate due to their longer average maturity (with loans usually ranging from three or four days to several months) and because of the marketing costs spent in finding buyers for these financial instruments. CDs and commercial paper usually are less popular in the short run than Federal funds and borrowings from the central bank's discount window when a depository institution needs money right away. Instead, the CD and commercial paper borrowing avenues are usually better for longer-term funding needs that stretch over several days or weeks. This is also generally the case with Eurocurrency deposits, which may require extra time for transaction completion.

The managers of banks and other depository institutions that regularly draw upon the money market for borrowed funds must follow changing interest rates minute by minute because the rate of interest is usually the principal expense in borrowing nondeposit funds. However, *noninterest* costs cannot be ignored in calculating the true cost of borrowing nondeposit funds, including the time spent by management and staff to find the best funds sources each time new money is needed. A good formula for doing cost comparisons among alternative sources of funds is as follows:

$$\text{Effective cost rate on deposit and nondeposit sources of funds} = \frac{\begin{array}{c}\text{Current interest} \\ \text{cost on amounts} + \\ \text{borrowed}\end{array}\begin{array}{c}\text{Noninterest costs} \\ \text{incurred} \\ \text{to access these funds}\end{array}}{\begin{array}{c}\text{Net investable funds raised} \\ \text{from this source}\end{array}}$$

where

$$\begin{array}{c}\text{Current interest cost} \\ \text{on amounts borrowed}\end{array} = \begin{array}{c}\text{Prevailing interest} \\ \text{rate in the money} \\ \text{market}\end{array} \times \begin{array}{c}\text{Amount of funds} \\ \text{borrowed}\end{array}$$

$$\begin{array}{c}\text{Noninterest costs to} \\ \text{access funds}\end{array} = \begin{array}{c}\text{Estimated cost} \\ \text{rate representing} \\ \text{staff time, facilities,} \\ \text{and transaction costs}\end{array} \times \begin{array}{c}\text{Amount of funds} \\ \text{borrowed}\end{array}$$

$$\begin{array}{c}\text{Net investable funds} \\ \text{raised}\end{array} = \begin{array}{c}\text{Total amount borrowed less legal reserve} \\ \text{requirements (if any), deposit insurance} \\ \text{assessments (if any), and funds placed} \\ \text{in nonearning assets}\end{array}$$

Note that the cost associated with attracting each funds source is compared to the net amount of funds raised after deductions are made (where necessary) for reserve requirements, deposit insurance fees, and that portion of borrowed funds diverted into such nonearning assets as excess cash reserves or fixed assets. We use *net investable funds* as the borrowing base because we wish to compare the dollar cost that must be paid out to attract borrowed funds relative to the dollar amount of those funds that can actually be used to acquire earning assets and cover the cost of fund-raising.

Let's see how the above formulas might be used to estimate the cost of borrowing funds. Suppose that Federal funds are currently trading at an interest rate of 6.0 percent. Moreover, management estimates that the marginal noninterest cost, in the form of personnel expenses and transactions fees, from raising additional monies in the Federal funds market is 0.25 percent. Suppose that a commercial bank will need $25 million to fund the loans it plans to make today, of which only $24 million can be fully invested due to other immediate cash demands. Then the effective annualized cost rate for Federal funds today would be calculated as follows:

$$\begin{array}{c}\text{Current interest cost} \\ \text{on federal funds}\end{array} = 0.06 \times \$25 \text{ million} = \$1.5 \text{ million}$$

$$\begin{array}{c}\text{Noninterest cost to} \\ \text{access Federal funds}\end{array} = 0.0025 \times \$25 \text{ million} = \$0.063 \text{ million}$$

$$\begin{array}{c}\text{Net investable} \\ \text{funds raised}\end{array} = \$25 \text{ million} - \$1 \text{ million} = \$24 \text{ million}$$

Therefore, the effective annualized Federal funds cost rate is

$$\frac{\$1.5 \text{ million} + \$0.063 \text{ million}}{\$24 \text{ million}} = 0.0651 \text{ or } 6.51 \text{ percent}$$

The bank in the above example would have to earn a net annualized return of at least 6.51 percent on the loans and investments it plans to make with these borrowed Federal funds just to break even.

Suppose the management of the bank discussed above decides to consider borrowing funds by issuing negotiable CDs that carry a current interest rate of 7.00 percent. Moreover, raising CD money costs this bank 0.75 percent in noninterest costs. Then the annualized cost rate incurred by this bank from selling CDs would be as follows:

$$\frac{\text{Effective CD}}{\text{cost rate}} = \frac{(0.07 \times \$25 \text{ million} + \$0.0075 \times \$25 \text{ million})}{\$24 \text{ million}}$$

$$= \frac{\$1.75 \text{ million} + \$0.1875 \text{ million}}{\$24 \text{ million}}$$

$$= 0.0807 \text{ or } 8.07 \text{ percent}$$

An additional expense is associated with selling CDs to raise the funds that the bank described above needs. CDs and other types of deposits received from the public carry a deposit insurance fee. This fee varies with the risk and capitalization of each bank or thrift institution whose deposits are insured by the Federal Deposit Insurance Corporation. In recent years the insurance fee has often been at or near zero due to the fact that the FDIC's insurance reserve has grown because of the relatively few failures and exceeded the level required by federal law of $1.25 in reserves for every $100 in insured deposits.

However, let's assume that the current FDIC insurance fee is $0.0027 per dollar of deposits—a fee sometimes charged the riskiest banks and thrifts in the U.S. system. (We should note as well that the FDIC requires a bank or thrift institution to pay this fee not just on the first $100,000 in a customer's deposit account but on the full face amount of each deposit received from the public.) Thus, the total insurance cost for the riskiest depository institutions on the $25 million we are talking about raising through selling CDs would be

$$\begin{array}{l}\text{Total deposits} \\ \text{received from} \\ \text{the public}\end{array} \times \begin{array}{l}\text{Insurance fee} \\ \text{per dollar}\end{array} = \$25 \text{ million} \times 0.0027$$

$$= \$67,500 \text{ or } \$0.0675 \text{ million}$$

If we deduct this fee from the new amount of CDs actually available for use, we get this:

$$\frac{\text{Effective CD}}{\text{cost rate}} = \frac{\$1.9375 \text{ million}}{\$24 \text{ million} - \$0.0675 \text{ million}}$$

$$= \frac{\$1.9375 \text{ million}}{\$23,925 \text{ million}} = 0.0810 \text{ or } 8.10 \text{ percent}$$

Clearly, issuing CDs would be more expensive for the bank in the above example than borrowing Federal funds. However, the CDs have the advantage of being available for several days or weeks, whereas Federal funds loans must often be repaid in 24 hours.

Functional cost analysis data assembled each year by the Federal Reserve banks indicates that nondeposit sources of funds generally are moderate in cost compared to other funding sources. Generally nondeposit sources of funds are more expensive than demand deposits but less expensive than time deposits. We must add a note of caution here, however, because the costs and the profits associated with nondeposit sources of funds tend to be more volatile from year to year than the cost and profitability of deposits. Nondeposit funds do have the advantage of *quick availability* compared to most types of deposits, but they are clearly not as stable a funding source for most depository institutions as time and savings deposits.

The Risk Factor The managers of financial institutions must consider at least two types of risk when selecting among different nondeposit sources. The first is **interest-rate risk**—the volatility of credit costs. All the interest rates shown in Table 12–10, except the Federal Reserve's discount rate, are determined by demand and supply forces in the open market and therefore are subject to erratic fluctuations. The shorter the term of the loan, the more volatile the prevailing market interest rate tends to be. Thus, most

In our discussion of determining how much each source of borrowed funds costs, we looked at each funding source separately. However, most borrowing institutions draw simultaneously on not one, but many different funds sources, including deposits, nondeposit borrowings, and owner's equity capital. Can we find a method for determining the cost of funding that somehow brings together all the sources of funding normally in use?

The answer is *yes.* Here we examine two of the most popular overall funds cost methods—the historical average cost approach and the pooled funds approach.

THE HISTORICAL AVERAGE COST APPROACH

This approach for determining how much funds cost looks at the past. It asks what funds the bank or other financial firm has raised to date and what they cost.

Sources of Funds Drawn Upon	Average Amount of Funds Raised (millions)	Average Rate of Interest Incurred	Total Interest Paid for Each Funds Source (millions)
Noninterest-bearing demand deposits	$ 100	0%	$ 0
Interest-bearing transaction deposits	200	7%	14
Savings accounts	100	5%	5
Time deposits	500	8%	40
Money market borrowings	100	6%	6
Total funds raised = $1,000		All interest costs = $65	

Then the average interest cost of deposits and money market borrowings is this:

$$\text{Weighted average interest expense} = \frac{\text{All interest paid}}{\text{Total funds raised}} = \frac{\$65}{\$1,000} = 6.5 \text{ percent}$$

But other operating costs, such as salaries and overhead, are incurred to attract deposits. If these are an estimated $10 million, we have

$$\text{Break-even cost rate on borrowed funds invested in earning assets} = \frac{\text{Interest + Other operating costs}}{\text{All earning assets}} = \frac{\$65 + \$10}{\$750} = 10 \text{ percent}$$

This cost rate is called *break even* because the borrowing institution must earn at least this rate on its earning assets (primarily loans and securities) just to meet the total operating costs of raising borrowed funds. But what about the borrowing institution's stockholders and their required rate of return (assumed here to be 12 percent after taxes)?

$$\text{Weighted average overall cost of capital} = \text{Break-even cost on borrowed funds} + \text{Before-tax cost of the stockholders' investment in the borrowing institution}$$

$$= \frac{\text{Break-even}}{\text{cost}} + \frac{\frac{\text{After-tax cost of}}{\text{stockholders'}}}{(1 - \text{Tax rate})} \times \frac{\frac{\text{Stockholders'}}{\text{investment}}}{\text{Earning assets}}$$

$$= 10 \text{ percent} + \frac{12 \text{ percent}}{(1 - 0.35)} \times \frac{\$100}{\$750} = 10 \text{ percent} + 2.5 \text{ percent}$$

$$= 12.5 \text{ percent}$$

Thus, 12.5 percent is the lowest rate of return over all fund-raising costs that the borrowing institution can afford to earn on its assets if its equity shareholders invest $100 million in the institution.

THE POOLED-FUNDS APPROACH

This method of costing borrowed funds looks at the future: What minimum rate of return are we going to have to earn on any future loans and security investments just to cover the cost of all new funds raised? Suppose our estimate for future funding sources and funding costs is as follows:

Profitable New Deposits and Nondeposit Borrowings	Dollars of New Deposit and Nondeposit Borrowings (millions)	Portion of New Borrowings That Will Be Placed in New Earning Assets	Dollar Amount That Can Be Placed in Earning Assets (millions)	Interest Expense and Other Operating Expenses of Borrowing Relative to Amounts Raised	All Operating Expenses Incurred (millions)
Interest-bearing transaction deposits	$100	50%	$ 50	8%	$ 8
Time deposits	100	60%	60	9%	9
New stockholders' investment in the institution	100	90%	90	13%	13
Total	$300		$200		$30

The overall cost of new deposits and other borrowing sources must be

$$\frac{\frac{\text{Pooled}}{\text{deposit and}}}{\frac{\text{nondeposit}}{\text{funds expense}}} = \frac{\frac{\text{All expected}}{\text{operating expenses}}}{\frac{\text{All new}}{\text{funds expected}}} = \frac{\$30 \text{ million}}{\$300 \text{ million}} = 10 \text{ percent}$$

But because only two-thirds of these expected new funds ($200 million out of $300 million raised) will actually be available to acquire earning assets,

$$\frac{\frac{\text{Hurdle}}{\text{rate of return}}}{\frac{\text{over all}}{\text{earning assets}}} = \frac{\frac{\text{All expected}}{\text{operating costs}}}{\frac{\text{Dollars available}}{\frac{\text{to place in}}{\text{earning assets}}}} = \frac{\$30 \text{ million}}{\$200 \text{ million}} = 15 \text{ percent}$$

Thus, the borrowing financial firm in the example above must earn *at least* 15 percent (before taxes), on average, on all the new funds it invests to fully meet its expected fund-raising costs.

Federal funds loans are overnight and, not surprisingly, this market interest rate tends to be the most volatile of all.

Management must also consider **credit availability risk.** There is no guarantee in any credit market that lenders will be willing and able to accommodate every borrower. When general credit conditions are tight, lenders may have limited funds to loan and may ration credit, confining loans only to their soundest and most loyal customers. Sometimes a financial firm may appear so risky to money market lenders that they will deny credit or make the price so high that its earnings will suffer. Experience has shown that the negotiable CD, Eurodollar, and commercial paper markets are especially sensitive to credit availability risks. Funds managers must be prepared to switch to alternative sources of credit and, if necessary, pay more for any funds they receive.

The Length of Time Funds Are Needed As we have seen, some funds sources cannot be relied on for immediate credit (such as commercial paper and Eurodollars). A manager in need of loanable funds this afternoon would be inclined to borrow in the Federal funds market. However, if funds are not needed for a few days, selling CDs or commercial paper becomes a more viable option. Thus, the term, or maturity, of the funds need plays a key role as well.

The Size of the Borrowing Institution The standard trading unit for most money market loans is $1 million—a denomination that often exceeds the borrowing requirements of the smallest financial institutions. For example, Eurodollar borrowings are in multiples of $1 million and go only to money-center commercial banks with the highest credit ratings. Large negotiable CDs from the largest banks and thrift institutions are preferred by most investors because there is an active secondary market for prime-rated CDs. Smaller depository institutions do not have the credit standing to be able to sell most large negotiable CDs. The same is true of commercial paper. In contrast, the Federal Reserve's discount window and the Federal funds market can make relatively small denomination loans that are suitable for smaller banks and other depository institutions.

Regulations Federal and state regulations may limit the amount, frequency, and use of borrowings by banks and thrift institutions. For example, CDs must be issued with maturities of at least seven days. The Federal Reserve banks limit excessive borrowing from the discount window, particularly by depository institutions that appear to display significant risk of failure. Other forms of borrowing may be subjected to legal reserve requirements by action of the Federal Reserve Board. For example, during the late 1960s and early 1970s, when the Federal Reserve was attempting to fight inflation with tight-money policies, it imposed legal reserve requirements for a time on Federal funds borrowings from nonbank sources, on repurchase agreements, and on commercial paper issued to purchase assets from affiliated lending institutions. While these particular requirements are not currently in force, it seems clear that in times of national emergency, government policy-makers would move swiftly to impose new controls, affecting both the costs and the risks associated with nondeposit borrowings.

Concept Check

12–22. What is the *funds gap?*

12–23. Suppose J. P. Morgan Chase Bank of New York discovers that projected new loan demand next week should total $325 million and customers holding confirmed credit lines plan to draw down $510 million in funds to cover their cash needs next week, while new deposits next week are projected to equal $680 million. The bank also plans to acquire $420 million in corporate and government bonds next week. What is the bank's projected funds gap?

12–24. What factors must the manager of a financial institution weigh in choosing among the various nondeposit sources of funding available today?

Summary

Although the principal funding source for banks and their closest competitors, thrift institutions, is still *deposits*, nearly all depository institutions today supplement the funds they attract through sales of deposits with nondeposit borrowings in the money and capital markets. In this chapter we explore the most important nondeposit funds sources and the factors that bear on the managerial decision about which source or sources of nondeposit funds to draw upon. The key points in the chapter include these:

- Today's heavy use of nondeposit borrowings by depository institutions arose with the development of *liability management*. Liability management, which began in earnest during the 1960s and 1970s and grew rapidly thereafter, calls upon the managers of financial institutions to actively manage their liabilities as well as their assets on the balance sheet and to use *interest rates* as the control lever. For example, when funds are short relative to an institution's need for them, additional funds can usually be attracted by raising the offer rate.

- The use of nondeposit borrowings as a key source of funds was given an added boost by the emergence of the *customer relationship doctrine*. This managerial strategy calls for putting the goal of satisfying the credit requests of all quality customers at the top of management's list, wherever possible. If deposits are inadequate to fund all quality loan requests, other sources of funds, including borrowings in the money and capital markets, should be used. Thus, the lending decision comes first, followed by the funding decision.

- One of the key sources of nondeposit funds today is the *Federal funds market*, where immediately available reserves are traded between financial institutions and usually returned within 24 hours. Borrowing from selected government agencies—in the United States, the *discount windows of the Federal Reserve banks* and *advances from the Federal Home Loan Banks*—has also grown rapidly in recent years and new and more lenient regulations have made this borrowing process easier.

- Other key funds sources include selling *negotiable jumbo ($100,000+) CDs* (mainly to corporate customers), borrowing *Eurocurrency deposits* from international banks offshore, issuing *commercial paper* in the open market through an affiliate or subsidiary corporation, executing *repurchase agreements* where loans collateralized by top-quality assets (usually governmental securities) are made available to borrowing institutions for a few hours or days, and *longer-term borrowings in the capital markets* through the issuance of subordinated debentures and other forms of longer-term debt.

- Before tapping nondeposit borrowings, however, the financial managers of banks and other depository institutions must estimate their funding requirements. One such estimate for a depository institution comes from the so-called *funds gap*, which is the spread between the current and expected volume of loans and investments and current and expected volume of deposit inflows.

- The particular nondeposit funds source(s) chosen by management usually rests upon such factors as (1) the relative cost of each nondeposit funding source; (2) the risk or dependability of each funds source; (3) the length of time funds will be needed; (4) the size of the borrowing institution and its funding needs; and (5) the content of government regulations affecting the fund-raising process.

- Among the most important government regulations bearing on the use of nondeposit funds are legal reserve requirements imposed by central banks around the world (requiring minimum amounts of liquidity on the balance sheets of depository institutions) and rules dictating the required content of contractual agreements when funds are loaned by one financial institution to another.

Key Terms

customer relationship
doctrine, *424*

liability management, *424*

federal funds market, *427*

repurchase agreements
(RPs), *430*

discount window, *432*

negotiable CD, *435*

Eurocurrency deposit, *437*

commercial paper
market, *438*

funds gap, *442*

interest-rate risk, *445*

credit availability risk, *448*

Problems and Projects

1. Robertson State Bank of Clayton decides to loan a portion of its reserves in the amount of $70 million held at the Federal Reserve Bank to Tenison National Security Bank for 24 hours. For its part, Tenison plans to make a 24-hour loan to a security dealer before it must return the funds to Robertson State Bank. Please show all the proper accounting entries for these transactions.

2. Masoner Savings, headquartered in a small community, holds most of its correspondent deposits with Flagg Metrocenter Bank, a money center institution. When Masoner has a cash surplus in its correspondent deposit, Flagg automatically invests the surplus in Federal funds loans to other money center banks. A check of Masoner's records this morning reveals a temporary surplus of $11 million for 48 hours. Flagg will loan this surplus for two business days to Secoro Central City Bank, which is in need of additional reserves. Please show the correct balance sheet entries to carry out this loan and to pay off the loan when its term ends.

3. Relgade National Bank secures primary credit from the Federal Reserve Bank of San Francisco in the amount of $32 million for a term of seven days. Please show the proper entries for granting this loan and then paying off the loan.

4. Itec Corporation purchases a 45-day negotiable CD with a $5 million denomination from Payson Guaranty Bank and Trust, bearing a 6.75 percent annual yield. How much in interest will the bank have to pay when this CD matures? What amount in total will the bank have to pay back to Itec at the end of 45 days?

5. International Commerce Bank borrows $125 million overnight through a repurchase agreement (RP) collateralized by Treasury bills. The current RP rate is 4.5 percent. How much will the bank pay in interest cost due to this borrowing?

6. National Commerce Bank of New York expects new deposit inflows next month of $330 million and deposit withdrawals of $275 million. The bank's economics department has projected that new loan demand will reach $621 million and customers with approved credit lines will need $266 million in cash. The bank will sell $480 million in securities, but plans to add $155 million in new securities to its portfolio. What is its projected funds gap?

7. Washington Mutual borrowed $150 million in Federal funds from J. P. Morgan Chase Bank in New York City for 24 hours to fund a 30-day loan. The prevailing Federal funds rate on loans of this maturity stood at 7.85 percent when these two institutions agreed on the loan. The funds loaned by Morgan were in the reserve deposit that bank keeps at the Federal Reserve Bank of New York. When the loan to Washington Mutual was repaid the next day, J. P. Morgan used $50 million of the returned funds to cover its own reserve needs and loaned $100 million in Federal funds to Texas Savings, Houston, for a two-day period at the prevailing Federal funds rate of 7.92 percent. With respect to these transactions, (*a*) construct T-account entries similar to those you encountered in this chapter, showing the original Federal funds loan and its repayment on the books of J. P. Morgan, Washington Mutual, and Texas Savings; and (*b*) calculate the total interest income earned by Morgan on both Federal funds loans.

8. BancOne of Ohio issues a three-month (90-day) negotiable CD in the amount of $14 million to Travelers Insurance Company at a negotiated annual interest rate of 8.47 percent (360-day basis). Calculate the value of this CD account on the day it

matures and the amount of interest income Travelers will earn. What interest return will Travelers Insurance earn in a 365-day year?

9. Banks and other lending affiliates within the holding company of Interstate National Bank are reporting heavy loan demand this week from companies in the southeastern United States that are planning a significant expansion of inventories and facilities before the beginning of the fall season. The holding company and its lead bank plan to raise $850 million in short-term funds this week, of which about $835 million will be used to meet these new loan requests. Federal funds are currently trading at 8.73 percent, negotiable CDs are trading in New York at 8.69 percent, and Eurodollar borrowings are available in London at all maturities under one year at 9.11 percent. One-month maturities of directly placed commercial paper carry market rates of 8.65 percent, while the primary credit discount rate of the Federal Reserve Bank of Richmond is currently set at 7.25 percent—a source that Interstate has used in each of the past two weeks. Noninterest costs are estimated at 0.25 percent for Fed funds, discount window borrowings, and CDs; 0.35 percent for Eurodollar borrowings; and 0.50 percent for commercial paper. Calculate the effective cost rate of each of these sources of funds for Interstate and make a management decision on what sources to use. Be prepared to defend your decision.

10. Hamilton Security Savings is considering the problem of trying to raise $80 million in money market funds to cover a loan request from one of its largest corporate customers, which needs a six-week loan. Money market interest rates are currently at the levels indicated below:

Federal funds, average for week just concluded	8.72%
Discount window of the Federal Reserve bank	7.00
CDs (prime rated, secondary market):	
One month	8.45
Three months	8.49
Six months	8.58
Eurodollar deposits (three months)	8.58
Commercial paper (directly placed):	
One month	8.55
Three months	8.42

Unfortunately, Hamilton's economics department is forecasting a substantial rise in money market interest rates over the next six weeks. What would you recommend to its funds management department regarding how and where to raise the money needed? Be sure to consider such cost factors as legal reserve requirements, regulations, and what happens to the relative attractiveness of each funding source if interest rates rise continually over the period of the proposed loan.

Alternative scenario:

What if Hamilton's economists are wrong and money market rates *decline* significantly over the next six weeks? How would your recommendation to the funds management department change on how and where to raise the funds needed?

11. Merchants National Bank has received $800 million in total funding, consisting of $200 million in checkable deposit accounts, $400 million in time and savings deposits, $100 million in money market borrowings, and $100 million in stockholders' equity. Interest costs on time and savings deposits are 9 percent, on average, while noninterest costs of raising these particular deposits equal approximately 2 percent of their dollar volume. Interest costs on checkable deposits average only 3 percent since many of

these deposits pay no interest, but noninterest costs of raising checkable accounts are about 7 percent of their dollar total. Money market borrowings cost Merchants an average of 10 percent in interest costs and 1 percent in noninterest costs. Management estimates the cost of stockholders' equity capital at 22 percent before taxes. (The bank is currently in the 35-percent corporate tax bracket.) When reserve requirements are added in, along with uncollected dollar balances, these factors are estimated to contribute another 15 percent to the cost of securing checkable deposits and 5 percent to the cost of acquiring time and savings deposits. Reserve requirements (on Eurodeposits only) and collection delays add an estimated 2 percent to the cost of the money market borrowings.

  a. Calculate Merchants' weighted average interest cost on total funds raised, figured on a before-tax basis.

  b. If the bank's earning assets total $700 million, what is its break-even cost rate?

  c. What is Merchants' overall historical weighted average cost of capital?

12. State Security Savings Association is considering funding a package of new loans in the amount of $400 million. Security has projected that it must raise $450 million in order to have $400 million available to make new loans. It expects to raise $325 million of the total by selling time deposits at an average interest rate of 8.75 percent. Noninterest costs from selling time deposits will add an estimated 0.45 percent in operating expenses. State Security expects another $125 million to come from noninterest-bearing transaction deposits, whose noninterest costs are expected to be 7.25 percent of the total amount of these deposits. What is the association's projected pooled-funds marginal cost? What hurdle rate must it achieve on its earning assets?

Internet Exercises

1. In terms of size, which banks in the U.S. financial system seem to rely most heavily on deposits as a source of funding and which on nondeposit borrowings and liability management? To provide an example for the numbers reported in Table 12–3, go to the FDIC's Institution Directory at **http://www3.fdic.gov/idasp/** and search by city and state to find a small bank holding company (BHC) located in your hometown or somewhere you enjoy visiting. Write down the BHC ID of your selected bank. Then go to **www3.fdic.gov/sdi/main.asp** to compare your small BHC with two larger BHCs, Bank of America (BHC ID 1073757) and J. P. Morgan Chase (BHC ID 1039502). Compare and contrast Deposits/Total Assets and Liabilities/Total Assets for the three BHCs to illustrate your point.

   If you need some help maneuvering in this site to create a report, read on. The process to create a report requires that you "Select the Number of Columns." You want to select "3" to develop the format to collect data for the most recent report. This provides three pull-down menus, each labeled Select One. In the columns select Bank Holding Company from the menu and go on to type in the BHC ID #. After defining the three columns click on Next. At this point, you focus on Report Selection, choosing to View and to do calculations in Percentages. Then you get to identify the information you want to collect before creating the report by clicking Next. You will find deposit and liability information in the Assets and Liabilities report.

2. You are interested in borrowing from the discount window of the Federal Reserve Bank in your area. Go to **www.frbdiscountwindow.org/** and find out the current interest rates at your FRB. What are they?

3. You are interested in borrowing from your Federal Home Loan Bank. First determine which district you are in and then go to the bank in that district and find the interest rates on FHLB advances. The following site will get you started: **www.fhlbanks.com**.

4. In this chapter you have been introduced to a number of instruments used for liability management. Repurchase agreements are always a challenge. To learn a little more about these instruments go to **http://www.rich.frb.org/pubs/instruments/ch6.html**. Who are the major participants in the RP market?

5. You have been introduced to the Eurodollar market. To learn a little more about this market go to **http://www.rich.frb.org/pubs/instruments/ch5.html**. For market participants, what are the three basic sources of risk associated with holding Eurodollars?

STANDARD
&POOR'S

S&P Market Insight Challenge

1. Use Standard & Poor's Market Insight website (**www.mhhe.com/edumarketinsight**) for this problem. The S&P Industry Survey "Banking" discusses the Federal Reserve's influence over the cost and availability of nondeposit funds sources. For a description of how the Fed's actions increase or decrease the money supply and affect the cost of funds to financial firms use the Industry tab in Market Insight, Educational Version. The drop-down menu provides subindustry selections among Diversified Banks and Regional Banks. After selecting one of these subindustry groupings you will find a recent S&P Industry Survey on Banking. Please download the banking survey and examine the section, "How the Industry Operates." Now describe the Federal Reserve System's influence on nondeposit liabilities.

2. Use Standard & Poor's Market Insight website (**www.mhhe.com/edumarketinsight**) for this problem. Nondeposit borrowings in the Federal funds market and from other money market sources have become more important among banks and thrift institutions in recent years. You can get an idea of the magnitude of this change by examining the most recent financial statements of the banks and thrifts represented on the website of S&P's Market Insight. Why do you think that major banks are drawing so heavily upon nondeposit liabilities today? Are there significant advantages in doing so? Significant risks?

REAL NUMBERS FOR REAL BANKS

Assignment for Chapter 12

YOUR BANK'S USE OF LIABILITY MANAGEMENT: A STEP BEYOND DEPOSITS

Liability management was first mentioned in Chapters 6 and 10 and further developed with the focus on sources of funds in Chapter 12. After deposits, where do bank managers go for funding? To the financial markets or, in the United States, to the Federal Reserve banks and Federal Home Loan banks. These types of nondeposit borrowing are described in detail in the beginning of this chapter and the interest rates paid for these funds are discussed in the latter part of the chapter. We will first look at liabilities to see what they reveal about our BHC's composition of sources of funds. Then we will explore the risk ratings for any implications concerning the market's evaluation of the BHC's risk exposure.

Part One: Collecting the Data

We have already collected most of the data available to examine nondeposit sources of funds. In Spreadsheet 2, Rows 21–25 are the nondeposit sources of funds. We add negotiable CDs and Eurodollar deposits to the nondeposit sources and we have the materials most often used in liability management. We will once again visit the FDIC's SDI website located at **www3.fdic.gov/sdi/main.asp** to collect two items from the Memoranda section of the Assets and Liabilities report that may provide further insights for your particular BHC and the peer group of large banks (more than $10 billion in assets). You will create the four-column report for your bank and the peer group across the two years. Access the Assets and Liabilities report using the pull-down menus and collect the percentage information for the two items listed below. Once again, you will enter the percentages as an extension of the information in Spreadsheet 2 in the designated cells.

(A142) Additional information about liabilities	Your Bank	Peer Group	Your Bank	Peer Group
Date (A143)	12/31/yy	12/31/yy	12/31/yy	12/31/yy
(A144)	Percentage of Total Assets			
Volatile liabilities (A145)	%	%	%	%
FHLB advances (A146)				

Selected References

For a fuller explanation of the workings of the Federal funds market, see:

1. Bennett, Paul, and Spence Hilton. "Falling Reserve Balances and the Federal Funds Rate." *Current Issues in Economics and Finance*, Federal Reserve Bank of New York 3, no. 5 (April 1997), pp. 1–6.

For a discussion of the new rules governing borrowings from the discount windows of the Federal Reserve banks and an explanation of borrowing from other central banks around the world, see:

2. Madigan, Brian F., and William R. Nelson. "Proposed Revision to the Federal Reserve's Discount Window Lending Programs." *Federal Reserve Bulletin*, July 2002, pp. 313–319.

To learn more about FHLB advances as an important source of funds for depository institutions, see:

3. Stojanovic, Dusan, Mark D. Vaughan, and Timothy J. Yeager. "FHLB Funding: How Secure Is The FDIC's Perch?" *Regional Economist*, Federal Reserve Bank of St. Louis, October 2000, pp. 4–9.

4. Thomson, James B. "Commercial Banks' Borrowing from the Federal Home Loan Banks." *Economic Commentary*, Federal Reserve Bank of Cleveland, July 2002.

Part Two: Analyzing the Data for Interpretation

A. Volatile liabilities include large-denomination time deposits, foreign-office deposits, Federal funds purchased, securities sold under agreements to repurchase, and other borrowings. These are the risk-sensitive sources used in liability management. You can compare the columns of row 145 to get a sense of the proper answers to the following questions: (1) Is your BHC increasing its reliance on liability management? (2) Is your bank using liability management more than its peers?

B. Once you have looked at the big picture using the aggregated measure of volatile liabilities to total assets, observe the comparative and trend differences of its components, especially FHLB advances, Federal funds purchased, and securities sold under agreements to repurchase as a proportion of total assets.

C. Write several paragraphs discussing your BHC's use of liability management from year to year and in comparison to its contemporaries.

Part Three: The Risk Associated with Your Banks' (BHC's) Marketable Liabilities: A Look at the Debt Ratings for Your Bank

A. Visit the website of an international ratings agency that covers financial institutions at **www.fitchibca.com**. Once there, read the definitions of the ratings that Fitch provides at **www.fitchibca.com/corporate/ratings/definitions/index .cfm**.

B. Then find your BHC and any subsidiaries (banks) that have issued liabilities by going back to **www.fitchibca.com** and clicking on the Banks and Securities Firms link, followed by the Issuer List link. Once you arrive at the Issuer List, go through the alphabetical list until you find the banks and BHC you have been following this semester. Then you can click on the Active Name link to acquire information about outstanding issues and their ratings.

C. Summarize and interpret the above information in one or two paragraphs describing the types of issues outstanding and the associated risk for the holders of these issues. Can you develop any rationales for the amount of volatile liabilities given the ratings?

www.mhhe.com/rose6e

5. Vaughan, Mark D., and David C. Wheelock. "Deposit Insurance Reform: Is It Deja Vu All Over Again?" *Regional Economist*, Federal Reserve Bank of St. Louis, October 2002, pp. 5–9.

For a discussion of the development and use of the negotiable CD, see:

6. Willernse, Rob J. "Large Certificates of Deposit." *Instruments of the Money Market*, Federal Reserve Bank of Richmond, 1986, pp. 36–52.

For an analysis of the causes and effects of Eurodollar borrowing, see:

7. Goodfriend, Marvin. "Eurodollars." *Instruments of the Money Market*, Federal Reserve Bank of Richmond, 1986, pp. 53–64.

8. Kreichen, Lawrence L. "Eurodollar Arbitrage." *Quarterly Review*, Federal Reserve Bank of New York, Summer 1982, pp. 10–22.

For an analysis of commercial paper as a borrowing instrument for banks and other depository institutions, see the following:

9. McCauley, Robert N., and Lauren A. Hargraves. "Eurocommercial Paper and U.S. Commercial Paper: Converging Money Markets?" *Quarterly Review*, Federal Reserve Bank of New York, Autumn 1987, pp. 24–35.

10. Rose, Peter S. "The Quest for Funds: New Directions in a New Market." *The Canadian Banker* 94, no. 5 (September/October 1987), pp. 46–55.

To discover more information about capital notes and other subordinated debt as a source of funds, see, for example:

11. Haubrich, Joseph. "Subordinated Debt: Tough Love for Banks?" *Economic Commentary*, Federal Reserve Bank of Cleveland, December 1998.

For an overview of recent trends on both sides of the banking industry's balance sheet, see especially:

12. Carlson, Mark, and Robert Perli. "Profits and Balance Sheet Developments at U.S. Commercial Banks in 2002." *Federal Reserve Bulletin*, June 2003, pp. 245–270.

13. McAndrews, James, and Samira Rajan. "The Timing and Funding of Fedwire Funds Transfers." *Economic Policy Review*, Federal Reserve Bank of New York, July 2000, pp. 17–32.

14. Spong, Kenneth, and Richard J. Sullivan. "The Outlook for the U.S. Banking Industry: What Does the Experience of the 1980s and 1990s Tell Us?" *Economic Review*, Federal Reserve Bank of Kansas City, Fourth Quarter 1999, pp. 65–88.

To learn more about the use of repurchase agreements in securing short-term funds and recent innovations in the RP market, see especially:

15. Fleming, Michael J., and Kenneth D. Garbade. "The Repurchase Agreement Refined: GCF Repo." *Current Issues in Economics and Finance*, Federal Reserve Bank of New York 9, no. 6 (June 2003), pp. 1–7.

CHAPTER THIRTEEN

Sources of Fee Income: Investment Banking, Security Trading, Insurance, Trust, and Other Revenue-Producing Services

Key Topics in This Chapter

- The Ongoing Search for Fee Income
- Investment Banking Services
- Mutual Funds and Other Investment Products
- Trust Services and Insurance Products
- Benefits of Product-Line Diversification
- Information Flows and Customer Privacy

Introduction

Banks and many of their competitors have faced an increasingly intense struggle in recent years to attract all the funds needed to make loans and investments and boost their revenues. Unfortunately, the struggle to attract deposits has sometimes been frustrated by the changing attitudes of the public regarding how and where they wish to place their savings and by intense competition among bank and nonbank depository institutions, such as credit unions and savings associations. Scores of banks and thrift institutions have found that deposit markets are not always friendly to them when they need more funds.

This is especially true when stock and bond prices are rising and customers may be shifting large amounts of their financial resources from savings deposits to investments in securities, as happened, for example, during much of the 1990s. Of course, security prices don't always rise; indeed, the opening of the 21st century demonstrated this painfully when stock values plummeted, leading to a resurgence in the growth of new deposits. However, whenever deposit growth does slow, bankers and other financial-service managers frequently are forced to uncover and aggressively pursue new sources of funds and new ways to generate revenue and income.

One of the most fertile fields for growth in future revenue on the part of banks and other financial firms appears to be **fee income**—revenues derived from charging customers for the particular financial services they use. Examples abound, including monthly service charges on checking accounts, commissions for providing insurance coverage for homes and businesses, membership fees for accepting and using a particular credit card, commissions for aiding customers with the purchase or sale of stock, and fees for providing financial advice to individuals and corporations, and so on, and so on.

Fee income is the most rapidly growing source of revenue for banks, thrift institutions, and selected other service providers. Some of this revenue comes from the sale of traditional services, such as checking and savings account charges, fees for the use of an automated teller machine (ATM), and commitment fees to extend a loan when the customer needs it. Indeed, much to the anger of some customers, fees on many traditional services, particularly deposits, not only have been multiplying, but, on average, are rising faster than the rate of inflation!

More recently, however, much of the fee income has come from nontraditional services—newer services that, traditionally, were not offered by a commercial bank, credit union, or other familiar financial firm for many years. Examples include commissions and fees from supplying corporations and governments with investment banking services, commissions and fees from the sale of investment products (including buying or selling stocks, bonds, shares in mutual funds, and the like on behalf of customers), fees for managing a customer's financial affairs and property through an affiliated trust company or trust department, and commissions and fees from the sale of insurance products (including life, health, and property/casualty insurance policies) and from insurance underwriting. This expansion of nontraditional services and the revenues they generate is part of the consolidation and convergence of financial-service industries and firms that has been going on now for many years, as we saw earlier in Chapter 1. Larger financial firms today can reach across industry boundaries to grab new fee-based service ideas and then take on the risks of offering these new services to their customers.

In some instances these nontraditional services appear to have a low correlation with more traditional revenue sources, thereby potentially helping to lower the overall risk of the offering institution. For example, if revenue from loans and deposits is falling because of a dip in the economy, perhaps revenues from the sale of bonds, mutual funds, and insurance policies may be rising. On balance, profits and income may not falter (or, at least, may decline by less) even in tough times. In brief, the drive among banks and competing financial firms to generate more fee income as an increasingly important revenue source springs from several sources:

- A desire to supplement traditional sources of funds (such as deposits) when these sources are inadequate.
- An effort to offset higher production costs by asking customers to absorb a larger share of the cost of both old and new financial services.
- A desire to reduce overall risk to the financial-service provider's cash flow by finding new sources of revenue not highly correlated with revenues from sales of traditional services.
- A goal to promote cross-selling of traditional and new services in order to further enhance revenue and income.

We turn now to look at several of these recently popular, nontraditional sources of revenue (fee income) for banks and some of their more aggressive competitors.

As bankers and many of their competitors have invaded new realms of financial service, especially in the securities and insurance industries, the World Wide Web has generally kept pace with supportive sites to convey information to bankers and other financial-service managers and their customers. Examples include URLs directed at securities management and developments in the securities markets, such as **www.globeadvisor.com**, **www.investorsgroup.com**, and **morningstar.com**. The Web also offers some information on trust activities of banks, which frequently involve handling and managing securities, through such sites as **encarta.msn.com**, which resembles an online encyclopedia.

The Securities Industry Association at **www.sia.com** has chimed in with its own perspectives on bank expansion into the securities trading field and what new federal and state laws allowing the convergence of banks and securities firms might mean. Moreover, the insurance industry has not been far behind with such sites as **www.namic.org** provided by the National Association of Mutual Insurance Companies. These sites look at what the sale of insurance by banks might mean for the public as well as for the insurance and banking industries.

Finally, the convergence of banking, securities dealers, insurance companies, and other financial-service industries in the wake of the passage of the landmark federal law, the Gramm-Leach-Bliley Act of 1999, has spawned an exploding controversy over the importance of protecting customer privacy as different financial firms share customer data with each other. That controversy has spawned important new regulations and volumes of discussion on the Web from such sites as the New York State Banking Department (at **www.banking.state.ny.us**), the American Bankers Association (at **www.aba.com**), and the Federal Deposit Insurance Corporation (at **www.fdic.gov**). Finally, toward the close of this chapter we discuss new privacy policy rules in the financial sector. Examples of financial institutions' privacy policy statements on the Web can be found at **www.americanexpress.com/privacy/** and **www.usbank.com/privacy%5fpledge.html**.

Sales of Investment Banking Services

Although commercial banks and their closest competitors have not been as successful with some of the fee-income services they have recently offered as they had hoped, one service that has been successful intermittently, particularly when the economy is expanding, is **investment banking.** Acting under the authority of the Gramm-Leach-Bliley Financial Services Modernization Act and earlier rulings by the Federal Reserve Board, many leading U.S. banking firms have recently either acquired or formed their own investment banking affiliates in order to serve corporations and governments around the world. Examples include Citigroup's acquisition of Salomon Brothers Smith Barney and Chase Manhattan's purchase of Hambrecht & Quist. The leading investment banks in the world today include Citigroup, J. P. Morgan Chase, Deutsche Bank, Morgan Stanley Dean Witter, Goldman Sachs, Merrill Lynch, Credit Suisse First Boston, Bear Stearns, BNP Paribus SA, and ABN Amro NV. Today 55 of more than 600 financial holding companies (FHCs) approved to operate in the United States control investment banking subsidiaries.

Investment bankers (IBs) are, first and foremost, financial advisers to corporations, governments, and other large institutions. IBs provide critical advice and direction to their clients on such important issues as these: Should we seek to raise new capital and, if so, where and how? Do we need to enter new market areas (including foreign markets) and, if so, how can we best accomplish this expansion strategy? Does our company need to acquire or merge with other firms and, if so, how and when is the best time to do so? Should we sell our company to another firm and, if so, what is our company worth?

Traditionally, the best-known and often the most profitable investment banking service is *security underwriting*—the purchase for resale of stocks, bonds, and other financial instruments in the money and capital markets on behalf of clients who need to raise new money.

Among the most profitable and, recently, most controversial of these underwriting services has been the volatile initial public offering (IPO) market in which scores of formerly privately held companies have gone public by offering new shares of stock, often leading to large speculative gains or losses during the first few hours of the sale.

Investment banking is substantially more risky (but also substantially more profitable, on average) than commercial banking. IBs must estimate, in advance, the probable value of the new securities they plan to purchase from their clients when the day arrives that those new securities must be offered to the public. Their hope is that the market price will move higher from the first day of sale—a hoped-for outcome that clearly may be spoiled by such random events as terrorism, war, and changes in government policy and regulation. If the IB misestimates and the market price plunges as the sale begins, the IB will be forced to absorb the resulting loss, which may mount into the hundreds of millions of dollars. Conversely, a strong rise in market price as the new security sale begins can magnify the IB's expected profits.

In addition to possible capital gains on security trading, IBs also charge fees and commissions for their various services. For example, in making markets for IPOs recently, some investment banks have charged underwriting fees ranging up to 4 percent of the amount of the securities brought to the market for sale. Thus, a relatively small $25 million offering of stock from a newly formed corporation might net the assisting IB a fee of a million dollars or more.

Research studies suggest that investment banking revenue and profitability is positively, but not highly, correlated with commercial banking revenues and profitability. Thus, there *may* be some significant product-line diversification effects that help to limit overall risk for a commercial banking company engaging in IB activity. Moreover, IB services clearly complement traditional lending services, allowing commercial banking firms to offer both conventional loans and security underwriting to customers seeking to raise new funds. Then, too, there may be economies in information gathering about clients to the extent that loan officers and investment bankers share information with each other.

Key URLs

If you are interested in a career in investment banking, see especially **www.careers-in-finance.com**. For more general information about investment banking, see **www.encyclopedia.com**.

As we saw earlier in Chapter 2, offering both commercial and investment banking services through the same financial-service firm was prohibited following passage of the Glass-Steagall Act in 1933. Only gradually, beginning in the 1980s, did this new service activity become available to the commercial banking community through a series of rulings by the Federal Reserve Board. With the passage of the Gramm-Leach-Bliley Act in the fall of 1999, the full range of IB services was opened up for adequately capitalized and well-managed commercial banking firms.

The long-lived prohibition against the two industries combining was fueled by the Depression-era U.S. Congress's belief that such a combination would pose several significant costs and risks, including

- Possibly forcing customers seeking loans to buy the securities the IB was trying to sell as a condition for getting a loan (i.e., tying contracts).
- Increasing the risk exposure of affiliated commercial banking firms due to the inherently volatile and cyclical behavior of IB activity, resulting in more bank failures.

Executives of the largest U.S. banks and other industry leaders countered these arguments successfully in the 1990s by pointing out that combined commercial banking–investment banking operations were readily available outside the United States and, as a result, foreign banking firms were capturing U.S. customers. They also argued that allowing commercial banks into investment banking would increase competition and lower client fees.

It is not yet clear, however, that the benefits alleged from this new service dimension for commercial banking have been completely satisfied, though commercial banks have

ETHICS IN BANKING

ETHICAL PROBLEMS APPEAR TO ABOUND IN THE INVESTMENT BANKING BUSINESS

The prospect of hundreds of millions of dollars in fines as a result of ethical breakdowns in the investment banking business looms on the horizon, causing many bankers to take a second and third look at their business practices and direction. Among the most serious allegations are that some security brokers and dealers have published distorted and false research information to get their customers to purchase securities the brokers and dealers most wanted to sell. Excessively optimistic research reports and performance predictions during the past decade appear to have "sold" thousands of customers who ultimately got burned when more objective information appeared in the financial marketplace.

One recent proposal to deal with this problem calls for investment banks to purchase security research reports from independent (and, hopefully, more objective) businesses. Another proposal calls for the creation of an independent research panel that would select research firms to supply unbiased security analysis, aimed principally at providing small investors with unbiased evaluations of security issuers. A major challenge for the Securities and Exchange Commission (SEC) and other regulatory institutions is how to set up effective firewalls that separate the security brokering and sales function from the security research function in a way that restores the confidence of the public in the fundamental quality and honesty of security brokers and dealers and the investment banking business.

transformed the investment banking industry, acquiring some of its largest firms and consolidating smaller IBs into larger ones that are international in scope. For one thing, IB services are still highly sensitive to fluctuations in the economy, often dropping off sharply in recessions. For example, between 2000 and 2002, security firms in the United States wiped out the jobs of more than 30,000 employees due to fewer merger deals and declining issues of new securities amidst a serious economic slowdown.

Moreover, allegations about some banks forcing their loan customers to sign "tying contracts"—compelling these customers to purchase IB-offered securities that they didn't need or possibly couldn't afford—as a condition for getting a loan surfaced as the new century began. At about the same time, serious charges emerged that some IBs were misleading investors by providing them with inaccurate information in order to promote sales of securities the firm was underwriting. Moreover, other allegations soon appeared regarding possible "spinning" activity—that is, some IBs may have given the directors and officers of favorite corporate clients special deals on purchasing certain IPO shares not available to other security buyers. These firms quickly came under scrutiny by the Securities and Exchange Commission and the bank regulatory agencies. Several IBs, including some of those recently acquired by commercial banking firms, were hit with heavy fines.

Selling Investment Products to Consumers

As the 1990s unfolded, many of the largest business and household depositors began moving their funds out of deposits at banks and thrift institutions into so-called **investment products**—stocks, bonds, mutual funds, annuities, and similar financial instruments that seemed to promise better returns than are available on many conventional bank and thrift deposits. In addition, the passing years have ushered in growing public concern over the lack of adequate savings for the retirement years, given today's longer average life spans. Then, too, yield curves have tended to be positively sloped in recent years, suggesting that longer-term financial assets, such as stocks and bonds, might ultimately deliver higher returns than relatively short-term deposits and build personal savings faster.

Accordingly, the public made massive adjustments in their investment portfolios over the past two decades. For example, between 1991 and 2003, checkable deposits and time

Key URL
To learn more about recent trends in the service fees charged by depository institutions in recent years, see especially **www.federal .reserve.gov/board docs/RptCongress**.

and savings accounts at U.S. banks and other depository institutions rose from about $3 trillion to just over $5 trillion, a respectable gain of about 74 percent, as Table 13–1 shows. However, the checkable deposit total held by commercial banks actually *fell* over this period even as savings deposits rose. Far more remarkable was the rapid expansion of several nondeposit investment products. For example, the public's holdings of shares in mutual funds soared more than 500 percent. Household investments in individual stocks climbed by about 60 percent, while retirement (pension) plan volume more than tripled.

The willingness of traditional bank and thrift institution customers to convert many of their conservative investments in deposits, most of which normally are protected by federal deposit insurance, into uninsured stocks, mutual funds, annuities, and other investment products surprised and shocked many members of the banking community. Banks and thrifts quickly began to develop investment products and to offer financial planning services, hoping to win back some of the lost deposits or, at least, to get their customers to carry out their purchases and sales of investment products through a depository institution rather than through nonbank competitors.

The most popular of the investment products sold recently have been shares in **mutual funds.** First set up in Great Britain in the 19th century, mutual funds came to the United States in the 1920s. By the opening of the 21st century, these investment companies served more than 90 million shareholders and held more than $6 trillion in customer savings.

Each share in a mutual fund permits an investor to receive a *pro rata* share of any dividends, interest payments, or other forms of income generated by a pool of stocks, bonds, or other securities that the fund holds. If a mutual fund is liquidated, each investor receives a portion of the total net asset value (NAV) of the fund after its liabilities are paid off, based on the number of shares each investor holds. Each fund has an announced investment purpose or objective, such as capital growth or the maximization of current income, and in the United States must register with the Securities and Exchange Commission (SEC) and provide investors with a prospectus describing its purpose, recent performance, and makeup. These investment pools have few employees. Instead, a board of directors, representing the stockholders, hires outside firms to provide most of the management expertise needed to guide the fund.

Key URLs
To uncover more information about mutual funds, see **www.mfea.com** and **www.ici.org**.

Mutual funds have been very attractive to many individuals and institutional investors because their long-run yields appear to be relatively high and most funds are well diversified, spreading the investor's risk exposure across many different types of stocks, bonds, and other financial instruments. Mutual funds offer the advantage of having a professional money manager who monitors daily the performance of each security held by the fund and constantly looks for profitable trading opportunities. For many small investors, who have neither the expertise nor the time to constantly watch the market, access to professional money management services can be a significant advantage. However, some authorities argue that mutual funds and other security brokers and dealers often engage in too much daily manipulation of security portfolios, running up their costs and reducing an investor's net return. Moreover, the sharp downturn in the stock market early in the 21st century sent many investors pulling their money out of mutual funds, with a substantial portion of these scurrying back to invest in traditional deposits. It also led to a substantial pullback in the number of banks and other financial-service providers that chose to offer investments in mutual funds and other services related to buying and selling securities.

Factoid
If you deposit in your bank account a check that you received from someone else and it proves to be uncollectible, are you likely to be charged a fee on such a returned item?
Answer: In the United States, yes; more than half of U.S. banks charge such a fee, which averages about $7. Does this seem OK to you? Why?

Passage of the Gramm-Leach-Bliley Act of 1999 granted banks, along with security firms and insurance companies, the right to apply to the Federal Reserve Board to become financial holding companies (FHCs) and thereby sponsor and distribute shares in all types of mutual funds. Most banks and selected other depository institutions are involved in the mutual fund business in at least two different ways. First, larger banking firms may offer *proprietary funds* through one of their affiliated companies. In this case the banking firm's

TABLE 13–1 Relative Growth of Deposits and Nondeposit Investment Products, 1991–2003**
(sales to households, businesses, and governments in the U.S. economy)

Source: Board of Governors of the Federal Reserve System, *Flow of Funds Accounts*, selected issues.

Financial Instruments Held	Billions of Dollars Acquired in													Percentage Changes 1991–2003***
	1991	1992	1993	1994	1995	1996	1997	1998	1999	2000	2001	2002	2003**	
Checkable and time and savings deposits held at banks and other depository institutions	$3002.2	$3029.4	$3262.7	$3199.5	$3316.6	$3504.0	$3937.0	$3934.4	$4135.4	$4381.7	$4798.6	$5085.3	$5220.2	73.9%
Corporate stock*	2577.9	2923.2	3216.6	3059.9	4160.9	4895.6	6302.5	7173.6	9197.3	7317.2	5888.4	4327.1	4165.9	61.6
Mutual fund shares	586.6	727.9	990.9	1047.4	1852.8	2342.4	2989.4	3613.1	4538.5	4434.6	4135.5	3639.4	3586.8	511.5
Life insurance reserves*	393.8	421.5	457.2	491.5	566.3	610.6	665.0	718.3	783.9	819.1	871.7	912.1	929.4	136.0
Pension fund reserves	2548.1	2726.1	3055.3	3186.5	5671.3	6325.1	7323.4	8209.0	9065.6	9075.1	8682.3	8014.2	7936.1	211.5
Investments in bank personal trusts	639.3	660.6	691.3	699.4	803.0	871.3	942.5	1001.0	1130.4	1019.4	912.0	840.9	806.3	26.1

*As reported by the household sector of the Federal Reserve's *Flow of Funds Accounts*.
**Year 2003 figures are for first quarter only.

staff will advise the fund about trading opportunities and will buy and sell shares at the request of its customers, working through an affiliated securities firm. Examples include Mellon Bank's Dreyfus Corporation with its extensive family of mutual funds, Bank of America's Nations Funds, BankOne's One Funds, and Wachovia's Evergreen Funds. Banking firms are permitted to (1) offer investment advice, normally the greatest source of fee income; (2) serve as transfer agent and custodian for mutual fund shares, keeping records of who owns shares and who is entitled to receive fund reports and earnings; and (3) execute the transactions dictated by the fund's investment adviser.

Alternatively, banking firms may offer *nonproprietary funds*. In this case the bank or other offering institution acts as a broker for an unaffiliated mutual fund or group of mutual funds but does not act as an investment advisor. Nonproprietary funds are organized, distributed, and managed by an unaffiliated company that may, however, rent lobby space inside a bank or thrift institution's branch offices or sell its shares through a broker who is related to the bank or other offering institution in some way. Usually the depository institution involved receives a fee or commission for any sales of shares in nonproprietary funds passing through its offices.

Some experts argue that proprietary funds have the advantage of providing a relatively continuous stream of income to a bank or other service provider, while fee income generated by sales of nonproprietary funds may fluctuate and is often quite small. Some banks and thrift institutions merely advertise access to nonproprietary funds without earning substantial fees from their sales. Nevertheless, advertising the availability of nonproprietary funds may serve to bring in customers and hopefully lead to selling them other services.

Certainly banks and thrift institutions that offer their customers access to mutual funds and other security investments can benefit from offering these products. There is at least the possibility of earning substantial fee income for brokerage and other related services, and some of that fee income may be less sensitive to interest-rate movements than are more traditional services, such as deposits and loans. In addition, many banks and other service providers appear to gain added prestige from offering their own (proprietary) mutual funds. Some CEOs argue that offering this service positions a bank or other offering institution well for the future, particularly with respect to those customers planning for their retirement and accumulating large amounts of savings.

A somewhat different investment product, **annuities,** comes in either fixed or variable form. *Fixed annuities* promise a customer who contributes a lump sum of savings a fixed rate of return over the life of the annuity contract. The fixed-rate annuity generates a continuous, level income stream to the customer or to his or her beneficiaries after a number of years have elapsed. Usually the customer pays no taxes on the annuity until he or she actually begins to receive the promised stream of income. *Variable annuities*, on the other hand, allow investors to invest a lump sum of money (perhaps $10,000 or more) in a basket of stocks, mutual funds, or other investments under a tax-deferred agreement, but there is no promise of a guaranteed or level rate of return. The customer can usually add more funds to the variable annuity contract as time goes by and then at some designated future point receive a stream of income payments whose amount is based upon the accumulated market value in the contract. If the prices of assets placed in the annuity's fund have declined in value, the customer (annuitant) may receive less income than expected. On the other hand, the annuitant may receive a larger income stream if the value of accumulated assets has risen.

Many annuity contracts promise death benefits so that if the customer dies, his or her heirs receive money based on the value of assets held in the contract. Some variable annuities promise a minimum rate of return, often based on the amount of initial investment, even if the market value of the contract's assets has fallen over time. One advantage for

STATE STREET BANK MAKES FEES PAY OFF

One of the best-known fee-focused banking companies in the world is State Street Corporation (**www.statestreet.com**), based in Boston. Years ago State Street phased out much of its traditional lending program and came to focus instead on fee-based services for the bulk of its revenue and income. Currently this bank has offices in more than 20 nations scattered around the globe.

State Street offers such key services as *asset management* (including the management of assets for other banks, pension plans, and mutual funds), *custodian services* (keeping track of the ownership of securities and delivering financial reports, interest earnings, and dividends to security holders), and *foreign exchange trading and risk management* on behalf of its larger corporate customers—to name just a few of State Street's wide array of financial-service offerings.

In terms of earnings, State Street is one of the most consistently profitable banks in the world, steadily growing its per-share core earnings and dividends paid to its shareholders, due in part to its emphasis on fee income rather than interest-sensitive loans as is true of most other banks. State Street Bank continues to expand its operations on the international front. Recently, for example, it announced the purchase of Deutsche Bank's custodian business, which would make it the largest recordkeeping and servicing agent for institutional investors on the planet.

selling banks and other service providers is that variable annuities often carry substantial annual fees. An annuity is the reverse of life insurance; instead of hedging against dying too soon, annuities are a hedge against living too long and outlasting one's savings. Recently insurance companies have been working with banks and thrift institutions to create proprietary variable annuities carrying the depository institution's label.

More than a thousand banking organizations—about one-fifth of the U.S. banking industry—were selling third-party or proprietary mutual funds and/or annuity plans as the new century began. Most of these sales (better than 90 percent) were made by multibillion-dollar banks, the industry's largest institutions. Unfortunately, not all of these product-line innovations have been particularly successful. For example, bank mutual fund and annuity sales recently have accounted for less than 5 percent of total bank fee (non-interest) income.

Somewhat more successful have been sales of shares in low-risk money market (short-term) mutual funds rather than sales of shares in longer-term stock and bond mutual funds, due, in part, to the close affinity between money market fund shares and money market deposits. U.S. banks' share of equity and bond funds sales reached a high of about 8 percent of all mutual fund sales in 1994 and has generally fallen since that time.

In part, these disappointing sales of many investment products offered by banks may be due to the record profits during much of the 1990s. With their earnings at record levels banks, in particular, felt less pressure to push hard on their investment products' sales. Bank sales fees also tend to be on the high side. At the same time regulators have placed bank and thrift sales of mutual funds and other investment products under intense scrutiny, while regulations applying to deposits, particularly deposit insurance fees and reserve requirements, have recently been lowered, making it more attractive and less costly to sell traditional deposits rather than the newer and more exotic savings instruments. Then, too, the start-up costs of mutual funds are high, especially the legal fees, and the minimum size fund needed to be really competitive may be $100 million or more in total assets, larger than many funds created in recent years.

Some banks have found other ways to profit from security sales today by serving as recordkeepers and processors for purchases and sales. Among the most famous of these institutions are the Bank of New York and, as the Real Banks, Real Decisions box explains, the State Street Bank of Boston, which provide such services as transferring the ownership of securities bought and sold, managing foreign stocks purchased by U.S. investors, and accounting for mutual fund sales of new shares and the redemption of already issued fund shares.

Several potential problems and risks are associated with sales of investment products. For one thing, their value is market determined and their performance can turn out to be highly disappointing, angering customers who may hold a bank or thrift institution offering the service to a higher standard of performance than it would a securities broker or dealer. Moreover, some banks and thrift institutions have become embroiled in costly lawsuits filed by disappointed customers who allege that they were misled about the risks associated with investment products. Banks and thrifts may run into *compliance* problems if they fail to properly register their investment product activities with the Securities and Exchange Commission or fail to comply with all the rules laid down by regulatory agencies, state commissions, and other legal bodies that monitor this market.

Current U.S. regulations require that customers must be told orally (and sign a document indicating that they were informed) that investment products are

1. Not insured by the Federal Deposit Insurance Corporation (FDIC).
2. Not a deposit or other obligation of a bank or thrift institution and not guaranteed by the offering institution.
3. Subject to investment risks, including possible loss of the principal value of the customer's investment.

These and other regulatory rules must be conspicuously displayed inside those offices of banks and thrift institutions where investment products are sold. Moreover, these products must be sold in an office area that is separate from the area where deposits are taken from the public. Bankers and thrift institution managers must demonstrate to government examiners that they are closely monitoring their investment products' sales practices, literally policing themselves in order to avoid serious problems that may adversely affect the public's confidence in these institutions. They must have blanket bond insurance coverage for their retail nondeposit sales and make only those sales recommendations to customers that are "suitable" for each customer's situation and needs. Finally, the names chosen for in-house mutual funds cannot be similar to the names of the banking firms sponsoring these funds because this might lead to confusion on the part of the public about the safety of investment products compared to the safety of federally insured deposits.

Concept Check

13–1. What services are provided by *investment banks* (IBs)? Who are their principal clients?

13–2. Why were U.S. commercial banks forbidden to offer investment banking services for several decades inside the United States? How did this affect the ability of U.S. banks to compete for underwriting business?

13–3. What advantages do commercial banks with investment banking affiliates appear to have over

competitors that do not offer investment banking services? What are the possible disadvantages?

13–4. What are *investment products?* What advantages might they bring to a depository institution choosing to offer these services?

13–5. What risks do investment products pose for the institutions that sell them? How might these risks be minimized or controlled?

Trust Services as a Source of Fee Income

Trust services—the management of property owned by customers, such as securities, land, buildings, and other investments—are among the oldest nondeposit products that banks and some of their closest competitors offer. There is evidence that offering professional trust services, including safeguarding and generating earnings from the prudent management of a customer's property, goes back nearly to the earliest origins of the banking and financial-services industry.

What is less well known to the public is the close tie between deposit taking by banks and offering trust services. A bank operating a trust department can be a major source of new deposits. Of course, not all banks have trust powers, which must be applied for from the bank's chartering agency or principal regulator, but most medium and large commercial banks and some thrift institutions do operate trust departments. Trust personnel are *not* permitted to share client information on those customers they serve with personnel in other parts of the financial firm.

Trust departments often generate very large deposits because they manage property (including deposits as well as other assets) for their customers, which usually include business firms, units of government, individuals and families, and charities and foundations. A trust officer—either instructed by a customer or on his or her own initiative—may place certain monies in a checking or a time deposit account for future use, such as to pay bills or to seek out a more favorable rate of return, on behalf of a client served by the trust department. Deposits placed in a bank by a trust department must be *fully secured*. Like any other deposit, they are covered by deposit insurance up to the legal insurance limit, and any amount over the insurance limit must be protected by investment-grade securities the bank holds while the deposit is present in the institution.

The trust business stretches back at least to the Middle Ages when landowners and other wealthy individuals (trustors) often chose to turn their property over to a manager (trustee), who would protect and control the use of that property for the benefit of its owner or owners. State-chartered U.S. banks have been allowed to provide trust services for many years, while national banks were granted the right to seek trust powers with passage of the Federal Reserve Act in 1913. For most of banking's history, trust departments were regarded as a needed service area for the benefit of a bank's customers, but trust operations were usually regarded as an unprofitable activity due to the large space and the highly skilled personnel required—usually a combination of portfolio managers, lawyers (particularly specialists in trust and tax law), and professional accountants—to serve trust customers. However, with the advent of government deregulation of the banking and financial system and the increasing tendency of banks to levy fees for their services, trust departments became increasingly popular as a source of fee income. For example, trust departments typically levy asset management (trustee) fees based upon the value of a customer's assets that they are called upon to manage and for filing tax reports. These fees are popular with bankers and other financial-service managers today because they are often less sensitive to fluctuations in market interest rates than are other revenue sources, such as interest on loans.

Trust departments function in a tremendous variety of roles. They routinely serve as executors or administrators of wills, identifying, inventorying, and protecting the property (estate) of a deceased person, ensuring that any unpaid bills are met and that the heirs of the deceased receive the income or assets to which they are entitled. Trust departments act as *agents* for companies that need to service security issues, such as by issuing new stock, paying stockholder dividends, and issuing or retiring bonds for client firms, and often manage the pension or retirement plans of both businesses and individuals. They also serve as

Key URLs
To learn more about the trust service activities of leading banking firms, see especially Wells Fargo & Co. at **www.wellsfargo.com/ com/corporatetrust**, the Bank of New York at **www.bankofny.com**, LaSalle Bank at **www.lasallebank.com/ trust/**, and Wachovia Bank at **www .wachovia.com**.

guardians of assets held for the benefit of minors or act on behalf of adult persons judged to be legally incompetent to manage their own affairs.

In fulfilling these many roles, trust departments promulgate basic trust agreements, contracts that grant a trust officer legal authority on behalf of a customer to invest funds, pay bills, and dispense income to persons or institutions with valid claims against the trust's assets. Many different types of trusts are permitted under the laws of different states, though the types and procedures often vary from state to state so that anyone desiring to enter into a trust agreement must consult state trust codes. More complex trust arrangements often require the services of an outside attorney as well.

Among the more popular kinds of trusts are *living trusts* or grantor revocable trusts, which allow bank trust officers to act on behalf of a living customer without a court order, generally help to avoid expensive probate proceedings if the property owner dies or becomes legally incompetent, and may be revoked or amended by the customer as desired. There are also *testamentary trusts*, which arise under a probated will and are often used to help save on estate taxes. If properly drawn, a testamentary trust can sometimes be used to protect a customer's property from the claims of creditors or beneficiaries who may make unreasonable demands that might prematurely exhaust the trust's assets. Other common types of trust agreements include *irrevocable trusts*, which allow wealth to be passed free of gift and estate taxes or may be used to allocate funds arising from court settlements or private contracts; *charitable trusts*, which support worthwhile causes, such as medical research, the arts, care of the needy, student scholarships, and orphanages; and *indenture trusts*, which usually collect, hold, and manage assets used to back an issue of securities by a corporation raising funds in the financial markets and then are employed to retire the securities on behalf of the issuing company when their term ends.

Clearly, trust departments perform a remarkable collection of roles and functions that are often unseen or unknown. However, their activities usually center upon establishing a *fiduciary relationship* with a customer, protecting that customer's property, making asset management and asset allocation decisions, planning a customer's estate and ensuring that estate property is passed in timely fashion to those entitled to its benefits under law, and assisting businesses in raising and managing funds and in providing retirement benefits to their employees. Trust departments must follow the terms of a trust or agency agreement and any court orders that have been issued. They are expected to be highly competent and diligent in their fiduciary and agency activities and are legally liable for losses due to negligence or for failure to act as a prudent decision maker would, intelligently pursuing the best interests of their customers. Trust departments have come to play vital and sometimes highly profitable roles in modern banks, including attracting a considerable volume of deposits. Moreover, many banks have used their trust departments to create mutual funds that grow rapidly in size and provide their trust customers with multiple investment options and permit a bank or other financial-service firm to achieve an efficient size mutual fund more quickly.

Historically, trust departments have been regarded as relatively staid and slow-moving operations. However, there has been a resurgence of trust activity in recent years as these units assist corporations with employee stock option plans (ESOPs), provide escrow agency and document custodial services, supply corporate cash and asset management needs, and serve as a conduit and recordkeeper for debt and equity securities offerings. Corporate trust departments at such leading banks as Wells Fargo Corporation, Wachovia, CIBC Mellon, HSBC Bank USA, and the Bank of New York have played leading roles in creating a global marketplace for mortgage instruments and other loan-backed security issues. This is one case where a nontraditional product line, *investment banking*, has helped to create demand for another product line, *trust services*, particularly for corporate customers seeking to protect their assets, control risk, and restructure or expand their capital base as a platform for future growth.

Sales of Insurance-Related Products

Not only have leading commercial bankers around the globe made heavy inroads into the investment banking business and into the field of brokering securities and annuities for their customers, but they also have begun to aggressively invade the insurance (risk management) business. One of the most famous of such banking–insurance alliances in modern history took place in the United States in 1998 when Citicorp, headquartered on the East Coast of the United States and considered one of the most innovative banks in the world, and Travelers Insurance Company, on America's West Coast, came together as a single corporate unit to cross-sell each other's products across the United States and around the globe (though Citicorp and Travelers later parted company in 2002). Citicorp and Travelers were by no means alone in their efforts to cross-sell financial services as bankers and insurance companies in Europe, Asia, Japan, and Canada moved closer together to share in the hoped-for benefits of conglomeration and convergence of different financial industries.

Types of Insurance Products Sold by Banks and Other Financial-Service Providers in Recent Years

The banking-insurance convergence trend that has emerged globally includes the brokering (sales) of **life insurance policies,** both through bank offices and through insurance agencies that can generate fees and commissions. These policies help to protect individuals, families, and businesses against loss in the event of a death and may also include a savings account component to prepare for future financial needs. In addition, banking and financial holding companies can now set up **life insurance underwriters** who hope to generate underwriting profits from managing insurable risks and collecting more in insurance premiums than they must pay out in insurance claims. Life insurance affiliates of bank and financial holding companies also frequently sell health insurance policies and retirement plans to individuals and businesses in return for premium payments, fees, and commissions from customers.

Bankers and many of their financial-service competitors have also begun to sell **property/casualty insurance policies,** not only through branch offices, but also through separately incorporated insurance agencies. Property/casualty insurers and insurance agents sell policies to their customers that cover an incredibly wide array of business and personal risks. For example, these policies deal with such risks as driving an automobile, operating a boat or ship, industrial accidents, illness and medical care costs, negligence or fraud in operating a business, damages to or negligence associated with owning a home, and protecting against losses due to changing interest rates and defaults on credit extended to others. **Property/casualty insurance underwriters** accept the risks involved in protecting lives and property from accidents, negligence, and other adverse events in the hope of earning more in premiums charged and from investments they make than the claims brought against them by policyholders.

New Rules Covering Insurance Sales by FDIC-Insured Depository Institutions

As bankers and many of their competitors have poured into the insurance products' business, concern over the possibility that customers may be misled or misinformed has greatly increased. For example, the public may conclude wrongly that insurance products offered by a bank or thrift institutions are covered by government-sponsored deposit insurance in case the customer suffers a loss. This concern in the United States led the key U.S. federal banking agencies—the Federal Reserve System, the Federal Deposit Insurance Corporation, the

DIVERSIFICATION THROUGH JOINT VENTURING: THE CASE OF WACHOVIA SECURITIES

In February 2003 Wachovia Corporation of Charlotte, North Carolina, one of the top 10-banks in the United States, announced an agreement with Prudential Financial, one of the world's leading insurance conglomerates, to create a new, jointly owned security brokerage firm. Combining existing brokerage units of these two financial giants, the new brokerage firm, called Wachovia Securities, was to be based in Richmond, Virginia, and would rank among the top five security brokers in the United States.

Wachovia's management viewed the new service unit as catering primarily to the investment needs of retail investors (individuals and families), partly counterbalancing the strong business-customer orientation of Wachovia Bank itself. The bank focuses primarily on the eastern United States, whereas the new brokerage firm may be able to reach across the entire continent, perhaps cross-selling many of the products the bank and its affiliates offer. Management also hopes the new combination will result in substantial cost savings by reducing staff and closing offices.

Clearly, the proposed new venture reflects management's belief that three major benefits, usually looked for in bank-nonbank financial firm combinations, will actually occur:

1. Economies of scale (size) for greater savings in operating costs and greater profit margins.
2. Product line diversification to reduce risk and expand revenue opportunities as the combination of old and new firms allows a wider range of services to be offered.
3. Geographic diversification to reduce risk and expand revenue opportunities that result from opening up new market areas and more fully penetrating existing markets as well.

In this instance the managements of Wachovia and Prudential may be correct in their estimates, but there is another side to this story. For example, both Fleet Boston Financial and U.S. Bancorp of Minneapolis have recently moved to dispose of their securities affiliates—Robertson Stephens Inc. in the case of Fleet and Piper Jaffrey in the case of U.S. Bancorp. Both bank holding companies found that their securities brokerage and underwriting units appeared to generate increased earnings volatility without the benefit of the cost savings they had hoped for. Only time will tell if the benefits of one-stop financial-service conglomerates suggested in financial theory really pan out in the real world.

Comptroller of the Currency, and the Office of Thrift Supervision—to issue consumer protection rules beginning in October 2001.

These rules call for mandatory disclosures on the part of depository institutions selling insurance products that stipulate

1. An insurance product or annuity is *not* a deposit or other obligation of a depository institution or its affiliate.
2. An insurance product or annuity sold by a depository institution in the United States is *not* insured by the FDIC, any other agency of the U.S. government, the depository institution, or its affiliates.
3. Insurance products or annuities may involve investment risk and possible loss of value.
4. U.S. depository institutions cannot base granting loans on the customer's purchase of an insurance product or annuity from a depository institution or any of its affiliates or on the customer's agreement not to obtain an insurance product or annuity from an unaffiliated entity.

Such disclosures to individuals and families, must be made both orally and in writing before completion of the sale of an insurance product. Moreover, the proposed new U.S.

rule requires written acknowledgment from the customer that these disclosures were received from the offering depository institution. Where practicable, a depository institution must keep insurance product sales activities physically separated from those areas within a bank or thrift institution where retail deposits are routinely taken from the public. Finally, employees who sell insurance-related products must be qualified and licensed as required by each state's insurance authorities.

The Alleged Benefits of Financial-Services Diversification

As we saw in Chapter 1, when two or more different industry types—such as banks and insurance companies—merge with each other, this strategic move is called **convergence.** One of the possible (but by no means guaranteed) benefits of industry convergence is the relatively low correlation that may exist between cash flows or revenues generated by the sale of traditional industry products (such as loans and deposits sold by banks) versus the sale of nontraditional products (such as banks selling automobile insurance coverage).

For example, Rose's study [12] of numerous bank and nonbank industries finds low positive and even negative correlations in cash flows between the banking industry and such financial-service industries as business and personal finance companies, security and commodity brokers and dealers, life and property/casualty insurers and insurance agencies, and real estate firms. Because the streams of revenue from these different product lines may move in different directions at different times, the overall impact of combining these different industries and products under one roof may be to stabilize combined cash flows and profitability. The risk of failure could also be reduced.

This potential consequence of the convergence of two or more financial-service industries is called the **product-line diversification effect.** Offering different services with different cash-flow variances over time tends to lower the overall risk of the financial firm.[1]

An Example of the Product-Line Diversification Effect

Let us briefly illustrate what could happen to overall institutional risk by combining traditional and nontraditional services in one organization. For example, suppose a banking company decides to add insurance services to its existing product menu. It expects to earn a 12 percent average return from sales of its traditional banking products and a 20 percent return from selling or underwriting insurance services. These two service lines are judged to be about equally risky in the variance of their cash flows (with a standard deviation of about 5 percent each), but the banking firm expects to receive 20 percent of its revenues from insurance sales and 80 percent from sales of traditional banking products. Suppose that cash flows from the two sets of services are negatively correlated over time with a correlation coefficient of –0.50.

---

[1] The *product-line diversification effect* refers to offering different services whose returns or cash flows are not perfectly correlated with each other, thereby reducing variability in the overall cash flows generated from sales of multiple services. As we will see in Chapter 18, there is a also a *geographic diversification effect,* which also can lead to reduced cash-flow risk for a bank or other financial firm serving several different geographic markets with different economic characteristics simultaneously; if one market is declining, other markets served may be on the rise, helping to stabilize overall cash flow. We need to keep in mind, however, that merely because a banking or other financial firm may be able to take advantage of product-line and/or geographic diversification, this does not guarantee that its overall risk exposure must necessarily decline. For example, management, feeling it is safer because of these two diversification effects, may take other steps, such as accepting more risky loans or reducing capital, that actually wind up making the institution even more risky than before.

What would happen to the bank's overall return from sales of traditional and nontraditional products in this case? Standard portfolio theory in finance suggests the following would happen to bank returns if the above assumptions turn out to be true:

$$
\begin{matrix}
\text{Expected return} \\
\text{from overall} \\
\text{service menu}
\end{matrix}
=
\begin{matrix}
\text{Proportion} \\
\text{of revenue} \\
\text{from traditional} \\
\text{services}
\end{matrix}
\times
\begin{matrix}
\text{Expected return} \\
\text{from traditional} \\
\text{services}
\end{matrix}
$$

$$
+
\begin{matrix}
\text{Proportion} \\
\text{of revenue} \\
\text{from nontraditional} \\
\text{services}
\end{matrix}
\times
\begin{matrix}
\text{Expected return} \\
\text{from nontraditional} \\
\text{services}
\end{matrix}
$$

In this example using the figures given previously,

$$
\begin{matrix}
\text{Expected} \\
\text{return from} \\
\text{the bank's overall} \\
\text{service menu}
\end{matrix}
= 0.80(12 \text{ percent}) + 0.20(20 \text{ percent}) = 13.6 \text{ percent}
$$

That return is a *higher* overall return than the bank would receive just from selling its traditional products, where the expected return is only 12 percent.

And what happens to the *risk* of return for this bank? The key relationship from finance theory is as follows:

$$
\begin{matrix}
\text{Variance of} \\
\text{overall return} \\
\text{from selling} \\
\text{traditional and} \\
\text{nontraditional} \\
\text{services}
\end{matrix}
=
\begin{matrix}
\text{Squared} \\
\text{proportion} \\
\text{of revenue} \\
\text{from traditional} \\
\text{services}
\end{matrix}
\times
\begin{matrix}
\text{Variance} \\
\text{of revenue} \\
\text{from traditional} \\
\text{services}
\end{matrix}
+
\begin{matrix}
\text{Squared} \\
\text{proportion} \\
\text{of revenue from} \\
\text{nontraditional} \\
\text{services}
\end{matrix}
$$

$$
\times
\begin{matrix}
\text{Variance} \\
\text{of revenue from} \\
\text{nontraditional} \\
\text{services}
\end{matrix}
+ 2 \times
\begin{matrix}
\text{Proportion} \\
\text{of revenue} \\
\text{from traditional} \\
\text{services}
\end{matrix}
\times
\begin{matrix}
(1 - \text{Proportion} \\
\text{of revenue} \\
\text{from} \\
\text{nontraditional} \\
\text{services})
\end{matrix}
\times
\begin{matrix}
\text{Correlation} \\
\text{of returns} \\
\text{between} \\
\text{traditional and} \\
\text{nontraditional} \\
\text{services}
\end{matrix}
$$

$$
\times
\begin{matrix}
\text{Standard} \\
\text{deviation} \\
\text{of return} \\
\text{from traditional} \\
\text{services}
\end{matrix}
\times
\begin{matrix}
\text{Standard} \\
\text{deviation} \\
\text{of return} \\
\text{from} \\
\text{nontraditional} \\
\text{services}
\end{matrix}
$$

In this instance, using the figures from the example above,

$$
\begin{matrix}
\text{Variance} \\
\text{of overall} \\
\text{return from} \\
\text{selling traditional} \\
\text{and} \\
\text{nontraditional} \\
\text{services}
\end{matrix}
=
\begin{matrix}
(0.80)^2(0.05)^2 + (0.20)^2(0.05)^2 \\
+2(0.80)(0.20)(-0.50)(0.05)(0.05)
\end{matrix}
$$

$$
= 13 \text{ percent}
$$

Potential Advantages of Combining Commercial Banking, Trust Services Management, Investment Banking, and Insurance Sales and Underwriting under the Same Financial Holding Company

Financial Holding Company (FHC)			
Commercial Banking	**Trust Services Management**	**Investment Banking**	**Insurance Sales and Underwriting**
Extending loans at interest Providing credit guarantees, payments services, liquidity and savings plans	Managing property Managing pension plans Recordkeeping and safekeeping Distributing new securities and interest and dividend payments on existing securities	Assisting clients with acquisitions and mergers Raising debt and equity capital for government and corporate clients (security underwriting) Brokering securities for clients	Providing risk management services for persons and property, pension plan management, cash management services, and long-term savings plans

The potential advantages of combining these financial-service activities under one corporate umbrella include supplementing traditional sources of funds and revenue with new funds and revenue sources, lowering the cost of service production and delivery through economies of scale (greater volume) and economies of scope (more intensive use of existing management and other productive resources), increased earnings stability, and reduced risk of failure through greater product-line and geographic diversification.

so the

$$\text{Overall standard deviation from selling traditional and nontraditional banking services} = \sqrt{13 \text{ percent}} = 3.06 \text{ percent}$$

Thus, the combined offering in this example of both traditional and nontraditional banking services serves to *lower* the bank's standard deviation of its overall return—a measure of the riskiness of the bank's overall rate of return—from an average of 5 percent to about 3 percent.

While this looks like a win–win situation—higher returns and lower overall risk with nontraditional products sold alongside traditional products—not everyone agrees that this result will occur. In fact, a recent study by Stiroh [13] from the Federal Reserve Bank of New York argues that cash flows or revenues from nontraditional products have become more volatile and more highly correlated with interest revenues from sales of traditional loans and investments, reducing any potential diversification benefits. Moreover, the same study finds evidence that noninterest revenue sources (particularly revenues generated by trading securities) often carry greater risk and lower risk-adjusted returns than do traditional interest-rate related sources of income. In short, the evidence on the real benefits, if any, of combining traditional and nontraditional financial services under one company remains mixed; the jury is still out on the real magnitude of the growth, profitability, and risk-reducing gains from the modern trend toward financial-services industry convergence.

Potential Economies of Scope

Another potential benefit from offering multiple services, such as traditional banking products (like deposits and loans) plus insurance, through the same financial firm is **economies of scope.** These potential cost savings arise because the same managerial, employee, and physical resources may be used to offer and provide *both* traditional and nontraditional products. Thus, expanding the number of different financial services offered may result in more efficient and intensive use of existing productive resources, lowering the overall cost of service production and delivery, and widening a financial firm's profit margin.

Nondeposit Services and Information Flows within the Banking or Financial Firm

Factoid
When you use an ATM to receive cash, under what circumstances are you most likely to pay a service fee for this service?
Answer: When you use an ATM belonging to a depository institution other than where you keep your deposit.

As banks and many of their competitors have evolved into more widely diversified financial-service firms offering investment, insurance, and other new services, they have become more and more like pure information-gathering, information-processing, and information-dispersing businesses. Indeed, even traditional services, such as savings deposits or checking accounts, represent little more than gathering and storing financial information and transmitting that information to others.

Moreover, by using the same information to offer more than one service to a customer, such as granting a loan and selling a life insurance policy to the same client, this development opens up potential new cost-saving economies. Financial service-providers can use the same customer data over and over again to generate revenue or cash flow, minimizing information costs per unit of service at the same time. Financial institutions are in a unique position in the economy to serve as a collection point for customer data and as an information processor and interpreter. By supplying credit and other information-based services that many customers regard as essential, financial firms generate valuable customer data that may be useful to a wide range of other businesses trying to deepen and expand their customer bases.

For example, nonbank businesses, whether affiliated with banks or not affiliated with banks, may seek to access bank-generated customer data and use it to enhance their own cash flow and market share. Indeed, some economists argue today that these potential information economies are literally the driving forces behind the mergers and acquisitions that are reshaping banking and other financial service industries today. Some financial firms see an inherent advantage in being affiliated with a bank, especially if it is too costly to attempt to purchase vital customer information from an independent provider.

As the 20th century drew to a close, several governments around the world, including federal and selected state governments inside the United States, decided that information gathering, processing, and especially information dispensing by banks and other financial firms might well become a source of either "good" or "evil" for the public. For example, banks with a wider array of bank and nonbank services to sell could use their customers' data files to generate more revenue productivity at low cost and become highly profitable, giving them a key economic advantage over other firms but also offering great potential for damage to their customers.

For example, suppose that medical data for a customer who is applying for life or health insurance coverage is shared with a bank where that customer is requesting a new home loan. Suppose the customer does have a serious medical problem and is denied insurance coverage. Denial of access to that one service could easily lead to denial of access to other financial services as well. The bank where the same customer applied for a home loan might use the adverse medical information uncovered by the insurance company to deny that loan. Moreover, this same adverse information might well be shared with other firms,

EXHIBIT 13–1
Key Items That Must Be Included in a Financial Firm's Privacy Policy and Be Sent to Its Customers at Least Once a Year

What kinds of information about customers the financial firm may share with other firms (e.g., the customer's income, marital status, credit history and credit rating, employment history, etc.).

What kinds of companies the customer's private information may be shared with (e.g., mortgage bankers, insurance agents, retailers, direct marketers, etc.).

What the customer can do to "opt out" of information sharing and tell the financial firm not to share his or her private data (e.g., by providing the customer a toll-free number to call, a website address to contact, or a special form to complete and send in to the firm).

A warning that some private information (such as data needed to carry out a transaction requested by the customer) can be shared even if the customer might wish otherwise.

resulting in the customer in question being "blacklisted" by many other service providers. Competition for a customer's business could be blunted by what is, in effect, coordinated and cooperative discrimination.

This very real possibility of personal damage from sharing data and the parallel problem of the outright invasion of personal privacy by businesses led to great controversy when the United States passed the Gramm-Leach-Bliley Act in 1999. As we recall from our earlier discussion of this new law in Chapters 2 and 3, the act allowed financial-service companies to share customer information among their affiliated firms and also with independently owned third parties provided customers did not expressly say "no" (or "opt out") of having their personal data distributed to others.

Subsequently, as the new century opened the federal banking and thrift agencies (including the Federal Reserve System, Comptroller of the Currency, Federal Deposit Insurance Corporation, and Office of Thrift Supervision) prepared new regulations to give customers a real chance to opt out of or at least limit the sharing of personal information. The first step was to draft regulations to protect **customer privacy** in sharing a customer's private data between unrelated financial-service providers, including banks, credit unions, finance and small-loan companies, thrift institutions, insurers and insurance agents, security brokers and dealers, and travel agents. This first set of new rules stipulated that when a customer applies to open a new account or access a new service he or she must be informed of the service provider's customer privacy policies. Moreover, at least once a year the customer must be reminded about the content of those privacy policies (see Exhibit 13–1).

If a customer objects to having his or her private data shared with other, unrelated businesses, such as telephone marketers, the service provider must tell the customer how to opt out of data sharing. If the customer fails to notify the service provider of his or her objections to sharing personal data, then the service firm can go ahead and share the customer's private information with others, even with outsiders.

Concept Check

12–6. What exactly are *trust services?*

12–7. How do trust services generate fee income and often deposits as well for banks and other financial institutions offering this service?

12–8. What types of *insurance products* do banks and a number of their competitors sell today? What advantages could these products offer banks and other depository institutions choosing to sell insurance services? Can you see any possible disadvantages?

12–9. What is *convergence? Product-line diversification? Economies of scope?* Why can they be of considerable importance for banks and other financial-service firms?

12–10. How can financial-service customers limit the sharing of their private data by different financial-service firms? In what ways could customer information sharing be useful for financial institutions and for their customers? What possible dangers does information sharing present?

Summary

In this chapter we have examined several of the newer services that many banks and some of their closest competitors have begun to offer in recent years, and we explored the reasons for this newest form of product-line (service) diversification among financial institutions. The most important points in the chapter include the following:

- Banks and a number of their strongest competitors are reaching beyond traditional industry boundaries to offer nontraditional products, such as life insurance, property/casualty insurance, investment banking, and brokerage of stocks, bonds, shares in mutual funds, and other securities. These nontraditional services have provided new sources of *fee income* for banks and other financial firms. They have also provided *product-line* (service) *diversification* to possibly lower risk and *economies of scope*, in which management, facilities, and other business resources are used more intensively and efficiently to generate revenue and income.

- Among the most important of the newer services offered by banks and other service providers is *investment banking*—providing advice to businesses, governments, and other institutions interested in expansion into new markets, pursuing mergers and acquisitions, or offering new debt and equity securities in the financial marketplace. When the economy is expanding, investment banking can be among the most profitable of financial services.

- Beginning in the 1990s hundreds of banks and other depository institutions began offering *investment products*, including the buying and selling of stocks, bonds, shares in mutual funds, and other financial instruments on behalf of their customers, generating commission and fee income in the process. Sales of these services also tend to soften the impact of the loss of deposits when customers are attracted away from depository institutions by perceived higher yields in the markets for stocks, bonds, and other investments.

- *Trust services*—the management of a customer's property and financial interests—are not new, especially in banking where many banks seek trust powers soon after they have been chartered. Trust departments provide a wide array of household and business trust services, including preparing wills and estate plans and managing the property of an individual or family, assisting companies with the creation and management of their employee pension plans, aiding corporations selling securities to the public (including keeping records of the ownership of any securities issued and dispensing payments on behalf of corporate clients), and numerous other specialized financial services. Trust services generate fee income and often attract new deposits to a bank or other depository institution.

- *Sales of insurance policies* and *the underwriting of insurance risks* have been added to the service menus of many larger bank and nonbank financial institutions, particularly since passage of the Gramm-Leach-Bliley Act, allowing the formation of financial holding companies. Sales of life insurance and property/casualty insurance policies to cover the financial risks of death, ill health, retirement, acts of negligence, and damage to personal and business property have generated substantial fees and commissions for banks and other financial firms offering these services. Larger banking organizations have also recently expanded into insurance underwriting in search of profits from investing and managing policyholder funds.

- As banks and their competitors have expanded into nontraditional product lines they have become premier information-gathering and information-processing businesses, collecting and disseminating extensive personal or inside data about their customers.

This information function helps banks and other financial firms devise new services more closely matched to each customer's service needs. However, it also carries risks (such as identity theft) to the customer whose private data may be shared with other businesses. Passage of the Gramm-Leach-Bliley Act of 1999 grants customers the opportunity to "opt out" of certain information sharing by banks and other financial firms.

Key Terms

fee income, *458*
investment banking, *459*
investment products, *461*
mutual funds, *462*
annuities, *464*
trust services, *467*
life insurance policies, *469*

life insurance
underwriters, *469*
property/casualty insurance
policies, *469*
property/casualty insurance
underwriters, *469*

convergence, *471*
product-line diversification
effect, *471*
economies of scope, *474*
customer privacy, *475*

Problems and Projects

1. Cotter National Bank has recently subscribed through a New York money center bank to an investment products service for its customers. Cotter will offer nonproprietary mutual funds to its customers as well as a variable annuity program for those interested in accumulating savings for retirement and to help with the costs of a college education for their children. The bank's marketing officer is struggling with several important issues, however, and needs your input and advice. For example,

   a. Is the bank likely to be better off offering a nonproprietary fund or should it attempt to help create a proprietary mutual fund service?

   b. What should Cotter do about setting up an investment products division within the bank to offer these two services? Are there any special requirements the bank needs to be aware of in designing the location of that new division, and how it will offer these services?

   c. What risks will the bank be confronted with when it actually begins offering these services? What kind of action plan might be designed to help minimize those risks and make Cotter National's program successful?

2. A banking company decides to expand its service menu to include the underwriting of new security offerings as well as offering traditional lending and deposit services. It discovers that the expected return and risk associated with these two sets of service offerings are as follows:

   Expected return from traditional banking services 10%
   Expected return from security underwriting 15%
   Standard deviation of return from traditional banking services 3%
   Standard deviation of return from security underwriting services 6%
   Correlation of returns between traditional banking and security
     underwriting services . . . . +0.25
   Proportion of revenues expected to be derived from:
     Traditional banking services 85%
     Security underwriting services 15%

   Please calculate the effects of the new service on the banking company's overall return and risk.

Internet Exercises

1. One of the most adventurous of bank service offerings in recent years has been the marketing of stock and bond mutual funds through banking companies. You will find offerings on many financial institution websites. For instances, visit **www.wachovia .com**; click the link for the Investing Center and explore types of investments. One group of mutual funds offered by Wachovia is managed by a subsidiary. What is the name of the subsidiary? Visit the subsidiary's website and see what types of funds it manages.

2. If you want to evaluate mutual funds, explore **www.morningstar.com**. Go to the Morningstar website; click the Funds button and then the Mutual Fund Quickrank link. What are the top five bond funds when measured by five-year annualized total return? What are the top five U.S. stock funds when measured by five-year annualized total return? How do the returns compare?

3. Banking and insurance companies have invaded each other's territory and share information. To gather more information about this growing trend toward convergence in banking and insurance firms, visit **www.financialservicesfacts.org/financial2/today/ convergence/**. Which banks and which insurance firms offer auto and homeowners insurance, life and health insurance, commercial insurance, and commercial banking services? What does this reveal to you?

4. If you are like millions of other financial-service customers, concerned about what financial-service companies may do with your private data, visit the Federal Trade Commission at **www.ftc.gov** and explore current regulations concerning privacy. Go to **www.ftc.gov/privacy/glbact/index.html** and summarize the financial privacy rule and the safeguards rule.

5. If, like millions of other financial-service customers, you are concerned about what your bank or other financial institution's privacy policy is, visit its website. You should find their privacy policy posted. Read the policy and print out a copy.

STANDARD &POOR'S

S&P Market Insight Challenge

1. Use Standard & Poor's Market Insight website (**www.mhhe.com/edumarketinsight**) for this problem. Investment banking and security brokerage activities are important sources of fee income for many financial-service businesses. In the S&P Industry Survey entitled "Investment Services," investment banking and brokerage services are classified by revenue source. For an up-to-date description of these particular revenue sources, click the Industry tab in S&P's Market Insight. The drop-down menu supplies the subindustry category of Investment Banking and Brokerage. Upon choosing this particular subindustry group, you will find a recent downloadable S&P Industry Survey on Investment Services. Download this survey and view the section, "How the Industry Operates," identifying and describing each source of revenue associated with investment banking and security brokerage.

2. Use Standard & Poor's Market Insight website (**www.mhhe.com/edumarketinsight**) for this problem. As you examine the financial-service providers on the S&P Market Insight, Educational version list, you will note that several of these firms have either commercial banking or insurance or investment banking affiliates. List which ones have affiliates or subsidiaries across these industry lines. Do any have all three of these industries represented among their affiliates or subsidiaries? Do these cross-industry affiliations carry any significant advantages for the companies involved? Has their performance really improved after these affiliations occurred? Why or why not?

REAL NUMBERS FOR REAL BANKS

Assignment for Chapter 13

YOUR BANK'S GENERATION OF FEE INCOME

After the passage of the Gramm-Leach-Bliley Act in 1999, financial holding companies were created and many institutions that wanted to broaden their activities and sources of income registered with the Federal Reserve. (In Chapter 3's assignment you determined whether your banking company is registered as a financial holding company.) The Gramm-Leach-Bliley Act also gave banks the go-ahead to expand beyond traditional banking activities within the individual banks. Chapter 13 describes the following nontraditional banking activities that can be used to generate noninterest fee income for financial institutions: (1) investment banking, (2) security trading, (3) insurance underwriting and sales, and (4) trust (fiduciary) activities. In this assignment, we will examine the types of noninterest income generated by your bank's service activities.

Part One: Collecting the Data

We will once again begin this assignment with a visit to the FDIC's SDI website located at **www3.fdic.gov/sdi/main.asp**. Once there, you will collect information from two reports, "Income and Expense" and "Additional Noninterest Income" for a comparative examination of the fee income generated by your bank compared to that of the peer group across two years. Access these reports using the pull-down menus and collect the percentage information for the items listed below. Once again the percentages will be entered as an extension of the information in Spreadsheet 2 in the designated cells. You will need to sum data to provide entries marked with * and **.

(A128)	Your Bank	Peer Group	Your Bank	Peer Group
Date (A129)	12/31/yy	12/31/yy	12/31/yy	12/31/yy
(A130)	Percentage of Average Assets			
Total noninterest income (A131)	%	%	%	%
(A132)	Bank (yyyy)	Peer (yyyy)	Bank (yyyy)	Peer (yyyy)
Fiduciary activities (A133)				
Service charges on deposit accounts (A134)				
Trading account gains and fees (A135)				
Investment banking, advisory, brokerage, and underwriting fees and commissions (A136)				
Venture capital revenue (A137)				
Net servicing and securitization income* (A138)				
Insurance commission fees and income (A139)				
Net gains (losses) on sales of assets (exc securities)** (A140)				
Other noninterest income (A141)				

*Is a sum of net servicing fees and net securitization income.

**Is a sum of net gains (losses) on sales of loans, net gains (losses) on sales of other real estate owned, and net gains (losses) on sales of other assets (excluding securities).

Part Two: Analyzing the Data for Interpretation

A. Extend Rows 128–131 to columns F, G, H, and I where you will calculate noninterest income as a percentage of total operating income (interest income plus noninterest income). For example, the formula for cell F131 would be B131/(B34 + B38) and the formula for cell I131 would be E131/(E34 + E38). Columns F–I should appear as follows:

Your Bank	Peer Group	Your Bank	Peer Group
12/31/yy	12/31/yy	12/31/yy	12/31/yy
Percentage of Total Operating Income			
(F131)%	(G131)%	(H131)%	(I131)%

B. Is noninterest income a significant component of total operating income? Is it more important for your bank than for the peer group? Has this changed across the years? Write one paragraph addressing these issues.

C. Use the chart function in Excel and the data by columns in rows 132 through 141 to create a group of four bar charts illustrating components of noninterest income for your BHC and its peer group over the two-year period. You will be able to select the block and create a single chart to be saved as one separate spreadsheet with just a few clicks of the mouse. To illustrate what you want to create, the chart containing information for NCC and its peer group

(continued)

REAL NUMBERS FOR REAL BANKS

Assignment for Chapter 13 *(continued)*

would appear as shown below (Note: if you have access to a color printer you will not have to transform graphics to be effective in black and white as we have done below):

D. Write one or two paragraphs interpreting your data and discussing your bank's generation of fee income relative to other large institutions (peer group) across the two-year

period. What types of activities have contributed to the fee income generated by your bank? What inferences can you make concerning the potential effects on risk exposure. You may want to incorporate tables using the Excel spreadsheets and reference these in your discussion.

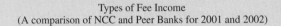

Types of Fee Income
(A comparison of NCC and Peer Banks for 2001 and 2002)

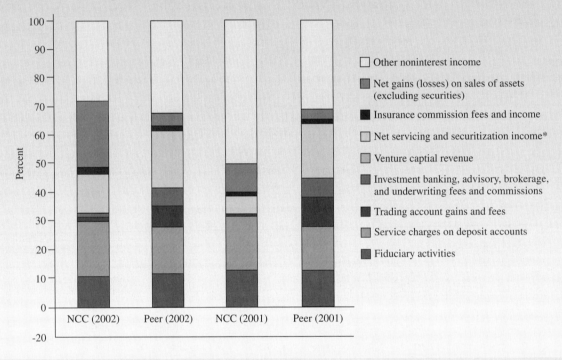

Selected References

For a discussion of fees charged for traditional deposit services, see:

1. Hannan, Timothy H. "Retail Fees of Depository Institutions, 1997–2001." *Federal Reserve Bulletin*, September 2002, pp. 405–413.

For a discussion of investment banking services, see:

2. Hayes, Samuel L. III, and Philip M. Hubbard. *Investment Banking.* Boston: Harvard Business School Press, 1990.

3. Helwege, Jean, and Nellie Lang. "Initial Public Offerings in Hot and Cold Markets." *Finance and Economics Discussion Series*, No. 2003-04, Board of Governors of the Federal Reserve System, Washington, D.C., 2003.

4. Henig, Peter D. "Warburg Who?" at www.redherring.com/insider/1999/0630/invwarburg.html.

For a discussion of the advantages and disadvantages for banks offering investment and insurance products, see:

5. Collins, Sean, and Phillip Mack. *Will Bank Proprietary Mutual Funds Survive? Assessing Their Viability Via Scope and Scale Estimates.* Finance and Discussion Series 95-52, Board of Governors of the Federal Reserve System, December 1995.

6. Federal Reserve System. *Retail Sales of Nondeposit Investment Products: Compliance Checklists.* Washington, D.C., July 1995.

7. Golter, Jay W. "Banks and Mutual Funds." *FDIC Banking Review,* August 1995, pp. 10–20.

8. Neely, Michelle Clark. "Banks and Mutual Funds: Hype or Hope?" *Monetary Trends,* Federal Reserve Bank of St. Louis, March 1997.

9. Engen, Eric M., and Andreas Lehnert. "Mutual Funds and the U.S. Equity Market." *Federal Reserve Bulletin,* December 2000, pp. 797–812.

10. Zinkewicz, Phil. "Trend Toward Banks Buying Agencies Gains Momentum." *Rough Notes Magazine,* 1998 (www.roughnotes.com).

For a detailed discussion of trust services, see:

11. Reed, Edward W., Richard V. Cotter, Edward K. Gill, and Richard K. Smith. *Commercial Banking,* 2nd ed. Englewood Cliffs, NJ: Prentice Hall, 1980.

For a discussion of product-line diversification in banking and financial services, see:

12. Rose, Peter S. "Diversification of the Banking Firm." *The Financial Review* 24, no. 2 (May 1989), pp. 251–280.

13. Stiroh, Kevin J. "Diversification in Banking: Is Noninterest Income the Answer?" *Staff Report No. 154,* Federal Reserve Bank of New York, 2002.

For a discussion of customer privacy issues in offering traditional and nontraditional financial services, see especially:

14. Zaretsky, Adam, M. "A New Universe in Banking after Financial Modernization." *The Regional Economist,* Federal Reserve Bank of St. Louis, April 2000, pp. 5–9.

www.mhhe.com/rose6e

CHAPTER FOURTEEN

The Management of Capital

Key Topics in This Chapter

- The Many Tasks of Capital
- Capital and Risk Exposures
- Types of Capital In Use
- Capital as the Centerpiece of Regulation
- Basel I and Basel II
- Planning to Meet Capital Needs

Introduction

In a book like this one all topics are important, all have a bearing upon the profitability and viability of banks and the institutions that compete with banks for the public's business. But some topics are clearly more important than others. *Capital* is one of those. Raising sufficient capital and retaining enough capital to protect the interests of depositors, borrowers, employees, owners, and the general public is one of the great challenges in bank management and in the management of many competing financial firms as well.

What is **capital?** For bankers and many of their competitors the word *capital* has a special meaning. It refers principally to the funds contributed by the owners of a financial firm. In the case of a commercial bank this means the stockholders—investors in the common and preferred stock that a banking firm has issued. In the case of banking's closest competitors, the thrift institutions, the "owners" may be stockholders if the thrift is a corporation or may be its customers in the case of a credit union or mutual savings bank or savings and loan association. (For a customer-owned thrift, capital consists of an accumulation of reinvested profits.)

What is it that the *owners* contribute? Their money—a portion of their wealth—is placed at the financial firm's disposal in the hope of earning a competitive rate of return on those contributed funds. Sometimes that desired rate of return on the wealth contributed by the owners emerges and sometimes it doesn't. Indeed, if the bank or other financial-service provider fails, the owners may lose everything they invested. Thus, capital consists mainly of owners' funds placed at risk in the pursuit of an expected rate of return commensurate with the risks accepted by the owners.

What form does the owner's investment in the bank or other financial institution take? As we will see in more detail later in this chapter, some of the owners' capital contribution takes the form of *purchases of stock*. Another important component consists of *annual earnings that the owners reinvest in the financial firm*, building up its reserves in the

Capital—how much banks and other financial firms actually hold and how much regulators should require that they hold—has been one of the most controversial topics in the history of the banking industry. Capital is expensive and, therefore, banks and competing financial institutions often seek to minimize the amount of capital they hold. In contrast, regulators operating in the public interest and concerned about bank safety often find themselves demanding more capital from the institutions they supervise. Agreements between bankers and regulators on this topic (and between one set of regulators and another) are often difficult to achieve.

The Basel Agreement on Bank Capital Standards, setting capital requirements for banks in many parts of the world, was an historic breakthrough in 1988 because so many nations were able to agree at the same time on a common set of standards and thereby "level the playing field" for most of the world's largest banking firms. Yet, the track record of problems with Basel, especially with financial managers finding clever ways to take advantage of a relatively rigid set of rules, has shown that, in a sense, the capital problem will never really be "solved" once and for all for banks and their competitors. Setting the amounts of capital financial institutions should hold is likely to be an ongoing process of interaction between bankers, regulators, and the free market.

If you wish to join the ongoing discussions on the Web regarding the Basel Agreement, its recent reforms, and what types of capital banks and similar institutions ought to hold, where can you go? One important site is the Bank for International Settlements (BIS): Publications at **http://www.bis .org/publ/** because the BIS was where the Basel Agreement on Bank Capital originated. Another potentially good source is Regulation Magazine at **http://www.cato.org/pubs/regulation/index .html**. You will also find technical discussions of key capital issues in the International Monetary Fund's Working Papers site at **http:// www.imf.org/external/pubs/cat/wp.cfm**. In addition, a number of the Federal Reserve Banks inside the United States publish working papers at their websites, and some of these discuss the capital issue. Examples include the Federal Reserve Bank of St. Louis Economics Working Paper series displayed at **http://www.stle.frb.org/research/wp** and the Federal Reserve Bank of Cleveland Economic Working Paper series at **http://www.clev.frb.org/ research/workpaper**.

hope that management will profitability invest those retained earnings, increasing the owners' future returns.

Why is capital so important in banking and financial-services management? There are many reasons, as we will see in the pages that follow. Capital performs such indispensable functions as supplying resources to start a new firm, creating a base of resources for future growth and expansion, providing a cushion of protection against risk (including the risk of failure), and promoting public confidence in the long-term viability and survival of a bank or other financial firm. Moreover, capital has become the centerpiece of banking supervision and regulation today—the lever that regulators of the industry can pull whenever the alarm bell sounds in an effort to prevent the collapse of a financial firm. Indeed, it is difficult to name anything else on the balance sheet of a bank or other institution that performs so many vital tasks. *Yes, capital is important.*

The Many Tasks Capital Performs

The capital accounts play several vital roles in supporting the daily operations and ensuring the long-run viability of banks and other financial intermediaries. In the first place, capital provides a cushion against the risk of failure by absorbing financial and operating losses until management can address the institution's problems and restore its profitability.

Second, capital provides the funds needed to charter, organize, and operate a bank or other financial firm before deposits or other sources of funds come flowing in. A new institution needs start-up funding to acquire land, build or lease facilities, purchase equipment, and hire officers and staff even before opening day.

Third, capital promotes public confidence and reassures creditors (including the depositors) concerning an institution's financial strength. Capital must also be strong enough to reassure borrowers that the bank or other lending institution will be able to meet their credit needs even if the economy turns down.

Fourth, capital provides funds for the organization's growth and the development of new services, programs, and facilities. For example, when a bank grows, it needs additional capital to support that growth and to accept the risks that come with offering new services and building new facilities. Most banks and other financial-service providers eventually outgrow the facilities they start with. An infusion of additional capital will permit a bank or other financial firm to expand into larger quarters or build additional branch offices in order to keep pace with its expanding market area and follow its customers with convenient service offerings.

Fifth, capital serves as a regulator of growth, helping to ensure that growth is sustainable in the long run. Both the regulatory authorities and the financial markets require that capital increases roughly in line with the growth of loans and other risky assets. Thus, the cushion to absorb losses is supposed to increase along with a financial institution's growing risk exposure. For example, a bank that expands its loans and deposits too fast will start receiving signals from the market and the regulatory community that its growth must be slowed or additional capital must be acquired.

Relatively recent research evidence suggests that capital has played a key role in the rapid growth of mergers among banks and other financial firms. For example, Peek and Rosengren [9] of the Federal Reserve Bank of Boston find evidence that hundreds of smaller banks have disappeared via merger because of burgeoning growth in large business loans (over $1 million each), which can only be made by bigger banks with stronger capital positions. Both banks' internal loan policies and federal bank regulations limit the maximum size of not fully secured loans made to a single borrower to no more than 15 percent of a bank's unimpaired capital and surplus, while fully collateralized loans are limited to no more than 25 percent of a federally chartered bank's unimpaired capital and surplus. Banks and other lenders whose capital fails to grow fast enough find themselves losing market share in the competition for the largest borrowing customers.

Finally, capital regulation has become an increasingly important tool to limit how much risk exposure banks and competing financial firms can accept. In this role capital not only tends to promote public confidence in the banking and financial system but also serves to protect the government's deposit insurance system from serious losses.

Capital and Risk

Capital and risk are intimately related to each other. Capital itself is mainly the funds contributed by the owners of a bank or other financial-service provider that have been placed there at the *owners' risk*—the risk that the institution will earn a less-than-satisfactory return on the owners' funds or may even fail, with the stockholders recovering little or nothing. The risks facing the owners are substantial. They include credit risk, liquidity risk, interest rate risk, operating risk, exchange risk, and crime risk.

Key Risks in Banking and Financial Institutions' Management

Credit Risk   There is, first of all, *credit risk*. For example, banks make loans and take on securities that are nothing more than promises to pay. When borrowing customers fail to make some or all of their promised interest and principal payments, these defaulted loans and securities result in losses that can eventually erode capital. Because owners' capital is usually no more than 10 percent of the volume of loans and risky securities (and often much less than that), it doesn't take too many defaults on loans and securities before capital simply becomes inadequate to absorb further losses. At this point, the bank or other financial firm fails and will close unless the regulatory authorities elect to keep it afloat until a buyer can be found.

Liquidity Risk Banks and other depository institutions encounter substantial *liquidity risk*—the danger of running out of cash when cash is needed to cover deposit withdrawals and to meet the credit requests of good customers. For example, if a bank cannot raise cash in timely fashion, it is likely to lose many of its customers and suffer a loss in earnings for its owners. If the cash shortage persists, it may lead to runs on the bank and ultimate collapse. The inability to meet liquidity needs at reasonable cost is often a prime signal that a financial institution is in serious trouble.

Interest Rate Risk Banks and their closest competitors also encounter risk to their *spread*—that is, the danger that revenues from earning assets will decline or that interest expenses will rise significantly, squeezing the spread between revenues and expenses and thereby reducing net income. Changes in the spread between revenues and expenses are usually related to either *portfolio management decisions* (i.e., changes in the composition of assets and liabilities) or *interest rate risk*—the probability that fluctuating interest rates will result in significant appreciation or depreciation in the value of and the return from the institution's assets. In recent years, banks and competing financial firms have found ways to reduce their interest rate risk exposure, but such risks have not been completely eliminated—nor can they be.

Filmtoid
What 1977 comedy revolves around two bank officers, played by Burgess Meredith and Richard Basehart, covering up employee embezzlement in the face of an on-site examination by regulators?
Answer: *The Great Bank Hoax*.

Operating Risk Financial-service providers also face significant **operating risk** due to possible breakdowns in quality control, inefficiencies in producing and delivering services, simple errors in judgment by management, fluctuations in the economy that impact the demand for each financial service, and shifts in competition as new suppliers of financial services enter or leave a particular financial firm's market area. These changes can adversely affect revenue flows, operating costs, and the value of the owner's investment in the institution (e.g., its stock price).

Exchange Risk Larger commercial banks and securities firms face **exchange risk** from their dealings in foreign currency. The world's most tradable currencies float with changing market conditions today. Banks and their international competitors trading in these currencies for themselves and their customers continually run the risk of adverse price movements on both the buying and selling sides of this market.

Crime Risk Finally, banks and other financial firms encounter significant **crime risk.** Fraud or embezzlement by employees or directors can severely weaken a financial institution and, in some instances, lead to its failure. In fact, the Federal Deposit Insurance Corporation lists fraud and embezzlement from insiders as one of the prime causes of recent bank closings. Moreover, the large amounts of money that banks keep in their vaults often prove to be an irresistible attraction to outsiders. As the famous outlaw Jesse James was reputed to have said when asked why he robbed banks, "because that's where the money is."

Robberies of depository institutions approached record levels during the 1970s and 1980s. These thefts were frequently a by-product of bankers' efforts to make their lobbies, drive-in windows, and teller machines more accessible to the public. While the 1990s brought a decline in the daily rate at which robberies were occurring, the extent and intensity of bank crime remain high by historical standards. The focus of robberies has shifted somewhat with changes in technology; theft from ATMs and from patrons using electronic networks has become one of the most problematic aspects of crime risk among depository institutions today.

Defenses against Risk

Of course, banks and competing financial firms are not devoid of protection against these many risks. In fact, there are several rings of defense that owners can rely upon to protect their institution's financial position. Among them are quality management, diversification, deposit insurance, and, ultimately, owners' capital.

Quality Management   One of these defenses is *quality management*—the ability of top-notch managers to move swiftly to deal with problems before they overwhelm a bank or other financial firm.

Diversification   Diversification of a financial institution's sources and uses of funds also has risk-reducing benefits. For example, banks generally strive to achieve two types of risk-reducing diversification: portfolio and geographic. **Portfolio diversification** means spreading out credit accounts and deposits among a wide variety of customers, including large and small business accounts, different industries, and households with a variety of sources of income and collateral. **Geographic diversification** refers to seeking out customers located in different communities or countries, which presumably will experience different economic conditions. These forms of diversification are most effective in reducing the risk of loss when cash flows from different groups of customers move in different patterns over time. Thus, declines in cash flow from one customer segment may be at least partially offset by increases in cash flow from other customer segments.

Deposit Insurance   Still another line of defense against the risks inherent in banking is *deposit insurance*. The Federal Deposit Insurance Corporation, established in the United States in 1934 and today protecting depositors holding up to $100,000 in any federally insured bank or thrift institution, was designed to promote public confidence in the banking system. While it has not stopped banks and thrifts from failing, the FDIC appears to have stopped runs on neighboring depository institutions when any one of them fails. Moreover, its power to examine banks and thrifts, issue cease and desist orders, levy civil money penalties, and seek criminal prosecution of violators of federal banking laws inhibits much risk taking by management and shareholders. This is why most industrialized countries today have some form of deposit insurance system.

Owners' Capital   When all else fails, it is *owners' capital* (net worth) that forms the ultimate defense against risk. Owners' capital absorbs losses from bad loans, poor securities investments, crime, and management misjudgment so that a bank or other financial firm can keep operating until its problems are corrected and its losses are recovered. Only when losses are so large that they overwhelm not only all the other defenses but also the owners' capital will the institution be forced to close its doors. Owners' capital is the last line of defense against failure. Thus, the greater the risk of failure, from whatever source, the more capital a financial institution should hold.

Types of Capital

Banks and other financial-service companies use several different types of capital:

1. **Common stock,** measured by the par (face) value of common equity shares outstanding, which pay a variable return depending on whether the issuing institution's board of directors votes to pay a dividend.

2. **Preferred stock,** measured by the par value of any shares outstanding that promise to pay a fixed rate of return (dividend rate); preferred stock may be perpetual, have only limited life, or be issued as trust preferred stock.

3. **Surplus,** representing the excess amount above each share of stock's par value paid in by the institution's shareholders.

4. **Undivided profits,** representing the net earnings that have been retained in the business rather than being paid out as dividends.

5. **Equity reserves,** representing funds set aside for contingencies such as legal action against the institution, as well as providing a reserve for dividends expected to be paid but not yet declared and a sinking fund to retire stock or debt in the future.

6. **Subordinated debentures,** representing long-term debt capital contributed by outside investors, whose claims legally follow (i.e., are subordinated to) the claims of depositors; these debt securities may carry a convertibility feature, permitting their future exchange for shares of stock.

7. **Minority interest in consolidated subsidiaries,** where the bank or other financial firm holds ownership shares in other businesses.

8. **Equity commitment notes,** which are debt securities repayable only from the sale of stock.

Relative Importance of the Different Sources of Capital

To get some idea of the relative importance of the different kinds of capital we examine the capital account for all U.S.-insured banks. Table 14–1 shows that these various sources of capital are by no means equal in importance. First, the *surplus* market value of all common and preferred stock above the stock's face or par value represents the largest proportion of U.S. bank capital, accounting for just over 40 percent of all long-term debt and equity capital. Close behind is *undivided profits* (or retained earnings) and capital reserves, representing just a fraction under 40 percent of U.S. banks' capitalization. The remaining 20 percent is divided up among all other types of capital, including *long-term debt* (subordinated notes and debentures) at close to 13 percent and the *par value of common stock* at almost 5 percent.

Preferred stock is relatively insignificant—less than 1 percent of the U.S. banking industry's capital—though preferred has increased in importance in recent years at larger banks and bank holding companies around the world. Bank preferred stock often carries floating dividend rates and a callability or redeemability feature that allows management to call in outstanding preferred shares and pay off the shareholders when it is financially advantageous to do so. However, bank preferred stock has been slow to win the confidence of

TABLE 14–1
Capital Accounts of
FDIC-Insured U.S.
Commercial Banks
(December 31, 2002)

Source: Federal Deposit
Insurance Corporation.

Forms of Capital	U.S. FDIC-Insured Commercial Banks	
	Amount in $ Billions	Percent of Total
Long-term debt capital:		
Subordinated notes and debentures	$ 94.7	12.8%
Equity capital:		
Common stock, par value	30.1	4.1
Perpetual preferred stock, par value	6.0	0.8
Surplus	320.2	43.1
Undivided profits and capital reserves	291.6	39.3
Total equity capital	$647.9	87.2%
Total long-term debt and equity capital	$742.6	100.0%

Note: Columns may not add to totals due to rounding.

many investors, in part because of bad experiences during the Great Depression of the 1930s when many troubled banks sold preferred shares just to stay afloat. Thus, many investors associate preferred stock with financial distress in banking.

A unique form of preferred stock that emerged recently is *trust preferred stock.* This hybrid type of equity capital is issued to investors through a trust company, and the funds raised are loaned to the bank using this capital-raising device. Thus, trust-issued preferred stock generates dividends that are tax deductible for the bank involved. As with other forms of preferred stock, the bank in question can miss making dividend payments and still avoid bankruptcy. Moreover, this unique form of stock is considered to be part of a bank's core (or Tier 1) capital for purposes of satisfying banking regulations (especially the Basel Agreement on Bank Capital rules discussed later in this chapter), making trust preferred stock cheaper than conventional types of common and preferred stocks. With all of the foregoing advantages, it's no wonder that many banks (especially the largest ones) have some trust preferred stock outstanding. However, a 2003 ruling by the Financial Accounting Standards Board (FASB) may significantly reduce the advantages of trust preferred stock for some issuing firms, requiring these companies to classify the trust preferred shares as debt and their payments to investors as interest payments rather than stock dividends.

Subordinated notes and *debentures* are a relatively small component of bank capital but a growing source of long-term funding for banks. Regulations require that these capital notes be subordinated to the claims of general creditors of the bank, including the depositors. Thus, if a bank closes and its assets are liquidated, the depositors have first claim on the proceeds and investors in debentures have a secondary claim. However, subordinated debtholders have a prior claim over common and preferred stockholders against the bank's earnings and assets.

Bank holding companies have issued substantial quantities of subordinated debt in recent years (especially to large institutional buyers such as pension funds and insurance companies). Frequently, such notes are callable shortly after issue and carry either fixed or floating interest rates (often tied to interest rates on government securities or short-term Eurodollar deposits). One distinct advantage of subordinated debt from a regulatory viewpoint is that it provides a form of *market discipline* for banks. Because federal insurance does not cover debt subordinated to deposits, investors in subordinated notes will demand higher yields on their securities due to the bank's acceptance of more risk. Holders of subordinated debt tend to be more risk sensitive than depositors and will therefore monitor bank behavior more closely, probably reducing the incidence of bank failure. Subordinated notes and debentures

generally can be issued successfully only by medium-size and larger banks and bank holding
companies whose credit standing is trusted by securities investors. Many securities dealers
simply refuse to handle small-bank debt issues because of the cost and risk involved.

The composition of capital is markedly different for the largest versus the smallest
banks. The smallest banks, for example, rely most heavily upon *retained earnings* (undivided profits) to build their capital positions and issue minuscule amounts of long-term
debt (subordinated notes and debentures). In contrast, the biggest banks rely principally
upon the surplus value of their stock sold in the financial marketplace, as well as retained
earnings, and also issue significant amounts of long-term debt capital. These differences
reflect, in part, the greater ability of the biggest banks to sell their capital securities in the
open market and attract thousands of investors, while the smallest institutions, having
only limited access to the financial markets, must depend principally upon their ability to
generate adequate income and retain a significant portion of those earnings in order to
build an acceptable capital cushion.

Nevertheless, it is generally the smallest banks that maintain the thickest cushion of
capital relative to their asset size. For example, at year-end 2002, the smallest American
banks (each holding less than $100 million in aggregate assets) posted an overall ratio of
total equity and debt capital to total assets of 11.1 percent, compared to a 9.9 percent
capital-to-asset ratio for medium-size banks (with assets totaling $100 million to $1 billion) and 10.6 percent for the largest U.S. FDIC-insured banks (whose asset holdings each
exceed $1 billion). Many authorities in the field believe that the smallest banking firms
should maintain larger capital-to-asset ratios because these smallest institutions are less
well diversified, both geographically and by product line, and, therefore, run a greater risk
of failing. Greater failure risk, in turn, poses a larger risk of loss to the government insurance fund that protects the public's deposits.

Concept Check

14–4. What forms of capital are in use today? What are
the key differences between the different types of
capital?

14–5. Measured by volume and percentage of total capital, what are the most important and least impor-

tant forms of capital held by U.S.-insured banks?
Why do you think this is so?

14–6. How do small banks differ from large banks in the
composition of their capital accounts and in the
total volume of capital they hold relative to their
assets? Why do you think these differences exist?

One of the Great Issues in the History of Banking: How Much Capital Is Really Needed?

How much capital a bank should hold has been one of the most controversial issues in
the history of the banking industry. Banks are at the center of the financial system. If they
fail because of a perceived shortage of capital, those failures could threaten the stability
of the whole financial system. Much of this historic controversy has evolved around two
questions:

1. Who should set capital standards for banks, the market or regulatory agencies?
2. What is a reasonable standard for bank capital?

Regulatory Approach to Evaluating Capital Needs

Reasons for Capital Regulation   The capital position of banks has been regulated for generations—longer than any other financial firm. Banks must meet minimum capital requirements before they can be chartered, and they must hold at least the minimum required level of capital throughout their corporate life. Regulatory agencies also indicate the forms of capital that are acceptable. As Wall [11] notes, the fundamental purposes of regulating bank capital are threefold:

1. To limit the risk of failures.
2. To preserve public confidence.
3. To limit losses to the federal government arising from deposit insurance claims.

The underlying assumption is that the private marketplace cannot accomplish all three of these objectives simultaneously because the market does not correctly price the impact of failures on the banking system's stability, nor is the market likely to accurately price the cost of bank failure to the deposit insurance fund.

Banks are unique in that they hold an unusually large proportion of short-term liabilities (especially demand deposits) that can be withdrawn immediately when public confidence falls. Few banks are in a position to liquidate their loan portfolios immediately when threatened with massive deposit withdrawals. Moreover, the managers of individual banks do not consider the possible external effects of their risk taking on other financial institutions, which may be dragged down by the collapse of neighboring institutions.

Large bank failures are a special problem, as Wall [11] observes. The failure of a big bank attracts significant media attention, causing depositors to raise questions about the soundness of *their* banks. Moreover, the largest banking organizations generally have a high proportion of nondeposit liabilities and large-denomination deposits that are not adequately covered by insurance. The failure of a large bank can have a greater impact on the government's deposit insurance fund than the failures of a considerable number of small insured banks and thrifts.

One of the damaging side effects of government-funded deposit insurance is that it lowers the normal level of vigilance among depositors over bank and thrift safety and risk taking. Feeling fully protected, most depositors do not monitor the risk of the depository institutions they patronize, nor do they penalize those banks that take on excessive risk by moving their funds to lower-risk institutions. This "moral hazard" feature of government-sponsored insurance encourages insured banks and thrift institutions to drive their capital-to-deposit ratios lower, thus exposing government insurance funds to even greater risk of loss.

Research Evidence   Considerable research has been conducted in recent years on the issue of whether the private marketplace or government regulatory agencies exert a bigger effect on bank risk taking and on capital decisions. The results of these studies are varied, but most find that the private marketplace is probably more important than government regulation in the long run in determining the amount and type of capital banks and other financial firms must hold. However, recently government regulation appears to have become nearly as important as the private marketplace by tightening capital regulations and imposing minimum capital requirements.

The financial markets do seem to react to the differential risk positions of banks by downgrading the debt and equity securities offered by riskier banking companies. However, as Eisenbeis and Gilbert [3] note, we are not at all sure market disciplining works as well for small and medium-size insured banks and thrifts whose securities are not as actively traded in the open market. Nor is it clear that the risk premiums the market imposes on lower-quality bank securities (in the form of lower prices and higher interest rates) are really large enough to discipline bank risk taking. Also, while the market may make efficient use of all the information it possesses, some of the most pertinent information needed to assess a bank's true level of risk exposure is hidden from the market and is known only to bank examiners.

Is a bank's capital-to-assets ratio significantly related to its probability of failure? Most research studies find little connection between capital ratios and the incidence of failure. For example, Santomero and Vinso [1] found that increased capital does not materially lower a bank's failure risk. Many banks would still fail even if their capital were doubled or tripled—a conclusion backed up by a study in New England by Peek and Rosengren [9], which found that four-fifths of banks failing there in the 1980s and early 1990s were classified by examiners as "well capitalized" before they failed. It is by no means certain that imposing higher capital requirements will reduce banking risk. As Wall [11] observes, banks confronted with higher capital requirements may take on more risk in other aspects of their operations in order to keep from earning lower returns.

Concept Check

14–7. What is the rationale for having the government set capital standards for banks and other financial institutions as opposed to letting the private marketplace set those standards?

14–8. What evidence does recent research provide on the role of the private marketplace in determining capital standards?

14–9. According to recent research, does capital prevent a bank or other financial institution from failing?

The Basel Agreement on International Bank Capital Standards: An Historic Contract among Leading Nations

While research evidence on the benefits and costs of imposing capital requirements on banks and other financial-service firms continues, the regulatory community has taken important steps in recent years to strengthen and improve government's role in assessing how much capital commercial banks really need and in making sure banks comply with government-imposed capital standards.

In 1988 the Federal Reserve Board, representing the United States, and representatives from other leading countries (including Belgium, Canada, France, Germany, Italy, Japan, the Netherlands, Spain, Sweden, Switzerland, the United Kingdom, and Luxembourg) announced agreement on new bank capital standards—usually referred to as the **Basel Agreement** for the city in Switzerland where this agreement was reached. The new Basel standards were to be applied uniformly to all banking institutions in their respective countries (with modifications for varying local conditions), even though the original guidelines were intended only for "internationally active" banks.

Formally approved in July 1988, the Basel capital rules were designed to encourage leading banks around the world to keep their capital positions strong, reduce inequalities in capital requirements among different countries to promote fair competition, and catch up with recent rapid changes in financial services and financial innovation (such as the enormous expansion of securitization and of the off-balance-sheet commitments banks have made in recent years). The new capital requirements were phased in gradually to allow bankers time to adjust. The full set of initial Basel standards went into effect in January 1993, though adjustments and modifications continued to be made for years, particularly in allowing or denying new capital instruments to be added, in changing the relative weights attached to various bank assets and types of capital, and in adjusting for different types of risk exposure. The Federal Reserve Board announced that the new capital guidelines would also apply, with small modifications, to the state-chartered member banks it examines regularly and to bank holding companies on a consolidated basis.

Basel I   The current Basel capital standards are known today as **Basel I.** Under the terms of Basel I, the various sources of bank capital were divided into two tiers:

Tier 1 capital (core capital) includes common stock and surplus, undivided profits (retained earnings), qualifying noncumulative perpetual preferred stock, minority interest in the equity accounts of consolidated subsidiaries, and selected identifiable intangible assets less goodwill and other intangible assets.[1]

Tier 2 capital (supplemental capital) includes the allowance (reserves) for loan and lease losses, subordinated debt capital instruments, mandatory convertible debt, intermediate-term preferred stock, cumulative perpetual preferred stock with unpaid dividends, and equity notes and other long-term capital instruments that combine both debt and equity features.

To determine each bank's *total regulatory capital*, regulators must deduct from the sum of Tier 1 and Tier 2 capital several additional items, including investments in unconsolidated subsidiaries, capital securities held by the bank that were issued by other depository institutions and are held under a reciprocity agreement, activities pursued by savings and loan associations that may have been acquired by a banking organization but are not permissible for national banks, and any other deductions that the bank's principal regulatory supervisor may demand.

---

[1] Banks are allowed to record an intangible asset known as *goodwill* on their balance sheets, which is an asset that arises when the stock of a bank or nonbank business is purchased for cash at a price that exceeds the firm's book value. The goodwill that an established banking firm has attracted by providing good service to its customers helps explain the extra market value the bank has as a going concern over its book value. Most regulatory agencies do *not* allow goodwill to count as bank capital. However, another intangible asset found in most banks is called *identifiable intangible assets*—intangibles other than goodwill; some portion of these intangibles *is* allowed to be counted as part of a bank's capital. One important identifiable intangible asset today is *mortgage servicing rights* (MSRSs), in which a bank can earn income by collecting and distributing loan payments and monitoring borrower compliance with the terms of loans.

Still another prominent identifiable intangible today is *purchased credit card relationships* (PCCRs). A bank or other financial firm buying into a credit card program acquires access to a new group of potential customers who may need future cash advances and other services that will generate expected profits for the bank in the future. Thus, PCCRs hold the promise of future income for a financial institution acquiring this intangible asset.

In February 1993 the Federal Reserve Board announced that purchased mortgage servicing rights (PMSRs) and PCCRs would be counted as qualifying intangible assets and would not have to be deducted from a bank's capital, provided they do not exceed 50 percent of Tier 1 capital with all intangibles included. Later, in 1997, federal regulators proposed that the limitation on the amount of mortgage servicing rights when combined with purchased credit card relationships (PCCRSs) be increased from 50 percent to 100 percent of Tier 1 capital. However, an added requirement was that PCCRs not exceed 25 percent of Tier 1 capital. Any amounts of PMSRs or PCCRs above the maximum allowable amount must be deducted from core capital. Moreover, PMSRs and PCCRs must be included in the calculation of a bank's total risk-weighted assets with a risk weight of 100 percent. Other identifiable intangibles must be deducted from Tier 1 capital and are not to be included in a bank's risk-weighted assets for purposes of determining its capital requirements.

Current capital requirements for a bank to qualify as adequately capitalized include these:

1. The ratio of core capital (Tier 1) to total risk-weighted assets must be at least 4 percent.
2. The ratio of total capital (the sum of Tier 1 and Tier 2 capital) to total risk-weighted assets must be at least 8 percent, with the amount of Tier 2 capital limited to 100 percent of Tier 1 capital.[2]

Calculating Risk-Weighted Assets under Basel I If a bank must compare its Tier 1 and Tier 2 capital to its total risk-weighted assets in order to determine if it is adequately capitalized, what exactly are *risk-weighted assets* under the terms of Basel I?

Each asset item on a bank's balance sheet and each off-balance-sheet commitment it has made are multiplied by a *risk-weighting factor* designed to reflect its credit risk exposure. Among the most closely watched off-balance-sheet items are standby letters of credit that banks issue to back the general-obligation notes and bonds of state and local governments and the loans and security issues of business firms and the long-term, legally binding credit commitments banks often make to their corporate customers.

Here is an example of how bankers can calculate their minimum required level of capital under Basel I standards. Suppose a bank has $6,000 in total capital, $100,000 in total assets, and the following balance sheet and off-balance-sheet (OBS) items:

Balance Sheet Items (Assets)	
Cash	$ 5,000
U.S. Treasury securities	20,000
Deposit balances held at domestic banks	5,000
Loans secured by first liens on 1- to 4-family residential properties	5,000
Loans to private corporations	65,000
Total balance sheet assets	$100,000
Off-Balance-Sheet (OBS) Items	
Standby letters of credit backing general-obligation debt issues of U.S. municipal governments	$ 10,000
Long-term, legally binding credit commitments to private corporations	20,000
Total off-balance-sheet items	$ 30,000

This bank's total capital to total balance-sheet assets ratio would be

$$\$6,000 \div \$100,000 = 6.00 \text{ percent}$$

However, the international capital standards are based upon risk-weighted assets, not total assets. To compute this bank's risk-weighted assets under Basel I, we may proceed as follows:

1. Compute the *credit-equivalent amount* of each off-balance-sheet (OBS) item. This figure is supposed to translate each OBS item into the equivalent amount of a direct loan considered to be of equal risk to the bank.

[2] The international capital standard permits subordinated debt with an original average maturity of at least five years to count toward required supplemental capital (Tier 2). The combined maximum amount of subordinated debt and intermediate-term preferred stock that qualifies as Tier 2 capital is limited to 50 percent of Tier 1 capital (net of goodwill and any other intangibles required to be deducted). Allowance for loan and lease losses also counts as supplemental capital, provided the loan-loss reserves are *general* (not specific) reserves and do not exceed 1.25 percent of a bank's risk-weighted assets. The components of Tier 2 capital are subject to the discretion of bank regulatory agencies in each nation covered by the Basel Agreement.

Off-Balance-Sheet (OBS) Items	Face Value		Conversion Factor		Credit Equivalent Amount
Standby letters of credit (SLCs) issued by bank to back municipal bonds and other direct credit substitutes, asset sales with recourse and repurchase agreements, and forward asset purchases	$10,000	×	1.00	=	$10,000
Long-term credit commitments made to private corporations	$20,000	×	0.50	=	$10,000

2. Multiply each balance sheet item and the credit-equivalent amount of each OBS item by its *risk weight*, as determined by the regulatory authorities. The weights given to each item in the bank's portfolio are 0 percent for cash, U.S. government securities, including GNMA mortgage-backed securities, and unconditionally cancelable credit commitments; 20 percent for deposits held at other banks and short-term self-liquidating trade-related contingencies; 50 percent for home mortgage loans and note-issuance facilities and credit commitments over one year; and 100 percent for corporate loans and credit commitments and all other claims on the private sector as well as bank premises and other fixed assets.

In the case of the bank we are using as an example, it would have the following risk-weighted assets:

0 Percent Risk-Weighting Category	
Cash	$ 5,000
U.S. Treasury securities	20,000
	$25,000 × 0 = $ 0

20 Percent Risk-Weighting Category	
Balances at domestic banks	$ 5,000
Credit-equivalent amounts of	10,000
SLCs backing bonds of U.S. municipalities	$15,000 × 0.20 = $ 3,000

50 Percent Risk-Weighting Category	
Loans secured by first liens on 1- to 4-family residential properties	$ 5,000 × 0.50 = $ 2,500

100 Percent Risk-Weighting Category	
Loans to private corporations	$65,000
Credit-equivalent amounts of long-term commitments to private corporations	10,000
	$75,000 × 1.00 = $75,000
Total risk-weighted assets held by this bank	$80,500

Calculating the Capital-to-Risk-Weighted Assets Ratio under Basel I   Once we know a bank's total risk-weighted assets and the total amount of its capital (Tier 1 + Tier 2) we can determine its capital adequacy ratio as required under the Basel I Agreement on International Capital Standards. The key formula is this:

$$\begin{array}{l} \text{Capital adequacy} \\ \text{ratio under the} \\ \text{Basel I Agreement} \\ \text{on International} \\ \text{Bank Capital Standards} \end{array} = \frac{\text{Total regulatory capital (or Tier 1 + Tier 2 Capital)}}{\text{Total risk-weighted assets}}$$

For the bank whose risk-weighted assets we just calculated above at $80,500, which currently has $6,000 in total regulatory capital, its capital adequacy ratio would be as follows:

$$\frac{\text{Total regulatory capital}}{\text{Total risk-weighted assets}} = \frac{\$6,000}{\$80,500} = 0.0745, \text{or } 7.45 \text{ percent}$$

Note that this bank's total-regulatory-capital-to-risk-weighted assets ratio of 7.45 percent is more than the required minimum for Tier 1 capital of 4 percent but below the combined Tier 1 plus Tier 2 capital requirement of 8 percent. Therefore, this bank would have to raise new capital to comply with the standards called for by Basel I.

Capital Requirements Attached to Derivatives

Recently, the Basel I capital standards were adjusted to take account of the risk exposure that banks face today from *derivatives*—futures, options, interest rate and currency swaps, interest rate cap and floor contracts, and other instruments designed to hedge against changing currency prices, interest rates, and positions in commodities. Many of these instruments expose a bank to *counterparty risk*—the danger that a customer the bank has entered into a contract with will fail to pay or to perform, forcing the bank to find a replacement contract with another party that may be less satisfactory.

One significant factor that limits risk exposure in many of these cases is that most futures and option contracts are traded on organized exchanges, such as the London International Financial Futures Exchange or the Chicago Mercantile Exchange, that guarantee the performance of each party to these contracts. Thus, if a bank's customer fails to deliver under an exchange-traded futures or options contract, the exchange involved will make delivery in full to the bank. In these instances banks would not normally be expected to post capital behind such exchange-traded contracts.

For other types of contracts, however, the revised Basel I required bankers, first, to convert each risk-exposed contract into its credit-equivalent amount as though it were a risky asset listed on a bank's balance sheet. Then, the credit-equivalent amount of each interest rate or currency contract is multiplied by a prespecified risk weight. Recent research suggests that interest rate contracts display considerably less risk exposure than do foreign-currency contracts. Accordingly, the Basel I credit-conversion factors for interest rate derivatives were set far lower than for contracts tied to the value of foreign currencies. For example, interest rate contracts with a maturity of one year or less were assigned a 0 credit-conversion factor, while rate contracts over one year carry a credit conversion factor of only 0.005 or 0.5 percent. In contrast, currency-based contracts one year or less to maturity carry a credit-conversion factor of 0.01 or 1 percent and those with maturities over one year have been assigned a credit-conversion factor of 0.05 or 5 percent.

In determining the credit-equivalent amounts of these off-balance-sheet contracts, Basel I required a banker to divide each contract's risk exposure to the bank into two categories: (1) potential market risk exposure and (2) current market risk exposure. *Potential market risk exposure* refers to the danger of loss at some future time if the customer who entered into a market-based contract with the bank fails to perform. In contrast, the *current market risk exposure* is designed to measure the risk of loss to the bank should a customer default today on its contract, which would compel the bank to replace the failed contract with a new one. Basel I required bankers to determine the current market value for a contract that is similar to the contract they have actually made with a customer in order to figure out the latter's replacement cost. Future cash flows expected under current contracts must be discounted back to their present values using today's interest rates, currency, or commodity prices to determine the value of such a contract in today's market.

Once the replacement cost of a contract was determined, the estimated potential market risk exposure amount was then added to the estimated current market risk exposure amount to derive the total credit-equivalent amount of each contract. This total is multiplied by the correct risk weight, which in most cases is 50 percent, or 0.50, to find the equivalent amount of risk-weighted bank assets represented by each contract. We then add this risk-weighted amount to all of a bank's other risk-weighted assets to derive its total on-balance-sheet and off-balance-sheet risk-weighted assets. As we saw in the preceding section, the total of all risk-weighted assets was then divided into each bank's total regulatory capital (Tier 1 plus Tier 2) to determine if it was adequately capitalized.

For example, consider again the bank whose risk-weighted assets we previously calculated to be $80,500. Suppose this bank has also entered into a $100,000 five-year interest rate swap agreement with one of its customers and a $50,000 three-year currency swap agreement with another customer. First, we multiply the face amount (notional value) of these two contracts by the appropriate credit conversion factor for each instrument—in this case, by 0.005 for the interest rate swap contract and by 0.05 for the currency swap contract—in order to find the bank's potential market risk exposure from each instrument. Second, we add the estimated replacement cost if suddenly the bank had to substitute new swap contracts at today's prices and interest rates for the original contracts. Let's assume these replacement costs amounted to $2,500 for the interest rate contract and $1,500 for the currency contract. Then:

Interest Rate and Currency Contracts	Face Amount of Contract	Conversion Factor for Potential Market Risk Exposure		Potential Market Risk Exposure		Current Market Risk Exposure (replacement cost)		Credit-Equivalent Volume of Interest Rate and Currency Contracts
Five-year interest rate swap contract	$100,000	× 0.005	=	$ 500	+	$2,500	=	$3,000
Three-year currency swap contract	$ 50,000	× 0.05	=	$2,500	+	$1,500	=	$4,000

The total credit-equivalent amount of both of these contracts combined is $7,000.

The final step is to multiply this total by the correct risk weight, which is 50 percent, or 0.50. This step gives the result:

$$\begin{array}{c}\text{Volume of risk-weighted assets}\\\text{represented by off-}\\\text{balance-sheet interest rate and}\\\text{currency contracts}\end{array} = \begin{array}{c}\text{Credit-equivalent}\\\text{volume of}\\\text{interest rate}\\\text{and currency contracts}\end{array} \times \begin{array}{c}\text{Credit}\\\text{risk}\\\text{weight}\end{array}$$

$$= \$7,000 \times 0.50 = \$3,500$$

EXAMPLES OF RISK WEIGHTS APPLIED TO BANK ASSETS AND OFF-BALANCE-SHEET ITEMS UNDER THE BASEL I AGREEMENT

A. Credit Risk Categories for Bank Assets on the Balance Sheet

Credit Risk Weights Used in the Calculation of a Bank's Risk Weighted Assets (percent of amount of each asset)	Assumed Amount of Credit Risk Exposure from Each Category of Bank Assets	Categories or Types of Bank Assets
0%	Zero credit risk	Cash; deposits at the Federal Reserve Banks; U.S. Treasury bills, notes, and bonds of all maturities; Government National Mortgage Association (GNMA) mortgage-backed securities; and debt securities issued by governments of the world's leading industrial countries belonging to the Organization for Economic Cooperation and Development (OECD).
20	Low credit risk	Checkbook float, interbank (correspondent) deposits, general obligation bonds and notes issued by states and local governments, securities issued or backed by U.S. government agencies, and mortgage-backed securities issued or guaranteed by the Federal National Mortgage Association (FNMA) or by the Federal Home Loan Mortgage Corporation (FHLMC).
50	Moderate credit risk	Residential (home) mortgage loans, selected multifamily housing loans that are well secured and perform adequately, and revenue bonds issued by state and local government units or agencies.
100	Highest credit risk	Commercial and industrial (business) loans, credit card loans, real property, investments in bank subsidiary companies, and all other assets not listed previously.

B. Credit Risk Categories for Off-Balance-Sheet Items

Conversion Factor for Converting Off-Balance-Sheet Items into Equivalent Amounts of On-Balance-Sheet Assets	Credit Risk Weights (percent)	Assumed Amount of Credit Risk	Categories or Types of Off-Balance-Sheet Items
0	0%	Zero or lowest credit risk	Loan commitments with less than one year to go, guarantees of federal government borrowings.
0.20	20	Low credit risk	Standby credit letters backing the issue of state and local government general obligation bonds.
0.20	100	Modest credit risk	Trade-based commercial letters of credit and bankers' acceptances.
0.50	100	Moderate credit risk	Standby credit letters guaranteeing a customer's future performance and unused bank loan commitments covering periods longer than a year.
1.00	100	Highest credit risk	Standby credit letters issued to back the repayment of commercial paper.

C. Credit Risk Categories for Derivatives and Other Market-Based Contracts Not Shown on a Bank's Balance Sheet

Conversion Factor for Converting Interest Rate and Currency Contracts into Equivalent Amounts of On-Balance-Sheet Assets	Credit Risk Weights (percent)	Assumed Amount of Credit Risk	Categories or Types of Off-Balance-Sheet Currency and Interest-Rate Contracts
0	50%	Lowest credit risk	Interest rate contracts one year or less to maturity.
0.005	50	Modest credit risk	Interest rate contracts over one year to maturity.
0.01	50	Moderate credit risk	Currency contracts one year or less to maturity.
0.05	50	Highest credit risk	Currency contracts over one year to maturity.

Source: Board of Governors of the Federal Reserve System.

To make use of this result let's return to our previous example. Recall that the bank we examined earlier held total regulatory capital of $6,000, and total risk-weighted assets of $80,500. Its total risk-weighted assets included total on-balance-sheet assets of $68,500 and off-balance-sheet standby credit letters and corporate loan commitments of $12,000. We now must add to these other assets the $3,500 in risk-weighted currency and interest rate contracts that we just determined. In this case the bank's ratio of total regulatory capital to risk-weighted assets would be as follows:

$$
\begin{aligned}
\text{Total regulatory capital} \div \text{Total risk-weighted assets} &= \frac{\text{Total (Tier 1 + Tier 2) capital}}{\substack{\text{Risk-weighted} \\ \text{on-balance-sheet} \\ \text{assets}} + \substack{\text{Risk-weighted} \\ \text{off-balance-sheet} \\ \text{assets}}} \\
&= \frac{\$6,000}{(\$68,500 + \$12,000 + \$3,500)} \\
&= \frac{\$6,000}{\$84,000} = 0.0714, \text{ or } 7.14 \text{ percent}
\end{aligned}
$$

We note that this bank is now substantially *below* the minimum total regulatory capital requirement of 8 percent of total risk-weighted assets as required by the Basel I Agreement. This capital-deficient bank will probably be compelled to dispose of some of its risky assets and to raise new capital through retained earnings or, perhaps, through sales of bank stock to bring its capital position up to the levels stipulated by Basel I. Notice, too, that we have only taken *credit risk* into account in the calculation of capital adequacy. We have not even considered the possibility of declines in the market value of assets on bank balance sheets due to increasing interest rates or falling currency or commodity prices. If regulators detected an excessive amount of risk exposure from these market forces, the bank would be asked to post even more capital than the $6,000 it already holds. In this instance this financial firm would face an even deeper capital deficiency than we calculated above and would be placed under considerable regulatory pressure to improve its capital position.

Bank Capital Standards and Market Risk   One of the most glaring holes in the original Basel Agreement was its failure to deal with *market risk*. The risk weights on bank assets mentioned previously were designed primarily to take account of credit risk—the danger that a borrowing customer might default on his or her loan. But banks also face significant *market risk*—the losses a bank may suffer due to adverse changes in interest rates, security prices, and currency and commodity prices. For example, banks are leading traders in foreign securities and overseas business property and can be severely damaged financially when foreign currency prices change (usually referred to as *exchange rate* or *currency risk*). In an effort to deal with these and other forms of market risk, the Basel Committee on Banking Supervision released new proposals in 1993 that would require banks facing greater exposure to market risk to hold larger amounts of capital relative to the size of their assets.

Market Risk and Value at Risk (VAR) Models   In January 1996 the Basel Committee on Banking Supervision formally approved a modification to the Basel I rules, permitting the largest banks to conduct internal risk measurement, and estimate the amount of capital necessary to cover *market risk*. Two years later regulators imposed capital requirements on the market risk exposure of the trading positions of the largest banks (those with trading accounts of more than $1 billion or that represent at least 10 percent of their total assets). Of particular concern was the potential loss to bank earnings and net worth (capital) if the market value of bank asset portfolios were to fall significantly.

Key URLs
Greater detail on
VAR and its link to
calculating bank capital
standards may be found
at such sites as **www
.creditmetrics.com,
www.defaultrisk.com,
www.riskmetrics.com,**
and **www.barclays
capital.com.**

Unique in the history of regulation, the revised Basel I rules allowed the largest banks to use their *own* preferred methods to determine the maximum loss they might sustain over a designated period of time—known as **value at risk (VAR) models.** VAR models attempt to measure the price or market risk of a portfolio of assets whose value may decline due to adverse movements in interest rates, stock prices, currency values, or commodity prices. These models provide a single number for an entire portfolio of assets, expressing the potential for loss over a specific time horizon with a given level of statistical confidence in the accuracy of the loss estimate.

For example, suppose a bank estimates that its trading portfolio's daily average value at risk is $100 million with a 99 percent level of confidence (equivalent to a 1 percent risk level). Then, if this VAR estimate of $100 million is correct, daily losses in portfolio value greater than $100 million should occur less than 1 percent of the time. An analysis of the bank's recent distribution of losses in its trading portfolio will indicate whether this estimate is reasonable or not. The higher the estimated VAR, the greater the amount of regulatory capital the bank must hold to offset this amount of market risk exposure.

The central elements of VAR include

1. An estimate of the maximum amount of loss in the bank's asset values that could occur at a specified level of risk (such as 1 percent).
2. An estimate of the time period over which the assets in question could be liquidated should market deterioration occur (for example, 24 hours for highly liquid assets or possibly two weeks in the case of assets that are more difficult to sell).
3. The confidence level that management attaches to its estimate of the probability of loss occurring in any given time period (such as 99 or 95 percent—the most commonly assumed confidence levels).

VAR analysis is usually most successful when assets are marketable, with a continuous price history, so that it is possible to estimate the likely volatility of each asset's value. Among the leaders in VAR modeling and measurement are CreditMetrics and RiskMetrics, both of which emerged during the 1990s under the leadership of J. P. Morgan.

Under the revised terms of Basel I, regulators determine the amount of capital a bank needs to cover its market risk exposure based upon a *multiple* of the bank's VAR estimate. Banks developing market risk assessment models that generate repeatedly poor estimates of risk exposure will be asked to hold more capital, thereby providing some incentive for bankers to do a better job assessing their institution's market risk exposure.

Possible Supplement to Basel I: Use of Debt Capital to Promote Greater Market Discipline of Bank Behavior Another idea that has recently been proposed as a supplement to Basel I and subsequent Basel agreements is to require the largest money center banks to periodically issue at least a minimal amount of *subordinated debt capital*. Recent research (e.g., Evanoff and Wall [13]) suggests that bank debt capital that is subordinated to the claims of a bank's depositors is highly sensitive to market investors' perceptions of bank risk. Thus, large banks issuing subordinated debt capital would be subject to greater *market discipline* if the marketplace perceives that the issuing bank has taken on excessive risk. One proposal calls for requiring the largest banks to sell a small amount of marketable, subordinated notes periodically each year to independent investors (not affiliated with the issuing bank). Because this long-term debt would not be guaranteed (even by the FDIC or other government insurance programs), buyers of these notes would be especially vigilant about the issuing banks' financial condition, resulting in higher borrowing costs if a bank's risk increased, which would signal regulators of possible trouble at the issuing bank. Thus, the financial marketplace could become an ally of bank regulators in encouraging safer practices and insuring that banks maintain adequate capital.

Key URL
Research on the risk
exposures of banks and
other financial firms
and the role of market
discipline in shaping
capital requirements
may be found at
www.frbsf.org.

As we will see shortly, the newest proposed version of the Basel Agreement on bank capital standards calls for greater use of the force of market discipline and also greater public disclosure to keep bank risk taking under control.

Basel II: A New Capital Accord Unfolding

Why Basel II Appears to Be Needed   Soon after the first Basel Agreement on bank capital was adopted, work began on the next "edition" of the international bank capital accord, known today as **Basel II.** Of special concern to bankers, regulatory agencies, and industry analysts was how to correct the obvious weaknesses of Basel I, particularly its insensitivity to *innovation* in the financial marketplace which is happening all the time.

Smart bankers found ways around many of Basel I's restrictions. For example, some bankers used *capital arbitrage* to increase their profitability and minimize their required levels of capital. These banking firms discovered that the broad asset risk categories in Basel I actually encompassed many different levels of risk exposure. For example, business loans and credit card loans were placed in the same risk category with the same weight even though credit card loans are often far riskier. However, because the risk weights were the same for *all* assets in the same risk category, a bank could simply sell off lower-risk assets and acquire more risky (but higher-yielding) assets without increasing its capital requirement. Thus, instead of making banks *less* risky, some parts of the Basel I system seemed to be encouraging them to become *more* risky.

Moreover, Basel I represented a "one size fits all" approach to capital regulation. It failed to recognize that no two banks are alike in terms of their risk profiles. Different banks have different risk exposure and, therefore, should use different models to estimate risk and be subject to different capital requirements.

As the 21st century opened, a rough draft of the next step, Basel II, appeared, and the Basel Committee on Bank Supervision agreed to several of its major provisions in July 2002. Under current plans, Basel II is expected to be gradually phased in and take full force sometime during 2006 or possibly later. Bankers are being encouraged to gradually adapt their policies and procedures so they will be ready for the new capital accord the first day it takes on full force.

Pillars of Basel II   The three "pillars" of Basel II are as follows:

1. *Minimum capital requirements* for each bank based on its own estimated risk exposure.
2. *Supervisory review* of each bank's risk-assessment procedures and the adequacy of its capital to ensure they are "reasonable" (with each bank covered by the new rules feeding its internal risk-exposure estimates into formulas created by the regulatory authorities to determine its own minimum capital requirement).
3. *Greater public disclosure* of each bank's true financial condition so that market discipline can become a powerful force compelling excessively risky banks to lower their risk exposure.

Internal Risk Assessment   The proposed Basel II agreement represents a revolutionary change in government regulatory philosophy. Banks will be permitted to measure their own risk exposure and determine how much capital they will need to meet that exposure, subject, of course, to review by the regulators to make sure those measurements and calculations are "reasonable." Moreover, participating banks are required to carry out their own repeated *stress testing* over the course of the business cycle, using a so-called internal-rating-based (IRB) approach, to ensure they are prepared for the possibly damaging impacts of ever-changing market conditions.

Key URLs
To gather more information about the development of Basel II's new capital rules, consult such sources as **www.bundesbank.de/ bank/bank_basel.ew .php.**, **www.bis.org/ publ/bcbsca.htm**, and **www.bis.org/press/ p020710.htm**.

The hope is that allowing each bank to assess its own risks and determine its own unique capital needs will promote greater flexibility in responding to changing market conditions and continuing innovation in the financial-services industry. Hopefully, Basel II will counteract one of the great weaknesses of the first Basel Accord—rigid rules that simply couldn't keep up with the ability of the largest financial institutions to develop new services and new methods. The fundamental goal of Basel II is to create a better alignment of capital regulations with the risks that international banks actually face in the modern world.

Operational Risk   One of the key innovations proposed for Basel II is requiring banks to hold capital to deal with *operational risk* in addition to credit and market risks. This type of risk exposure includes such things as losses from employee fraud, product flaws, accounting errors, computer breakdowns, and natural disasters (such as storms and earthquakes) that may damage a bank's physical assets and reduce its ability to communicate with its customers. To lower their capital requirement, bankers must demonstrate that they are using effective measures to reduce operational risk, including purchasing adequate insurance coverage, maintaining back-up service capability, conducting effective internal audits, and developing quality contingency plans and management information systems. Banks subject to Basel II will be asked to estimate the probability of adverse operating risk events and the potential losses these many generate.

Basel II and Credit Risk Models   Paralleling the development of VAR models to estimate market risk exposure and calculate required levels of capital has been the recent rapid rise of **credit risk models.** These computer algorithms attempt to measure the bank or other financial firm's exposure to default or, at least, to credit downgrading due to changes in the quality of its risky assets (especially business, credit card, and home mortgage loans). Credit risk models estimate potential losses to a lender should customers fail to pay off their loans as promised ("default mode" models) or, in broader ("multistate") models, should the credit rating of loan customers decline. Such changes would tend to lower the resale value of loans and reduce the probability of full-value recovery for the lender.

Conversely, if customers' credit ratings improve and the probability of loan default goes down, loan values tend to rise, as does the overall value and quality of bank loan portfolios. To detect such changes, most banks and other lenders use both *external* credit ratings provided by such vendors as Moody's or Standard & Poor's and their own *internal* risk-rating system to assign loans to various risk categories. Credit risk models provide a basis for estimating how much *capital* may be necessary to cover potential loan losses or credit downgrades and still protect the solvency of the lending institution.

Credit risk models are likely to be used much more heavily in the future when Basel II is in full force. Under Basel I, minimum capital requirements remain the same for most types of loans regardless of credit rating. When Basel II arrives, however, minimum capital requirements will probably vary significantly with credit quality. One example that the FDIC cited recently (see FDIC News Release PR-3-2003, January 14, 2003) shows a AAA-rated commercial loan under Basel II bearing a projected minimum capital requirement as low as $0.37 or as high as $4.45 per $100 loaned. If the loan is BBB rated, however, its minimum capital requirement may range from as low as $1.01 to as high as $14.13. In contrast, Basel I's minimum capital requirement for such a loan remains fixed at $8 per $100. Clearly, Basel II, as currently proposed, is much more sensitive to credit risk than is its predecessor.

A Dual (Large-Bank, Small-Bank) Set of Rules   Basel II is expected to adopt one set of capital rules for the largest multinational banks and another set for smaller banking firms. Regulators are especially concerned that small banks could be overwhelmed by the

A COMPARISON OF THE CHANGING RULES FOR INTERNATIONAL REGULATION OF BANK CAPITAL

Features of Basel I Rules (as formally adopted in 1988):

- Identified the principal types of capital that are acceptable to regulators (including Tier 1 or core capital and Tier 2 or supplemental capital) and was the first formal capital standard to take into account risk exposure from off-balance-sheet (OBS) transactions.

- Focused primarily upon credit or default risk inherent in the assets on a bank's balance sheet and among off-balance-sheet items (such as derivative contracts and credit commitments), with market risk exposure from changing interest rates, currency, and commodity prices added later.

- Determined individual banks' capital requirements using the same formula and the same set of risk weights (a "one size fits all" approach).

- Applied the same minimum capital requirements to all banks in participating countries (including a 4 percent minimum ratio of Tier 1 capital to total risk-weighted assets and an 8 percent minimum ratio of Tier 1 plus Tier 2 capital to total risk-weighted assets).

Features of Basel II Rules (scheduled for implementation in full force in 2006 or somewhat later):

- Provides for greater sensitivity to arbitrage and innovation in the financial marketplace, which demands more flexible bank capital rules than Basel I allowed.

- Recognizes that different banks have different risk exposures, may have to employ different methods to assess their own unique risk exposures, and may be subject to different capital requirements (including different rules for large versus small banking firms).

- Broadens the types of risk considered in determining capital requirements and establishes minimum capital requirements for credit, market, and operational risks. The result of this and other changes is that Basel II is substantially more risk sensitive than Basel I.

- Requires each bank to develop in-house risk-management models and stress tests for assessing its own degree of risk exposure (VAR or value at risk) under a variety of different marketplace scenarios.

- Requires each bank to determine its own capital requirements based on its own calculated risk exposure, subject to review for "reasonableness" by regulatory authorities.

- Promotes greater public disclosure of each bank's true financial condition so that greater market discipline is applied to banks perceived to be taking on excessive risk.

heavy burdens of gathering risk-exposure information and performing complicated risk calculations. Then, too, if the adoption of Basel II results in *lowering* the capital requirements of many of the largest banks (as some experts expect), this "bifurcated" system could create a competitive disadvantage for smaller banking firms. It is expected that smaller institutions will be able to continue to use simpler and more standardized approaches in determining their capital requirements and risk exposures, paralleling the rules under Basel I.

Remaining Problems with the Implementation of Basel II The Basel II plan is by no means perfect at this stage. It was released as a consultative paper in April 2003 and stimulated many public comments—both pro and con. Major questions and issues remain to be resolved. First, the technology of risk measurement still has a long way to go before Basel II is fully implemented. For example, some forms of risk (such as operational risk), as of yet, have *no generally accepted measurement scale*. In these instances we don't know exactly how to calculate the amount of risk exposure present and how that exposure may be changing over time.

Then, too, there is the complex issue of *risk aggregation*. How do we add up the different forms of risk exposure in order to get an accurate picture of a bank's total risk exposure? Clearly, the different forms of risk being considered in Basel II must be quantified in some way so we can combine them into one corporate risk index that guides us in figuring out how much regulatory capital a given bank needs to have.

Moreover, what should we do about the *business cycle*? It is likely that most banks will face greater risk exposure (at least when it comes to credit risk) in the middle of an economic recession than they will in a period of economic expansion. This implies that most banks will need greater amounts of capital when the economy is down. But how much? Is it possible that some forms of risk will be rising and while others are falling over the course of the business cycle? Again, the problem of risk aggregation comes into play.

Finally, some bankers and financial experts have expressed concern about *improving regulator competence*. As the technology of advanced risk-management models moves forward, regulators must be trained to keep up so they can assess the accuracy and effectiveness of the different risk models and risk-measurement procedures each bank has adopted. This means that the regulatory community must change along with changes in the financial-services industry.

Concept Check

14–10. What are the most popular financial ratios regulators use to assess the adequacy of bank capital today?

14–11. What is the difference between core (or Tier 1) capital and supplemental (or Tier 2) capital?

14–12. A bank reports the following items on its latest balance sheet: allowance for loan and lease losses, $42 million; undivided profits, $81 million; subordinated debt capital, $3 million; common stock and surplus, $27 million; equity notes, $2 million; minority interest in subsidiaries, $4 million; mandatory convertible debt, $5 million; identifiable intangible assets, $3 million; and noncumulative perpetual preferred stock, $5 million. How much does the bank hold in Tier 1 capital? In Tier 2 capital? Does the bank have too much Tier 2 capital?

14–13. What changes in the regulation of bank capital were brought into being by the Basel Agreement? What is Basel I? Basel II?

14–14. First National Bank reports the following items on its balance sheet: cash, $200 million; U.S. government securities, $150 million; residential real estate loans, $300 million; and corporate loans, $350 million. Its off-balance-sheet items include standby credit letters, $20 million, and long-term credit commitments to corporations, $160 million. What are First National's total risk-weighted assets? If the bank reports Tier 1 capital of $30 million and Tier 2 capital of $20 million, does it have a capital deficiency?

14–15. How is the Basel Agreement likely to affect a bank's choices among assets it would like to acquire?

14–16. What are the most significant differences between Basel I and Basel II? Explain the importance of the concepts of internal risk assessment, VAR, and market discipline.

Changing Capital Standards inside the United States

Inside the United States, regulatory agencies stress the need for strong bank capital positions before they will approve the offering of new services or the establishment or acquisition of new offices or subsidiary firms. Strongly capitalized commercial banks will be allowed to venture into new fields (such as investment banking or insurance underwriting) and expand geographically. Banks with weak capital face more regulatory pressure and will be restricted in their activities until they improve their capital positions. The underlying rationale for "capital-based supervision" is that banks will be less likely to fail or take on excessive risk if their owners are forced to place more of their own money at risk. In effect, the more capital backing a bank's activities, the more its stockholders will likely exercise quality control over the bank's operations. However, there are limits on how much capital regulators can demand from banks. Demanding too much capital throttles back a bank's ability to lend funds profitably in order to support economic growth and, other factors held equal, tends to lower the bank's overall return on equity (ROE), making it less attractive to capital market investors and more difficult to raise new capital in the future.

Several new capital rules created recently by U.S. regulatory agencies were mandated by the FDIC Improvement Act passed by Congress in November 1991. This law requires federal regulators to take "prompt corrective action" (or PCA) when an insured depository institution's capital falls below acceptable levels. Section 131 of the act allows regulators to impose tougher restrictions on an insured bank or thrift institution as its capital level declines, such as prohibiting the payment of management fees or stockholder dividends. If an institution's ratio of tangible equity capital to total assets drops to 2 percent or less, a bank or thrift is considered "critically undercapitalized," and it can be placed in conservatorship or receivership within 90 days unless the institution's principal regulator and the FDIC determine that it would be in the interest of the public and the deposit insurance fund to allow the troubled institution to continue under present ownership and management. To avoid seizure, the bank or thrift institution must have a positive net worth and demonstrate that it is actually improving its condition.

In the fall of 1992 the FDIC and the other federal regulators created five capital-adequacy categories for banks and thrift institutions for purposes of implementing prompt corrective action when a bank or thrift becomes inadequately capitalized. These five categories describe how well capitalized each bank or thrift is:

A. *Well capitalized*—a U.S. depository institution in this category has a ratio of total capital to risk-weighted assets of at least 10 percent, a ratio of Tier 1 (or core) capital to risk-weighted assets of at least 6 percent, and a leverage ratio (Tier 1 capital to average total assets) of at least 5 percent. A well-capitalized bank or thrift faces *no* significant regulatory restrictions on its expansion.

B. *Adequately capitalized*—a U.S. depository institution in this group has a minimum ratio of total capital to risk-weighted assets of at least 8 percent, a ratio of Tier 1 capital to risk-weighted assets of at least 4 percent, and a leverage ratio of at least 4 percent. Such an institution cannot accept broker-placed deposits without regulatory approval.

C. *Undercapitalized*—a U.S. bank or thrift that fails to meet one or more of the capital minimums for an adequately capitalized depository institution is considered undercapitalized and is subject to a variety of mandatory or discretionary regulatory restrictions, including limits on the dividends and management fees it is allowed to pay, on access to the Federal Reserve's discount window, on its maximum asset growth rate, on the expansion of its facilities or services, or on any proposed merger unless approval is obtained in advance from federal regulators. Such a bank or thrift is subject to increased monitoring and must pursue a plan for capital recovery.

D. *Significantly undercapitalized*—a U.S. depository institution belonging to this group possesses a ratio of total capital to risk-weighted assets of less than 6 percent, a Tier 1 capital to risk-weighted assets ratio of under 3 percent, and a leverage ratio average of less than 3 percent. A bank or thrift in this category is subject to all the restrictions faced by undercapitalized institutions plus other restrictions such as mandatory prohibitions on paying bonuses and raises to senior officers without regulator approval, limits on deposit interest rates that may be paid, and, in some cases, mandatory merger.

E. *Critically undercapitalized*—this category applies to those U.S. depository institutions whose ratio of tangible equity capital to total assets is 2 percent or less (where tangible

Key URLs
To learn more about the capital requirements of U.S. banks and thrift institutions see especially the following websites: **www.fdic.gov**, **www.occ.treas.gov**, and **www.ots.treas.gov**.

equity includes common equity capital and cumulative perpetual preferred stock minus most forms of intangible assets). Banks and thrifts in this lowest capital group face all the restrictions applying to undercapitalized institutions plus required regulator approval for such transactions as granting loans to highly leveraged borrowers, making changes in their charter or bylaws, paying above-market interest rates on deposits, changing their accounting methods, or paying excessive compensation or bonuses to consultants or staff. A critically undercapitalized institution may be prevented from paying principal and interest on its subordinated debt and will be placed in conservatorship or receivership if its capital level is not increased within a prescribed time limit.

In recent years the FDIC has analyzed the financial reports of federally insured depository institutions and found that over 90 percent of U.S. banks and thrifts fall in either the *well-capitalized* or *adequately capitalized* groups. Regulators have repeatedly concluded that the American banking system must be in reasonably good shape. Unfortunately, this conclusion usually is based upon the book values of assets reported by the nation's banks and thrifts and on the book value of their capital, not on market values, and could turn out to be an exaggeration of the industry's true condition. Only time will tell.

Planning to Meet Capital Needs

Facing regulatory pressures to maintain adequate capital, commercial banks and many of their competitors are increasingly recognizing the need to plan for their long-range capital needs and to raise new capital as they grow from internal and external sources.

Raising Capital Internally

In most years, the principal source of capital is from earnings kept inside of most financial institutions rather than paid out to their stockholders. Internally generated capital has the advantage of not having to depend on the open market for funds, thus avoiding flotation costs. Not only is internal capital generally less expensive to raise, but it also does not threaten existing stockholders with loss of control—that is, it avoids dilution of their share of ownership and their earnings per share of stock held. For example, if a financial firm chooses to sell stock, some shares may be sold to new stockholders, who will then be entitled to share in any future earnings and to vote on policies. However, internal capital has the disadvantage of being fully taxable by the federal government and being significantly affected by changing interest rates and economic conditions not controllable by management.

Dividend Policy Relying on the growth of net earnings to meet capital needs means that a decision must be made concerning the amount of earnings retained in the business versus the amount to be received by stockholders in the form of dividends. That is, the board of directors and management must agree on the appropriate *retention ratio*—current retained earnings divided by current after-tax net income—which then determines the *dividend payout ratio*—current dividends to stockholders divided by current after-tax net income.

The retention ratio is of great importance to management. A retention ratio set too low (and, therefore, a dividend payout ratio set too high) results in slower growth of internal capital, which may increase failure risk and retard the expansion of earning assets. A retention ratio set too high (and, therefore, a dividend payout ratio set too low) can result in a cut in the stockholders' dividend income. Other factors held constant, such a cut would reduce the market value of the stock issued by a bank or other corporate financial institution. The optimal dividend policy is one that maximizes the value of the stockholders' investment. New stockholders will be attracted and existing stockholders retained if the rate of return on owners' equity capital at least equals returns generated by other investments of comparable risk.

It is particularly important for management to try to achieve a *stable* dividend track record. If the bank's or other financial institution's dividend payout ratio is kept relatively constant, interested investors will perceive less risk in their dividend payments and the institution will look more attractive to investors. As a study of commercial banks by Keen [5] suggests, bank stock prices typically drop quickly after a dividend cut is announced. This not only disappoints current stockholders but also discourages potential buyers of equity shares, making it more difficult to raise new capital in the future.

How Fast Must Internally Generated Funds Grow? A key factor affecting management's decision about an appropriate retention ratio and dividend payout ratio is how fast the bank or other financial firm can allow its assets, especially loans, to grow so that its existing ratio of capital assets is protected from erosion. In other words, how fast must earnings grow to keep the capital-to-assets ratio of a bank or other financial firm protected if it continues paying the same dividend rate to its stockholders?

The following formula helps management and the board of directors answer such questions:

$$\textbf{Internal capital growth rate,} \text{ or Retained earnings} \tag{1}$$
$$\div \text{ Equity capital} = \text{ROE} \times \text{Retention ratio}$$
$$= \frac{\text{Net income after taxes}}{\text{Equity capital}} \times \frac{\text{Retained earnings}}{\text{Net income after taxes}}$$

The reader will recall the ROE relationship discussed in Chapter 5:

$$\text{ROE} = \text{Profit margin} \times \text{Asset utilization} \times \text{Equity multiplier} \tag{2}$$

Then it must be true that

$$\begin{matrix}\text{Internal} \\ \text{capital} \\ \text{growth rate}\end{matrix} = \begin{matrix}\text{Profit} \\ \text{margin}\end{matrix} \times \begin{matrix}\text{Asset} \\ \text{utilization}\end{matrix} \times \begin{matrix}\text{Equity} \\ \text{multiplier}\end{matrix} \times \begin{matrix}\text{Retention} \\ \text{ratio}\end{matrix} \tag{3}$$

or

$$\frac{\text{Retained earnings}}{\text{Equity capital}} = \frac{\text{Net income}}{\substack{\text{after taxes} \\ \text{Operating revenue}}} \times \frac{\text{Operating revenue}}{\text{Total assets}} \tag{4}$$
$$\times \frac{\text{Total assets}}{\text{Equity capital}} \times \frac{\text{Retained earnings}}{\substack{\text{Net income} \\ \text{after taxes}}}$$

This formula shows that if we want to increase internally generated capital, we must increase net earnings (through a higher profit margin, asset utilization ratio, and/or equity multiplier) or increase the earnings retention ratio, or both.

To illustrate the use of this formula, imagine that the management of a bank has forecast a return on equity (ROE) of 10 percent for this year and plans to pay the bank's stockholders 50 percent of any net earnings the bank earns. How fast can assets grow without reducing its current ratio of total capital to total assets? Equation 1 above yields

$$\text{ICGR} = \text{ROE} \times \text{Retention ratio} = 0.10 \times 0.50 = 5 \text{ percent}$$

Thus, this bank's assets cannot grow more than 5 percent under the assumptions made. Otherwise, the bank's capital-to-assets ratio will fall. If it falls far enough, the regulatory authorities will insist that the bank increase its capital.

To take one more example, suppose a commercial bank's assets are forecast to grow 10 percent this year. What options are open to management in terms of an earnings rate, measured by ROE, and an earnings retention ratio if the current ratio of capital to total assets is to be preserved? There are, of course, numerous possibilities that the formula above will generate, as revealed in the following table. For example, if management can boost the bank's return on equity to 20 percent, it can pay out 50 percent of its net after-tax income, retain the other 50 percent, and still protect its current capital-to-assets ratio. With an ROE of 10 percent, however, this bank must retain *all* of its current earnings. It should also be clear that if ROE falls below 10 percent, the bank's capital-to-assets ratio must decline as well, even if it retains all of its current income. In this instance, management may find the regulators insisting on raising more capital from outside the bank to offset a poor earnings record.

Example: If a commercial bank's assets are expected to grow at a 10 percent rate this year, what combination of return on equity and retention rate for earnings will preserve its current capital-to-assets ratio?

$$\text{Forecasted asset growth rate of 10 percent} = \text{ROE} \times \text{Retention ratio}$$

0.10	= 0.20	×	0.50
0.10	= 0.15	×	0.67
0.10	= 0.10	×	1.00

Raising Capital Externally

If a bank or other financial firm does need to raise capital from outside sources, it has several options: (1) selling common stock, (2) selling preferred stock, (3) issuing capital notes, (4) selling assets, (5) leasing certain fixed assets, especially buildings and (6) swapping stock for debt securities. Which alternative management chooses will depend primarily on the impact each source would have on returns to the stockholders, usually measured by earnings per share (EPS). Other key factors to consider are the institution's risk exposure, the impact on control of the institution by its existing stockholders, the state of the market for the assets or securities being sold, and regulations.

Issuing Common Stock The sale of equity shares is generally the most expensive way to raise external capital, considering flotation costs and the greater risk to earnings that stockholders face compared to debtholders. Unless the existing stockholders can absorb all the new shares, a new stock issue may dilute control of a bank or other financial firm and its EPS unless the bank can earn more on the funds raised than their cost of issue. Issuing stock also reduces the degree of leverage a financial institution can employ. The offsetting advantage, however, is that increasing the amount of ownership shares increases future borrowing capacity.

Issuing Preferred Stock The sale of preferred stock is, like the sale of common stock, generally among the more expensive sources of capital. Because preferred shareholders have a prior claim on earnings over holders of common equity, dividends to the common stockholder may be lower after preferred shares are issued. However, preferred stock has an advantage over debt in the form of greater flexibility (because dividends need not be paid), and newly issued preferred shares add future borrowing capacity for a bank or other corporate financial-service firm.

Moreover, as we saw earlier in this chapter, new hybrid forms of preferred shares (such as trust preferred stock) have appeared recently that carry lower cost and conform to bank regulatory standards.

Issuing Subordinated Notes and Debentures The advantage of subordinated debt is the generation of increased financial leverage to boost EPS if more can be earned on borrowed funds than their cost. Moreover, interest payments on debt securities are tax deductible. However, debt adds to failure risk and earnings risk and may make it more difficult to sell stock in the future.

Selling Assets and Leasing Facilities Occasionally, banks and other financial service providers sell all or a portion of their office facilities and lease back from the new owner space to carry on their operations. Such a transaction usually creates a substantial inflow of cash (which is reinvested at current interest rates) and a sizable addition to net worth as well, strengthening the selling institution's capital position without actual change of title.

The most successful sale-and-leaseback transactions have occurred where inflation and economic growth have significantly increased current property values over the book value of the property recorded on the balance sheet. When faster write-offs of commercial real estate are possible, the economic incentive from selling and leasing back property can be most attractive. However, this potentially attractive feature was dimmed a bit in 1986 with passage of the Tax Reform bill. This law lengthened real estate depreciation requirements for most structures, thus requiring management to evaluate their real estate transactions more in terms of their economic benefits rather than their tax benefits. However, the leasing bank usually receives substantial amounts of cash at low cost, increasing its earnings.

Many depository institutions in recent years have *sold assets* to improve their capital-to-assets ratios. They have also frequently slowed the growth of more risky assets and redistributed some of their assets toward lower-risk investments so that their risk-weighted assets decline. A related strategy is to avoid booking loans, thereby avoiding an increase in assets and capital requirements, by referring loan customers to alternative sources of outside funds, such as securitizations or standby credit agreements (as described, for example, in Chapter 8).

One recent innovation, called a *script issue*, recognizes that while some assets (particularly buildings) may have appreciated in market value well beyond their book value, management may have no desire to sell those assets. A script issue creates property revaluation reserves to capture the difference between the market value and book value of selected assets, and these reserves are capitalized to give shareholders bonus shares of stock. The new shares increase equity capital but do not dilute ownership or reduce the value of stock already issued.

Swapping Stock for Debt Securities In recent years a number of commercial banking organizations have undertaken stock-for-debt swaps. For example, a bank may have $2 million in subordinated debentures on its balance sheet, issued at an interest cost of 8 percent. Following conventional practice, these bonds are recorded at their issue price (book value). If interest rates have risen recently, say to 10 percent, these notes may now have a *market value* of just $1 million. By selling new stock in the amount of $1 million and buying back the notes at their current market price, the bank is able to remove a $2 million debt from its balance sheet. From the regulators' perspective, the swapping institution has strengthened its capital and saved the cost of future interest payments on the notes. Moreover, most debt issues have a sinking fund requirement, which requires annual payments into the fund to retire the bonds. These future cash outlays are no longer needed after a stock-for-debt swap is completed.

Choosing the Best Alternative for Raising Outside Capital The choice of which method to use in raising outside capital should be made on the basis of a careful financial analysis of the alternatives and their effects on a financial firm's earnings per share. Table 14–2 gives an example of a commercial bank that needs to raise $20 million in external capital. The institution currently has 8 million shares of common stock outstanding at a $4-per-share par value and has total assets of close to $1 billion, with $60 million in equity capital. If this bank can generate total revenue of about $100 million and hold operating expenses to no more than $80 million, it should have about $10.8 million in earnings left after taxes. If management elects to raise the needed $20 million in new

TABLE 14–2
Methods of Raising
External Capital for a
Bank

Income or Expense Item	Sell Common Stock at $10 per Share	Sell Preferred Stock Promising an 8 Percent Dividend at $20 per Share	Sell Capital Notes with a 10 percent Coupon Rate
Estimated revenues	$100 million	$100 million	$100 million
Estimated operating expenses	80	80	80
Net revenues	20	20	20
Interest expense on capital notes	—	—	2
Estimated before-tax net income	20	20	18
Estimated income taxes (35%)	7	7	6.3
Estimated after-tax net income	13	13	11.7
Preferred stock dividends	—	1.6	—
Net income available to common stockholders	$13 million	$11.4 million	$11.7 million
Earnings per share of common stock	$1.30	$1.43	$1.46
	(10 million shares)	(8 million shares)	(8 million shares)

Note: Initially the bank has 8 million shares of common stock outstanding, with a $4-per-share par value.

capital by issuing 2 million new equity shares, each at a net price of $10, the common stockholders will receive $1.30 in earnings per share.

Is the issue of common stock the *best* alternative for this bank? Not if its goal is to maximize earnings per share. For example, management finds that it could issue preferred stock, bearing an 8 percent dividend, at $20 per share. If the board of directors elects to declare an annual dividend on these preferred shares, this will drain $1.6 million ($20 million × 0.08) each year from earnings that would normally flow to the common stockholders. But it will still leave $11.6 million for holders of the 8 million in common shares, or a dividend rate of $1.43 per share. Thus, the preferred stock route would yield this bank's common stockholders $0.13 more in dividends per share than would the issue of additional common stock.

Management also discovers that it could sell $20 million in subordinated capital notes bearing a 10 percent coupon rate. While the bank must pay $2 million in interest annually on these notes, this still leaves almost $12 million left over after all expenses (including taxes). When distributed among the 8 million common shares, this will yield $1.46 per share. Clearly, the best of the three capital-raising options in this example is *issuing debt capital notes*. Moreover, the capital notes carry no voting power, so the current stockholders retain control.

Concept Check

14–17. What steps should be part of any plan for meeting a long-range need for capital?

14–18. How does dividend policy affect the need for capital?

14–19. What is the ICGR and why is it important to the management of a financial firm?

14–20. Suppose that a bank has a return on equity capital of 12 percent and that its retention ratio is 35 percent. How fast can this bank's assets grow without reducing its current ratio of capital to assets?

Suppose that the bank's earnings (measured by ROE) drop unexpectedly to only two-thirds of the expected 12 percent figure. What would happen to the bank's ICGR?

14–21. What are the principal sources of external capital for a bank or other corporate financial institution?

14–22. What factors should management consider in choosing among the various sources of external capital?

Summary

In the history of banking there are few more controversial issues than those surrounding *capital*. A long-standing debate among bankers, regulators, and financial analysts concerns how much and what types of capital banks should hold. Not only the definition and concept of capital but also our views on the proper role for capital in controlling the behavior of banks and other financial firms are changing. Among the key points in this chapter are the following:

- The term *capital* in the banking and financial-services field refers to the funds contributed by the *owners*—money invested in a bank or other financial firm and placed at risk in the hope of earning a competitive rate of return. Banks are corporations and their owners are shareholders—investors in common and preferred stock, while for some other financial firms, such as credit unions and mutual savings banks, the owners are customers who invest their deposits in the institution and capital is an accumulation of reinvested profits.

- Capital consists principally of common and preferred stock, surplus (the excess value of stock over its par value), reserves for contingencies, undivided profits, equity reserves, minority interest in consolidated subsidiaries, and equity commitment notes. Most banks and other financial firms don't have all of these types of instruments in their capital account. The most important capital sources include stock, surplus, undivided profits, and equity reserves. However, increasingly in recent years banks and some thrifts have issued long-term debt subordinated to the claims of depositors, which is also recognized as capital by most regulatory agencies.

- Capital is the ultimate line of defense against failure and bankruptcy, giving the bank or other financial firm time to respond to the various kinds of risks that it faces and return to profitability again. Capital also supplies long-term money to get a new bank or other financial institution started, provides a base for future growth, and promotes public confidence in each financial firm and in the financial system.

- The volume of capital a bank or other regulated financial institution holds and the makeup of its capital account are determined by both *regulation* and the *financial marketplace*. Because not all of the information on the true condition of banks and other regulated firms is normally released to the public, the private marketplace alone may not be completely reliable as an effective regulator in promoting the public interest, creating a role for government regulation of each institution's capital account.

- Capital requirements today are set by regulatory agencies in each nation and, for banks in more than 100 nations today, under rules laid out in the Basel Agreement on International Bank Capital Standards—one of the first successful efforts in history to impose common rules on banks in many different countries. These government agencies set minimum capital requirements and assess the capital adequacy of the banks and other financial firms they regulate.

- Capital regulation aimed primarily at the largest international banks formally began in 1988 with a formal agreement known as Basel I. This set of international rules requires many of the largest commercial banks to separate their on-balance-sheet and off-balance-sheet assets and commitments into risk categories and to multiply each asset by its appropriate risk weight to determine total risk-exposed assets. The ratio of total regulatory capital outstanding relative to total risk-weighted assets and off-balance-sheet commitments is a key indicator of the strength of each bank's capital position. There are minimum capital adequacy ratios that all banks must meet.

- Weaknesses in the Basel I international agreement, especially its inability to respond to change and innovation in the financial marketplace, has led to a draft Basel II agreement, scheduled to be phased in and take full force sometime in 2006 or somewhat later. This new approach to capital management and regulation will require the largest banking firms to conduct a continuing internal assessment of their risk exposures, including stress testing, and to calculate their required level of capital. Thus, each participating bank will have its own unique capital requirements based on its own unique risk profile. Smaller banks will likely use a simpler, standardized approach to determining their minimum capital requirements identical to, or at least similar to, the rules of Basel I.

- Banks and other financial firms in need of additional capital have several different sources to draw upon, including internal and external sources of funds. The principal internal source is retained earnings. The principal external sources include (a) selling common stock; (b) selling preferred stock; (c) issuing capital notes; (d) selling assets; (e) leasing fixed assets; and (f) swapping stock for debt.

- Choosing among the various sources of capital requires the management of a financial institution to consider the relative cost and risk of each capital source, the institution's overall risk exposure, the potential impact of each source on returns to the shareholders, government regulations, and the demands of investors in the private marketplace.

Key Terms

capital, 483
operating risk, 486
exchange risk, 486
crime risk, 486
portfolio diversification, 487
geographic
diversification, 487
common stock, 488
preferred stock, 488
surplus, 488

undivided profits, 488
equity reserves, 488
subordinated
debentures, 488
minority interest in
consolidated
subsidiaries, 488
equity commitment
notes, 488
Basel agreement, 492

Basel I, 493
tier 1 capital, 493
tier 2 capital, 493
value at risk (VAR)
models, 501
Basel II, 502
credit risk models, 503
internal capital growth
rate, 508

Problems and Projects

1. Harrison Savings Association has forecast the following performance ratios for the year ahead. How fast can Harrison allow its assets to grow without reducing its ratio of equity capital to total assets, assuming its performance holds reasonably steady over its planning period?

Profit margin of net income over operating revenue	0.0875
Asset utilization (operating revenue ÷ assets)	0.0963
Equity multiplier	15.22X
Net earnings retention ratio	0.4000

2. Using the formulas developed in this chapter and in Chapter 5 and the information that follows, calculate the ratios of total capital to total assets for the banking firms listed below. What relationship among these banks' return on assets, return on equity capital, and capital-to-assets ratios did you observe? What implications or recommendations would you draw for the management of each of these banks?

Name of Bank	Net After-Tax Income ÷ Total Assets (or ROA)	Net After-Tax Income ÷ Total Equity Capital (or ROE)
First National Bank of Domen	0.0149	0.125
Security National Bank	0.0070	0.125
Ilsher State Bank	0.0082	0.1005
Mercantile Bank and Trust Company	0.0037	0.1005
Westlake National Trust	−0.0045	−0.0500

3. Using the following information for Premier Western National Bank, calculate that bank's required level of capital based on the new international capital standards discussed in this chapter. Does the bank have sufficient capital under the terms of the Basel I Agreement?

On-Balance-Sheet Items (Assets)		Off-Balance-Sheet Items	
Cash	$ 2.5 million	Standby credit letters backing municipal bonds	$18.1 million
U.S. Treasury securities	25.6		
Deposit balances due from other banks	4.0	Long-term binding commitments to corporate customers	40.2 million
Loans secured by first lines on residential property (1- to 4-family dwellings)	8.7	Total of all off-balance-sheet items	$58.3 million
Loans to corporations	108.4		
Total assets	$149.2 million	Total capital	$10.5 million

4. Crossroads Savings has been told by examiners that it needs to raise an additional $8 million in long-term capital. Its outstanding common equity shares total 7.5 million, each bearing a par value of $1. This thrift institution currently holds total assets of nearly $2 billion, with $105 million in total equity. During the coming year, the thrift's economist has forecast operating revenues of $175 million, of which operating expenses will absorb 96 percent.

Among the options for raising capital considered by management are (*a*) selling $8 million in common stock, or 320,000 shares at $25 per share; (*b*) selling $8 million in preferred stock bearing a 9 percent annual dividend yield at $12 per share; or (*c*) selling $8 million in 10-year capital notes with a 10 percent coupon rate. Which option would be of most benefit to the stockholders? What happens if operating revenues increase more than the forecast? Cite examples of the consequences. What happens if there is a slower-than-expected volume of revenues (only $125 million instead of $175 million)? Please explain.

5. Please calculate Willow River National Bank's total risk-weighted assets, based on the following items that the bank reported on its latest balance sheet. Does the bank appear to have a capital deficiency?

Cash	$ 120 million
Domestic interbank deposits	240 million
U.S. government securities	450 million
Residential real estate loans	370 million
Commercial loans	520 million
Total assets	$1,700 million
Total liabilities	$1,569 million
Total capital	$ 136 million

Off-balance-sheet items include

Standby credit letters	$ 75 million
Long-term loan commitments to private companies	180 million

6. Suppose that Willow River National Bank, whose balance sheet is given in problem 5, reports the forms of capital shown in the following table as of the date of its latest financial statement. What is the total dollar volume of the bank's Tier 1 capital? Tier 2 capital? According to the data given in problems 5 and 6, does Willow River National Bank have a capital deficiency?

Common stock (par value)	$18 million
Surplus	22 million
Undivided profits	84 million
Allowance for loan losses	75 million
Subordinated debt capital	40 million
Intermediate-term preferred stock	12 million

7. Please indicate which items appearing on the following bank financial statements would be classified under the terms of the Basel Agreement as (*a*) Tier 1 capital and (*b*) Tier 2 capital.

Allowance for loan and lease losses	Subordinated debt capital instruments with an original average maturity of at least five years
Subordinated debt under two years to maturity	Common stock
Intermediate-term preferred stock	Equity notes
Qualifying noncumulative perpetual preferred stock	Undivided profits
Cumulative perpetual preferred stock with unpaid dividends	Mandatory convertible debt
	Minority interest in the equity accounts of consolidated subsidiaries

8. Under the terms of the Basel I Agreement, what *risk weights* apply to the following on-balance-sheet and off-balance-sheet items for a bank?

Residential real estate loans	Credit card loans
Cash	Standby letters of credit for municipal
Commercial loans	bonds
U.S. Treasury securities	Long-term commitments to make
Deposits held at other banks	corporate loans
GNMA mortgage-backed	Currency derivative contracts
securities	Interest-rate derivative contracts
Standby credit letters for	Short-term (under one year) loan
commercial paper	commitments
Federal agency securities	Bank real property
Municipal general obligation bonds	Bankers' acceptances
Investments in subsidiaries	Municipal revenue bonds
FNMA or FHLMC issued	Reserves on deposit at the Federal
or guaranteed securities	Reserve banks

Internet Exercises

1. You are the CFO of a large corporation that is reevaluating the depository institutions it relies upon for financial services. Since your company will maintain deposits in excess of $100,000, you want to make sure that the institutions you rely upon are well capitalized. Compare the total capital to risk-weighted assets, the Tier 1 capital to risk-weighted assets, and the leverage ratio for the following four banks: Bank of America (BHC ID 1073757), J. P. Morgan Chase (BHC ID 1039502), National City Corp (BHC ID 1069125, and Wachovia (BHC ID 1073551). This is easily accomplished at **www3.fdic.gov/sdi/main.asp** where you can create a report for the four BHCs.

   If you need some help maneuvering around this site to create a report, read on. The process to create a report requires you to select the number of columns. You want to select "4" to develop the format to collect data for the most recent report. This provides four pull-down menus, each labeled Select One. In the columns select Bank Holding Company from the menu and go on to type in the BHC ID #. After defining the four columns click on Next. At this point you focus on Report Selection, choosing to view and to do calculations in percentages. Then you get to identify the information you want to collect before creating the report by clicking Next. You will find the "Performance and Conditions" report to be quite helpful. Are all the institutions well capitalized? Which institution has the highest capital ratios?

2. You are moving to Philadelphia and two savings associations have been recommended by soon-to-be colleagues. They are Washington Savings Association (OTS Docket #29281) and United Savings Banks (OTS Docket # 28836). You thought you would compare their capital adequacy, which is easily accomplished at **www3.fdic.gov/sdi/main.asp** where you can create a report for the two savings associations. If you need some help maneuvering around this site to create a report continue reading. The process to create a report requires you to select the number of columns. You want to select "2" to develop the format to collect data for the most recent report. This provides two pull-down menus, each labeled Select One. In the columns select Single Institution from the menu and go on to type in the OTS Docket Number. After defining the two columns, click on Next. At this point you focus on Report Selection, choosing to view and to do calculations in percentages. Then you get to identify the information you want to collect before creating the report by clicking Next. You will

find the "Performance and Conditions" report to be helpful. What capital adequacy category is appropriate?

3. The Basel Agreement is always evolving. Visit **http://www.bis.org/publ/bcbsca.htm** to find out what the current state of the new agreement is. What are the key issues?

STANDARD &POOR'S

S&P Market Insight Challenge

1. Use Standard & Poor's Market Insight website (**www.mhhe.com/edumarketinsight**) for this problem. Capital levels capture the abilities of depository institutions to sustain losses and are very important to regulatory agencies watching this industry. For an up-to-date view of capital levels in the banking and thrift industries, please use the Industry tab in S&P's Market Insight and the drop-down menu to select among the subindustry choices of Diversified Banks, Regional Banks, and Thrifts & Mortgage Finance. By choosing among these subgroups, you will be able to access the S&P Industry Survey on Banking and the Survey on Savings and Loans. Please download both surveys and explore the sections, "How to Analyze a Bank" and "How to Analyze a Savings and Loan Company," with particular focus on the capital adequacy issue. Compare and contrast the most recent capital levels posted by commercial banks and thrift institutions.

2. Use Standard & Poor's Market Insight website (**www.mhhe.com/edumarketinsight**) for this problem. One of the most important topics in this chapter centers around the historic Basel Agreement on standards for bank capital. Basel I established minimum capital requirements for all banks in participating countries based on Tier 1 and Tier 2 capital and the risk-weighted assets of each bank. How well capitalized do some of the banks that have filed financial reports with Market Insight appear to be, measured relative to Basel's requirements? Do you see any apparent weaknesses? Are there other facts you'd like to know before relying exclusively on the capital ratios you have just calculated to make a judgment?

REAL NUMBERS FOR REAL BANKS   Assignment for Chapter 14

YOUR BANK'S CAPITAL: THE CUSHION FOR LOSSES AND FUNDS FOR GROWTH

Chapter 14 describes the management of capital in a depository institution and the tasks capital performs. Capital serves as a cushion for both operating and financial losses. The regulators have capital adequacy requirements that depository institutions must meet to continue operations. This chapter describes how to calculate three different capital adequacy ratios that are then used to place an institution in one of five capital adequacy categories. Each capital adequacy category determines permissible activities. For instance, for a bank holding company to be certified as a financial holding company (FHC) as outlined in the Gramm-Leach-Bliley Act, all the banks within the holding company must be *well capitalized.*

Part One of this assignment examines the capital ratios in aggregate for the depository institutions in your BHC. Another role of capital is to support the growth of an institution. In this chapter we learn to calculate the internal capital growth rate (ICGR). The internal capital growth rate is how fast the bank can allow its assets to grow without reducing its capital-to-assets ratio. In Part Two we will calculate ICGRs and discuss the growth opportunities or limitations.

Part One: Regulatory Capital Adequacy

A. **Data Collection:** For this part, you will once again access data at the FDIC's website located at **www3.fdic.gov/sdi/main.asp** for your BHC. Use SDI to create a two-column report of your bank's information—a column for each year. In this part of the assignment, for Report Selection use the pull-down menu to select Assets and Liabilities and view this in dollars. In the Memoranda section you will find the dollar amount (in 000s) of Tier One equity. Then go on to look at the "Performance and Condition Ratios" report, where you will find the three capital ratios computed for you. (What a nice surprise, given the tedious process of calculating risk-weighted assets.) Enter the data in Spreadsheet 1 as follows.

Maturity & repricing data for debt securities: (A86)	12/31/yyyy	12/31/yyyy
Tier 1 (core) capital (A87)	$	$
Core capital (leverage) ratio (A88)	%	%
Tier 1 risk-based capital ratio (A89)	%	%
Total risk-based capital ratio (A90)	%	%
Risk-weighted assets (to be calculated from above) (A91)	$	$

B. With the information you have collected, you can calculate the dollar amount of risk-weighted assets.

C. Using the information in rows 88–90 determine the capital adequacy category of the aggregation of banks (BHC as defined by the FDIC's SDI) for each year.

D. Compare columns of rows 87–91.

E. Utilizing the above information, write one or two paragraphs about your bank's capital adequacy and any changes you have observed between the two years.

Part Two: Evaluating the Internal Capital Growth Rate

A. Calculation of ICGR: The chapter concludes with a discussion of raising capital internally and externally. Review Equations 1–4 on calculating the ICGR. You have already calculated ROE and have the information needed to calculate the retention ratio in Spreadsheet 1. Use the formula function in Excel to calculate the entries for Columns B and C, Rows 93–95.

Growth of Assets: (A92)	12/31/yyyy	12/31/yyyy
Retention ratio (A93)		
Internal capital growth rate (A94)		
Growth of assets over the last calendar year (A95)		

B. Write one paragraph interpreting the above information and discussing the potential for your bank's growth.

Selected References

The following studies discuss the factors contributing to bank failure:

1. Santomero, Anthony M., and Joseph D. Vinso. "Estimating the Probability of Failure for Commercial Banks and the Banking System." *Journal of Banking and Finance 1* (1977), pp. 185–205.
2. Short, Eugene D.; Gerald P. O'Driscoll, Jr.; and Franklin D. Berger. "Recent Bank Failures: Determinants and Consequences." *Proceedings of a Conference on Bank Structure and Competition*, Federal Reserve Bank of Chicago, 1985.

These studies present an overview of the market's role in influencing bank capital positions:

3. Eisenbeis, Robert A., and Gary G. Gilbert. "Market Discipline and the Prevention of Bank Problems and Failure." *Issues in Bank Regulation 3* (Winter 1985), pp. 16–23.
4. Flannery, Mark J. "Using Market Information in Prudential Bank Supervision: A Review of the U.S. Empirical Evidence." *Journal of Money, Credit and Banking 30* (1998), pp. 273–305.
5. Keen, Howard, Jr. "The Impact of a Dividend Cut Announcement on Bank Share Prices." *Journal of Bank Research*, Winter 1983, pp. 274–81.
6. Kwan, Simon. "The Promise and Limits of Market Discipline in Banking." *FRBSF Economic Letter*, Federal Reserve Bank of San Francisco, No. 2002-36, December 13, 2002.
7. ———. "Bank Security Prices and Market Discipline." *FRBSF Economic Letter*, Federal Reserve Bank of San Francisco, No. 2002-37, December 20, 2002.

For a discussion of capital adequacy standards, their effects, and recent changes, see the following:

8. Eubanks, Walter W. "Risk-Based Capital and Regulatory Enforcement." *CRS Review*, May/June 1991, pp. 16–18.
9. Peek, Joe, and Eric S. Rosengren. "Have Borrower Concentration Limits Encouraged Bank Consolidation?" *New England Economic Review*, Federal Reserve Bank of Boston, January/February 1997, pp. 37–47.
10. ———. "How Well Capitalized Are 'Well-Capitalized' Banks?" *New England Economic Review*, September/October 1997, pp. 41–50.
11. Wall, Larry D. "Regulation of Banks' Equity Capital." *Economic Review*, Federal Reserve Bank of Atlanta, November 1985, pp. 4–18.

For a discussion of steps taken to broaden the Basel Agreement on international bank capital standards to take account of market risk and interest rate risk, see especially the following:

12. Board of Governors of the Federal Reserve System, Study Group on Subordinated Notes and Debentures. "Using Subordinated Debt as an Instrument of Market Discipline." *Staff Study 172*, Washington, D. C., December 1999.
13. Evanoff, Douglas D., and Larry D. Wall. "Subordinated Debt and Bank Capital Reform." *Working Paper Series 00-7*, Federal Reserve Bank of Chicago, August 2000.
14. Federal Deposit Insurance Corporation. *Final Rule Amending Risk-Based Capital Requirements to Incorporate Market Risk*. October 10, 1996.
15. Hambrich, Joseph G. "Subordinated Debt: Tough Love for Banks?" *Economic Commentary*, Federal Reserve Bank of Cleveland, December 1998.
16. Hendricks, Daryll. "Evaluation of Value-at-Risk Models Using Historical Data." *Economic Policy Review*, Federal Reserve Bank of New York, April 1996, pp. 39–69.

17. Hendricks, Daryll, and Beverly Hirtle. "Bank Capital Requirements for a Market Risk: The Internal Models Approach." *Economic Policy Review*, Federal Reserve Bank of New York, December 1997, pp. 1–12.

18. Jordan, John S. "Pricing Bank Stocks: The Contribution of Bank Examinations." *New England Economic Review*, Federal Reserve Bank of Boston, May–June 1999, pp.39–53.

19. Marshall, David, and Subu Venkatarainan. "Bank Capital for Market Risk: A Study in Incentive-Compatible Regulation." *Chicago Fed Letter*, No. 104 (April 1996), pp. 1–3.

20. Stevens, Ed. "Evolution in Banking Supervision." *Economic Commentary*, Federal Reserve Bank of Cleveland, March 1, 2000.

For more information about Basel II and the issues it raises see especially these sources:

21. Lopez, Jose A. "What Is Operational Risk?" *FRBSF Economic Letter*, Federal Reserve Bank of San Francisco, 2002-02 (January 25, 2002).

22. ———. "How Financial Firms Manage Risk." *FRBSF Economic Letter*, Federal Reserve Bank of San Francisco, No. 2003-03, February 14, 2003.

23. ———. "Modeling Credit Risk for Commercial Loans." *FRBSF Economic Letter*, Federal Reserve Bank of San Francisco, 2001-12, April 27, 2001.

24. Powell, Donald E. "Statement on the New Basel Accord," presented before the Subcommittee on Domestic and International Monetary Policy, Trade, and Technology of the Committee on Financial Services, U.S. House of Representatives, February 27, 2003.

25. Santomero, Anthony M. "Process and Progress in Risk Management." *Business Review*, Federal Reserve Bank of Philadelphia, First Quarter 2003, pp. 1–5.

26. Study Group on Disclosure. "Improving Public Disclosure in Banking." *Staff Study 173*, Board of Governors of the Federal Reserve System, March 2000, pp. 1–35.

27. Hendricks, Daryll. "Evaluation of Value-at-Risk Models Using Historical Data." *Economic Policy Review*, Federal Reserve Bank of New York, April 1996, pp. 39–70.

28. Hirtle, Beverly J.; Mark Levonian; Marc Saidenberg; Stefan Walter; and David Wright. "Using Credit Risk Models for Regulatory Capital: Issues and Options." *Economic Policy Review*, Federal Reserve Bank of New York, March 2001, pp. 19–35.

For a detailed discussion of the U.S. capital regulatory policy, known as PCA or "prompt corrective action" for banks and thrift institutions, this source is especially helpful:

29. Shibut, Lynn; Tim Critchfield; and Sarah Bohn. "Differentiating among Critically Undercapitalized Banks and Thrifts." *FDIC Banking Review* 15, no. 2 (2003) pp. 1–38.

PART FIVE

Providing Loans to Businesses and Consumers

Lending to customers is the centerpiece of banking as it is for many nonbank lending firms, such as finance companies and credit unions. Loans are the main component of assets for most banks and for other business and consumer lenders. For these institutions, loans usually are the principal source of operating revenue and the chief source of risk exposure. Lenders fail for many reasons, but at or near the top of the list are bad loans.

Loans are "the reason to be" for most banks and competing lenders. Loans define their principal role in the community, whether that community is a small town or reaches around the globe. There is a crucial interaction between the lending function and the economic welfare of communities. Credit fuels economic expansion. Experts have often commented that you can tell very quickly which communities are served by banks and other lenders that aggressively market loans—evidence of economic growth is usually everywhere in the form of new homes, new businesses, new schools, and the like.

As in every other area of the financial-services business today, however, competition presses in on all sides of the lending function. For example, bank business lending programs are challenged by aggressive nonbank business lenders (such as GE Capital and Commercial Credit) and credit underwriters (like Merrill Lynch and Goldman Sachs). Bank household loan programs are challenged by the rapidly growing credit programs advertised by credit unions, savings and loans, consumer finance companies (such as Household Finance), and credit card lenders (like Capital One and MBNA).

No bank or competing lender can afford not staying on top of its loan portfolio all the time. This requires lenders to create management policies that spell out what types of loans are to be made and on what terms. Bankers, in particular, watch their ratio of total loans to total assets, aware that increases in their loans-to-assets ratio promise more revenue but also more risk. They must also keep a close eye on their ratio of loans to capital. Regulators limit loan growth severely unless capital grows apace to protect those who place their savings with the banking industry.

As we will see in this section, innovation is changing the lending business in unprecedented ways. More loans are finding their way into the resale market or into loan pools off the balance sheet. This allows banks and other regulated lenders to avoid having to raise more expensive capital and makes them appear less risky. In the future, more banks and financial holding companies are likely to be engaged in merchant banking, not only extending loans to their best business customers but also taking equity (ownership) positions in many of the firms to whom they lend.

Our focus in this part proceeds in steps. We look first at loan policies and procedures to shape a lender's loan portfolio in the desired direction and train loan officers to make good decisions. Then we turn to business loans—their types, how they can be evaluated to control risk, and how they are priced to generate adequate revenue. Finally, we examine household lending in order to see how consumer loans are made and explore the extensive regulations that impact household lending today.

CHAPTER FIFTEEN

Lending Policies and Procedures

Key Topics in This Chapter

- Types of Loans Banks Make
- Factors Affecting the Mix of Loans Made
- Regulation of Lending
- Creating a Written Loan Policy
- Steps in the Lending Process
- Loan Review and Loan Workouts

Introduction

J. Paul Getty, once the richest man in the world, observed: "If you owe the bank $100, that's your problem. If you owe the bank $100 million, that's the bank's problem." To be sure, lending to businesses, governments, and individuals is one of the most important services banks and their closest competitors provide, and it is also among the riskiest.

However, risky or not, the principal reason banks and many competing lenders are issued charters of incorporation by state and national governments is to make loans to their customers.[1] Banks, thrift institutions, and other chartered lenders are expected to support their local communities with an adequate supply of credit for all legitimate business and consumer financial needs and to price that credit reasonably in line with competitively determined market interest rates.

Indeed, making loans to fund consumption and investment spending is the principal economic function of banks and their closest competitors. How well a lender performs in fulfilling the lending function has a great deal to do with the economic health of its region, because loans support the growth of new businesses and jobs within the lender's trade territory. Moreover, loans often seem to convey positive information to the marketplace about a borrower's credit quality, enabling a borrower whose loan is approved to obtain more and perhaps somewhat cheaper funds from other sources as well.

Despite all the benefits of lending for both the institutions that make loans and for their customers, the lending process bears careful internal and external monitoring at all times. When a bank or other lender gets into serious financial trouble, its problems usually spring from loans that have become uncollectible due to mismanagement, illegal manipulation, misguided lending policies, or an unexpected economic downturn. No wonder,

---

[1] Portions of this chapter are based upon Peter S. Rose's article in *The Canadian Banker* (5) and are used with the permission of the publisher.

then, that when examiners appear at a bank or other regulated lending institution they conduct a thorough review of its loan portfolio. Usually this involves a detailed analysis of the documentation and collateral for the largest loans, a review of a sample of small loans, and an evaluation of loan policies to ensure they are sound and prudent in order to protect the public's funds.

Types of Loans

What *types* of loans do banks and many of their closest competitors make? The answer, of course, is that banks make a wide variety of loans to a wide variety of customers for many different purposes—from purchasing automobiles and buying new furniture, taking dream vacations, or pursuing college educations to constructing homes and office buildings. Fortunately, we can bring some order to the diversity of lending by grouping loans according to their *purpose*—what customers plan to do with the proceeds of their loans. At least once each year, the Federal Reserve System, the FDIC, and the Comptroller of the Currency require each U.S. bank and thrift institution to report the composition of its loan portfolio by purpose of loan on a report form known as Schedule A, attached to its balance sheet. Table 15–1 summarizes the major items reported on Schedule A for all U.S. commercial banks as of December 31, 2002.

We note from Table 15–1 that bank loans may be divided into seven broad categories of loans, delineated by their purposes:

1. **Real estate loans,** which are secured by real property—land, buildings, and other structures—and which include short-term loans for construction and land development and longer-term loans to finance the purchase of farmland, homes, apartments, commercial structures, and foreign properties.

TABLE 15–1
Loans Outstanding for All U.S.-Insured Commercial Banks as of December 31, 2002 (consolidated domestic and foreign offices)

Source: Federal Deposit Insurance Corporation.

Bank Loans Classified by Purpose	Amount for All FDIC-Insured U.S. Banks ($ billions)	Percentage of Loan Portfolio		
		Percentage of Total Loans for all FDIC-Insured U.S. Banks	Smallest U.S. Banks (less than $100 million in total assets)	Largest U.S. Banks (over $1 billion in total assets)
Real estate loans[a]	$2068.0	49.7%	60.1%	46.2%
Loans to depository institutions[b]	133.5	3.2	0.1	3.8
Loans to finance agricultural production	46.8	1.1	10.3	0.5
Commercial and industrial loans[c]	912.0	21.9	16.8	22.9
Loans to individuals[d]	703.6	16.9	11.4	18.3
Miscellaneous loans[e]	137.0	3.3	1.0	3.7
Lease financing receivables	162.5	3.9	0.3	4.6
Total (gross) loans and leases shown on U.S. banks' balance sheet	$4163.4	100.0%	100.0%	100.0%

[a]Construction and land development loans; loans to finance one- to four-family homes; multifamily residential property loans; nonfarm, nonresidential property loans; foreign real estate loans.

[b]Loans to commercial banks and other foreign and domestic depository institutions and acceptances of other banks.

[c]Credit to construct business plant and equipment; loans for business operating expenses; loans for other business uses, including international loans and acceptances.

[d]Loans to purchase automobiles; credit cards; mobile home loans; loans to purchase consumer goods; loans to repair and modernize residences; all other personal installment loans; single-payment loans; and other personal loans.

[e]Includes loans to foreign governments and state and local governments and acceptances of other banks. Columns may not add exactly to totals due to rounding error.

The World Wide Web has opened up a whole new world of learning possibilities for both experienced and new loan officers. It provides notices of special training sessions available through various professional organizations, instructions about how to apply for loans at private and governmental institutions, and job openings for those interested in becoming loan officers and credit analysts.

Among the most prominent of the websites on lending education are those sponsored by the Risk Management Association or RMA (formerly known as Robert Morris Associates), which advertises lending seminars and other educational products at its principal website at **www.rmahq.org**. Interesting information on possible loan officer careers may often be found at **financial-jobs.com** and at Loan Officers and Counselors: Occupational Outlook Handbook at **www.bls.gov/oco/ocos018.htm**.

As we note later in this chapter, one of the most powerful forces affecting lending today is regulation, and there are several good websites on the rules that govern the lending process. For example, the Federal Financial Institutions Examination Council (FFIEC) maintains an FFIEC Press Releases website at **www.ffiec.gov/press.htm**. You can also go to the main websites of the Federal Deposit Insurance Corporation (**www.fdic.gov**) and the Federal Reserve System (**www.federalreserve.gov**) to check their information about new and existing regulatory rules. Both the World Bank and the International Monetary Fund Libraries have combined their lists of holdings particularly beneficial to international lenders at **jolis.worldbankimflib.org/external.htm**.

To learn more about the terminology of lending, go to sites such as **www.bcpl.net/~ibcnet/terms.html** maintained by the Baltimore County Public Library. Finally, the risk of extending loans has prompted several regulatory agencies to develop guidelines that help lending institutions control this major source of risk in the industry. One example is the Basel Committee, established by leading central banks around the world, which has sponsored several papers on credit risk management. These may be viewed at the Bank for International Settlements site at **www.bis.org**.

Factoid
In the most recent years which financial institution has been the number one lender in the U.S. economy?
Answer: Commercial banks, followed by insurance companies.

2. **Financial institution loans,** including credit to banks, insurance companies, finance companies, and other financial institutions.

3. **Agricultural loans,** extended to farm and ranch operations to assist in planting and harvesting crops and to support the feeding and care of livestock.

4. **Commercial and industrial loans,** granted to businesses to cover such expenses as purchasing inventories, paying taxes, and meeting payrolls.

5. **Loans to individuals,** including credit to finance the purchase of automobiles, mobile homes, appliances, and other retail goods, to repair and modernize homes, cover the cost of medical care and other personal expenses, either extended directly to individuals or indirectly through retail dealers.

6. *Miscellaneous loans,* which include all those loans not listed above, including securities' loans.

7. *Lease financing receivables,* where the lender buys equipment or vehicles and leases them to its customers.

Of the loan categories shown, the largest in dollar volume is real estate loans, accounting for close to half of total bank loans. The next largest category is commercial and industrial (C&I) loans, representing about one-quarter of the total, followed by loans to individuals and families, accounting for about one-sixth of all loans federally insured U.S. commercial banks make.

Factors Determining the Growth and Mix of Loans

While Table 15–1 indicates the relative amounts of different kinds of loans for the whole U.S. banking industry, the mix usually differs quite markedly from institution to institution. One of the key factors in shaping an individual lender's loan portfolio is the profile of *characteristics of the market area* it serves. Each lender must respond to the particular demands for credit arising from customers in its own market. For example, a bank serving a suburban community with large numbers of single-family homes and small retail stores will normally have mainly residential real estate loans, automobile loans, and credit for the purchase of home appliances and for meeting household expenses. In contrast, a lender situated in a central city surrounded by office buildings, department stores, and manufacturing establishments will typically devote the bulk of its loan portfolio to business loans designed to stock shelves with inventory, purchase equipment, and meet payrolls.

Of course, banks and other lenders are not totally dependent on the local areas they serve for *all* the loans they acquire. They can purchase whole loans or pieces of loans from other lenders, share in loans with other lenders (known as *participations*), or even use credit derivatives to offset the economic volatility inherent in loans from their trade territory (as we saw in Chapter 8, for example). These steps can help reduce the risk of loss if the local areas served incur severe economic problems. However, most banks and other lenders are chartered by government authorities primarily to service selected markets and, as a practical matter, most of their loan applications will come from these areas.

Lender size is also a key factor shaping the composition of a loan portfolio. For example, the volume of capital held by a bank or thrift institution determines its *legal lending limit* to a single borrower. Larger banks are often **wholesale lenders,** devoting the bulk of their credit portfolios to large-denomination loans to corporations and other business firms. Smaller banks, on the other hand, tend to emphasize **retail credit,** in the form of smaller-denomination personal cash and installment loans and home mortgage loans extended to individuals and families, as well as smaller business loans to farms and ranches.

Table 15–1 reveals some of the differences between the largest and smallest U.S. banks in loan portfolio mix. The smallest banks (under $100 million in total assets) are more heavily committed to real estate and agricultural loans compared to the largest banking firms (over $1 billion in assets), which are more heavily committed to commercial loans and loans to individuals. The *experience and expertise of management* in making different types of loans also shape the composition of a loan portfolio, as does the lending institution's *loan policy,* which prohibits its loan officers from making certain kinds of loans.

Loan mix at any particular institution depends heavily upon the *expected yield* that each loan offers compared to the yields on all other assets the lender could acquire. Other factors held equal, a lender would generally prefer to make loans bearing the highest expected returns after all expenses and the risk of loan losses are taken into account. One way lenders can assess this yield versus cost factor is to set up a cost accounting system that considers all expected revenues along with the direct and indirect costs of making each type of loan. For banks that don't possess their own sophisticated cost accounting systems, the Federal Reserve banks have created a program called *Functional Cost Analysis* (FCA), which collects data on bank assets, income, expenses, and service volume and calculates an estimated yield and cost for loans and other service functions.

Concept Check

15–1. In what ways does a bank's lending function affect the economy of its community or region?

15–2. What are the principal types of loans made by banks?

15–3. What factors appear to influence the growth and mix of loans held by a lending institution?

15–4. A bank's cost accounting system reveals that its losses on real estate loans average 0.45 percent of loan volume and its operating expenses from making these loans average 1.85 percent of loan volume. If the gross yield on real estate loans is currently 8.80 percent, what is the bank's net yield on these loans?

Examination of recent Functional Cost Analysis reports by the Federal Reserve banks suggests that gross yields (i.e., total revenue received divided by loan volume) typically have been exceptionally high for credit card loans, installment loans (mainly to households and smaller businesses), and real estate loans. However, when *net yields* (with expenses and loss rates deducted from revenues received) are calculated, real estate and commercial loans rank high relative to other loan types, helping to explain their popularity among bankers and other lenders.

Lender size appears to have a significant influence on the net yield from different kinds of loans. Smaller banks, for example, seem to average higher net returns from granting real estate and commercial loans, whereas larger banks appear to have a net yield advantage in making credit card loans to households. Of course, *customer size* as well as lender size can affect relative loan yields. For example, the largest banks make loans to the largest corporations where loan rates are relatively low due to generally lower risk and the force of competition; in contrast, small banks loan money primarily to the smallest-size businesses, whose loan rates tend to be much higher than those for large corporate loans. Thus, it is not too surprising that the net yields on commercial loans tend to be higher among the smallest banks.

As a general rule, a bank or other lending institution should make those types of loans for which it is the *most efficient producer*. For example, the Fed's Functional Cost Analysis program suggests that the largest banks have a cost advantage in making nearly all types of real estate and installment loans. Medium-size and large banks are generally the lowest-cost producers of credit card loans. While the smallest banks appear to have few cost advantages relative to larger banks for almost any type of loan, these smaller lending institutions are frequently among the most effective at controlling loan losses, perhaps because they often have better knowledge of their customers.

Regulation of Lending

Commercial banks are among the most closely regulated of all lending institutions. Not surprisingly, the mix, quality, and yield of the loan portfolio of any bank is heavily influenced by the character and depth of the *regulation* that it faces. Any loans made are subject to examination and review and many are restricted or even prohibited by law.

For example, banks are frequently prohibited from making loans collateralized by their own stock. Real estate loans granted by a U.S. national bank cannot exceed the bank's capital and surplus or 70 percent of its total time and savings deposits, whichever is greater. A loan to a single customer normally cannot exceed 15 percent of a national bank's unimpaired capital and surplus account. The lending limit may be further increased to 25 percent of unimpaired capital and surplus if the loan amount exceeding the 15 percent limit is fully secured by marketable securities.

Loans to a bank's officers extended for purposes other than funding education or the purchase of a home or that are not fully backed by U.S. government securities or deposits are limited to the greater of 2.5 percent of the bank's capital and unimpaired surplus or $25,000, but cannot be more than $100,000. State-chartered banks face similar restrictions on insider loans in their home states and from the Federal Deposit Insurance Corporation. The Sarbanes-Oxley Act of 2002 requires that loans to insiders be priced at market rather than being subsidized by the lending institution.

The Community Reinvestment Act (1977) requires all banks to make "an affirmative effort" to meet the credit needs of individuals and businesses in their trade territories so that no areas of the local community are discriminated against in seeking access to bank credit. Moreover, under the Equal Credit Opportunity Act (1974), no individual can be

Key URL
To get a better view of government regulation of lending, see especially **www.fdic.gov/regulations/safety/manual**.

denied credit because of race, sex, religious affiliation, age, or receipt of public assistance. Disclosure laws, such as the federal Truth-in-Lending Act (1968), require that the household borrower be quoted the "true cost" of a loan, as reflected in the annual percentage interest rate (APR) and all required charges and fees for obtaining credit, *before* the loan agreement is signed.[2]

In the field of international lending, special regulations have appeared in recent years in an effort to reduce the risk exposure associated with granting loans overseas. In this field, banks often face significant political risk from foreign governments passing restrictive laws or seizing foreign-owned property, and substantial business risk due to lack of information and knowledge concerning foreign markets. U.S. law in the form of the International Lending and Supervision Act requires U.S. banks to report to regulatory agencies and make public any credit exposures to a single country that exceed 15 percent of their primary capital or 0.75 percent of their total assets, whichever is the smaller of the two. This law also imposes restriction on the fees banks may charge a troubled international borrower to restructure a loan.

The quality of a bank's loan portfolio and the soundness of its lending policies are the areas federal and state bank examiners look at most closely when examining the institution. Under the Uniform Financial Institutions Rating System used by federal bank examiners, each banking firm is assigned a numerical rating based on the quality of its asset portfolio, including its loans. The examiner assigns one of these ratings:

1 = strong performance
2 = satisfactory performance
3 = fair performance
4 = marginal performance
5 = unsatisfactory performance

The better a bank's asset-quality rating, the less frequently it will be subject to review and examination by federal banking agencies.

Examiners generally look at all loans above a designated minimum size and at a random sample of small loans. Loans that are performing well but have minor weaknesses because the lender has not followed its own loan policy or has failed to get full documentation from the borrower are called *criticized loans*. Loans that appear to contain significant weaknesses or that represent what the examiner regards as a dangerous concentration of credit in one borrower or in one industry are called *scheduled loans*. A scheduled loan is a warning to management to monitor that credit carefully and to work toward reducing the lender's concentrated risk exposure from it.

When an examiner finds some loans that carry an immediate risk of not paying out as planned, these credits are *adversely classified*. Typically, examiners will place adversely classified loans into one of three groupings: (1) *substandard loans*, where the loans' margin of protection is inadequate due to weaknesses in collateral or in the borrower's repayment abilities; (2) *doubtful loans*, which carry a strong probability of an uncollectible loss to the lending institution; and (3) *loss loans*, which are regarded as uncollectible and not suitable to be called bankable assets. A common procedure for examiners is to multiply the total of all substandard loans by 0.20, the total of all doubtful loans by 0.50, and the total of all loss loans by 1.00, then sum these weighted amounts and compare their grand total with the lender's sum of loan-loss reserves and equity capital. If the weighted sum of all adversely classified loans appears too large relative to loan-loss reserves and equity capital, examin-

---

[2] See Chapter 17 for a more detailed discussion of antidiscrimination and disclosure laws applying to bank loans to individuals.

ETHICS IN BANKING

FINDING WAYS AROUND LOAN REGULATIONS

One of the most common ethical problems surrounding the lending of money arises when lenders seek loopholes around laws and regulations that govern the granting of loans. These rules are designed to prevent excessive risk taking in what normally is the riskiest part of the banking business and to ensure fairness in making credit available to all qualified customers.

One of the most frequent violations centers around legal lending limits, which restrict the amount of credit that can be extended to a single customer. The purpose of this limiting rule is to prevent a lending institution from becoming too dependent upon the financial condition of one or a handful of borrowers, any of which may fail and cause the lender to fail as well.

In one notable case in Mississippi in 2002, a former bank CEO pled guilty to charges of making false statements on bank records. Among other allegations brought by the Federal Deposit Insurance Corporation (FDIC) and law-enforcement authorities, the bank CEO allowed favored customers to go beyond legal lending limits and receive excess amounts of credit. These transactions allegedly were covered up by changing the names attached to various loans. The CEO's bank ultimately collapsed. In this instance the U.S. Attorney's Office brought criminal charges and sought several million dollars in fines to help the FDIC and other creditors recover their money.

Source: Federal Deposit Insurance Corporation, News Release, October 17, 2000.

ers will demand changes in the lender's policies and procedures or, possibly, require additions to loan-loss reserves and capital. Financial institutions that disagree with examiner classifications of their loans can appeal these examiner rulings.

Of course, the quality of loans and other assets is only one dimension of a lender's performance that is rated under the Uniform Financial Institutions Rating System. Numerical ratings are also assigned based on examiner judgment of capital adequacy, management quality, earnings record, liquidity position, and sensitivity to market risk exposure. All five dimensions of performance are combined into one overall numerical rating, popularly referred to as the **CAMELS rating.** The letters in CAMELS are derived from

Capital adequacy
Asset quality
Management quality
Earnings record
Liquidity position
Sensitivity to market risk

Banks and thrift institutions whose overall CAMELS rating is toward the low, riskier end of the numerical scale—an overall rating of 4 or 5—are examined more frequently than the highest-rated institutions, those with ratings of 1, 2, or 3.

One final note on the examination process today: Rapidly changing technology and the emergence of very large financial institutions appear to have weakened the effectiveness of traditional examination procedures. An added problem is that examinations tend to occur no more frequently than once a year and the decay in the quality of examination information over time can be quite rapid, especially among weakly performing or poorly managed lending institutions. Accordingly, regulators are beginning to turn more toward *market forces* as a better long-run approach to monitoring behavior and encouraging lenders to manage their institutions prudently. The new emerging emphasis in examination is to rely more and more upon "private market discipline" in which such factors as borrowing costs, stock prices, and other market values are used as "signals" as to how well a lender is performing and to help examiners determine if they need to take a close look at

Key URL
For an interesting source of information about trends in lending and loan policies, see the Senior Loan Officer Opinion Survey at **www.federalreserve.gov/boarddocs/snloansurvey.**

how a lending institution displaying adverse market signals is managing its loans and protecting the public's funds.[3]

Establishing a Written Loan Policy

One of the most important ways a bank or other lending institution can make sure its loans meet regulatory standards and are profitable is to establish a *written loan policy*. Such a policy gives loan officers and management specific guidelines in making individual loan decisions and in shaping the overall loan portfolio. The actual makeup of a lender's loan portfolio should reflect what its loan policy says. Otherwise, the loan policy is not functioning effectively and should be either revised or more strongly enforced by senior management.

What should a written loan policy contain? The examinations manual, which the Federal Deposit Insurance Corporation gives to new examiners, suggests the most important elements of a well-written loan policy. These elements are as follows:

1. A goal statement for the loan portfolio (i.e., statement of the characteristics of a good loan portfolio in terms of types, maturities, sizes, and quality of loans).
2. Specification of the lending authority given to each loan officer and loan committee (measuring the maximum amount and types of loan that each employee and committee can approve and what signatures are required).
3. Lines of responsibility in making assignments and reporting information within the loan department.
4. Operating procedures for soliciting, reviewing, evaluating, and making decisions on customer loan applications.
5. The required documentation that is to accompany each loan application and what must be kept in the lender's credit files (required financial statements, security agreements, etc.).
6. Lines of authority within the lending institution detailing who is responsible for maintaining and reviewing the institution's credit files.
7. Guidelines for taking, evaluating, and perfecting loan collateral.
8. A presentation of policies and procedures for setting loan interest rates and fees and the terms for repayment of loans.
9. A statement of quality standards applicable to all loans.
10. A statement of the preferred upper limit for total loans outstanding (i.e., the maximum ratio of total loans to total assets allowed).
11. A description of the lending institution's principal trade area, from which most loans should come.
12. A discussion of the preferred procedures for detecting, analyzing, and working out problem loan situations.

Concept Check

15–5. Why is lending so closely regulated by state and federal authorities?

15–6. What is the CAMELS rating and how is it used?

15–7. What should a good written loan policy contain?

---

[3] In order to more closely monitor the condition of banks and thrifts between regular examinations the regulatory agencies today use *off-site monitoring* systems. For example, the FDIC employs SCOR—the Statistical CAMELS Off-Site Rating—which forecasts future CAMELS ratings quarterly, based on 12 key financial ratios tracking equity capital, loan loss exposure, earnings, liquid assets, and loan totals. See especially Collier et al. [14].

Other authorities would add to this list such items as specifying what loans the lender would prefer *not* to make, such as loans to support the construction of speculative housing or loans to support leveraged buyouts (LBOs) of companies by a small group of insiders who typically make heavy use of debt to finance the purchase, as well as a list of preferred loans (such as short-term business inventory loans that are self-liquidating).

A written loan policy statement carries a number of advantages for the lending institution adopting it. It communicates to employees working in the loan department what procedures they must follow and what their responsibilities are. It helps the lender move toward a loan portfolio that can successfully blend *multiple objectives,* such as promoting profitability, controlling risk exposure, and satisfying regulatory requirements. Any exceptions to the written loan policy should be fully documented, and the reasons why a variance from the loan policy was permitted should be listed. While any written loan policy must be flexible due to continuing changes in economic conditions and regulations, violations of loan policy should be infrequent events.

Steps in the Lending Process

Most loans to individuals arise from a direct request from a customer who approaches a member of the lender's staff and asks to fill out a loan application. Business loan requests, on the other hand, often arise from contacts the loan officers and sales representatives make as they solicit new accounts from firms operating in the lender's market area. Sometimes loan officers will call on the same company for months before the customer finally agrees to give the lending institution a try by filling out a loan application. Most loan department personnel fill out a customer contact report similar to the one shown in Table 15–2 when they visit a potential new customer's place of business. This report is updated after each subsequent visit, giving the next loan officer crucial information about a prospective client before any other personal contacts are made.

Once a customer decides to request a loan, an interview with a loan officer usually follows, giving the customer the opportunity to explain his or her credit needs. That interview is particularly important because it provides an opportunity for the loan officer to assess the customer's *character* and *sincerity of purpose.* If the customer appears to lack sincerity in acknowledging the need to adhere to the terms of a loan, this must be recorded as a strong factor weighing against approval of the loan request.

If a business or mortgage loan is applied for, a loan officer often makes a *site visit* to assess the customer's location and the condition of the property and to ask clarifying questions. The loan officer may contact other creditors who have previously loaned money to this customer to see what their experience has been. Did the customer fully adhere to previous loan agreements and, where required, keep satisfactory deposit balances? A previous payment record often reveals much about the customer's character, sincerity of purpose, and sense of responsibility in making use of credit extended by a lending institution.

If all is favorable to this point, the customer is asked to submit several crucial documents the lender needs in order to fully evaluate the loan request, including complete financial statements and, in the case of a corporation, board of directors' resolutions authorizing the negotiation of a loan with the lender. Once all documents are on file, the lender's credit analysis division conducts a thorough financial analysis of the applicant aimed at determining whether the customer has sufficient cash flow and backup assets to repay the loan. The credit analysis division then prepares a brief summary and recommendation, which goes to the appropriate loan committee for approval. On larger loans, members of the credit analysis division may give an oral presentation and discussion will ensue between staff analysts and the loan committee over the strong and weak points of a loan request.

TABLE 15–2

Sample Customer
Contact Report
(results of previous
calls on this
customer)

Name of customer: _____

Address:_____ Telephone: ( )_____

Lender personnel making the most recent contact: _____

Names of employees making previous contacts with this customer:_____

_____

Does this customer currently use our services? _____ Yes _____ No

Which ones?_____

If no, has the customer used any of our services in the past? _____

If a business firm, what officials or principals with the customer's firm have been contacted by
our institution?

_____

If an individual, what is the customer's occupation? _____

If a business firm, what line of business is the customer in? _____

Approximate annual sales: $ _____ Size of labor force: _____

With whom does the customer bank at present? _____

What problems (if any) does the customer report having with his/her current banking
relationship?

_____

What services does this customer use at present? (Please check)

_____ Line of credit   _____ Letters of credit

_____ Term loan   _____ Funds transfers

_____ Checkable deposits   _____ Cash management services

_____ CDs and other time accounts   _____ Trust services

What services does this customer *not* use currently that might be useful to him or her?

_____

Describe the results of the most recent contact with this customer: _____

_____

Recommended steps to prepare for the next call (e.g., special information needed, additional

personnel needed): _____

_____

If the loan committee approves the customer's request, the loan officer or the credit committee will usually check on the property or other assets to be pledged as collateral in order to ensure that the lending institution has immediate access to the collateral or can acquire title to the property involved if the loan agreement is defaulted. This is often referred to as *perfecting* the lender's claim to collateral. Once the loan officer and the loan committee are satisfied that both the loan and the proposed collateral are sound, the note and other documents that make up a loan agreement are prepared and are signed by all parties to the agreement.

Is this the end of the process? Can the loan officer put the signed loan agreement on the shelf and forget about it? Hardly! The new agreement must be monitored continuously to ensure that the terms of the loan are being followed and that all required payments of principal and interest are being made as promised. For larger commercial credits, the loan officer will visit the customer's business periodically to check on the firm's progress and to see what other services the customer may need. Usually a loan officer or other staff member places information about a new loan customer in a computer file known as a *customer profile*. This file shows what services the customer is currently using and contains other information required by management to monitor a customer's progress and financial service needs.

Credit Analysis: What Makes a Good Loan?

The division or department responsible for analyzing and making recommendations on the fate of most loan applications is the *credit department*. Experience has shown that this department must satisfactorily answer three major questions regarding each loan application:

1. Is the borrower *creditworthy*? How do you know?
2. Can the loan agreement be properly *structured and documented* so that the lending institution and its customers who supply it with funds are adequately protected and the customer has a high probability of being able to service the loan without excessive strain?
3. Can the lender *perfect* its claim against the assets or earnings of the customer so that, in the event of default, the lender's funds can be recovered rapidly at low cost and with low risk?

Let's look in turn at each of these three key issues in the "yes" or "no" decision a lending institution must make on every loan request.

Is the Borrower Creditworthy?

The question that must be dealt with before any other is whether or not the customer can *service the loan*—that is, pay out the credit when due, with a comfortable margin for error. This usually involves a detailed study of six aspects of the loan application: *character, capacity, cash, collateral, conditions,* and *control*. All must be satisfactory for the loan to be a good one from the lender's point of view. (See Table 15–3.)

Character The loan officer must be convinced that the customer has a well-defined *purpose* for requesting credit and a serious intention to repay. If the officer is not sure exactly why the customer is requesting a loan, this purpose must be clarified to the lender's satisfaction. Once the purpose is known, the loan officer must determine if it is consistent with the lending institution's current loan policy. Even with a good purpose, however, the loan officer must determine that the borrower has a responsible attitude toward using borrowed funds, is truthful in answering questions, and will make every effort to repay what is owed. Responsibility, truthfulness, serious purpose, and serious intention to repay all monies owed make up what a loan officer calls *character*. If the loan officer feels the customer is insincere in promising to use borrowed funds as planned and in repaying as agreed, the loan should *not* be made, for it will almost certainly become a problem credit.

Capacity The loan officer must be sure that the customer requesting credit has the authority to request a loan and the legal standing to sign a binding loan agreement. This customer characteristic is known as the *capacity* to borrow money. For example, in most states a minor (e.g., under age 18 or 21) cannot legally be held responsible for a credit

TABLE 15-3 The Six Basic Cs of Lending

Source: Peter S. Rose, "Loans in a Troubled Economy," *The Canadian Banker*, *ICB Review* 90, no. 3 (June 1983), p. 55.

Character	Capacity	Cash	Collateral	Conditions	Control
Customer's past payment record	Identity of customer and guarantors	Take-home pay for an individual, the past earnings, dividends, and sales record for a business firm	Ownership of assets	Customer's current position in industry and expected market share	Applicable laws and regulations regarding the character and quality of acceptable loans
Experience of other lenders with this customer	Copies of Social Security cards, driver's licenses, corporate charters, resolutions, partnership agreements, and other legal documents	Adequacy of past and projected cash flow	Vulnerability of assets to obsolescence	Customer's performance vis-à-vis comparable firms in the same industry	Adequate documentation for examiners who may review the loan
Purpose of loan	Description of history, legal structure, owners, nature of operations, products, and principal customers and suppliers for a business borrower	Availability of liquid reserves	Liquidation value of assets	Competitive climate for customer's product	Signed acknowledgments and correctly prepared loan documents
Customer's track record in forecasting business or personal income		Turnover of payables, accounts receivable, and inventory	Degree of specialization in assets	Sensitivity of customer and industry to business cycles and changes in technology	Consistency of loan request with lender's written loan policy
Credit rating		Capital structure and leverage	Liens, encumbrances, and restrictions against property held	Labor market conditions in customer's industry or market area	Inputs from noncredit personnel (such as economists or political experts) on the external factors affecting loan repayment
Presence of cosigners or guarantors of the proposed loan		Expense controls	Leases and mortgages issued against property and equipment	Impact of inflation on customer's balance sheet and cash flow	
		Coverage ratios	Insurance coverage	Long-run industry or job outlook	
		Recent performance of borrower's stock and price-earnings (P/E) ratio	Guarantees and warranties issued to others	Regulations, political and environmental factors affecting the customer and/or his or her job, business, and industry	
		Management quality	Lender's relative position as creditor in placing a claim against borrower's assets		
		Recent accounting changes	Probable future financing needs		

agreement; thus, the lender would have great difficulty collecting on such a loan. Similarly, the loan officer must be sure that the representative from a corporation asking for credit has proper authority from the company's board of directors to negotiate a loan and sign a credit agreement binding the corporation. Usually this can be determined by obtaining a copy of the resolution passed by a corporate customer's board of directors, authorizing the company to borrow money. Where a business partnership is involved, the loan officer must ask to see the firm's partnership agreement to determine which individuals are authorized to borrow for the firm. A loan agreement signed by unauthorized persons could prove to be uncollectible and, therefore, result in substantial losses for the lending institution.

Cash   This key feature of any loan application centers on the question: Does the borrower have the ability to generate enough **cash**—in the form of *cash flow*—to repay the loan? In general, borrowing customers have only three sources to draw upon to repay their loans: (*a*) cash flows generated from sales or income, (*b*) the sale or liquidation of assets, or (*c*) funds raised by issuing debt or equity securities. Any of these sources may provide sufficient cash to repay a loan. However, lenders have a strong preference for *cash flow* as the principal source of loan repayment because asset sales can weaken a borrowing customer and make the lender's position as creditor less secure. Moreover, shortfalls in cash flow are common indicators of failing businesses and troubled loan relationships. This is one reason current banking regulations require that the lender document the cash flow basis for approving a loan.

What is **cash flow?** In an accounting sense, it is usually defined as follows:

$$\text{Cash flow} = \begin{matrix} \text{Net Profits} \\ \text{(or total} \\ \text{revenues less} \\ \text{all expenses)} \end{matrix} + \begin{matrix} \text{Noncash Expenses} \\ \text{(especially} \\ \text{depreciation)} \end{matrix}$$

This is often called *traditional cash flow* and can be further broken down into this form:

$$\text{Cash flow} = \begin{matrix} \text{Sales Revenues} - \text{Cost of Goods Sold} - \text{Selling, General and} \\ \text{Administrative Expenses} - \text{Taxes Paid in Cash} + \text{Noncash Expenses} \end{matrix}$$

with all of the above items (except noncash expenses) figured on the basis of actual cash inflows and outflows instead of on an accrual basis.

In this slightly expanded format, traditional cash flow measures point to at least five major areas loan officers should look at carefully when lending money to business firms or other institutions. These are the key areas:

1. The level of and recent trends in sales revenue (which reflect the quality and public acceptance of products and services).
2. The level of and recent changes in cost of goods sold (including inventory costs).
3. The level of and recent trends in selling, general, and administrative expenses (including the compensation of management and employees).
4. Any tax payments made in cash.
5. The level of and recent trends in noncash expenses (led by depreciation expenses).

Adverse movements in *any* of these key sources and uses of cash demand inquiry and satisfactory resolution by a loan officer.

A more recent and, in some ways, more revealing approach to measuring cash flow is often called the *direct cash flow method* or sometimes *cash flow by origin*. It answers the simple but vital question: *Why* is cash changing over time? This method divides cash flow into its three principal sources:

1. *Net cash flow from operations* (the borrower's net income expressed on a cash rather than an accrual basis).
2. *Net cash flow from financing activity* (which tracks cash inflows and outflows associated with selling or repurchasing borrower-issued securities).
3. *Net cash flow from investing activities* (which examines outflows and inflows of cash resulting from the purchase and sale of the borrower's assets).

This method of figuring cash flow and its components can be extremely useful in ferreting out the recent sources of a borrower's cash flow. For example, most lenders would prefer that most incoming cash come from operations (sales of product or service). If, on the other hand, a substantial proportion of incoming cash arises instead from the sale of assets (investing activities) or from issuing debt (financing activities), the borrower may have even less opportunity to generate cash in the future, presenting any prospective lender with added risk exposure if a loan is granted. Some accountants and financial analysts use another definition:

$$\text{Cash flow} = \frac{\text{Net profits} + \text{Noncash expenses} + \text{Additions to accounts payable}}{- \text{Additions to inventories and accounts receivable}}$$

One of the benefits of this latter definition of cash flow is that it helps to focus a loan officer's attention on those facets of a customer's business that reflect the quality and experience of its management and the strength of the market the customer serves. A borrowing customer that stays afloat through heavy use of trade credit (accounts payable), is piling up large inventories of unsold goods, or is having difficulty collecting from its own credit customers (accounts receivable) is likely to be a problem credit. Most lenders would hesitate to commit their scarce reserves to such a customer without the good prospect of a turnaround in the customer's circumstances. In short, the loan officer's evaluation of a borrower's cash flow involves asking and answering such important questions as these: Is there a history of steady growth in earnings or sales? Is there a high probability that such growth will continue to support the loan? Current borrower income and the borrower's income history are important pieces of evidence in answering such questions and in making a lending decision.

Collateral   In assessing the *collateral* aspect of a loan request, the loan officer must ask, Does the borrower possess adequate net worth or own enough quality assets to provide adequate support for the loan? The loan officer is particularly sensitive to such features as the age, condition, and degree of specialization of the borrower's assets. Technology plays an important role here as well. If the borrower's assets are technologically obsolete, they will have limited value as collateral because of the difficulty of finding a buyer for those assets should the borrower's income falter.

Conditions   The loan officer and credit analyst must be aware of recent trends in the borrower's line of work or industry and how changing economic conditions might affect the loan. A loan can look very good on paper, only to have its value eroded by declining sales or income in a recession or by the high interest rates occasioned by inflation. To assess industry and economic conditions, most lenders maintain files of information—newspaper clippings, magazine articles, and research reports—on the industries represented by their major borrowing customers.

Control   The last factor in assessing a borrower's creditworthy status is control, which centers on such questions as whether changes in law and regulation could adversely affect the borrower and whether the loan request meets the lender's and the regulatory authorities' standards for loan quality. For example, a few years ago passage of the windfall profits tax in the United States made a number of energy companies somewhat less desirable as borrowing customers because that tax absorbed a substantial proportion of their current cash flow.

Can the Loan Agreement Be Properly Structured and Documented?

The six Cs of credit aid the loan officer and the credit analyst in answering the broad question: Is the borrower creditworthy? Once that question is answered, however, a second issue must be faced: Can the proposed loan agreement be structured and documented to satisfy the needs of both borrower and lender?

The loan officer is responsible to both the borrowing customer and the depositors or other creditors as well as the stockholders and must seek to satisfy the demands of *all*. This requires, first, the drafting of a loan agreement that meets the borrower's need for funds with a comfortable repayment schedule. The borrower must be able to comfortably handle any required loan payments, because the lender's success depends fundamentally on the success of its customers. If a major borrower gets into trouble because it is unable to service a loan, the lending institution may find itself in serious trouble as well. Proper accommodation of a customer may involve lending more or less money than requested (because many customers do not know their own financial needs), over a longer or shorter period than requested. Thus, a loan officer must be a financial counselor to customers as well as a conduit for their loan applications.

A properly structured loan agreement must also protect the lender and those the lender represents—principally depositors, other creditors, and stockholders—by imposing certain restrictions (covenants) on the borrower's activities when these activities could threaten the recovery of the lender's funds. The process of recovering the lender's funds—when and where the lender can take action to get its funds returned—also must be carefully spelled out in a loan agreement.

Can the Lender Perfect Its Claim against the Borrower's Earnings and Any Assets That May Be Pledged as Collateral?

Reasons for Taking Collateral   While large corporations, and other borrowers with impeccable credit ratings often borrow unsecured (with no specific collateral pledged behind their loans except their reputation and ability to generate earnings), most borrowers at one time or another will be asked to pledge some of their assets or to personally guarantee the repayment of their loans. Getting a pledge of certain borrower assets as collateral behind a loan really serves two purposes for a lender. If the borrower cannot pay, the pledge of collateral gives the lender the right to seize and sell those assets designated as loan collateral, using the proceeds of the sale to cover what the borrower did not pay back. Secondly, collateralization of a loan gives the lender a psychological advantage over the borrower. Because specific assets may be at stake (such as the customer's automobile or home), a borrower feels more obligated to work hard to repay his or her loan and avoid losing valuable assets. Thus, the third key question faced with many loan applications is, Can the lender *perfect* its claim against the assets or earnings of a borrowing customer?

The goal of a lender taking collateral is to precisely *define* which borrower assets are subject to seizure and sale and to *document* for all other creditors to see that the lender has a legal claim to those assets in the event of nonperformance on a loan. When a lender holds a claim against a borrower's assets that stands superior to the claims of other lenders and to the borrower's own claim, we say that lender's claim to collateral has been *perfected*. Lending institutions have learned that the procedures necessary for establishing a perfected claim on someone else's property differ depending on the nature of the assets

Key URLs
For an overview of modern loan risk evaluation techniques see, for example, **www.riskmetrics.com/ rm.html** and **www .defaultrisk.com**.

pledged by the borrower and depending on the laws of the state or nation where the assets reside. For example, a different set of steps is necessary to perfect a claim if the lender has actual possession of the assets pledged (e.g., if the borrower pledges a deposit already held in the bank or lets the lender hold some of the customer's stocks and bonds) as opposed to the case where the borrower retains possession of the pledged assets (e.g., an automobile). Yet another procedure must be followed if the property pledged is real estate—land and buildings.

Common Types of Loan Collateral Examples of the most popular assets pledged as collateral for loans and what is usually done to legally attach those assets in order to collateralize a loan are listed here.

Accounts Receivable. The lender takes a security interest in the form of a stated percentage (usually somewhere between 40 and 90 percent) of the face amount of accounts receivable (sales on credit) shown on a business borrower's balance sheet. When the borrower's credit customers send in cash to retire their debts, these cash payments are applied to the balance of the borrower's loan. The lending institution may agree to lend still more money as new receivables arise from the borrower's sales to its customers, thus allowing the loan to continue as long as the borrower has need for credit and continues to generate an adequate volume of sales and credit repayments.

Factoring. A lender can purchase a borrower's accounts receivable based upon some percentage of their book value. The percentage figure used depends on the quality and age of the receivables. Moreover, because the lender takes over ownership of the receivables, it will inform the borrower's customers that they should send their payments to the purchasing institution. Usually the borrower promises to set aside funds in order to cover some or all of the losses that the lending institution may suffer from any unpaid receivables.

Inventory. In return for a loan, a lender may take a security interest against the current amount of inventory of goods or raw materials a business borrower owns. Usually a lending institution will advance only a percentage (30 to 80 percent is common) of the estimated market value of a borrower's inventory in order to leave a substantial cushion in case the inventory's value begins to decline. The inventory pledged may be controlled completely by the borrower, using a so-called *floating lien* approach. Another option, often used for auto and truck dealers or sellers of home appliances, is called *floor planning*, in which the lender takes temporary ownership of any goods placed in inventory and the borrower sends payments or sales contracts to the lender as the goods are sold.[4]

Real Property. Following a title search, appraisal, and land survey, a lending institution may take a security interest in land and/or improvements on land owned by the borrower and record its claim—a *mortgage*—with a government agency in order to warn other lenders that the property has already been pledged (i.e., has a lien against it) and to help defend the original lender's position against claims by others.

---

[4] Lenders seeking closer control over a borrower's inventory will often employ a technique called *warehousing* in which the goods are stored and monitored by the lender or by an independent agent working to protect the lender's interest. (The warehouse site may be in a location away from the borrower's place of business—a *field warehouse.*) As the inventory grows, warehouse receipts are issued to the lending institution, giving it a legal claim against the warehoused goods or materials. The lender will make the borrower a loan equal to some agreed-upon percentage of the expected market value of the inventory covered by the warehouse receipts. When the public buys goods from the borrowing firm, the lender surrenders its claim so the company's product can be delivered to its customers. However, the customer's cash payments go straight to the lending institution to be applied to the loan's balance. Because of the potential for fraud or theft, loan officers may inspect a business borrower's inventory periodically to ensure that the loan is well secured and that proper procedures for protecting and valuing inventory are being followed.

For example, public notice of a mortgage against real estate may be filed with the county courthouse or tax assessor/collector in the county where the property resides. The lender may also take out title insurance and insist that the borrower purchase insurance to cover damage from floods and other hazards, with the lending institution receiving first claim on any insurance settlement that is made.

Personal Property. Lenders often take a security interest in automobiles, furniture and equipment, jewelry, securities and other forms of personal property a borrower owns. A *financing statement* may be filed with state or local government offices in those cases where the borrower keeps possession of any personal property pledged as collateral during the term of a loan. To be effective, the financing statement must be signed by both the borrower, and an officer of the lending institution. On the other hand, a *pledge agreement* may be prepared (but will usually not be publicly filed) if the lender or its agent holds the pledged property, giving the lending institution the right to control that property until the loan is repaid in full. In July 2001, 46 states adopted new rules under the Uniform Commercial Code (UCC) affecting how banks and other lenders can perfect liens and how borrowers file collateral statements. The four remaining states came on board with the new regulations in 2002. Specifically, Article 9 of the UCC now requires all financial statements that detail collateral associated with a loan to be filed in one location—the secretary of state's office in the debtor's home state. Previously, these financial statements were filed inside the United States in the local area where a loan's collateral was situated, most often in county court houses or county recorder's offices.

Personal Guarantees. A pledge of the stock, deposits, or other personal assets held by the major stockholders or owners of a company may be required as collateral to secure a business loan. Guarantees are often sought in lending to smaller businesses or to firms that have fallen on difficult times. Then, too, getting pledges of personal assets from the owners of a business firm gives the owners an additional reason to want their firm to prosper and to repay their loan.

Other Safety Devices to Protect a Loan Many loan officers argue that the collateral a customer pledges behind a loan is just one of the safety zones that a lending institution must wrap around the funds it has loaned for adequate protection. As Exhibit 15–1 indicates, most loan officers prefer to have at least two safety zones—ideally, three—around the funds they have placed at risk with the customer. The primary safety zone is income or cash flow, the preferred source from which the customer will repay the loan. The

EXHIBIT 15–1
Safety Zones
Surrounding the
Funds Loaned
by a Bank

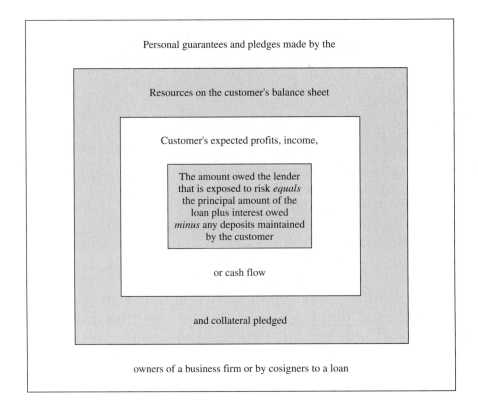

Personal guarantees and pledges made by the

Resources on the customer's balance sheet

Customer's expected profits, income,

The amount owed the lender
that is exposed to risk *equals*
the principal amount of the
loan plus interest owed
minus any deposits maintained
by the customer

or cash flow

and collateral pledged

owners of a business firm or by cosigners to a loan

second consists of strength on the customer's balance sheet, in the form of assets that can be pledged as collateral or liquid assets that can be sold for cash in order to fill any gaps in the customer's cash flow. Finally, the outer safety zone consists of guarantees from a business firm's owners to support a loan to their firm or from third-party cosigners who pledge their personal assets to back another person's loan.

Sources of Information about Loan Customers

A lender often relies heavily on outside information to assess the character, financial position, and collateral of a loan customer (see Table 15–4). Such an analysis begins with a review of information the borrower supplies in the loan application. How much money is being requested? For what purpose? What other obligations does the customer have? What assets might be used as collateral to back up the loan?

The lending institution may contact other lenders to determine their experience with this customer. Were all scheduled payments in previous loan agreements made on time? Were deposit balances kept at high enough levels? In the case of a household borrower, the local or regional *credit bureau* will be contacted to ascertain the customer's credit history. How much was borrowed previously and how well were those earlier loans handled? Is there any evidence of slow or delinquent payments? Has the customer ever declared bankruptcy?

Most business borrowers of any size carry credit ratings on their bonds and other debt securities and on the firm's overall credit record. Moody's and Standard & Poor's assigned ratings reflect the probability of default on bonds and shorter-term notes. Dun & Bradstreet provides overall credit ratings for several thousand corporations. It and other firms

Key URLs

Among the most important websites for financial data and analysis of firms and industries of particular use to loan officers are Dun and Bradstreet at **www.dnb.com** and RMA at **http:// rmaweb.rmahq.org/** (see Annual Statement Studies link).

TABLE 15–4
Some Outside
Sources of
Information
Frequently Used in
Loan Analysis

Consumer Information
Local or regional credit bureaus
Customer financial statements
Experience of other lenders with this customer
The World Wide Web, especially items listed under consumer or household loans and under types of personal or family loans, such as auto loans, boat loans, and home mortgage loans

Business Information
New York Times and *New York Times Index*
The World Wide Web, especially under the different categories of business loans, such as small business loans, term loans, revolving credit, and working capital loans

Government Information
Moody's Government Manual
Government budget reports
Credit rating agencies
The World Wide Web, especially under the names of regulatory agencies, such as the Federal Reserve System, the Federal Deposit Insurance Corporation (FDIC), and the Federal Financial Institutions Examination Council (FFIEC)

General Economic Information
Local newspapers
Local chamber of commerce
The World Wide Web, especially under websites maintained by the Board of Governors of the Federal Reserve System and the 12 Federal Reserve banks, the U. S. Department of Commerce, the U. S. Treasury Department, and the Bureau of Labor Statistics

and organizations, such as Risk Management Associates (RMA), provide benchmark operating and financial ratios for whole industries so that the borrower's particular operating and financial ratios in any given year can be compared to industry standards.

One of the most widely consulted sources of data on business firm performance is Risk Management Associates, founded as RMA in Philadelphia in 1914 to exchange credit information among business lending institutions and to organize conferences and publish educational materials to help train loan officers and credit analysts. While RMA began in the United States, its members have now spread over much of the globe with especially active groups in Canada, Great Britain and Western Europe, Hong Kong, and Mexico. RMA publishes several respected journals and studies, including *Creative Considerations, Lending to Different Industries*, and the *RMA Journal*, to help inform and train credit decision makers.

Another popular RMA publication is its *Annual Statement Studies: Financial Ratio Benchmarks*, which provides financial performance data on businesses grouped by industry type and by size category. Loan officers who are members of RMA submit financial performance information based on data supplied by their borrowing business customers. RMA then groups this data and calculates average values for selected performance ratios. Among the ratios published by RMA and grouped by industry and firm size are

Current assets to current liabilities (the current ratio).

Current assets minus inventories to current liabilities (the quick ratio).

Sales to accounts receivable.

Cost of sales to inventory (the inventory turnover ratio).

Earnings before interest and taxes to total interest payments (the interest coverage ratio).

Fixed assets to net worth.

Total debt to net worth (the leverage ratio).

Profits before taxes to total assets and to tangible net worth.

Total sales to net fixed assets and to total assets.

RMA also calculates common-size balance sheets (with all major asset and liability items expressed as a percentage of total assets) and common-size income statements (with profits and operating expense items expressed as a percentage of total sales) for different size groups of firms within an industry. Recently the association began publishing a second volume of its statement studies series called *Annual Statement Studies: Industry Default Probabilities and Cash Flow Measures*, which reports on the risk exposure of about 450 different industries, estimates default probabilities for one- and five-year intervals, and tracks at least four different measures of cash flow—a key element in any lending decision.

Finally, RMA currently offers lenders a Windows-based version of its statement studies series, called COMPARE2, which permits a credit analyst or loan officer to do a *spreadsheet analysis*—arraying the loan customer's financial statements and key financial and operating ratios over time relative to industry averages based upon data from more than 130,000 different businesses. COMPARE2 enables a loan officer to counsel his or her borrowing customer, pointing out any apparent weaknesses in the customer's financial or operating situation compared to industry standards. It also reports on recent developments in each of about 450 different industries. This credit analysis routine is also available to business firms planning to submit a loan request to a bank or other lending institution so business owners can personally evaluate their firm's financial condition from the lender's perspective.

A similar array of industry data is provided by Dun & Bradstreet Credit Services. This credit-rating agency collects information on approximately 3 million firms in 800 different business lines (captured by Standard Industrial Classifications, or SIC, codes). D&B prepares detailed financial reports on individual borrowing companies for its subscribers. For each firm reviewed, the D&B *Business Information Reports* provide a credit rating, a brief financial and management history of the firm, a summary of recent balance sheet and income and expense statement trends, a listing of any major loans known to be still outstanding against the firm, its terms of trade, the names of its key managers, and the location and condition of the firm's facilities. Dun & Bradstreet also prepares an *Industry Norm Book*, containing annual financial and operating data for firms grouped by industry for the most recent year and the past three years. D&B calculates 14 key ratios measuring efficiency, profitability, and solvency, as well as common-size balance sheets and income statements (with each entry expressed as a percent of total assets or total net sales) for the medium-size, or typical, firm and for the uppermost and lowest quartiles of firms in each industry.

In evaluating a credit application, the loan officer must look beyond the customer to the economy of the local area for smaller loan requests and to the national or international economy for larger credit requests. Many loan customers are especially sensitive to the fluctuations in economic activity known as the *business cycle*. For example, auto dealers, producers of farm and other commodities, home builders, and security dealers and brokers face cyclically sensitive markets for their goods and services. This does not mean that banks and other lending institutions should not lend to such firms. Rather, they must be aware of the vulnerability of some of their borrowers to cyclical changes and structure loan terms to take care of such fluctuations in economic conditions. Moreover, for all business borrowers it is important to develop a forecast of future industry conditions. The loan officer must determine if the customer's projections for the future conform to the outlook for the industry as a whole. Any differences in outlook must be explained before a final decision is made about approving or denying a loan request.

Parts of a Typical Loan Agreement

The Note   When a bank or other lending institution grants a loan to one of its customers, such an extension of credit is always accompanied by a *written contract* with several different parts. First, the **note,** signed by the borrower, specifies the principal amount
of the loan. The face of the note will also indicate the interest rate attached to the principal amount and the terms under which repayment must take place (including the dates
on which any installment payments are due).

Loan Commitment Agreement   In addition, larger business loans and home mortgage
loans often are accompanied by **loan commitment agreements,** in which the lender
promises to make credit available to the borrower over a designated future period up to a
maximum amount in return for a commitment fee (usually expressed as a percentage—
such as 0.5 percent—of the maximum amount of credit available). This practice is common in the extension of short-term business credit lines, where, for example, a business
customer may draw against a maximum $1 million credit line as needed over a given pe-
riod (such as six months).

Collateral   Loans may be either secured or unsecured. Secured loans have a pledge of
some of the borrower's property behind them (such as a home or an automobile) as **collateral** that may have to be sold if the borrower has no other way to repay the lender. Unsecured loans have no specific borrower assets pledged behind them; these loans rest largely
on the reputation and estimated earning power of the borrower. Secured loan agreements
include a section describing any assets that are pledged as collateral to protect the lender's
interest, along with an explanation of how and when the lending institution can take possession of the collateral in order to recover its funds. For example, an individual seeking
an auto loan usually must sign a *chattel mortgage* agreement, which means that the borrower temporarily assigns the vehicle's title to the lender until the loan is paid off.

Covenants   Most formal loan agreements also contain **restrictive covenants,** which are
usually one of two types: *affirmative* or *negative*.

1. *Affirmative covenants* require the borrower to take certain actions, such as periodically
   filing financial statements with the lending institution, maintaining insurance coverage on the loan and on any collateral pledged, and maintaining specified levels of liquidity and equity.
2. *Negative covenants* restrict the borrower from doing certain things without the lender's
   approval, such as taking on new debt, acquiring additional fixed assets, participating in
   mergers, selling assets, or paying excessive dividends to stockholders.

Borrower Guaranties or Warranties   In most loan agreements, the borrower specifically *guarantees* or **warranties** that the information supplied in the loan application is
true and correct. The borrower may also be required to pledge personal assets—a house,
land, automobiles, and so on—behind a business loan or against a loan that is consigned
by a third party. Whether collateral is posted or not, the loan agreement must identify
who or what institution is responsible for the loan and obligated to make payment.

Events of Default   Finally, most loans contain a section listing **events of default,** specifying what actions or inactions by the borrower would represent a significant violation of
the terms of the loan agreement and what actions the lender is legally authorized to take
in order to secure the recovery of its funds. The events-of-default section also clarifies
who is responsible for collection costs, court costs, and attorney's fees that may arise from
litigation of the loan agreement.

Key URL
For more information
about loan accounting
and disclosure of
problem loans in an
international setting,
see especially
www.bis.org/publ.

Loan Review

What happens to a loan agreement after it has been endorsed by the borrower and the lending institution? Should it be filed away and forgotten until the loan falls due and the borrower makes the final payment? Obviously that would be a foolish thing for any lender to do because the conditions under which each loan is made are constantly changing, affecting the borrower's financial condition and his or her ability to repay a loan. Fluctuations in the economy weaken some businesses and increase the credit needs of others, while individuals may lose their jobs or contract serious health problems, imperiling their ability to repay any outstanding loans. The loan department must be sensitive to these developments and periodically review *all* loans until they reach maturity.

While most lenders today use a variety of different **loan review** procedures, a few general principles are followed by nearly all lending institutions. These include

1. Carrying out reviews of all types of loans on a periodic basis—for example, routinely examining the largest loans outstanding every 30, 60, or 90 days, along with a random sample of smaller loans.
2. Structuring the loan review process carefully to make sure the most important features of each loan are checked, including
   a. The record of borrower payments to ensure that the customer is not falling behind the planned repayment schedule.
   b. The quality and condition of any collateral pledged behind the loan.
   c. The completeness of loan documentation to make sure the lender has access to any collateral pledged and possesses the full legal authority to take action against the borrower in the courts if necessary.
   d. An evaluation of whether the borrower's financial condition and forecasts have changed, which may have increased or decreased the borrower's need for credit.
   e. An assessment of whether the loan conforms to the lender's loan policies and to the standards applied to its loan portfolio by examiners from the regulatory agencies.
3. Reviewing the largest loans most frequently because default on these credit agreements could seriously affect the lender's own financial condition.
4. Conducting more frequent reviews of troubled loans, with the frequency of review increasing as the problems surrounding any particular loan increase.
5. Accelerating the loan review schedule if the economy slows down or if the industries in which the lending institution has made a substantial portion of its loans develop significant problems (e.g., the appearance of new competitors or shifts in technology that will demand new products and new delivery methods).

Loan review is not a luxury but a necessity for a sound lending program. It not only helps management spot problem loans more quickly but also acts as a continuing check on whether loan officers are adhering to their institution's own loan policy. For this reason, and to promote objectivity in the loan review process, many of the largest lenders separate their loan review personnel from the loan department itself. Loan reviews also aid senior management and the lender's board of directors in assessing the institution's overall exposure to risk and its possible need for more capital in the future.

Handling Problem Loan Situations

Inevitably, despite the safeguards most lenders build into their loan programs, some loans will become *problem loans*. Usually this means the borrower has missed one or more promised payments or the collateral pledged behind a loan has declined significantly in value. While each problem loan situation is somewhat different, several features common to most such situations should warn a lending institution that troubles have set in (see Table 15–5):

1. Unusual or unexplained delays in receiving promised financial reports and payments or in communicating with bank personnel.
2. For business loans, any sudden change in methods used by the borrowing firm to account for depreciation, make pension plan contributions, value inventories, account for taxes, or recognize income.
3. For business loans, restructuring outstanding debt or eliminating dividends, or experiencing a change in the customer's credit rating.
4. Adverse changes in the price of a borrowing customer's stock.
5. Net earnings losses in one or more years, especially as measured by returns on the borrower's assets (ROA), or equity capital (ROE), or earnings before interest and taxes (EBIT).
6. Adverse changes in the borrower's capital structure (equity/debt ratio), liquidity (current ratio), or activity levels (e.g., the ratio of sales to inventory).
7. Deviations of actual sales or cash flow from those projected when the loan was requested.

TABLE 15–5
Warning Signs of Weak Loans and Poor Lending Policies

Source: Federal Deposit Insurance Corporation, *Bank Examination Policies*, Washington, D.C., selected years.

The manual given to bank and thrift examiners by the FDIC discusses several telltale indicators of problem loans and poor bank lending policies:

Indicators of a Weak or Troubled Loan	Indicators of Inadequate or Poor Lending Policies
Irregular or delinquent loan payments	Poor selection of risks among borrowing customers
Frequent alterations in loan terms	
Poor loan renewal record (with little reduction of principal each time the loan is renewed)	Lending money contingent on possible future events (such as a merger)
	Lending money because a customer promises a large deposit
Unusually high loan rate (perhaps an attempt to compensate the lender for a high-risk loan)	Failure to specify a plan for the liquidation of loans
Unusual or unexpected buildup of the borrowing customer's accounts receivable and/or inventories	High proportion of loans made to borrowers outside the lender's trade territory
Rising debt-to-net-worth (leverage) ratio	Incomplete credit files
Missing documentation (especially missing customer financial statements)	Substantial self-dealing credits (loans to insiders—employees, directors, or stockholders)
Poor-quality collateral	
Reliance on reappraisals of assets to increase the borrowing customers' net worth	Tendency to overreact to competition (making poor loans to keep customers from going to competing lending institutions)
Absence of cash flow statements or projections	Lending money to support speculative purchases
Customer reliance on nonrecurring sources of funds to meet loan payments (e.g., selling buildings or equipment)	Lack of sensitivity to changing economic conditions

LENDING AND ECONOMIC GROWTH

In the late 1990s governments and investors around the world became concerned about economic developments in Asia, particularly in such leading Asian nations as Korea, Indonesia, Japan, Thailand, Malaysia, and Hong Kong. As several economies in the region weakened and the international value of several Asian currencies sagged, many economists and financial analysts began to point to the crucial role played by *lending*—the extension of credit—in determining the health of *any* economy. When loan quality declines, lenders typically respond by cutting back on the new loans they plan to make and also refuse a higher portion of customer requests for loan renewals. As the supply of credit declines, business invest-ment spending and spending by consumers begin to fall, caus-ing rising unemployment and eventual economic stagnation if loan volume continues to fall.

The foregoing chain of events is particularly likely to hap-pen in those countries where banks account for the majority of assets and loans in the financial system. Moreover, several countries around the world recently have made the mistake of directing their banks to lend to government-favored projects or to support troubled firms in struggling industries rather than letting the private marketplace direct the flow of credit toward those borrowers and investment projects offering the highest expected returns. At the same time, banks with troubled loans were frequently permitted to keep those loans on their books at full face value and to delay recognition of declining values of land, stock prices, and other assets (called "regulatory for-bearance"). Recent developments in portions of Asia and in other corners of the world remind us that *credit* can be a pow-erful force for good in a nation's economy, stimulating eco-nomic activity and creating new jobs, but if poorly managed, fluctuations in the supply and quality of loans can lead to seri-ous economic distress.

Factoid
What are the principal causes of failure among banks and thrift institutions?
Answer: Bad loans, management error, criminal activity, and adverse economic conditions.

8. Sudden, unexpected, and unexplained changes in deposit balances maintained by the customer.

What should a lender do when a loan is in trouble? Experts in **loan workouts**—the process of recovering funds from a problem loan situation—suggest the following key steps:

1. Lenders must always keep the goal of loan workouts firmly in mind: to maximize the chances for full recovery of funds.

2. Rapid detection and reporting of any problems with a loan are essential; delay often worsens a problem loan situation.

3. The loan workout responsibility should be separate from the lending function to avoid possible conflicts of interest for the loan officer.

4. Loan workout specialists should confer with the troubled customer *quickly* on possible options, especially for cutting expenses, increasing cash flow, and improving manage-ment control. Precede this meeting with a preliminary analysis of the problem and its possible causes, noting any special workout problems (including the presence of com-peting creditors). Develop a preliminary plan of action after determining the lending institution's risk exposure and the sufficiency of loan documents, especially any claims against the customer's collateral other than that held by the lender.

5. Estimate what resources are available to collect the troubled loan, including the esti-mated liquidation values of assets and deposits.

6. Loan workout personnel should conduct a tax and litigation search to see if the bor-rower has other unpaid obligations.

7. For business borrowers, loan personnel must evaluate the quality, competence, and integrity of current management and visit the site to assess the borrower's property and operations.

8. Loan workout professionals must consider all reasonable alternatives for cleaning up the troubled loan, including making a new, temporary agreement if loan problems appear to be short-term in nature or finding a way to help the customer strengthen cash flow (such as reducing expenses or entering new markets) or to infuse new capital into

the business. Other possibilities include finding additional collateral; securing endorsements or guarantees; reorganizing, merging, or liquidating the firm; or filing a bankruptcy petition.

Of course, the preferred option nearly always is to seek a revised loan agreement that gives both the lending institution and its customer the chance to restore normal operations. Indeed, loan experts often argue that even when a loan agreement is in serious trouble, the customer may not be. This means that a properly structured loan agreement rarely runs into irreparable problems. However, an improperly structured loan agreement can contribute to a borrower's financial problems and be a cause of loan default.

Concept Check

15–12. What sources of information are available today that loan officers and credit analysts can use in evaluating a customer loan application?

15–13. What are the principal parts of a loan agreement? What is each part designed to do?

15–14. What is *loan review?* How should a loan review be conducted?

15–15. What are some warning signs to management that a problem loan may be developing?

15–16. What steps should a lender go through in trying to resolve a problem loan situation?

Summary

This chapter has focused on lending policies and procedures and the many different types of loans that banks and other leaders offer to their customers. It makes these key points:

- Making loans is the principal *economic function* of banks and competing lending institutions. Loans support communities and nations by providing credit to finance the development of new businesses, sustain existing activities, and create jobs for individuals so that incomes and living standards can grow over time.

- Lending is also *risky*, because loan quality is affected by both external and internal factors. *External factors* include changes in the economy, natural disasters, and regulations imposed by government. *Internal factors* affecting loan risk include management errors, illegal manipulation, and weak or ineffective lending policies.

- The risk of loss in the lending function is at least partially controlled by (*a*) *government regulation* and (*b*) *internal policies and procedures*. Regulatory agencies such as the FDIC send out teams of examiners to investigate the lending policies and procedures and the quality of loans within each lending institution. Among depository institutions today a five-point CAMELS rating system is used to evaluate the performance and risk exposure of lenders based upon the quantity and quality of their capital, assets, management, earnings, liquidity, and sensitivity to market risk.

- Risk is also controlled by creating and following written policies and procedures for processing each credit request. Written loan policies should describe the types of loans the lender will and will not make, the desired terms for each type of loan, the necessary documentation before approval is granted, how collateral is to be evaluated, desired pricing techniques, and lines of authority for loan approvals.

- Lenders consider multiple factors in approving or denying each loan request: (1) *character* (including loan purpose and borrower honesty); (2) *capacity* (especially the legal authority of the borrower to sign a loan agreement); (3) *cash* (including the adequacy of income or cash flow); (4) *collateral* (including the quality and quantity of assets to backstop a loan); (5) *conditions* (including the state of the economy); and (6) *control* (including compliance with the lender's loan policy and with regulations).

- Most lending decisions center around three key issues: (1) Is the borrower creditworthy and how do you know? (2) Can the loan agreement be properly structured to protect the lender and the public's funds? (3) Can a claim against the borrower's assets or earnings be perfected in the event of loan default?
- Finally, a sound lending program must make provision for the periodic review of all outstanding loans. When this *loan review* process turns up problem loans, they may be turned over to a *loan workout* specialist who must investigate the causes of the problem and work with the borrower to find a solution that maximizes the chances for recovery of funds.

Key Terms

real estate loans, *524*
financial institution loans, *525*
agricultural loans, *525*
commercial and industrial loans, *525*
loans to individuals, *525*
wholesale lenders, *526*

retail credit, *526*
CAMELS rating, *529*
cash, *535*
cash flow, *535*
note, *543*
loan commitment agreements, *543*

collateral, *543*
restrictive covenants, *543*
warranties, *543*
events of default, *543*
loan review, *544*
loan workouts, *546*

Problems and Projects

1. The lending function of depository institutions is highly regulated and this chapter gives some examples of the structure of these regulations for national banks. In this problem you are asked to apply those regulations to Green Tree National Bank (GTNB). GTNB has the following sources of funds: $100 million in capital and surplus, $100 million in demand deposits, $600 million in time and savings deposits, and $200 million in subordinated debt.

   a. What is the maximum dollar amount of real estate loans that GTNB can grant?

   b. What is the maximum dollar amount GTNB may lend to a single customer?

2. Karakee V. Corporation, seeking renewal of its $12 million credit line, reports the data in the following table (in millions of dollars) to Whelington National Bank's loan department. Please calculate the measures of the firm's cash flow as defined earlier in this chapter. What trends do you observe and what are their implications for the decision to renew or not renew the firm's line of credit?

	20X1	20X2	20X3	20X4	Projections for Next Year
Accounts receivable	$ 5.1	$ 5.5	$ 5.7	$ 6.0	$ 6.4
Inventories	8.0	8.2	8.3	8.6	8.9
Accounts payable	7.9	8.4	8.8	9.5	9.9
Depreciation and other noncash expenses	11.2	11.2	11.1	11.0	10.9
Net profits	4.4	4.6	4.9	4.1	3.6

3. Silsbee Manufacturing and Service Company holds a sizable inventory of dishwashers and dryers, which it hopes to sell to retail dealers over the next six months. These appliances have a total estimated market value currently of $16,357,422. The firm also reports accounts receivable currently amounting to $8,452,876. Under the guidelines for taking collateral discussed in this chapter, what is the *minimum* size loan or credit line Silsbee is likely to receive from its principal lender? What is the *maximum* size loan or credit line Silsbee is likely to receive?

4. Under which of the six Cs of credit discussed in this chapter does each of the following pieces of information belong?

   a. First National Bank discovers there is already a lien against the fixed assets of one of its customers asking for a loan.

   b. Xron Corporation has asked for a type of loan its lender normally refuses to make.

   c. John Selman has an excellent credit rating.

   d. Smithe Manufacturing Company has achieved higher earnings each year for the past six years.

   e. Consumers Savings Association's auto loan officer asks a prospective customer, Harold Ikels, for his driver's license.

   f. Merchants Center National Bank is concerned about extending a loan for another year to Corrin Motors because a recession is predicted in the economy starting within the next quarter of the year.

   g. Wes Velman needs an immediate cash loan and has gotten his brother, Charles, to volunteer to cosign the note should the loan be approved.

   h. ABC Finance Company checks out Mary Earl's estimate of her monthly take-home pay with Mary's employer, Bryan Sims Doors and Windows.

   i. Hillsoro Bank and Trust would like to make a loan to Pen-Tab Oil and Gas Company but fears a long-term decline in oil and gas prices.

   j. First State Bank of Jackson seeks the opinion of an expert on the outlook for sales growth and production in Mexico before granting a loan to a Mexican manufacturer of auto parts.

   k. The history of Membres Manufacture and Distributing Company indicates the firm has been through several recent changes of ownership and there has been a substantial shift in its principal suppliers and customers in recent years.

   l. Frank Evans, loan officer of Home and Office Savings Bank, has decided to review the insurance coverages maintained by its borrowing customer, Plainsman Wholesale Distributors.

5. Butell Manufacturing has an outstanding $11 million loan with Citicenter Bank for the current year. As required in the loan agreement, Butell reports selected data items to the bank each month. Based on the following information, is there any indication of a developing *problem loan?* About what dimensions of the firm's performance should Citicenter Bank be concerned?

	Current Month	One Month Ago	Two Months Ago	Three Months Ago	Four Months Ago
Cash account (millions of dollars)	$33	$57	$51	$44	$43
Projected sales (millions of dollars)	$298	$295	$294	$291	$288
Stock price per share (monthly average)	$6.60	$6.50	$6.40	$6.25	$6.50
Capital structure (equity/debt ratio in percent)	32.8%	33.9%	34.6%	34.9%	35.7%
Liquidity ratio (current assets/current liabilities)	1.10x	1.23x	1.35x	1.39x	1.25x
Earnings before interest and taxes (EBIT; in millions of dollars)	$15	$14	$13	$11	$13
Return on assets (ROA; percent)	3.32%	3.25%	2.98%	3.13%	3.11%
Sales revenue (millions of dollars)	$290	$289	$290	$289	$287

Butell has announced within the past 30 days that it is switching to new methods for calculating the depreciation of its fixed assets and for valuing its inventories. The firm's board of directors is planning to discuss at its next meeting early next month a proposal to reduce stock dividends in the coming year.

6. Identify which of the following restrictive loan covenants are *affirmative* and which are *negative* covenants:

   a. Nige Trading Corporation must pay no dividends to its shareholders above $3 per share without express lender approval.

   b. HoneySmith Company pledges to fully insure its production line equipment against loss due to fire, theft, or adverse weather.

   c. Soft-Tech Industries cannot take on new debt without notifying its principal lending institution first.

   d. PennCost Manufacturing must file comprehensive financial statements each month with its principal bank.

   e. Dolbe King Company must secure lender approval prior to increasing its stock of fixed assets.

   f. Crestwin Service Industries must keep a minimum current (liquidity) ratio of 1.5× under the terms of its loan agreement.

   g. Dew Dairy Products is considering approaching Selwin Farm Transport Company about a possible merger but must first receive lender approval.

7. Please identify which of the six basic Cs of lending—character, capacity, cash, collateral, conditions, and control—applies to each of the loan factors listed here:

Insurance coverage	Asset liquidation
Competitive climate for customer's product	Inflation outlook
	Adequate documentation
Credit rating	Changes in accounting standards
Corporate resolution	Written loan policy
Liquid reserves	Coverage ratios
Asset specialization	Purpose of loan
Driver's license	Laws and regulations that apply to the making of loans
Expected market share	
Economists' forecasts	Wages in the labor market
Business cycle	Changes in technology
Performance of comparable firms	Obsolescence
Guarantees/warranties	Liens
Expense controls	Management quality
Inventory turnover	Leverage
Projected cash flow	History of firm
Experience of other lenders	Customer identity
Social Security card	Payment record
Price-earnings ratio	Partnership agreement
Industry outlook	Accounts receivable turnover
Future financing needs	Accounts payable turnover

Internet Exercises

1. If you wanted to find out about regulations applying to bank lending, where would you look on the Web? Why do you think this area has become so important lately? (See, for example, **www.ffiec.gov.**)

2. If you wanted to find out more about the evaluation of loan portfolios during onsite examinations, the FDIC provides an online copy of its Division of Supervision Manual of Examination Policies at **www.fdic.gov/regulations/safety/manual**. Go to this site and find the link for Loan Classifications, then answer the following question: What are "special mention" loans?

3. Are you interested in becoming a loan officer? A credit analyst? Go to the Bureau of Labor Statistics' site at **www.bls.gov/oco/ca/cas027.htm** and read about the banking industry. What is the outlook for positions as loan officers and credit analysts? What could you expect in terms of earnings?

4. Suppose you were hired as a consultant by a lending institution's loan department to look at the quality of its controls designed to minimize credit risk. You know this lender is concerned that its principal government supervisory agency is going to take a hard look shortly at how the loan department is managed and the risks in its loan portfolio. Where on the Internet could you look to find some guidelines on how to control and manage credit risk? List two or three suggestions for credit risk control that you found at the website or sites you investigated. For example, you may wish to check **www.fdic.gov** and **www.bis.org**.

STANDARD &POOR'S

S&P Market Insight Challenge

1. Use Standard & Poor's Market Insight website (**www.mhhe.com/edumarketinsight**) for this problem. The S&P Industry Survey covering the banking industry discusses commercial banks' earnings from loans. For a very recent description of the banking industry's loan portfolio please click on the Industry tab in Market Insight and use the drop-down menu to select a subindustry group, such as diversified banks or regional banks. Upon choosing one of these groups, you will encounter a recent S&P Industry Survey on Banking. Download the banking survey and proceed to the section, "How the Industry Operates." What is the composition of the typical bank's loan portfolio? What is the most recent dollar amount of aggregate loans held by all FDIC-insured commercial banks?

2. Use Standard & Poor's Market Insight website (**www.mhhe.com/edumarketinsight**) for this problem. Lending lies at the heart of banking and its closest financial-service competitors, but also usually represents the greatest risk a banker can accept. Using the information in this chapter and in Chapters 4 and 5, develop a list of indicators of loan quality that could be used to assess the riskiness of an individual bank's loan portfolio. Now apply these loan quality indicators to the most recent loan portfolio information available for some of the banks contained in S&P's Market Insight, Educational Version. Which Insight banks appear to have the strongest and the weakest loan quality? What are the implications of your findings for the management of these institutions? How confident are you in the loan-quality indicators you developed?

REAL NUMBERS FOR REAL BANKS

Assignment for Chapter 15

YOUR BANK'S LOAN PORTFOLIO: LOANS CLASSIFIED BY PURPOSE

Chapter 15 is an overview of lending with a focus on policies and procedures. Table 15–1 illustrates the composition of the industry's (all FDIC-insured U.S. banks) loan portfolio, highlighting the differences between small banks (less than $100 million in total assets) and large banks (more than $1 billion in total assets). In this assignment we will be doing a similar analysis for your banking company compared to the peer group of very large banks (more than $10 billion in total assets).

Trend and Comparative Analysis

A. **Data Collection:** In the assignment for Chapter 5, we collected information for gross loans and leases and net loans and leases. Now we will further break down gross loans and leases based on purpose. Use SDI to create a four-column report of your bank's information and the peer group information across years. For report selection, you will access the "Net Loans and Leases" report. We suggest that you continue to collect percentage information for ease of entry. Enter this data into Spreadsheet 2 as follows:

Gross Loans and Leases	Your Bank	Peer Group	Your Bank	Peer Group
Date(A88)	12/31/yy	12/31/yy	12/31/yy	12/31/yy
Real estate loans	%	%	%	%
Loans to depository institutions and acceptances of other banks				
Farm loans				
Commercial and industrial loans				
Loans to individuals				
Lease financing receivables				
All other loans**				

**Note: All other loans in this context must be calculated as total other loans and leases minus lease financing receivables minus loans to depository institutions and acceptances of other banks.

B. Use the chart function in Excel and the data by columns in rows 62 through 63 to create four pie charts illustrating the loan portfolio composition by purpose for the BHC you chose earlier and its peer group. Your pie charts should include titles and labels. For instance, the following is a pie chart for National City Corp for 12/31/02:

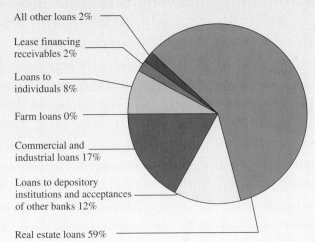

NCC Loan Composition by Purpose (12/31/02)

All other loans 2%

Lease financing receivables 2%

Loans to individuals 8%

Farm loans 0%

Commercial and industrial loans 17%

Loans to depository institutions and acceptances of other banks 12%

Real estate loans 59%

C. Interpreting the above information, write approximately one page about the composition of your bank's loan portfolio. Has the composition changed across time? How does the composition of your bank's loan portfolio compare to other very large banks (your peer group)? Use your pie charts as graphics and incorporate them in the discussion. The above pie chart was included by creating a text box and copying the Excel spreadsheet into the text box.

Selected References

See the following sources for additional information on the content and contributions of a written loan policy:

1. Malone, Robert B. "Written Loan Policies." *Journal of Commercial Bank Lending*, June 1976, pp. 18–24.

2. Mott, Hubert C. "Establishing Criteria and Concepts for a Written Credit Policy." *Journal of Commercial Bank Lending*, April 1977, pp. 2–16.

For a review of procedures for identifying and working out problem loan situations, see the following:

3. Eyring, Joseph R. "Five Key Steps for a Successful Workout Program." *Journal of Commercial Bank Lending*, December 1984, pp. 28–35.

4. NeMer, Gary. "Analysis of Problem Loan Alternatives for Secured Lenders." *Journal of Commercial Bank Lending*, October 1982, pp. 38–52.

5. Rose, Peter S. "Loans in Trouble in a Troubled Economy." *Canadian Banker and ICB Review* 90, no. 3 (June 1983), pp. 52–57.

6. ————. "Serving Loan Customers in Mexico: How U.S. Banks Manage Credit Risk." *Journal of Lending and Credit Risk Management*, October 1996, pp. 27–35.

7. Taylor, Jeremy D. "Understanding Industry Risk: Parts 1, 2, and 3." *Journal of Lending and Credit Risk Management*, August, September, and October 1996.

For a discussion of the impact of changing technology on lending, see these sources:

8. McGinnis, Patricia. "The Place of Technology in Generating Credit Opportunities." *Journal of Lending and Credit Risk Management*, June 1977, pp. 15–29.

9. Rose, Peter S. "Lenders and the Internet." *Journal of Lending and Credit Risk Management*, June 1997, pp. 31–40.

10. Spong, Kenneth, and Richard J. Sullivan. "The Outlook for the U.S. Banking Industry: What Does the Experience of the 1980s and 1990s Tell Us?" *Economic Review*, Federal Reserve Bank of Kansas City, Fourth Quarter 1999, pp. 65–83.

For a fuller discussion of the examination process and its relationship to lending, these are especially helpful:

11. Greenspan, Alan. Speech before the 2000 Financial Markets Conference, Federal Reserve Bank of Atlanta, by the Chairman of the Federal Reserve Board, Sea Island, Georgia, October 16, 2000.

12. Hirtle, Beverly J., and Jose A. Lopez. "Supervisor Information and the Frequency of Bank Examinations." *Economic Policy Review*, Federal Reserve Bank of New York, April 1999, pp. 1–19.

For a discussion of the linkages between lending and other financial-service activities and the growth of the economy, see:

13. Levine, Ross. "More on Finance and Growth: More Finance, More Growth?" *Review*, Federal Reserve Bank of St. Louis, July/August 2003, pp. 31–46.

For an overview of recent developments in off-site examination tools and examiner ratings, see especially:

14. Collier, Charles, Sean Forbush, Daniel A. Nuxoll, and John O'Keefe. "The SCOR System of Off-Site Monitoring: Its Objectives, Functioning, and Performance." *FDIC Banking Review* 15, no. 3 (2003), pp. 17–32.

Lending to Business Firms and Pricing Business Loans

Key Topics in This Chapter

- Types of Business Loans: Short-Term and Long-Term
- Analyzing Business Loan Requests
- Collateral and Contingent Liabilities
- Sources and Uses of Business Funds
- Pricing Business Loans
- Customer Profitability Analysis

Introduction

The great American author and humorist Mark Twain observed: "A banker is a fellow who lends his umbrella when the sun is shining and wants it back the minute it begins to rain." Many troubled businesses seeking credit in recent years might agree with Mr. Twain. Indeed, securing the large amounts of credit that many businesses require can be a complicated and challenging task because bankers usually take a close look at business borrowers and their loan requests. Moreover, business loans—often called *commercial and industrial* or *C&I loans*—rank among the most important assets that commercial banks and their closest competitors (such as finance companies like GE Capital and Commercial Credit Corporation) hold.

Indeed, a glance at the most recent balance sheet for all U.S. insured banks combined reveals that fully a quarter of their loan portfolio is devoted to business or C&I loans. Moreover, this percentage of the total loan portfolio does not include many commercial real estate loans and loans to other financial institutions that banks make but classify elsewhere on their balance sheets. This is why any discussion of the methods and procedures used in analyzing and granting loans usually begins with a discussion of commercial lending.

In this chapter we look at the many different types of business or commercial and industrial loans that banks and some of their closest competitors make. We also explore the process for evaluating business loans based on an interesting example from the energy industry. Finally, the chapter examines some of the most popular and widely used techniques for pricing loans extended to business customers.

Commercial (or business) loans were the earliest form of lending banks did in their more than 2,000-year-old history. Later in the 20th century finance companies, insurance firms, and thrift institutions entered the business lending field. Today loan officers skilled in evaluating the credit of businesses are usually among the most experienced and highest-paid people in the financial services field, along with security underwriters.

The World Wide Web has multiplied information sites focusing on various aspects of business credit in recent years. For example, there are sites focused on lending to *(a)* smaller businesses, such as SBA: Financing Your Business at **www.sba.gov/sbaloan/7a.html**, and The ABCs of Borrowing at **www.howtoadvice.com/borrowing**; *(b)* large international corporate and institutional customers at **jolis.worldbankimflib.org/external.htm**; and *(c)* asset-based borrowing (such as factoring accounts receivable) at **www.factors.net**.

Business loan officers have a big job today just keeping up with changing trends in the nature and technology of commercial credit. The Web also aids them in this educational area through such sites as those maintained by the Risk Management Association at **www.rmahq.org** and Quick Start at **www.quick-start.net**.

Finally, business loan pricing has always been a challenge for loan officers, but never more so than in the current era when so much loan pricing is market driven and intensely competitive. Loan officers in the commercial field often tap such sites as the Loan Pricing Corporation, which contains financial information on the performance of the commercial loan market, at **www.loanpricing.com**. For commercial loan rates tied directly to money and capital market interest rates, such data sources as the Federal Reserve's H.15 Statistical Release on Selected Interest Rates at **www.bog.frb.fed.us/release/h15/current** can help business loan officers spot trends in credit costs. It will assist them to profitably and competitively price a loan, not just for today's market, but for the life of a loan contract.

Types of Business Loans

Banks, finance companies, and competing business lenders grant many different types of commercial loans. Among the most widely used forms of business credit are the following:

Key URL
To learn more about helpful procedures in applying for small business loans, see, in particular, **www.business.com/directory**.

Short-Term Business Loans

- Self-liquidating inventory loans
- Working capital loans
- Interim construction financing
- Security dealer financing
- Retailer and equipment financing
- Asset-based loans (accounts receivable financing, factoring, and inventory financing)
- Syndicated loans

Long-Term Business Loans

- Term loans to support the purchase of equipment, rolling stock, and structures
- Revolving credit financing
- Project loans
- Loans to support acquisitions of other business firms

Short-Term Loans to Business Firms

Self-Liquidating Inventory Loans

Historically, commercial banks have been the leaders in extending short-term credit to businesses. In fact, until World War II banks granted mainly **self-liquidating loans** to business firms. These loans usually were used to finance the purchase of inventory—raw materials or finished goods to sell. Such loans take advantage of the normal *cash cycle* in a business firm:

1. Cash (including borrowed cash) is spent to acquire inventories of raw materials and semifinished or finished goods.
2. Goods are produced or shelved and listed for sale.
3. Sales are made (often on credit).
4. The cash received (immediately or later from credit sales) is then used to repay the self-liquidating loan.

In this case, the term of the loan begins when cash is needed to purchase inventory and ends (perhaps in 60 to 90 days) when cash is available in the firm's account to write the lender a check for the balance of its loan.

While banks today make a far wider array of business loans than just simple self-liquidating credits, the short-term loan—frequently displaying many of the features of self-liquidation—continues to account for at least half of all bank loans to business firms. In fact, most business loans cover only a few weeks or months and are usually related closely to the borrower's need for short-term cash to finance purchases of inventory or to cover production costs, the payment of taxes, interest payments on bonds and other debt, and dividend payments to stockholders.

There is some concern in the banking and commercial finance industries today that traditional inventory loans are on the decline. Thanks to the development of just in time (JIT) and supply chain management techniques businesses can continuously monitor their inventory levels and more quickly replace missing items. Reflecting this trend, inventory-to-sales ratios have recently been declining in many industries. Thus, there appears to be less need for traditional inventory financing and many businesses are experiencing lower inventory financing costs. In the future, lenders will be forced to develop other saleable services in order to replace potential losses in inventory-loan revenues as new software-driven technology speeds up ordering and shipment, allowing businesses to get by with leaner in-house stocks of goods and raw materials.

Working Capital Loans

Key URL
If you wanted to learn more about the regulations applicable to loans for small businesses and for minority groups (including loans made to minority-owned businesess) where could you go? See the educational pamphlets available at **www .federalreserve.gov**.

Working capital loans provide businesses with short-run credit, lasting from a few days to about one year. Working capital loans are most often used to fund the purchase of inventories in order to put goods on shelves or to purchase raw materials; thus, they come closest to the traditional self-liquidating loan described previously.

Frequently the working capital loan is designed to cover seasonal peaks in the business customer's production levels and credit needs. For example, a clothing manufacturer anticipating heavy demand in the fall for back-to-school clothes and winter wear will require short-term credit in the late spring and summer to purchase inventories of cloth and hire additional workers to increase output in order to have clothes ready for shipment to retailers during the August to December period. The clothing manufacturer's bank or other lender can set up a line of credit stretching from six to nine months, permitting that manufacturer to draw upon the credit line as needed over this period. The amount of the line is determined from the manufacturer's estimate of the maximum amount of funds that will be needed at any point during the six to nine-month term of the loan. Such loans are frequently renewed under the provision that the borrower pay off all or a significant portion of the loan before renewal is granted.

Normally, working capital loans are secured by accounts receivable or by pledges of inventory and carry a floating interest rate on the amounts actually borrowed against the approved credit line. A commitment fee is charged on the unused portion of the credit line and sometimes on the entire amount of funds made available. **Compensating deposit balances** may be required from the customer. These include required deposits whose minimum size is based on the size of the credit line (e.g., 1 to 5 percent of the credit line) and required deposits equal to a stipulated percentage of the total amount of credit actually used by the customer (e.g., 15 to 20 percent of actual drawings against the line).

Interim Construction Financing

A popular form of secured short-term lending is the **interim construction loan,** used to support the construction of homes, apartments, office buildings, shopping centers, and other permanent structures. Although the structures involved are permanent, the loans themselves are temporary. They provide builders with the funds needed to hire workers, rent or lease construction equipment, purchase building materials, and develop land. But once the construction phase is over, this short-term loan usually is paid off with a longer-term mortgage loan issued by another lender, such as an insurance company or pension fund. In fact, many banks and other commercial lenders will not lend money to a builder or land developer until that customer has secured a mortgage loan commitment to take over the long-term financing of a project once its construction is completed. Recently, some commercial banks have issued "minipermanent" loans, providing funding for construction and the early operation of a project for as long as five to seven years.

Security Dealer Financing

Dealers in government and private securities need short-term financing to purchase new securities and carry their existing portfolios of securities until they are sold to customers or reach maturity. Such loans are readily granted by many of the largest banks and other commercial lenders because of their high quality—often backed by pledging the dealer's holdings of government securities as collateral. Moreover, many loans to securities dealers are so short—overnight to a few days—that the lender can quickly recover its funds or make a new loan at a higher interest rate if the credit markets have tightened up.

A closely related type of loan is extended to *investment banking firms* to support their underwriting of new corporate bonds, stocks, and government debt. Such issues of securities occur when investment bankers help their business clients finance a merger or the acquisition of another firm, assist in taking a company public (that is, issuing new stock to broaden an existing business's capital base and open its ownership shares to purchase by any interested investor), or aid in launching a completely new venture. Once the investment banker is able to sell these new securities to investors in the capital market, the loan plus any interest owed is repaid.

Banks and other security firms also lend directly to businesses and individuals buying stocks, bonds, options, and other financial instruments. Margin requirements enforced in the United States by the Federal Reserve Board usually limit such loans to no more than *half* the amount of the security or securities being acquired (under Regulation U). However, in an effort to aid the market for small business capital, the Fed ruled in December 1997 that selected lenders could loan up to 100 percent of the purchase price of "small cap" stocks that are listed by NASDAQ.

Retailer and Equipment Financing

Banks and finance companies support installment purchases of automobiles, home appliances, furniture, business equipment, and other durable goods by financing the receivables that dealers selling these goods take on when they write installment contracts to cover customer purchases. In turn, these contracts are reviewed by banks and other lending institutions with whom the dealers have established credit relationships. If they meet acceptable credit standards, the contracts are purchased by lenders at an interest rate that varies with the risk level of each borrower, the quality of collateral pledged, and the term of each loan.

In the case of dealers selling automobiles, business and electronic equipment, furniture, and other durable goods, lenders may agree to finance the dealer's whole inventory through what is called *floor planning.* The lender agrees to extend credit to the dealer so he or she can place an order with a manufacturer to ship goods for resale. Most such loans are for 90-day terms initially and may be renewed for one or more 30-day periods. In return for the loan the dealer signs a security agreement, giving the lending institution a lien against the goods in the event of nonpayment. At the same time the manufacturer is authorized to ship goods to the dealer and to bill the lender for their value. Periodically, the lender will send an agent to check the goods on the dealer's floor to determine what is selling and what remains unsold. As goods are sold, the dealer sends a check to the lender for the manufacturer's invoice amount for each item bought from the dealer, known as a "pay-as-sold" agreement.

If the lending institution's agent visits the dealer and finds any items sold off for which the lender has not received payment (known as "sold out of trust"), a check will be requested immediately for those particular items. If the dealer fails to pay, the lender may be forced to repossess the goods and return some or all of them to the manufacturer for credit. Floor planning agreements typically include a loan-loss reserve, which is built up from the interest earned as borrowers repay their installment loans and is reduced if any loans are defaulted. Once the loan-loss reserve reaches a predetermined level, the dealer receives rebates for a portion of the interest earned on the installment contracts.

Asset-Based Financing

An increasing portion of short-term lending by banks and other lenders in recent years has consisted of **asset-based loans**—credit secured by the shorter-term assets of a firm that are expected to roll over into cash in the future. Key business assets used for many of these loans are accounts receivable and inventories of raw materials or finished goods. The lender commits funds against a specific percentage of the book value of outstanding credit accounts or against inventory. For example, it may be willing to loan an amount equal to 70 percent of a firm's current accounts receivable (i.e., all those credit accounts that are not past due). Alternatively, it may make a loan for 40 percent of the business customer's current inventory of goods on the shelf or sitting in a warehouse. As accounts receivable are collected or inventory is sold, a portion of the cash proceeds flow to the lending institution to retire the loan.

In most loans collateralized by accounts receivable and inventory, the borrowing firm retains title to the assets pledged, but sometimes title is passed to the lender, which then assumes the risk that some of those assets will not pay out as expected. The most common example of this arrangement is **factoring,** where the bank, finance company, or other lender actually takes on the responsibility of collecting the accounts receivable of one of its business customers. Because the lender incurs both additional expense and additional risk with a factored loan, it typically assesses a higher discount rate and lends a smaller fraction of the book value of the customer's accounts receivable.

Syndicated Loans

A type of large corporate loan that is increasingly used today is the **syndicated loan.** This is typically a loan or loan package extended to a corporation by a group of banks and other institutional lenders. These loans may be "drawn" by the borrowing company, with the funds used to support business operations or commercial expansion, or "undrawn," serving as lines of credit to back a security issue or other venture. Banks and other lenders engage

Key URL
If you would like to
learn more about
syndicated loans,
see especially **www
.federalreserve.gov/
releases/snc/default
.htm.**

in syndicated loans both to spread (and, thereby, reduce) the heavy risk exposures of these large loans, often involving hundreds of millions or billions of dollars in credit for each loan, and to earn fee income. An example of this type of fee income is facility fees to open a credit line or a commitment fee to keep a line of credit available for a period of time on undrawn syndicated loans.

Many syndicated loans are traded in the secondary (resale) market and usually carry a coupon or interest rate based upon the benchmark rate, LIBOR—the London Interbank Offered Rate on Eurodollar deposits. These coupon rates in recent years have generally ranged from 100 to 400 basis points over LIBOR, while the loans themselves usually have a light to medium credit quality grade and may be either short-term or long-term in maturity.

As reported by R. Alton Gilbert [2] of the Federal Reserve of St. Louis, beginning in the 1970s the federal bank regulatory agencies in the United States annually conduct surveys of syndicated loans called shared national credits (SNCs), which bring together at least three lending institutions and total a minimum of $20 million each. Because of the size and character of SNCs, federal bank examiners look at these loans very carefully, searching particularly for those that appear to be *classified credits*—that is, weak loans that are rated, in the best case, *substandard, doubtful* if somewhat weaker, or, in the worst case, an outright *loss* that must be written off the books. Interestingly enough, Gilbert points out that the majority of classified SNCs appear to be held, not by banks, but by nonbank lenders (such as finance and investment companies), which often take on subinvestment-grade syndicated loans or buy distressed loans from other lenders in the hope of scoring exceptional returns.

Long-Term Loans to Business Firms

Term Business Loans

Term loans are designed to fund long- and medium-term business investments, such as the purchase of equipment or the construction of physical facilities, covering a period longer than one year. Usually the borrowing firm applies for a lump-sum loan based on the budgeted cost of its proposed project and then pledges to repay the loan in a series of installments.

Thus, term loans look to the flow of future earnings of a business firm to amortize and retire the credit. The schedule of installment payments is usually structured with the borrower's normal cycle of cash inflows and outflows firmly in mind. For example, there may be "blind spots" built into the repayment schedule, so no installment payments will be due at those times of the year when the customer is normally short of cash. Some term loan agreements do not call for repayments of principal until the end of the loan period. For example, in a "bullet loan" only interest is paid periodically, with the principal due when the loan matures.

Term loans normally are secured by *fixed assets* (e.g., plant or equipment) owned by the borrower and may carry either a fixed or a floating interest rate. That rate is normally higher than on shorter-term business loans due to the lender's greater risk exposure from such loans. The probability of default or other adverse changes in the borrower's position is certain to be greater over the course of a long-term loan. For this reason, loan officers and credit analysts pay attention to several different dimensions of a business customer's term loan application: (1) the qualifications of the borrowing firm's management, (2) the quality of its accounting and auditing systems, (3) whether or not the customer conscientiously files periodic financial statements, (4) whether the customer is willing to agree not to pledge assets to other creditors, (5) whether adequate insurance will be secured, (6) whether the customer is excessively exposed to the risk of changing technology,

SMALL BUSINESS LENDING: IS IT ON THE DECLINE IN BANKING?

One of the most controversial forms of lending today focuses on "small businesses"—the firms with the smallest volume of sales (perhaps up to $5 or $10 million in annual sales revenue). This is an important group of businesses. Most firms start out as small businesses and many depend upon bank credit for their start and to support their continued growth. Equally important, small business hiring accounts for most of the new job opportunities created in the economy each year.

However, the consolidating banking industry *may* be reducing the availability of credit for small businesses. For example, recent evidence suggests that those banks most heavily involved in merger activity tend to grow their small business loan portfolios more slowly than nonmerging banks. In recent years some of the largest bank holding companies have experienced a decline in the proportion of their portfolio devoted to small business credit. This *might* suggest that the small business sector could run into a "credit crunch" in the future if the banking sector continues to move toward fewer, but larger banks.

We must be cautious, though, because the available evidence is mixed. Even though some larger banks have recently reduced the *proportion* of their portfolios devoted to small business loans, the *total amount of credit* provided to small firms may actually be rising as banking consolidates. For example, if a bank's loan portfolio grows from $100 million to $200 million, while at the same time the percentage of its loan portfolio devoted to small businesses drops from 10 percent to 8 percent, the *total* amount of small business credit actually *rises*—from $10 million (or 0.10 × $100 million) to $16 million (or $200 million × 0.08). Many small businesses may actually benefit.

To be sure, large banks often have difficulty making small business loans because of the absence of loan standardization (which drives up costs) and their occasional lack of "personalized" service. However, the jury is still out as to whether small business lending will rise or fall in the future as banking becomes concentrated in the largest banks. (For further discussion on this issue see Katherine Samolyk and Christopher Richardson, "Bank Consolidation and Small Business Lending within Local Markets," *FDIC Working Paper Series 2003–02,* Federal Deposit Insurance Corporation, Washington, D.C., 2003.)

(7) the length of time before a proposed long-term project will generate positive cash flow, (8) trends in market demand, and (9) the strength of the customer's net worth position.

Revolving Credit Financing

A **revolving credit line** allows a business customer to borrow up to a prespecified limit, repay all or a portion of the borrowing, and reborrow as necessary until the credit line matures. One of the most flexible of all forms of business loans, revolving credit is often granted without specific collateral to secure the loan and may be short-term or cover a period as long as three, four, or five years. This form of business financing is particularly popular when the customer is highly uncertain about the timing of future cash flows or about the exact magnitude of his or her future borrowing needs. Revolving credit helps even out fluctuations in the business cycle for a firm, allowing it to borrow extra cash in economic recessions when sales are down, and to repay during boom periods when internally generated cash is more abundant. Where the lender is legally obligated to honor every customer request for funds up to the limit of the line, the lending institution normally will charge a *loan commitment fee* either on the unused portion of the credit line or, sometimes, on the entire amount of revolving credit available for customer use.

Loan commitments are usually of two types. The most common is a *formal loan commitment,* which is a contractual promise to lend to a customer up to a maximum amount of money at a set interest rate or rate markup over the prevailing base loan rate (prime or LIBOR). In this case, the lender can renege on its promise to lend only if there has been a "material adverse change" in the borrower's financial condition or if the borrower has not fulfilled some provision of the lender's commitment contract. A second, looser form of loan commitment is a *confirmed credit line,* where the lending institution indicates its approval of a customer's request for credit in an emergency, though the price of such a credit line may not be set in advance and the customer may have little intention to draw upon the credit line, using it instead as a guarantee to back up a loan obtained elsewhere. These looser commitments typically go only to top-credit-rated firms and are usually priced much lower than formal loan commitments. They help borrowers get advance approval for loans so they can access credit quickly and send favorable signals to other possible providers of credit.

One form of business revolving credit that has grown rapidly in recent years is the use of *credit cards*. Many small businesses today have come to depend upon credit cards as a source of operating capital, thus avoiding having to get approval for every loan request. Unfortunately, the interest rates charged usually are very high and if a personal card is used, the business borrower winds up being personally liable for the business's debts.

Long-Term Project Loans

The most risky of all business loans are **project loans**—credit to finance the construction of fixed assets designed to generate a flow of revenue in future periods. Prominent examples include oil refineries, pipelines, mines, power plants, and harbor facilities. The risks surrounding such projects are both large and numerous: (1) large amounts of funds, often several billion dollars' worth, are involved; (2) the project being funded may be delayed by weather or the shortage of building materials; (3) laws and regulations in the region or country where the project is under construction may change in a way that adversely affects the completion or cost of the project; and (4) interest rates may change, adversely affecting either the lender's return on the loan (many of which are made with fixed rates of interest) or the ability of the project's sponsors to repay (if the loan carries a floating rate). Project loans are usually granted to several companies jointly sponsoring a large project. Due to their size and risk, they are often shared by several lenders.

Project loans may be granted on a *recourse basis*, in which the lender can recover funds from the sponsoring companies if the project does not pay out as planned. At the other extreme, the loan may be extended on a nonrecourse basis, in which there are no sponsor guarantees; the project stands or falls on its own merits. In this case, the lender faces significant risks and, typically, demands a high contract loan rate to compensate for them. Many such loans require that the project's sponsors pledge enough of their own capital to see the project through to completion.

Concept Check

16–1. What special problems does business lending present to the management of a bank or other business lending institution?

16–2. What are the essential differences among working capital loans, open credit lines, asset-based loans, term loans, revolving credit lines, interim financing, project loans, and acquisition loans?

Loans to Support Acquisitions of Other Business Firms

The 1980s and 1990s ushered in an explosion of loans to finance mergers and acquisitions of businesses before these loans began slowing appreciably as the 21st century opened. Among the most noteworthy of these acquisition credits are **LBOs,** or *leveraged buyouts* of firms by small groups of investors, often led by managers inside the firm who believe their firm is undervalued in the marketplace. A targeted company's stock price could be driven higher, it is usually argued, if its new owners can bring more aggressive management techniques to bear, including selling off some of its assets in order to generate more revenue.

These insider purchases have often been carried out by highly optimistic groups of investors, who are willing to borrow heavily (often 90 percent or more of the LBOs are financed by debt) in the belief that revenues can be raised higher than debt-service costs through superior management. Frequently the optimistic assumptions behind LBOs have turned out to be wrong and many of these loans have become delinquent when economic conditions faltered.

Analyzing Business Loan Applications

In making business loans, the lender's margin for error is relatively narrow. Many business loans are of such large denomination that the lending institution itself may be at risk if the loan goes bad. Moreover, competition for the best business customers reduces the spread between the yield on such loans and the cost of funds, labor, taxes, and overhead, which the lender must pay in order to make these loans. For most business credits, the lender must commit roughly $100 in loanable funds for each $1 earned after all costs, including taxes. This is a modest *reward-to-risk* ratio, which means that business lenders need to take special care, particularly with loans that carry large denominations and, therefore, large risk exposure. With such a small reward-to-risk ratio, it doesn't take many business loan defaults to seriously erode the lender's profits.

As we noted in Chapter 15, most loan officers like to build several layers of protection around a business loan agreement to ensure return of loan principal and expected interest earnings by the end of the loan agreement. Typically, this requires finding two or three sources of funds the business borrower could draw upon to repay the loan. The most common sources of repayment for business loans are the following:

1. The business borrower's profits or cash flow.
2. Business assets pledged as collateral behind the loan.
3. A strong balance sheet with ample amounts of marketable assets and net worth.
4. Guarantees given by the business, such as drawing on the owners' personal property to backstop a loan.

Notice that each of these potential sources of repayment for a loan involves an analysis of customer financial statements, especially balance sheets and income statements. Let's turn to these two basic business financial statements and look at them as a loan officer would.

Analysis of a Business Borrower's Financial Statements

Analysis of the financial statements of a business borrower typically begins when the lender's credit analysis department prepares an analysis over time of how the key figures on the borrower's financial statement have changed (usually during the last three, four, or five years). An example of such an historical analysis for an oil and gas company, Black Gold, Inc., is shown in Table 16–1. It presents balance sheets for the last four years and income statements for the same time period.

Note that these financial statements include both dollar figures and percentages of total assets (in the case of the balance sheet) and total sales (in the case of the income statement). These percentage figures, often called *common-size ratios*, show even more clearly than the dollar figures on each financial statement the most important financial trends experienced by this or any other business loan customer. These percentage-composition ratios control for differences in size of firm, permitting the loan officer to compare a particular business customer with other firms and with the industry as a whole. The common-size ratios most often used to help analyze a business borrower's financial statements include the following:

Important Balance Sheet Percentage-Composition Ratios

Percentage Composition of Assets	**Percentage Composition of Total Liabilities and Net Worth**
Cash/Total assets	Accounts payable/Total liabilities and net worth (= total assets)
Marketable securities/Total assets	Notes payable/Total liabilities and net worth
Accounts receivable/Total assets	Taxes payable/Total liabilities and net worth
Inventories/Total assets	Total current liabilities/Total liabilities and net worth
Fixed assets, net of depreciation/Total assets	Long-term debt obligations (including long-term bank loans)/Total liabilities and net worth
Other (miscellaneous) assets/Total assets	Other liabilities/Total liabilities and net worth
	Total net worth/Total liabilities and net worth

Important Income Statement Percentage-Composition Ratios

Percentage Composition of Total Income (gross revenues or sales)

Cost of sales/Sales
Gross profit/Sales
Labor costs (wages, salaries, and fringe benefits)/Sales
Selling, administrative, and other expenses/Sales
Depreciation expenses/Sales
Other operating expenses/Sales
Net operating profit/Sales
Interest expense on borrowed funds/Sales
Net income before taxes/Sales
Income taxes/Sales
Net income after taxes/Sales

Comparative analysis of changes in these ratios for the recent past helps the loan officer determine any developing weaknesses in loan protection, such as decreases in assets that might be pledged as collateral or a reduction in earning power of the borrowing firm. For example, we can analyze the percentage composition statements showing assets, liabilities, and equity capital for Black Gold, Inc., as reported in Table 16–1. Based on these percentage composition statements, would Black Gold represent a good risk for the bank it has approached for a loan?

In this case Black Gold is asking the bank for a $5 million working capital line of credit tied to a borrowing base of assets, in the guise of accounts receivable and inventory, in anticipation of a sharp upturn in oil and gas prices. Black Gold currently owes $3.9 million to another bank with whom it has had a relationship for several years, but now the company has expressed considerable unhappiness with its current banking relationship and wants to establish a new relationship. Sometimes a business customer's unhappiness springs from poor or inadequate service provided by its current bank or other financial service provider; on other occasions, however, unhappiness with a banking relationship arises

TABLE 16–1 Historical Analysis of the Financial Statements of Black Gold, Inc.
(dollar figures in millions)

	Black Gold's Balance Sheets Arrayed in a Spreadsheet							
	Most Recent Year		One Year Ago		Two Years Ago		Three Years Ago	
Balance Sheet Items	Dollar Value	Percentage of Total	Dollar Value	Percentage of Total	Dollar Value	Percentage of Total	Dollar Value	Percentage of Total
Assets								
Cash	$ 1.0	3.6%	$ 1.3	4.5%	$ 1.7	5.7%	$ 2.2	6.9%
Marketable securities	0.5	1.8	0.8	2.8	1.0	3.3	___	0.0
Accounts receivable	**8.3**	**29.6**	**7.4**	**25.5**	**6.2**	**20.7**	4.1	12.8
Inventories	**5.2**	**18.6**	**4.5**	**15.5**	**3.4**	**11.3**	2.3	7.2
Total current assets	$15.0	53.6	$14.0	48.3	$12.3	41.0	$ 8.6	26.9
Fixed assets, gross	19.4	69.3	20.2	69.7	21.5	71.7	22.4	70.0
Less: Accumulated depreciation	10.1	36.8	9.2	31.7	8.0	26.7	5.1	15.9
Fixed assets, net	9.3	33.2	11.0	37.9	13.5	45.0	17.3	54.1
Other assets	3.7	13.2	4.0	13.8	4.2	14.0	6.1	19.1
Total assets	$28.0	100.0%	$29.0	100.0%	$30.0	100.0%	$32.0	100.0%
Liabilities and Equity								
Accounts payable	$ 1.3	4.6%	$ 1.2	4.1%	$ 0.8	2.7%	$ 1.0	3.1%
Notes payable	3.9	13.9	3.4	11.7	3.2	10.7	1.7	8.4
Taxes payable	0.1	0.4	0.2	0.7	0.1	0.3	0.8	2.3
Total current liabilities	$ 5.3	18.9	$ 4.8	16.6	$ 4.1	13.7	$ 4.5	14.1
Long-term debt	**12.2**	**43.6**	**13.2**	**45.5**	**12.5**	**41.6**	**11.4**	**35.6**
Other liabilities	0.0	0.0	0.4	−1.4	3.5	11.7	6.1	19.1
Total liabilities	$17.5	62.5%	$18.4	63.4%	$20.1	67.0%	$22.0	68.8%
Common stock	1.0	3.6	1.0	3.4	1.0	3.3	1.0	3.1
Paid-in surplus	3.0	10.7	3.0	10.3	3.0	10.0	3.0	9.4
Retained earnings	6.5	23.2	6.6	22.8	5.9	19.7	6.0	18.8
Total net worth	10.5	37.5	10.6	36.6	9.9	33.0	10.0	31.3

	Black Gold's Income Statement							
	Most Recent Year		One Year Ago		Two Years Ago		Three Years Ago	
Income Statement Items	Dollar Value	Percentage of Total	Dollar Value	Percentage of Total	Dollar Value	Percentage of Total	Dollar Value	Percentage of Total
Net Sales	**$32.0**	**100.0%**	**$30.0**	**100.0%**	**$28.0**	**100.0%**	**$31.0**	**100.0%**
Less: Cost of goods sold	**18.0**	**56.3**	**16.0**	**53.3**	**15.0**	**53.6**	**14.0**	**45.2**
Gross profits	$14.0	43.8	$14.0	46.7	$13.0	46.4	$17.0	54.8
Less: Selling, administrative, and other expenses	9.0	28.1	9.0	30.0	8.0	28.6	11.0	35.5
Less: Depreciation expenses	3.0	9.4	3.0	10.0	3.0	10.7	2.0	6.5
Net operating income	$ 2.0	6.3	$ 2.0	6.7	$ 2.0	7.1	$ 4.0	12.9
Less: Interest expense on borrowed funds	2.0	6.3	1.0	3.3	2.0	7.1	2.0	6.5
Net income before taxes	0.0	0.0	1.0	3.3	0.0	0.0	2.0	6.5
Less: Income taxes	0.1	0.3	0.3	1.0	0.1	0.4	0.2	0.6
Net income after taxes	($ 0.1)	(0.3)%	$ 0.7	2.3%	($ 0.1)	(3.6)%	$ 1.8	5.8%

because the business customer is in trouble and its current lending institution is simply trying to work its way out of a troubled situation, either by demanding payment on current loans or by refusing to accommodate new credit requests. One of a loan officer's tasks is to find out as much as possible about a business customer's current banking relationships and why they are or are not working out.

Careful examination of Table 16–1 suggests that the loan officer involved in this case would have several important questions to ask this customer. For example, Black Gold's net income after taxes and net income as a percentage of total net sales has been negative in two of the last four years. Its sales revenues have been essentially flat over the past four years, while the cost of goods sold, both in dollar terms and relative to net sales, has risen significantly over the past four years. Moreover, if this loan is to be secured by accounts receivable and inventory, the loan officer clearly has reason to be concerned, because the dollar amount and percentage of total assets of both of these balance sheet items have risen sharply. And, the firm's short-term (current) liabilities have risen as well.

Financial Ratio Analysis of a Customer's Financial Statements

Information from balance sheets and income statements is typically supplemented by financial ratio analysis. By careful selection of items from a borrower's balance sheets and income statements, the loan officer can shed light on such critical areas in business lending as (1) a borrowing customer's *ability to control expenses;* (2) a borrower's *operating efficiency* in using resources to generate sales and cash flow; (3) the *marketability* of the borrower's product line; (4) the *coverage* that earnings provide over a business firm's financing cost; (5) the borrower's *liquidity position,* indicating the availability of ready cash; (6) the borrower's track record of *profitability* or net income; (7) the amount of *financial leverage* (or debt relative to equity capital) a business borrower has taken on; and (8) whether a borrower faces significant *contingent liabilities* that may give rise to substantial claims in the future.

The Business Customer's Control over Expenses

A barometer of the quality of a business firm's management is how carefully it monitors and controls its expenses and how well its earnings—the primary source of cash to repay a loan in most cases—are likely to be protected and grow. Selected financial ratios, usually computed by credit analysts to monitor a firm's expense control program, include the following:

Wages and salaries/Net sales

Overhead expenses/Net sales

Depreciation expenses/Net sales

Interest expense on borrowed funds/Net sales

Cost of goods sold/Net sales

Selling, administrative, and other expenses/Net sales

Taxes/Net sales

A loan officer confronted with several of these expense-control measures for Black Gold, Inc., would probably have serious doubts about the firm's management quality and its earnings prospects for the future, as shown in Table 16–2. Some of Black Gold's expense ratios—selling, administrative, and other expenses and taxes relative to net sales—have declined; however, the rest have either held steady or risen as a percentage of the firm's net sales. In fact, it is Black Gold's inability to reduce its overall expenses in the face of a relatively flat sales record that has caused its net earnings generally to decline over the past

TABLE 16–2

Expense-Control
Ratios for Black
Gold, Inc.

	Most Recent Year	One Year Ago	Two Years Ago	Three Years Ago
Cost of goods sold ÷ net sales	56.3%	53.5%	53.6%	45.2%
Selling, administrative, and other expenses ÷ net sales	28.1	30.0	28.6	35.5
Depreciation expenses ÷ net sales	9.4	10.0	10.7	6.5
Interest expense on borrowed funds ÷ net sales	6.3	3.3	7.1	6.5
Taxes ÷ net sales	0.3	1.0	0.4	0.6

four years. The loan officer working on this case will need some highly convincing arguments from the customer to demonstrate that the firm's future expense and net earnings picture will improve.

Operating Efficiency: Measure of a Business Firm's Performance Effectiveness

It is also useful to look at a business customer's operating efficiency. How effectively are assets being utilized to generate sales and cash flow for the firm and how efficiently are sales converted into cash? Important financial ratios here include these:

Annual cost of goods sold/Average inventory (or inventory turnover ratio)

Net sales/Net fixed assets

Net sales/Accounts and notes receivable

Net sales/Total assets

Average collection period =
Accounts receivable ÷ Annual credit sales ÷ 360

In the case of Black Gold, what do these efficiency ratios show? Clearly, as Table 16–3 reveals, some measures of Black Gold's efficiency show nothing conclusive, while others tell a story of deteriorating efficiency in the management of key assets, particularly accounts receivable. Moreover, *inventory turnover*—an indicator of management's effectiveness in controlling the size of the firm's inventory position—has shown a declining trend.[1]

The *average collection period,* or accounts receivable turnover ratio, for Black Gold reveals a disturbing trend. The collection period ratio reflects the firm's effectiveness in collecting cash from its credit sales and provides evidence on the overall quality of the firm's credit accounts. A lengthening of the average collection period suggests a rise in past-due credit accounts and poor collection policies. Clearly, this has happened to Black Gold: Its average collection period has almost doubled in the past four years, rising from 47.6 days to 93.4 days. The loan officer would certainly ask why this has occurred and what steps the firm was taking to bring the turnover of its receivables back into line.

The ratio measuring *turnover of fixed assets* indicates how rapidly sales revenues are being generated as a result of using up the firm's plant and equipment (net fixed assets) to

---

[1] In general, the higher a firm's inventory ratio, the better it is for banks and other creditors, because this ratio shows the number of times during a year that the firm turns over its investment in inventories by converting those inventories into goods sold. When the inventory turnover ratio is too low it may indicate poor customer acceptance of the firm's products or ineffective production and inventory control policies. Too high an inventory turnover ratio could reflect underpricing of the firm's product or inadequate stocks of goods available for sale, with frequent stockouts, which drives customers away.

TABLE 16–3
Efficiency Ratios
for Black Gold, Inc.

	Most Recent Year	One Year Ago	Two Years Ago	Three Years Ago
Inventory turnover ratio: Annual cost of goods sold ÷ average inventory	3.46×	3.56×	4.41×	6.09×
Average collection period: Accounts receivable ÷ annual sales ÷ 360*	93.4 days	88.8 days	79.7 days	47.6 days
Turnover of fixed assets: Net sales ÷ net fixed assets	3.44×	2.73×	2.07×	1.79×
Turnover of total assets: Net sales ÷ total assets	1.14×	1.03×	0.93×	0.97×

*360 days is used for ease of computation in calculating this ratio.

produce goods or services. In this instance, Black Gold's fixed-asset turnover is rising, but there is little cause for comfort because a quick check of the balance sheet in Table 16–1 shows that the primary reason for rising fixed-asset turnover is a declining base of plant and equipment. Black Gold is either selling some of its fixed assets to raise cash or simply not replacing depreciated worn-out plant and equipment. Black Gold's management has asked for a $5 million line of credit in anticipation of increasing sales, but it is doubtful that the firm could handle these sales increases even if they occurred, given its declining base of productive fixed assets. A similar trend is reflected in the turnover ratio of total assets, which is rising for the same reasons.

Marketability of the Customer's Product or Service

In order to generate adequate cash flow to repay a loan, the business customer must be able to market goods, services, or skills successfully. A lender can often assess public acceptance of what the business customer has to sell by analyzing such factors as the growth rate of sales revenues, changes in the business customer's share of the available market, and the *gross profit margin* (GPM), defined as

$$\text{GPM} = \frac{\text{Net sales} - \text{Cost of goods sold}}{\text{Net sales}}$$

A closely related and somewhat more refined ratio is the *net profit margin* (NPM):[2]

$$\text{NPM} = \frac{\text{Net income after taxes}}{\text{Net sales}}$$

What has happened to the GPM and NPM of Black Gold, Inc.? Clearly, as revealed in Table 16–4, both GPM and NPM are on a downward trend. This trend tips off the loan officer to several actual or potential problems, including potentially inappropriate pricing policies, expense control problems, and market deterioration.

---

[2] The *gross profit margin* (GPM) measures both market conditions—demand for the business customer's product or service and how competitive a marketplace the customer faces—and the strength of the business customer in its own market, as indicated by how much the market price of the firm's product or service exceeds the customer's unit cost of production and delivery. The *net profit margin* (NPM), on the other hand, indicates how much of the business customer's profit from each dollar of sales survives after all expenses are deducted, reflecting both the effectiveness of the firm's expense control policies and the competitiveness of its pricing policies.

ETHICS IN BANKING

ALLEGED TYING ARRANGEMENTS WOULD IMPOSE UNFAIR BURDENS ON BUSINESS LOAN CUSTOMERS

When the Glass-Steagall Act was passed in 1933, one of its targets was "tying" arrangements between commercial and investment banks and their business customers. These arrangements often enabled commercial banks lending money to one of their corporate customers to compel that customer, as a condition for getting approval of a loan, to purchase securities that the bank's investment underwriting unit was trying to sell. The customer didn't intend to purchase the heavily promoted securities but felt pressured to do so in order to get the credit he or she needed.

Alternatively, some corporate customers were told that their chances of getting the bank's continued advice and support would be enhanced if they purchased other services, such as cash management or trust services. In some cases, the additional services purchased were either not needed or

were priced above market levels. For this and other reasons, the U.S. Congress acted during the 1930s to separate the commercial banking (lending) and investment banking (security underwriting and brokerage) industries.

Passage of the Gramm-Leach-Bliley (Financial Services Modernization) Act in 1999 reversed the restrictions imposed by Glass-Steagall. The new law allowed commercial banking and investment banking firms to acquire each other along with other financial-service providers. Perhaps, predictably, charges of "tying" arrangements soon emerged across the markets. Most of the allegations against some of Wall Street's leading banks and securities dealers centered upon alleged ties between loan approvals and sales of heavily promoted securities, reminiscent of the Glass-Steagall Act and the 1930s era. Officials of the Securities and Exchange Commission, the Federal Reserve System, and other agencies have expressed doubt that such practices are widespread but have promised a full investigation.

TABLE 16–4
Gross and Net Profit Margins of Black Gold, Inc.

	Most Recent Year	One Year Ago	Two Years Ago	Three Years Ago
Gross profit margin (GPM)	43.8%	46.7%	46.4%	54.8%
Net profit margin (NPM)	−0.3	2.3	−3.6	5.8

Coverage Ratios: Measuring the Adequacy of Earnings

Coverage refers to the protection afforded creditors of a firm based on the amount of the firm's earnings. The best-known coverage ratios include the following:

$$\text{Interest coverage:} \quad \frac{\text{Income before interest and taxes}}{\text{Interest payments}}$$

$$\text{Coverage of interest and principal payments:} \quad \frac{\text{Income before interest and taxes}}{\left[\text{Interest payments} + \dfrac{\text{Principal repayments}}{1 - \text{Firm's marginal tax rate}}\right]}$$

$$\text{Coverage of all fixed payments:} \quad \frac{\text{Income before interest, taxes, and lease payments}}{\text{Interest payments} + \text{Lease payments}}$$

Note that the second of these coverage ratios adjusts for the fact that repayments of the principal of a loan are *not* tax deductible, while interest and lease payments are generally tax-deductible expenses in the United States.

What has happened to Black Gold's coverage ratios? During the current year, Black Gold must pay back $930,000 of its long-term debt; it also owes $3.9 million in short-term

TABLE 16–5
Coverage Ratios for
Black Gold, Inc.

	Most Recent Year	One Year Ago	Two Years Ago	Three Years Ago
Interest coverage	1.0×	2.0×	1.0×	2.0×
Coverage of interest and principal payments	0.29×	0.22×	0.32×	0.43×

notes payable. One year ago it paid back $1 million in long-term debt, while two and three years ago it paid back $1.1 million and $1.3 million in long-term obligations, respectively. As Table 16–5 shows, Black Gold's interest coverage is weak. Its earnings are barely adequate to cover its interest payments, and once repayments of principal are thrown in, Black Gold's earnings are simply inadequate to cover both its interest and principal payments. The firm must content itself with less debt (and use more owners' equity) to finance itself, find ways to boost its earnings, or lengthen its debt through restructuring so that current debt service payments are reduced. Perhaps all three steps need to be taken. The loan officer should offer counsel to this customer concerning these alternatives and suggest how the firm might strengthen its coverage ratios to increase its chances of securing a loan.

Liquidity Indicators for Business Customers

Key URLs

The quality and condition of commercial loans made in the United States are periodically surveyed in the Federal Reserve's Senior Loan Officer Opinion Survey (the results are reported at **www.federalreserve.gov/boarddocs/snloansurvey**) and the FDIC's Regional Outlook Survey at **www.fdic.gov/bank/analytical/regional**.

The borrower's liquidity position reflects his or her ability to raise cash in timely fashion at reasonable cost, including the ability to meet loan payments when they come due.[3] Popular measures of liquidity include the following:

$$\text{Current ratio} = \frac{\text{Current assets}}{\text{Current liabilities}}$$

$$\text{Acid-test ratio} = \frac{\text{Current assets} - \text{Inventory}}{\text{Current liabilities}}$$

$$\text{Net liquid assets} = \frac{\text{Current}}{\text{assets}} - \frac{\text{Inventories of}}{\text{raw materials}} - \frac{\text{Current}}{\text{liabilities}}$$
$$\text{or goods}$$

$$\text{Net working capital} = \text{Current assets} - \text{Current liabilties}$$

The concept of **working capital** is important because it provides a measure of a firm's ability to meet its short-term debt obligations from its holdings of current assets.

What has happened to Black Gold's liquidity position? The firm made substantial progress in building up its liquidity two years ago, when current assets covered current liabilities three times over. Since that time, however, Black Gold's current and acid-test ratios have dipped significantly (see Table 16–6). The only bright spots in the firm's liquidity picture are the recent expansion in its working capital of $9.7 million and its relatively stable net liquid asset position. However, when we carefully examine the causes of

---

[3] An individual, business firm, or government is considered *liquid* if it can convert assets into cash or borrow immediately spendable funds precisely when cash is needed. Liquidity is a short-run concept in which time plays a key role. For that reason, most measures of liquidity focus on the amount of *current assets* (cash, marketable securities, accounts receivable, inventory, prepaid expenses, and any other assets that normally roll over into cash within a year's time) and *current liabilities* (accounts payable, notes payable, taxes payable, and other short-term claims against the firm, including any interest and principal payments owed on long-term debt that must be paid during the current year).

TABLE 16–6
Changes in Liquidity
at Black Gold, Inc.

	Most Recent Year	One Year Ago	Two Years Ago	Three Years Ago
Current ratio: Current assets ÷ current liabilities	2.83×	2.92×	3.00×	1.91×
Acid-test ratio: (Current assets − inventories) ÷ current liabilities	1.85×	1.98×	2.17×	1.40×
Working capital (= current assets − current liabilities)	$9.7 mil.	$9.2 mil.	$8.2 mil.	$4.1 mil.
Net liquid assets (= current assets − inventories − current liabilities)	$4.5 mil.	$4.7 mil.	$4.8 mil.	$1.8 mil.

this working capital gain, we discover that it has been brought about largely by selling off a portion of the firm's fixed assets (plant and equipment) and through the use of debt. Neither of these events is likely to be well received by the loan officers or credit analysts.

Banks and other commercial lenders are especially sensitive to changes in a business loan customer's liquidity position because it is through the conversion of liquid assets, including the cash account, that loan repayments usually come. Erosion in a firm's liquidity position increases the risk that the lender will have to attach the customer's other assets to recover its funds. Such a step is usually time-consuming, costly, and uncertain in its outcome. If the bank in this case ultimately decides to make a loan to Black Gold, it will almost certainly insist on covenants in the loan agreement requiring the firm to strengthen its liquid reserves.

We should note, as Haubrich and Cabral dos Santos [4] observe, that liquidity can also have a "dark side." A business borrower with too many assets tied up in liquid form, rather than in income-producing assets, loses opportunities to boost returns. Excess liquidity also invites dishonest managers and employees to "take the money and run." Clearly, a loan officer must be wary of extremes in customer performance and ask for explanations whenever performance extremes are found.

Profitability Indicators

The ultimate standard of performance in a market-oriented economy is how much net income remains for the owners of a business firm after all expenses (except stockholder dividends) are charged against revenue. Most loan officers will look at both pretax net income and after-tax net income to measure the overall financial success or failure of a prospective borrower relative to comparable firms in the same industry. Popular bottom-line indicators of the financial success of business borrowers include

Before-tax net income ÷ total assets, net worth, or total sales
After-tax net income ÷ total assets, net worth, or total sales

How profitable has Black Gold been? Table 16–7 summarizes key profitability trends for this oil and gas firm. Clearly, there is little cause for comfort for the loan officer handling this credit application. Black Gold's earnings began a long-term decline two to three years ago, and there is little evidence to suggest that a turnaround is in sight. The firm's management has predicted an upturn in sales, which may result also in an earnings upturn. However, the loan officer must be satisfied that the prospects for such a recovery are truly bright. Of course, the loan might be granted if sufficient collateral were available that could be sold to recover the lending bank's funds. But most loan officers would find this a poor substitute for earnings and cash flow in repaying a loan.

TABLE 16–7
Profitability Trends at
Black Gold, Inc.

	Most Recent Year	One Year Ago	Two Years Ago	Three Years Ago
Before-tax net income ÷ total assets	0.0%	3.4%	0.0%	6.3%
After-tax net income ÷ total assets	−0.4	2.4	−0.3	5.6
Before-tax net income ÷ net worth	0.0	9.4	0.0	20.0
After-tax net income ÷ net worth	−1.0	6.6	−1.0	18.0

TABLE 16–8
Leverage Trends at
Black Gold, Inc.

	Most Recent Year	One Year Ago	Two Years Ago	Three Years Ago
Leverage ratio: Total liabilities ÷ total assets	62.5%	63.4%	67.0%	68.8%
Total liabilities ÷ net worth	1.67×	1.74×	2.03×	2.20×
Capitalization ratio: Long-term debt ÷ long-term debt plus net worth	53.7%	55.5%	55.8%	53.3%
Debt-to-sales ratio: Total liabilities ÷ net sales	54.7%	61.3%	71.8%	71.0%

The Financial Leverage Factor as a Barometer of a Business Firm's Capital Structure

Any lender of funds is concerned about how much debt a borrower has taken on in addition to the loan being sought. The term *financial leverage* refers to the use of debt in the hope that the borrower can generate earnings that exceed the cost of debt, thereby increasing the potential return to a business firm's owners (stockholders). Key financial ratios used to analyze any borrowing business's credit standing and use of financial leverage are as follows:

$$\text{Leverage ratio} = \frac{\text{Total liabilities}}{\text{Total assets}}$$

$$\text{Capitalization ratio} = \frac{\text{Long-term debt}}{\text{Total long-term liabilities and net worth}}$$

$$\text{Debt-to-sales ratio} = \frac{\text{Total liabilities}}{\text{Net sales}}$$

What has happened to Black Gold's leverage, or debt position? As shown in Table 16–8, Black Gold's leverage ratio has improved in the most recent period, with assets and net worth generally growing somewhat faster than the firm's debt. Moreover, its mix of long-term funding sources—debt and equity capital—has been relatively constant, while total liabilities have declined relative to sales. Much of the firm's funding has come from sources other than debt, such as depletion of fixed assets and a buildup in such current assets as accounts receivable and inventory.

Exhibit 16–1 summarizes the key ratios bank loan officers use to analyze a business borrower's financial condition, while Table 16–9 summarizes the ratios that highlight Black Gold's current standing.

TABLE 16–9
Summary of Key
Financial Ratios
Showing Trends
in the Financial
Condition
of Black Gold, Inc.

Financial Ratio Categories and Key Ratio Measures	Values in Most Recent Year	Financial Ratios for Black Gold:		
		One Year Ago	Two Years Ago	Three Years Ago
Expense Control Measures				
Cost of goods sold/Net sales	56.3%	53.5%	53.6%	45.2%
Selling, administrative, and other expenses/Net sales	28.1	30.0	28.6	35.5
Depreciation expenses/Net sales	9.4	10.0	10.7	6.5
Interest expense on borrowed funds/Net sales	6.3	3.3	7.1	6.5
Taxes/Net sales	0.3	1.0	0.4	0.6
Operating Efficiency Measures				
Annual cost of goods sold/Average inventory	3.46×	3.56×	4.41×	6.09×
Average receivables collection period	93.4 days	88.8 days	79.7 days	47.6 days
Net sales/Net fixed assets	3.44×	2.73×	2.07×	1.79×
Net sales/Total assets	1.14×	1.03×	0.93×	0.97×
Marketability of Product or Service Measures				
Gross profit margin (GPM)	43.8%	46.7%	46.4%	54.8%
Net profit margin (NPM)	−0.3	2.3	−3.6	5.8
Coverage Measures				
Interest coverage	1.0×	2.0×	1.0×	2.0×
Coverage of interest and principal payments	0.29×	0.22×	0.32×	0.43×
Liquidity Measures				
Current assets/Current liabilities (current ratio)	2.83×	2.92×	3.00×	1.91×
Acid-test ratio (Current assets less inventories/Current liabilities)	1.85×	1.98×	2.17×	1.40×
Working capital (current assets less current liabilities)	$9.7 mil.	$9.2 mil.	$8.2 mil.	$4.1 mil.
Net liquid assets (current assets less inventories less current liabilities)	$4.5 mil.	$4.7 mil.	$4.8 mil.	$1.8 mil.
Profitability Measures				
Before-tax net income/Total assets	0.0%	3.4%	0.0%	6.3%
After-tax net income/Total assets	−0.4	2.4	−0.3	5.6
Before-tax net income/Net worth	0.0	9.4	0.0	20.0
After-tax net income/Net worth	−1.0	6.6	−1.0	18.0
Leverage or Capital Structure Measures				
Leverage ratio (Total liabilities divided by total assets)	62.5%	63.4%	67.0%	68.8%
Total liabilities/Net worth	1.67×	1.74×	2.03×	2.20×
Capitalization ratio (Long-term debt divided by long-term debt plus net worth)	53.7%	55.5%	55.8%	53.3%
Debt-to-sales ratio (Total liabilities divided by net sales)	54.7%	61.3%	71.8%	71.0%

EXHIBIT 16–1

Summary of Key Ratios Used to Analyze a Business Loan Customer's Financial Condition

Expense Control Measures
Wages and salaries/Net sales
Overhead expenses/Net sales
Depreciation expenses/Net sales
Interest expenses on borrowed funds/Net sales
Cost of goods sold/Net sales
Selling, administrative, and other expenses/Net sales
Taxes/Net sales

Operating Efficiency Measures
Annual cost of goods sold/Average inventory
Net sales/Total assets
Net sales/Net fixed assets
Net sales/Accounts and notes receivable
Average receivables collection period

Liquidity Indicators or Measures
Current assets/Current liabilities (or coverage ratio)
Current assets less inventory/Current liabilities (or acid-test ratio)
Net liquid assets (or current assets less inventories of raw materials or goods less current liabilities)
Net working capital (Current assets less current liabilities)

Measures of a Business Customer's Product or Service
Gross profit margin (net sales less cost of goods sold divided by net sales)
Net profit margin (net income after taxes/ net sales)

Coverage Measures
Interest coverage (income before interest and taxes divided by interest payments)
Coverage of interest and principal payments (income before interest and taxes divided by interest payments and principal payments over 1 minus the firm's marginal tax rate)
Coverage of all fixed payments (income before interest, taxes, and lease payments divided by interest plus lease payments)

Leverage Factor (or Capital Structure) Measures
Total liabilities/Total assets (or leverage ratio)
Long-term debt/Total long-term liabilities and net worth (or capitalization ratio)
Total liabilities/Net sales (or debt-to-sales ratio)

Comparing a Business Customer's Performance to the Performance of Its Industry

Key URLs
For detailed information on how industries are classified today for economic and financial analysis using the Standard Industrial Classification (SIC) and North American Industrial Classification System (NAICS) codes see especially the U.S. Bureau of Labor Statistics (**www.bls .gov**) and the U.S. Census Bureau (**www.census.gov/epcd/ www/naics.html**).

It is standard practice among loan officers to compare each business customer's performance to the performance of the customer's entire industry. Several organizations work to aid loan officers in gathering industrywide data; two of the most famous and widely used are these:

Dun & Bradstreet Industry Norms and Key Business Ratios, which provides 14 business and financial ratios for industries containing over 18 million businesses for up to three years, including common-size balance sheets and income statements, dollar totals for sales and selected other accounts, and such key performance ratios as return on assets and net worth, turnover of accounts receivable and inventory, liabilities and fixed assets to net worth, and current assets to current liabilities. (See, for example, **www.bizminer.com**.)

RMA Annual Statement Studies, which assembles data provided by loan officers and their customers for over 640 industries (listed by their SIC and NAICS codes) from six different U.S. regions. Includes 16 common-size financial ratios based on the composition of the balance sheet and income statement, divides this information into six asset and sales size groups, presents average industry performance levels as well as upper and lower quartiles of performance, and is available by book (often found in library reference departments), to subscribers online in the form of industry profiles, and via CD Rom. (See **www.rmahq.org/Ann_Studies/asstudies.html**.)

Black Gold is classified as a member of the crude oil and natural gas extraction industry (SIC Code 1311 and NAICS code 211111). Generally, Black Gold's performance places it *below* industry standards (means or medians) in terms of several of the key performance ratios we have examined in the preceding sections. The loan officer would want to discuss with Black Gold's management the reasons for the firm's lagging performance and how management proposes to raise Black Gold's ranking within its own industry.

Contingent Liabilities

Types of Contingent Liabilities   Usually not shown on customer balance sheets are other potential claims against the borrower that loan officers must be aware of, such as these:

1. Guarantees and warranties behind the business firm's products.
2. Litigation or pending lawsuits against the firm.
3. Unfunded pension liabilities the firm will likely owe its employees in the future.
4. Taxes owed but unpaid.
5. Limiting regulations.

These **contingent liabilities** can turn into actual claims against the firm's assets and earnings at a future date, reducing the funds available to repay a loan. The loan officer's best move in this circumstance is, first, to ask the customer about pending or potential claims against the firm and then to follow up with his or her own investigation, checking courthouse records, public notices, and newspapers. It is far better to be safe and well informed than to repose in blissful ignorance. In a case like Black Gold, the loan officer would routinely check into possible contingent liabilities.

Environmental Liabilities   A new contingent liability that has increasingly captured lenders' concerns is the issue of possible lender liability for *environmental damage* under the terms of the Comprehensive Environmental Response, Compensation, and Liability Act and its Super Fund Amendments. These federal laws make current and past owners of contaminated property, current and prior operators of businesses located on contaminated property, and those who dispose of or transport hazardous substances potentially liable for any cleanup costs associated with environmental damage. (Most states have enacted similar environmental damage and cleanup laws.) Other federal government laws that establish liability for the creation, transportation, storage, and disposal of environmentally dangerous substances include the Resource Conservation and Recovery Act, the Clean Water Act, the Clean Air Act, and the Toxic Substance Control Act.

In 1990 a federal appeals court in the Fleet Factors case ruled that a lender could be held liable for cleanup of hazardous wastes spilled by a firm to whom it had loaned money if the lender was "significantly involved" in the borrower's decision making on how to dispose of hazardous wastes.[4] Faced with this and other court decisions, many lenders felt compelled to scrutinize closely the pollution hazards of any property pledged as collateral upon which they might have the right to foreclose. In an effort to give lenders guidelines on how to evaluate their environmental risks, the U.S. Environmental Protection Agency (EPA) issued a lender liability rule in 1992, defining a "security interest exemption" that creditors could take advantage of when taking possession of polluted property. The EPA guidelines state that a lender holding "indicia of ownership" (such as a deed of trust, lien, or mortgage) can be exempted from any environmental liability associated with the owner's property provided that the lender takes certain steps. For one thing lenders must not participate in the management of the borrower's property and must take action primarily to protect the credit they have extended to the borrower rather than treating their interest in the borrower's property as a long-term investment. If the lender forecloses on

---

[4] See especially *United States* v. *Fleet Factor Corp.,* 901 F.2d 1550, and, for a similar decision, see *United States* v. *Maryland Bank & Trust Co.,* 632 F.Supp. 573.

INTERNAL CREDIT RATING SYSTEMS FOR BUSINESS LENDING: HOW BANKERS RATE THEIR BUSINESS LOAN CUSTOMERS

Many banks have developed internal credit-risk rating systems that assess the credit quality of a business firm when it applies for a loan and are used periodically to reevaluate a customer with an existing loan to determine if credit quality has at least been maintained. There are many differences in these credit rating systems from bank to bank. Some rate business borrowers according to their potential for profitability for the lender in order to help price a loan, measure the borrower's sensitivity to stress, or spot developing payout problems before things get out of hand. Among the loans usually subjected to internal ratings are commercial and industrial loans and loan commitments, commercial leases, real estate loans, foreign loans, and loans to financial institutions.

Among the key borrower characteristics considered in assigning internal credit-quality grades are firm size, book or market value of equity, liquidity on the balance sheet, borrower access to funds sources other than the bank, historical and projected earnings, operating cash flow, interest coverage, financial leverage, borrower's position and condition relative to its industry, quality of financial statements (for example: are they audited?), and country of domicile. Many large banks use both *external* (e.g., Moody's or Standard & Poor's) and *internal* rating systems to double-check raters' judgment calls.

Credit rating systems are changing rapidly, with greater emphasis today on profitability analysis and borrower sensitivity to risk. The Basel Accord on bank capital (discussed in Chapter 14) is now encouraging banks to measure the credit quality of their whole loan portfolio in order to determine how much capital is needed to cover credit risk. (See especially William F. Treacy and Mark S. Carey, "Credit Risk Rating at Large U.S. Banks," *Federal Reserve Bulletin,* November 1998, pp. 897–921.)

polluted property, it must post that property for sale within 12 months after securing marketable title. A lender can (*a*) require that a borrower perform an environmental assessment of his or her own property; (*b*) require that polluted property be cleaned up; (*c*) inspect and monitor the borrower's property; and (*d*) demand in writing that a borrower comply with all environmental laws and regulations.

In February 1993 the Federal Deposit Insurance Corporation issued guidelines to help federally supervised depository institutions develop an *environmental risk assessment program,* which government examiners will review each time a bank or thrift institution is examined. A senior officer inside each institution must be appointed to implement and administer procedures for protecting against loss from environmental damage. Each depository institution is supposed to establish a training program for its staff, develop procedures for evaluating the environmental risks present in loans collateralized by a customer's property, and put in place safeguards to shield the institution from environmental liability. A business borrower like Black Gold—an oil and gas company—would be carefully scrutinized for possible environmental liabilities.

Preparing Statements of Cash Flows from Business Financial Statements

Besides balance sheets and income statements, loan officers like to see a third accounting statement from a business borrower—the **Statement of Cash Flows.** This statement, required by the Financial Accounting Standards Board (FASB), is usually readily available from borrowers. It provides insights into how and why a firm's cash balance has changed. While a comparison of balance sheets for two consecutive periods reveals whether cash has increased or decreased and income statements identify revenues and expenses leading

TABLE 16–10
Statement of Cash Flows for Black Gold, Inc. (figures in millions of dollars)

Most Recent Year	Source of Information
Cash Flows from Operations	
Net income (loss)	($0.1) *Most recent income statement (IS)*
Adjustments to Reconcile Net Income	
Add: Depreciation	$3.0 *Most recent income statement*
Changes in Assets and Liabilities	
Add: Decrease in other assets	$0.3 *Comparison of consecutive balance sheets (CBSs)*
Add: Increase in accounts payable	$0.1 *Comparison of consecutive balance sheets*
Subtract: Increase in accounts receivable	($0.9) *Comparison of consecutive balance sheets*
Subtract: Increase in inventories	($0.7) *Comparison of consecutive balance sheets*
Subtract: Decrease in taxes payable	(<u>$0.1</u>) *Comparison of consecutive balance sheets*
Net Cash Flow from Operations	$1.6
Cash Flows from Investment Activities	
Purchase of new machinery	($1.3) Acquisition cost (can be derived from CBSs after adjusting for all other changes)
Redemption of marketable securities	<u>$0.3</u> Book value of securities sold (CBSs) + gains (IS) – losses(IS)
Net Cash Flow from Investment Activities	($1.0)
Cash Flows from Financing Activities	
Increase in notes payable	$0.5 *Comparison of consecutive balance sheets*
Repayment of long-term debt	($1.0) *Comparison of consecutive balance sheets*
Repayment of other liabilities	($0.4) *Comparison of consecutive balance sheets*
Subtract: Dividends paid	<u>$0.0</u> *Difference between net income (IS) and change in retained earnings (CBSs)*
Net Cash Flow from Financing Activities	(<u>$0.9</u>)
Increase (decrease) in cash for the year	($0.3) *Sum of net cash flow from operations, investments, and financing activities. Entry should check with comparison of consecutive balance sheets.*

to the bottom line of net income, lenders often want to know more about cash flows. For example: *Will the borrower be able to generate sufficient cash to support its production and sales activities and still be able to repay the lender? Why is the cash position of the borrower changing over time and what are the implications of these changes for the lender?*

The Statement of Cash Flows illustrates how cash receipts and disbursements are generated by operating activities, investing activities, and financing activities. The fundamentals of the process are to identify all activities that generate or necessitate cash and then to group them based on whether they originated with operations, investments, or financing. Table 16–10 provides an illustration of the Statement of Cash Flows for Black Gold's most recent year prepared using the following format:

Cash Flow by Origin = Net Cash Flow from Operations
 (focusing upon the normal flow
 of production, inventories, and sales)
 + Net Cash Flow from Investing Activities
 (focusing upon the purchase and sale of assets)
 + Net Cash Flow from Financing Activities
 (including the issuance of debt)

The most important of these activities are the operations of a firm. The operating cash flows may be identified using either a direct method or an indirect method. FASB recommends the direct method; however, the indirect method, which we will illustrate using Black Gold, Inc, is used more frequently. As introduced in Chapter 15 the traditional (direct) measure of operating cash flows is this:

$$\begin{aligned}
\text{Traditional (Direct) Operating} &= \text{Net Cash Flow from Operations} + \text{Noncash Expenses} \\
\text{Cash Flow Measure} &\quad \text{(measured on a cash, not an accrual, basis)} \\
&= \text{Net Sales Revenue} - \text{Cost of Goods Sold} - \text{Selling,} \\
&\quad \text{General and Administrative Expenses} - \text{Taxes} \\
&\quad \text{Paid in Cash} + \text{Noncash Expenses (especially} \\
&\quad \text{depreciation)}
\end{aligned}$$

The income statement, which we associate with operations, is created using accrual rather than cash-basis accounting. The indirect method for calculating operating cash flows begins with net income from the income statement and shows the reconciliation of this figure to that of operating cash flows:

$$\begin{aligned}
\text{Indirect Operating} &= \text{Net Income} + \text{Noncash Expenses} + \text{Losses} \\
\text{Cash Flow Measure} &\quad \text{from the sale of assets} - \text{Gains from the sale of assets} \\
&\quad - \text{Increases in assets associated with operations} + \text{Increases in} \\
&\quad \text{current liabilities associated with operations} - \text{Decreases} \\
&\quad \text{in current liabilities associated with operations} + \text{Decreases in} \\
&\quad \text{current assets associated with operations}
\end{aligned}$$

This equation begins with net income and adds back noncash expenses, such as depreciation. Then it adjusts for gains or losses from the sale of assets that are incorporated on the income statement in order to group them with investing activities. Finally, it adds all changes on the balance sheet that generate cash (i.e., decreases in accounts receivable, decreases in inventory, decreases in other assets, increases in accounts payable, and increases in accrued items) and subtracts all changes on the balance sheet that require cash (i.e., increases in accounts receivable, increases in inventory, increases in other assets, decreases in accounts payable, and decreases in accrued items). This process is illustrated as cash flows from operations for Black Gold in Table 16–10.

The second section of the Statement of Cash Flows describes the inflows and outflows associated with the acquisition and disposition of assets used in operations. The cash flows associated with investing activities include all purchases and sales of securities and long-term assets, such as plant and equipment. While some notion of these activities can be gleaned from the changes in marketable securities and fixed assets on consecutive balance sheets and gains and losses recorded on the income statement, the Statement of Cash Flows directs attention to the actual funds needed or provided. Typically healthy, growth-oriented firms are investing in fixed assets to support operations. At the end of the most recent year, Black Gold wrote off $2 million in refinery equipment that was fully depreciated, but no longer serviceable. As a partial replacement they purchased equipment costing $1.3 million. While this investment in fixed assets required funds, Black Gold generated some $300,000 in funds by cashing in Treasury bills as they matured.

The third and final section of the Statement of Cash Flows reports financing activities. Cash inflows include the short- and long-term funds provided by lenders and owners, while cash outflows include the repayment of borrowed funds, dividends to owners, and the repurchasing of outstanding stock. In terms of cash inflows from financing activities, Black Gold increased notes payable by $500,000. Their cash outflows included the repayment of $1.4 million in long-term debt and other liabilities.

Let's examine more closely the Statement of Cash Flows in Table 16–10, compiled by the accountants at Black Gold, Inc., and supplied to the loan officer in the Black Gold case. This statement shows clearly how Black Gold supported its production and delivery of oil and gas over the past year. The funds to support Black Gold's activities were generated by drawing down liquidity (cash and marketable securities), through short-term borrowings (accounts and notes payable) and by postponing the replacement of equipment. These sources of cash inflow suggest the company may be exhausting its liquidity and capacity to borrow, casting doubts regarding its ability to repay future borrowings.

Clearly, Black Gold cannot continue deferring the replacement of assets. Claiming a noncash expense of $3 million for plant and equipment on their income statement, management wrote off $2.1 million of fully depreciated fixed assets that had "bit the dust," while only purchasing the necessities for $1.3 million. The firm needs to develop *new* sources of funding (preferably through expanded sales and net income) to remain viable in the long run. Black Gold's management must present a convincing argument to the loan officer on how the firm will improve its sales and net earnings.

The cash outflows for Black Gold summarized in Table 16–10 reveal that funds amounting to $4.3 million were used to increase accounts receivable and inventories, purchase essential new equipment, and repay long-term debt and other liabilities. The loan officer will examine closely the build-up of accounts receivable and inventories for quality and marketability because these assets can be hard to liquidate in a down market. On a brighter note, the $1.4 million that went to pay off long-term debt and other liabilities is a positive development. This reduction in debt helped to increase Black Gold's future borrowing capacity.

Pro Forma Statements of Cash Flows and Balance Sheets

Not only is it useful to look at historical data in a Statement of Cash Flows, but it is also important to estimate the business borrower's future cash flows and statement of financial condition. Lenders often have the customer prepare these *pro forma* statements, and then credit analysts within the lending institution will prepare their own version of these forecasts for comparison purposes.

Table 16–11 shows a pro forma balance sheet and Statement of Cash Flows for Black Gold, Inc. To no one's surprise, Black Gold has predicted a rosy future for its oil and gas operations. Net sales are forecast to increase 10 percent, resulting in positive net income of $100,000, while Black Gold's total assets are predicted to climb from $28 to $31.8 million within the coming year. The predicted positive earnings would help to boost the firm's retained earnings account and thereby strengthen its equity capital. At the same time the cash account is forecast to return to its level of two or three years ago at $2 million by the end of the current year. For additional liquidity, the firm forecasts adding $1 million to its holdings of marketable securities—a readily available liquidity reserve—and the less-liquid receivables and inventory accounts allegedly will be worked down (each by $0.4 million) through improved credit collection methods and better pricing and restocking policies.

Not only will the decline in plant and equipment be halted, Black Gold's management estimates, but also $4 million in new fixed assets will be added to replace obsolete or worn-out facilities. According to Table 16–11, the firm is planning to expand its net fixed assets (plant and equipment) shown on the pro forma balance sheet by $1 million. This would be accomplished by claiming a depreciation expense of $3 million, purchasing new assets of $4 million, while writing off the $3 million of fully depreciated assets that will be disposed of with neither gains nor losses accruing. Black Gold's management also plans to acquire other (miscellaneous) assets of $1.6 million, and pay off $200,000 of its outstanding long-term debt.

TABLE 16–11   **Pro Forma Balance Sheet and Statement of Cash Flows for Black Gold, Inc.** (figures in millions of dollars)

Items from the Balance Sheet	Actual Balance Sheet at End of Most Recent Year	Pro Forma Balance Sheet One Year from Now	Items from the Balance Sheet	Actual Balance Sheet at End of Most Recent Year	Pro Forma Balance Sheet One Year from Now
Asset items:			**Liabilities and net worth items:**		
Cash account	$ 1.0	$ 2.0	Accounts payable	$ 1.3	$ 1.4
Marketable securities	0.5	1.5	Notes payable	3.9	5.0
Accounts receivable	8.3	7.9	Taxes payable	0.1	0.5
Inventories held	5.2	4.8	Current liabilities	5.3	6.9
Current assets	15.0	16.2			
			Long-term debt obligations	12.2	12.0
Net fixed assets	9.3	10.3	Other liabilities	0.0	2.3
Other assets	3.7	5.3	Common stock outstanding	1.0	1.0
Total assets	$28.0	$31.8	Paid-in surplus	3.0	3.0
			Retained earnings	6.5	6.6
			Total liabilities and net worth	$28.0	$31.8

Pro Forma Cash Flows One Year from Now		Pro Forma Cash Flows One Year from Now	
Cash Flows from Operations		**Cash Flows from Investment Activities**	
Net income (loss)	$0.1	Purchase of new machinery	($4.0)
Adjustments to reconcile net income		Purchase of marketable securities	($1.0)
Add: Depreciation	$3.0	**Net cash flow from investment activities**	($5.0)
Changes in assets and liabilities			
Add: Decrease in accounts receivable	$0.4	**Cash flows from financing activities**	
Add: Decrease in inventories	$0.4	Increase in notes payable	$1.1
Add: Increase in accounts payable	$0.1	Repayment of long-term debt	($0.2)
Add: Increase in taxes payable	$0.4	Funds from other liabilities	$2.3
Subtract: Increase in other assets	($1.6)	Dividends paid	$0.0
Net cash flow from operations	$2.8	**Net cash flow from financing activities**	$3.2
		Increase (decrease) cash for the year	$1.0

Effect of the proposed loan: Black Gold proposes to pay off the $3.9 million note owed to its former bank with the $5 million it is requesting in new bank credit. If the loan is approved as requested, its cash account would rise by $1 million to $2 million and its notes payable account would increase by $1.1 million to $5 million, reflecting the amount owed the firm's new lender.

These cash outflows reportedly are to be covered by decreasing accounts receivable by $0.4 million, decreasing inventories by $0.4 million, increasing accounts payable by $0.1 million, increasing taxes payable by $0.4 million, increasing notes payable (to be provided by the lending bank) by $1.1 million, and increasing other (unspecified) liabilities by $2.3 million. Because the additional debt could weaken the lending bank's claim against this customer, should it make the loan and that loan ultimately becomes a problem credit, the loan officer will want to find out exactly why and how this proposed additional debt capital would be raised and assess its possible adverse consequences for the lender.

What will make possible all these adventurous plans for restructuring and rebuilding Black Gold's assets and capital? As Table 16–11 shows in the notes payable account, the firm is relying heavily on its $5 million credit request from the bank to pay off its outstanding $3.9 million in short-term notes and to provide an additional $1.1 million in new cash to strengthen its assets and help fuel the projected gains in its net income. Are these forecasts reasonable? That, of course, is the decision the loan officer and, ultimately, the bank's loan committee must make. Experienced loan officers know that, in most cases, the customer is more optimistic and far less objective about the future than a lender can afford to be.

A key factor shaping this customer's future performance will be what happens to energy prices in the global market. The lender would be well advised to carry out a *simulation analysis* of this customer's future financial condition, assuming an array of different possible oil and gas prices (and, therefore, net sales figures) and seeing what the consequences are for the firm's pro forma balance sheet, income statement, and statement of cash flows. Armed with this information, the loan committee can move toward a more satisfactory credit decision based on its assessment of the most likely future conditions in the global energy market.

The Loan Officer's Responsibility to the Lending Institution and the Customer

There is an understandable tendency on the part of many readers to look at the foregoing figures for Black Gold and simply say *no*. This proposed loan as requested does not appear to many analysts to have reasonable prospects for being repaid, given Black Gold's recent trends in sales revenue, expenses, cash flow, and net earnings. But it is at this point that the credit analyst and the loan officer *may* part company. A loan officer must look beyond the immediate facts to the broader, longer-term aspects of the customer relationship. Denial of this loan request will almost certainly lose this customer's business (including any deposits the company may have placed with the lending institution) and probably lose the personal accounts of some stockholders and employees of Black Gold as well. Other firms in the same or related industries may also be discouraged from applying to this lender for coverage of their credit needs.

Lending institutions cannot stay in business for long by making bad loans of this size, but they also must be cautious about flatly turning away large corporate accounts without at least exploring the possibilities for establishing some sort of customer relationship. That sort of policy soon leads to loss of market share and may ultimately damage bottom-line earnings. Many experienced loan officers argue that a better long-run business loan policy is to *find some way to help a business customer* under terms the lender feels adequately protect its funds and its reputation in the marketplace. This doesn't necessarily mean extending a loan where the risks appear unacceptable. Helping the customer may mean, instead, offering to provide noncredit services, such as cash management services, advice on a proposed merger, or assistance with a new security offer the customer may be planning.

Yet another possible option to be explored is a counteroffer on the proposed loan that is small enough and secured well enough to adequately protect the lender. In the case of Black Gold, Inc., the bank is confronted with a request for a $5 million credit line—an amount that is considerably more than the loan officer is likely to be willing to grant, given this customer's apparent financial and operating weaknesses. Suppose, however, that the loan officer, with the approval of the loan committee, proposes the following alternative plan to this customer:

> The bank will extend a $1.5 million line of credit for six months, with the line to be cleaned up at the end of that period. If all payments on this credit are satisfactorily made and there is no further deterioration in the customer's financial position, the bank will renew the credit line on a quarterly basis. Any drawings against the line will be secured by a lien against all unencumbered fixed assets of the firm, 70 percent of all accounts receivable that are current, and 40 percent of the value of all inventories held. The bank will be granted a first lien against any new fixed assets acquired by the firm. Interest payments will be assessed monthly. The customer agrees to hold a deposit with the bank equal to

EARNINGS DECEPTION BY BORROWING BUSINESSES: WHAT SHOULD LOAN OFFICERS DO?

As the 21st century dawned, the credit markets were rocked by stories of corporate fraud and deception as several leading borrowing businesses inflated their earnings to attract capital and lower the cost of their loans. Many corporations, even those not committing outright fraud, have created their own earnings measures, reporting to lenders and the public such questionable numbers as "pro forma," "street," or "operating" earnings, while burying lower, but more generally accepted (GAAP) earnings measures in out of the way places in their reports. These "engineered" earnings figures often omit unfavorable items, inflating revenues and understating expenses.

Loan officers today must be especially conscious of earnings-inflation devices used by some of their biggest business customers. The well-trained loan officer today asks lots of questions about businesses' financial statements, including these:

- How exactly were earnings or income computed?
- What expense items have been excluded from earnings estimates and why?
- How are pension plan expenses and returns calculated?
- How are employee stock options (ESOPs) accounted for?
- How did your firm treat losses on assets, corporate restructuring charges, and other extraordinary expenses?

Recently several leading companies, such as General Motors, General Electric, Coca-Cola, and Procter & Gamble, have revised their reporting methods to include the expensing of employee stock options, more transparent treatment of pension plan returns and obligations, and more conservative handling of extraordinary business expenses. Unfortunately, many business borrowers still have not yet responded to the public and regulators' call for accurate and honest financial reports.

Note: See, for example, John B. Carlson and Erkin Y. Sahinoz, "Measures of Corporate Earnings: What Number Is It?" *Economic Commentary,* Federal Reserve Bank of Cleveland, February 1, 2003.

---

20 percent of the amount of any actual drawings against the line and 5 percent of the amount of any unused portion of the line.

In addition, the customer agrees to file monthly reports on the status of sales, expenses, net income, accounts receivable, and inventory and to file quarterly audited balance sheet and income statements. Any changes in the management of the firm or any sales of plant and equipment, merger agreements, or liquidations must be approved in advance by the bank. The customer will maintain at least the current levels of the firm's leverage and liquidity ratios, and any significant deviations from the firm's projections or any significant changes in the firm's financial and operating position will be reported to the bank immediately. Any failure to conform to the terms of this agreement by the customer will make the loan immediately due and payable.

An agreement of this sort offers protection to the lending bank in a number of ways. For example, Black Gold has an estimated $2 million in unmortgaged fixed assets and plans to acquire an additional $1 million in new equipment. Added protection is provided by the conservative percentages of accounts receivable and inventory the bank would take as collateral and by the required compensating balances (deposits) the customer would retain with the bank. In the event of a default on this loan, the bank could exercise its *right of offset* and take control of these deposits in order to repay the balance due on the loan. Interest must be paid monthly, which means the bank will recover a substantial portion of its expected interest income early in the loan's term, further reducing the bank's income risk associated with this credit. Any action by the customer or adverse change in the customer's position that leads to a violation of the loan agreement gives the bank legal grounds to take possession of the firm's assets pledged behind the loan and sell those assets to recover the loan's proceeds and any unpaid interest.

Black Gold may well decline this agreement, particularly because (*a*) it gives the customer much less money than requested ($1.5 million instead of $5 million), (*b*) the loan funds are offered for a shorter term than requested (six months instead of one year), and

(c) the agreement places *many* restrictions on the freedom of Black Gold's management decision making and flexibility. But the key point is this: *If the customer says "no" to this proposal by the lender, it is the customer, not the lending institution, who is declining to establish a relationship.* The lender has demonstrated a willingness to help meet at least a portion of the customer's financing needs. Moreover, good lending policy calls for the loan officer to assure the customer that, *even if he or she turns down the lender's offer, the lending institution still stands ready at any future time to try to work with that customer to find a suitable service package that will satisfy both parties.*

The alert reader will note that we said nothing in the foregoing draft loan agreement about what *rate of interest* the loan should bear. The loan rate, too, can be shaped in such a way that it further protects and compensates the lender for any risks incurred. We turn next to this important loan pricing issue.

Concept Check

16–3. What aspects of a business firm's financial statements do loan officers and credit analysts examine carefully?

16–4. What aspect of a business firm's operations is reflected in its ratio of cost of goods sold to net sales? In its ratio of net sales to total assets? In its GPM ratio? In its ratio of income before interest and taxes to total interest payments? In its acid-test ratio? In its ratio of before-tax net income to net worth? In its ratio of total inabilities to net sales? What are the principal limitations of these ratios?

16–5. What are contingent liabilities and why might they be important in deciding whether to approve or disapprove a business loan request?

16–6. What is cash-flow analysis and what can it tell us about a business borrower's financial condition and prospects?

16–7. What is a pro forma statement of cash flows and what is its purpose?

16–8. Should a loan officer ever say "no" to a business firm requesting a loan? Please explain when and where.

Pricing Business Loans

One of the most difficult tasks in lending is deciding how to *price* a loan.[5] The lender wants to charge a high enough interest rate to ensure that each loan will be profitable and compensate the lending institution fully for the risks involved. However, the loan rate must also be low enough to accommodate the business customer in such a way that he or she can successfully repay the loan and not be driven away to another lender or into the open market for credit. The more competition the lender faces for a customer's loan business, the more it will have to keep the price of that loan at a reasonable level. Indeed, in a loan market characterized by intense competition, the lender is a price *taker*, not a price setter. With deregulation of banking and financial services under way in many nations, deregulated competition has significantly narrowed the profit margins many lenders are able to earn, making correct pricing of loans even more imperative today than in the past.

The Cost-Plus Loan Pricing Method

In pricing a business loan, management must consider the cost of raising loanable funds and the operating costs of running the lending institution. This means that lenders must know what their costs are in order to consistently make profitable, correctly priced loans

---

[5] This section is based upon Peter S. Rose's article [18], which appeared originally in *The Canadian Banker* and is used by permission of the publisher.

of any type. There is no substitute for a well-designed *management information system* when it comes to pricing loans.

The simplest loan-pricing model assumes that the rate of interest charged on any loan includes four components: (1) the cost to the lender of raising adequate funds to lend, (2) the lender's nonfunds operating costs (including wages and salaries of loan personnel and the cost of materials and physical facilities used in granting and administering a loan), (3) necessary compensation paid to the lender for the degree of default risk inherent in a loan request, and (4) the desired profit margin on each loan that provides the lending institution's stockholders with an adequate return on their capital. A loan pricing scheme of this sort is often called **cost-plus loan pricing.** Thus:

$$
\begin{array}{c}
\text{Loan} \\
\text{interest} \\
\text{rate}
\end{array}
=
\begin{array}{c}
\text{Marginal} \\
\text{cost of raising} \\
\text{loanable funds} \\
\text{to lend to} \\
\text{the borrower}
\end{array}
+
\begin{array}{c}
\text{Nonfunds} \\
\text{operating} \\
\text{costs}
\end{array}
+
\begin{array}{c}
\text{Estimated} \\
\text{margin to} \\
\text{compensate for} \\
\text{default risk}
\end{array}
+
\begin{array}{c}
\text{Desired} \\
\text{profit} \\
\text{margin}
\end{array}
$$

Each of these components can be expressed in annualized percentage terms relative to the amount of the loan.

For example, suppose a bank has a loan request from one of its corporate customers for $5 million (as in the Black Gold case discussed earlier in this chapter). If the bank must sell negotiable CDs in the money market at an interest rate of 5 percent to fund this loan, the marginal cost of loanable funds for this particular loan will be 5 percent. Nonfunds operating costs to analyze, grant, and monitor this loan are estimated at 2 percent of the $5 million request. The credit department may recommend adding 2 percent of the amount requested to compensate for the risk that the loan will not be repaid on time. Finally, the bank may desire a 1 percent profit margin over and above the financial, operating, and risk-related costs of this loan. Thus, this loan will be offered to the borrower at an annual rate of 10 percent (= 5 percent + 2 percent + 2 percent + 1 percent). In contrast, the expected return on a loan depends not only on the rate of return the borrower promises to pay, but also on the probability the borrower will default on some or all of the payments required in the loan contract.

The Price Leadership Model

One of the drawbacks of the cost-plus loan pricing model is its assumption that a lending institution accurately knows what its costs are. This is often not the case. Lenders today are usually multiproduct businesses that often face great difficulty in trying to properly allocate operating costs among the many different services each offers. Moreover, the cost-plus pricing method implies that a lender can price a loan with little regard for the competition posed by other lenders. For the vast majority of loans today this is simply not true. Competition will impact the lender's desired profit margin on a loan; in general, the more intense the competition, the thinner the profit margin becomes.

These limitations of the cost-plus approach have led to a form of **price leadership** in the banking industry, which began among leading money center banks more than 60 years ago. During the Great Depression of the 1930s, major commercial banks established a uniform base lending fee known as the **prime rate,** sometimes called the *base* or reference rate, supposedly at that time the lowest rate charged the most creditworthy customers on short-term, working capital loans. The actual loan rate charged any particular customer would be determined by the following formula:

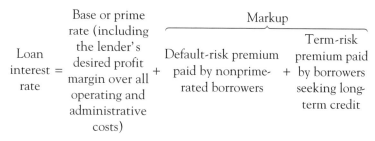

For example, a medium-sized business customer asking for a three-year loan to purchase new equipment might be assessed an annual loan rate of 12 percent, consisting of a prime (or base) rate of 8 percent plus 2 percent for default risk and another 2 percent for term risk because of the long-term character of the loan. Longer-term loans are assigned a term-risk premium because lending over a longer period of time exposes the lender to more opportunities for loss than does an otherwise comparable short-term loan. Assignment of risk premiums is one of the most difficult aspects of loan pricing, with a wide variety of different risk-adjustment methods in use. Copeland [21] suggests assigning loan-quality *grades* according to the following schedule:

Risk Category	Risk Premium	Risk Category	Risk Premium
No risk	0.00%	Special-mention	1.50%
Minimal risk	0.25	Substandard	2.50
Standard risk	0.50	Doubtful	5.00

Many observers would argue, however, that a loan classified as *doubtful* or even *substandard* simply doesn't belong in the loan portfolio of a bank or other regulated lending institution.

The risk premiums attached to loans are often referred to collectively as the *markup*. Lending institutions can expand or contract their loan portfolios simply by contracting or expanding their loan-rate markups. Many lenders prefer, however, simply to vary their loan rejection rates rather than changing either their base rate or their markups.[6]

In the United States today, the *prevailing prime rate* is considered to be the most common base rate figure announced by the majority of the 25 largest banks (measured by asset size) that publish their loan rates regularly. Prime rates used by other, generally smaller U.S. banks and other lending institutions often differ from the prevailing prime. For many years, the prime rate was changed only infrequently, requiring a resolution voted upon by each bank's board of directors. However, the advent of inflation and more volatile interest rates gave rise to a *floating* prime rate, tied to changes in such important money market interest rates as the 90-day commercial paper rate and the 90-day CD rate. With floating primes, major corporate borrowers with impeccable credit ratings might be permitted to borrow, for example, at a prime rate one half a percentage point above the most recent commercial paper rate or at a spread of one-half a percentage point above the most recent four-week average CD rate.

---

[6] Charging high-risk borrowers the full risk premium that their perceived risk to the lender seems to warrant is not always wise. Indeed, such a policy may increase the chances that a borrower will default on a loan agreement, resulting in the lender's earning a return on such a loan that is even less than earned on prime-quality loans. For example, if an A-rated borrower is charged a prime interest rate of 6 percent and a high-risk borrower is assessed a loan rate of 12 percent, the second borrower may feel compelled to adopt high-risk business strategies with small chance of success in an attempt to meet such high required loan payments. These high-risk business strategies may lead to default, sharply lowering the lender's actual return. This is why most lending institutions use *both* price (loan rate) and credit rationing (i.e., denying some loans regardless of price) to regulate the size and composition of their loan portfolios.

Two different floating prime rate formulas were soon developed by leading money center banks: (1) the prime-plus method and (2) the times-prime method. For example, a borrowing corporate customer might be quoted a short-term *prime-plus-2* loan rate of 12 percent when the prime rate stands at 10 percent. Alternatively, this customer might be quoted a *1.2 times-prime rate*, that is,

$$\text{Loan interest rate} = 1.2 \text{ (prime rate)} = 1.2 \text{ (10 percent)} = 12 \text{ percent}$$

While these two formulas may lead to the same initial loan rate, as in the previous example, they lead to very different loan rates when interest rates change and the borrower has a floating-rate loan.

For example, in a period of *rising* interest rates, the times-prime method causes the customer's loan rate to rise faster than the prime-plus method. If interest rates *fall*, the customer's loan rate declines more rapidly under the times-prime method. For example, if the prime rate rises from 10 percent to 15 percent, the customer's loan rate in our example increases from 12 percent to 17 percent with the prime-plus method and from 12 percent to 18 percent with the times-prime method. However, if prime drops from 10 percent to 8 percent, the prime-plus method yields a 10 percent loan rate, while the times-prime approach yields only 9.6 percent.

Recent research by Dueker [15] and others suggests that the prime rate may be an *asymmetric interest rate*. This means that banks and other lenders tend to raise the prime rate (and, thus, charge borrowers more) more readily than they lower their prime rate (and charge borrowing customers less). The slower downward adjustment of loan rates based on prime implies, for example, that borrowers heavily dependent upon banks for credit pay relatively higher interest costs than businesses that can bypass institutional lenders and tap the capital markets for funds. Thus, more bank-dependent borrowers may be more vulnerable to business cycles and more likely to fail during cyclical downturns in the economy.

During the 1970s, the supremacy of the prime rate as a base for business loans was challenged by **LIBOR**—the London Interbank Offered Rate—on short-term Eurodollar deposits, which range in maturity from a few days to a few months. As time has passed, more and more leading banks and other large commercial lenders have switched to LIBOR-based loan pricing due to the growing use of Eurodollars as a source of loanable funds. A second cause was the spreading internationalization of the banking and financial system, with foreign banks entering many domestic loan markets, including Canada and the United States. LIBOR offered a common pricing standard for all banks, both foreign and domestic, and gave customers a common basis for comparing the terms on loans offered by different lenders.

As an example of LIBOR-based pricing, we note that in mid-2003 prevailing interest rates on three-month Eurodollar deposits in London fluctuated in a range of about 1.20 to 1.30 percent (annual rate). For example, during the week ended May 30, 2003, leading international banks in London were quoting a three-month average LIBOR of 1.20 percent. Therefore, a large corporation borrowing short-term money for, say, 90 days from a domestic or foreign bank might be quoted an interest rate on a multimillion dollar loan of

$$\begin{matrix} \text{LIBOR-based} \\ \text{loan rate} \end{matrix} = \text{LIBOR} + \text{Default-risk premium} + \text{Profit margin}$$

$$= 1.20\% + 0.125\% + 0.125\% = 1.45\%$$

For longer-term loans stretching over several months or years the lender might add a term-risk premium to the above formula to compensate for the added risk of a longer term commitment to its business customer. For example, a one-year loan based on a one-year LIBOR rate of 1.50% would be this:

LOAN TERMS FOR BUSINESS BORROWERS—WHAT FEDERAL RESERVE SURVEYS TELL US

The Federal Reserve System collects information on business loans granted by 348 domestically chartered U.S. commercial banks and 50 U.S. branches and agencies of foreign banks each quarter of the year. Recent loan surveys suggest that most business loans tend to be (or have) these characteristics:

1. Short maturities (under one year) rather than long maturities by a wide margin.

2. The more numerous short-term loans to businesses average about 30 days to maturity, with long-term (over-one-year) bank business loans approaching an average of about 45 months to maturity.

3. Fixed interest rates when granted for shorter loan maturities and floating interest rates for longer-maturity business loans due to the latter's increased interest rate risk.

4. Base loan rates tied most often to the Federal funds interest rate, foreign money market rates (such as LIBOR), the prime rate, or other base rates.

5. Higher loan rates when loan maturity is longer in order to compensate the lender for added term risk associated with a longer-term loan.

6. Higher loan rates on smaller denomination business loans (especially for credits under $1 million in size).

7. Secured by collateral more often if the loans carry longer maturities or have smaller denominations.

Recent research suggests that older firms, the longer the borrower–lender relationship, and the purchase of additional services from the same lender tend either to result in a lower loan rate or tend to reduce the chances of a loan denial. Also, audited firms appear to pay somewhat lower loan rates than unaudited firms and business borrowers that successfully complete loan transactions often get lower loan rates on subsequent borrowings and usually get monitored less frequently.

Key URL
To learn about the Federal Reserve's quarterly survey of terms of business lending, see **www. federalreserve.gov/ releases/e2/**.

$$\begin{aligned} \text{LIBOR-based loan rate} &= \text{LIBOR} + \text{Default risk preimum} \\ &\quad + \text{Term-risk premium} + \text{Profit margin} \\ &= 1.50\% + 0.125\% + 0.25\% + 0.125\% = 2.00\% \end{aligned}$$

Below-Prime Market Pricing

Factoid
Measured by the volume of business loans made by banks operating in the United States, which base interest rate is most heavily used to price these loans—a foreign interest rate or a domestic interest rate?
Answer: A foreign interest rate (usually LIBOR).

Further modifications to the prime or LIBOR-based loan pricing systems were made in the 1980s and 1990s when **below-prime pricing** became important. In the United States, for example, many banks announced that some large corporate loans covering only a few days or weeks would be made at low money market interest rates (such as the Federal funds rate used on domestic interbank loans of reserves) plus a very small margin (perhaps one-eighth to one-quarter of a percentage point) to cover risk exposure and profit margin.

Thus, if we can borrow Federal funds in today's market for 2.50 percent and a top-quality business customer requests a 30-day $10 million credit line, we may choose to make the loan at 2.75 percent (or 2.50 percent to cover the money market cost of borrowing + 0.25 percent markup for risk and profitability). The result is a short-term loan rate one or more percentage points *below* the posted prime rate, diminishing the importance of the prime rate as a reference point for business loans.

Not surprisingly, as the prime rate became less important and some market interest rates became more volatile, many major banks dropped the use of formulas linking prime to open-market interest rates. However, the prime rate continues to be important as a pricing method for smaller business loans, consumer credit, and construction loans. Thus, a two-tiered business loan market has emerged. Loans to small and medium-size businesses

BANKERS TRUST AND GE CAPITAL: LETTING THE MARKETPLACE ASSESS BUSINESS CREDIT RISK

Recently such prominent commercial lenders as Bankers Trust (now a unit of Germany's Deutsche Bank), JP Morgan Chase, and GE Capital have led the financial-services industry in developing new methods for dealing with the risks of lending. Extensive computer programs have appeared to analyze customer financial reports, calculate key performance ratios, and process current information from the financial marketplace in order to more accurately assess a business customer's risk exposure.

One of the key features of these new risk assessment programs is heavier reliance on *signals from the private marketplace,* using the market as a *credit monitor.* When a business borrower's stock price falls or the interest yields attached to that borrower's outstanding bonds and commercial paper increase, many loan officers ask: What is the cause? Is the market signaling that this particular customer presents more risk to its lenders? If so, credit requests from this business customer must be priced higher.

In short, many commercial loan rates today are tied very closely to changing borrower circumstances as monitored by the marketplace. A market signal of greater risk sparks an upward adjustment in current and future loan rates, raising the size of the risk premium attached to the base loan rate. As we saw in Chapter 8, commercial lenders may also further shelter their institution from risk by purchasing credit derivatives. This newer approach to commercial lending reflects not only improved technology in the risk assessment field, but also the growing use of loan syndications by lenders, bringing in new investors to share in large loans who often demand greater risk protection.

are usually based on prime or some other widely recognized base rate, while large-denomination business loans increasingly are based on national and international (such as LIBOR) money market interest costs at the time the loan is made. The narrow margins (markups) on such loans have spurred wider use of loan participations, with banks more actively sharing their biggest loans, generating fee income, and moving at least a portion of these credits to lenders with lower funding costs.

Customer Profitability Analysis

As bankers developed more comprehensive information systems to keep track of their services and costs, a new loan pricing technique appeared, known as **customer profitability analysis** (CPA). This loan-pricing method begins with the assumption that the lender should take the whole customer relationship into account when pricing each loan request. CPA focuses on the rate of return from the entire customer relationship, calculated from the following formula:

$$\begin{array}{l}\text{Net before-tax rate}\\\text{of return to the}\\\text{lender from the whole}\\\text{customer relationship}\end{array} = \frac{\begin{array}{c}\text{Revenue from}\\\text{loans and other}\\\text{services provided}\\\text{to this customer}\end{array} - \begin{array}{c}\text{Expenses from}\\\text{providing loans}\\\text{and other services}\\\text{to this customer}\end{array}}{\begin{array}{c}\text{Net loanable funds used in excess of this}\\\text{customer's deposits}\end{array}}$$

Revenues paid in to the lender by a customer may include loan interest, commitment fees, fees for cash management services, and data processing charges. *Expenses* incurred on behalf of the customer may include wages and salaries of the lender's employees, credit investigation costs, interest accrued on deposits, account reconciliation and processing costs (including checks paid, loan and deposit recordkeeping and collection, and lockbox services), and loanable funds' acquisition costs. *Net loanable funds* are the amount of credit used by the customer minus his or her average collected deposits (adjusted for required reserves).

In effect, then, the amount of loanable funds each customer uses over and above those funds he or she supplies to the lending institution is evaluated. If the calculated net rate of return from the entire relationship with the customer is *positive*, the loan request will probably be approved, because the lender will be earning a premium over *all* expenses incurred (including a competitive rate of return to its shareholders). If the calculated net return is *negative*, the loan request may be denied or the lender may seek to raise the loan rate or increase the prices of other services requested by the customer in order to continue the relationship on a profitable basis. Customers who are perceived to be more risky are expected to return to the lending institution a higher calculated net rate of return. Customer profitability analysis (CPA) applied to the loan request of Black Gold, Inc., considered in the previous chapter, can be illustrated in the following example.

An Example of Annualized Customer Profitability Analysis

Problem   A bank is considering granting a $1.5 million line of credit for six months to Black Gold, Inc., an energy company. Assuming Black Gold uses the full line and keeps a 20 percent compensating deposit with the bank, the following bank revenues and expenses should result from dealing with this customer:

Sources of Revenue Expected to Be Supplied by This Customer	
Interest income from loan (12%, six months)	$ 90,000
Loan commitment fees (1%)	15,000
Fee for managing customer's deposits	45,000
Funds transfer charges	5,000
Fees for trust services and recordkeeping	61,000
Total annualized revenues expected	$ 216,000
Costs Expected to Be Incurred in Serving This Customer	
Deposit interest owed to the customer (10%)	$ 15,000
Cost of funds raised to lend this customer	80,000
Activity costs for this customer's accounts	25,000
Cost of funds transfers for this customer	1,000
Cost of processing the loan	3,000
Recordkeeping costs	1,000
Total annualized expenses	$ 125,000
Net Amount of the Bank's Reserves Expected to Be Drawn upon by This Customer This Year	
Average amount of credit committed to customer	$1,500,000
Less: Average customer deposit balances (net of required reserves)	−270,000
Net amount of loanable reserves committed to customer	$1,230,000

$$\begin{array}{l}\text{Annual before-tax rate} \\ \text{of return over costs} \\ \text{from the entire} \\ \text{lender–customer relationship}\end{array} = \frac{\text{Revenue expected} - \text{Cost expected}}{\text{Net amount of loanable funds supplied}}$$

$$= \frac{(\$216,000 - \$125,000)}{\$1,230,000} = 0.074 \text{ or } 7.4\%$$

Interpretation: If the net rate of return from the entire lender–customer relationship is *positive*, the proposed loan is *acceptable* because all expenses have been met. If the calculated net rate of return is negative, however, the proposed loan and other services provided to the customer are not correctly priced as far as the lender is concerned. The greater the perceived risk of the loan, the higher the net rate of return the lender should require.

Earnings Credit for Customer Deposits In calculating how much in revenues a customer generates for the bank or other lending institution, many lenders give the customer credit for any earnings received from investing the balance in the customer's deposit account in earning assets. Of course, it would be unwise to include the full amount of the customer's deposit in calculating any earnings from investing deposit money because a depository institution has to post reserve requirements, and a substantial portion of the customer's deposit balance may consist of *float* arising from checks written by the customer against his or her account but not yet charged against the account. Most depository institutions calculate the actual amount of *net investable funds* provided by a customer's deposit and the earnings credit for a customer using some version of the following formulas:

$$\begin{pmatrix} \text{Net} \\ \text{investable} \\ \text{(usable)} \\ \text{funds for} \\ \text{the lender} \end{pmatrix} = \begin{pmatrix} \text{Customer's} \\ \text{average} \\ \text{deposit} \\ \text{balance} \end{pmatrix} - \begin{pmatrix} \text{Average} \\ \text{amount} \\ \text{of float} \\ \text{in the} \\ \text{account} \end{pmatrix} - \begin{pmatrix} \text{Required} & & \text{Net} \\ \text{legal} & & \text{amount of} \\ \text{reserves} & \times & \text{collected} \\ \text{behind} & & \text{funds in the} \\ \text{the deposit} & & \text{account} \end{pmatrix}$$

$$\begin{pmatrix} \text{Amount of} \\ \text{earnings credited} \\ \text{to the customer} \end{pmatrix} = \begin{pmatrix} \text{Annual} \\ \text{earnings} \\ \text{rate} \end{pmatrix} \times \begin{pmatrix} \text{Fraction of the year} \\ \text{funds are available} \\ \text{from the deposit} \end{pmatrix} \times \begin{pmatrix} \text{Net investable} \\ \text{(usable) funds} \end{pmatrix}$$

For example, suppose a commercial customer posts an average deposit balance this month of $1,125,000. Float from uncollected checks accounts for $125,000 of this balance, yielding net collected funds of $1 million. If this is a checking account at a large bank, for example, the applicable legal reserve requirement will be 10 percent. After negotiation with the customer, the bank has decided to give this customer credit for an annual interest return from use of the customer's deposit equal to the average 91-day Treasury bill rate (assumed here to be 6.60 percent). In this instance, the customer's net usable (investable) funds and earnings credit will be as follows:

$$\begin{pmatrix} \text{Net investable} \\ \text{(usable) funds} \\ \text{for the bank} \end{pmatrix} = \$1,125,000 - \$125,000 - (.10 \times \$1,000,000) = \$900,000$$

$$\begin{pmatrix} \text{Amount of earnings} \\ \text{credit to this customer} \end{pmatrix} = 6.60 \text{ percent} \times \frac{1}{12} \times \$900,000 = \$4,950$$

Therefore, in constructing a summary of revenues and expenses from all the lender's dealings with this customer, the lender would give the customer credit on the revenue side for $4,950 earned last month from investing the customer's deposits in earning assets.

The Future of Customer Profitability Analysis Customer profitability analysis has become increasingly sophisticated and more encompassing in recent years. Detailed accounting statements showing sources of revenue and expenses from servicing each major customer have been developed. Often the borrowing company itself, its subsidiary firms, major stockholders, and top management are all consolidated into one profitability analysis statement so that the lender receives a comprehensive picture of the *total* customer relationship. The consolidation approach can determine if losses suffered from servicing one account are, in fact, made up by another account that is part of the same overall customer relationship. Automated CPA systems permit lenders to plug in alternative loan and deposit pricing schedules to see which pricing schedule works best for both the customer and the lending institution. As Knight [16] observes, CPA can also be used to identify the most profitable types of customers and loans and the most successful loan officers.

Concept Check

16–9. What methods are in use today to price business loans?

16–10. Suppose a bank estimates that the marginal cost of raising loanable funds to make a $10 million loan to one of its corporate customers is 4 percent, its nonfunds operating costs to evaluate and offer this loan are 0.5 percent, the default-risk premium on the loan is 0.375 percent, a term-risk premium of 0.625 percent is to be added, and the

bank's desired profit margin is 0.25 percent. What loan rate should be quoted this borrower? How much interest will the borrower pay in a year?

16–11. What are the principal strengths and weaknesses of the different loan-pricing methods in use today?

16–12. What is *customer profitability analysis?* What are its advantages for the borrowing customer and the lender?

Summary

In this chapter we have explored the many types of loans that banks and some of their closest competitors (including finance companies, insurance firms, security dealers, and thrift institutions) extend to businesses today. The key points in this chapter included the following:

- Business loans are often divided into *short-term* (under one year) and *long-term* (more than a year to maturity). A similar, but sometimes more meaningful classification divides these credits into *working capital loans*—usually short-term credits aimed principally at funding purchases of business inventories, meeting payrolls, paying taxes, and covering other temporary expenses—and *term loans*—typically employed to fund permanent additions to working capital or to plant and equipment.

- There are numerous varieties of working capital and term loans, including *seasonal open credit lines* to deal with fluctuating demand for products and services during the year; *dealer financing* to cover the acquisition of appliances, equipment, and vehicles subsequently sold to business and household customers; *asset-based loans*, which are focused upon or backed by specific real and financial assets; *revolving credit*, which allows borrowings, pay downs, and reborrowings continually until the revolver's term expires; and *project loans* to construct and install new plant and equipment.

- The evaluation of each business loan application usually involves one or more *loan officers*, who contact and negotiate with the customer; one or more *credit analysts*, who evaluate the customer's financial strengths and weaknesses; and a *loan committee* or *loan administrator*, who must ultimately approve or deny the requested credit.

- Among the more important credit evaluation techniques used today are (1) *composition analysis of borrower financial statements* (including the use of common-size balance sheets and income statements); (2) *financial ratio analysis* (including ratio measures of expense control, efficiency, coverage, profitability, liquidity, and leverage); and (3) actual and pro forma *statements of cash flows*.

- Several different methods for pricing business loans have appeared over the years, including *cost-plus* loan pricing, *price leadership* loan pricing, *below-prime loan pricing*, and *customer profitability analysis*. Many business loans today are priced directly off money market interest rates (such as LIBOR or the prevailing federal funds, CD, or commercial paper rates), with narrow profit margins reflecting intense competition for the best business customers.

- There is also a growing trend toward pricing business credit based on the *total relationship* between lender and borrower (including all the services the customer purchases from the lender and the costs of all the services provided) rather than pricing each requested loan independent of what other services the customer uses.

Key Terms

self-liquidating loans, 556
working capital loans, 557
compensating deposit balances, 558
interim construction loan, 558
asset-based loans, 559
factoring, 559
syndicated loan, 559

term loans, 560
revolving credit line, 561
project loans, 562
LBOs, 562
working capital, 570
contingent liabilities, 575
Statement of Cash Flows, 576

cost-plus loan pricing, 584
price leadership, 584
prime rate, 584
LIBOR, 586
below-prime pricing, 587
customer profitability analysis, 588

Problems and Projects

1. From the following descriptions please identify what *type* of business loan is being discussed.

   a. A temporary credit supports the construction of homes, apartments, office buildings, and other permanent structures.

   b. A loan is made to an automobile dealer to support the shipment of new cars to the dealer's showroom floor.

   c. Credit extended on the basis of a business's accounts receivable.

   d. The term of an inventory loan is being set to match the exact length of time needed to generate sufficient cash to repay the loan.

   e. Credit is extended for up to one year to purchase raw materials and cover a seasonal peak need for cash.

   f. A government security dealer requires credit to add new government bonds to his security portfolio.

   g. Credit is granted for a term longer than a year to support the purchase of plant and equipment.

   h. A group of investors wishes to take over a firm using debt financing and improve its management and its earnings.

   i. A business firm receives a three-year line of credit against which it can borrow, repay, and borrow again if necessary during the loan's three-year term.

   j. Credit is extended to support the construction of a toll road.

2. As a new credit trainee for Evergreen National Bank, you have been asked to evaluate the financial position of a medium-size manufacturing corporation, Hamilton Steel Castings, which has asked for renewal of and an increase in its six-month credit line. Hamilton now requests a $7 million credit line, and you must draft your first credit opinion for a senior credit analyst. Unfortunately, Hamilton just changed management, and its financial report for the last six months was not only late but also garbled. As best as you can tell, its sales, assets, operating expenses, and liabilities for the six-month period just concluded display the following patterns (figures in millions of dollars):

	January	February	March	April	May	June
Net sales	$48.1	$47.3	$45.2	$43.0	$43.9	$39.7
Cost of goods sold	27.8	28.1	27.4	26.9	27.3	26.6
Selling, administrative, and other expenses	19.2	18.9	17.6	16.5	16.7	15.3
Depreciation	3.1	3.0	3.0	2.9	3.0	2.8
Interest cost on borrowed funds	2.0	2.2	2.3	2.3	2.5	2.7
Expected tax obligation	1.3	1.0	0.7	0.9	0.7	0.4

Total assets	24.5	24.3	23.8	23.7	23.2	22.9
Current assets	6.4	6.1	5.5	5.4	5.0	4.8
Net fixed assets	17.2	17.4	17.5	17.6	18.0	18.0
Current liabilities	4.7	5.2	5.6	5.9	5.8	6.4
Total liabilities	15.9	16.1	16.4	16.5	17.1	17.2

You have been reassured by several analysts in the department that this is an easy account with which to start your career. Hamilton has a 16-year relationship with the bank and has routinely received and paid off a credit line of $4 to $5 million. Actually, the credit department has already decided to approve the request, which goes to the bank's loan committee this afternoon. The department's senior analyst tells you to prepare because you will be asked for your opinion of this loan request (though you have been led to believe the loan will be approved anyway, because Hamilton's president serves on Evergreen's board of directors).

What will you recommend if asked? Is there any reason to question the latest data supplied by this customer? Could other factors be at work that you do not yet understand about this customer's business? How could you find out in the short time available? If this loan request is granted, what do you think the customer will do with the funds?

3. From the data given in the following table, please construct as many of the financial ratios discussed in this chapter as you can and then indicate what dimension of a business firm's performance each ratio represents.

Business Assets		Annual Revenue and Expense Items	
Cash account	$ 10	Net sales	$680
Accounts receivable	95	Cost of goods sold	520
Inventories	108	Wages and salaries	61
Fixed assets	301	Interest expense	18
Miscellaneous assets	96	Overhead expenses	29
	610	Depreciation expenses	15
Liabilities and Equity		Selling, administrative,	
Short-term debt:		and other expenses	30
Accounts payable	83	Before-tax net income	7
Notes payable	107*	Taxes owed	2
Long-term debt (bonds)	325*	After-tax net income	5
Miscellaneous liabilities	15		
Equity capital	80		

*Annual principal payments on bonds and notes payable total $55. The firm's marginal tax rate is 35 percent.

4. Chamrod Corporation has placed a term loan request with its bank and submitted the following balance sheet entries for the year just concluded and the pro forma balance sheet expected by the end of the current year. Construct a pro forma Statement of Cash Flows for the current year using the consecutive balance sheets and some additional needed information. The forecast net income for the current year is $175 million with $50 million being paid out in dividends. The depreciation expense for the year will be $100 million and planned expansions will require the acquisition of $258 million in fixed assets at the end of the current year. As you examine the pro forma Statement of Cash Flows, do you detect any changes that might be of concern either to the bank's credit analyst, loan officer, or both?

Chamrod Corporation
(all amounts in millions of dollars)

	Assets at the End of the Most Recent Year	Assets Projected for the End of the Current Year		Liabilities and Equity at the End of the Most Recent Year	Liabilities and Equity Projected for the End of the Current Year
Cash	$ 532	$ 417	Accounts payable	$ 970	$1,030
Accounts receivable	1,018	1,225	Notes payable	2,733	2,950
Inventories	894	973	Taxes payable	327	216
Net fixed assets	2,740	2,898	Long-term debt obligations	872	931
Other assets	66	87	Common stock	85	85
			Undivided profits	263	388
Total assets	$5,250	$5,600	Total liabilities and equity capital	$5,250	$5,600

5. Which of the dimensions of a business firm's financial and operating performance do each of the following ratios measure?

Average collection period

Gross profit margin

Current ratio

Total liabilities/Total assets

Overhead expenses/Net sales

Income before interest, taxes, and lease payments/(Interest plus lease payments)

After-tax net income/Net worth

Unfunded pension liabilities

Annual cost of goods sold/Average inventory

Net sales/Net fixed assets

Depreciation expenses/Net sales

Total liabilities/Net sales

Cost of goods sold/Net sales

Interest coverage

Before-tax net income/Total assets

Net sales/Total assets

Net income after taxes/Net sales

Current assets less current liabilities

Acid-test ratio

Long-term debt/(Total long-term liabilities and net worth)

Interest expense on borrowed funds/Net sales

After-tax net income/Total sales

Net sales/Accounts and notes receivable

Percentage change in stock price

6. As a loan officer for Enterprise National Bank, you have been responsible for the bank's relationship with USF Corporation, a major producer of remote-control devices for activating television sets, VCRs, and other audio-video equipment. USF has just filed a request for renewal of its $10 million line of credit, which will cover approximately 10 1/2 months. USF also regularly uses several other services sold by the bank. Using the most recent year as a guide, you estimate that the expected revenues from this commercial loan customer and the expected costs of serving this customer will consist of the following:

Expected Revenues		Expected Costs	
Annual interest income from the requested loan (assuming a loan rate of prime + 1 percent, or 11% this month)	$1,100,000	Interest paid on customer deposits (9%)	$ 25,000
		Cost of funds raised	975,000
Loan commitment fee (1%)	100,000	Account activity costs	19,000
Deposit management fees	4,500	Wire transfer costs	1,300
Wire transfer fees	3,500	Loan processing costs	12,400
Fees for agency services	8,800	Recordkeeping costs	4,500

The bank's credit analysts have estimated the customer will keep an average deposit balance of $2,125,000 for the year in which the line is active. What is the expected net rate of return from this proposed loan renewal if the customer actually draws down the full amount of the requested line? What decision should the bank make under the foregoing assumptions? If you decide to turn down this request, under what assumptions regarding revenues, expenses, and customer-maintained deposit balances would you be willing to make this loan?

7. In order to help fund a loan request of $10 million for one year from one of its best customers, Chilton Westover Bank sold negotiable CDs to its business customers in the amount of $6 million at a promised annual yield of 8.75 percent and borrowed $4 million in the Federal funds market from other banks at today's prevailing interest rate of 8.40 percent.

    a. Would you come to a different conclusion regarding this loan request if the customer insisted on opening a time deposit account bearing a 9.25 percent interest rate (instead of 9 percent) and the cost of other funds raised to make this loan rose from $975,000 to $1,065,000, while the prime rate fell to 9.50 percent? Why or why not?

    b. At what loan rate does the bank merely break even on this customer relationship, assuming all other revenues and costs remain unchanged?

    c. At what interest cost level does the bank break even on this customer relationship, assuming the prime rate and all other revenues and costs are held constant?

    Credit investigation and recordkeeping costs to process this loan application were an estimated $25,000. The Credit Analysis Division recommends a minimal 1 percent risk premium on this loan and a minimal profit margin of one-fourth of a percentage point. The bank prefers using cost-plus loan pricing in these cases. What loan rate should it charge?

8. Many loans to larger domestic and foreign corporations are quoted today at small risk premiums and profit margins over the London Interbank Offered Rate (LIBOR) on short-term Eurodollar deposits. Englewood Bank has a $15 million loan request for working capital to fund accounts receivable and inventory from one of its largest corporate customers, APEX Exports. The bank offers its customer a floating-rate loan for 90 days with an interest rate equal to LIBOR on 30-day Eurodeposits (currently trading at a rate of 9.25) plus a one-quarter percentage point markup over LIBOR. APEX, however, wants the loan at a rate of 1.014 times LIBOR. If the bank agrees to this loan rate request, what interest rate will attach to the loan if it is made today? How does this compare with the loan rate the bank wanted to charge? What does this customer's request reveal about the borrowing firm's interest rate forecast for the next 90 days?

9. Five weeks ago, RJK Corporation borrowed from the commercial finance company that employs you as a loan officer. At that time, the decision was made (at your personal urging) to base the loan rate on below-prime market pricing, using the average weekly Federal funds interest rate as the money market borrowing cost. The loan was quoted to RJK at the Federal funds rate plus a three-eighths percentage point markup for risk and profit.

    Today, this five-week loan is due, and RJK is asking for renewal of the loan at money market borrowing cost plus one-fourth of a percentage point. You must assess whether the finance company did as well on this account using the Federal funds rate as the index of borrowing cost as it would have done by quoting RJK the prevailing CD rate, the commercial paper rate, the Eurodollar deposit rate, or possibly the prevailing rate on U.S. Treasury bills plus a small margin for risk and profitability. To assess what would have happened (and might happen over the next five weeks if the loan is renewed at a small margin over any of the money market rates listed above), you have assembled these data from a recent issue of the *Federal Reserve Bulletin:*

Weekly Averages of Money Market Rates over the Most Recent 5 Weeks					
Money Market Interest Rates	**Week 1**	**Week 2**	**Week 3**	**Week 4**	**Week 5**
Federal funds	8.72%	8.80%	8.69%	8.46%	8.46%
Commercial paper (one-month maturity)	8.55	8.63	8.53	8.43	8.40
CDs (one-month maturity)	8.54	8.58	8.50	8.40	8.35
Eurodollar deposits (three-month maturity)	8.58	8.56	8.60	8.43	8.38
U.S. Treasury bills (three-month, secondary market)	7.60	7.77	7.74	7.67	7.60

What conclusion do you draw from studying the behavior of these common money market base rates for business loans? Should the RJK loan be renewed as requested, or should the lender press for a different loan pricing agreement? Please explain your reasoning. If you conclude that a change is needed, how would you explain the necessity for this change to the customer?

10. RCB Corporation has posted an average bank deposit balance this past month of $270,500. Float included in this one-month average balance has been estimated at $73,250. Required legal reserves are 3 percent of net collected funds. What is the amount of net investable (usable) funds available to the bank?

   Suppose RCB's bank agrees to give RCB credit for an annual interest return of 5.75 percent on the net investable funds the company provides the bank. Measured in total dollars, how much of an earnings credit from the bank will RCB earn?

Internet Exercises

1. If you are a business lender and your assignment has recently been changed from making large corporate loans to small business lending—an area where you have almost no experience—you will want to become familiar with the Small Business Administration at **www.sba.gov/financing**. There you will find information about SBA loan programs. What is the Basic 7(a) Loan Program? How does this program benefit the lender?

2. As a small business lender, you have a customer that is an exporter and needs working capital on a short-term basis. Are there special loan programs available through the SBA that would be useful? See **www.sba.gov/financing**. What four unique requirements are associated with the applicable loan program?

3. What is *factoring?* Visit **www.cfa.com** and click on the button, "What is asset based lending?" What types of factoring are described at this link? Describe three types of factoring arrangements.

4. Business lenders are made, not born. Visit **www.rmahg.org**. Click on the "About RMA" button. What is the objective of RMA? Describe its eMentor product.

5. What market interest rates are most widely used as base rates to price commercial loans? Go to **www.federalreserve.gov/releases/** and look at weekly releases of selected interest rates. What was the one-month Eurodollar deposit (London) rate for the week of May 16, 2003? What was the prime rate for the week of May 14, 2003?

6. If you wanted to know more about the details of business loans, you might visit **www.loanpricing.com**. Go there and click on the link for the most recent U.S. lead arranger league tables. Who were the top three arrangers by volume? What were the volumes? Who were the top three arrangers by number of deals? How many deals did they do?

STANDARD &POOR'S

S&P Market Insight Challenge

1. Use Standard & Poor's Market Insight website (**www.mhhe.com/edumarketinsight**) for this problem. In the S&P industry survey devoted to banking, loan quality is graphically portrayed using such account items as nonperforming assets, loss reserves, provision for loan losses, and net charge-offs. For an up-to-date graphic, click on the Industry tab in S&P's Market Insight. The drop-down menu you encounter supplies the subindustry groups labeled Diversified Banks and Regional Banks. Upon selecting one of these subindustries you will uncover a recent S&P industry survey on banking, which you should download to examine the section, "Industry Trends." Print out the graphic illustration of loan quality that you find and describe and interpret recent loan-quality trends.

2. Use Standard & Poor's Market Insight website (**www.mhhe.com/edumarketinsight**) for this problem. The biggest loan category, measured in dollars, for most money-center banks today is usually commercial and industrial (business) loans. Examining some of the leading banks for which Market Insight, Educational Version, provides data, reports, and stories, see if you can determine what major kinds of business loans these banks typically grant. Do the banks differ in the make-up of the business loans they usually extend? Why is this so? Are the Insight banks active small business lenders? How do you know?

www.mhhe.com/rose6e

REAL NUMBERS FOR REAL BANKS

Assignment for Chapter 16

YOUR BANK'S OFFERINGS OF C&I LOANS TO SMALL AND LARGE FIRMS

The focus of Chapter 16 is business lending. The chapter opens with descriptions of the types of short-term and long-term loans financial institutions offer to business firms. The process of creating and maintaining these loans is the core of this chapter, which concludes with an examination of pricing business loans. In this assignment, we will be visiting our bank's website and exploring the types of loans offered to small businesses and large corporations. Terminology is not always consistent; hence, the descriptions become important in understanding a bank's offerings. Don't be intimidated when you encounter terms that are not familiar.

Part One: Small Business Loans

A. Visit your banking company's website. If you do not know the URL, use a search engine such as **www.google.com** or **www.alltheweb.com** to locate the website. Once you arrive at the website, look for small business services, lending in particular. Read everything you can about the instruments the bank offers the small business borrower, keeping in mind the basic types of C&I loans described in this chapter.

B. What types of short-term credit does the lender offer the small business customer? What types of long-term products are available?

C. Write approximately one page describing the loan products for the small business customer and assess the website's effectiveness in providing this information.

Part Two: Corporate Loans

A. Return to the home page for your banking company and look for corporate services. At this point, you are interested in instruments that will show up as C&I loans on your bank's balance sheet and that represent financing for the corporate customer. Read everything you can about the instruments offered to the large business borrower, once again keeping in mind the basic types of C&I loans described in this chapter. Websites typically provide lots of information for corporate borrowers and often mix in other services with the loan products. (Remember, fee-generating services are not the focus of this assignment.)

B. What types of short-term credit does the institution offer the corporate customer? What types of long-term products are available? Do you see any syndicated loans?

C. Write approximately one page describing the loan products for the large business customer and assess the website's effectiveness in providing this information.

Selected References

The following studies discuss risks inherent in business lending:

1. Former, John B. "What the New CERCLA Rule Means for Lenders." *The Bankers Magazine*, May/June 1993, pp. 51–58.

2. Gilbert, R. Alton. "Exposure of U.S. Banks to Problem Syndicated Loans." *Monetary Trends*, Federal Reserve Bank of St. Louis, December 2002.

3. Graber, Ned W. "The EPA's New CERCLA Rule: An Aid, Not a Remedy." *The Bankers Magazine*, January/February 1993, pp. 43–58.

4. Haubrich, Joseph G., and Joãn Cabral dos Santos. "The Dark Side of Liquidity." *Economic Commentary*, Federal Reserve Bank of Cleveland, September 15, 1997.

5. McElroy, John M. "Issues in Lending—How to Document Equipment Lease Financings." *The Journal of Lending and Credit Risk Management*, October 1996, pp. 50–56.

6. Osterberg, William P. "LBOs and Conflicts of Interest." *Economic Commentary*, Federal Reserve Bank of Cleveland, August 15, 1989, pp. 1–4.

The following are studies of factors that may predict business failures or troubled loans:

7. Altman, Edward I.; G. Haldeman; and P. Nurajanan. "Zeta Analysis: A New Model to Identify the Bankruptcy Risk of Corporations." *Journal of Banking and Finance 1* (1977), pp. 29–54.

8. Carlson, John B., and Erkin Y. Sahinoz. "Measures of Corporate Earnings: What Number Is Best?" *Economic Commentary*, Federal Reserve Bank of Cleveland, February 1, 2003.

9. Taylor, Jeremy D. "Understanding Industry Risk: Part 3." *The Journal of Lending and Credit Risk Management*, October 1996, pp. 14–26.

Discussion of the changing structure of the business loan market may be found in these sources:

10. Berger, Allen N., and Gregory F. Udell. "The Institutional Memory Hypothesis and the Procyclicality of Bank Lending Behavior," *Finance and Economics Discussion Series*, Board of Governors of the Federal Reserve System, 2003–02, February 2003.

11. Saidenberg, Marc R., and Philip E. Strahan. "Are Banks Still Important for Financing Large Businesses?" *Current Issues in Economics and Finance*, Federal Reserve Bank of New York 5, no. 12 (August 1999) pp. 1–6.

12. Strahan, Philip E., and James P. Weston. "Small Business Lending and the Changing Structure of the Banking Industry." *Journal of Banking and Finance* 22, nos. 2–6 (1998), pp. 821–45.

See the following for good discussions of loan pricing techniques:

13. Avery, Robert B., and Allen N. Berger. "Loan Commitments and Bank Risk Exposure." *Journal of Banking and Finance* 15 (1991), pp. 173–79.

14. Blackwell, David W., and Drew B. Winters. "Banking Relationships and the Effect of Monitoring on Loan Pricing." *The Journal of Financial Research* XX, no. 2 (Summer 1997), pp. 275–89.

15. Dueker, Michael J. "Are Prime Rate Changes Asymmetric?" *Review*, Federal Reserve Bank of St. Louis, September/October 2000, pp. 33–40.

16. Knight, Robert E. "Customer Profitability Analysis—Part 1: Alternative Approaches toward Customer Profitability." *Monthly Review*, Federal Reserve Bank of Kansas City, April 1975, pp. 11–20.

17. McElroy, John M. "Issues in Lending—How to Document Equipment Lease Financings." *The Journal of Lending and Credit Risk Management*, October 1996, pp. 50–56.

18. Rose, Peter S. "Loan Pricing in a Volatile Economy." *The Canadian Banker* 92, no. 5 (October 1985), pp. 44–49.

19. Samolyk, H. "Small Business Credit Markets: Why Do We Know So Little about Them?" *FDIC Banking Review* X, no. 2 (1997), pp. 14–32.

For a discussion of the role of supply-chain management, just-in-time, and other business production and ordering techniques in altering the demand for business credit, see especially the following:

20. McCarthy, Jonathan, and Egon Zakrajsek. "Inventory Dynamics and Business Cycles." *Finance and Economics Discussion Series*, Working Paper 2003–26, Washington, D.C.: Board of Governors of the Federal Reserve System, June 2003.

For a discussion of risk grades in helping to set commercial loan rates, see in particular:

21. Copeland, Timothy S. "Aspects to Consider in Developing a Loan-Pricing Microcomputer Model." *The Magazine of Bank Administration*, August 1983, pp. 32–34.

22. Treacy, William F., and Mark S. Carey. "Credit Risk Rating at Large U.S. Banks." *Federal Reserve Bulletin*, November 1998, pp. 897–921.

www.mhhe.com/rose6e

Consumer Loans, Credit Cards, and Real Estate Lending

Key Topics in This Chapter

- Types of Loans for Individuals and Families
- Unique Characteristics of Consumer Loans
- Evaluating a Consumer Loan Request
- Credit Cards and Credit Scoring
- Disclosure Rules and Discrimination
- Loan Pricing and Refinancing

Introduction

Statesman, philosopher, and scientist Benjamin Franklin once observed: "If you would know the value of money go and try to borrow some." Over the past couple of generations millions upon millions of consumers (individuals and families) have tried to do just that—borrow money—in order to supplement their income and enhance their life style. Apparently most have succeeded. Consumer debt is one of the fastest growing forms of borrowing money around the globe, reaching more than $7 trillion in volume in the United States alone as the 21st century opened.

Just as consumer borrowing has become a key driving force in the financial marketplace today, so have the banks making these loans. Bankers have emerged in recent decades to become dominant providers of credit to individuals and families. Of course, things didn't start out that way—for most of their history banks largely ignored household borrowers, allowing credit unions, savings associations, and finance companies to move in and capture this important marketplace, while banks concentrated on their business customers.

In part, the modern dominance of banks in lending to households stems from their growing reliance on individuals and families for their chief source of funds—checkable and savings deposits. Many households today would be hesitant to deposit their money in a bank unless they believed there was a good chance they will also be able to borrow from that same institution when they need a loan. Then, too, recent research suggests that consumer credit is among the most profitable services a bank can offer.

However, banking services directed at consumers can also be among the most costly and risky financial products that a bank sells because the financial condition of individuals and families can change so quickly due to illness, loss of employment, or other family tragedies. Lending to households, therefore, must be managed with care and sensitivity to the special challenges they represent. Moreover, profit margins on many consumer loans have narrowed appreciably as leading finance companies like Household Finance and GMAC, key savings associations like Washington Mutual, and thousands of aggressive credit unions have grown to seriously challenge the dominance of banks in this field.

In this chapter we examine the types of consumer and real-estate-centered loans lenders typically make and see how they evaluate household loan customers. We also explore the broad dimensions of the enormously significant credit card market, which accounts for a major share of consumer loans today. In addition, the chapter examines the powerful role of regulation in the consumer financial-services field as federal and state governments have become major players in setting the rules that govern this important market. Finally, we examine the pricing of consumer and real estate loans in a financial-services marketplace where the battle for household borrowers has become intense and many institutional casualties are strewn along the way.

Types of Loans Granted to Individuals and Families

Several different types of consumer loans are available, and the number of credit plans to accommodate consumers' financial needs is growing in the wake of deregulation of financial institutions in the United States and in many other industrialized countries. We can classify consumer loans by *purpose*—what the borrowed funds will be used for—or by *type of loan*—for example, whether the borrower must repay in installments or repay in one lump sum when the loan comes due. One popular classification scheme for consumer loans combines both loan types and loan purposes.

For example, loans to individuals and families may be divided into two groups, depending upon whether they finance the purchase of new homes with a *residential mortgage loan* or whether they finance other, nonhousing consumer activities (vacations, purchases of automobiles, etc.) through *nonresidential loans*. Second, within the nonresidential category, consumer loans are often divided into subcategories based on type of loan—*installment* loans, *noninstallment* loans and *revolving credit* loans (including the familiar credit-card loan). We will look at the nature of these consumer loan types more closely in the paragraphs that follow and in subsequent sections of this chapter.

Residential Mortgage Loans

Credit to finance the purchase of a home or to fund improvements on a private residence comes under the general label of **residential mortgage loans.** The purchase of residential property in the form of houses and multifamily dwellings (including duplexes, triplexes, and apartment buildings) usually gives rise to a long-term loan, typically bearing a term of 15 to 30 years and secured by the property itself. Such loans may carry either a fixed interest rate or a variable (floating) interest rate that changes periodically with a specified base rate (such as the market yield on 10-year U.S. government bonds) or a national mortgage interest rate (for example, the Federal Home Loan Bank Board's average home mortgage yield). A commitment fee, typically 1 to 2 percent of the face amount of the loan, is routinely charged up front to assure the borrower that a residential loan will be available for a stipulated period. Although banks are the leading residential mortgage lenders today, several other important lenders in this market include savings associations and savings banks, credit unions, finance companies, and insurance companies as well as the mortgage banking subsidiaries of financial holding companies.

One of the most rapidly growing forms of credit in recent years are those loans that flow to individuals, families, and small (often home-based) businesses. This field of lending covers a broad beachhead of literally hundreds of loan-supported purchases, from buying a new automobile, financing a new home, and purchasing furniture and appliances on credit to funding vacations and sending children to college.

Because loan officers in this area have to know so much about so many different things, the World Wide Web has become important to many of them. For example, they may use the Web in some instances to call up consumer credit reports (from such credit rating agencies as Experian at **www.experian.com** or Transunion at **www.transunion.com**) in order to speed the loan decision-making process.

As discussed later in this chapter, the loan evaluation technique of "credit scoring" has become extremely popular because of its speed, statistical advantages, and nondiscriminatory features. The Web has kept abreast of developments in the credit-scoring field through such websites as Fair, Isaac, and Company, at **www.fairisaac.com** and Experian Scorex at **www.experian-scorex.com**, which contribute to the development and dissemination of credit-scoring models.

Finally, lenders need all the help they can get in pricing consumer loans, and the World Wide Web is one of the information sources they use heavily today. For example, in pricing loans and figuring a customer's required payments, lenders can turn to such popular websites as Financial Power Tools at **www.financialpowertools.com** and to HSH Associates, financial publishers, at **homeplans.hsh.com**. The latter site can help both loan officers and consumers seeking loan information, figuring amortization rates, and determining credit grades, prepayment schedules, and possible loan interest rates.

Nonresidential Loans

In contrast to residential mortgage loans, nonresidential loans to individuals and families include installment loans and noninstallment (or single-payment) loans and a hybrid form of credit extended through credit cards (usually called revolving credit).

Installment Loans   Short-term to medium-term loans, repayable in two or more consecutive payments (usually monthly or quarterly), are known as **installment loans.** Such loans are frequently employed to buy big-ticket household items (e.g., automobiles, recreational vehicles, furniture, and home appliances) or to consolidate existing household debts.

Noninstallment Loans   Short-term loans individuals and families draw upon for immediate cash needs that are repayable in a lump sum when the borrower's note matures are known as *noninstallment loans*. Such loans may be for relatively small amounts—for example, $500 or $1,000—and include charge accounts that often require payment in 30 days or some other relatively short time period. Noninstallment loans may also be made for a short period (usually six months or less) to wealthier individuals and may be quite large, often ranging from $5,000 to $25,000. Noninstallment loans are frequently used to cover the cost of vacations, medical care, the purchase of home appliances, and auto and home repairs.

Credit Card Loans and Revolving Credit

One popular form of consumer credit today is accessed via credit cards issued by VISA, MasterCard, Discover, and several smaller bank and nonbank credit card companies. Credit cards offer their holders access to either installment or noninstallment credit because the customer can charge a purchase on the account represented by the card and pay off the

Factoid
Who makes more credit card loans than any other originator of such loans in the United States?
Answer: Commercial banks do, followed by finance companies and thrifts.

THE CREDIT CARD MARKET: IS DOMINANCE FADING? HOW CAN BANK EARNINGS BE PROTECTED?

For many years the credit card market has been dominated by VISA and MasterCard, and these two leaders have also captured a major share of the more rapidly growing debit card market. Included in the associations representing these two card systems are such leading banking firms as Bank of America, Wells Fargo, and Bank One. But that dominance and the relatively high rates of return on credit card services that thousands of banks participating in these two systems have received in the past may have peaked out. For the management of many leading banks today the key issue is: *What do we do next?*

In 2001 the U.S. Department of Justice successfully sued VISA and MasterCard, charging anti-competitive behavior as the two dominant card systems tried to exclude member banks from also issuing American Express and Discover cards to their customers—a decision now under appeal. In the spring of 2003, Wal-Mart, Sears, and other retailers sued the two market leaders in federal court for insisting that retailers accept VISA and MasterCard debit cards and pay the fees these two networks require for clearing customer transactions despite the availability of cheaper payments networks. At about the same time, a California court ordered VISA and MasterCard to refund nearly $800 million to customers for not fully disclosing their extra fees on overseas credit card transactions. This bad news comes at a time when credit card sales are slowing and card profit margins appear to be thinning.

Where do the many banks in these systems go from here? Their managements are wrestling with the choices—charging higher user fees for late payments, cash advances, and the like? Shifting more weight to the debit card market or into home equity credit lines, both now substantially outstripping credit card growth? Adopting marketing innovations, such as smart cards, affinity cards offering bonuses for trading with selected merchants, or multifunction cards that provide multiple services? Reaching into distant markets (such as Europe and Asia) where current account balances average much lower? Pushing sales to college students? If you were a bank manager what would you do?

charge in one billing period, escaping any finance charge, or choose to pay off the purchase price gradually, incurring a monthly finance charge that is based on an annual rate usually ranging from about 10 percent to 24 percent and sometimes more.

Card companies find that *installment users* of credit cards are far more profitable due to the interest income they generate than are noninstallment users, who quickly pay off their charges before interest can be assessed. Banks and other card providers also earn discount fees (usually 1 to 7 percent of credit card sales) from the merchants who accept their cards. So rapid has been the acceptance of bank-issued and other charge cards that close to two trillion are estimated to be in use today around the globe.

Credit cards offer *convenience* and a *revolving line of credit* that the customer can access whenever the need arises. Card-service providers have found, however, that careful management and control of their credit card programs is vital due to the relatively high proportion of delinquent borrowers and the large number of cards that have been stolen and used fraudulently. There is evidence that significant economies of scale pervade the credit card field because, in general, only the largest card operations are consistently profitable. Nevertheless, the future of the credit card appears to be relatively secure because of advancing technology that will eventually give most cardholders access to a full range of financial services, including savings and payments accounts.

While the credit card market is heavily concentrated among a handful of leaders—VISA and MasterCard, in particular—new varieties of card plans, such as Citibank's AT&T Universal, Fleet Platinum Visa, and MBNA's Elite Rewards Platinum, are aggressively expanding to offer no-interest or very low-interest programs to attract consumers willing to transfer their account balances from competing programs. However, once the no-interest or low-interest period ends, most card programs plan a jump in interest rates to 10 percent or higher. The purpose of this aggressive marketing effort is traceable to recent slower growth in the credit card market.

New Credit Card Regulations

New credit card regulations appeared early in 2003 as the chief U.S. regulators of depository institutions—the Office of the Comptroller of the Currency, the Federal Reserve System, the Federal Deposit Insurance Corporation, and the Office of Thrift Supervision—moved to slow the expansion of credit card offers to customers with low credit ratings. Regulators expressed concern that many weak household borrowers were being carried on the books of credit card lenders for months even when their payments were woefully behind schedule. Some lenders allegedly had adopted the policy of liberalizing credit terms so that delinquent borrowers would continue to run up charges and fees with little hope of eventual repayment.

Indeed, there was evidence that many customers were charged very high card fees but asked to make low minimum payments, resulting in "negative amortization" of their credit-card debt. This meant that rather than paying down their debts, many troubled credit-card customers found themselves owing still more over time due to late payment fees, over-credit-limit charges, and such. In January 2003 U.S. bank regulatory agencies warned credit card lenders that federal examiners would begin looking for excessive use of fees and unreasonably liberal credit terms that appeared to "doom" many low-credit-rated customers to making payments indefinitely without hope of retiring their debts. Regulators began to pressure U.S. lenders to make sure that the majority of their credit card borrowers were set up in repayment plans that would normally result in complete repayment of balances owed within 60 months.

Debit Cards: A Partial Substitute for Credit Cards?

Debit cards—plastic that may be used to pay for goods and services, but not to extend credit—are today one of the fastest growing of all household financial services, substantially exceeding the recent growth of credit cards. Currently the credit card market is about triple the size of the debit card market, but debit cards are growing more than three times as fast as credit cards. Among the leading firms offering these plastic substitutes for writing checks, paying cash, or presenting a credit card to pay for purchases of goods and services are First Data Corp, VISA USA Inc., and MasterCard International Inc.

Debit cards are a convenient method of paying *now* and a vehicle for making deposits into and withdrawals from ATMs. These cards are also used to facilitate check cashing and to establish a customer's identity. Close relatives of the debit card, especially popular in Europe today, are so-called "smart cards" that carry balances that can be spent electronically in stores and shopping centers until the balance entered on the card is fully used up. Prepaid or niche cards, offered by such institutions as MasterCard International, VISA USA, and Comdata Corp., are now emerging that, like smart cards, are also preloaded with cash. One of the most common uses of these newest card types is by employers who may pay employees by filling their cards with salary money each month or prepay employee travel expenses.

Debit cards enforce discipline on consumers who, when using such a card, must pay immediately without borrowing money. They save both the customer and the banker time and paperwork compared to the use of checks. Moreover, bankers and other financial firms have found them to be an additional source of fee income without the high losses associated with default and theft that often accompany traditional credit cards.

CREDIT CARD SERVICE PRODUCTION AND COSTS

Banks and other lenders offering credit card services have had to adapt to powerful forces in the credit card market in recent years. Among the key factors affecting this important financial service today are the following:

- Credit card programs carry strong *economies of scale* in service production and delivery; only the largest-volume programs tend to survive and record positive profitability. Small programs, on average, have poor or even negative profitability due to excess operating costs.

- *Cost control* is the key to profitable card programs, especially in the areas of marketing, recordkeeping and account processing, and losses due to fraud and theft (which are among the fastest-growing costs today). Credit card providers are beginning to exploit new identification technology (such as finger and hand prints and retinal scanning) to provide greater protection from fraud and theft losses.

- Over time the credit card industry has tended to *concentrate in the hands of fewer leading programs,* such as MasterCard and VISA. The combined result of greater concentration and increased consumer demand has, up to recently, sharply boosted profits. (For example, in 2002 the return on assets [ROA] of credit card lenders was about three times the banking industry's average ROA.)

- However, *competition has been intensifying recently* with banks (such as Citigroup) and nonbanks (such as GE Consumer Finance) fighting it out in multiple markets around the globe. The credit card business is slowing and margins seem to be falling.

- If competition has increased, one propelling force is the *increasing sophistication of consumers* in recognizing differences in price and service quality among competing programs, taking advantage of cards offering the lowest rates and fees, and transferring account balances ("surfing") wherever and whenever interest rates look more favorable.

- *Law and regulation are playing bigger roles in the credit card field* today because of allegations of overcharging customers, attempts to stifle competition, and excessive borrowing by thousands of customers who can ill afford to do so. One key regulatory innovation in the United States requires full and readable disclosures in the form of a Schumer Box (which must inform account holders about finance charges, grace periods, card balance calculations, and any fees that might be assessed).

Rapid Consumer Loan Growth   Whatever their category, most types of consumer loans have grown explosively in recent years, fed by a growing economy and intense competition among consumer lenders. For examples, household debt grew in the United States from less than 70 percent of family disposable income in 1985 to more than 100 percent of personal disposable income in 2003. Home mortgage loan growth was the fastest of all consumer loan categories, rising from less than 43 percent of U.S. disposable personal income in 1985 to about two-thirds of that measure of household income in 2003.

Characteristics of Consumer Loans

By and large, bankers, thrift institutions, finance companies, and other household lenders regard consumer loans as profitable credits with "sticky" interest rates. That is, they are typically priced well above the cost of funding them, but their contract interest rates usually don't change with market conditions during the life of the loan as do interest rates on most business loans today, though flexible-rate consumer credit appears to be growing. This means that most consumer loans are exposed to interest rate risk if their funding cost rises high enough. However, consumer loans are usually priced so high (i.e., with a sufficiently large risk premium built into the loan rate) that market interest rates on borrowed loanable funds and default rates on the loans themselves would have to rise substantially before most consumer credits would become unprofitable.

Why are interest rates so high on most consumer loans? One key reason is revealed by the Functional Cost Analysis (FCA) program conducted by the Federal Reserve banks. This cost accounting system suggests that consumer loans are among the most costly and most risky to make per dollar of loanable funds of any of the loans that most lending institutions grant to their customers. Consumer loans also tend to be *cyclically sensitive*. They rise in periods of economic expansion when consumers are generally more optimistic about the future. On the other hand, when the economy turns down into a recession, many individuals and families become more pessimistic about the future and reduce their borrowings accordingly.

Household borrowings appear to be relatively *interest inelastic:* Consumers are often more concerned about the size of monthly payments required by a loan agreement than the interest rate charged (though, obviously, the contract interest rate on a loan influences the size of its required payments). While the level of the interest rate is often not a significant conscious factor among household borrowers, both education and income levels *do* materially influence consumers' use of credit. Individuals with higher incomes tend to borrow more in total and relative to the size of their annual incomes. Those households in which the principal breadwinner has more years of formal education also tend to borrow more heavily relative to their level of income. For these individuals and families, borrowing is often viewed as a tool to achieve a desired standard of living rather than as a safety net to be used only in emergencies.

Concept Check

17–1. What are the principal differences among residential loans, nonresidential installment loans, noninstallment loans, and credit card or revolving loans?

17–2. Why do interest rates on consumer loans typically average higher than on most other kinds of loans?

Evaluating a Consumer Loan Application

Character and Purpose The key factors in analyzing any consumer loan application are the *character* of the borrower and the borrower's *ability to pay*. The loan officer must be assured that the borrowing customer feels a keen sense of moral responsibility to repay a loan fully and on time. Moreover, the borrower's income level and valuable assets (such as holdings of securities or savings deposits) must be sufficient to reassure the loan officer that the customer has the ability to repay the loan with a comfortable margin for safety. For this reason, a consumer loan officer nearly always checks with the national or regional **credit bureau** concerning the customer's credit history. These institutions hold files on most individuals who, at one time or another, have borrowed money, indicating their record of repayment and credit rating.

Often the fundamental character of the borrower is revealed in the *purpose* of the loan request. The loan officer must ask: Has the customer clearly stated what he or she plans to do with the money? Is the stated purpose of the loan consistent with the lender's written loan policy? Is there evidence of a sincere intention to repay any funds borrowed? Some senior loan officers counsel new loan officers to visit with each customer where this is practical because such conversations often reveal flaws in character and sincerity that have a direct bearing on the likelihood of loan repayment. When there is time, experienced loan officers may fill out the loan application rather than letting the borrowing customer do it alone. By asking the customer pertinent questions as the application is being filled out, a skilled lender often can make a better call on whether the customer's loan request meets the lender's quality standards. The customer's spoken answers may be far more revealing about character and sincerity of purpose than information extracted from a computer file.

Unfortunately, economic pressures encouraging automation in the consumer lending process have led most consumer lending institutions to spend less time with the customer. Information gathering and loan evaluation increasingly are being turned over to computer programs. The result is that many consumer loan officers today know very little about the character traits of their customers beyond the information called for on a credit application, which may be faxed or telephoned in or sent via computer terminal.

In the case of a borrower without a credit record or with a poor track record of repaying loans, a **cosigner** may be requested to support repayment. Technically, if the borrower defaults on a cosigned loan agreement, the cosigner is obligated to make good on the loan. However, many lenders regard a cosigner mainly as a psychological device to encourage repayment of the loan, rather than as a real alternative source of security. The borrower may feel a stronger moral obligation to repay the loan knowing the cosigner's credit rating also is on the line.

Income Levels   Both the *size* and *stability* of an individual's income are considered important by consumer loan officers. They generally prefer the customer to report *net salary*, or *take-home pay*, as opposed to gross salary, and may check with the customer's employer to verify the accuracy of customer-supplied income figures, length of employment, residence address, and Social Security number.

Deposit Balances   An indirect measure of income size and stability is the *daily average deposit balance* maintained by the customer, which the loan officer may verify with the depository institution involved. In most states, certain lenders are granted the **right of offset** against the customer's deposit as additional protection against the risks of consumer lending. This right permits the lender to call a loan that is in default and seize any checking or savings deposits the customer may hold in order to recover its funds. However, the customer normally must be notified at least 10 days in advance before this right is exercised, which can result in funds disappearing before the lending institution can recover any portion of its loan.

Employment and Residential Stability   Among the many factors considered by experienced consumer loan officers is *duration of employment*. Most lenders are not likely to grant a sizable loan to someone who has held his or her present job for only few weeks or months. *Length of residence* is also frequently analyzed because the longer a person stays at one address, the more stable his or her personal situation is presumed to be. Frequent changes of address can be a strong negative factor in deciding whether to grant a loan.

Pyramiding of Debt   Consumer loan officers are especially sensitive to evidence that debt is piling up relative to a consumer's monthly or annual income. *Pyramiding of debt*— where the individual draws credit at one lending institution to pay another—is frowned upon by loan officers, as are high or growing credit card balances and frequent returned checks drawn against the customer's deposit account. These items are viewed as indicators of the customer's money management skill. Customers lacking these basic skills may be unable to avoid taking on too much debt and getting themselves in serious trouble with their creditors.

How to Qualify for a Consumer Loan   Are there ways to improve one's chances of getting a loan? One positive factor is *home ownership* or, for that matter, ownership of any form of real property, such as land or buildings. Even if such property is not posted as collateral behind a loan, it conveys the impression of stability and good money management skills. Having a telephone is also important as a sign of stability and a low-cost way for the lender's collections department to contact the borrower in case of trouble. Another positive factor is maintaining *strong deposit balances*. Not only do above-average deposit levels suggest a financially disciplined individual determined to meet his or her obligations, but also the lender may be able to profitably use those deposits to fund other loans.

The most important thing to do, however, is to answer all the loan officer's questions truthfully. Consumer loan officers often look for *inconsistencies* on a loan application as a sign the borrower is untruthful or, at best, forgetful. For example, a Social Security or personal ID number often reveals what geographic area a person comes from. Does the borrower's Social Security number match his or her personal history as indicated on the loan application? Are the borrower and his or her employer located at the addresses indicated? Is the amount reported as take-home pay or annual income the same as what the employer reports? Has the customer reported all debts outstanding, or does a credit check reveal many unreported obligations the customer has forgotten or simply walked away from?

The Challenge of Consumer Lending Consumer loans are not easy to evaluate. For one thing, it is often easier for individuals to conceal pertinent information bearing on the payout of a loan (such as their health or future employment prospects) than for most businesses (whose loan applications are frequently accompanied by audited financial statements). Moreover, a business firm usually can more easily adjust to ill health, injury, or financial setbacks than can individuals. The default rate on consumer loans usually is several times higher than that for many types of commercial loans. The key features of consumer loans that help the loan officer hold down potential losses are that most are small in denomination and often secured by marketable collateral, such as an automobile.

Example of a Consumer Loan Application

We can illustrate some of the most important types of information a consumer loan officer gathers and what these bits of information are designed to reveal by examining the sample loan application shown in Table 17–1. This is a credit application to finance the purchase of a new automobile, one of the most common and normally one of the more profitable and secure types of loans made by a bank, finance company, credit union, or other auto lender. The customer, J. B. Skylark, is trading in a used car in order to purchase a new Ford Taurus. The trade-in value and down payment will cover nearly 20 percent of the purchase price, and the lender is asked to cover the remainder (80 percent) of the automobile's price. The lending institution will take a *chattel mortgage* against the vehicle in order to gain the legal right to repossess it if the loan is defaulted. As long as car prices remain fairly stable or increase, the lender's funds should be reasonably well secured.

However, character, stability, and adequate disposable income (not heavily burdened with fixed debt obligations and taxes) are important components of any consumer loan request, and these elements raise serious questions about this particular loan request. Skylark has been at his present address for only 10 months and stayed at his previous address in another city for just one year. He has worked only eight months for his present employer. Many lenders prefer borrowing customers who have resided or worked in their market area for at least one year, which is often considered a sign of reliability. The loan officer must decide if Skylark's residential and employment situation comes close enough to the lending institution's standards in this regard.

The Skylarks' annual gross income is slightly above average and, for both husband and wife, amounts to almost $39,000 or about $30,000 in total take-home pay. The family has debt obligations amounting to $103,000 which appears to be high—about three times their annual (gross) income—but includes their home mortgage loan. Most home mortgage

Factoid
Who are the two leading automobile lenders in the United States?
Answer: Commercial banks and finance companies.

TABLE 17–1
A Typical Consumer
Loan Application

Credit application submitted by <u>J. P. L. Skylark V</u> on <u>December 1, this year</u> to the First National Bank of Collridge.

Applicant's street address: <u>3701 Elm Street</u>

City of residence: <u>Orangeburg</u>   State and Zip Code: <u>CA 77804</u>

Purpose of the requested loan: <u>To purchase a new car for personal and family use</u>

Desired term of loan: <u>5 years</u>

For auto loan requests, please fill in the following information:

    Auto is <u>X</u> New <u>   </u> Used.   Year: <u>Current</u>

    Make: <u>Ford Taurus</u>

    Model: <u>4-Door Sedan</u>   Vehicle identification no. <u>8073617</u>

    The vehicle is equipped with: <u>Air conditioning, automatic transmission, power steering, power brakes, AM/FM stereo, CD player, automatic door locks.</u>

Vehicle to be traded in: <u>Chevrolet Monte Carlo</u>   Model: <u>4-door Sedan</u>

Age of vehicle: <u>8 years</u>

Vehicle identification no. <u>6384061</u>

Optional equipment on trade-in vehicle: <u>Air conditioning, automatic transmission, power brakes, power steering, AM/FM radio</u>

Details of the proposed purchase:

Purchase price quoted by seller:	$18,750
Cash down payment to be made:	$ 1,575
Value of trade-in vehicle:	$ 3,500
Total value put down:	$ 5,075
Unpaid portion of purchase price:	$13,675
Other items covered in the loan:	$ 650
Total amount of credit requested:	**$14,325**

Customer information:

Social Security no. <u>671-66-8324</u>

Birthdate: <u>2/21/73</u>

Time at present address: <u>10 months</u>   Phone no. <u>965-1321</u>

Previous home address: <u>302 W. Solar St., Casio City, California</u>

How long at previous address: <u>1 year</u>

Driver's license no. and state: <u>A672435 California</u>

Number of dependents: <u>3</u>

Current employer: <u>Hometown Warehouse Co.</u>

(continued)

TABLE 17–1
Continued

Length of employment with current employer: 8 months

Nature of work: Drive truck, load merchandise, keep books

Annual salary: $26,000   Employer's phone no. 963-8417

Other income sources: Investments, Trust Fund

Annual income from other sources: $5,000

Debts owed (including home mortgage): $103,000

Monthly debt payments: $1,140

Nearest living relative (not spouse): Elsa Lyone   Phone: 604-682-7899

   Address: 6832 Willow Ave., Amera, OK, 73282

Does the applicant want the lender to consider spouse's income in evaluating this loan?

  __X__ Yes _____ No

Spouse's current annual income: $7,800

Name of spouse's employer: Dimmitt Savings and Security Association

Occupation: Secretary   Length of employment: 8 months

   The information I have given in this credit application is true and correct to the best of my
   knowledge. I am aware that the lender will keep this credit application regardless of whether
   or not the loan is approved. The lender is hereby granted permission to investigate my credit
   and employment history for purpose of verifying the information submitted with this credit
   application and for evaluating my credit status.

Customer's signature: J. P. Skylark

Date signed: 12/1/current year

lenders would find a debt to income ratio of two and one-half to three times not unusual by today's standards.

The monthly payments on this debt *are* on the high side, however, at just over $1,140 (including the home mortgage payment). Monthly debt payments already account for more than a third of monthly gross income, not counting the payments of $225 per month that the requested car loan will require. Many lenders prefer to see a required-monthly-payment-to-income ratio no more than 25 to 30 percent. However, the bulk of the family's debt and debt service payments are on their home and, in a reasonably strong local real estate market, the value of that home would provide adequate security for the lender. Moreover, the Skylarks seem to have adequate insurance coverage and hold at least some liquid financial investments in the form of stocks, bonds, and other securities. The loan officer's check with both Mr. and Mrs. Skylark's employers revealed that they both have good prospects for continued employment.

The Skylarks' loan application is for a reasonable purpose, consistent with this bank's loan policy, and the family's reported income high enough to suggest a reasonably strong probability that the loan would be repaid. Accordingly, the loan officer accepted their application and proceeded to check out the Skylark's credit record. When the report from the credit bureau arrived on-screen minutes later, however, the loan officer saw very quickly that there was a serious problem with this loan application. Unfortunately, as

TABLE 17–2
Sample Credit
Bureau Report

E-Z Credit Bureau Report on J.P.L. Skylark, SSN 671-66-8324
Credit bureau address: 8750 Cafe Street, San Miguel, CA 87513
607-453-8862
Credit items as of: *6/15/Current Year*

Name of Creditor	Maximum Term Credit	Amount Owed	Outstanding Balance	Past Due	Monthly Payments	Status
Windcrest Deluxe Apts.	Six months	$ 610	$ 610	$610	$305	Past due
VISA	Open	$1,680	$1,540	$250	$125	Past due
MasterCard	Open	$1,435	$1,250	$176	$ 88	Past due
First State Bank of Slyvon	Six months	$ 750	$ 150	$150	$ 75	Past due
Kinney's Furniture Mart and Emporium	One year	$ 847	$ 675	—	$ 34	Current
First National Bank of Orangeburg	One year	$2,500	$ 675	—	$120	Current
Saint Barrio Hospital and Medical Clinic	Open	$ 160	$ 160	—	—	Charged off

Key URLs
To find out more about the information credit bureaus provide consumer lenders you may wish to contact the 3 largest credit bureaus in the U.S. at **www.experian.com**, **www.equifax.com**, and **www.transunion.com**.

shown in Table 17–2, the Skylarks had a mixed credit record, with at least five instances of delinquent or unpaid bills. The other debts were essentially as reported on the loan application with only minor discrepancies. At best, the loan officer would ask the Skylarks about these unreported debts, but more likely this loan request will simply be turned down due to an unacceptable credit record. The loan officer clearly would be justified in having doubts about this borrower's sense of judgment and responsibility in borrowing and repaying borrowed funds.

The Equal Credit Opportunity Act requires U.S. banks and selected other consumer lending institutions to notify their credit customers in writing when they deny a loan request. They must give *reasons* for the denial, and where a credit bureau report is used, the customer must be told where that credit bureau is located. This way the customer can verify his or her credit record and demand that any errors found in the report be corrected. Table 17–3 shows the credit denial report form given to the Skylarks and the reasons they were given on why their loan was turned down. In this case, the loan officer cited the unpaid debts and the relatively short period of time the Skylarks had held their current jobs. A good feature of this particular denial form is that the customer is cordially invited to use other services at the lending institution and to reapply if his or her financial situation improves.

An acceptable consumer loan request will display evidence of (*a*) the stability of the borrower's employment or residence location; (*b*) the accuracy and consistency of information the borrower supplies; (*c*) the legitimacy of the borrower's purpose for borrowing money; and (*d*) the borrower's personal money management skills. It is when a household application is weak in one or two of these features that loan officers face tough decisions and increasingly today rely on some sort of objective credit rating system to make good lending decisions. The ultimate decision to accept or deny any particular loan request depends on the expected return and risk of that proposed loan relative to the expected returns and risks of other possible investments the lender might make or has already made, management's attitude toward risk, and the lender's standing in the eyes of the regulatory community.

TABLE 17–3
Statement of Denial, Termination, or Change on a Customer Credit Application

First National Bank of Collridge

Statement to: <u>Mr. J. P. L. Skylark</u>
     Customer's Name

    <u>3701 Elm Street</u>   <u>Orangeburg, CA 77804</u>
    Customer's residence address City   State

Statement date: <u>6/18/current year</u>

Credit requested by customer: <u>$14,325, 5-year auto installment loan</u>

Action taken by the bank on the request: <u>Loan denied</u>

Unfortunately, the bank cannot approve the amount and terms of credit you have asked for as of the date indicated above. The reason(s) for our denial of your requested loan are: <u>Past-due loans and inadequate length of employment</u>

Our investigation of your credit request included a credit report from: <u>E-Z Credit Bureau, 8750 Cafe Street, San Miguel, CA 87513.</u> Federal law allows you to obtain, upon submission of a written request, a copy of the information that led to a denial of this credit request.

If you believe you have been discriminated against in obtaining credit because of your race, color, religion, sex, national origin, marital status, legal age, receipt of public assistance, or exercise of rights under the Consumer Credit Protection Act, you may apply to the principal federal regulatory agency for this bank, which is the Comptroller of the Currency, U.S. Treasury Department, Washington, D.C. 20219.

Please let me or the other employees of our bank know at any time in the future if we can assist you with other services this bank offers. We value your friendship and your business and would like to be of assistance to you in meeting your personal banking needs. Please consider submitting another loan request in the future if the situation that led to the denial of this credit request improves.

       Sincerely,

          <u>W. A. Numone</u>
          William A. H. Numone III
          Senior Vice President
          Personal Banking Division

Credit Scoring Consumer Loan Applications

Most lenders today use **credit scoring** to evaluate the loan applications they receive from consumers. In fact, major credit card systems, such as Master Card and VISA, use these systems routinely to evaluate their credit card applicants, while growing numbers of banks and other lenders are using credit-scoring models to evaluate auto, home equity, first mortgage, and business loans. Many insurance companies also use scoring systems today to help them evaluate new policyholders and the risks these prospective customers might present to the insurer.

Credit-scoring systems have the advantage of being able to handle a large volume of credit applications quickly with minimal labor, thus reducing operating costs, and they may be an effective substitute for the use of judgment among inexperienced loan officers, thus helping to control bad-debt losses. Many customers like the convenience and speed with which their credit applications can be handled by automated credit-scoring systems. Often the customer can phone in a loan request or fill out an Internet application, and in a matter of minutes the lender can dial up that customer's credit bureau report through its online computer network and reach a quick decision on the customer's request (now within eight minutes, on average, for auto loan requests).

Credit-scoring systems are usually based on discriminant models or related techniques, such as logit or probit models or neural networks, in which several variables are used jointly to establish a numerical score for each credit applicant. If the applicant's score exceeds a critical cutoff level, he or she is likely to be approved for credit in the absence of other damaging information. If the applicant's score falls below the cutoff level, credit is likely to be denied in the absence of mitigating factors. Among the most important variables used in evaluating consumer loans are credit bureau ratings, home ownership, income bracket, number and type of deposit accounts owned, type of occupation, and time in current job.

The basic theory of credit scoring is that lenders and statisticians can identify the financial, economic, and motivational factors that separate good loans from bad loans by observing large groups of people who have borrowed in the past. Moreover, it assumes that the same financial and other factors that separated good from bad loans in the past will, with an acceptable risk of error, separate good from bad loans in the future. Obviously, this underlying assumption can be wrong if the economy or other factors change abruptly, which is one reason good credit scoring systems are frequently retested and revised as more sensitive predictors are identified.

Scoring systems usually select between 7 and 12 items from a customer's credit application and assign each a point value from 1 to 10. For example, examination of a sample of consumer credit accounts might show that the factors in the following table on page 615 were important in separating good loans (i.e., those that paid out in timely fashion) from bad loans (i.e., where repayment was seriously delayed or not made at all).

The highest score a customer could have in the eight-factor credit-scoring system that follows is 430 points. The lowest possible score is 90 points. Suppose the lender finds that, of those past-approved loan customers scoring 280 points or less, 40 percent (or 1,200) became bad loans that had to be written off as a loss. These losses averaged $600 per credit account, for a total loss of $720,000. Of all the good loans made, however, only 10 percent (300) scored 280 points or less under this scoring system. At $600 per loan, these low-scoring good loans amounted to $180,000. Therefore, if a loan officer uses 280 points as the *criterion score*, or *break point*, the lender will save an estimated $720,000 minus $180,000, or $540,000, by following the decision rule of making only those loans where the credit applicant scores higher than 280 points. If the lender's future loan-loss experience is the same, denying all loan applications scoring 280 points or less will reduce loss accounts by about 40 percent and reject just 10 percent of the good loan customers. Management can experiment with other criterion scores to determine which cutoff point yields the greatest net savings in loan losses for the lending institution's consumer credit program.

Let's suppose the lending institution finds that 280 points is indeed the optimal break point for maximum savings from loan losses. The lender's consumer credit history could be further analyzed to find out what influence the *amount of credit* extended to a customer has upon the lender's loan-loss experience. The lender might find that the following point-scoring schedule on page 616 results in the largest net savings from consumer credit losses.

Clearly, such a system removes personal judgment from the lending process and reduces the lender's decision time from hours to minutes. It does run the risk, however, of alienating those customers who feel the lending institution has not fully considered their financial situation and the special circumstances that may have given rise to their loan request. There is also the danger of being sued by a customer under federal antidiscrimination laws (such as the Equal Credit Opportunity Act) if race, gender, marital status, or other discriminating factors prohibited by statute or court rulings are used in a scoring system. Federal regulations allow the use of age or certain other personal characteristics as discriminating factors if the lender can show that these factors *do* separate, at a statistically significant level, good from bad loans and that the scoring system is frequently statistically tested and revised to take into account recent changes in actual credit experience. The burden of proof is on the lender to demonstrate that its credit scoring system successfully identifies quality loan applications at a statistically significant level.

**Predictive Factors in an Example
of a Credit Scoring Model and Their Point Values**

Factors for Predicting Credit Quality	Point Value
1. Customer's occupation or line of work:	
Professional or business executive	100
Skilled worker	80
Clerical worker	70
Student	50
Unskilled worker	40
Part-time employee	20
2. Housing status:	
Owns home	60
Rents home or apartment	40
Lives with friend or relative	20
3. Credit rating:	
Excellent	100
Average	50
No record	20
Poor	00
4. Length of time in current job:	
More than one year	50
One year or less	20
5. Length of time at current address:	
More than one year	20
One year or less	10
6. Telephone in home or apartment:	
Yes	20
No	00
7. Number of dependents reported by customer:	
None	30
One	30
Two	40
Three	40
More than three	20
8. Deposit accounts held:	
Both checking and savings	40
Savings account only	30
Checking account only	20
None	00

Frequent verification and revision of a credit-scoring system is not only wise from a legal and regulatory point of view, but it also mitigates the biggest potential weakness of such systems—their inability to adjust quickly to changes in the economy and in family lifestyles. An inflexible credit evaluation system can be a deadly menace to a lending institution's consumer loan program, driving away sound consumer credit requests, ruining the lender's reputation in the communities it serves, and adding unacceptably high credit risks to the loan portfolio.

Point-Scoring Schedule of Approved Credit Amounts

Point Score Value or Range	Credit Decision
280 points or less	Reject application
290–300 points	Extend credit up to $1,000
310–330 points	Extend credit up to $2,000
340–360 points	Extend credit up to $3,000
370–380 points	Extend credit up to $4,000
390–400 points	Extend credit up to $6,000
410–430 points	Extend credit up to $10,000

The FICO Scoring System

The most famous of all credit scoring systems currently in widespread use is known as FICO, developed and sold by Fair Isaac Corporation. Fair Isaac's credit scoring system calculates scores for millions of consumers worldwide and provides these scores to credit bureaus, lending institutions, and individuals who file a request. Fair Isaac also provides programs for individuals and families that suggest how they can improve their FICO score and, thereby, gain access to more credit or access credit more cheaply. A FICO score simulator allows individuals to estimate what would happen to their FICO score if certain changes were made in their personal financial profile. Many borrowers check their FICO rating before they seek a large loan (such as a home mortgage) in order to assess their chances of getting approved.

Key URLs

To learn more about FICO credit scoring, see especially **www.fairisaac.com** and **www.myfico.com**.

FICO scores range from 300 to 850, with higher values denoting less credit risk to lenders. To a lending institution, an individual with a lower FICO score implies a lower probability of timely repayment if the lender should grant a loan and, therefore, a loan is less likely to be granted. However, all lending institutions do not adopt the same cutoff score for loan approval so that a good score for one lender may not be a good mark for another. It is an individual lender's decision.

While Fair Isaac provides the public only general information about its scoring systems, its credit scores are based on five different types of information (arrayed from most important to least important):

1. The borrower's payment history.
2. The amount of money owed.
3. The length of a prospective borrower's credit history.
4. The nature of the new credit being requested.
5. The types of credit the borrower has already used.

Fair Isaac also indicates what elements of a borrower's background—especially age, race, color, sex, religion, marital status, employment history and salary, and residential location—are *not* considered in establishing a FICO score. It confines the list of factors considered in its credit scoring system to those items usually available in each customer's credit bureau report. FICO scores are recalculated as new information comes in about a credit user. The hallmarks of the system are speed, objectivity, and impartiality, which make this system especially useful for closely regulated financial institutions.

Concept Check

17–3. What features of a consumer loan application should a loan officer examine most carefully?

17–4. How do credit-scoring systems work?

17–5. What are the principal advantages to a lending institution of using a credit-scoring system to evaluate consumer loan applications?

17–6. Are there any significant disadvantages to a credit-scoring system?

17–7. In the credit-scoring system presented in this chapter, would a loan applicant who is a skilled worker, lives with a relative, has an average credit rating, has been in his or her present job and at his or her current address for exactly one year, has four dependents and a telephone, and holds a checking account be likely to receive a loan? Please explain why.

17–8. What is FICO and what does it do for lenders? Why is this credit-scoring system so popular today?

Laws and Regulations Applying to Consumer Loans

Numerous laws and regulations limiting the activities of consumer lending institutions have been enacted during the past four decades. The principal federal laws fall into two broad groups: (1) **disclosure rules,** which mandate telling the consumer about the cost and other terms of a loan, lease agreement, or other financial service; and (2) **antidiscrimination laws,** which prevent categorizing loan customers according to their age, sex, race, or other irrelevant factors and denying credit to anyone solely because of membership in one or more of these groups. Many lenders view such rules as burdensome and out of step with technological and service innovations. They are also a constant challenge to the enforcement powers of the regulatory community, which is burdened with numerous complaints and questions of interpretation. Yet, the flow of adequate financial information to consumers is becoming more and more vital in the wake of government deregulation of the financial sector, which has been accompanied by greater risk for both financial institutions and their customers.

Customer Disclosure Requirements

One of the most prominent pieces of federal legislation in the consumer services field is the **Truth-in-Lending Act,** passed in 1968 by the U.S. Congress and simplified in 1981 through passage of the Truth-in-Lending Simplification and Reform Act. The Federal Reserve Board has prepared Regulation Z to implement these truth-in-lending laws. The express purpose of truth in lending is to promote the informed use of credit among consumers by requiring full disclosure of credit terms and costs. Lenders must tell customers the annual percentage rate (APR, or actuarial, rate) on the loan requested, the total dollar amount of all finance charges, and, in the case of home mortgage loans, the required fees for approvals, closing costs, and other loan-related expenses.

Amendments to Truth in Lending in 1970 and 1974 gave rise to the Fair Credit Reporting Act and the Fair Credit Billing Act. The former expressly grants consumers access to their credit files, usually kept by credit bureaus. The **Fair Credit Reporting Act** authorizes individuals and families to review their credit files for accuracy and to demand an investigation and correction of any inaccuracies. The law requires a credit agency to correct these inaccuracies promptly and to allow the consumer to insert a brief statement of explanation for any damaging items displayed in the file. Moreover, it severely restricts access to consumer credit files, requiring an individual's written consent.

The **Fair Credit Billing Act** of 1974 permits consumers to dispute billing errors with a merchant or credit card company and receive a prompt investigation of billing disputes. The consumer may withhold payment on the disputed portions of a bill and cannot be reported as delinquent or forced to pay interest penalties until the dispute is settled. Any creditor who does not respond to a consumer's inquiry about a bill or, having responded, does not investigate and attempt to resolve the matter must ultimately forfeit the disputed charge (up to a maximum of $50). A 30-day notice to customers is required before a lending institution or merchant can alter credit charges or service fees.

The *Fair Credit and Charge-Card Disclosure Act* requires that customers applying for credit cards be given early written notice (usually before a credit card is used for the first time) about required fees to open or to renew a credit account. Also, if an existing credit card account is about to be renewed and a fee for renewal is charged, the customer must receive written notice in advance. The consumer must also be told if there is any change in credit card insurance coverage or fees. These rules are designed especially for credit cards granted to customers following solicitations made by direct mail, by telephone, or through advertisements that reach the general public.

Finally, if a credit customer gets behind in his or her loan payments, the **Fair Debt Collection Practices Act** limits how far a creditor or credit collection agency can go in pressing that customer to pay up. For example, a bill collector is not allowed to "harass" a debtor or use misrepresentation to obtain information about or gain access to a debtor. Calls placed at unusual times or to a debtor's place of work are illegal if made without the debtor's permission; nor can a bill collector legally disclose the purpose of the call to someone other than the debtor. These debt collection rules are enforced in the United States by the Federal Trade Commission.

Outlawing Credit Discrimination

Access to credit is an essential ingredient of the good life for the average family today. Recognition of this fact led the U.S. Congress during the 1970s to outlaw discrimination in the granting of credit based on age, sex, race, national origin, religion, location of residence, or receipt of public assistance. The **Equal Credit Opportunity Act** prohibits lenders from asking certain questions of a customer, such as the borrower's age or race. (An exception is made for home mortgage loans so that the federal government can collect information on who is or is not receiving mortgage credit to determine if discrimination is being practiced in this vital loan area.) Also, the loan officer cannot ask about other income sources beyond wage and salary income unless the customer voluntarily supplies this information.

The **Community Reinvestment Act** (CRA) is designed to prevent a lender of funds from arbitrarily marking out certain neighborhoods deemed undesirable and refusing to lend to people whose addresses place them in the excluded area. The CRA requires each lending institution to delineate the *trade territory* it plans to serve and to offer all of its services without discrimination to all residents in that particular trade territory. The lender's board of directors must review annually the definition of trade territory that management has chosen to see if it is still valid. Moreover, each lending institution's performance in making an affirmative effort to serve the credit and other financial-service needs of its trade territory is evaluated by federal examiners (known as a CRA *rating*). The regulatory authorities take a lender's CRA rating into account when it applies to establish a new branch office or close a branch, requests approval of a merger or acquisition, or requests permission to offer new services.

ETHICS IN BANKING

IDENTITY THEFT CHALLENGES BOTH FINANCIAL INSTITUTIONS AND THEIR CUSTOMERS

The fastest rising crime against individuals and families today is *identity theft*—the deliberate attempt to make unauthorized use of someone else's Social Security number, deposit account number, or other personal data in order to fraudulently obtain money or credit. So rapid is the rise of this crime, which claims about half a million victims a year in the U.S. alone, that it has taken on the character of an epidemic.

Unless an individual or family is alert virtually all of the time and aware of what's happening to their accounts each month, identity theft can be difficult to detect and costly to recover from. It is also a big challenge to banks, credit card companies, and other financial-service providers which increasingly today wind up "holding the bag" for the losses, now approaching an estimated $5 billion annually.

Examples of identity theft abound. Thus far, the largest such theft ever uncovered occurred in New York in 2001 and 2002. A gang of individuals managed to penetrate the internal records of a company supplying credit reports to lenders in the region. One member of the gang secretly downloaded credit reports and passed them to other members of the gang, who sold the information on the streets. Recipients of that informa-

tion then requested new credit cards, obtained new checkbooks, and even secured new ATM cards bearing the stolen identities and promptly moved to empty each victim's account. Law enforcement authorities estimated that more than 30,000 individuals and families had their private information lifted and sold before state and federal authorities made arrests.

To stop or at least slow down the identity-theft epidemic the Federal Trade Commission and other regulatory agencies have been advising consumers to zealously protect their Social Security, credit card, and savings account numbers, checkbooks, and other private information sources. Especially important is to avoid giving out identifying numbers over the phone.

Because of the potential credit losses and damage to customers' good will, bankers and other financial-service providers have put together extensive customer-alert programs that urge account holders to review their checking and savings accounts at least once a month and immediately report any discrepancies. This process has been made somewhat easier with electronic banking services that allow customers to check their accounts daily from home or office. Bankers and many of their competitors now check picture IDs (for example: driver's licenses) when a customer seeks to withdraw funds from an account or to open a new account.

In August 1989, Title XII of the Financial Institutions Reform, Recovery, and Enforcement Act required the federal banking agencies to *publish* the CRA ratings of banks and thrift institutions so their customers would be aware of which lenders were providing broad-based support to their local communities. Each covered lending institution must place its CRA performance evaluation in a public file at its head office and in at least one office in each community that the lender serves within 30 days of receiving the examiner's report. This public file must be open for customers to inspect during regular business hours and the lender must provide copies (for a reasonable fee) to anyone requesting materials in the file.

CRA ratings are based on 12 "assessment factors" that examiners review when they visit a bank or other covered lender, including the lender's effort to communicate with members of the local community concerning their credit needs, its participation in government-related housing programs, the geographic distribution of loans the lender has made, and any evidence of illegal credit discrimination. Federal examiners assign one of four different CRA ratings: outstanding (O), satisfactory (S), needs to improve (N), or substantial noncompliance (SN). Absent reasonable cause for an earlier investigation, small depository institutions with outstanding CRA ratings are exempt from CRA examinations for as long as five years, thus reducing the cost burden of these examinations.

A recent study by one of the authors [7] finds that banks receiving a grade of O—the highest CRA rating—have earned it by first carefully *documenting* their community-oriented activities. They periodically survey their employees who are active in the local community to be able to document their strong community involvement when regulators ask

Factoid
Which major bank
inside the United States
was the first to establish
a separate department
for granting loans
to households
(consumers)?
Answer: First National
City Bank of New York
(later Citibank).

for evidence on their community activities. Top-rated banks also frequently survey their customers to determine customer perceptions about the quality of the bank's services and to keep up with changing customer service needs. Banks with the highest community service ratings often get involved with local programs to provide affordable housing, hold seminars to counsel small businesses and new home buyers on how to apply for loans, and monitor the geographic distribution of their loans to make sure certain areas of the community are not systematically being shut out in their access to financial services.

Laws that supplement the provisions of the Community Reinvestment Act are the Home Mortgage Disclosure Act, the Fair Housing Act, and the Financial Institutions Reform, Recovery, and Enforcement Act. The former requires that banks and other institutional mortgage lenders publicly disclose at least once a year the areas of urban communities in which they have granted residential mortgage loans and home improvement loans. The Fair Housing Act prohibits discrimination in the sale, leasing, or financing of housing because of color, national origin, race, religion, or sex. The Financial Institutions Reform, Recovery, and Enforcement Act requires lending institutions to report the race, sex, and income of all those individuals *applying* for mortgage loans so that federal regulatory agencies can more easily detect possible discrimination in home mortgage lending.

These laws do not tell banks and other financial institutions *who* should receive credit. Rather, they require each lending institution to focus on the facts pertinent to each individual loan application, case by case, and prevent lenders from lumping their customers into categories (such as by age, sex, or race) and making credit decisions solely on the basis of group membership.

Predatory Lending and Subprime Loans

Recent regulatory concerns over consumer lending practices have been very much in the news. One of the most controversial practices is known today as **predatory lending**—an abusive practice among some lenders, often associated with home mortgage and home equity loans. This usually consists of granting so-called **subprime loans** to borrowers with below-average credit records and, in the eyes of the regulatory community at least, charging excessive fees and interest rates for these lower-quality loans. Subprime loans tend to go to borrowers with a record of delinquent payments, previously charged-off loans, bankruptcies, or court judgments to be paid off.

Some predatory lenders may insist on unnecessary and expensive loan insurance in amounts well beyond what is needed to cover actual loan risk. The excessive loan insurance costs and higher interest rates may result in unaffordable payments for weak borrowers. This kind of abusive lending practice can increase the chances that low-credit-rated borrowers will lose their homes.

In 1994 the U.S. Congress passed the Home Ownership and Equity Protection Act, which was aimed at protecting home buyers from loan agreements they couldn't afford to carry. Loans with annual percentage rates (APR) of 10 percentage points or more above the yield on comparable maturity U.S. Treasury securities and closing fees above 8 percent of the loan amount were defined as "abusive." When those high rates are charged, the consumer has a minimum of six days (three days before plus three days after a home loan closing) to decide whether or not to proceed with the transaction. If a credit-granting institution fails to properly disclose the costs and risks or includes prohibitive terms in a loan agreement, the borrower has up to three years to rescind the transaction, and creditors may be liable for damages.

Subprime lending is a difficult field to regulate. It can open the door to predatory lending practices in the pursuit of higher returns. However, the subprime market also opens up opportunities for access to credit among those households that may be unable to access credit any other way.

Real Estate Loans

Banks, thrift institutions, credit unions, and finance and insurance companies, to name a few financial institutions, make real estate loans to fund the acquisition of real property: homes, apartment complexes, shopping centers, office buildings, warehouses, and other physical structures, as well as land. Real estate lending is a field unto itself, possessing important differences from other types of loans. These credits may be either short-term **construction loans,** paid out within months as a building project is completed, or long-term mortgages that may stretch out 25 to 30 years in order to provide permanent financing for the acquisition or improvement of real property. Whatever their maturity, real estate loans have been one of the most rapidly growing areas of lending over the past decade, climbing at a double-digit growth rate and reaching nearly a third of all bank assets as the 21st century began. Unfortunately, such loans can be among the riskiest forms of credit to extend to customers.

Differences between Real Estate Loans and Other Loans

Real estate loans differ from most other kinds of loans in several key respects. First, the average size of a real estate loan is usually much larger than the average size of other loans, especially consumer loans and small business loans. Moreover, certain mortgage loans, mainly on single-family homes, tend to have the longest maturities (from about 15 years to 30 years) of any loan made. Long-term lending of this sort carries considerable risk for the lending institution because many things can happen—including adverse changes in economic conditions, interest rates, and the financial health of the borrower—over the term of such a loan.

With most other types of loans, the projected cash flow or income of the borrower is most important in the decision to approve or deny a loan application. With real estate lending, however, the condition and value of the property that is the object of the loan are nearly as important as the borrower's income. In real estate lending, competent property appraisal is vitally important to the decision on a loan request. Such appraisals must conform to industry and government standards, particularly if it is likely that the mortgage will subsequently be sold in the secondary market.

One such regulation is the Federal National Mortgage Association's (FNMA, or Fannie Mae) requirement that any home mortgage loans acquired must come from borrowers whose monthly house payment (including loan principal and interest, taxes, and insurance) does not exceed 28 percent of their monthly gross income and the sum of whose regular monthly payments (including housing costs) does not exceed 36 percent of their monthly gross income. The maturity of the home mortgage loan cannot be less than 10 years or more than 30 years, and the property must be appraised by a Fannie Mae–approved appraiser. FNMA regulations also stipulate that the borrower's credit report cannot be more than 90 days old.

Filmtoid
What 1989 film documentary reveals the negative effects the closure of a GM plant had on the property values in Flint, Michigan, and the inability of laid-off workers to meet debt obligations?
Answer: *Roger and Me.*

While rules such as these represent a burden to the home mortgage lender, they bring an offsetting benefit because loans conforming to these regulatory standards usually can be sold quite readily in the secondary market to other financial institutions or to government agencies such as Fannie Mae or Ginnie Mae (i.e., the Government National Mortgage Association, or GNMA). Frequently a lending institution will package its mortgage loans into GNMA-sponsored loan pools and sell securities as claims against those pools to investors, thereby raising funds to make still more loans.

Changes in regulations and the shifting fortunes of different financial institutions have resulted in major changes in bank and nonbank firms making mortgage loans. While commercial banks often prefer to make shorter-term property loans (especially construction loans), the mortgage banking subsidiaries of bank holding companies now account for a major portion of all home mortgage loans. These subsidiary firms have strong market contacts and can usually resell any home mortgage loans they make in short order to long-distance mortgage lenders, such as life insurers, savings banks, or foreign investors. Mortgage subsidiaries usually establish short-term "warehouse lines" at other lending institutions in order to provide them with adequate funding to carry the mortgages they originate or buy until they sell those same loans to other investors.

Factors in Evaluating Applications for Real Estate Loans

In evaluating real estate loan applications, loan officers must consider the following points:

1. The amount of the down payment planned by the borrower relative to the purchase price of mortgaged property is a critical factor in determining how safe a mortgage loan is from the lender's point of view. In general, the higher the ratio of loan amount to purchase price, the less incentive the borrower has to honor all the terms of the loan because the borrower has less equity in the property. When mortgages reach 90 percent or more of the property's purchase price, mortgage insurance becomes important and the lender must place added emphasis on assessing the borrower's character and sense of responsibility.

2. Real property loans often bring in other business (such as deposits and future property-improvement loans) from the borrowing customer. Therefore, they should be viewed in the context of a *total relationship* between borrower and lender. For example, the lender might be willing to give a mortgage loan customer a somewhat lower loan rate in return for a pledge that the customer will use other financial services and keep substantial deposits at the lending institution.

3. Deposit stability is a key factor for a bank or thrift institution in deciding what volume and type of real estate loans it should make. Lenders with more stable deposits usually can be more aggressive with their real estate lending programs and reach for longer-term, higher-yielding loans.

4. Home mortgage loans require the real estate loan officer to consider carefully the following aspects of the credit application:

    a. Amount and stability of the borrower's income, especially relative to the size of the mortgage loan and the size of the payments required.

    b. The borrower's available savings and where the borrower will obtain the required down payment. If the down payment is made by drawing down savings significantly, the customer has fewer liquid assets available for future emergencies, such as paying off the mortgage if someone in the family becomes ill or loses a job.

    c. The borrower's track record in caring for and managing property. If the mortgaged property is not properly maintained, the lender may not fully recover the loaned funds in a foreclosure and sale.

d. The outlook for real estate sales in the local market area in case the property must be repossessed. In a depressed local economy with substantial unemployment, many houses, apartments, and business structures are put up for sale, with few active buyers. The lender could wait a long time for the return of its funds.

e. The outlook for interest rates if the home mortgage loan carries a floating rate. While the secondary market for floating-rate mortgage loans has improved in recent years, fixed-rate home mortgages are still easier to sell.

During the 1970s and 1980s, severe problems appeared in the real estate loan portfolios of many U.S. banks and other home mortgage lenders. Several of the largest banks in the United States, for example, foreclosed on and sold substantial commercial and residential properties at deeply discounted prices. In response to these problems, Congress enacted Title XI of the Financial Institutions Reform, Recovery, and Enforcement Act of 1989. Title XI requires the use of state-certified or licensed appraisers for real estate loans that come under the regulatory authority of the federal banking and thrift supervisory agencies. The four chief federal regulators of banks and thrifts have recently ruled that certified or licensed appraisals are required for most real estate loans that exceed $250,000 in amount. (Renewals of existing loans are generally exempt from specific appraisal requirements.) For smaller-denomination real estate loans, a lender must follow "prudent" evaluation standards and document in writing its valuation of any property that is the basis for a real estate loan, including the assumptions upon which estimated property values are based.

Further tightening of standards and regulations surrounding real estate loans occurred when Congress passed the National Affordable Housing Act in 1990. This law and its supporting regulations require that applicants for mortgage loans must be given a disclosure statement indicating whether the servicing rights (i.e., the right to collect payments from the borrower) could be transferred to another institution that borrowers will have to deal with during the life of their loan. In an effort to reduce the loss of homes through foreclosure, Congress stipulated that lenders must tell borrowers delinquent in repaying their mortgage loans if the lender counsels home owners or knows of any nonprofit organizations that provide such counseling.

Concept Check

17–12. In what ways is a real estate loan unique compared to other kinds of bank loans?

17–13. What factors should a banker or other lender consider in evaluating real estate loan applications?

Home Equity Lending

In the United States, the 1986 Tax Reform Act opened up even wider the rapidly growing field of **home equity loans.** Under these credit programs, home owners whose residence has appreciated in value can use the *equity* in their homes—the difference between a home's estimated market value and the amount of the mortgage loans against it—as a borrowing base. Thus, if a home was purchased for $100,000 and has a $70,000 mortgage loan against it today and, due to inflation and growing demand for housing, its market value is now $120,000, the home owner will have a *borrowing base* of about $50,000 (i.e., $120,000 – $70,000). This base might be drawn upon as collateral for a $50,000 loan to remodel the home, to purchase a second home, or for some other legitimate purpose.

Two main types of home equity loans are in use today. The first is the *traditional home equity loan,* which is a closed-end credit covering a specific period of months and years and is used mainly for home improvements. Traditional equity credits are normally repaid in equal installments, quarterly or monthly, and are most frequently secured by a second mortgage against the borrower's home.

Many lenders have recently seized upon the home equity loan opportunity by offering consumers a second and newer type of home equity loan—*lines of credit against their home's borrowing base*. They usually determine the credit limit on these home equity lines by taking a percentage of the appraised value of the borrowing customer's home (say, 75 percent) and subtracting the amount the customer still owes on the existing mortgage loan. That is:

Appraised value of home	$150,000
Times percentage allowed	×75%
Equals percentage of home's appraised value	$112,500
Minus balance still owed on home mortgage	−60,500
Equals maximum credit line available to customer	$ 52,000

The maximum loan amount allowed may be adjusted based on the customer's income and other debts incurred plus his or her past repayment record with other loans.

These credit lines can be used for any legitimate purpose, not just housing-related expenditures—for example, to purchase an automobile or finance a college education. Moreover, many of these credit lines are revolving credits, which means the customer can borrow up to the maximum amount of the loan, repay all or a portion of the amount borrowed, and borrow again up to the stipulated maximum amount any number of times until the credit line matures, which usually occurs at some point within 5 to 10 years. Because home equity–based credit tends to be longer term and more secure, it often carries a lower loan rate and longer payout period, thus reducing the borrower's installment payments below the required payments on more conventional consumer loans. Traditional home equity loans normally are priced using longer-term interest rates, while home equity credit lines often have interest rates tied closely to short-term rates, such as the yield on U.S. Treasury bills or the prime lending rate.

Demographically speaking, home equity borrowers tend to be more affluent than the average homeowner. They report higher levels of personal income and more equity in their homes. Home equity borrowers also tend to be older customers with a longer period of home ownership and a longer record of employment. Most home equity customers are in their late 40s or older; many are in retirement or near retirement and have substantially paid off their first home mortgage. Most equity loans are used to pay for home improvements, to repay old installment loans, to finance an education, to fund vacations, or to cover medical costs.

Loan officers need to exercise great care with home equity loan requests. For one thing, they rest on the assumption that housing prices will not decline significantly. Yet there is ample historical evidence that economic downturns and rising unemployment can flood local housing markets with homes for sale, rapidly depressing prices. While in most states a lender can repossess a home pledged as collateral for a loan, often the lending institution has difficulty selling the home for a price that recoups all its funds plus all the costs incurred in making and servicing the loan and in taking possession of the collateral. There is also room to question the wisdom of using an appreciating asset, such as a house, to purchase an asset not likely to appreciate, such as an automobile, furniture, and appliances. Loan officers must exercise care in granting such credit requests, lending only a portion (perhaps no more than 60 or 70 percent in riskier markets) of the home's estimated equity value in order to allow an adequate cushion should real estate markets turn down.

Moreover, strict regulations at the federal level, stemming from the Competitive Equality in Banking Act of 1987 and the Home Equity Loan Consumer Protection Act of 1988, require lenders to put an interest rate cap on how high loan rates can go on floating-rate home equity loans. Lenders must also provide their customers with information on all loan charges and significant risks under a required Truth in Lending Act disclosure statement. The consumer's overriding risk is that the lender would be forced to repossess his or her home. Not only does such an event destroy customer relationships and result in adverse publicity for the lending institution, but it may also saddle the lender with an asset that could be difficult to sell.

The Consumer Protection Act of 1988 prohibits a home equity lender from arbitrarily canceling a loan and demanding immediate payment. However, if the lender can show that the customer has committed fraud or misrepresentation, has failed to pay out the loan as promised, or has not kept up the value of the property involved, collection of the loan can be accelerated. The home equity loan customer, then, has little choice but to pay up or surrender the home that was pledged as collateral, unless protected in some way by law.

The Changing Environment for Consumer and Real Estate Lending

Powerful forces are reshaping the extension of credit to individuals and families today. For one thing, the population is *aging* rapidly in the United States, Japan, and other industrialized nations. As people grow older, they tend to make *less* use of credit and to pay down their outstanding debt obligations. This suggests that the total demand for consumer credit per capita eventually may fall, forcing consumer lenders to fight hard for profitable consumer loan accounts. Moreover, deregulation has brought more lenders into the consumer credit field. Financial institutions hoping to protect their revenues in this field will need to construct their fee schedules carefully.

A related trend in consumer lending—*point-of-sale loans*—also reflects changes going on in the population to whom lenders market their consumer credit services. More loan customers today demand speed and convenience in the lending process. Many consumers want credit available instantly when they are making purchases rather than having to drive to a bank or other lending institution to request a loan. Many lenders today are offering indirect loans through dealers in autos, home appliances, and other big-ticket items, so that the dealer prepares a credit agreement and phones or faxes the borrowing customer's information to the lender seeking quick approval. Other lending institutions are offering *preapproval credit programs* where the customer phones in or mails credit information to the lender and gets approval for a loan before a purchase is made. In this instance the store or dealer where the customer makes a purchase can simply verify with the lending institution that a loan has already been approved.

These newer approaches sharply reduce the need to enter a bank or other financial firm and result in more indirect lending at the point at which a sale is being made, rather than direct lending to the customer at the branch office of a bank or other lending institution. The result is lower transactions cost and greater convenience for the customer, but lenders must be alert to the added risks involved in making quick credit decisions and the possible loss of direct relationships with their customers.

Yet another controversial trend in consumer lending centers upon the recent explosion in personal bankruptcy filings inside the United States. During the past decade U.S. court filings for personal bankruptcy status have soared to well over a million a year under a widening array of options granted by federal and state laws (including Chapters 7, 11, and 13 of the federal bankruptcy code). In order to keep pace with this upsurge in personal bankruptcies, consumer lenders have had to become intimately acquainted with the provisions of federal and state bankruptcy codes. Unfortunately, bankruptcy laws present serious challenges to consumer lending institutions.

For example, a substantial proportion of household assets may be exempt from liquidation in order to help bankrupt individuals recover financially. A married couple may be able to shelter under federal bankruptcy protection up to $40,000 in such personal assets as the equity in a home, household furniture and appliances, a car, retirement accounts, and any equipment used in the debtor's job. A few states have passed statutes allowing even more assets to be sheltered from creditors, and federal law permits a debtor filing bankruptcy to switch to state bankruptcy rules where this change would be beneficial. Nearly a third of the states, however, have adopted more conservative rules that shelter fewer debtor assets than does federal law.

The federal bankruptcy code specifies the rules under which a troubled debtor's personal assets can be sold, with the proceeds allocated to the individual's creditors. The Bankruptcy Act directs the courts to approve a repayment plan that allows a debtor to gradually pay off his or her creditors, who may not repossess or foreclose on any of the debtor's assets as long as court-approved payments are being made. The results serve to make consumer lenders more cautious about borderline loan requests and encourage lenders to include higher-risk premiums in their consumer loan rates, which could price many lower-income borrowers out of the market for household credit.

Concept Check

17–14. What is home equity lending, and what are its advantages and disadvantages for banks and other consumer lending institutions?

17–15. How is the changing age structure of the population likely to affect consumer loan programs?

What other forces are reshaping household lending today?

17–16. What challenges have U.S. bankruptcy laws provided consumer lenders when it comes to liquidating the assets of defaulting borrowers?

Pricing Consumer and Real Estate Loans: Determining the Rate of Interest and Other Loan Terms

A financial institution prices every consumer loan by setting an interest rate, maturity, and terms of repayment that both the lender and customer find comfortable. While many consumer loans are short term, stretching over a few weeks or months, long-term loans to purchase automobiles, home appliances, and new homes may stretch from one or two years all the way out to 25 or 30 years. Indeed, in some cases, such as with automobile loans, consumer loan maturities have been extended in recent years as higher product prices have encouraged lenders to grant longer periods of loan repayment so that consumers can afford the monthly payments. A loan officer will usually work with a customer, proposing different loan maturities until a repayment schedule is found that, when taking into consideration the consumer's other debt obligations, fits both current and projected household income. Competition among consumer credit suppliers is also a powerful factor shaping consumer loan rates today. Where lenders face intense competition for loans, interest rates tend to be driven down closer to loan production costs.

The Interest Rate Attached to Nonresidential Consumer Loans

The Cost-Plus Model

Many consumer loans are priced off some base or cost rate, with a profit margin and compensation for risk added. For example, the rate on a consumer installment loan may be figured from the *cost-plus model:*

$$
\begin{array}{c}
\text{Loan rate} \\
\text{paid by the} \\
\text{consumer}
\end{array}
=
\begin{array}{c}
\text{Lender's cost} \\
\text{of raising} \\
\text{loanable} \\
\text{funds}
\end{array}
+
\begin{array}{c}
\text{Nonfunds operating} \\
\text{cost (including} \\
\text{wages and salaries} \\
\text{of lender personnel)}
\end{array}
$$

$$
+
\begin{array}{c}
\text{Premium for} \\
\text{risk of} \\
\text{customer} \\
\text{default}
\end{array}
+
\begin{array}{c}
\text{Premium for term} \\
\text{risk with a} \\
\text{longer-term loan}
\end{array}
+
\begin{array}{c}
\text{Desired} \\
\text{profit} \\
\text{margin}
\end{array}
$$

Lending institutions use a wide variety of methods to determine the actual loan rates they will offer to their customers. Among the most popular methods for calculating consumer loan rates are the annual percentage rate (or APR), the simple interest method, the discount rate, and the add-on rate method.

Annual Percentage Rate   Under the terms of the Truth-in-Lending Act, lenders must give the household borrower a statement specifying the **annual percentage rate (APR)** for a proposed loan. The APR is the internal rate of return (annualized) that equates expected total payments with the amount of the loan. It takes into account how fast the loan is being repaid and how much credit the customer will actually have use of during the life of the loan.

For example, suppose a consumer borrows $2,000 for a year, paying off the loan in 12 equal monthly installments, including $200 in interest cost. Each month the borrower makes a payment of $183.33 in principal and interest. The periodic interest rate may be found using a financial calculator or spreadsheet such as Excel and then annualized by multiplying it by the number of periods in one year in order to get the APR. You are looking for the periodic rate of return associated with 12 payments of $183.33 that have a present value (amount received at time of loan) of $2,000. The rate calculated is 1.4974 percent per month,[1] which equates to an APR of 17.97 percent (1.4974 × 12). APRs are easily determined using financial calculators and financial functions in spreadsheets that have been programmed with algorithms to solve the equations that lack explicit solutions. Before such advances in technology, the Federal Reserve System prepared rate tables for loan officers to use when the loan rate was calculated using another method, such as simple interest. Providing the APR allows borrowers to compare a particular loan rate with the loan rates offered by other lenders. Comparing loan rates encourages individuals to shop around for credit.

For another APR example, suppose that you, as the loan officer, quote your customer an APR of 12 percent on a one-year loan of $1,000 to be repaid monthly. The customer asks, *How much will I pay in finance charges under the terms of this loan?* To provide the answer to this question, you must determine the monthly payments for a 12-month (period) loan for $1,000 (present value) at a periodic rate of 1 percent (12%/12). Using a financial calculator or spreadsheet, you find that the monthly payment is $88.85.[2] The sum of all payments over the life of the loan is $1,066.20 (88.85 × 12) where $1,000 is the loan principal. The total finance charge to the customer is $1,066.20 − $1,000 = $66.20 over the life of the loan.

On the other hand, suppose the customer is told he or she must pay $260 in finance charges to get a $2,000 loan for 24 months. This means the consumer makes payments of

---

[1] Using a TI BAII plus financial calculator where N = 12, I/Y = ?, PV = 2,000, Pmt = − 188.33, and FV = 0, the periodic rate of return is 1.4974%.

[2] This is calculated using N = 12, I/Y = 1%, PV = 1,000, Pmt = ?, and FV = 0.

$94.17 (2,260/24). What APR is this customer being quoted? The periodic rate for 24 monthly payments of $94.17 with a present value of $2,000 is 1.002 percent.[3] The APR is the periodic rate annualized (1.002 × 12) or 12.02 percent. Clearly, this customer is being quoted a 12 percent annual percentage loan rate (APR).

Simple Interest   The **simple interest** approach, like the APR, also adjusts for the length of time a borrower actually has use of credit. If the customer is paying off a loan gradually, the simple interest approach determines the declining loan balance, and that reduced balance is then used to determine the amount of interest owed.

For example, suppose the customer asks for $2,000 for a year at a simple interest rate of 12 percent in order to purchase some furniture. If none of the principal of this loan is to be paid off until the year ends, the interest owed by the customer is as follows:

$$\text{Interest owed} = \text{Principal} \times \text{Rate} \times \text{Time}$$

or

$$I = \$2,000 \times 0.12 \times 1 = \$240$$

At maturity the customer will pay the bank $2,240, or $2,000 in principal plus $240 in interest.

Now assume instead that the loan principal is to be paid off in four quarterly installments of $500 each. The interest owed in each quarter will be as follows:

First quarter:	$I = \$2,000 \times 0.12 \times 1/4$
	$I = \$60$
Second quarter:	$I = \$1,500 \times 0.12 \times 1/4$
	$I = \$45$
Third quarter:	$I = \$1,000 \times 0.12 \times 1/4$
	$I = \$30$
Fourth quarter:	$I = \$500 \times 0.12 \times 1/4$
	$I = \$15$
Total interest owed:	$= \$60 + \$45 + \$30 + \$15$
	$= \$150$

Total payments due are as follows:

First quarter:	$\$500 + \$60 = \$560$
Second quarter:	$\$500 + \$45 = \$545$
Third quarter:	$\$500 + \$30 = \$530$
Fourth quarter:	$\underline{\$500 + \$15 = \$515}$
Total payments due:	$\$2,000 + \$150 = \$2,150$

Clearly, with simple interest the customer saves on interest as the loan approaches maturity.

The Discount Rate Method   While most consumer loans allow the customer to pay off the interest owed, as well as the principal, gradually over the life of a loan, the **discount rate method** requires the customer to pay interest up front. Under this approach, interest is deducted *first*, and the customer receives the loan amount *less* any interest owed.

For example, suppose the loan officer offers a consumer $2,000 at a 12 percent loan rate. The $240 in interest ($2,000 × 0.12) is deducted from the loan principal; the borrower receives as a deposit available for spending $2,000 minus $240, or $1,760. When the

---

[3] 1.002 percent is obtained using N = 24, I/Y = ?, PV = −2,000, Pmt = 94.17, and FV = 0.

Insights and Issues

loan matures, however, the customer must pay back the full $2,000. The borrower's effective loan rate is

$$\frac{\text{Discount}}{\text{loan rate}} = \frac{\text{Interest owed}}{\text{Net amount of credit received}} = \frac{\$240}{\$1,760} = 0.136, \text{ or } 13.6 \text{ percent}$$

The Add-On Loan Rate Method One of the oldest loan rate calculation methods is known simply as the **add-on method** because any interest owed is added to the principal amount of the loan before the customer is told what the required installment payments will be. For example, if the customer requests $2,000 and is offered a 12 percent add-on interest rate and a repayment plan of 12 equal monthly installments, the total payments due will be $2,000 in principal plus $240 in interest, or $2,240. Each monthly payment will be $186.67 ($2,240 ÷ 12), consisting of $166.67 in loan principal and $20 in monthly interest. Because the borrower has only about $1,000, on average, available during the year, the effective loan rate is approximately two times 12 percent or 24 percent. Only if the loan is paid off in a single lump sum at the end will the add-on rate equal the simple interest rate. Otherwise, the consumer is paying a higher effective loan rate than he or she is being quoted.

Rule of 78s   A rule of thumb used to determine how much interest income a lender is entitled to accrue at any point in time from a loan that is being paid out in monthly installments is known as the **Rule of 78s.** This is particularly important when a borrower pays off a loan early and may, therefore, be entitled to a rebate of some of the interest charges associated with the loan. The rule of 78s arises from the fact that the sum of the digits 1 through 12 is 78 (that is $1 + 2 + 3 + . . . + 10 + 11 + 12 = 78$). To determine the borrowing customer's interest rebate from early repayment of an installment loan, total the digits for the months remaining on the loan and divide that sum by 78. For example, suppose a consumer requests a one-year loan to be repaid in 12 monthly installments, but is able to repay the loan after only nine months. This customer would be entitled to receive back as an interest rebate

$$\frac{1 + 2 + 3}{1 + 2 + \cdots + 11 + 12} \times 100 = \frac{6}{78} \times 100 = 7.69 \text{ percent}$$

of the total finance charges on the loan. The lender is entitled to keep 92.31 percent of those finance charges in this example.

Use of Variable Rates on Consumer Loans

Many installment and lump-sum payment loans to families and individuals are made with fixed interest rates rather than with floating rates that change with credit market conditions. However, due to the volatility of interest rates a greater number of floating-rate consumer loans have appeared in recent years. When floating-rate consumer loans are issued, their contract rates are often tied to the prime (commercial) loan rate, to U.S. Treasury bill rates, or to other published interest rates in what is often called *base rate* pricing.

For example, in January 2003 the majority of the largest U.S. banks were quoting a prime lending rate of 4.25 percent. A consumer borrowing to finance a vacation or to repay some medical bills might be quoted an initial loan rate of:

$$\begin{matrix} \text{Floating} \\ \text{prime-based} \\ \text{consumer} \\ \text{loan rate} \end{matrix} = \begin{matrix} \text{Prime} \\ \text{or base} + \\ \text{rate} \end{matrix} \begin{matrix} \text{Risk} \\ \text{premium} \end{matrix} = \begin{matrix} 4.25 \\ \text{percent} \end{matrix} + \begin{matrix} 3 \\ \text{percent} \end{matrix} = \begin{matrix} 7.25 \\ \text{percent} \end{matrix}$$

Concept Check

17–17. What options does a loan officer have in pricing consumer loans?

17–18. Suppose a customer is offered a loan at a discount rate of 8 percent and pays $75 in interest at the beginning of the term of the loan. What net amount of credit did this customer receive? Suppose you are told that the effective rate on this loan is 12 percent. What is the average loan amount the customer has available during the year?

17–19. See if you can determine what APR you are charging a consumer loan customer if you grant the customer a loan for five years, payable in monthly installments, and the customer must pay a finance charge of $42.74 per $100.

17–20. If you quote a consumer loan customer an APR of 16 percent on a $10,000 loan with a term of four years that requires monthly installment payments, what finance charge must this customer pay?

CONSUMER LOAN RATES: RECENT SURVEYS AND WHAT THEY REVEAL

Recently the Federal Reserve Board began surveying banks and finance companies for the loan rates they quote (as well as for selected other loan terms, such as maturity, loan-to-value ratios, and the average amount financed) for automobile loans and for personal credit. An example of the recent loan terms quoted on these different loan types is shown below.

Terms on Popular Consumer Loans
(Data for February 2003)

Type of Loan and Lending Institution	Average Annual Loan Rate (in percent)	Type or Characteristic of Loan	Survey Average Values
Commercial banks:		Average maturity of loans in months:	
48-month new car loan	7.11%	New car loans	59.2 mo.
24-month personal loan	11.62	Used car loans	57.7 mo.
Credit cards:		Loan-to-value ratios:	
All accounts	13.20	New car loans	97.0%
Accounts assessed interest	12.85	Used car loans	99.0
Auto finance companies:		Amount financed in dollars:	
New car loans	3.99	New car loans	$24,864
Used car loans	10.43	Used car loans	14,231

Source: Survey by the Board of Governors of the Federal Reserve System.

Surveying the table above reveals some interesting associations between consumer loan rates and other features of a consumer loan, such as maturity, cost, and risk. We notice, for example, that credit card loans, which are among the riskiest in terms of both loan default and losses due to fraud, tend to carry the highest average interest rates. Automobile loans are generally cheaper than personal loans (even though the latter tend to have shorter maturities) because auto loans are secured by marketable collateral—the automobile itself—whereas many personal loans are either unsecured by any specific collateral or have collateral pledged that is more difficult to sell.

We note also that new car loan rates tend to be lower than used car loan rates. The newer the vehicle, the easier it generally is to sell should the borrower be unable to repay, and lenders find that new car owners tend to take better care of their vehicles. Moreover, used cars have been rising rapidly in price due to heavier demand. Moreover, car rental companies have tended to keep their fleets for longer periods, so the supply of used cars from this traditional source has diminished. As a result, many used car loans are now extended for maturities that equal or exceed new car loan maturities, and lenders have been willing to extend a larger percentage of a used car's purchase price in the form of a loan.

Overall, there is evidence that consumers have recently become much more sensitive to differences in loan rates on different types of loans offered by different lending institutions. Indeed, even the smallest consumer borrowers with little financial education are now increasingly shopping around and learning to refinance everything from automobile, mobile home, and home mortgage loans to credit card obligations. The result is narrower spreads on consumer loans and greater consolidation among consumer lending institutions.

If the prime rate subsequently moves upward to 6 percent, then the consumer's new loan rate would be

$$\frac{\text{Floating prime-based}}{\text{consumer loan rate}} = 6 \text{ percent } + 3 \text{ percent } = 9 \text{ percent}$$

Quite obviously, if the lending institution controls the base rate itself, the lender could change the base and the loan rate itself anytime it wishes. Because this could be grossly unfair to borrowers, most regulatory agencies insist that the base rate being used *not* be under the lender's direct control. In the previous example, the prime rate quoted in *The Wall Street Journal* and other widely read financial news sheets is based on an average of top-quality loan rates quoted by at least 75 percent of the 30 largest banks in the United States. Thus, it would be difficult for any one lender to arbitrarily reset its prime rate irrespective of market conditions simply to jack up the loan rates paid by its customers.

Interest Rates on Home Mortgage Loans

For nearly half a century, stretching from the Great Depression of the 1930s into the 1970s, most loans to finance the purchase of new homes were **fixed-rate mortgages (FRMs)**—that is, they carried fixed terms, especially a *fixed interest rate* that the borrower could rely upon. In the early 1970s, the pressure of inflation and more volatile interest rates gave rise to adjustable-rate home mortgage loans. Then in 1981, both the Comptroller of the Currency and the Federal Home Loan Bank Board authorized the offering of **adjustable-rate mortgages (ARMs)** for all U.S. federally chartered depository institutions.

The popularity of ARMs may be attributed to aggressive marketing of these loans by lenders seeking to make the yields on their earning assets more responsive to market interest rate movements. Many lending institutions have offered teaser rates that are significantly below loan rates on FRMs. Because ARMs often carry lower initial interest rates than traditional fixed-rate mortgages, they allow more individuals and families to qualify for a home mortgage loan. Some home mortgage lenders have offered *cap rates* on ARMs. For example, the lender may agree not to raise the loan rate more than two percentage points in any given year or more than five percentage points over the life of the loan, no matter how high other interest rates in the economy go.

Whether a customer takes out an FRM or an ARM, the loan officer must determine what the initial loan rate will be and, therefore, what the monthly payments will be. Each monthly payment on a home mortgage loan reduces a portion of the principal of the loan and a portion of the interest owed on the total amount borrowed. With the majority of mortgage loan contracts today, monthly payments early in the life of the loan go mainly to pay interest. As the loan gets closer to maturity, the monthly payments increasingly are devoted to reducing the loan's outstanding principal.

Loan officers and customers may determine if a mortgage loan is affordable by figuring the required monthly payment given the interest rate the mortgage lender will charge. Such problems are applications of the time value of money that would usually be calculated using a financial calculator or spreadsheet. The formula for monthly payments is as follows:

$$\text{Customer's monthly mortgage payment} = \frac{\text{Amount of loan principal} \times \left(\dfrac{\text{Annual loan rate}}{12}\right) \times \left(1 + \dfrac{\text{Annual loan rate}}{12}\right)^{t \times 12}}{\left[\left(1 + \dfrac{\text{Annual loan rate}}{12}\right)^{t \times 12} - 1\right]}$$

The required monthly payment for a \$50,000, 25-year mortgage loan calculated at the fixed rate of 12 percent is \$526.61.[4] The total in payments over the life of the loan is

---

[4] Using a financial calculator (TI Ball Plus), N = 25 × 12, I = 12%/12, PV = −50,000, PMT = ?, and FV = 0.

$526.61 \times 25 \times 12 = \$157,983$. If you subtract the $50,000 in principal, you will find that the borrower will pay $107,983 in interest over the life of the loan. The actual monthly payment on the loan just described normally will vary somewhat from year to year even with an FRM due to changes in property taxes, dwelling insurance, and other fees that typically are included in each monthly installment payment on a home mortgage.

In the foregoing example we calculated the required monthly payments on a fixed-rate mortgage. We can, of course, use the same method to calculate the required monthly payment on an adjustable rate mortgage loan by simply plugging in a new interest rate each time that interest rates change. For example, assume that, as in the previous FRM example, the initial loan rate for an ARM is also 12 percent. However, after one year (i.e., 12 monthly payments) has elapsed, the mortgage loan rate rises to 13 percent. In this case the customer's monthly payments would increase to $563.30:[5]

$$
\begin{matrix} \text{Each} \\ \text{monthly} \\ \text{payment} \end{matrix} = \frac{\$49,662.30 \times \left(\dfrac{0.13}{12}\right) \times \left(1 + \dfrac{0.13}{12}\right)^{24 \times 12}}{\left(1 + \dfrac{0.13}{12}\right)^{24 \times 12} - 1} = \$563.30
$$

The above example assumes that the loan rate increased to 13 percent beginning with the 13th monthly payment. Note that after one year the principal of the loan (which originally stood at $50,000) had dropped to $49,662.30 due to the monthly payments made during the first 12 months of the loan.[6] When considering whether or not to approve a customer's request for an adjustable-rate loan, the loan officer must decide whether a rise in interest rates is likely and whether the customer has sufficient budget flexibility and future earnings potential to handle the varying loan payments than can exist with an adjustable-rate loan.

Charging the Customer Mortgage Points   Home mortgage loan agreements often require borrowers to pay an additional charge up front called **points.** This extra charge is determined by multiplying the amount of the home mortgage loan by a specific percentage figure. For example, suppose the borrower seeks a $100,000 home loan and the lender assesses the borrower an up-front charge of two points. In this case the home buyer's extra charge would be

$$
\begin{matrix} \text{Dollar amount} \\ \text{of points} \\ \text{charged on} \\ \text{a home} \\ \text{mortgage} \\ \text{loan} \end{matrix} = \begin{matrix} \text{Amount} \\ \text{of the} \\ \text{mortgage} \\ \text{loan} \end{matrix} \times \begin{matrix} \text{Number} \\ \text{of points} \\ \text{charged} \\ \text{by the} \\ \text{lender} \end{matrix} = \$100,000 \times 0.02 = \$2,000
$$

By requiring the borrower to pay something extra over and above the interest owed on his or her home loan, a lender can earn a higher effective interest rate on a loan than just the loan rate itself. This extra yield can be found by deducting from the amount of the mortgage loan the dollar amount of points charged and by adding the dollar amount of points to the interest owed on the loan. In this instance we would argue that the borrower has available for his or her use, not the full amount of the mortgage loan, but rather the loan amount *less* the points assessed by the lending institution.

---

[5] Using the financial calculator once again, N = 24 × 12, I = 13%/12, PV = 49,662.30, PMT = ?, and FV = 0.

[6] The $49,662.30 is calculated using N = 24 × 12, I = 12%/12, PV = ?, PMT = 526.61, and FV = 0.

For example, suppose a borrower is assessed two points on a 20-year home mortgage loan amounting to $100,000 and bearing an interest rate of 7 percent. Deducting the $2,000 in points (or $100,000 × 0.02) from the $100,000 loan amount tells us that the borrower has only $98,000 in credit available. This raises the borrower's effective interest rate from 7 percent to about 7.26 percent and thereby generates a higher effective yield for the lender.

Home Mortgage Refinancings and the Impact of Record Low Loan Rates

The high sensitivity of the home mortgage market to changing loan rates was amply demonstrated as the 21st century opened. Mortgage loan rates in the United States plunged to 40-year lows, pushed downward by a weakened economy. In 2001 alone approximately 7 million homes were refinanced, resulting in $1.2 trillion in new home mortgage debt.

Of course, low home loan interest rates were not the only factor fueling this recent upsurge in individual and family borrowing. Most of the home loans carried tax-deductible interest expenses not available through other types of loans. Many households also took advantage of the record low interest rates to convert longer-term home mortgage loans into shorter-term loans, hoping to save thousands of dollars in interest cost over the life of their mortgage borrowings. Indeed, 15-year home mortgage loans rose to a volume roughly two or three times that of 30-year home mortgage lending during the refinancing boom that opened the 21st century.

Concept Check

17–21. What differences exist between ARMs and FRMs?

17–22. How is the loan rate figured on a home mortgage loan? What are the key factors or variables?

17–23. What are *points?* What is their function?

17–24. Why did home mortgage real estate loans soar to record levels as the 21st century opened?

Summary

Lending to consumers and the making of real estate loans have been among the most popular financial services offered by bankers and their financial-service competitors in recent years. Among the most important points discussed in this chapter are the following:

- Loans and other financial services extended to households represent one of the most important sources of financial-service revenues and deposits today as banks, credit unions, savings associations, and finance companies all compete aggressively for the consumer's account.

- Consumer credit represents an important supplement to business credit services, providing financial institutions with a more diversified customer base and helping to reduce the exposure of lenders to the impact of business cycles when revenues expand and contract over periods of months or years.

- Consumer and real-estate-centered lending presents special challenges to loan officers due to higher-than-average default rates related to the vulnerability of individuals and families to loss of employment, illness, divorce and other adverse circumstances.

- The keys to successful consumer and real estate lending today center on the ability to process large volumes of credit requests quickly so the household borrower receives a fast decision from the lender. Automation has become a powerful force with the use of *credit-scoring systems* to mathematically evaluate each household's credit capacity and credit bureaus that give lenders quick access to consumer credit histories.

- Loans and other financial services sold to households have increasingly been shaped by federal and state regulations designed to promote (*a*) fuller disclosure of prices and other contract terms and (*b*) greater fairness in the marketplace, outlawing discrimination on the basis of race, sex, religion, and other irrelevant factors. These laws and regulations serve to promote competition, encourage households to shop for credit, and, hopefully at least, lead to more informed household decision making.

- Real estate loans are most often directed at households seeking places to live, including single-family homes and other dwellings. Real estate credit provides the financial resources to support the construction of homes, condominiums, apartments, shopping centers, office buildings, and other forms of real property. Banks and many of their competitors make both short-term mortgage credit (usually in the form of construction loans) and long-term mortgages available to businesses and households. Officers and staff of real estate lending institutions must have multiple skills in assessing property values, real estate law, and the regulations that surround this field. More than any other type of loan, real-estate lending depends heavily on judging the value and outlook for a loan's collateral.

- Pricing consumer and real estate loans is challenging as several different loan pricing techniques have emerged. With so many different methods available for calculating loan interest rates and other credit terms, confusion abounded for lenders and customers until the Truth in Lending Act was passed in the United States, requiring the lender to disclose the *APR* (annual percentage rate) that applies to a customer's loan, yielding a common standard for customers to compare one proposed loan against another.

- A trend today is toward more *market-sensitive loan rates* in this field in order to reduce interest-rate risk on the part of consumer and real estate lenders, particularly in the latter field where fixed-rate and adjustable-rate mortgage loans compete against each other for the customer's allegiance. In the case of adjustable-rate credit, loan officers must be especially careful in deciding whether a borrowing customer has sufficient budgetary flexibility to be able to adjust to variable loan payments, especially if interest rates are expected to rise during the life of a loan.

Key Terms

www.mhhe.com/rose6e

Problems and Projects

1. The Childress family has applied for a $5,000 loan for home improvements, especially to install a new roof and add new carpeting. Bob Childress is a welder at Ford Motor Co., the first year he has held that job, and his wife sells clothing at Wal-Mart. They have three children. The Childresses own their home, which they purchased six months ago, and have an *average* credit rating, with some late bill payments. They have a telephone, but hold only a checking account with a bank and a few bonds. Mr. Childress has a $35,000 life insurance policy with a cash surrender value of $1,100. Suppose the lender uses the credit scoring system presented in this chapter and denies all credit applications scoring fewer than 360 points. Is the Childress family likely to get the loan?

2. Mr. and Mrs. Napper are interested in funding their children's college education by taking out a home equity loan in the amount of about $24,000. Eldridge National Bank is willing to extend a loan, using the Nappers' home as collateral. Their home has been appraised at $110,000, and Eldridge has a policy of allowing a customer to use no more than 70 percent of the appraised value of a home as a borrowing base. The Nappers still owe $60,000 on the first mortgage against their home. Is there enough residual value left in the Nappers' home to support their loan request? How could the lender help them meet their credit needs?

3. Arthur Renfro has just been informed by a finance company that he can access a line of credit of no more than $28,000 based upon the equity value in his home. Renfro still owes $30,500 on a first mortgage against his home and $11,500 on a second mortgage claim against the home, which was incurred last year to repair the roof and driveway. If the appraised value of Renfro's residence is $95,000, what percentage of the home's estimated market value is the lender using to determine Renfro's maximum available line of credit?

4. Which federal law or laws applies to each of the situations described below?

   a. A loan officer asks an individual requesting a loan about her race.

   b. A bill collector called Jim Jones three times yesterday at his work number without first asking permission.

   c. Sixton National Bank has developed a special form to tell its customers the finance charges they must pay to secure a loan.

   d. Consumer Savings Bank has just received an outstanding rating from federal examiners for its efforts to serve all segments of its trade territory.

   e. Presage State Bank must disclose once a year the areas in the local community where it has made home mortgage and home improvement loans.

   f. Reliance Credit Card Company is contacted by one of its customers in a dispute over the amount of charges the customer made at a local department store that accepts the company's credit cards.

   g. Amy Imed, after requesting a copy of her credit bureau report, discovers several errors in the report and demands a correction.

5. James Smithern has asked for a $3,500 loan from Beard Center National Bank to repay some personal expenses. The bank uses a credit-scoring system to evaluate such requests, which contains the following discriminating factors along with their associated point weights in parentheses:

   Credit Rating (excellent, 3; average, 2; poor or no record, 0)
   Time in Current Job (five years or more, 6; one to five years, 3)
   Time at Current Residence (more than 2 years, 4; one to two years, 2; less than one year, 1)

Telephone in Residence (yes, 1; no, 0)
Holds Account at Bank (yes, 2; no, 0).

The bank generally grants a loan if a customer scores 9 or more points. Mr. Smithern has an average credit rating, has been in his current job for three years and at his current residence for two years, has a telephone, but has no account at the bank. Is James Smithern likely to receive the loan he has requested?

6. Singleton Savings Bank, in reviewing its credit card customers, finds that of those customers who scored 40 points or less on its credit-scoring system, 35 percent (or a total of 10,615 credit customers) turned out to be delinquent credits, resulting in a total loss. This group of bad credit card loans averaged $1,200 in size per customer account. Examining its successful credit accounts Singleton finds that 12 percent of its good customers (or a total of 3,640 customers) scored 40 points or less on the bank's scoring system. These low-scoring but good accounts generated about $1,500 in revenues each. If Singleton's credit card division follows the decision rule of granting credit cards only to those customers scoring more than 40 points and future credit accounts generate about the same average revenues and losses, about how much can the bank expect to save in net losses?

7. The T. Williams family purchased its three-bedroom home for $97,000 on the outskirts of San Francisco 10 years ago. The initial mortgage loan on the house was for $70,500, but has now been paid down to $53,800. Currently, comparable homes in the same neighborhood are selling on the market for about $185,000. What is the family's *borrowing base* that might be drawn upon as collateral for a home equity loan?

   Suppose a lender proposes to offer a credit line based upon two-thirds of the home's current appraised value. What is the maximum credit line the lender will make available to the Williams family?

8. The Vaud family needs some extra funds to put their two children through college starting this coming fall and to buy a new computer system for a part-time home business. They are not sure of the current market value of their home, though comparable four-bedroom homes are selling for about $210,000 in the neighborhood. The Van Nuys Federal and Merchants Savings Association will loan 80 percent of the property's appraised value, but the Vauds still owe $142,000 on their home mortgage and a home improvement loan combined. What maximum amount of credit is available to this family should it elect to seek a home equity credit line?

9. San Carlos Bank and Trust Company uses a credit-scoring system to evaluate most consumer loans that amount to more than $2,500. The key factors used in its scoring system are as follows:

Borrower's length of employment in his/her present job:		Credit bureau report:	
More than one year	6 points	Excellent	8 points
Less than one year	3 points	Average	5 points
Borrower's length of time at current address:		Below average or no record	2 points
More than 2 years	8 points	Credit cards currently active:	
One to two years	4 points	One card	6 points
Less than one year	2 points	Two cards	4 points
Borrower's current home situation:		More than two cards	2 points
Owns home	7 points	Deposit account(s) with bank:	
Rents home or apartment	4 points	Yes	5 points
Lives with friend or relative	2 points	No	2 points

The Mulvaney family has two wage earners who have held their present jobs for 18 months. They have lived at their current street address for one year, where they rent on a six-month lease. Their credit report is excellent but shows only one previous charge. However, they are actively using two credit cards right now to help with household expenses. Yesterday, they opened an account at San Carlos and deposited $250. The Mulvaneys have asked for a $4,500 loan to purchase a used car and some furniture. The bank has a cutoff score in its scoring system of 30 points. Would you make this loan for two years, as they have requested? Are there factors not included in the scoring system that you would like to know more about? Please explain.

10. William Crenshaw has asked for a personal loan of $4,500. Crenshaw wants to keep the principal of the loan for a full year and pay the interest at that time. However, the credit union reviewing this loan application insists on monthly amortization of the loan, with a 13 percent annual interest rate. Under these terms, how much interest will Crenshaw pay in a year? How much interest would he have paid if he had gotten the loan on his preferred terms?

11. Frank Petrel wants to start his own business, an auto repair shop. He has asked his bank for a $10,000 new-venture loan. The bank has a policy of making *discount-rate* loans in these cases if the venture looks good, but at an interest rate of prime plus 2. (The prime rate is currently posted at 12.5 percent.) If Mr. Petrel's loan is approved for the full amount requested, what net proceeds will he have to work with from this loan? What is the effective interest rate on this loan for one year?

12. The Robbins family has asked for a 20-year mortgage in the amount of $60,000 to purchase a home. At a 10 percent loan rate, what is the required monthly payment?

13. James Alters received a $1,500 loan last month with the intention of repaying the loan in 12 months. However, Alters now discovers he has the cash to repay the loan right now after making just one payment. What percentage of the total finance charge is Alters entitled to receive as a rebate and what percentage of the loan's finance charge is the lender entitled to keep?

14. Constance Homer is planning to start a small business and has asked Slidell Corners State Bank for a $10,000 loan. The bank agrees to Ms. Homer's business proposal and indicates it will give Constance $9,400 when the loan begins and collect $600 in interest up front. What is the effective interest rate on this loan?

15. The Lindal family has been planning a vacation to Europe for the past two years. Stilwater Savings Association agrees to advance a loan of $2,500 to finance the trip provided the Lindals pay the loan back in 12 equal monthly installments during the current year. Stilwater will charge an add-on loan rate of 12 percent. How much in interest will the Lindals pay under the add-on rate method? What is the amount of each required monthly payment? What is the effective loan rate in this case?

16. Joseph Nework's request for a three-year automobile loan for $10,000 has been approved. Reston Center Bank will require equal monthly installment payments for 36 months until the loan is fully retired. The bank tells Joseph that he must pay a total of $2,217 in finance charges to receive this loan. What is the loan's APR?

17. Kyle Ellisor has asked for a 30-year mortgage to purchase a home on Long Island. The purchase price is $260,000, of which Ellisor must borrow $225,000 to be repaid in monthly installments. If Kyle can get this loan for an APR of 14 percent, how much in total finance charges must he pay?

18. Mary Perland is offered a $1,200 loan for a year to be paid back in equal quarterly installments of $300 each. If Mary is offered the loan at 8 percent simple interest, how much in total interest charges will she pay? Would Mary be better off (in terms of lower interest cost) if she were offered the $1,200 at 6 percent simple interest with

only one principal payment when the loan reaches maturity? What advantage would this second set of loan terms have over the first set of loan terms?

19. Bill and Sue Rogers are negotiating with their local bank to secure a mortgage loan in order to buy their first home. With only a limited down payment available to them, Bill and Sue must borrow $80,000. Moreover, the bank has assessed them one and a half points on the loan. What is the dollar amount of points they must pay to receive this loan? How much home mortgage credit will they actually have available for their use?

20. Dresden Bank's personal loan department quotes Mr. Angelo a finance charge of $6.06 for each $100 in credit the bank is willing to extend to him for a year (assuming the balance of the loan is to be paid off in 12 equal installments). What APR is the bank quoting Mr. Angelo? How much would he save per $100 borrowed if he could retire the loan in six months?

Internet Exercises

1. What is credit scoring? Visit **www.fairisaac.com** and look for an article by Jed Graham entitled, "Fair, Isaac Makes More Use of Its Analytical Minds." You will find it as an article listed under News. Describe this IT company's role in credit scoring.

2. How does the Web help a consumer loan officer determine a customer's credit rating and credit history? For an example, go to **www.experian.com** and see Business Services. What products and services does this firm have to offer the banker?

3. Go to **nt.mortgage101.com/partner-scripts/1038.asp** to find the meaning of such real estate lending terms as *adjustable-rate mortgage*, *points*, and *home equity credit*. Provide the definition for each of the above terms.

4. What methods and tools are available on the Web to aid in pricing consumer loans and real estate credit? See, for example, **www.financialpowertools.com**. Use the auto loan calculator to calculate the monthly payments on a 48-month car loan given that the purchase price is $23,000; the down payment is $1,200; the trade-in value of the customer's current vehicle is $5,000, but $4,000 is still owed; nontaxable fees are $40.00, sales tax is 7 percent, and the interest rate is 5 percent.

5. Why is regulation so important in the personal loan area? For some insights regarding this issue, visit **www.hud.gov** and **www.ffiec.gov**. At **www.hud.gov/groups/lenders .cfm** find the meaning of and concerns associated with *predatory lending*. At **www .ffiec.gov** determine the purpose of the Home Mortgage Disclosure Act (HMDA).

S&P Market Insight Challenge

**STANDARD
&POOR'S**

1. Use Standard & Poor's Market Insight website (**www.mhhe.com/edumarketinsight**) for this problem. Savings and loan associations have focused on home mortgage loans since their inception. For an up-to-date view of S&Ls' share of today's mortgage origination market, click the Industry tab in S&P's Market Insight. A drop-down menu reveals the subindustry category Thrifts & Mortgage Finance. By choosing this category you will be able to access the S&P Industry Survey on Savings and Loans. Please download this particular survey and explore the section entitled "Industry Trend." What is happening to the thrifts' share of mortgage originations? Can you explain why?

2. Use Standard & Poor's Market Insight website (**www.mmhe.com/edumarketinsight**) for this problem. Who are the leading lending institutions in making credit available to consumers (individuals and families)? S&P's Market Insight contains a significant number of major household lenders, including Household International, Capital One Financial, and Bank of America. See if you can determine the ratio of consumer loans to total loans for each of these institutions and other leading household lenders on the Insight list. Why do the consumer loan to total loan ratios differ so much among these institutions? Do they also differ in the kinds of consumer loans they make? Why? What forms of risk does consumer lending present to these particular institutions?

REAL NUMBERS FOR REAL BANKS   Assignment for Chapter 17

YOUR BANK'S PROVISION OF CREDIT TO INDIVIDUALS AND FAMILIES

Chapter 17 explores consumer loans, credit cards, and real estate lending. In this assignment we look at how regulators categorize loans to individuals and families. We will use this information to evaluate the changing composition of your bank's retail loan portfolio across years and relative to other large banks.

Trend and Comparative Analysis

A. **Data Collection:** In the assignment for Chapter 15, we did a breakdown of gross loans and leases based on purpose.

Retail loans were allocated to either the real estate loan category or to the loans to individuals category. In this assignment we will go back to the SDI at **www3.fdic .gov/sdi/main.asp** and collect more detailed information on these loans. This entails using SDI to create a four-column report of your bank's information and peer group information across years. For Report Selection, you will access the Net Loans and Leases and 1–4 Family Residential Net Loans and Leases reports to collect percentage information as detailed below. Enter this data into Spreadsheet 2 as follows:

Loans to Individuals and Families (A158)	Your Bank	Peer Group	Your Bank	Peer Group
Date (A159)	12/31/yy	12/31/yy	12/31/yy	12/31/yy
Multifamily residential real estate (A160)	%	%	%	%
1–4 family residential loans: Secured by first liens (A161)				
1–4 family residential loans: Secured by junior liens (A162)				
1–4 family residential loans: Home equity loans (A163)				
Credit cards and related plans** (A164)				
Other loans to individuals (A165)				

**Note: On this line we have summed the two individual items of credit cards and related plans.

B. Use the chart function in Excel and the data by columns in rows 160 through 165 to create four pie charts illustrating the break-down of loans to individuals and families. Your pie charts should include titles and labels. For instance, the following is a pie chart for National City Corp (NCC) for 12/31/02:

Loans to Individuals and Families (NCC 12-31-02)

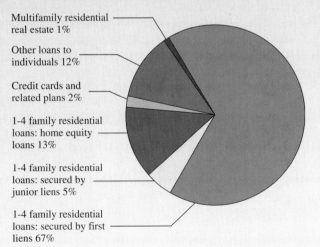

Multifamily residential real estate 1%

Other loans to individuals 12%

Credit cards and related plans 2%

1-4 family residential loans: home equity loans 13%

1-4 family residential loans: secured by junior liens 5%

1-4 family residential loans: secured by first liens 67%

C. Write approximately one page about the types of loans your bank makes to individuals and families. Has the composition changed across time? How does the composition of your bank's retail loan portfolio compare to other very large banks (your peer group)? Can you make any inferences concerning credit risk and/or interest rate risk exposure? Use your pie charts as graphics and incorporate them in the discussion. The above pie chart was inserted using a text box and then copying the Excel spreadsheet into the text box.

Selected References

For an analysis of the risks in consumer lending, see the following:

1. Aizcorbe, Ana M.; Arthur B. Kennickell; and Kevin B. Moore. "Recent Changes in U.S. Family Finances: Evidence from the 1998 and 2001 Survey of Consumer Finances." *Federal Reserve Bulletin*, January 2003, pp. 1–32.

2. Canner, Glenn B., and Charles A. Luckett. "Home Equity Lending." *Federal Reserve Bulletin*, May 1989, pp. 333–44.

See the following studies for further discussion of real estate lending procedures and practices:

3. Comptroller of the Currency, Federal Deposit Insurance Corporation, Board of Governors of the Federal Reserve System, and Office of Thrift Supervision. "Interagency Advisory on Mortgage Banking." Press release, February 25, 2003.

4. Noon, H. Richard. "Residential Mortgage Lending and Mortgage Loan Warehousing." In *The Bankers' Handbook*, 3rd ed. Homewood, IL.: Richard D. Irwin, 1989.

5. Reavis, Charles G., Jr. "Lending on Income Property." In *The Bankers' Handbook*, 3rd ed. Homewood, IL.: Richard D. Irwin, 1989.

For an overview of consumer credit laws and their impact, see the following:

6. Day, George S., and William K. Brandt. "Consumer Research and the Evaluation of Information Disclosure Requirements: The Case of Truth in Lending." *Journal of Consumer Research*, June 1974, pp. 21–32.

7. Rose, Peter S. "The Performance of Outstanding CRA-Rated Banks." *Bankers Magazine*, September/October 1994, pp. 53–59.

For a discussion of the role of technology in modern consumer lending, see these sources:

8. Avery, Robert B.; Raphael W. Bostic; Paul S. Calem; and Glenn B. Canner. "Credit Risk, Credit Scoring, and the Performance of Home Mortgages." *Federal Reserve Bulletin*, July 1996, pp. 621–48.

9. Bruene, Jim. "Online Profitability: Just a Credit Application Away?" *The Journal of Lending and Credit Risk Management*, June 1997, pp. 52–63.

10. Canner, Glenn B.; Thomas A. Durkin; and Charles A. Luckett. "Recent Developments in Home Equity Lending." *Federal Reserve Bulletin*, April 1998, pp. 241–51.

11. Henson, Andrea; Wayne Passmore; and Roger Sparks. "Credit Scoring and Mortgage Securitization: Do They Lower Mortgage Rates?" *Finance and Economics Discussion Series* 2000–44, Board of Governors of the Federal Reserve System, 2.11, 2000.

12. Mester, Loretta J. "What's the Point of Credit Scoring?" *Business Review*, Federal Reserve Bank of Philadelphia, September/October 1997, pp. 3–16.

To learn more about credit bureaus and their services, see the following:

13. Avery, Robert B.; Paul S. Calem; and Glenn B. Canner. "An Overview of Consumer Data and Credit Reporting." *Federal Reserve Bulletin*, February 2003, pp. 48–73.

14. Federal Deposit Insurance Corporation. "Credit History 101: The ABCs of Credit Reporting and Credit Scores." *Consumer News*, Winter 2002–2003.

For discussions of the pricing and calculation of consumer loan rates, see the following:

15. Avery, Robert B.; Raphael W. Bostic; and Glenn B. Canner. "CRA Special Lending Programs." *Federal Reserve Bulletin,* November 2000, pp. 711–31.

16. ———. "The Performance and Profitability of CRA-Related Lending." *Economic Commentary,* Federal Reserve Bank of Cleveland, November 2000.

17. Henson, Andrea; Wayne Passmore; and Roger Sparks. "Credit Scoring and Mortgage Securitization: Do They Lower Mortgage Rates?" *Finance and Economics Discussion Series* 2000–44, Board of Governors of the Federal Reserve System, 2.11, 2000.

PART SIX

The Path of Expansion for Banks and Competing Financial-Service Providers

Banks must not only be profitable, but they also must grow relative to their competitors. Otherwise, they may face a buyout from competitors and simply disappear. Growth is also an indicator of how well their customer base is being served. Banks and other financial firms that are growing tend to have a more satisfied customer base.

However, there are many ways for a financial-service provider to grow. For example, it can develop and launch *new customer-service facilities* in old and new market areas, increasing customer convenience and attracting new funds. Today these new facilities may be traditional physical structures—new offices staffed by customer-oriented person-nel—or automated electronic facilities that reach out to ever more distant customers at any hour of the day or night and at significantly lower cost. Electronic facilities also are somewhat less regulated than chartering new banks and building new brick and mortar branch offices, which adds to their growing economic advantage.

Banks and their competitors can also grow by *merger and acquisition*. Prominent exam-ples include Chase Manhattan's acquisition of J. P. Morgan and Bank of America's pend-ing acquisition of FleetBoston Financial Corp, the leading bank based in New England. There have been more than 9,000 bank mergers in the United States over the past two decades. As a result the industry is experiencing massive *consolidation*—fewer but larger financial-service providers. The 100 largest U.S. banks control more than half of the industry's assets. In theory, this tends to lower costs through economies of scale and spreads risk.

Alternatively, banks and their financial competitors can reach out and acquire other businesses with different product lines. One prominent example of recent vintage is the acquisition of Household Finance, one of the top consumer finance companies in the world, by HSBC of London, one of the largest banks on the planet. At the same time, banking's competitors—principally securities firms and insurers—have acquired banks, thrifts, and other financial-service providers. These acquisitions have led to *convergence*, as different types of financial firms invade each other's product lines, blurring the dis-tinction between banking and nonbanking activities. These changes have been facili-tated by the spread of interstate banking in the United States and by the rise of the European Community and Asia's vast new markets.

Banks and their competitors can more easily reach around the globe today, establishing communications links with their customers in distant markets or acquiring financial firms abroad and inheriting an established customer base. International expansion offers numerous potential benefits, including greater geographic diversification and staying abreast of customers expanding overseas.

Of course, international expansion is not without its challenges for banks and their competitors—new cultures, new languages, new regulations, and new currencies must all be dealt with. In short, bank expansion into foreign markets solves some problems and gives rise to new ones, as we will see in this final part of the text.

CHAPTER EIGHTEEN

Creating and Managing Service Outlets: New Charters, Branches, and Electronic Facilities

Key Topics in This Chapter

- Chartering New Financial-Service Institutions
- The Performance of New Banks
- Establishing Full-Service Branches
- In-Store Branching
- Establishing Limited-Service Facilities
- The Internet and Online Banking

Introduction

There is an old joke that claims bank drive-in windows were invented in order to permit cars to occasionally visit their true owner—the bank! While bankers have developed many unique service-delivery facilities for many different reasons, checking up on the cars they finance is usually not one of them! Rather, bank service facilities are usually established today for the *convenience* of bank customers.

For example, customers want to be able to access their checking and savings accounts and access loans at a time and place that conveniently answers their daily needs. For most of the history of banks and other financial-service providers, "convenience" has meant *location*. Businesses and consumers have preferred to buy the services supplied by a bank or other financial institution located in the same community or neighborhood rather than from a financial institution situated across town, in another state, or from another region or nation.

However, customers' views about what is "convenient" are changing rapidly with the growing use of the Internet, home and office computers, cell phones, fax machines, automated tellers dispensing cash and accepting deposits, point-of-sale terminals in retail stores, and credit cards that grant access to an instant loan any time and any place without requiring lender approval of every purchase. These newer technologies for storing and transmitting financial information have eroded the significance of physical location

If you wanted to charter a new bank today, where would you go to get help with such an important project? In the United States both the Comptroller of the Currency's Office in the U.S. Treasury Department (at **www.occ.treas.gov**) and many of the states have set up websites to help you get organized in order to submit a new bank charter application and start a new bank. (See, for example, Organizing a New State Bank in the State of New York Banking Department at **www.banking.state.ny.us**.) Thrift institutions are also chartered by the states and, at the federal level, by the Office of Thrift Supervision in the U.S. Treasury Department at **www.ots.treas.gov**.

Information on different types of auxiliary financial-service facilities (for example, branch offices and automated teller machines) shows up in several places on the World Wide Web. For example: the rapid rise of automated tellers to well over 100,000 in the United States alone is tracked in such sites as ATM Magazine at **www.atmmagazine.com/** and through discussions of ATM fees and surcharges at **www.atmsurcharges.com** and **www.bankrate.com/brm/rate/atm_chk_home.asp**.

Finally, the Internet has become a fast-growing automated advertising and service delivery channel for offering banking and other financial services. Not surprisingly, space on the Web devoted to Internet banking and financial services has exploded accordingly. Among the more popular sites recently have been the Online Banking Report (OBR): Internet Strategies for Financial Institutions at **www.onlinebankingreport.com**; Internet Fraud—What to Watch For and How to Deal With It at **www.internetfraud.usdoj.gov**; True Web Banks and Credit Unions by OBR, which lists banks and credit unions providing Internet services at **www.onlinebankingreport.com** (see the Quick Jump Menu for True Web Banks). Other key sites exploring online banking issues include **www.bank security.com** and **www.bankersonline.com/roadmaps/roadmaps.html** (see Internet Banking Information links).

(geography) as the main determinant of which financial firm a customer chooses today. In the modern world *timely access* to financial services, not just the physical location of service facilities, becomes the key indicator of customer convenience. For example, it may be faster and easier to request a loan over the telephone or through an online application or a fax machine from hundreds of miles away than it is to visit a financial-service provider situated only blocks away, but reachable only by weaving your way through traffic jams and crowded parking lots, and open only during "regular business hours."

However, for some important financial services today—especially checking accounts, smaller savings deposits, safety deposit boxes, and consumer and small business loans—*physical presence* is still of considerable importance to many customers. This is especially true when something goes wrong with a service account. For example, when a customer discovers that his or her account is overdrawn or when the customer's estimate of an account balance does not agree with the bank or other financial institution that holds that account and checks begin to bounce, the presence of a nearby service facility becomes very important. Thus, for many financial services and especially when special problems arise, the convenient physical location of a financial-service provider is still a valued commodity to many customers.

In deciding how they will respond to customers' changing demands for timely access to services, bankers and other financial-service providers today have several options to choose from:

1. *Chartering new financial institutions.*
2. *Establishing new full-service branch offices*, offering most or perhaps all the services that are also available from the home office.
3. *Setting up limited-service facilities*, including drive-in and walk-up teller windows, self-service terminals inside branch offices, automated teller machines (both those on the

premises of banks and thrifts and those situated in remote locations, such as shopping centers, airports, or retail shops), point-of-sale terminals in retail stores and shops, telephone connections, home and office computers linked to a financial institution's computer through the Internet, and other electronic media.

In the sections that follow we examine each of these options for delivering financial services conveniently to customers.

Chartering a New Bank or Other Financial-Service Institution

No one can start a bank or other major financial firm inside the United States (and in many other nations as well) without the express approval of federal or state authorities, and sometimes both. This is particularly true for banks and other depository institutions (such as credit unions and savings associations).

For example, in the case of commercial banks, the public's need for a new bank in a particular location must be demonstrated and the honesty and competence of its organizers and proposed management established. Sufficient protection against failure must be provided in the form of equity capital pledged by the founding stockholders. Usually they must supply enough start-up capital (currently in the $2 million to $10 million range) to cover several years (usually at least the initial three years) and show that the proposed new institution will achieve adequate levels of profitability.

Why is all this required for new banks? Government chartering agencies believe that banks need special scrutiny for several reasons: (1) they are the principal institutions holding the public's savings, and unregulated chartering activity might result in excessive numbers of poorly capitalized banks that fail; (2) banks are at the heart of the payments process to support trade and commerce, so their failure could disrupt business activity; and (3) banks create more money (immediate spending power) than any other financial institution, which suggests that chartering too many banks might result in excessive money creation and inflation. Although there is considerable debate about the validity of these arguments, they constitute the key rationale for the elaborate structure of cradle-to-grave regulation and restrictions on entry that characterize most banking systems today. Many of the same arguments have been used to justify current state and federal restrictions on the chartering of new thrift institutions, security dealers, insurance companies, and finance companies.

The Bank Chartering Process in the United States

Only the banking commissions in each of the 50 states and the **Office of the Comptroller of the Currency** (OCC)—a division of the Treasury Department—can issue a **charter of incorporation** to start a new U.S. bank. Generally speaking, federal standards for receiving a bank charter are more rigorous than the rules of the **state banking commissions.** However, organizers often seek a federal bank charter for the added prestige it conveys in the minds of customers, especially large depositors.

An additional check on the bank chartering policies of the state banking commissions is provided by the **Federal Deposit Insurance Corporation (FDIC).** Most newly formed banks immediately seek FDIC insurance for their deposits in order to strengthen public confidence in the new institution. Moreover, the banking laws of most states require a new bank to obtain federal deposit insurance certification before a state banking commission will issue its charter of incorporation. The FDIC must be convinced that the new bank is likely to be managed prudently before it will issue a certificate of insurance.[1]

The choice between pursuing a federal or a state charter usually comes down to weighing the benefits and costs of each for the particular bank and location the organizers have in mind. The key pros and cons include the following:

Benefits of Applying for a Federal (National) Bank Charter

- It brings added prestige due to stricter regulatory standards, which may help attract larger corporate and individual deposits.
- In times of trouble the technical assistance supplied to a struggling bank by national bank authorities may be of better quality, giving the troubled bank a better chance of long-run survival.

Benefits of Applying for a State Bank Charter

- It may be easier and less costly to secure a state charter.
- The bank need not join the Federal Reserve System and, therefore, avoids having to buy and hold low-yielding Federal Reserve stock.
- Many states allow a bank to lend a higher percentage of its capital to a single borrower, while national banks can lend unsecured only up to 15 percent of their capital and surplus to a single borrowing customer.
- State-chartered banks may be able to make certain types of loans (e.g., loans on unimproved land) or offer certain services (e.g., real estate brokerage) that national banks may not be able to offer.

Concept Check

18–1. Why is the physical location or physical presence of a bank still important to many customers despite recent advances in long-distance communications technology?

18–2. Why is the creation (chartering) of new banks closely regulated? What about nonbank financial firms?

18–3. What do you see as the principal benefits and costs of government regulation of the number of financial-service charters issued?

18–4. Who charters new banks in the United States? New thrift institutions?

18–5. What key role does the FDIC play in the chartering process?

18–6. What are the advantages of having a national bank charter? A state bank charter?

Questions Regulators Usually Ask the Organizers of a New Bank

It is instructive to look at the types of information chartering authorities demand before approving or denying a bank charter application. A sample of the questions the Comptroller of the Currency asks on applications to charter new national banks follows. These criteria are often used by organizers and chartering agencies to assess a new financial firm's prospects for success:

[1] In March 2002 the FDIC, the OCC, and the Office of Thrift Supervision (OTS) issued a uniform application form—the "Interagency Charter and Federal Deposit Insurance Application"—to be used by financial institutions to apply for a national bank or federal savings association charter or for federal deposit insurance. The purpose of the new form is to simplify the chartering process, especially for federally chartered depository institutions. (See, for example, **www.fdic.gov**.)

Factoid
Does being "easy" in allowing new bank charters in your state result in more bank failures?
Answer: A study by De Young at the Chicago Fed suggests liberal chartering states have no more failures, on average, than those with restrictive chartering policies. (See WP-00-09 at the Federal Reserve Bank of Chicago.)

1. What are the population and geographic boundaries of the primary service area (PSA) from which the new banking firm is expected to generate 75 percent or more of its loans and deposits? The PSA must have enough businesses and households to ensure an adequate customer base for the new institution.

2. How many competing banks, savings and loans, credit unions, finance companies, and insurance companies granting loans are located within the service area of the proposed new financial institution? The organizers must include information on competitors' services, hours of operation, and distances from the proposed bank. The more intense local competition is, the more difficult it is for a new financial firm to attract customers.

3. What are the number, types, and sizes of businesses in the service area? New banks and other new financial-service providers depend heavily on the demands of businesses for commercial deposit services and for loans to stock their shelves with inventories and to purchase business equipment.

4. What are the traffic patterns in the proposed bank's service area, the adequacy of its roads and highways, and any geographic barriers to the flow of traffic? Most new financial-service firms (and their branch offices and other service facilities) are situated along major routes of travel for commuters going to work and to shopping areas and schools, providing greater customer convenience.

5. Specifically, what is happening to population growth, incomes, types of occupations represented, educational levels, and the age distribution of residents in the proposed service area? The presence of well-educated residents in the local area implies higher incomes and greater use of financial services.

6. The organizers are asked to describe the banking history of the local community, the frequency with which new banks and other financial firms have been added to the area, and their track record of performance. The rapid growth of banks and other financial institutions in the local area and good profitability among these institutions suggests that the proposed new financial institution might also become profitable and experience good growth.

7. Who is to own any stock issued by the proposed bank; especially, what amount will be held by the organizers, directors, and officers. The chartering agency wants to be sure the bank can raise adequate capital to support its future growth and protect its depositors, and it likes to see evidence of a broad base of support among local residents.

8. What is the business and banking experience of the organizers and senior management of the new institution? Successful businesspeople on the bank's board and staff will help attract new credit and deposit accounts.

9. What are the organizers' projections for total deposits, loans, revenues, operating expenses, and net income for the first three to five years of the proposed bank's operation? The quality of these projections will shed light on how much the organizers of a proposed new financial firm know about the banking business.

The answers to these questions are often supported by a detailed economic analysis of the local market, prepared by an economist or professional business analyst. Frequently, local businesses and households are surveyed on the possible need for a new bank. If existing banks in the area protest the award of a new charter, a public hearing may be held in which the organizers will submit testimony concerning (1) why there is a public need for the new institution, (2) whether the new bank is likely to be profitable (usually within three years), and (3) whether there is adequate business in the local area to support both the new bank and existing financial institutions without increasing the probability of failure.

The organizers usually establish **public need** by pointing out either that local banks and other financial-service providers are not conveniently located to businesses and residents in the area or that existing financial institutions fail to offer some key services, such as business equipment loans or trust services. However, the public-need factor in chartering decisions appears to have become somewhat less important in recent years. Under the feasibility standard adopted by the Comptroller of the Currency during the 1980s, applicants for a national bank charter are asked for a detailed business plan and are required to demonstrate that skilled management will be hired for the new institution. If the organizers pledge sufficient capital and the business plan and proposed management appear to be adequate, a new charter is likely to be issued.

Concept Check

18–7. What kinds of information must the organizers of new national banks provide the Comptroller of the Currency in order to get a charter? Why could this information be important?

18–8. What is the meaning of *public need* as it applies to chartering new banks? Why is the "public need" aspect of a charter application less important today than in the past?

Factors Weighing on the Decision to Seek a New Bank Charter

Filmtoid

What 1998 romantic comedy, starring Meg Ryan and Tom Hanks, illustrates the effects of competition in a less-regulated market when a small owner-operated book store fails because it cannot compete in terms of price with the "large-box" book store? **Answer:** *You've Got Mail.*

Filing a bank charter application is a costly process in most of the United States. The organizers of a new bank must carefully analyze their business prospects and answer several key questions regarding external and internal factors that might affect the new institution's chances for success.

1. External factors include
   a. *The level of local economic activity.* Is it high enough to generate sufficient deposit and loan demand to support a new bank? Often measured by the volume of retail sales, personal income, bank debits (i.e., local check volume), and number of households and businesses in the service area.
   b. *Growth of local economic activity.* Is the local market area growing fast enough to generate additional deposits and loans so that the new institution can grow to an efficient size? Often measured by trends in total deposits and loans, retail sales, bank debits, population growth, construction activity, and school enrollments.
   c. *The need for a new bank.* Has the local population grown or moved into new areas not currently receiving convenient financial services? Often measured by population per bank or per banking office, recent earnings and deposit growth of existing banks, number and size of new residential construction projects (apartments, single-family homes, etc.).
   d. *The strength and character of local competition in supplying financial services.* How many competing financial institutions are there and how aggressive are they in advertising their services? This is often measured by the number of bank offices relative to area population and the number of other financial institutions offering checkable accounts, savings plans, consumer loans, and business credit.
2. Internal factors include
   a. *Qualifications and contacts of the organizers.* Do the organizers have adequate depth of experience? Is their reputation in the local community strong enough to attract customers?

    b. *Management quality.* Have the organizers been able to find a chief executive officer with adequate training and experience in bank management? Will the organizing group be able to find and pay competent management and staff to fill the new institution's key posts?

    c. *Pledging of capital to cover the cost of filing a charter application and getting under way.* Is the net worth position of the organizers strong enough to meet the initial capitalization requirements imposed by regulation and cover consulting and legal fees? Because the chartering process covers many months and may wind up in court before the new financial firm is allowed to open, do the organizers have sufficient financial strength to see the project through to its completion?

Volume and Characteristics of New Bank Charters

Factoid
Are newly chartered banks more or less likely to fail than established banks?
Answer: A study by De Young at the Federal Reserve Bank of Chicago suggests that, on average, they are less likely to fail during their first four years, more likely to fail for a time thereafter, and eventually have a failure rate matching that of established banks.

In view of all the foregoing questions and issues and their associated costs and risks, it may come as no surprise that only a fraction of the businesspeople who consider starting a new bank or other financial firm ultimately submit formal applications for new charters. Yet, surprisingly, the number of new banks and other depository institutions being chartered in the United States recently has accelerated, averaging a hundred or more per year, due, in part, to the displacement of many bank officers who lost their jobs when their former institutions were merged and to public demand for more personalized service sometimes not available from large, established banking firms.

Clearly, merely getting charter approval does not end the challenges facing a new bank's organizers and management. Following charter approval, stock can be legally offered to the public through a so-called *offering memorandum* that describes the charter's business plan, management, and the rights and terms of the stock sale. In the United States a Deposit Insurance Application usually must be filed with the FDIC after the charter application is approved. Corporate bylaws must be adopted, operating policies drafted, and bonding and insurance secured for bank employees. Added to these costs are the riskiness of a new venture, and the burdens imposed by regulation.

Where are most newly chartered banks located? What types of markets do new banks serve? Analysis of recent charter approvals suggests that most new U.S. banks are chartered in relatively large urban areas where, presumably, expected rates of return on the organizers' investments are the highest. For example, Rose and Fry [3] found that new charter markets had a median population of close to 200,000, and their population growth rate was approximately double the total U.S. population growth rate. As population increases relative to the number of banking organizations operating in a given state, increased numbers of new charters are issued. Presumably, many bank organizers view population growth as a proxy for growth in the demand for financial services. The faster *total bank assets* in a state grow, the greater the probability of chartering new banking institutions there, presumably because the success of area banks leads new-bank organizers to expect success when their bank is chartered. In contrast, increases in the *bank concentration ratio* tend to reduce chartering activity in a state by 20 to 30 percent. This suggests that substantial numbers of bank organizers fear having to take on a dominant bank or other dominant financial firm in their chosen area. Still, no one has found convincing evidence that new banks or other financial firms are overwhelmed by their competition, nor can they be driven from most local markets if they are willing to compete.

How Well Do New Banks Perform?[2]

Launching a new banking organization or other financial firm entails considerable risk. There is no guarantee that the new institution will survive and prosper. Deregulation of the financial sector has brought scores of new competitors into traditional banking markets. Moreover, existing financial firms have a decided advantage over newly chartered institutions in their greater experience, greater size, and well-established reputations. How successful, in general, are new banking firms?

Research findings are generally optimistic. Most new financial firms grow, in terms of total deposits, at a moderate to rapid rate, initially attracting funds from their organizers, from business associates of the organizers, and from customers dissatisfied with other banks. In fact, Motter [9] observed in a study of newly chartered national banks that increases in loan accounts tended to outstrip gains in deposits as customers denied loans by other lending institutions moved quickly to sound out the credit policies of the new institution in town. Despite a track record of loan losses that generally exceeded those of established banks, most new banks were profitable within two years of opening their doors.

In a review of new banks formed in Massachusetts, Shea [5] found that early monitoring and control of operating expenses are vital for a new bank to be successful. It must carve out a solid niche in the local community that differentiates it from other financial-service providers in the minds of customers. Nevertheless, the majority of new banks became profitable in their second or third year of operation. Consistent with this finding, De Young [1] discovered that new banks are less likely to fail than established banks.

Research suggests that the early performance of a new bank is strongly tied to the experience, financial strength, and market contacts of those who put the organization together. Selby [4], for example, found that the volume of deposits generated by the banks' first board of directors accounted for a major share of deposits brought in during the initial year of operation. This finding emphasizes the need to find organizers who have successfully operated other businesses. Moreover, the growth of income in the local market, especially household after-tax income and business sales, appears to be positively related to new bank growth.

Numerous research studies have shown that chartering new banks has competitive effects that generally serve the public interest. Most such studies (e.g., Fraser and Rose [6], Motter [9], and McCall and Peterson [8]) have looked at small cities and rural communities served by one, two, or three banks in which a new competitor is suddenly chartered by either state or federal authorities. Generally, existing banks in these smaller communities have stepped up their lending activities and become more active in attracting funds through deposit sales after a new financial firm has entered, suggesting that local residents gained better service. Evidence on whether the prices of financial services were reduced or the yields paid to savings account customers increased is decidedly mixed, however. Most studies find *few* price effects from the entry of new competitors. However, a review of the intrusion of New York City banks into neighboring counties, by Motter and Carson [10], uncovered a tendency for loan rates to fall following the entry of additional competition.

---

[2] Portions of this section are based on Peter S. Rose's article in *The Canadian Banker* [7] and are used with permission.

E-BANKING AND E-COMMERCE

CHARTERING INTERNET BANKS

Both the federal government and many states authorize the banks they supervise to offer Internet banking services or even charter an Internet-only bank (a "virtual bank"). The concern of most regulators is that an application to offer Internet services or to form a new electronic bank (1) be backed by a sound business plan to help insure that the new venture succeeds (especially because many Internet ventures are not yet profitable); and (2) provide adequate safeguards for the bank's records and its customers' accounts and transactions from "hackers" and others unauthorized to invade the privacy of the bank and its customers.

A good example of the rules and regulations that apply to Internet banks may be found at the website established by the Comptroller of the Currency (OCC) (**www.occ.treas.gov/corpbook/group 4/public/pdf/internetnbc.pdf**), which details the rules for establishing a new Internet bank with a national (federal) charter. The OCC allows Internet-only banks to receive charters as well as banks with more traditional facilities that also want a Web-based service delivery channel, provided the proposed bank or bank Web service unit "may reasonably be expected to operate successfully and in a safe and sound manner."

Organizers of Internet banks, like those of any bank that applies for a national charter, must consist of a group of at least five people who will serve as the Internet bank's initial board of directors. These organizers must be U.S. citizens and in good standing in the banking and business community. The OCC places no express limits on the electronic devices or facilities that may be used to produce and deliver services, provided banking services are delivered in a way that conforms to all banking laws and the procedures are "safe, sound, and secure."

National banks may operate or provide "information only" websites; "transactional" websites that enable customers to access their accounts, purchase goods and services, apply for loans, pay bills, and transfer funds; wireless service channels; and home and office banking through personal computers. A key issue for the future centers on which of these electronic banking approaches is likely to be profitable and, therefore, economically viable in the long run. At this point none of these different service delivery routes has convincingly demonstrated consistent profitability.

Concept Check

18–9. What are the key factors the organizers of a new bank should consider before deciding to seek a charter?

18–10. Where are most new banks chartered in the United States?

18–11. How well do most new banks perform for the public and for their owners?

Establishing Full-Service Branch Offices: Choosing Locations and Designing New Branches[3]

When an established bank, thrift institution, or other financial firm wishes to enter new markets or when its valued customers move, the most important vehicle for market entry in the modern era has been the creation of new **branch offices,** offering many, if not all, the services that are also available from the home office. Branches are usually much cheaper to establish than chartering whole new financial service corporations. Less capital is required, the application for new branch offices in most states is far less detailed than

---

[3] Portions of this section are based on Peter S. Rose's article on bank branching in *The Canadian Banker* [18] and are used with permission.

that usually required for a proposed new corporate charter, and there is usually much less duplication of staff because a new branch doesn't normally require a full slate of officers and operations personnel as a whole new bank would, for example.

The number of full-service branch offices of depository institutions in the United States has grown from just over 10,000 in 1960 to more than 78,000 by 2003. FDIC-insured commercial banks operated about 66,000 branch offices, while nonbank savings institutions reported operating another 12,000-plus branch facilities. These figures do not count the even greater numbers of limited-service facilities, such as automated cash-dispensing machines (ATMs), which total more than 140,000 in the United States alone.

The location, design, and services offered by a branch office depend, first, upon the preferences of customers and, secondly, on the preferences of management and employees. *Both* customer-friendly and worker-friendly branch offices are needed. Marketing research studies suggest that most customers rate an atmosphere of *confidentiality* and *privacy* in carrying out their personal transactions as the most important features of new branch offices. And customers and employees seem also to rank *efficiency* high in describing the arrangement of an ideal branch office—service departments and workstations should be easily reachable for both customers and employees.

BancOne of Columbus, Ohio, is an industry leader in designing and testing new ideas for the design of branch offices and other customer service facilities. When the customer enters one of its newer branches, he or she may be confronted with such eye-catching features as neon lights that highlight what financial services each department offers and direct customers' attention to daily specials (i.e., merchandising graphics). To further ease customer anxiety, there is an information desk near the entrance to help confused customers find the service counters that best meet their needs. Visually attractive advertisements confront customers waiting in the lobby to meet with financial service representatives. More recently, BancOne has developed both full-service branches—providing traditional services (such a loans and deposits) and new services (such as travel planning, insurance, and financial counseling)—and specialized branches ("boutiques") that supply services specifically geared to their local area (such as savings and investment products for retired customers). Other branch-office innovators include Wells Fargo, Bank of America, Washington Mutual Inc., and Charter One Financial Inc. The message of these recent innovations seems reasonably clear: Customers, particularly new customers, need guidance on where to go and what services are available inside each branch office. Otherwise, they will soon become frustrated and go elsewhere.

Desirable Sites for New Branches

Among the most desirable sites for full-service branch offices today are those with at least some of the following characteristics:

1. Heavy traffic count (for example, 30,000 to 40,000 cars per day), indicating a large flow of vehicular traffic (and potential customers) passing near the proposed site, but even at peak times (e.g., on Friday afternoons) customers must be able to easily see and access the office and its drive-in windows.

2. Large numbers of retail shops and stores present in the surrounding neighborhood, which usually generate a substantial volume of loan and deposit business.

3. Local populations that are of above-average age (particularly those individuals 45 years of age and older) who often have substantial amounts of savings and need a variety of different financial services.

4. A surrounding area that encompasses substantial numbers of business owners, managers, and professional men and women at work or in residence.

5. A steady or declining number of service facilities operated by financial-service competitors, leaving a substantial volume of business that a new branch office might be able to attract.

6. Above-average population growth, usually favorable to establishing a branch office in a local area.

7. Above-average population density (i.e., a greater number of persons per square mile around the proposed site).

8. A target ratio of

$$\begin{array}{c} \text{Population} \\ \text{per branch} \\ \text{office} \end{array} = \dfrac{\begin{array}{c}\text{Total population in the} \\ \text{area to be served}\end{array}}{\begin{array}{c}\text{Number of branch offices} \\ \text{present in the area}\end{array}}$$

In the United States, for example, there is an average of about 4,000 people per branch office. However, some other nations have much higher average population-per-branch ratios. For example, Austria and Germany have more than 10,000 people per bank branch, while Japan has more than 8,000 people per branch office. The larger the population served by each office, the more financial services are likely to be purchased, expanding revenues and enhancing the efficiency of operations.

9. Above-average levels of household income, with higher-income groups usually offering branch offices the opportunity to sell more services.

Key URLs
To discover what's happening in the design of new bank branches, see such web locations as **www.idanetwork.org** and **http://webi .wharton.upenn.edu/ research**.

For branch offices designed primarily to attract *deposits,* the key branch sites to look for are usually neighborhoods with relatively high median incomes, heavy concentrations of retail stores and shops, older-than-average resident populations, and high proportions of homeowners rather than renters. On the other hand, financial firms seeking more *checking accounts* through their branches generally should enter neighborhoods with high levels of individual and family incomes as well as areas where shopping centers and retail stores are concentrated. Higher levels of *savings deposits* are usually to be found in local markets where there is an above-average proportion of older heads of households (including retired individuals and families) and where there is a large proportion of residents who own their own homes.

For branches primarily created to generate *loan demand from household customers,* residential areas with a heavy proportion of young families and substantial new home construction, along with concentrations of retail stores and shopping centers and high traffic flow, are particularly desirable locations. In contrast, *commercial loan demand* is usually focused upon central city office locations where a lending institution's credit analysts, management information systems personnel, and loan approval committees are normally housed.

Expected Rate of Return The decision of whether or not to establish a branch office is a *capital-budgeting decision,* requiring a large initial cash outflow (cost) to fund the purchase or lease of property and to begin operations. Branches are usually created with the expectation that future net cash inflows (NCF) will be large enough to guarantee the bank or other financial firm an acceptable return, E(r), on its invested capital. That is, management can estimate expected return from the opening of a new branch facility from this formula:

$$
\begin{array}{c}
\text{Cash outflow to} \\
\text{fund the establishment} \\
\text{of a new branch} \\
\text{office}
\end{array}
= \frac{\text{NCF}_1}{[1 + E(r)]^1} + \frac{\text{NCF}_2}{[1 + E(r)]^2} + \cdots
\tag{1}
$$

$$
+ \frac{\text{NCF}_n}{[1 + E(r)]^n}
$$

where a new branch will be judged to be economically viable if its expected return, $E(r)$, equals or exceeds the minimum acceptable return (k) to the offering financial firm's stockholders; that is, $E(r) \geq k$. For example, if a new branch office is expected to cost \$3 million to acquire the site and install the necessary equipment to begin operations and to generate \$600,000 in annual cash inflow net of all operating expenses for 10 years, the branch's expected return will be found from this formula:

$$
\$3,000,000 = \frac{\$600,000}{[1 + E(r)]^1} + \frac{\$600,000}{[1 + E(r)]^2} + \cdots + \frac{\$600,000}{[1 + E(r)]^{10}}
$$

Using a financial calculator, we find that the proposed branch's expected return, $E(r)$, is 15.1 percent.[4]

If the shareholders' minimum acceptable rate of return is 10 percent, this branch project appears to be economically viable. Of course, the return actually earned from the investment in each branch depends upon the demand for its services in the communities it serves, the quality of its management and staff, and the cost in capital and other resources necessary to operate the branch.

Geographic Diversification   When considering possible locations for new branches, management should consider not only the expected rate of return, $E(r)$, from each new branch location, but also (*a*) the variance around that expected return, $\sigma^2[E(r)]$, which is due mainly to fluctuations in economic conditions in the area served by the branch, and (*b*) the covariance, COV, of expected returns from the proposed new branch, existing branches, and other assets previously established or acquired by the offering institutions, $\{COV[E(r_i), E(R_j)]\}$. The impact of a new branch's expected return (R_B) on the offering institution's overall or total return (R_T) from its existing branches and other assets (R_{OA}) can be found from

$$
E(R_T) = W \times E(R_B) + (1 - W) \times E(R_{OA})
\tag{2}
$$

where W is the proportion of total resources to be invested in new branch B and $(1 - W)$ is the proportion of the offering institution's resources invested in all of its other branches and other assets (OA). The marginal impact of a new branch on overall risk, measured by the variance of its total return (R_T), is

$$
\sigma^2(R_T) = W^2\sigma^2(R_B) + (1 - W)^2\, \sigma^2(R_{OA}) + 2W\,(1 - W)\, COV(R_B, R_{OA})
\tag{3}
$$

where

$$
COV(R_B, R_{OA}) = \rho_{B,OA} \times \sigma_B \times \sigma_{OA}
$$

---

[4] A financial calculator such as the Texas Instruments BAII Plus is used to calculate the expected return where N = 10, I/Y = ?, PV = −3,000,000, Pmt = 600,000, and FV = 0.

with $\rho_{B,OA}$ representing the correlation coefficient between the expected return from the proposed new branch and the returns from other branches and assets of the offering institution, σ_B the standard deviation of the proposed new branch's expected return, and σ_{OA} the standard deviation of return from other assets held by the offering financial firm.

To see the usefulness of these formulas, let's suppose the management of a commercial bank knows the following return and risk information about a proposed new branch office project:

$$E(R_B) = 15 \text{ percent} \qquad \sigma(R_B) = 3 \text{ percent}$$
$$E(R_{OA}) = 10 \text{ percent} \qquad \sigma(R_{OA}) = 3 \text{ percent}$$

Suppose the proposed new branch would represent 25 percent of this bank's total assets, meaning the bank's other branches and assets must represent the remaining 75 percent of its total assets. That is,

$$W = 0.25$$
$$\text{and}$$
$$(1 - W) = 0.75$$

and the new branch's returns are *negatively* related to the returns from the bank's other assets, specifically

$$\rho_{B,A} = -0.40$$

Using formula (2), this bank's expected return after investing in the new branch B would be

$$E(R_T) = 0.25 \,(15 \text{ percent}) + 0.75 \,(10 \text{ percent}) = 11.25 \text{ percent}$$

The total risk carried by the bank after adding the new branch would be

$$\sigma^2(R_T) = (0.25)^2 \,(3 \text{ percent})^2 + (0.75)^2 \,(3 \text{ percent})^2$$
$$+ \, 2(0.25)(0.75)(-0.40)(3 \text{ percent})(3 \text{ percent})$$

Then,

$$\sigma^2(R_T) = 4.28 \text{ percent}$$

or

$$\sigma(R_T) = 2.07 \text{ percent}$$

The foregoing calculations show us that not only would the proposed new branch increase this bank's total rate of return from all of its assets (increasing R_T from 10 percent to 11.25 percent) but the proposed new branch's negative return correlation with existing branch offices and other assets also lowers the bank's standard deviation of its total return from 3 percent to just over 2 percent, producing a **geographic diversification** effect that reduces overall risk exposure.

Thus, it is not always optimal for management to choose only those branch sites offering the highest expected returns. Risk and the covariance of a proposed new branch's expected return with the expected returns from other assets must also be considered. If two branches cost about the same to construct and generate about the same expected returns, management would most likely choose that branch location that is situated in a more stable local economy so that the variability about the branch's expected return is lower. Moreover, if two branch sites have similar construction costs, expected returns, and return variances, management is usually better off to select that site whose expected return has a low positive or even a negative covariance with the returns expected from the financial firm's other branches. Such a choice would tend to lower the overall risk from the institution's whole portfolio of service facilities.

Branch Regulation

Regulation in the United States recently has made it more difficult to close full-service branch offices of depository institutions. The FDIC Improvement Act of 1991, for example, requires a U.S. bank or thrift institution to notify its principal regulatory agency and its customers at least 90 days before a branch office is to be closed and to post a conspicuous notice of the plan to close at the branch site at least 30 days prior to closing. Moreover, the Community Reinvestment Act of 1977 requires banks and thrifts to make an effort to reach all segments of their communities with services, which often makes it difficult to receive permission to close a branch in neighborhoods where customer volume and deposits may be declining but there are few other financial-service outlets available.

The Changing Role of Branches

Many analysts see the roles played by branch offices evolving in new directions today. For example, in the banking industry, where there is a strong *sales orientation*, branch offices represent the bank's "eyes and ears" in local areas that help the organization identify the largest and potentially most profitable customers and link them to the bank's most profitable services. Also, branches appear to offer the greatest opportunities for *cross-selling*, where each customer is offered a package of financial services that fully meets his or her needs. Most automated facilities do not appear to be as effective at cross-selling multiple services as full-service branch offices are.

This concept of making branches as *sales oriented* as possible explains why a growing number of branch offices today are specially configured to maximize sales opportunities. For example, the low-profit, but heavily used teller stations now are frequently placed at the rear of branch office lobbies so that customers going to the teller windows must pass by departments advertising other fee-generating services. Customers waiting in their cars at drive-in windows today are often confronted with signs advertising loans and other services and with loudspeakers that, over a backdrop of soft music, remind them of new service options. Moreover, branch office hours increasingly are being set to match local customers' shopping and recreational schedules. For example, New Jersey's Commerce Bancorp provides customer access to its branches on Sundays. Of course, the new sales-oriented strategy of branch banking assumes that all employees in each branch office are trained to know about all the services the financial firm offers and are taught to look for every opportunity to sell more services to their customers.

Branch offices are coming to be viewed today less as mere deposit gatherers and more as sources of free-generating service sales and for booking profitable assets. In a sense, financial-service branches are struggling today to become more like other retail stores, where the goal is to sell customers as many products as possible, while minimizing operating costs. Increasingly, this objective has meant the substitution of as much automation as possible in place of personnel and office space.

One of the keys to branch office profitability is to apply the latest information technology and thereby lower personnel costs, moving operations personnel and those who must review and approve customer loan requests—that is, those personnel not needed for direct selling to the consumer—to a centrally located operations center. Customer self-service terminals are becoming more readily available so that customers themselves can readily obtain price quotations on new services, get copies of forms and legal documents, monitor their own accounts, and even schedule appointments with staff. However,

Key URL
How long does it take
to install an in-store
bank branch? Normally
at least two months.
However, Bank of
America has developed
a special kit that can
have one up and
running in about three
days! See especially
**www.conway.com/
sshighlites/0697/511
.htm**.

automation on this scale demands that the financial-service branches of the future be much larger in size, perhaps averaging $75 million to $100 million in accounts served instead of the $10 million to $50 million size range so prevalent today. In many cases this will require consolidation of smaller branches into fewer large branch offices with fewer and more productive employees serving customers.

In-Store Branching

More financial-service branches in the future are likely to be located inside shopping centers, supermarkets, and other stores, selling not just loans and savings deposits and cashing checks, but also marketing a full range of fee-based services through sales-oriented employees. The in-store branches operated recently by Wells Fargo are one example. **In-store branches** typically are much less costly to build and maintain, costing as little as one-fourth the expense incurred in constructing and operating a stand-alone branch, usually operate over longer hours (including weekends and holidays, which often are more convenient times for wealthier customers and those with heavy workweek schedules), and experience more traffic flow than conventional branches as customers enter stores to buy groceries, hardware, and apparel and usually pass right by the financial firm's service counters. While there is evidence that fewer loans typically arise from in-store branches than from stand-alone branches, deposit volume is often heavier at in-store sites, which frequently attract the store's own deposit of its daily cash receipts and the personal accounts of store employees.

By 1996 supermarket bank branches numbered close to 4,400, representing about 7.7 percent of all commercial bank branches in the United States. Store branch environments present their own challenges and problems, however. For one thing they usually require aggressive marketing strategies in order to get shoppers "in a banking mood." Moreover, in-store branches usually have no drive-in windows. To be successful, an in-store branch operation must seek close cooperation with store owners and employees (including joint advertising and promotion activities). It helps greatly if the store mentions the financial-service provider in its advertising and if public announcements are made periodically during operating hours, reminding shoppers of the financial firm's presence in the store. For example, some retail stores and banks have engaged in cooperative promotional campaigns—for example, offering customers who open a deposit account free merchandise from the store.

Bankers and other financial-service managers of the future are going to have to be more creative than in the past in seeking out new sites in which to locate profitable branch offices. For example, Harris Trust of Chicago has pioneered branches in apartment complexes, while Phoenix's Valley National Bank (now Bank One) operated a rent-free branch for a few hours each day in a senior citizens' retirement home. Other financial-service branches have recently appeared in factories and hospitals in an attempt to bring the financial-service provider closer to locations where current and potential customers reside, work, or enjoy leisure time.

In sort of a "reverse approach" to in-store branching there is a developing trend toward inviting other popular vendors inside bank branch offices. For example, a couple of New York banking firms, Charter One Financial and North Fork Bancorp, are creating branch facilities that have Starbucks' coffee shops inside. These bankers are looking for ways to increase the volume of customer traffic inside their new branches. While about four-fifths or more of all bank customers, on average, trek into bank branches at least once a month, the frequency of customer visits to bank branch offices appears to have been declining for more than a decade, due, in part, to other (especially electronic) transaction options recently made available to customers.

Establishing and Monitoring Limited-Service Facilities

The high cost of chartering new banks and other financial firms and of setting up and operating full-service branch offices has led recently to a steady expansion of limited-service facilities: automated teller machines (ATMs), point-of-sale terminals, telephones, online computer service outlets, and drive-in facilities. Even though full-service branches continue to be the main delivery channel for most customers and services, online household banking customers have risen from about 4 million to close to 30 million in five years. Thus, the most successful bank service delivery systems today are *multichannel*—combining both full-service branches and electronic, limited-service facilities within the same banking firm.

Point-of-Sale Terminals   Computer facilities in retail shops and stores that permit a customer to instantly pay for goods and services electronically by deducting the cost of each purchase directly from his or her account are known as **point-of-sale** (POS) **terminals.** The customer presents an encoded *debit card* to the store clerk who inserts it into a computer terminal connected to the bank or other financial firm's computer system. The customer's account is charged for the purchase and funds are automatically transferred to the store's deposit account.

Current point-of-sale networks are about equally divided between online and offline POS systems. The latter accumulate all of a customer's transactions until day's end and then the total of all transactions is subtracted from the customer's account. In contrast, online systems deduct each purchase as it is made from the customer's account. Costwise, banks and other providers would generally prefer offline POS systems, but online systems appear to reduce the frequency of customer overdrafts and, thus, may be less costly in the long run.

POS terminals are increasing rapidly all over the world. In the United States the number of POS terminals climbed during the 1990s from 50,000 to over 100,000 as the 21st century opened. The majority of the recently installed POS terminals have appeared in gasoline stations and supermarkets. Among the market leaders in this field are MasterCard and VISA, which sell their point-of-sale systems under the trade names MAESTRO and INTERLINK.

Customer resistance to POS usage appears to be fading, and their future growth is expected to be quite rapid. Service providers must work to overcome several disadvantages for the customer, such as loss of checkbook float (because loss of funds occurs the same day), computer problems that can generate costly mistakes, and the absence of canceled checks, which give customers handy written receipts for tax purposes. However, checking account fees are on the rise, which eventually may make POS terminals more economically attractive for more customers.

Automated Tellers (ATMs)   An **ATM** combines a computer terminal, recordkeeping system, and cash vault in one unit, permitting customers to enter a bank or other financial firm's bookkeeping system with either a plastic card containing a personal identification number (PIN) or by punching a special code number into a computer terminal linked to the bank's computerized records 24 hours a day. Once access is gained into the bank's system, cash withdrawals may be made up to prespecified limits, and deposits, balance inquiries, and bill paying may take place. With ATMs taking over more routine services like cashing checks, the personnel of a bank or other financial-service firm have more time to sell other services and help those customers who have special service needs. The average ATM processes about 200 transactions per day, though some handle more than 600 customer requests per day.

Where did ATMs begin? The forerunner of all the modern-day machines began operations at a branch office of Britain's Barclays Bank in 1967. This first automatic cash dispenser could only accommodate customer cash withdrawals, however; no other services were provided. Most bankers at the time expected that customers would use this pioneering automated device only when full-service offices were not open. One of the earliest visitors to Barclays new machine was the U.S. entrepreneur B. J. Meredith. When Meredith's own firm showed no immediate interest in producing these new machines, he contacted his famous relative, Don Meredith, a former professional football quarterback. Together with other investors, the Merediths set up a new firm, Docutel, Inc., to manufacture ATMs. The first Docutel automated teller was set up at Citizens and Southern National Bank in Atlanta. Soon, banks and other depository institutions worldwide were asking for these new machines and competing manufacturers, such as Diebold and IBM, became active suppliers to the financial marketplace.

ATMs today frequently offer such diverse products as bus and train tickets; postage stamps; passes to athletic events, concerts, and movies; gift certificates; and purchase payments at retail shops. Today ATMs are frequently shared by several depository institutions in order to lower costs and are networked with hundreds of other machines to offer customers full access to their accounts while traveling. Though expensive to purchase and install, ATMs save on employee salaries, utility bills, and maintenance costs. Diebold, Inc., a world leader in electronic banking, estimates that an ATM costs at least $30,000, on average, while the cost of opening a full-service branch averages close to $1 million or more.

U.S. banks spend at least $5 billion a year on ATMs and more than 140,000 are currently operating in the United States with thousands more available in Canada, Japan, and Western Europe. About half of all U.S. households possess at least one ATM access card. U.S. ATMs handle 5 to 6 billion financial transactions annually and bring in about $1 billion a year in industry revenues. Access fees, if they exist, are normally cheaper (averaging about 30 cents per cash withdrawal) if a customer uses an ATM owned by his or her depository institution. However, fees are more common if you use another institution's ATM that is networked to your financial-service provider because most depository institutions charge each other an interchange fee; if a fee is charged, customers must be informed in advance under the 1999 Gramm-Leach Bliley Act. ATM service providers that do assess their customers user fees often employ *conditional pricing schedules*. For example, if the customer's deposit balance drops below $1,000, a fee of 25 to 50 cents may be assessed per ATM transaction; otherwise, customer access may be free.

As Neeley [16] observes, charging an ATM usage fee is highly controversial. Recently the two largest automated teller networks in the United States—PLUS and Cirrus—decided to let the owners of ATMs that are part of their two national networks charge noncustomers a surcharge for ATM use. Several regional systems also began to charge for their ATM services. In part, the recent appearance of higher fees reflects the pattern of ATM usage today—with just over 85 percent of all transactions consisting of cash withdrawals from accounts, while deposits into accounts represent only about 10 percent of all ATM transactions. Other potential fee-generating uses are limited at present even though many ATMs have the capability to dispense such items as theater tickets, postage stamps, mutual fund shares, and traveler's checks. Then, too, because banks and other service providers belonging to an ATM network pay "interchange fees" (ranging from 50 cents to about $2.00) to the network's owners, these fees often are passed along to customers in the form of surcharges. Customers can generally escape these fees only by sticking to their own service provider's ATMs or by using human tellers inside the lobby or accessed through drive-in windows. However, these surcharge fees may put smaller financial firms that own few machines at a disadvantage, encouraging customers seeking to avoid ATM fees to transfer

ETHICS IN BANKING

ELECTRONIC BANKING USHERS IN ITS OWN ETHICAL ISSUES

Automated banking facilities, such as home and office computer banking and automated teller machines (ATMs), have brought numerous benefits to banks and other financial firms and to their customers. Transactions costs are lower and convenience is greater for both depository institutions and their customers, who also benefit from greater speed and accuracy.

Unfortunately, electronic banking has brought with it real ethical issues, particularly an upsurge in *computer crime*. Hackers have, on occasion, broken into financial-service computer systems and transferred funds to their own accounts or disrupted bank information systems, removed or rerouted critical information, and laundered money across international borders.

One of the most frequent targets of criminals today is ATMs, which contain stocks of cash to accommodate customers who need immediate spending money. These machines are often situated in remote locations where customers have been robbed while using them or had their account numbers stolen, or the machines themselves have been pillaged, uprooted and carried away, or, in a few cases, blown up with dynamite to get to the cash inside.

A unique twist on the ATM route to illegal cash emerged in 2001 and 2002. This case involved two Colorado banks, one of which failed and was acquired by the other. These banks contracted with the owner of a business to operate ATMs in order to serve the banks' customers and provide armored car services to safely transport cash. Soon, the business owner began removing some of the banks' cash that he was transporting, using that cash to cover his own business expenses. This process went on for more than a year. According to the Federal Deposit Insurance Corporation (FDIC), the pilfered money was never repaid, resulting in sizeable losses to the banks involved and to the FDIC when it resolved the failure of one of the two banks. (The FDIC estimated its losses at more than $9 million.) The ATM/armored car service provider was ultimately arrested and convicted of multiple counts of fraud.

To be sure, even as banking technology improves and becomes more sophisticated, so does the creativeness of those who would steal money from banks and other financial-service firms and subvert legitimate banking transactions.

Source: Federal Deposit Insurance Corporation, news release, October 17, 2002.

their accounts to the largest financial institutions, which operate more machines in more locations. These fees may be especially damaging to low-income consumers who often have few full-service branch offices in their neighborhoods but may have ATMs nearby.

During the past two decades, many banks and other depository institutions have moved to lower their operating costs by adding ATMs onto their full-service branch offices and by simultaneously reducing the number of personnel and the amount of rented space inside each branch office. For example, Zimmerman [23] reported several years ago that Manufacturers Hanover Trust in New York City added new ATMs to three of its least profitable branch offices, making them semiautomated branches. The bank was able to cut the number of staff members working in these particular branches in half and sharply reduce rental costs.

One important consideration with automation, however, is the amount of downtime ATMs often experience. If no human tellers are available and the bank or other service provider has only one ATM on site and it is not working, customers become frustrated and may take their business elsewhere. This is why many financial institutions install multiple ATMs at the same site and often replace their old machines frequently.

Automated tellers generally rank high in resource efficiency: they call for only a limited commitment of resources, particularly staff. ATMs process many more transactions per month than human tellers (an average of about 6,400 for ATMs compared to about 4,300 transactions per month per human teller) and do so at lower cost per transaction (automated teller transactions cost an average of about $3.75 per customer per month versus an average of about $4.38 per customer per month for a full-service branch office). On a per-transaction basis, the same transaction that costs an average of about 36 cents through an ATM costs about $1.06 through a human teller. This is why some large banking firms

Factoid

Service fees from the use of ATMs normally are greatest when a customer uses the ATMs belonging to a bank other than his or her own. These out-of-network ATM fees currently are growing faster than the rate of inflation.

(such as Bank One) have experimented with charging service fees if a customer uses a human teller for a transaction that could be handled more cheaply through an ATM.

However, automated tellers and other limited-service facilities do *not* rank high among those customers interested in personalized service (particularly among older customers), nor do they rank high in their ability to sell peripheral services, such as enticing customers to take out a car loan or purchase a savings or retirement plan. Depository institutions that put their ATMs outside or away from branch office lobbies often find that this move sharply diminishes their ability to sell other services. Moreover, many customers view limited-service facilities as less safe due to the frequent incidence of crime—robbery and even murder of customers in an effort to steal their cash or to get hold of their personal identification numbers so that a thief can access the customer's account at will. Automated facilities frequently attract crime because about three-quarters of all transactions carried out through these machines are cash withdrawals. Video and central station monitoring, along with privacy screens, extensive lighting systems, and built-in alarms, are popular methods today for increasing ATM safety and security.

How do banks and other service providers decide whether to add a new ATM to the services they currently offer? The basic answer is that they estimate the cash savings the new machine is likely to generate if customers use the ATM instead of writing a check or going to a human teller, translate the estimated volume of future savings into their present value, and then compare the estimated present value of savings against the cash outlay required to purchase and install the new machine. For example, standard new ATMs today may cost in the range of $40,000 to $50,000 each and may cost another $30,000 to $40,000 to install, depending on location and other factors. Let's suppose the total cash outlay will be $80,000 for a bank considering installing a new cash machine. After analyzing its check-processing costs, the bank estimates that it will save $1.00 for each check that is not written because customers will use the machine instead. Suppose the machine is expected to last for 10 years and handle 30,000 cash transactions per year. At $1.00 in savings per transaction, the total annual volume of savings should be approximately $30,000. The cost of capital the bank will incur to raise new funds to finance the ATM's purchase and installation is estimated to be 14 percent based upon the bank's risk exposure and expected future earnings. Therefore, we have:

$$\begin{matrix} \text{Net} \\ \text{present} \\ \text{value of} \\ \text{the new ATM} \end{matrix} = \begin{matrix} \text{Present value of} \\ \text{the stream of} \\ \text{cash savings from} \\ \text{the new ATM} \\ \text{discounted} \\ \text{at 14\%} \end{matrix} - \begin{matrix} \text{The total} \\ \text{cash outlay} \\ \text{for the} \\ \text{new ATM} \end{matrix}$$

$$\$76,483 = \$156,483^5 - \$80,000$$

Because the new machine generates a net present value (NPV) of + $76,483 for the bank, thus adding value to the institution's balance sheet, management would be likely to proceed with this project.

In closing, however, we must note that ATMs are not necessarily profitable for all banks and other service providers. For example, because ATMs are available 24 hours a day, customers may use these machines more frequently and for smaller transactions than they would with a human teller. If the customer needs cash for a movie on Friday night and for dinner on Sunday, he or she may access an ATM Friday afternoon for $30 and then drive to the ATM again on Sunday for another $50 to pay for dinner. In contrast, customers may

[5] The present value of the stream of cash savings from the new ATM is calculated using a financial calculator where N = 10, I/Y = 14%, PV = ?, Pmt = −30,000, and FV = 0.

visit a human teller in the branch office lobby or drive-in center on Friday and withdraw $80 for the whole weekend. Moreover, customers show little hesitation to use ATMs for their cash withdrawals but then use a human teller when it's time to deposit a payroll check, thus requiring the financial-service provider to have *both* teller machines and human tellers available during regular business hours. Then, too, the widening use of surcharge fees for ATM use may cause some customers to reduce their usage of automated tellers in favor of human tellers, pushing up operating costs once again. A recent study conducted at the Federal Reserve Board concluded that the cost of operating ATMs has exceeded the income they generate by more than $10,000 annually per machine.

Automated Loan Machines (ALMs) One interesting self-service device that has been tested recently is an **ALM**, or automated loan machine. These computer terminals permit a customer to apply for a loan by inputting certain information into the terminal, such as a Social Security number and driver's license number. The customer may also be asked a series of questions to verify his or her identity and credit standing. ALMs may have access to a database that includes the customer's driving record from the state motor vehicle division and the customer's credit report. If the machine grants the loan applied for (which normally ranges from about $500 to perhaps $5,000 to $10,000), the customer may be asked to sign for the loan on an electronic pad and then either receive a check or have the amount recorded in his or her deposit account.

Loan machines offer the prospect of saving substantial amounts of money in making smaller size consumer and business loans. Unfortunately, ALMs do not yet allow for flexibility in evaluating customers who may have past credit problems or no credit history, but who are now good-quality credit customers who deserve special consideration. They also do not permit lenders to personally interview their customers, make judgments about the customers' character, or maximize the opportunity to sell other services.

Self-Service Terminals As the decade of the 1990s began, several banks in New England set up self-service terminals, allowing customers on their own to open new accounts, transfer funds between accounts, order checks, stop payment on checks previously issued, and get information on the terms of other services their banks offer. Some financial firms have added telephones and video screens so that customers with self-service problems or other questions can dial up an employee for information day or night. Self-service machines linked to financial-service personnel offer the prospect of providing fully automated service centers around the clock, seven days a week, at substantially lower cost than at traditional, fully staffed branch offices that often needlessly duplicate both personnel and equipment.

Home and Office Online Banking Giving customers access to financial services—via telephone, computer terminals, TV monitors, or other electronic devices from their own home or office or while traveling or shopping—seems to be slowly gaining ground once again after a disappointing start during the 1980s and early 1990s. Many experts see home and office online banking or banking while in motion as the ultimate end point in the long-term evolution of financial-service facilities. Someday, they predict, nearly all financial transactions initiated by customers will arise from the customer's own location, be it at home, in an automobile or airplane, at work, or in a shopping mall or restaurant, at any hour of the day or night. Systems to allow customers to make computer purchases over the Internet or, alternately, through television sets are already in place.

Many banks and other service providers are developing highly automated telephone centers today that help their customers satisfy their demands for services without having to walk inside a branch office, get out of a car, or even open a car window to approach an ATM. Some experts argue that the *telephone* will be the key financial-service delivery

E-BANKING AND E-COMMERCE

ACHs AND CHECKS: THE TIDE IS TURNING, BUT SLOWLY

Every day millions of dollars flow across the United States as businesses, households, and governments pay their bills and depository institutions collect those funds and route them into the correct accounts. Some institutions and individuals pay by check—still the most popular route, accounting for nearly 60 percent of the value of all payments made in the United States—and others by currency and coin, money orders, and credit and debit cards. A third route—accounting for just over 10 percent of all payments, but gaining ground—is *the direct deposit of funds electronically* (most of these monies sent via FedLine, the Federal Reserve's electronic payments network). At work daily routing these "electronic dollars" to the accounts of their rightful owners is a nationwide network of automated clearinghouses (ACHs).

ACHs permit businesses to electronically deposit their employees' paychecks and permit households and businesses to make regular payments on their mortgages and other loans and to pay utility bills and other recurring costs via computer, thereby avoiding checks and other, less-convenient payment methods. The hard fact to explain, however, is why electronic transactions have not taken over the American payments system. In Europe they nearly have (with some countries reporting that close to two-thirds of their payments move electronically). *Why is the American experience so different?*

A recent article by economist Joanna Stavins of the Federal Reserve Bank of Boston may offer an answer. For one thing, Americans are reluctant to give up their checkbooks, probably because the price usually charged for this service is well below its true cost. Many depositories fear losing their checking account customers if they were to raise checkbook fees to cover all the costs of paying by check.

Another problem centers on the high cost of equipment to make electronic payments possible. Bankers, for example, cannot be sure an adequate volume of their customers will choose the electronic payments route after they have invested in the proper equipment, nor can they accurately predict how many other depository institutions will join them online, thereby making the service more valuable to customers. Thus, the success of such an investment depends not just on the institution making the investment, but on competitors and other outsiders (a phenomenon called "network externality"). In the United States, which has a much more decentralized banking system than does Europe, the outcome of such an investment is more uncertain. Therefore, many U.S. financial firms have postponed offering full electronic services.

Note: See especially Joanna Stavins, "Perspective on Payments," *Regional Review*, Federal Reserve Bank of Boston, First Quarter 2003, pp. 6–9.

Factoid
U.S. customers using Web banking services totaled more than 25 million in 2003.

channel for the future because so many different services can be marketed, delivered, and verified via telephone. And with increasing use of cell phones in automobiles and on the street, and portable computer keyboards, the more traditional drive-in windows and walk-up windows have come to look less convenient and efficient than many customers once thought they were.

The emergence of Internet-only banking companies in the last decade of the 20th century might have seemed to forecast the eventual demise of neighborhood branch offices with their huge demands on bank resources. However, the managers of electronic banking facilities and online banks, such as National Interbank and Juniper Financial, have discovered that not having convenient neighborhood branch offices can prove to be a business obstacle, especially in attracting the public's deposits. Customers of these online financial firms in many cases have had to mail in their deposits and drive to automated teller machine locations to obtain the spendable cash they need. They sometimes complain about their inability to speak with bank representatives in order to straighten out problems. Most online bankers have found that they must compensate their customers when they don't offer neighborhood offices by promising higher interest rates on the electronic accounts they do attract.

By the beginning of the 21st century several online banks with no neighborhood offices began to look around for effective substitutes. One strategy has been to approach chain stores, such as Mail Boxes Etc., and ask to "piggyback" on their numerous neighborhood

Use of the Internet as a Financial-Service Delivery Medium

Factoid
Online financial-service customers can be served at substantially lower cost than those customers served in person, through ATMs, or over the telephone.

Increasingly, large and small banks and other financial-service providers are establishing Web "branches." Many of these institutions sell selected services via their **Internet service sites,** such as bill paying, funds transfer, balance inquiries, and mortgage and consumer loans, and acquaint customers with other services that are available from the main office. Some financial firms include maps on their websites so customers can not only find where nearby offices are located but also what locations within each branch office offer certain services. Several "virtual banks" have recently appeared that exist only on the Internet and plan to survive from the fees they can earn by electronically collecting and dispensing customer funds.

FINANCIAL SERVICES MOST COMMONLY OFFERED VIA THE INTERNET

These services include making payments (especially paying recurring bills or employing bill presentment systems where the customer is shown a bill on the computer screen and electronic payment options appear), checking on account balances, moving funds between accounts, comparing loan and deposit interest rates, and getting access to application forms for loans, deposits, and other services.

Advantages for Banks and Other Financial-Service Providers   The Internet is a low-cost source of information and a service delivery vehicle available at any time anywhere so that customers can be served around the globe. The cost to establish and maintain a website is relatively low when compared to building, equipping, and staffing a traditional branch office. Online services are available 24 hours a day, 365 days a year, and usually offer consistently accurate transactions. Internet customers find the financial-service provider rather than the financial firm searching for customers. A final advantage is that customer use is measurable, and it's easier to get customer feedback on service quality, pricing, and problems than at a busy brick and mortar branch office.

Factoid
Bankers generally prefer online customers especially because these particular customers tend to hold larger-than-average deposit balances and purchase multiple services.

Disadvantages   Among the toughest problems are protecting customer privacy and heading off crime, such as by using private dial-ups, breaking transactions into small bundles, or using coded data so that thieves have a tougher time breaking in. As the Internet's popularity continues to grow, so does the threat of slowdowns and "hacker"-imposed system crashes. In addition, the Internet is not a warm and inviting medium through which a financial-services manager can easily get to know and recognize his or her clients. Many customers do not yet have compatible electronic systems, and the cost of being able to link up may be prohibitive to some potential customers. Finally, competition on the Internet is not limited by geography; thousands of financial-service providers across the country and around the world are vying for each customer's accounts.

outlets. Others, such as ING Direct in Canada, have begun to build their own neighborhood locations. In ING's case, a string of cafes was created in Canada, Europe, and the United States to offer customers food, drink, and comfortable surroundings, attracting dollar-valued and Euro-valued deposits. The United States may, however, be the biggest challenge for the growers of online banking businesses because it still possesses one of the world's lowest ratios of online customers relative to the total number of Internet shoppers.

Financial-Service Facilities of the Future

Despite continually advancing technology, most experts seem to agree that the total number of financial-service offices industrywide will probably not decline significantly; indeed, the total of all financial-service facilities may continue to grow in the future if the population desiring to use these services continues to increase. However, the design and function of most financial-service facilities are likely to evolve into new configurations—more wholly or partially automated facilities with broader self-service capability and more service facilities in non-stand-alone locations inside or adjacent to other stores and shops. Future facilities will also likely include information-accessing equipment that is so portable

POSSIBLE INTERNET USES

Banks and other financial-service providers can use the Internet for advertising, conducting customer surveys, giving customers a detailed description of service facilities, checking transactions on behalf of a customer, conducting business 24 hours a day, and granting speedy access to service application forms. The Internet can also promote conversations between customers and financial firms to improve services because it makes it easier to gather customer complaints and solicit customer evaluation of services offered.

WAYS TO PROMOTE CUSTOMER INTERNET USE

Banks and other financial institutions should use the Internet to emphasize safety, promote Web services at every opportunity, and revise their websites as often as possible to hold customer interest. They should survey customers frequently about quality, satisfaction, and availability of services and allow customers to download information about services and service facilities. The Web can promote customer dialogue to resolve problems through e-mail and telephone conversations.

Bankers and other financial-service managers need to ask themselves several key questions when planning to offer services via the Internet and in designing their websites and electronic communications systems. For example,

- Is the financial institution doing a good job describing its service offerings and explaining how a customer can access those services?
- Is the institution concerned enough about security and privacy to take significant steps to protect its customers?
- Does the institution provide a way for the public to get questions answered and problems solved?
- Does the financial firm identify someone specifically (by name) that the customer can contact with questions and problems?
- Does the bank or other service provider give the customer enough information to evaluate its current financial condition, data that would matter especially to large account holders and stockholders?
- Does the financial firm provide a way for job seekers to find out about career opportunities with the institution?
- Is the bank or other financial institution willing to invest in state-of-the-art Internet functionality to stay competitive in a marketplace of thousands of traditional and nontraditional financial-service providers?

that financial-service outlets will be able to visit or accompany the customer, wherever he or she goes, rather than requiring the customer to visit them.

Finally, the use of so-called "digital cash" will permit customers to be their own financial-service branches for certain routine transactions. Bank customers will be able to carry a pocketsize computer terminal to register payments for goods and services and to transfer funds as needed or carry a "smart card," which is an electronic purse holding a specified amount of electronic money to spend. When all the customer's electronic money is spent on purchases of goods and services, the card can be electronically "refilled" again and again with digital cash in order to support future purchases. But, even with these service innovations, there is still likely to be a significant role for traditional full-service branch offices geared to the special service needs of the neighborhoods and communities they serve, helping customers plan for the future with the aid of a broad menu of financial-service offerings and expert financial advice.

Whatever form future bank service facilities take, however, each branch office and limited-service facility will have to continually prove its worth in generating revenues and net earnings for banks and their competitors. Financial firms of the future are likely to

Key URLs
To learn more about website banking and its services, see such sites as **www.bankof america.com/billpay**, **www.sterlingbank.com**, and **www.bitsinfo.org**.

follow the lead of many retail stores in evaluating the success of their branch offices and limited-service facilities in terms of profits and costs per square foot. Future service facilities will have to combine a retail, sales-oriented environment with customer-friendly automation and still be flexible enough to deal with continuing product innovation. No longer can branches and limited-service facilities be just deposit gatherers; they must also be aggressive fee generators, selling credit, money management, and planning services to businesses and individuals as well as traditional savings plans. And the roles of branch managers will change as well; they must spend more time on the street generating new business (i.e., becoming highly sales oriented) by calling regularly on prospective clients and building stronger links to their communities.

Concept Check

18–12. Why is the establishment of new branch offices usually favored over the chartering of new banks and other financial firms as a vehicle for delivering financial services?

18–13. What factors are often considered in evaluating possible sites for new branch offices?

18–14. What changes are occurring in the design of, and the roles played by, bank branch offices? Please explain why these changes are occurring.

18–15. What laws and regulations affect the creation of new bank and thrift branches and the closing of existing branches? What advantages and what problems can the closing of a bank or thrift branch office create?

18–16. What new and innovative sites have been selected for new branch offices in recent years? Why have these sites been chosen by many finan-

cial firms? Do you have any ideas about other new branch sites that you believe should be considered?

18–17. What are POS terminals and where are they usually located?

18–18. What services do ATMs provide? What are the principal limitations of ATMs as a service provider? Should ATMs carry fees? Why?

18–19. What are self-service terminals and what advantages do they have for financial institutions and their customers?

18–20. What financial services are currently available on the Internet? What problems have bankers encountered in trying to offer Internet services?

18–21. How can banks and other financial firms better promote their Internet service options?

Summary

In this chapter we examined the major types of service outlets banks and other financial firms use today to deliver their services to the public. We examined these key points:

- *Convenience*—timely access to financial services—is a key factor in determining how customers choose which bank or other financial-service firm to use. Advances in communications technology allow customers to reach financial firms over great distances so that timely access today does not necessarily mean that service providers need to locate their service outlets in the same communities where their customers live and work.

- Nevertheless, for services where significant and costly problems may occur (such as checking accounts) the nearby presence of the financial-service provider remains appealing to many customers, especially households and small businesses.

- The key types of financial-service outlets used today include (1) chartering new banks and other corporate service providers; (2) establishing new full-service branch offices; or (3) setting up limited-service facilities, such as automated teller machines, point-of-sale terminals, Internet service channels, telephone centers, and electronically coded cards. Each type of service facility has its own unique advantages and disadvantages and appeals to different customer groups.

- If a financial-service provider elects to charter a new corporation, applications must be submitted to federal or state regulatory authorities. In the case of commercial banks in the United States, the individual states and the Comptroller of the Currency in Washington, D.C., can issue charters of incorporation. For thrift institutions, both the states and the federal Office of Thrift Supervision can award charters to organizing groups.

- Newly chartered banks and closely related financial firms generally are profitable within two to three years and depend heavily on the local business contacts of the organizers, the expansion of population and income in their principal service area, and the intensity of competition.

- Less costly than chartering new financial firms is the creation of full-service branch offices, usually set up in areas of high traffic volume. Other key factors in locating service facilities are population density, retail and wholesale sales, and industrial development. Traditional branches are stand-alone facilities that provide most of the same services as a financial institution's home office. More recently, limited-service facilities set up in prime shopping areas have helped to reduce operating costs from offering high-volume services.

- Internet sites generally operate at only a fraction of the cost of services provided through traditional brick and mortar branch offices. Unfortunately those facilities that are the cheapest to operate—for example, automated teller machines and websites—are often the least effective at cross-selling additional services. Whatever service facilities move to dominance in the future, these delivery vehicles are likely to be scrutinized more closely for performance and efficiency and configured for marketing multiple services more effectively.

Key Terms

Office of the Comptroller of the Currency, 647
charter of incorporation, 647
state banking commissions, 647

Federal Deposit Insurance Corporation (FDIC), 647
public need, 649
branch offices, 653
geographic diversification, 657

in-store branches, 659
point-of-sale terminals, 660
ATM, 660
ALM, 664
Internet service sites, 666

Problems and Projects

1. A group of businessmen and women from the town of Papillon are considering filing an application with the state banking commission to charter a new bank. Due to a lack of current banking facilities within a 10-mile radius of the community, the organizing group estimates that the initial banking facility would cost about $2.5 million to build along with another $700,000 in other organizing expenses and would last for about 20 years. Total revenues are projected to be $210,000 the first year, while total operating expenses are projected to reach $180,000 in year 1. Revenues are expected to increase 8 percent annually after the first year, while expenses will grow an estimated 7 percent annually after year 1. If the organizers require a minimum of a 10 percent annual rate of return on their investment of capital in the proposed new bank, are they likely to proceed with their charter application given the above estimates?

2. Luvel Savings and Loan is considering the establishment of a new branch office at the corner of Lafayette and Connecticut Avenues. The savings association's economics department projects annual operating revenues of $1.25 million from fee income generated by service sales and annual branch operating expenses of $680,000. The cost of

procuring the property is $1.66 million and branch construction will total an estimated $2.32 million; the facility is expected to last 16 years. If the savings and loan has a minimum acceptable rate of return on its invested capital of 12 percent, will Luvel likely proceed with this branch office project?

3. Sullivan Bank of Commerce estimates that building a new branch office in the newly developed Guidar residential township will yield an annual expected return of 12 percent with an estimated standard deviation of 4 percent. The bank's marketing department estimates that cash flows from the proposed Guidar branch will be mildly positively correlated (with a correlation coefficient of +0.30) with the bank's other sources of cash flow. The expected annual return from the bank's existing facilities and other assets is 11 percent with a standard deviation of 3 percent. The branch will represent just 10 percent of Sullivan's total assets. Will the proposed branch increase Sullivan's overall rate of return? Its overall risk?

4. The following statistics and estimates were compiled by First Saving Bank of Eastlin regarding a proposed new branch office and the bank itself:

Branch office expected return = 16%
Standard deviation of return = 5%
Bank's overall expected return = 12%
Standard deviation of bank's return = 2%
Branch asset value as a percentage
  of total bank assets = 15%
Correlation of net cash flows
  for branch and bank as a whole = +0.35

What will happen to the savings bank's total expected return and overall risk if the proposed new branch project is adopted?

5. First National Bank of Huron is considering installing three ATMs in its westside branch. The new machines are expected to cost $48,000 apiece. Installation costs will amount to about $32,000 per machine. Each machine has a projected useful life of 10 years. Due to rapid growth in the westside district, these three machines are expected to handle 180,000 cash transactions per year. On average, each cash transaction is expected to save 42 cents in check processing costs. If First National has a 12 percent cost of capital, should the bank proceed with this investment project?

6. First State Security Bank is planning to set up its own web page to advertise its location and services on the Internet and to offer customers selected service options, such as paying recurring households bills, verifying account balances, and dispensing deposit account and loan application forms. What factors should First State take into account as it plans its own web page and Internet service menu? How can the bank effectively differentiate itself from other banks currently present on the Internet? How might the bank be able to involve its own customers in designing its website and pricing its Internet service package?

Internet Exercises

1. If you need information about new charters for financial institutions, the place to look is the website of the chartering agency. For national banks, that would be the OCC at **www.occ.treas.gov**. You will find the Comptroller's Licensing Manual for Charters at **www.occ.treas.gov/corpbook/group4/public/pdf/charters.pdf**. Summarize the organizing group's role in seeking a charter for a new bank.

2. Suppose your bank is considering the construction of an in-store branch. Visit **www.intbantec.com/** for information from a company that designs and installs such

branches. Click on the Branch Design button. What is the difference between a storefront and a workplace branch?

3. If you want to stay abreast of the newest developments in the ATM field, visit **http://www.atmmarketplace.com**. If you are comparison shopping for ATMs for your institution, go to **www.atmmarketplace.com/buyersguide.php** and compare the features of three different ATMs. Print your comparison page.

4. Which U.S. banks and credit unions offer full Internet services? Visit **www.onlinebankingreport.com** and use the quick jump menu to access True Web Banks. Do a search based on your state. How many such banks are in your state?

5. What should you do if you suspect you may have become the victim of Internet fraud? Visit **www.internetfraud.usdoj.gov**. This site also provides information on possible types of Internet fraud. Review one of the four general tips on possible Internet fraud schemes found at this site.

STANDARD &POOR'S

S&P Market Insight Challenge

Use Standard & Poor's Market Insight website (**www.mhhe.com/edumarketinsight**) for this problem. While both banking and thrift industries are consolidating, charters for *new* depository institutions are still being issued. For up-to-date information concerning the profiles of these two industries, utilize the Industry tab in S&P's Market Insight. When you encounter the drop-down menu, you will see the subindustry groups labeled Diversified Banks, Regional Banks, and Thrifts & Mortgage Finance. By choosing these particular industry groupings, you will bring up the S&P Industry Survey covering banking and the survey devoted to savings and loans. Please download these surveys and read through the sections marked "Industry Profile" and "Industry Trends." What information were you able to collect on the number of new charters issued? What factors appear to influence the issuance of new charters in the banking and thrift field? Do you think the recent rapid growth of electronic service delivery channels (such as ATMs and the Internet) has affected chartering activity? In what ways?

www.mhhe.com/rose6e

REAL NUMBERS FOR REAL BANKS   Assignment for Chapter 18

A LOOK AT YOUR BANK'S USE OF BRANCHES, ATMS AND OTHER SERVICE OUTLETS FOR EXPANSION

While the overall number of BHCs and banks is decreasing, the number of newly chartered banks, branch offices, and ATMs is on the rise. In this assignment we will assess the changing structure of the BHC you have followed since Chapter 1.

An Examination of New Offices

A. Go to the FDIC's Institution Directory at **http://www3.fdic.gov/idasp/** and do a search for your bank holding company (BHC) using the BHC ID. This search will produce a list of bank and thrift subsidiaries. If you click on the active certificate links, additional information will appear and you will be able to pull up a current list of offices for that bank. A list of all offices associated with that bank will appear, accompanied with information on location, codes identifying the type of office, and the date established. You will want to focus your attention on new offices established since January 1, 2000. Collect information on the type of office, location (city, state), and date established for all new offices of each bank within your bank holding company.

B. In aggregate, how many new offices has your BHC established? What are the types of offices it has created? (Note that the codes are defined using their active link.) Where are the new offices located?

C. Compose several paragraphs discussing your bank's expansion using different types of offices and evaluating its strategy. Note: Your bank may have established limited new offices if it has focused on expansion via mergers and acquisitions, the topic for Chapter 19.

Selected References

For information on how new banks perform, see the following studies:

1. De Young, Robert. "For How Long Are Newly Chartered Banks Financially Fragile?" *Working Paper Series*, Research Department, Federal Reserve Bank of Chicago, September 2000.

2. Hunter, William C., and Aruna Srinivasan. "New Banks Control Their Own Future." *Economics Update*, Federal Reserve Bank of Atlanta 3, no. 3 (March 1990), pp. 1–2.

3. Rose, Peter S., and Clifford L. Fry. "Entry into U.S. Banking Markets: Dimensions and Implications of the Charter Process." Paper presented at the Western Finance Association Meetings, Honolulu, Hawaii, June 1976.

4. Selby, Edward. "The Role of Director Deposits in New Bank Growth." *Journal of Bank Research*, Spring 1981, pp. 60–61.

5. Shea, Maurice, P., III. "New Commercial Banks in Massachusetts." *New England Business Review*, Federal Reserve Bank of Boston, September 1967, pp. 2–9.

For studies of how new banks affect existing institutions, see the following:

6. Fraser, Donald R., and Peter S. Rose. "Bank Entry and Bank Performance." *The Journal of Finance* 27 (March 1972), pp. 65–78.

7. Rose, Peter S. "Competition and the New Banks." *The Canadian Banker and ICB Review* 84, no. 4 (July/August 1977), pp. 61–66.

For a discussion of the reasons for and impact of entry regulation in banking, see these studies:

8. McCall, Allan S., and Manfred D. Peterson. *The Impact of De Novo Commercial Bank Entry.* Working paper no. 76–7, Federal Deposit Insurance Corporation, 1976.

9. Motter, David C. "Bank Formation and the Public Interest." *The National Banking Review* 2 (March 1967), pp. 299–350.

10. Motter, David C., and Dean Carson. "Bank Entry and the Public Interest: A Case Study." *The National Banking Review* 1 (June 1964), pp. 469–512.

11. Federal Deposit Insurance Corporation. *Tips for Safe Banking over the Internet.* Washington, D.C., September 2000.

For a review of factors bearing on establishing new branches, limited-service facilities, and Internet services, the following sources are helpful:

12. Berger, Allen N. *The Economic Effects of Technological Progress: Evidence from the Banking Industry.* Finance and Economics Discussion Series, Board of Governors of the Federal Reserve System, Washington, D.C., 2002-50.

13. Board of Governors of the Federal Reserve System. *The Future of Retail Electronic Payments Systems: Industry Interviews and Analysis.* Staff Study 175, Washington, D.C., 2002.

14. Comptroller of the Currency. *The Internet and the National Bank Charter.* Washington, D.C., January 2001.

15. Garry, Michael. "Money in the Bank." *Progressive Grocer,* December 1991, pp. 62–65.

16. Neeley, Michelle Clark. "What Price Convenience? The ATM Surcharge Debate." *Regional Economist,* Federal Reserve Bank of Boston, July 1997, pp. 5–9.

17. Radecki, Lawrence J., and John Wenninger. "Paying Electronic Bills Electronically." *Current Issues in Economics and Finance,* Federal Reserve Bank of New York 5, no. 1 (January 1999), pp. 1–6.

18. Rose, Peter S. "The Bank Branch: Which Way to the Future?" *The Canadian Banker* 43, no. 6 (December 1986), pp. 40–50.

19. Stefanadis, Chris. "Why Hasn't Electronic Bill Presentment and Payment Taken Off?" *Current Issues in Economics and Finance,* Federal Reserve Bank of New York, July/August 2002.

20. Wenninger, John. "The Emerging Role of Banks in E-Commerce." *Current Issues in Economics and Finance,* Federal Reserve Bank of New York 6, no. 3 (March 2000), pp. 1–5.

21. Williams, Christopher. "Banks Go Shopping for Customers." *Regional Economist,* Federal Reserve Bank of St. Louis, October 1997, pp. 12–13.

22. Zdanowicz, John S. "Applying Portfolio Theory to Branch Selection." *Journal of Retail Banking* 13, no. 4 (Fall 1991), pp. 25–28.

23. Zimmerman, Kim. "Automation Helps Struggling Branch Double Deposits." *Bank Systems and Equipment* 25, no. 9 (September 1988), pp. 90–91.

CHAPTER NINETEEN

Mergers and Acquisitions: Managing the Process

Key Topics in This Chapter

- Merger Trends in the United States and Abroad
- Motives for Merger
- Selecting a Suitable Merger Partner
- U.S. and European Merger Rules
- Making a Merger Successful
- Research on Merger Motives and Outcomes

Introduction

In many nations around the globe, a wave of mergers between large and small banks, securities firms, insurance companies, and other financial-service providers has been under way for several years. In the United States banking and financial services has consistently ranked in the top five of all U.S. industries in the number of merger transactions year after year. Since 1980 more than 9,000 mergers among U.S. insured commercial banks have occurred, along with acquisitions of hundreds of thrift institutions (savings and loans and savings banks) over the same time period. Worldwide, more than 10,000 financial-service companies were merged or acquired in the world's 13 leading industrialized nations between 1990 and 2001.

These numerous marriages among financial-service institutions reflect the great forces of consolidation and convergence that have been dramatically reshaping the financial-services industry in the current era, driven by intense competition, the lifting of restrictive government rules (deregulation), and the continuing search for the optimal size financial-services organization that will operate at lowest cost with sufficient geographic and product-line diversification to reduce risk.

Our purpose in this chapter is to more fully understand the merger process in banking and financial services. We will explore the legal, regulatory, and economic factors that bankers and other financial-service managers should consider before pursuing a merger or acquisition. We will examine the available research evidence on the benefits and costs of these corporate combinations for both investors and the public.

The banking and financial services industry worldwide is being reshaped by mergers and acquisitions as smaller financial institutions combine to produce larger ones, spanning countries and continents. Some of the largest banking companies have combined with securities dealers, insurance companies, merchant bankers, and other nonbank entities to become highly diversified financial-service producers. However, while mergers and acquisitions worldwide have numbered in the thousands in recent years, not all are successful investment transactions. Indeed, more and more management teams are turning to the World Wide Web to help plan their mergers and acquisitions and to track the success or lack of success of those mergers and acquisitions that have already occurred.

Among the most popular websites in this field are SNL Financial's sites for mergers and acquisitions by banks and thrifts (**www.snl.com/bank/manda/**), by firms in nonbank financial-services industries (**www.snl.com/financial_svc/manda/**), and by insurance firms (**www.snl.com/insurance**). Other interesting sites touching on merger and acquisition trends in financial services include **www.innercitypress.org/bankbeat.html**, which contains news stories on mergers, layoffs, and changing regulations. Research on the impact of mergers and acquisitions conducted at the Federal Reserve Bank of St. Louis is often presented at the site **research.st.louisfed.org/wp/**, while questions and answers concerning the effects of bank merger activity may be found at **www.aba/com/Industry+Issues/ECO_Mergers_QA.htm**. The consolidation that the scores of acquisitions and mergers bring to the banking and financial-services industry every year is traced out in stories at **search.news.yahoo.com/search/news** (do a full coverage search on bank mergers) and at **www.cato.org** (search on mergers).

Mergers on the Rise

While mergers and acquisitions have swept through the entire financial-services sector in recent years, banking mergers and acquisitions have been the most numerous and widely publicized of these transactions. Many of the mergers sweeping through banking in recent decades reflect lower legal barriers that previously prohibited or restricted bank expansion.

For example, in the United States both state and federal laws prohibited or restricted interstate banking in the United States until the 1980s, when new state laws allowing banks and bank holding companies to cross state lines appeared. Then, in 1994, the U.S. Congress passed the Riegle-Neal Interstate Banking Act, which permitted bank holding companies to reach for bank acquisitions nationwide, subject only to broad limits in the proportion of insured deposits any single banking corporation could control and allowed nationwide branching. These new federal and state laws opened the floodgates to true nationwide banking for the first time in American history.

The merger wave in financial services received yet another legislative boost inside the United States when the Gramm-Leach-Bliley (Financial Services Modernization) Act of 1999 was passed (discussed in more detail in Chapters 2 and 3). The new GLB law opened wide the gates for bank–nonbank financial-service combinations. It permits banks, insurance companies, and security firms to acquire each other, increasing the opportunities for relatively large financial firms to diversify their product lines and reduce their dependence upon a limited menu of services. However, as Rhoades [32] and Piloff [30] have observed, while GLB may offer the prospect of reducing U.S. financial firms' risk exposure, it doesn't appear to hold great promise for major improvements in operating efficiency among banks and many of their financial-service competitors.

A massive merger wave involving leading banks, insurance companies, securities firms, and other financial-service providers swept through Europe during the 1990s, accompanying the formation and expansion of the European Community (EC). Competition among

CONSOLIDATION AND CONVERGENCE IN THE FINANCIAL SERVICES MARKETPLACE

Two of the dominant trends in the banking and financial services sector in recent years have been consolidation and convergence. *Consolidation* refers to a declining population of businesses in any one industry. Banking, security brokering, insurance, and several other financial-service industries have experienced this trend in recent years as they become dominated by fewer, but much larger businesses, largely through mergers and acquisitions. *Convergence,* on the other hand, refers to the movement of two or more industries toward each other, so that different firms wind up offering many of the same services. Convergence also often occurs through mergers and acquisitions as firms reach across industry boundaries to acquire business units with different service menus, though it can also take place through innovation and service diversification within an individual financial firm.

Listed below are some of the largest mergers and acquisitions of financial firms in recent years, some leading to *consolidation* in banking and some to *convergence* of bank and nonbank firms:

Examples of Consolidating Mergers and Acquisitions in Banking

Dai-Ichi Kangyo Bank, Fuji Bank, and Industrial Bank of Japan combined into Mizuho Holdings Inc. in 2001 to form the world's largest bank (in assets).

First Union Bank of Charlotte, North Carolina, acquired Wachovia Bank in 2001, creating the fourth largest U.S. commercial bank (in assets).

Wells Fargo Bank of California acquired Norwest Corp. of Ohio, a leading Midwest U.S. banking firm, in 1998.

Examples of Converging Mergers and Acquisitions among Bank and Nonbank Firms

Household Finance, a consumer-oriented finance company, was acquired by HSBC of London, one of the world's top five banks, in November 2002.

Allianz AG, the world's largest insurance company, acquired Dresdner Bank, one of Germany's largest commercial banks, in 2001.

Citicorp merged with Travelers Group, a major insurance carrier, to form Citigroup in 1998, then the world's second largest banking company (in assets).

European financial firms is becoming ever more intense, leading to continuing mergers and acquisitions, particularly in France, Germany, Italy, and Spain. However, financial-service mergers in Europe slowed somewhat as the 21st century opened due to a slow-growth economy, credit quality problems, and several European governments attempting to protect their home banks from acquisition by outsiders.

Asia and Japan followed Europe with a growing number of mergers involving mainly banks, insurers, and securities firms. These corporate combinations were being pieced together in an effort to shore up credit quality problems, fend off the ravages of deflation and sluggish national economies, and compete with powerful U.S. and European banks expanding across the Asian landscape. Table 19–1 lists other examples of recent international banking and financial-service mergers.

In the United States a similar convergence and consolidation trend has brought banks into common ownership with security and commodity broker-dealer firms, finance companies, insurance agencies and underwriters, credit card companies, thrift institutions, and numerous other nonbank service providers. Examples include Citicorp's 1998 merger with

Factoid
Where do most bank mergers take place in the United States?
Answer: In the southeastern United States (including such states as Alabama, Florida, Georgia, and the Carolinas).

TABLE 19–1
Recent Leading
International Bank
Mergers and
Acquisitions

Acquiring Institution	Acquired Institution	Year
Mizuho Holdings, Inc., Japan	Dai-Ichi Kangyo Bank, Fuji Bank, and the Industrial Bank of Japan	2001
Sumitomo Mitsui Banking Corporation, Japan	Sakura Bank and Sumitomo Bank	2001
HSBC Holdings PLC, Great Britain	Credit Commercial de France	2001
Banco Santander, S.A., Spain	Banco de Estado de Sao Paulo, Brazil	2000
ABN Amro Holdings, N.V.	Michigan National Corp., United States	2000
Deutsche Bank, AG, Germany	Bankers Trust Company, United States	1999

TABLE 19–2
Some of the Largest
Bank Mergers and
Acquisitions
in U.S. History

Acquiring Institution	Acquired Institution	Year
Bank of America, North Carolina	FleetBoston Financial	2003
Chase Manhattan Corp., New York	J. P. Morgan & Co., New York	2000
Fleet Financial Group, Massachusetts	BankBoston Corp., Massachusetts	1999
Travelers Group, California	Citicorp, New York	1998
NationsBank, North Carolina	Bank America, California	1998
Nations Bank, North Carolina	Barnett Banks, Florida	1997

Travelers Insurance, Inc., creating one of the largest financial-service providers in the world; Bank One's acquisition of credit card leader First USA; and Summit Bancorp's purchase of the thrift institution, Collective Bankcorp. Moreover, after passage of the Gramm-Leach-Bliley Act in November 1999, nonbank financial service firms have gobbled up some banks on their own. One example is the Federal Reserve Board's May 2000 approval of the proposed acquisition of U.S. Trust Corporation, then the 12th largest commercial banking organization in New York, by security broker/dealer Charles Schwab Corporation of San Francisco. Table 19–2 lists some of the largest bank mergers in U.S. history.

The current merger wave in banking and among other financial-service industries is unlikely to end soon, and its effects will be long lasting. The public will be confronted in the future with fewer, but larger financial-service organizations that will pose stronger competition for banks and other financial firms not joining the acquisition and merger trend. In this chapter, we examine the nature, causes, and effects of mergers and acquisitions. We will look at the laws and regulations that shape these corporate combinations and the factors that are important in selecting a merger partner.

The Motives behind the Rapid Growth of Banking and Financial-Service Mergers

As Table 19–3 illustrates, mergers usually occur because (1) the stockholders (owners) involved expect to increase their wealth (value per share of stock) or perhaps reduce their risk exposure, thus increasing their welfare; (2) management expects to gain higher salaries and employee benefits, greater job security, or greater prestige from managing a larger firm; or (3) both stockholders and management may reap benefits from a merger. There may be other motives as well. Let's take a closer look at some of the most powerful merger motives that appear to have been at work in recent years in the banking and financial-services sector.

TABLE 19–3 Possible Motives for Mergers and Acquisitions among Banks and Other Financial-Service Firms

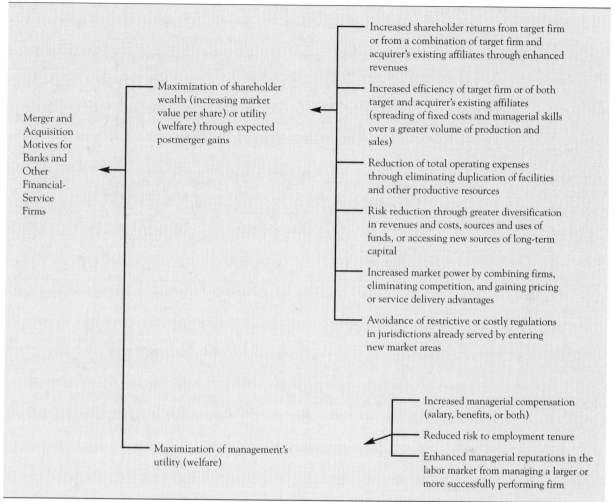

Profit Potential To most authorities in the field the recent upsurge in bank and nonbank financial-service mergers—averaging several hundred a year in the United States alone—reflects the expectation of the stockholders that **profit potential** will increase once the merger is completed. If the acquiring organization has more aggressive management than the firm it acquires, revenues and earnings may rise as markets are more fully exploited and new services developed. This is especially true of interstate or international mergers where many new markets are entered, opening up much greater new revenue potential. Moreover, if the acquiring firm's management is better trained than the management of the acquired institution, the efficiency of the merged organization may increase, resulting in more effective control over operating expenses. Either way—through reduced expenses or expanded revenues—mergers can improve profit potential. Other factors held equal, the value of a merging firm's stock may rise, increasing the welfare of its stockholders.

Risk Reduction Alternatively, many partners to mergers anticipate reduced **cash flow risk** and reduced **earnings risk** as well. The lower risk may arise from the fact that mergers increase the overall size and prestige of an organization, open up new markets with different economic characteristics from markets already served, or make possible the offering of new services whose cash flows are different in timing from the cash flows generated by existing services. For example, many European bank mergers in recent years (pursued by such leading banks as ABN AMRO and Verenigte Spaar-Bank) appear to have been motivated by the search for "complementarity" in services. Thus, a wholesale-oriented bank pursues a retail-oriented bank or a bank allies itself with an insurance company in an effort to broaden the menu of services offered the public, thereby reducing risk exposure from relying upon too narrow a lineup of services. Therefore, mergers can help to *diversify* the combined organization's sources of cash flow and earnings, resulting in a more stable financial firm able to withstand wide fluctuations in economic conditions and in the competitive environment of the industry.

Filmtoid
What 1999 British film concludes with the ING Group of the Netherlands acquiring London's Barings Bank, which has gone "belly-up" due to the risk exposure of Nick Leeson's futures trading operation in Singapore?
Answer: *Rogue Trader*

Rescue of Failing Institutions   The failure of a company is often a motive for merger. For example, many bank mergers have been encouraged by the FDIC and other bank and thrift regulatory agencies as a way to conserve scarce federal deposit insurance reserves and avoid an interruption of customer service when a depository institution is about to fail. One of the most prominent examples was the acquisition of First City Bancorporation of Texas in January 1993 by Chemical Bank of New York. In this case a well-managed and capital-strong banking company saw an opportunity to acquire substantial assets (about $6.6 billion) and deposits (close to $4.4 billion) with only a limited capital investment (less than $350 million). Following passage of the Garn–St Germain Depository Institutions Act (1982) and the Competitive Equality in Banking Act (1987), bank holding companies operating in the United States were allowed to reach across state lines to acquire failing banks and thrifts. Finally, with the enactment of the Financial Institutions Reform, Recovery, and Enforcement Act of 1989, Congress voted to allow bank holding companies to acquire even healthy thrift institutions anywhere inside the United States, subject to regulatory approval.

Tax and Market-Positioning Motives   Many mergers arise from expected **tax benefits,** especially where the acquired firm has earnings losses that can be used to offset taxable profits of the acquirer (Weston and Chung [19]). There may also be **market-positioning benefits,** in which a merger will permit the acquiring institution to acquire a base in a completely new market. For example, acquiring an existing bank, rather than chartering a new banking firm with new personnel, can significantly reduce the cost of positioning in a new market. Further expansion in the form of branching or future mergers can subsequently take place, with the most recently acquired bank as a base of operations. A good example of this merger motive is the recently announced acquisition of FleetBoston Financial Corp in New England by Bank of America Corp., with the latter seeking to purchase or open branches in numerous areas across the United States where there is strong market growth potential. The B of A/Fleet merger would result in a single banking-facilities network of close to 6,000 branches and roughly 17,000 ATMs.

These market-positioning mergers are likely to accelerate in the future now that the Riegle-Neal Interstate Banking Act has become law in the United States and recent banking directives have been passed by the European Economic Community to more freely allow banks to cross state and national boundaries, make acquisitions, and purchase or establish new branch offices. Moreover, Germany's Commerzbank, ING Group of the Netherlands, and Allianz AG Holdings have recently bought sizeable ownership shares in Korean banks to further position themselves in the developing financial markets of Asia, opening up potential new sources of revenue and earnings.

The Cost Savings or Efficiency Motive   Large-scale staff reductions and savings from eliminating duplicate facilities have followed in the wake of some of the largest mergers in the financial-services sector. For example, in April 1992 Bank of America merged with Security Pacific to create what was then the second largest banking firm in the United States. After the merger, close to 500 branch offices were targeted for closure with projected savings of more than a billion dollars. Similarly, when insurer Allianz acquired Germany's Dresdner Bank in 2001, Dresdner's staff was cut by 8,000 (or about 16 percent of its labor force) in an effort to save money. The search for **cost savings** (economies of scale) were also uncovered in a survey by Lausberg and Rose [28, 29] of the massive merger wave occurring in European banking during the 1980s and 1990s. Of the 107 European bank merger events examined, the single most important merger motivation was the desire to reduce operating costs, followed by a plan to diversify into new markets as part of an internationalization strategy.

We must be cautious about making too much of this efficiency or cost savings factor in explaining the recent rash of banking and financial-services mergers, however. Most mergers are of the *market extension* type, which means the institutions involved don't overlap much or at all in terms of geographic area served. Thus, closing duplicate office facilities is less possible. In fact, to the surprise of many experts, branch offices are expanding in the banking industry, not contracting, even as the massive bank merger wave is unfolding. For example, as Rhoades [32] points out, while the number of banks operating in the United States fell from about 14,400 in 1980 to about 8,700 as the 21st century approached, the number of branch offices swelled to more than 70,000, and the number of ATMs soared even higher to more than 140,000. What these numbers suggest is that some customers, especially households and smaller businesses, appear to demand a local banking connection. This limits how far bankers can go in closing down what they feel is "unneeded" service space.

Mergers as a Device for Reducing Competition   Yet another possible explanation for hundreds, if not thousands, of recent mergers may be the wish to lower the degree of competition in the marketplace. When two competitors are allowed to merge, the public is served by fewer rivals for their business. Service quality may diminish, and prices and profits may rise. At least consistent with this merger explanation is the rapid rise in financial services industry concentration under way all over the globe, including the United States nationally and in some American towns and cities. For example, as Rhoades [32] observes, the 100 largest U.S. banks jumped from holding a 47 percent share of total industry deposits in 1980 to about 71 percent in 1998. While much less of an overall increase in concentration is evident in local markets, there are reports of greater concentration in the largest U.S. metropolitan areas and in some urban and rural market areas. If true, there is the potential from this merger motive for damage to the public. More aggressive prosecution of the antitrust laws, as we will discuss later in this chapter, will need to be considered.

Other Merger Motives   Management may believe a merger will result in increased capacity for growth, maintaining the acquiring institution's historic growth rate. Moreover, a merger enables a lending institution to expand its loan limit to better accommodate corporate customers. This is a particularly important factor in markets where the lender's principal business customers may be growing more rapidly than the lending institution itself (as noted by Peek and Rosengren [24]).

Mergers often give smaller institutions access to capable new management, which is always in short supply. For example, in the commercial banking industry large banking companies recruit on college campuses and often hire through employment agencies in major metropolitan areas. Smaller, outlying banks have fewer market contacts to help find managerial talent, and they may not be able to afford top-quality personnel. The same is true of access to costly new electronic technology. For example, the merger of First Union Corp. of North Carolina and CoreStates Financial Corp. of Pennsylvania in 1998 appeared to be driven, in part, by CoreStates' need for upgraded computer systems to more efficiently handle its retail consumer accounts.

Merger Motives That Executives and Employees Identify In a study by Prasad and Prasad [31], senior executives from 25 of the largest banking firms in the United States were asked what factors they consider in choosing target banks to acquire. The most prominent feature mentioned was *quality of management*. Several officers of leading banks said they preferred merger partners whose managements were compatible with their own. Other key factors mentioned in identifying desirable institutions to acquire were profitability (especially return on assets), efficiency of operations, and maintenance of market share.

Concept Check

19–1. Exactly what is a merger?

19–2. Why are there so many mergers each year in the banking industry? In other financial-services industries?

19–3. What factors seem to motivate most mergers?

Selecting a Suitable Merger Partner

How can management and the owners of a bank or other financial firm decide if a proposed merger is good for the organization? The answer involves measuring both the costs and benefits of a proposed merger. Because the acquiring and acquired institutions may have different reasons for pursuing a merger, this is not an easy cost–benefit calculation. Even so, the most important goal of any merger should be to increase the *market value* of the surviving firm so that its stockholders receive higher returns on the funds they have invested. Stockholders deserve a return on their investment commensurate with the risks they have taken on.

For example, a merger is beneficial to the stockholders of a bank in the long run if it increases the bank's stock price per share. The value (price) of a bank's stock, like the stock of any other corporation, depends upon these factors:

1. The expected stream of future dividends flowing to the stockholders.
2. The discount factor applied to the future stock dividend stream, based on the rate of return required by the capital markets on investments of comparable risk.

Specifically,

$$\text{Market price per share of stock} = \sum_{t}^{\infty} \frac{D_t}{(1 + c)^t}$$

where annual expected dividends per share are represented by D_t and c is the opportunity cost rate on capital invested in projects that expose investors to comparable risk. Clearly, if a proposed merger increases expected future stockholder dividends or lowers investors' required rate of return from the organization by reducing its risk, or combines the two, the bank or other corporate financial institution's stock will *rise* in price and its stockholders will benefit from the transaction.

How might a merger increase expected future earnings or reduce the level of risk exposure? One possibility is by *improving operating efficiency*—that is, by reducing operating cost per unit of output. A bank or other financial firm might achieve greater efficiency by consolidating its operations and eliminating unnecessary duplication. Thus, instead of two separate planning and marketing programs, two separate auditing staffs, and so forth, the merged institution may be able to get by with just one. Existing resources—land, labor, capital, and management skills—may be used more efficiently if new production and service delivery methods (such as automated equipment) are used, increasing the volume of services produced with the same number of inputs.

Another route to higher earnings is to enter new markets or offer new services via merger. Entry into new markets can generate *geographic diversification* if the markets entered have different economic characteristics from those markets already served. Alternatively, a merger may allow banks and other financial firms with different packages of services to combine their service menus, expanding the service options presented to their customers. This is *product-line diversification*. Both forms of diversification tend to stabilize cash flow and net earnings, presenting the stockholders with less risk and probably increasing the market value of their stock. Ideally, merger-minded managers want to find an acquisition target whose earnings or cash flow is negatively correlated (or displays a low positive correlation) with the acquiring organization's cash flows.

For many bankers and other financial-service managers, a major consideration in any proposed merger is its probable impact on the earnings per share (EPS) of stock of the surviving firm. Will EPS improve after the merger, making the new combined institution's stock more attractive to investors in the financial marketplace? Stockholders of the firm to be acquired are usually asking the same question: If we exchange our stock in the old institution for the stock of the acquiring firm, will our EPS rise?

Generally speaking, the stockholders of both acquiring and acquired institutions will experience a gain in earnings per share of stock if (*a*) a company with a higher stock-price-to-earnings (P-E) ratio acquires a company with a lower P-E ratio and (*b*) combined earnings do not fall after the merger. In this instance, earnings per share will rise even if the acquired institution's stockholders are paid a reasonable premium for their shares.

For example, suppose the stockholders of Bank A, whose current stock price is $20 per share, agree to acquire Bank B, whose stock is currently valued at $16 per share. If Bank A earned $5 per share of stock on its latest report and B also earned $5 per share, they would have the following P-E ratios:

$$\text{A's P-E ratio} = \frac{\$20 \text{ price per share}}{\$5 \text{ earnings per share}} = 4$$

$$\text{B's P-E ratio} = \frac{\$16 \text{ price per share}}{\$5 \text{ earnings per share}} = 3.2$$

Suppose, too, that these two banks had, respectively, 100,000 shares and 50,000 shares of common stock outstanding and that Bank A reported net earnings of $500,000, while B posted net earnings of $250,000. Thus, their combined earnings would be $750,000 in the most recent year.

If the shareholders of Bank B agree to sell out at B's current stock price of $16 per share, they will receive 4/5 ($16/$20) of a share of stock in Bank A for each share of B's stock. Thus, a total of 40,000 shares of Bank A (50,000 Bank B shares × 4/5) will be issued to the stockholders of Bank B to complete the merger. The combined organization will then have 140,000 shares outstanding. If earnings remain constant after the merger, the stockholders' earnings per share will be

$$\frac{\text{Earnings}}{\text{per share}} = \frac{\begin{array}{c}\text{Combined}\\\text{earnings}\end{array}}{\begin{array}{c}\text{Shares of}\\\text{stock outstanding}\end{array}} = \frac{\$750,000}{140,000} = \$5.36$$

which is clearly higher than the $5 per share that Bank A and Bank B each earned for their shareholders before they merged.

As long as the acquiring institution's P-E ratio is larger than the acquired firm's P-E ratio, there is room for paying the acquired company's shareholders at least a moderate **merger premium** to sweeten the deal. A merger premium expressed in percentage terms can be calculated from this formula:

$$\text{Merger premium (in percent)} = \frac{\begin{array}{l}\text{Aquired firm's} \\ \text{current stock} \\ \text{price per share}\end{array} + \begin{array}{l}\text{Additional amount} \\ \text{paid by the acquirer} \\ \text{for each share of the} \\ \text{acquired firm's stock}\end{array}}{\text{Acquired firm's current stock price}} \times 100$$

For example, suppose that despite the difference in current market value between Bank A's and Bank B's stock (i.e., $20 versus $16 per share), Bank A's shareholders agree to offer B's shareholders a bonus of $4 per share (i.e., a merger premium of [$16 + $4]/$16 = 1.25, or 125 percent). This means B's stockholders will exchange their stock for Bank A's shares with an **exchange ratio** of 1:1. Therefore, B's shareholders, who currently hold 50,000 shares in Bank B, will wind up holding 50,000 shares in Bank A. The combined organization will have 150,000 shares outstanding. If earnings remain at $750,000 following the merger, the consolidated banking organization will be able to maintain its earnings per share at the current level of $5 (i.e., $750,000/150,000 shares).

Unfortunately, paying merger premiums can get out of hand. Until recently, merger premiums ranging from 150 to 250 percent had become commonplace, and they often yielded disappointing results for the stockholders long after these mergers were consummated. For example, suppose B's shareholders are offered a merger premium of 150 percent—that is, they are paid $24 per share for stock currently valued at $16 (or [$16 + $8]/$16 = 1.5). This means B's stockholders will get 6/5 of a share ($24/$20) in the acquiring organization, Bank A, for every share of Bank B's stock they now hold. When the exchange is made on these terms, there will be 60,000 new shares of Bank A (6/5 × 50,000 of B's shares), or a total of 160,000 shares for the combined banking firm. If total earnings do not fall but remain close to $750,000, the merged bank will report the following earnings per share:

$$\text{EPS} = \$750,000 \div 160,000 = \$4.69$$

Clearly, the earnings per share of the merged firm will have declined due to the **dilution of ownership** created by offering the acquired bank's stockholders an excessive number of new shares relative to the value of their old shares.

If the ratio of the stock price to the earnings of the firm to be acquired is greater than the P-E ratio for the acquiring firm, the combined firm's EPS will fall below its original level, a victim of spreading available earnings over more shares of stock, or earnings dilution. For example, suppose Bank A, with a P-E ratio of 4 (or a $20 price per share/$5 in EPS) and 100,000 shares of stock outstanding, attempts to acquire Bank B, with a P-E ratio of 5 (i.e., $25 share price/$5 in EPS) and 50,000 shares of stock issued. Assume that total earnings after the merger ($750,000) match the banks' combined earnings before the merger. If A's stockholders agree to grant B's owners 1.25 shares ($25 price per share for B's stock ÷ $20 per share for A's stock) in the merged bank for each share of stock they presently hold, the new bank will have 62,500 new shares (i.e., 1.25 × 50,000 of B's shares) added to the 100,000 the acquiring bank already has outstanding. The merged firm will then have earnings per share of

$$\text{EPS} = \$750,000 \div 162,500 \text{ shares} = \$4.62$$

which is substantially less than the $5 in earnings per share that Bank A posted before this merger. There is a significant dilution of earnings in this case because of the greater P-E ratio of the acquired bank and because so many new shares were issued to pay the high merger premiums promised to the acquired institution's shareholders.

The financial success of a merger, then, depends heavily on the comparative dollar amounts of earnings reported by the two participating organizations and their relative price-earnings ratios. For example, the immediate change in earnings per share from the merger of Bank A and Bank B depends on this ratio:

$$\frac{\text{Price per share of Bank A's stock}}{\text{Current net earnings of Bank A}} \div \frac{\text{Price per share of Bank B's stock}}{\text{Current net earnings of Bank B}}$$

Of course, even if EPS goes down right after the merger, the transaction may still be worth pursuing if future earnings are expected to grow faster as a result of the acquisition. If significantly greater efficiency and cost savings result over the long run, the effects of paying a higher price (in new stock that must be handed over to the acquired institution's shareholders) will be more than made up eventually. Standard financial management practice calls for analyzing what will happen to the combined organization's EPS under different possible scenarios of future earnings and stock prices. If it takes too long to recover the cost of an acquisition according to the projected path of EPS, management of the acquiring institution should look elsewhere for a merger target.

The Merger and Acquisition Route to Growth

Whatever its motives, each merger is simply a financial transaction that results in the acquisition of one or more firms by another institution. The acquired firm (usually the smaller of the two) gives up its charter and adopts a new name (usually the name of the acquiring organization). The assets and liabilities of the acquired firm are added to those of the acquiring institution.[1] A merger normally occurs after the managements of the acquiring and acquired organizations have struck a deal. The proposed transaction must then be ratified by the board of directors of each organization and possibly by a vote of each firm's common stockholders.[2]

If the stockholders approve (usually by at least a two-thirds majority), the unit of government that issued the original charter of incorporation must be notified, along with any regulatory agencies that have supervisory authority over the institutions involved. For example, in the United States the federal banking agencies have 30 days to comment on the merger of two federally supervised banks and there is a 30-day period for public comments as well. Public notice that a merger application has been filed must appear three times over a 30-day period, at approximately two-week intervals, in a newspaper of general circulation serving the communities where the main offices of the banks involved are located. The U.S. Justice Department can bring suit if it believes competition would be significantly reduced after the proposed merger.

In deciding whether or not to merge, management and the board of directors of the acquiring firm often consider many characteristics of the targeted institution. The

---

[1] Two or more firms may also *consolidate* their assets to form one institution, with all participating firms giving up their former identities to become parts of a larger organization. Consolidations are much less common in banking and financial services than mergers, however.

[2] In a purchase and assumption transaction, two-thirds of the shareholders of the acquired firm must approve; however, usually no shareholder vote of approval is required by stockholders of the acquiring institution, nor is shareholder approval usually required when a firm engages in a partial liquidation of its assets (e.g., a bank or thrift institution selling some of its branch offices).

principal factors examined by most merger analysts fall into six broad categories: (1) the firm's history, ownership, and management; (2) the condition of its balance sheet; (3) the firm's track record of growth and operating performance; (4) the condition of its income statement and cash flow; (5) the condition and prospects of the local economy served by the targeted institution; and (6) the competitive structure of the market in which the firm operates (as indicated by any barriers to entry, market shares, and degree of market concentration).

In addition to the foregoing items, many acquirers will look at these factors as well:

1. The comparative management styles of the merging organizations.
2. The principal customers the targeted institution serves.
3. Current personnel and employee benefits.
4. Compatibility of accounting and management information systems among the merging companies.
5. Condition of the targeted institution's physical assets.
6. Ownership and earnings dilution before and after the proposed merger.

A thorough evaluation of any proposed corporate merger before it occurs is absolutely essential, as recent experience has shown.

Methods of Consummating Merger Transactions

Mergers usually take place employing one of two methods: (*a*) pooling of interests or (*b*) purchase accounting. For mergers begun before July 1, 2001, the Financial Accounting Standard Board (FASB) permitted the use of the *pooling of interests* approach in which the merger partners merely sum the volume of their assets, liabilities, and equity in the amounts recorded just before their merger takes place. The result, clearly, is a merged firm displaying a simple combined total of all the merger partners' assets, liabilities, and equity in one combined balance sheet. The income statement of the newly consolidated firm will reflect the income and expenses of both firms added together for the full period of time covered by the income and expense statement as though the merging businesses had been one company when the income statement began.

In contrast, under *purchase accounting* the firm to be acquired is valued at its purchase price and that price is added to the total assets of the acquirer. The purchase method requires that the acquiring and acquired firms be handled on a different basis so it is important to know who is acquiring whom. The acquirer records the acquisition at the price paid to the stockholders of the acquired company, first valuing the acquired firm at market plus goodwill, if the acquisition price and market value are different.

Goodwill is an intangible asset usually arising from a merger transaction where the purchase price of the merger target is larger than the difference between the fair value of its assets minus any liabilities taken on. The Financial Accounting Standards Board (specifically, in FASB 142) labels goodwill as the "intangible synergies" of a combined financial firm resulting from a merger. As Carlson and Perli [34] observe, with the rapid pace of banking industry consolidation in recent years goodwill on bank balance sheets has virtually exploded, growing at more than 30 percent annually to climb just over 1 percent of total industry assets during the past decade. While FASB used to require goodwill to be amortized (and, thus, gradually disappear) over its useful life (not to exceed 40 years), the Standards Board has recently changed its mind and now goodwill need not be amortized as long as it doesn't become impaired due to deterioration in a merging company's financial strength. In contrast to the purchase accounting approach to mergers where goodwill is permitted, no goodwill is figured in when using the pooling of interest approach.

Another way to view the merger process is to determine exactly what the acquirer is buying in the transaction: assets or shares of stock. Mergers are generally carried out by using either (1) the purchase of assets or (2) the purchase of common stock. With the **purchase-of-assets method,** the acquiring institution buys all or a portion of the assets of the acquired institution, using either cash or its own stock. In purchase-of-assets mergers, the acquired institution usually distributes the cash or stock to its shareholders in the form of a liquidating dividend, and the acquired organization is then dissolved. With some asset purchase deals, however, the institution selling its assets may continue to operate as a separate, but smaller, corporation.

With the **purchase-of-stock method,** on the other hand, the acquired firm ceases to exist; the acquiring firm assumes *all* of its assets and liabilities. While cash may be used to settle either type of merger transaction, in the case of commercial banks regulations require that all but the smallest mergers and acquisitions be paid for by issuing additional stock of the acquirer. Moreover, a stock transaction has the advantage of not being subject to taxation until the stock is sold, while cash payments are usually subject to immediate taxation. Stock transactions trade current gains for future gains that are expected to be larger if everything goes as planned.[3]

The most frequent kind of merger in banking today involves **wholesale** (large metropolitan) **banks** merging with smaller **retail banks.** This lets money center banks gain access to relatively low-cost, less interest-sensitive consumer accounts and channel those deposited funds into profitable corporate loans. Most financial-firm takeovers are friendly— readily agreed to by all parties—although a few are *hostile,* resisted by existing management and stockholders. Not long ago in the acquisition of Irving Trust by Bank of New York, for example, the management and directors of Irving created obstacle after obstacle, legal and financial, to this corporate marriage before the courts finally cleared it to proceed.

Regulatory Rules for Bank Mergers in the United States

Mergers have transformed the commercial banking industry more than any other type of financial-services industry. In this section we take a close look at the government rules applying to bank mergers in the United States.

Two sets of rules generally govern the mergers of banks and other financial firms: (1) decisions by courts of law and (2) statutes enacted by legislators, reinforced by regulations. In the United States, for example, the Sherman Antitrust Act of 1890 and the Clayton Act of 1914 forbid mergers that would result in monopolies or significantly lessen competition in any industry. Whenever any such merger is proposed, it must be challenged in court by the U.S. Department of Justice.

Inside the United States the most important law affecting the mergers and acquisitions of commercial banks is the **Bank Merger Act of 1960.** This law requires each merging bank to request approval from its principal federal regulatory agency before a merger can take place. For national banks, this means applying to the Comptroller of the Currency for prior approval. For insured state-chartered banks that are members of the Federal Reserve System, the Fed's approval is required. Insured, state-chartered nonmember institutions must gain approval from the Federal Deposit Insurance Corporation.

Under the terms of the Bank Merger Act, each federal agency must give top priority to the **competitive effects** of a proposed merger. This means estimating the probable effects

---

[3] Merger transactions involving banks and other financial firms generally must be accounted for in accordance with Accounting Principles Board Opinion No. 16 (APB No. 16). The difference between the purchase price and the fair value of net assets acquired in mergers should be treated as an intangible asset in accordance with generally accepted accounting principles (GAAP).

of a merger on the pricing and availability of banking services in the local community and on the degree of concentration of deposits or assets in the largest depository institutions in the local market. Thus, current merger laws in banking rest on three premises: (1) the *cluster of products* offered by a bank is the relevant product line to be considered in a merger or acquisition; (2) the relevant market to be concerned about, in most instances, is *local* (counties or metropolitan areas); and (3) the *structure* of the local market (usually measured by degree of concentration) is the principal determining factor in how much competition already exists and how a merger might damage or aid that competition. Where concentration is high—that is, where the largest depository institutions control a dominant share of local deposits or assets—the risk of damaging competition is greater, and the merger is less likely to win regulatory approval unless the merging institutions agree to *divest* some of their affiliated banks and branches. For example, in 1992 Bank America was allowed to acquire Security Pacific Corp. only after agreeing to divest itself of 213 branch offices in five states, holding almost $9 billion in deposits.

Key URL
To learn more about law and regulation in the banking sector, see, for example, **http:// library.findlaw.com/ articles**.

Moreover, the *trend* in concentration also comes under close scrutiny from the regulatory agencies. Markets that have recently experienced increasing concentration ratios or declining numbers of financial-service suppliers are less likely to see mergers approved than are markets where concentration is falling. Other factors that must be weighed include the financial history and condition of the merging institutions, the adequacy of their capital, their earnings prospects, strength of management, and the convenience and needs of the community to be served. Mergers with anticompetitive effects cannot go unchallenged by federal authorities unless the applicant can show that such combinations would result in significant **public benefits.** Among the possible benefits are providing financial services where none are conveniently available and rescuing a failing financial institution whose collapse would have damaging effects on the public welfare.

The federal supervisory agencies prefer to approve mergers that will enhance the financial strength of the institutions involved. Regulators repeatedly emphasize the need for improving management skills and strengthening equity capital. The existence of such laws and regulations creates a barrier for any merger that would lead to substantial changes in market share and market concentration, possibly damaging competition in the local (county or metropolitan) market. This creates a dilemma for aggressive financial firms. Expansion-minded management and stockholders must distinguish proposed combinations that are likely to be challenged by the government, resulting in expensive legal battles, from those that are likely to sail through with few problems. It should be noted that the large majority of merger applications filed—usually more than 90 percent—are approved. However, this high approval rate reflects a good deal of screening out of unacceptable mergers through informal conferences between merger-minded financial institutions and regulatory officials.

Justice Department Guidelines

To reduce the legal uncertainties in the merger process, the U.S. Department of Justice issued formal guidelines for merger applicants in 1968. The initial **Justice Department Merger Guidelines** were quite restrictive. They required firms operating in markets judged to be highly concentrated, with only limited competition, to acquire primarily *foothold businesses* (i.e., those having a small or insignificant market share) or to enter such markets *de novo* (i.e., start a new firm). In June 1982, the Reagan administration authorized more liberal merger guidelines. These rules permitted combinations that would probably have been challenged by the Justice Department under the old guidelines. The Justice Department further modified its merger guidelines in 1992, including the special guidelines for bank mergers and the mergers of selected other financial institutions that we operate under today.

The degree of *concentration* in a market is measured by the proportion of assets or deposits controlled by the largest institutions serving that market. Presumably, if the largest firms control a substantial share of market assets or deposits, anticompetitive behavior (including collusive agreements) is more likely, resulting in damage to the public from excessive prices and poor service quality. The Justice Department guidelines require calculation of the **Herfindahl-Hirschman Index** (HHI) as a summary measure of *market concentration*. HHI reflects the proportion of total assets, deposits, or sales accounted for by each firm serving a given market. Each firm's market share is squared, and HHI is calculated as the sum of squared market shares for all firms serving a specific market area. Thus, the Herfindahl-Hirschman index is derived from this formula:

$$HHI = \sum_{i=1}^{k} A_i^{2}$$

where A_i represents the percentage of market-area deposits or assets controlled by the *i*th bank or other financial firm in the market, and there are k banks or other financial firms in total serving the market. We note from this formula that the Herfindahl index reflects *both* the number of institutions in the market and the concentration of deposits or assets in the largest financial-service institutions and assigns heavier weight (by squaring each firm's market share) to those institutions commanding the biggest market shares.

For example, suppose that a small local banking market contains four commercial banks having the deposits and deposit market shares shown in the following table:

Bank Deposits and Market Shares in Edgecroft County			
Name of Banking Firm	Deposits in Latest Annual Report	Market Shares of Total Deposits (A_i)	Square of Each Bank's Market Share (A_i^2)
First Security National Bank	**$245 million**	50.8%	2,580.6
Edgecroft National Bank	113 million	23.4	547.6
Lincoln County State Bank	69 million	14.3	204.5
Edgecroft State Bank and Trust Co.	55 million	11.4	130.0
Totals	$482 million	100.0%	3,462.7

In this case:

$$HHI = \sum A_i^{2} = 3,462.7 \text{ points}$$

HHI may vary from 10,000 (i.e., 100^2)—a monopoly position, where the leading firm is the market's sole supplier—to near zero for unconcentrated markets. In theory, the smaller the value of HHI, the less one or a few firms dominate any given market and the more equally are market shares distributed among firms. The more nearly firms are equal in size, the more competitive the relevant market is usually assumed to be and the less likely is anticompetitive behavior.

Under Department of Justice guidelines, any merger that would (*a*) result in a postmerger HHI of less than 1,800 or (*b*) change the value of the HHI in the relevant market area by less than 200 points would not likely be challenged by the Justice Department because, in the government's view, the merged firm would not gain enough market power to significantly damage the public welfare. However, when a proposed merger appears to yield a Herfindahl index exceeding these guidelines (i.e., the HHI in the relevant market would be more than 1,800 and rise by more than 200 points), the Justice Department considers such a market "highly concentrated." Proposed mergers in highly concentrated markets may draw a Justice Department challenge in federal court unless the department's lawyers and economists can find evidence of extenuating circumstances.

Consider the above example in which we calculated the market shares of commercial banks in Edgecroft County, where HHI equaled 3,462.7 points. According to the Justice Department's guidelines, Edgecroft would be a "highly concentrated market" (provided that Justice confined its definition of the relevant banking market to the local county itself and did not bring in surrounding areas that have more banks, as often happens where cities span several counties). The biggest bank in Edgecroft, First Security National, holds a 50.8 percent market share. First Security would have a difficult time gaining approval for a merger with any other Edgecroft bank. (The largest bank in the county is more than twice as large as its nearest competitor, and the smallest bank has only an 11 percent market share.) Indeed, it would be difficult for any commercial bank mergers to take place inside the Edgecroft market because of its highly concentrated status and because no matter which two of the four banks might wish to merge with each other, the resulting change in HHI would be relatively large. (As an example, if the two smallest banks merged, their combined market share would be 25.7 percent, which, when squared, is 660.5 points. The HHI for the market would climb more than 300 points, from 3,462.7 to 3,788.7, following this merger.) However, a bank outside the Edgecroft market might well be able to merge with one of the Edgecroft banks in what is known as a *market extension merger*. This would leave the local market's HHI unchanged and would not reduce the number of alternative suppliers of banking services to the public.

Extenuating circumstances are frequently considered in approving those mergers that lead to only moderate increases in market concentration. These mitigating factors may include the ease with which new firms can enter the same market, the conduct of firms already present in the market, the types of products involved and the terms under which they are being sold, and the type and character of buyers in the relevant market area.

In recent years, the Justice Department has liberalized its standards for judging the anti-competitive effects of bank mergers. One device Justice has used to carry out this more liberal attitude is to include *nonbank financial institutions* in the calculation of some concentration ratios for local markets. Including at least a portion of the deposits held by savings and loans, credit unions, and other financial institutions in the total deposits of a local market area lowers the market share held by each bank. Thus, fewer financial-services mergers will appear to damage competition and more mergers will receive federal approval, other factors held equal. However, recent research (see, for example, Kwast, Starr-McCluer, and Wolken [27]) suggests that in most local markets banks continue to be the principal financial-service provider to households and small businesses, especially for checking and savings services and for credit.

The Merger Decision-Making Process by U.S. Federal Regulators

U.S. federal bank regulatory agencies must apply the standards imposed by the Bank Merger Act and the Justice Department Merger Guidelines to all merger proposals. Each merger application is reviewed (*a*) by staff economists and attorneys working for the federal banking agencies to assess the potential impact of the proposed merger on competition and (*b*) by officials of the agencies' examination and supervision department to assess the merger's probable impact on the financial condition and future prospects of the banks involved.

The Bank Merger Act also requires the federal agency that is the merging banks' principal supervisor to assess the effect of the proposed merger on public convenience and the public's need for an adequate supply of financial services at reasonable prices. The agency involved must review the banks' records to determine if they have made an affirmative effort to serve all segments of the population in their trade area without discrimination.

This assessment is required under the terms of the Community Reinvestment Act (CRA) of 1977, which forbids banks and selected other financial firms from *redlining*—that is, marking off certain neighborhoods within their trade area and declining to extend financial services (especially credit) to residents of those neighborhoods. Compliance with this affirmative action law has become more important to federal regulators with the passage of time.

As we saw in Chapter 17, federal examiners must review each bank's community service record each time they examine a bank's financial records and award a CRA rating, ranging from "outstanding" down to "substantial noncompliance." Any bank that has a low CRA rating runs the risk of having its proposed merger denied by the federal banking agencies. Recently an additional regulatory hurdle has been imposed on merging banks and selected other financial firms in the form of the Home Mortgage Disclosure Act (HMDA). This law requires selected lenders making home mortgage loans to report periodically the geographic distribution and other features of their home loans so that regulatory authorities can look for any evidence of discrimination against individuals and families seeking loans to purchase new homes on the basis of race, ethnic origins, neighborhood location, or other illegal factors. Home mortgage lenders that appear to have practiced discriminatory lending practices face an uphill battle in trying to win approval of a proposed merger.

Finally, one element of regulator decision-making that has figured prominently in large U.S. bank mergers as the 1990s ended and a new century began was the growing use of *divestiture*. As more banks and other financial firms merge, fewer are left and the merger process is more likely to eliminate direct competitors with many overlapping markets. To preserve and protect competition, regulators have increasingly demanded that large merging banking firms sell their offices in those local markets where the merging institutions compete with each other. Among the most prominent mergers inside the United States where participating banks were ordered to sell off some of their offices were the 1992 merger of BankAmerica Corp. with Security Pacific Corp. (where about 200 offices were divested), the 1997 merger of Nations Bank with Barnett Banks (where nearly 125 offices were traded away), and Fleet Financial Group's 1999 merger with Bank Boston Corp. (where more than 300 offices were divested). Many experts in the field believe the divestiture tool will continue to be heavily used in banking as mergers swallow up ever larger financial-service competitors.

Merger Rules in Europe

The recent formation of the European Union (EU) has resulted in a wave of mergers on that continent. Partly as a result, the European Commission—an executive body of the EU currently based in Brussels—has emerged as a key arbiter of mergers involving European businesses. Because the European Commission cannot break apart a merger after that combination has already occurred (unlike the U.S. Justice Department), the Brussels commission has recently become aggressive in denying some companies permission to merge if the proposed combination would lead to "collective dominance" in a given market.

The doctrine of *collective dominance* suggests that if a significant European market would become so concentrated as a result of a proposed merger or mergers that only about four firms would come to dominate that market, then the European Commission might well vote to block any further market concentration, even if non-European firms were involved. While, thus far, banking and financial services in Europe do not appear to be as heavily concentrated as are several other European industries, there is little question that a strong consolidation trend in financial services is under way in the EU and may soon lead to significant regulatory challenges. Anticipating this possibility, European and non-European financial firms are surveying their industry for potential merger candidates before the "regulator's axe" becomes a significant factor inside Europe's markets (for example, American Express Company recently acquired Threadneedle Asset Management Holdings). In 2002 the United States and the European Union agreed to work toward joint review of mergers involving multinational businesses in order to avoid conflicting merger decisions when a U.S. and a European firm propose to combine their ownership and resources.

Making a Success of a Merger

As we will see later in this chapter when we review the record of actual postmerger outcomes, many mergers simply do not work. A variety of factors often get in the way of mergers' success, including poor or ill-prepared management, a mismatch of corporate cultures and styles, excessive prices paid by the acquirer for the acquired firm, a failure to take into account the customers' feelings and concerns, and a lack of strategic "fit" between the combining companies so that nothing really meshes smoothly with minimal friction and the merged institution finds that it cannot move forward as a cohesive and effective competitor.

Recent experience and research have suggested a few helpful steps that improve the chances for a desirable merger performance outcome, including these:

1. Acquirer, know thyself! Every financial-service company that is intent on growth through merger must thoroughly evaluate its own financial condition, track record of performance, strengths and weaknesses of the markets it already serves, and strategic objectives. Such an analysis can help management and stockholders identify strengths and weaknesses and clarify whether a merger could really help to magnify each participating institution's strengths and compensate for its weaknesses.

2. Get organized for a detailed analysis of possible new markets to enter and institutions to acquire. Banks and other financial firms that are merger focused should create a management/shareholder team (including outside consultants, such as investment banking specialists) with the skills needed to successfully evaluate potential new markets, potential acquisitions, and their apparent strengths and weaknesses.

   Favorable markets to enter typically show a track record of above-average but stable growth in incomes and business sales, a somewhat older-than-average population with a high proportion of professional workers and business owners and managers, moderate to low inflation with stable currency prices, moderate competition, and a favorable regulatory environment that does not hinder bank expansion or the development of new banking services. Desirable institutional targets, on the other hand, show evidence of persistent earnings growth and market acceptance of the services they offer (as measured by the growth of assets and deposits and a rising market share), a strong capital base, facilities and equipment that are functioning well and are up to date, evidence of close monitoring and control over operating costs, and complementary goals between acquiring and acquired institutions.

3. Establish a realistic price for the target firm based on a careful assessment of its projected future earnings discounted by a capital cost rate that fully reflects the risks of the target market and target firm and reflects all prospective costs that will have to be met by the acquiring firm (such as closing or upgrading poorly located or inadequately equipped branch offices, replacing outdated or incompatible management information systems, educating inadequately trained staff to handle new services, and correcting salary disparities that may exist between the two merging organizations).

4. Once a merger is agreed upon, create a combined management team with capable managers from both acquiring and acquired firms that will direct, control, and continually

Key URL
Additional information about choosing the right merger target may be found at numerous web locations, such as **www.yaledailynews .com/article.asp ?AID=8420.**

SELLING OFF BRANCH OFFICES TO GAIN APPROVAL FOR A MERGER: *DIVESTITURE*

For several decades now banks and thrift institutions that operate branch offices in local neighborhoods have sometimes been asked to *divest* themselves of some of their offices in order to secure regulators' approval for their proposed mergers with other depository institutions. This type of request typically has come from such agencies as the U.S. Department of Justice, the Federal Reserve Board, the Comptroller of the Currency, and the Federal Trade Commission in an effort to promote competition.

For example, in a market dominated by three commercial banks, if two of them merge, all of their branches then become part of one banking firm. Consumers in that market now have only two banking alternatives. Worse still, in a given local neighborhood there may only be branch offices of the two merging institutions present which, after the merger, results in neighborhood residents having just one local banking service option.

Accordingly, in recent years several bank and thrift mergers have been approved by regulators only if some of the branch offices of the acquired depository institution are sold off to a third party. Examples of banks confronted with this divestiture decision have included BankAmerica Corporation in its merger with Security Pacific Corporation in 1992, NationsBank Corporation in its acquisition of Barnett Banks, Inc. in 1998, and Banc One Corporation in its acquisition of First Chicago NBD, also in 1998. In the BankAmerica–Security Pacific merger case, 187 branches were sold to other banks not involved in that merger.

What happened to the branch offices disposed of? Did they survive or did all of their depositors leave? A recent study by Steven Piloff of the Federal Reserve Board finds that, in general, the branches disposed of did well. Initially, they faced a "runoff" around the time of their sale because some depositors apparently wanted to follow their old bank even after it was acquired by a larger institution, didn't trust the new owner of the branches, or perhaps used the occasion to make a change they may have been planning all along.

After the initial "runoff," growth in deposits resumed at a pace comparable to that of other branch offices. Interestingly, the larger the bank purchasing these branches, the faster the divested branches tended to grow, perhaps because larger depositories are more familiar to the public, offer more services, or manage their new offices more effectively. Overall, the *divestiture* requirement to promote banking and thrift competition appears to have worked reasonably well.

See especially Steven J. Piloff, "What's Happened at Divested Bank Offices? An Empirical Analysis of Antitrust Divestitures in Bank Mergers," *Finance and Economics Discussion Series,* Federal Reserve Board, no. 60, Washington, D.C. 2002.

assess the quality of progress toward the consolidation of the two organizations into a single effective unit.

5. Establish a reporting and communications system between senior management, branch and line managers, and staff that promotes rapid two-way communication of goals, operating problems, and ideas for improved technology and procedures so that employees at all levels feel involved in the merger, are convinced that effort and initiative will be rewarded, and believe they have a contribution to make toward the merger's ultimate success.

6. Create communications channels for both employees and customers to promote (1) understanding of why the merger was pursued, and (2) what the consequences are likely to be for both anxious customers and employees who may fear interruption of service, loss of jobs, higher service fees, the disappearance of familiar faces inside the institution, and other changes. This may require setting up customer and employee "hot lines" to calm concerned people and give them the direction and assurances they seek.

7. Set up customer advisory panels to evaluate and comment upon the merged institution's community image, service and marketing effectiveness, efforts to recognize loyal customers, pricing schedules, and general helpfulness to customers.

The foregoing steps, even if faithfully followed, do not promise successful mergers, but they will increase the probability that a merger will proceed smoothly and possibly achieve its long-range goals.

Concept Check

19–4. What factors should a bank or other financial firm consider when choosing a good merger partner?

19–5. What factors must the regulatory authorities consider when deciding whether to approve or deny a merger?

19–6. When is a market too concentrated to allow a merger to proceed? What could happen if a merger

were approved in an excessively concentrated market area?

19–7. What steps that management can take appear to contribute to the chances for success in a merger? Why do you think many mergers produce disappointing results?

Research Findings

What is the track record of mergers involving banks and other types of financial firms? What impact do they have on the public and upon stockholders? A number of studies over the years have addressed these questions. In general, the results are mixed—some positive and some negative effects. Other challenging problems—such as establishing a solid base in a new market—are often resolved successfully through the merger route, however.

The Financial Impact

A recent study by Rose [17], which looked at the earnings impact of approximately 600 national bank mergers, found *no* significant differences in profitability between merging and comparably sized nonmerging banks serving the same local markets. In fact, this study showed that the acquired institutions were significantly more profitable than their acquirers in the returns earned for their stockholders. However, the acquired firms were significantly less profitable than comparable-size nonmerging banks serving the same markets, perhaps giving rise to the expectation among stockholders and management involved in these mergers that such combinations would help to improve earnings.

Studies by Pettway and Trifts [9] and by Darnell [20] tend to confirm this picture of relatively poor profit performance. Darnell found that most bank mergers involved payment by the acquiring banks of substantial premiums over book value to shareholders of the acquired banks. Moreover, these merger premiums tended to rise as more mergers occurred because there were usually fewer remaining banks to buy. The observations of Pettway and Trifts and of Darnell suggest the existence of factors unrelated to profit operating behind many bank mergers.

There is some evidence that the stockholders of interstate banking companies acquiring banks across state lines have scored slightly positive abnormal returns on their stock when these acquisitions were announced. For example, a study by Millon-Cornett and De [7] examined selected interstate bank acquisitions and found that the shareholders of both acquiring and the acquired banks reaped positive returns higher than would be expected from the risk incurred by their stockholders. And, both Millon-Cornett and Tehranian [8] and Spong and Shoenhair [13] found improvements in bank performance after interstate mergers were concluded, including increased earnings, better cost control, greater employee productivity, and faster growth. Rose [12] also found that interstate banking companies tend to gain greater local and statewide market shares of deposits and loans (but not earnings) when they acquire banks across state lines. However, Goldberg and Hanweck [4] found neither gains in statewide shares nor any edge in profitability over noninterstate banks.

Factoid
Do mergers seem to improve bank performance? Not according to the Federal Reserve Bank of San Francisco, which finds only that, in some instances, operating costs are lowered. See especially **www.frbsf.org/econrsrch/workingp/wp99-10.pdf**.

Concept Check

19–8. What does recent research evidence tell us about the impact of most mergers in the financial sector?

19–9. Does it appear that most mergers among banking firms serve the public interest?

Do bankers involved in mergers generally regard their efforts as successful? A survey by Rose [17] of nearly 600 U.S. bank mergers occurring from 1970 to 1985 asked that very question of the CEOs involved. Overall, no more than two-thirds of these merging institutions believed they had fulfilled their merger expectations. For example, in only about half the cases investigated did profits, growth, market share, or market power actually increase and risk and operating costs fall. Roughly one-third of those seeking more qualified management apparently did *not* find it. However, CEOs at a substantial majority of the merging institutions (at least 80 percent) believed that their banks' capital base had improved and they were now a more efficient organization.

Unfortunately, as another study by Rose [10] suggests, there are absolutely no guarantees that any merger will be successful, just as there never is any guarantee of benefits from any other type of capital investment. Rose's study of 572 U.S. acquiring banking institutions, purchasing nearly 650 other banks, found a nearly symmetric distribution of earnings outcomes from mergers—roughly half registering positive earnings gains and about half displaying negative earnings results. Among the institutions experiencing positive earnings gains, lower operating costs, greater employee productivity, faster growth, and greater concentration (perhaps implying less competition) in the markets where the headquarters offices of banks examined were located appeared to account for the greater earnings achieved. Thus, a significant portion of higher postmerger returns appeared to be due to increases in postmerger market concentration. This latter outcome suggests that, in some cases at least, the public may be paying higher prices for banking and financial services than would prevail in less concentrated (more competitive) markets. If so, regulatory agencies need to take a closer look at any proposed mergers for possible evidence of significant changes in the competitive climate within merger-active market areas.

Finally, an extensive study on an international scale by Amel, Barnes, Panetta, and Salles [1], published recently by the Federal Reserve Board, covers the effects of mergers among commercial banks, insurance companies, and securities firms in leading industrialized countries. The study finds that mergers and acquisitions in the financial sector (especially among commercial banks and insurance companies) often do seem to produce operating cost savings (economies of scale), though only up to a relatively small size of firm. However, there is often little or no evidence of substantial cost reductions among larger financial firms or of any improvements in managerial quality.

The Public Benefits

In what ways does the *public* benefit from mergers? Most studies that have looked at this issue find few real public benefits. For example, the survey by Rose [16] discussed earlier asked the CEOs of merging U.S. banks whether there had been any increase in hours of operation in order to provide the public with better access to banking facilities. Fewer than 20 percent of the merging institutions reported any increase in hours of operation. About one-third changed their pricing policies, but the most common change was a price *increase* following merger, particularly in checking account service fees, loan interest rates, deposit interest rates, and safe-deposit box fees. This result is echoed by Kohn [23], Bacon [2], and Snider [18], who all found that banking firms absorbed in a merger tend to have their prices changed to match those of the acquiring organization.

One factor that appears to keep price increases following mergers under some restraint, at least, is *population migration.* As Kiser [6] observes, loan and deposit interest rates tend to be more favorable to customers in areas where substantial numbers of households are relocating and, because of this movement, are compelled to seek out new banks for the financial services they need. Unfortunately, the majority of households move infrequently and, usually, to a nearby location, keeping their working relationship with the same banks and other financial-service firms. This fact of life appears to give merging banks and other service providers more latitude to raise service prices and limit competition.

On the positive side, there is no convincing evidence that the public has suffered from a decline in service quality or availability following most mergers. In fact, Kaufman's study [22] of Elkhart, Indiana, where two of three banks in town merged, found that the majority of businesses and consumers surveyed believed that service quality had gone up following this merger. Kohn [23] found no evidence of a loss of local funding in a study of banking and thrift mergers in New York State, while Jones and Laudadio [21] suggested that mergers may significantly lower the bank failure rate. This notion was reinforced by Rose [11] whose study of 84 large bank holding companies making interstate acquisitions of banks found that diversifying bank operations into at least four states or two different economic regions of the United States could stabilize asset and equity returns, reduce the chances of insolvency, and lead to lower operating costs.

One negative impact of mergers among commercial banks has been detected in some of the most recent studies (e.g., Karcesle, Ongena, and Smith [26]), especially for business customers who are heavily dependent upon their banks for credit. On average, business borrowers of merger-targeted banks appear to lose some of their returns and equity value. The reason may be that the borrowing customers' relationships with their lending institution may be threatened when new owners take over. In contrast, business customers that can more easily switch lenders in the wake of a merger seem to be less harmed (in terms of their rate of return or value) by mergers than are customers who can't easily switch the lending institutions with which they deal.

Finally, there may be an unexpected pro-competitive aspect to merger activity among financial-service providers. A recent study by Seelig and Critchfield published by the FDIC [33] explores an apparent connection between bank and thrift mergers inside a given market area and an increase in charters to form *new* banks and thrift institutions in that same market. These researchers find that mergers tend to stimulate *de novo* entry, suggesting, perhaps, that new competitors are more likely to appear in those market areas where merger activity is perceived to be changing the balance of power. No one is exactly sure why this increase in *de novo* entry occurs—perhaps mergers anger some customers who readily switch their accounts to new banks and thrifts or mergers lead to cost cutting, firing some employees who then start new financial-service institutions.

Summary

Mergers and acquisitions of bank and nonbank financial firms have been a major vehicle for change in the financial-services industry for many decades. This chapter has explored these key points regarding the merger and acquisition process in banking and financial services:

- Mergers and acquisitions in the financial-services field have absorbed thousands of banks, thrift institutions, securities firms, insurance companies, finance companies, and other financial-service firms in recent years. Among the driving forces behind these corporate combinations are changes in legislation and regulation, intense competition among financial-service providers, and the continuing search for greater operating efficiency and reduction of costs and risk exposure.

- Mergers in the banking industry, in particular, have been powerfully influenced by changing legislation and regulation as governments around the world have moved to loosen the rules governing the financial marketplace. In the United States the passage of the Riegle-Neal Interstate Banking Act during the 1990s and numerous state laws during the 1980s gradually opened up the possibility of nationwide banking through mergers and acquisitions. As the 1990s drew to a close, the Gramm-Leach-Bliley (Financial Services Modernization) Act permitted merger combinations among banks, security firms, and insurance companies. Parallel financial-service mergers and acquisitions unfolded at about the same time in Europe as the European Union established a common currency and financial system.

- While government deregulation has opened up substantial opportunities for banking and financial-service mergers, key economic and financial forces have encouraged the managers and owners of financial firms to take advantage of these new opportunities. Among the powerful economic and financial forces at work has been the movement of customers to distant markets, encouraging financial-service firms to expand in order to follow and retain those customers. Moreover, mergers and acquisitions have proven to be a less expensive route for company expansion than has the creation of new financial firms or the construction of chains of new branch offices. Finally, the possibility of risk reduction through the processes of geographic diversification (expansion into new market areas) and product-line diversification (expansion into new types of services) has lured many bankers and other financial-service managers to seek out promising acquisition targets.

- Despite recent deregulation, significant government rules still surround the merger process. A prominent example in the United States is the Bank Merger Act of 1960 and its many subsequent amendments. Under the terms of this law, proposed mergers involving banking firms must be approved or denied by each institution's principal federal regulatory agency—the Comptroller of the Currency for national banks, the Federal Deposit Insurance Corporation for U.S.-insured banking firms not members of the Federal Reserve System, or the Federal Reserve for state-chartered banking companies that have established membership in the Federal Reserve System.

- Merger laws in the United States require the Department of Justice (DOJ) to evaluate the competitive effects of any proposed merger among financial institutions just as it does for proposed combinations of nonfinancial companies. The Department can file suit in federal court to stop any proposed merger that, in its judgment, would have an adverse impact on competition, thereby harming the public interest.

- Mergers and acquisitions among financial firms are capital investment decisions and, as such, must be carefully examined for their potential economic benefits and costs. If the expected returns are less than the minimum returns sought by each firm's stockholders, the proposed transaction is not likely to be pursued unless other mitigating factors intervene. The key to successful mergers among banks and other financial firms involves carefully assessing the strengths and weakness of both the acquirer and the proposed acquisition target and designing a strategy to maximize any synergies that may emerge once the merger is under way.

- Current research on the impact of mergers among banks and other financial-service firms comes to very mixed conclusions. While most financial-service mergers appear to be profitable, many are either unprofitable or fall disappointingly short of their premerger objectives. Moreover, the majority of cases offer meager evidence of public benefits. For example, service charges and fees often rise, rather than fall, following the completion of a merger transaction. However, the menu of financial services offered to the public frequently increases once a merger or acquisition is completed.

Key Terms

profit potential, 679
cash flow risk, 679
earnings risk, 679
tax benefits, 680
market-positioning
benefits, 680
cost-savings
(efficiency), 681
merger premium, 684

exchange ratio, 684
dilution of ownership, 684
purchase-of-assets
method, 687
purchase-of-stock
method, 687
wholesale banks, 687
retail banks, 687

Bank of Merger Act
of 1960, 687
competitive effects, 687
public benefits, 688
Justice Department Merger
Guidelines, 688
Herfindahl-Hirschman
Index, 689

**Problems
and Projects**

1. Evaluate the impact of the following proposed mergers upon the *postmerger earnings per share* of the combined organization:

   a. An acquiring bank reports that the current price of its stock is $18 per share and the bank earns $6 per share for its stockholders; the acquired bank's stock is selling for $15 per share and that bank is earning $5 per share. The acquiring institution has issued 200,000 shares of common stock, whereas the acquired institution has 100,000 shares of stock outstanding. Stock will be exchanged in this merger transaction exactly at its current market price. Most recently, the acquiring bank turned in net earnings of $1,200,000 and the acquired banking firm reported net earnings of $300,000. Following this merger, combined earnings of $1,600,000 are expected.

   b. The bank to be acquired is currently earning $14 per share, and its acquirer is reporting earnings of $12 per share. The acquired firm's stock is trading in today's market at $24 per share, while the acquiring firm's stock exchanges today for $20 per share. The acquired institution has 75,000 shares outstanding; the acquiring institution, on the other hand, has issued 80,000 shares of common stock. The combined organization is expected to earn $900,000; before the merger, the acquired bank posted net earnings of $400,000 and the acquiring bank tallied net earnings of $600,000. If the stock will be traded at the going market price to effect this merger, what will postmerger earnings per share be?

2. Under the following scenarios, calculate the *merger premium* and the *exchange ratio*:

   a. The acquired corporate savings and loan association's stock is selling in the market today at $8 per share, while the acquiring institution's stock is trading at $12 per share. The acquiring firm's stockholders have agreed to extend to shareholders of the target firm a bonus of $4 per share. The acquired thrift has 30,000 shares of common stock outstanding, and the acquiring institution has 50,000 common equity shares. Combined earnings after the merger are expected to remain at their premerger level of $1,250,000 (where the acquiring firm earned $1,000,000 and the acquired institution $250,000).

   b. The acquiring firm reports that its common stock is selling in today's market at $30 per share. In contrast, the acquired institution's equity shares are trading at $24 per share. To make the merger succeed, the acquired firm's shareholders will be given a bonus of $2 per share. The acquiring institution has 120,000 shares of common stock issued and outstanding, while the acquired firm has issued 40,000 equity shares. The acquiring firm reported premerger annual earnings of $850,000, and the acquired institution earned $150,000. After the merger, earnings are expected to decline to $900,000. Is there any evidence of dilution of ownership or earnings in either merger transaction?

3. The Silverton metropolitan area is presently served by five large branch banks with total deposits as follows:

	Current Deposits
Silverton National Bank	$854 million
Silverton County Merchants Bank	605 million
Commerce National Bank of Silverton	383 million
Rocky Mountain Trust Company	211 million
Security National Bank and Trust	107 million

Calculate the Herfindahl-Hirschman Index (HHI) for the Silverton metropolitan area. Suppose that Rocky Mountain Trust Company and Security National Bank propose to merge. What would happen to the HHI in the metropolitan area? Would the U.S. Department of Justice be likely to approve this proposed merger? Would your conclusion change if the Silverton County Merchants Bank and the Rocky Mountain Trust Company planned to merge?

4. Langley Savings Association has just received an offer to merge from Courthouse County Bank. Langley's stock is currently selling for $40 per share. The shareholders of Courthouse County agree to pay Langley's stockholders a bonus of $10 per share. What is the merger premium in this case? If Courthouse County's shares are now trading for $65 per share, what is the exchange ratio between the equity shares of these two institutions? Suppose that Langley has 10,000 shares and Courthouse County has 30,000 shares outstanding. How many shares in the merged firm will Langley's shareholders wind up with after the merger? How many total shares will the merged company have outstanding?

5. The city of Wanslow is served by three banks, which recently reported deposits of $234 million, $182 million, and $67 million, respectively. Calculate the Herfindahl index for the Wanslow market area. If the second and third largest banks merge, what would the postmerger Herfindahl index be? Under the Department of Justice guidelines discussed in the chapter, would the Justice Department be likely to challenge this merger?

6. In which of the situations described in the accompanying table do the stockholders of both acquiring and acquired firms experience a gain in earnings per share of stock as a result of a merger?

	P-E Ratio of Acquiring Firm	P-E Ratio of Acquired Firm	Premerger Earnings of Acquiring Firm	Premerger Earnings of Acquired Firm	Combined Earnings after the Merger
A.	5	3	$ 750,000	$425,000	$1,200,000
B.	4	6	$ 470,000	$490,000	$ 850,000
C.	8	7	$ 890,000	$650,000	$1,540,000
D.	12	12	$1,615,000	$422,000	$2,035,000

7. Please list the steps that you believe should contribute positively to success in a merger transaction in the financial-services sector. What management decisions or goals? On average, what proportion of mergers among financial firms would you expect would be likely to achieve the goals of management and/or the owners and what proportion would likely fall well short of the mergers' objectives? Why?

Internet Exercises

1. You are interested in the mergers and acquisitions that are reshaping the banking and financial services industry in the United States and abroad. Visit **www.innercitypress. org/bankbeat.html** and you will get more recent banking news than you want to read in one sitting. If you are using Internet Explorer, click Edit button, then use the Find command to look for the word *merger*. What are the newsworthy merger announcements?

2. *Consolidation* refers to a declining population of businesses in any one industry. Visit **www.financialservicesfacts.org/financial/** and explore the link on consolidation. Discuss the number of financial-service mergers by industry.

3. *Convergence* refers to the movement of two or more industries over time toward each other, resulting in different firms offering many of the same services. Visit **www.financial servicesfacts.org/financial/** and explore the link on convergence. How do the service offerings of large commercial banks compare with securities firms? How do commercial banks compare with insurance firms?

4. Which ingredients appear to be associated with a successful bank merger or acquisition? Go to **www.snl.com/bank/manda/** and read one of the latest merger and acquisition stories. What are the important factors?

5. Which ingredients appear to be associated with a successful nonbank financial-services merger or acquisition? Go to **www.snl.com/financial_svc/manda/** and read one of the latest merger and acquisition stories. What are the important factors?

STANDARD &POOR'S

S&P Market Insight Challenge

1. Use Standard & Poor's Market Insight website (**www.mhhe.com/edumarketinsight**) for this problem. The banking and thrift industries have been in a consolidation mode—fewer but larger companies—for years. Recent information concerning acquisitions and mergers in these industries may be found using the Industry tab in S&P's Market Insight, Educational Version. A drop-down menu displays such industry groups as Diversified Banks, Regional Banks, and Thrifts & Mortgage Finance. By choosing these particular industry groups you will be able to find the S&P Industry Survey on Banking as well as the survey covering savings and loans. Please download both of these industry surveys and explore the parts labeled "Industry Profile" and "Industry Trends." Please describe the most recent trends in mergers and discuss their underlying motivations.

2. Use Standard & Poor's Market Insight website (**www.mhhe.com/edumarketinsight**) for this problem. Please examine closely the list of bank holding companies, investment banking or security/broker dealer firms, finance companies, and life and property/ casualty insurers listed on S&P's Market Insight, Educational Version. Which of these companies have engaged in a significant merger or acquisition within the past three years? Which have been acquired themselves within that time span by a bank or nonbank business? (Prominent examples include Citigroup, HSBC Holdings PLC, Bank of America, Salomon Smith Barney, Aetna Life and Casualty, and Household International among many others on the Insight list.)

3. Use Standard & Poor's Market Insight website (**www.mhhe.com/edumarketinsight**) for this problem. As this chapter relates, business mergers and acquisitions, including those in the financial sector, frequently result in disappointing financial and operating performance. Can you cite any examples in the financial-services group of firms on Market Insight experiencing disappointing postmerger or postacquisition performance? What reasons can you cite for the disappointing performance results?

REAL NUMBERS FOR REAL BANKS

Assignment for Chapter 19

A LOOK AT YOUR BANK'S USE OF MERGERS FOR EXPANSION

The overall number of BHCs and banks is decreasing due to consolidation within the industry and convergence across the different financial services industries. In this assignment we will examine the history of your bank in the context of mergers and acquisitions. With mergers and acquisitions, the acquisition may take place through the BHC or one of its subsidiary banks.

AN EXAMINATION OF HOW YOUR BANK EVOLVED

A. You will need to go back to your informational spreadsheet created in Chapter 2 and view the names of the banks listed as part of your BHC. You will want to check the history of the BHC and each bank. Go to the National Information Center at **www.ffiec.gov/nic/** and click on the Institution History button. This brings up a screen where you

can search for BHCs and banks. (Hint: with National City Corp, if I type in "National City" I will access the BHC and all the banks that begin with National City.) Focus on all mergers occurring since January 1, 2000. Collect information on your BHC and each bank within your BHC, who acquired who and when, noting the state of the target institution.

B. Choose one or more acquisitions and search for press releases on your BHC's website.

C. Focusing on the chosen acquisition, go to a search engine such as **www.alltheweb.com** and do a news search.

D. Using the data you found and the press releases and any news articles collected, compose several paragraphs describing your BHC's acquisitions and providing inferences concerning your BHC's merger strategy. Remember to reference your sources of information.

Selected References

For analyses of how mergers affect the performance of banks and similar organizations please see the following:

1. Amel, Dean; Colleen Barnes; Fabio Panetta; and Carmelo Salles. "Consolidation and Efficiency in the Financial Sector: A Review of the International Evidence." *Finance and Economics Discussion Series*, Study 2002-47, Board of Governors of the Federal Reserve System, 2002.

2. Bacon, Peter W. *A Study of Bank Mergers in Marion County, Indiana, 1945 to 1966.* Staff Memorandum, Research Department, Federal Reserve Bank of Chicago, October 1967.

3. Dick, Astrid A. "Market Structure and Quality: An Application to the Banking Industry." *Finance and Economics Discussion Series*, No. 2003-14, Board of Governors of the Federal Reserve System, 2003.

4. Goldberg, L. G., and G. A. Hanweck. "What Can We Expect from Interstate Banking?" *Journal of Banking and Finance* 12 (1988), pp. 51–67.

5. Hughes, Joseph P.; William L. Lang; Loretta J., Mester; Choon-Geol Moon; and Michael S. Pagano. "Do Bankers Sacrifice Value to Build Financial Empires?" *Working Paper 02-2*, Federal Reserve Bank of Philadelphia, 2002.

6. Kiser, Elizabeth K. "Household Switching Behavior at Depository Institutions: Evidence from Survey Data." *Working Paper*, Board of Governors of the Federal Reserve System, August 14, 2002.

7. Millon-Cornett, M., and S. De. "Common Stock Returns in Corporate Takeover Bids: Evidence of Interstate Bank Mergers." *Journal of Banking and Finance* 15 (1991), pp. 273–95.

8. Millon-Cornett, M., and H. Tehranian. "Changes in Corporate Performance Associated with Bank Acquisitions." *Journal of Financial Economics* 31 (1992), pp. 211–34.

9. Pettway, Richard, and J. W. Trifts. "Do Banks Overbid When Acquiring Failed Banks?" *Financial Management* 14 (Summer 1985), pp. 5–15.

10. Rose, Peter S. "The Distribution of Outcomes from Corporate Mergers: The Case of Commercial Banking." *Journal of Accounting, Auditing, and Finance* X, no. 2 (March 1995).

11. ———. "The Diversification and Cost Effects of Interstate Banking." *Financial Review* 31, no. 2 (May 1996). pp. 431–52.

12. ———. *The Local and Statewide Market Share Advantages of Interstate Banking Firms.* Unpublished paper, Texas A&M University, September 1997.

13. Spong, Kenneth, and J. D. Shoenhair. "Performance of Banks Acquired on an Interstate Basis." *Financial Industry Perspectives*, Federal Reserve Bank of Kansas City, December 1992, pp. 15–23.

These studies treat merger regulations and laws:

14. Powell, Donald E. Speech by the Chairman of the Federal Deposit Insurance Corporation before the American Bankers Association Annual Meeting in Phoenix, Arizona, October 8, 2002.

15. Rose, Peter S. "Merger Mania, Banking Style." *The Canadian Banker* 90, no. 5 (1984), pp. 38–44.

16. ———. "Improving Regulatory Policy for Mergers: An Assessment of Bank Merger Motivations and Performance Effects." *Issues in Bank Regulation* 9, no. 3 (Winter 1987), pp. 32–39.

17. ———. "The Impact of Mergers in Banking: Evidence from a Nationwide Sample of Federally Chartered Banks." *Journal of Economics and Business* 39, no. 4 (November 1987), pp. 289–312.

18. Snider, Thomas E. "The Effect of Merger on the Lending Behavior of Rural Banks in Virginia." *Journal of Bank Research*, Spring 1973, pp. 52–57.

19. Weston, J. Fred, and Kwang S. Chung. "Do Mergers Make Money?" *Mergers and Acquisitions*, Fall 1983, pp. 40–48.

For an analysis of the terms under which bank mergers take place, see the following:

20. Darnell, Jerome C. "Bank Mergers: The Prices Paid for Merger Partners." *Business Review*, Federal Reserve Bank of Philadelphia, July 1973, pp. 16–25.

For a review of the public interest aspects of financial-service mergers, see the following:

21. Jones, J. C. H., and L. Laudadio. "Canadian Bank Mergers, The Public Interest, and Public Policy." *Banca Nazionale del Lavoro*, 1973, pp. 109–40.

22. Kaufman, George G. "Customers View a Bank Merger—Before and After Surveys." *Business Conditions*, Federal Reserve Bank of Chicago, July 1989, pp. 5–8.

23. Kohn, Ernest. *Branch Banking, Bank Mergers, and the Public Interest.* New York State Banking Department, 1964.

24. Peek, Joe, and Eric S. Rosengren. "Have Borrower Concentration Limits Encouraged Bank Consolidation?" *New England Economic Review*, Federal Reserve Bank of Boston, January/February 1997, pp. 37–47.

25. Rose, Peter S. "Convenience and Needs: A Survey of Holding Company Bank Services." *Issues in Bank Regulation* 6, no. 3 (Winter 1988), pp. 26–31.

For a discussion of planning for mergers, see these studies:

26. Karcesle, Jason; Steven Ongena; and David C. Smith. *The Impact of Bank Consolidation on Commercial Borrower Welfare*. International Finance Discussion Papers, Board of Governors of the Federal Reserve System, No. 679, Washington, D.C., September 2000.

27. Kwast, Myron L.; Martha Starr-McCluer; and John D. Wolken. *Market Definition and the Analysis of Antitrust in Banking*. Finance and Economics Discussion Series No. 1997–52, Board of Governors of the Federal Reserve System, Washington, D.C., 1997.

28. Lausberg, Carsten, and Peter S. Rose. "Merger Motives in European Banking: Results of an Empirical Study." *Bank Archive* 43 no. 3 (1995), pp. 177–86.

29. ———. "Managing Bank Mergers." *Bank Archive* 45 (June 1997), pp. 423–27.

30. Piloff, Steven J. "Multimarket Contact in Banking." *Review of Industrial Organization* 14 (March 1999), pp. 163–82.

31. Prasad, Rose M., and S. Benjamin Prasad. "Strategic Planning in Banks: Senior Executives' Views." *International Journal of Management* 6, no. 4 (December 1989), pp. 435–41.

32. Rhoades, Stephen A. *Bank Mergers and Banking Structure in the United States, 1980–98*. Staff Study 174, Board of Governors of the Federal Reserve System, August 2000.

For an exploration of possible linkages between bank and thrift merger activity and the chartering of new (de novo) banks and thrift institutions, see especially this source:

33. Seelig, Steven A., and Tim Critchfield. "Merger Activity as a Determinant of *De Novo* Entry into Urban Banking Markets." *Working Paper 2003–01*, Federal Deposit Insurance Corporation, Washington, D.C., April 2003.

For a discussion of new rules regarding the treatment of goodwill in mergers among banks and other institutions see especially:

34. Carlson, Mark, and Roberto Perli. "Profits and Balance Sheet Developments at U.S. Commercial Banks in 2002." *Federal Reserve Bulletin,* June 2003, pp. 243–270.

CHAPTER TWENTY

International Banking Service Options

Key Topics in This Chapter

- Types of International Banking Organizations
- Regulation of International Banking
- Foreign Banking Activity in the United States
- Services Provided by International Banks
- Managing Currency Risk Exposure
- Future Problems and Market Opportunities

Introduction

Commercial banks were not only among the first financial institutions to appear in recorded history but also were among the first financial firms to venture into international markets and offer their services in distant locations. The first banks were located principally in global trading centers around the Mediterranean Sea, including Athens, Cairo, Jerusalem, and Rome, aiding merchants in financing shipments of raw materials and goods for sale and exchanging one nation's coin for that of another in order to assist travelers. Much later, during the colonial period of American history, foreign banks based in Europe entered the Americas and met a large share of the financing needs of American businesses.

United States banks established a significant beachhead in Europe and elsewhere around the globe as the 20th century opened. This was followed by a dramatic expansion in the 1950s and 1960s as American banks set up branch offices, subsidiaries, and joint ventures with local firms in hundreds of foreign markets. This period of foreign expansion by U.S. financial institutions was directed mainly at the commercial centers of Western Europe, the Middle East, and South and Central America. During the 1970s and 1980s American banks expanded their presence around the Pacific Rim, especially in Japan, Hong Kong, and Singapore. American, European, and Japanese multinational banks played a key role in investing the huge amounts of funds flowing to petroleum producers as world oil prices rose. American banks were also called upon to help finance the huge trade deficits that the United States incurred in purchasing a growing number of goods and services from abroad.

For a time, during the 1980s, the torch of leadership in international banking passed to the Japanese, whose banks established strong beachheads in London, New York, and other major financial centers around the globe. At the same time, growth of international banking firms in the United States and Western Europe slowed markedly. Intensified competition,

Banking and its principal financial-service competitors are expanding their service marketing boundaries in all directions on nearly all the world's continents. One reason is the continuing search for higher revenues, lower operating costs, and reduced risk exposure through geographic diversification. Another is that bankers and other financial-service managers long ago learned to follow their best customers in order to keep their business, whether those customers move across town, across the nation, or across the ocean.

Because banking and its principal competitors in the securities, insurance, and finance company industries are now truly international in scope, these financial-market competitors are more difficult to keep track of as crucial service providers. The World Wide Web has become a vital tool to keep up with foreign developments affecting banking and financial services, and it has enabled banks and their competitors to work faster in responding to their increasingly far-flung customer base. Among the most widely used information sources available on the Web to keep bankers globally informed is the Bank for International Settlements (BIS) at **www.bis.org**. The BIS is an international organization designed to promote cooperation among central banks and agencies pursuing monetary and financial stability.

If you click on **www.bis.org/cbanks.htm**, you will find links to the central banks of more than 130 countries. Other key bank-related agencies on the global stage include the International Bank for Reconstruction and Development at **www.worldbank.org/** (click on the IBRD link) and the World Bank and International Monetary Fund libraries at **jolis.worldbankimflib.org/external.htm**.

Various private institutions also have gone on the Web to provide information for international bankers and the customers they serve. These include the Institute of International Bankers (composed of multinational banking organizations active in the United States) at **www.iib.org**; the Bank of Montreal, which has compiled information on international economics (at **www.bmo.com/economic**); and NewsNow Newslink which offers updated news links on international banking and finance at **www.newsnow.co.uk** (choose topics for newsfeed). For those readers who may have an interest in possible job opportunities in international banking and related fields, there is **www.bankstaffers.com**.

spurred on by deregulation among the governments of Great Britain, the United States, and other nations and by significant advances in communications technology, forced many international bank and nonbank financial firms to reduce their physical presence in foreign markets in order to cut operating expenses. Moreover, many of their principal credit customers, especially nations like Argentina and Brazil, were experiencing serious economic problems, fueling the retrenchment of international banking around the globe.

As the 21st century approached, leadership in banking and financial services passed once again to American and European banks and many of their nonbank financial-service competitors, led by such giants as Citigroup, Bank of America, HSBC, UBS/Swiss Bank, J. P. Morgan Chase, Britain's Barclays PLC, ING Group of the Netherlands, and Germany's Deutsche Bank. International financial services today continue to be vitally important sources of revenue and earnings for leading bank and nonbank firms around the world.

In this chapter we take a close look at the organizational forms, services, problems, and challenges facing large international banking and financial-service organizations today.[1]

---

[1] Portions of this chapter are based on Peter S. Rose's article in *The Canadian Banker* [5] and are used with the permission of the publisher.

EXHIBIT 20–1

Types of International Banking Organizations and Facilities

International Banking Service Options

Types of Foreign Banking Organizations

In their pursuit of business around the world, banks use a wide variety of *organizational structures* to deliver services to their international customers (as illustrated in Exhibit 20–1).

Representative Offices   The simplest organizational presence for a bank active in foreign markets is the **representative office,** a limited-service facility that can market the services supplied by the home office and identify new customers but does not take deposits or book loans. These offices are established to supply support services both to the parent bank and to its customers.

Agency Offices   Somewhat more complete than the representative office is an **agency office,** which in many jurisdictions does not take deposits from the public (though New York agencies, for example, often do take deposits), but extends commitments to make or purchase loans, provides seasonal and revolving credit agreements, issues standby letters of credit, provides technical assistance and advice to customers (primarily corporations and governments), administers their cash accounts, and assists with customer security trading.

Branch Offices   The most common organizational unit for most international banks is the **branch office,** normally offering a full line of services. Foreign branches are *not* separate legal entities, but merely the local office that represents a single large financial-service corporation. They can accept deposits from the public subject to the regulations of the country where they are located and may escape some of the rules for deposit taking faced by branches of the same bank in its home country. For example, the branch offices of U.S. banks overseas do not have to post legal reserve requirements or pay FDIC insurance fees on the deposits they take abroad.

Subsidiaries   When an international bank acquires majority ownership of a separate, legally incorporated foreign bank, the foreign bank is referred to as a **subsidiary** of the international bank. Because the subsidiary possesses its own charter and capital stock, it will not necessarily close down if its principal owner fails. Similarly, a subsidiary bank can be closed without a substantial adverse effect on the international bank that owns it (as happened in the Philippines when a subsidiary of New York's Citicorp closed). Subsidiaries may be used instead of branches because local regulations may prohibit or restrict branching or because of tax advantages. Also, many international banks prefer to acquire an existing firm overseas that already has an established customer base.

Joint Ventures A bank that is particularly concerned about risk exposure in entering a new foreign market, lacks the necessary expertise and customer contacts abroad, or wishes to offer services prohibited to banks alone may choose to enter into a **joint venture** with a foreign bank or nonbank firm, sharing both profits and expenses.

Edge Act Corporations **Edge Acts** are separate domestic U.S. companies owned by a U.S. or foreign bank, but located outside the home state of the bank that owns them. These subsidiary corporations are limited primarily to international or foreign business transactions. Federal legislation passed at the end of World War I permitted banks large enough to post the required capital to apply for Edge Act charters from the Federal Reserve Board.

Agreement Corporations These business corporations are subsidiaries of a bank organized under Section 25 of the Federal Reserve Act. Agreement corporations must devote the bulk of their activities to serving international customers and carrying out international transactions, similar to Edge Act corporations.

IBFs An **international banking facility (IBF)** is a creation of U.S. banking regulations, first authorized by the Federal Reserve Board in 1981. IBFs are simply computerized account records that are not a part of the domestic U.S. accounts of the bank that operates the IBF. They must be domiciled inside U.S. territory and their activities must focus upon international commerce. Deposits placed in an IBF are exempt from U.S. deposit reserve requirements and deposit insurance fees. IBFs may be operated by either U.S.-chartered banks or by banks foreign to the United States.

Shell Branches In order to escape the burden of regulation, many international banks have established special foreign offices that merely record the receipt of deposits and other international transactions. These **shell branches** may contain little more than a desk and a telephone or fax machine where deposits from the worldwide Eurocurrency markets are booked to avoid deposit insurance assessments, reserve requirements, and other costs incurred when a domestic bank accepts deposits. Many large international banks have operated shell branches for years in such attractive offshore locations as the Bahamas and the Grand Cayman Islands.

Export Trading Companies (ETCs) In 1982, the U.S. Congress passed the **Export Trading Company Act** (ETCA), which allowed U.S. banking firms and Edge Act corporations to create **export trading companies** (ETCs). According to Federal Reserve Board regulations, these specialized firms must receive over half of their income from activities associated with exporting goods and services from the United States. Once established, an ETC can offer such services as export insurance coverage, transportation and warehousing of salable products, trade financing, and research into the possibility of exploiting markets abroad.

Concept Check

20–1. What organizational forms do international banks use to reach their customers?

20–2. Why are there so many different types of international organizations in the banking and financial institutions' sector?

Regulation of International Banking

International banking activities are closely regulated by both home and host countries all over the globe. However, a strong trend today is toward deregulation of banking and the related fields of securities brokerage and securities underwriting. An increasing number of nations today recognize the necessity of coordinating their regulatory activities so that eventually all banks and some of their closest competitors serving international markets will operate under similar rules, called *harmonization*.

Goals of International Banking Regulation

International banking activities are regulated for many of the same reasons that shape domestic banking regulations. There is an almost universal concern for *protecting the safety of depositor funds,* which usually translates into laws and regulations restricting bank risk exposure and rules specifying minimum amounts of owners' equity capital to serve as a cushion against operating losses. Regulations frequently limit nonbanking business activities to avoid excessive risk taking and criminal activity, as in the famous Bank of Credit and Commerce International (BCCI) case in the early 1990s. Then, too, to the extent that international banks can create money through their lending and deposit-creating activities, international banking activity is regulated to *promote stable growth in money and credit* in order to avoid threats to economic health in individual nations.

However, many international banking regulations are unique to the international field itself—that is, they don't apply to most domestic banking activity. For example, *foreign exchange controls* prohibit the export of domestic currency in order to protect a nation against loss of its foreign currency reserves, which might damage its prospects for repaying international loans and purchasing goods and services abroad. Another instance would be rules that *restrict the outflow of scarce capital* that some governments see as vitally necessary for the health of their domestic economies. There is also a strong desire in many parts of the world to *protect domestic financial institutions and financial markets from foreign competition.* Many countries prefer to avoid international entanglements and excessive dependence on other countries for vital raw materials and other goods and services. This isolationist philosophy often leads to outright prohibition of outsiders from entry into full-service banking and may also restrict the international operations of domestic banks.

Expansion and Regulation of Foreign Bank Activity in the United States

Beginning in the 1970s and continuing to the present day, foreign banks have sought a solid foothold inside the United States, attracted by the huge size of the common market formed by the 50 states, the relative economic and political stability inside the United States, and the expansion of foreign banks' own customers inside U.S. territory (e.g., foreign-owned auto and electronics firms setting up manufacturing plants on American soil). As recently as 1991, about 560 U.S. branches and agencies were operated by about 300 foreign-owned banks, holding more than $400 billion in assets. By the spring of 2003 more than 525 agencies, branches, and other foreign-owned banking facilities were situated within the United States, with more than $1.3 trillion in total assets under their control.

These foreign-owned banking facilities were controlled by about 225 corporate banking families, led by such familiar international banking giants as Barclays and the Royal Bank of Scotland in Great Britain, Credit Lyonnais from France, and Deutsche Bank of Germany. These foreign-owned banking facilities included about 240 branch banking offices, just over 150 representative offices, 76 U.S.-chartered banks that were majority owned by foreign banking organizations, and just over 50 nondeposit-taking agency

TABLE 20–1 Foreign Banking Offices in the United States: Assets, Loans, and Deposits*

Source: Board of Governors of the Federal Reserve System, *Flow of Funds Accounts* and *The Federal Reserve Bulletin*, selected issues.

Item	Dollar Amounts In Billions at Year-End								
	1995	1996	1997	1998	1999	2000	2001	2002	2003**
Total financial assets held by foreign banks in the U.S.	$666.3	$714.8	$811.3	$806.5	$750.9	$789.4	$791.9	$801.1	$835.7
Percent of all financial assets held by U.S.-chartered banks	20.19%	20.89%	21.7%	19.8%	16.9%	16.5%	15.8%	14.8%	15.19%
Total loans held by foreign banks in the U.S.	$303.9	$339.9	$368.6	$369.6	$333.8	$392.8	$367.2	$355.2	$365.3
Percent of total loans held by U.S.-chartered banks	13.2%	13.99%	13.9%	12.7%	10.6%	11.49%	10.49%	9.4%	9.7%
Total deposits held by foreign banks in the U.S.	$138.2	$193.3	$243.2	$275.6	$331.4	$334.1	$392.2	$364.2	$371.9
Percent of total deposits held by U.S.-chartered banks	5.79%	7.59%	8.99%	9.4%	10.8%	10.2%	10.99%	9.5%	9.5%

*Includes branches and agencies of foreign banks, Edge Act and agreement corporations, New York investment companies (through second quarter of 1996), and American Express Bank.
**2003 figures are for the first quarter of the year.

Key URLs

Two of the chief sources of international banking statistics today are the Bank for International Settlements at **www.bis.org/publ** and the Federal Reserve System at **www .federalreserve.gov**.

offices. Most of these foreign-owned banking facilities were based in New York, with substantial additional units centered in San Francisco, Los Angeles, Chicago, and Atlanta.

Although the expansion of foreign bank activity inside the United States was rapid during the 1970s and 1980s, led by the Japanese, the growth of this segment of the industry has been more volatile and uncertain in recent years. For example, according to data provided by the Federal Reserve's *Flow of Funds Accounts*, the total *financial* assets held by foreign banks inside their U.S. facilities peaked at just over $800 billion in 1997 and 1998 before declining to about $750 billion as the 20th century closed, only to begin rising again to about $835 billion in 2003. As Table 20–1 indicates, the percentage of U.S. bank assets held by foreign banks dropped from about 20 percent of the total assets of all U.S.-chartered banks in 1995 to only about 15 percent in 2003.

Similarly, *loans* extended by foreign banks in U.S. markets peaked in 2000 at almost $400 billion and then fell back to about $365 billion in 2003. This pattern of relatively slow and unsteady growth in foreign-bank-controlled assets and loans inside the United States may be attributed to multiple causes, including a slowdown in the world economy; government deregulation of domestic U.S. banks, which has permitted these institutions to be more aggressive competitors and to recapture some market share previously lost to foreign financial firms; and weakness in several major foreign banks (especially those based inside Japan).

In contrast, *deposits* held by foreign banks operating in the United States rose rapidly from about $140 billion in 1995 to nearly $400 billion in 2003. Thus, foreign banks have more than doubled their deposit market share in the United States during the past decade. These foreign-owned institutions attracted large amounts of money-market CDs from U.S. customers fleeing a volatile stock market and fearful about spreading corporate bankruptcies and rising unemployment. For many foreign-owned banks these American deposits were vitally needed to shore up faltering economies and financial systems back home.

The International Banking Act of 1978 The expansion of foreign banking activity inside America's borders led to strong pressure on the U.S. Congress by domestic banking groups and, eventually, to passage of the **International Banking Act** (IBA) of 1978—the first major federal law regulating foreign bank activity in the United States. The IBA's key components were as follows:

- It required branches and agency offices of foreign banks to secure federal licenses for their U.S. operations.
- It restricted foreign branching within the United States, requiring each bank to designate a home state and follow that state's branching rules just as American banks must do.
- It stipulated that deposits accepted at the U.S. branch or agency offices of foreign banks holding $1 billion or more in consolidated assets are subject to legal reserve requirements determined by the Federal Reserve Board.
- It made U.S. branches of foreign banks eligible for deposit insurance under stipulated conditions and granted them access to certain Federal Reserve services, such as the ability to borrow from the Federal Reserve banks.

The Foreign Bank Supervision Enhancement Act of 1991 On December 19, 1991, Congress amended the IBA with passage of the **Foreign Bank Supervision Enhancement Act.** The new law placed tighter controls on foreign bank operations in the United States. Applications from foreign banks to expand their U.S. banking activities must be reviewed and approved by the Federal Reserve Board. Service offerings of foreign banks are basically limited to the same list of banking services that U.S. national banks are permitted to offer. Moreover, no foreign bank can accept retail deposit accounts of less than $100,000 from the public unless it first obtains insurance coverage from the FDIC. Any foreign bank desiring to acquire more than 5 percent of the voting shares of a U.S. bank company must first seek Federal Reserve Board approval.

The Federal Reserve System must also review how thoroughly foreign banks are supervised by their home countries. If the Federal Reserve Board determines that regulation and supervision of a foreign bank by that bank's home nation is inadequate, the Fed can deny that foreign bank permission to establish a branch, agency, or representative office inside United States territory or to start or acquire any U.S. subsidiary firms. Moreover, the Board can terminate the operations of a foreign bank in the United States if it finds that bank has violated U.S. laws, engaged in unsafe or unsound banking practices inside U.S. territory, or is not being operated in a manner consistent with the public interest. The 1991 law empowered the Fed to examine the U.S. offices and affiliates of any foreign bank and stipulated that the Federal Reserve Board must be notified a minimum of 30 days in advance if a foreign bank wishes to close any of its U.S. offices.

New Capital Regulations for Major Banks Worldwide

The spread of foreign banks into the United States and of U.S. banks into other nations, coupled with serious international debt problems, soon led to new regulatory standards for the capital that international banks must hold as a buffer against risk. First, in November 1983, the U.S. Congress passed the **International Lending and Supervision Act,** which required federal regulatory agencies to prepare new capital and lending rules for U.S.-supervised banks. Specifically, the 1983 law required American banks to restrict the size of fees charged for rescheduling payments on loans made overseas in order to avoid excessive burdens on debtor countries, report their foreign loan exposures to individual countries to bank examiners, and hold adequate capital and special reserves to protect depositors against possible losses on foreign loans.

Soon after these rules were implemented, negotiations began between the United States and other leading nations to determine if international cooperation in banking

RUSSIAN BANKING: RECOVERY AND RENEWAL

The Russian banking system experienced the equivalent of a Chernobyl nuclear meltdown in 1998. Hundreds of banks failed and thousands of Russian depositors lost confidence in their banking system, many stashing their cash in the proverbial cookie jar rather than risking the loss of still more of their savings.

However, a *new* banking system is emerging out of the ashes of the old as aggressive managers pursue what remains of a potentially lucrative market, especially among young adults, many of whom have high-paying jobs and need sources of credit and a fast and efficient way to pay for their purchases (including credit and debit cards). New banking market leaders have emerged, such as the domestic institutions known as Alfa Bank and Moscow Credit Bank as well as Citibank from the United States. There is also an aggressive expansion of customer-service facilities under way, including new branch offices, more ATM machines, and growing use of online banking services. Russia's great size, projected economic growth, and "underbanked" population appear to offer great marketing opportunities for aggressive international banks willing to take the leap.

regulation was possible. Finally, on July 15, 1988, representatives of 12 nations announced an agreement in Basel, Switzerland, on common bank capital standards. The **Basel Agreement,** as we saw earlier in Chapter 14, called for all banks to achieve a minimum total-capital-to-total risk-adjusted assets ratio of 8 percent. The announced purpose of the Basel Agreement was twofold: (1) to strengthen international banks, thereby strengthening public confidence in them; and (2) to remove inequalities in regulation between nations that contribute to competitive inequalities between their banks. In the wake of the Basel Agreement, many leading banks announced plans to raise new capital and sell off assets to improve their capital-asset ratios.

Concept Check

20–3. What are the principal goals of international banking regulation?

20–4. What were the key provisions of the U.S International Banking Act of 1978 and the International Lending and Supervision Act of 1983?

20–5. Explain what the Basel Agreement is and why it is so important.

Customer Services Supplied by Banks in International Markets

Customers active in foreign markets require a wide variety of services, ranging from credit and the execution of payments to the provision of marketing advice and assistance (see, for example, Table 20–2). The variety of services international banks and their strongest competitors offer has expanded significantly in response to evolving customer needs and intense international competition.

Making Foreign Currencies Available for Customer and Proprietary Transactions

International banks supply foreign currency—**FOREX**—services to their customers. Many of their customers require sizable quantities of spendable currencies to pay for imported goods and raw materials, to purchase foreign securities, and to complete mergers and

TABLE 20–2
Key Customer
Services Offered by
International Banks

The International Bank Service Menu	
Supplying foreign currencies for customer transactions	Supplying long- and short-term credit and credit guarantees (direct loans, note issuance facilities, Europaper, ADRs, etc.)
Hedging against foreign currency risk (currency futures and options, forward contracts, and swaps)	Payments and cash management services (acceptances, letters of credit, and other drafts)
Security underwriting for corporate customers (bond, note, and stock issues)	Savings or thrift instruments (CDs, savings accounts, pension programs)
Hedging against interest-rate risk (interest-rate swaps, caps, financial futures, and options)	Foreign marketing assistance for customers (foreign market analysis and trade financing)

acquisitions. Other customers may receive on a regular basis large amounts of foreign currency or foreign-currency–denominated deposits from businesses and individuals abroad who buy their products or purchase their securities. These foreign funds must be exchanged for domestic currency to help the customer meet his or her own cash needs. International banks routinely hold working balances of those foreign currencies most in demand by their customers.

Top Trading Firms Operating in Today's Global Currency Markets

Citigroup, Inc.	UBS Warburg	J. P. Morgan Chase & Company
Deutsche Bank AG	Morgan Stanley Group	Goldman Sachs Group, Inc.
Credit Suisse-First Boston Corp.	ABN AMRO Bank	HSBC Holdings PLC

Recently there has been a sharp increase in FOREX trading activity among leading commercial and investment bank dealers due to increased volatility of leading currencies, especially the U.S. dollar. Trading volume now exceeds a trillion dollars a day and is climbing, making this market one of the largest on the planet. Somewhat unique is the recent upsurge in *proprietary trading* where dealers speculate for themselves on trends in the prices of selected currencies. Revenues from currency trading seem to behave somewhat differently than revenues from other services, frequently improving while other markets are down. However, bid-ask spreads among currency dealers have narrowed substantially in today's marketplace, which solidly favors the highest-volume trading businesses.

Hedging against Foreign Currency Risk Exposure

Customers who receive or dispense large amounts of foreign currencies look to international banks for protection against *currency risk*—the potential for loss due to fluctuations in currency prices (exchange rates). But customers are not the only ones who face currency risk; international banks themselves also must deal with substantial currency risk.

Currency risks arise most often in international banking when (*a*) making foreign-currency–denominated loans to their customers, (*b*) issuing foreign-currency–denominated IOUs (such as deposits) to raise new funds, (*c*) purchasing foreign-issued securities, or (*d*) trading in foreign currencies for a bank's own currency position as

JAPAN'S ECONOMIC PROBLEMS AND REFORM OF THE JAPANESE FINANCIAL SYSTEM

Early in the 21st century, Japan's economy and financial system continued to struggle after a decade of drastic economic and financial dislocation, marked by faltering consumption and investment spending, rising unemployment, declining stock and real property values, and deterioration in bank profitability and capital accompanied by serious loan losses. Desperate to find effective countermeasures to these truly serious economic problems, the Bank of Japan pushed key interest rates down close to zero in an effort to stimulate borrowing and spending and, ultimately, set in motion a period of economic recovery. A rescue plan for the nation's banks was launched late in the 1990s, though it could not prevent substantial numbers of bank failures.

These problems have been all the more perplexing because a decade or so earlier the Japanese economy was the envy of much of the rest of the world. Its economic and financial system was characterized by surging stock prices and real estate values; a massive balance of payments surplus with the rest of the world, which seemingly couldn't get enough Japanese cars, stereos, TVs, and other items; and an incredibly high domestic savings rate, which led to massive foreign investments, including buying numerous businesses, land, and stocks and bonds inside the United States. By the late 1980s at least 16 of the world's top 20 banks were Japanese banks, and these banks were, by far, the leading foreign banking entities in the United States, representing over 60 percent of all foreign bank assets in the United States and responsible for nearly a fifth of all domestic U.S. business loans.

All of these positive trends of the 1980s were turned around during the 1990s and early in the 21st century. Japanese stocks fell to less than a quarter of their peak values, while land prices plummeted to a third of their earlier heights. These massive declines led to the collapse of hundreds of bank and non-bank firms, which were pulled down by the combined assault of bad loans, falling stock and real estate prices, and rapidly eroding capital cushions. Because many Japanese banks hold a huge volume of corporate stock associated with loans to their borrowing customers and also have large amounts of "paper" capital in the form of estimated future tax credits, they have relatively weak defenses against the recent huge losses in the value of their loans and investments. Moreover, the Japanese government has been sluggish and deeply divided about how to address the nation's economic problems, rescue the banking system, and avoid more job losses.

An added problem is suggested by recent research evidence (e.g., Smith [21]) which finds that Japanese banks tend to be less sensitive to risk and underprice their loans compared to foreign banks lending inside Japan. Partly as a result, Japanese banks seem to attract somewhat riskier borrowers than do competing foreign banks. This risk-exposure problem

well as the currency needs of its customers. The *net exposure* of a bank or of one of its customers to fluctuations in the value of any particular currency can be determined from the following equation:

$$
\begin{aligned}
\begin{array}{c} \text{Net exposure to} \\ \text{risk from any} \\ \text{one currency} \end{array} =
&\overbrace{\left[\begin{array}{c} \text{Assets held that are} \\ \text{denominated in the} \\ \text{currency} \end{array} - \begin{array}{c} \text{Liabilities issued in} \\ \text{the currency} \end{array} \right]}^{\text{Net foreign-currency–denominated assets}} \\
+ &\overbrace{\left[\begin{array}{c} \text{Volume of the} \\ \text{currency purchased} \end{array} - \begin{array}{c} \text{Volume of the} \\ \text{currency sold} \end{array} \right]}^{\text{Net position in foreign currency}}
\end{aligned}
$$

An international bank or bank customer with a *positive* net exposure in a given foreign currency—that is, whose net foreign-currency–denominated assets plus its net foreign-currency position is greater than zero—is said to be *net long* in that particular currency. This condition may arise because the bank or its customer has more foreign-currency–denominated assets than liabilities, has purchased more of a foreign currency than it has

appears to be exacerbated by weak marketplace disciplining of Japanese bank behavior (in part, because most deposits are fully covered by insurance) and the lack of agreement among Japanese lawmakers and regulators as to how to deal with their nation's financial problems. In short, the troubled condition of the Japanese banking sector apparently is not solely the result of a struggling economy, but also reflects weak financial-management practices.

In need of more capital to offset loan losses that may amount to more than a fourth of the nation's gross domestic product (GDP), several of Japan's leading banks have pulled back from international banking activities and declared themselves to be domestic banking firms once again. Pleas for government help in the form of injections of new bank capital led the Japanese government to become proactive in using taxpayer funds to shore up the domestic financial system beginning in 1998 and 1999, though banks and other financial firms receiving aid had to pledge to make fundamental changes in their operations and financing, including cleaning up bad loans and searching for new sources of private capital. Evidence began to mount as the new century opened that some of these pledges were not being met, and leading banks like Mizuho Financial Group, Sumitomo Mitsui Financial Group, Mitsubishi Tokyo, Resona Holdings, and UFJ Holdings Inc. worked hard to maintain the public's confidence.

At the same time, the Japanese government began borrowing heavily to flood the economy with liquidity, lower interest rates, and shore up deeply depressed stock and bond markets. The Bank of Japan pledged to keep interest rates at historic lows and to purchase the depressed stock of some Japanese companies from the banks that held these shares. In the wake of these expensive measures to rescue Japan's economy and financial system, the nation's public debt mushroomed to over 100 percent of its GDP.

Troubled Japanese banks were asked to scale back their overseas ventures in hopes of shoring up the domestic supply of credit. However, in today's open international economy this has had the effect of transferring some of Japan's problems to other nations, especially in Asia. The withdrawal of many Japanese banks from foreign credit markets served to exacerbate the so-called "Asian crisis" of the late 1990s as property values and income plummeted for a time in South Korea, Thailand, Indonesia, and other Asian economies. On the other side of the coin, however, if the Japanese economy begins a strong recovery as the 21st century unfolds, it will not only greatly strengthen the domestic banking system and those Japanese banks that remain viable, but it will also help recapitalize much of the remainder of Asia and foster economic growth there and in other parts of the world.

Key URL
To learn about the Japanese banking and financial system, see especially www.zenginkyo.or.jp.

Factoid
Internet-based banks got their start in Japan in the year 2000 with the creation of *Japan Net Bank*, backed by Sumitomo Mitsui Banking Corporation, Fujitsu, and Nippon Life Insurance.

sold, or both. If the currency involved declines in value in the foreign exchange markets relative to the value of the domestic currency, the bank or its customer will suffer a loss due to its net long position in that particular currency.

On the other hand, a bank or bank customer may have a *negative* net exposure in a given foreign currency, indicating that its net foreign-currency–denominated assets plus net foreign-currency position is less than zero. This may occur because the bank's or the customer's liabilities in a given foreign currency are greater than its assets denominated in that same currency, or the volume of the currency sold exceeds the amount purchased or both. In this instance the international bank or its customer is said to be in a *net short* position in that particular currency. If the currency involved increases in value against the international bank's or the customer's home currency, a loss will occur in a net short position. In general, the more volatile a given currency is, the greater the possibility for scoring gains or for experiencing losses from any given foreign currency position.

Research evidence (see, for example, Hopper [12]) suggests that currency exchange rates are not consistently predictable and show no reliable connection to such fundamental factors as money supply growth and output in different countries—two forces that finance theory suggests should help to explain relative currency-price movements. Accordingly, international banks typically employ a wide variety of currency-hedging techniques to help shelter their own and their customers' currency risk exposure. The most widely used of these currency-risk management techniques include forward contracts, currency futures contracts, currency options, currency warrants, and currency swaps.

Forward Contracts   For example, international banks may use **forward contracts,** in which a customer anticipating a future need to make currency purchases will work through the bank to negotiate a contract with another party calling for the delivery of currency at a stipulated price on a specific future date. Customers needing currency will agree to accept a specific amount of currency on a given future day for a price set today.

On the other hand, customers expecting to *receive* currency will often seek out contracts to sell that currency at a prespecified price. Because the price is set at the opening of a forward contract, the customer is protected from currency risk no matter which way currency prices go. If the customer is uncertain of the future date and the amount of currency involved, the international bank may provide an *option forward contract*, in which the customer receives the right, but not the obligation, to deliver or take delivery of specific currencies on a future date at an agreed-upon exchange rate.

Currency Futures Contracts   An increasingly popular alternative to the forward contract among banks and their customers is a **currency futures contract.** These contractual agreements between buyer and seller promise delivery of stipulated currencies at a specified price on or before a terminal date. The two basic futures contract types are long hedges and short hedges.

Long hedges in currency futures are designed to protect an international bank's customer from increases in the price of the currency the customer must eventually acquire. They are particularly useful for *importers*, because payment for goods received often must be made in

The nations of North, South and Central America offer great prospects for international bank expansion because of their burgeoning populations and valuable natural resources to promote industrialization and the growth of production and income. Several of these nations—Mexico, Canada, Brazil, Venezuela, and Argentina—rank among the countries having the highest current and projected real economic growth.

However, this region of the globe presents its own unique challenges to international banking. Political instability and volatile economies and financial systems have plagued the region for generations, evidenced most recently by the collapse or near-collapse of the banking and financial system in Argentina and Brazil late in the 1990s and early in the 21st century.

Nevertheless, there are signs that this region is becoming more integrated with the rest of the world and that broad changes affecting the banking and financial systems globally are also occurring in the Americas. Examples include the opening up of domestic banking and financial systems to entry by foreign financial units (especially in Argentina and Mexico where foreign banking companies own the top domestic banking firms), the gradual lifting of state ownership and controls over banking, fewer restrictions on trade and the flow of capital, increased use of automated financial-services technology, and, through mergers and acquisitions, a shift in financial structure toward fewer, but much larger financial-service units.

Among the leading international banks and financial firms with a strong presence in Central and South America and Mexico are Citigroup, J. P. Morgan Chase, and Merrill Lynch from the United States, ABN AMRO from the Netherlands, Banco Espiritu Santo of Portugal, and Banco Bilbao Vizcaya Argentaria (BBV) and Banco Santander Central Hispano (STD), both based in Spain and now among the key players in both Europe and Latin America.

the foreign exporter's home currency, and a rise in the exchange rate between the exporter's home currency and the importer's home currency can quickly eliminate any expected profit on the sale of goods. Under a long hedge contract, the customer pledges to take delivery of currency at contract maturity for price X. If currency prices subsequently rise, the customer can go back to the currency futures market and sell similar currency futures contracts at the new higher price, Y. This cancels out the customer's obligation to take delivery of currency and, at the same time, generates a trading profit on each contract equal to the price difference $(Y - X)$ less any commission charged and taxes. Profits made on currency futures help to offset any loss that arises when the customer must actually acquire the currency and pay for the imported goods.

Alternatively, many international bank customers, especially those *exporting* goods, find *short-hedge* futures contracts useful. These agreements require the customer to pledge delivery of a stipulated currency at a guaranteed price, X, to a counterparty on the maturity date. If currency prices subsequently fall, the customer can enter the futures market again on or before the first contract's maturity date and buy similar contracts at the lower price, Y, thus eliminating the responsibility to deliver currency. A profit is earned on each contract first sold and then bought equal to $X - Y$ (minus taxes and transactions costs).

Other Tools for Reducing Currency Risk

The Development of Currency Options   The so-called **currency option** gives a buyer the right, though not the obligation, to either deliver or take delivery of a designated currency or foreign-currency–denominated futures contract at a set price any time before the option expires. Thus, unlike the forward market, where delivery must take place on a certain date, actual delivery may not occur in the option market. Currency options include both spot and futures options.

Factoid
In Japan, the second largest economy in the world, banks play a considerably larger role than in the United States and in many other industrialized economies, accounting for about 60 percent of all fund-raising and all loans made. Therefore, troubles in the Japanese banking industry can have very profound effects on the rest of the Japanese economy.

Exchange-traded currency options on futures contracts have been growing rapidly in recent years. These contracts depend for their value on the underlying futures contract, which in turn depends on the price of the currency itself. When the price of a currency rises, the nearest-term currency futures contract also rises in price. An international bank holding sizable assets denominated in that currency can reduce the risk of loss from falling currency spot prices by selling currency futures or by buying put options or selling call options for that same currency.

Call currency options give their holder the right to purchase currency or currency futures contracts at a fixed price any time before the option expires. *Put* currency options represent the right to sell currency or currency futures contracts at a specified price on or before the published expiration date. For example, a call on euro futures contracts at a strike price of $0.92 gives the buyer of this call option the right to buy a contract calling for delivery of euros at a price of $0.92 to the buyer. If the market price of euro futures climbs above $0.92 per euro, the call option is said to be "in the money," and its buyer will exercise his or her option and take delivery of euro futures contracts at a price of $0.92. On the other hand, if euro futures stay below a strike price of $0.92, the call option will go unexercised because the buyer of the call can purchase futures contracts more cheaply in the market; in this case, the call option would be "out of the money." Generally, a put option is needed to protect against a fall in currency prices, whereas call options protect against loss from rising currency prices.

The advantage of the currency option is that it limits downside risk but need not reduce upside profits. The purchase price of a currency option is normally low enough to permit even small firms to participate in currency-hedging activities, and the currency option is a more flexible instrument than many other currency-hedging tools.

Currency Swaps   Finally, currency risk can be reduced with **currency swaps.** A currency swap is a contract between two parties—often two borrowers who have borrowed money denominated in different currencies—to exchange one currency for another and thereby help reduce the risk of loss as currency prices change. For example, a U.S. corporation (Company A) may have received a loan denominated in pounds and will need pounds when it must make payments on its pound-denominated loan. A's swap partner is Company B, which is called the *counterparty* to the currency swap. B is based in Great Britain but has a loan in dollars from a U.S. bank. Clearly, Company A has easy access to dollars but needs pounds when its loan payments come due, while Company B has easy access to pounds but needs dollars to make its loan payments. Under the terms of a straight currency swap Company B pays out pounds to Company A and receives, in turn, dollars from Company A when loan payments must be made. (See Exhibit 20–2.)

EXHIBIT 20–2
A Straight
Currency Swap

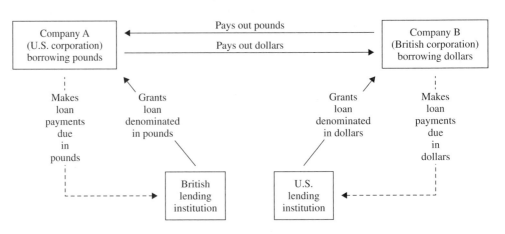

What's the great advantage of a currency swap? It makes it much easier and more efficient for a borrower to tap the international financial markets for loanable funds, borrowing in whatever type of currency-denominated loan results in the best deal for the borrower. Another advantage, unlike so many other currency risk-hedging tools, is that currency swaps can be set up to cover long periods of time (stretching into years, if necessary) as opposed to other risk-hedging tools, like futures and options, which generally have short horizons. Moreover, while other hedging tools are often highly standardized in form and, therefore, rigid and inflexible, a currency swap can be tailored to conform to the two swap partners' specific financial needs.

For an international bank currency swaps offer several advantages, for example:

- International banks are heavy borrowers in a variety of foreign currencies and can enter into swap contracts to reduce their own currency risk exposure.
- International banks can generate fee income by arranging currency swaps for their customers, serving as a currency swap dealer, and generate additional fee income by ensuring that either or both swap partners will fulfill the terms of their contract, serving as a currency swap guarantor.

The swap contract market has become one of the largest financial markets in the world, helping businesses and governments hedge risk and even giving some of the world's largest central banks a new instrument to trade in and help in shaping money and credit conditions to strengthen and stabilize their home nations' economies. Thus, swap contracts have truly become a global financial instrument, fostering trade and commerce, protecting against risk, and assisting policymakers.

Supplying Customers with Short- and Long-Term Credit or Credit Guarantees

International banks are the leading source of credit for multinational corporations and many governmental units at home and abroad. They provide both short- and long-term financing for the purchase of raw materials and for meeting payrolls, constructing buildings, and other important projects.

Note Issuance Facilities   Most international bank loans are short-term business credits carrying floating interest rates that are usually tied to some international base rate or reference rate. The most popular rate of this type is LIBOR, the London Interbank Offered Rate on borrowings of short-term Eurodollar deposits between international banks. Increasingly in recent years, however, international banks have provided credit guarantees for their customers' borrowings in the open market. One of the most popular of these is the **note issuance facility (NIF).** NIFs are primarily medium-term credit agreements between international banks and their larger corporate and governmental customers. The NIF customer is authorized to periodically issue short-term notes, each of which usually comes due in 90 to 180 days, over a stipulated period (such as five years). International banks pledge to either buy up any notes not bought by other investors or to grant supplemental loans based on LIBOR or on some other reference interest rate. In most cases, the customer's notes are in large denominations (e.g., $1 million U.S. or larger).

Europaper   International banks have also played a key role in the **Eurocommercial paper (ECP)** market, where multinational corporations raise short-term credit covering weeks or months. This short-term loan market is centered in London's financial district and has attracted international banks and nonfinancial corporations as investors. While most ECP borrowers are based outside the United States, a growing cadre of U.S. companies whose credit ratings are not strong enough to crack the U.S. commercial paper

Factoid
What type or category of loan held by the foreign offices of U.S. banks has the biggest dollar volume?
Answer: Commercial and industrial (business) loans, which account for more than half of all loans held by U.S. banks' foreign offices. Loans to individuals are a distant second.

CHINA—HIGH PROFILE TARGET FOR ENTRY BY INTERNATIONAL BANKS AND OTHER FINANCIAL INSTITUTIONS

International banks continually scour the globe looking for new markets and promising opportunities for lending money and attracting new funds. Over the past decade China—both the People's Republic on the Chinese mainland and Taiwan offshore—have appeared to be especially promising business targets. Leading international banking institutions like Citigroup, Merrill Lynch, J. P. Morgan Chase, HSBC Holdings PLC, Morgan Stanley, and Deutsche Bank appear to see great potential for long-run expansion given China's huge population, vast resources, and low labor costs.

Among the most attractive features of today's Chinese marketplace is limited domestic competition because many state-owned businesses are weak and lack the expertise necessary to compete successfully with experienced foreign companies. Then, too, China is today among the fastest-growing industrialized economies as Europe and the Americas struggle with relatively slow growth. Finally, China is gradually deregulating its banking system, stock exchanges, and manufacturing sec-

tor, permitting foreign investors to slowly acquire a bigger market share. Foreign banks have been promised eventual open access to China's domestic financial-service markets as part of China's new membership in the World Trade Organization (WTO).

Among the key areas of opportunity for the globe's multinational investment banks are China's stock exchanges and its markets for currency trading, commercial lending, and insurance services. Of particular interest in the current period is the sharp rise in nonperforming loans held by China's biggest state banks, which include the Industrial & Commercial Bank of China, China Construction Bank, the Bank of China, and the Agricultural Bank of China. If packaged properly, many of these troubled loans (which by various estimates range from $400 to $700 billion or about 25 to perhaps 50 percent of total loans outstanding) can be sold to international investors, creating a lucrative new market for the sale of risky securities—an area where European and American banks have specialized expertise. China will become even more of an attractive business target when its national currency, the yuan, becomes freely convertible into other leading global currencies.

market or who need to sell longer-maturity paper are successfully placing their notes in the Europaper market. A recent spur to this market has come from financial deregulation in Japan, which permits Japanese bank affiliates abroad to underwrite international commercial paper, while both Japanese and non-Japanese firms have recently been allowed to issue and buy yen-denominated commercial paper. International banks are heavy buyers of ECP for themselves and their investing customers and are also among the leading sellers of ECP issues. For example, Citicorp Investment Bank Ltd., and Swiss Banking Corporation International have accounted for more than a quarter of all international paper sold to investors in recent years.

American Depository Receipts   A related form of assistance U.S. banks provide to selected foreign credit customers is the **American depository receipt (ADR)**—a receipt issued by a U.S. international bank that makes it easier for a foreign business borrower to sell its securities to U.S. investors. In essence, an ADR is a negotiable instrument representing an ownership interest in the stock or other securities of a non-U.S. company. A U.S. international bank agrees to hold the securities issued and to sell investors the ADRs as claims against those securities.

When the security issuer approves of such an arrangement, the ADR is said to be "sponsored" by the issuer. However, an international bank can simply choose to package any foreign securities that might be of interest to U.S. investors and sell ADRs without issuer approval, resulting in "unsponsored" depository receipts. ADRs may or may not be registered with the U.S. Securities and Exchange Commission (unsponsored ADRs are exempt from registration requirements) and sold on a U.S. securities exchange. One of their main attractions for U.S. investors is the absence of currency risk since the value of a foreign security represented by an ADR is transformed by this instrument into U.S. dollars. Moreover, American investors can diversify their portfolios more easily by buying

ADRs and usually recover their funds more quickly by liquidating an ADR than by trying to sell a foreign-issued security.

Supplying Payments and Thrift (Savings) Instruments to International Customers

Payments Services   International banks are essential to the functioning of global trade and commerce through the offering of *payments and thrift instruments*. Not only do they provide foreign currencies for a customer making cash payments overseas, but they also can transfer the ownership of deposits through the global correspondent banking system. International banks issue and accept drafts in payment for purchases of goods and services across national borders.

These irrevocable commitments of a bank to pay may be in the form of *sight drafts,* due and payable upon presentation, or *time drafts,* payable only on a specific future date, usually just long enough for goods to be shipped to another country. Time drafts usually arise when an importer requests its bank to issue a *letter of credit,* guaranteeing that the bank will pay a certain exporter of goods if the importer fails to do so. The exporter may then draw through one of its correspondent banks a bill for payment, which is presented to the importer's bank for acceptance and eventual payment. International banks also issue traveler's checks denominated in foreign currencies and will cable or wire funds anywhere a customer designates.

Savings (Thrift) Services   International banks encourage *thrift*—short-term and long-term savings—by their customers. Most of these savings instruments are certificates of deposit (CDs)—interest-bearing receipts for funds deposited in a bank. While CDs were developed to be fixed-rate savings instruments, a sizable minority carry floating interest rates tied to movements of a specific base rate (such as LIBOR). Each day, major international banks post sets of CD rates for the most popular deposit maturities, posting higher or lower rates based on their need for funds.

The tremendous success of this bank funds-raising instrument led to an expansion of the CD concept around the world in the form of the EuroCD, a deposit sold in million-dollar units, first in London and eventually reaching all major financial centers. Today, most EuroCDs are issued by branches of the largest U.S., Japanese, Canadian, European, and British clearing banks. Large-denomination EuroCDs traded in the interbank market are often called *tap CDs,* while packages of smaller-denomination EuroCDs sold to a wide range of investors are called *tranche CDs.* While most Eurodollars are fixed-rate deposits, floating-rate CDs (FRCDs) and floating-rate notes (FRNs) are also issued to protect investors and borrowers against interest rate risk. These flexible-rate investments tend to be medium- to long-term in maturity, ranging from about 1 year to about 5 years in the case of FRCDs and to about 20 years for FRNs, with the attached interest rates typically adjusted every three to six months to reflect current interest rate movements.

Underwriting Customer Note and Bond Issues in the Eurobond Market

The development of note issuance facilities (NIFs) by international banks, discussed earlier, is but one example of the growing role of international banks in *underwriting new securities issues* in the open market. Another example is the **Eurobond market,** where borrowers issue bonds outside their home country. One reason for the growth of such a market was the increasing number of U.S. corporations, led by firms the size of Ford Motor Co. and Campbell Soup Co., that decided to tap Eurobonds to fund their overseas ventures. When U.S. interest rates rise, even purely domestic firms may find that Eurobond borrowings look cheaper by comparison. Leading banks active in this market include Lloyds Bank

Factoid
Which do you suppose is biggest—the revenue from loans held at the foreign offices of U.S. banks or the interest expense on the deposits held at these foreign offices? **Answer:** They are often close in amount but deposit interest has often outstripped loan revenue at U.S banks' foreign offices in recent years, quite unlike the situation inside the United States where loan revenue received usually outstrips deposit interest paid out to customers.

PLC, J. P. Morgan Chase, and Citigroup. In an effort to broaden the market's appeal for the future, recent innovations have sometimes appeared. Among them are debt securities denominated in European currency units (ECUs), representing currencies issued by various European countries.

Protecting Customers against Interest-Rate Risk

International banks have been called upon in growing numbers to help protect their customers against *interest-rate risk*—the risk of loss due to adverse interest-rate movements. Borrowers contract for loans whose interest rates float with changes in market conditions. Thus, rising interest rates increase the customer's borrowing cost and threaten to erode the profit margin on investment projects supported by borrowing. Conversely, the international bank's customer may suffer a loss in the event interest rates fall if the customer's funds are invested in deposits with floating interest yields or in other short-maturity investments that must be renewed at lower interest rates. Similarly, a customer with a fixed-rate loan fails to benefit from lower market interest rates unless steps are taken to cover that eventuality.

Interest-Rate Swaps   International banks can help their customers limit interest-rate risk exposure by arranging **interest-rate swaps.** As described in Chapter 7, these contractual agreements require each party to pay all or a portion of the interest bill owed on the other party's loan. Not only do interest-rate swaps usually reduce interest expense for each party, but they also permit each swap partner to more accurately balance cash inflows generated by its assets with cash outflows traceable to its liabilities.

Interest-Rate Caps   International banks also limit the interest-rate risk exposure of borrowing customers by imposing caps (maximum rates) on a customer loan in return for a fee. For example, the customer requesting a $100 million loan with an interest rate based on LIBOR may ask for a 10 percent interest-rate cap so that a rise in market interest rates does not send the loan rate above 10 percent. Such caps transfer interest-rate risk from the borrowing customer to the international bank and often carry a stiff fee to compensate the bank for its added risk exposure.

Financial Futures and Options   International banks are also active in assisting their customers with trading in financial futures and option contracts. For example, if the customer faces substantial loss from a *rise* in interest rates, then a *short* futures hedge (as described in Chapter 7) can be used to offset any loss due to a higher loan rate; alternatively, a *put* option could be employed. The prospect of customer losses from *falling* interest rates, on the other hand, could be hedged through a *long* (or buying) futures hedge or through the use of a *call* option.

Helping Customers Market Their Products through Export Trading Companies

An increasingly popular device for aiding customers to sell their goods abroad is the *export trading company* (ETC), developed originally by the Japanese. ETCs research foreign markets, identify firms in those foreign markets that could distribute products, and then provide or arrange the funding, insurance, and transportation needed to move goods to market. While larger U.S. manufacturers have also developed extensive foreign trading operations, thousands of smaller U.S. firms have not maximized their opportunities in export markets, in part due to a lack of adequate market research and few contacts abroad.

ETCs have been developed by leading money center banks in the United States and by dozens of smaller U.S. regional and community banks. Leading U.S. institutions launching

Key URLs

What trends are reshaping international banking today and in the future? See, for example, **www.bis.org/review** and **www.lacefinancial.com**.

ETC operations at various times include Bank of America, Bankers Trust Co. (now affiliated with Deutsche Bank), J. P. Morgan Chase Corp., Citigroup, and Fleet Boston (now scheduled for merger with the Bank of America). Despite widespread interest, however, the growth of export trading activity via ETCs based in the United States has been disappointing thus far. To be sure, external developments have played a major role in limiting ETC activities, particularly the difficulties many less-developed countries have faced in finding resources to pay for imports from the United States and in servicing their international debt. Lack of bank management experience with the ETC form of organization and lack of distribution channels and market data from abroad have proven to be major hurdles, especially for smaller banks.

U.S. banks have also complained of heavy capitalization requirements, regulatory limits on credit extended from banks to their ETC affiliates, and legal restrictions on the proportion of income that must come from exporting activities. For example, at least 51 percent of ETC income must come from U.S. exporting activities, and a U.S. international bank can invest no more than 5 percent of its consolidated capital in an ETC nor lend more than 10 percent of its capital to its own ETC.

Future Problems for International Banks

Growing Customer Use of Securities Markets to Raise Funds

International banks today face an ongoing challenge to their lending business—namely growing competition from securities markets and securities dealers for the fund-raising needs of their customers. When many international loans developed severe repayment problems during the 1980s and 1990s, many international banks withdrew substantial resources from the global credit markets. Securities houses were quick to seize this opening and provide a conduit for borrower offerings of notes and bonds in the Eurocurrency markets. Later, large insurance companies, finance companies, and other large nonbank financial institutions joined the competition to attract borrowers away from banks and assist them in their access to the open market to sell securities and raise new capital. While international banks have purchased many of these securities themselves, they have been forced to settle for slower growth or even declines in their credit-providing business, with smaller earnings margins on the credit they do extend to international borrowers.

Whether international banks can regain or even maintain their share of global business credit depends on current and future regulations that control their risk-taking worldwide, changing public attitudes regarding the safety and soundness of these multinational

TABLE 20–3

Leading International Banks and Bank Holding Companies around the Globe	
Mizuho Holdings, Japan	J. P. Morgan Chase, United States
Citigroup Inc., United States	Bank of America, United States
Sumitomo Mitsui Banking Company, Japan	Credit Suisse, Switzerland
Deutsche Bank, Germany	UFJ Holdings, Japan
Mitsubishi Tokyo Financial Group, Japan	Royal Bank of Scotland, United Kingdom
UBS, Switzerland	ABN Amro Bank, the Netherlands
BNP Paribus, France	Barclays Bank PLC, United Kingdom
HSBC Holdings PLC, United Kingdom	Societe Generale de France

Leading Nonbank Financial Firms Competing with International Banks (including insurance companies, securities dealers and brokers, finance companies, and credit card companies)	
Allianz, Germany*	Merrill Lynch, United States
American International Group, United States	Goldman Sachs, United States
Morgan Stanley, United States	Prudential Financial, United States
Federal National Mortgage Association (FNMA), United States**	Nomura Holdings, Japan
	MetLife, United States
Federal Home Loan Mortgage Corporation, United States**	Swiss Reinsurance, Switzerland
	Lehman Brothers, United States
GE Capital Corporation, United States	Zurich Financial Services, Switzerland
AXA, France*	American Express Co, United States

Notes: *Insurance companies with banking affiliates.
**Mortgage banking companies.

institutions, and the aggressiveness of their principal competitors in the international marketplace—securities dealers, insurance firms, and finance companies—who are also intent on widening their shares of the lucrative international corporate financing market. Indeed, as Table 20–3 reflects, several of the world's largest securities dealers and insurance companies have grown and expanded their service menus to compete with many of the globe's biggest banks. Challenged as never before, international banks today must work hard to find new sources of revenue and capital to meet the potent competition posed by other banks and by nonbank financial-service institutions—for example, by selling their superior ability at credit evaluation, at packaging loans and securities for resale, and at creating credit guarantees in support of their customers' global financial-service needs.

Developing Better Methods for Assessing Risk in International Lending

International Loan Risks   The greatest source of risk for most international banks lies in granting foreign loans. Foreign lending is generally more risky than domestic lending because information sources overseas are often less reliable than those at home, it's easier to monitor a loan made nearby rather than one made thousands of miles away, and the court systems needed to enforce contracts and conduct bankruptcy proceedings are often absent in the international arena. This added risk associated with international loans is often called *country risk*. A related form of international lending risk, called *sovereign risk*, occurs when a foreign government takes actions that interfere with the repayment of an international loan, such as by repudiating all foreign debt obligations, appropriating private property, or suspending loan payments for a time to conserve the home government's foreign exchange reserves. The result is that financial institutions choosing to lend abroad must analyze both the individual borrower and the country and government where the borrower resides.

Possible Solutions to Troubled International Loans   Troubled foreign loans, like problem domestic loans, may be *restructured* so that a new loan agreement is put together to replace the old loan agreement. The new loan usually assesses the borrower a lower interest rate and grants a longer maturity until final payment in return for a restructuring fee paid to the lender. The net cost (or *concessionality*) of such a loan to the lender is usually measured by the difference in present value of the original loan versus the (usually lower) present value of the newly restructured loan. Alternatively, a troubled loan can be sold in the secondary market for international loans that has grown up since the early 1980s and is centered around commercial banks and security dealers in New York and London. Many international banks have found buyers for discounted international loans among large corporations, other banks, and wealthy investors seeking speculative investments with potential for high returns. Selling international loans removes these credits from the balance sheet, provides funding for new assets, and may raise the value of the selling bank's stock.

Still another method used by international banks to deal with troubled international credits is to write off all or a portion of a foreign loan, recognizing that loan as a probable loss. The result is a credit against taxes that, in effect, shares the loan loss between the international bank's shareholders and the government.

Another alternative is for international banks to accept *exit bonds* in lieu of loan repayments. These debt securities are typically valued below the loans they replace and usually require lower or longer-term debt-service payments. Exit bonds may be backed by government securities or other acceptable collateral. For example, during the 1990s the U.S. Treasury Department announced plans to sell zero-coupon U.S. government bonds to Mexico at prices below their market value in order to support a refinancing agreement worked out between the government of Mexico and leading international banks. Mexico could use these bonds, issued as part of the so-called Brady Plan, to pay off exit bonds issued to international banks lending to that nation. Other nations, including Argentina, Brazil, and the Philippines, converted some of their loans into Brady bonds bearing longer maturities and lower interest rates than the original bank loans. These swaps of Brady bonds for loans were frequently supported by the central bank of the country where the borrower resides, providing a high-quality loan guarantee.

In most cases, a *combination* of remedies for troubled international loans has been used. The package of remedies may include restructuring delinquent loans and rescheduling their interest and principal payments, supplemental financial support by the International Monetary Fund (IMF) and other international agencies, stimulation of exports, and reduction of imports by indebted nations in an effort to buy time so these countries can move toward debt retirement and a stronger domestic economy.

Factoid
Of all the problems confronting international banks today at the opening of the 21st century, what problem appears to be the biggest of them all?
Answer:
Nonperforming loans, threatening international bank revenues, net earnings, and long-run survivability.

International Loan Risk Evaluation Systems   There is little argument today with the proposition that banks engaged in international lending need to develop improved methods for analyzing the quality and soundness of international loans before they are made and better methods for monitoring international borrower performance after loans are granted. Several risk evaluation systems are in use today.

For example, the *checklist approach* lists economic and political factors believed to be significantly correlated with loan risk, such as military conflicts, balance-of-payments deficits, and rising unemployment. Comparative weights may be applied to each factor on the list, or all may be equally considered in the international loan evaluation process. The weights may take the form of statistical or mathematical probabilities, leading to the calculation of an index value for default risk. Changes in the index value then become part of an early warning loan evaluation system. The listed items may be supplemented by field reports from bank personnel with firsthand knowledge of the debtor country.

THE EXPANDING EUROPEAN UNION (EU) AND ITS IMPLICATIONS FOR INTERNATIONAL BANKERS

The unification of Europe has been a lengthy historical drama, following centuries of war and political and economic turmoil. A key milestone in the decades-long process of establishing the European Union (EU) took place in 1992 when the Maastricht Treaty on European Union was adopted. Among the most controversial of its provisions was a call for the creation of a single European currency (the euro); a common central bank (the ECB); and the integration of foreign policies, judicial and legal systems, and domestic affairs. Maastricht set in motion the rules for each nation to become a member state of the European Community (EC), provided it could jump over the tough hurdles Maastricht laid down.

Initially, in January 1999, 11 nations joined the European Union (EU) in launching the new community, establishing the euro as the Union's common currency unit, and creating a national banking system led by a new European Central Bank. The 11 nations forming the initial common monetary system (later expanding to 12 nations) included Austria, Belgium, Finland, France, Germany, Ireland, Italy, Luxembourg, the Netherlands, Portugal, and Spain. Eventually other nations—such as Denmark and the United Kingdom—that made up the original European Union formed under the Maastricht Treaty are expected to join the new common money and credit system. Moreover, several other nations inside Europe and on its fringes have applied to join the EU, some as early as 2004, including the Czech Republic, Cypress, Estonia, Hungary, Latvia, Malta, Lithuania, Poland, Slovakia, and Slovenia.

Perhaps the greatest consequence of the EU for international bankers is the creation of a single banking market spreading across most of Western Europe. The new European *single banking market* is shaped by several guiding rules that govern all member states of the union:

A. Each member country will keep its own regulatory agencies and will be the chief supervisor of banks headquartered in each nation's territory, no matter how far these banks extend into other European Community member states.

B. While bank regulatory rules may differ across European nations, all member states must maintain minimal regulatory standards so that banks from each country face a relatively level playing field and will not have a strong incentive to leave a European nation with tough rules and migrate to another member nation with more lenient rules.

C. The principle of "national treatment" generally applies: regardless of what EU member country a bank uses as its headquarters, when it enters a new European state, it is subject to the same rules as domestic banks operating there. An individual EU member state can impose restrictions on international banks entering its territory from another member nation, but its own banks then may be subject to the same restrictions. The principle of national treatment gives nations a powerful incentive to keep regulations as simple and as relatively equal as possible.

D. The principle of "mutual recognition" was also adopted by selected nations with the formation of the new European system. A nation can allow an entering foreign bank to continue offering the same services it is allowed to offer in its home country even if domestic banks are not allowed to do so. This principle tends to give foreign banks a compet-

Factoid

Which nation today seems to promise both the most rapid economic growth but also the greatest barriers to foreign bank entry? **Answer:** The Peoples' Republic of China.

An alternative approach, which uses expert opinion in making a determination, is the *Delphi method.* Business analysts, economists, and experts in international law are assembled, and their separate, independently derived risk evaluations of a country are compiled and shared with each member of the expert panel. Panel members are then given an opportunity to revise their earlier assessments of a country's risk exposure. The final report is prepared as a consensus view of the amount of an individual country's risk exposure.

One serious problem with both of these approaches is timeliness. Significant changes in default-risk exposure may occur well before any of the calculated indexes or group opinion surveys pick it up. More recently, advanced statistical methods (including discriminant analysis) have been applied to country risk problems (as noted by Melvin and Schlagenhauf [2]). Linear modeling techniques have been constructed that attempt to classify international loans into those that will be successfully repaid versus those that will require debt rescheduling or will be defaulted outright based upon key preselected predictor variables.

Among the most popular predictor variables to measure the risk exposure of loans to a particular country are growth of the domestic money supply (an indicator of possible future inflation and currency devaluations), the ratio of real investment to gross national or gross domestic product (which measures a nation's future ability to be productive), the ratio of

itive edge over domestic banks if there are great differences in banking rules from nation to nation.

E. Under the Second Banking Directive of 1993, the term *banking* was defined in one way across the whole community, so that all European banks can offer a common set of services (referred to as *universal banking*). These common services include deposit taking; lending; financial leasing; providing payments services; supplying guarantees and credit commitments; trading in money market instruments, securities, currencies, financial futures, options, and other interest-bearing or interest-rate hedging instruments; aiding issuers of new securities; advising on acquisitions and mergers; brokering funds; granting portfolio advice and management services, supplying safekeeping services; and providing credit references.

F. All EC member states agree to a single passport so that any international bank from a member nation can conduct business in any other member nation in whatever form it views as giving it the best advantage, including the possibility of setting up a new branch or subsidiary firm or possibly merging with another bank without facing domestic restrictions.

G. All member states must offer some form of deposit insurance, which may be government run or supervised, as in Belgium, Finland, France, and Italy, or privately owned, as in Austria, Germany, Ireland, Luxembourg, the Netherlands, Portugal, and Spain. Depositors of failed banks must be reimbursed within three months. A member nation could establish an insurance system where insurance fees are assessed against all banks and funds are accumulated to deal with future bank failures (as in the United States) or a different system could be adopted where member banks are assessed charges only after a failure actually occurs.

H. All banks within the EU are to have identical capital standards that mirror the Basel International Capital Standards (discussed more fully in Chapter 14) in order to avoid giving some European banks significant advantages over others.

I. No EU bank is permitted to loan to a single client more than 25 percent of its capital position, a provision designed to ensure that each bank has a diversified loan portfolio with limited risk exposure.

Bank entry across national borders within the EU is free and open, and all depositors have at least some form of insurance protection. Overall, the few research studies that have been conducted suggest that competition has increased and at least some banking services now seem to be available at lower prices. However, many steps still need to be taken to level the playing field throughout the EU, particularly in such areas as taxation, governmental subsidies, labor laws, and excess capacity in the banking industry.

Selected References: James R. Barth, Daniel E. Nolle, and Tara N. Rice, *Commercial Banking Structure, Regulation, and Performance: An International Comparison,* Economics Working Paper 97-6, Office of the Comptroller of the Currency, Washington, D.C., 1997; and Neil B. Murphy, "European Union Financial Developments: The Single Market, the Single Currency, and Banking," *FDIC Banking Review* 13, no. 1 (2000), pp. 1–18.

interest and debt amortization payments to total exports (which compares required debt payments to the principal source for generating foreign exchange reserves to repay debt—a nation's exports), and the ratio of total imports to a nation's foreign exchange reserves (which measures a country's spending abroad relative to the availability of foreign exchange reserves to pay for that spending). However, controversy has continued to swirl around the usefulness of these advanced statistical models due to delays in the reporting of key data, the importance of hard-to-capture random events (such as labor strikes or political revolutions), and instability over time in the relative importance of the different predictor variables used in country-risk models.

Recently published country-risk indicators have become popular aids for bank loan officers trying to evaluate an international loan. One such widely used indicator is the *Euromoney Index*, published by *Euromoney* magazine. *Euromoney*'s country-risk index is based upon a variety of economic and political variables, including access to bank and open-market financing sources, credit ratings, and the international borrower's default history. Another popular indicator of country risk today is the *Institutional Investor Index* (III), published by *Institutional Investor* magazine. The III is derived from a survey of loan officers who work for multinational banks and submit their rankings of each nation as to its probability of default.

Credit-quality indicators are often supplemented by market price information arising from sales of international loans. The prices of debt (loans or bonds) issued by various countries and traded in New York and London's secondary market for international debt provide a daily barometer of how the market as a whole views the risk exposure from each borrowing country. Several international dealers provide the latest price quotes on those foreign loans currently available for sale.

Adjusting to New Market Opportunities Created by Deregulation and New International Agreements

International financial markets are passing through dramatic change as deregulation in one nation after another and international treaties open up new financial service opportunities. Inside the United States the federal government moved in 1994 to allow nationwide acquisitions of American banks by holding companies to open up the opportunity for interstate branch banking. Five years later, the U.S. Congress voted to permit banks, insurance companies, and security dealers to acquire each other through the creation of financial holding companies. These same privileges were extended to foreign banks, making the United States a more attractive market for expanding international banks, security dealers, insurance companies, and other global financial-service providers.

Opportunities Created by NAFTA   In November 1993 the United States government gave final approval to the North American Free Trade Agreement (NAFTA), setting in motion a gradual opening up of Mexico's financial system to outside entry by banks and other financial-service firms from Canada and the United States. The Mexican banking market has become attractive for outside entry because Mexico's banks and nonbank service firms have not moved aggressively to serve such important customer groups as small businesses and households, in part because they are still recovering from the stultifying effects of prior government ownership. The government's earlier seizure of the banking system has retarded the modernization of Mexico's banks. However, NAFTA permits only *gradual* entry through separately capitalized subsidiaries into Mexico by outside banks and nonbank financial service companies, carrying over into the 21st century in an attempt to protect domestic financial-service providers from being overwhelmed by heavyweight Canadian, U.S., European, and Asian financial companies before at least some of the Mexican firms are strong enough to fight their own battles. Meanwhile, the members of NAFTA are considering expansion to include Chile and other member nations, granting still more marketing opportunities for leading international banks.

Opportunities in the European Community and in Eastern Europe   An even larger and more challenging expansion opportunity lies in the continuing integration of the European Union (EU) and the opening up of Eastern Europe and the nations from the former Soviet Union to privatization of property, new businesses, and free markets. Trade barriers are due to be further reduced and eventually eliminated among the member nations of the EU as the 21st century unfolds, under the leadership of a unified European central bank and common monetary system. When combined with now-independent Eastern Europe, the eastern and western European regions boast a population significantly larger than the United States.

However, marketing success across the European continent as a whole appears to demand a significant local presence throughout Europe. Merely setting up a bank or other firm without building a local network of distributors carries little chance of long-term success, particularly in wresting market share from resident competitors and from U.S. financial firms that have had a significant presence there for many years.

Projections by the International Monetary Fund (IMF) have recently identified a set of nations whose projected growth in total real production and income ranks them at or near the top. If these projections turn out to be correct, international bankers and other financial-service managers are likely to consider these parts of the globe as strong potential marketing targets. Included in this group are these nations:

China	The Philippines
India	Russia
Indonesia	Singapore
Ireland	South Korea
Malaysia	Taiwan
Mexico	Turkey

Do you think the IMF is correct in its projections? Why? What risks do these nations appear to present to the international banking community?

Source: The International Monetary Fund, Washington, D.C.

Opportunities in Asia as Barriers Erode   Finally, one of the most promising geographic areas for future expansion by international banks and other financial-service providers lies in Asia, especially in such rapidly growing nations as China, Hong Kong, Indonesia, South Korea, Thailand, and Vietnam. The huge populations of these countries represent business opportunities of historic proportions for those international banks, securities dealers, equity funds, and other financial-service acquirers positioned to take advantage of them. Moreover, the cultural and legal barriers that have prevented consumers and businesses from buying financial products popular in the Western World—such as credit cards, life insurance policies, stocks and bonds, and retirement plans—appear to be eroding as several international banks have moved aggressively to establish strong toeholds in the Asian marketplace.

Factoid
Which Asian nation has the greatest number of separately incorporated commercial banks relative to the size of its population?
Answer: Taiwan with more than 50 different banking companies.

One example of this foreign "invasion" of Asian markets is J. P. Morgan Chase's recent successful effort to secure licenses inside China to supply currency services to Chinese businesses and to provide trading in China's national monetary unit, the yuan, for foreign businesses seeking deals inside China. Moreover, China is committed under its recently signed agreement with the World Trade Organization to allow foreign banking firms to sell retail financial services throughout the nation according to an agreed-upon timetable. Other recent examples of foreign financial-services expansion throughout Asia and nearby nations include the 1999 acquisition of majority ownership by U.S.-based Newbridge Capital Ltd of Korea First Bank and the purchase by U.S.-based Farallon Capital of a controlling position in Indonesia's PT Bank Central Asia. Other leading buyers of shares in Asian financial firms include Citigroup, HSBC Holdings, Standard Chartered Bank of Great Britain, and the Carlyle Group in the United States.

However, major overhaul is needed to sweep away the stringent barriers China and other Asian nations have erected to protect their own banking institutions and to fully privatize the ownership of domestic businesses in the region so that foreign buyers can more easily bid for control. Reforms of this type have been slow to occur in Japan and on the Asian continent, in part due to concerns over foreign control and the potential destruction of local culture and customs. Moreover, the progress made thus far could easily be reversed, causing foreign investors substantial losses.

SPECIAL BANKS GRANTING MICROCREDIT AROUND THE GLOBE

Most, but not all, banks in foreign markets are large financial institutions, granting multimillion-dollar loans. Beginning in the mid-1970s a new type of banking firm emerged in Bangladesh and is now active in more than 30 countries with over a million clients. This bank's loans average only $100 to $200 in size and are granted to individuals (mostly women and minorities) to start and sustain small businesses, including such ventures as making chairs, clothing, and clay pots, caring for children, providing cleaning services, and operating scores of other small ventures.

As the Federal Reserve Bank of Dallas reports, these micro lenders are called Grameen banks, reflecting the Bengali word for "village." They have spread into such diverse nations as India, Mexico, the Philippines, and the United States in order to provide credit to grassroots businesses run by people struggling to overcome poverty. The Grameen Foundation in Washington, D.C., provides advice and support for many of these microbanks all over the world. Many U.S. banking firms support similar credit programs as part of their community development activities.

See especially Diana Mendoza, "Microcredit Means Macro Opportunity," *Banking and Community Perspectives,* Federal Reserve Bank of Dallas, Special Issue, 2003, pp. 1–4.

Concept Check

20–13. This chapter focuses on three major problem areas that international banks must deal with in the future. What are these three areas?

20–14. What different approaches to country-risk evaluation have international banks developed in recent years?

20–15. What different regions around the globe today appear to offer the greatest opportunities for expansion for international banks? Why do you think this is so?

Key URLs
For further information on Grameen banks see especially **www.planfund.org** and **www. dallasfed.org**.

The Need for Careful Planning   These international marketing challenges will demand careful bank planning, particularly the formulation of global long-range investment strategies. These plans must take into account subtle differences in language, customs, and legal systems. Above all else, there must be *organizational flexibility* that permits rapid response to new banking opportunities as new local markets open up and early recognition of developing problems when existing markets deteriorate or new regulatory barriers appear.

Summary

In this chapter we have explored the development of international banking and the many services banks and many of their largest nonbank financial-service competitors offer in international markets today. Among the key points covered in the chapter are the following:

- International banking has been practiced for centuries in the Middle East and Western Europe as bankers emerged to provide business loans and exchange currencies to aid merchants and foreign travelers. Within the past century U.S., European, and, more recently, Japanese and Asian banks have grown to play leading roles on the international scene.

- In order to expand abroad, international banks and many of their closest competitors have used a wide variety of different organizational forms. Examples include *representative offices* (which facilitate the flow of information between financial firms and their overseas customers), *agencies* (which provide selected financial services such as customer credit and liquidity needs), *branch offices* (which offer many of the same services that an international bank's home office provides), and *affiliated companies* and *joint ven-*

tures (which often supply key supporting services such as insurance, marketing, and security trading). Frequently the different organizational forms are used to avoid burdensome banking regulations in a particular country.

- International banking services today cover a wide variety of customer needs, such as supplying foreign currencies, providing hedging services to deal with currency and interest-rate risk, supplying credit and credit guarantees in order to fund trade and capital expansion, helping customers tap the Eurocurrency and Eurobond markets to raise new capital, supplying cash management services, and providing assessments of foreign marketing opportunities.

- The *regulation* of international banking and financial services remains a powerful force shaping global finance and trade. Nations vary greatly in the scope and content of their laws and regulations surrounding the financial-services sector. The managers of internationally focused banks and other financial firms have often taken advantage of these regulatory discrepancies between nations, entering those market areas where regulation is less of a burden (often referred to as *regulatory arbitrage*).

- One of the most significant regulatory trends is *government deregulation* among leading industrial nations, giving international banks and their nonbank competitors more latitude to expand abroad. Prominent examples include the passage of the Gramm-Leach-Bliley (GLB) Act in the United States, allowing banks to combine with insurance and securities firms, and the opening of a common financial and currency system in Europe, facilitating mergers within the European financial sector.

- Recently *international regulatory cooperation* among nations has become more common so that all international banks and other financial firms may eventually face the same set of rules. One of the best examples is the Basel Agreement, enforcing common capital standards among the world's leading banks.

- Nevertheless, serious problems confront the international banking and financial services sector today due to the inherent risks in this field. Foreign expansion often presents financial-service providers with new government restrictions; new credit, currency, and interest-rate risks; new cultural standards and practices; and less quality information upon which to base business decisions than usually is available in domestic markets. New emerging trade blocs and more open economies in Europe, North America, and Asia are creating new marketing opportunities today, but also major new challenges for international banking firms and their financial-service competitors.

Key Terms

representative office, *707*
agency office, *707*
branch office, *707*
subsidiary, *707*
joint venture, *708*
Edge Acts, *708*
international banking facility (IBF), *708*
shell branches, *708*
Export Trading Company Act, *708*
export trading companies, *708*

International Banking Act, *710*
Foreign Bank Supervision Enhancement Act, *711*
International Lending and Supervision Act, *711*
Basel Agreement, *712*
FOREX, *712*
forward contracts, *716*
currency futures contract, *716*

currency option, *717*
currency swaps, *718*
note issuance facility (NIF), *719*
Eurocommercial paper (ECP), *719*
American depository receipt (ADR), *720*
Eurobond market, *721*
interest-rate swaps, *722*

Problems and Projects

1. Pacific Trading Company purchased Canadian dollars yesterday in anticipation of a purchase of electric equipment through a Canadian supply house. However, Pacific was contacted this morning by a Japanese trading company that says equipment closer to its specifications is available in 48 hours from an electronics manufacturer in Osaka. A phone call to Pacific's bank this morning indicated that another of the bank's customers, a furniture importer located in San Francisco, purchased a comparable amount of yen in order to pay for an incoming shipment from Tokyo, only to discover that the shipment will be delayed until next week. Meanwhile, the furniture company must pay off an inventory loan tomorrow that it received 30 days ago from Toronto-Dominion Bank.

   Which of the instruments described in this chapter would be most helpful to these two companies? Construct a diagram that illustrates the transaction you, as an international banker, would recommend to these two firms to help solve their current problems.

2. Nelson Sporting Goods has ordered a shipment of soccer equipment from a manufacturer and distributor in Munich. Payment for the shipment (which is valued at $3.5 million U.S.) must be made in euros that have changed in value in the last 30 days from 1.0268 euros/$ to 1.0592 euros/$. If this trend is expected to continue, would you as Nelson's banker recommend that this customer use a currency futures hedge? Why or why not?

3. U.S. Signal Q Corporation will import new wooden toys from a French manufacturer this week at a price of 200 euros per item for eventual distribution to retail stores. The current euro–dollar exchange rate is 1.01 euros per U.S. dollar. Payment for the shipment will be made by Signal Q next month, but euros are expected to appreciate significantly against the dollar. Signal Q asks its bank, Southern Merchants Bank, N.A., for advice on what to do. What kind of futures transaction could be used to deal with this problem faced by Signal Q Corporation? Futures contracts calling for delivery of euros next month are priced currently at 1.04 euros per dollar and are expected to be priced next month at 0.99 euros per dollar.

4. Maesen Hardware Manufacturing Corporation regularly ships tools to the United States to retail hardware outlets from its shipping warehouse in Stuttgart, Germany. Its normal credit terms call for full payment in U.S. dollars for the hardware it ships within 90 days of the shipment date. However, Maesen must convert all U.S. dollars received from its customers into euros in order to compensate its local workers and suppliers. Maesen has just made a large shipment to retail dealers in the United States and is concerned about a forecast just received from its local bank that the U.S. dollar–euro exchange rate will fall sharply over the next month. The current euro–U.S. dollar exchange rate is 1.07 euros per dollar. However, the local bank's current forecast calls for the exchange rate to fall to 1.03 euros per dollar, so that Maesen will receive substantially less in euros for each U.S. dollar it receives in payment for its tools. Please explain how Maesen Corporation, with the aid of its bank, could use currency futures to offset at least a portion of its projected loss due to the expected change in the euro–dollar exchange rate.

5. Hilgarde International Mercantile Guaranty Corporation has made a $15 million investment in a stamping mill located in northern Germany and fears a substantial decline in the euro's current spot price from $0.98 to $0.95, lowering the value of the firm's capital investment. Hilgarde's principal U.S. bank advises the firm to use an appropriate option contract to help reduce Hilgarde's risk of loss due to currency risk.

   What currency option contract would you recommend to deal with this situation? Explain why the option contract you have selected would help to reduce the firm's currency risk exposure.

6. Sogo International Bank of Japan holds U.S. dollar-denominated assets of $394 million and dollar-denominated liabilities of $587 million, has purchased U.S. dollars in the currency markets amounting to $66 million, and sold U.S. dollars totaling $24 million. What is Sogo's *net* exposure to risk from fluctuations in U.S. dollar prices relative to the bank's domestic currency? Under what circumstances could Sogo lose if dollar prices change relative to the yen?

7. Suppose that Westminster Bank has a net long position in U.S. dollars of $8 million, dollar-denominated liabilities of $115 million, U.S. dollar purchases of $268 million, and dollar sales of $173 million. What is the current value of the bank's dollar-denominated assets? Suppose the U.S. dollar's exchange value rises against the pound. Is Westminster likely to gain or lose? Why?

Internet Exercises

1. Why are banks more prone to cross national borders today and even span continents to acquire other financial service providers? Visit the Institute of International Bankers website at **www.iib.org**. Click on the Institute's Annual Global Survey covering the activities of more than 40 countries. Choose a country of interest to you and read the synopsis at the end of the survey. What are some key issues for your country?

2. You want some current news on international banks. Visit **www.newsnow.co.uk** and use the newsfeed to locate banking topics within business and finance news. Read an article from a country other than the United States. What were the major issues discussed in this article?

3. Suppose you want some detailed information about central banks outside the United States. Visit **www.bis.org/cbanks.htm**. What is the URL for the central bank of the European Union? Hong Kong? Thailand?

4. To get an idea of the internationalization of some of our large banks, visit Citigroup's Country website at **www.citigroup.com/citigroup/global/index.htm**. Describe its presence in Morocco, Saudi Arabia, and Finland.

STANDARD &POOR'S S&P Market Insight Challenge

Use Standard & Poor's Market Insight website (**www.mhhe.com/edumarketinsight**) for this problem. S&P's Market Insight, Educational Version has a number of foreign bank and financial-service firms listed in its inventory of financial-service providers. Examples include Mitsubishi Financial Group, HSBC Holdings PLC, and Barclays PLC, among others represented in the Insight collection. Most of these foreign financial corporations have a solid presence in the United States, the European Community, Japan, and selected Asian markets. Which are significantly represented in all four of these areas of the globe? With what financial services? What advantages might this bring to those banks and other financial firms with the broadest global representation?

REAL NUMBERS FOR REAL BANKS

Assignment for Chapter 20

YOUR BANK'S USE OF FOREIGN OFFICES

Chapter 20 explores the services and issues involved with foreign banks operating in the United States and U.S. banks operating abroad. One way that U.S. banks can operate abroad is through foreign offices. This chapter describes the different types of offices, and they will be the focus of this assignment. First we will collect and examine the data to see how foreign offices affect our BHC's balance sheet. Then we will look at the number, types, and location of foreign offices associated with the BHC you have chosen.

Part One: Trend and Comparative Analysis of the Contribution of Foreign Offices to your BHC's Report of Condition

A. Data Collection: In this assignment we return to the SDI at **www3.fdic.gov/sdi/main.asp** and collect data from the net loans and leases and total deposits reports. This entails using SDI to create a four-column report of your bank's information and the peer group information across years. You are to collect the two items listed below and enter this data into Spreadsheet 2 as follows:

Loans to Individuals and Families (A167)	Your Bank	Peer Group	Your Bank	Peer Group
Date (A168)	12/31/yy	12/31/yy	12/31/yy	12/31/yy
Total loans and leases in foreign offices (A169)	%	%	%	%
Deposits held in foreign offices (A170)				

B. Write one paragraph about the contributions of foreign offices to operations. Has your BHC focused more or less attention on foreign offices? Has your BHC moved into foreign markets using offices more or less than other very large banks (your peer group)?

Part Two: How Your BHC Used Foreign Offices to Expand Internationally

A. Go to the FDIC's Institution Directory at **http://www3.fdic .gov/idasp/**, and do a search for your bank holding company (BHC) using the BHC ID. This search will produce a list of bank and thrift subsidiaries. If you click on the active

certificate links, additional information will appear and you will be able to pull up a current list of offices for that bank. At the bottom of the list of all offices associated with that bank you'll find information on location, codes identifying the type of office, and the date foreign offices were established. You will want to focus your attention on the number of foreign offices, their types, and their locations. Collect this information for each bank belonging to the bank holding company you have chosen.

B. Compose several paragraphs discussing your banking company's expansion internationally and evaluate their strategy to expand or not.

Selected References

For excellent discussions of assessing risk in international lending, see the following:

1. Denison, Daniel R. "A Pragmatic Model for Country Risk Analysis." *Journal of Commercial Bank Lending*, March 1984, pp. 29–37.

2. Melvin, Michael, and Don Schlagenhauf. "A Country Risk Index: Econometric Formulation and an Application to Mexico." *Economic Inquiry*, 1984, pp. 601–19.

For an analysis of the recent activities of U.S. banks in international markets, see these studies:

3. Houpt, James V. *International Trends for U.S. Banks and Banking Markets*. Staff Study no. 156, Board of Governors of the Federal Reserve System, May 1988.

4. Pardee, Scott E. "Internationalization of Financial Markets." *Economic Review*, Federal Reserve Bank of Kansas City, February 1987, pp. 3–7.

5. Rose, Peter S. "The Quest for Funds: New Directions in a New Market." *The Canadian Banker* 94, no. 5 (September/October 1987), pp. 46–55.

For an analysis of the expansion of Japanese banking abroad, see these articles:

6. Frankel, Allen B., and Paul B. Morgan, "Deregulation and Competition in Japanese Banking." *Federal Reserve Bulletin*, August 1992, pp. 579–93.

7. Japanese Bankers Association. *Japanese Banks 2001*. Zenginkyo, Tokyo, Japan, 2002. (See also www.zenginkyo.or.jp.)

8. Rose, Peter S. *Japanese Banking and Investment in the United States: An Assessment of Their Impact upon U.S. Markets and Institutions*. New York: Quorum Books, 1991.

These studies discuss international debt crises and currency hedging tools:

9. Kawaller, Ira G. "Options on Currency Futures." *The Bankers Magazine*, January/ February 1987, pp. 20–22.

10. Truman, Edwin M. "U.S. Policy on the Problems of International Debt." *Federal Reserve Bulletin*, November 1989, pp. 727–35.

For an explanation of U.S. regulations on foreign banks, see:

11. Misback, Anan E. "The Foreign Bank Supervision Enhancement Act of 1991." *Federal Reserve Bulletin*, January 1993, pp. 1–10.

For an analysis of banking and financial problems in Europe and Asia, see:

12. Hopper, Gregory P. "What Determines the Exchange Rate: Economic Factors or Market Sentiment?" *Business Review*, Federal Reserve Bank of Philadelphia, September/ October 1997, pp. 17–29.

13. Huh, Chan. "Banking System Developments in the Four Asian Tigers." *Economic Letter*, Federal Reserve Bank of San Francisco, No. 97-22 (August 8, 1997), pp. 1–3.

14. Peek, Joe, and Eric S. Rosengren. "Japanese Banking Problems: Implications for Lending in the United States." *New England Economic Review*, Federal Reserve Bank of Boston, January/February 1999.

15. ———. "Determinants of the Japan Premium: Actions Speak Louder than Words." Working Paper 98–99, Federal Reserve Bank of Boston, 1998.

For a discussion of recent foreign bank expansion inside the United States, see:

16. Lopez, Jose A. "Patterns in the Foreign Ownership of U.S. Banking Assets." *Economic Letter*, Federal Reserve Bank of San Francisco, November 2000.

For an overview of Japan's efforts at reform of its banking and financial system, see:

17. Cargill, Thomas. "Japan Passes Again on Fundamental Financial Reform." *FRBSF Economic Letter*, No. 2002-28, Federal Reserve Bank of San Francisco, September 2002.

18. Glick, Reuven. "Financial Issues in the Pacific Basin Region." *FRBSF Economic Letter*, No. 2002-38, Federal Reserve Bank of San Francisco, December 2002.

For an overview of international banking trends in North and South America, see especially these studies:

19. Haar, Jerry. "The Changing Landscape of Financial Services in Latin America's Large Emerging Markets." *Working Paper Series No. 15*, The Dante B. Fascell North-South Center, University of Miami, July 2003.

www.mhhe.com/rose6e

20. Zhang, Frank X. "What Did the Credit Market Expect of Argentina's Default? Evidence from Default Swap Data." *Finance and Economics Discussion Series No. 2003-25*, Division of Research and Statistics, Federal Reserve Board, Washington, D.C., April 16, 2003.

Recent research on the risk management practices of Japanese banks may be found in the following article:

21. Smith, David C. "Loans to Japanese Borrowers." *International Finance Discussion Papers*, Board of Governors of the Federal Reserve System, 2003.

Using a Financial Calculator

Time Value of Money (TVM): Application of Formula Using Financial Calculators and Spreadsheets

$$PV = \sum_{t=1}^{N} \frac{Pmt_t}{(1+I)^t} + \frac{FV_N}{(1+I)^N}$$

Where:

Calculator notation (Excel notation)

N (nper) = number of periods.

I (rate) = periodic rate.

PV (PV) = Present Value (Price/Value Today)

Pmt (pmt) = annuity cash flow to be paid at the end of each period.

FV (FV) = Future Value (Sale or redemption price of security to be paid at the end of N periods).

Basics for using Excel formula functions: Excel automatically prompts you for information, after you choose one of the following functions:

- ❖ FV(rate,nper,pmt,pv,type)
- ❖ PV(rate,nper,pmt,fv,type)
- ❖ NPER(rate,pmt,pv,fv,type)
- ❖ PMT(rate,nper,pv,fv,type)
- ❖ RATE(nper,pmt,pv,fv,type)

Basics for using the TI BAII Plus to determine values of TVM variables

- ❖ Using the TVM registers for calculations: Enter value then press register key (shown below) for storage. [N] [I/Y] [PV] [PMT] [FV]
- ❖ After entering information into TVM registers press [CPT] and the TVM key for your solution.

Housekeeping functions

- ❖ For accuracy, set your calculator to display all possible decimal places: [2nd] [format] [9] [ENTER]
- ❖ Assume only one pmt per period. (Your calculator will arrive set at 12 pmts) [2nd] [P/Y] [1] [ENTER]
- ❖ After each problem, make sure you clear your time value of money (TVM) registers: [2nd] [CLR TVM]

Troubleshooting: When solving for N or I/Y, cash inflows (i.e., Pmt and FV) must have opposite signs of cash outflows (i.e., PV), otherwise your calculator will return "Error".

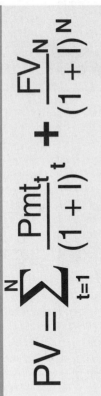

Calculating the Present Value of Cash Flows
(Using TI BAII Plus Financial Calculator and Excel Financial Functions)

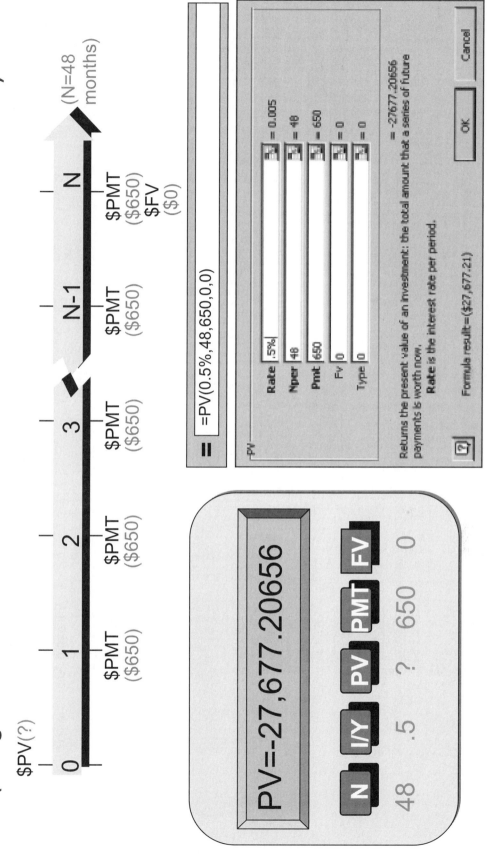

Example: Calculate the Present Value (i.e., the loan amount) of monthly payments of $650 for 4 years (48 months) discounted at an annual rate of 6% compounded monthly (monthly periodic interest rate is 6%/12=.5%).

Calculating the Future Value of Cash Flows
(Using TI BAII Plus Financial Calculator and Excel Financial Functions)

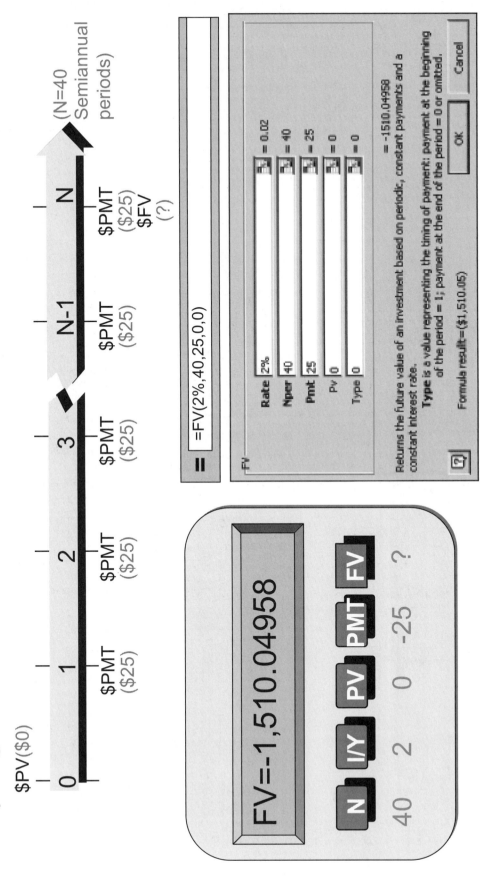

Example: Calculate the Future Value of a $25 annuity where semiannual payments are invested at an annual rate of 4% compounded semiannually (the semiannual periodic interest rate is 4%/2=2%) for 20 years (40 semiannual periods).

Calculating the Annual Percentage Rate (APR)
(Using TI BAII Plus Financial Calculator and Excel Financial Functions)

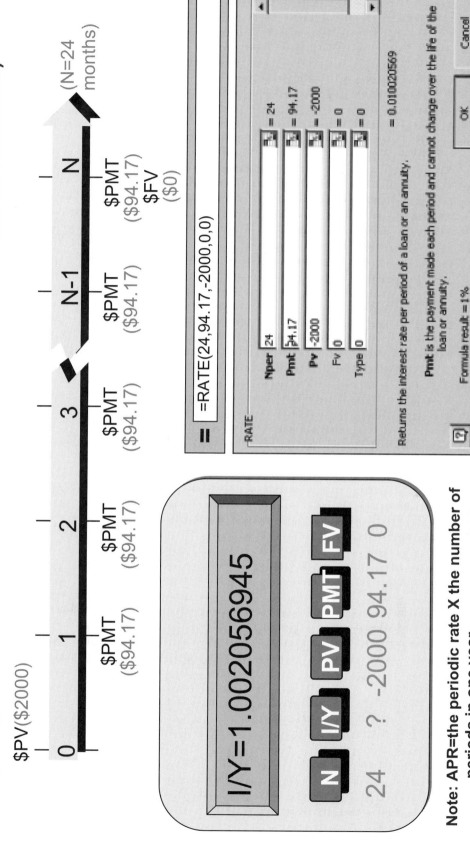

$PV($2000)

0	1	2	3		N-1	N

$PMT
($94.17)

$PMT
($94.17)

$PMT
($94.17)

$PMT
($94.17)

$PMT
($94.17)
$FV
($0)

(N=24 months)

= =RATE(24,94.17,-2000,0,0)

RATE

Nper 24 = 24

Pmt 94.17 = 94.17

Pv -2000 = -2000

Fv 0 = 0

Type 0 = 0

= 0.0100020569

Returns the interest rate per period of a loan or an annuity.

Pmt is the payment made each period and cannot change over the life of the loan or annuity.

Formula result = 1%

OK   Cancel

I/Y=1.0020056945

N   I/Y   PV   PMT   FV

24   ?   -2000   94.17   0

Note: APR=the periodic rate X the number of periods in one year
APR=1.0020569 X 12 = 12.02%

Example: Calculate the APR for a customer who borrows $2000 (PV), agreeing to monthly payments of $94.17 over the next 24 months.

A

account party The customer who requests a standby letter of credit from a bank or other lender of funds.

add-on method A procedure for calculating a consumer's loan rate in which interest is assessed on the full principal of an installment loan.

adjustable-rate mortgages (ARMs) Loans against real property whose interest rate periodically adjusts to changes in market interest rates.

affiliated banks Banks whose stock has been acquired by a holding company.

agency offices International banking offices that provide credit and other nondeposit services.

agency theory An explanation of the risk-taking behavior of individuals and institutions that focuses on the parties to a principal–agent contract in which any agent may seek to optimize his or her position at the expense of the principal(s) involved.

agricultural loans Credit extended to farm and ranch operations to assist in planting and harvesting crops and to care for and market livestock.

ALMs Automated loan machines that allow a customer to enter selected bits of information and receive a loan of cash if the machine's programmed credit standards are met.

American depository receipt (ADR) A receipt issued by a U.S. bank that makes it easier for a foreign business borrower to sell its securities in the United States.

annual percentage rate (APR) Interest rate on a loan that the U.S. Truth and Lending Act requires to be quoted to a household consumer seeking a loan.

annuities An investment product sold by many banks and other financial firms today in which the customer invests his or her savings under the terms of a contract that promises a stream of income in the future (either fixed or variable in amount).

antidiscrimination laws Laws that prevent the grouping of loan customers into categories according to their age, sex, race, national origin, location of residence, religious affiliation, or receipt of public assistance and that prohibits the denial of a loan to anyone solely because of membership in one or more of these groups.

asset-based loans Loans secured by a business firm's assets, particularly accounts receivable and inventory.

asset-liability management The process of decision making to control a bank or other financial institution's exposure to interest-rate risk.

asset liquidity management A strategy for meeting liquidity needs, in which liquid funds are stored in readily marketable assets that can be quickly converted into cash as needed.

asset management A management strategy that regards the volume and mix of a bank or other financial firm's sources of funds as determined largely by the wishes of its customers and calls for management to concentrate on controlling assets, rather than on managing liabilities, in order to meet liquidity needs and other goals.

asset utilization The ratio of total operating revenues to total assets, measuring the average yield on assets.

assignments A form of loan sale in which ownership of a loan is transferred to the loan buyer who then has a direct claim against the borrower.

ATMs Automated teller machines through which a customer can access his or her deposit account, make loan payments, or obtain information and other services.

B

balanced liquidity management The combined use of both asset management and liability management to cover liquidity needs.

bank The financial intermediary that offers the widest range of financial services—especially credit, savings, and payment services—and performs the widest range of financial functions of any business firm in the economy.

bank discount rate The method by which yields on Treasury bills and other money market securities are calculated using par value and a 360-day year to determine the appropriate discount rate or yield.

bank holding company A corporation chartered for the purpose of holding the stock (equity shares) of one or more banks.

Bank Holding Company Act U.S. law that brought bank holding company organizations under comprehensive federal regulation.

Bank Merger Act of 1960   A law passed by the U.S. Congress that requires each merging bank to notify its principal federal regulatory agency of a pending merger and requests federal approval before the merger can be completed.

bankers' acceptance   A bank's written promise to pay the holder of the acceptance a designated amount of money on a specific future date.

bankers' banks   Regional service firms, often created as joint ventures by groups of banks and other financial firms, in order to facilitate the delivery of certain customer services, such as the rapid transfer and investment of customer funds and the execution of orders to buy or sell securities.

Basel Agreement   A negotiated agreement between bank regulatory authorities in the United States, Canada, Great Britain, Japan, and eight other nations in western Europe to set common capital requirements for all banks under their jurisdiction.

Basel I   The first official agreement between the United States, Belgium, Canada, France, Germany, Italy, Japan, the Netherlands, Sweden, Switzerland, the United Kingdom, and Luxembourg, formally approved in Basel, Switzerland, in 1988 and imposing common minimum capital requirements on banks headquartered in these countries.

Basel II   The version of the Basel accord on bank capital requirements designed to succeed Basel I, permitting banks to employ their own internal risk-assessment methods and calculate their own minimum capital requirements as well as mandating periodic stress testing to estimate the impact of changing market conditions on each bank's financial position.

basic (lifeline) banking   Low-cost deposits and other services that are designed to meet the needs of customers of limited means.

below-prime pricing   Interest rates on loans set below the prevailing prime rate, usually based on the level of key money market interest rates (such as the current market rate on Federal funds or Eurodollar deposits).

beneficiary   The party who will receive payment under a financial guarantee if certain events occur, such as default on a loan.

board of directors   The committee elected by the stockholders to set policy and oversee the performance of a bank or other business.

Board of Governors   The center of authority and decision making within the Federal Reserve System; the board must contain no more than seven persons, each selected by the president of the United States and

confirmed by the U.S. Senate for a term not exceeding 14 years.

branch banking   An arrangement in which a bank offers a full range of services from multiple locations, including a head office and one or more branch offices.

branch offices   Full-service units operated by a business that is headquartered in another location.

business risk   The probability that the economy will turn down into a recession, with reduced demand for loans, deposits, and other products and services.

C

call risk   The danger that an investor in loans or securities will experience a lower-than-expected rate of return due to the issuer of the loans or securities calling in these instruments and retiring them early before they reach maturity.

CAMELS rating   A system that assigns a numerical rating to a bank or thrift based on examiner judgment regarding its capital adequacy, asset condition, management quality, earnings record, liquidity position, and sensitivity to market risk.

capital   Long-term funds contributed to a bank or other financial institution primarily by its owners, consisting mainly of stock, reserves, and retained earnings.

capital market instruments   Investment securities that reach maturity over periods longer than one year.

capital risk   The probability that a financial institution or one of its borrowing customers will fail, exhausting its capital.

cash   This term is one of the six Cs of credit, which loan officers should review in any loan application, referring to the generation of income or cash flow by a borrowing customer.

cash flow   Often measured by the net income plus noncash expenses (such as depreciation) of a business loan customer.

cash flow analysis   An analytical approach to measuring the volume and composition of cash inflows and cash outflows experienced or expected by a borrowing customer.

cash flow risk   The danger that cash flows may fluctuate widely due to economic conditions, service mix, and other factors; a merger may help to reduce this risk by combining organizations and service packages that have different cash flow patterns over time.

cash management services   A service in which a financial firm agrees to handle cash collections and cash disbursements for a business firm and to invest any temporary cash surpluses in interest-bearing securities until those funds are needed.

certificate of deposit (CD)   An interest-bearing receipt for the deposit of funds in a bank or nonbank thrift institution for a specified period of time.

charter of incorporation   A license to open and operate a commercial bank or other business, issued by either the commission of the state where the firm is to be located or the Comptroller of the Currency (for federally chartered banks) inside the United States.

clearing balances   Deposits held with the Federal Reserve banks by depository institutions to help clear checks for payment and collection and that allow the depository institutions using Federal Reserve services to earn interest credits on these balances in order to help offset the cost of Fed services.

collateral   A borrower's possession of adequate net worth, quality assets, or other items of value that give added support to his or her ability to repay a loan.

commercial and industrial loans   Credit granted to businesses to help cover purchases of inventory, plant, and equipment and to meet other operating expenses.

commercial paper   Short-term, unsecured IOUs offered to investors in the money market by major corporations with the strongest credit ratings.

commercial paper market   Market where short-term notes with maturities ranging from three or four days to nine months are traded, issued by well-known banking and nonbanking companies for the purpose of raising working capital.

common stock   Type of capital measured by the par value of all common equity shares outstanding that pays a variable return to its owners after all expenses and other claims are met.

Community Reinvestment Act   Federal law passed in 1977 requiring covered depository institutions to make "an affirmative effort" to serve all segments of their trade territory without discrimination.

compensating deposit balances   Required deposits a customer must keep with a lender as a condition for getting a loan.

competitive effects   The aspect of a merger or acquisition between two or more financial institutions that will have an impact on interfirm rivalry, either reducing or increasing competition in the markets served by the firms involved; this impact of a merger or acquisition is, under current federal law, the most important factor federal regulatory agencies must weigh in deciding to approve or deny any proposed acquisitions or mergers.

Competitive Equality in Banking Act   Legislation that authorized recapitalization of the Federal Savings and Loan Insurance Corporation to deal more effectively with failing savings and loan associations, required depository institutions to provide more information to their customers on when credit is given for deposited funds, and placed a moratorium on the creation of nonbank banks and the offering of insurance, securities, and real estate services by commercial banks operating inside the United States.

Comptroller of the Currency (or Administrator of National Banks)   The federal government agency, a part of the U.S. Treasury Department, that awards charters for new national banks in the United States and also supervises and regularly examines all existing national banks.

conditional pricing   Establishing minimum-size account balances and charging a lower or even zero fee if the customer's deposit balance climbs *above* that required minimum but a higher fee if the average balance falls *below* the required minimum amount.

conglomerates   Corporations that bring together a wide variety of different businesses and product lines under common ownership.

construction loans   Short-term loans designed to fund the building of new structures and then be paid off and replaced with a longer-term mortgage loan once the construction phase of the project has ended.

contingent liabilities   Debt obligations that will not come due unless certain events occur, such as borrower default or the exercise of product warranties.

contingent obligation   A financial instrument whose issuer pledges to pay if certain events (such as default on a loan) occur; for example, federal deposit insurance is a contingent obligation of the government, payable if a bank or thrift institution fails.

convergence   The bringing together of firms from different industries to create conglomerate firms offering multiple services.

convexity   The rate of change in an asset's price or value varies with the level of interest rates or yields.

core capital   Permanent capital of a bank, consisting mainly of common stock, surplus, retained earnings, and equity reserves.

core deposits   A stable and predictable base of deposited funds, usually supplied by households and smaller businesses, that is not highly sensitive to movements in market interest rates but tends to remain loyal to the depository institution.

corporate bonds   Debt securities issued by private corporations with original maturities longer than five years.

corporate governance   The network of relationships between a corporation's board of directors and members of its management team that help to define who has control over what issues and who makes pivotal decisions within the organization.

corporate notes   Debt securities issued by private corporations with original maturities of five years or less.

correspondent banking   A system of formal and informal relationships among large and small depository institutions established to facilitate the exchange of certain services, such as the clearing of checks and the exchange of information.

cosigner   A person obligated to support the repayment of a loan by a borrower who either has no credit record or has such a poor track record of repaying loans that he or she cannot get a loan without the support of the cosigner.

cost-benefit loan pricing   A method for pricing loans that adds all costs of making a loan and compares those costs to all expected revenues generated by a loan.

cost-plus deposit pricing   Charging customers for the full cost or a significant portion of the total cost of any deposit services they use.

cost-plus loan pricing   Figuring the rate of interest on a loan by adding together all interest and noninterest costs associated with making the loan plus margins for profit and risk.

cost savings (efficiency)   A motivation for mergers that rests on the possibility that by combining two or more institutions together, overall operating expenses will be reduced, creating the possibility of a rise in net income for the combined (merged) institution.

credit availability risk   The possibility that lenders may not have the funds to loan or be willing to accommodate every qualified borrower when credit is requested.

credit bureau   A business firm that keeps data files on people who have borrowed money, indicating their previous record of loan repayments.

credit default swaps   Financial agreements that permit a lender to protect itself against credit (default risk) by receiving compensation from a counterparty to help offset excessive loan losses or excessive fluctuations in loan revenue.

credit derivatives   Financial contracts that are designed to protect a lending institution against loss due to defaults on its loans or security holdings.

credit enhancement   A contract in which a financial institution promises to back up the credit of another firm.

credit life insurance   An insurance policy that guarantees repayment of a loan if a borrower dies or is disabled before his or her loan is paid off.

credit option   An agreement between a lending institution and an option writer that is designed to protect a lender against possible loss due to declines in the value of some of its assets or to prevent a significant rise in borrowing costs should the borrower's credit rating be lowered or other events occur that result in higher fund-raising costs.

credit risk   The probability that the issuer of a loan or security will fail and default on any promised payments of interest or principal or both.

credit risk models   Analytical tools, including computer programs, designed to assess the level of default risk associated with a loan customer seeking to borrow funds or the default-risk exposure of a whole portfolio of loans or other assets.

credit scoring   The use of a discriminant equation to classify loan applicants according to the probability of their repaying their loans, based on customer characteristics such as their credit rating or length of employment.

credit swap   A financial contract designed to reduce the risk of default on loans by having two lending institutions exchange a portion of their expected loan payments with each other.

credit unions   Nonprofit depository institutions that make loans to and accept deposits only from their members who must share a common bond (such as working for the same employer).

crime risk   The danger of fraud, embezzlement, robbery, or other crimes that could result in loss for a financial institution.

currency exchange   Trading one form of currency (such as dollars) for another (such as francs or pesos) in return for a fee; one of the first services offered when the banking industry began centuries ago.

currency futures contract   Agreement between a buyer and a seller of foreign currencies that promises delivery of a stipulated currency at a specified price on a specific date in the future.

currency option   Contract giving the option holder the right, but not the obligation, to deliver or take delivery of a specific currency at a set price on or before the contract's expiration date.

currency swaps   Agreements between two or more parties who need to borrow foreign currency that help to protect each of them against changes in currency prices by agreeing to exchange payments denominated in different currencies.

customer privacy   Protecting the personal information that customers supply to their financial-service providers so that customers are not damaged by the release of their private data to outside parties.

customer profitability analysis   A method for evaluating a customer's loan request that takes into account all revenues and expenses associated with serving that particular customer and calculates an expected net return over all costs incurred from serving the customer.

customer relationship doctrine   The management strategy whose first priority is making loans to all those customers who meet the lender's quality standards and from whom positive earnings are expected.

D

demand deposit   Checking account services that permit depositors to write drafts in payment for goods and services that the depository institution involved must honor immediately upon presentation.

de novo bank   A newly chartered banking corporation.

Depository Institutions Deregulation and Monetary Control Act   Law passed in the United States in 1980 requiring that federal interest rate ceilings on deposits sold to the public be phased out so that deposit interest rates could more closely reflect prevailing market conditions; it also authorized the offering of NOW accounts throughout the United States, which pay an explicit interest return to the customer and have third-party payment powers.

dilution of ownership   The degree to which the proportionate share of ownership held by the current owners of a firm is reduced when additional equity shares are issued to new stockholders or to the shareholders of a firm that is being acquired.

disclosure rules   Laws and regulations that mandate telling the consumer about financing costs and other essential terms of a loan or lease agreement.

discount brokerage services   A service designed to assist customers with purchases and sales of securities at relatively low brokerage fees.

discounting commercial notes   The process of making loans to local merchants who use IOUs received from their customers as collateral.

discount rate method   The procedure used to assess interest on a loan in which interest is deducted up front at the beginning of the loan and the customer receives for his or her use the full principal of the loan less the interest assessed.

discount window   Department within each Federal Reserve bank that lends legal reserves to eligible institutions for short periods of time.

dual banking system   A system of banking regulation in which both federal and state authorities have significant regulatory powers and supervisory responsibilities over the activities of commercial banks.

duration   A present-value weighted measure of the maturity of an individual security or portfolio of securities in which the timing and amount of *all* cash flows expected from the security or portfolio of securities are considered.

duration gap   The difference between the duration of an institution's assets and the duration of its liabilities.

duration gap management   A strategy or technique used by the management of a bank or other financial institution to achieve a desired spread between the duration of its assets and the duration of its liabilities in order to control the institution's interest-rate risk exposure.

E

earnings risk   The danger that earnings may fluctuate widely due to changes in economic conditions, demand for services, mix of services offered, or other factors; a merger between two or more organizations may dampen this form of risk by bringing together different revenue sources with different cash flow patterns over time.

economies of scope   Employing the same management, staff, and facilities to offer multiple products or services, thereby helping to reduce the per-unit cost of production and delivery of goods or services.

Edge Acts   Subsidiary companies of a banking organization that must devote the majority of their activities to transactions involving international trade and commerce; establishment of these subsidiaries must be approved by the Federal Reserve Board.

efficiency   An indicator of how well management and staff have been able to keep the growth of revenues and income ahead of rising operating costs.

Equal Credit Opportunity Act   Legislation passed by the U.S. Congress in 1974 that prohibits lenders from asking certain questions of a borrowing household customer, such as his or her age, race, or religion, and from denying a loan based solely upon a credit applicant's age, race, religion, ethnic origins, receipt of public assistance, or similar characteristics.

equipment leasing services   The purchase of equipment on behalf of a customer in order to lease the equipment to that customer in return for a series of lease payments.

equity commitment notes   Type of bank capital in the form of debt securities that is repayable only from the future sale of bank stock.

equity multiplier   The ratio of total assets to total equity capital.

equity reserves   Type of capital representing funds set aside for contingencies such us losses on assets, lawsuits, and other extraordinary events, as well as providing a reserve for dividends expected to be paid out to stockholders but not yet declared and a sinking fund to be used to retire stock or debt capital instruments in the future.

Eurobond market   An institution that brings together sellers of bonds issued outside their home country and interested buyers in one or more other nations.

Eurocommercial paper (ECP)   Short-term notes issued by multinational corporations and sold to investors in one or more countries that permit these corporations to borrow funds for a few days, weeks, or months.

Eurocurrency deposit   Deposits denominated in a currency different from the currency of the home country of the bank where they are created.

events of default   A section contained in most loan agreements listing what actions or omissions by a borrower would represent a violation of the terms of the agreement and what action the lender is legally authorized to take in response.

exchange ratio   The number of shares of stock in the acquiring firm that stockholders of the acquired firm will receive for each share they hold.

exchange risk   The probability of loss because of fluctuating currency prices in international markets.

expense preference   An approach to the management of a firm in which managers draw upon the resources of the firm to provide them with personal benefits (such as lavish offices, country club memberships, etc.) not needed to produce and sell products, thereby raising the cost of production and reducing returns to the firm's owners; an

agency cost problem in which the interests of the managers of a firm take precedence over the interests of its owners.

Export-Import Bank   A lender of funds created by the U.S. government to aid with export-import financing and to make loans that support the development of overseas markets.

export trading companies (ETCs)   Organizational devices to aid customers in selling their goods abroad, particularly the products of smaller businesses, by creating a subsidiary firm to help with foreign marketing and the financing of exports.

Export Trading Company Act   Law passed by the U.S. Congress in 1982 that allowed U.S. banks to make direct investments in export trading companies to help their U.S. business customers sell goods and services abroad.

F

factoring   Sale of the shorter-term assets of a business firm that are expected to roll over into cash in the near term, such as accounts receivable and inventory, in order to raise more working capital.

Fair Credit Billing Act   Law enacted by the U.S. Congress in 1974 that permits consumers to dispute alleged billing errors committed by a merchant or credit card company and requires that consumers receive a prompt investigation of any billing disputes under penalty of forfeiture of at least a portion of the amount billed.

Fair Credit Reporting Act   Law that authorizes U.S. consumers to review their credit records, as reflected in the files of a credit bureau, for accuracy and to demand the investigation and correction of any inaccuracies.

Fair Debt Collection Practices Act   Law passed by the U.S. Congress limiting how far a creditor can go in pressing a loan customer to pay up.

FDIC Improvement Act   A law passed by the U.S. Congress in 1991 to recapitalize the Federal Deposit Insurance Corporation and exercise closer regulation over troubled banks and other depository institutions.

federal agency securities   Marketable notes and bonds sold by agencies owned by or started by the federal government, such as the Federal National Mortgage Association (FNMA) or the farm credit agencies.

Federal Deposit Insurance Corporation (FDIC)   The U.S. government agency that guarantees the repayment of the public's deposits in U.S. banks and thrifts up to a maximum of $100,000 and assesses insurance premiums that must be paid by depositories offering federally insured deposits.

Federal funds market   A domestic source of reserves in which a depository institution can borrow the excess reserves held by other institutions; also known as *same-day money* because these funds can be transferred instantaneously by wire from the lending institution to the borrowing institution.

Federal Open Market Committee (FOMC)   Composed of the members of the Federal Reserve Board and the presidents of the Federal Reserve banks, the FOMC sets money and credit policies for the Federal Reserve System and oversees the conduct of open market operations, the Federal Reserve's chief policy tool.

Federal Reserve Bank   A quasi-public U.S. institution created in 1913 by the Federal Reserve Act that provides financial services, such as check clearing, to depository institutions in the region served by each individual Federal Reserve Bank.

Federal Reserve System   The federal agency that serves as a "lender of last resort" for depository institutions in need of temporary loans and is charged by the U.S. Congress to monitor and control the growth of money and credit and stabilize credit market conditions and the economy.

fiduciary relationship   An agreement between a financial institution and its customer in which the institution becomes responsible for managing the customer's funds or other property.

finance companies   Financial institutions that extend credit to businesses and individuals, either through direct loans or through purchasing accounts receivable from their customers, and raising loanable funds principally through borrowing in the money and capital markets.

financial advisory services   A range of services that may include investment advice, the preparation of tax returns, and help with recordkeeping; business customers often receive aid in checking on the credit standing of prospective customers unknown to them and assistance in evaluating marketing opportunities abroad.

financial boutiques   Banks and other financial-service companies that offer a limited set of services to selected customer groups.

financial futures   Contracts calling for the delivery of specific types of securities at a set price on a specific future date.

financial guarantees   Instruments used to enhance the credit standing of a borrower in order to help lower the borrower's credit costs by pledging to reimburse a lender if the borrower fails to pay.

financial holding companies (FHCs)   Corporations that control one or more financial institutions and, perhaps,

other businesses as well; under the terms of the Gramm-Leach-Bliley Act of 1999 banks, insurance companies, security dealers, and selected other financial firms may be acquired and brought under common ownership through a financial holding company organization.

financial institution loans   Both long- and short-term credit extended to banks, insurance companies, and other financial institutions.

Financial Institutions Reform, Recovery, and Enforcement Act   U.S. law passed in 1989 that authorized bank holding companies to acquire healthy savings and loan associations and restructured the FDIC, dividing its insurance fund into a Bank Insurance Fund (BIF) to cover U.S. commercial bank deposits and a Savings Associations' Insurance Fund (SAIF) to insure the deposits of U.S.-based savings and loan associations and other thrifts.

fixed-rate mortgages (FRMs)   Loans against real property whose rate of interest does not change during the life of the loan.

Foreign Bank Supervision Enhancement Act   U.S. law, passed in 1991, giving the Federal Reserve Board greater regulatory powers over foreign banks operating in the United States, including the power to close a foreign bank's U.S. facilities if found to be inadequately supervised or operated in an unsafe manner.

FOREX   Foreign currencies and foreign-currency–denominated deposits offered by international banks to aid their customers who trade and travel abroad.

forward contracts   Agreements that can be used when a customer anticipates a future need to acquire foreign currency or expects to receive foreign currency; a financial institution negotiates a contract with another party on behalf of its customer, fixing the price at which currency is exchanged and specifying a date on which the currency will be delivered.

full-service branch   A branch office that offers all or most of the same services that the firm's head office also offers.

full-service interstate banking   The establishment of banks or bank branches across state lines by individual banking organizations that offer a complete menu of banking services.

Funds-Flow Statement   A financial statement that shows where funds have come from and how they have been used over a specific time period.

funds gap   The difference between current and projected credit and deposit flows that creates a need for raising additional reserves or for profitably investing any excess reserves that may arise.

funds management   Combining asset and liability management strategies in order to achieve a financial institution's goals and meet its liquidity needs more effectively.

G

Garn-St Germain Depository Institutions Act   A U.S. deregulation law, passed in 1982, that permitted nonbank thrift institutions to become more like commercial banks in the services they could offer and allowed all federally regulated depository institutions to offer deposits competitive with money market mutual fund share accounts.

geographic diversification   Spreading out credit accounts and deposits among customers located in different communities, regions, or countries in order to reduce the overall risk of loss to a bank or other lending institution.

Glass-Steagall Act   Law passed by the U.S. Congress in 1933 that legally mandated the separation of commercial and investment banking, imposed interest rate ceilings on bank deposits, authorized the creation of the Federal Deposit Insurance Corporation, and granted federally chartered banks the power to branch throughout a state, provided that state grants similar powers to its own state-chartered banks.

Gramm-Leach-Bliley (Financial Services Modernization) Act   A U.S. federal law approved in 1999 permitting common ownership of banks, securities firms, and insurers through financial holding companies or subsidiaries if well capitalized and well managed and granted regulatory approval.

H

hedge funds   Private partnerships that sell shares to only a limited group of investors in order to invest in a wide variety of assets and derivative instruments in the hope of achieving exceptional returns regardless of the direction the market subsequently moves.

Herfindahl-Hirschman Index   A summary measure of market concentration used by the U.S. Justice Department, in which the assets of each firm serving a given market are squared and the squared market shares of all firms are then summed to derive a single index number reflecting the degree of concentration of assets in the largest firms.

holding period yield (HPY)   A rate of discount bringing the current price of a security into line with its stream of expected cash inflows and its expected sale price at the end of the investor's holding period.

home equity loans   Credit extended to an individual or family on the basis of the spread or gap between the estimated market value of a home and the amount of mortgage loans outstanding against the property.

I

inflation risk   The probability that the prices of goods and services (including the interest rate on borrowed funds and the cost of personnel and other productive resources) will rise or that the value of assets will be eroded due to rising prices, lowering the expected return on invested capital.

installment loans   Credits that are repayable in two or more consecutive payments, usually on a monthly or quarterly basis.

in-store branches   Branch offices located in a grocery store or other retail outlet.

insurance policies   Contracts that guarantee payment if the customer dies, becomes disabled, or suffers loss of property or earning power.

interest rate cap   Ceiling interest rate imposed on a loan designed to protect the borrower from an unacceptable rise in the interest cost of that loan.

interest rate collar   A combination of an interest rate cap and an interest rate floor; puts brackets around the movement of a loan rate so that it cannot rise above the cap or fall below the floor.

interest rate floor   Minimum interest rate below which the interest cost of a loan normally cannot fall, thus protecting the lender from additional lost revenue if market interest rates move lower.

interest rate option   A contract that either (1) grants a holder of securities or loans the right to place (put) those instruments with another investor at a specified exercise price before the option expires or (2) allows an investor to take delivery of securities or other financial instruments (call) from another investor at a specified price on or before the option's expiration date.

interest rate risk   The probability that rising or falling interest rates will adversely affect the margin of interest revenues over interest expenses or result in decreasing the value of net worth.

interest rate swaps   Agreements that enable two different borrowers of funds to aid each other by exchanging some of the most favorable features of their loans; usually the two participating institutions exchange interest rate payments in order to reduce their borrowing costs and better balance their inflows and outflows of funds.

interest sensitive   An asset or liability item that can be repriced as market interest rates change.

interest-sensitive gap management   Management techniques that usually require a computer analysis of the maturities and repricing opportunities associated with interest-bearing assets, deposits, and money market borrowings in order to determine when and by how much a financial institution is exposed to interest rate risk.

interim construction loan   Secured short-term lending to support the construction of homes, apartments, office buildings, shopping centers, and other permanent structures.

internal capital growth rate   The rate of growth of net earnings that remain inside a firm rather than being paid out to its stockholders; this growth rate depends on a firm's return on equity and its dividend policies.

International Banking Act   Law passed by the U.S. Congress in 1978 that brought foreign banks operating in the United States under federal regulation for the first time; it required foreign banking offices taking deposits from the public to post reserve requirements and allowed them to apply for federal deposit insurance coverage.

international banking facility (IBF)   Computerized account records that are kept separate from a U.S. bank's domestic accounts and that keep track primarily of international or overseas transactions.

International Lending and Supervision Act   Law passed by the U.S. Congress in 1983 that requires U.S. banks to hold stipulated minimum amounts of capital and that sets standards for making, evaluating, and restructuring overseas loans.

Internet banking   The offering of information and selected services through the World Wide Web by banks and similar financial-service firms.

Internet service sites   Computer files or pages set up on the World Wide Web to advertise services or offer selected service options to Web users.

investment banking services   A bank's offer to underwrite a corporate or institutional customer's securities in order to aid that customer in raising funds.

investment products   Sales of mutual funds, annuities, and other nondeposit instruments offered through the bank's service delivery facilities, either with the aid of an

affiliate or offered by an unrelated financial services company but sold through the bank's service facilities.

J

joint venture   Cooperative service production and delivery between banks or between banks and nonbank firms in order to provide a wider array of customer services at a profit.

Justice Department Merger Guidelines   Standards for evaluating the impact of a proposed merger on the concentration of assets or deposits in a given market area; the Justice Department uses these standards to help it decide whether to sue to block a proposed merger that might damage competition.

L

Lagged reserve accounting (LRA)   An accounting system begun by the Federal Reserve in 1984 for calculating each depository institution's legal reserve requirement, in which the reserve computation and reserve maintenance periods for transaction deposits are not exactly the same.

LBOs (leveraged buyouts)   Contractual agreements in which a company or small group of individual investors purchases a business or buys a portion of a business firm's assets with heavy use of debt and relatively little equity capital and relies on increased earnings after the business is taken over to retire the debt.

legal reserves   Assets that by law must be held behind deposits or other designated liabilities; in the United States, these assets consist of vault cash and deposits at the Federal Reserve banks.

letter of credit   A legal notice in which a financial institution guarantees the credit of one of its customers who is borrowing from another institution.

liability management   Use of borrowed funds to meet liquidity needs, in which a financial institution attracts the volume of liquidity it needs by raising or lowering the rate of interest it is willing to pay on borrowed funds.

LIBOR   The London Interbank Offered Rate on short-term Eurodollar deposits, which is used as a common basis for quoting loan rates to corporations and other large borrowers.

life and property casualty insurers   Firms selling risk protection to their customers in an effort to offset financial losses related to death, ill health, negligence, storm damage, and other adverse events.

life insurance policies   Contracts that promise cash payments to beneficiaries when the death of a policyholder occurs.

life insurance underwriters   Companies that manage the risks associated with paying off life insurance claims and collecting premium payments from life insurance policyholders.

liquid asset   Any asset that meets three conditions: (1) price stability, (2) ready marketability, and (3) reversibility.

liquidity   Access to sufficient immediately spendable funds at reasonable cost exactly when those funds are needed.

liquidity gap   The amount by which the sources and uses of liquidity do not match.

liquidity indicators   Certain bellwether financial ratios (e.g., total loans outstanding divided by total assets) that are used to estimate liquidity needs and to monitor changes in liquidity position.

liquidity risk   The probability that an individual or institution will be unable to raise cash precisely when cash is needed at reasonable cost and in the volume required.

loan commitment agreements   Promises to provide credit to a customer in the future, provided certain conditions are met.

loan option   A device to lock in the amount and cost of borrowing for a designated time period by allowing a customer to borrow at a guaranteed interest rate, regardless of any subsequent changes in market interest rates, until the option expires.

loan participation   Agreement under which a lender will share a large loan with one or more other lenders in order to provide the borrower with sufficient funds and reduce risk exposure to any one lending institution.

loan review   A process of periodic investigation of all outstanding loans to make sure each loan is paying out as planned, all necessary documentation is present, and loan officers are following the institution's loan policy.

loan sales   A form of investment banking in which the lender trades on his or her superior ability to evaluate the creditworthiness of borrowers and sells some of the loans the lender has made to other investors who value the lender's expertise in assessing credit quality.

loans to individuals   Credit extended to households to finance the purchase of automobiles and appliances, medical and personal expenses, and other household needs.

loan strip   The sale of a portion of a large loan for a short period of time, usually for period less than the loan's remaining time to maturity.

loan workouts   Activity within a lending institution that focuses on delinquent loans and that tries to develop and implement strategies designed to recover as much as possible from troubled borrowers.

M

market-penetration deposit pricing   Offering high interest rates (often well above current market levels) or charging low or zero customer fees in order to bring in as many new deposit customers as possible.

market-positioning benefits   A motive for conducting a merger between two or more firms, in which the firms involved anticipate gaining access to important new markets not previously served or securing a stronger foothold in markets currently served.

market risk   The potential for loss due to rising or falling interest rates; the danger that changing interest rates may force a financial institution to accept substantial losses on any assets that must be sold or acquired or on any funds that must be borrowed or repaid.

maturity gap   The difference between the average maturity of a bank or other financial-service firm's assets and the average maturity of its liabilities.

McFadden-Pepper Act   Legislation passed by the U.S. Congress in 1927 that allows national banks to branch within the city where they are headquartered if the laws of the state involved do not forbid such branches.

member bank   A commercial bank that has joined the Federal Reserve System and is subject to its rules and regulations; includes all national banks as well as state-chartered banks that elect to join the Federal Reserve System.

merchant banks   Banks that often provide not only all the consumer and commercial services a regular bank provides but also offer credit, investment, and consulting services in an attempt to satisfy all the financial service needs of their clients; usually these banks invest a substantial share of their own equity capital in a customer's commercial project.

merger premium   A bonus offered to the shareholders of a firm to be acquired, consisting of an amount of cash or stock in the acquiring institution that exceeds the current market value of the acquired firm's stock.

minority interest in consolidated subsidiaries   Partial ownership interest that a bank or other financial firm holds in other business firms.

monetary policy   A central bank's primary job, which involves making sure that the banking and financial system functions smoothly and that the supply of money and credit from that system contributes to the nation's economic goals.

money market deposit accounts (MMDAs)   Short-maturity deposits having a term of only a few days, weeks, or months and on which the offering depository institution can pay any competitive interest rate over designated short intervals of time; these deposits also have limited checking account powers.

money market instruments   Investment securities that reach maturity within one year and are noted for their low credit risk and ready marketability.

money position manager   Managerial position that is responsible for ensuring that the institution maintains an adequate level of legal reserves to meet its reserve requirements as set by law and also has access to sufficient quantities of reserves to accommodate customer demand and meet other cash needs.

mortgage-backed bond   A debt instrument representing a claim against the interest and principal payments generated by a pool of mortgage loans.

mortgage banking companies   Financial-service firms that acquire mortgage loans for eventual resale to longer-term lenders (e.g., insurance companies and pension funds).

multibank holding companies   A type of holding company that holds stock in more than one bank.

municipal bonds   Debt obligations issued by states, cities, counties, and other local governmental units.

mutual funds   Investment companies that attract savings from the public and invest those funds in a pool of stocks, bonds, and other financial instruments, with each saver receiving a share of the earnings generated by the pool of financial instruments.

N

National Credit Union Administration   A federal regulatory agency set up during the 1930s as a result of passage of the Federal Credit Union Act in the United States to charter and supervise federal credit unions.

negotiable CD   A type of interest-bearing deposit that may be sold to other investors in the secondary market any number of times before it reaches maturity.

net interest margin   The spread between interest income and interest expense divided by either total assets or total earning assets.

net liquidity position   The difference between the volume of liquid funds available and the demand for liquid funds.

net profit margin   The ratio of net income after taxes divided by total operating revenues.

networking   The sharing of facilities for the movement of funds and financial information between financial-service providers.

nonbank banks   Financial-service firms that either offer checking account services or grant commercial loans, but not both.

noninterest margin   The spread between noninterest income and noninterest expenses divided by total assets or total earning assets.

note   A written contract between a borrowing customer and a lender describing the responsibilities of both parties.

note issuance facility (NIF)   A medium-term credit agreement between an international bank and its larger corporate and governmental credit customers, where the customer is authorized to periodically issue short-term notes, each of which usually comes due and is retired in 90 to 180 days, over a stipulated contract period (such as five years), with the bank pledging to buy any notes the customer cannot sell to other investors.

NOW accounts   Savings deposits against which a customer can write negotiable drafts (checks) but that reserve the depository institution's right to insist on prior notice before the customer withdraws his or her funds.

O

Office of the Comptroller of the Currency   See Comptroller of the Currency.

Office of Thrift Supervision A federal regulatory agency inside the U.S. Treasury Department that is authorized to charter and supervise thrift institutions, including savings and loan associations and savings banks.

open market operations (OMO) Purchases and sales of securities—in most cases, direct obligations of the government—that are designed to move reserves and interest rates toward levels desired by a central bank (such as the Federal Reserve System).

operating risk The danger of loss due to fluctuating earnings and cash flows from business operations.

opportunity cost Forgone income that is not earned because idle funds have not been invested in earning assets; also, the yield available on the next best alternate use of an individual or institution's funds.

organizational forms The structure of operations, facilities, and personnel within a bank or other financial firm that enables it to produce and deliver financial services.

P

participation loans Purchases of loans by a third party, not part of the original loan contracts.

passbook savings deposits Accounts sold to household customers in small denominations along with a small booklet or computer statement showing the account's current balance, interest earnings, deposits, and withdrawals.

pledging Backing deposits owed to the federal government and local units of government by requiring the financial institutions holding those deposits to hold designated high-quality (low-risk) assets (usually government securities of various types) that could be sold to recover government funds if the depository institution fails.

point-of-sale (POS) terminals Computer equipment in stores to allow electronic payments for goods and services.

points An up-front fee often charged a borrower taking on a home mortgage, which is determined by multiplying the loan amount by the number of percentage points assessed the borrower.

portfolio diversification Spreading out credit accounts and deposits among a wide variety of customers, including many large and small businesses, different industries, and households in order to reduce the lender's risk of loss.

portfolio immunization An interest-rate hedging device that permits a financial institution to reduce loss in the value of its assets or in the value of its net worth due to changing interest rates by equating the average duration of its assets to the average duration of its liabilities.

portfolio shifting Selling selected securities, often at a loss, to offset taxable income from other sources and to restructure a financial firm's asset portfolio to one that is more appropriate for current market conditions.

predatory lending Granting loans to weaker borrowers and charging them excessive fees and interest rates, increasing the risk of their defaulting on those loans.

preferred stock Type of capital measured by the par value of any shares outstanding that promise to pay their owners a fixed rate of return or (in the case of variable-rate preferred) a rate determined by an agreed-upon formula.

prepayment risk A risk carried by many securitized assets in which some of these assets (usually loans) are paid off early and the investor receiving those prepayments may be forced to reinvest the prepaid funds at lower current market yields, resulting in a lower than expected overall return from investing in securitized assets.

price leadership A method for setting loan rates that looks to leading lending institutions to set the base loan rate.

primary capital The sum of total equity capital, the allowance for possible loan losses, mandatory convertible debentures, and minority interests in consolidated subsidiaries, minus intangible assets other than purchased loan-servicing rights.

prime rate An administered interest rate on loans quoted by leading banks and usually set by a vote of each bank's board of directors; the interest rate that the public usually thinks is the best (lowest) rate for loans and that a bank quotes to its biggest and best customers (principally large corporations).

product-line diversification Offering multiple financial services in order to reduce the risk associated with declining revenues and income from any one service offered.

profitability An important indicator of performance, it represents the rate of return a financial firm or other business has been able to generate from using the resources at its command in order to produce and sell services.

profit potential A motive for carrying out a merger, in which the shareholders of either the acquiring firm, the acquired firm, or both anticipate greater profits due to greater revenues or lower operating costs after the merger is completed.

project loans Credit designed to finance the construction of fixed assets associated with a particular investment project that is expected to generate a flow of revenue in future periods sufficient to repay the loan and turn a profit.

property-casualty insurance policies Contracts that pledge reimbursement of policyholders for personal injuries, property damage, and other losses incurred in return for policyholder premium payments.

public benefits Aspect of a merger or holding-company acquisition application in which merging or acquiring financial firms must show how the transaction will improve the quality, availability, or pricing of services offered to the public.

public need One of the criteria used by governmental agencies to determine whether a new bank, branch, or other financial service unit should be approved for a charter, which focuses on whether or not an adequate volume and variety of financial services are available conveniently in a given market area.

purchase-of-assets method A method for completing a merger in which the acquiring institution buys all or a portion of the assets of the acquired organization, using either cash or its own stock to pay for the purchase.

purchase-of-stock method A method for carrying out a merger in which the acquired firm usually ceases to exist because the acquiring firm assumes all of its assets and liabilities.

R

real estate brokerage services A service that assists customers in finding homes and other properties for sale or for rent.

real estate loans Credit secured by real property, including short-term credit to support building construction and land development, and longer-term credit to support the purchase of residential and commercial structures.

relationship pricing Basing fees charged a customer on the number of services and the intensity of use of those services that the customer purchases.

Report of Condition A bank or thrift institution's balance sheet, which lists the assets, liabilities, and equity capital (owners' funds) held by or invested in the depository institution at any single point in time; reports of condition must be filed periodically with regulatory agencies.

Report of Income A bank or thrift's income statement, which indicates how much revenue has been received and what expenses have been incurred over a specific period of time; reports of income must be filed periodically with regulatory agencies.

representative office The simplest organizational presence for an international bank in foreign markets, consisting of limited-service facilities that can market services supplied by the home office and identify new customers but usually cannot take deposits or make decisions on the granting of loans.

repurchase agreement (RP) A money market instrument that involves the temporary sale of high-quality assets (usually government securities) accompanied by an agreement to buy back those assets on a specific future date at a predetermined price or yield.

reserve computation period A period of time established by the Federal Reserve System for certain depository institutions over which the daily average amounts of various deposits are computed to determine each institution's legal reserve requirement.

reserve maintenance period According to federal law and regulation, a period of time spanning two weeks, during which a bank or qualifying thrift institution must hold the daily average amount of legal reserves it is required by law to hold behind its deposits and other reservable liabilities.

residential mortgage loans Credit to finance the purchase of homes or fund improvements on private residences.

retail banks Consumer-oriented banks that sell the majority of their services to households and smaller businesses.

retail credit Smaller-denomination loans extended to individuals and families as well as to smaller businesses.

restrictive covenants Parts of a loan agreement, specifying actions the borrower must take or must not take for a loan agreement to remain in force.

retirement plans Financial plans offered by various financial institutions that accumulate and manage the savings of customers until they reach retirement age.

revolving credit line A financing arrangement that allows a business customer to borrow up to a specified limit, repay all or a portion of the borrowing, and reborrow as necessary until the credit line matures.

Riegle-Neal Interstate Banking and Branching Efficiency Act Federal law passed in 1994 that permits bank holding companies to acquire banks nationwide and authorized interstate branching and mergers beginning June 1, 1997.

right of offset   The legal authority of a lender that has extended a loan to one of its customers to seize any checking or savings deposits the customer may hold with the lender in order to recover the lender's funds.

ROA   Return on total assets as measured by the ratio of net income after taxes to total assets.

ROE   Return on equity capital invested in a bank or other corporation by its stockholders, measured by after-tax net income divided by total equity capital.

Rule of 78s   A method for calculating rebates of interest payments to be returned to a customer if a loan is retired early.

S

safekeeping   A bank or other financial institution's practice of holding precious metals, securities, and other valuables owned by its customers in secure vaults.

Sarbanes-Oxley Accounting Standards Act   Federal law passed in the United States in 2002 deigned to prohibit public companies from publishing false or misleading financial reports and creating an accounting standards board to oversee the practices of the accounting and auditing professions.

savings and loan associations   Depository institutions that concentrate the majority of their assets in the home mortgage loan area and rely mainly on savings deposits as their principal source of funding.

savings deposits   Interest-bearing funds left with a bank or thrift institution for a period of weeks, months, or years (with no minimum required maturity under U.S. regulations).

secondary capital   The sum of all forms of temporary capital, including limited-life preferred stock, subordinated notes and debentures, and mandatory convertible debt instruments not eligible to be counted as primary capital.

Securities and Exchange Commission   A federal oversight board created by the Securities and Exchange Act of 1934 that requires public companies to file financial reports and disclose relevant information about their financial condition to the public and to prevent the issuance of fraudulent or deceptive information in the offering of new securities to the public.

securitization   Setting aside a group of income-earning assets and issuing securities against them in order to raise new funds.

securitized assets   Loans placed in an income-generating pool against which securities are issued in order to raise new funds.

security brokerage   Offering customers a channel through which to buy or sell stocks, bonds, and other securities at low transactions cost instead of having to go through a security broker or dealer.

security brokers and dealers   Financial firms engaged in buying and selling stocks, bonds, and other securities on behalf of their customers and providing underwriting services for new issues of stocks and debt securities as well as financial advice regarding market conditions and other financial matters.

security underwriting   A service provided by investment banks to corporate and governmental customers in which new securities issued by a customer are purchased by the investment bank and sold in the money and capital markets in the hope of earning a profitable spread.

self-liquidating loans   Business loans, usually to support the purchase of inventories, in which the credit is gradually repaid by the borrowing customer as inventory is sold.

service differentiation   Creating perceptions in the minds of customers that a particular financial firm's services are of better quality, are more conveniently available, or differ in some other significant way from similar services offered by competitors.

servicing rights   Rights retained by a lender selling a loan in which the lender continues to collect interest payments from the borrower and monitors the borrower's compliance with loan terms on behalf of the purchaser of the loan.

shell branches   Booking offices located offshore from the United States that record international transactions (such as taking deposits) and escape many regulatory restrictions that limit the activities of domestic offices.

simple interest   A method for calculating the interest rate on a loan that adjusts for the declining balance on a loan and uses a formula, principal times interest times time, to determine the amount of interest owed.

sources and uses of funds method   Approach developed for estimating liquidity requirements that examines the expected sources of liquidity (for a bank, principally its deposits) and the expected uses of liquidity (principally its loans) and estimates the net difference between funds sources and uses over a given period of time in order to aid liquidity planning.

Sources and Uses of Funds Statement   Financial reports on a business customer showing changes in assets and liabilities over a given period of time.

standby letter of credit (SLC)   Popular type of financial guarantee in which the issuer of the letter guarantees the beneficiary of the letter that a loan he or she has made will be repaid.

state banking commissions   Boards or commissions appointed by governors or legislators in each of the 50 states that are responsible for issuing new bank charters and supervising and examining state-chartered banks.

state insurance commissions   Regulatory bodies created by state law in each of the 50 U.S. states that regulate life and property/casualty insurance companies selling their policies to the public in an effort to ensure adequate service to the public at reasonable cost.

Statement of Cash Flows   A financial report often constructed by credit analysts or by borrowing customers that shows a prospective borrower's sources of cash flowing in and flowing out and the actual or projected net cash flow available to repay a loan or other obligation.

Statement of Stockholders' Equity   A financial statement that shows what changes have occurred in a bank or other business's capital account (where the owners have invested their funds) over a specified time period.

stockholders   The owners of a business who hold one or more shares of common and/or preferred stock issued by their corporation and elect its board of directors.

stripped security   A debt security whose promised interest payments and promised repayments of principal are separated from each other; each of these promised payment streams becomes the basis for issuing new securities in the form of interest-only (IO) and principal-only (PO) discount obligations.

structure of funds method   Method of estimating liquidity requirements that depends on a detailed analysis of deposit and loan customers and how the levels of their deposits and loans are likely to change over time.

subordinated debentures (or notes)   Type of capital represented by debt instruments whose claim against the borrowing institution legally follows the claims of depositors but comes ahead of the stockholders.

subprime loans   Credit granted to borrowers whose credit rating is considered to be weak or below average, often due to a prior record of delinquent payments, bankruptcy, or other adverse developments.

subsidiary   A corporation operated by international banks that is used to sell bank and nonbank services overseas and is often set up or acquired because bank branch offices may be prohibited in some foreign markets or because of tax advantages or other factors.

super NOWs   Savings accounts that usually promise a higher interest return than regular NOW accounts but often impose restrictions on the number of drafts (checks) or withdrawals the depositor is allowed to make.

supplemental capital   Secondary forms of capital, such as debt securities and limited-life preferred stock, that usually have a definite maturity and are not, therefore, perpetual funding instruments.

surplus   Type of capital representing the excess amount above each share of stock's par value paid in by stockholders when they purchased their shares.

sweep accounts   Contracts executed between a depository institution and some of its deposit customers that allow the institution to transfer funds (usually overnight) out of the customers' checking accounts into their savings deposits or into other types of deposits that do not carry legal reserve requirements.

syndicated loan   A loan or line of credit extended to a business firm by a group of lenders in order to reduce the credit risk exposure to any single lending institution.

T

tax benefits   Ways to save on a potential tax obligation by investing in tax-exempt earning assets, incurring tax-deductible expenses, or accruing income losses that help offset taxable income from loans or other income sources.

tax swapping   A process in which lower-yielding securities may be sold at a loss that is deductible from ordinary taxable income, usually to be replaced by securities bearing more favorable returns.

term loans   Credit extended for longer than one year and designed to fund longer-term business investments, such as the purchase of equipment or the construction of new physical facilities.

thrift deposits   Accounts whose principal purpose is to provide an interest-bearing outlet for customer savings—that is, a place for the customer to store liquid purchasing power at interest until needed.

Tier 1 capital   Core capital for a banking firm that includes common stock, undivided profits, selected preferred stock and intangible assets, and minority interest in subsidiary businesses.

Tier 2 capital   Supplemental long-term funds for a bank, including allowance for loan and lease losses, subordinated debt capital, selected preferred stock, and equity notes.

time deposits   Interest-bearing accounts with stated maturities, which may carry penalties in the form of lost interest earnings or reduction of principal if early withdrawal occurs.

transaction deposit   A deposit service in which checks or drafts against the deposit may be used to pay for purchases of goods and services.

Treasury bill   A direct obligation of the U.S. government that must mature within one year from date of issue.

Treasury bonds   The longest-term U.S. Treasury debt securities, with original maturities beyond 10 years.

Treasury notes   Coupon instruments issued by the U.S. government, with original maturities from more than 1 year to a maximum of 10 years, which promise investors a fixed rate of return.

trust services   Management of property and other valuables owned by a customer under a contract (the trust agreement) in which the bank serves as trustee and the customer becomes the trustor during a specified period of time.

Truth-in-Lending Act   Law passed by the U.S. Congress in 1968 that promotes the informed use of credit among consumers by requiring full disclosure of credit terms and costs.

Truth-in-Savings Act   Law passed by the U.S. Congress in 1991 that requires depository institutions to fully disclose the prices and other terms offered on deposit services so that customers can more easily compare deposit plans offered by different service providers.

U

underwriting   Buying new securities from the businesses that issued them and attempting to resell those securities at a profit to other investors.

underwriting property/casualty insurance risks
Companies that attempt to profit from collecting policyholder premiums that exceed cash outflows to pay off policyholder claims for injuries and damages.

undivided profits   Type of bank capital representing the net earnings of a bank that have been retained in the business rather than being paid out as dividends to the bank's stockholders.

Uniform Bank Performance Report (UBPR)   A compilation of financial and operating information, periodically required to be submitted to federal banking agencies, which is designed to aid regulators and financial analysts in analyzing a U.S. bank's financial condition.

unit banks   Banks that offer the full range of their services from one office, though a small number of services (such as taking deposits or cashing checks) may be offered from limited-service facilities, such as drive-up windows and ATMs.

USA Patriot Act   Federal law passed in the United States in the fall of 2001 requiring banks and selected other financial institutions to verify the identity of customers opening new accounts and to report any suspicious activities to a division of the U.S. Treasury Department.

V

value at risk (VAR) models   A statistical framework for measuring an asset portfolio's exposure to changes in market prices or market rates of interest over a given time period, subject to a given probability level.

virtual banks   Banking firms chartered by federal or state authorities to offer financial services to the public exclusively online.

W

warranties   A section within a loan agreement in which a borrower affirms to the lender that the information he or she supplies is true and correct.

wholesale banks   Large metropolitan banks that offer financial services mainly to corporations and other large institutions.

wholesale lenders   Lending institutions that devote the bulk of their credit portfolios to large-denomination loans extended to corporations and other relatively large business firms and institutions.

working capital   The current assets of a business firm (consisting principally of cash, accounts receivable, inventory, and other assets normally expected to roll over into cash within a year); some authorities define working capital as equal to current assets minus current liabilities.

working capital loans   Loans that provide businesses with short-term credit lasting from a few days to one year and that are often used to fund the purchase of inventories in order to put goods on shelves or to purchase raw materials.

Y

yield curve   A graphic picture of how interest rates vary with different maturities of securities as viewed at a single point in time.

yield to maturity (YTM)   The expected rate of return on a debt security held until its maturity date is reached, based on the security's purchase price, promised interest payments, and redemption value at maturity.